DATE DUE

Notes
on the
New Testament

Albert Barnes

Edited by

Robert Frew

I CORINTHIANS

BAKER BOOK HOUSE
Grand Rapids, Michigan 49506

BARNES' NOTES

Heritage Edition

Fourteen Volumes 0834-4

When ordering by ISBN (International Standard Book Number), numbers listed above should be preceded by 0-8010-.

Reprinted from the 1884-85 edition published by Blackie & Son,
London, edited by Robert Frew

Reprinted 1983 by Baker Book House Company

ISBN : 0-8010-0846-8

Printed and bound in the United States of America

INTRODUCTION

CORINTH was properly a small dynasty, or territory in Greece, bounded on the east by the gulf of Saron ; on the south by the kingdom of Argos ; on the west by Sicyon ; and on the north by the kingdom of Megaris, and upper part of the isthmus and bay of Corinth, the latter of which is now called the Golfo de Lepanto, or the gulf of Lepanto. This tract, or region, not large in size, possessed a few rich plains, but was in general uneven, and the soil of an indifferent quality. The city of Corinth was the capital of this region. It stood near the middle of the isthmus, which in the narrowest part was about six miles wide, though somewhat wider where Corinth stood. Here was the natural *carrying place*, or portage from the Ionian sea on the west, to the Ægean on the east. Many efforts were made by the Greeks, and afterwards by the Romans, to effect a communication between the Ægean and Adriatic seas by cutting across this isthmus ; and traces still remain of these attempts. Means were even contrived for transporting vessels across. This isthmus was also particularly important as it was the key of the Peloponnesus, and attempts were often made to fortify it. The city had two harbours,—Lechæum on the gulf of Corinth, or sea of Crissa on the west, to which it was joined by a double wall, twelve stadia, or about a mile and a half in length ; and Cenchrea, or the sea of Saron on the east, distant about seventy stadia, or nearly nine miles. It was a situation therefore peculiarly favourable for commerce, and highly important in the defence of Greece.

The city is said to have been founded by Sisyphus, long before the siege of Troy, and was then called Ephyra. The time when it was founded is, however, unknown. The name *Corinth*, was supposed to have been given to it from Corinthus, who, by different authors, is said to have been the son of Jupiter, or of Marathon, or of Pelops, who is said to have rebuilt and adorned the city.

The city of Corinth was built at the foot of a high hill, on the top of which stood a citadel. This hill, which stood on the south of the city, was its defence in that quarter, as its sides were extremely steep. On the three other sides it was protected by strong and lofty ramparts. The circumference of the city proper was about forty stadia, or five miles. Its situation gave it great commercial advantages. As the whole of that region was mountainous and rather barren, and as the situation gave the city extraordinary commercial advantages, the inhabitants early turned their attention to commerce, and amassed great wealth. This fact was, to no inconsiderable extent, the foundation of the luxury, effeminacy, and vices for which the city afterwards became so much distinguished.

The merchandise of Italy, Sicily, and the western nations, was landed at Lech æum on the west ; and that of the islands of the Ægean sea, of Asia Minor, and of the Phœnicians, and other oriental nations, at Cenchrea on the east. The city of Corinth thus became the mart of Asia and Europe ; covered the sea with its ships, and formed a navy to protect its commerce. It was distinguished by building galleys and ships of a new and improved form; and its naval force procured it respect from other nations. Its population and its wealth was thus increased by the influx of foreigners. It became a city rather distinguished by its wealth, and naval force, and commerce, than by its military achievements, though it produced a few of the most valiant and distinguished leaders in the armies of Greece.

Its population was increased and its character somewhat formed from another circumstance. In the neighbourhood of the city the *Isthmian games* were celebrated, which attracted so much attention, and which drew so many strangers from distant parts of the world. To those games, the apostle Paul not infrequently refers, when recommending Christian energy and activity. See Note, 1 Cor. ix. 24, 26, 27; comp. Heb. xii. 1.

From these causes, the city of Corinth became eminent among all ancient cities for wealth, and luxury, and dissipation. It was the mart of the world. Wealth flowed into it from all quarters. Luxury, amusement, and dissipation, were the natural consequents, until it became the most gay and dissolute city of its times, —*the Paris of antiquity.*

There was another cause which contributed to its character of dissoluteness and corruption. I refer to its religion. The principal deity worshipped in the city was Venus ; as Diana was the principal deity worshipped at Ephesus; Minerva at Athens, &c. Ancient cities were devoted usually to some particular god or goddess, and were supposed to be under their peculiar protection. See Note, Acts xiv. 13. Corinth was devoted, or dedicated thus to the goddess of love, or licentious passion ; and the effect may be easily conceived. The temple of Venus was erected on the north side or slope of the Acrocorinthus, a mountain about half a mile in height on the south of the city, and from the summit of which a magnificent prospect opened on the north to Parnassus and Helicon, to the eastward the island of Ægina and the citadel of Athens, and to the west the rich and beautiful plains of Sicyon. This mountain was covered with temples and splendid houses ; but was especially devoted to Venus, and was the place of her worship. Her shrine appeared above those of the other gods; and it was enjoined by law, that one thousand beautiful females should officiate as courtesans, or public prostitutes, before the altar of the goddess of love. In a time of public calamity and imminent danger, these women attended at the sacrifices, and walked with the other citizens singing sacred hymns. When Xerxes invaded Greece, recourse was had to their intercession to avert the impending calamity. They were supported chiefly by foreigners ; and from the avails of their vice a copious revenue was derived to the city. Individuals, in order to ensure success in their undertakings, vowed to present to Venus a certain number of courtesans, which they obtained by sending to distant countries. Foreign merchants were attracted in this way to Corinth ; and in a few days would be stripped of all their property. It thus became a proverb, " It is not for every one to go to Corinth,"—(οὐ παντὸς ἀνδρὸς εἰς Κόρινθον ἐστὶν ὁ πλους.) The effect of this on the morals of the city can be easily understood. It became the most gay, dissipated, corrupt, and ultimately the most effeminate and feeble portion of Greece. It is necessary to make these statements, because they go to show the exceeding grace of God in collecting a church in such a city, the power of the gospel in overcoming the strongest and most polluted passions of our nature; and because no small part of the irregularities which arose in the church at Corinth, and which gave the apostle occasion to write this epistle, were produced by this prevailing licentiousness of the people ; and by the fact, that gross and licentious passions had received the countenance of law and the patronage of public opinion. See chap. v. vii. See article *Lais* in the Biographical Dictionaries.

Though Corinth was thus dissipated and licentious in its character, yet it was also distinguished for its refinement and learning. Every part of literature was cultivated there, so that before its destruction by the Romans, Cicero (pro lege Man. cap. v.) scrupled not to call it totius Græciæ lumen—the light of all Greece.

Corinth was, of course, exposed to all the changes and disasters which occurred to the other cities of Greece. After a variety of revolutions in its government, which it is not necessary here to repeat, it was taken by the Roman consul L. Mummius, 147 years before Christ. The riches which were found in the city were immense. During the conflagration, it is said that all the metals which were there were melted and run together, and formed that valuable compound which was so much celebrated as Corinthian brass. Others, however, with more probability, say that the Corinthian artists were accustomed to form a metal, by a mixture of brass with small quantities of gold and silver, which was so brilliant as to cause the extraordinary estimate in which this metal was held. Corinth, however, was again rebuilt. In the time of Julius Cesar, it was colonised by his order, and soon again resumed something of its former magnificence. By the Romans the whole of Greece was divided into two provinces, Macedonia and Achaia. Of the latter Corinth was the capital ; and this was its condition when it was visited by Paul. With its ancient splendour, it also soon relapsed into its former dissipation and licentiousness ; and when Paul visited it, it was perhaps as dissolute as at any former period of its history. The subsequent history of Corinth it is not necessary to trace. On the division of the Roman empire, it fell, of course, to the eastern empire, and when this was overthrown by the Turks, it came into their hands, and it remained under their dominion until the recent revolution in Greece. It still retains its ancient name ; but with nothing of its ancient grandeur. A single temple, itself dismantled, it is said, is all that remains, except the ruins, to mark the site of one of the most splendid cities of antiquity. For the authorities of these statements, see Travels of Anacharsis, vol. iii. pp. 369 —388 ; Edin. Ency. art. Corinth ; Lemprière's Classical Dictionary, and Bayle's Dictionary, art. Corinth.

§ 2. *The Establishment of the Church at Corinth.*

The apostle Paul first visited Corinth about A. D. 52, (Lardner,) See Acts xviii. 1. He was then on his way from Macedonia to Jerusalem. He had passed some time at Athens, where he had preached the gospel, but not with such success as to warrant him to remain, or to organize a church ; see Notes on Acts xvii. He was alone at Athens, having expected to have been joined there by Silas and Timothy, but in that he was disappointed ; Acts xvii. 15 ; comp. xviii. 5. He came to Corinth alone, but found Aquila and Priscilla there, who had lately come from Rome, and with them he waited the arrival of Silas and Timothy. When they arrived, Paul entered on the great work of preaching the gospel in that splendid and dissipated city, first to the Jews, and when it was rejected by them, then to the Greeks ; Acts xviii. 5, 6. His feelings when he engaged in this work, he has himself stated in 1 Cor. xvi. 2—5. (see Note on that place.) His embarrassments and discouragements were met by a gracious promise of the Lord that he would be with him, and would not leave him ; and that it was his purpose to collect a church there ; see Note on Acts xviii. 9, 10. In the city, Paul remained eighteen months, (Acts xviii. 11,) preaching without molestation, until he was opposed by the Jews under Sosthenes their leader, and brought before Gallio. When Gallio refused to hear the cause, and Paul was discharged, it is said, that he remained there yet " a good while," (Acts xviii. 18,) and then sailed into Syria.

Of the size of the church that was first organised there, and of the general character of the converts, we have no other knowledge than that which is con tained in the epistle. There is reason to think that Sosthenes, who was the principal agent of the Jews in arraigning Paul before Gallio, was converted, (see 1 Cor. i. 1.) and perhaps some other persons of distinction ; but it is evident that the church was chiefly composed of those who were in the more humble walks of life ; see Notes on 1 Cor. i. 26—29. It was a signal illustration of the grace of God, and the power of the gospel, that a church was organized in that city of gayety, fashion, luxury, and licentiousness ; and it shows that the gospel is adapted to meet and overcome all forms of wickedness, and to subdue all classes of people to itself. If a church was established in the gay and dissolute capital of Achaia, then there is not now a city on earth so gay and so profligate that the same gospel may not meet its corruptions, and subdue it to the cross of Christ. Paul subsequently visited Corinth about A. D. 58, or six years after the establishment of the church there. He passed the winter in Greece—doubtless in Corinth and its neighbourhood, on his journey from Macedonia to Jerusalem, the fifth time in which he visited the latter city. During this stay at Corinth he wrote the epistle to the Romans. See the introduction to the Epistle to the Romans.

§ 3. *The time and place of writing the first Epistle to the Corinthians.*

It has been uniformly supposed that this epistle was written at Ephesus. The circumstances which are mentioned incidently in the epistle itself, place this beyond a doubt. The epistle purports to have been written, not like that to the Romans, without having been at the place to which it was written, but *after* Paul had been at Corinth. " I, brethren, *when I came unto you*, came not with excellency of speech," &c. chap. ii. 1. It also purports to have been written when he was about to make another visit to that church ; chap. iv. 19, " But I will come to you shortly, if the Lord will." Chap. xvi. 5, " Now I will come to you when I pass through Macedonia, for I do pass through Macedonia." Now the history in the Acts of the Apostles informs us, that Paul did in fact visit Achaia, and doubtless Corinth twice ; see Acts xviii. 1, &c. ; xx. 1—3. The same history also informs us that it was from Ephesus that Paul went into Greece ; and as the epistle purports to have been written a short time before that journey, it follows, to be consistent with the history, that the epistle must have been written while he was at Ephesus. The narrative in the Acts also informs us, that Paul had passed two years in Ephesus before he set out on his second journey into Greece.

With this supposition, all the circumstances relating to the place where the apostle then was which are mentioned in this epistle agree. " If after the manner of men, I have fought with beasts at Ephesus, what advantageth it me, if the dead rise not?" chap. xv. 32. It is true, as Dr. Paley remarks, (*Horæ Paulinæ*,) that the apostle might say this wherever he was ; but it was much more natural, and much more to the purpose to say it, if he was at Ephesus at the time, and in the midst of those conflicts to which the expression relates. " The churches of Asia salute you," chap. xvi. 19. It is evident from this, that Paul was near those churches, and that he had intercourse with them. But Asia, throughout the Acts of the Apostles, and in the epistles of Paul, does not mean commonly the whole of Asia, nor the whole of Asia Minor, but a district in the interior of Asia Minor, of which Ephesus was the capital ; see Note, Acts ii. 9 ; vi. 9 ; xvi. 6 ; xx. 16. " Aquila and Priscilla salute you," chap. xvi. 19. Aquila and Priscilla were at Ephesus during the time in which I shall endeavour to show this epistle was written, Acts xviii. 26. It is evident, if this were so, that the epistle was written at Ephesus. " But I will tarry at Ephesus until Pentecost," chap. xvi. 8. This is almost an express declaration that he was at Ephesus when the epistle was written. " A great and effectual door is opened to me, and there are many adversaries," chap. xvi. 9. How well this agrees with the history, may be seen by comparing it with the account in Acts, when Paul was at Ephesus. Acts xix. 20, " So mightily grew the word of God and prevailed." That there were " many adversaries," may be seen from the account of the same period in Acts xix. 9, " But when divers were hardened, and believed not, but spake evil of that way before the multitude, he departed from them and separated the disciples," Comp. Acts xix. 23—41. From these circumstances, it is put beyond controversy, that the epistle was written from Ephesus. These circumstantial, and undesigned coincidences, between a letter written by Paul and an independent history by Luke, is one of those strong evidences so common in genuine writings, which go to show that neither is a forgery. An impostor in forging a history like that of the Acts, and then writing an epistle, would not have thought of these coincidences, or introduced them in the manner in which they occur here. It is perfectly manifest that the notes of the time, and place, and circumstances in the history, and in the epistle, were not introduced to correspond with each other, but have every appearance of genuineness and truth. See Paley's Horæ Paulinæ, on this epistle.

The circumstances which have been referred to in regard to the *place* where this epistle was written, serve also to fix the *date* of its composition. It is evident, from chap. xvi. 8, that Paul purposed to tarry at Ephesus until Pentecost. But this must have been written and sent away *before* the riot which was raised by Demetrius (Acts xix. 23—41), for immediately after that Paul left Ephesus and went to Macedonia, Acts xx. 1, 2. The reason why Paul purposed to remain in Ephesus until Pentecost, was, the success which he had met with in preaching the gospel, chap. xvi. 9. But after the riot excited by Demetrius, this hope was in a measure defeated, and he soon left the city. These circumstances serve to fix the time when this epistle was written to the interval which elapsed between what is recorded in Acts xix. 22, 23. This occurred about A. D. 56 or 57. Pearson and Mill place the date in the year 57 ; Lardner, in the spring of the year 56.

It has never been doubted that Paul was the author of this epistle. It bears his name ; has internal evidence of having been written by him, and is ascribed to him by the unanimous voice of antiquity. It has been made a question, however, whether this was the *first* letter which Paul wrote to them ; or whether he had previously written an epistle to them which is now lost. This inquiry has been caused by what Paul says in 1 Cor. v. 9, " I wrote unto you in an epistle," &c. Whether he there refers to another epistle, which he wrote to them before this, and which they had disregarded ; or whether to the previous chapters of this epistle ; or whether to a letter to some other church which they had been expected to read, has been made a question. This question will be considered in the Note on that verse.

§ 4. *The Occasion on which this Epistle was written.*

It is evident that this epistle was written in reply to one which had been addressed by the church at Corinth to Paul ; 1 Cor. vii. 1, " Now concerning the things whereof ye wrote unto me," &c. That letter had been sent to Paul while at Ephesus, by the hands of Stephanas, and Fortunatus, and Achaicus, who had come to consult with him respecting the state of the church at Corinth, 1 Cor. xvi. 17, 18. In addition to this, Paul had heard various reports of certain disorders which had been introduced into the church at Corinth, and which required his attention and correction. Those disorders, it seems, as was natural, had not been mentioned in the letter which they sent to him, but he had heard of them incidentally by some members of the family of Chloe, 1 Cor. i. 11. They pertained to the following subjects. (1.) The divisions which had arisen in the church by the popularity of a teacher who had excited great disturbance, (1 Cor. i. 12, 13.) Probably this teacher was a Jew by birth, and not improbably of the sect of the Sadducees (2 Cor. xi. 22), and his teaching might have been the occasion why in the epistle Paul entered so largely into the proof of the doctrine of the resurrection from the dead, 1 Cor. xv. (2.) The Corinthians, like all other Greeks, were greatly in danger of being deluded, and carried away by a subtile philosophy, and by a dazzling eloquence, and it is not improbable that the false teacher there had taken advantage of this, and made it the occasion of exciting parties, and of creating a prejudice against Paul, and of undervaluing his authority because he had made no pretensions to these endowments. It was of importance, therefore, for Paul to show the true nature and value of their philosophy, and the spirit which should prevail in receiving the gospel, chap. i. 18—31. ii. iii. (3.) Paul's authority had been called in question as an apostle, and not improbably by the false teacher, or teachers, that had caused the parties which had been originated there. It became necessary, therefore, for him to vindicate his authority, and show by what right he had acted in organizing the church, and in the directions which he had given for its discipline and purity. chap. iv. ix. (4.) A case of incest had occurred in the church which had not been made the subject of discipline, chap. v. This case was a flagrant violation of the gospel ; and yet it is not improbable that it had been palliated, or vindicated by the false teachers ; and it is certain that it excited no shame in the church itself. Such cases were not regarded by the dissolute Corinthians as criminal. In a city dedicated to Venus, the crimes of licentiousness had been openly indulged, and this was one of the sins to which they were particularly exposed. It became necessary, therefore, for Paul to exert his apostolic authority, and to remove the offender in this case from the communion of the church, and to make him an example of the severity of Christian discipline. (5.) The Corinthians had evinced a litigious spirit, a fondness for going to law, and for bringing their causes before heathen tribunals, to the great scandal of religion, instead of endeavouring to settle their difficulties among themselves. Of this the apostle had been informed, and this called also for his authoritative interposition, chap. vi. 1—8. (6.) Erroneous views and practices had arisen, perhaps, under the influence of the false teachers, on the subject of temperance, chastity, &c. To the vices of intemperance, licentiousness, and gluttony, the Corinthian Christians from their former habits, and from the customs of their countrymen, were particularly exposed. Those vices had been judged harmless, and had been freely indulged in, and it is not improbable that the views of the apostle had been ridiculed as unnecessarily stern, and severe, and rigid. It became necessary, therefore, to correct their views, and to state the true nature of the Christian requirements, chap. vi. 8—20. (7.) The apostle having thus discussed those things of which he had incidentally heard, proceeds to notice particularly the things respecting which they had consulted him by letter. Those were, (a) *Marriage,* and the duties in regard to it in their circumstances, chap. vii. (b.) *The eating of things offered to idols,* chap. viii. In order to enforce his views of what he had said on the duty of abstaining from the use of certain food, if it was the occasion of giving offence, he shows them (chap. ix.) *that it was the great principle on which he had acted in his ministry ;* that he was not imposing on them any thing which he did not observe himself ; that though he had full authority as an apostle to insist on *a support* in preaching, yet for the sake of peace, and the prosperity of the church, he had voluntarily relinquished his *rights,* and endeavoured by all means to save some, chap. ix. By this example, he seeks to persuade them to a course of life as far as possible from a life of gluttony, and fornication, and self-indulgence, and to assure them that although they had been highly favoured, as the Jews had been also, yet like them, they might also fall, chap. x. 1—12. These principles he illustrates by a reference to their joining in feasts, and celebrations with idols, and the dangers to which they would subject themselves by so doing; and concludes that it would be *proper* in those circumstances wholly to abstain from partaking of the meat offered in sacrifice to idols if it were known to be such. This was to be done on the principle that no offence was to be given. And thus the *second* question referred to him was disposed of, chap. x. 13—33. In connection with this, and as an illustration of the principle on which he acted, and on which he wishes them to act, that of promoting mutual edification, and avoiding offence he refers (chap. xi.) to two other subjects, the one, the proper relation of the woman to the man, and the general duty of her being in subjection to him, (chap. xi. 1—16 ;) and the other, a far more important matter, the proper mode of celebrating the Lord's supper, chap. xi. 17—34. He had been led to speak of this, probably, by the discussion to which he had been invited on the subject of their *feasts,* and the discussion of *that* subject naturally led to the consideration of the much more important subject of their mode of celebrating the Lord's supper. That had been greatly abused to purposes of riot, and disorder, and abuse, which had grown directly out of their former views and habits in public festivals. Those views and habits they had transferred to the celebration of the eucharist. It became necessary, therefore, for the apostle to correct those views, to state the true design of the ordinance, to show the consequences of an improper mode of celebration, and to endeavour to reform them in their mode of observing it, chap. xi. 17—34. (c) Another subject which had probably been submitted to him in the letter was, the nature of spiritual gifts ; the design of the power of speaking with tongues, and the proper order to be observed in the church on this subject. These powers seem to have been imparted to the Corinthians in a remarkable degree ; and like most other things had been abused to the promotion of strife and ambition ; to pride in their possession, and to irregularity and disorder in their public assemblies. This whole subject the apostle discusses, (chap. xii. xiii. xiv.) He states the design of imparting this gift ; the use which should be made of it in the church, the necessity of due subordination in all the members and officers ; and in a chapter unequalled in beauty in any language, (chap. xiii.) shows the inferiority of the highest of these endowments to a kind, catholic spirit—to the prevalence of charity, and thus endeavours to allay all contentions and strifes for ascendancy, by the prevalence of the spirit of LOVE. In connection with this (chap. xiv.) he reproves the abuses which had arisen on *this* subject, as he had done on others, and seeks to repress all disorders. (8.) A very important subject, the apostle reserved to the close of the epistle— the resurrection of the dead. (chap. xv.) *Why* he chose to discuss it in this place, is not known. It is quite probable that he had not been *consulted* on this subject in the letter which had been sent to him. It is evident, however, that erroneous opinions had been entertained on the subject, and probably inculcated by the religious teachers at Corinth. The philosophic minds of the Greeks we know were much disposed to deride this doctrine (Acts xvii. 32), and in the Corinthian church it had been either called in question, or greatly perverted, chap. xv. 12. That the same body would be raised up had been denied, and the doctrine that came to be believed was, probably, simply that there would be a future state, and that the only resurrection was the resurrection of the soul from sin, and that this was past ; comp. 2 Tim. ii. 18. This subject the apostle had not before taken up, probably because he had not been consulted on it, and because it would find a more appropriate place *after* he had reproved their disorders, and answered their questions. After all those discussions, after examining all the opinions and practices that prevailed among them, it was proper *to place the great argument for the truth of the religion which they all professed on a permanent foundation, and to close the epistle by reminding them, and proving to them that the religion which they professed, and which they had so much abused, was from heaven.* The proof of this was the resurrection of the Saviour from the dead. It was indispensable to hold that in its obvious sense, and holding that, the truth of their own resurrection was demonstrated, and the error of those who denied it was apparent. (9.) Having touched this demonstration, the apostle closes the epistle (chap. xvi.) with some miscellaneous directions and salutations.

§ 5. *Divisions of the Epistle.*

THE divisions of this epistle, as of the other books of the Bible, into chapters and verses, is arbitrary, and often not happily made. See the Introduction to the Notes on the Gospels. Various divisions of the epistle have been proposed in order to present a proper analysis to the mind. The division which is submitted here is one that arises from the previous statement of the scope and design of the epistle, and will furnish the basis of my analysis. According to this view, the body of this epistle may be divided into three parts, viz.—

I. The discussion of irregularities and abuses prevailing in the church at Corinth, of which the apostle had incidentally learned by report, chap. i.—vi.

II. The discussion of various subjects which had been submitted to him in a letter from the church, and of points which grew out of those inquiries, chap. vii.—xiv.

III. The discussion of the great doctrine of the resurrection of Christ—the foundation of the hope of man—and the demonstration arising from that, that the Christian religion is true, and the hopes of Christians well founded, chap. xv. (See the " Analysis" prefixed to the Notes.)

§ 6. *The Messengers by whom this Epistle was sent to the Church at Corinth, and its success.*

It is evident that Paul felt the deepest solicitude in regard to the state of things in the church at Corinth. Apparently as soon as he had heard of their irregularities and disorders through the members of the family of Chloe (chap. i. ii.) he had sent Timothy to them, if possible to repress the growing dissensions and irregularities ; 1 Cor. iv. 17. In the mean time the church at Corinth wrote to him to ascertain his views on certain matters submitted to him (1 Cor. vii. 1), and the reception of this letter gave him occasion to enter at length into the subject of their disorders and difficulties. Yet he wrote the letter under the deepest solicitude about the manner of its reception, and its effect on the church, 2 Cor. ii. 4, " For out of much affliction and anguish of heart I wrote unto you with many tears," &c. Paul had another object in view which was dear to his heart, and which he was labouring with all diligence to promote, which was the collection which he proposed to take up for the poor and afflicted saints at Jerusalem ; see Notes, Rom. xv. 25, 26. This object he wished to press at this time on the church at Corinth ; 1 Cor. xvi. 1—4. In order, therefore, to ensure the success of his letter, and to facilitate the collection, he sent *Titus* with the letter to the church at Corinth, with instructions to have the collection ready, 2 Cor. vii. 7, 8, 13, 15. This collection, Titus was requested to finish ; 2 Cor. viii. 6. With Titus, Paul sent another brother, perhaps a member of the church at Ephesus (2 Cor. xii. 8), a man whose praise, Paul says, was in all the churches, and who had been already designated by the churches to bear the contribution to Jerusalem, 2 Cor. viii. 18, 19. By turning to Acts xxi. 29, we find it incidentally mentioned that " Trophimus an Ephesian" was with Paul in Jeru-salem, and undoubtedly this was the person here designated. This is one of the undesigned coincidences between Paul's epistle and the Acts of the Apostles, of which Dr. Paley has made so much use in his *Horæ Paulinæ* in proving the genuineness of these writings. Paul did not deem it necessary or prudent for him to go himself to Corinth, but chose to remain in Ephesus. The letter to Paul (1 Cor. vii. 1) had been brought to him by Stephanas, Fortunatus, and Achaicus (1 Cor. xvi. 17), and it is probable that they accompanied Titus and the other brother with him who bore Paul's reply to their inquiries.

The success of this letter was all that Paul could desire. It had the effect to repress their growing strifes, to restrain their disorders, to produce true repent-ance, and to remove the person who had been guilty of incest in the church. The whole church was deeply affected with his reproofs, and engaged in hearty zeal in the work of reform, 2 Cor. vii. 9—11. The authority of the apostle was recognised, and his epistle read with fear and trembling, 2 Cor. vii. 15. The act of discipline which he had required on the incestuous person was inflicted by the whole church, 2 Cor. ii. 6. The collection which he had desired (1 Cor. xvi. 1—4), and in regard to which he had boasted of their liberality to others, and ex-pressed the utmost confidence that it would be liberal (2 Cor. ix. 2, 3), was taken up agreeably to his wishes, and their disposition on the subject was such as to furnish the highest satisfaction to his mind, 2 Cor. vii. 13, 14. Of the suc-cess of his letter, however, and of their disposition to take up the collection, Paul was not apprised until he had gone into Macedonia, where Titus came to him, and gave him information of the happy state of things in the church at Corinth, 2 Cor. vii. 4—7, 13. Never was a letter more effectual than this was, and never was authority in discipline exercised in a more happy and successful way.

General Character and Structure of the Epistle.

THE general style and character of this Epistle is the same as in the other writings of Paul. See Introduction to the Epistle to the Romans. It evinces the same strong and manly style of argument and language, the same structure of sentences, the same rapidity of conception, the same overpowering force of language and thought, and the same characteristics of temper and spirit in the author. The main difference between the style and manner of this epistle, and the other epistles of Paul, arises from the scope and design of the argument. In the epistle to the Romans, his object led him to pursue a close and connected train of argumentation. In this, a large portion of the epistle is occupied with *reproof*, and it gives occasion for calling into view at once the *authority* of an apostle, and the spirit and manner in which reproof is to be administered. The reader of this epistle cannot but be struck with the fact, that it was no part of Paul's character to show indulgence to sin; that he had no design to flatter; that he neither " cloaked nor concealed transgression;" that in the most open, firm, and manly manner possible, it was his purpose to rebuke them for their disorders, and to repress their growing irregularities. At the same time, however, there is full opportunity for the display of tenderness, kindness, love, charity, and for Christian instruction an opportunity for pouring forth the deepest feelings of the human heart—an opportunity which Paul never allowed to escape unimproved. Amidst all the severity of reproof, there is the love of friendship; amidst the rebukes of an apostle, the entreaties and tears of a father. And we here contemplate Paul, not merely as the profound reasoner, not simply as a man of high intellectual endowments, but as evincing the feelings of the man, and the sympathies of the Christian.

Perhaps there is less difficulty in understanding this epistle than the epistle to the Romans. A few passages indeed have perplexed all commentators, and are to this day not understood. See chap. v. 9: xi. 10: xv. 29. But the general meaning of the epistle has been much less the subject of difference of interpretation. The reasons have probably been the following. (1.) The subjects here are more numerous, and the discussions more brief. There is, therefore, less difficulty in following the author than where the discussion is protracted, and the manner of his reasoning more complicated. (2.) The subjects themselves are far less abstruse and profound than those introduced into the epistle to the Romans. There is, therefore, less liability to misconception. (3.) The epistle has never been made the subject of theological warfare. No system of theology has been built on it, and no attempt made to press it into the service of abstract dogmas. It is mostly of a practical character, and there has been, therefore, less room for contention in regard to its meaning. (4.) No false and unfounded theories of philosophy have been attached to this epistle, as have been to the epistle to the Romans. Its simple sense, therefore, has been more obvious, and no small part of the difficulties in the interpretation of that epistle are wanting in this. (5.) The apostle's design has somewhat varied his style. There are fewer complicated sentences, and fewer parentheses, less that is abrupt and broken, and elliptical, less that is rapid, mighty, and overpowering in argument. We see the point of a reproof at once, but we are often greatly embarrassed in a complicated argument. The xvth chapter, however, for closeness and strength of argumentation, for beauty of diction, for tenderness of pathos, and for commanding and overpowering eloquence, is probably unsurpassed by any other part of the writings of Paul, and unequalled by any other composition. (6.) It may be added, that there is less in this epistle that opposes the native feelings of the human heart, and that humbles the pride of the human intellect, than in the epistle to the Romans. One great difficulty in interpreting that epistle has been that the doctrines relate to those high subjects that rebuke the pride of man, demand prostration before his Sovereign, require the submission of the understanding and the heart to God's high claims, and throw down every form of self-righteousness. While substantially the same features will be found in all the writings of Paul, yet his purpose in this epistle led him less to dwell on those topics than in the epistle to the Romans. The result is, that the *heart* more readily acquiesces in these doctrines and reproofs, and the general strain of this epistle; and as the *heart* of man has usually more agency in the interpretation of the Bible than the understanding, the obstacles in the way of a correct exposition of this epistle are proportionably fewer than in the epistle to the Romans.

The same spirit, however, which is requisite in understanding the epistle to the Romans, is demanded here. In all Paul's epistles, as in all the Bible, a spirit of candour, humility, prayer, and industry is required. The knowledge of God's truth is to be acquired only by toil, and candid investigation. The mind that is filled with prejudice is rarely enlightened. The proud, unhumbled spirit seldom receives benefit from reading the Bible, or any other book. He acquires the most complete, and the most profound knowledge of the doctrines of Paul, and of the Book of God in general, who comes to the work of interpretation with the most humble heart; and the deepest sense of his dependence on the aid of that Spirit by whom originally the Bible was inspired. For "the meek will he guide in judgment, and the meek will he teach his way," Ps. xxv. 9.

EPISTLE TO THE CORINTHIANS

CHAPTER 1.

PAUL, called *a to be* an apostle of Jesus Christ through the

a Rom. 1. 1.

will of God, and Sosthenes *b our* brother.

2 Unto the church of God which

b Mat. 12. 38.

CHAPTER I.

1. *Paul, called to be an apostle.* See Notes, Rom. i. 1. ¶ *Through the will of God.* Not by human appointment, or authority, but in accordance with the will of God, and his command. That *will* was made known to him by the special revelation granted to him at his conversion, and call to the apostleship; Acts ix. Paul often refers to the fact that he had received a direct commission from God, and that he did not act on his own authority; comp. Gal. i. 11, 12; 1 Cor. ix. 1—6; 2 Cor. xi. 22—33; xii. 1—12. There was a special reason why he commenced this epistle by referring to the fact that he was divinely called to the apostleship. It arose from the fact that his apostolic authority had been called in question by the false teachers at Corinth. That this was the case is apparent from the general strain of the epistle, from some particular expressions (2 Cor. x. 8—10); and from the fact that he is at so much pains throughout the two epistles to establish his divine commission. ¶ *And Sosthenes.* Sosthenes is mentioned in Acts xviii. 17, as "the chief ruler of the synagogue" at Corinth. He is there said to have been beaten by the Greeks before the judgment-seat of Gallio because he was a Jew, and because he had joined with the other Jews in arraigning Paul, and had thus produced disturbance in the city; see Note on this place. It is evident that at that time he was not a Christian. When he was converted, or why he left Corinth and was now with Paul at Ephesus, is unknown. Why Paul associated him

with himself in writing this epistle is not known. It is evident that Sosthenes was not an apostle, nor is there any reason to think that he was inspired. Some circumstances are known to have existed respecting Paul's manner of writing to the churches, which may explain it. (1.) He was accustomed to employ an amanuensis or scribe in writing his epistles, and the amanuensis frequently expressed his concurrence or approbation in what the apostle had indicted; see Note, Rom. xvi. 22, comp. Col. iv. 18 "*The salutation* by the hand of Paul," 2 Thess. iii. 17; 1 Cor. xvi. 21. It is possible that Sosthenes might have been employed by Paul for this purpose. (2.) Paul not unfrequently associated others with himself in writing his letters to the churches, himself claiming authority as an apostle; and the others expressing their concurrence; 2 Cor. i. 1. Thus in Gal. i. 1, "all the brethren" which were with him, are mentioned as united with him in addressing the churches of Galatia; Phil. i. 1; Col. i. 1; 1 Thess. i. 1. (3.) Sosthenes was well known at Corinth. He had been the chief ruler of the synagogue there. His conversion would, therefore, excite a deep interest, and it is not improbable that he had been conspicuous as a preacher. All these circumstances would render it proper that Paul should associate him with himself in writing this letter. It would be bringing in the testimony of one well known as concurring with the views of the apostle, and tend much to conciliate those who were disaffected towards him.

is at Corinth, *a* to them *b* that are sanctified *c* in Christ Jesus, called *d* *to be* saints, with all that in

a Acts 18. 1.　　b Jude 1.　　c John 17.19.

2. *Unto the church of God which is at Corinth.* For an account of the time and manner in which the church was established in Corinth, see the Introduction, and Notes on Acts xviii. 1—17. The church is called " the church of God," because it has been founded by his agency, and was devoted to his service. It is worthy of remark, that although great disorders had been introduced into that church; though there were separations and erroneous doctrines; though there were some who gave evidence that they were not sincere Christians, yet the apostle had no hesitation in applying to them the name of a church of God. ¶ *To them that are sanctified.* To those who are made holy. This does not refer to the profession of holiness, but implies that they were *in fact* holy. The word means that they were *separated* from the mass of heathens around them, and devoted to God and his cause. Though the word used here (ἡγιασμένοις) has this idea of *separation* from the mass around them, yet it is separation on account of their being *in fact*, and not in profession merely, different from others, and truly devoted to God; see Note, Rom. i. 7. ¶ *In Christ Jesus.* That is, *by* (ἐν) the agency of Christ. It was by his authority, his power, and his Spirit, that they had been separated from the mass of heathens around them, and devoted to God; comp. John xvii. 19. ¶ *Called* to be *saints.* The word *saints* does not differ materially from the word *sanctified* in the former part of the verse. It means those who are *separated* from the world, and set apart to God as holy. The idea which Paul introduces here is, that they became such because they were *called* to be such. The idea in the former part of the verse is, that this was done "by Christ Jesus;" here he says that it was because they were *called* to this privilege. He doubtless means to say that it was not by any native tendency

every place call *e* upon the name of Jesus Christ our Lord, both theirs and ours:

d 2 Tim.1.9; 1 Pet.1.15.　　e 2 Tim.2.22.

in themselves to holiness, but because God had called them to it. And this calling does not refer merely to an external invitation, but it was that which was made *effectual* in their case, or that on which the fact of their being saints could be predicated; comp. ver. 9; see 2 Tim. i. 9; " Who hath saved us, and called us with an holy calling, not according to our works, but according to his own purpose and grace," &c.; 1 Pet. i. 15; Note, Rom. i. 6, 7; viii. 28; Eph. iv. 1; 1 Tim. vi. 12; 1 Pet. ii. 9. ¶ *With all*, &c. This expression shows, (1.) That Paul had the same feelings of attachment to all Christians in every place; and (2.) That he expected that this epistle would be read, not only by the church at Corinth, but also by other churches. That this was the uniform intention of the apostle in regard to his epistles, is apparent from other places; comp. 1 Thess. v. 27; " I charge you by the Lord that this epistle be read unto all the holy brethren;" Col. iv. 16; " And when this epistle is read among you, cause that it be read also in the church of the Laodiceans." It is evident that Paul expected that his epistles would obtain circulation among the churches; and it was morally certain that they would be soon transcribed, and be extensively read.—The ardent feelings of Paul embraced all Christians in every nation. He knew nothing of the narrowness of exclusive attachment to *sect.* His heart was full of love, and he loved, as we should, all who bore the Christian name, and who evinced the Christian spirit. ¶ *Call upon the name of Jesus Christ.* To call upon *the name* of any person, in Scripture language, is to call on the person himself; comp. John iii. 18; Note, Acts iv. 12. The expression "*to call upon the name*" (ἐπικαλουμένοις), to invoke the name, implies worship, and prayer; and proves, (1.) That the Lord Jesus is an object of worship; and (2.) That

3 Grace *a be* unto you, and peace from God our Father, and *from* the Lord Jesus Christ.

4 I thank *b* my God always on your behalf, for the grace of

a 1 Pet.1.2. *b* Rom.1.8.

God which is given you by Jesus Christ;

5 That in every thing ye are enriched by him, in all utterance, *c* and *in* all knowledge;

c 2 Cor.8.7.

---

one characteristic of the early Christians, by which they were known and distinguished, was their calling upon the name of the Lord Jesus, or their offering worship to him. That it implies worship, see Note on Acts vii. 59; and that the early Christians called on Christ by prayer, and were distinguished by that, see the Note on Acts vii. 50, and compare Note, Acts i. 24, also Acts ii. 21; ix. 13; xxii. 16; 2 Tim. ii. 22. ¶ *Both theirs and ours.* The Lord of all—both Jews and Gentiles—of *all* who profess themselves Christians, of whatever country or name they might have originally been. Difference of nation or birth gives no pre-eminence in the kingdom of Christ, but all are on a level, having a common Lord and Saviour; comp. Eph. iv. 5.

3. *Grace be unto you*, &c.; see Note, Rom. i. 7.

4. *I thank my God*, &c. No small part of this epistle is occupied with reproofs for the disorders which had arisen in the church at Corinth. Before proceeding, however, to the specific statement of those disorders (ver. 10, seq.), the apostle *commends* them for the attainments which they had really made in divine knowledge, and thus shows that he was disposed to concede to them all that he could. It was no part of the disposition of Paul to withhold commendation where it was due. On the contrary, as he was disposed to be faithful in reproving the errors of Christians, he was no less disposed to commend them when it could be done; comp. Note, Rom. i. 8. A willingness to commend those who do well is as much in accordance with the gospel, as a disposition to reprove where it is deserved; and a minister, or a parent, may frequently do as decided good by judicious commendation as by reproof, and much more than by fault-finding and harsh

crimination. ¶ *On your behalf.* In respect to you; that God has conferred these favours on you. ¶ *For the grace of God.* On account of the favours which God has bestowed on you through the Lord Jesus. Those favours are specified in the following verses. For the meaning of the word *grace*, see Note, Rom. i. 7.

5. *That in every thing.* In every respect, or in regard to all the favours conferred on any of his people. You have been distinguished by him in all those respects in which he blesses his own children. ¶ *Ye are enriched by him;* comp. Note, Rom. ii. 4. The meaning of this expression is, "you *abound* in these things; they are conferred abundantly upon you." By the use of this word, the apostle intends doubtless to denote *the fact* that these blessings had been conferred on them abundantly; and also that this was a *valuable endowment*, so as to be properly called *a treasure*. The mercies of God are not only conferred abundantly on his people, but they are a bestowment of inestimable value; comp. 2 Cor. vi. 10. ¶ *In all utterance.* With the power of speaking various languages ($\grave{\epsilon}\nu$ $\pi\alpha\nu\tau\grave{\iota}$ $\lambda\acute{o}\gamma\psi$). That this power was conferred on the church at Corinth, and that it was highly valued by them, is evident from chap. xiv ; comp. 2 Cor. viii. 7. The power of speaking those languages the apostle regarded as a subject of thanksgiving, as it was a proof of the divine favour to them; see chap. xiv. 5, 22, 39. ¶ *And in all knowledge.* In the knowledge of divine truth. They had understood the doctrines which they had heard, and had intelligently embraced them. This was not true of *all* of them, but it was of the body of the church; and the hearty commendation and thanksgiving of the apostle for these favours, laid the foundation for the remarks which he

6 Even as the testimony of Christ was confirmed in you.

7 So that ye come behind in

a Tit.2.13.   1 *revelation.*

no gift; waiting *a* for the [1] coming of our Lord Jesus Christ:

8 Who shall also confirm *b* you

b 1 Thess.3.13; 5.23,24.

had subsequently to make, and would tend to conciliate their minds, and dispose them to listen attentively, even to the language of reproof.

6. *Even as.* Καϑὼς. The force of this expression seems to be this, "The gospel of Christ was at first established among you by means of the miraculous endowments of the Holy Ghost. Those same endowments are still continued among you, and *now* furnish evidence of the divine favour, and of the truth of the gospel to you, *even as—i. e.* in the same measure as they did when the gospel was first preached." The power to speak with tongues, &c.; (chap.xiv.) would be a *continued miracle,* and would be a demonstration to them then of the truth of Christianity as it was at first. ¶ *The testimony of Christ.* The gospel. It is here called "the testimony of Christ," because it bore witness to Christ—to his divine nature, his miracles, his Messiahship, his character, his death, &c. The message of the gospel consists in bearing witness to Christ and his work; see chap. xv. 1—4; 2 Tim. i. 8. ¶ *Was confirmed.* Was established, or proved. It was proved to be divine, by the miraculous attestations of the Holy Spirit. It was confirmed, or made certain to their souls by the agency of the Holy Spirit, sealing it on their hearts. The word translated *confirmed* (ἐβεβαιώϑη), is used in the sense of establishing, confirming, or demonstrating by miracles, &c.; in Mark xvi. 20; comp. Heb. xiii. 9; Phil. i. 7. ¶ *In you* (ἐν ὑμῖν). Among you as a people, or in your hearts. Perhaps the apostle intends to include both. The gospel had been established among them by the demonstrations of the agency of the Spirit in the gift of tongues, and had at the same time taken deep root in their hearts, and was exerting a practical influence on their lives.

7. *So that.* God has so abundantly endowed you with his favours. ¶ *Ye come behind* (ὑστερεῖσϑαι). You are

not wanting, or deficient. The word is usually applied to destitution, want, or poverty; and the declaration here is synonymous with what he had said, ver. 5, that they abounded in every thing. ¶ *In no gift.* In no favour, or gracious endowment. The word used here (χαρίσμα), does not refer necessarily to extraordinary and miraculous endowments, but includes also *all* the kindnesses of God towards them in producing peace of mind, constancy, humility, &c. And the apostle meant evidently to say that they possessed, in rich abundance, all those endowments which were bestowed on Christians. ¶ *Waiting for.* Expecting, or looking for this coming with glad and anxious desire. This was, certainly, *one* of the endowments to which he referred, to wit, that they had grace given them earnestly to desire, and to wait for the second appearing of the Lord Jesus. An earnest wish to see him, and a confident expectation and firm belief that he will return, is an evidence of a high state of piety. It demands strong faith, and it will do much to elevate the feelings above the world, and to keep the mind in a state of peace. ¶ *The coming,* &c. Gr. The revelation—(τὴν ἀποκάλυψιν)—the manifestation of the Son of God. That is, waiting for his return to judge the world, and for his approbation of his people in that day. The earnest expectation of the Lord Jesus became one of the marks of early Christian piety. This return was promised by the Saviour to his anxious disciples, when he was about to leave them; John xiv. 3. The promise was renewed when he ascended to heaven; Acts i. 11. It became the settled hope and expectation of Christians that he would return; Tit. ii. 13; 2 Pet. iii 12; Heb. ix. 28. And with the earnest prayer that he would quickly come, John closes the volume of inspiration; Rev. xxii. 20, 21.

8. *Who shall also confirm you.* Who

unto the end, *that ye may be* blameless in the day of our Lord Jesus Christ:

shall establish you in the hopes of the gospel. He shall make you *firm* (βεβαιώσει) amidst all your trials, and all the efforts which may be made to shake your faith, and to remove you from that firm foundation on which you now rest. ¶ *Unto the end.* That is, to the coming of the Lord Jesus Christ. He would keep them to the end of life in the path of holiness, so that at the coming of the Lord Jesus they might be found blameless; comp. John xiii. 1. The sense is, that they should be kept, and should not be suffered to fall away and perish;—and this is one of the many places which express the strong confidence of Paul that those who are true Christians shall be preserved unto everlasting life; comp. Phil. i. 6. ¶ *That ye may be blameless,* The word rendered *blameless* (ἀνεγκλήτους;) does not mean perfect, but properly denotes those against whom there is no charge of crime; who are unaccused, and against whom there is no ground of accusation. Here it does not mean that they were personally perfect, but that God would so keep them, and enable them to evince a Christian character, as to give evidence that they were his friends, and completely escape condemnation in the last day, see Notes on Rom. viii. 39, 34. There is no man who has not his faults; no Christian who is not conscious of imperfection; but it is the design of God so to keep his people, and so to justify and sanctify them through the Lord Jesus, that the church may be presented "a glorious church, without spot or wrinkle" (Eph. v. 37) in the day of judgment. ¶ *In the day, &c.* In the day when the Lord Jesus shall come to judge the world; and which will be called *his* day, because it will be the day in which *he* will be the great and conspicuous object, and which is especially appointed to glorify him; see 2 Thess. i. 10, "Who shall come to be glorified in his saints, and to be admired in all them that believe."

9 God *is* faithful, by whom ye were called unto the fellowship *a* of his Son Jesus Christ our Lord.

a 1 John 1.3.

9. *God* is *faithful.* That is, God is true, and constant, and will adhere to his promises. He will not deceive. He will not promise, and then fail to perform; he will not commence any thing which he will not perfect and finish. The object of Paul in introducing the idea of the *faithfulness* of God here, is to show the reason for believing that the Christians at Corinth would be kept unto everlasting life. The evidence that they will persevere depends on the fidelity of God; and the argument of the apostle is, that as they had been called *by him* into the fellowship of his Son, his faithfulness of character would render it certain that they would be kept to eternal life. The same idea he has presented in Phil. i. 6, "Being confident of this very thing, that he which hath begun a good work in you, will also perform it until the day of Jesus Christ." ¶ *Ye were called.* The word "called" here does not refer merely to *an invitation* or an *offer of life,* but to the effectual influence which had been put forth; which had inclined them to embrace the gospel Note, Rom. viii. 30; ix. 12; see Mark ii 17; Luke v. 32; Gal. i. 6; v. 8, 13; Eph. i. 4; Col. iii. 15. In this sense the word often occurs in the Scriptures, and is designed to denote a power, or influence that goes forth *with* the external invitation, and that makes it effectual. That power is the agency of the Holy Spirit. ¶ *Unto the fellowship of his Son.* To participate with his Son Jesus Christ; to be *partakers* with him; see Notes, John xv. 1—8. Christians participate with Christ, (1.) In his feelings and views; Rom. viii. 9. (2.) In his trials and sufferings, being subjected to temptations and trials similar to his; 1 Pet. iv. 13, "But rejoice, inasmuch as ye are partakers of Christ's sufferings;" Col. i. 24; Phil. iii. 10. (3.) In his *heirship* to the inheritance and glory which awaits him; Rom. viii. 17, " And if children, then heirs, heirs of God and joint heirs with Christ;" I

10 Now I beseech you, brethren, by the name of our Lord Jesus Christ, *a* that ye all speak the same thing, and *that* there be

a John 17.19.

Pet. i. 4. (4.) In his triumph in the resurrection and future glory; Mat. xix. 28, " Ye which have followed me, in the regeneration when the Son of man shall sit on the throne of his glory, ye also shall sit upon twelve thrones, judging the twelve tribes of Israel;" John xiv. 19, " Because I live, ye shall live also;" Rev. iii. 21, " To him that overcometh will I grant to sit with me in my throne, even as I also overcame, and am set down with my Father in his throne."

[Immediately on our union to Christ, we have fellowship with him, in all the blessings of his purchase. This communion or fellowship *with* him is the necessary result of our union *to* him. On the saint's union to Christ, see supplementary Note on Rom. viii. 10. page 176.]

From all this, the argument of the apostle is, that as they *partake* with Christ in these high privileges, and hopes, and promises, they will be kept by a faithful God unto eternal life. God is faithful to his Son; and will be faithful to all who are united to him. The argument for the perseverance of the saints is, therefore, sure.

10. *Now I beseech you, brethren.* In this verse the apostle enters on the discussion respecting the irregularities and disorders in the church at Corinth, of which he had incidentally heard; see ver. 11. The first of which he had incidentally learned, was that which pertained to the divisions and strifes which had arisen in the church. The consideration of this subject occupies him to ver. 17; and as those divisions had been caused by the influence of philosophy, and the ambition for distinction, and the exhibition of popular eloquence among the Corinthian teachers, this fact gives occasion to him to discuss that subject at length (chap. i. 17—31; xi.); in which he shows that the gospel did not depend for its success on the reasonings of philosophy, or the persuasions of eloquence. This part of the subject he commences with the language of entreaty. " I beseech you, brethren"—the language of affectionate exhortation rather than of stern command. Addressing them as his brethren, as members of the same family with himself, he conjures them to take all proper measures to avoid the evils of schism and of strife. ¶ *By the name.* By the authority of his name; or from reverence for him as the common Lord of all. ¶ *Of our Lord Jesus Christ.* The reasons why Paul thus appeals to his name and authority here, may be the following. (1.) Christ should be regarded as the supreme head and leader of all his church. It was improper, therefore, that the church should be divided into portions, and its different parts enlisted under different banners. (2.) " The whole family in heaven and earth should be named" after him (Eph. iii. 15), and should *not* be named after inferior and subordinate teachers. The reference to "the venerable and endearing name of Christ here, stands beautifully and properly opposed to the various human names under which they were so ready to enlist themselves."—*Doddridge.* " There is scarce a word or expression that he [Paul] makes use of, but with relation and tendency to his present main purpose; as here, intending to abolish the names of leaders they had distinguished themselves by, he beseeches them by the name of Christ, a form that I do not remember he elsewhere uses."—*Locke.* (3.) The prime and leading thing which Christ had enjoined on his church was *union* and mutual love (John xiii. 34; xv. 17), and for this he had most earnestly prayed in his memorable prayer; John xvii. 21—23. It was well for Paul thus to appeal to the name of Christ— the sole head and Lord of his church. and the friend of union, and thus to rebuke the divisions and strifes which had arisen at Corinth. ¶ *That ye all speak the same thing.* " That ye hold the same doctrine."—*Locke.* This exhortation evidently refers to their holding and expressing the same reli-

no [1] divisions among you; but *that* ye be perfectly joined together in the same mind and in the same judgment.

1 *schisms.*

gious sentiments, and is designed to rebuke that kind of contention and strife which is evinced where different opinions are held and expressed. To "speak the same thing" stands opposed to speaking different and conflicting things; or to controversy, and although *perfect* uniformity of opinion cannot be expected among men on the subject of religion any more than on other subjects, yet on the great and fundamental doctrines of Christianity, Christians may be agreed; on all points in which they differ they may evince a good spirit; and on all subjects they may *express* their sentiments in the language of the Bible, and thus "speak the same thing." ¶ *And* that *there be no divisions among you.* Greek, σχίσματα, *schisms.* No divisions into contending parties and sects. The church was to be regarded as one and indivisible, and not to be rent into different factions, and ranged under the banners of different leaders; comp. John ix. 16; 1 Cor. xi. 18; xii. 25. ¶ *But that ye be perfectly joined together* (ἦτε δὲ κατηρτισμένοι). The word here used and rendered "perfectly joined together," denotes properly to restore, mend, or repair that which is rent or disordered (Mat. iv 21, Mark i. 19), to amend or correct that which is *morally* evil and erroneous (Gal. vi. 1), to render perfect or complete (Luke vi. 40), to fit or adapt any thing to its proper place so that it shall be complete in all its parts, and harmonious, (Heb. xi. 5); and thence to compose and settle controversies, to produce harmony and order. The apostle here evidently desires that they should be united in feeling; that every member of the church should occupy his appropriate place, as every member of a well proportioned body, or part of a machine has its appropriate place and use; see his wishes more fully expressed in chap. xii. 12—31. ¶ *In the same mind* (νοΐ); see Rom. xv. 5. This cannot mean that they

11 For it hath been declared unto me of you, my brethren, by them *which are of the house* of Chloe, that there are contentions among you.

were to be united in precisely the same shades of opinion, which is impossible —but that their minds were to be disposed towards each other with mutual good will, and that they should live in harmony. The word here rendered *mind*, denotes not merely the intellect itself, but that which is *in* the mind—the thoughts, counsels, plans; Rom. xi. 34; xiv. 5; 1 Cor. ii. 16; Col. ii. 18. *Bretschneider.* ¶*And in the same judgment* (γνώμη). This word properly denotes science, or knowledge; opinion, or sentiment; and sometimes, as here, the purpose of the mind, or *will.* The sentiment of the whole is, that in their understandings and their volitions, they should be united and kindly disposed towards each other. Union of feeling is possible even where men differ much in their views of things. They may love each other much, even where they do not see alike. They may give each other credit for honesty and sincerity, and may be willing to suppose that others *may be right,* and *are honest* even where their own views differ. The foundation of Christian union is not so much laid in uniformity of intellectual perception as in right feelings of the heart. And the proper way to produce union in the church of God, is not to *begin* by attempting to equalize all *intellects* on the bed of Procrustes, but to produce supreme love to God, and elevated and pure Christian love to all who bear the image and the name of the Redeemer.

11. *For it hath been declared unto me.* Of the contentions existing in the church at Corinth, it is evident that they had not informed him in the letter which they had sent; see chap. vii. 1, comp. the Introduction. He had incidentally heard of their contentions. ¶ *My brethren.* A token of affectionate regard, evincing his love for them, and his deep interest in their welfare, even when he administered a needed rebuke. ¶ Of the house *of*

12 Now this I say, that every one of you saith, I am of Paul; and I of Apollos; *a* and I of Cephas; *b* and I of Christ.

a Acts 19.1.

b John 1.42.

Chloe. Of the family of Chloe. It is most probable that Chloe was a member of the church at Corinth, some of whose family had been at Ephesus when Paul was, and had given him information of the state of things there. Who those members of her family were, is unknown. Grotius conjectures that they were Stephanas, Fortunatus, and Achaicus, mentioned in chap. xvi. 17, who brought the letter of the church at Corinth to Paul. But of this there is no certain evidence; perhaps not much probability. If the information had been obtained from them, it is probable that it would have been put in the letter which they bore. The probability is that Paul had received this information before they arrived.

12. *Now this I say.* This is what I mean; or, I give this as an instance of the contentions to which I refer. ¶ *That every one of you saith.* That you are divided into different factions, and ranged under different leaders. The word translated "that" (ὅτι) might be translated here, *because,* or *since,* as giving a reason for his affirming (ver. 11) that there were contentions there. "Now I say that there are contentions, *because* you are ranged under different leaders," &c.—*Calvin.* ¶ *I am of Paul.* It has been doubted whether Paul meant to affirm that the parties had actually taken the names which he here specifies, or whether he uses these names as illustrations, or suppositions, to show the absurdity of their ranging themselves under different leaders. Many of the ancient interpreters supposed that Paul was unwilling to specify the real names of the false teachers and leaders of the parties, and that he used these names simply by way of illustration. This opinion was grounded chiefly on what he says in chap. iv. 6, "And these things, brethren, I have *in a figure* transferred to myself and to Apollos for your sakes," &c. But in this place Paul is not referring so particularly to the factions or parties existing in the church, as he is to the necessity of modesty and humility; and in order to enforce this, he refers to himself and Apollos to show that even those most highly favoured should have a low estimate of their importance, since all *their* success depends on God; see chap. iii. 4—6. It can scarcely be doubted that Paul here meant to say that there were parties existing in the church at Corinth, who were called by the names of himself, of Apollos, of Cephas, and of Christ. This is the natural construction; and this was evidently the information which he had received by those who were of the family of Chloe. *Why* the parties were ranged under *these* leaders, however, can be only a matter of conjecture. Lightfoot suggests that the church at Corinth was composed partly of Jews and partly of Gentiles; see Acts xviii. The Gentile converts, he supposes, would range themselves under Paul and Apollos as their leaders; and the Jewish under Peter and Christ. Paul was the apostle to the Gentiles, and Peter particularly the apostle to the Jews (Gal. ii. 7); and this circumstance might give rise to the division. Apollos succeeded Paul in Achaia, and laboured successfully there; see Acts xviii. 27, 28. These two original parties might be again sub-divided. A part of those who adhered to Paul and Apollos might regard Saul with chief veneration, as being the founder of the church as the instrument of *their* conversion, as the chief apostle, as signally pure in his doctrine and manner; and a part might regard Apollos as the instrument of *their* conversion, and as being distinguished for eloquence. It is evident that the main reason why Apollos was regarded as the head of a faction was on account of his extraordinary eloquence, and it is probable that his followers might seek particularly to imitate him in the graces of popular elocution. ¶ *And I of Cephas,* Peter; comp. John i. 42. He was regarded particularly as the

13 Is Christ divided? was Paul crucified for you, or were ye baptized in the name of Paul?

apostle to the Jews; Gal. ii. 7. He had his own peculiarity of views in teaching, and it is probable that his teaching was not regarded as entirely harmonious with that of Paul; see Gal. ii. 11—17. Paul had everywhere among the Gentiles taught that it was not necessary to observe the ceremonial laws of Moses; and, it is probable, that Peter was regarded by the Jews as the advocate of the contrary doctrine. Whether Peter had been at Corinth is unknown. If not, they had heard of his name, and character; and those who had come from Judea had probably reported him as teaching a doctrine on the subject of the observance of Jewish ceremonies unlike that of Paul. ¶ *And I of Christ.* Why this sect professed to be the followers of Christ, is not certainly known. It probably arose from one of the two following causes. (1.) Either that they had been in Judea and had seen the Lord Jesus, and thus regarded themselves as particularly favoured and distinguished: or, (2.) More probably because they refused to call themselves by any inferior leader, and wished to regard Christ alone as their head, and possibly prided themselves on the belief that they were more conformed to him than the other sects.

13. *Is Christ divided?* Paul, in this verse, proceeds to show the impropriety of their divisions and strifes. His general argument is, that Christ alone ought to be regarded as their head and leader, and that his claims, arising from his crucifixion, and acknowledged by their baptism, were so pre-eminent that they could not be divided, and the honours due to him should not be rendered to any other. The apostle, therefore, asks, with strong emphasis, whether Christ was to be regarded as divided? Whether this single supreme head and leader of the church, had become the head of different contending factions? The strong absurdity of supposing that, showed the impropriety of their ranging themselves under different banners and leaders. ¶ *Was Paul cru-*

cified for you? This question implies that the crucifixion of Christ had an influence in saving them which the sufferings of no other one *could* have, and that those sufferings were in fact the peculiarity which distinguished the work of Christ, and rendered it of so much value. The atonement was the grand, crowning work of the Lord Jesus. It was through this that *all* the Corinthian Christians had been renewed and pardoned. That work was so pre-eminent that it could not have been performed by another. And as they had *all* been saved by that alone; as they were alike dependent on his merits for salvation, it was improper that they should be rent into contending factions, and ranged under different leaders. If there is any thing that will recall Christians of different names and of contending sects from the heat of strife, it is the recollection of the fact that they have been purchased by the same blood, and that the same Saviour died to redeem them all. If this fact could be kept before their minds, it would put an end to angry strife everywhere in the church, and produce universal Christian love. ¶ *Or were ye baptized in the name of Paul.* Or, *into,* or *unto* the name of Paul; see Note, Mat. xxviii. 19. To be baptized *into,* or *unto* any one is to be devoted to him, to receive and acknowledge him as a teacher, professing to receive his rules, and to be governed by his authority.—*Locke.* Paul here solemnly reminds them that their *baptism* was an argument why they should not range themselves under different leaders. By that, they had been solemnly and entirely devoted to the service of the only Saviour. "Did I ever," was the implied language of Paul, "baptize in my own name? Did I ever pretend to organize a sect, announcing myself as a leader? Have not I always directed you to that Saviour into whose name and service you have been baptized?" It is remarkable here, that Paul refers to himself, and not to Apollos or Peter.

14 I thank God that I baptized none of you but Crispus *a* and Gaius; *b*

a Acts 18.8.   *b* Rom.16.23; 3 John 1,&c.

He does not insinuate that the claims of Apollos or Peter were to be disparaged, or their talents and influence to be undervalued, as a jealous rival would have done; but he numbers himself first, and alone, as having no claims to be regarded as a religious leader among them, or the founder of a sect. Even he, the founder of the church, and their spiritual father, had never desired or intended that they should call themselves by *his* name; and he thus showed the impropriety of their adopting the name of *any* man as the leader of a sect.

14. *I thank God*, &c. Why Paul did not himself baptize, see in ver. 17. To him it was now a subject of grateful reflection that he had *not* done it. He had not given any occasion for the suspicion that he had intended to set himself up as a leader of a sect or party. ¶ *But Crispus.* Crispus had been the chief ruler of the synagogue at Corinth; Acts xviii. 8. ¶ *And Gaius.* Gaius resided at Corinth, and at his house Paul resided when he wrote the epistle to the Romans; Rom. xvi. 23. It is also possible that the third epistle of John was directed to this man; see 3 John 1. And if so, then probably Diotrephes (3 John 9), who is mentioned as one who loved "to have the pre-eminence," had been one cause of the difficulties at Corinth. The other persons at Corinth had been probably baptized by Silas and Timothy.

15. *Lest any should say.* Lest any of those who had been baptized should pervert his design, and say that Paul had baptized them unto himself; or, lest any others should, with any appearance of truth, say that he had sought to make disciples to himself. The Ethiopic version renders this, "that ye should not say we were baptized in his name." Many of the ancient MSS. read this, "lest any should say that *ye were baptized* into my name." *Mill.*

15 Lest any should say that I had baptized in mine own name.
16 And I baptized also the

16. *And I baptized also the household.* The family. Whether there were any infants in the family, does not appear. It is certain that the family was among the first converts to Christianity in Achaia, and that it had evinced great zeal in aiding those who were Christians; see chap. xvi. 15.—From the manner in which Paul mentions this, it is probable that Stephanas did not reside at Corinth when he was baptized, though he might have subsequently removed there. "I baptized none *of you* (ver. 14.)—*i. e.* none of those who permanently dwelt at Corinth, or who were members of the original church there, but Crispus and Gaius—but I baptized also the family of Stephanas, *now* of your number."—Or it may mean, "I baptized none of you *who are adult members of the church*, but Crispus and Gaius, though I also baptized the *family* of Stephanas." If this be the true interpretation, then it forms an argument to prove that Paul practised household baptism, or the baptism of the families of those who were themselves believers. Or the expression may simply indicate a *recollection* of the true circumstances of the case—a species of *correction* of the statement in ver. 14, "I recollect now also that I baptized the family of Stephanas." ¶ *Household* (οἶκον). The house; the family. The word comprises the whole family, including adults, domestics, slaves, and children. It includes, (1.) The *men* in a house, (Acts vii. 10; 1 Tim. iii. 4, 5, 12;) (2.) *Domestics*, (Acts x. 2; xi. 14; xvi. 15. 31; 1 Tim. iii. 4;) (3.) *The family* in general; Luke x. 5; xvi. 27. *Bretschneider.* It was the custom, doubtless, for the apostles to baptize the entire *household*, whatever might be the age, including domestics, slaves, and children. The head of a family gave up the entire *household* to God.

[That adult domestics and slaves were baptized without *personal* profession or other

household of Stephanas; *a* besides, I know not whether I baptized any other.

17 For Christ sent me not to

baptize, but to preach the gospel : not with wisdom *b* of ¹ words, lest the cross of Christ should be made of none effect.

a chap. 16.15,17.

b chap. 2.1,4,13.   1 or *speech.*

evidence of faith, is incredible. The word *αικος* indeed includes domestics as well as children, out while the latter must have been admitted on the profession of their parents, it is reasonable to suppose that the former would be received solely on their own.]

¶ *Of Stephanas.* Who Stephanas was, is not known. The Greek commentators say that he was the jailer of Philippi, who, after he had been baptized (Acts xvi. 33), removed with his family to Corinth. But of this there is no certain evidence. ¶ *Besides.* Besides these. ¶ *I know not,* &c. I do not know whether I baptized any others who are *now* members of that church. Paul would, doubtless, recollect that he had baptized others in other places, but he is speaking here particularly of Corinth This is not to be urged as an argument against the *inspiration* of Paul, for (1.) It was not the design of inspiration to free the memory from defect in ordinary transactions, or in those things which were not to be received for the instruction of the church; (2.) The meaning of Paul may simply be, "I know not who of the original members of the church at Corinth may have removed, or who may have died; I know not who may have removed *to* Corinth from other places where I have preached and baptized, and consequently I cannot know whether I may not have baptized *some* others of your present number." It is evident, however, that if he had baptized any others, the number was small.

17. *For Christ sent me not to baptize.* That is, not to baptize as my main business. Baptism was not his principal employment, though he had a commission in common with others to administer the ordinance, and occasionally did it. The same thing was true of the Saviour, that he did not personally baptize, John iv. 2. It is probable that the business of baptism

was intrusted to the ministers of the church of inferior talents, or to those who were connected with the churches permanently, and not to those who were engaged chiefly in travelling from place to place. The reasons of this may have been, (1.) That which Paul here suggests, that if the apostles had themselves baptized, it might have given occasion to strifes, and the formation of parties, as those who had been baptized by the apostles might claim some superiority over those who were not. (2.) It is probable that the rite of baptism was preceded or followed by a course of instruction adapted to it, and as the apostles were travelling from place to place, this could be better intrusted to those who were to be with them as their ordinary religious teachers. It was an advantage that those who imparted this instruction should also administer this ordinance. (3.) It is not improbable, as Doddridge supposes, that the administration of this ordinance was intrusted to inferiors, because it was commonly practised by immersion, and was attended with some trouble and inconvenience, while the time of the apostles might be more directly occupied in their main work. ¶ *But to preach the gospel.* As his main business; as the leading, grand purpose of his ministry. This is the grand object of all ministers. It is not to build up a sect or party; it is not to secure simply the *baptism* of people in this or that communion; it is to make known the glad tidings of salvation, and call men to repentance and to God. ¶ *Not with wisdom of words* (*ουκ εν σοφια λογου*). Not in wisdom of *speech.* Margin. The expression here is a Hebraism, or a form of speech common in the Hebrew writings, where a noun is used to express the meaning of an adjective, and means *not in wise words or discourse.* The *wisdom* here mentioned, refers, doubtless, to that which was common among the Greeks, and which was so highly valued. It included the following things:—(1.) Their subtle and learned mode of disputation, or that which was practised in their schools of philosophy. (2.) A graceful and winning eloquence; the arts by which they sought to commend their sentiments, and to win others to their opinions. On this also the Greek rhetoricians greatly valued themselves, and this, probably, the false teachers endeavoured to imitate. (3.) That which is elegant and finished in literature, in style and composition. On this the Greeks greatly valued themselves, as the Jews did on miracles and wonders; comp. ver. 22. The apostle means to say, that the success of the gospel did not depend on these things; that he had not sought them; nor had he exhibited them in his preaching. His doctrine and his manner had not been such as to appear wise to the Greeks; and he had not depended on eloquence or philosophy for his success. Longinus (on the Sublime) enumerates Paul among men distinguished for eloquence; but it is probable that he was not distinguished for the graces of *manner* (comp. 2 Cor. x. 1. 10), so much as the strength and power of his reasoning.

Paul here introduces a *new* subject of discourse, which he pursues through this and the two following chapters—the effect of philosophy on the gospel, or the estimate which ought to be formed in regard to it. The *reasons* why he introduces this topic, and dwells upon it at such a length, are not perfectly apparent. They are supposed to have been the following. (1.) He had incidentally mentioned his own preaching, and his having been set apart particularly to that; verse 17. (2.) His authority, it is probable, had been called in question by the false teachers at Corinth. (3.) The ground of this, or the reason why they undervalued him, had been probably, that he had not evinced the eloquence of manner and the graces of oratory on which they so much valued themselves. (4.) They had depended for their success on captivating the Greeks by the charms of graceful rhetoric and the

refinements of subtle argumentation (5.) In every way, therefore, the deference paid to rhetoric and philosophy in the church, had tended to bring the pure gospel into disrepute; to produce faction; and to destroy the authority o, the apostle. It was necessary, therefore, thoroughly to examine the subject, and to expose the real influence of the philosophy on which they placed so high a value. ¶ *Lest the cross of Christ.* The simple doctrine that Christ was crucified to make atonement for the sins of men. This was the peculiarity of the gospel; and on this doctrine the gospel depended for success in the world. ¶ *Should be made of none effect.* Should be rendered vain and ineffectual. That is, lest the success which might attend the preaching of the gospel should be attributed to the graces of eloquence, the charms of language, or the force of human argumentation, rather than to its true cause, the preaching of Christ crucified; or lest the *attempt* **to** recommend it by the charms of eloquence should divert the attention from the simple doctrines of the cross, and the preaching be really vain. The preaching of the gospel depends for its success on the simple power of its truths, borne by the Holy Spirit to the hearts of men; and not on the power of argumentation, and the charms of eloquence. To have adorned the gospel with the charms of Grecian rhetoric, would have obscured its wisdom and efficacy, just as the gilding of a diamond would destroy its brilliancy. True eloquence, and real learning and sound sense, are not to be regarded as valueless; but their use in preaching is to convey the truth with plainness; to fix the mind *on* the pure gospel; and to leave the conviction on the heart that this system is the power of God. The design of Paul here cannot be to condemn true eloquence and just reasoning, but to rebuke the vain parade, and the glittering ornaments, and dazzling rhetoric which were objects of so much esteem in Greece. A real belief of the gospel, a simple and natural statement of its sublime truths, will admit of, and prompt to, the most manly and noble kind of eloquence.

18 For the preaching of the cross is to them *a* that perish foolishness; but unto us which are saved it is the power *b* of God.

a 2 Cor.2.15. | *b* Rom.1.16.

The highest powers of mind, and the most varied learning, may find ample scope for the illustration and the defence of the simple doctrines of the gospel of Christ. But it does not *depend* for its success on these, but on its pure and heavenly truths, borne to the mind by the agency of the Holy Spirit.

18. *For the preaching of the cross.* Greek, "the *word* (ὁ λόγος) of the cross;" *i. e.* the doctrine of the cross; or the doctrine which proclaims salvation only through the atonement which the Lord Jesus Christ made on the cross. This cannot mean that the statement that Christ died as a martyr on a cross, appears to be foolishness to men; because, if that was all, there would be nothing that would appear contemptible, or that would excite their opposition more than in the death of any other martyr. The statement that Polycarp, and Ignatius, and Paul, and Cranmer died as martyrs, does not appear to men to be foolishness, for it is a statement of an historical truth, and their death excites the high admiration of all men. And if, in the death of Jesus on the cross, there had been nothing more than a mere martyr's death, it would have been equally the object of admiration to all men. But the "preaching of the cross" must denote more than that; and must mean, (1.) That Christ died as an atoning sacrifice for the sins of men, and that it was this which gave its peculiarity to his sufferings on the cross. (2.) That men can be reconciled to God, pardoned, and saved only by the merits and influence of this atoning sacrifice. ¶ *To them that perish* (τοῖς μὲν ἀπολλυμένοις). To those who are about to perish, or to those who have a character fitting them for destruction; *i. e.* to the wicked. The expression stands in contrast with those who are "saved," *i. e.* those who have seen the beauty of the cross of Christ, and who have fled to it for salvation. ¶ *Foolishness.* Folly. That

is, it appears to them to be contemptible and foolish, or unworthy of belief. To the great mass of the Jews, and to the heathen philosophers, and indeed, to the majority of the men of this world, it has ever appeared foolishness, for the following reasons. (1.) The humble origin of the Lord Jesus. They despise him that lived in Nazareth; that was poor; that had no home, and few friends, and no wealth, and little honour among his own countrymen. (2.) They despise him who was put to death, as an impostor, at the instigation of his own countrymen, in an ignominious manner on the cross—the usual punishment of slaves. (3.) They see not why there should be any particular efficacy in his death. They deem it incredible that he who could not save himself should be able to save them; and that glory should come from the ignominy of the cross. (4.) They are blind to the true beauty of his personal character; to the true dignity of his nature; to his power over the sick, the lame, the dying, and the dead; they see not the bearing of the work of atonement on the law and government of God; they believe not in his resurrection, and his present state of exalted glory. The world looks only at the fact, that the despised man of Nazareth was put to death on a cross, and smiles at the idea that such a death could have any important influence on the salvation of man.—It is worthy of remark, also, that to the ancient philosophers this doctrine would appear still more contemptible than it does to the men of these times. Every thing that came from Judea, they looked upon with contempt and scorn; and they would spurn above all things else the doctrine that they were to expect salvation only by the crucifixion of a Jew. Besides, the account of the crucifixion has now lost to us no small part of its reputation of ignominy. Even around the cross there is conceived to be no small amount of honour and glory. There is now a sacredness

19 For it is written, *a* I will
destroy the wisdom of the wise,

and will bring to nothing the understanding of the prudent.

a Isa.29.14; Jer.8.9.

about it from religious associations ;
and a reverence which men in Christian lands can scarcely help feeling
when they think of it. But to the
ancients it was connected with every
idea of ignominy. It was the punishment of slaves, impostors, and vaga-
bonds; and had even a greater degree
of disgrace attaohed to it than the gal-
lows has with us. With them, therefore, the death on the cross was associated with the idea of all that is
shameful and dishonourable; and to
speak of salvation only by the sufferings and death of a crucified man, was
fitted to excite in their bosoms only
unmingled scorn. ¶ *But unto us which
are saved.* This stands opposed to
"them that perish." It refers, doubtless, to Christians, as being *saved* from
the power and condemnation of sin;
and as having a prospect of eternal salvation in the world to come. ¶ *It is
the power of God.* See Note, Rom. i.
16. This may either mean that the
gospel is called "the power of God,"
because it is the *medium* through
which God exerts his power in the
salvation of sinners ; or, the gospel is
adapted to the condition of man, and
is efficacious in renewing him and sanctifying him. It is not an inert, inactive letter, but is so fitted to the understanding, the heart, the hopes, the
fears of men, and all their great constitutional principles of action, that it
actually overcomes their sin, and diffuses peace through the soul. This efficacy is not unfrequently attributed to
the gospel. John xvii. 17; Heb. iv.
12; Jam. i. 18; 1 Pet. i. 22, 23.—When
the gospel, however, or the preaching
of the cross, is spoken of as effectual
or powerful, it must be understood of
all the agencies which are connected
with it; and does not refer to simple,
abstract propositions, but to the truth
as it comes attended with the influences which God sends down to accompany it. It includes, therefore, the
promised agency of the Holy Spirit,
without which it would not be effectual.

But the agency of the Spirit is designed
to give efficacy to that which is *really*
adapted to produce the effects, and not
to act in an arbitrary manner. All the
effects of the gospel on the soul—in
regeneration, repentance, faith, sanctification ;—in hope, love, joy, peace,
patience, temperance, purity, and
devotedness to God, are only such *as
the gospel is fitted to produce.* It has a
set of truths and promises just *adapted*
to each of these effects; just fitted to
the soul by him who knows it; and
adapted to *produce* just these results.
The Holy Spirit secures their influence
on the mind : and is the grand living
agent of accomplishing just what the
truth of God is *fitted originally* to produce. Thus the preaching of the cross
is "the power of God;" and every
minister may present it with the assurance that he is presenting, not "a cun-
ningly devised fable," but a system
really fitted to save men ; and yet, that
its reception by the human mind
depends on the promised presence of
the Holy Spirit.

19. *For it is written.* This passage is quoted from Isa. xxix. 14. The
Hebrew of the passage, as rendered in
the English version is, "the wisdom
of their wise *men* shall perish, and the
understanding of their prudent *men*
shall be hid." The version of the
LXX. is, "I will destroy the wisdom
of the wise, and the understanding of
the prudent I will hide" (χρύψω), corresponding substantially with the quotation by Paul. The sense in the
Hebrew is not materially different.
The meaning of the passage as used
by Isaiah is, that such was the iniquity
and stupidity of "Ariel" (Isa. xxix.
1), that is, Jerusalem, that God
would so execute his judgments as to
confound their wise men. and overwhelm those who boasted of their
understanding. Those in whom they
had confided, and on whom they relied,
should appear to be bereft of their
wisdom; and they should be made
conscious of their own want of coun-

20 Where *a is* the wise? where *is* the scribe? where *is* the disputer

a Isa.33.18.

of this world? hath not God made foolish *b* the wisdom of this world?

b Isa.44.25.

sel to meet and remove the impending calamities. The apostle does not affirm that this passage in Isaiah refers to the times of the gospel. The contrary is manifestly true. But it expresses a general principle of the divine administration—*that the coming forth of God is often such as to confound human prudence ; in a manner which human wisdom would not have devised ; and in such a way as to show that he is not dependent on the wisdom of man.* As such, the sentiment is applicable to the gospel ; and expresses just the idea which the apostle wished to convey—that the wisdom of the wise should be confounded by the plan of God; and the schemes of human devising be set at naught. ¶ *I will destroy.* That is, I will abolish; or will not be dependent on it ; or will show that my plans are not derived from the counsels of men. ¶ *The wisdom of the wise.* The professed wisdom of philosophers. ¶ *And will bring to nothing.* Will show it to be of no value in this matter. ¶ *The prudent.* The men professing understanding ; the sages of the world. We may remark, (1.) That the plan of salvation was not the contrivance of human wisdom. (2.) It is *unlike* what men have themselves devised as systems of religion. It did not occur to the ancient philosophers; nor has it occurred to the modern. (3.) It may be expected to excite the opposition, the contempt, and the scorn of the wise men of this world; and the gospel makes its way usually, not with their friendship, but in the face of their opposition. (4.) Its success is such as to confound and perplex them. They despise it, and they see not its secret power; they witness its effects, but are unable to account for them. It has always been a question with philosophers why the gospel met with such success; and the various accounts which have been given of it by its enemies, show how much they have been embarrassed. The most-elabo-

rate part of Gibbon's "Decline and Fall of the Roman Empire," is contained in his attempt to state the causes of the early propagation of Christianity, in chap. xv. xvi.; and the obvious failure of the account shows how much the mind of the philosophic sceptic was embarrassed by the fact of the spread of Christianity. (5.) The reception of the gospel demands an humble mind; Mark x. 15. Men of good sense, of humble hearts, of childlike temper, embrace it; and they see its beauty, and are won by its loveliness, and controlled by its power. They give themselves to it ; and find that it is fitted to save their souls. (6.) In this, Christianity is like all science. The discoveries in science are such as to confound the wise in their own conceits, and overthrow the opinions of the prudent, just as much as the gospel does, and thus show that both are from the same God—the God who delights to pour such a flood of truth on the mind as to overwhelm it in admiration of himself, and with the conviction of its own littleness. The profoundest theories in science, and the most subtle speculations of men of genius, in regard to the causes of things, are often overthrown by a few simple discoveries—and discoveries which are at first despised as much as the gospel is. The invention of the telescope by Galileo was to the theories of philosophers and astronomers, what the revelation of the gospel was to the systems of ancient learning, and the deductions of human wisdom. The one confounded the world as much as the other ; and both were at first equally the object of opposition or contempt.

20. *Where* is *the wise?* Language similar to this occurs in Isa. xxxiii. 18, "Where is the scribe? where is the receiver? where is he that counted the towers?" Without designing to *quote* these words as having an original reference to the subject now under

21 For *a* after that, in the wisdom of God, the world by

wisdom knew not God, it pleased God by the foolishness of

a Luke 10.21; Rom.1.20,22,28.

consideration, Paul uses them as any man does language where he finds words with which he or his readers are familiar, that will convey his meaning. A man familiar with the Bible, will naturally often make use of Scripture expressions in conveying his ideas. In Isaiah the passage refers to the deliverance of the people from the threatened invasion of Sennacherib. The 18th verse represents the people as meditating on the threatened terror of the invasion; and then in the language of exultation and thanksgiving at their deliverance, saying, "where is the wise man that laid the plan of destroying the nation? Where the Inspector General (see my Note on the passage in Isaiah), employed in arranging the forces? Where the receiver (marg. the *weigher*), the paymaster of the forces? Where the man that counted the towers of Jerusalem, and calculated on their speedy overthrow? All baffled and defeated; and their schemes have all come to naught." So the apostle uses the same language in regard to the boasted wisdom of the world in reference to salvation. It is all baffled, and is all shown to be of no value. ¶ *The wise* (σοφός). The sage. At first the Greek men of learning were called *wise men* (σοφοί), like the magicians of the East. They afterwards assumed a more *modest* appellation, and called themselves the *lovers of wisdom* (φιλόσοφοι), or *philosophers*. This was the name by which they were commonly known in Greece, in the time of Paul. ¶ *Where is the scribe?* (γραμματεύς). The scribe among the Jews was a learned man, originally employed in transcribing the law, but subsequently the term came to denote a learned man in general. Among the Greeks the word was used to denote a public notary; or a transcriber of the laws; or a secretary. It was a term, therefore, nearly synonymous with a man of learning; and the apostle evidently

uses it in this sense in this place. Some have supposed that he referred to the Jewish men of learning here; but he probably had reference to the Greeks. ¶ *Where is the disputer of this world?* The acute and subtle sophist of this age. The word *disputer* (συζητητής), properly denotes one who *inquires* carefully into the causes and relations of things; one who is a subtle and abstruse investigator. It was applied to the ancient sophists and disputants in the Greek academies; and the apostle refers, doubtless, to them. The meaning is, that in all their professed investigations, in all their subtle and abstruse inquiries, they had failed of ascertaining the way in which man could be saved; and that God had devised a plan which had baffled all their wisdom, and in which their philosophy was disregarded. The term *world,* here (αἰῶνος), refers, probably, not to the world as a physical structure—though Grotius supposes that it does—but to that *age* —the disputer of that *age*, or generation—an age eminently wise and learned. ¶ *Hath not God made foolish,* &c. That is, has he not by the originality and superior efficacy of his plan of salvation, poured contempt on all the schemes of philosophers, and evinced their folly? Not only without the aid of those schemes of men, but in opposition to them, he has devised a plan for human salvation that evinces its efficacy and its wisdom in the conversion of sinners, and in destroying the power of wickedness. Paul here, possibly, had reference to the language in Isa. xliv. 25. God "turneth wise men backward, and maketh their knowledge foolish."

21. *For after that* (ἐπειδὴ). Since, or seeing that it is true that the world by wisdom knew not God. After all the experience of the world it was ascertained that men would never by their own wisdom come to the true knowledge of God, and it pleased him to devise another plan for salvation.

preaching to save them that believe.

22 For the Jews require a sign *a*
and the Greeks seek after wisdom:

a Mat.12.38,&c.

¶ *In the wisdom of God.* This phrase
is susceptible of two interpretations.
(1.) The first makes it refer to "the
wisdom of God" evinced in the works
of creation—the demonstration of his
existence and attributes found there,
and, according to that, the apostle
means to say, that the world by a survey of the works of God did not know
him; or were, notwithstanding those
works, in deep darkness. This interpretation is adopted by most commentators—by Lightfoot, Rosenmüller, Grotius, Calvin, &c. According
to this interpretation, the word ἰ (*in*)
is to be translated *by* or *through.* (2.)
A second interpretation makes it refer
to the wise arrangement or government of God, by which this was permitted. "For when, by the wise
arrangement or government of God;
after a full and fair trial of the native,
unaided powers of man, it was ascertained that the true knowledge of
God would not be arrived at by man,
it pleased him," &c. This appears to
be the correct interpretation, because
it is the most obvious one, and because
it suits the connection best. It is,
according to this, a *reason* why God
introduced a new method of saving
men. This may be said to have been
accomplished by a plan of God, which
was *wise*, because, (1.) It was desirable that the powers of man should be
fully tried before the new plan was
introduced, in order to show that it
was not dependent on human wisdom,
that it was not originated by man, and
that there was really need of such an
interposition. (2.) Because *sufficient
time* had been furnished to make the
experiment. An opportunity had
been given for four thousand years,
and still it had failed. (3.) Because
the experiment had been made in the
most favourable circumstances. The
human faculties had had time to ripen
and expand; one generation had had
an opportunity of profiting by the
observation of its predecessor; and
the most mighty minds had been
brought to bear on the subject. If

the sages of the east, and the profound
philosophers of the west, had not been
able to come to the true knowledge
of God, it was in vain to hope that
more profound minds could be brought
to bear on it, or that more careful
investigation would be bestowed on it.
The experiment had been fairly made,
and the result was before the world;
see Notes on Rom. i. ¶ *The world.*
The men of the world; particularly
the philosophers of the world. ¶ *By
wisdom.* By their own wisdom, or
by the united investigations of the
works of nature. ¶ *Knew not God.*
Obtained not a true knowledge of him.
Some denied his existence; some
represented him under the false and
abominable forms of idol worship;
some ascribed to him horrid attributes; *all* showed that they had no
true acquaintance with a God of
purity, with a God who could pardon
sin, or whose worship conduced to
holiness of life; see Notes, Rom. i.
¶ *It pleased God.* God was disposed,
or well pleased. The plan of salvation originated in his good pleasure,
and was such as his wisdom approved.
God *chose* this plan, so unlike all the
plans of men. ¶ *By the foolishness of
preaching.* Not "by foolish preaching," but by the preaching of the
cross, which was regarded as foolish
and absurd by the men of the world.
The plan is wise, but it has been
esteemed by the mass of men, and was
particularly so esteemed by the Greek
philosophers, to be egregiously foolish
and ridiculous; see Note, ver. 18.
¶ *To save them that believe.* That
believe in the Lord Jesus Christ; see
Note, Mark xvi. 16. This was the
peculiarity and essence of the plan of
God, and this has appeared to the
mass of men to be a plan devoid of
wisdom and unworthy of God. The
preaching of the cross which is thus
esteemed foolishness, is made the
means of saving them, because it sets
forth God's only plan of mercy, and
states the way in which lost sinners
may become reconciled to God.

23 But we preach Christ crucified, unto the Jews a stumbling-
block, *a* and unto the Greeks foolishness;

a Isa. 8.14; 1 Pet. 2.8.

22. *For the Jews require a sign.*
A miracle, a prodigy, an evidence of
divine interposition. This was the
characteristic of the Jewish people.
God had manifested himself to them
by miracles and wonders in a remarkable manner in past times, and they
greatly prided themselves on that fact,
and always demanded it when any new
messenger came to them, professing
to be sent from God. This propensity they often evinced in their intercourse with the Lord Jesus; Mat.
xii. 38; xvi. 1; Mark viii. 11; Luke
xi. 16; xii. 54—56. Many MSS.,
instead of "sign" here in the singular,
read *signs* in the plural; and Griesbach has introduced that reading into
the text. The sense is nearly the
same, and it means that it was a characteristic of the Jews to demand the
constant exhibition of miracles and
wonders; and it is also implied here,
I think, by the reasoning of the apostle, that they believed that the communication of such signs to them as
a people, would secure their salvation,
and they therefore despised the simple
preaching of a crucified Messiah.
They expected a Messiah that should
come with the exhibition of some stupendous signs and wonders from heaven (Mat. xii. 38, &c., as above);
they looked for the displays of amazing power in his coming, and they
anticipated that he would deliver them
from their enemies by mere power;
and they, therefore, were greatly
offended (ver. 23), by the simple doctrine of a crucified Messiah. ¶ *And
the Greeks,* &c. Perhaps this means
the heathen in general, in opposition
to the Jews; Note, Rom. i. 16. It
was, however, peculiarly the characteristic of the Greek philosophers.
They seek for schemes of philosophy
and religion that shall depend on
human wisdom, and they therefore
despise the gospel.
23. *But we.* We who are Christian
preachers make Christ crucified the
grand subject of our instructions and

our aims in contradistinction from the
Jew and the Greek. *They* seek, the
one miracles, the other wisdom, *we*
glory only in the cross. ¶ *Christ crucified.* The word Christ, the anointed,
is the same as the Hebrew name Messiah. The *emphasis* in this expression
is on the word *crucified.* The Jews
would make the Messiah whom they
expected no less an object of glorifying
than the apostles, but they spurned the
doctrine that he was to be *crucified.*
Yet in that the apostles boasted; proclaiming him crucified, or *having been
crucified* as the only hope of man. This
must mean more than that Christ was
distinguished for moral worth, more
than that he died as a martyr; because if
that were all, no reason could be given
why *the cross* should be made so prominent an object. It must mean that
Christ was crucified for the sins of men,
as an atoning sacrifice in the place of
sinners. "We proclaim a crucified
Messiah as the only redeemer of lost
men." ¶ *To the Jews a stumbling-block.*
The word *stumbling-block* (σκάνδαλον)
means properly any thing in the way
over which one may fall; then any
thing that gives offence, or that causes
one to fall into sin. Here it means
that to the Jews, the doctrine that the
Messiah was to be crucified gave great
offence; excited, irritated, and exas-
perated them; that they could not
endure the doctrine, and treated it
with scorn. Comp. Note, Rom. ix. 33;
1 Pet. ii. 8. It is well known that to
the Jews no doctrine was more offensive than this, that the Messiah was to
be put to death, and that there was to
be salvation in no other way. It was
so in the times of the apostles, and it
has been so since. They have, therefore, usually called the Lord Jesus, by
way of derision, תלוי *Tolvi, the man
that was hanged,* that is, on a cross;
and Christians they have usually denominated, for the same reason, עבדי תלוי
*Abdai Tolvi,—servants of the man that
was hanged.* The reasons of this feeling are obvious. (1.) They had looked

24 But unto them which are called, both Jews and Greeks, Christ the ^a power of God, and the wisdom of God.

a ver.18.

for a magnificent temporal prince; but the doctrine that their Messiah was crucified, dashed all their expectations. And they regarded it with contempt and scorn, just in proportion as their hopes had been elevated, and these high expectations cherished. (2.) They had the common feelings of all men, the native feelings of pride, and self-righteousness, by which they rejected the doctrine that we are dependent for salvation on one who was crucified. (3.) They regarded Jesus as one given over by God for an enormous attempt at imposition, as having been justly put to death; and the object of the curse of the Almighty. Isa. liii. 4, "We did esteem him stricken, smitten or God." They endeavoured to convince themselves that he was the object of the divine dereliction and abhorrence; and they, therefore, rejected the doctrine of the cross with the deepest feelings of detestation. ¶ *To the Greeks.* To the Gentiles in general. So the Syriac, the Vulgate, the Arabic, and the Æthiopic versions all read it. The term *Greek* denotes all who were not Jews; thus the phrase, "the Jews and the Greeks" comprehended the whole human family, ver. 22. ¶ *Foolishness.* See Note on ver. 18. They regarded it as folly, (1.) Because they esteemed the whole account a fable, and an imposition; (2.) It did not accord with their own views of the way of elevating the condition of man; (3.) They saw no efficacy in the doctrine, no tendency in the statement that a man of humble birth was put to death in an ignominious manner in Judea, to make men better, or to receive pardon. (4.) They had the common feelings of unrenewed human nature; blind to the beauty of the character of Christ, and blind to the design of his death; and they therefore regarded the whole statement as folly. We may remark here, that the feelings of the Jews and of the Greeks on this subject, are the common feelings of men. Everywhere sinners have the same views of the cross; and everywhere the human heart, if left to itself,

rejects it, as either a stumbling-block or as folly. But the doctrine should be preached, though it is an offence, and though it appears to be folly. It is the only hope of man; and by the preaching of the cross alone can sinners be saved.

24. *But unto them which are called.* To all true Christians. Note, ver. 9. ¶ *Both Jews and Greeks.* Whether originally of Jewish or Gentile extraction, they have here a common, similar view of the crucified Saviour. ¶ *Christ the power of God.* Christ *appears* to them as the power of God; or it is through him that the power of salvation is communicated to them. Note, ver. 18. ¶ *And the wisdom of God.* The way in which God evinces *his* wisdom in the salvation of men. They see the plan to be *wise.* They see that it is adapted to the end. They see it to be fitted to procure pardon, and sanctification, and eternal life. It is God's wise plan for the salvation of men; and it is *seen* by those who are Christians, to be *adapted* to this end. They see that there is a beauty in his character; an excellency in his doctrines; and an efficacy in his atonement, to secure their salvation.—We may remark on this verse, (1.) That when men become Christians, their hearts are changed. The views of Christians are here represented as diametrically opposite to those of other men. To one class, Christ is a stumbling-block; to others, folly; to Christians he is full of beauty. But those views of the Christian, can be obtained only by a change of heart. And the change from regarding an object or being as *foolishness* to regarding it as full of beauty, must be a radical and a mighty change. (2.) All Christians have similar views of the Saviour. It matters not whether they were Jew or Greek; it matters not whether they were born in a northern or southern clime—"whether an Indian or an African sun has burned upon them;" whether they speak the same or different languages; whether they were born amidst the same or different

25 Because the foolishness of God is wiser than men ; and the weakness of God is stronger than men.

denominations of Christians; whether in the same or different countries; or whether they are men in the same or different Christian communities, they have the same views of the Saviour. They see him to be the power and the wisdom of God. They are united in him, and therefore united to each other ; and should regard themselves as belonging to the same family, and as bound to the same eternal home. (3.) There is *real efficacy* in the plan of salvation. It is a scheme of power. It is adapted to the end, and is admirably fitted to accomplish the great effects which God designs to accomplish. It is not a scheme intended to show its own imbecility, and the need of another and an independent agent to accomplish the work. All the effects which the Holy Ghost produces on the soul, are such, and *only* such, as the truth of the gospel is *adapted* to produce in the mind. The gospel is God's plan of putting forth *power* to save men. It seizes upon great elements in human nature ; and is adapted to enlist them in the service of God. It is just *fitted* to man as a being capable of reasoning and susceptible of emotion ; as a being who may be influenced by hope and fear ; who may be excited and impelled to duty by conscience, and who may be roused from a state of lethargy and sin by the prospect of eternal life, and the apprehension of eternal death. *As such* it should always be preached —as a system *wise*, and *adapted* to the great end in view, as a system most powerful, and "mighty to the pulling down of strong holds."

25. *Because the foolishness of God.* That which God appoints, requires, commands, does, &c., which appears to men to be foolish. The passage is not to be understood as affirming that it is *really* foolish or unwise : but that it appears so to men.—Perhaps the apostle here refers to those parts of the divine administration where the wisdom of the plan is not seen ; or where the reason of what God does is concealed. ¶ *Is wiser than men.* Is better adapted

to accomplish important ends,and more certainly effectual than the schemes of human wisdom. This is especially true of the plan of salvation—a plan apparently foolish to the mass of men—yet indubitably accomplishing more for the renewing of men, and for their purity and happiness, than all the schemes of human contrivance. They have accomplished nothing towards men's salvation ; this accomplishes every thing, They have always failed ; this never fails. ¶ *The weakness of God.* There is really no weakness in God, any more than there is folly. This must mean, therefore, the things of his appointment which *appear* weak and insufficient to accomplish the end. Such are these facts—that God should seek to save the world by Jesus of Nazareth, who was supposed unable to save himself (Mat. xxvii. 40—43); and that he should expect to save men by the gospel, by its being preached by men who were without learning, eloquence, wealth, fame, or power. The instruments were feeble; and men judged that this was owing to the weakness or want of power in the God who appointed them. ¶ *Is stronger than men.* Is able to accomplish more than the utmost might of man. The feeblest agency that God puts forth—so feeble as to be esteemed weakness—is able to effect more than the utmost might of man. The apostle here refers particularly to the work of redemption ; but it is true every where. We may remark, (1.) That God often effects his mightiest plans by that which seems to men to be weak and even foolish. The most mighty revolutions arise often from the slightest causes ; his most vast operations are often connected with very feeble means. The revolution of empires ; the mighty effects of the pestilence ; the advancement in the scien · ces, and arts, and the operations of nature, are often brought about by means apparently as little fitted to accomplish the work as those which are employed in the plan of redemption. (2.) God is great. If his feeb-

26 For ye see your calling, brethren, how that not *a* many wise men

a Zeph.3.12; John 7.48.

after the flesh, not many mighty not many noble, *are called:*

lest powers put forth, surpass the mightiest powers of man, how great must be his might. If the powers of man who rears works of art ; who levels mountains and elevates vales; if the power which reared the pyramids, be as nothing when compared with the feeblest putting forth of divine power, how mighty must be his arm ! How vast that strength which made, and which upholds the rolling worlds ! How safe are his people in his hand ! And how easy for him to crush all his foes in death !

26. *For ye see your calling.* You know the general character and condition of those who are Christians among you, that they have not been generally taken from the wise, the rich, and the learned, but from humble life. The design of the apostle here is, to show that the gospel did not depend for its success on human wisdom. His argument is, that *in fact* those who were blessed by it had not been of the elevated ranks of life mainly, but that God had shown his power by choosing those who were ignorant, and vicious, and abandoned, and by reforming and purifying their lives. The verb " ye see" (βλέπετε), is ambiguous, and may be either in the indicative mood, as our translators have rendered it, " ye do see ; you are well apprised of it, and know it," or it may be in the imperative, "see; contemplate your condition;" but the sense is substantially the same. –*Your calling* (τὴν κλῆσιν) means 'those who are called" (ver. 9) ; as "the circumcision" means those who are circumcised. Rom. iii. 30. The ense is, " look upon the condition of those who are Christians." ¶ *Not many wise men.* Not many who are regarded as wise ; or who are ranked with philosophers. This supposes that there were *some* of that description, though the mass of Christians were then, as now, from more humble ranks of life. That there were *some* of high rank and wealth at Corinth who became Christians, is well known. Crispus

and Sosthenes, rulers of the synagogue there (Acts xviii, 8, 17; Comp. 1 Cor i. 1); Gaius, a rich, hospitable man (Rom. xvi. 23); and Erastus the chancellor of the city of Corinth (Rom. xvi. 23), had been converted and were members of the church. Some have supposed (*Macknight*) that this should be rendered "not many mighty, wise, &c. *call you;* that is, God has not employed the wise and the learned to *call* you into his kingdom." But the sense in our translation is evidently the correct interpretation. It is the *obvious* sense ; and it agrees with the design of the apostle, which was to show that God had not consulted the wisdom, and power, and wealth of men in the establishment of his church. So the Syriac and the Vulgate render it. ¶ *According to the flesh.* According to the maxims and principles of a sensual and worldly policy; according to the views of men when under the influence of those principles ; *i. e.* who are unrenewed. The flesh here stands opposed to the spirit ; the views of the men of this world in contradistinction from the wisdom that is from above. ¶ *Not many mighty* Not many men of power; or men sustaining important *offices* in the state. Comp, Rev. vi. 15. The word may refer to those who wield power of any kind, whether derived from office, from rank, from wealth, &c. ¶ *Not many noble.* Not many of illustrious birth, or descended from illustrious families—εὐγενεῖς, *well-born.* In respect to each of these classes, the apostle does not say that there were no men of wealth, and power, and birth, but that the mass or body of Christians was not composed of such. They were made up of those who were in humble life. There were a few, indeed, of rank and property, as there are now; but then, as now, the great mass was composed of those who were from the lower conditions of society. The rea. son why God had chosen his people from that rank is stated in ver. 29.— The character of many of those who

27 But God *a* hath chosen the foolish things of the world, to confound the wise ; and God hath chosen the weak things of the world, to

confound the things which are mighty ;

28 And base things of the world, and things which are de-

a Ps.8.2; Mat.11.25.

'omposed the church at Corinth before the conversion, is stated in chap. vi. 9—11, which see.

27. *But God hath chosen.* The fact of their being in the church at all was the result of his choice. It was owing entirely to his grace. ¶ *The foolish things.* The things esteemed foolish among men. The expression here refers to those who were destitute of learning, rank, wealth, and power, and who were esteemed as fools, and were despised by the rich and the great. ¶ *To confound.* To bring to shame; or that he might make them ashamed ; *i. e.* humble them by showing them how little he regarded their wisdom ; and now little their wisdom contributed to the success of his cause. By thus overlooking them, and bestowing his favours on the humble and the poor ; by choosing his people from the ranks which they despised, and bestowing on them the exalted privilege of being called the sons of God, he had poured dishonour on the rich and the great, and overwhelmed them, and their schemes of wisdom, with shame. It is also true, that those who are regarded as fools by the wise men of the world are able often to confound those who boast of their wisdom ; and that the arguments of plain men, though unlearned except in the school of Christ ; of men of sound common sense under the influence of Christian principles, have a force which the learning and talent of the men of this world cannot gainsay or resist. They have *truth* on their side; and truth, though dressed in a humble garb, is more mighty than error, though clothed with the brilliancy of imagination, the pomp of declamation, and the cunning of sophistry. ¶ *And the weak things.* Those esteemed weak by the men of the world. ¶ *The mighty.* The great ; the noble ; the learned.

28. *And base things of the world.*

Those things which by the world are esteemed ignoble. Literally, those which are not of noble, or illustrious birth (τὰ ἀγνῆ). ¶ *Things which are despised.* Those which the world regards as objects of contempt; comp. Mark ix. 12; Luke xviii. 19; Acts iv. 11. ¶ Yea. The introduction of this word by the translators does nothing to illustrate the sense, but rather enfeebles it. The language here is a striking instance of Paul's manner of expressing himself with great strength. He desires to convey in the strongest terms, the fact, that God had illustrated his plan by choosing the objects of least esteem among men. He is willing to admit *all* that could be said on this point. He says, therefore, that he had chosen the things of ignoble birth and rank—the base things of the world; but this did not fully express his meaning. He had chosen objects of contempt among men ; but this was not strong enough to express his idea. He adds, therefore, that he had chosen those things which were absolutely *nothing*, which had no existence ; which could not be supposed to influence him in his choice. ¶ *And things which are not* (τὰ μὴ ὄντα). That which is nothing; which is worthless; which has no existence; those things which were below contempt itself ; and which, in the estimation of the world, were passed by as having no existence ; as not having sufficient importance to be esteemed worthy even of the slight notice which is implied in contempt. For a man who despises a thing must at least notice it, and esteem it worth *some* attention. But the apostle here speaks of things *beneath* even that slight notice; as completely and totally disregarded, as having no existence. The language here is evidently that of hyperbole (comp. Note, John xxi. 25). It was a figure

:pised, hath God chosen, *yea,* and things which are not, to bring to naught things that are ;

a Rom.3.27.

of speech common in the East, and not unusual in the sacred writings; comp. Isa. xl. 17.

All nations before him are as nothing
And they are counted to him less than nothing and vanity.

See also Rom. iv. 17, "God, who—calleth those things which be not, as though they were." This language was strongly expressive of the estimate which the Jews fixed on the Gentiles, as being a despised people, as being in fact *no* people; a people without laws, and organization, and religion, and privileges; see Hos. i. 10; ii. 23; Rom. ix. 25; 1 Pet. ii. 10. "When a man of rank among the Hindoos speaks of low-caste persons, of notorious profligates, or of those whom he despises, he calls them *alla-tha-var-kal, i. e. those who are not.* The term does not refer to life or existence, but to a quality or disposition, and is applied to those who are vile and abominable in all things. "My son, my son, go not among them *who are not.*" "Alas! alas! those people are all *alla-tha-varkal.*" When wicked men prosper, it is said, "this is the time for those *who are not.*" "Have you heard that those *who are not* are now acting righteously?" Vulgar and indecent expressions are also called, "words that are not." To address men in the phrase *are not,* is provoking beyond measure."—*Roberts,* as quoted in Bush's Illustrations of Scripture. ¶ *To bring to naught.* To humble and subdue. To show them how vain and impotent they were. ¶ *Things that are.* Those who on account of their noble birth, high attainments, wealth, and rank, placed a high estimate on themselves and despised others.

29. *That no flesh.* That no men; no class of men. The word *flesh* is often thus used to denote men. Mat. xxiv. 22; Luke iii. 6; John xvii. 2; Acts ii. 17; 1 Pet. i. 24, &c.

---

29 That *a* no flesh should glory in his presence.

30 But of him are ye in *b*

b 2 Cor.5.17; Eph.1.3,10.

¶ *Should glory.* Should boast; Rom. iii. 27. ¶ *In his presence.* Before him. That man should *really* have nothing of which to boast; but that the whole scheme should be adapted to humble and subdue him. On these verses we may observe, (1.) That it is to be expected that the great mass of Christian converts will be found among those who are of humble life—and it may be observed also, that true virtue and excellence; sincerity and amiableness; honesty and sincerity, are usually found there also. (2.) That while the mass of Christians are found there, there *are* also those of noble birth, and rank, and wealth, who become Christians. The aggregate of those who from elevated ranks and distinguished talents have become Christians, has not been small. It is sufficient to refer to such names as Pascal, and Bacon, and Boyle, and Newton, and Locke, and Hale, and Wilberforce, to show that religion can command the homage of the most illustrious genius and rank. (3.) The *reasons* why those of rank and wealth do not become Christians, are many and obvious. (*a*) They are beset with peculiar temptations. (*b*) They are usually satisfied *with* rank and wealth, and do not feel their need of a hope of heaven. (*c*) They are surrounded with objects which flatter their vanity, which minister to their pride, and which throw them into the circle of alluring and tempting pleasures. (*d*) They are drawn away from the means of grace and the places of prayer, by fashion, by business, by temptation. (*e*) There is something about the pride of learning and philosophy, which usually makes those who possess it unwilling to sit at the feet of Christ; to acknowledge their dependence on any power; and to confess that they are poor, and needy, and blind, and naked before God. (4.) The gospel is designed to produce humility, and *to* place all men on a

Christ Jesus, who of God is made unto us *a* wisdom, and righteous-

ness, *b* sanctification, *c* and redemption : *d*

a Eph.1.17; Col.2.3.

b Isa.45.24; Jer.23.5,6; Rom.4.25.
c John 17.19.　　　　d Eph.1.7.

level in regard to salvation. There is no royal way to the favour of God. No monarch is saved because he is a monarch; no philosopher because he is a philosopher; no rich man because he is rich; no poor man because he is poor. All are placed on a level. All are to be saved in the same way. All are to become willing to give the entire glory to God. All are to acknowledge him as providing the plan, and as furnishing the grace that is needful for salvation. God's design is to bring down the pride of man, and to produce everywhere a willingness to acknowledge *him* as the fountain of blessings and the God of all.

30. *But of him.* That is, by his agency and power. It is not by philosophy; not from ourselves; but by his mercy. The apostle keeps it prominently in view, that it was not of their philosophy, wealth, or rank that they had been raised to these privileges, but of God as the author. ¶ *Are ye.* Ye are what you are by the mercy of God. 1 Cor. xv. 10. You owe your hopes to him. The emphasis in this verse is to be placed on this expression, " are ye." You are Christians, not by the agency of man, but by the agency of God.

[See the supplementary Note on Rom. viii. 10, page 176.]

¶ *In Christ Jesus.* Note, ver. 4. By the medium, or through the work of Christ, this mercy has been conferred on you. ¶ *Who of God.* From God (ἀπὸ Θεοῦ). Christ is given to us *by* God, or appointed *by* him to be our wisdom, &c. God originated the scheme, and God gave him for this end. ¶ *Wisdom.* That is, he is to us the source of wisdom; it is by him that we are made wise. This cannot mean that his wisdom becomes strictly and properly ours; that it is set over to us, and reckoned as our own, for that is not true. But it must mean simply, that Christians have become *truly wise* by the agency, the teaching, and the work of Christ. Philo-

sophers had attempted to become wise by their own investigations and inquiries. But Christians had become wise by the work of Christ; that is, it had been by his instructions that they had been made acquainted with the true character of God ; with his law; with their own condition ; and with the great truth that there was a glorious immortality beyond the grave. None of these truths had been obtained by the investigations of philosophers, but by the instructions of Christ. In like manner it was that through him they had been made practically wise unto salvation. Comp. Col. ii. 3, " In whom are hid all the treasures of wisdom and knowledge." He is the great agent by whom we become truly wise. Christ is often represented as eminently wise, and as the source of all true wisdom to his people. Isa. xi. 1; Mat. xiii. 54; Luke ii. 40, 52 ; 1 Cor. i. 24; iii. 10. " Ye are wise in Christ." Many commentators have supposed that the beautiful description of wisdom, in Prov. viii. is applicable to the Messiah. Christ may be said to be made wisdom to us, or to communicate wisdom, (1.) Because he has in his own ministry instructed us in the true knowledge of God, and of those great truths which pertain to our salvation. (2.) Because he has by his word and spirit led us to see our true situation, and made us "wise unto salvation." He has turned us from the ways of folly, and inclined us to walk in the path of true wisdom. (3.) Because he is to his people now the source of wisdom. He enlightens their mind in the time of perplexity; guides them in the way of truth ; and leads them in the path of real knowledge. It often happens that obscure and ignorant men, who have been taught in the school of Christ, have more true and real knowledge of that which concerns their welfare, and evince more real practical wisdom, than can be learned in all the schools of philosophy and learning on the earth. It is wise for a sinful and dying creature to prepare for eternity. But none but those who are instructed by the Son of God, become thus wise. ¶ *And righteousness.* By whom we become righteous in the sight of God. This declaration simply affirms that we become righteous through him, as it is affirmed that we become wise, sanctified, and redeemed through him. But neither of the expressions determine any thing as to the *mode* by which it is done. The leading idea of the apostle, which should never be lost sight of, is that the Greeks by their philosophy did *not* become truly wise, righteous, sanctified, and redeemed; but that this was accomplished through Jesus Christ. But *in what way* this was done, or by what process or mode, is not here stated; and it should be no more *assumed* from this text that we became *righteous* by the imputation of Christ's righteousness, than it should be that we became wise by the *imputation* of his wisdom, and sanctified by the imputation of his holiness. If this passage would prove one of these points, it would prove all. But as it is absurd to say that we became wise by the imputation of the personal wisdom of Christ, so this passage should not be brought to prove that we became righteous by the imputation of his righteousness. Whatever may be the truth of that doctrine, this passage does not prove it.

[The same objection is advanced by Whitby. "They who say that Christ is made our righteousness by his righteousness imputed to us, have the same reason to say also, that he is made our wisdom, by his wisdom imputed to us,"—to which Mr. Scott has replied, that "there might be some weight in this objection, if this were the only passage of Scripture, by which those who hold imputed righteousness prove their doctrine; if there were any other passages in the sacred oracles which even seem to countenance the notion of imputed wisdom, &c.; and if the nature of the case were not essentially different. Another may pay my debt, and allow me to receive the wages which he has earned, or the reward to which his services entitle him ; thus his payment and his labour may be set down to my account, or imputed to me for my adequate advantage. But who can have wisdom, health or liberty, by imputation?"—*Scott's Commen-*

tary. For a full discussion of the doctrine of imputation, see the supplementary Notes on Rom. i. 17 ; iv. 3 ; v. 12, 21 ; pages 31, 96, 114.] By turning to other parts of the New Testament to learn in what way we are made righteous through Christ, or in what way he is made unto us righteousness ; we learn that it is in two modes, (1.) Because it is by his merits alone that our sins are pardoned, and we are justified, and treated as righteous (see Note, Rom. iii. 26, 27); and (2.) Because by his influence, and work, and Spirit, and truth, we are made personally holy in the sight of God. The former is doubtless the thing intended here, as sanctification is specified after. The apostle here refers simply to the *fact,* without specifying the *mode* in which it is done. That is to be learned from other parts of the New Testament. Comp. Note, Rom. iv. 25. The doctrine of justification is, that God regards and treats those as righteous who believe on his Son, and who are pardoned on account of what he has done and suffered. The several steps in the process may be thus stated. (1.) The sinner is by nature exposed to the wrath of God. He is lost and ruined. He has no merit of his own. He has violated a holy law, and that law condemns him, and he has no power to make an atonement or reparation. He can never be pronounced a *just* man on his own merits. He can never *vindicate* his conduct, as a man can do in a court of justice where he is unjustly accused, and so be pronounced just. (2.) Jesus Christ has taken the sinner's place, and died in his stead. He has honoured a broken law ; he has rendered it consistent for God to pardon. By his dreadful sufferings, endured in the sinner's place, God has shown his hatred of sin, and his willingness to forgive. His truth will be vindicated, and his law honoured, and his government secured, if now he shall pardon the offender when penitent. As he endured these sorrows for others, and not for himself, they can be *so* reckoned, and *are* so judged by God. All the *benefits* or *results* of that atonement, therefore, as it was made for others, can be applied to

31 That, according as it is writ-

a Jer.9.23,24.

:hem, and all the advantage of such substitution in their place, can be made over to them, as really as when a man pays a note of hand for a friend; or when he pays for another a ransom. The price is reckoned *as* paid for them, and the *benefits* flow to the debtor and the captive. It is not reckoned that *they* paid it, for that is not true; but that it was done *for* them, and the benefit may be theirs, which *is* true. (3.) God has been pleased to promise that these benefits may be conferred on him who believes in the Saviour. The sinner is *united* by faith to the Lord Jesus, and is so adjudged, or reckoned. God *esteems* or judges him to be a believer according to the promise. And so believing, and so repenting, he deems it consistent to pardon and justify him who is so united to his Son by faith. He is justified, not by the *act* of faith; not by any merits of his own, but by the merits of Christ. He has no other ground, and no other hope. Thus he is *in fact* a pardoned and justified man; and God so reckons and judges. God's law is honoured, and the sinner is pardoned and saved; and it is now as consistent for God to treat him as a righteous man, as it would be if he had never sinned—since there is as high honour shown to the law of God, as there would have been had he been personally obedient, or had he personally suffered its penalty. And as, through the death of Christ, the same *results* are secured in upholding God's moral government as would be by his condemnation, it is *consistent* and *proper* for God to forgive him and treat him as a righteous man; and to do so accords with the infinite benevolence of his heart. ¶ *And sanctification.* By him we are sanctified or made holy. This does not mean, evidently, that his personal holiness is reckoned to us, but that by his work applied to our hearts, we become personally sanctified or holy. Comp. Eph. iv. 24. This is done by the agency of his Spirit applying *truth* to the mind (John xvii. 19), by the aid

ten, *a* He that glorieth, let him glory in the Lord.

which he furnishes in trials, temptations, and conflicts, and by the influence of hope in sustaining, elevating and purifying the soul. All the *truth* that is employed to sanctify, was taught primarily by him; and all the *means* that may be used are the purchase of his death, and are under his direction; and the Spirit by whose agency Christians are sanctified, was sent into the world by him, and in answer to his prayers. John xiv. 16; xv.26. ¶ *And redemption* (ἀπολύτρωσις). For the meaning of this word, see Note, Rom. iii. 24. Here it is evidently used in a larger sense than it is commonly in the New Testament. The things which are specified above, "justification and sanctification," are a part of the work of redemption. Probably the word is used here in a wide sense, as denoting the whole *group*, or class of influences by which we are brought at last to heaven; so that the apostle refers not only to his atonement, but to the work by which we are *in fact* redeemed from death, and made happy in heaven. Thus in Rom. viii. 23, the word is applied to the resurrection, " the *redemption* of the body." The sense is, "it is by Christ that we are redeemed; by him that an atonement is made; by him that we are pardoned; by him that we are delivered from the dominion of sin, and the power of our enemies; and by him that we shall be rescued from the grave, and raised up to everlasting life." Thus the whole work depends on him; and no part of it is to be ascribed to the philosophy, the talent, or the wisdom of men. He does not merely *aid* us; he does not complete that which is imperfect; he does not come in to do a part of the work, or to supply our defects; but it is *all* to be traced to him. See Col. ii. 10, " And ye are complete in him."

31. *As it is written.* This is evidently a quotation made from Jer. ix 23, 24. It is not made literally; but the apostle has *condensed* the sense of the prophet into a few words, and

CHAPTER II.

AND I, brethren, when I came to you, came not *a* with excel-

a ver. 4, 13.

lency of speech or of wisdom, declaring unto you the testimony of God.

---

has retained essentially his idea. ¶ *He that glorieth.* He that boasts or exults. ¶ *In the Lord.* Not ascribing his salvation to human abilities, or learning, or rank, but entirely to God. And from this we see, (1.) That the design of the plan of salvation is to exalt God in view of the mind. (2.) That the design is to make us humble; and this is the design also of all his works no less than of the plan of salvation. All just views of the creation tend to produce true humility. (3.) It is an evidence of piety when we are thus disposed to exalt God, and to be humble. It shows that the heart is changed; and that we are truly disposed to honour him. (4.) We may rejoice in God. We have no strength, and no righteousness of which to boast; but we may rejoice in him. He is full of goodness and mercy. He is able to save us. He can redeem us out of the hand of all our enemies. And when we are conscious that we are poor, and feeble, and helpless; when oppressed with a sense of sin, we may rejoice in him as our God; and exult in him as our Saviour and Redeemer. True piety will delight to come and lay every thing at his feet, and whatever may be our rank, or talent, or learning, we shall rejoice to come with the temper of the humblest child of poverty, and sorrow, and want, and to say, " not unto us, not unto us, but unto thy name give glory for thy mercy, and for thy truth's sake," Ps. cxv. 1.

' Not to our names, thou only just and true,
Not to our worthless names is glory due ;
Thy power and grace, thy truth and justice
　　claim
Immortal honours to thy sovereign name."
　　　　　　　　　　　　　　　Watts.

CHAPTER II.

The design of this chapter is the same as the concluding part of chap. i. (ver. 17—31), to show that the gospel does not depend for its success on human wisdom, or the philosophy of

men. This position the apostle further confirms, (1.) ver. i—5, By a reference to his own example, as having been successful among them, and yet not endowed with the graces of elocution, or by a commanding address; yet (2.) Lest it should be thought that the gospel was real folly, and should be contemned, he shows in the remainder of the chapter (ver. 6 —16), that it contained *true* wisdom ; that it was a profound scheme— rejected, indeed, by the men of the world, but *seen* to be wise by those who were made acquainted with its real nature and value, ver. 5 16.

The first division of the chapter (ver. 1—5), is a continuation of the argument to show that the success of the gospel does not depend on human wisdom or philosophy. This he proves, (1.) By the fact that when he was among them, though his preaching was attended with success, yet he did not come with the attractions of human eloquence, ver. 1. (2.) This was in accordance with his purpose, not designing to attempt any thing like that, but having another object, ver. 2. (3.) In fact he had *not* evinced that, but the contrary, ver. 3, 4. (4.) His design was that their conversion should not *appear* to have been wrought by human wisdom or eloquence, but to have been manifestly the work of God, ver. 5.

1. *And I, brethren.* Keeping up the tender and affectionate style of address. ¶ *When I came unto you.* When I came at first to preach the gospel at Corinth. Acts xviii. 1, &c. ¶ *Came not with excellency of speech.* Came not with graceful and attractive eloquence. The apostle here evidently alludes to that nice and studied choice of language ; to those gracefully formed sentences, and to that skill of arrangement in discourse and argument which was so much an object of regard with the Greek rhetoricians. It is probable that Paul

2 For 1 determined not to know any thing among you, save *a* Jesus Christ, and him crucified.

a Gal.6.14.

was never much distinguished for these (comp. 2 Cor. x. 10), and it is certain he never made them an object of intense study and solicitude. Comp. ver. 4, 13. ¶ *Or of wisdom.* Of the wisdom of this world ; of that kind of wisdom which was sought and cultivated in Greece. ¶ *The testimony of God.* The testimony or the witnessing which God has borne to the gospel of Christ by miracles, and by attending it everywhere with his presence and blessing. In ver. 6, the gospel is called " the testimony of Christ ;" and here it may either mean the witness which the gospel bears to the true character and plans of God ; or the witnessing which God had borne to the gospel by miracles, &c. The gospel contains the testimony of God in regard to his own character and plans ; especially in regard to the great plan of redemption through Jesus Christ. Several MSS. instead of "testimony of God," here read " the mystery of God." This would accord well with the scope of the argument ; but the present reading is probably the correct one. See *Mill.* The Syriac version has also *mystery.*

2. *For I determined.* I made a resolution. This was my fixed, deliberate purpose when I came there. It was not a matter of accident, or chance, that I made Christ my great and constant theme, but it was my deliberate purpose. It is to be recollected that Paul made this resolution, knowing the peculiar fondness of the Greeks for subtle disquisitions, and for graceful and finished elocution ; that he formed it when his own mind, as we may judge from his writings, was strongly inclined by nature to an abstruse and metaphysical kind of discussion, which could not have failed to attract the attention of the acute and subtle reasoners of Greece ; and that he made it when he must have been fully aware that the theme which he had chosen to dwell upon would be

3 And I was with you in weakness, and in fear, and in much trembling.

certain to excite derision and contempt. Yet he formed, and adhered to this resolution, though it might expose him to contempt ; and though they might reject and despise his message. ¶ *Not to know.* The word *know* here (ειδιναι) is used probably in the sense of *attend to, be engaged in,* or *regard.* I resolved not to give my time and attention while among you to the laws and traditions of the Jews ; to your orators, philosophers, and poets ; to the beauty of your architecture or statuary ; to a contemplation of your customs and laws, but to *attend* to this only—making known the cross of Christ. The word (ειδω) to know, is sometimes thus used. Paul says that he designed that this should be the only thing on which his mind should be fixed ; the only object of his attention ; the only object on which he there sought that knowledge should be diffused. Doddridge renders it " appear to know." ¶ *Any thing among you.* Any thing while I was with you. Or, any thing that may exist among you, and that may be objects of interest to you. I resolved to know nothing of it, whatever it might be. The former is, probably, the correct interpretation. ¶ *Save Jesus Christ.* Except Jesus Christ. This is the only thing of which I purposed to have any knowledge among you. ¶ *And him crucified.* Or, "*even* (και) him that was crucified." He resolved not only to make the *Messiah* the grand object of his knowledge and attention there, but EVEN a *crucified* Messiah ; to maintain the doctrine that the Messiah *was to be* crucified for the sins of the world ; and that he who *had been* crucified was *in fact* the Messiah. See Note, chap. i. 23. We may remark here, (1.) That this should be the resolution of every minister of the gospel. This is *his* business. It is not to be a politician ; not to engage in the strifes and controversies of men ; it is not to be a good farmer, or scholar merely; not to mingle with his people in festive circles and enjoyments; not to be a man of taste and philosophy, and distinguished mainly for refinement of manners; not to be a profound philosopher or metaphysician, but to make Christ crucified the grand object of his attention, and seek always and everywhere to make him known. (2.) He is not to be ashamed anywhere of the humbling doctrine that Christ was crucified. In this he is to glory. Though the world may ridicule; though philosophers may sneer; though the rich and the gay may deride it, yet this is to be the grand object of interest to him, and at no time, and *in no society* is he to be ashamed of it. (3.) It matters not what are the amusements of society around him; what fields of science, of gain, or ambition, are open before him, the minister of Christ is to know Christ and him crucified alone. If he cultivates science, it is to be that he may the more successfully explain and vindicate the gospel. If he becomes in any manner familiar with the works of art, and of taste, it is that he may more successfully show *to* those who cultivate them, the superior beauty and excellency of the cross. If he studies the plans and the employments of men, it is that he may more successfully meet them *in* those plans, and more successfully speak to them of the great plan of redemption (4.) The preaching of the cross is the only kind of preaching that will be attended with success. That which has in it much respecting the divine mission, the dignity, the works, the doctrines, the person, and the atonement of Christ, will be successful. So it was in the time of the apostles; so it was in the Reformation; so it was in the Moravian missions; so it has been in all revivals of religion. There is a power about that kind of preaching which philosophy and human reason have not. "Christ is God's great ordinance" for the salvation of the world; and we meet the crimes and alleviate the woes of the world, just in proportion as we hold the cross up as appointed to overcome the one, and

to pour the balm of consolation into the other.

3. *And I was with you.* Paul continued there at least a year and six months. Acts xviii. 11. ¶ *In weakness.* In conscious feebleness; diffident of my own powers, and not trusting to my own strength. ¶ *And in fear, and in much trembling.* Paul was sensible that he had many enemies to encounter (Acts xviii. 6.): and he was sensible of his own natural disadvantages as a public speaker, 2 Cor. x. 10. He knew too, how much the Greeks valued a manly and elegant species of oratory; and he, therefore, delivered his message with deep and anxious solicitude as to the success. It was at this time, and in view of these circumstances, that the Lord spoke to him by night in a vision, and said, "be not afraid, but speak, and hold not thy peace; for I am with thee, and no man shall set on thee to hurt thee; for I have much people in this city," Acts xviii. 9, 10. If Paul was conscious of weakness, well may other ministers be; and if Paul sometimes trembled in deep solicitude about the result of his message, well may other ministers tremble also. It was in such circumstances, and with such feelings, that the Lord met him to encourage him.—And it is when other ministers feel thus, that the promises of the gospel are inestimably precious. We may add, that it is then, and then only, that they are successful. Notwithstanding all Paul's fears, he was successful there. And it is commonly, perhaps always, when ministers go to their work conscious of their own weakness; burdened with the weight of their message; diffident of their own powers; and deeply solicitous about the result of their labours, that God sends down his Spirit, and converts sinners to God. The most successful ministers have been men who have evinced most of this feeling; and most of the revivals of religion have commenced, and continued, just as ministers have preached, conscious of their own feebleness, distrusting their own powers, and looking to God for aid and strength.

4. *And my speech.* The word *speech*

4 And my speech and my preaching *was* not with [1] enticing words of [a] man's wisdom, but in demon-

stration [b] of the Spirit and of power:

5 That your faith should not

---

1 or, *persuasible.*   *a* 2 Pet.1.16.

b 1 Thess.1.5.

---

here—if it is to be distinguished from *preaching*—refers, perhaps, to his more private reasonings ; his preaching to his public discourses. ¶ *Not with enticing words.* Not with the persuasive reasonings (πειϑοῖς λόγοις) of the wisdom of men. Not with that kind of oratory that was adapted to captivate and charm ; and which the Greeks so much esteemed. ¶ *But in demonstration.* In the showing (ἀπο-δείξει) ; or in the testimony or evidence which the Spirit produced. The meaning is, that the Spirit furnished the evidence of the divine origin of the religion which he preached, and that it did not depend for its proof on his own reasonings or eloquence. The proof, the demonstration which the Spirit furnished was, undoubtedly, the miracles which were wrought; the gift of tongues ; and the remarkable conversions which attended the gospel.—The word *Spirit* here refers, doubtless, to the Holy Spirit; and Paul says that this Spirit had furnished demonstration of the divine origin and nature of the gospel. This had been by the gift of tongues (chap. i. 5—7. Comp. chap. xiv.), and by the effects of his agency in renewing and sanctifying the heart. ¶ *And of power,* That is, of the power of God (ver. 5) ; the divine power and efficacy which attended the preaching of the gospel there. Comp. 1 Thess. i. 5.— The *effect* of the gospel is the evidence to which the apostle appeals for its truth. That effect was seen, (1.) In the conversion of sinners to God of all classes, ages, and conditions, when all human means of reforming them was vain. (2.) In its giving them peace, joy, and happiness; and in its transforming their lives. (3.) In making them different men—in making the drunkard sober ; the thief honest ; the licentious pure ; the profane reverent ; the indolent industrious ; the harsh and unkind, gentle and kind ; and the wretched happy.

(4.) In its diffusing a mild and pure influence over the laws and customs of society; and in promoting human happiness everywhere.—And in regard to this evidence to which the apostle appeals, we may observe, (1.) That is a kind of evidence which any one may examine, and which no one can deny. It does not need laboured, abstruse argumentation, but it is everywhere in society. Every man has witnessed the effects of the gospel in reforming the vicious, and no one can deny that it has this power. (2.) It is a mighty display of the power of God. There is no more striking exhibition of his power over mind than in a revival of religion. There is no where more manifest demonstration of his presence than when, in such a revival, the proud are humbled, the profane are awed, the blasphemer is silenced, and the profligate, the abandoned, and the moral—are converted unto God, and are led as lost sinners to the same cross, and find the same peace. (3.) The gospel has thus evidenced from age to age that it is from God. Every converted sinner furnishes such a demonstration; and every instance where it produces peace, hope, joy, shows that it is from heaven.

5. *That your faith.* That is, that your belief of the divine origin of the Christian religion. ¶ *Should not stand.* Greek, " should not *be ;*" that is, should not rest upon this; or be sustained by this. God intended to furnish you a firm and solid demonstration that the religion which you embraced was from him ; and this could not be if its preaching had been attended with the graces of eloquence, or the abstractions of refined metaphysical reasoning. It would then appear to rest on human wisdom. ¶ *In the power of God.* In the evidence of divine power accompanying the preaching of the gospel. The power of God would attend the exhibition of truth everywhere ; and would be a

' stand in the wisdom of men, but in the power of God.

1 be.

demonstration that would be irresistible that the religion was not originated by man, but was from heaven. That power was seen in changing the heart; in overcoming the strong propensities of our nature to sin; in subduing the soul; and making the sinner a new creature in Christ Jesus. Every Christian has thus, in his own experience, furnished demonstration that the religion which he loves is from God, and not from man. Man could not subdue these sins; and man could not so entirely transform the soul. And although the unlearned Christian may not be able to investigate all the evidences of religion; although he cannot meet all the objections of cunning and subtle infidels, although he may be greatly perplexed and embarrassed by them, yet he may have the fullest proof that he loves God, that he is different from what he once was; and that all this has been accomplished by the religion of the cross. The blind man that was made to see by the Saviour (John x.), might have been wholly unable to tell how his eyes were opened, and unable to meet all the cavils of those who might doubt it, or all the subtle and cunning objections of physiologists, but of one thing he certainly could not doubt, that "whereas he was blind, he then saw;" John x. 25. A man may have no doubt that the sun shines, that the wind blows, that the tides rise, that the blood flows in his veins, that the flowers bloom, and that this could not be except it was from God, while he may have no power to explain these facts; and no power to meet the objections and cavils of those who might choose to embarrass him. So men may know that their hearts are changed; and it is on this ground that no small part of the Christian world, as in every thing else, depend for the most satisfactory evidence of their religion. On this ground humble and unlearned Christians have been often willing to go to the stake as martyrs—just as a humble and unlearned patriot is will-

6 Howbeit we speak wisdom among them *a* that are perfect:

a Phil.3.15.

ing to die for his country. He *loves* it; and he is willing to die for it. A Christian *loves* his God and Saviour; and is willing to *die* for his sake.

6. *How be it.* But (δὲ). This commences the *second* head or argument in this chapter, in which Paul shows that if human wisdom *is* wanting in his preaching, it is not devoid of true, and solid, and even divine wisdom.— *Bloomfield.* ¶ *We speak wisdom.* We do not admit that we utter foolishness. We have spoken of the foolishness of preaching (chap. i. 21); and of the estimate in which it was held by the world (chap. i. 22—28); and of our own manner among you as not laying claim to human learning or eloquence; but we do not design to admit that we have been really speaking folly. We have been uttering that which is truly wise, but which is seen and understood to be such only by those who are qualified to judge—by those who may be denominated "perfect," that is, those who are fitted by God to understand it. By "wisdom" here, the apostle means that system of truth which he had explained and defended—the plan of salvation by the cross of Christ. ¶ *Among them that are perfect* (ἐν τοῖς τελείοις). This word "perfect" is here evidently applied to Christians, as it is in Phil. iii. 15, "Let us therefore as many as be perfect, be thus minded." And it is clearly used to denote those who were advanced in Christian knowledge; who were qualified to understand the subject; who had made progress in the knowledge of the mysteries of the gospel; and who thus saw its excellence. It does not mean here that they were *sinless,* for the argument of the apostle does not bear on that inquiry, but that they were qualified to understand the gospel in contradistinction from the gross, the sensual, and the carnally minded, who rejected it as foolishness. There is, perhaps, here an allusion to the heathen *mysteries,* where those who had been fully initiated were said to be *perfect*—fully instructed in those

yet not the wisdom of this world, nor of the princes of this world that come to *a* naught:

7 But we speak the wisdom

a Ps. 33.10.

of God in a mystery, *even* the hidden *b* wisdom, which God ordained before the world unto our glory:

b Eph. 3.5,9.

rites and doctrines. And if so, then this passage means, that those only who have been fully instructed in the knowledge of the Christian religion, will be qualified to see its beauty and its wisdom. The gross and sensual do not see it, and those only who are enlightened by the Holy Spirit are qualified to appreciate its beauty and its excellency. ¶ *Not the wisdom of the world.* Not that which this world has originated or loved. ¶ *Nor of the princes of this world.* Perhaps intending chiefly here the rulers of the Jews; see ver. 8. They neither devised it, nor loved it, nor saw its wisdom; ver. 8. ¶ *That come to naught.* That is, whose plans fail; whose wisdom vanishes; and who themselves, with all their pomp and splendour, come to nothing in the grave; comp. Isa. xiv. All the plans of human wisdom shall fail; and this which is originated by God only shall stand.

7. *But we speak.* We who have preached the gospel. ¶ *The wisdom of God.* We teach or proclaim the wise plan of God for the salvation of men; we make known the divine wisdom in regard to the scheme of human redemption. This plan was of God, in opposition to other plans which were of men. ¶ *In a mystery, even the hidden* wisdom (ἐν μυστηρίῳ τὴν ἀπο-κεκρυμμένην). The words "even" and "wisdom" in this translation have been supplied by our translators; and the sense would be more perspicuous if they were omitted, and the translation should be literally made, " We proclaim the divine wisdom hidden in a mystery.' The apostle does not say that their *preaching* was mysterious, nor that their doctrine was unintelligible, but he refers to the fact that this wisdom had been *hidden in a mystery* from men until that time, but was *then* revealed by the gospel. In other words, he does not say that what they then declared was hidden in a mystery, but

that they made known the divine wisdom which *had been* concealed from the minds of men. The word *mystery* with us is commonly used in the sense of that which is beyond comprehension; and it is often applied to such doctrines as exhibit difficulties which we are not able to explain. But this is not the sense in which it is commonly used in the Scriptures; see Note, Mat. xiii. 11; comp. Campbell on the Gospels, Diss. ix. part i. The word properly denotes that which is *concealed* or *hidden;* that which has not yet been made known; and is applied to those truths which until the revelation of Jesus Christ were *concealed* from men, which were either *hidden* under obscure types and shadows or prophecies, or which had been altogether unrevealed, and unknown to the world. The word stands opposed to that which is *revealed,* not to that which is in itself plain. The doctrines to which the word relates may be in themselves clear and simple, but they are hidden *in* mystery until they are revealed. From this radical idea in the word *mystery,* however, it came also to be applied not only to those doctrines which *had not* been made known, but to those also which were in themselves deep and difficult: to that which is enigmatical and obscure; 1 Cor. xiv. 2; 1 Tim. iii. 16. It is applied also to the secret designs and purposes of God; Rev. x. 7. The word is most commonly applied by Paul to the secret and long concealed design of God to make known his gospel to the Gentiles; to break down the wall between them and the Jews; and to spread the blessings of the true religion everywhere; Rom. xi. 25; xvi. 25; Eph. i. 9; iii. 9; vi. 19. Here, it evidently means the beauty and excellency of the person and plans of Jesus Christ, but which were IN FACT unknown to the princes of this world. It does not imply, of necessity, that they *could* not have understood them,

8 Which none of the princes of this world knew: for ^a had they

a Luke 23.34.

known *it*, they would not have crucified the Lord of glory.

---

nor that they were unintelligible, but that, *in fact*, whatever was the cause, they were concealed from them. Paul says (ver. 8), that *had* they known his wisdom, they would not have crucified him—which implies at least that it was not in itself unintelligible; and he further says, that this mystery had been revealed to Christians by the Spirit of God, which proves that he does not here refer to that which is in itself unintelligible; ver. 10. "The apostle has here especially in view the all-wise counsel of God for the salvation of men by Jesus Christ, in the writings of the Old Testament only obscurely signified, and to the generality of men utterly unknown."— *Bloomfield.* ¶ *Which God ordained.* Which plan, so full of wisdom, God appointed in his own purpose before the foundation of the world; that is, it was a plan which from eternity he determined to execute. It was not a *new* device; it had not been got up to serve an occasion; but it was a plan laid deep in the eternal counsel of God, and on which he had his eye for ever fixed. This passage proves, that God had a plan, and that this plan was eternal. This is all that is involved in the doctrine of eternal decrees or purposes. And if God had a plan about this, there is the same reason to think that he had a plan in regard to all things. ¶ *Unto our glory.* In order that we might be honoured or glorified. This may refer either to the honour which was put upon Christians in this life, in being admitted to the privileges of the sons of God; or more probably to that "eternal weight of glory" which remains for them in heaven; 2 Cor. iv. 17. One design of that plan was to raise the redeemed to "glory, and honour, and immortality." It should greatly increase our gratitude to God, that it was a subject of eternal design; that he always has cherished this purpose; and that he has loved us with such love, and sought our happiness and salvation with such intensity, that in order to accomplish it, he was will-

ing to give his own Son to die on a cross.

8. *Which none of the princes.* None of those rulers who were engaged in the crucifixion of the Messiah, referring both to the Jewish rulers, and the Roman governor. ¶ *Knew.* They did not perceive or appreciate the excellency of his character, the wisdom of his plan, the glory of his scheme of salvation. Their ignorance arose from not understanding the prophecies, and from an unwillingness to be convinced that Jesus of Nazareth had been truly sent by God. In Acts iii. 17, Peter says that it was through ignorance that the Jews had put him to death; see Note on this place. ¶ *For had they known* it. Had they fully understood his character, and seen the wisdom of his plan, and his work, they would not have put him to death; see Note on Acts iii. 17. Had they seen the hidden wisdom in that plan—had they understood the glory of his real character, the truth respecting his incarnation, and the fact that he was the long expected Messiah of their nation, they would not have put him to death. It is incredible that they would have crucified their Messiah, knowing and believing him to be such. They *might* have known it, but they were unwilling to examine the evidence. They expected a *different* Messiah, and were unwilling to admit the claims of Jesus of Nazareth. For *this* ignorance, however, there was no excuse. If they had not a full knowledge, it was their own fault. Jesus had performed miracles which were a complete attestation to his divine mission (John v. 36; x. 25); but they closed their eyes on those works, and were unwilling to be convinced.—God always gives to men sufficient demonstration of the truth, but they close their eyes, and are *unwilling* to believe. This is the sole reason why they are not converted to God and saved. ¶ *They would not have crucified.* It is perfectly manifest that the Jews would not have crucified their own Messiah, *knowing him to be*

9 But, as it is written, *a* Eye
hath not seen, nor ear heard,

a Isa. 64. 4.

such. He was the hope and expectation of their nation. All their desires
were centered in him. And to him
they looked for deliverance from all
their foes. ¶ *The Lord of glory.* This
expression is a Hebraism, and means
"the glorious Lord;" or the "Messiah." Expressions like this, where a
noun performs the office of an adjective, are common in the Hebrew language.—Grotius supposes that the
expression is taken from that of "the
King of glory," in Ps. xxiv. 7—9.

> Lift up your heads, O ye gates,
> Be ye lift up, ye everlasting doors,
> And the King of glory shall come in.
> Who is this King of glory?
> JEHOVAH, strong and mighty
> JEHOVAH, mighty in battle.
> Lift up your heads, O ye gates;
> Lift them up, ye everlasting doors;
> And the King of glory shall come in.
> Who is this King of glory?
> JEHOVAH of hosts, he is the King of glory.

God is called "the God of glory" in
Acts vii. 2.—The fact that this appellation is given to JEHOVAH in the Old
Testament, and to the Lord Jesus
in the verse before us, is one of those
incidental circumstances which show
how the Lord Jesus was estimated by
the apostles : and how familiarly they
applied to him names and titles which
belong only to God. The foundation of this appellation is laid in his
exalted perfections; and in the honour
and majesty which he had with the
Father before the world was; John
xvii. 1—5.
9. *But as it is written.* This passage is quoted from Isa. lxiv. 4. It is
not quoted literally; but the sense
only is given. The words are found in
the apocryphal books of Elijah; and
Origen and Jerome supposed that
Paul quoted from those books. But
it is evident that Paul had in his eye
the passage in Isaiah ; and intended
to apply it to his present purpose.
These words are often applied by commentators and others to the future
life, and are supposed by them to be
descriptive of the state of the blessed
there. But against the supposition
that they refer directly to the future

neither have entered into the heart
of man, the things which God

state, there are insuperable objections.
(1.) The first is, that the passage in
Isaiah has no such reference. In that
place it is designed clearly to describe
the blessedness of those who were
admitted to the divine favour ; who
had communion with God ; and to
whom God manifested himself as their
friend. That blessedness is said to be
superior to all that men elsewhere
enjoy; to be such as could be found
no where else but in God. See Isa.
lxiv. 1, 4, 5, 8. It is used there, as
Paul uses it, to denote the happiness
which results from the communication
of the divine favour to the soul. (2.)
The object of the apostle is not to
describe the future state of the
redeemed. It is to prove that those
who are Christians have true wisdom
(ver. 6, 7); or that they have views of
truth, and of the excellence of the plan
of salvation which the world has not,
and which those who crucified the
Lord Jesus did not possess. The thing
which he is describing here, is not
merely the *happiness* of Christians,
but their views of the *wisdom* of the
plan of salvation. They have views of
that which the eyes of other men have
not seen; a view of wisdom, and
fitness, and beauty which can be found
in no other plan. It is true that this
view is attended with a high degree of
comfort; but the comfort is not the
immediate thing in the eye of the
apostle. (3.) The declaration in ver.
10, is conclusive proof that Paul does
not refer to the happiness of heaven.
He there says that God *has* revealed
these things to Christians by his Spirit.
But if *already* revealed, assuredly it
does not refer to that which is *yet* to
come. But although this does not
refer *directly* to heaven, there may be
an application of the passage to a
future state in an *indirect* manner,
which is not improper. If there are
such manifestations of wisdom in the
plan here; if Christians see so much
of its beauty here on earth ; and if
their views so far surpass all that the
world sees and enjoys, how much

hath prepared for them that love him.

10 But ^a God hath revealed *them* unto us by his Spirit: for the

greater and purer will be the manifestations of wisdom and goodness in the world of glory. ¶ *Eye hath not seen.* This is the same as saying, that no one had ever fully perceived and understood the value and beauty of those things which God has prepared for his people. All the world had been strangers to this until God made a revelation to his people by his Spirit. The blessedness which the apostle referred to had been unknown alike to the Jews and the Gentiles. ¶ *Nor ear heard.* We learn the existence and quality of objects by the external senses; and those senses are used to denote any acquisition of knowledge. To say that the eye had not seen, nor the ear heard, was, therefore, the same as saying that it was not known at all. All men had been ignorant of it. ¶ *Neither have entered into the heart of man.* No man has conceived it; or understood it. It is new; and is above all that man has seen, and felt, and known. ¶ *The things which God hath prepared.* The things which God "has held in reserve" *(Bloomfield);* that is, what God has appointed in the gospel for his people. The thing to which the apostle here refers particularly, is the wisdom which was revealed in the gospel; but he also intends, doubtless, to include *all* the provisions of mercy and happiness which the gospel makes known to the people of God. Those things relate to the pardon of sin; to the atonement, and to justification by faith; to the peace and joy which religion imparts; to the complete and final redemption from sin and death which the gospel is fitted to produce, and which it will ultimately effect. In all these respects, the blessings which the gospel confers, surpass the full comprehension of men; and are infinitely beyond all that man could know or experience without the religion of Christ. And if on earth the gospel confers such blessings on its friends, how much higher and purer shall be the joys which it shall bestow in heaven!

10. *But God hath revealed* them. That is, those elevated views and enjoyments to which men everywhere else had been strangers, and which have been under all other forms of religion unknown, have been communicated to us by the revelation of God. —This verse commences the *third* part of this chapter, in which the apostle shows *how* these truths, so full of wisdom had been communicated to Christians. It had not been by any native endowments of theirs; not by any strength of faculties, or powers. but solely by revelation from God, ¶ *Unto us.* That is, first to the apostles; secondly, to all Christians —to the church and the world *through* their inspired instructors: and third, to all Christians by the illuminating agency of the Spirit on their hearts. The connection shows that he did not mean to confine this declaration to the apostles merely, for his design was to show that *all* Christians had this knowledge of the true wisdom. It was true that this was revealed in an eminent manner to the apostles, and through their inspired preaching and writings; but it is also true, that the same truths are communicated by the agency of the same Spirit to all Christians; John xvi. 12—14. No truth is now communicated to Christians which was not revealed to and by the inspired writers; but the *same* truths are imparted by means of their writings, and by the illumination of the Spirit to all the true friends of God. ¶ *By his Spirit.* By the Holy Spirit, that was promised by the Saviour. John xiv. 26; xv. 26, 27; xvi. 7—14. This proves, (1.) That men by nature are not able to discover the deep things of God—the truths which are needful to salvation. (2.) That the apostles were inspired by the Holy Ghost; and if so, then the Scriptures are inspired. (3.) That all Christians are the subjects of the teaching of the Holy Spirit; that these truths are made known to them

Spirit searcheth all things, yea, the deep *a* things of God.

a Rom.11.33.

11 For what *b* man knoweth the things of a man, save the

b Prov.14.10.

by his illumination ; and that but for this, they would remain in the same darkness as other men. ¶ *For the Spirit.* The Holy Spirit, or the Spirit of God; see ver. 11. ¶ *Searcheth.* This word does not fully express the force of the original (ἐρευνᾷ). It means to search accurately, diligently, so as fully to understand; such profound research as to have thorough knowledge. So David uses the Hebrew word חקר in Ps. cxxxix. 1. So the word is used to denote a careful and accurate investigation of secret and obscure things, in 1 Pet. i. 11. Comp. John vii. 52 ; Rom. viii. 27 ; Rev. ii. 23, where it is used to denote that profound and accurate search by which the desires and feelings of the *heart* are known—implying the most profound knowledge of which we can have any conception ; see Prov. xx. 27. Here it means, that the Holy Spirit has an intimate knowledge of all things. It is not to be supposed that he *searches,* or *inquires* as men do who are ignorant ; but that he has an intimate and profound knowledge, such as is usually the *result* of a close and accurate search. The *result* is what the apostle means to state—the accurate, profound, and thorough knowledge, such as usually attends research. He does not state the *mode* in which it is obtained ; but the fact. And he uses a word more emphatic than simple *knowledge,* because he designs to indicate that his knowledge is profound, entire, and thorough. ¶ *All things.* All subjects ; all laws ; all events ; all beings. ¶ *The deep things of God.* He has a thorough knowledge of the hidden counsels or purposes of God ; of all his plans and purposes. He sees all his designs. He sees all his councils ; all his purposes in regard to the government of the universe, and the scheme of salvation. He knows all whom God designs to save ; he sees all that they need ; and he sees how the plan of God is fitted to their salvation.—This pas-

sage proves, (1.) That the Spirit is, in some respects, *distinct* from the Father, or from him who is here called God. Else how could he be said to *search* all things, even the deep purposes of God ? To *search* implies *action, thought, personality.* An attribute of God cannot be said to *search.* How could it be said of the justice, the goodness, the power, or the wisdom of God that it *searches,* or *acts?* To search, is the action of an intelligent agent, and cannot be performed by an attribute. (2.) The Spirit is omniscient. He searches or clearly understands "all things"—the very definition of omniscience. He understands all the profound plans and counsels of God. And how can there be a higher demonstration of omniscience than to *know God?*—But if omniscient, the Holy Spirit is divine—for this is one of the incommunicable attributes of God ; 1 Chron. xxviii. 9 ; Psal. cxxxix. 1 ; Jer. xvii. 10. (3.) He is not a distinct *being* from God. There is a *union* between him and God, such as may be compared to the union between a man and his soul, ver. 11. God is one ; and though he subsists as Father, Son, and Spirit, yet he is one God, Deut. vi. 4.—This passage is, therefore, a very important, and a decisive one in regard to the personality and divinity of the Holy Spirit.

11. *For what man,* &c. The design of this is, to *illustrate* what he had just said by a reference to the way in which man acquires the knowledge of himself. The purpose is to show that the Spirit has an *exact* and *thorough* knowledge of the things of God ; and this is done by the very striking thought that no man can know his own mind, his own plans and intentions, but himself—his own spirit. The essential idea is, that no man can know another ; that his thoughts and designs can only be known by himself, or by his own spirit ; and that unless he chooses to reveal them to others,

spirit of man which is in him? even so ^a the things of God knoweth no man, but the Spirit of God.

a Rom.11.33,34.

they cannot ascertain them. So of God. No man can penetrate his designs; and unless he chooses to make them known by his Spirit, they must for ever remain inscrutable to human view. ¶ *The things of a man.* The "deep things"—the hidden counsels, thoughts, plans, intentions. ¶ *Save the spirit of man,* &c. Except his own mind; *i. e.* himself. No other man can fully know them. By the spirit of man here, Paul designs to denote the human soul—or the intellect of man. It is not to be supposed that he here intends to convey the idea that there is a perfect resemblance between the relation which the soul of man bears to the man, and the relation which the Holy Spirit bears to God. The illustration is to be taken in regard to the point immediately before him—which is, that no one could know and communicate the deep thoughts and plans of God except his Spirit—just as no one could penetrate into the intentions of a man, and fully know them, but himself. The passage proves, therefore, that there is a knowledge which the Spirit has of God, which no man, no angel can obtain, just as every man's spirit has a knowledge of his own plans which no other man can obtain; that the Spirit of God can *communicate* his plans and deep designs, just as a man can communicate his own intentions; and consequently, that while there is a *distinction* of some kind between the Spirit of God and God, as there is a distinction which makes it proper to say that a man has an intelligent soul, yet there is such a profound and intimate knowledge of God by the Spirit, that he must be equal with him; and such an intimate union, that he can be called "the Spirit of God," and be one with God, as the human soul can be called "the spirit of the man," and be one with him. In all respects we are not to suppose that there is a simi-

12 Now we have received, not ^b the spirit of the world, but the Spirit which is of God: that ^c we might know the things

b Rom.8.15.　　*c* 1 John 5.20.

larity. In these points there is.—It may be added that the *union,* the *oneness* of the Spirit of God with God, is no more absurd or inexplicable than the union of the spirit of man with the man; or the *oneness* of the complex person made up of body and soul, which we call *man.* When men have explained all the difficulties about *themselves*—in regard to their own bodies and spirits, it will be time to advance objections against the doctrines here stated in regard to God. ¶ *Even so.* To the same extent; in like manner. ¶ *The things of God.* His deep purposes and plans. ¶ *Knoweth no man.* Man cannot search into them—any more than one man can search the intentions of another.

12. *Now we have received.* We who are Christians; and especially we, the apostles. The following verse shows that he had himself and the other apostles chiefly in view; though it is true of all Christians that they have received, not the spirit of this world, but the spirit which is of God. ¶ *Not the spirit of this world.* Not the wisdom and knowledge which this world can give—not the learning and philosophy which were so much valued in Greece. The views of truth which we have, are not such as this world gives, but are such as are communicated by the Spirit of God. ¶ *But the Spirit which is of God.* We are under the teachings and influence of the Holy Spirit. ¶ *That we might know.* That we might fully understand and appreciate. The Spirit is given to us in order that we might fully understand the favours which God has conferred on us in the gospel. It was not only necessary that God should grant the blessings of redemption by the gift of his Son, but, such was the hardness and blindness of the human heart, it was needful that he should grant his Holy Spirit also, that men might be brought fully to see and appreciate the

that are freely given to us of God.

value of those favours. For men do not see them by nature ; neither does any one see them who is not enlightened by the Holy Spirit of God. ¶ *The things that are freely given us.* That are conferred on us as a matter of grace or favour. He here refers to the blessings of redemption—the pardon of sin, justification, sanctification, the divine favour and protection, and the hope of eternal life.—These things we *know;* they are not matters of conjecture ; but are surely and certainly confirmed to us by the Holy Spirit. It is possible for all Christians to know and be fully assured of the truth of those things, and of their interest in them.

13. *Which things we speak.* Which great, and glorious, and certain truths, we, the apostles, preach and explain. ¶ *Not in the words which man's wisdom teacheth.* Not such as human philosophy or eloquence would dictate. They do not have their origin in the devices of human wisdom, and they are not expressed in such words of dazzling and attractive rhetoric as would be employed by those who pride themselves on the wisdom of this world. ¶ *But which the Holy Ghost teacheth.* That is, in the words which the Holy Ghost imparts to us. Locke understands this as referring to the fact that the apostles used "the language and expressions" which the Holy Ghost had taught in the revelations of the Scriptures. But this is evidently giving a narrow view of the subject. The apostle is speaking of the whole course of instruction by which the deep things of God were made known to the Christian church ; and all this was not made known in the very words which were already contained in the Old Testament. He evidently refers to the fact that the apostles were themselves under the direction of the Holy Spirit, in the words and doctrines which they imparted ; and this passage is a full proof that they laid claim to divine inspiration. It is further observable that

13 Which things also we speak, not *a* in the words which man's

a chap. 1. 17.

he says, that this was done in such "words" as the Holy Ghost taught, referring not to the doctrines or subjects merely, but to the manner of expressing them. It is evident here that he lays claim to an inspiration in regard to the words which he used, or to the manner of his stating the doctrines of revelation. Words are the signs of thoughts ; and if God designed that his truth should be accurately expressed in human language, there must have been a supervision over the *words* used, that such should be employed, and such only, as should accurately express the sense which he intended to convey. ¶ *Comparing spiritual things with spiritual* (πνευματικοῖς πνευματικὰ συγκρίνοντες). This expression has been very variously interpreted ; and is very difficult of explanation. Le Clerc renders it "speaking spiritual things to spiritual men." Most of the fathers rendered it "comparing the things which were written by the Spirit of the Old Testament with what is now revealed to us by the same Spirit, and confirming our doctrine by them." Calvin renders the word "*comparing*" by *fitting,* or adapting (*aptare*), and says that it means "that he adapted spiritual things to spiritual men, while he accommodated words to the thing ; that is, he tempered that celestial wisdom of the Spirit with simple language, and which conveyed by itself the native energy of the Spirit." Thus, says he, he reproved the vanity of those who attempted to secure human applause by a turgid and subtle mode of argument. Grotius accords with the fathers, and renders it, "explaining those things which the prophets spake by the Spirit of God, by those things which Christ has made known to us by his Spirit." Macknight renders it, "explaining spiritual things in words taught by the Spirit." So Doddridge. — The word rendered "comparing" (συγκρίνοντες), means properly to collect, join, mingle, unite together ; then to separate or distin-

wisdom teacheth, but which the Holy Ghost teacheth; comparing spiritual things with spiritual.

14 But the natural man receiveth *a* not the things of the Spirit of God; for they are foolishness

a Matt.13,11,&c; Rom.8.5,7.

guish parts of things and unite them into one; then to judge of the qualities of objects by carefully separating or distinguishing; then to *compare* for the purpose of judging, &c. As it means to compare one thing with another for the purpose of explaining its nature, it comes to signify to *interpret*, to *explain ;* and in this sense it is often used by the LXX. as a translation of פתר *Phathar*, to open, unfold, explain. (See Gen. xl. 8, 16, 22; xli. 12, 15); also of פשר, to explain (Num. xv. 32); and of the Chaldee פשר, (Dan. v. 13, 17). See also Dan. ii. 4—7, 9, 16, 24, 26, 30, 36, 45; iv. 3, 4, 6, 16, 17; v. 7, 8, 13, 16, 18, 20; vii. 16, in all which places the noun συγκρισις, is used in the same sense. In this sense the word is, doubtless, used here, and is to be interpreted in the sense of *explaining, unfolding.* There is no reason, either in the word here used, or in the *argument* of the apostle, why the sense of *comparing* should be retained. ¶ *Spiritual things* (πνευματικα). Things, doctrines, subjects that pertain to the teaching of the Spirit. It does not mean things *spiritual* in opposition to *fleshly ;* or *intellectual* in opposition to things pertaining to *matter ;* but spiritual as the things referred to were such as were wrought, and revealed by the Holy Spirit—his doctrines on the subject of religion under the new dispensation, and his influence on the heart. ¶ *With spiritual* (πνευματικοις). This is an adjective; and may be either masculine or neuter. It is evident, that some noun is understood. That may be either, (1.) ανθρωποις, *men*—and then it will mean "to spiritual men"—that is, to men who are enlightened or taught by the Spirit; and thus many commentators understand it; or, (2.) It may be λογοις, *words*—and then it may mean, either that the "spiritual things" were explained by "words" and illustrations drawn from the writings of the Old

Testament, inspired by the Spirit—as most of the fathers, and many moderns understand it; or that the "things spiritual" were explained by words which the Holy Spirit *then* communicated, and which were adapted to the subject—simple, pure, elevated; not gross, not turgid, not distinguished for rhetoric, and not such as the Greeks sought, but such as became the Spirit of God communicating great, sublime, yet simple truths to men. It will then mean "explaining *doctrines* that pertain to the Spirit's teaching and influence in *words* that are taught by the same Spirit, and that are fitted to convey in the most intelligible manner those doctrines to men." Here the idea of the Holy Spirit's present agency is kept up throughout; the idea that *he* communicates the doctrine, and the mode of stating it to man.—The supposition that λογοις, *words*, is the word understood here, is favoured by the fact that it occurs in the previous part of this verse. And if this be the sense, it means that the words which were used by the apostles were pure, simple, unostentatious, and undistinguished by display—such as became *doctrines* taught by the Holy Spirit, when communicated in *words suggested* by the same Spirit.

14. *But the natural man* (ψυχικος, δε ανθρωπος). The word *natural* here stands opposed evidently to *spiritual.* It denotes those who are governed and influenced by the natural instincts; the animal passions and desires, in opposition to those who are influenced by the Spirit of God. It refers to unregenerate men; but it has also not merely the idea of their being unregenerate, but that of their being influenced by the animal passions or desires. See Note on chap. xv. 44. The word *sensual* would correctly express the idea. The word is used by the Greek writers to denote that which man has in common with the brutes—to denote that they are under

unto him : neither can he know *them*, because they are spiritually discerned.

a Prov.28.5.

15 But he *a* that is spiritual ¹ judgeth all things, yet he him· self ² is judged of no man.

1 or, *discerneth.*   2 or, *discerned.*

the influence of the senses, or the mere animal nature, in opposition to reason and conscience.—*Bretschneider.* See 1 Thess. v. 23. Here it denotes that they are under the influence of the senses, or the animal nature, in opposition to being influenced by the Spirit of God. Macknight and Doddridge render it "the animal man." Whitby understands by it the man who rejects revelation, the man who is under the influence of carnal wisdom. The word occurs but six times in the New Testament; 1 Cor. xv. 44, 44, 46; James iii. 15: Jude 19. In 1 Cor. xv. 44, 44, 46, it is rendered "natural," and is applied to the body as it exists before death, in contradistinction from that which shall exist after the resurrection—called a spiritual body. In James iii. 15, it is applied to wisdom, "This wisdom — is earthly, *sensual,* devilish." In Jude 19, it is applied to *sensual* persons, or those who are governed by the senses in opposition to those who are influenced by the Spirit: "These be they who separate themselves, *sensual,* having not the Spirit." The word here evidently denotes those who are under the influence of the senses; who are governed by the passions and the animal appetites, and natural desires; and who are uninfluenced by the Spirit of God. And it may be observed that this was the case with the great mass of the heathen world, even including the philosophers. ¶ *Receiveth not* (οὐ δέχεται), does not *embrace* or *comprehend* them. That is, he rejects them as folly; he does not perceive their beauty, or their wisdom; he despises them. He loves other things better. A man of intemperance does not receive or love the arguments for temperance ; a man of licentiousness, the arguments for chastity; a liar, the arguments for truth. So a sensual or worldly man does not receive or love the arguments for religion. ¶ *The things of the Spirit of God.*

The doctrines which are inspired by the Holy Spirit, and the things which pertain to his influence on the heart and life. The things of the Spirit of God here denote all the things which the Holy Spirit produces. ¶ *Neither can he know them.* Neither can he understand or comprehend them. Perhaps, also, the word *know* here implies also the idea of *loving,* or *approving* of them, as it often does in the Scripture. Thus to know the Lord often means to love him, to have a full, practical acquaintance with him. When the apostle says that the animal or sensual man cannot know those things, he may have reference to one of two things. Either, (1.) That those doctrines were not discoverable by human wisdom, or by any skill which the natural man may have, but were to be learned only by revelation. This is the main drift of his argument, and this sense is given by Locke and Whitby. Or, (2.) He may mean that the sensual, the unre· newed man cannot perceive their beauty and their force, even *after* they are revealed to man, unless the mind is enlightened and inclined by the Spirit of God. This is probably the sense of the passage. This is the simple affirmation of *a fact*—that while the man remains sensual and carnal, he cannot perceive the beauty of those doctrines. And this *is* a simple and well known fact. It is a truth—universal and lamentable— that the sensual man, the worldly man, the proud, haughty, and self-confident man ; the man who gives the influence of his animal appetites— licentious, false, ambitious, and vain —*does not* perceive any beauty in Christianity. So the intemperate man perceives no beauty in the arguments for temperance; the adulterer, no beauty in the arguments for chastity; the liar, no beauty in the arguments for truth. It is a simple fact, that while he is intemperate, or licen· tious, or false, he *can* perceive no beauty in these doctrines. But this does not prove that he has no natural faculties for perceiving the force and beauty of these arguments; or that he *might* not apply his mind to their investigation, and be brought to embrace them; or that he *might* not abandon the love of intoxicating drinks, and sensuality, and falsehood, and be a man of temperance, purity, and truth. He has all the natural faculties which are requisite in the case; and all the inability is his *strong love* of intoxicating drinks, or impurity, or falsehood. So of the sensual sinner. While he thus remains in love with sin, he cannot perceive the beauty of the plan of salvation, or the excellency of the doctrines of religion. He needs just the *love* of these things, and the *hatred* of sin. He needs to cherish the influences of the Spirit; to *receive* what He has taught, and not to reject it through the love of sin; he needs to yield himself to their influences, and then their beauty will be seen. The passage here *proves* that *while* a man is thus sensual, the things of the Spirit will appear to him to be folly; it proves nothing about his ability, or his natural faculty, to see the excellency of these things, and to turn from his sin. It is the affirmation of a simple fact everywhere discernible, that the natural man *does* not perceive the beauty of these things; that while he remains in that state he *cannot;* and that if he is ever brought to perceive their beauty, it will be by the influence of the Holy Spirit. Such is his love of sin, that he never *will* be brought to see their beauty except by the agency of the Holy Spirit. "For wickedness perverts the judgment, and makes men err with respect to practical principles; so that no one can be wise and judicious who is not good." *Aristotle*, as quoted by Bloomfield.

¶ *They are spiritually discerned.* That is, they are perceived by the aid of the Holy Spirit enlightening the mind and influencing the heart.

[The expression ψυχικὸς ἄνθρωπος has given rise to much controversy. Frequent attempts have been made to explain it, merely of the animal or sensual man. If this be the true sense, the doctrine of human depravity, in as

far at least as this text may be supposed to bear upon it, is greatly invalidated. The apostle would seem to affirm only, that individuals, addicted to the gross indulgences of sense, are incapable of discerning and appreciating spiritual things. Thus a large exception would be made in favour of all those who might be styled intellectual and moral persons, living above the inferior appetites, and directing their faculties to the candid investigation of truth. That the phrase, however, is to be explained of the natural or *unregenerate* man, whether distinguished for intellectual refinement, and external regard to morals, or degraded by animal indulgence, will appear evident from an examination of the passage. The word in dispute comes from ψυχη, which though it primarily signify the breath or animal life, is by no means confined to that sense, but sometimes embraces the mind or soul "as distinguished both from man's body and from his πνευμα, or spirit, breathed into him immediately by God".—*See Parkhurst's Greek Lexicon.* The etymology of the word does not necessarily require us, then, to translate it "sensual." The context therefore alone must determine the matter. Now the "natural man" is there opposed to the spiritual man, the ψυχικὸς to the πνευματικὸς, and if the latter be explained of "him who is enlightened by the Holy Spirit"—who is regenerate—the former must be explained of him who is *not* enlightened by that Spirit,—who is still in a state of nature; and will thus embrace a class far more numerous than the merely sensual part of mankind. Farther; the general scope of the passage demands this view. The Corinthians entertained an excessive fondness for human learning and wisdom. They loved philosophical disquisition and oratorical display, and may therefore have been impatient of the "unenticing words" of Paul. To correct their mistaken taste, the apostle asserts and proves the utter insufficiency of human wisdom, either to discover spiritual things, or to appreciate them when discovered. He exclaims "where is the *wise?*—where is the scribe?—where is the disputer of this world?—hath not God made foolish the wisdom of this world?" chap. i. 17, 31. Now it would be strange indeed, if in bringing his argument to a conclusion, he should simply assert, that *sensual* men were incapable of spiritual discernment. So lame and impotent a conclusion is not to be attributed to the apostle. The disputed phrase, therefore, must be understood of all unregenerate persons, however free from gross sin, or eminent in intellectual attainment. Indeed it is the *proud wisdom* of the world, and not its sensuality, that the apostle throughout has chiefly in view. Add to all this; that the simplicity of the gospel has *in reality* met with more bitter opposition and pointed scorn, from men of worldly wisdom,

16 For who *a* hath known the mind of the Lord, that he [1] may instruct him? But we have [b] the mind of Christ?

a Isa.40.13; Jer. 23.18.

1 *shall.*   b John 17.8.

thán from men of the sensual class. Of the former *especially* is it true that they have counted the gospel "foolishness" and contemptuously rejected its message.

Of this natural man it is affirmed that he *cannot* know the things of the Spirit of God. He *can* know them *speculatively*, and may enlarge on them with great accuracy and beauty, but he cannot know them so as to approve and receive. Allowing the incapacity to be moral, not natural or physical, that is to say, it arises from *disinclination or perversion of will:* still the spiritual perception *is* affected by the fall, and whether that be directly or indirectly through the will, matters not, *as far as the fact is concerned. It* remains the same. The mind of man when applied to spiritual subjects, has not now the same discernment it originally had, and as our author remarks, if ever it is brought to perceive their beauty, it must be by the agency of the Spirit. See the supplementary Note on Rom. viii. 7; page 174.]

15. *But he that is spiritual.* The man who is enlightened by the Holy Spirit in contradistinction from him who is under the influence of the *senses* only. ¶ *Judgeth.* Gr. *Discerneth.* (margin); the same word as in the previous verse. It means that the spiritual man has a discernment of those truths in regard to which the sensual man was blind and ignorant. ¶ *All things.* Not absolutely all things; or not that he is omniscient; but that he has a view of those things to which the apostle had reference—that is, to the things which are revealed to man by the Holy Spirit. ¶ *Yet he himself is judged.* Greek, as in the margin, "is discerned;" that is, his feelings, principles, views, hopes, fears, joys, cannot be fully understood and appreciated by any natural or sensual man. He does not comprehend the principles which actuate him ; he does not enter into his joys; he does not sympathize with him in his feelings. This is a matter of simple truth and universal observation. The reason is added in the following verse,—that as the Christian is influenced by the Lord and as the natural man does not know him, so he cannot know him who

is influenced by him ; that is the Christian.

16. *For who hath known*, &c. This passage is quoted from Isa. xl. 13. The interrogative form is a strong mode of denying that *any* one has ever known the mind of the Lord. The argument of Paul is this, " No one can understand God. No one can fully comprehend his plans, his feelings, his views, his designs. No one by nature, under the influence of sense and passion, is either disposed to investigate his truths, or loves them when they are revealed. But the Christian is influenced by God. He has his Spirit. He has the mind of Christ; who had the mind of God. He sympathizes with Christ; he has his feelings, desires, purposes, and plans. And as no one can fully understand God by nature, so neither can he understand him who is influenced by God, and is like him; and it is not to be wondered at that he regards the Christian religion as folly, and the Christian as a fool. ¶ *The mind of Christ.* The views, feelings, and temper of Christ. We are influenced by his Spirit.

REMARKS.

1st. Ministers of the gospel should not be too anxious to be distinguished for excellency of speech or language, ver. 1. Their aim should be to speak the simple truth, in language pure and intelligible to all. Let it be remembered, that if there ever was any place where it would be proper to seek such graces of eloquence, it was Corinth. If in any city now, or in any refined and genteel society it would be proper, it would have been proper in Corinth. Let this thought rebuke those, who, when they preach to a gay and fashionable auditory, seek to fill their sermons with ornament rather than with solid thought; with the tinsel of rhetoric, rather than with pure language. Paul was *right* in his course; and was *wise.* True taste abhors meretricious ornaments, as much as the gospel does. And the man who is called to preach in a rich and fashionable congregation, should remember, that he is stationed there not to please the ear, but to save the soul; that his object is not to display his talent or his eloquence, but to rescue his hearers from ruin. This purpose will make the mere ornaments of rhetoric appear small. It will give seriousness to his discourse; gravity to his diction; unction to his eloquence; heart to his arguments; and success to his ministry.

2d. The purpose of every minister should be like that of Paul, to preach Christ and him crucified only. See Note on ver. 2.

3d. If Paul trembled at Corinth in view of dangers and difficulties; if he was conscious of his own weakness and feebleness, then we should learn also to be humble. He is not much in danger of erring who imitates the example of this great apostle. And if he who had received a direct commission from the great Head of the church, and who was endowed with such mighty powers, was modest, unassuming, and diffident, then it becomes ministers of the gospel now, and all others to be humble also. We should not, indeed, be afraid of men; but we should be modest, humble, and lowly; much impressed, as if conscious of our mighty charge; and anxious to deliver just such a message as God will approve and bless.

Would I describe a preacher, such as Paul,
Were he on earth, would hear, approve, and
    own,
Paul should himself direct me. I would trace
His master-strokes, and draw from his design.
I would express him simple, grave, sincere;
In doctrine uncorrupt; in language plain;
And plain in manner, decent, solemn, chaste,
And natural in gesture: much impress'd
Himself, as conscious of his awful charge;
And anxious mainly that the flock he feeds
May feel it too. Affectionate in look,
And tender in address, as well becomes
A messenger of grace to guilty men.
                                    Task, B. ii.

Our aim should be to commend our message to every man's conscience; and to do it with humility towards God, and deep solicitude; with boldness towards our fellow men—respect-

fully towards them—but still resolved to tell the truth, ver. 3.

4th. The faith of Christians does not stand in the wisdom of man. Every Christian has evidence in his own heart, in his experience, and in the transformation of his character, that none but God could have wrought the change on his soul. His hopes, his joys, his peace, his sanctification, his love of prayer, of the Bible, of Christians, of God, and of Christ, are all such as nothing could have produced but the mighty power of God. All these bear marks of their high origin. They are the work of God on the soul. And as the Christian is fully conscious that these are not the *native* feelings of his heart—that if left to himself he would never have had them; so he has the fullest demonstration that they are to be traced to a divine source. And can he be mistaken about their existence? Can a man doubt whether he *has* joy, and peace, and happiness? Is the infidel to tell him coolly that he must be mistaken in regard to the existence of these emotions, and that it is all delusion? Can a child doubt whether it loves a parent; a husband whether he loves his wife; a friend, a friend; a man, his country? And can he doubt whether this emotion produces joy? And can a man doubt whether he loves God? Whether he has different views from what he once had? Whether he has peace and joy in view of the character of God, and the hope of heaven? And by what right shall the infidel tell him that he is mistaken, and that all this is delusion? How can *he* enter into the soul, and pronounce the man who professes to have these feelings mistaken? What should we think of the man who should tell a wife that she did not love her husband; or a father that he did not love his children? How *can* he know this? And, in like manner, how *can* an infidel and a scoffer say to a Christian, that all his hopes and joys, his love and peace are delusion and fanaticism? The truth is, that the great mass of Christians are just as well satisfied of the truth of religion, as they are of their own existence; and that a Christian will die for his love to the Saviour, just as he will die for his wife, and children, and country. Martyrdom in the one case is on the same principle as martyrdom in the other. Martyrdom in either, is noble and honourable, and evinces the highest qualities and principles of the human mind.

5th. Christians are influenced by true wisdom, ver. 6. They are not fools; though they appear to be to their fellow men. They see a *real* beauty and wisdom in the plan of redemption which the world does not discern. It is not the wisdom of this world; but it is the wisdom which looks to eternity. Is a man a fool who acts with reference to the future? Is he a fool who believes that he shall live to all eternity, and who regards it as proper to make preparation for that eternity? Is he a fool who acts as if he were to die—to be judged—to enter on an unchanging destiny? Folly is manifested in closing the eyes on the reality of the condition; not in looking at it as it is. The man who is sick, and who strives to convince himself that he is well; the man whose affairs are in a state of bankruptcy, and who is unwilling to know it, is a fool. The man who is willing to know all about his situation, and to act accordingly, is a wise man. The one represents the conduct of a sinner, the other that of a Christian. A man who should see his child drowning, or his house on fire, or the pestilence breathing around him, and be unconcerned, or *dance* amidst such scenes, would be a fool or a madman. And is not the sinner who is gay and thoughtless over the grave and over *hell* equally foolish and mad? And if there be a God, a heaven, a Saviour, and a hell; if men are to die, and to be judged, is he not wise who acts *as if* it were so, and who lives accordingly? While Christians, therefore, may not be distinguished for the wisdom of this world—while many are destitute of learning, science, and eloquence, they *have* a wisdom which shall survive when all other is vanished away.

6th. All the wisdom of this world shall come to nought, ver. 6. What

will be the value of political sagacity, when all governments shall come to an end but the divine government? What the value of eloquence, and graceful diction, when we stand at the judgment seat of Christ? What the value of science in this world, when all shall be revealed with the clearness of noon-day? How low will appear *all* human attainments in that world, when the light of eternal day shall be shed over all the works of God? How little can human science do to advance the eternal interests of man? And how shall all fade away in the future world of glory—just as the feeble glimmering of the stars fades away before the light of the morning sun! How little, therefore, should we pride ourselves on the highest attainments of science, and the most elevated distinctions of learning and eloquence.

7th. God has a purpose in regard to the salvation of men, ver. 7. This scheme was ordained before the world. It was not a new device. It was not the offspring of chance, an accident, or an *after thought*. It was because God purposed it *from eternity*. God has a plan; and this plan contemplates the salvation of his people. And it greatly enhances the value of this benevolent plan in the eyes of his people, that it has been the object of *the eternal earnest desire and purpose of God.* How much a gift is enhanced in value from the fact that it has been long the purpose of a parent to bestow it; that he has toiled for it; that he has made arrangements for it; and that this has been the chief object of his efforts and his plan for years. So the favours of eternal redemption are bestowed on Christians as the fruit of the eternal purpose and desire of God. And how should our hearts rise in gratitude to him for his unspeakable gift!

8th. One great and prominent cause of sin is the fact that men are blind to the reality and beauty of spiritual objects. So it was with those who crucified the Lord, ver. 8. Had they seen his glory as it was, they would not have crucified him. And so it is now. When men blaspheme God, they see not his excellency; when they revile religion, they know not its real value ; when they break the laws of God, they do not fully discern their purity and their importance. It is true they are wilfully ignorant, and their crime is often enhanced by this fact ; but it is equally true that "they know not what they do." For such poor, blinded, deluded mortals, the Saviour prayed ; and for such we should all pray. The man that curses God, has no just sense of what he is doing. The man who is profane, and a scoffer, and a liar, and an adulterer, has no just sense of the awful nature of his crime ; and is an object of commiseration—while his *sin* should be *hated*—and is a proper subject of prayer.

9th. Men are often committing the most awful crimes when they are unconscious of it. ver. 8. What crime could compare with that of crucifying the only Son of God ? And what crime could be attended with more dreadful consequences to its perpetrators ? So of sinners now. They little know what they do ; and they little know the consequences of their sins. A man may curse his Maker, and say it is in sport ! But how will it be regarded in the day of judgment ? A man may revile the Saviour ! But how will it appear when he dies ? It is a solemn thing to trifle with God and with his laws. A man is safer when he sports on a volcano, or when he makes a jest of the pestilence or the forked lightnings of heaven, than when he sports with religion and with God ! In a world like this, men should be serious and fear God. A single deed, like that of the crucifixion of Christ, may be remembered, when all the circumstances of sport and mockery shall have passed away— remembered when the world shall be destroyed, and stars and suns shall rush to ruin.

10th. Christians have views of the beauties of religion, and have consolations arising from these views, which the world has not, ver. 9. They have different views of God, of Christ, of heaven, of eternity. They see a beauty in all these things, and a wisdom in the plan of salvation, which

the men of the world do not see. The contemplations of this beauty and wisdom, and the evidence which they have that they are interested in all this, gives them a joy which the world does not possess. They see what the eye has not elsewhere seen ; they enjoy what men elsewhere have not enjoyed ; and they are elevated to privileges which men elsewhere do not possess. On earth they partake of happiness which the world never can give, and in heaven they shall partake of the fulness of that joy—of pleasures there which the eye had not before seen, nor the ear heard, nor the heart of man conceived. Who would not be a Christian ?

11th. The Holy Ghost is in some sense distinct from the Father. This is implied in his action as an agent— in searching, knowing, &c. ver. 10, 11. An attribute ; a quality, does not search and know.

12th. The Holy Spirit is divine. None can know God but one equal to himself. If the Spirit intimately knows the wisdom, the goodness, the omniscience, the eternity, the power of God, he must be divine. No created being can have this intelligence, ver. 10, 11.

13th. Christians are actuated by a different spirit from the men of this world, ver. 12. They are influenced by a regard to God and his glory. The men of the world are under the influence of pride, avarice, sensuality, ambition, and vain glory.

14th. The sinner does not perceive the beauty of the things of religion. To all this beauty he is blind. This is a sober and a most melancholy fact. Whatever may be the cause of it, the fact is undeniable and sad. It is so with the sensualist ; with the men of avarice, pride, ambition, and licentiousness. The gospel is regarded as folly, and is despised and scorned by the men of this world. This is true in all places, among all people, and at all times. To this there are no exceptions in human nature ; and over this we should sit down and weep.

15th. The *reason* of this is, that men love darkness. It is not that they are destitute of the natural faculties for

CHAPTER III.

A ND I, brethren, could not speak
unto you as *a* unto spiritual,

but as unto carnal, *even* as unto
babes *b* in Christ.

a chap. 2.14,15.　　　　*b* Heb.5.12,13; 1 Pet.2.2.

loving God, for they have as strong
native powers as those who become
Christians. It is because they *love
sin*—and this simple fact, carried out
into all its bearings, will account for
all the difficulties in the way of the
sinner's conversion. There is nothing
else; and

16th. We see here the value of the
influences of the Spirit. It is by this
Spirit alone that the mind of the
Christian is enlightened, sanctified,
and comforted. It is by Him alone
that he sees the beauty of the religion
which he loves; it is by His influence
alone that he differs from his fellow
men. And no less important is it for
the sinner. Without the influences of
that Spirit his mind will always be in
darkness, and his heart will always
hate the gospel. How anxiously,
therefore, should he cherish His influences! How careful should he be not
to grieve Him away!

17th. There is a difference between
Christians and other men. One is
enlightened by the Holy Spirit, the
other not; one sees a beauty in religion, to the other it is folly; the one
has the mind of Christ, the other has
the spirit of the world; the one dis-
cerns the excellency of the plan of
salvation, to the other all is darkness
and folly. How could beings differ
more in their moral feelings and views
than do Christians and the men of
this world?

CHAPTER III.

THE design of this chapter is substantially the same as the former. It
is to reprove the pride, the philosophy, the vain wisdom on which the
Greeks so much rested; and to show
that the gospel was not dependent on
that for its success, and that that had
been the occasion of no small part of the
contentions and strifes which had
arisen in the church at Corinth. The
chapter is occupied mainly with an
account of his own ministry with
them; and seems designed to meet an
objection which either *was* made, or
could have been made by the Corin-

thians themselves, or by the false
teacher that was among them. In
chap. ii. 12—16, he had affirmed that
Christians were in fact under the
influence of the Spirit of God; that
they were enlightened in a remarkable
degree; that they understood all
things pertaining to the Christian
religion. To this, it either was, or
could have been objected that Paul,
when among them, had not instructed
them fully in the more deep and abstruse points of the gospel; and that he
had confined his instructions to the
very rudiments of the Christian religion. Of this, probably the false
teachers who had formed parties
among them, had taken the advantage, and had pretended to carry the
instruction to a much greater length,
and to explain many things which
Paul had left unexplained. Hence
this division into parties. It became
Paul, therefore, to state why he had
confined his instructions to the rudiments of the gospel among them—and
this occupies the first part of the
chapter, v. 1—11. The *reason* was,
that they were not prepared to receive
higher instruction, but were carnal,
and he could not address them as
being prepared to enter fully into the
more profound doctrines of the Christian religion. The *proof* that this was
so, was found in the fact that they had
been distracted with disputes and
strifes, which demonstrated that they
were not prepared for the higher
doctrines of Christianity. He then
reproves them for their contentions,
on the ground that it was of little
consequence by what instrumentality they had been brought to the
knowledge of the gospel, and that
there was no occasion for their strifes
and sects. ALL success, whoever was
the instrument, was to be traced to
God (ver. 5—7), and the fact that one
teacher or another had first instructed
them, or that one was more eloquent
than another, should not be the foundation for contending sects. God was
the source of all blessings. Yet in

order to show the real nature of his own work, in order to meet the whole of the objection, he goes on to state that he had done the most important part of the work in the church himself. He had laid the foundation; and all the others were but rearing the superstructure. And much as *his* instructions might appear to be elementary, and unimportant, yet it had been done with the same skill which an architect evinces who labours that the foundation may be well laid and firm, ver. 10, 11. The others who had succeeded him, whoever they were, were but builders upon this foundation. The foundation had been well laid, and they should be careful how they built on it, ver. 12—16. The mention of this fact—that he had laid the foundation, and that that foundation was Jesus Christ, and that they had been reared upon that as a church, leads him to the inference (ver. 16, 17), that they should be holy as the temple of God; and the conclusion from the whole is, (1.) That no man should deceive himself, of which there was so much danger (ver. 18—20); and, (2.) That no Christian should glory in men, for all things were theirs. It was no matter who had been their teacher on earth, all belonged to God; and they had a common interest in the most eminent teachers of religion, and they should rise above the petty rivalships of the world, and rejoice in the assurance that all things belonged to them, ver. 21—23.

1. *And I, brethren.* See chap. ii. 1. This is designed to meet an implied objection. He had said (chap. ii. 14—16) that Christians were able to understand all things. Yet, they would recollect that he had not addressed them as such, but had confined himself to the more elementary parts of religion when he came among them. He had not entered upon the abstruse and difficult points of theology—the points of speculation in which the subtle Greeks so much abounded and so much delighted. He now states the reason why he had not done it. The reason was one that was most humbling to their pride; but it

was the true reason, and faithfulness demanded that it should be stated. It was, that they were *carnal*, and not qualified to understand the deep mysteries of the gospel; and the *proof* of this was unhappily at hand. It was too evident in their contentions and strifes, that they were under the influence of carnal feelings and views. ¶ *Could not speak unto you as unto spiritual.* "I could not regard you as spiritual—as qualified to enter into the full and higher truths of the gospel; I could not regard you as divested of the feelings which influence carnal men—the men of the world, and I addressed you accordingly. I could not discourse to you as to far-advanced and well-informed Christians. I taught you the *rudiments* only of the Christian religion." He refers here, doubtless, to his instructions when he founded the church at Corinth. See Note, chap. ii. 13—15. ¶ *But as unto carnal.* The word *carnal* here (σαρκινοῖς) is not the same which in chap. ii. 14, is translated *natural* (ψυχικὸς). *That* refers to one who is unrenewed, and who is wholly under the influence of his sensual or animal nature, and is no where applied to Christians. *This* is applied here to Christians—but to those who have much of the remains of corruption, and who are imperfectly acquainted with the nature of religion; babes in Christ. It denotes those who still evinced the feelings and views which pertain to the flesh, in these unhappy contentions, and strifes, and divisions. "The works of the flesh are hatred, variance, emulations, wrath, strife, seditions, envyings" (Gal. v. 20, 21); and these they had evinced in their divisions; and Paul knew that their danger lay in this direction, and he therefore addressed them according to their character. Paul applies the word to himself (Rom. vii. 14), "for I am carnal;" and here it denotes that they were as yet under the influence of the corrupt passions and desires which the flesh produces. ¶ *As unto babes in Christ.* As unto those recently born into his kingdom, and unable to understand the profounder doctrines of the Christian religion. It is a com-

2 I have fed you with milk, and not with meat: for hitherto ^a ye were not able *to bear it*, neither yet now are ye able.

3 For ye are yet carnal: for whereas ^b *there is* among you envy-

ing, and strife, and ¹ divisions, are ye not carnal, and walk ² as men?

4 For while one saith, I ^c am of Paul; and another, I *am* of Apollos; are ye not carnal?

5 Who then is Paul, and who *is*

a John 16.12.   *b* James 3.16.   1 or, *factions*.   2 *according to man*.   *c* chap.1.12.

mon figure to apply the term infants and children to those who are feeble in understanding, or unable, from any cause, to comprehend the more profound instructions of science or religion.

2. *I have fed you with milk.* Paul here continues the metaphor, which is derived from the custom of feeding infants with the lightest food. Milk here evidently denotes the more simple and elementary doctrines of Christianity—the doctrines of the new birth, of repentance, faith, &c. The same figure occurs in Heb. v. 11—14; and also in classical writers. See Wetstein. ¶ *And not with meat.* Meat here denotes the more sublime and mysterious doctrines of religion. ¶ *For hitherto.* Formerly, when I came among you, and laid the foundations of the church. ¶ *Not able* to bear it. You were not sufficiently advanced in Christian knowledge to comprehend the higher mysteries of the gospel. ¶ *Neither yet now,* &c. The reason why they were not then able he proceeds immediately to state.

3. *For ye are yet carnal.* Though you are Christians, and are the friends of God in the main, yet your divisions and strifes show that you are yet, in some degree, under the influence of the principles which govern the men of this world. Men who are governed solely by the principles of this world, evince a spirit of strife, emulation and contention; and just so far as you are engaged in strife, just so far do you show that you are governed by their principles and feelings. ¶ *For whereas.* In proof that you are carnal I appeal to your contentions and strifes. ¶ *Envying* (ζῆλος), zeal; used here in the sense of *envy*, as it is in James iii. 14, 16. It denotes, properly, any *fervour* of mind (from ζέω), and may be applied to any exciting and agitating passion. The envy here referred to,

was that which arose from the superior advantages and endowments which some claimed or possessed over others. Envy everywhere is a fruitful cause of strife. Most contentions in the church are somehow usually connected with envy. ¶ *And strife.* Contention and dispute. ¶ *And divisions.* Dissensions and quarrels. The margin correctly renders it *factions.* The idea is, that they were split up into parties, and that those parties were embittered with mutual recriminations and reproaches, as they always are in a church. ¶ *And walk as men.* Marg. *according to man.* The word *walk* is used often in the Scriptures in the sense of *conduct* or *act.* You *conduct* as men, *i. e.* as men commonly do; you evince the same spirit that the great mass of men do. Instead of being filled with love; of being united and harmonious as the members of the same family ought to be, you are split up into factions as the men of the world are.

4. *For while one saith,* &c.; see Note, chap. i. 12.

5. *Who then is Paul,* &c.; see Notes, chap. i. 13. Why should a party be formed which should be named after Paul? What has he done or taught that should lead to this? What eminence has *he* that should induce any to call themselves by his name? He is on a level with the other apostles; and all are but ministers, or servants, and have no claim to the honour of giving names to sects and parties. God is the fountain of all your blessings, and whoever may have been the *instrument* by whom you have believed, it is improper to regard them as in any sense the fountain of your blessings, or to arrange yourselves under their name. ¶ *But ministers.* Our word *minister,* as now used, does not express the proper force of this word. We in applying it to preachers of the

Apollos, but ministers by whom ye believed, even *a* as the Lord gave to every man?

a Rom.12.3,6; 1 Pet.4.11.

gospel do not usually advert to the original sense of the word, and the reasons why it was given to them. The original word ($\delta\iota\acute{\alpha}\kappa o\nu o\iota$) denotes properly *servants* in contradistinction from *masters* (Mat. xx. 26; xxiii. 11; Mark ix. 35; x. 43); and denotes those of course who are in an inferior rank of life. They had not command, or authority, but were subject to the command of others. It is applied to the preachers of the gospel because they are employed in the *service* of God; because they go at his command, and are subject to his control and direction. They have not original authority, nor are they the source of influence or power. The idea here is, that they were the mere instruments or servants by whom God conveyed all blessings to the Corinthians; that they as ministers were on a level, were engaged in the same work, and that therefore, it was improper for them to form parties that should be called by their names. ¶ *By whom.* Through whom ($\delta\iota'$ $\tilde{\omega}\nu$), by whose instrumentality. They were not the original source of faith, but were the mere servants of God in conveying to them the knowledge of that truth by which they were to be saved. ¶ *Even as the Lord gave to every man.* God is the original source of faith; and it is by his influence that any one is brought to believe; see Note, Rom. xii. 3, 6. There were diversities of gifts among the Corinthian Christians, as there are in all Christians. And it is here implied, (1.) That all that any one had was to be traced to God as its author; (2.) That he is a sovereign, and dispenses his favours to all as he pleases; (3.) That since *God* had conferred those favours, it was improper for the Corinthians to divide themselves into sects and call themselves by the name of their teachers, for *all* that they had was to be traced to God alone. This idea, that *all* the gifts and graces which Christians had, were to be traced to God alone, was one which

6 I have planted, Apollos watered; but God *b* gave the increase.

b chap.15.10.

the apostle Paul often insisted on; and if this idea had been kept before the minds and hearts of all Christians, it would have prevented no small part of the contentions in the church, and the formation of no small part of the sects in the Christian world.

6. *I have planted.* The apostle here compares the establishment of the church at Corinth to the planting of a vine, a tree, or of grain. The figure is taken from agriculture, and the meaning is obvious. Paul established the church. He was the first preacher in Corinth; and if any distinction was due to any one, it was rather to him than to the teachers who had laboured there subsequently; but he regarded himself as worthy of no such honour as to be the head of a party, for it was not himself, but God who had given the increase. ¶ *Apollos watered.* This figure is taken from the practice of watering a tender plant, or of watering a garden or field. This was necessary in a special manner in eastern countries. Their fields became parched and dry from their long droughts, and it was necessary to irrigate them by artificial means. The sense here is, that Paul had laboured in establishing the church at Corinth; but that subsequently Apollos had laboured to increase it, and to build it up. It is certain that Apollos did not go to Corinth until after Paul had left it; see Acts xviii. 18; comp. 27. ¶ *God gave the increase.* God caused the seed sown to take root and spring up; and God blessed the irrigation of the tender plants as they sprung up, and caused them to grow. This idea is still taken from the husbandman. It would be vain for the farmer to sow his seed unless God should give it life. There is no life in the seed, nor is there any inherent power in the earth to make it grow. God only, the giver of all life, can quicken the germ in the seed, and make it live. So it would be in vain for the farmer to water his plant unless God should

7 So then neither *a* is he that planteth any thing, neither he that watereth, but God that giveth the increase.

a John 15.5; 2 Cor.12 9—11.

8 Now he that planteth and he that watereth are one : and every man *b* shall receive his own reward according to his own labour.

b Ps.62.12; Rev.22.12.

bless it. There is no living principle in the water ; no inherent power in the rains of heaven to make the plant grow. It is *adapted*, indeed, to this, and the seed would not germinate if it was not planted, nor grow if it was not watered ; but the life is still from God. He arranged these means, and he gives life to the tender blade, and sustains it. And so it is with the word of life. It has no inherent power to produce effect by itself. The power is not in the naked word, nor in him that plants, nor in him that waters, nor in the heart where it is sown, but in God. But there is a *fitness* of the means to the end. The word is adapted to save the soul. The seed must be sown or it will not germinate. Truth must be sown in *the heart*, and the heart must be prepared for it—as the earth must be ploughed and made mellow, or it will not spring up. It must be cultivated with assiduous care, or it will produce nothing. But still it is all of God—as much so as the yellow harvest of the field, after all the toils of the husbandman is of God. And as the farmer who has just views, will take no praise to himself because his corn and his vine start up and grow after all his care, but will ascribe all to God's unceasing, beneficent agency ; so will the minister of religion, and so will every Christian, after all their care, ascribe all to God.

7. *Any thing.* This is to be taken *comparatively.* They are nothing in comparison with God. Their agency is of no importance compared with his ; see Note, chap. i. 28. It does not mean that their agency ought not to be performed ; that it is not important, and indispensable in its place ; but that the honour is due to God.—Their agency *is* indispensable. God *could* make seed or a tree grow if they were not planted in the earth. But he does not do it. The agency of the husbandman is indispensable in the ordinary operations of his providence. If he

does not plant, God will not make the grain or the tree grow. God *blesses* his labours ; he does not work a miracle. God attends *effort* with success ; he does not interfere in a miraculous manner to accommodate the *indolence* of men. So in the matter of salvation. The efforts of ministers would be of no avail without God. They could do nothing in the salvation of the soul unless He should give the increase. But *their* labours are as indispensable and as necessary, as are those of the farmer in the production of a harvest. And as every farmer could say, "my labours are *nothing* without God, who alone can give the increase," so it is with every minister of the gospel.

8. *Are one* (ἕν εἰσιν). They are not the same person ; but they are *one* in the following respects : (1.) They are *united* in reference to the same work. Though they are engaged in different things—for planting and watering are different kinds of work, yet it is one in regard to the end to be gained. The employments do not at all *clash*, but tend to the same end. It is not as if one planted, and the other was engaged in pulling up. (2.) Their work is *one*, because one is as necessary as the other. If the grain was not planted there would be no use in pouring water there ; if not watered, there would be no use in planting. The work of one is as needful, therefore, as the other ; and the one should not undervalue the labours of the other. (3.) They are *one* in regard to God. They are *both* engaged in performing one work ; God is performing another. There are not three parties or portions of the work, but two. They two perform one part of the work ; God *alone* performs the other. Theirs would be useless without him ; he would not ordinarily perform his without their performing their part. They *could* not do his part if they would—as they cannot make a plant *grow ;* he *could* perform their

9 For we are labourers to- ¹ husbandry, *ye are* God's build-
gether *a* with God: ye are God's ing. *b*

a 2 Cor.6.1.

1 or, *tillage*.   *b* Heb.3.6; 1 Pet.2.5.

part—as *he* could plant and water without the farmer; but it is not in accordance with his arrangements to do it. ¶ *And every man.* The argument of the apostle here has reference only to ministers; but it is equally true of all men, that they shall receive their proper reward. ¶ *Shall receive.* In the day of judgment, when God decides the destiny of men. The decisions of that day will be simply determining what every moral agent *ought* to receive. ¶ *His own reward.* His fit, or proper (τον ίδιον) reward; that which pertains to him, or which shall be a proper expression of the character and value of his labour. The word *reward* (μισθόν) denotes properly that which is given by contract for service rendered; an equivalent in value for services or for kindness; Note, Rom. iv. 4. In the Scriptures it denotes pay, wages, recompense given to day-labourers, to soldiers, &c. It is applied often, as here, to the retribution which God will make to men in the day of judgment; and is applied to the *favours* which he will then bestow on them, or to the *punishment* which he will inflict as the reward of their deeds. Instances of the former sense occur in Mat. v. 12; vi.; Luke vi. 23, 35; Rev. xi. 18; of the latter in 2 Pet. ii. 13, 15.—In regard to the righteous, it does not imply *merit*, or that they deserve heaven; but it means that God will render to them that which, according to the terms of his new covenant, he has promised, and which shall be a fit expression of his acceptance of their services. It is *proper*, according to these arrangements, that they should be blessed in heaven. It would *not* be proper that they should be cast down to hell.— Their original and their sole *title* to eternal life is the grace of God through Jesus Christ; the *measure*, or *amount* of the favours bestowed on them there, shall be according to the services which they render on earth. A parent may resolve to divide his estate among

his sons, and their title to *any* thing may be derived from his mere favour, but he may determine that it shall be divided *according* to their expressions of attachment, and to their obedience to him.

9. *For we are labourers together with God* (Θεοῦ γὰρ ἐσμεν συνεργοί). We are God's co-workers. A similar expression occurs in 2 Cor. vi. 1, "We then as workers together with him," &c. This passage is capable of two significations: *first*, as in our translation, that they were co-workers with God; engaged with him in his work, that he and they co-operated in the production of the effect; or that it was a *joint-work;* as we speak of a partnery, or of joint-effort among men. So many interpreters have understood this. If this is the sense of the passage, then it means that as a farmer may be said to be a co-worker with God when he plants and tills his field, or does that without which God would not work in that case, or without which a harvest would not be produced, so the Christian minister co-operates with God in producing the same result. He is engaged in performing that which is indispensable to the end; and God also, by his Spirit, co-operates with the same design. If this be the idea, it gives a peculiar sacredness to the work of the ministry, and indeed to the work of the farmer and the vinedresser. There is no higher honour than for a man to be engaged in doing the same things which God does, and participating with him in accomplishing his glorious plans. But doubts have been suggested in regard to this interpretation. (1.) The Greek does not of necessity imply this. It is literally, not we are his co-partners, but we are his fellow-labourers, *i. e.* fellow-labourers in his employ, under his direction --as we say of servants of the same rank they are fellow-labourers of the same master, not meaning that the master was engaged in working *with*

10 According ^a to the grace of God

a Rom. 12. 3.

them, but that *they* were fellow-labourers one with another in his employment. (2.) There is no expression that is parallel to this. There is none that speaks of God's operating *jointly* with his creatures in producing the *same* result. They may be engaged in regard to the same end; but the sphere of God's operations and of their operations is distinct. God does one thing; and they do another, though they may contribute to the same result. The sphere of God's operations in the growth of a tree is totally distinct from that of the man who plants it. The man who planted it has *no* agency in causing the juices to circulate; in expanding the bud or the leaf; that is, in the proper work of God.—In 3 John 8, Christians are indeed said to be "fellow-helpers to the truth" (συνεργοὶ τῇ ἀληθείᾳ); that is, they operate with the truth, and contribute by their labours and influence to that effect. In Mark also (xvi. 20), it is said that the apostles "went forth and preached everywhere, the Lord working with them" (τοῦ κυρίου συνεργοῦντος), where the phrase means that the Lord co-operated with them by miracles, &c. The Lord, by his own proper energy, and in his own sphere, contributed to the success of the work in which they were engaged. (3.) The main design and scope of this whole passage is to show that God is all— that the apostles are nothing; to represent the apostles not as joint-workers with God, but as working by themselves, and God as alone giving efficiency to all that was done. The idea is, that of depressing or humbling the apostles, and of exalting God; and this idea would not be consistent with the interpretation that they were *joint*-labourers with him. While, therefore, the Greek would bear the interpretation conveyed in our translation, the sense *may* perhaps be, that the apostles were joint-labourers with each other in God's service; that they were united in their work, and that God was all in all; that they were like servants employed *in* the service of a

master, without saying that the master participated with them in their work. This idea is conveyed in the translation of Doddridge, "we are the fellow-labourers of God." So Rosenmüller. Calvin, however, Grotius, Whitby, and Bloomfield, coincide with our version in the interpretation. The Syriac renders it "We work with God." The Vulgate, "We are the aids of God." ¶ *Ye are God's husbandry* (γεώργιον); margin, *tillage*. This word occurs no where else in the New Testament. It properly denotes a *tilled* or *cultivated field;* and the idea is, that the church at Corinth was the field on which *God* had bestowed the labour of tillage, or culture, to produce fruit. The word is used by the LXX. in Gen. xxvi. 14, as the translation of מִקְנֶה, "For he had *possession* of flocks," &c.; in Jer. xli. 23, as the translation of צֶמֶד, *a yoke;* and in Prov. xxiv. 30; xxxi. 16, as the translation of שָׂדֶה, *a field;* "I went by the *field* of the slothful," &c. The sense here is, that all their culture was of God; that as a church they were under his care; and that all that had been produced in them was to be traced to his cultivation. ¶ *God's building.* This is another metaphor. The object of Paul was to show that *all* that had been done for them had been really accomplished by God. For this purpose he first says that they were God's cultivated field; then he changes the figure; draws his illustration from architecture, and says, that they had been *built* by him as an architect rears a house. It does not rear itself; but it is reared by another. So he says of the Corinthians, "Ye are the building which God erects." The same figure is used in 2 Cor. vi. 16, and Eph. ii 21; see also Heb. iii. 6; 1 Pet. ii. 5. The idea is, that God is the supreme agent in the founding and establishing of the church, in all its gifts and graces.

10. *According to the grace of God.* By the favour of God which is given to me. All that Paul had done had been by the mere favour of God. His appointment was from him; and all

master-builder, I have laid the foundation, and another buildeth thereon.

But let every man take heed how he buildeth thereupon.

the skill which he had shown, and all the agency which he had employed, had been from him. The architectural figure is here continued with some striking additions and illustrations. By the " grace of God" here, Paul probably means his apostleship to the Gentiles, which had been conferred on him by the mere favour of God, and all the wisdom, and skill, and success which he had evinced in founding the church. ¶ *As a wise master-builder.* Gr. *Architect.* The word does not imply that Paul had any pre-eminence over his brethren, but that he had proceeded in his work as a skilful architect, who secures first a firm foundation. Every builder begins with the foundation ; and Paul had proceeded in this manner in laying first a firm foundation on which the church could be reared. The word *wise* here means skilful, judicious ; comp. Mat. vii. 24. ¶ *I have laid the foundation. What* this foundation was, he states in ver. 11. The meaning here is, that the church at Corinth had been at first established by Paul ; see Acts xviii. 1, &c. ¶ *And another.* Other teachers. I have communicated to the church the first elements of Christian knowledge. Others *follow out* this instruction, and edify the church. The discussion here undergoes a slight change. In the former part of the chapter, *Christians* are compared to a building ; here the *doctrines* which are taught in the church are compared to various parts of a building. *Grotius.* See similar instances of translation in Mat. xiii ; Mark iv. John x. ¶ *But let every man,* &c. Every man who is a professed teacher. Let him be careful what instructions he shall give to a church that has been founded by apostolic hands, and that is established on the only true foundation. This is designed to guard against false instruction and the instructions of false teachers. Men should take heed what instruction they give to a church, (1.) Because of the fact that the church belongs to God, and they should be cautious what directions they give to

it ; (2.) Because it is important that Christians should not only be on the true foundation, but that they should be fully instructed in the nature of their religion, and the church should be permitted to rise in its true beauty and loveliness ; (3.) Because of the evils which result from false instruction. Even when the foundation is firm, incalculable evils will result from the want of just and discriminating instruction. Error sanctifies no one. The effect of it even on the minds of true Christians is to mar their piety ; to dim its lustre ; and to darken their minds. No Christian can enjoy religion except under the full-orbed shining of the word of truth ; and every man, therefore, who gives false instruction, is responsible for all the darkness he causes, and for all the want of comfort which true Christians under his teaching may experience. (4.) Every man must give an account of the nature of his instructions ; and he should therefore "take heed to himself, and his doctrine" (1 Tim. iv. 16) ; and preach *such* doctrine as shall bear the test of the great day. And from this we learn, that it is important that the church should be built on the true foundation ; and that it is scarcely less important that it should be built up in the knowledge of the truth. Vast evils are constantly occurring in the church for the want of proper instruction to young converts. Many seem to feel that provided the foundation be well laid, that is all that is needed. But the grand thing which is wanted at the present time, is, that those who *are* converted should, as soon as possible, be instructed FULLY in the nature of the religion which they have embraced. What would be thought of a farmer who should plant a tree, and never water or trim it ; who should plant his seed, and never cultivate the corn as it springs up ; who should sow his fields, and then think that all is well, and leave it to be overrun with weeds and thorns? Piety is often stunted, its early shootings blighted, its rapid growth checked,

11 For other foundation can no man lay than that is laid, *a* which is Jesus Christ.

a Isa.28.16; Mat.16.18; Eph.2.20; 2 Tim.2.19.

12 Now if any man build upon this foundation gold, silver, precious stones, wood, hay, stubble;

for the want of early culture in the church. And perhaps there is no one thing in which pastors more frequently fail than in regard to the culture which ought to be bestowed on those who are converted—especially in early life. Our Saviour's views on this were expressed in the admonition to Peter, "Feed my lambs," John xxi. 15.

11. *For other foundation.* It is *implied* by the course of the argument here, that *this* was the foundation which had been laid at Corinth, and on which the church there had been reared. And it is *affirmed* that no other foundation can be laid. A foundation is that on which a building is reared : the foundation of a church is the *doctrine* on which it is established; that is, the doctrines which its members hold—those truths which lie at the basis of their hopes, and by embracing which they have been converted to God. ¶ *Can no man lay.* That is, there *is* no other true foundation. ¶ *Which is Jesus Christ.* Christ is often called the foundation; the stone; the corner stone on which the church is reared; Isa. xxviii. 16; Mat. xxi. 42; Acts iv. 11; Eph. ii. 20; 2 Tim. ii. 19; 1 Pet. ii. 6. The meaning is, that no true church can be reared which does not embrace and hold the true doctrines respecting him —those which pertain to his incarnation, his divine nature, his instructions, his example, his atonement, his resurrection, and ascension. The reason why no true church can be established without embracing the truth as it is in Christ is, that it is by him only that men can be saved; and where *this* doctrine is wanting, all is wanting that enters into the essential idea of a church. The fundamental doctrines of the Christian religion must be embraced, or a church cannot exist; and where those doctrines are denied, no association of men can be recognised as a church of God. Nor can the foundation be modified or shaped so as to suit the wishes of men. It must

be laid as it is in the Scriptures; and the superstructure must be reared on that alone.

12. *Now if any man.* If any teacher in the doctrines which he inculcates; or any private Christian in the hopes which he cherishes. The main discussion doubtless, has respect to the teachers of religion. Paul carries forward the metaphor in this and the following verses with respect to the building. He supposes that the *foundation* is laid; that it is a true foundation; that the essential doctrines in regard to the Messiah are the real basis on which the edifice is reared. But, he says, that even admitting that, it is a subject of vast importance to attend to the kind of structure which shall be reared on that; whether it shall be truly beautiful, and valuable in itself, and such as shall abide the trial of the last great day; or whether it be mean, worthless, erroneous, and such as shall at last be destroyed. There has been some difference of opinion in regard to the interpretation of this passage, arising from the question whether the apostle designed to represent *one* or *two* buildings. The former has been the more common interpretation, and the sense according to that is, "the true foundation is laid; but on that it is improper to place vile and worthless materials. It would be absurd to work them in with those which are valuable; it would be absurd to work in, in rearing a building, wood, and hay, and stubble, with gold, and silver, and precious stones; there would be a want of concinnity and beauty in this. So in the spiritual temple. There is an impropriety, an unfitness, in rearing the spiritual temple, to interweave truth with error; sound doctrine with false." See Calvin and Macknight. Grotius renders it, " Paul feigns to himself an edifice, partly regal, and partly rustic. He presents the image of a house whose walls are of marble, whose columns are made partly of gold and partly of

silver, whose beams are of wood, and whose roof thatched with straw." Others, among whom are Wetstein, Doddridge, Rosenmüller, suppose that he refers to *two* buildings that might be reared on this foundation—either one that should be magnificent and splendid; or one that should be a rustic cottage, or mean hovel, thatched with straw, and made of planks of wood. Doddridge paraphrases the passage, " *If any man build,* I say, *upon this foundation,* let him look to the materials and the nature of his work; whether he raise a stately and magnificent temple upon it, adorned as it were like the house of God at Jerusalem, with gold and silver, and large, beautiful, and costly stones; or a mean hovel, consisting of nothing better than planks of wood roughly put together, and thatched with hay and stubble. That is, let him look to it, whether he teach the substantial, vital truths of Christianity, and which it was intended to support and illustrate; or set himself to propagate vain subtilties and conceits on the one hand, or legal rites and Jewish traditions on the other; which although they do not entirely destroy the foundation, disgrace it, as a mean edifice would do a grand and extensive foundation laid with great pomp and solemnity." This probably expresses the correct sense of the passage. The foundation may be well laid; yet *on* this foundation an edifice may be reared that shall be truly magnificent, or one that shall be mean and worthless. So the true foundation of a church may be laid, or of individual conversion to God, in the true doctrine respecting Christ. That church or that individual *may be* built up and adorned with all the graces which truth is fitted to produce; or there may be false principles and teachings superadded; doctrines that shall delude and lead astray; or views and feelings cultivated *as* piety, and believed *to be* piety, which may be no part of true religion, but which are mere delusion and fanaticism. ¶ *Gold, silver.* On the meaning of these words it is not necessary to dwell; or to lay too much stress. Gold is the emblem of that which is valuable and precious,

and may be the emblem of that truth and holiness which shall bear the trial of the great day. In relation to the figure which the apostle here uses, it may refer to the fact that columns or beams in an edifice might be gilded; or perhaps, as in the temple, that they might be solid gold, so as to bear the action of intense heat; or so that fire would not destroy them.—So the precious doctrines of truth, and all the feelings, views, opinions, habits, practices, which truth produces in an individual or a church, will bear the trial of the last great day. ¶ *Precious stones.* By the stones here referred to, are not meant *gems* which are esteemed of so much value for ornaments, but beautiful and valuable marbles. The word *precious* here ($\tau\iota\mu\iota\nu s$) means those which are obtained at a *price,* which are costly and valuable; and is particularly applicable, therefore, to the costly marbles which were used in building. The figurative sense here does not differ materially from that conveyed by the silver and gold. By this edifice thus reared on the true foundation, we are to understand, (1.) The true doctrines which should be employed to build up a church—doctrines which would bear the test of the trial of the last day; and, (2.) Such views in regard to piety, and to duty; such feelings and principles of action, as should be approved, and seen to be genuine piety in the day of judgment. ¶ *Wood.* That might be easily burned. An edifice reared of wood instead of marble, or slight buildings, such as were often put up for temporary purposes in the east—as cottages, places for watching their vineyards, &c.; see my Note, on Isa. i. 8. ¶ *Hay, stubble.* Used for thatching the building, or for a roof. Perhaps, also, grass was sometimes employed in some way to make the walls of the building. Such an edifice would burn readily; would be constantly exposed to take fire. By this is meant, (1.) Errors and false doctrines, such as will not be found to be true in the day of judgment, and as will then be swept away; (2.) Such practices and mistaken views of piety, as shall grow out of false doctrines and

13 Every man's work shall be made manifest : for the day shall declare it, because it shall ¹ be

1 is.

revealed by fire; and the ᵃ fire shall try every man's work, of what sort it is.

a Zech.13.9; 2 Pet.1.7; 4.12.

errors.—The foundation may be firm. Those who are referred to may be building on the Lord Jesus, and may be true Christians. Yet there is much error among those who are not Christians. There are many things *mistaken* for piety which will yet be seen to be false. There is much enthusiasm, wildfire, fanaticism, bigotry; much affected humility; much that is supposed to be orthodoxy; much regard to forms and ceremonies; to " days, and months, and times, and years" (Gal. iv. 10); much over-heated zeal, and much precision, and solemn sanctimoniousness ; much regard for external ordinances where the heart is wanting, that shall be found to be false, and that shall be swept away in the day of judgment.

13. *Every man's work shall be made manifest.* What every man has built on this foundation shall be seen. Whether he has held truth or error; whether he has had correct views of piety or false ; whether what he has done has been what he *should* have done or not. ¶ *For the day.* The day of judgment. The great day which shall reveal the secrets of all hearts, and the truth in regard to what every man has done. The event will show what edifices on the true foundation are firmly, and what are weakly built. *Perhaps* the word *day* here may mean *time* in general, as we say, " time will show—'' and as the Latin adage says, *dies docebit;* but it is more natural to refer it to the day of judgment. ¶ *Because it shall be revealed by fire.* The work, the edifice which shall be built on the true foundation shall be made known amidst the fire of the great day. The *fire* which is here referred to, is doubtless that which shall attend the consummation of all things—the close of the world. That the world shall be destroyed by fire, and that the solemnities of the judgment shall be ushered in by a universal conflagration, is fully and frequently revealed. See Isa. lxvi. 15 ;

2 Thess. i. 8 ; 2 Pet. iii. 7, 10, 11. The burning fires of that day, Paul says, shall reveal the character of every man's work, as fire sheds light on all around, and discloses the true nature of things. It may be observed, however, that many critics suppose this to refer to the fire of persecution, &c. *Macknight.* Whitby supposes that the apostle refers to the approaching destruction of Jerusalem. Others, as Grotius, Rosenmüller, &c. suppose that the reference is to *time* in general; it shall be declared ere long; it shall be seen whether those things which are built on the true foundation, are true by the test of time, &c. But the most natural interpretation is that which refers it to the day of judgment. ¶ *And the fire shall try every man's work.* It is the property of fire to test the qualities of objects. Thus, gold and silver, so far from being destroyed by fire, are purified from dross. Wood, hay, stubble, are consumed. The power of fire to try or test the nature of metals, or other objects, is often referred to in the Scripture. Comp. Isa. iv. 4 : xxiv. 15 ; Mal. iii. 2 ; 1 Pet. i. 7. It is not to be supposed here that the material fire of the last day shall have any tendency to purify the soul, or to remove that which is unsound; but that the investigations and trials of the judgment shall remove all that is evil, as fire acts with reference to gold and silver. As they are not burned but purified ; as they pass unhurt through the intense heat of the furnace, so shall all that is genuine pass through the trials of the last great day, of which trials the burning world shall be the antecedent and the emblem. That great day shall show what is genuine and what is not.

14. *If any man's work abide,* &c. If it shall appear that he hast taught the true doctrines of Christianity, and inculcated right practices and views of piety, and himself cherished right feelings : if the trial of the great day, when the real qualities of all objects shall be

14 If any man's work abide which he hath built thereupon, he shall receive a reward.

15 If any man's work shall be burned, he shall suffer loss : but

he himself shall be saved ; yet so [a] as by fire.

16 Know ye not that ye [b] are the temple of God, and *that* the Spirit of God dwelleth in you?

a Zech. 3.2; Jude 23.

b 2 Cor.6.16.

known, shall show this. ¶ *He shall receive a reward.* According to the nature of his work. See Note on ver. 8. This refers, I suppose, to the proper rewards on the day of judgment, and not to the honours and the recompense which he may receive in this world. If *all* that he has taught and done shall be proved to have been genuine and pure, then his reward shall be in proportion.

15. *If any man's work shall be burned.* If it shall not be found to bear the test of the investigation of that day—as a cottage of wood, hay, and stubble would not bear the application of fire. If his doctrines have not been true; if he has had mistaken views of piety; if he has nourished feelings which *he* thought were those of religion; and inculcated practices which, however well meant, are not such as the gospel produces; if he has fallen into error of opinion, feeling, practice, however conscientious, yet he shall suffer loss. ¶ *He shall suffer loss.* (1.) He shall *not* be elevated to as high a rank and to as high happiness as he otherwise would. That which he supposed would be regarded as acceptable by the Judge, and rewarded accordingly, shall be stripped away, and shown to be unfounded and false : and in consequence, he shall not obtain those elevated rewards which he anticipated. This, compared with what he expected, may be regarded as a loss. (2.) He shall be injuriously affected by this for ever. It shall be a *detriment* to him to all eternity. The effects shall be felt in all his residence in heaven—not producing misery but attending him with the consciousness that he *might* have been raised to superior bliss in the eternal abode.— The phrase here literally means, "he shall be mulcted." The word is a law term, and means that he shall be fined, *i. e.* he shall suffer detriment. ¶ *But*

he himself shall be saved. The apostle all along has supposed that the true foundation was laid (ver. 11), and if that is laid, and the edifice is reared upon that, the person who does it shall be safe. There may be much error, and many false views of religion, and much imperfection, still the man that is building on the true foundation shall be safe. His errors and imperfections shall be removed, and he may occupy a lower place in heaven, but he shall be safe. ¶ *Yet so as by fire* (ὡς διὰ πυρός). This passage has greatly perplexed commentators; but probably without any good reason. The apostle does not say that Christians will be doomed to the fires of purgatory; nor that they will pass through fire; nor that they will be exposed to pains and punishment at all; but he *simply carries out the figure* which he commenced, and says that they will be saved, *as if* the action of fire had been felt on the edifice on which he is speaking. That is, as fire would consume the wood, hay, and stubble, *so* on the great day every thing that is erroneous and imperfect in Christians shall be removed, and that which is true and genuine shall be preserved as *if* it had passed through fire. Their whole character and opinions shall be investigated; and that which is good shall be approved; and that which is false and erroneous be removed. The idea is not that of a man whose house is burnt over his head and who escapes through the flames, nor that of a man who is subjected to the pains and fires of purgatory; but that of a man who had been spending his time and strength to little purpose; who had built, indeed, on the true foundation, but who had reared so much on it which was unsound, and erroneous, and false, that he himself would be saved with great difficulty, and with the loss of much of that reward which he had expected, *as if* the fire had passed over him and his works. The simple idea, therefore, is, that that which is genuine and valuable in his doctrines and works, shall be rewarded, and the man shall be saved: that which is not sound and genuine, shall be removed, and he shall suffer loss. Some of the fathers, indeed, admitted that this passage taught that all men would be subjected to the action of fire in the great conflagration with which the world shall close; that the wicked shall be consumed; and that the righteous are to suffer, some more and some less, according to their character. On passages like this, the Romish doctrine of purgatory is based. But we may observe, (1.) That this passage does not necessarily or naturally give any such idea. The interpretation stated above is the *natural* interpretation, and one which the passage will not only bear, but which it demands. (2.) *If* this passage *would* give any countenance to the absurd and unscriptural idea that the souls of the righteous at the day of judgment are to be re-united to their bodies, in order to be subjected to the action of intense heat, to be brought from the abodes of bliss and compelled to undergo the burning fires of the last conflagration, still it would give no countenance to the still more absurd and unscriptural opinion that those fires have been and are still burning; that all souls are to be subjected to them; and that they can be removed only by masses offered for the dead, and by the prayers of the living. The idea of danger and peril is, indeed, in this text; but the idea of personal salvation is retained and conveyed.

16. *Know ye not*, &c. The apostle here carries forward and completes the figure which he had commenced in regard to Christians. His illustrations had been drawn from architecture; and he here proceeds to say that Christians are that building (see ver. 9): that they were the sacred temple which God had reared; and that, therefore, they should be pure and holy. This is a practical application of what he had been before saying. ¶ *Ye are the temple of God.* This

is to be understood of the *community* of Christians, or of the church, as being the place where God dwells on the earth. The idea is derived from the mode of speaking among the Jews, where they are said often in the Old Testament to be the temple and the habitation of God. And the allusion is probably to the fact that God dwelt by a visible symbol—*the Shechinah*—in the temple, and that his abode was there. As he dwelt there among the Jews; as he had there a temple—a dwelling place, so he dwells among Christians. *They* are his temple, the place of his abode. His residence is with them; and he is in their midst. This figure the apostle Paul several times uses, 1 Cor. vi. 19; 2 Cor. vi. 16; Eph. ii. 20—22. A great many passages have been quoted by Elsner and Wetstein, in which a virtuous mind is represented as the temple of God, and in which the obligation to preserve that inviolate and unpolluted is enforced. The figure is a beautiful one, and very impressive. A *temple* was an edifice erected to the service of God. The temple at Jerusalem was not only most magnificent, but was regarded as most sacred; (1.) From the fact that it was devoted to his service; and (2.) From the fact that it was the peculiar residence of Jehovah. Among the heathen also, temples were regarded as sacred. They were supposed to be *inhabited* by the divinity to whom they were dedicated. They were regarded as inviolable. Those who took refuge there were safe. It was a crime of the highest degree to violate a temple, or to tear a fugitive who had sought protection there from the altar. So the apostle says of the Christian community. They were regarded as *his* temple—God dwelt among them—and they should regard themselves as holy, and as consecrated to his service. And so it is regarded as a species of sacrilege to violate the temple, and to devote it to other uses, 1 Cor. vi. 19; see ver. 17. ¶ *And* that *the Spirit of God.* The Holy Spirit, the third person of the Trinity. This is conclusively proved by 1 Cor. vi. 19, where he is called "the Holy Ghost." ¶ *Dwelleth in*

17 If any man [1] defile the temple of God, him shall God destroy; for the temple of God is holy, which *temple* ye are.

1 or, *destroy*.

18 Let no man deceive himself. [a] If any man among you seemeth to be wise in this world, let him become a fool, that he may be wise.

a Prov.26,12.

you. As God dwelt formerly in the tabernacle, and afterwards in the temple, so his Spirit now dwells among Christians.—This cannot mean, (1.) That the Holy Spirit is *personally united* to Christians, so as to form a personal union; or, (2.) That there is to Christians any communication of his nature or personal qualities; or, (3.) That there is any union of *essence*, or *nature* with them, for God is present in all places, and can, *as* God, be no more present at one place than at another. The only sense in which he can be peculiarly present in any place is by his *influence*, or *agency*. And the idea is one which denotes agency, influence, favour, peculiar regard; and in that sense only can he be present with his church. The expression must mean, (1.) That the church is the seat of his operations, the field or abode on which he acts on earth; (2.) That his *influences* are there, producing the appropriate effects of his agency, love, joy, peace, long-suffering, &c.; (Gal. v. 22, 23); (3.) That he produces there consolations, that he sustains and guides his people; (4.) That they are regarded as dedicated or consecrated to him; (5.) That they are especially *dear* to him —that he loves them, and thus makes his abode with them. See Note, John xiv. 23.

["These words import the actual presence and inhabitation of the Spirit himself. The fact is plainly attested, but it is mysterious, and cannot be distinctly explained. In respect of his essence, he is as much present with unbelievers as with believers. His dwelling in the latter must therefore signify, that he manifests himself, in their souls, in a peculiar manner; that he exerts there his gracious power, and produces effects which other men do not experience—We may illustrate his presence with them, as distinguished from his presence with men in general, by supposing the vegetative power of the earth to produce, in the surrounding region, only common and worthless plants, but to throw out, in a select

spot, all the riches and beauty of a cultivated garden."—*Dick's Theol. Vol. III.* p. 287.]

17. *If any man defile,* &c. Or, *destroy, corrupt* ($\phi\vartheta\epsilon\iota\rho\epsilon\iota$). The Greek word is the same in both parts of the sentence. "If any man *destroy* the temple of God, God shall *destroy* him." This is presented in the form of an adage or proverb. And the truth here stated is based on the fact that the temple of God was inviolable. That temple was holy; and if any man subsequently destroyed it, it might be presumed that God would destroy him. The figurative sense is, "If any man by his doctrines or precepts shall pursue such a course as *tends* to destroy the church, God shall severely punish him. ¶ *For the temple of God is holy.* The temple of God is to be regarded as sacred and inviolable. This was unquestionably the common opinion among the Jews respecting the temple at Jerusalem; and it was the common doctrine of the Gentiles respecting their temples. Sacred places were regarded as inviolable; and this general truth Paul applies to the Christian church in general.—Locke supposes that Paul had particular reference here to the false teachers in Corinth. But the expression, "if any man," is equally applicable to all other false teachers as to him. ¶ *Which* temple *ye are.* This proves that though Paul regarded them as lamentably corrupt in some respects, he still regarded them as a true church—as a part of the holy temple of God.

18. *Let no man deceive himself.* The apostle here proceeds to make a practical application of the truths which he had stated, and to urge on them humility, and to endeavour to repress the broils and contentions into which they had fallen. Let no man be puffed up with a vain conceit of his own wisdom, for this had been the real cause of all the evils which

19 For the wisdom of this world is foolishness with God : for it is

they had experienced. Grotius renders this, "See that you do not attribute too much to your wisdom and learning, by resting on it, and thus deceive your own selves." "All human philosophy," says Grotius, "that is repugnant to the gospel is but vain deceit."—Probably there were many among them who would despise this admonition as coming from Paul, but he exhorts them to take care that they did not deceive themselves. We are taught here, (1.) The danger of self-deception—a danger that besets all on the subject of religion. (2.) The fact that false philosophy is the most fruitful source of self-deception in the business of religion. So it was among the Corinthians; and so it has been in all ages since. ¶ *If any man among you.* Any teacher, whatever may be his rank or his confidence in his own abilities; or any private member of the church. ¶ *Seemeth to be wise.* Seems to himself; or is thought to be, has the credit, or reputation of being wise. The word *seems* (δοκεῖ) implies this idea—if any one seems, or is supposed to be a man of wisdom ; if this is his reputation ; and if he seeks that this should be his reputation among men. See instances of this construction in Bloomfield. ¶ *In this world.* In this *age,* or *world* (ἐν τῷ αἰῶνι τούτῳ). There is considerable variety in the interpretation of this passage among critics. It may be taken either with the preceding or the following words. Origen, Cyprian, Beza, Grotius, Hammond, and Locke, adopt the latter method, and understand it thus, "If any man among you thinks himself to be wise, let him not hesitate to be a fool in the opinion of this age in order that he may be truly wise."— But the interpretation conveyed in our translation, is probably the correct one. "If any man has the reputation of wisdom among the men of this generation, and prides himself on it," &c. If he is esteemed wise in the sense in which the men of this world are, as a philosopher, a man of science, learning, &c. ¶ *Let him become a*

fool. (1.) Let him be willing to be regarded as a fool. (2.) Let him sincerely embrace this gospel, which will inevitably expose him to the charge of being a fool. (3.) Let all his earthly wisdom be esteemed in his own eyes as valueless and as folly in the great matters of salvation. ¶ *That he may be wise.* That he may have true wisdom—that which is of God.— It is implied here, (1.) That the wisdom of this world will not make a man truly wise. (2.) That a *reputation* for wisdom may contribute nothing to a man's true wisdom, but may stand in the way of it. (3.) That for such a man to embrace the gospel it is necessary that he should be willing to cast away dependence on his own wisdom, and come with the temper of a child to the Saviour. (4.) That to do this will expose him to the charge of folly, and the derision of those who are wise in their own conceit. (5.) That true wisdom is found only in that science which teaches men to live unto God, and to be prepared for death and for heaven—and that science is found only in the gospel.

19. *For the wisdom of this world.* That which is esteemed to be wisdom by the men of this world on the subject of religion. It does not mean that true wisdom is foolishness with him. It does not mean that science, and prudence, and law—that the knowledge of his works—that astronomy, and medicine, and chemistry, are regarded by him as folly, and as unworthy the attention of men. God is the friend of truth on all subjects ; and he requires us to become acquainted with his works, and commends those who search them, Ps. xcii. 4 ; cxi. 2. But the apostle refers here to that which was esteemed to be wisdom among the ancients, and in which they so much prided themselves, their vain, self-confident, and false opinions on the subject of religion ; and especially those opinions when they were opposed to the simple but sublime truths of revelation. See Note, chap. i. 20, 21. ¶ *Is foolishness with God.* Is esteemed by him

written, *a* He taketh the wise in their own craftiness.

20 And again, *b* The Lord knoweth the thoughts of the wise, that they are vain.

a Job 5.13.   *b* Ps.94.11.

to be folly. Note, chap. i. 20.–24. ¶ *For it is written,* &c. Job v. 13. The word rendered "taketh" here denotes to clench with the fist, gripe, grasp. And the sense is, (1.) However crafty, or cunning, or skilful they may be ; however self-confident, yet that they cannot deceive or impose upon God. He can thwart their plans, overthrow their schemes, defeat their counsels, and foil them in their enterprises, Job v. 12. (2.) He does it by their own cunning or craftiness. He allows them to involve themselves in difficulties or to entangle each other. He makes use of even their own craft and cunning to defeat their counsels. He allows the plans of one wise man to come in conflict with those of another, and thus to destroy one another. Honesty in religion, as in every thing else, is the best policy; and a man who pursues a course of conscientious integrity may expect the protection of God. But he who attempts to carry his purposes by craft and intrigue—who depends on skill and cunning instead of truth and honesty, will often find that he is the prey of his own cunning and duplicity.

20. *And again,* Ps. xciv. 11. ¶ *The Lord knoweth.* God searches the heart. The particular thing which it is here said that he knows, is, that the thoughts of man are vain. They have this quality ; and this is that which the psalmist here says that God sees. The affirmation is not one respecting the *omniscience* of God, but with respect to what God sees of the nature of the thoughts of the wise. ¶ *The thoughts of the wise.* Their plans, purposes, designs. ¶ *That they are vain.* That they lack real wisdom ; they are foolish ; they shall not be accomplished as they expect ; or be seen to have that wisdom which they now suppose they possess.

21 *Therefore,* &c. Paul here pro-

21 Therefore let *o* no man glory in men: for all things are yours ;

22 Whether Paul, or Apollos, or Cephas, or the world, or life, or

c Jer.9.23,24.

ceeds to apply the principles which he had stated above. Since all were ministers or servants of God ; since God was the source of all good influences ; since, whatever might be the pretensions to wisdom among men, it was all foolishness in the sight of God, the inference was clear, that no man should glory in man. They were all alike poor, frail, ignorant, erring, dependent beings. And hence, also, as *all* wisdom came from God, and as Christians partook *alike* of the benefits of the instruction of the most eminent apostles, they ought to regard this as belonging to them in common, and not to form parties with these names at the head. ¶ *Let no man glory in men;* see chap. i. 29 ; comp. Jer. ix. 23, 24. It was common among the Jews to range themselves under different leaders—as Hillel and Shammai ; and for the Greeks, also, to boast themselves to be the followers of Pythagoras, Zeno, Plato, &c. The same thing began to be manifest in the Christian church; and Paul here rebukes and opposes it. ¶ *For all things are yours.* This is a *reason* why they should not range themselves in parties or factions under different leaders. Paul specifies what he means by "all things" in the following verses. The sense is, that since they had an interest in all that could go to promote their welfare ; as they were *common* partakers of the benefits of the talents and labours of the apostles ; and as they belonged to Christ, and all to God, it was improper to be split up into factions, *as if* they derived any *peculiar* benefit from one set of men, or one set of objects. In Paul, in Apollos, in life, death, &c. they had a *common* interest, and no one should boast that he had any special proprietorship in any of these things.

22. *Whether Paul, or Apollos.* The

death, or things present, or things to come; all are yours;

23 And ye *a* are Christ's; and Christ *is* God's.

a Rom.14.8.

sense of this is clear. Whatever advantages result from the piety, self-denials, and labours of Paul, Apollos, or any other preacher of the gospel, are *yours*—you have the benefit of them. One is as much entitled to the benefit as another; and all partake alike in the results of their ministration. You should therefore neither range yourselves into parties with their names given to the parties, nor suppose that one has any *peculiar* interest in Paul, or another in Apollos. Their labours belonged to the church in general. *They* had no partialities—no rivalship—no desire to make parties. They were united, and desirous of promoting the welfare of the *whole* church of God. The doctrine is, that ministers belong to the church, and should devote themselves to its welfare; and that the church enjoys, in common, the benefits of the learning, zeal, piety, eloquence, talents, example of the ministers of God. And it may be observed, that it is no small privilege thus to be permitted to regard *all* the labours of the most eminent servants of God as designed for our welfare; and for the humblest saint to feel that the labours of apostles, the self-denials and sufferings, the pains and dying agonies of martyrs, have been for *his* advantage. ¶ *Or Cephas.* Or Peter. John i. 42. ¶ *Or the world.* This word is doubtless used, in its common signification, to denote the things which God has made; the universe, the things which pertain to this life. And the meaning of the apostle probably is, that all things pertaining to this world which God has made—all the events which are occurring in his providence were so far *theirs*, that they would contribute to their advantage, and their enjoyment. This general idea may be thus expressed: (1.) The world was made by God their common Father, and they have an interest in it as *his* children, regarding it as the work of his hand, and seeing

him present in all his works. Nothing contributes so much to the true *enjoyment* of the world—to comfort in surveying the heavens, the earth, the ocean, hills, vales, plants, flowers, streams, in partaking of the gifts of Providence, as this feeling, that *all* are the works of the Christian's Father, and that *they* may all partake of these favours as his children. (2.) The frame of the universe is sustained and upheld for their sake. The universe is kept by God; and one design of God in keeping it is to protect, preserve, and redeem his church and people. To this end he defends it by day and night; he orders all things; he keeps it from the storm and tempest; from flood and fire; and from annihilation. The sun, and moon, and stars—the times and seasons, are all thus ordered, that his church may be guarded, and brought to heaven. (3.) The course of providential events are ordered for their welfare also, Rom. viii. 28. The revolutions of kingdoms—the various persecutions and trials, even the rage and fury of wicked men, are all overruled, to the advancement of the cause of truth, and the welfare of the church. (4.) Christians have the promise of *as much* of this world as shall be needful for them; and in this sense "the world" is theirs. See Matt. vi. 33; Mark x. 29, 30; 1 Tim. iv. 8, "Godliness is profitable for all things, having promise of the life that now is, and of that which is to come." And such was the result of the long experience and observation of David, Ps. xxxvii. 25, "I have been young, and now am old; yet have I not seen the righteous forsaken, nor his seed begging bread." See Isa. xxxiii. 16. ¶ *Or life.* Life is theirs, because (1.) They *enjoy* life. It is *real* life to them, and not a vain show. They live for a *real* object, and not for vanity. Others live for parade and ambition—Christians live for the great purposes of life; and life to them has reality, as being a state preparatory to another and a higher world. Their life is not an endless circle of unmeaning ceremonies—of false and hollow pretensions to friendship—of a vain pursuit of happiness, which is never found, but is passed in a manner that is rational, and sober, and that truly deserves to be called *life*. (2.) The various events and occurrences of life shall all tend to promote their welfare, and advance their salvation. ¶ *Death*. They have an *interest*, or *property* even in death, usually regarded as a calamity and a curse. But it is theirs, (1.) Because they shall have *peace* and support in the dying hour. (2.) Because it has no terrors for them. It shall take away nothing which they are not willing to resign, (3,) Because it is the avenue which leads to their rest; and it is *theirs* just in the same sense in which we say that " this is *our* road" when we have been long absent, and are inquiring the way to our homes. (4.) Because they shall triumph over it. It is subdued by their Captain, and the grave has been subjected to a triumph by his rising from its chills and darkness. (5.) Because death is the means—the occasion of introducing them to their rest. It is the *advantageous circumstance* in their history, by which they are removed from a world of ills, and translated to a world of glory. It is to them a source of inexpressible *advantage*, as it translates them to a world of light and eternal felicity; and it may truly be called *theirs*. ¶ *Or things present, or things to come.* Events which are now happening, and all that can possibly occur to us, Note, Rom. viii. 38. All the calamities, trials, persecutions—all the prosperity, advantages, privileges of the present time, and all that shall yet take place, shall tend to promote our welfare, and advance the interests of our souls, and promote our salvation. ¶ *All are yours.* All shall tend to promote your comfort and salvation.

23. *And ye are Christ's.* You belong to him; and should not, therefore, feel that you are devoted to any earthly leader, whether Paul, Apollos, or Peter. As you belong to Christ by redemption, and by solemn dedication to his service, so you should feel that you are his alone. You are his property—his people—his friends. You should regard yourselves as such, and feel that you all belong to the same family, and should not, therefore, be split up into contending factions and parties. ¶ *Christ is God's.* Christ is the mediator between God and man. He came to do the will of God. He was and is still devoted to the service of his Father. God has a proprietorship in all that he does, since Christ lived, and acted, and reigns to promote the glory of his Father. The argument here seems to be this, " You belong to Christ; and he to God. You are bound, therefore, not to devote yourselves to a *man*, whoever he may be, but to Christ, and to the service of that one true God, in whose service even Christ was employed. And as Christ sought to promote the glory of his Father, so should you in all things." This implies no inferiority of nature of Christ to God. It means only that he was employed in the service of his Father, and sought his glory— a doctrine every where taught in the New Testament. But this does not imply that he was inferior in his nature. A son may be employed in the service of his father, and may seek to advance his father's interests. But this does not prove that the son is inferior in nature to his father. It proves only that he is inferior in *some* respects—in office. So the Son of God consented to take an inferior office or rank; to become a mediator, to assume the form of a servant, and to be a man of sorrows; but this proves nothing in regard to his original rank or dignity. That is to be learned from the numerous passages which affirm that in nature he was equal with God. See Note, John i. 1.

REMARKS.

1st. Christians when first converted may be well compared to infants, ver. 1. They are in a new world. They just open their eyes on truth They see new objects; and have new objects of attachment. They are feeble, weak, helpless. And though they often have high joy, and even great self-confidence, yet they are in themselves ignorant and weak, and in need of constant teaching. Christians should not only possess the spirit, but they should feel that they are *like* children. They are like them not only in their temper, but in their ignorance, and weakness, and helplessness.

2d. The instructions which are imparted to Christians should be adapted to their capacity, ver. 2. Skill and care should be exercised to adapt that instruction to the wants of tender consciences, and to those who are feeble in the faith. It would be no more absurd to furnish strong food to the new born babe than it is to present some of the higher doctrines of religion to the tender minds of converts. The *elements* of knowledge must be first learned ; the tenderest and most delicate food must first nourish the body.—And perhaps in nothing is there more frequent error than in presenting the higher, and more difficult doctrines of Christianity to young converts, and *because* they have a difficulty in regard to them, or because they even reject them, pronouncing them destitute of piety. Is the infant destitute of life because it cannot digest the solid food which nourishes the man of fifty years? Paul adapted *his* instructions to the delicacy and feebleness of infantile piety; and those who are like Paul will feed with great care the lambs of the flock. All young converts should be placed under a course of instruction adapted to *their* condition, and should secure the careful attention of the pastors of the churches.

3d. Strife and contention in the church is proof that men are under the influence of carnal feelings. No matter what is the *cause* of the contention, the very fact of the existence of such strife is a proof of the existence of such feelings somewhere, ver. 3, 4. On what side soever the original fault of the contention may be, yet its existence in the church is always proof that *some*—if not all—of those who are engaged in it are under the influence of carnal feelings. Christ's kingdom is designed to be a kingdom of peace and love; and divisions and contentions are always attended with evils, and with injury to the spirit of true religion.

4th. We have here a rebuke to that spirit which has produced the existence of sects and parties, ver. 4. The practice of naming sects after certain men, we see, began early, and was as early rebuked by apostolic authority. Would not the same apostolic authority rebuke the spirit which now calls one division of the church after the name of Calvin, another after the name of Luther, another after the name of Arminius! Should not, and will not all these divisions yet be merged in the high and holy name of Christian? Our Saviour evidently supposed it possible that his church should be one (John xvii. 21—23); and Paul certainly supposed that the church at Corinth might be so united. So the early churches were; and is it *too much* to hope that some way may yet be discovered which shall break down the divisions into sects, and *unite* Christians both in feeling and in name in spreading the gospel of the Redeemer every where? Does not every Christian sincerely desire it? And may there not yet await the church *such* a union as shall concentrate all its energies in saving the world? How much effort, how much talent, how much wealth and learning are now wasted in contending with other denominations of the great Christian family! How much would this wasted—and worse than wasted wealth, and learning, and talent, and zeal do in diffusing the gospel around the world! Whose heart is not sickened at these contentions and strifes; and whose soul will not breathe forth a pure desire to Heaven that the time may soon come when all these contentions shall die away, and when the voice of strife shall be hushed; and when the united host of God's elect shall go forth to subdue the world to the gospel of the Saviour?

5th. The *proper* honour should be paid to the ministers of the gospel. ver. 5—7. They should not be put in the place of God; nor should their services, however important, prevent the supreme recognition of God in the conversion of souls. God is to be all and in all.—It is proper that the ministers of religion should be treated with respect (1 Thess. v. 12, 13); and ministers have a right to expect and to desire the affectionate regards of those who are blessed by their instrumentality. But Paul—eminent and successful as he was—would do nothing that would diminish or obscure the singleness of view with which the agency of God should be regarded in the work of salvation. He regarded himself as nothing compared with God; and his highest desire was that God in all things might be honoured.

6th. God is the source of all good influence, and of all that is holy in the church. He only gives the increase. Whatever of humility, faith, love, joy, peace, or purity we may have, is all to be traced to him. No matter who plants, or who waters, God gives life to the seed; God rears the stalk, God expands the leaf; God opens the flower and gives it its fragrance; and God forms, preserves, and ripens the fruit. So in religion. No matter who the minister may be; no matter how faithful, learned, pious, or devoted, yet if any success attends his labours, it is all to be traced to God. This truth is never to be forgotten; nor should any talents, or zeal, however great, ever be allowed to dim or obscure its lustre in the minds of those who are converted.

7th. Ministers are on a level, ver. 8, 9. Whatever may be their qualifications or their success, yet they can claim no pre-eminence over one another. They are fellow labourers— engaged in one work, accomplishing the same object, though they may be in different parts of the same field. The man who plants is as necessary as he that waters; and both are inferior to God, and neither could do any thing without him.

8th. Christians should regard themselves as a holy people, ver. 9. They are the cultivation of God. All that they have is from him. His own agency has been employed in their conversion; his own Spirit operates to sanctify and save them. Whatever they have is to be traced to God; and they should remember that they are, therefore, consecrated to him.

9th. No other foundation can be laid in the church except that of Christ, ver. 10, 11. Unless a church is founded on the true doctrine respecting the Messiah, it is a false church, and should not be recognised as belonging to him. There can be no other foundation, either for an individual sinner, or for a church. How important then to inquire whether we are building our hopes for eternity on this tried foundation! How faithfully should we examine this subject lest our hopes should all be swept away in the storms of divine wrath! Matt. vii. 27, 28. How deep and awful will be the disappointment of those who suppose they have been building on the true foundation, and who find in the great day of judgment that all has been delusion!

10th. We are to be tried at the day of judgment, ver. 13, 14. All are to be arraigned, not only in regard to the foundation of our hopes for eternal life, but in regard to the superstructure,—the nature of our opinions and practices in religion. Every thing shall come into judgment.

11th. The trial will be such as to test our character. All the trials through which we are to pass are designed to do this. Affliction, temptation, sickness, death, are all intended to produce this result, and all have a tendency to this end. But, pre-eminently is this the case with regard to the trial at the great day of judgment. Amidst the light of the burning world, and the terrors of the judgment; under the blazing throne, and the eye of God, every man's character shall be seen, and a just judgment shall be pronounced.

12th. The trial shall remove all that is impure in Christians, ver. 14. They shall then see the truth; and in that world of truth, all that was erroneous in their opinions shall be corrected. They shall be in a world where fanaticism cannot be mistaken for the love of truth, and where enthusiasm cannot be substituted for zeal. All true and real piety shall there abide; all which is false and erroneous shall be removed.

13th. What a change will then take place in regard to Christians. *All* probably cherish *some* opinions which are unsound; all indulge in *some* things now supposed to be piety, which will not then bear the test. The great change will then take place from impurity to purity; from imperfection to perfection. The very passage from this world to heaven will secure this change; and what a vast revolution will it be thus to be ushered into a world where all shall be pure in sentiment; all perfect in love.

14th. Many Christians may be much disappointed in that day. Many who are now zealous for *doctrines*, and who pursue with vindictive spirit others who differ from them, shall then "suffer loss," and find that the *persecuted* had more real love of truth than the *persecutor*. Many who are now filled with zeal, and who denounce the comparatively leaden and tardy pace of others; many whose bosoms glow with rapturous feeling, and burn, as they suppose, with a seraph's love, shall find that *all* this was not piety—that animal feeling was mistaken for the love of God; and that a zeal for sect, or for the triumph of a party, was mistaken for love to the Saviour; and that the kindlings of an ardent imagination had been often substituted for the elevated emotions of pure and disinterested love.

15th. Christians, teachers, and people should examine themselves, and see what *is* the building which they are rearing on the true foundation. Even where the foundation of a building is laid broad and deep, it is of much importance whether a stately and magnificent palace shall be reared on it, suited to the nature of the foundation, or whether a mud-walled and a thatched cottage shall be all. Between the foundation and the edifice in the one case there is the beauty of proportion and fitness; in the other there is incongruity and unfitness. Who would lay such a deep and broad

foundation as the basis on which to rear the hut of the savage or the mud cottage of the Hindoo? Thus in religion. The foundation to all who truly believe in the Lord Jesus is broad, deep, firm, magnificent. But the superstructure — the piety, the advancement in knowledge, the life, is often like the cottage that is reared on the firm basis—that every wind shakes, and that the fire would soon consume. As the *basis* of the Christian hope is firm, so should the superstructure be large, magnificent, and grand.

16th. Christians are to regard themselves as holy and pure, ver. 16, 17. They are the temple of the Lord —the dwelling place of the Spirit. A temple is sacred and inviolable. So should Christians regard themselves. They are dedicated to God. He dwells among them. And they should deem themselves holy and pure; and should preserve their minds from impure thoughts, from unholy purposes, from selfish and sensual desires. They should be in all respects such as will be the fit abode for the Holy Spirit of God. How pure should men be in whom the Holy Spirit dwells! How single should be their aims! How constant their self-denials! How single their desire to devote all to his service, and to live always to his glory! How heavenly should they be in their feelings; and how should pride, sensuality, vanity, ambition, covetousness, and the love of gayety, be banished from their bosoms! Assuredly in God's world there should be *one* place where he will delight to dwell—one place that shall remind of heaven, and that place should be the church which has been purchased with the purest blood of the universe.

17th. We see what is necessary if a man would become a Christian, ver. 18. He must be willing to be esteemed a fool; to be despised; to have his name cast out as evil; and to be regarded as even under delusion and deception. Whatever may be his rank, or his reputation for wisdom, and talent, and learning, he must be willing to be regarded as a fool by his former associates and companions; to cast off all reliance on his own wis-

CHAPTER IV.

LET a man so account of us, as of the ministers *a* of

a 2 Cor.6.4.

dom; and to be associated with the poor, the persecuted, and the despised followers of Jesus. Christianity knows no distinctions of wealth, talent, learning. It points out no royal road to heaven. It describes but one way; and whatever contempt an effort to be saved may involve us in, it requires us to submit to that, and even to rejoice that our names are cast out as evil.

18th. This is a point on which men should be especially careful that they are not deceived, ver. 18. There is nothing on which they are more likely to be than this. It is not an easy thing for a proud man to humble himself; it is not easy for men who boast of their wisdom to be willing that their names should be cast out as evil. And there is great danger of a man's flattering himself that he is willing to be a Christian, who would *not* be willing to be esteemed a fool by the great and the gay men of this world. He still intends to be a Christian and be saved; and yet to keep up his reputation for wisdom and prudence. Hence every thing in religion which is not consistent with such a reputation for prudence and wisdom he rejects. Hence he takes sides with the world. As far as the world will admit that a man ought to attend to religion he will go. Where the world would pronounce any thing to be foolish, fanatical, or enthusiastic, he pauses. And his religion is not shaped by the New Testament, but by the opinions of the world.—Such a man should be cautious that he is not deceived. All *his* hopes of heaven are probably built on the sand.

19th. We should not overvalue the wisdom of this world, ver. 18, 19. It is folly in the sight of God. And we, therefore, should not over-estimate it, or desire it, or be influenced by it. True wisdom on any subject we should not despise; but we should especially value that which is connected with salvation.

20th. This admonition is of especial

Christ, and stewards of the mysteries of God.

2 Moreover, it is required in

applicability to ministers of the gospel. They are in special danger on the subject; and it has been by *their* yielding themselves so much to the power of speculative philosophy, that parties have been formed in the church, and that the gospel has been so much corrupted.

21st. These considerations should lead us to live above contention, and the fondness of party. Sect and party in the church are not formed by the love of the pure and simple gospel, but by the love of some philosophical opinion, or by an admiration of the wisdom, talents, learning, eloquence, or success of some Christian teacher. Against this the apostle would guard us; and the considerations presented in this chapter should elevate us above all the causes of contention and the love of sect, and teach us to love as brothers all who love our Lord Jesus Christ.

22d. Christians have an interest in all things that can go to promote their happiness. Life and death, things present and things to come—all shall tend to advance their happiness, and promote their salvation; ver. 21—23.

23d. Christians have nothing to fear in death. Death is theirs, and shall be a blessing to them. Its sting is taken away, and it shall introduce them to heaven. What have they to fear? Why should they be alarmed? Why afraid to die? Why unwilling to depart and to be with Christ?

24th. Christians should regard themselves as devoted to the Saviour. They are his, and he has the highest conceivable claim on their time, their talents, their influence, and their wealth. To him, therefore, let us be devoted, and to him let us consecrate all that we have.

CHAPTER IV.

THIS chapter is a continuation of the subject discussed in those which go before, and of the argument which closes the last chapter. The proper division would have been at ver. 6.

stewards, *a* that a man be found faithful.

a Luke 12.42; Tit.1.7; 1 Pet.4.10.

The design of the first six verses is to show the real estimate in which the apostles ought to be held as the ministers of religion. The remainder of the chapter (ver. 7—21) is occupied in setting forth further the claims of the apostles to their respect in contradistinction from the false teachers, and in reproving the spirit of vain boasting and confidence among the Corinthians. Paul (ver. 7) reproves their boasting by assuring them that they had no ground for it, since all that they possessed had been given to them by God. In ver. 8, he reproves the same spirit with cutting irony, as if they claimed to be eminently wise.—Still further to reprove them, he alludes to his own self-denials and sufferings, as contrasted with *their* ease, and safety, and enjoyment, ver. 9 —14. He then shows that his labours and self-denials in their behalf, laid the foundation for his speaking to them with authority as a father, ver. 15, 16. And to show them that he claimed that authority over them as the founder of their church, and that he was not afraid to discharge his duty towards them, he informs them that he had sent Timothy to look into their affairs (ver. 17), and that himself would soon follow; and assures them that he had *power* to come to them with the severity of Christian discipline, and that it depended on *their* conduct whether he should come with a rod, or with the spirit of meekness and love, ver. 21.

1. *Let a man.* Let all; let this be the estimate formed of us by each one of you. ¶ *So account of us.* So think of us, the apostles. ¶ *As the ministers of Christ.* As the servants of Christ. Let them form a true estimate of us and our office—not as the head of a faction; not as designing to form parties, but as unitedly and entirely the servants of Christ; see chap. iii. 5. ¶ *And stewards.* Stewards were those who presided over the affairs of a family, and made provision for it, &c.; see Note, Luke xvi. 1. It was an office of much responsibility;

3 But with me it is a very small thing that I should be

and the apostle by using the term here seems to have designed to elevate those whom he seemed to have depreciated in chap. iii. 5. ¶ *Of the mysteries of God.* Of the gospel; Note, chap. ii. 7. The office of steward was to provide those things which were necessary for the use of a family. And so the office of a minister of the gospel, and a steward of its mysteries, is to dispense such instructions, guidance, counsel, &c., as may be requisite to build up the church of Christ; to make known those sublime truths which are contained in the gospel, but which had not been made known before the revelation of Jesus Christ, and which are, therefore, called *mysteries*. It is implied in this verse, (1.) That the office of a minister is one that is *subordinate* to Christ—they are his servants. (2.) That those in the office should not attempt to be the head of sect or party in the church. (3.) That the office is honourable as that of a steward is ; and, (4.) That Christians should endeavour to form and cherish *just* ideas of ministers; to give them their *true* honour; but not to overrate their importance.

2. *Moreover, &c.* The fidelity required of stewards seems to be adverted to here, in order to show that the apostles acted from a higher principle than a desire to please man, or to be regarded as at the head of a party; and they ought so to esteem them as bound, like all stewards, to be faithful to the master whom they served. ¶ *It is required,* &c. It is expected of them; it is the *main* or *leading* thing in their office. Eminently in that office fidelity is required as an indispensable and cardinal virtue. Fidelity to the master, faithfulness to his trust, as THE virtue which by way of eminence is demanded there. In other offices other virtues may be particularly required. But here fidelity is demanded. This is required particularly because it is an office of trust; because the master's goods are at his disposal; because there is so much opportunity for the

judged of you, or of man's [1] judg-ment; yea, I judge not mine own self:

1 *day*.

4 For I know nothing by my-self; *a* yet am I not hereby jus-

a Ps.143.2.

steward to appropriate those goods to his own use, so that his master cannot detect it. There is a strong similarity between the office of a steward and that of a minister of the gospel. But it is not needful here to dwell on the resemblance. The idea of Paul seems to be, (1.) That a minister, like a steward, is devoted to his master's service, and should regard himself as such. (2.) That he should be faithful to that trust, and not abuse or violate it. (3.) That he should not be judged by his fellow-stewards, or fellow-ser vants, but that his main desire should be to meet with the approbation of his master.—A minister should be faithful for obvious reasons. Because, (*a*) He is appointed by Jesus Christ; (*b*) Because he must answer to him; (*c*) Because the honour of Christ, and the welfare of his kingdom is entrusted to him; and (*d*) Because of the importance of the matter committed to his care; and the importance of fidelity can be measured only by the consequences of his labours to those souls in an eternal heaven or an eter-nal hell.

3. *But with me*. In my estimate; in regard to myself. That is, I esteem it a matter of no concern. Since I am responsible as a steward to my mas-ter only, it is a matter of small concern what *men* think of me, provided I have his approbation. Paul was not insensible to the good opinion of men. He did not despise their favour or court their contempt. But this was not the principal thing which he regarded; and we have here a noble elevation of pur-pose and of aim, which shows how direct was his design to serve and please the master who had appointed him to his office. ¶ *That I should be judged*. The word rendered *judged* here properly denotes to examine the qualities of any person or thing; and sometimes, as here, to express the result of such examination or judgment. Here it means to *blame* or *condemn*. ¶ *Of you*. By you. Dear as you are to me as a church and a people, yet

my main desire is not to secure your esteem, or to avoid your censure, but to please my master, and secure his approbation. ¶ *Or of man's judg-ment*. Of *any* man's judgment. What he had just said, that he esteemed it to be a matter not worth regarding, whatever might be their opinion of him, might seem to look like arro-gance, or appear as if he looked upon *them* with contempt. In order to avoid this construction of his language, he here says that it was not because he despised them, or regarded their opin-ion as of less value than that of others, but that he had the same feelings in regard to all men. Whatever might be their rank, character, talent, or learning, he regarded it as a matter of the least possible consequence what they thought of him. He was answer-able not to them, but to his Master; and he could pursue an independent course whatever they might think of his conduct. This is designed also evidently to reprove them for seeking so much the praise of each other. The Greek here is " of man's *day*," where *day* is used, as it often is in Hebrew, to denote the day of trial; the day of judgment; and then simply judgment. Thus the word ‎‏יום‏‎ *day* is used in Job xxiv. 1; Ps. xxxvii. 13; Joel i. 15; ii. 1; iv. 19; Mal. iii. 19. ¶ *Yea, I judge not my own self*. I do not attempt to pro-nounce a judgment on myself. I am conscious of imperfection, and of being biased by self-love in my own favour. I do not feel that my judgment of myself would be strictly impartial, and in all respects to be trusted. Favour-able as may be my opinion, yet I am sensible that I may be biased. This is designed to soften what he had just said about their judging him, and to show further the little value which is to be put on the judgment which man may form. " If I do not regard my own opinion of myself as of high value, I cannot be suspected of undervaluing you when I say that I do not much regard your opinion; and if I do not estimate highly my *own* opinion of

tified : but he that judgeth me is the Lord.

5 Therefore judge *a* nothing before the time, until the Lord

a Mat.7.1.

myself, then it is not to be expected that I should set a high value on the opinions of others."—God only is the infallible judge; and as we and our fellow-men are liable to be biased in our opinions, from envy, ignorance, or self-love, we should regard the judgment of the world as of little value.

4. *For I know nothing by myself.* There is evidently here an ellipsis to be supplied, and it is well supplied by Grotius, Rosenmüller, Calvin, &c. "I am not conscious of *evil*, or *unfaithfulness* to myself; that is, in my ministerial life." It is well remarked by Calvin, that Paul does not here refer to the whole of his life, but only to his apostleship. And the sense is, "I am conscious of integrity in this office. My own mind does not condemn me of ambition or unfaithfulness. Others may accuse me, but I am not conscious of that which should condemn me, or render me unworthy of this office." This appeal Paul elsewhere makes to the integrity and faithfulness of his ministry. So his speech before the elders of Ephesus at Miletus; Acts xx. 18, 19, 26, 27; comp. 2 Cor. vii. 2; xii. 17. It was the appeal which a holy and faithful man could make to the integrity of his public life, and such as every minister of the gospel *ought* to be able to make. ¶ *Yet am I not hereby justified.* I am not justified *because* I am not conscious of a failure in my duty. I know that God the judge may see imperfections where I see none. I know that I may be deceived; and therefore, I do not pronounce a judgment on myself as if it were infallible and final. It is not by the consciousness of integrity and faithfulness that I expect to be saved; and it does not follow that I claim to be free from all personal blame. I know that partiality to ourselves will often teach us to overlook many faults that others may discern in us. ¶ *He that judgeth me is the Lord.* By his judgment I am to abide; and by his

come, who *b* both will bring to light the hidden things of darkness, and will make manifest the counsels of the hearts : and then

b Rom.2.16; Rev.20.2.

judgment I am to receive my eternal sentence, and not by my own view of myself. He searcheth the hearts. He may see evil where I see none. I would not, therefore, be self-confident; but would, with humility, refer the whole case to him. Perhaps there is here a gentle and tender reproof of the Corinthians, who were so confident in their own integrity; and a gentle admonition to them to be more cautious, as it was *possible* that the Lord would detect faults in them where they perceived none.

5. *Therefore.* In view of the danger of being deceived in your judgment, and the impossibility of certainly knowing the failings of the heart. ¶ *Judge nothing.* Pass no decided opinion; see Note, Mat. vii. 1. The apostle here takes occasion to inculcate on them an important lesson—one of the leading lessons of Christianity —not to pass a harsh opinion on the conduct of any man, since there are so many things that go to make up his character which we cannot know; and so many secret failings and motives which are all concealed from us. ¶ *Until the Lord come.* The Lord Jesus at the day of judgment, when all secrets shall be revealed, and a true judgment shall be passed on all men. ¶ *Who both will bring to light;* see Note, Rom. ii. 16. ¶ *The hidden things of darkness.* The secret things of the heart which have been hidden as it were in darkness. The subsequent clause shows that this is the sense. He does not refer to the deeds of night, or those things which were wrought in the secret places of idolatry, but to the secret designs of the heart; and perhaps means gently to insinuate that there were many things about the character and feelings of his enemies which would not well bear the revelations of that day. ¶ *The counsels of the hearts.* The purposes, designs, and intentions of men. All their plans shall be made known in that day. And

shall every man have praise of God.

6 And these things, brethren, I have in a figure transferred to myself and *to* Apollos for your

it is a most fearful and alarming truth, that no man can conceal his purposes *beyond* the day of judgment. ¶ *And then shall every man have praise of God.* The word here rendered *praise* (ἔπαινος) denotes in this place *reward*, or that which is *due* to him; the just sentence which ought to be pronounced on his character. It does not mean as our translation would imply, that every man will then receive the divine approbation—which will not be true; but that every man shall receive what is due to his character, whether good or evil. So Bloomfield and Brotschneider explain it. Hesychius explains it by *judgment* (κρίσις). The word must be limited in its signification according to the subject or the connection. The passage teaches, (1.) That we should not be guilty of harsh judgment of others. (2.) The reason is, that we cannot know their feelings and motives. (3.) That all secret things will be brought forth in the great day, and nothing be concealed *beyond* that time. (4.) That every man shall receive justice there. He shall be treated as he ought to be. The destiny of no one will be decided by the opinions of men; but tho doom of all will be fixed by God. How important is it, therefore, that we be prepared for that day; and how important to cherish such feelings, and form such plans, that they *may* be developed without involving us in shame and contempt!

6. *And these things.* The things which I have written respecting religious teachers (chap. ii. 5, 6, 22), and the impropriety of forming sects called after their names. ¶ *I have in a figure transferred to myself and Apollos.* The word here used (μετεσχημάτισα) denotes, properly, to put on another form or figure; *to change* (Phil. iii. 21, "who shall *change* our vile body"); to *transform* (2 Cor. xi. 13, "*transforming* themselves into the apostles of Christ"); and then to apply in the way of a figure of speech. This may

sakes; that ye might learn in us not to think *of men* above that which is written, that no one of you be puffed up for one against another.

mean that neither Paul, Apollos, or Peter, were set up among the Corinthians as heads of parties, but that Paul here made use of their names to show how improper it *would* be to make *them* the head of a party, and hence, how improper it was to make *any* religious teacher the head of a party; or Paul may mean to say that he had mentioned himself and Apollos *particularly*, to show the impropriety of what had been done; since, if it was improper to make *them* heads of parties, it was much more so to make inferior teachers the leaders of factions. Locke adopts the former interpretation. The latter is probably the true interpretation, for it is evident from chap. i. 12, 13, that there *were* parties in the church at Corinth that were called by the names of Paul, and Apollos, and Peter; and Paul's design here was to show the impropriety of this by mentioning *himself, Apollos,* and *Peter*, and thus by transferring the whole discussion from *inferior* teachers and leaders to show the impropriety of it. He might have argued against the impropriety of following other leaders. He might have mentioned their names. But this would have been invidious and indelicate. It would have excited *their* anger. He therefore says that he had transferred it all to himself and Apollos; and it *implied* that if it were improper to split themselves up into factions with *them* as leaders, much more was it improper to follow others; *i. e.* it was improper to form parties at all in the church. "I mention this of *ourselves;* out of delicacy I forbear to mention the names of others."—And this was one of the instances in which Paul showed great *tact* in accomplishing his object, and avoiding offence. ¶ *For your sakes.* To spare your feelings; or to show you in an inoffensive manner what I mean. And particularly by this that you may learn not to place an inordinate value on men. ¶ *That ye might*

7 For who [1] maketh thee to differ *from another?* and what[a] hast thou that thou didst not receive?

1 *distinguished thee.*

Now if thou didst receive *it,* why dost thou glory, as if thou hadst not received *it?*

a James 1.17.

learn in us. Or *by* our example and views. ¶ *Not to think,* &c. Since you see the plan which we desire to take; since you see that we who have the rank of apostles, and have been so eminently favoured with endowments and success, do not wish to form parties, that you may also have the same views in regard to others. ¶ *Above that which is written.* Probably referring to what he had said in chap. iii. 5—9, 21; iv. 1. Or it *may* refer to the general strain of Scripture requiring the children of God to be modest and humble. ¶ *That no one of you be puffed up.* That no one be proud or exalted in self-estimation above his neighbour. That no one be disposed to look upon others with contempt, and to seek to depress and humble them. They should regard themselves as brethren, and as all on a level. The *argument* here is, that if Paul and Apollos did not suppose that *they* had a right to put themselves at the head of parties, *much less* had any of them a right to do so. The *doctrine* is, (1.) That parties are improper in the church; (2.) That Christians should regard themselves as on a level; and, (3.) That no one Christian should regard others as beneath him, or as the object of contempt.

7. *For who maketh,* &c. This verse contains a *reason* for what Paul had just said; and the reason is, that all that any of them possessed had been derived from God, and no endowments whatever, which they had, could be laid as the foundation for self-congratulation and boasting. The apostle here doubtless has in his eye the teachers in the church of Corinth, and intends to show them that there was no occasion of pride or to assume pre-eminence. As all that they possessed had been given of God, it could not be the occasion of boasting or self-confidence. ¶ *To differ from another.* Who has *separated* you from another; or who has made you superior to others. This may refer to every thing

in which one was superior to others, or distinguished from them. The apostle doubtless has reference to those attainments in piety, talents, or knowledge by which one teacher was more eminent than others. But the same question may be applied to native endowments of mind; to opportunities of education; to the arrangements by which one rises in the world; to health; to property; to piety; to eminence and usefulness in the church. It is God who makes one, in any of these respects, to differ from others; and it is especially true in regard to personal piety. Had not *God* interfered and made a difference, all would have remained alike under sin. The race would have together rejected his mercy; and it is only by his distinguishing love that *any* are brought to believe and be saved. ¶ *And what hast thou.* Either talent, piety, or learning. ¶ *That thou didst not receive.* From God. By whatever means you have obtained it, it has been the gift of God. ¶ *Why dost thou glory,* &c. Why dost thou boast as if it were the result of your own toil, skill or endeavour. This is not designed to discourage human exertion; but to discourage a spirit of vain-glory and boasting. A man who makes the most painful and faithful effort to obtain any thing good, will, if successful, trace his success to God. He will still feel that it is God who gave him the disposition, the time, the strength, the success. And he will be *grateful* that he was enabled to make the effort; not vain, or proud, or boastful, because that he was successful. This passage states a general doctrine, that the reason why one man differs from another is to be traced to God; and that this fact should repress all boasting and glorying, and produce true humility in the minds of Christians. It may be observed, however, that it is as true of intellectual rank, of health, of wealth, of food, of raiment, of liberty, of peace, as it is of

8 Now ye are full, now ye are rich, *a* ye have reigned as kings without us : and I would to God

a Rev.3.17.

religion, that *all* come from God; and as this fact which is so obvious and well known, does not repress the exertions of men to preserve their health and to obtain property, so it should not repress their exertions to obtain salvation. God governs the world on the same good principles every where ; and the fact that he is the source of all blessings, should not operate to discourage, but should prompt to human effort. The hope of his aid and blessing is the only ground of encouragement in *any* undertaking.

8. *Now ye are full,* It is generally agreed that this is spoken in *irony,* and that it is an indignant sarcasm uttered against the false and self-confident teachers in Corinth. The design is to contrast them with the apostles; to show how self-confident and vain the false teachers were, and how laborious and self-denying the apostles were; and to show to them how little claim *they* had to authority in the church, and the *real* claim which the apostles had from their self-denials and labours. The whole passage is an instance of most pungent and cutting sarcasm, and shows that there *may* be occasions when irony may be proper, though it should be rare. An instance of cutting irony occurs also in regard to the priests of Baal, in 1 Kings xviii. 27. The word translated "ye are full" (*κεκορεσμένοι*) occurs only here, and in Acts xxvii. 38, " And when they had eaten enough." It is usually applied to a feast, and denotes those who are satiated or satisfied. So here it means, "You think you have enough. You are satisfied with your conviction of your own knowledge, and do not feel your need of any thing more." ¶ *Ye are rich.* This is presenting the same idea in a different form. "You esteem yourselves to be rich in spiritual gifts, and graces, so that you do not feel the necessity of any more." ¶ *Ye have reigned as kings.* This is simply carrying forward the idea before stated;

ye did reign, that we also might reign with you.

9 For I think, that God hath

but in the form of a *climax.* The first metaphor is taken from persons *filled with food ;* the second from those who are so *rich* that they do not feel their want of more; the third from those who are raised to a *throne,* the highest elevation, where there was nothing further to be reached or desired. And the phrase means, that they had been fully satisfied with their condition and attainments, with their knowledge and power, that they lived like rich men and princes—revelling, as it were, on spiritual enjoyments, and disdaining all foreign influence, and instruction, and control. ¶ *Without us.* Without our counsel and instruction. You have taken the whole management of matters on yourselves without any regard to our advice or authority. You did not feel your need of our aid; and you did not regard our authority. You supposed you could get along as well without us as with us. ¶ *And I would to God ye did reign.* Many interpreters have understood this as if Paul had really expressed a wish that they were literal princes, that they might afford protection to him in his persecution and troubles. Thus Grotius, Whitby, Locke, Rosenmüller, and Doddridge. But the more probable interpretation is, that Paul here drops the *irony,* and addresses them in a sober, earnest manner. It is the expression of a wish that they were as truly happy and blessed as they thought themselves to be. " I wish that you *were* so abundant in all spiritual improvements ; I wish that you *had* made such advances that you could be represented as full, and as rich, and as princes, needing nothing, that when I came I might have nothing to do but to partake of your joy." So Calvin, Lightfoot, Bloomfield. It implies, (1.) A *wish* that they were truly happy and blessed; (2.) A doubt implied whether they *were* then so; and, (3.) A desire on the part of Paul to *partake* of their real and true joy, instead

set forth us the ¹ apostles last, as
it were appointed to death : for
we *a* are made a ² spectacle unto

1 or, *the last apostles.*

of being compelled to come to them
with the language of rebuke and admonition; see ver. 19, 21.

9. *For I think.* It seems to me.
Grotius thinks that this is to be taken
ironically, as if he had said, "It seems
then that God has designed that we,
the apostles, should be subject to contempt and suffering, and be made poor
and persecuted, while you are admitted
to high honours and privileges." But
probably this is to be taken as a *serious*
declaration of Paul, designed to show
their actual condition and trials, while
others were permitted to live in enjoyment.   Whatever might be *their* condition, Paul says that the condition of
himself and his fellow-labourers was
one of much contempt and suffering;
and the inference seems to be, that
they ought to doubt whether they were
in a right state, or had any occasion for
their self-congratulation, since they so
little resembled those whom God had
set forth. ¶ *Hath set forth.* Has
showed us; or placed us in public view.
¶ *The apostles last.* Marg. or, *the
last apostles* (τοὺς ἀποστόλους ἐσχάτους).
Grotius supposes that this means in
the lowest condition; the humblest
state; a condition like that of beasts.
So Tertullian renders it.   And this
interpretation is the correct one if the
passage be ironical.   But Paul may
mean to refer to the custom of bringing forth those in the amphitheatre at
the *conclusion* of the spectacles who
were to fight with other men, and who
had no chance of escape.   These inhu-
man games abounded every where;
and an allusion to them would be well
understood, and is indeed often made
by Paul; comp. 1 Cor. ix. 26 ; 1 Tim.
vi. 12 ; 2 Tim. iv. 7; see Seneca Epis.
chap. vii.   This interpretation receives
support from the words which are used
here, "God hath exhibited," "spectacle," or *theatre*, which are all applicable to such an exhibition.   Calvin,
Locke, and others, however, suppose
that Paul refers to the fact that he
was the *last* of the apostles ; but this

the world, and to angels, and to
men.

10 We *are* fools for Christ's

a Heb.10 33.   2 *theatre.*

interpretation does not suit the connection of the passage. ¶ *As it were*
(ὡς).   Intimating the *certainty* of
death. ¶ *Appointed unto death* (ἐπι-
θανατίους).   Devoted to death.   The
word occurs no where else in the New
Testament.   It denotes the certainty
of death, or the fact of being destined
to death; and implies that such were
their continued conflicts, trials, persecutions, that it was morally certain
that they would terminate *in* their
death, and only *when* they died, as the
last gladiators on the stage were destined to contend until they should die.
This is a very strong expression; and
denotes the continuance, the constancy, and the intensity of their sufferings in the cause of Christ. ¶ *We
are made a spectacle.*   Marg. *theatre*
(θέατρον).   The theatre, or amphitheatre of the ancients was composed
of an *arena*, or level floor, on which
the combatants fought, and which was
surrounded by circular seats rising
above one another to a great height,
and capable of containing many
thousand spectators.   Paul represents
himself as on this arena or stage, contending with foes, and destined to
death.   Around him and above him
are an immense host of men and angels,
looking on at the conflict, and await-
ing the issue.   He is not alone or
unobserved.   He is made public; and
the universe gazes on the struggle.
Angels and men denote the universe,
as gazing upon the conflicts and
struggles of the apostles.   It is a vain
inquiry here, whether he means good
or bad angels.   The expression means
that he was *public* in his trials, and
that this was exhibited to the universe.
The whole verse is designed to convey
the idea that God had, for wise purposes, appointed them in the sight of
the universe, to pains, and trials, and
persecutions, and poverty, and want,
which would terminate only in their
death; see Heb. xii. 1, &c.   What
these trials were he specifies in the
following verses.

sake, but ye *are* wise in Christ ; we *are* weak, but ye *are* strong ; ye *are* honourable, but we are de-spised.

---

10. We are *fools*. This is evidently ironical. "We are doubtless foolish men, but ye are wise in Christ. We, Paul, Apollos, and Barnabas, have no claims to the character of wise men—we are to be regarded as fools, unworthy of confidence, and unfit to instruct ; but you are full of wisdom." ¶ *For Christ's sake* (διὰ Χριστὸν.) On account of Christ ; or in reference to his cause, or in regard to the doctrines of the Christian religion. ¶ *But ye are wise in Christ.* The phrase "*in* Christ," does not differ in signification materially from the one above; "for Christ's sake." This is wholly ironical, and is exceedingly pungent. "You, Corinthians, boast of your wisdom and prudence. You are to be esteemed very wise. You are unwilling to submit to be esteemed fools. You are proud of your attainments. We, in the mean time, who are apostles, and who have founded your church, are to be regarded as fools, and as unworthy of public confidence and esteem." The whole design of this irony is to show the folly of their boasted wisdom. That they only should be wise and prudent, and the apostles fools, was in the highest degree absurd; and this absurdity the apostle puts in a strong light by his irony. ¶ *We* are *weak*. We are timid and feeble, but you are daring, bold and fearless. This is irony. The very reverse was probably true. Paul was bold, daring, fearless in declaring the truth, whatever opposition it might encounter ; and probably many of them were timid and time-serving, and endeavouring to avoid persecution, and to accommodate themselves to the prejudices and opinions of those who were wise in their own sight ; the prejudices and opinions of the world. ¶ *Ye* are *honourable*. Deserving of honour and obtaining it. Still ironical. You are to be esteemed as worthy of praise. ¶ *We* are *despised* (ἄτιμοι). Not only actually contemned, but worthy to be so. This was irony also. And the design was to show

them how foolish was their self-confidence and self-flattery, and their attempt to exalt themselves.

11. *Even unto this present hour.* Paul here drops the irony, and begins a serious recapitulation of his actual sufferings and trials. The phrase here used "unto this present hour" denotes that these things had been incessant through all their ministry. They were not merely at the commencement of their work, but they had continued and attended them everywhere. And even then they were experiencing the same thing. These privations and trials were still continued, and were to be regarded as a part of the apostolic condition. ¶ *We both hunger and thirst.* The apostles, like their master, were poor, and in travelling about from place to place, it often happened that they scarcely found entertainment of the plainest kind, or had money to purchase it. It is no dishonour to be poor, and especially if that poverty is produced by doing good to others. Paul might have been rich, but he chose to be poor for the sake of the gospel. To enjoy the luxury of doing good to others, we ought to be willing to be hungry and thirsty, and to be deprived of our ordinary enjoyments. ¶ *And are naked.* In travelling, our clothes become old and worn out, and we have no friends to replace them, and no money to purchase new. It is no discredit to be clad in mean raiment if that is produced by self-denying toils in behalf of others. There is no honour in gorgeous apparel ; but there is real honour in voluntary poverty and want, when produced in the cause of benevolence. Paul was not ashamed to travel, to preach, and to appear before princes and kings, in a soiled and worn-out garment, for it was worn out in the service of his Master, and Divine Providence had arranged the circumstances of his life. But how many a minister now would be ashamed to appear in such clothing ! How many professed Christians are ashamed

11 Even unto this present hour we both hunger and thirst, and are naked, *a* and are buffeted, and have no certain dwelling-place.

a Rom. 8. 35.   *b* Acts 20. 34.

to go to the house of God because they cannot dress well, or be in the fashion, or outshine their neighbours! If an apostle was willing to be meanly clad in delivering the message of God, then assuredly *we* should be willing to preach, or to worship him in such clothing as he provides. We may add here, what a sublime spectacle was here; and what a glorious triumph of the truth. Here was Paul with an impediment in his speech; with a personage small and mean rather than graceful; and in a mean and tattered dress; and often in chains, yet delivering truth before which kings trembled, and which produced every where a deep impression on the human mind. Such was the power of the gospel *then!* And such triumph did the truth then have over men. See Doddridge. ¶ *And are buffeted.* Struck with the hand; Note, Mat. xxvi. 67. Probably it is here used to denote harsh and injurious treatment in general; comp. 2 Cor. xii. 7. ¶ *And have no certain dwelling-place.* No fixed or permanent home. They wandered to distant lands; threw themselves on the hospitality of strangers, and even of the enemies of the gospel; when driven from one place they went to another; and thus they led a wandering, uncertain life, amidst strangers and foes. They who know what are the comforts of home; who are surrounded by beloved families; who have a peaceful and happy fire-side; and who enjoy the blessings of domestic tranquillity, may be able to appreciate the trials to which the apostles were subjected. All this was for the sake of the gospel; all to purchase the blessings which we so richly enjoy.

12. *And labour, &c.* This Paul often did. See Note, Acts xviii. 3; compare Acts xx. 34; 1 Thess. ii. 9. 2 Thess. iii. 8. ¶ *Being reviled.* That they were often reviled or reproached, their history every where shows. See the Acts of the Apostles.

12 And labour, *b* working with our own hands: being reviled, *c* we bless; being persecuted, we suffer it: 13 Being defamed, we entreat:

c Matt. 5. 44; Acts 7. 60.

They were reviled or ridiculed by the Gentiles as Jews; and by all as Nazarenes, and as deluded followers of Jesus; as the victims of a foolish superstition and enthusiasm. ¶ *We bless.* We return good for evil. In this they followed the explicit direction of the Saviour; see Note, Matt. v. 44. The *main* idea in these passages is, that they were reviled, were persecuted, &c. The other clauses, "we bless," "we suffer it," &c. seem to be thrown in *by the way* to show how they bore this ill treatment. As if he had said "we are reviled; and what is more, we bear it patiently, and return good for evil." At the same time that he was recounting his trials, he was, therefore, incidentally *instructing* them in the nature of the gospel, and showing how their sufferings were to be borne; and how to illustrate the excellency of the Christian doctrine. ¶ *Being persecuted.* Note, Matt. v. 11. ¶ *We suffer it.* We sustain it; we do not revenge it; we *abstain* from resenting or resisting it.

13. *Being defamed.* Greek, Blasphemed, *i. e.* spoken of and to, in a harsh, abusive, and reproachful manner. The original and proper meaning of the word is to speak in a reproachful manner of any one, whether of God or man. It is usually applied to God, but it may also be used of men. ¶ *We entreat.* Either God in their behalf, praying him to forgive them, or we entreat them to turn from their sins, and become converted to God. Probably the latter is the sense. They besought them to examine more candidly their claims instead of reviling them; and to save their souls by embracing the gospel instead of destroying them by rejecting it with contempt and scorn. ¶ *We are made.* We became; we are so regarded or esteemed. The word here does not imply that there was any positive agency in *making* them

we are made as the filth of the earth, *and are* the off-scouring *a* of all things unto this day.

14 I write not these things to

a Lam.3.45.

sname you, but as my beloved sons *b* I warn *you.*

15 For though ye have ten thousand instructors in Christ, yet *have*

b 1 Thess.2.11.

zuch, but simply that they were in fact so regarded. ¶ *As the filth of the earth.* It would not be possible to employ stronger expressions to denote the contempt and scorn with which they were every where regarded. The word *filth* (περικαθαρματα) occurs nowhere else in the New Testament. It properly denotes filth, or that which is collected by sweeping a house, or that which is collected and cast away by purifying or cleansing any thing; hence any vile, worthless, and contemptible object. Among the Greeks the word was used to denote the victims which were offered to *expiate crimes,* and particularly men of ignoble rank, and of a worthless and wicked character, who were kept to be offered to the gods in a time of pestilence, to appease their anger, and to *purify* the nation. Bretschneider and Schleusner. Hence it was applied by them to men of the most vile, abject, and worthless character. But it is not certain that Paul had any reference to that sense of the word. The whole force of the expression may be met by the supposition that he uses it in the sense of that filth or dirt which is collected by the process of cleansing or scouring any thing, as being vile, contemptible, worthless. So the apostles were regarded. And by the use of the word *world* here, he meant to say that they were regarded as the most vile and worthless men which the *whole world* could furnish; not only the refuse of Judea, but of all the nations of the earth. As if he had said "more vile and worthless men could not be found on the face of the earth." ¶ And are *the off-scouring of all things.* This word (περιψημα) occurs no where else in the New Testament. It does not differ materially from the word rendered *filth.* It denotes that which is rubbed off by scouring or cleaning any thing; and hence any thing vile or worthless; or a vile and worthless man. This term

was also applied to vile and worthless men who were sacrificed or thrown into the sea as an expiatory offering, as it were to purify the people. Suidas remarks that they said to such a man, "be then our περιψημα," our redemption, and then flung him into the sea as a sacrifice to Neptune. See Whitby, Calvin, Doddridge. ¶ *Unto this day.* Continually. We have been constantly so regarded. See ver. 11.

14. *To shame you.* It is not my design to put you to shame by showing you how little you suffer in comparison with us. This is not our design, though it may have this effect. I have no wish to make you ashamed, to appear to triumph over you or merely to taunt you. My design is higher and nobler than this. ¶ *But as my beloved sons.* As my dear children. I speak as a father to his children, and I say these things for your good. No father would desire to make his children ashamed. In his counsels, entreaties, and admonitions, he would have a higher object than that. ¶ *I warn you.* I do not say these things in a harsh manner, with a severe spirit of rebuke: but in order to *admonish* you, to suggest counsel, to instil wisdom into the mind. I say these things not to make you blush, but with the hope that they may be the means of your reformation, and of a more holy life. No man, no minister, ought to reprove another merely to overwhelm him with shame, but the object should always be to make a brother better; and the admonition should be so administered as to have this end, not sourly or morosely, but in a kind, tender, and affectionate manner.

15. *For though ye have ten thousand instructors.* Though you may have or though you should have. It matters not how many you have, yet it is still true that I only sustain the relation to you of spiritual father, and whatever respect it is proper for you to have

ye not many fathers ; for in Christ
Jesus I have begotten you through
the gospel.

16 Wherefore, I beseech you, be
ye followers of me.

17 For this cause have I sent

toward them, yet there is a peculiar
right which I have to admonish you,
and a peculiar deference which is due
to me, from my early labours among
you, and from the fact that you are
my spiritual children. ¶ *Instructers.*
Gr. Pedagogues; or those who conducted children to school, and who
superintended their conduct out of
school hours. Hence those who had
the care of children, or teachers in
general. It is then applied to instructers of any kind. ¶ *In Christ.* In the
Christian system or doctrine. The
authority which Paul claims here, is
that which a *father* has in preference
to such an instructer. ¶ *Not many
fathers.* Spiritual fathers. That is,
you have but one. You are to remember that however many teachers you
have, yet that I alone am your spiritual father. ¶ *In Christ Jesus.* By
the aid and authority of Christ. I
have begotten you by preaching his
gospel and by his assistance. ¶ *I
have begotten you.* I was the instrument of your conversion. ¶ *Through
the gospel.* By means of the gospel;
by preaching it to you, that is, by the
truth.

16. *Wherefore.* Since I am your
spiritual father. ¶ *Be ye followers of
me.* Imitate me; copy my example;
listen to my admonitions. Probably
Paul had particularly in his eye their
tendency to form parties ; and here
admonishes them that *he* had no disposition to form sects, and entreats
them in this to imitate his example.
A minister should always so live as
that he can, without pride or ostentation, point to his own example ; and
entreat his people to imitate him.
He should have such a confidence in
his own integrity; he should lead such
a blameless life : and *he should be
assured that his people have so much
evidence of his integrity,* that he can
point them to his own example, and

unto you Timotheus, who is my
beloved son and faithful in the
Lord, who shall bring you into
remembrance of my ways which be
in Christ, as I teach everywhere in
every church.

entreat them to live like himself.
And to do this, he should live a life of
piety, and should furnish such evidence of a pure conversation, that
his people may have reason to regard
him as a holy man.

17. *For this cause.* In order to
remind you of my doctrines and my
manner of life. Since I am hindered
from coming myself, I have sent a
fellow labourer as my messenger, well
acquainted with my views and feelings,
that he might do what I would do if I
were present. ¶ *Have I sent unto
you Timotheus.* Timothy, the companion and fellow labourer of Paul.
This was probably when Paul was at
Ephesus. He sent Timothy and
Erastus into Macedonia, probably
with instructions to go to Corinth if
convenient. Yet it was not quite
certain that Timothy would come to
them, for in chap. xvi. 10, he expresses a doubt whether he would. Paul
was probably deeply engaged in Asia,
and did not think it proper then for
him to leave his field of labour. He
probably supposed also, that Timothy,
as his ambassador, would be able to
settle the difficulties in Corinth as
well as if he were himself present.
¶ *My beloved son.* In the gospel.
See Acts xvi. 1—3; 1 Tim. i. 2. He
supposed, therefore, that they would
listen to him with great respect.
¶ *And faithful in the Lord.* A true
Christian and a faithful servant of
Christ ; and who is, therefore, worthy
of your confidence. ¶ *Of my ways.*
My doctrine, my teaching, my mode
of life. ¶ *Which be in Christ.* That
is, my Christian life : my ministry ; or
my conduct as a Christian and a follower of the Saviour. ¶ *As I teach
everywhere,* &c. This was designed
probably to show them that he taught
them no new or peculiar doctrines ;
he wished them simply to conform to
the common rules of the churches,

18 Now some are puffed up, as though I would not come to you.

19 But I will come to you shortly, if *a* the Lord will; and will know, not the speech of them which are puffed up, but *b* the power.

a James 4.15.   *b* Gal.2.6.

20 For the kingdom *c* of God *is* not in word, but in power.

21 What will ye? shall *d* I come unto you with a rod, or in love, and *in* the spirit of meekness?

c Rom.14.17.   *d* 2 Cor.13.10.

and to be like their Christian brethren every where. The Christian church is founded every where on the same doctrines; is bound to obey the same laws; and is fitted to produce and cherish the same spirit. The same spirit that was required in Ephesus or Antioch, was required at Corinth; the same spirit that was required at Corinth, at Ephesus, or at Antioch, is required now.

18. *Now some are puffed up.* They are puffed up with a vain confidence; they say that I would not dare to come; that I would be afraid to appear among them, to administer discipline, to rebuke them, or to supersede their authority. Probably he had been detained by the demand on his services in other places, and by various providential hinderances from going there, until they supposed that he stayed away from fear. And possibly he might apprehend that they would think he had sent Timothy because he was afraid to come himself. Their conduct was an instance of the haughtiness and arrogance which men will assume when they suppose they are in no danger of reproof or punishment.

19. *But I will come.* It is from no fear of them that I am kept away; and to convince them of this I will come to them speedily. ¶ *If the Lord will.* If the Lord permit; if by his providence he allows me to go. Paul regarded the entering on a journey as dependent on the will of God; and felt that God had all in his hand. No purpose should be formed without a reference to his will; no plan without feeling that he can easily frustrate it and disappoint us; see James iv. 15. ¶ *And will know.* I will examine; I will put to the test; I will fully understand. ¶ *Not the speech,* &c. Not their vain and empty boasting; not their confident assertions, and their

self-complacent views. ¶ *But the power.* Their real power. I will put their power to the proof: I will see whether they are able to effect what they affirm; whether they have more real power than I have. I will enter fully into the work of discipline, and will ascertain whether they have such authority in the church, such a power of party and of combination, that they can resist me, and oppose my administration of the discipline which the church needs. "A passage," says Bloomfield, "which cannot, in nerve and vigour, or dignity and composed confidence, be easily paralleled, even in Demosthenes himself."

20. *For the kingdom of God.* The reign of God in the church (Note, Mat. iii. 2); meaning here, probably, the power or authority which was to be exercised in the government and discipline of the church. Or it may refer to the manner in which the church had been established. "It has not been set up by empty boasting; by pompous pretensions; by confident assertions. Such empty boasts would do little in the great work of founding, governing, and preserving the church; and unless men have some higher powers than this they are not qualified to be religious teachers and guides." ¶ *But in power.* (1.) In the miraculous power by which the church was established—the power of the Saviour and of the apostles in working miracles. (2.) In the power of the Holy Ghost in the gift of tongues, and in his influence on the heart in converting men; Note, chap. i. 18. (3.) In the continual power which is needful to protect, defend, and govern the church. Unless teachers showed that they had *such* power, they were not qualified for their office.

21. *What will ye.* It depends on yourselves how I shall come. If you lay aside your contentions and strifes;

if you administer discipline as you should; if you give yourselves heartily and entirely to the work of the Lord, I shall come, not to reprove or to punish, but as a father and a friend. But if you do not heed my exhortations or the labours of Timothy; if you still continue your contentions, and do not remove the occasions of offence, I shall come with severity and the language of rebuke. ¶ *With a rod.* To correct and punish. ¶ *In the spirit of meekness.* Comforting and commending instead of chastising. Paul intimates that this depended on themselves. They had the power, and it was their duty to administer discipline; but if they would not do it, the task would devolve on him as the founder and father of the church, and as intrusted with power by the Lord Jesus to administer the severity of Christian discipline, or to punish those who offended by bodily suffering; see chap. v. 5; chap. xi. 30. See also the case of Ananias and Sapphira (Acts v. 1, &c.), and of Elymas the sorcerer. (Acts xiii. 10, 11.)

REMARKS.

1st. We should endeavour to form a proper estimate of the Christian ministry; ver. 1. We should regard ministers as the servants of Jesus Christ, and honour them for their Master's sake; and esteem them also in proportion to their fidelity. They are entitled to respect as the ambassadors of the Son of God; but that respect also should be in proportion to their resemblance of him and their faithfulness in their work. They who love the ministers of Christ, who are like him, and who are faithful, love the Master that sent them; they who hate and despise them despise him; see Mat. x. 40—42.

2d. Ministers should be faithful; ver. 2. They are the stewards of Christ. They are appointed by him. They are responsible *to* him. They have a most important trust—more important than any other stewards, and they should live in such a manner as to receive the approbation of their master.

3d. It is of little consequence what the world thinks of us; ver. 3. A good name is on many accounts desirable;

but it should not be the leading consideration; nor should we do any thing *merely* to obtain it. Desirable as is a fair reputation, yet the opinion of the world is not to be too highly valued; for, (1.) It often misjudges; (2.) It is prejudiced for or against us; (3.) It is not to decide our final destiny; (4.) To desire that simply, is a selfish and base passion.

4th. The esteem even *of friends* is not to be the leading object of life; ver. 2. This is valuable, but not so valuable as the approbation of God. Friends are partial, and even where they do not approve our course, if we are conscientious, we should be willing to bear with their disapprobation. A good conscience is every thing. The approbation even of friends cannot help us in the day of judgment.

5th. We should distrust ourselves; ver. 3, 4. We should not pronounce too confidently on our motives or our conduct. We may be deceived. There may be much even in our own motives that may elude our most careful inquiry. This should teach us humility, self-distrust, and charity. Knowing our *own* liableness to mis-judge ourselves, we should look with kindness on the faults and failings of others.

6th. We see here the nature of the future judgment; ver. 5. (1.) The hidden things of darkness will be brought out—all the secret crimes, and plans, and purposes of men will be developed. All that has been done in secret, in darkness, in the night, in palaces and in prisons, will be developed. What a development will take place in the great day when the secret crimes of a world shall be revealed; and when all that has now escaped the notice of men, and the punishment of courts, shall be brought out! (2.) Every man's secret thoughts shall be revealed. There will be no concealment then. All that we have devised or desired; all the thoughts that we have forgotten, shall there be brought out to noon-day. How will the sinner tremble when *all* his thoughts are made known! Suppose, unknown to him, some person had been writing down all that a man has *thought* for a day, a week, or a year, and should begin to *read* it to him. Who is there that would not hang his head with shame, and tremble at such a record? Yet at the day of judgment the thoughts of *the whole life* will be revealed. (3.) Every man shall be judged as he *ought* to be. God is impartial. The man that *ought* to be saved will be; the man that *ought not* will not be. How solemn will be the *impartial trial of the world!* Who can think of it but with alarm!

7th. We have no occasion for pride or vain-boasting; ver. 7. All that we have of beauty, health, wealth, honour, grace, has been given to us by God. For what he has given us we should be grateful; but it should not excite pride. It is, indeed, valuable *because* God gives it, and we should remember his mercies, but we should not boast. We have nothing to boast of. Had we our deserts, we should be driven away in his wrath, and made wretched. That any are out of hell is matter of thankfulness; that one possesses more than another proves that God is a sovereign, and not that we are more worthy than another, or that there is by nature any ground of preference which one has over another.

8th. Irony and sarcasm are sometimes lawful and proper; ver. 8—10. But it is not often as safe as it was in the hands of the apostle Paul. Few men can regulate the talent properly; few should allow themselves to indulge in it. It is *rarely* employed in the Bible; and it is rarely employed elsewhere where it does not do injury. The cause of truth can be usually sustained by sound argument; and that which cannot be thus defended is not worth defence. Deep wounds are often made by the severity of wit and irony; and an indulgence in this usually prevents a man from having a single friend.

9th. We see from this chapter what religion has cost; ver. 9—13. Paul states the sufferings that he and the other apostles endured in order to establish it. They were despised, and persecuted, and poor, and regarded as the refuse of the world. The Christian religion was founded on the blood of its author, and has been reared amidst the sighs and tears of its friends. All its early advocates were subjected to persecution and trial; and to engage in this work involved the certainty of being a martyr. We enjoy not a blessing which has not thus been purchased; and which has not come to us through the self-denials and toils of the best men that the earth has known. Persecution raged around all the early friends of the church; and it rose and spread while the fire of martyrdom spread, and while its friends were everywhere cast out as evil, and called to bleed in its defence.

10th. We have here an illustrious instance of the manner in which reproach, and contempt, and scorn should be borne; ver. 12, 13. The apostles imitated the example of their Master and followed his precepts. They prayed for their enemies, persecutors, and slanderers. There is nothing but religion that can produce this spirit; and this can do it always. The Saviour evinced it; his apostles evinced it; and all *should* evince it, who profess to be its friends.—We may remark, (1.) This is not produced by nature. It is the work of grace alone. (2.) It is the very spirit and genius of Christianity to produce it. (3.) Nothing but religion will enable a man to bear it, and will produce this temper and spirit. (4.) We have an instance here of what *all* Christians should evince. All should be in this like the apostles. All should be like the Saviour himself.

11th. We have an argument here for the truth of the Christian religion. The argument is founded on the fact that the apostles were willing to suffer so much in order to establish it.—They professed to have been eye-witnesses of what they affirmed. They had nothing to gain by spreading it if it was not true. They exposed themselves to persecution on this account, and became willing to die rather than deny its truth.—Take, for example, the case of the apostle Paul. (1.) He had every prospect of honour and of wealth in his own country. He had been liberally educated, and had the confidence of his countrymen. He might have risen to the highest station

CHAPTER V.

IT is reported commonly *that there is* fornication among you, and such fornication as is not so much as named among the Gentiles, that [a] one should have his father's wife.

a Deut.27.20.

of trust or influence. He had talents which would have raised him to distinction anywhere. (2.) He could not have been mistaken in regard to the events connected with his conversion; Acts ix. The scene, the voice, the light, the blindness, were all things which could not have been counterfeited. They were open and public. They did not occur "in a corner." (3.) He had no earthly motive to change his course. Christianity was despised when he embraced it; its friends were few and poor; and it had no prospect of spreading through the world. It conferred no wealth; bestowed no diadem; imparted no honours; gave no ease; conducted to no friendship of the great and the mighty. It subjected its friends to persecution, and tears, and trials, and death. What should *induce* such a man to make such a change? Why should Paul have embraced this, but from a conviction of its truth? How could he be convinced of that truth except by some argument that should be *so strong* as to overcome his hatred to it, make him willing to renounce all his prospects for it; to encounter all that the world could heap upon him, and even death itself, rather than deny it? But such a religion had a higher than any earthly origin, and must have been from God.

12th. We may expect to suffer reproach. It has been the common lot of all, from the time of the Master himself to the present. Jesus was reproached; the apostles were reproached; the martyrs were reproached, and we are not to be surprised that ministers and Christians are called to like trials now. It is enough "for the disciple that he be as his Master, and the servant as his Lord."

CHAPTER V.

THIS chapter is entirely occupied with a notice of an offence which existed in the church at Corinth. and with a statement of the measures which the apostle expected them to pursue in regard to it. Of the existence of this offence he had been informed, probably by "those of the house of Chloe," chap. i. 11, and there is reason to suppose that they had not even alluded to it in the letter which they had sent to him asking advice; see chap. vii. 1; comp. the Introduction. The apostle (ver. 1) reproves them for tolerating a species of licentiousness which was not tolerated even by the heathens; he reproves them (ver. 2) for being puffed up with pride even while this scandal existed in their church; he ordered them forthwith to purify the church by removing the incestuous person (ver. 4, 5); and exhorted them to preserve themselves from the influence which a single corrupt person might have, operating like leaven in a mass; (ver. 6, 7.) Then, lest they should mistake his meaning, and suppose that by commanding them not to keep company with licentious persons (ver. 9), he meant to say, that they should withdraw from all intercourse with the heathen who were known to be idolaters and corrupt, he says that that former command was not designed to forbid *all* intercourse with them, (ver. 9—12); but that he meant his injunction now to extend particularly to such as were professed members of the church; that they were not to cut off all intercourse with society at large because it was corrupt; that if any man professed to be a Christian and yet was guilty of such practices they were to disown him (ver. 11); that it was not his province, nor did he assume it, to judge the heathen world which was *without* the church (ver. 12); but that this was entirely consistent with the view that he had a right to exercise discipline *within* the church, on such as professed to be Christians; and that therefore, they were bound to put away that wicked person.

1. *It is reported.* Gr. It is heard. There is a rumour. That rumour had been brought to Paul, probably by the

2 And ye are puffed up, and have not rather mourned, *a* that

a 2 Cor.7.7.

he that hath done this deed might be taken away from among you.

members of the family of Chloe, chap. i. 11. ¶ *Commonly* ("Ολως). Every where. It is a matter of common fame. It is so public that it cannot be concealed; and so certain that it cannot be denied. This was an offence, he informs us, which even the heathen would not justify or tolerate; and, therefore, the report had spread not only in the churches, but even among the heathen, to the great scandal of religion.—When a report obtains *such* a circulation, it is certainly time to investigate it, and to correct the evil. ¶ That there is *fornication.* See Note, Acts xv. 20. The word is here used to denote incest; for the apostle immediately explains the nature of the offence. ¶ *And such fornication,* &c. An offence that is not tolerated or known among the heathen. This greatly aggravated the offence, that in a Christian church a crime should be tolerated among its members which even gross heathens would regard with abhorrence. That this offence was regarded with abhorrence by even the heathens has been abundantly proved by quotations from classic writers. See Wetstein, Bloomfield, and Whitby. Cicero says of the offence, expressly, that "it was an incredible and unheard of crime." Pro Cluen. 5. 6.—When Paul says that it was not "so much as named among the Gentiles," he doubtless uses the word (ὀνομάζεται) in the sense of *named with approbation, tolerated,* or *allowed.* The crime was known in a few instances, but chiefly of those who were princes and rulers; but it was no where regarded with approbation, but was always treated as abominable wickedness. All that the connection requires us to understand by the word "*named*" here is, that it was not tolerated or allowed; it was treated with abhorrence, and it was, therefore, more scandalous that it was allowed in a Christian church.— Whitby supposes that this offence that was tolerated in the church at Corinth gave rise to the scandals

that were circulated among the heathen respecting the early Christians, that they allowed of licentious intercourse among the members of their churches. This reproach was circulated extensively among the heathen, and the primitive Christians were at much pains to refute it. ¶ *That one should have.* Probably as his wife; or it may mean simply that he had criminal intercourse with her. Perhaps some man had parted with his wife, on some account, and his son had married her, or maintained her for criminal intercourse. It is evident from 2 Cor. vii. 12, that the person who had suffered the wrong, as well as he who had done it, was still alive.—Whether this was marriage or concubinage, has been disputed by commentators, and it is not possible, perhaps, to determine. See the subject discussed in Bloomfield.

2. *And ye are puffed up.* Note, chap. iv. 18. You are filled with pride, and with a vain conceit of your own wisdom and purity, notwithstanding the existence of this enormous wickedness in your church. This does not mean that they were puffed up, or proud *on account* of the existence of this wickedness, but they were filled with pride *notwithstanding,* or in spite of it. They *ought* to have been a humbled people. They *should* have mourned, and should have given their first attention to the removal of the evil. But instead of this, they had given indulgence to proud feeling, and had become elated with a vain confidence in their spiritual purity. Men are always elated and proud when they have the least occasion for it. ¶ *And have not rather mourned,* &c. Have not rather been *so* afflicted and troubled as to take the proper means for removing the offence. The word *mourn* here is taken in that large sense. Ye have not been *so much* afflicted—so troubled with the existence of this wickedness, as to take the proper measures to remove the offender.—Acts of discipline in the

3 For I verily, as absent *a* in body, but present in spirit, have ¹ judged already, as though I were

Col.2.5.   1 or, *determined.*

present *concerning* him that hath so done this deed ;

4 In the name *b* of our Lord

b 2 Cor.2.9,10.

church should always commence with *mourning* that there is occasion for it. It should not be *anger*, or pride, or revenge, or party feeling, which prompt to it. It should be deep *grief* that there is occasion for it ; and tender compassion for the offender. ¶ *Might be taken away.* By excommunication. He should not, while he continues in this state, be allowed to remain in your communion.

3. *For I verily.* But I, whatever it may cost me; however you may esteem my interference ; and whatever personal ill-will may be the result towards me, have adjudged this case to be so flagrant as to demand the exercise of discipline, and since the church to whom it belongs have neglected it, I use the authority of an apostle, and of a spiritual father, in directing it to take place. This was not a formal sentence of excommunication ; but it was the declared opinion of an apostle that such a sentence *should* be passed, and an *injunction* on the church to exercise this act of discipline. ¶ *As absent in body.* Since I am not personally present with you, I express my opinion in this manner. I am absent in body from you, and cannot, therefore, take those steps in regard to it which I could were I present. ¶ *But present in spirit.* My heart is with you; my feelings are with you; I have a deep and tender interest in the case; and I judge *as if* I were personally present. Many suppose that Paul by this refers to a power which was given to the apostles, though at a distance, to discern the real circumstances of a case by the gift of the Spirit. Comp. Col. ii. 5; 2 Kings v. 26; vi. 12. (Whitby, Doddridge, &c.) But the phrase does not demand this interpretation. Paul meant, probably, that though he was absent, yet his mind and attention had been given to this subject; he felt as deeply as though he were present, and would act in the same

way. He had, in some way, been fully apprized of all the circumstances of the case, and he felt it to be his duty to express his views on the subject. ¶ *Have judged already.* Margin, *Determined* (κέκρικα). I have made up my mind ; have decided, and *do* decide. That is, he had determined what *ought* to be done in the case. It was a case in which the course which ought to be pursued was plain, and on this point his mind was settled. What that course should be he states immediately. ¶ *As though I were present.* As though I had a personal knowledge of the whole affair, and were with you to advise.—We may be certain that Paul had the fullest information as to this case ; and that the circumstances were well known. Indeed, it was a case about *the facts* of which there could be no doubt. They were everywhere known (ver. 1), and there was no need, therefore, to attempt to establish them by formal proof.

4. *In the name*, &c. By the authority; or in the behalf; or acting by his commission or power. 2 Cor. ii 10. See Note, Acts iii. 6. This does not refer to Paul alone in declaring his opinion, but means that they were to be assembled in the name of the Lord Jesus, and that they were to proceed to exercise discipline by his authority. The idea is, that the authority to administer discipline is derived from the Lord Jesus Christ, and is to be exercised in his name, and to promote his honour. ¶ *When ye are gathered together.* Or, " You being assembled in the name of the Lord Jesus." This is to be connected with the previous words, and means, (1.) That they were to be assembled for the purpose of administering discipline ; and (2.) That this was to be done in the name and by the authority of the Lord Jesus. ¶ *And my spirit*, ver. 3. As if I were with you; that is, with my declared opinion ;

Jesus Christ, when ye are gathered together, and my spirit, with the power *a* of our Lord Jesus Christ,

a Mat.16.19; John 20.23.

knowing what I would advise, were I one of you; or, I being *virtually* present with you by having delivered my opinion. It cannot mean that Paul's soul would be really present with them, but that, knowing his views and feelings, and what he would do, and knowing his love for them, they could act as if he were there. This passage proves that discipline belongs to the church itself; and so deep was Paul's conviction of this, that even *he* would not administer it, without their concurrence and action. And if Paul would not do it, and in a case too where bodily pains were to be inflicted by miraculous agency, assuredly no other ministers have a right to assume the authority to administer discipline without the action and the concurrence of the church itself.

[The general doctrine of the New Testament is that the government of the church is invested, not in the people or church members at large, but in certain rulers or office-bearers, 1 Cor. xii. 28; Eph. iv. 11, 12; 1 Thess. v. 12, 13; Heb. xiii. 7; 1 Tim. v. 17. We find these elders or rulers existing in every church to which our attention is directed, while the people are continually exhorted to yield a willing submission to their authority. Now the passage under review must be explained in consistency with the analogy of truth, or the general scope of Scripture on the subject. It is unwise to build our conclusion on an insulated text. But, in reality, the language of the apostle, in this place, when fairly examined, gives no countenance to the idea that the judicial power of the church resides in the people. The case of the incestuous man was *judged by the apostle himself* previous to the transmission of his letter to the Corinthian church, which was therefore enjoined, not to adjudicate on the matter, but simply to give effect to the decision of Paul. " I verily *have judged already* concerning him who hath done this deed; in the name of our Lord Jesus Christ," &c. If it be still demanded why then were the people to assemble? the answer is obvious. It was necessary that the sentence should be published, where the crime had been committed, that the members of the church might concur in it, and withdraw from the

5 To deliver *b* such an one unto Satan for the destruction of the flesh, that the *c* spirit may be saved in the day of the Lord Jesus.

b 1 Tim.1.20.　　*c* chap.11.32.

society of the guilty person. The simple fact of the people being assembled, is no proof that they were judges.

Yet candour requires us to state that the words in the third verse, *ηδη κεκρικα* (I have already judged) are supposed by some to intimate, not the delivering of an authoritative sentence, but the simple expression of an opinion in regard to what *ought* to be done. This, however, seems neither consistent with the scope of the passage, nor with just ideas of apostolical authority. The apostles had " the care of all the churches, with power to settle matters of faith and order, to determine controversies, and exercise the rod of discipline on all offenders, whether pastors or flock; 1 Cor. v. 3—6; 2 Cor. x. 8; xiii. 10."]

¶ *With the power*, &c. This phrase is to be connected with the following verse. " I have determined what ought to be done. The sentence which I have passed is this. You are to be assembled in the name and authority of Christ. I shall be virtually present. And you are to deliver such a one to Satan, *by the power of our Lord Jesus Christ.*" That is, it is to be done by you; and the *miraculous* power which will be evinced in the case will proceed from the Lord Jesus. The word *power* (*δυναμις*), is used commonly in the New Testament to denote some miraculous and extraordinary power, and here evidently means that the Lord Jesus would put forth such a power in the infliction of pain and for the preservation of the purity of his church.

5. *To deliver.* This is the sentence which is to be executed. You are to deliver him to Satan, &c. ¶ *Unto Satan.* Beza, and the Latin fathers, suppose that this is only an expression of excommunication. They say, that in the Scriptures there are but two kingdoms recognised—the kingdom of God, or the church, and the kingdom of the world, which is regarded as under the control of Satan; and that to exclude a man from one is to subject him to the dominion of the other. There is some foundation for this

6 Your glorying *a* is not good.
Know ye not that a little leaven
b leaveneth the whole lump?

a James 4.16.

opinion; and there can be no doubt
that *excommunication* is here intended,
and that, *by* excommunication, the
offender was in some sense placed
under the control of Satan. It is
further evident that it is here supposed that by being thus placed under
him the offender would be subject to
corporal inflictions by the agency of
Satan, which are here called the
"destruction of the flesh." Satan is
elsewhere referred to as the author of
bodily diseases. Thus in the case of
Job, Job ii. 7. A similar instance is
mentioned in 1 Tim. i. 20, where Paul
says he had delivered Hymeneus and
Alexander to "Satan, that they might
learn not to blaspheme." It may be
observed here that though this was to
be done by the concurrence of the
church, as having a right to administer discipline, yet it was directed by
apostolic authority; and there is no
evidence that this was the usual form
of excommunication, nor ought it now
to be used. There was evidently
miraculous power evinced in this case,
and that power has long since ceased
in the church. ¶ *For the destruction
of the flesh.* We may observe here,
(1.) That this does not mean that the
man was *to die* under the infliction of
the censure, for the object was to
recover him; and it is evident that,
whatever he suffered as the consequence of this, he survived it, and
Paul again instructed the Corinthians
to admit him to their fellowship, 2
Cor. ii. 7. (2.) It was designed to
punish him for licentiousness of life—
often called in the Scriptures one of
the sins, or works of the flesh (Gal.
v. 19), and the design was that the
punishment should follow *in the line
of the offence*, or be a just retribution
—as punishment often does. Many
have supposed that by the "destruction of the flesh" Paul meant only the
destruction of his fleshly appetites or
carnal affections; and that he supposed
that this would be effected by the act
of excommunication. But it is very

7 Purge out therefore the old
leaven, that ye may be a new
lump, as ye are unleavened. For

b Luke 13.21.

evident from the Scriptures that the
apostles were imbued with the power
of inflicting diseases or bodily calamities for crimes. See Acts xiii. 11 ; 1
Cor. xi. 30. What this bodily malady
was, we have no means of knowing.
It is evident that it was not of very
long duration, since when the apostle
exhorts them (2 Cor. ii. 7) again to
receive him, there is no mention made
of his suffering then under it.—This
was an extraordinary and miraculous
power. It was designed for the
government of the church in its
infancy, when every thing was fitted
to show the direct agency of God ;
and it ceased, doubtless, with the
apostles. The church now has no
such power. It cannot now work
miracles ; and all its discipline now is
to be *moral* discipline, designed not to
inflict bodily pain and penalties, but
to work a moral reformation in the
offender. ¶ *That the spirit may be
saved.* That his soul might be saved ;
that he might be corrected, humbled,
and reformed by these sufferings, and
recalled to the paths of piety and virtue. This expresses the true design
of the discipline of the church, and it
ought *never* to be inflicted but with a
direct intention to benefit the offender, and to save the soul. Even when
he is cut off and disowned, the design
should not be vengeance, or punishment merely, but it should be to recover him and save him from ruin. ¶ *In
the day of the Lord Jesus.* The day
of judgment when the Lord Jesus
shall come, and shall collect his people to himself.

6. *Your glorying.* Your boasting ;
or confidence in your present condition, as if you were eminent in purity
and piety. ¶ *Is not good.* Is not
well, proper, right. Boasting is never
good; but it is especially wrong when,
as here, there is an existing evil that
is likely to corrupt the whole church.
When men are disposed to boast, they
should at once make the inquiry whether there is not some sin indulged in,

even Christ ^a our passover is ¹ sacrificed for us:

a Isa.53.7; 1 Pet.1.19; Rev.5.6,12.   1 or, *slain.*

on account of which they should be humbled and subdued. If all individual Christians, and all Christian churches, and all men of every rank and condition, would look at things as they are, they would never find occasion for boasting. It is only when we are blind to the realities of the case, and overlook our faults, that we are disposed to boast. The reason why this was improper in Corinth, Paul states—that any sin would tend to corrupt the whole church, and that therefore they ought not to boast until that was removed. ¶ *A little leaven,* &c. A small quantity of leaven or yeast will pervade the entire mass of flour, or dough, and diffuse itself through it all. This is evidently a proverbial saying. It occurs also in Gal. v. 9. Comp. Note, Matt. xiii. 33. A similar figure occurs also in the Greek classic writers.—By *leaven* the Hebrews metaphorically understood whatever had the power of *corrupting,* whether doctrine, or example, or any thing else. See Note, Matt. xvi. 6. The sense here is plain. A single sin indulged in, or allowed in the church, would act like leaven—it would pervade and corrupt the whole church, unless it was removed. On this ground, and for this reason, discipline should be administered, and the corrupt member should be removed.

7. *Purge out therefore,* &c. Put away; free yourselves from. ¶ *The old leaven.* The apostle here takes occasion, from the mention of *leaven,* to exhort the Corinthians to put away vice and sin. The figure is derived from the custom of the Jews in putting away leaven at the celebration of the passover. By the *old* leaven he means vice and sin; and also here the person who had committed the sin in their church. As the Jews, at the celebration of the passover, gave all diligence in removing leaven from their houses —searching every part of their dwellings with candles, that they might remove every particle of leavened bread from their habitations—so the

8 Therefore let us keep ² the feast, ^b not with old leaven, neither

2 or, *holy day.*   b Ex.13.6.

apostle exhorts them to use all diligence to search out and remove all sin. ¶ *That ye may be a new lump.* That you may be like a new mass of flour, or dough, before the leaven is put into it. That you may be pure. and free from the corrupting principle. ¶ *As ye are unleavened.* That is, as ye are bound by your Christian profession to be unleavened, or to be pure. Your very *profession* implies this, and you ought, therefore, to remove all impurity, and to become holy. Let there be no impurity, and no mixture inconsistent with that holiness which the gospel teaches and requires. The apostle here does not refer merely to the case of the incestuous person, but he takes occasion to exhort them to put away *all* sin. Not only to remove this occasion of offence, but to remove *all* impurity, that they might become entirely and only holy. The doctrine is, that Christians are by their profession holy, and that therefore they ought to give all diligence to remove every thing that is impure. ¶ *For even Christ,* &c. As the Jews, when their paschal lamb was slain, gave great diligence to put away all leaven from their dwellings, so we Christians, since *our* passover is slain, ought to give the like diligence to remove all that is impure and corrupting from our hearts.—There can be no doubt here that the paschal lamb was a type of the Messiah; and as little that the leaven was understood to be emblematic of impurity and sin. and that their being required to put it away was intended to be an emblematic action designed to denote that all sin was to be removed and forsaken. ¶ *Our passover.* Our *paschal lamb,* for so the word πάσχα usually signifies. The sense is, "We Christians have a paschal lamb; and that lamb is the Messiah. And as the Jews, when *their* paschal lamb was slain, were required to put away all leaven from their dwellings, so *we,* when *our* paschal lamb is slain, should put away all sin from our hearts and

ther with the *a* leaven of malice and wickedness, but with the

a Mat.16.6,12.

from our churches." This passage proves that Paul meant to teach that Christ had *taken the place* of the paschal lamb—that that lamb was designed to adumbrate or typify him—and that consequently when *he* was offered, the paschal offering was designed to cease. Christ is often in the Scriptures compared to a *lamb.* See Isa. liii. 7; John i. 29; 1 Pet. i. 19; Rev. v. 6, 12. ¶ *Is sacrificed for us.* Margin, Or *slain* (ἐτυθη). The word θύω may mean simply to slay or kill; but it is also used often in the sense of making a sacrifice as an expiation for sin; Acts xiv. 13, 18; 1 Cor. x. 20; comp. Gen. xxxi. 54; xlv. 1; Ex. iii. 18; v. 3, 8, 17; viii. 8, 25—29; xiii. 15; xx. 24; 2 Chron. xv. 26, where it is used as the translation of the word הבז, to sacrifice. It is used as the translation of this word no less than ninety-eight times in the Old Testament, and perhaps always in the sense of a *sacrifice,* or bloody offering. It is also used as the translation of the Hebrew word הבט, and שחט, to kill, &c. in Ex. xii. 21; 1 Kings xi. 19; xxv. 11; 2 Chron. xxix. 22, &c.; in all in eleven places in the Old Testament. It is used in a similar sense in the New Testament, in Matt. xxii. 4; Luke xv. 23, 27, 30; John x. 10; Acts x. 13; xi. 7. It occurs no where else in the New Testament than in the places which have been specified.—The true sense of the word here is, therefore, to be found in the doctrine respecting the passover. That that was intended to be a sacrifice for sin is proved by the nature of the offering, and by the account which is every where given of it in the Old Testament. The paschal lamb was slain as a sacrifice. It was slain in the temple; its blood was poured out as an offering; it was sprinkled and offered by the priests in the same way as other sacrifices; see Ex. xxiii. 18; xxxiv. 25; 2 Chron. xxx. 15, 16. And if so, then this passage means that Christ was offered *as a sacrifice for sin*—in accordance with the num-

unleavened *bread* of sincerity and truth.

erous passages of the New Testament, which speak of his death in this manner (see Note, Rom. iii. 25); and that his offering was designed to take the place of the paschal sacrifice, under the ancient economy. ¶ *For us.* For us who are Christians. He died in our stead; and as the Jews, when celebrating *their* paschal feast, put away all leaven, so *we,* as Christians, should put away all evil from our hearts, since that sacrifice has now been made once for all.

8. *Let us keep the feast.* Margin, *Holy day* (ἑορτάζωμεν). This is language drawn from the paschal feast, and is used by Paul frequently to carry out and apply his illustration. It does not mean literally the paschal supper here—for that had ceased to be observed by Christians—nor the Lord's supper particularly; but the sense is "As the Jews when they celebrated the paschal supper, on the slaying and sacrifice of the paschal lamb, put away all leaven—as emblematic of sin—so let us, in the slaying of *our* sacrifice, and in all the duties, institutions and events consequent thereon, put away all wickedness from our hearts as individuals, and from our societies and churches. Let us engage in the service of God by putting away all evil." ¶ *Not with the old leaven.* Not under the influence, or in the indulgence of the feelings of corrupt and unrenewed human nature.—The word *leaven* is very expressive of that former or *old* condition, and denotes the corrupt and corrupting passions of our nature before it is renewed. ¶ *The leaven of malice.* Of unkindness and evil—which would *diffuse* itself, and pervade the mass of Christians. The word *malice* (κακίας) denotes *evil* in general. ¶ *And wickedness.* Sin; evil. There is a *particular* reference here to the case of the incestuous person. Paul means that *all* wickedness should be put away from those who had been saved by the sacrifice of their *Passover,* Christ; and, therefore, this sin in a special manner.

9 I wrote unto you in an epistle *a* not to company with fornicators:

10 Yet not altogether with the fornicators of this world, or

a Eph.5.11 ; 2 Thess.3.14.

¶ *But with the unleavened* bread, &c. That is, with sincerity and truth. Let us be sincere, and true, and faithful ; as the Jews partook of bread unleavened, which was emblematic of purity, so let us *be* sincere and true. It is implied here that this could not be done unless they would put away the incestuous person.—No Christians can have, or give evidence of sincerity, who are not willing to put away all sin.

9. *I wrote unto you.* I have written (*έγραψα*). This word may either refer to this epistle, or to some former epistle. It simply denotes that he *had* written to them, but whether in the former part of this, or in some former epistle which is now lost, cannot be determined by the use of this word. ¶ *In an epistle* (*έν τῇ ἐπιστολῇ*). There has been considerable diversity of opinion in regard to this expression. A large number of commentators as Chrysostom, Theodoret, Oecumenius, most of the Latin commentators, and nearly all the Dutch commentators — suppose that this refers to the same epistle, and that the apostle means to say that in the former part of this epistle (ver. 2) he had given them this direction. And in support of this interpretation they say that *τῇ* here is used for *ταυτη*, and appeal to the kindred passages in Rom. xvi. 2 ; Col. iv. 6; 1 Thess. v. 27; 2 Thess. iii. 3, 4. Many others—as Grotius, Doddridge, Rosenmüller, &c.—suppose it to refer to some other epistle which is now lost, and which had been sent to them before their messengers had reached him. This epistle might have been very brief, and might have contained little more than this direction. That this is the correct opinion, may appear from the following considerations, viz: (1.) It is the *natural* and *obvious* interpretation—one that would strike the great mass of men. It is just such an expression as Paul *would* have used on the supposition that he *had* written a previous epistle. (2.)

It is the very expression which he uses in 2 Cor. vii. 8, where he is referring to this epistle as one which he had sent to them. (3.) It is not true that Paul had in any former part of this epistle given this direction. He had commanded them to remove an incestuous person, and such a command might seem to imply that they ought not to keep company with such a person; but it was not a general command *not* to have intercourse with them. (4.) It is altogether probable that Paul would write more letters than we have preserved. We have but fourteen of his remaining. Yet he laboured many years; founded many churches; and had frequent occasion to write to them. (5.) We know that a number of books have been lost which were either inspired or which were regarded as of authority by inspired men. Thus the books of Jasher, of Iddo the seer, &c., are referred to in the Old Testament, and there is no improbability that similar instances may have occurred in regard to the writers of the New Testament. (6.) In ver. 11, he expressly makes a distinction between the epistle which he was then writing and the former one. " But now," *i. e.* in this epistle, " I have written (*έγραψα*) to you," &c. an expression which he would not use if ver. 9, referred to the *same* epistle. These considerations seem to me to be unanswerable, and to prove that Paul had sent another epistle to *them* in which he had given this direction. (7.) This opinion accords with that of a very large number of commentators. As an instance, Calvin says, " The epistle of which he here speaks, is not now extant. Nor is it to be doubted that many others have perished; but it is sufficient that these survive to us which the Lord saw to be needful." If it be objected that this may affect the doctrine of the inspiration of the New Testament, since it is not to be supposed that God would suffer the

with the covetous, or extortioners, or with idolaters; for then must ye needs go out of the world.

writings of inspired men to be lost, we may reply, (*a*) That there is no evidence that these writings were inspired. Paul often makes a distinction in regard to his own words and doctrines, as inspired or uninspired (see chap. vii.); and the same thing may have occurred in his writings. (*b*) This does not affect the inspiration of the books which remain, even on the supposition that those which were lost were inspired. It does not prove that these are not from God. If a man loses a guinea it does not prove that those which he has *not* lost are counterfeit or worthless. (*c*) If inspired, they may have answered the purpose which was designed by their inspiration—and then have been suffered to be lost—as *all* inspired *books* will be destroyed at the end of the world. (*d*) It is to be remembered that a large part of the *discourses* of the inspired apostles, and even the Saviour himself (John xxi. 25), have been lost. And why should it be deemed any more wonderful that inspired *books* should be lost than inspired *oral teaching?* Why more wonderful that a brief letter of Paul should be destroyed than that numerous discourses of him "who spake as never man spake," should be lost to the world? (*e*) We should be thankful for the books that remain, and we may be assured that all the truth that is needful for our salvation has been preserved and is in our hands. That *any* inspired books have been preserved amidst the efforts which have been made to destroy them *all*, is more a matter of wonder than that a few have been lost, and should rather lead us to gratitude that we have them than to grief that a few, probably relating to local and comparatively unimportant matters, have been destroyed. ¶ *Not to company, &c.* Not to associate with; see Eph. v. 11; 2 Thess. iii. 14. This, it seems, was a *general* direction on the subject. It referred to *all* who had this character. But the direction which he *now* (ver. 11) proceeds to give, relates to a dif-

ferent matter—the proper degree of intercourse with those who were *in the church.*

10. *Yet not altogether, &c.* In my direction not "to company" with them, I did not mean that you should refuse *all* kinds of intercourse with them; that you should not treat them with civility, or be engaged with them in any of the transactions of life, or in the ordinary intercourse of society between man and man, for this would be impossible—but that you should not *so* associate with them as to be esteemed to belong to them, or so as to be corrupted by their example. You are not to make them companions and friends. ¶ *With the fornicators.* Most heathen were of this description, and particularly at Corinth. See the Introduction to this epistle. ¶ *Of this world.* Of those who are out of the church; or who are not professed Christians. ¶ *Or with the covetous.* The avaricious; those greedy of gain. Probably his direction in the former epistle had been that they should avoid them. ¶ *Or extortioners.* Rapacious persons; greedy of gain, and oppressing the poor, the needy, and the fatherless, to obtain money. ¶ *Or an idolater.* All the Corinthians before the gospel was preached there worshipped idols. ¶ *Then must ye needs, &c.* It would be necessary to leave the world. The world is full of such persons. You meet them every where. You cannot avoid them in the ordinary transactions of life, unless you either destroy yourselves, or withdraw wholly from society. This passage shows, (1.) That that society was *full* of the licentious and the covetous, of idolaters and extortioners. (Comp. Notes, Rom. i.) (2.) That it is not right either to take our own lives to avoid them, or to withdraw from society and become monks; and therefore, that the whole monastic system is contrary to Christianity; and, (3.) That it is needful we should have *some* intercourse with the men of the world; and to have dealings with them as

11 But now I have written unto you not to keep company,

if *a* any man that is called a brother be a fornicator, or covetous, or an

a Rom.16.17; 2 John 10.

neighbours, and as members of the community. *How far* we are to have intercourse with them is not settled here. The general principles may be, (1.) That it is only so far as is necessary for the purposes of good society, or to show kindness to them as neighbours and as members of the community. (2.) We are to deal *justly* with them in all our transactions. (3.) We may be connected with them in regard to the things which *we have in common*—as public improvements, the business of education, &c. (4.) We are to endeavour to do them good, and for *that* purpose we are not to shun their society. But, (5.) We are not to make them our companions; or to associate with them *in* their wickedness, or *as* idolaters, or covetous, or licentious; we are not to be known as partakers with them in these things. And for the same reason we are not to associate with the gay *in* their gayety; with the proud *in* their pride; with the fashionable *in* their regard to fashion; with the friends of the theatre, the ball-room, or the splendid party, *in* their attachment to these amusements. In all these things we are to be separate; and are to be connected with them only in those things which we may have *in common* with them, and which are not inconsistent with the holy rules of the Christian religion. (6.) We are not *so* to associate with them as to be corrupted by their example; or so as to be led *by* that example to neglect prayer and the sanctuary, and the deeds of charity, and the effort to do good to the souls of men. We are to make it a great point that our *piety* is not to suffer by that intercourse; and we are never to do any thing, or conform to any custom, or to have any such intercourse with them as to *lessen* our growth in grace; divert our attention from the humble duties of religion; or mar our Christian enjoyment.

11. *But now.* In this epistle. This shows that he had written a former letter. ¶ *I have written to you.*

Above. I have *designed* to give this injunction that you are to be entirely separated from one who is a professor of religion and who is guilty of these things. ¶ *Not to keep company.* To be wholly separated and withdrawn from such a person. Not to associate with him in any manner. ¶ *If any man that is called a brother.* Any professing Christian; any member of the church. ¶ *Be a fornicator,* &c. Like him who is mentioned, ver. 1. ¶ *Or an idolater.* This must mean those persons who while they professed Christianity still attended the idol feasts, and worshipped there. Perhaps a *few* such may have been found who had adopted the Christian profession hypocritically. ¶ *Or a railer.* A reproachful man; a man of coarse, harsh, and bitter words: a man whose characteristic it was to *abuse* others; to vilify their character, and wound their feelings. It is needless to say how much this is contrary to the spirit of Christianity, and to the example of the Master, "who when he was reviled, reviled not again." ¶ *Or a drunkard.* Perhaps there might have been some then in the church, as there are now, who were addicted to this vice. It has been the source of incalculable evils to the church; and the apostle, therefore, solemnly enjoins on Christians to have no fellowship with a man who is intemperate. ¶ *With such an one no not to eat.* To have no intercourse or fellowship with him of any kind; not to do any thing that would seem to acknowledge him as a brother; with such an one not even to eat at the same table. A similar course is enjoined by John; 2 John 10, 11. This refers to the intercourse of common life, and not particularly to the communion. The true Christian was wholly to disown such a person, and not to do any thing that would seem to imply that he regarded him as a Christian brother. It will be seen here that the rule was much more strict in regard to one who professed to be a Christian than to those who

idolator, or a railer, or a drunkard, or an extortioner; with such an one no not to eat.

12 For what have I to do to judge them also that are without? *a* do not ye judge them that are within?

a Mark 4.11.

were known and acknowledged heathens. The reasons may have been, (1.) The necessity of keeping the church pure, and of not doing any thing that would seem to imply that Christians were the patrons and friends of the intemperate and the wicked. (2.) In respect to the heathen, there could be no danger of its being supposed that Christians regarded them as brethren, or showed to them any more than the ordinary civilities of life; but in regard to those who professed to be Christians, but who were drunkards, or licentious, if a man was on terms of intimacy with them, it would seem as if he acknowledged them as brethren and recognised them as Christians. (3.) This entire separation and withdrawing from *all* communion was necessary in these times to save the church from scandal, and from the injurious reports which were circulated. The heathen accused Christians of all manner of crime and abominations. These reports were greatly injurious to the church. But it was evident that currency and plausibility would be given to them if it was known that Christians were on terms of intimacy and good fellowship with heathens and intemperate persons. Hence it became necessary to withdraw *wholly* from them; to withhold even the ordinary courtesies of life; and to draw a line of total and entire separation. Whether this rule in its utmost strictness is demanded now, since the nature of Christianity is known, and since religion cannot be in *so much* danger from such reports, may be made a question. I am inclined to the opinion that the ordinary civilities of life may be shown to such persons: though certainly nothing that would seem to *recognise* them as Christians. But as neighbours and relatives; as those who may be in distress and want, we are assuredly not forbidden to show towards them the offices of kindness and com-

passion. Whitby and some others, however, understand this of the communion of the Lord's supper, and of that only.

12. *For what have I to do*, &c. I have no authority over them; and can exercise no jurisdiction over them. All my rules, therefore, must have reference only to those who are within the church. ¶ *To judge.* To pass sentence upon; to condemn; or to punish. As a Christian apostle I have no jurisdiction over them. ¶ *Them also that are without.* Without the pale of the Christian church; heathens; men of the world; those who did not profess to be Christians. ¶ *Do not ye judge,* &c. Is not your jurisdiction as Christians confined to those who are *within* the church, and professed members of it? *Ought* you not to exercise discipline there, and inflict punishment on its unworthy members? Do you not in fact thus exercise discipline, and separate from your society unworthy persons—and ought it not to be done in this instance, and in reference to the offender in your church?

13. *But them,* &c. They who are unconnected with the church are under the direct and peculiar government of God. They are indeed sinners, and they deserve punishment for their crimes. But it is not *ours* to pronounce sentence upon them, or to inflict punishment. God will do that. *Our* province is in regard to the church. We are to judge these; and these alone. All others we are to leave entirely in the hands of God. ¶ *Therefore.* Gr. *And* (χαί). "Since it is yours to judge the members of your own society, do you exercise discipline on the offender and put him away." ¶ *Put away from among yourselves.* Excommunicate him; expel him from your society. This is the utmost power which the church has; and this the church is bound to exercise on all those who have openly offended against the laws of Jesus Christ.

13 But them that are without God judgeth. Therefore put away *a* from

a Mat.18.17.

among yourselves that wicked person.

REMARKS.

1st. A public rumour with regard to the existence of an offence in the church should lead to discipline. This is due to the church itself that it may be pure and uninjured; to the cause, that religion may not suffer by the offence; and to the individual, that he may have justice done him, and his character vindicated if he is unjustly accused; or that if guilty he may be reclaimed and reformed.—Offences should not be *allowed* to grow until they become scandalous; but when they *do*, every consideration demands that the matter should be investigated; ver. 1.

2d. Men are often filled with pride when they have least occasion for it; ver. 2. This is the case with individuals—who are often elated when their hearts are full of sin—when they are indulging in iniquity; and it is true of churches also, that they are most proud when the reins of discipline are relaxed, and their members are cold in the service of God, or when they are even living so as to bring scandal and disgrace on the gospel.

3d. We see in what way the Christian church should proceed in administering discipline; ver. 2. It should not bo with harshness, bitterness, revenge, or persecution. It should be with *mourning* that there is necessity for it, with *tenderness* toward the offender; with *deep grief* that the cause of religion has been injured; and with *such grief* at the existence of the offence as to lead them to prompt and decided measures to remove it.

4th. The exercise of discipline belongs to the church itself; ver. 4. The church at Corinth was to be assembled with reference to this offence, and was to remove the offender. Even Paul, an apostle, and the spiritual father of the church, did not claim the authority to remove an offender except *through* the church. The church was to take up the case; to act on it; to pass the sentence; to excommunicate

the man. There could scarcely be a stronger proof that the power of discipline is *in* the church, and is not to be exercised by any independent individual, or body of men, foreign to the church, or claiming an independent right of discipline. If *Paul* would not presume to exercise such discipline independently of the church, assuredly no minister, and no body of ministers have any such right now. Either by themselves in a collective congregational capacity, or through their representatives in a body of elders, or in a committee appointed by them; every church is *itself* to originate and execute all the acts of Christian discipline over its members. [See the Supplementary note on ver. 4].

5th. We see the *object* of Christian discipline; ver. 5. It is not revenge, hatred, malice, or the mere exercise of power that is to lead to it; it is *the good of the individual* that is to be pursued and sought. While the church endeavours to remain pure, its aim and object should be mainly to correct and reform the offender, that his spirit may be saved. When discipline is undertaken from any other motive than this; when it is pursued from private pique, or rivalship, or ambition, or the love of power; when it seeks to overthrow the influence or standing of another, it is wrong. The salvation of the offender and the glory of God should prompt to all the measures which should be taken in the case.

6th. We see the danger of indulging in *any* sin—both in reference to ourselves as individuals, or to the church; ver. 6. The smallest sin indulged in will spread pollution through the whole body, as a little leaven will effect the largest mass.

7th. Christians should be pure; ver. 7, 8. Their Saviour—their paschal lamb, was pure; and he died that they might be pure. He gave himself that his people might be holy; and by all the purity of his character; by all the labours and self-denials of his life; by all his sufferings and groans in our behalf, are we called on to be holy.

8th. We are here presented with directions in regard to our intercourse with those who are not members of the church; ver. 10. There is nothing that is more difficult to be understood than the duty of Christians respecting such intercourse. Christians often feel that they are in danger from it, and are disposed to withdraw almost entirely from the world. And they ask with deep solicitude often, what course they are to pursue? Where shall the line be drawn? How far shall they go? And where shall they deem the intercourse with the world unlawful or dangerous?—A few remarks here as rules may aid us in answering these questions.

(I.) Christians are not *wholly* to withdraw from intercourse with the people of this world. This was the error of the monastic system, and this error has been the occasion of innumerable corruptions and abominations in the papal church.—They are not to do this because,

(*a*) It is impossible. They must needs then, says Paul, go out of the world.

(*b*) Because religion is not to be regarded as dissocial, and gloomy, and unkind.

(*c*) Because they have many interests in common with those who are unconnected with the church, and they are not to abandon them. The interests of justice, and liberty, and science, and morals, and public improvements, and education, are all interests in which they share in common with others.

(*d*) Many of their best friends—a father, a mother, a son, a daughter, may be out of the church, and religion does not *sever* those ties, but binds them more tenderly and closely.

(*e*) Christians are inevitably connected in commercial dealings with those who are not members of the church; and to cease to have *any* connection with them would be to destroy their own business, and to throw themselves out of employment, and to break up society.

(*f*) It would prevent the possibility

of doing much good either to the bodies or the souls of men. The poor, the needy, and the afflicted are, many of them, out of the church, and they have a claim on the friends of Christ, and on their active beneficence.

(*g*) It would break up and destroy the church altogether. Its numbers are to be increased and replenished from age to age by the efforts of Christians; and this demands that Christians should have *some* intercourse with the men of the world whom they hope to benefit.

(*h*) An effort to withdraw wholly from the world injures religion. It conveys the impression that religion is morose, severe, misanthropic; and all *such* impressions do immense injury to the cause of God and truth.

(II.) The *principles* on which Christians should regulate their intercourse with the world, are these:

(*a*) They are not to be conformed to the world; they are not to do any thing that shall countenance the views, feelings, principles of the world *as such*, or as distinguished from religion. They are not to do any thing that would show that they *approve* of the peculiar fashions, amusements, opinions of the people of the world; or to leave the impression that *they* belong to the world.

(*b*) They are to do justice and righteousness to every man, whatever may be his rank, character, or views. They are not to do any thing that will be calculated to give an unfavourable view of the religion which they profess to the men of the world.

(*c*) They are to discharge with fidelity all the duties of a father, husband, son, brother, friend, benefactor, or recipient of favours, towards those who are out of the church; or with whom they may be connected.

(*d*) They are to do good to all men —to the poor, the afflicted, the needy, the widow, the fatherless.

(*e*) They are to endeavour so to live and act—so to converse, and so to form their plans as to promote the salvation of all others. They are to seek their spiritual welfare; and to endeavour by example, and by conversation; by exhortation and by all the means in

CHAPTER VI.

DARE any of you, having a matter against another, go to their power to bring them to the knowledge of Christ. For this purpose they are kept on the earth instead of being removed to heaven; and to this object they should devote their lives.

9th. We see from this chapter who are *not* to be regarded as Christians, whatever may be their professions; ver. 11. A man who is, (1.) a fornicator; or, (2.) COVETOUS; or, (3.) an idolater; or, (4.) a *railer*; or, (5.) a drunkard; or, (6.) an *extortioner*, is not to be owned as a Christian brother. Paul has placed the covetous man, and the railer, and extortioners, in most undesirable company. They are ranked with fornicators and drunkards. And yet how many such persons there are in the Christian church—and many, too, who would regard it as a special insult to be ranked with a drunkard or an adulterer. But in the eye of God both are alike unfit for his kingdom, and are to be regarded as having no claims to the character of Christians.

10th. God will judge the world, ver. 12, 13. The world that is *without* the church—the mass of men that make no profession of piety, must give an account to God. They are travelling to his bar; and judgment in regard to them is taken into God's own hands, and he will pronounce their doom. It is a solemn thing *to be judged* by a holy God; and they who have no evidence that they are Christians, should tremble at the prospect of being soon arraigned at his bar.

CHAPTER VI.

THE main design of this chapter is to reprove the Corinthians for the practice of going to law before heathen courts, or magistrates, instead of settling their differences among themselves. It seems that after their conversion they were still in the habit of carrying their causes before heathen tribunals, and this the apostle regarded as contrary to the genius and spirit of the Christian religion, and as tending to expose religion to contempt in the eyes of the men of the world. He, therefore, (ver. 1—7,) reproves this law before the unjust, and not before the saints?

2 Do ye not know that the saints practice, and shows them that their differences should be settled among themselves. It seems also that the spirit of litigation and of covetousness had led them in some instances to practice fraud and oppression of each other, and he, therefore, takes occasion (ver. 8—11) to show that this was wholly inconsistent with the hope of heaven and the nature of Christianity.

It would seem, also, that some at Corinth had not only indulged in these and kindred vices, but had actually defended them. This was done by plausible, but sophistical arguments, drawn from the strong passions of men; from the fact that the body was made for eating and drinking, &c. To these arguments the apostle replies in the close of the chapter, (ver. 12—20,) and especially considers the sin of fornication, to which they were particularly exposed in Corinth, and shows the heinousness of it, and its entire repugnance to the pure gospel of Christ.

1. *Dare any of you.* The *reasons* why the apostle introduced this subject here may have been, (1.) That he had mentioned the subject of *judging* (chap. v. 13), and that naturally suggested the topic which is here introduced; and, (2.) This might have been a prevailing evil in the church of Corinth, and demanded correction. The word *dare* here implies that it was inconsistent with religion, and improper. "*Can* you do it; is it proper or right; or do you presume so far to violate all the principles of Christianity as to do it." ¶ *Having a matter.* A subject of litigation; or a suit. There may be differences between men in regard to property and right, in which there shall be no blame on either side. They may both be desirous of having it equitably and amicably adjusted. It is not a *difference* between men that is in itself wrong, but it is the spirit with which the difference is adhered to, and the unwillingness to have justice done that is so often wrong. ¶ *Against*

a shall judge the world ? and if the world shall be judged by you, are

a Dan.7.22; Mat.19.28: Jude 14,15; Rev.20.4.

ye unworthy to judge the smallest matters ?

---

another. Another member of the church. A Christian brother. The apostle here directs his reproof against the *plaintiff*, as having the choice of the tribunal before which he would bring the cause. ¶ *Before the unjust.* The heathen tribunals; for the word *unjust* here evidently stands opposed to the saints. The apostle does not mean that they were always unjust in their decisions, or that equity could in no case be hoped from them, but that they were classed in that division of the world which was different from the saints, and is synonymous with *unbelievers*, as opposed to believers. ¶ *And not before the saints.* Before Christians. Can you not settle your differences among yourselves as Christians, by leaving the cause to your brethren, as arbitrators, instead of going before heathen magistrates? The Jews would not allow any of their causes to be brought before the Gentile courts. Their rule was this, " He that tries a cause before the judges of the Gentiles, and before their tribunals, although their judgments are as the judgments of the Israelites, so this is an ungodly man," &c. Maimon, Hilch, Sanhedrim, chap. xxvi. § 7. They even looked on such an action as as bad as profaning the name of God.

2. *Do ye not know,* &c. The object of this verse is evidently to show that Christians were qualified to determine controversies which might arise among themselves. This the apostle shows by reminding them that they shall be engaged in determining matters of much more moment than those which could arise among the members of a church on earth; and that if qualified for that, they must be regarded as qualified to express a judgment on the questions which might arise among their brethren in the churches. ¶ *The saints.* Christians, for the word is evidently used in the same sense as in ver. 1. The apostle says that they knew this, or that this was so well established a doctrine that none could

doubt it. It was to be admitted on all hands. ¶ *Shall judge the world.* A great variety of interpretations has been given to this passage. Grotius supposes it means that they shall be *first* judged by Christ, and then act as *assessors* to him in the judgment, or join with him in condemning the wicked; and he appeals to Mat. xix. 28 ; Luke xxii. 30, where Christ says that they which have followed him should "sit on thrones judging the twelve tribes of Israel." See Note on Mat. xix. 28. Whitby supposes that it means that Christians are to judge or condemn the world by their example, or that there shall be Christian magistrates, according to the prophecy of Isaiah (xlix. 23), and Daniel (vii. 18). — Rosenmüller supposes it means that Christians are to judge the errors and sins of men pertaining to religion, as in chap. ii. 13, 16 ; and that they ought to be able, therefore, to judge the smaller matters pertaining to this life. Bloomfield, and the Greek fathers, and commentators, suppose that this means, that the saints will furnish matter to *condemn* the world; that is, by their lives and example they shall be the occasion of the greater condemnation of the world. But to this there are obvious objections. (1.) It is an unusual meaning of the word *judge.* (2.) It does not meet the case before us. The apostle is evidently saying that Christians will occupy so high and important a station in the work of judging the world that they ought to be regarded as qualified to exercise judgment on the things pertaining to this life ; but the fact that their holy lives shall be the occasion of the deeper condemnation of the world does not seem to furnish any plain reason for this.—To the opinion, also, of Whitby, Lightfoot, Vitringa, &c. that it refers to the fact that Christians would be magistrates, and governors, &c. according to the predictions of Isaiah and Daniel, there are obvious objections. (1.) The judgment to

3 Know ye not that we shall judge angels? how much more things that pertain to this life?

which Paul in this verse refers is different from that pertaining to things of this life (ver. 3), but the judgment which Christian magistrates would exercise, as such, would relate to them. (2.) It is not easy to see in this interpretation how, or in what sense, the saints shall judge the angels, ver. 3. The common interpretation, that of Grotius, Beza, Calvin, Doddridge, &c. is that it refers to the future judgment, and that Christians will in that day be employed in some manner in judging the world. That this is the true interpretation, is apparent for the following reasons. (1.) It is the *obvious* interpretation—that which will strike the great mass of men, and is likely, therefore, to be the true one. (2.) It accords with the account in Mat. xix. 28, and Luke xxii. 30. (3.) It is the only one which gives a fair interpretation to the declaration that the saints should judge angels in ver. 3. If asked *in what way* this is to be done, it may be answered, that it may be meant simply that Christians shall be exalted to the right hand of the Judge, and shall encompass his throne; that they shall assent to, and approve of his judgment, that they shall be elevated to a post of honour and favour, AS IF they were associated with him in the judgment. They shall then be regarded as his friends, and express their approbation, and that *with a deep sense of its justice,* of the condemnation of the wicked. Perhaps the idea is, not that they shall *pronounce* sentence, which will be done by the Lord Jesus, but that they shall then be qualified to see the justice of the condemnation which shall be passed on the wicked; they shall have a clear and distinct view of the case; they shall even see the propriety of their everlasting punishment, and shall not only approve it, but be qualified to enter into the subject, and to pronounce upon it intelligently. And the argument of the apostle is, that if they would be qualified to pronounce on the eternal doom of men and angels; if they had such views of jus-

tice and right, and such integrity as to form an opinion and express it in regard to the everlasting destiny of an immense host of immortal beings, assuredly they ought to be qualified to express their sense of the smaller transactions in this life, and pronounce an opinion between man and man. ¶ *Are ye unworthy.* Are you disqualified. ¶ *The smallest matters.* Matters of least consequence—matters of little moment, scarcely worth naming compared with the great and important realities of eternity. The "smallest matters" here mean, the causes, suits, and litigations relating to property, &c.

3. *Shall judge angels.* All the angels that shall be judged, good or bad. Probably the reference is to fallen angels, as there is no account that holy angels will then undergo a trial. The sense is, "Christians will be qualified to see the justice of even the sentence which is pronounced on fallen angels. They will be able so to embrace and comprehend the nature of law, and the interests of justice, as to see the propriety of their condemnation. And if they can so far enter into these important and eternal relations, assuredly they ought to be regarded as qualified to discern the nature of justice *among men,* and to settle the unimportant differences which may arise in the church." Or, perhaps, this may mean that the saints shall in the future world be raised to a rank in some respects more elevated than even the angels in heaven. (Prof. Stuart.) In what respects they will be thus elevated, if this is the true interpretation, can be only a matter of conjecture. It may be supposed that it will be because they have been favoured by being interested in the plan of salvation—a plan that has done so much to honour God; and that *to have been* thus saved by the *immediate* and *painful* intervention of the Son of God, will be a higher honour than all the privileges which beings *can* enjoy who are innocent themselves.

4 If then ye have judgments of things pertaining to this life, set them to judge who are least esteemed in the church.

5 I speak to your shame. Is it so, that there is not a wise man among you? no, not one that shall be able to judge between his brethren?

---

4. *Ye have judgments.* Causes; controversies; suits. ¶ *Things pertaining to this life.* Property, &c. ¶ *Set them to judge,* &c. The verb translated set (καθιζετε) may be either in the imperative mood, as in our translation, and then it will imply a command; or it may be regarded as in the indicative, and to be rendered interrogatively, "Do ye set or appoint them to judge who are of little repute for their wisdom and equity?" *i. e.* heathen magistrates. The latter is probably the correct rendering, as according to the former no good reason can be given why Paul should command them to select as judges those who had little repute for wisdom in the church. Had he designed this as a command, he would doubtless have directed them to choose their most aged, wise and experienced men, instead of those "least esteemed." It is manifest, therefore, that this is to be read as a question: "Since you are abundantly qualified yourselves to settle your own differences, do you employ the heathen magistrates, in whom the church can have little confidence for their integrity and justice?" It is designed, therefore, as a severe reproof for what they had been accustomed to do; and an implied injunction that they should do it no more. ¶ *Who are least esteemed* (ἐξουθενημένους). Who are *contemned*, or regarded as of no value or worth; in whose judgment and integrity you can have little or no confidence. According to the interpretation given above of the previous part of the verse this refers to the heathen magistrates—to men in whose virtue, piety and qualifications for just judgment Christians could have little confidence; and whose judgment *must* be regarded as in fact of very little value, and as very little likely to be correct. That the heathen magistrates were in general very corrupt there can be no doubt. Many of them were men of abandoned charac-

ter, of dissipated lives, men who were easily bribed, and men, therefore, in whose judgment Christians could repose little confidence. Paul reproves the Corinthians for going before them with their disputes when they could better settle them themselves. Others, however, who regard this whole passage as an *instruction* to Christians to appoint those to determine their controversies who were least esteemed, suppose that this refers to the *lowest orders* of judges among the Hebrews; to those who were least esteemed, or who were almost despised; and that Paul directs them to select *even* them in preference to the heathen magistrates. See Lightfoot. But the objection to this is obvious and insuperable. Paul would not have recommended this class of men to decide their causes, but would have recommended the selection of the most wise and virtuous among them. This is proved by ver. 5, where, in directing them to settle their matters among themselves, he asks whether there is not a "*wise* man" among them, clearly proving that he wished their difficulties adjusted, not by the most obscure and the least respected members of the church, but by the most wise and intelligent members. ¶ *In the church.* By the church. That is, the heathen magistrates evince such a character as not to be worthy of the confidence of the church in settling matters of controversy.

5. *I speak to your shame.* I declare that which is a reproach to you, that your matters of dispute are carried before heathen tribunals. ¶ *Is it so, &c.* Can it be that in the Christian church—the church collected in refined and enlightened Corinth—there is not a single member so wise, intelligent and prudent that his brethren may have confidence in him, and refer their causes to him? Can this be the case in a church that boasts so much of its wisdom, and that prides itself so

6 But brother goeth to law with brother, and that before the unbelievers.

7 Now therefore there is utterly a fault among you, because ye go to law one with another. Why do

much in the number and qualifications of its intelligent members?

6. *But brother,* &c. One Christian goes to law with another. This is designed as a reproof. This was wrong, (1.) Because they ought rather to take wrong and suffer themselves to be injured (ver. 7); (2.) Because they might have chosen some persons to settle the matter by arbitration without a formal trial; and, (3.) Because the civil constitution would have allowed them to have settled all their differences without a law-suit. Josephus says that the Romans (who were now masters of Corinth) permitted the Jews in foreign countries to decide private affairs, where nothing capital was in question, among themselves. And Dr. Lardner observes, that the Christians might have availed themselves of this permission to have settled *their* disputes in the same manner. Credibility, vol. i. p. 165.

7. *There is utterly a fault.* There is *altogether* a fault; or you are entirely wrong in this thing. ¶ *That ye go to law,* &c. That is, in the sense under discussion, or before heathen magistrates. This was the point under discussion, and the interpretation should be limited to this. Whatever may be the propriety or impropriety of going to law before Christian magistrates, yet the point which the apostle refers to was that of going to law before heathens. The passage, therefore, should not be interpreted as referring to *all* litigation, but only of that which was the subject of discussion. The apostle says that that was wholly wrong; that they ought by no means to go with their causes against their fellow Christians before heathen magistrates; that *whoever* had the right side of the question, and *whatever* might be the decision, *the thing itself* was unchristian and wrong; and that rather than dishonour religion by a trial or suit of this kind they ought to be willing to *take* wrong, and to suffer any personal and private injustice. The argument is, that great-

er evil would be done to the cause of Christ by the fact of Christians appearing before a heathen tribunal with their disputes than could result to either party from the injury done by the other.— And this is probably *always* the case; so that although the apostle refers here to heathen tribunals the same reasoning, on the principle, would apply to Christians carrying their causes into the courts at all. ¶ *Why do ye not rather take wrong?* Why do ye not suffer yourself to be injured rather than to dishonour the cause of religion by your litigations? They *should* do this, (1.) Because religion requires its friends to be willing to suffer wrong patiently; Prov. xx. 22; Mat. v. 39, 40; Rom. xii. 17, 19; 1 Thess. v. 15. (2.) Because great injury results to the cause of religion from such trials. The private wrong which an individual would suffer, in perhaps all cases, would be a less evil on the whole than the *public* injury which is done to the cause of piety by the litigations and strifes of Christian brethren before a civil court. (3.) The differences among Christians could be adjusted among themselves, by a reference to their brethren. In ninety-nine cases of a hundred, the decision would be more likely to be just and satisfactory to all parties from an amicable reference, than from the decisions of a civil court. In *the very few* cases where it would be otherwise, it would be better for the individual to suffer, than for the cause of religion to suffer. Christians *ought* to love the cause of their Master more than their own individual interest. They ought to be more afraid that the cause of Jesus Christ would be injured than that they should be a few pounds poorer from the conduct of others, or than that they should individually suffer in their character from the injustice of others. ¶ To *be defrauded?* Receive injury; or, suffer a loss of property. Grotius thinks that the word "take wrong" refers to personal insult; and

ye not rather take *a* wrong? why do ye not rather *suffer yourselves to* be defrauded ? *b*

8 Nay, ye do wrong, and defraud, and that *your* brethren.

9 Know ye not that the unrighte-

the word "defrauded" refers to injury in property. Together, they are probably designed to refer to all kinds of injury and injustice. And the apostle means to say, that they had better submit to any kind of injustice than carry the cause against a Christian brother before a heathen tribunal. The doctrine here taught is that Christians ought by no means to go to law with each other before a heathen tribunal; that they ought to be willing to suffer any injury from a Christian brother rather than do it. And by *implication* the same thing is taught in regard to the duty of all Christians, *that they ought to suffer any injury to their persons and property rather than dishonour religion by litigations before civil magistrates.* It may be asked then whether law suits are never proper; or whether courts of justice are *never* to be resorted to by Christians to secure their rights? To this question we may reply, that the discussion of Paul relates only to Christians, when both parties are Christians, and that it is designed to prohibit such an appeal to courts by them. If *ever* lawful for Christians to depart from this rule, or for Christians to appear before a civil tribunal, it is conceived that it can be only in circumstances like the following. (1.) Where two or more Christians may have a difference, and where they know not what *is* right, and what the law is in a case. In such instances there may be a reference to a civil court to determine it—to have what is called *an amicable suit,* to ascertain from the proper authority what the law is, and what is justice in the case. (2.) When there are causes of difference between Christians and the men of the world. As the men of the world do not acknowledge the propriety of submitting the matter to the church, it may be proper for a Christian to carry the matter before a civil

tribunal. Evidently, there is no other way, in such cases, of settling a cause; and this mode may be resorted to not with a spirit of revenge, but with a spirit of love and kindness. Courts are instituted for the settlement of the rights of *citizens,* and men by becoming Christians do not alienate their rights as citizens. Even these cases, however, might commonly be adjusted by a reference to impartial men, better than by the slow, and expensive, and tedious, and often irritating process of carrying a cause through the courts (3.) Where a Christian is *injured* in his person, character, or property, he has a right to seek redress. Courts are instituted for the protection and defence of the innocent and the peaceable against the fraudulent, the wicked, and the violent. And a Christian owes it to his country, to his family, and to himself, that the man who has injured him should receive the proper punishment. The peace and welfare of the community demand it. If a man murders my wife or child, I owe it to the laws and to my country, to justice and to God, to endeavour to have the law enforced. So if a man robs my property, or injures my character, I may owe it to *others* as well as to myself that the law in such a case should be executed, and the rights of others also be secured. But in all these cases, a Christian should engage in such prosecutions not with a desire of revenge, not with the love of litigation, but with the love of justice, and of God, and with a mild, tender, candid and forgiving temper, with a real desire that the opponent may be benefited, and that all *his* rights also should be secured; comp. Notes on Rom. xiii.

8. *Nay, ye do wrong,* &c. Instead of enduring wrong patiently and cheerfully, they were themselves guilty of injustice and fraud. ¶ *And that* your *brethren.* Your fellow Christians.

ous shall not inherit the kingdom of God? Be not deceived; neither *a* fornicators, nor idolaters, nor

a Gal.5.19—21; Eph.5.4,5; Heb.12.14; 13.4;

adulterers, nor effeminate, nor abusers of themselves with mankind,

Rev.22. 15.

As if they had injured those of their own family—those to whom they ought to be attached by most tender ties. The offence in such cases is aggravated, not because it is in itself any worse to injure a Christian than another man, but because it shows a deeper depravity, when a man overcomes all the ties of kindness and love, and injures those who are near to him, than it does where no such ties exist. It is for this reason that parricide, infanticide, &c. are regarded everywhere as crimes of peculiar atrocity, because a child or a parent must have sundered all the tenderest cords of virtue before it could be done.

9. *Know ye not, &c.* The apostle introduces the declaration in this verse to show the *evil* of their course, and especially of the injustice which they did one to another, and their attempt to enforce and maintain the evil by an appeal to the heathen tribunals. He assures them, therefore, that the unjust could not be saved. ¶ *The unrighteous.* The unjust (ἄδικοι)—such as he had just mentioned—they who did *injustice* to others, and attempted to do it under the sanction of the courts. ¶ *Shall not inherit.*—Shall not possess; shall not enter into. The kingdom of heaven is often represented as an *inheritance*; Mat. xix. 29; xxv. 34; Mark x. 17; Luke x. 25; xviii. 18; 1 Cor. xv. 50; Eph. i. 11, 14; v. 5. ¶ *The kingdom of God.* Cannot be saved; cannot enter into heaven; see Note, Mat.iii. 2. This *may* refer either to the kingdom of God in heaven; or to the church on earth—most probably the former. But the sense is the same essentially, whichever is meant. The man who is not fit to enter into the one is not fit to enter into the other. The man who is fit to enter the kingdom of God on earth, shall also enter into that in heaven. ¶ *Be not deceived.* A most important direction to be given to all. It implies, (1.) That they were *in*

danger of being deceived. (*a*) Their own *hearts* might have deceived them. (*b*) They might be deceived by their false opinions on these subjects. (*c*) They might be in danger of being deceived by their *leaders,* who perhaps held the opinion that some of the persons who practised these things could be saved. (2.) It implies, that there was *no necessity* of their being deceived. They might know the truth. They might easily understand these matters. It *might* be plain to them that those who indulged in these things could not be saved. (3.) It implies that it was of high *importance* that they should *not* be deceived. For, (*a*) The soul is of infinite value. (*b*) To lose heaven—to be *disappointed* in regard to that, will be a tremendous loss. (*c*) To inherit hell and its woes will be a tremendous curse. O how anxious should all be that they be not deceived, and that while they *hope* for life they do not sink down to everlasting death! ¶ *Neither fornicators;* see Gal, v. 19—21; Eph. v. 4, 5; Heb. xii. 14; xiii. 4. Note, Rom. i. 29. ¶ *Nor effeminate* (μαλακοί). This word occurs in Mat. xi. 8, and Luke vii. 25, where it is applied to clothing, and translated " *soft* raiment;" that is, the light, thin garments worn by the rich and great. It occurs no where else in the New Testament except here. Applied to morals, as it is here, it denotes those who give themselves up to a soft, luxurious, and indolent way of living; who make self-indulgence the grand object of life; who can endure no hardship, and practise no self-denial in the cause of duty and of God. The word is applied in the classic writers to the Cinædi, the Pathics, or Catamites; those who are given up to wantonness and sensual pleasures, or who are kept to be prostituted to others. Diog. Laer. vii. 5, 4. Xenoph. Mem. iii. 7. 1. Ovid Fast. iv. 342. The connection here seems to demand such an interpreta-

10 Nor thieves, nor covetous, nor drunkards, nor revilers, nor extortioners, shall inherit the kingdom of God.

11 And such *a* were some of you;

a Eph.2.1,2; 5.8; Col.3.7; Tit.3.3—6.

tion, as it occurs in the description of vices of the same class—sensual and corrupt indulgences.—It is well known that this vice was common among the Greeks—and particularly prevailed at Corinth. ¶ *Abusers of themselves with mankind* (ἀρσενοκοῖται). Pæderastæ or Sodomites. Those who indulged in a vice that was common among all the heathen ; see Notes, Rom. i. 27. 10. *Nor covetous ;* see Note, chap. v. 10. It is remarkable that the apostle always ranks *the covetous* with the most abandoned classes of men. ¶ *Nor revilers.* The same word which in chap. v. 11, is rendered *railer;* see Note on that place. ¶ *Nor extortioners;* Note, chap. v. 11. ¶ *Shall inherit.* Shall enter ; shall be saved, ver. 9.

11. *And such.* Such drunkards, lascivious, and covetous persons. This shows, (1.) The exceeding grace of God that could recover even *such* persons from sins so debasing and degrading. (2.) It shows that we are not to despair of reclaiming the most abandoned and wretched men. (3.) It is well for Christians to look back on what they once were. It will produce (*a*) humility, (*b*) gratitude, (*c*) a deep sense of the sovereign mercy of God, (*d*) an earnest desire that others may be recovered and saved in like manner ; comp. Eph. ii. 1, 2 ; v. 8 ; Col. iii. 7 ; Tit. iii. 3, 6.—The *design* of this is to remind them of what they were, and to show them that they were now under obligation to lead better lives—by all the mercy which God had shown in recovering them from sins so degrading, and from a condition so dreadful. ¶ *But ye are washed;* Heb. x. 22. Washing is an emblem of purifying. They had been made pure by the Spirit of God. They had been, indeed, baptized, and their baptism was an emblem of purifying, but the thing here particularly referred to

but ye are washed, *b* but ye are sanctified, *c* but ye are justified *d* in the name of the Lord Jesus, and by the Spirit of our God.

12 All things are lawful unto me

b Heb.10.22.   *c* Heb.2.11.
d Rom.8.30.

is not baptism, but it is something that had been done by the Spirit of God, and must refer to his agency on the heart in cleansing them from these pollutions. Paul here uses *three* words, *washed, sanctified, justified,* to denote the various agencies of the Holy Spirit by which they had been recovered from sin. The first, that of *washing,* I understand of that work of the Spirit by which the process of purifying was *commenced* in the soul, and which was especially signified in baptism—the work of regeneration or conversion to God. By the agency of the Spirit the defilement of these pollutions had been washed away or removed— as filth is removed by ablution.—The agency of the Holy Ghost in regeneration is elsewhere represented by washing, Tit. iii. 5, " The washing of regeneration." comp. Heb. x. 22. ¶ *Ye are sanctified.* This denotes the progressive and advancing process of purifying which succeeds regeneration in the Christian. Regeneration is the commencement of it—its close is the perfect purity of the Christian in heaven ; see Note, John xvii. 17. It does not mean that they were *perfect*—for the reasoning of the apostle shows that this was far from being the case with the Corinthians ; but that the work was advancing, and that they were in fact under a process of sanctification. ¶ *But ye are justified.* Your sins are pardoned, and you are accepted as righteous, and will be treated as such on account of the merits of the Lord Jesus Christ ; see Note, Rom. i. 17 ; iii. 25, 26 ; iv. 3. The apostle does not say that this was *last* in the order of *time,* but simply says that this was done to them. Men are justified *when* they believe, and when the work of sanctification commences in the soul. ¶ *In the name of the Lord Jesus.* That is, by the Lord Jesus; by his authority, appointment, influence;

but all things are not [1] expedient : all things are lawful for me, but I

1 or, *profitable.*

Note, Acts iii. 6. All this had been accomplished *through* the Lord Jesus; that is, in his name remission of sins had been proclaimed to them (Luke xxiv. 47) ; and by his merits all these favours had been conferred on them. ¶ *And by the Spirit of our God.* The Holy Spirit. All this had been accomplished by *his* agency on the heart. —This verse brings in the whole subject of redemption, and states in a most emphatic manner the various stages by which a sinner is saved, and by this single passage, a man may obtain all the essential knowledge of the plan of salvation. All is *condensed* here in few words. (1.) He is by nature a miserable and polluted sinner —without merit, and without hope. (2.) He is renewed by the Holy Ghost, and washed by baptism. (3.) He is justified, pardoned, and accepted as righteous, through the merits of the Lord Jesus alone. (4.) He is made holy—becomes sanctified—and more and more like God, and fit for heaven. (5.) All this is done by the agency of the Holy Ghost. (6.) The *obligation* thence results that he should lead a holy life, and forsake sin in every form. 12. *All things are lawful unto me.* The apostle here evidently makes a transition to another subject from that which he had been discussing—a consideration of the *propriety* of using certain things which had been esteemed lawful. The expression, "all things are lawful," is to be understood as used by those who palliated certain indulgences, or who vindicated the vices here referred to, and Paul designs to reply to them. His reply follows. He had been reproving them for their vices, and had specified several. It is not to be supposed that they would indulge in them without some show of defence ; and the declaration here has much the appearance of a proverb, or a common saying—that all things were lawful ; that is, " God has formed all things for our use, and there can be no evil if we use them." By the phrase " all things " here, perhaps,

will not be brought under the power [a] of any.

a chap.9.27.

may be meant *many* things ; or things in general ; or there is nothing in itself unlawful. That there were many vicious persons who held this sentiment there can be no doubt ; and though it cannot be supposed that there were any in the Christian church who would openly advocate it, yet the design of Paul was to *cut up* the plea altogether *wherever it might be urged,* and to show that it was false and unfounded. The particular things which Paul here refers to, are those which have been called *adiaphoristic,* or indifferent ; *i. e.,* pertaining to certain meats and drinks, &c. With this Paul connects also the subject of fornication—the subject particularly under discussion. *This* was defended as " lawful," by many Greeks, and was practised at Corinth ; and was the vice to which the Corinthian Christians were particularly exposed. Paul designed to meet *all* that could be said on this subject ; and to show them that these indulgences could *not* be proper for Christians, and could not in *any* way be defended.— We are not to understand Paul as admitting that fornication is in any case lawful ; but he designs to show that the practice cannot possibly be defended in any way, or by any of the arguments which had been or could be used. For this purpose, he observes, (1.) That *admitting* that all things were lawful, there were many things which ought not to be indulged ; (2.) That *admitting* that they were lawful, yet a man ought not to be under the power of any improper indulgence, and should abandon any habit when it had the mastery. (3.) That fornication was positively wrong, and against the very nature and essence of Christianity, ver. 13—20. ¶ *Are not expedient.* This is the first answer to the objection. Even should we admit that the practices under discussion are lawful, yet there are many things which are not expedient ; that is, which do not *profit,* for so the word ($\sigma\nu\mu\phi\epsilon\rho\epsilon\iota$) properly signifies ; they are injurious

13 Meats *a* for the belly, and the belly for meats : but God shall

a Matt.15.17,20; Rom.14.17.

and hurtful. They might injure the body; produce scandal; lead others to offend or to sin. Such was the case with regard to the use of certain meats, and even with regard to the use of wine. Paul's rule on this subject is stated in 1 Cor. viii. 13. That if these things did injury to others, he would abandon them for ever; even though they were in themselves lawful; see Note on chap. viii. and on Rom. xiv. 14 —23. There are many customs which, perhaps, cannot be strictly proved to be unlawful or sinful, which yet do injury in some way if indulged in; and which as their indulgence can do no good, should be abandoned. Any thing that does evil—however small —and no good, should be abandoned at once. ¶ *All things are lawful.* Admitting this; or even on the supposition that all things are in themselves right. ¶ *But I will not be brought under the power.* I will not be subdued by it; I will not become the *slave* of it. ¶ *Of any.* Of any custom, or habit, no matter what it is. This was Paul's rule ; the rule of an independent mind. The principle was, that even admitting that certain things were in themselves right, yet his grand purpose was *not to be the slave of habit,* not to be subdued by any practice that might corrupt his mind, fetter his energies, or destroy his freedom as a man and as a Christian. We may observe, (1.) That this is a good rule to act on. It was Paul's rule (1 Cor. ix. 27), and it will do as well for us as for him. (2.) It is the true rule of an independent and noble mind. It requires a high order of virtue; and is the only way in which a man may be useful and active. (3.) It may be applied to *many things* now. Many a Christian and Christian minister *is a slave;* and is completely under the *power* of some habit that destroys his usefulness and happiness. He is the SLAVE of indolence, or carelessness, or of some VILE HABIT—as the use of tobacco, or of wine. He has not independence

destroy both it and them. Now the body *is* not for *b* fornication,

b 1 Thess.4.3,7.

enough to break the cords that bind him; and the consequence is, that life is passed in indolence, or in self-indulgence, and time, and strength, and property are wasted, and religion blighted, and souls ruined. (4.) The man that has not courage and firmness enough to act on this rule should doubt his piety. If he is a voluntary slave to some idle and mischievous habit, how can he be a Christian! If he does not love his Saviour and the souls of men enough to break off from such habits which he knows are doing injury, how is he fit to be a minister of the self-denying Redeemer?

13. *Meats for the belly,* &c. This has every appearance of being an adage or proverb. Its meaning is plain. " God has made us with appetites for food; and he has made food adapted to such appetites, and it is right, therefore, to indulge in luxurious living." The word *belly* here (κοιλία) denotes the *stomach ;* and the argument is, that as God had created the natural appetite for food, and had created food, it was right to indulge in eating and drinking to any extent which the appetite demanded. The word *meats* here (βρώματα) does not denote animal food particularly, or flesh, but *any kind* of food. This was the sense of the English word formerly. Matt. iii. 4; vi. 25 ; ix. 10 ; x. 10; xiv. 9, &c. ¶ *But God shall destroy.* This is the reply of Paul to the argument. This reply is, that as both are so soon to be destroyed, they were unworthy of the care which was bestowed on them, and that attention should be directed to better things. It is unworthy the immortal mind to spend its time and thought in making provision for the body which is soon to perish. And especially a man should be willing to abandon indulgences in these things when they tended to injure the mind, and to destroy the soul. It is unworthy a mind that is to live for ever, thus to be anxious about that which is so soon to be destroyed in the grave. We may observe here, (1.)

but for the Lord, *a* and the Lord *b* for the body.

14 And God *c* hath both raised

a Rom.12.1.   *b* Eph.5.23.

This *is* the great rule of the mass of the world. The pampering of the appetites is the great purpose for which they live, and the only purpose. (2.) It is folly. The body will soon be in the grave; the soul in eternity. How low and grovelling is the passion which leads the immortal mind always to anxiety about what the body shall eat and drink! (3.) Men should act from higher motives. They should be thankful for *appetites* for food; and that God *provides* for the wants of the body; and should eat to obtain strength to serve him, and to discharge the duties of life. Man often degrades himself below—far below—the brutes in this thing. *They* never pamper their appetites, or *create artificial* appetites. Man, in death, sinks to the same level; and all the record of his life is, that "he lived to eat and drink, and died as the brute dieth." How low is human nature fallen! How sunken is the condition of man! ¶ *Now the body* is *not,* &c. "But (δὲ) the body is not designed for licentiousness, but to be devoted to the Lord." The remainder of this chapter is occupied with an argument against indulgence in licentiousness—a crime to which the Corinthians were particularly exposed. See the Introduction to this epistle. It cannot be supposed that any members of the church would indulge in this vice, or would vindicate it; but it was certain, (1.) That it was *the* sin to which they were particularly exposed; (2.) That they were in the midst of a people who *did* both practise and vindicate it; comp. Rev. ii. 14, 15. Hence the apostle furnished them with *arguments* against it, as well to *guard* them from temptation, as to enable them to meet those who did defend it, and also to settle the morality of the question on an immovable foundation. The *first* argument is here stated, that the body of man was designed by its Maker to be devoted to him, and should be consecrated to the purposes of a pure and

up the Lord, and will also raise up us by his own power.

15 Know ye not that your bodies

c Rom.6.5,8.

holy life. We are, therefore, bound to devote our animal as well as our rational powers to the service of the Lord alone. ¶ *And the Lord for the body.* "The Lord is in an important sense for the body, that is, he acts, and plans, and provides for it. He sustains and keeps it; and he is making provision for its immortal purity and happiness in heaven. It is not right, therefore, to take the body, which is nourished by the kind and constant agency of a holy God, and to devote it to purposes of pollution." That there is a reference in this phrase to the resurrection, is apparent from the following verse. And as God will exert his mighty power in raising up the body, and will make it glorious, it ought not to be prostituted to purposes of licentiousness.

14. *And God hath both raised up,* &c. This is the *second* argument against indulgences in this sin. It is this. "We are united to Christ. God has raised him from the dead, and made his body glorified. Our bodies will be like his (comp. Phil. iii. 21); and since our body is to be raised up by the power of God; since it is to be perfectly pure and holy, and since this is to be done by his agency, it is wrong that it should be devoted to purposes of pollution and lust." It is unworthy (1.) Of our *connection* with that pure Saviour who has been raised from the dead—the image of our resurrection from the death and defilements of sin (comp. Notes, Rom. vi. 1—12); and (2.) Unworthy of the hope that our bodies shall be raised up to perfect and immortal purity in the heavens. No argument could be stronger. A deep sense of our union with a pure and risen Saviour, and a lively hope of immortal purity, would do more than all other things to restrain from licentious indulgences.

15, 16. *Know ye not,* &c. This is the *third* argument against licentiousness. It is, that we as Christians are united to Christ (comp. Notes, John

are the members *a* of Christ? shall I then take the members of Christ, and make *them* the members of an harlot? God forbid!

16 What! know ye not that he which is joined to an harlot is one

a Eph.5.30.

body? for two, *b* saith he, shall be one flesh.

17 But he that is joined unto the Lord is one *c* spirit.

18 Flee *d* fornication. Every sin that a man doeth is without

b Gen.2.24; Matt.19.5.   *c* John 17.21—23; Eph.4.4.   *d* Pro.6.25—32; 7.24—27.

---

xv. 1, &c.); and that it is abominable to take the members of Christ and subject them to pollution and sin. Christ was pure—wholly pure. We are professedly united to him. We are bound therefore to be pure, as he was. Shall that which is a part, as it were, of the pure and holy Saviour, be prostituted to impure and unholy embraces? ¶ *God forbid!* Note, Rom. iii. 4. This expresses the deep abhorrence of the apostle at the thought. It needed not *argument* to show it. The whole world revolted at the idea; and language could scarcely express the abomination of the very thought. ¶ *Know ye not,* &c. This is designed to confirm and strengthen what he had just said. ¶ *He which is joined.* Who is *attached* to; or who is connected with. ¶ *Is one body.* That is, is to be regarded as one; is closely and intimately united. Similar expressions occur in classic writers. See Grotius and Bloomfield. ¶ *For two, saith he,* &c. This Paul *illustrates* by a reference to the formation of the marriage connection in Gen. ii. 14. He cannot be understood as affirming that that passage had original reference to illicit connections; but he uses it for purposes of illustration. God had declared that the man and his wife became one; in a similar sense in unlawful connections the parties became one.

17. *But he that is joined to the Lord.* The true Christian, united by faith to the Lord Jesus; see John xv. 1, seq. ¶ *Is one spirit.* That is, in a sense similar to that in which a man and his wife are one body. It is not to be taken literally; but the sense is, that there is a close and intimate union; they are united in feeling, spirit, intention, disposition. The argument is beautiful. It is, " As the union of souls is more important than that of bodies; as that union is

more lasting, dear, and enduring than any union of body with body can be, and as our union with him is with a Spirit pure and holy, it is improper that we should *sunder* that tie, and break that sacred bond, by being joined to a harlot. The union with Christ is more intimate, entire, and pure than that can be between a man and woman; and *that* union should be regarded as sacred and inviolable." O, if all Christians felt and regarded this as they should, how would they shrink from the connections which they often form on earth! Comp. Eph. iv. 4.

18. *Flee fornication.* A solemn command of God—as explicit as any that thundered from mount Sinai. None can disregard it with impunity —none can violate it without being exposed to the awful vengeance of the Almighty. There is force and emphasis in the word *flee* (φεύγατε). Man should *escape* from it; he should not stay to *reason* about it; to debate the matter; or even to *contend* with his propensities, and to try the strength of his virtue. There are some sins which a man can *resist ;* some about which he can reason without danger of pollution. But this is a sin where a man is *safe* only when he flies; free from pollution only when he refuses to entertain a thought of it ; secure when he seeks a victory by flight, and a conquest by retreat. Let a man turn away from it without reflection on it and he is safe. Let him think, and reason, and he may be ruined. " The very passage of an impure thought through the mind leaves pollution behind it." An argument on the subject often leaves pollution; a description ruins; and even the presentation of motives *against* it may often fix the mind with dangerous inclination on the crime. There is no way of avoid-

the body; but he that committeth fornication sinneth against his own body.

19 What! know ye not that your [a] body is the temple of the Holy Ghost *which is* in you which

a 2 Cor.6.16.   b Rom.14.7,8.

ye have of God, and ye are not [b] your own ?

20 For ye are bought [c] with a price: therefore glorify [d] God in your body, and in your spirit which are God's.

c Acts 20.28; 1 Pet.1.18,19; Rev.5.9.
d 1 Pet.2.9.

---

ing the pollution but in the manner prescribed by Paul; there is no man safe who will not follow his direction. How many a young man would be saved from poverty, want, disease, curses, tears, and hell, could these TWO WORDS be made to blaze before him like the writing before the astonished eyes of Belshazzar (Dan. v.), and could they terrify him from even the *momentary* contemplation of the crime. ¶ *Every sin,* &c. This is to be taken *comparatively.* Sins in general ; the common sins which men commit do not *immediately* and directly affect the *body,* or waste its energies, and destroy life. Such is the case with falsehood, theft, malice, dishonesty, pride, ambition, &c. They do *not* immediately and directly impair the constitution and waste its energies. ¶ *Is without the body.* Does not immediately and directly affect the body The more immediate effect is on the mind ; but the sin under consideration produces an immediate and direct effect on the body itself. ¶ *Sinneth against his own body.* This is the *fourth* argument against indulgence in this vice, and it is more striking and forcible. The sense is, " It wastes the bodily energies ; produces feebleness, weakness, and disease ; it impairs the strength, enervates the man, and shortens life." Were it proper, this might be *proved* to the satisfaction of every man by an examination of the effects of licentious indulgence. Those who wish to see the effects stated, may find them in Dr. Rush on the Diseases of the Mind. Perhaps no single sin has done so much to produce the most painful and dreadful diseases, to weaken the constitution, and to shorten life as this. Other vices, as gluttony and drunkenness, do this also, and all sin has *some* effect

in destroying the body, but it is true of this sin in an eminent degree.

19. *What! know ye not,* &c. This is the *fifth* argument against this sin The Holy Ghost dwells in us ; our bodies are his temples ; and they should not be defiled and polluted by sin ; Note, chap. iii. 16, 17. As this Spirit is *in* us, and as it is *given* us by God, we ought not to dishonour the gift and the giver by pollution and vice. ¶ *And ye are not your own* This is the *sixth* argument which Paul uses. We are purchased; we belong to God ; we are his by redemption ; by a precious price paid ; and we are bound, therefore, to devote ourselves, body, soul, and spirit, as he directs, to the glory of his name, not to the gratification of the flesh ; see Note, Rom. xiv. 7, 8.

20. *For ye are bought.* Ye Christians are *purchased :* and by right of purchase should therefore be employed as he directs This doctrine is often taught in the New Testament, and the argument is often urged that, therefore, Christians should be devoted to God ; see chap. vii. 23 ; 1 Pet. i. 18, 19 ; ii. 9 ; 2 Pet. ii. 1 ; Rev. v. 9 ; see Note on Acts xx. 28. ¶ *With a price* ($\tau\iota\mu\tilde{\eta}$). A *price* is that which is *paid* for an article, and which, in the view of the seller, is a fair compensation, or a valuable consideration why he should part with it; that is the price paid is as valuable to him as the thing itself would be. It may not be the same thing either in quality or quantity, but it is that which to him is a sufficient consideration why he should part with his property. When an article is bought for a valuable consideration, it becomes wholly the property of the purchaser. He may keep it, direct it, dispose of it. Nothing else is to be allowed to control it

without his consent.—The language here is figurative. It does not mean that there was strictly a *commercial* transaction in the redemption of the church, a literal *quid pro quo*, for the thing spoken of pertains to moral government, and not to commerce. It means, (1.) That Christians have been redeemed, or recovered to God; (2.) That this has been done by a *valuable consideration*, or that which, in his view, was a full equivalent for the sufferings that they would have endured if they had suffered the penalty of the law; (3.) That this valuable consideration was the blood of Jesus, as an atoning sacrifice, an offering, a ransom, which *would accomplish the same great ends in maintaining the truth and honour of God, and the majesty of his law, as the eternal condemnation of the sinner would have done;* and which, therefore, may be called, *figuratively*, the price which was paid. For if the same ends of justice could be accomplished by his atonement which *would* have been by the death of the sinner himself, then it was consistent for God to pardon him. (4.) Nothing else could or would have done this. There was no *price* which the sinner could pay, no atonement which *he* could make; and consequently, if Christ had not died, the sinner would have been the slave of sin, and the servant of the devil for ever. (5.) As the Christian is thus purchased, ransomed, redeemed, he is bound to devote himself to God only, and to keep his commands, and to flee from a licentious life. ¶ *Glorify God.* Honour God; live to him; see Note, Matt. v. 16; John xii. 28; xvii. 1. ¶ *In your body*, &c. Let your entire person be subservient to the glory of God. Live to him; let your life tend to his honour. No stronger arguments could be adduced for purity of life, and they are such as all Christians must feel.

REMARKS.

1st. We see from this chapter (ver. 1—8.) the evils of law-suits, and of contentions among Christians. Every law-suit between Christians is the means of greater or less dishonour to the cause of religion. The contention and strife; the time lost and the money wasted; the hard feelings engendered, and bitter speeches caused; the ruffled temper, and the lasting animosities that are produced, always injure the cause of religion, and often injure it for years. Probably no law-suit was ever engaged in by a Christian that did not do *some* injury to the cause of Christ. Perhaps *no* law-suit was ever conducted between Christians that ever did any good to the cause of Christ.

2d. A contentious spirit, a fondness for the agitation, the excitement, and the strife of courts, is inconsistent with the spirit of the gospel. Religion is retiring, peaceful, calm. It seeks the peace of all, and it never rejoices in contentions.

3d. Christians should do nothing that will tend to injure the cause of religion in the eye of the world, ver. 7, 8. How much better is it that I should lose a few pounds, than that my Saviour should lose his honour! How much better that my purse should be empty of glittering dust, even by the injustice of others, than that a single gem should be taken from his diadem! And how much better even that I should lose all, than that *my* hand should be reached out to pluck away one jewel, by my misconduct, from his crown! Can silver, can gold, can diamonds be compared in value to the honour of Christ and of his cause?

4th. Christians should *seldom* go to law, even with others; never, if they can avoid it. Every other means should be tried first; and the law should be resorted to only when all else fails. How few law-suits there would be if man had no bad passions! How seldom is the law applied to from the simple love of justice; how seldom from pure benevolence; how seldom for the glory of God! In nearly *all* cases that occur between men, a friendly reference to others would settle all the difficulty ; always if there were a right spirit between the parties. Comparatively *few* suits at law will be approved of, when men come to die; and the man who has had the least to do with the law, will have the least, usually, to regret when he enters the eternal world.

5th. Christians should be honest—strictly honest—always honest, ver. 8. They should do justice to all; they should defraud none. Few things occur that do more to disgrace religion than the suspicions of *fraud*, and overreaching, and deception, that often rest on professors of religion. How can a man be a Christian, and not be an honest man? Every man who is not strictly honest and honourable in his dealings, should be regarded, whatever may be his pretensions, as an enemy of Christ and his cause.

6th. The unholy cannot be saved, ver. 9, 10. So God has determined; and this purpose cannot be evaded or escaped. It is fixed; and men may think of it as they please, still it is true that there are large classes of men who, if they continue such, cannot inherit the kingdom of God. The fornicator, the idolater, the drunkard, and the covetous, cannot enter heaven. So the Judge of all has said, and who can unsay it? So he has decreed, and who can change his fixed decree? And so it should be. What a place would heaven be if the drunkard, and the adulterer, and the idolater were there! How impure and unholy would it be! How would it destroy all our hopes, dim all our prospects, mar all our joys, if we were told that they should sit down with the just in heaven! Is it not one of our fondest hopes that heaven will be pure, and that *all* its inhabitants shall be holy? And *can* God admit to his eternal embrace, and treat as his eternal friend, the man who is unholy; whose life is stained with abomination; who loves to corrupt others; and whose happiness is found in the sorrows, and the wretchedness, and vices of others? No; religion is pure, and heaven is pure; and whatever men may think, of one thing they may be assured, that the fornicator, and the drunkard, and the reviler shall not inherit the kingdom of God.

7th. If none of these *can* be saved as they are, what a host are travelling down to hell! How large a part of every community is made up of such persons! How vast is the number of drunkards that are known! How vast the host of extortioners, and of covetous men, and revilers of all that is good! How many curse their God and their fellow men! How difficult to turn the corner of a street without hearing an oath! How necessary to guard against the frauds and deceptions of others! How many men and women are known to be impure in their lives! In all communities how much does this sin abound! and how many shall be revealed at the great day as impure, who are now unsuspected! how many disclosed to the universe as all covered with pollution, who now boast even of purity, and who are received into the society of the virtuous and the lovely! Verily, the broad road to hell is thronged! And verily, the earth is pouring into hell a most dense and wretched population, and rolling down a tide of sin and misery that shall fill it with groans and gnashing of teeth for ever.

8th. It is well for Christians to reflect on their former course of life, as contrasted with their present mercies, ver. 11. Such were they, and such they would still have been but for the mercy of God. Such as is the victim of uncleanness and pollution, such as is the profane man and the reviler, such we should have been but for the mercy of God. That alone has saved us, and that only can keep us. How should we praise God for his mercy, and how are we bound to love and serve him for his amazing compassion in raising us from our deep pollution, and saving us from hell?

9th. Christians should be pure; ver. 11—19. They should be above suspicion. They should avoid the appearance of evil. No Christian can be *too* pure; none can feel too much the obligation to be holy. By every sacred and tender consideration God urges it on us; and by a reference to our own happiness as well as to his own glory, he calls on us to be holy in our lives.

10th. May we remember that we are not our own; ver. 20. We belong to God. We have been ransomed by sacred blood. By a reference to the

CHAPTER VII.

NOW concerning the things whereof ye wrote unto me:

value of that blood; by all its preciousness and worth; by all the sighs, and tears, and groans that bought us; by the agonies of the cross, and the bitter pains of the death of God's own Son, we are bound to live to God, and to him alone. When we are tempted to sin, let us think of the cross. When Satan spreads out his allurements, let us recall the remembrance of the sufferings of Calvary, and remember that all these sorrows were endured that *we* might be pure. O how would sin appear were we *beneath* the cross, and did we feel the warm blood from the Saviour's open veins trickle upon us! Who would *dare* indulge in sin there? Who *could* do otherwise than devote himself, body, and soul, and spirit, unto God?

CHAPTER VII.

THIS chapter commences the *second* part or division of this epistle, or, *the discussion of those points which had been submitted to the apostle in a letter from the church at Corinth, for his instruction and advice.* See the Introduction to the epistle. The letter in which they proposed the questions which are here discussed, has been lost. It is manifest that, if we now had it, it would throw some light on the *answers* which Paul has given to their inquiries in this chapter. The *first* question which is discussed (ver. 1—9) is, whether it were lawful and proper to enter into the marriage relàtion. How this question had arisen, it is not now possible to determine with certainty. It is probable, however, that it arose from disputes between those of Jewish extraction, who held not only the lawfulness but the importance of the marriage relation, according to the doctrines of the Old Testament, and certain followers or friends of some Greek philosophers, who might have been the advocates of celibacy. But *why* they advocated that doctrine is unknown. It is known, however, that many even of the Greek philosophers, among whom were Lycurgus, Thales, Antiphanes, and Socrates (see Gro-

It is good for a man not to touch a woman.

2 Nevertheless, *to avoid* fornica-

tius), thought that, considering "the untractable tempers of women, and how troublesome and fraught with danger was the education of children," it was the part of wisdom not to enter into the marriage relation. From them may have been derived the doctrine of celibacy in the Christian church; a doctrine that has been the cause of so much corruption in the monastic system, and in the celibacy of the clergy among the papists. The Jews, however, everywhere defended the propriety and duty of marriage. They regarded it as an ordinance of God. And to this day they hold that a man who has arrived to the age of twenty years, and who has not entered into this relation, unless prevented by natural defects, or by profound study of the law, sins against God. Between these two classes, of those in the church who had been introduced there from these two classes, the question would be agitated whether marriage was lawful and advisable.

Another question which, it seems, had arisen among them was, whether it was proper to continue *in* the married state in the existing condition of the church, as exposed to trials and persecutions; or whether it was proper for those who had become converted, to continue their relations in life with those who were unconverted. This the apostle discusses in ver. 10—24. Probably many supposed that it was unlawful to live with those who were not Christians; and they thence inferred that the relation which subsisted *before* conversion should be dissolved. And this doctrine they carried to the relation between master and servant, as well as between husband and wife. The general doctrine which Paul states in answer to this is, that the wife was not to depart from her husband (ver. 10); but if she did, she was not at liberty to marry again, since her former marriage was still binding; ver. 11. He added that a believing man, or Christian, should not put away his

tion, let every man have his own wife, and let every woman have her own husband.

3 Let the ^a husband render unto the wife due benevolence : and likewise also the wife unto the husband

a Ex.21.10 ; 1 Pet.3.7.

unbelieving wife (ver. 12), and that the relation *should* continue, notwithstanding a difference of religion ; and that *if* a separation ensued, it should be in a peaceful manner, and the parties were not at liberty to marry again; ver. 13—17. So, also, in regard to the relation of master and slave. It was not to be violently sundered. The relations of life were not to be broken up by Christianity ; but every man was to remain in that rank of life in which he was when he was converted, unless it could be changed in a peaceful and lawful manner; ver. 18—24.

A *third* subject submitted to him was, whether it was advisable, in existing circumstances, that the unmarried virgins who were members of the church should enter into the marriage relation ; ver. 25—40. This the apostle answers in the remainder of the chapter. The *sum* of his advice on that question is, that it would be *lawful* for them to marry, but that it was not then advisable; and that, at all events, they should so act as to remember that life was short, and so as not bo too much engrossed with the affairs of this life, but should live for eternity. He said that though it was *lawful*, yet, (1.) In their present distress it might be unadvisable; ver. 26. (2.) That marriage tended to an increase of care and anxiety, and it might not be proper *then* to enter into that relation; ver. 32—35. (3.) That they should live to God; ver. 29—31. (4.) That a man should not be oppressive and harsh towards his daughter, or towards one under his care; but that, if it would be severe in him to *forbid* such a marriage, he should allow it; ver. 36. And, (5.) That on the whole it was advisable, under existing circumstances, *not* to enter into the marriage relation ; ver. 38—40.

1. *Now, concerning, &c.* In reply to your inquiries. The first, it seems, was in regard to the propriety of marriage ; that is, whether it was lawful and expedient. ¶ *It is good.* It is

well. It is fit, convenient, or, it is suited to the present circumstances, or, the thing itself is well and expedient in certain circumstances. The apostle did not mean that marriage was unlawful, for he says (Heb. xiii. 4) that "marriage is honourable in all." But he here admits, with one of the parties in Corinth, that it was well, and proper in some circumstances, not to enter into the marriage relation ; see ver. 7, 8, 26, 28, 31, 32. ¶ *Not to touch a woman.* Not to be connected with her by marriage. Xenophon (Cyro. b. 1) uses the same word (ἅπτω, *to touch*) to denote marriage ; comp. Gen. xx. 4, 6 ; xxvi. 11; Prov. vi. 29.

2. *Nevertheless.* But (δὶ). Though this is to be admitted as proper where it can be done, when a man has entire control of himself and his passions, and though in present circumstances it would be expedient, yet it may be proper also to enter into the marriage connection. ¶ To avoid *fornication.* Gr. On account of (διὰ) fornication. The word fornication is used here in the large sense of licentiousness in general. For the sake of the purity of society, and to avoid the evils of sensual indulgence, and the corruptions and crimes which attend an illicit intercourse, it is proper that the married state should be entered. To this vice they were particularly exposed in Corinth. See the Introduction. Paul would keep the church from scandal. How much evil, how much deep pollution, how many abominable crimes would have been avoided, which have since grown out of the monastic system, and the celibacy of the clergy among the papists, if Paul's advice had been followed by all professed Christians ! Paul says that marriage is honourable, and that the relations of domestic life should be formed to avoid the evils which would otherwise result. The world is the witness of the evils which flow from the neglect of his advice. Every community where

4 The wife hath not power of her own body, but the husband : and likewise also the husband hath not power of his own body, but the wife.

5 Defraud ye not one another,

a Joel 2.16.

the marriage tie has been lax and feeble, or where it has been disregarded or dishonoured, has been full of pollution, and it ever will be. Society is pure and virtuous, just as marriage is deemed honourable, and as its vows are adhered to and preserved. ¶ *Let every man,* &c. Let the marriage vow be honoured by all. ¶ *Have his own wife.* And one wife to whom he shall be faithful. Polygamy is unlawful under the gospel ; and divorce is unlawful. Let every man and woman, therefore, honour the institution of God, and avoid the evils of illicit indulgence.

3. *Let the husband,* &c. " Let them not imagine that there is any virtue in living separate from each other, as if they were in a state of celibacy."— *Doddridge.* They are bound to each other ; in every way they are to evince kindness, and to seek to promote the happiness and purity of each other. There is a great deal of *delicacy* used here by Paul, and his expression is removed as far as possible from the *grossness* of heathen writers. His meaning is plain ; but instead of using a *word* to express it which would be indelicate and offensive, he uses one which is not indelicate in the slightest degree. The word which he uses (*εὔνοιαν, benevolence*) denotes kindness, good-will, affection of mind. And by the use of the word "due" (*ὀφειλομένην*), he reminds them of the sacredness of their vow, and of the fact that in person, property, and in every respect, they belong to each other. It was *necessary* to give this direction, for the contrary might have been regarded as proper by many who would have supposed there was special virtue and merit in living separate from each other ;—as facts have shown that many *have* imbibed such an idea :—and it was not possible to give the rule with

except *it be* *a* with consent for a time, that ye may give yourselves to fasting and prayer; and come together again, that *b* Satan tempt you not for your incontinency.

6 But I speak this by per-

b 1 Thess.3.5.

more *delicacy* than Paul has done. Many MSS., however, instead of "due benevolence," read *ὀφειλὴν, a debt,* or *that which is owed ;* and this reading has been adopted by Griesbach in the text. Homer, with a delicacy not unlike the apostle Paul, uses the word *φιλότητα, friendship,* to express the same idea.

4. *The wife hath not power,* &c. By the marriage covenant that power, in this respect, is transferred to the husband. ¶ *And likewise, also, the husband.* The equal rights of husband and wife, in the Scriptures, are everywhere maintained. They are to regard themselves as united in most intimate union, and in most tender ties.

5. *Defraud ye not,* &c. Of the right mentioned above. Withdraw not from the society of each other. ¶ *Except it be with consent.* With a mutual understanding, that you may engage in the extraordinary duties of religion ; comp. Ex. xix. 15. ¶ *And come together again,* &c. Even by mutual consent, the apostle would not have this separation to be perpetual : since it would expose them to many of the evils which the marriage relation was designed to avoid. ¶ *That Satan,* &c. That Satan take not advantage of you, and throw you into temptation, and fill you with thoughts and passions which the marriage compact was designed to remedy.

6. *But 1 speak this by permission,* &c. It is not quite certain whether the word "this" (*τοῦτο*), in this verse, refers to what precedes, or to what follows. On this commentators are divided. The more natural and obvious interpretation would be to refer it to the preceding statement. I am inclined to think that the more natural construction is the true one, and that Paul refers to what he had said in ver. 5. Most recent commentators,

mission, *and* not of commandment.

7 For I would that all men
were even as I myself. But

as Macknight and Rosenmüller, however, suppose it refers to what follows,
and appeal to similar places in Joel
i. 2; Ps. xlix. 2; 1 Cor. x. 23. Calvin supposes it refers to what was said
in ver. 1. ¶ *By permission* (συγγνώμην).
This word means *indulgence*, or *permission*, and stands opposed to that
which is expressly enjoined; comp.
ver. 25. " I am *allowed* to say this;
I have no express command on the
subject; I give it as my opinion; I
do not speak it directly under the
influence of divine inspiration;" see
ver. 10, 25, 40. Paul here does not
claim to be under inspiration in these
directions which he specifies. But this
is no argument against his inspiration
in general, but rather the contrary.
For, (1.) It shows that he was an
honest man, and was disposed to state
the exact truth. An impostor, pretending to inspiration, would have
claimed to have been *always* inspired.
Who ever heard of a *pretender* to
divine inspiration admitting that in
any thing he was not under divine
guidance? Did Mahomet ever do
this? Do impostors now ever do it?
(2.) It shows that in other cases, where
no exception is made, he *claimed* to
be inspired. These few exceptions,
which he expressly makes, prove that
in everywhere else he claimed to be
under the influence of inspiration. (3.)
We are to suppose, therefore, that in
all his writings where he makes no
express exceptions, (and the exceptions are *very few* in number,) Paul
claimed to be inspired. Macknight,
however, and some others, understand
this as mere *advice*, as an inspired man,
though not as a command. ¶ *Not of
commandment*. Not by express instruction from the Lord; see ver. 25.
I do not claim in this to be under the
influence of inspiration ; and my counsel here may be regarded, or not, as
you may be able to receive it.
  7. *For I would*, &c. I would prefer.
¶ *That all men*, &c. That Paul was
unmarried is evident from 1 Cor. ix. 5.
But he does not refer to this fact here.
When he wishes that all men were like

himself, he evidently does not intend
that he would prefer that all should
be unmarried, for this would be against
the divine institution, and against his
own precepts elsewhere. But he would
be glad if all men had control over
their passions and propensities as he
had; had the gift of continence, and
could abstain from marriage when circumstances of trial, &c., would make it
proper. We may add, that when Paul
wishes to exhort to any thing that is
difficult, he usually adduces *his own
example* to show that *it may be done;*
an example which it would be well for
all ministers to be able to follow.
¶ *But every man hath his proper gift.*
Every man has his own peculiar talent,
or excellence. One man excels in one
thing, and another in another. One
may not have this particular virtue,
but he may be distinguished for another
virtue quite as valuable. The *doctrine*
here is, therefore, that we are not to
judge of others by ourselves, or measure
their virtue by ours. We may excel
in some one thing, they in another.
And because they have not *our* peculiar
virtue, or capability, we are not to condemn or denounce them; comp. Mat.
xix. 11, 12. ¶ *Of God.* Bestowed by
God either in the original endowments
and faculties of body or mind, or by his
grace. In either case it is the gift of
God. The virtue of continence is his
gift as well as any other; and Paul had
reason, as any other man must have, to
be thankful that God had conferred it
on him. So if a man is naturally amiable, kind, gentle, large-hearted, tender, and affectionate, he should regard
it as the gift of God, and be thankful
that he has not to contend with the
evils of a morose, proud, haughty, and
severe temper. It is true, however,
that all these virtues may be greatly
strengthened by discipline, and that
religion gives vigour and comeliness
to them all. Paul's virtue in this was
strengthened by his resolution; by his
manner of life; by his frequent fastings and trials, and *by the abundant
employment* which God gave him in
the apostleship. And it is true still,

a every man hath his proper gift of God, one after this manner, and another after that.

8 I say therefore to the unmarried and widows, It is good for them if they abide even as I.

a Mat.19.11,12.

that if a man is desirous to overcome the lusts of the flesh, industry, and hardship, and trial, and self-denial will enable him, by the grace of God, to do it. *Idleness* is the cause of no small part of the corrupt desires of men; and God kept Paul from these, (1.) By giving him enough *to do;* and, (2.) By giving him enough *to suffer.*

8. *It is good for them.* It may be advisable, in the present circumstances of persecution and distress, not to be encumbered with the cares and anxieties of a family; see ver. 26, 32 —34. The word *unmarried* (ἀγάμοις) may refer either to those who had never been married, or to widowers. It here means simply those who were at that time unmarried, and his reasoning applies to both classes. ¶ *And to widows.* The apostle specifies these, though he had not specified *widowers* particularly. The reason of this distinction seems to be, that he considers more particularly the case of those females who had never been married, in the close of the chapter, ver. 25. ¶ *That they abide.* That they remain, in the present circumstances, unmarried; see ver. 26.

9. *But if they cannot contain.* If they have not the gift of continence; if they cannot be secure against temptation; if they have not strength of virtue enough to preserve them from the danger of sin, and of bringing reproach and scandal on the church. ¶ *It is better.* It is to be preferred. ¶ *Than to burn.* The passion here referred to is often compared to a fire; see Virg. Æn. iv. 68. It is better to marry, even with all the inconveniences attending the marriage life in a time of distress and persecution in the church (ver. 26), than to be the prey of raging, consuming, and exciting passions.

10. *And unto the married.* This

9 But if they cannot contain, let *b* them marry: for it is better to marry than to burn.

10 And unto the married I command, *yet* not I, but the Lord, Let *c* not the wife depart from *her* husband:

b 1 Tim.5.14.   *c* Mal.2.14-16; Mat.19.6-9.

verse commences the *second* subject of inquiry; to wit, whether it was proper, in the existing state of things, for those who *were* married to continue this relation, or whether they ought to separate. The *reasons* why any may have supposed that it was best to separate, may have been, (1.) That their troubles and persecutions might be such that they might judge it best that families should be broken up; and, (2.) Probably many supposed that it was unlawful for a Christian wife or husband to be connected at all with a heathen and an idolater. ¶ *I command, yet not I, but the Lord.* Not I so much as the Lord. This injunction is not to be understood as *advice* merely, but as a solemn, divine command, from which you are not at liberty to depart. Paul here professes to utter the language of inspiration, and demands obedience. The express command of "the Lord" to which he refers, is probably the precept recorded in Mat. v. 32, and xix. 3—10. These precepts of Christ asserted that the marriage tie was sacred and inviolable. ¶ *Let not the wife depart,* &c. Let her not prove faithless to her marriage vows; let her not, on any pretence, desert her husband. Though she is a Christian, and he is not, yet let her not seek, on that account, to be separate from him.— The law of Moses did not permit a wife to divorce herself from her husband, though it was sometimes done (comp. Mat. x. 12); but the Greek and Roman laws allowed it.—*Grotius.* But Paul here refers to a formal and legal separation before the magistrates, and not to a voluntary separation, without intending to be formally divorced. The reasons for this opinion are, (1.) That such divorces were known and practised among both Jews and heathens. (2.) It was important

11 But and if she depart, let her remain unmarried, or be reconciled to *her* husband: and let not the husband put away *his* wife.

12 But to the rest speak I, not

a the Lord: If any brother hath a wife that believeth not, and she be pleased to dwell with him, let him not put her away.

13 And the woman which hath

a Ezra 10.11, &c.

to settle the question whether they were to be allowed in the Christian church. (3.) The claim would be set up, probably, that it might be done. (4.) The question whether a *voluntary separation* might not be proper, where one party was a Christian, and the other not, he discusses in the following verses, ver. 12—17. Here, therefore, he solemnly repeats the law of Christ, that *divorce*, under the Christian economy, was not to be in the power either of the husband or wife.

11. *But and if she depart.* If she have withdrawn by a rash and foolish act; if she has attempted to dissolve the marriage vow, she is to remain unmarried, or be reconciled. She is not at liberty to marry another. This may refer, I suppose, to instances where wives, ignorant of the rule of Christ, and supposing that they had a right to separate themselves from their husbands, had rashly left them, and had supposed that the marriage contract was dissolved. Paul tells them that this was impossible; and that *if* they had so separated from their husbands, the pure laws of Christianity did not recognise this right, and they must either be reconciled to their husbands, or remain alone. The marriage tie was so sacred that it could not be dissolved by the will of either party. ¶ *Let her remain unmarried.* That is, let her not marry another. ¶ *Or be reconciled to her husband.* Let this be done, if possible. If it cannot be, let her remain unmarried. It was a *duty* to be reconciled if it was possible. If not, she should not violate her vows to her husband so far as to marry another. It is evident that this rule is still binding, and that no one who has separated from her husband, whatever be the cause, unless there be a regular divorce, according to the law

of Christ (Mat. v. 32), can be at liberty to marry again. ¶ *And let not the husband;* see Note, Mat. v. 32. This right, granted under the Jewish law, and practised among all the heathen, was to be taken away wholly under the gospel. The marriage tie was to be regarded as sacred; and the tyranny of man over woman was to cease.

12. *But to the rest.* "I have spoken in regard to the duties of the unmarried, and the question whether it is right and advisable that they should marry, ver. 1—9. I have also uttered the command of the Lord in regard to those who are married, and the question whether separation and divorce were proper. Now in regard to *the rest of the persons and cases* referred to, I will deliver my opinion." *The rest,* or remainder, here referred to, relates particularly to the cases in which one party was a Christian and the other not. In the previous verses he had delivered the solemn, explicit law of Christ, that *divorce* was to take place on neither side, and in no instance, except agreeably to the law of Christ; Mat. v. 32. That was settled by divine authority. In the subsequent verses he discusses a different question; whether a *voluntary separation* was not advisable and proper when the one party was a Christian and the other not. The word *rest* refers to these instances, and the questions which would arise under this inquiry. ¶ *Not the Lord;* Note, ver. 6. "I do not claim, in this advice, to be under the influence of inspiration; I have no express command on the subject from the Lord; but I deliver my opinion as a servant of the Lord (ver. 40), and as having a right to offer advice, even when I have no express command from God, to a church which I have founded, and which has consulted me on the sub-

a husband that believeth not, and if he be pleased to dwell with her, let her not leave him.

14 For the unbelieving husband is sanctified by the wife, and the unbelieving wife is sanctified by the husband; else were your children unclean; but now *a* are they holy.

a Mal.2.15,16.

ject." This was a case in which both he and they were to follow the principles of Christian prudence and propriety, when there was no express commandment. Many such cases may occur. But few, perhaps none, can occur, in which some Christian principle shall not be found, that will be sufficient to direct the anxious inquirer after truth and duty. ¶ *If any brother.* Any Christian. ¶ *That believeth not.* That is not a Christian; that is a heathen. ¶ *And if she be pleased.* If it seems best to her; if she consents; approves of living together still. There might be many cases where the wife or the husband, that was not a Christian, would be so opposed to Christianity, and so violent in their opposition, that they would not be willing to live with a Christian. When this was the case, the Christian husband or wife could not prevent the separation. When this was *not* the case, they were not to seek a separation themselves. ¶ *To dwell with him.* To remain in connection with him as his wife, though they differed on the subject of religion. ¶ *Let him not put her away.* Though she is a heathen, though opposed to his religion, yet the marriage vow is sacred and inviolable. It is not to be sundered by any change which can take place in the opinions of either party. It is evident that if a man were at liberty to dissolve the marriage tie, or to discard his wife when his own opinions were changed on the subject of religion, that it would at once destroy all the sacredness of the marriage union, and render it a nullity. Even, therefore, when there is a difference of opinion on the vital subject of religion, the tie is not dissolved; but the only effect of religion should be, to make the converted husband or wife more tender, kind, affectionate, and faithful than they were before; and all the more so as their partners are without the hopes of the gospel, and

as they may be won to love the Saviour, ver. 16.

13. *Let her not leave him.* A change of phraseology from the last verse, to suit the circumstances. The wife had not power to *put away* the husband, and expel him from his own home; but she might think it her duty to be separated from him. The apostle counsels her not to do this; and this advice should still be followed. She should still love her husband and seek his welfare; she should be still a kind, affectionate, and faithful wife; and all the more so that she may show him the excellence of religion, and win him to love it. She should even bear much, and bear it long; nor should she leave him unless her life is rendered miserable, or in danger; or unless he wholly neglects to make provision for her, and leaves her to suffering, to want, and to tears. In such a case no precept of religion forbids her to return to her father's house, or to seek a place of safety and of comfort. But even then it is not to be a separation on account of a difference of religious sentiment, but for brutal treatment. Even then the marriage tie is not dissolved, and neither party are at liberty to marry again.

14. *For the unbelieving husband.* The husband that is not a Christian; who still remains a heathen, or an impenitent man. The apostle here states *reasons* why a separation should not take place when there was a difference of religion between the husband and the wife. The first is, that the unbelieving husband is sanctified by the believing wife. And the *object* of this statement seems to be, to meet an objection which might exist in the mind, and which might, perhaps, be urged by some. "Shall I not be *polluted* by such a connection? Shall I not be defiled, in the eye of God, by living in a close union with a heathen, a sinner, an enemy of God, and an opposer of the gospel?" This objec-

tion was natural, and is, doubtless, often felt. To this the apostle replies, " No ; the contrary may be true. The connection produces a species of sanctification, or diffuses a kind of holiness over the unbelieving party by the believing party, so far as to render their children holy, and therefore it is improper to seek for a separation."
¶ *Is sanctified* (ἠγίασται). There has been a great variety of opinions in regard to the sense of this word. It does not comport with my design to state these opinions. The usual meaning of the word is, to make holy ; to set apart to a sacred use ; to consecrate, &c ; see Note, John xvii. 17. But the expression cannot mean here, (1.) That the unbelieving husband would become holy, or be a Christian, *by the mere fact of a connection with* a Christian, for this would be to do violence to the words, and would be contrary to facts every where ; nor, (2.) That the unbelieving husband *had been* sanctified by the Christian wife (Whitby), for this would not be *true* in all cases ; nor, (3.) That the unbelieving husband would gradually become more favourably inclined to Christianity, by observing its effects on the wife (according to Semler) ; for, though this might be true, yet the apostle was speaking of something *then*, and which rendered their children at that time holy ; nor, (4.) That the unbelieving husband *might* more easily be sanctified, or become a Christian, by being connected with a Christian wife (according to Rosenmüller and Schleusner), because he is speaking of something in the connection which made the children holy ; and because the word ἁγιάζω is not used in this sense elsewhere. But it is a good rule of interpretation, that the words which are used in any place are to be limited in their signification by the connection ; and all that we are required to understand here is, that the unbelieving husband was sanctified *in regard to the subject under discussion;* that is, in regard to the question whether it was proper for them to live together, or whether they should be separated or not. And the sense may be, " They are by the marriage tie one flesh. They are indissolubly united by the ordinance of God. As they are one by his appointment, as they have received his sanction to the marriage union, and as one of them is holy, so the other is to be regarded as sanctified, or made *so* holy by the divine sanction to the union, that it is proper for them to live together in the marriage relation." And in proof of this, Paul says if it were *not* so, if the connection was to be regarded as impure and abominable, then their children were to be esteemed as illegitimate and unclean. But now they were *not* so regarded, and *could* not so be ; and hence it followed that they might lawfully continue together. So Calvin, Beza, and Doddridge interpret the expression. ¶ *Else were your children unclean* (ἀκάθαρτα). Impure ; the opposite of what is meant by holy. Here observe, (1.) That this is a reason why the parents, one of whom was a Christian and the other not, should not be separated ; and, (2.) The reason is founded on the fact, that *if* they were separated. the offspring of such a union must be regarded as illegitimate, or unholy ; and, (3.) It *must* be improper to separate in such a way, and for such a reason, because even *they* did not believe, and could not believe, that their children were defiled, and polluted, and subject to the shame and disgrace attending illegitimate children. This passage has often been interpreted, and is often adduced to prove that children are "federally holy," and that they are entitled to the privilege of baptism on the ground of the faith of one of the parents. But against this interpretation there are insuperable objections. (1.) The phrase " federally holy" is unintelligible, and conveys no idea to the great mass of men. It occurs no where in the Scriptures, and what can be meant by it ? (2.) It does not accord with the scope and design of the argument. There is not one word about baptism here ; not one allusion to it ; nor does the argument in the remotest degree bear upon it. The question was not whether children

should be baptized, but it was whether there should be a separation between man and wife, where the one was a Christian and the other not. Paul states, that *if* such a separation should take place, it would *imply* that the marriage was improper; and *of course* the children must be regarded as unclean. But how would the supposition that they were federally holy, and the proper subjects of baptism, bear on this? Would it not be equally true that it was proper to baptize the children whether the parents were separated or not? Is it not a doctrine among Pedobaptists every where, that the children are entitled to baptism on the faith of *either* of the parents, and that that doctrine is not affected by the question here agitated by Paul? Whether it was proper for them to live together or not, was it not equally true that the child of *a* believing parent was to be baptized? But, (3.) The supposition that this means that the children would be regarded as *illegitimate* if such a separation should take place, is one that accords with the whole scope and design of the argument. "When one party is a Christian and the other not, shall there be a separation?" This was the question. "No," says Paul; "if there *be* such a separation, it must be because the marriage *is improper;* because it would be wrong to live together in such circumstances." What would follow from this? Why, that all the children that have been born since the one party became a Christian, must be regarded as having been born while a connection existed that was improper, and unchristian, and unlawful, and of course they must be regarded as illegitimate. But, says he, you do not *believe* this yourselves. It follows, therefore, that the connection, even according to your own views, is proper. (4.) This accords with the meaning of the word *unclean* ($\dot{\alpha}\kappa\dot{\alpha}\vartheta\alpha\rho\tau\alpha$). It properly denotes that which is impure, defiled, idolatrous, unclean (*a*) In a Levitical sense; Lev. v. 2. (*b*) In a moral sense. Acts x. 28; 2 Cor. vi. 17; Eph. v. 5. The word will appropriately express the sense of illegitimacy;

and the argument, I think, evidently requires this. It may be summed up in a few words. "Your separation would be a proclamation to all that you regard the *marriage* as invalid and improper. From this it would follow that the offspring of such a marriage would be illegitimate. But *you* are not prepared to admit this; you do not believe it. Your children you esteem to be legitimate, and they are so. The marriage tie, therefore, should be regarded as binding, and separation unnecessary and improper." See, however, Doddridge and Bloomfield for a different view of this subject.—I believe infant baptism to be proper and right, and an inestimable privilege to parents and to children. But a good cause should not be made to rest on feeble supports, nor on forced and unnatural interpretations of the Scriptures. And such I regard the usual interpretation placed on this passage. ¶ *But now are they holy.* Holy in the same sense as the unbelieving husband is *sanctified* by the believing wife; for different forms of the same word are usual. That is, they are legitimate. They are not to be branded and treated as bastards, as they would be by your separation. *You* regard them as having been born in lawful wedlock, and they *are* so; and they should be treated as such by their parents, and not be exposed to shame and disgrace by your separation.

The Note of Dr. Doddridge, to which the author has candidly referred his readers, is here subjoined: "On the maturest and most impartial consideration of this text, I must judge it to refer to infant baptism. Nothing can be more apparent, than that the word "holy" signifies persons who might be admitted to partake of the distinguishing rites of God's people; comp. Exod. xix. 6; De. vii. 6; xiv. 2; xxvi. 19; xxxiii. 3; Ezra ix. 2, with Isa. xxxv. 8; lii. 1; Acts x. 28. And as for the interpretation which so many of our brethren the Baptists have contended for, that *holy* signifies *legitimate*, and *unclean*, *illegiti.mate* (not to urge that this seems an unscriptural sense of the word,) nothing can be more evident than that the argument will by no means bear it; for it would be proving a thing by itself *idem peridem* to argue, that the converse of the parents was lawful because the children were not bastards, whereas all

15 But if the unbelieving depart, let him depart. A brother or a sister is not under bondage in such *cases:* but God hath called *a* us [1] to peace.

16 For what knowest thou, O

a Rom.12.18; 14.19; Heb.12.14. 1 *in.*

who thought the converse of the parents unlawful, must think that the children were illegitimate."

The sense of the passage seems to be this : Christians are not to separate from their unconverted partners, although the Jews were commanded to put away their strange or heathen wives; because the unbelieving party is so far sanctified by the believing party, that the marriage connection is quite *lawful for Christians. There is nothing in the Christian religion that forbids it.* Otherwise, argues the Apostle, your children would be unclean, just as the offspring of unequal and forbidden marriages among the Jews, was unclean, and therefore denied the privilege of circumcision ; whereas your infants, as appears from their right to baptism, acknowledged in all the churches, are holy, just as the Jewish children who had a right to circumcision were holy, not *internally* but externally and legally, in consequence of their covenant relation to God. Or briefly thus.—Do not separate. The marriage is quite lawful for Christians, otherwise your children could not be reckoned holy, in the sense of having a right to the seal of the ovenant, *i. e.* baptism. The argument for infant baptism is indeed incidental, but not the less strong on that account. And to say there is no allusion whatever to that subject is a mere begging of the question.

To evade this conclusion in favour of infant baptism, the Baptists have strenuously contended, that the proper sense of "holy" is legitimate or lawfully born. But, 1. The word in the original (ἁγιος) does not in a single instance bear this sense. The question is not what sense *may* possibly be attached to the term, but what *is* its real meaning. It is on the other hand, very frequently used in the sense assigned to it by Doddridge and others. 2. According to this view (viz. of legitimacy), the apostle is made gravely to tell the Corinthians, that the marriage, in the supposed case, was lawful in a *civil sense,* a thing which they could not possibly doubt, and which must have been *equally true if both parties had been unbelieving.* It is incredible that the Corinthians should wish or need to be informed on any such point ? But if we call to mind what has been noticed above, concerning the command, binding the Jews to dissolve their unequal marriages, and to treat the offspring of them as unclean (Ezra x. 3.), we can easily imagine the Corinthians anxious to ascertain whether the Christian religion had retained any such injuction. No, says the apostle, you see your children are holy, as the

children of equal or allowed marriage among the Jews were. Therefore you need have no scruples on the point ; you require not to separate. Any obscurity that rests on the passage arises from inattention to the Jewish laws, and to the senses in which the Jews used the words " unclean" and " holy." In primitive times these terms, applied to children, would be readily understood, without any explanation such as is needed now. 3. As Doddridge in the above Note has acutely remarked, the supposition that the apostle proves the lawfulness of the marriage in a civil sense, from the legitimacy of the children, makes him argue in a circle. The thing to be proven, and the proof, are in reality one and the same. If the Corinthians knew that their children were legitimate, how could they think of applying to Paul on a subject so simple as the legality of of their marriages. It is as if they had said, " We know that our children are legitimate. Inform us if our marriages are legal !"

15. *But if the unbelieving depart.* If they choose to leave you. ¶ *Let him depart.* You cannot prevent it, and you are to submit to it patiently, and bear it as a Christian. ¶ *A brother or a sister is not under bondage,* &c. Many have supposed that this means that they would be at liberty to marry again when the unbelieving wife or husband had gone away; as Calvin, Grotius, Rosenmüller, &c. But this is contrary to the strain of the argument of the apostle. The sense of the expression "is not bound," &c. is, that *if* they forcibly depart, the one that is left is not bound by the marriage tie to make provision for the one that departed ; to do acts that might be prejudicial to religion by a violent effort to compel the departing husband or wife to live with the one that is forsaken ; but is at liberty to live separate, and should regard it as proper so to do. ¶ *God hath called us to peace.* Religion is peaceful. It would prevent contentions and broils. This is to be a grand principle. If it cannot be obtained by living together, there should be a peaceful separation ; and *where* such a separation has taken place, the one

wife, whether thou shalt save *a thy* husband? or how [1] knowest thou,

O man, whether thou shalt save *thy* wife?

a 1Pet.3.1,2.   1 *what.*

which has departed should be suffered to remain separate in peace. God has called us to live in peace with all if we can. This is the general principle of religion on which we are always to act. In our relation to our partners in life, as well as in all other relations and circumstances, this is to guide us. Calvin supposes that this declaration pertains to the former part of this verse; and that Paul means to say, that if the unbelieving depart, he is to be suffered to do so peaceably rather than to have contention and strife, for God has called us to a life of peace.

16. *For what knowest thou*, &c. The apostle here assigns a *reason* why the believing party should not separate from the other needlessly, or why he should not desire to be separated. The reason is, the possibility, or the probability, that the unbelieving party might be converted by the example and entreaties of the other. ¶ *Whether then*, &c. How do you know *but* this may be done? Is there not a possibility, nay a probability of it, and is not this a sufficient reason for continuing together? ¶ *Save thy husband.* Gain him over to the Christian faith; be the means of his conversion and salvation; comp. Rom. xi. 26.—We learn from this verse, (1.) That there is a possibility that an unbelieving partner in life may be converted by the example of the other   (2.) That this should be an object of intense interest to the Christian husband or wife, because (*a*) It will promote the happiness of the other; (*b*) It will promote their usefulness; (*c*) It will be the means of blessing their family, for parents should be *united* on the subject of religion, and in their example and influence in training up their sons and daughters; and (*d*) Because the salvation of a beloved husband or wife should be an object of intense interest, (3.) This object is of so much importance that the Christian should be

willing to submit to much, to bear much, and to bear long, in order that it may be accomplished. Paul said that it was desirable even to live with a heathen partner to do it; and so also it is desirable to bear much, very much, with even an unkind and fretful temper, with an unfaithful and even an intemperate husband, or with a perverse and peevish wife, if there is a prospect that they may be converted. (4.) This same direction is elsewhere given; 1 Pet. iii. 1, 2.   (5.) It is often done. It is not hopeless. Many a wife has thus been the means of saving a husband; many a husband has been the means of the salvation of the wife.—In regard to the *means* by which this is to be hoped for, we may observe that it is not by a harsh, fretful, complaining temper; it is to be by kindness, and tenderness, and love. It is to be by an exemplification of the excellency of religion by example; by patience when provoked, meekness when injured, love when despised, forbearance when words of harshness and irritation are used, and by showing *how* a Christian *can* live, and what is the true nature of religion; by kind and affectionate conversation when alone, when the heart is tender, when calamities visit the family, and when the thoughts are drawn along by the events of Providence towards death. Not by harshness or severity of manner, is the result to be hoped for, but by tender entreaty, and mildness of life, and by prayer. Pre eminently this is to be used. When a husband will not hear, God can hear; when he is angry, morose, or unkind, God is gentle, tender, and kind; and when a husband or a wife turn away from the voice of gentle entreaty. God's ear is open, and God is ready to hear and to bless. Let one thing guide the life. We are never to cease to set a Christian example; never to cease to live as a Christian should live; never to cease to pray fervently to the God of grace, that the partner

17 But as God hath distributed to every man, as *a* the Lord hath called every one, so let him walk. And *b* so ordain I in all churches.

18 Is any man called being circumcised? let him not become uncircumcised. Is any called in uncircumcision? *c* let him not be circumcised.

19 Circumcision *d* is nothing,

a ver.20,24.   *b* chap.4.17; 2 Cor.11.28.   *c* Acts 15.1,&c.; Gal.5.2,&c.;   *d* Gal.5.6. 6.15.

of our lives may be brought under the full influence of Christian truth, and meet us in the enjoyments of heaven.

17. *But as God hath distributed,* &c. As God hath *divided* (ἐμέρισεν); *i. e.* given, imparted to any one. As God has given grace to every one. The words εἰ μὴ denote simply *but* in the beginning of this verse. The apostle here introduces a new subject; or an inquiry varying somewhat from that preceding, though of the same general nature. He had discussed the question whether a husband and wife ought to be separated on account of a difference in religion. He now says that the general principle there stated ought to rule everywhere; that men who become Christians ought not to seek to change their condition or calling in life, but to remain in that situation in which they were when they became Christians, and show the excellence of their religion IN that particular calling. The *object* of Paul, therefore, is to preserve order, industry, faithfulness in the relations of life, and to show that Christianity does not design to break up the relations of social and domestic intercourse. This discussion continues to ver. 24. The phrase " as God hath distributed " refers to the *condition* in which men are placed in life, whether as rich or poor, in a state of freedom or servitude, of learning or ignorance, &c. And it implies that *God* appoints the lot of men, and orders the circumstances of their condition; that religion is not designed to interfere *directly* with this; and that men should seek to show the real excellence of religion in the particular sphere in which they may have been placed by divine providence *before* they became converted. ¶ *As the Lord hath called every one.* That is, in the condition or circumstances in which any one is when he is called by

the Lord to be a Christian. ¶ *So let him walk. In* that sphere of life; in that calling (ver. 20); in that particular relation in which he was, let him remain, unless he can consistently change it for the better, and THERE let him illustrate the true beauty and excellence of religion. This was designed to counteract the notion that the fact of embracing a new religion dissolved the relations of life which existed before. This idea probably prevailed extensively among the Jews. Paul's object is to show that the gospel, instead of dissolving those relations, only strengthened them, and enabled those who were converted the better to discharge the duties which grow out of them. ¶ *And so ordain I,* &c. This is no peculiar rule for you Corinthians. It is the universal rule which I everywhere inculcated. It is not improbable that there was occasion to insist everywhere on this rule, and to repress disorders which might have been attempted by some who might suppose that Christianity dissolved the former obligations of life.

18. *Is any man called?* Does any one become a Christian? Note, chap. i. 26. ¶ *Being circumcised.* Being a native-born Jew, or having become a Jewish proselyte, and having submitted to the initiatory rite of the Jewish religion. ¶ *Let him not become uncircumcised.* This could not be literally done. But the apostle refers here to certain efforts which were made to remove the marks of circumcision which were often attempted by those who were ashamed of having been circumcised. The practice is often alluded to by Jewish writers, and is described by them; comp. 1 Mac. i. 15. It is not decorous or proper here to show how this was done. The process is described in Cels. de Med. vii. 25; see Grotius and Bloomfield.

and uncircumcision is nothing, but the keeping *a* of the commandments of God.

a John 15.14; 1 John 2.3.

¶ *Is any called in uncircumcision?* A Gentile, or one who had not been circumcised. ¶ *Let him not be circumcised.* The Jewish rites are not binding, and are not to be enjoined on those who have been converted from the Gentiles ; see Notes, Rom. ii. 27—30.

19. *Circumcision is nothing*, &c. It is of no consequence in itself. It is not that which God requires now. And the mere external rite can be of no consequence one way or the other. The heart is all; and that is what God demands ; see Note, Rom. ii. 29. ¶ *But the keeping of the commandments of God Is* something, *is* the main thing, *is* every thing ; and this can be done whether a man is circumcised or not.

20. *Let every man abide.* Let him remain or continue. ¶ *In the same calling.* The same occupation, profession, rank of life. We use the word *calling* in the same sense to denote the occupation or profession of a man. Probably the original idea which led men to designate a profession as a *calling* was the belief that *God* called every man to the profession and rank which he occupies; that is, that it is by his *arrangement*, or *providence*, that he occupies that rank rather than another. In this way every man has a *call* to the profession in which he is engaged as really as ministers of the gospel ; and every man should have as clear evidence that *God* has *called* him to the sphere of life in which he moves as ministers of the gospel should have that God has called *them* to their appropriate profession. This declaration of Paul, that every one is to remain in the same occupation or rank in which he was when he was converted, is to be taken in a general and not in an unqualified sense. It does not design to teach that a man is in *no* situation to seek a *change* in his profession when he becomes pious. But it is intended to

20 Let every man abide *b* in the same calling wherein he was called. 21 Art thou called *being* a ser-

b Prov.27.8.

show that religion was the friend of order ; that it did not disregard or disarrange the relations of social life; that it was fitted to produce *contentment* even in an humble walk, and to prevent repinings at the lot of those who were more favoured or happy. That it did not design to prevent *all* change is apparent from the next verse, and from the nature of the case. *Some* of the circumstances in which a change of condition, or of calling, may be proper when a man is converted, are the following. (1.) When a man is a *slave*, and he can obtain his freedom, ver. 21. (2.) When a man is pursuing a *wicked* calling or course of life when he was converted, even if it is lucrative, he should abandon it as speedily as possible. Thus if a man is engaged, as John Newton was, in the slave-trade, he should at once abandon it. If he is engaged in the manufacture or sale of ardent spirits, he should at once forsake the business, even at great personal sacrifice, and engage in a lawful and honourable employment ; see Note, Acts xix. 19. No considerations can justify a continuance in a course of life like this after a man is converted. No consideration can make a business which is " evil, and only evil, and that continually," proper or right. (3.) Where a man can increase his usefulness by choosing a new profession. Thus the usefulness of many a man is greatly promoted by his leaving an agricultural, or mechanical employment; or by his leaving the bar, or the mercantile profession, and becoming a minister of the gospel. In such situations, religion not only *permits* a man to change his profession, but it *demands* it ; nor will God smile upon him, or bless him, unless the change is made. An opportunity to become more useful imposes an obligation to change the course of life. And no man is permitted to *waste* his life and talents in a mere scheme of money-making, or

vant ? care *a* not for it : but if thou mayest be made free, use *it* rather.

a Heb.13.5.

22 For he that is called in the Lord, *being* a servant, is *b* the

b John 8.36; Rom.6.18,22.

in self-indulgence, when by changing his calling he can do more for the salvation of the world.

21. *Being a servant* (δ:ῦλος). A slave. Slaves abounded in Greece, and in every part of the heathen world. Athens, *e. g.*, had, in her best days, twenty thousand freemen, and four hundred thousand slaves. See the condition of the heathen world on this subject illustrated at length, and in a very learned maner, by Rev. B. B. Edwards, in the Bib. Repository for Oct. 1835, pp. 411—436. It was a very important subject to inquire what *ought* to be done in such instances. Many slaves who had been converted might argue that the institution of slavery was contrary to the rights of man ; that it destroyed their equality with other men ; that it was cruel, and oppressive, and unjust in the highest degree; and that therefore they ought not to submit to it, but that they should burst their bonds, and assert their rights as freemen. In order to prevent restlessness, uneasiness, and insubordination ; in order to preserve the peace of society, and to prevent religion from being regarded as disorganizing and disorderly, Paul here states the principle on which the slave was to act. And by referring to this case, which was the strongest which could occur, he designed doubtless to inculcate the duty of order, and contentment in general in all the other relations in which men might be when they were converted. ¶ *Care not for it.* Let it not be a subject of deep anxiety and distress ; do not deem it to be disgraceful; let it not affect your spirits; but be content in the lot of life where God has placed you. If you can in a proper way obtain your freedom, do it ; if not let it not be a subject of painful reflection. In the sphere of life where God by his providence has placed you, strive to evince the Christian spirit, and show that you are able to bear the sorrows and endure the

toils of your humble lot with submission to the will of God, and so as to advance *in* that relation the interest of the true religion. *In* that calling do your duty, and evince always the spirit of a Christian. This duty is often enjoined on those who were servants, or slaves : Eph. vi. 5 ; Col. iii. 22 ; 1 Tim. vi. 1 ; Tit. ii. 9 ; 1 Pet. ii. 18. This duty of the slave, however, does not make the oppression of the master right or just, any more than the duty of one who is persecuted or reviled to be patient and meek makes the conduct of the persecutor or reviler just or right ; nor does it prove that the master has a *right* to hold the slave as *property*, which can never be right in the sight of God ; but it requires simply that the slave should evince, even in the midst of degradation and injury, the spirit of a Christian, just as it is required of a man who is injured in any way, to bear it as becomes a follower of the Lord Jesus. Nor does this passage prove that a slave ought not to *desire* freedom if it can be obtained, for this is supposed in the subsequent clause. Every human being has a right to desire to be free, and to seek liberty. But it should be done in accordance with the rules of the gospel ; so as not to dishonour the religion of Christ, and so as not to injure the true happiness of others, or overturn the foundations of society. ¶ *But if thou mayest be free.* If thou canst (δύνασαι), if it is in your power to become free. That is, if your master or the laws set you free ; or if you can purchase your freedom ; or if the laws can be changed in a regular manner. If freedom *can* be obtained in *any* manner that is not *sinful.* In many cases a Christian master might set his slaves free ; in others, perhaps, the laws might do it ; in some, perhaps, the freedom of the slave might be purchased by a Christian friend. In all these instances it would be proper to embrace the opportunity of becoming free. The

Lord's [1] freeman ; likewise also he that is called, *being* free, is *a* Christ's servant.

1 *made free.*   *a* Ps.116.16; 1 Pet.2.16.

23 Ye are bought *b* with a price ; be not ye the servants of men.

b chap.6.20; 1 Pet.1.18,19.

apostle does not speak of insurrection, and the whole scope of the passage is *against* an attempt on their part to obtain freedom by force and violence. He manifestly teaches them to remain in their condition, to bear it patiently and submissively, and *in* that relation to bear their hard lot with a Christian spirit, unless their freedom could be obtained without *violence* and *bloodshed.* And the same duty is still binding. Evil as slavery is, and always evil, and only evil, yet the Christian religion requires patience, gentleness, forbearance; not violence, war, insurrection, and bloodshed. Christianity would teach *masters* to be kind, tender, and gentle; to liberate their slaves, and to change the laws so that it may be done; to be *just* towards those whom they have held in bondage. It would *not* teach the slave to rise on his master, and imbrue his hands in his blood; to break up the relations of society by violence; or to dishonour his religion by the indulgence of the feelings of revenge and by murder. ¶ *Use* it *rather.* Avail yourselves of the privilege if you can, and be a freeman. There are disadvantages attending the condition of a slave, and if you can escape from them in a proper manner, it is your privilege and your duty to do it.

22. *For he that is called in the Lord.* He that is called *by* the Lord ; he that becomes a Christian. ¶ *Being a servant.* A slave when he is converted. ¶ *Is the Lord's freeman.* Marg. *Made free* (ἀπελεύθερος). Is manumitted, made free, endowed with liberty by the Lord. This is designed evidently to comfort the heart of the slave, and to make him contented with his condition; and it is a most delicate, happy, and tender argument. The sense is this. " You are blessed with freedom from the bondage of sin by the Lord. You were formerly a slave to sin, but now you are liberated. *That* bondage was far more grievous,

and far more to be lamented than the bondage of the body. But from that long, grievous, and oppressive servitude you are now free. Your condition, even though you are a slave, is far better than it was before; nay, *you* are now the true freeman, the freeman of the Lord. Your spirit is free; while those who are not slaves, and perhaps your own masters, are even now under a more severe and odious bondage than yours. You should rejoice, therefore, in deliverance from the greater evil, and be glad that in the eye of God you are regarded as *his* freeman, and endowed by him with more valuable freedom than it would be to be delivered from the bondage under which you are now placed. Freedom from sin is the highest blessing that can be conferred on men; and if *that* is yours, you should little regard your external circumstances in this life. You will soon be admitted to the eternal liberty of the saints in glory, and will forget all your toils and privations in this world." ¶ *Is Christ's servant.* Is the *slave* (δοῦλος;) of Christ ; is bound to obey law, and to submit himself, as you are, to the authority of another. This too is designed to promote *contentment* with his lot, by the consideration that *all* are bound to obey law; that there is no such thing as absolute independence ; and that, since law *is* to be obeyed, it is not degradation and ignominy to submit to those which God has imposed on us by his providence in an humble sphere of life. Whether a freeman or a slave, we are bound to yield obedience to law, and everywhere must obey the laws of God. It is not, therefore, degradation to submit to *his* laws in a state of servitude, though these laws come to us through an earthly master. In this respect, the slave and the freeman are on a level, as *both* are required to submit to the laws of Christ; and, even if freedom could be obtained, there is no

24 Brethren, let[a] every man, wherein he is called, therein abide with God.

25 Now concerning virgins I

a ver.17,20.

have no commandment [b] of the Lord ; yet I give my judgment, as one that hath obtained mercy of the Lord to be faithful [c]

b ver.6,10,40.   *c* 1 Tim 1.12.

---

such thing as absolute independence. This is a very beautiful, delicate and happy argument: and perhaps no consideration could be urged that would be more adapted to produce contentment. 23. *Ye are bought with a price.* Though you are slaves to men, yet you have been purchased for God by the blood of his Son ; Note, chap. vi. 20. You are, therefore, in his sight of inestimable worth, and are bound to be his. ¶ *Be not ye the servants of men.* That is, "Do not *regard yourselves as the slaves* OF MEN. Even in your humble relation of life, even as servants under the laws of the land, regard yourselves as the servants of God, as obeying and serving him *even in this relation.* since *all* those who are bought with a price—all Christians, whether bond or free—are in fact the servant (slaves, δοῦλοι) of God, ver. 22. *In* this relation, therefore, esteem yourselves as the servants of God, as bound by his laws, as subject to him, and as really serving him, while you yield all proper obedience to your master." Rosenmüller, Grotius, and some others, however, think that this refers to Christians in general; and that the apostle means to caution them against subjecting themselves to needless rites and customs which the false teachers would impose on them. Others have supposed (as Doddridge) that it means that they should not sell themselves into slavery; but assuredly a caution of this kind was not needful. The view given above I regard as the interpretation demanded by the connection. And in this view it would promote contentment, and would even prevent their taking any improper measures to disturb the relations of social life, by the high and solemn consideration that even *in* that relation they were in common with all Christians, the true and real servants of God. They belonged to God, and they should serve *him.*

In all things which their masters commanded, that were in accordance with the will of God, and that could be done with a quiet conscience, they were to regard themselves as serving God; if at any time they were commanded to do that which God had forbidden, they were to remember that they were the servants OF GOD, and that he was to be obeyed rather than man.

24. *Brethren, &c.*; see Note, v. 20.

25. *Now concerning virgins.* This commences the *third* subject on which the opinion of Paul seems to have been asked by the church at Corinth —whether it was proper that those who had unmarried daughters, or wards, should give them in marriage. The reason why this question was proposed may have been, that many in the church at Corinth were the advocates of celibacy, and this, perhaps, on two grounds. (1.) Some may have supposed that, in the existing state of things—the persecutions and trials to which Christians were exposed — it would be advisable that a man who had unmarried daughters, or wards, should keep them from the additional cares and trials to which they would be exposed with a family ; and, (2.) Some may have already been the advocates for celibacy, and have maintained that that state was more favourable to piety, and was altogether to be preferred. It is known that that opinion had an early prevalence, and gave rise to the establishment of *nunneries* in the papal church ; an opinion that has everywhere been attended with licen'tiousness and corruption. It is not improbable that there may have been advocates for this opinion even in the church of Corinth ; and it was well, therefore, that the authority of an apostle should be employed to sanction and to honour the marriage union. ¶ *I have no commandment, &c.* No positive, express revelation ; see Notes

26 I suppose therefore that this is good for the present [1] distress ; *I say,* that *a it is* good for a man so to be.

27 Art thou bound unto a wife ?

seek not to be loosed. Art thou loosed from a wife ? seek not a wife.

28 But and if thou marry, thou *b* hast not sinned ; and if a virgin marry, she hath not sinned. Never-

1 or, *necessity.*　　　*a* ver.1,8.

b Heb.13.4.

on ver. 6, 10. ¶ *Yet I give my judgment.* I give my opinion, or advice ; see Note, ver. 6. ¶ *As one that hath obtained mercy of the Lord.* As a Christian ; one who has been pardoned, whose mind has been enlightened, and who has been endued with the grace of God. ¶ *To be faithful.* Faithful to my God. As one who would not give advice for any selfish, or mercenary, or worldly consideration ; as one known to act from a desire to honour God, and to seek the best interests of the church, even though there is no explicit command. The advice of *such* a man—a devoted, faithful, self-denying, experienced Christian—is entitled to respectful deference, even where there is no claim to inspiration. Religion qualifies to give advice ; and the advice of a man who has no selfish ends to gratify, and who is known to seek supremely the glory of God, should not be disregarded or slighted. Paul had a special claim to give this advice, because he was the founder of the church at Corinth.

26. *I suppose.* I think ; I give the following advice. ¶ *For the present distress.* In the present state of trial. The word *distress* (ἀνάγκην, *necessity*) denotes calamity, persecution, trial, &c. ; see Luke xxi. 23. The word rendered *present* (ἐνεστῶσαν) denotes that which *urges on,* or that which at that time presses on, or afflicts. Here it is implied, (1.) That at that time they were subject to trials so severe as to render the advice which he was about to give proper ; and, (2.) That he by no means meant that this should be a *permanent arrangement* in the church, and of course it cannot be urged as an argument for the monastic system. What the *urgent distress* of this time was, is not certainly known. If the epistle was written about A. D. 59 (see the Introduction), it was in

the time of Nero ; and probably he had already begun to oppress and persecute Christians. At all events, it is evident that the Christians at Corinth were subject to some trials which rendered the cares of the marriage life undesirable. ¶ It is *good for a man so to be.* The emphasis here is on the word *so* (οὕτως) ; that is, it is best for a man to conduct *in the following manner ;* the word *so* referring to the advice which follows. " I advise that he conduct in the following manner, to wit." Most commentators suppose that it means *as he is ; i. e.,* unmarried ; but the interpretation proposed above best suits the connection. The advice given is in the following verses.

27. *Art thou bound unto a wife ?* Art thou already married ? Marriage is often thus represented as a *tie,* a *bond,* &c. ; see Note, Rom. vii. 2. ¶ *Seek not to be loosed.* Seek not a *dissolution* (λύσιν) of the connection, either by divorce or by a separation from each other ; see Notes on ver. 10—17. ¶ *Art thou loosed from a wife ?* Art thou unmarried ? It should have been rendered *free from* a wife ; or art thou single ? It does not imply of necessity that the person had been married, though it *may* have that meaning, and *signify* those who had been separated from a wife by her death. There is no necessity of supposing that Paul refers to persons who had divorced their wives. So Grotius, Schleusner, Doddridge, &c.

28. *Thou hast not sinned.* There is no express command of God on this subject. The counsel which I give is mere advice, and it may be observed or not as you shall judge best. Marriage is honourable and lawful ; and though there may be circumstances where it is *advisable* not to enter into this relation, yet there is no law which prohibits it. The same advice

theless such shall have trouble in the flesh : but I spare you.

29 But this I say, brethren, the

---

would be proper now, if it were a time of persecution ; or if a man is poor, and cannot support a family ; or if he has already a dependent mother and sisters to be supported by him, it would be well to follow the advice of Paul. So also when the cares of a family would take up a man's time and efforts; when *but* for this he might give himself to a missionary life, the voice of wisdom may be in accordance with that of Paul ; that a man may be free from these cares, and may give himself with more undivided interest and more successful toil to the salvation of man. ¶ *Such shall have trouble in the flesh.* They shall have anxiety, care, solicitude, trials. Days of persecution are coming on, and you may be led to the stake, and in those fiery trials your families may be torn asunder, and a part be put to death. Or you may be poor, and oppressed, and driven from your homes, and made wanderers and exiles, for the sake of your religion. ¶ *But I spare you.* I will not dwell on the melancholy theme. I will not pain your hearts by describing the woes that shall ensue. I will not do any thing to deter you from acting as you deem right. If you choose to marry, it is lawful; and I will not imbitter your joys and harrow up your feelings by the description of your future difficulties and trials. The word *flesh* here denotes outward circumstances in contradistinction from the mind. They might have peace of mind, for religion would furnish that ; but they would be exposed to poverty, persecution, and calamity.

29. *But this I say.* Whether you are married or not, or in whatever condition of life you may be, I would remind you that life hastens to a close, and that its grand business is to be prepared to die. It matters little in what condition or rank of life we are, if we are ready to depart to another and a better world. ¶ *The time* is *short.* The time is *contracted,*

time. *a is* short : it remaineth that both they that have wives be as though they had none :

a 1 Pet.4.7; 2 Pet.3.8,9.

---

drawn into a narrow space (συνεσταλμένος). The word which is here used is commonly applied to the act of *furling* a sail, *i. e.*, reducing it into a narrow compass ; and is then applied to any thing that is reduced within narrow limits. Perhaps there was a reference here to the fact that the time was *contracted,* or made short, by their impending persecutions and trials. But it is always equally true that time is short. It will soon glide away, and come to a close. The idea of the apostle here is, that the plans of life should all be formed in view of this truth, THAT TIME IS SHORT. No plan should be adopted which does not contemplate this ; no engagement of life made when it will not be appropriate to think of it ; no connection entered into when the thought "time is short," would be an unwelcome intruder; see 1 Pet. iv. 7; 2 Pet. iii. 8, 9. ¶ *It remaineth* (τὸ λοιπόν). The remainder is ; or this is a consequence from this consideration of the shortness of time. ¶ *Both they that have wives,* &c. This does not mean that they are to treat them with unkindness or neglect, or fail in the duties of love and fidelity. It is to be taken in a general sense, that they were to live above the world, that they were not to be unduly attached to them that they were to be ready to part with them ; and that they should not suffer attachment to them to interfere with any duty which they owed to God. They were in a world of trial ; and they were exposed to persecution ; and as Christians they were bound to live entirely to God, and they ought not, therefore, to allow attachment to earthly friends to alienate their affections from God, or to interfere with their Christian duty. In one word, they ought to be *just as faithful to God,* and *just as pious,* in every respect, as if they had no wife and no earthly friend. Such a consecration to God is difficult, but not impossible. Our earthly attachments and cares

30 And they that weep, as though they wept not ; and they that rejoice, as though they rejoiced not;

and they that buy, as though they possessed not ;

31 And they that use this world,

draw away our affections from God, but they need not do it. Instead of being the occasion of *alienating* our affections from God, they should be, and they might be, the means of binding us more firmly and entirely to him and to his cause. But alas, how many professing Christians live *for* their wives and children only, and not *for* God *in* these relations ! how many suffer these earthly objects of attachment to alienate their minds from the ways and commandments of God, rather than make them the occasion of uniting them more tenderly to him and his cause !

30. *And they that weep.* They who are afflicted. ¶ *As though they wept not.* Restraining and moderating their grief by the hope of the life to come. *The general idea in all these expressions is, that in whatever situation Christians are, they should be dead to the world, and not improperly affected by passing events.* It is impossible for human nature *not* to feel when persecuted, maligned, slandered, or when near earthly friends are taken away. But religion will calm the troubled spirit; pour oil on the agitated waves; light up a smile in the midst of tears; cause the beams of a calm and lovely morning to rise on the anxious heart; silence the commotions of the agitated soul, and produce joy even in the midst of sorrow. Religion will keep us from immoderate grief, and sustain the soul even when in distress nature forces us to shed the tear of mourning. Christ sweat great drops of blood, and Christians often weep; but the heart may be calm, peaceful, elevated, confident in God in the darkest night and the severest tempest of calamity. ¶ *And they that rejoice.* They that are happy; they that are prospered; that have beloved families around them ; that are blessed with success, with honour, with esteem, with health. They that have occasion of rejoicing and gratitude. ¶ *As though they re-*

joiced not. Not rejoicing with excessive or immoderate joy. Not with riot or unholy mirth. Not satisfied *with* these things; though they may rejoice *in* them. Not forgetting that they must soon be left; but keeping the mind in a calm, serious, settled, thoughtful state, in view of the fact that all these things must soon come to an end. O how would this thought silence the voice of unseemly mirth ; How would it produce calmness, serenity, heavenly joy, where is now often unhallowed riot; and true peace, where now there is only forced and boisterous revelry ! ¶ *As though they possessed not.* It is right to buy and to obtain property. But it should be held with the conviction that it is by an uncertain tenure, and must soon be left. Men may give a deed that shall secure from their fellow men ; but no man can give a title that shall not be taken away by death. Our lands and houses, our stocks and bonds and mortgages, our goods and chattels, shall soon pass into other hands. Other men will plough our fields, reap our harvests, work in our shops, stand at our counters, sit down at our firesides, eat on our tables, lie upon our beds. Others will occupy our places in society, have our offices, sit in our seats in the sanctuary. Others will take possession of our gold, and appropriate it to their own use; and *we* shall have no more interest in it, and no more control over it, than our neighbour has now, and no power to eject the man that has taken possession of our houses and our lands. Secure therefore as our titles are, safe as are our investments, yet how soon shall we lose *all* interest in them by death; and how ought this consideration to induce us to live above the world, and to secure a treasure in that world where no thief approaches, and no moth corrupts.

31. *And they that use this world.* That make a necessary and proper use of it to furnish raiment, food.

as not abusing *it :* for the fashion *a* of this world passeth away.

32 But I would have you with out carefulness. He that is un-

a Ps.39.6;James4.14;1Pet.4.7;1John2.17.

clothing, medicine, protection, &c. It is right so to *use* the world, for it was made for these purposes. The word *using* here refers to the lawful use of it (χρώμενοι). ¶ *As not abusing* it. (καταχρώμενοι). The preposition κατα, in composition here has the sense of *too much, too freely,* and is taken not merely in an intensive sense, but to denote evil, the *abuse* of the world. It means that we are not to use it *to excess ;* we are not to make it a mere matter of indulgences, or to make that the main object and purpose of our living. We are not to give our appetites to indulgence; our bodies to riot; our days and nights to feasting and revelry. ¶ *For the fashion of this world* (τὸ σχῆμα.) The form, the appearance. In 1 John ii. 17, it is said that "the world passeth away and the lust thereof." The word "fashion" here is probably taken from the shifting scenes of the drama; where, when the scene changes, the imposing and splendid pageantry passes off. The form, the fashion of the world is like a splendid, gilded pageant. It is unreal and illusive. It continues but a little time; and soon the scene changes, and the fashion that allured and enticed us now passes away, and *we* pass to other scenes. ¶ *Passeth away* (παράγει). Passes off like the splendid, gaudy, shifting scenes of the stage. What a striking description of the changing, unstable, and unreal pageantry of this world! Now it is gay, splendid, gorgeous, lovely; to-morrow it is gone, and is succeeded by new actors and new scenes. Now all is busy with one set of actors; to-morrow a new company appears, and again they are succeeded by another, and all are engaged in scenes that are equally changing, vain, gorgeous, and delusive. A similiar idea is presented in the well known and beautiful description of the great British dramatist :—

married *b* careth for the things that *1* belong to the Lord, how he may please the Lord :

33 But he that is married careth

b 1Tim.5.5.　　　1 *of the Lord,* as ver.34.

" All the world's a stage,
And all the men and women merely players.
They have their exits and their entrances,
And one man in his time plays many parts."

If such be the character of the scenes in which we are engaged, how little should we fix our affections on them, and how anxious should we be to be prepared for the *real* and *unchanging* scenes of another world !

32. *But I would have you.* I would advise you to such a course of life as should leave you without carefulness My advice is regulated by that wish, and that wish guides me in giving it ¶ *Without carefulness* (ἀμερίμνους). Without anxiety, solicitude, care ; without such a necessary attention to the things of this life as to take off your thoughts and affections from heavenly objects ; see Notes on Mat. vi. 25—31. ¶ *Careth for the things that belong to the Lord.* Marg. " The things of the Lord ;" the things of religion. His attention is not distracted by the cares of this life ; his time is not engrossed, and his affections alienated by an attendance on the concerns of a family, and especially by solicitude for them in times of trial and persecution. He can give his *main attention* to the things of religion. He is at leisure to give his chief thoughts and anxieties to the advancement of the Redeemer's kingdom. Paul's own example showed that this was the course which *he* preferred ; and showed also that in some instances it was lawful and proper for a man to remain unmarried, and to give himself entirely to the work of the Lord. But the divine commandment (Gen. i. 28), and the commendation everywhere bestowed upon marriage in the Scriptures, as well as the nature of the case, show that it was not designed that celibacy should be general.

33. *Careth for the things of the world.* Is under a necessity of giving

for the things that are of the world, how he may please *his* wife.

34 There is difference *also* between a wife and a virgin. The unmarried woman careth for the things of the Lord, that she may be holy both in body and in spirit:

---

attention to the things of the world ; or cannot give his undivided attention and interest to the things of religion. This would be especially true in times of persecution. ¶ *How he may please his wife.* How he may gratify her ; how he may accommodate himself to her temper and wishes, to make her happy. The apostle here plainly intimates that there would be *danger* that the man would be *so* anxious to gratify his wife, as to interfere with his direct religious duties. This may be done in many ways. (1.) The *affections* may be taken off from the Lord, and bestowed upon the wife. *She* may become the object of even improper attachment, and may take the place of God in the affections. (2.) The *time* may be taken up in devotion to her, which should be given to secret prayer, and to the duties of religion. (3.) She may demand his *society* and *attention* when he ought to be engaged in doing good to others, and endeavouring to advance the kingdom of Christ. (4.) She may be gay and fashionable, and may lead him into improper expenses, into a style of living that may be unsuitable for a Christian, and into society where his piety will be injured, and his devotion to God lessened ; or, (5.) She may have erroneous opinions on the doctrines and duties of religion ; and a desire to please her may lead him insensibly to modify his views, and to adopt more lax opinions, and to pursue a more lax course of life in his religious duties. Many a husband has thus been injured by a gay, thoughtless, and imprudent wife; and though that wife *may be* a Christian, yet her course may be such as shall greatly retard his growth in grace, and mar the beauty of his piety.

34. *Between a wife and a virgin,* Between a woman that is married and one that is unmarried. The apostle says that a similar difference between the condition of her that is married and her that is unmarried takes place, which had been observed between the married and the unmarried *man.* The Greek word here ($\mu\epsilon\mu\epsilon\rho\iota\sigma\tau\alpha\iota$) may mean, *is divided,* and be rendered, " the wife and the virgin are *divided* in the same manner;" *i. e.* there is the same difference in their case as exists between the married and the unmarried man. ¶ *The unmarried women,* &c. Has more advantages for attending to the things of religion ; has fewer temptations to neglect her proper duty to God ¶ *Both in body and in spirit.* Entirely holy ; that she may be entirely devoted to God. Perhaps in her case the apostle mentions the "body," which he had not done in the case of the man, because her temptation would be principally in regard to that —the danger of endeavouring to decorate and adorn her person to please her husband. ¶ *How she may please* her *husband.* The apostle here intends, undoubtedly, to intimate that there were dangers to personal piety in the married life, which would not occur in a state of celibacy ; and that the unmarried female would have greater opportunities for devotion and usefulness than if married. And he intimates that the married female would be in danger of losing her zeal and marring her piety, by attention to her husband, and by a constant effort to please him. Some of the ways in which this might be done are the following. (1.) As in the former case (ver. 33), her *affections* might be transferred from God to the partner of her life. (2.) Her *time* will be occupied by an attention to him and to his will ; and there would be danger that that attention would be allowed to interfere with her hours of secret retirement and communion with God. (3.) Her time will be necessarily broken in upon by the cares of a family, and she should therefore guard with peculiar vigilance, that

but she that is married [a] careth for the things of the world, how she may please *her* husband.

a Luke 10.40-42.

35 And this I speak for your own profit ; not that I may cast a snare upon you, but for that

she may *redeem* time for secret communion with God. (4.) The time which she before gave to benevolent objects, may now be given to please her husband. Before her marriage she may have been distinguished for zeal, and for active efforts in every plan of doing good ; subsequently, she may lay aside this zeal, and withdraw from these plans, and be as little distinguished as others. (5.) Her piety may be greatly injured by false notions of what should be done to please her husband. If he is a worldly and fashionable man, she may seek to please him by " gold, and pearls, and costly array." Instead of cultivating the ornament of " a meek and quiet spirit," her main wish may be to decorate her person, and render herself attractive by the adorning of her *person* rather than of her *mind*. (6.) If he is opposed to religion, or if he has lax opinions on the subject, or if he is sceptical and worldly, she will be in danger of relaxing in *her* views in regard to the strictness of Christianity, and of becoming conformed to his. She will insensibly become *less* strict in regard to the Sabbath, the Bible, the prayer meeting, the Sabbath-school, the plans of Christian benevolence, the *doctrines* of the gospel. (7.) To please him, she will be found in the gay circle,—perhaps in the assembly room, or even the theatre, or amidst companies of gayety and amusement, and will forget that she is professedly devoted only to God. And, (8.) She is in danger, as the result of all this, of forsaking her old religious friends, the companions of purer, brighter days, the humble and devoted friends of Jesus ; and of seeking society among the gay, the rich, the proud, the worldly. Her piety thus is injured ; she becomes worldly and vain, and less and less like Christ ; until heaven, perhaps, in mercy smites her idol, and he dies, and leaves her again to the blessed-

ness of single-hearted devotion to God. O ! how many a Christian female has thus been injured by an unhappy marriage with a gay and worldly man ! How often has the church occasion to mourn over piety that is dimmed, benevolence that is quenched, zeal that is extinguished by devotion to a gay and worldly husband ! How often does humble piety weep over such a scene ! How often does the cause of sacred charity sigh ! How often is the Redeemer wounded in the house of his friends ! And O how often does it become NECESSARY for God to interpose, and to remove by death the object of the affection of his wandering child, and to clothe her in the habiliments of mourning, and to bathe her cheeks in tears, that " by the sadness of the countenance her heart may be made better." Who can tell how many a widow is made such from this cause ; who can tell how much religion is injured by thus stealing away the affections from God ?

35. *For your own profit.* That you may avail yourselves of all your advantages and privileges, and pursue such a course as shall tend most to advance your personal piety and salvation. ¶ *Not that I may cast a snare upon you.* The word rendered *snare* (βρόχον) means a cord, a rope, a bond ; and the sense is, that Paul would not *bind* them by any rule which God had not made ; or that he would not restrain them from that which is lawful, and which the welfare of society usually requires. Paul means, that his object in his advice was their welfare ; it was not by any means to bind, fetter, or restrain them from any course which would be for their real happiness, but to promote their real and permanent advantage. The idea which is here presented by the word *snare*, is usually conveyed by the use of the word *yoke* (Mat. xi. 29 ; Acts xv. 10 ; Gal. v. 1), and sometimes by the word *burden* ; Mat. xxiii. 4 ; Acts xv. 28. ¶ *But*

which is comely, and that ye may attend upon the Lord without distraction.

36 But if any man think that he behaveth himself uncomely toward his virgin, if she pass the

flower of *her* age, and need so require, let him do what he will he sinneth not: let them marry.

37 Nevertheless he that standeth steadfast in his heart, having no necessity, but hath power over his

---

for that which is comely (εὔσχημον). Decorous, fit, proper, noble. For that which is best *fitted* to your present condition, and which, on the whole, will be best, and most for your own advantage. There would be a fitness and propriety in their pursuing the course which he recommended. ¶ *That ye may attend on the Lord.* That you may engage in religious duties and serve God. ¶ *Without distraction.* Without being drawn away (ἀπερισπάστως); without care, interruption, and anxiety. That you may be free to engage with undivided interest in the service of the Lord.

36. *That he behaveth himself uncomely.* Acts an unbecoming part, imposes an unnecessary, painful, and improper constraint, crosses her inclinations which are in themselves proper. ¶ *Toward his virgin.* His daughter, or his ward, or any unmarried female committed to his care. ¶ *If she pass the flower of* her *age.* If she pass the marriageable age and remains unmarried. It is well known that in the east it was regarded as peculiarly dishonourable to remain unmarried; and the authority of a father, therefore, might be the means of involving his daughter in shame and disgrace. When this would be the case, it would be wrong to prohibit her marriage. ¶ *And need so require.* And she ought to be allowed to marry. If it will promote her happiness, and if she would be unhappy, and regarded as dishonoured, if she remained in a state of celibacy. ¶ *Let him do what he will.* He has the *authority* in the case, for in the east the *authority* resided with the father. He may either give her in marriage or not, as he pleases. But in this case it is advisable that she should marry. ¶ *He sinneth not.* He errs not; he will do nothing positively wrong in the case. Marriage is lawful, and in this case it is advisable, and

he may consent to it, for the reasons above stated, without error or impropriety.

37. *Nevertheless.* But. The apostle in this verse states *some* instances where it would *not* be proper to give a daughter in marriage; and the verse is a kind of summing up of all that he had said on the subject. ¶ *That standeth steadfast in his heart,* &c. Most commentators have understood this of the father of the virgin, and suppose that it refers to his purpose of keeping her from the marriage connection. The phrase to stand steadfast, is opposed to a disposition that is vacillating, unsettled, &c., and denotes a man who has command of himself, who adheres to his purpose, a man who has *hitherto* adhered to his purpose, and to whose happiness and reputation it is important that he should be known as one who is not vacillating, or easily moved. ¶ *Having no necessity.* Where there is nothing in *her* disposition or inclination that would make marriage necessary, or when there is no *engagement* or *obligation* that would be violated if she did not marry. ¶ *But hath power over his own will.* Hath power to do as he pleases; is not bound in the case by another. When there is no *engagement*, or *contract*, made in childhood, or promise made in early life that would bind him. Often daughters were espoused, or promised when they were very young, and in such a case a man would be bound to adhere to his engagement; and much as he might *desire* the reverse, and her celibacy, yet he would not have power over his own will, or be at liberty to withhold her. ¶ *And hath so decreed in his heart.* Has so *judged*, determined, resolved. ¶ *That he will keep his virgin.* His daughter, or ward, in an unmarried state. He has *power* and *authority* to do it, and if he does it he will not sin. ¶ *Doeth well.* In

own will, and hath so decreed in his heart that he will keep his virgin, doeth well. *a*

38 So then, *a* he that giveth *her* in marriage doeth well; but he

a ver.28.

that giveth *her* not in marriage doeth better.

39 The wife *b* is bound by the law as long as her husband liveth: but if her husband be dead, she is

b Rom.7.2.

either of these cases, he does well. If he has a daughter, and chooses to retain her in an unmarried state, he does well or right.

38. *Doeth well.* Does right; violates no law in it, and is not to be blamed for it. ¶ *Doeth better.* Does that which is on the whole to be preferred, if it can be done. He more certainly, in the present circumstances, consults her happiness by withholding her from the marriage connection than he could by allowing her to enter it.

39. *The wife is bound,* &c.; see Notes, Rom. vii. 2. ¶ *Only in the Lord.* That is, only to one who is a Christian; with a proper sense of her obligations to Christ, and so as to promote his glory. The apostle supposed that could not be done if she were allowed to marry a heathen, or one of a different religion. The same sentiment he advances in 2 Cor. vi. 14, and it was his intention, undoubtedly, to affirm that it was proper for a widow to marry no one who was not a Christian. The reasons at that time would be obvious. (1.) They could have no sympathy and fellow-feeling on the most important of all subjects, if the one was a Christian and the other a heathen; see 2 Cor. vi. 14, 15, &c. (2.) If she should marry a heathen, would it not be showing that she had not as deep a conviction of the importance and truth of her religion as she ought to have? If Christians were required to be " separate," to be "a peculiar people," not "to be conformed to the world," how could these precepts be obeyed if the society of a heathen was voluntarily chosen, and if she became united to him for life? (3.) She would in this way greatly hinder her usefulness; put herself in the control of one who had no respect for her religion, and who would demand her time and attention, and thus interfere with her attendance on the public and private duties of religion, and the

offices of Christian charity. (4.) She would thus greatly endanger her piety. There would be danger from the opposition, the taunts, the sneers of the enemy of Christ; from the secret influence of living with a man who had no respect for God; from his introducing her into society that was irreligious, and that would tend to mar the beauty of her piety, and to draw her away from simple-hearted devotion to Jesus Christ. And do not these *reasons* apply to similar cases now? And if so, is not the law still binding? Do not such unions now, as really as they did then, place the Christian where there is no mutual sympathy on the subject dearest to the Christian heart? Do they not show that she who forms such a union has not as deep a sense of the importance of piety, and of the pure and holy nature of her religion as she ought to have? Do they not take time from God and from charity; break up plans of usefulness, and lead away from the society of Christians, and from the duties of religion? Do they not expose often to ridicule, to reproach, to persecution, to contempt, and to pain? Do they not often lead into society, by a desire to please the partner in life, where there is no religion, where God is excluded, where the name of Christ is never heard, and where the piety is marred, and the beauty of simple Christian piety is dimmed? *And if so,* are not such marriages contrary to the law of Christ? I confess, that this verse, to my view, proves that all such marriages are a violation of the New Testament; and if they are, they should not on *any* plea be entered into; and it will be found, in perhaps nearly *all* instances, that they are disastrous to the piety of the married Christian, and the occasion of ultimate regret, and the cause of a loss of comfort, peace, and usefulness in the married life.

at liberty to be married to whom she will; only *a* in the Lord.

40 But she is happier if she so

a 2 Cor.6.14.

40. *If she so abide.* If she remain a widow even if she could be married to a Christian. ¶ *After my judgment.* In my opinion; ver. 25. ¶ *And I think also that I have the Spirit of God.* Macknight and others suppose that this phrase implies entire certainty; and that Paul means to affirm that in this he was clear that he was under the influence of inspiration. He appeals for the use of the term (δωκῶ) to Mark x. 32; Luke viii. 18; 1 Cor. iv. 9; viii. 2; xi. 16; Heb. iv. 1, &c. But the word does not usually express absolute certainty. It implies a doubt; though there may be a strong persuasion or conviction; or the best judgment which the mind can form in the case; see Mat. vi. 7; xxvi. 53; Mark vi. 49; Luke viii. 18; x. 36; xii. 51; xiii. 24; xxii. 24; Acts xvii. 18; xxv. 27; 1 Cor. xvi. 12, 22, &c. It implies here a belief that Paul was under the influence of the infallible Spirit, and that his advice was such as accorded with the will of God. Perhaps he alludes to the fact that the teachers at Corinth deemed themselves to be under the influence of inspiration, and Paul said that he judged also of himself that he was divinely guided and directed in what he said.—*Calvin.* And as Paul in this could not be mistaken; as his *impression* that he was under the influence of that Spirit was, in fact, a *claim* to divine inspiration, so this advice should be regarded as of divine authority, and as binding on all. This interpretation is further demanded by the circumstances of the case. It was necessary that he should assert divine authority to counteract the teaching of the false instructors in Corinth; and that he should interpose that authority in prescribing rules for the government of the church there, in view of the *peculiar* temptations to which they were exposed.

REMARKS.

We learn from this chapter,

1st. The sacredness of the marriage union; and the nature of the feelings

abide, after *b* my judgment: and I think *c* also that I have the Spirit of God.

b ver.25.   *c* 2 Pet.3.15,16.

with which it should be entered; ver. 1—13. On a most delicate subject Paul has shown a seriousness and delicacy of expression which can be found in no other writings, and which demonstrate how pure his own mind was, and how much it was filled with the fear of God. In all things his aim is to promote purity, and to keep from the Christian church the innumerable evils which everywhere abounded in the pagan world. The marriage connection should be formed in the fear of God. In all that union, the parties should seek the salvation of the soul; and so live as not to dishonour the religion which they profess.

2d. The duty of labouring earnestly for the conversion of the party in the marriage connection that may be a stranger to piety; ver. 16. This object should lie very near the heart; and it should be sought by all the means possible. By a pure and holy life; by exemplifying the nature of the gospel; by tenderness of conversation and of entreaty; and by fidelity in all the duties of life, we should seek the conversion and salvation of our partners in the marriage connection. Even if both are Christians, this great object should be one of constant solicitude —to advance the piety and promote the usefulness of the partner in life.

3d. The duty of contentment in the sphere of life in which we are placed; ver. 18, &c. It is no disgrace to be poor, for Jesus chose to be poor. It is no *disgrace*, though it is a calamity, to be a slave. It is no disgrace to be in an humble rank of life. It is disgraceful only to be a sinner, and to murmur and repine at our allotment. God orders the circumstances of our life; and they are well ordered when under the direction of his hand. The great object should be to do right in the relation which we sustain in life. If poor, to be industrious, submissive, resigned, virtuous; if rich, to be grateful, benevolent, kind. If a slave or a servant, to be faithful, kind, and obedient; using liberty, if it can be lawfully obtained; resigned, and calm, and gentle, if by the providence of God such must continue to be the lot in life.

4th. The duty of preserving the order and regularity of society; ver. 20—23. The design of the gospel is not to produce insubordination or irregularity. It would not break up society; does not dissolve the bonds of social life; but it cements and sanctifies the ties which connect us with those around us. It is designed to promote human happiness; and that is promoted, not by resolving society into its original elements; not by severing the marriage tie, as atheists would do; not by teaching children to disregard and despise their parents, or the common courtesies of life, but by teaching them to maintain inviolate all these relations. Religion promotes the interests of society; it does not, like infidelity, dissolve them. It advances the cause of social virtue; it does not, like atheism, retard and annihilate it. Every Christian becomes a better parent, a more affectionate child, a kinder friend, a more tender husband or wife, a more kind neighbour, a better member of the community.

5th. Change in a man's calling should not be made from a slight cause. A Christian should not make it unless his former calling were wrong, or unless he can by it extend his own usefulness. But when that can be done, he *should* do it, and do it with out delay. If the course is wrong, it should be forthwith abandoned. No consideration can make it right to continue it for a day or an hour: no matter what may be the sacrifice of property, it should be done. If a man is engaged in the slave-trade, or in smuggling goods, or in piracy, or highway robbery, or in the manufacture and sale of poison, it should be at once and for ever abandoned. And in like manner, if a young man who is converted can increase his usefulness by changing his plan of life, it should be done as soon as practicable. If by becoming a minister of the gospel he can be a more useful man, every consideration demands that he should leave *any* other profession, however

lucrative or pleasant, and submit to the self-denials, the cares, the trials, and the toils which attend a life devoted to Christ in the ministry in Christian or pagan lands. Though it should be attended with poverty, want, tears, toil, or shame, yet the single question is, "Can I be more useful to my Master there than in my present vocation?" If he *can* be, that is an indication of the will of God which he cannot disregard with impunity.

6th. We should live above this world; ver. 29, 30. We should partake of all our pleasures, and endure all our sufferings, with the deep feeling that we have here no continuing city and no abiding place. Soon all our earthly pleasures will fade away; soon all our earthly sorrows will be ended. A conviction of the shortness of life will tend much to regulate our desires for earthly comforts, and will keep us from being improperly attached to them; and it will diminish our sorrows by the prospect that they will soon end.

7th. We should not be immoderately affected with grief; ver. 30. It will all soon end, in regard to Christians. Whether our tears arise from the consciousness of our sins or the sins of others; whether from persecution or contempt of the world; or whether from the loss of health, property, or friends, we should bear it all patiently, for it will soon end; a few days, and all will be over; and the *last* tear shall fall on our cheeks, and the *last* sigh be heaved from our bosom.

8th. We should not be immoderate in our joy, ver. 30. Our highest earthly joys will soon cease. Mirth, and the sound of the harp and the viol, the loud laugh and the song will soon close. What a change should this thought make in a world of gayety, and mirth, and song! It should not make men gloomy and morose; but it should make them serious, calm, thoughtful. O, did all feel that death was near, that the solemn realities of eternity were approaching, what a change *would* it make in a gay and thoughtless world! How would it close the theatre and the ball-room; how would it silence the jest, the

CHAPTER VIII.

NOW as touching things offered ^a unto idols, we know that

a Acts 15.10,19.

jeer, and the loud laugh; and how would it diffuse seriousness and calmness over a now gay and thoughtless world! "Laughter is mad," says Solomon; and in a world of sin, and sorrow, and death, assuredly seriousness and calm contemplation are demanded by every consideration.

9th. What an effect would the thought that "time is short," and that "the fashion of this world passeth away," have on the lovers of wealth! It would, (1.) Teach them that property is of little value. (2.) That the possession of it can constitute no distinction beyond the grave: the rich man is just as soon reduced to dust, and is just as offensive in his splendid mausoleum, as the poor beggar. (3.) A man feeling this, would be led (or *should* be) to make a good use of his property on earth. See Note, Luke xvi. 1—9. (4.) He would be led to seek a better inheritance, an interest in the treasures that no moth corrupts, and that never fade away. Note, Matt. vi. 20. This single thought, that the fashion of this world is soon to pass away—an idea which no man can doubt or deny—if allowed to take firm hold of the mind, would change the entire aspect of the world.

10th. We should endeavour so to live in all things as that our minds should not be oppressed with undue anxiety and care, ver. 32. In all our arrangements and plans, and in all the relations of life, our grand object should be to have the mind free for the duties and privileges of religion. We should seek not to be encumbered with care; not to be borne down with anxiety; not to be unduly attached to the things of this life.

11th. We should enter into the relations of life so as not to interfere with our personal piety or usefulness, but so as to promote both, ver. 32—35. All our arrangements should be so formed as that we may discharge our religious duties, and promote our usefulness to our fellow men. But, alas,

we all have knowledge. ^b Knowledge ^c puffeth up, but charity ^d edifieth.

b Rom.14.14,22.　　c Isa 47.10.　　d chap xiii.

how many enter into the marriage relation with unchristian companions, whose active zeal is for ever quenched by such a connection! How many form commercial connections or partnerships in business with those who are not Christians, where the result is to diminish their zeal for God, and to render their whole lives useless to the church! And how much do the cares of life, in all its relations, interfere with simple-hearted piety, and with the faithful discharge of the duties which we owe to God and to a dying world! May God of his mercy enable us so to live in all the relations of life as that our usefulness shall not be retarded but augmented; and so to live that we can see without one sigh of regret the "fashion of this world pass away;" our property or our friends removed; or even the magnificence of the entire world, with all its palaces, and temples, and "cloud-capped towers," passing away amidst the fires that shall attend the consummation of all things!

CHAPTER VIII.

IN this chapter another subject is discussed, which had been proposed by the church at Corinth for the decision of the apostle: *Whether it was right for Christians to partake of the meat that had been offered in sacrifice to idols?* On this question there would be doubtless a difference of opinion among the Corinthian Christians. When those sacrifices were made to heathen gods, a part of the animal was given to the priest that officiated, a part was consumed on the altar, and a part (probably the principal part) was the property of him who offered it. This part was either eaten by him at home, as food which had been in some sense consecrated or blessed by having been offered to an idol; or it was partaken of at a feast in honour of the idol; or it was in some instances exposed for sale in the market in the same way as other meat. Whether, therefore, it would be right to partake of that food, either when invited to the house of a heathen friend, or when it was exposed for sale in the market, was a question which could not but present itself to a conscientious Christian. The *objection* to partaking of it would be, that to partake of it either in the temples or at the feasts of their heathen neighbours, would be to lend their countenance to idolatry. On the other hand, there were many who supposed that it was always lawful, and that the scruples of their brethren were needless. Some of their arguments Paul has alluded to in the course of the chapter : they were, that an idol was nothing in the world ; that there was but one God, and that every one must know this ; and that, therefore, there was no danger that any worshipper of the true God could be led into the absurdities of idolatry, ver. 4—6. To this the apostle replies, that though there *might* be this knowledge, yet, (1.) Knowledge sometimes puffed up, and made us proud, and that we should be careful lest it should lead us astray by our vain self-confidence, ver. 1, 2, 7. (2.) That *all* had not that knowledge (ver. 7) ; and that they even then, notwithstanding all the light which had been shed around them by Christianity, and notwithstanding the absurdity of idolatry, still regarded an idol as a real existence, as a god, and worshipped it as such ; and that it would be highly improper to countenance in any way that idea. He left the inference, therefore, that it was not proper, *from this argument*, to partake of the sacrifices to idols.

A second argument in favour of partaking of that food is alluded to in ver. 8, to wit, that it must be in itself a matter of indifference ; that it could make no difference before God, where all depended on *moral* purity and holiness of heart, whether a man had eaten *meat* or not ; that we were really no better or worse for it ; and that, therefore, it was proper to partake of that food. To this Paul replies, (1.) That though this was true, as an abstract proposition, yet it might be the occasion of leading others into sin,

ver. 9. (2.) That the effect on a weak brother would be to lead him to suppose that an idol *was* something, and to confirm him in his supposition that an idol should have some regard, and be worshipped in the temple, ver. 10. (3.) That the consequence might be, that a Christian of little information and experience might be drawn away and perish, ver. 11. (4.) That this would be to sin against Christ, if a feeble Christian should be thus destroyed, ver. 12. And, (5.) That as for himself, if indulgence in meat was in any way the occasion of making another sin, he would eat no meat as long as the world stood (ver. 13) ; since to abstain from *meat* was a far less evil than the injury or destruction of an immortal soul.

1. *Now as touching.* In regard to ; in answer to your inquiry whether it is right or not to partake of those things. ¶ *Things offered unto idols.* Sacrifices unto idols. Meat that had been offered in sacrifice, and then either exposed to sale in the market, or served up at the feasts held in honour of idols, at their temples, or at the houses of their devotees. The priests, who were entitled to a part of the meat that was offered in sacrifice, would expose it to sale in the market ; and it was a custom with the Gentiles to make feasts in honour of the idol gods on the meat that was offered in sacrifice ; see ver. 10, of this chapter, and chap. x. 20, 21. Some Christians would hold that there could be no harm in partaking of this meat any more than any other meat, since an idol was nothing ; and others would have many scruples in regard to it, since it would seem to countenance idol worship. The request made of Paul was, that he should settle some *general principle* which they might all safely follow. ¶ *We know.* We admit ; we cannot dispute ; it is so plain a case that no one can be ignorant on this point. Probably these are the words of the Corinthians, and perhaps they were contained in the letter which was sent to Paul. They would affirm that they were not ignorant in regard to the nature of idols ; they were well assured that they were

nothing at all; and hence they seemed to *infer* that it might be right and proper to partake of this food anywhere and every where, even in the idol temples themselves ; see ver. 10. To this Paul replies in the course of the chapter, and particularly in ver. 7. ¶ *That we all have knowledge.* That is, on this subject; we are acquainted with the true nature of idols, and of idol worship; we *all* esteem an idol to be nothing, and cannot be in danger of being led into idolatry, or into any improper views in regard to this subject by participating of the food and feasts connected with idol worship This is the statement and argument of the Corinthians. To this Paul makes *two* answers. (1.) In a *parenthesis* in ver. 1—3, to wit, that it was not safe to rely on mere *knowledge* in such a case, since the effect of mere knowledge was often to puff men up and to make them proud, but that they ought to act rather from "charity," or love; and, (2.) That though the mass of them might have this knowledge, yet that *all* did not possess it, and they might be injured, ver. 7. Having stated this argument of the Corinthians, that all had knowledge, in ver. 1, Paul then in a parenthesis states the usual effect of knowledge, and shows that it is not a safe guide, ver. 1—3. In ver. 4, he *resumes* the statement (commenced in ver. 1) of the Corinthians, but which, in a mode quite frequent in his writings, he had broken off by his parenthesis on the subject of knowledge; and in ver. 4—6, he states the argument more at length; concedes that there was to them but one God, and that the majority of them must know that; but states in ver. 7, that *all* had not this knowledge, and that those who *had* knowledge ought to act so as not to injure those who had not. ¶ *Knowledge puffeth up.* This is the beginning of the parenthesis. It is the reply of Paul to the statement of the Corinthians, that all had knowledge. The sense is, "Admitting that you all have knowledge ; that you know what is the nature of an idol, and of idol worship ; yet mere *knowledge* in this case is not a safe

guide ; its effect *may* be to puff up, to fill with pride and self-sufficiency, and to lead you astray. *Charity*, or love, as well as knowledge, should be allowed to come in as a guide in such cases, and will be a safer guide than mere knowledge." There had been some remarkable proofs of the impropriety of relying on mere *knowledge* as a guide in religious matters among the Corinthians, and it was well for Paul to remind them of it. These pretenders to uncommon wisdom had given rise to their factions, disputes, and parties, (see chap. i. ii. iii.) ; and Paul now reminds them that it was not safe to rely on such a guide. And it is no more safe now than it was then. Mere *knowledge*, or science, when the *heart* is not right, fills with pride ; swells a man with vain self-confidence and reliance in his own powers, and very often leads him entirely astray. Knowledge combined with right feelings, with pure principles, with a heart filled with love to God and men, may be trusted : but not mere intellectual attainments ; mere abstract science ; the mere cultivation of the intellect. Unless the *heart* is cultivated *with* that, the effect of knowledge is to make a man a pedant ; and to fill him with vain ideas of his own importance; and thus to lead him into error and to sin. ¶ *But charity edifieth.* Love (ἡ ἀγάπη); so the word means; and so it would be well to translate it. Our word *charity* we now apply almost exclusively to alms-giving, or to the favourable opinion which we entertain of others when they seem to be in error or fault. The word in the Scripture means simply *love.* See Notes on chap. xiii. The sense here is, " Knowledge is not a safe guide, and should not be trusted. *Love* to each other and to God, true Christian affection, will be a safer guide than mere knowledge. Your conclusion on this question should not be formed from mere abstract *knowledge;* but you should ask what LOVE to others— to the peace, purity, happiness, and salvation of your brethren—would demand. If *love* to them would prompt to this course, and permit you

2 And if *a* any man think that he knoweth any thing, he knoweth nothing yet as he ought to know.

a Rom.11.25; Gal.6.3; 1 Tim.6 3,4.

3 But if any man love God, the same is known *b* of him.

4 As concerning therefore the

b Nah.1.7; 2 Tim.2.19.

to partake of this food, it should be done ; if not, if it would injure them, whatever mere *knowledge* would dictate, it should *not* be done." The doctrine is, that love to God and to each other is a better guide in determining what to do than mere knowledge. And it is so. It will prompt us to seek the welfare of others, and to avoid what would injure them. It will make us tender, affectionate, and kind ; and will better tell us *what* to do, and *how* to do it in the best way, than all the abstract knowledge that is conceivable. The man who is influenced by love, ever pure and ever glowing, is not in much danger of going astray, or of doing injury to the cause of God. The man who relies on his knowledge is heady, high-minded, obstinate, contentious, vexatious, perverse, opinionated ; and most of the difficulties in the church arise from such men. Love makes no difficulty, but heals and allays all : mere knowledge heals or allays none, but is often the occasion of most bitter strife and contention. Paul was wise in recommending that the question should be settled by *love;* and it would be wise if all Christians would follow his instructions.

2. And if any think, &c. The connection and the scope of this passage require us to understand this as designed to condemn that vain conceit of knowledge, or self-confidence, which would lead us to despise others, or to disregard their interests. " If any one is conceited of his knowledge, is so vain, and proud, and self-confident, that he is led to despise others, and to disregard their true interests, he has not yet learned the very first elements of true knowledge as he ought to learn them. True knowledge will make us humble, modest, and kind to others. It will not puff us up, and it will not lead us to overlook the real happiness of others." See Rom. xi. 25. *¶ Any thing.* Any matter pertaining to science, morals,

philosophy, or religion. This is a general maxim pertaining to all *pretenders* to knowledge. *¶ He knoweth nothing yet, &c.* He has not known what is most necessary to be known on the subject; nor has he known the true use and design of knowledge, which is to edify and promote the happiness of others. If a man has not *so* learned any thing as to make it contribute to the happiness of others, it is a proof that he has never learned the true design of the first elements of knowledge. Paul's design is to induce them to seek the welfare of their brethren. Knowledge, rightly applied, will promote the happiness of all. And it is true now as it was then, that if a man is a *miser* in knowledge as in wealth ; if he lives to accumulate, never to impart ; if he is filled with a vain conceit of his wisdom, and seeks not to benefit others by enlightening their ignorance, and guiding them in the way of truth, he has never learned the true use of science, any more than the man has of wealth who always hoards, never gives. It is valueless unless it is diffused, as the light of heaven would be valueless unless diffused all over the world, and the waters would be valueless if always preserved in lakes and reservoirs, and never diffused over hills and vales to refresh the earth.

3. But if any man love God. If any man is truly attached to God ; if he seeks to serve him, and to promote his glory. The sense seems to be this. " There is no true and real knowledge which is not connected with love to God. This will prompt a man also to love his brethren, and will lead him to promote their happiness. A man's course, therefore, is not to be regulated by mere knowledge, but the grand principle is love to God and love to man. Love edifies ; love promotes happiness ; love will prompt to what is right ; and love will secure the approbation of God." Thus explained, this difficult verse accords

eating of those things that are offered in sacrifice unto idols, we know that an idol *a* *is* nothing in

a Isa.41.24.

the world, and that *there is* none other *b* God but one.

5 For though there be that are

b Deut.4.39; Isa.44.8,24.

with the whole scope of the parenthesis, which is to show that a man should not be guided in his intercourse with others by mere knowledge, however great that may be; but that a safer and better principle was *love*, *charity* (*ἀγάπη*), whether exercised towards God or man. Under the guidance of this, man would be in little danger of error, Under the direction of mere *knowledge* he would never be sure of a safe guide; see chap. xiii. ¶ *The same is known of him.* The words " is known " (*ἔγνω-σται*) I suppose to be taken here in the sense of " is approved by God; is loved by him; meets with his favour," &c. In this sense the word *known* is often used in the Scriptures. Note, Matt. vii. 23. The sense is, " If any man acts under the influence of sacred charity, or love to God, and consequent love to man, he will meet with the approbation of God. He will seek his glory, and the good of his brethren; he will be likely to do right; and God will approve of his intentions and desires, and will regard him as his child. Little distinguished, therefore, as he may be for human knowledge, for that science which puffs up with vain self-confidence, yet he will have a more truly elevated rank, and will meet with the approbation and praise of God. This is of more value than mere knowledge, and this love is a far safer guide than any mere intellectual attainments." So the world would have found it to be if they had acted on it; and so Christians would always find it.

4. *As concerning therefore,* &c. The parenthesis closes with ver. 3. The apostle now proceeds to the real question in debate, and *repeats* in this verse the question, and the admission that all had knowledge. The *admission* that all had knowledge proceeds through ver. 4, 5, and 6; and in ver. 7 he gives the answer to it. In ver. 4—6 *every thing* is admitted by Paul which they asked in regard to the real

extent of their knowledge on this subject; and in ver. 7 he shows that even on the ground of this admission, the conclusion would not follow that it was right to partake of the food offered in sacrifice in the temple of an idol. ¶ *The eating of those things,* &c, Whether it is right to eat them. Here the question is varied somewhat from what it was in ver. 1, but substantially the same inquiry is stated. The question was, whether it was right for Christians to eat the meat of animals that had been slain in sacrifice to idols. ¶ *We know,* ver. 1. We Corinthians know; and Paul seems fully to admit that they had all the knowledge which they claimed, ver. 7. But his object was to show that even *admitting* that, it would not follow that it would be right to partake of that meat. It is well to bear in mind that the *object* of their statement in regard to knowledge was, to show that there could be no impropriety in partaking of the food. This argument the apostle answers in ver. 7. ¶ *That an idol is nothing.* Is not the true God; is not a proper object of worship. We are not so stupid as to suppose that the block of wood, or the carved image, or the chiseled marble is a real intelligence, and is conscious and capable of receiving worship, or benefiting its votaries. We fully admit, and know, that the whole thing is delusive; and there can be no danger that, by partaking of the food offered in sacrifice to them, we should ever be brought to a belief of the stupendous falsehood that they *are* true objects of worship, or to deny the true God. There is no doubt that the more intelligent heathen had this knowledge; and doubtless nearly all Christians possessed it, though a few who had been educated in the grosser views of heathenism might still have regarded the idol with a superstitious reverence. For whatever might have been the knowledge of statesmen and

a called gods, whether in heaven or in earth, (as there be gods many and lords many,)

a John 10.34,35.

6 But as to us *b there is but* one God, the Father, of whom *are* all things, and we in [1] him ; and one

b Mal.2.10; Eph.4.6.   1 or, for.

philosophers on the subject, it was still doubtless true that the great mass of the heathen world *did* regard the dumb idols as the proper objects of worship, and supposed that they were inhabited by invisible spirits — the gods. For purposes of state, and policy, and imposition, the lawgivers and priests of the pagan world were careful to cherish this delusion ; see ver. 7. ¶ *Is nothing.* Is delusive; is imaginary. There may have been a reference here to the name of an idol among the Hebrews. They called idols —רֵּלִילִים (*Elilim*), or in the singular אֱלִיל (*Elil*), vain, null, nothing-worth, nothingness, vanity, weakness, &c.; indicating their vanity and powerlessness ; Lev. xxvi. 1 ; 1 Chron. xvi. 26 ; Isa. ii. 8 ; x. 10 ; xix. 11, 13, 20; xxxi. 7 ; Ps. xc. 5 ; Ezek. xxx. 13 ; Hab. ii. 18 ; Zech. xi. 17, &c. ¶ *In the world.* It is nothing at all ; it has no power over the world ; no real existence anywhere. There *are* no such gods as the heathens pretend to worship. There is but *one* God ; and that fact is known to us all. The phrase " in the world " seems to be added by way of emphasis, to show the *utter* nothingness of idols ; to explain in the most emphatic manner the belief that they had no real existence. ¶ *And that there is none other God but one.* This was a great cardinal truth of religion ; see Note, Mark xii. 29 ; comp. Deut. vi. 4, 5. To keep this great truth in mind was the grand object of the Jewish economy ; and this was so plain, and important, that the Corinthians supposed that it must be admitted by all. Even though they should partake of the meat that was offered in sacrifice to idols, yet they supposed it was not possible that any of them could forget the great cardinal truth that there was but one God.

5. *That are called gods.* Gods so called. The heathens everywhere worshipped multitudes, and gave to them

the name of gods. ¶ *Whether in heaven.* Residing in heaven, as a part of the gods were supposed to do. Perhaps, there may be allusion here to the sun, moon, and stars ; but I rather suppose that reference is made to the celestial deities, or to those who were supposed to *reside* in heaven, though they were supposed occasionally to visit the earth, as Jupiter, Juno, Mercury, &c. ¶ *Or in earth.* Upon the earth ; or that reigned particularly over the earth, or sea, as Ceres, Neptune, &c. The ancient heathens worshipped some gods that were supposed to dwell in heaven ; others that were supposed to reside on earth ; and others that presided over the inferior regions, as Pluto, &c. ¶ *As there be gods many* (ὥσπερ), &c. As there are, in fact, many which are so called or regarded. It is a fact that the heathens worship many whom they esteem to be gods, or whom they regard as such. This cannot be an admission of Paul that they were truly gods, and ought to be worshipped ; but it is a declaration that they *esteemed* them to be such, or that a *large number* of imaginary beings were thus adored. The emphasis should be placed on the word *many* , and the design of the parenthesis is, to show that the number of these that were worshipped was not a few, but was immense ; and that they were *in fact* worshipped as gods, and allowed to have the influence over their minds and lives which they *would* have if they were real ; that is, that the *effect* of this popular belief was to produce just as much fear, alarm, superstition, and corruption, as though these imaginary gods had a real existence. So that though the more intelligent of the heathen put no confidence in them, yet the effect on the great mass was the same as if they had had a real existence, and exerted over them a real control. ¶ *And lords many* (κύριοι πολλοί). Those who had

Lord Jesus Christ, by whom *a* *are* all things, and we by him.

a John 1.3; Heb.1.2.

a *rule* over them ; to whom they submitted themselves ; and whose laws they obeyed. This name *lord* was often given to their idol gods. Thus among the nations of Canaan their idols was called בַּעַל (*Baal*, or *lord*), the tutelary god of the Phenicians and Syrians ; Judg. viii. 33 ; ix. 4, 46. It is used here with reference to the *idols*, and means that the laws which they were supposed to give in regard to their worship had *control* over the minds of their worshippers.

6. *But to us.* Christians. We acknowledge but one God, Whatever the heathen worship, we know that there is but one God ; and he alone has a right to rule over us. ¶ *One God, the Father.* Whom we acknowledge as the Father of all ; Author of all things ; and who sustains to all his works the relation of a father. The word " Father " here is not used as applicable to the first person of the Trinity, as distinguished from the second, but is applied to God *as* God ; not as the Father in contradistinction from the Son, but to the divine nature as such, without reference to that distinction—the Father as distinguished from his offspring, the works that owe their origin to him. This is manifest, (1.) Because the apostle does not use the correlative term " Son " when he comes to speak of the " one Lord Jesus Christ ; " and (2.) Because the scope of the passage requires it. The apostle speaks of *God*, of the divine nature, the one infinitely holy Being, as sustaining the relation of Father *to his creatures.* He produced them, He provides for them. He protects them, as a father does his children. He regards their welfare ; pities them in their sorrows ; sustains them in trial ; shows himself to be their friend. The name *Father* is thus given frequently to God, as applicable to the one God, the divine Being ; Ps. ciii. 13 ; Jer. xxxi. 9 ; Mal. i. 6 ; ii. 10 ; Matt. vi. 9 ; Luke xi. 2, &c. In other places it is applied to the first person of the Trinity as distinguished from

7 Howbeit *there is* not in every man that knowledge : for some

the second ; and in these instances the correlative *Son* is used, Luke x. 22 ; xxii. 42 ; John i. 18 ; iii. 35 ; v. 19— 23, 26, 30, 36 ; Heb. i. 5 ; 2 Pet. i. 17, &c. ¶ *Of whom* (ἐξ οὗ). From whom as a fountain and source ; by whose counsel, plan, and purpose. He is the great source of all ; and all depend on him. It was by his purpose and power that all things were formed, and *to* all he sustains the relation of a Father. The *agent* in producing all things, however, was the Son, Col. i. 16 ; Note, John i. 3. ¶ *Are all things.* These words evidently refer to the whole work of creation, as deriving their origin from God, Gen. i. 1. Every thing has thus been formed in accordance with his plan ; and all things now depend on him as their Father. ¶ *And we.* We Christians. We are what we are by him. We owe our existence to him ; and by him we have been regenerated and saved. It is owing to his counsel, purpose, agency, that we have an existence ; and owing to him that we have the hope of eternal life. The leading idea here is, probably, that to God Christians owe their hopes and happiness. ¶ *In him* (εἰς αὐτόν) ; or rather *unto* him : that is, we are formed *for* him, and should live to his glory. We have been made what we are, as Christians, that we may promote his honour and glory. ¶ *And one Lord*, &c. One Lord in contradistinction from the " *many* lords " whom the heathens worshipped. The word *Lord* here is used in the sense of *proprietor*, ruler, governor, or king ; and the idea is, that Christians acknowledge subjection to *him alone*, and not to *many* sovereigns, as the heathens did. Jesus Christ is the Ruler and Lord of his people. They acknowledge their allegiance to him as their supreme Lawgiver and King. They do not acknowledge subjection to *many* rulers, whether imaginary gods or men ; but receive their laws from him alone. The word " Lord " here does not imply of necessity any inferiority to God ; since it is a term which is frequently applied to God himself. The idea in the passage is, that from God, the Father of all, we derive our existence, and all that we have ; and that we acknowledge *immediate* and *direct* subjection to the Lord Jesus as our Lawgiver and Sovereign. From him Christians receive their laws, and to him they submit their lives. And this idea is so far from supposing *inferiority* in the Lord Jesus to God, that it rather supposes equality ; since a right to give laws to men, to rule their consciences, to direct their religious opinions and their lives, can appropriately appertain only to one who has equality with God. ¶ *By whom,* &c. (δι᾽ οὖ). By whose *agency ;* or through whom, as the agent. The word "*by*" (δι᾽) stands in contradistinction from "*of*" (ἐξ) in the former part of the verse ; and obviously means, that, though "all things" derived their existence *from* God as the fountain and author, yet it was "*by*" the agency of the Lord Jesus. This doctrine, that the Son of God was the great agent in the creation of the world, is elsewhere abundantly taught in the Scriptures ; see Note, John 1. 3. ¶ *Are all things.* The universe ; for so the phrase τὰ πάντα properly means. No words could better express the idea of the universe than these ; and the declaration is therefore explicit that the Lord Jesus created all things. Some explain this of the "new creation;" as if Paul had said that *all things* pertaining to our salvation were from him. But the objections to this interpretation are obvious. (1.) It is not the natural signification. (2.) The phrase "all things" naturally denotes the universe. (3.) The scope of the passage requires us so to understand it. Paul is not speaking of the new creature ; but he is speaking of the question whether there is more than one God, one Creator, one Ruler over the wide universe. The heathen said there was ; Christians affirmed that there was not. The scope, therefore, of the passage requires us to understand this of the vast material uni-

verse ; and the obvious declaration here is, that the Lord Jesus was the Creator of all. ¶ *And we.* We Christians (1 Pet. i. 21) ; or, we as men ; we have derived our existence "*by*" (δι᾽) or *through* him. The expression will apply either to our original creation, or to our hopes of heaven, as being *by* him ; and is equally true respecting both. Probably the idea is, that *all* that we have, as men and as Christians, our lives and our hopes, are *through* him and by his agency. ¶ *By him* (δι᾽ αὐτοῦ). By his agency. Paul had said, in respect to God the Father of all, that we were *unto* (εἰς) him ; he here says that in regard to the Lord Jesus, we are *by* (δι᾽) him, or by his agency. The sense is, " God is the author, the former of the plan ; the source of being and of hope ; and we are to live *to* him : but Jesus is the *agent* by whom all these things are made, and through whom they are conferred on us." Arians and Socinians have made use of this passage to prove that the Son was inferior to God ; and the argument is, that the *name* God is not given to Jesus, but another name implying inferiority ; and that the design of Paul was to make a *distinction* between God and the Lord Jesus. It is not the design of these Notes to examine opinions in theology ; but in reply to this argument we may observe, briefly, (1.) That those who hold to the divinity of the Lord Jesus do not deny that there is a *distinction* between him and the Father : they fully admit and maintain it, both in regard to his eternal existence (*i. e.* that there is an eternal distinction of persons in the Godhead) and in regard to his office as mediator. (2.) The term "Lord," given here, does not of necessity suppose that he is inferior to God. (3.) The *design* of the passage supposes that there was equality in some respects. God the Father and the Lord Jesus sustain relations to men that in some sense correspond to the "many gods" and the "many lords" that the heathen adored ; but they were equal in nature. (4.) The work of creation is expressly in this passage ascribed to the Lord Jesus. But the work of creation can-

with conscience of the idol unto this hour, eat *it* as a thing offered unto an idol ; and their conscience being weak is defiled.

a Rom.14.17.

8 But meat *a* commendeth us not to God : for neither if we eat, [1] are we the better ; neither if we eat not, [2] are we the worse.

1 or, *have we the more.* 2 or, *have we the less.*

---

not be performed by a creature. There can be no delegated *God*, and no delegated *omnipotence*, or delegated infinite wisdom and omnipresence. The work of creation implies divinity ; or it is impossible to prove that there *is* a God : and if the Lord Jesus made " ALL THINGS," he must be God.

7. *Howbeit.* But. In the previous verses Paul had stated the argument of the Corinthians—that they *all* knew that an idol was nothing; that they worshipped but one God; and that there could be no danger of their falling into idolatry, even should they partake of the meat offered in sacrifice to idols. Here he replies, that though this might be *generally* true, yet it was not universally ; for that some were ignorant on this subject, and supposed that an idol had a real existence, and that to partake of that meat would be to confirm them in their superstition. The *inference* therefore is, that on their account they should abstain; see ver. 11—13. ¶ There is *not*, &c. There are some who are weak and ignorant; who have still remains of heathen opinions and superstitious feelings. ¶ *That knowledge.* That there is but one God ; and that an idol is nothing. ¶ *For some with conscience of the idol.* From conscientious regard *to* the idol; believing that an idol god has a real existence; and that his favour should be sought, and his wrath be deprecated. It is not to be supposed that converted men would regard idols as the *only* God; but they might suppose that they were *intermediate* beings, good or bad angels, and that it was proper to seek their favour or avert their wrath. We are to bear in mind that the heathen were exceedingly ignorant ; and that their former notions and superstitious feelings about the gods whom their fathers worshipped, and whom they had adored, would not soon leave them, even on their conversion to Christianity. This is just one instance, like

thousands, in which former erroneous opinions, prejudices, or superstitious views may influence those who are truly converted to God, and greatly mar and disfigure the beauty and symmetry of their religious character. ¶ *Eat it as a thing*, &c. As offered to an idol who was entitled to adoration; or as having a right to their homage. They supposed that some invisible spirit was present with the idol; and that his favour should be sought, or his wrath averted by sacrifice. ¶ *And their conscience being weak.* Being unenlightened on this subject; and being too weak to withstand the temptation in such a case. Not having a conscience sufficiently clear and strong to enable them to resist the temptation ; to overcome all their former prejudices and superstitious feelings ; and to act in an independent manner, as if an idol were nothing. Or their conscience was morbidly sensitive and delicate on this subject : they might be disposed to do right, and yet not have sufficient knowledge to convince them that an idol was nothing, and that they ought not to regard it. ¶ *Is defiled.* Polluted ; contaminated. By thus countenancing idolatry he is led into sin, and contracts guilt that will give him pain when his conscience becomes more enlightened ; ver. 11, 13. From superstitious reverence of the idol, he might think that he was doing right ; but the effect would be to lead him to a conformity to idol worship that would defile his conscience, pollute his mind, and ultimately produce the deep and painful conviction of guilt. The general reply, therefore, of Paul to the first argument in favour of partaking of the meat offered in sacrifice to idols is, that *all* Christians have not full knowledge on the subject; and that to partake of that might lead them into the sin of idolatry, and corrupt and destroy their souls.

8. *But meat commendeth us not to*

9 But take heed lest by any means this [1] liberty *a* of yours become a stumbling-block to them that are weak.

1 or, *power.*   *a* Rom.14.13,20; Gal.5.13.·

10 For if any man see thee which hast knowledge sit at meat in the idol's temple, shall not the conscience of him which is weak

God. This is to be regarded as the view presented by the Corinthian Christians, or by the advocates for partaking of the meat offered in sacrifice to idols. The sense is, "Religion is of a deeper and more spiritual nature than a mere regard to circumstances like these. God looks at the heart. He regards the motives, the thoughts, the moral actions of men. The mere circumstance of eating *meat,* or abstaining from it, cannot make a man better or worse in the sight of a holy God. The acceptable worship of God is not placed in such things. It is more spiritual; more deep; more important. And *therefore,*" the inference is, "it cannot be a matter of much importance whether a man eats the meat offered in sacrifice to idols, or abstains." To this argument the apostle replies (ver. 9—13), that, although this might be true in itself, yet it might be the occasion of leading others into sin, and it would *then* become a matter of *great importance* in the sight of God, and should be in the sight of all true Christians. The word "commendeth" (πιρίστησι) means properly to introduce to the favour of any one, as a king or ruler; and here means to *recommend* to the favour of God. God does not regard this as a matter of importance. He does not make his favour *depend* on unimportant circumstances like this. ¶ *Neither if we eat.* If we partake of the meat offered to idols. ¶ *Are we the better.* Margin, *Have we the more.* Gr. Do we abound (περισσεύομεν); that is, in moral worth or excellence of character; see Note, Rev. xiv. 17. ¶ *Are we the worse.* Margin, *Have we the less.* Greek, Do we lack or want (ὑστερούμεθα); that is, in moral worth or excellence.

9. *But take heed.* This is the reply of Paul to the argument of the Corinthians in ver. 8. "Though all that you say should be admitted to be true, as it must be; though a man *is* neither morally better nor worse for partaking

of meat or abstaining from it; yet the grand principle to be observed is, so to act as not to injure your brethren. Though you may be no better or worse for eating or not eating, yet if your conduct shall injure others, and lead them into sin, *that* is a sufficient guide to determine you what to do in the case. You should abstain entirely. It is of far more importance that your brother should *not* be led into sin, than it is that you should partake of meat which you acknowledge (ver. 8) is in itself of no importance." ¶ *Lest by any means* (μή πως). You should be careful that by no conduct of yours your brother be led into sin. This is a general principle that is to regulate Christian conduct in all matters that are in themselves indifferent. ¶ *This liberty of yours.* This which you claim as a right; this power which you have, and the exercise of which is in itself lawful. The *liberty* or power (ἐξουσία) here referred to was that of partaking of the meat that was offered in sacrifice to idols; ver. 8. A man may have a *right* abstractly to do a thing, but it may not be prudent or wise to exercise it. ¶ *Become a stumbling-block.* An occasion of sin; Note, Mat. v. 29; also Note, Rom. xiv. 13. See that it be not the occasion of leading others to sin, and to abandon their Christian profession; ver. 10. ¶ *To them that are weak.* To those professing Christians who are not fully informed or instructed in regard to the true nature of idolatry, and who still may have a superstitious regard for the gods whom their fathers worshipped.

10. *For if any man.* Any Christian brother who is ignorant, or any one who might otherwise become a Christian. ¶ *Which hast knowledge.* Who are fully informed in regard to the real nature of idol worship. You will be looked up to as an example. You will be presumed to be partaking of this feast in honour of the idol. You will thus encourage him, and he will

be [1] emboldened to eat those things which are offered to idols;

11 And through thy knowledge

1 edified.

shall the weak brother perish, for whom Christ died?

12 But [a] when ye sin so against

a Mat. 25. 40, 45.

partake of it with a conscientious regard to the idol. ¶ *Sit at meat.* Sitting down to an entertainment in the temple of the idol. Feasts were often celebrated, as they are now among the heathen, in honour of idols. Those entertainments were either in the temple of the idol, or at the house of him who gave it. ¶ *Shall not the conscience of him which is weak.* Of the man who is not fully informed, or who still regards the idol with superstitious feelings; see ver. 7. ¶ *Be emboldened.* Margin, *Edified* (οἰκοδομηθήσεται). Confirmed; established. So the word *edify* is commonly used in the New Testament; Acts ix. 31. Rom. xiv. 19; Eph. iv. 12; 1 Thess. v. 11. The sense here is, "Before this he had a superstitious regard for idols. He had the remains of his former feelings and opinions. But he was not *established* in the belief that an idol was any thing; and his superstitious feelings were fast giving way to the better Christian doctrine that they were nothing. But *now*, by your example, he will be fully *confirmed* in the belief that an idol *is* to be regarded with respect and homage. He will see you in the very temple, partaking of a feast in honour of the idol; and he will infer not only that it is right, but that it is a matter of conscience with you, and will follow your example."

11. *And through thy knowledge.* Because you *knew* that an idol was nothing, and that there could be really no danger of falling into idolatry from partaking of these entertainments. You will thus be the means of deceiving and destroying him. The *argument* of the apostle here is, that if *this* was to be the result, the duty of those who *had* this knowledge was plain. ¶ *Shall the weak brother.* The uninformed and ignorant Christian. That it means a real Christian there can be no doubt. For (1.) It is the *usual* term by which Christians are designated—the endearing name of *brother;* and (2.) The scope of the passage

requires it so to be understood; see Note, Rom. xiv. 20. ¶ *Perish.* Be destroyed; ruined; lost; Note, John x. 28. So the word ἀπολεῖται properly and usually signifies. The sense is, that the *tendency* of this course would be to lead the weak brother into sin, to apostacy, and to ruin. But this does not prove that any who were truly converted should apostatize and be lost; for (1.) There may be a *tendency* to a thing, and yet that thing may never happen. It may be arrested, and the event not occur. (2.) The *warning* designed to prevent it may be effectual, and be the means of saving. A man in a canoe floating down the Niagara river may have a *tendency* to go over the falls; but he may be hailed from the shore, and the hailing may be effectual, and he may be saved. The call to him was *designed* to save him, and actually had that effect. So it may be in the warnings to Christians. (3.) The apostle does not say that any true Christian would be lost. He puts a question; and affirms that if *one* thing was done, *another might* follow. But this is not affirming that any one *would* be lost. So I might say that *if* the man *continued* to float on towards the falls of Niagara, he would be destroyed. If one thing was done, the other would be a consequence. But this would be very different from a statement that a man *had actually* gone over the falls, and been lost. (4.) It is elsewhere abundantly proved that no one who has been truly converted will apostatize and be destroyed; see Notes, John x. 28; comp. Note, Rom. viii. 29, 30. ¶ *For whom Christ died.* This is urged as an argument why we should not do any thing that would tend to destroy the souls of men. And no stronger argument could be used. The argument is, that we should not do any thing that would tend to frustrate the work of Christ, that would render the shedding of his blood vain. The *possibility* of doing this is urged; and that

the brethren, and wound their weak conscience, ye sin against Christ.

13 Wherefore, if meat make

my brother to offend, I will eat no flesh while the world standeth, lest *a* I make my brother to offend.

a chap.9.22.

bare possibility should deter us from a course of conduct that might have this tendency. It is an appeal drawn from the deep and tender love, the sufferings, and the dying groans of the Son of God. If *he* endured so much to *save* the soul, assuredly we should not pursue a course that would tend to *destroy* it. If he *denied* himself so much to *redeem*, we should not, assuredly, be so fond of self-gratification as to be unwilling to abandon any thing that would tend to *destroy*. 12. *But when ye sin so against the brethren.* This is designed further to show the evil of causing others to sin; and hence the evil which might arise from partaking of the meat offered to idols. The word *sin* here is to be taken in the sense of *injuring, offending, leading into sin.* You violate the law which requires you to love your brethren, and to seek their welfare, and thus you sin against them. Sin is properly against God; but there may be a course of injury pursued against men, or doing them injustice or wrong, and this is *sin* against them. Christians are bound to do right towards all. ¶ *And wound their weak conscience.* The word *wound* here (τύπτοντες, *smiting, beating*) is taken in the sense of *injure.* Their consciences are ill-informed. They have not the knowledge which you have. And by your conduct they are led farther into error, and believe that the idol *is* something, and is to be honoured. They are thus led into sin, and their conscience is more and more perverted, and oppressed more and more with a sense of guilt. ¶ *Ye sin against Christ.* Because (1.) Christ has commanded you to love them, and seek their good, and not to lead them into sin, and (2.) Because they are so intimately united to Christ (Notes, John xv. 1, &c.) that to offend them is to offend him; to injure the members is to injure the head; to destroy their souls is to pain his heart and to injure

his cause; Note, Mat. x. 40; comp. Luke x. 16.

13. *Wherefore.* As the conclusion of the whole matter. ¶ *If meat, &c.* Paul here proposes his own views and feelings, or tells them how he would act in order to show them how they should act in these circumstances. ¶ *Make my brother to offend.* Lead him into sin; or shall be the cause of leading him into error and guilt. It does not mean, if the eating of meat should *enrage* or *irritate* another; but if it is the occasion of his being led into transgression. How this might be done is stated in ver. 10. ¶ *I will eat no flesh, &c.* My eating meat is a matter of comparative unimportance. I can dispense with it. It is of much less importance to me than happiness, a good conscience, and salvation are to my brother. And the law of love therefore to him requires me to deny myself rather than to be the occasion of leading him into sin. This is a noble resolution; and marks a great, disinterested, and magnanimous spirit. It is a spirit that seeks the good of all; that can deny itself; that is supremely anxious for the glory of God and the salvation of man, and that can make personal comfort and gratification subservient to the good of others. It was the principle on which Paul always acted; and is the very spirit of the self-denying Son of God. ¶ *While the world standeth.* Greek, For ever. The phrase 'I will *never* eat meat' would express the idea. ¶ *Lest I make, &c.* Rather than lead him into sin, by my indulging in eating meat offered in sacrifice to idols.

REMARKS.

This chapter is very important, as it settles some *principles* in regard to the conduct of Christians; and shows how they should act in reference to things that are *indifferent;* or which in themselves can be considered as neither right nor wrong; and in reference to those things which may be considered in themselves as *right* and *lawful*, but whose indulgence might injure others. And from the chapter we learn,—

1st. That Christians, though they are truly converted, yet may have many erroneous views and feelings in reference to many things, ver. 6. This was true of those converted from ancient heathenism, and it is true of those who are *now* converted from heathenism, and of all young converts. Former opinions, and prejudices, and even superstitions, abide long in the mind, and cast a long and withering influence over the regions of Christian piety. The morning dawn is at first very obscure. The change from night to daybreak is at first scarcely perceptible. And so it may be in conversion. The views which a heathen entertained from his childhood could not at once be removed. The influence of corrupt opinions and feelings, which a sinner has long indulged, may *travel over* in his conversion, and may long endanger his piety and destroy his peace. Corrupt and infidel thoughts, associations of pollution, cannot be destroyed at once; and we are not to expect from a child in the Christian life, the full vigour, and the elevated principle, and the strength to resist temptation, which we expect of the man matured in the service of the Lord Jesus. This should lead us to *charity* in regard to the imperfections and failings of young converts; to a willingness to aid and counsel them; to *carefulness* not to lead them into sin; and it should lead us *not* to expect the same amount of piety, zeal, and purity in converts from degraded heathens, which we expect in Christian lands, and where converts have been trained up under all the advantages of Sabbath-schools and Bible-classes.

2d. Our opinions should be formed, and our treatment of others regulated, not by abstract *knowledge*, but by love, ver. 1. A man is usually much more likely to act *right* who is influenced by charity and love, than one who is guided by simple knowledge,

or by self-confidence. One is humble, kind, tender towards the frailties of others, sensible himself of infirmity, and is *disposed* to do right; the other may be vain, harsh, censorious, unkind, and severe. Knowledge is useful; but for the practical purposes of life, in an erring and fallen world, love is more useful; and while the one often leads astray, the other seldom errs. Whatever *knowledge* we may have, we should make it a point from which we are never to depart, that our opinions of others, and our treatment of them, should be formed under the influence of love.

3d. We should not be self-confident of our wisdom, ver. 2. Religion produces humility. Mere knowledge may fill the heart with pride and vanity. True knowledge is not inconsistent with humility; but it must be joined with a *heart* that is right. The men that have been most eminent in knowledge have also been distinguished for humility; but the *heart* was right; and they saw the folly of depending on mere knowledge.

4th. There is but one God, ver. 4—6. This great truth lies at the foundation of all true religion; and yet is so simple that it may be known by all Christians, however humble, and is to be *presumed* to be known by all. But though simple, it is a great and glorious truth. To keep this before the minds of men was one great purpose of all God's revelations; and to communicate it to men is now the grand object of all missionary enterprises. The world is full of idols and idolaters; but the knowledge of this simple truth would change the moral aspect of the entire globe. To spread this truth should be the great aim and purpose of all true Christians; and when this truth *is* spread, the idols of the heathen will fall to the dust.

5th. Christians acknowledge one and only one Lord, ver. 6. He rules over them. His laws bind them. He controls them. He has a right to them. He can dispose of them as he pleases. They are not their own; but are bound to live entirely to him, and for the promotion of his cause.

6th. It becomes Christians to exercise continual care, lest their conduct, even in things which are in themselves lawful, should be the occasion of leading others into sin, ver. 9. Christians very often pursue a course of conduct which may not be in itself unlawful, but which may lead others who have not their intelligence, or strength of principle, into error. One man may be safe where another man is in danger. One man may be able to resist temptations which would entirely overcome another. A course of life may, perhaps, be safe for a man of years and of mature judgment, which would be ruinous to a young man. And the grand principle here should be, not to do that, even though it may be lawful itself, which would be the occasion of leading others into sin.

7th. We see here the importance and the power of example, ver. 10, 11. Nothing is of more value than a correct Christian example. And this applies particularly to those who are in the more elevated ranks of life, who occupy stations of importance, who are at the head of families, colleges, and schools. The ignorant will be likely to follow the example of the learned; the poor of the rich; those in humble life will imitate the manners of the great. Even in things, therefore, which may not be in themselves unlawful in these circumstances, they should set an example of self-denial, of plainness, of abstinence, for the sake of those beneath them. They should so live that it would be safe and right for all to imitate their example. Christ, though he was rich, yet so lived that *all* may safely imitate him; though he was honoured of God, and exalted to the highest office as the Redeemer of the world, yet he lived so that all in every rank may follow him; though he had all power, and was worshipped by angels, yet so lived that he might teach the most humble and lowly *how* to live; and so lived that it is safe and proper for all to live as he did. So should every monarch, and prince, and rich man; every noble, and every learned man; every man of honour and office; every master of a family, and every

man of age and wisdom, live that all others may learn of them *how* to live, and that they may safely walk in their footsteps.

8th. We have here a noble instance of the principles on which Paul was willing to act, ver. 13. He was willing to deny himself of any gratification, if his conduct was likely to be the occasion of leading others into sin. Even from that which was in itself lawful he would abstain for ever, if by indulgence he would be the occasion of another's falling into transgression. But how rare is this virtue! How seldom is it practised! How few Christians and Christian ministers are there who deny themselves any gratification in things in themselves right, lest they should induce others to sin! And yet this is the grand principle of Christianity; and this should influence and guide all the professed friends and followers of Christ. This *principle* might be applied to many things in which many Christians now freely indulge, and *if* applied, would produce great and important changes in society. (1.) Entertainments and feasts which, perhaps, you may be able to *afford* (that is, *afford* in the supposition that what you have is *yours*, and not the Lord's), may lead many of those who cannot afford it to imitate you, and to involve themselves in debt, in extravagance, in ruin. (2.) You might *possibly* be safe at a festival, at a public dinner, or in a large party; but your *example* would encourage others where they would *not* be safe; and yet, how could you reply should they say that you were there, and that they were encouraged by you? (3.) On the supposition that the use of wine and other fermented liquors may be in themselves lawful, and that you *might* be safe in using them, yet *others* may be led by your example to an improper use of them, or contract a taste for stimulating drinks that may end in their ruin. Would it be right for *you* to continue the use of wine in such circumstances? Would Paul have done it? Would he not have adopted the noble principle in this chapter, that he would not touch it while the

CHAPTER IX.

A M I not an apostle? am I not free? have I not *a* seen Jesus

Christ our Lord? are not ye my work *b* in the Lord?

a Acts 9.3,17.   *b* chap.4.15.

world stands, if it led him to sin? (4.) You might be safe in a party of amusement, in the circle of the gay, and in scenes of merriment and mirth. I say you *might* be, though the supposition is scarcely *possible* that Christian piety is ever safe in such scenes, and though it is certain that Paul or the Saviour would not have been found there. But how will it be for the young, and for those of less strength of Christian virtue? Will they be safe there? Will they be able to guard against these allurements as you could? Will they not be led into the love of gayety, vanity, and folly? And what would Paul have done in such cases? What would Jesus Christ have done? What should Christians now do? This single principle, if fairly applied, would go far to change the aspect of the Christian world. If all Christians had Paul's delicate sensibilities, and Paul's' strength of Christian virtue, and Paul's willingness to deny himself to benefit others, the aspect of the Christian world would soon change. How many practices now freely indulged in would be abandoned! And how soon would every Christian be seen to set such an example that all others could safely follow it !

CHAPTER IX.

THE apostle had in chap. viii. 13, mentioned his willingness to deny himself if he might be the means of benefitting others. On this principle he had acted ; and on this he purposed to act. The mention of this principle of action seems to have led him to a further illustration of it in his own case, and *in* the illustration to meet an objection that had been urged against him at Corinth ; and the scope of this chapter seems to have been not only to give an *illustration* of this principle (see chap. ix. 27), but to show that this principle on which he acted would account for his conduct when with them, and would meet all the objections which had been made against his apostleship.

These objections seem to have been, (1.) That he had not seen Jesus Christ ; and therefore *could* not be an apostle ; ver. 1. (2.) That he did not live like the other apostles, that he was unmarried, was a solitary man, and a wanderer, and was unlike the other apostles in his mode of life, not indulging as apostles *might* do in the ordinary comforts of life ; ver. 4, 5. (3.) That he and Barnabas were compelled to labour for their support, and were *conscious*, therefore, that they had no pretensions to the apostolic office ; ver. 6. And (4.) That the fact that he was unsupplied ; that he did not apply to Christians for his maintenance ; that he did not urge this as a *right*, showed that he was conscious that he had no claims to the apostolic character and rank.

To all this he replies in this chapter, and the main drift and design of his reply is, to show that he acted on the principle suggested in chap. viii. 13, that of denying himself ; and consequently, that though he had a *right* to maintenance, yet that the fact that he did not *urge* that right was no proof that he was not sent from God, but was rather a proof of his being actuated by the high and holy principles which *ought* to influence those who were called to this office. In urging this reply, he shows,—

(1.) That he *had* seen Jesus Christ, and had this qualification for the office of an apostle ; ver. 1.

(2.) That he had the power like others to partake of the common enjoyments of life, and that his *not* doing it was no proof that he was not an apostle ; ver. 4.

(3.) That he was not prohibited from entering the domestic relations as others had done, but had the right to enjoy the same privileges if he chose; and that his *not* doing it was no proof that he was not an apostle, but was an instance of his denying himself for the good of others ; ver. 5.

(4.) That he was not under a *necessity* of labouring with his own hands, but that he might have required support as others did ; that his labouring was only another instance of his readiness to deny himself to promote the welfare of others ; ver. 6.

This sentiment he illustrates through the remainder of the chapter by showing that he had a *right* to support in the work of the apostleship, and that his not insisting on it was an instance of his being willing to deny himself that he might do good to others ; that he did not *urge* this right because to do that might injure the cause (ver. 12, 15) ; and that whether he received support or not, he was bound to preach the gospel. In this he shows (*a*) (ver. 7—10, 13) That *God* gave him the *right* to support if he chose to exercise it ; (*b*) That it was *equitable* that he should be supported (ver. 11) ; (*c*) That the Lord had ordained this as a general law, that they which preached the gospel should live by it (ver. 14) ; (*d*) That he had not chosen to avail himself of it because it might do injury (ver. 12, 15) ; (*e*) That necessity was laid upon him at all events to preach the gospel (ver. 16) ; (*f*) That if he did this without an earthly reward, he would be rewarded in heaven in a distinguished manner (ver. 17, 18) ; (*g*) That he had made it the grand principle of his life, not to make money, but to save souls, and that he had sought this by a course of continued self-denial (ver. 19—22) ; (*h*) That all this was done for the sake of the gospel (ver. 23) ; and (*i*) That he had a grand and glorious object in view, which required him, after the manner of the Athletae, to keep his body under, to practise self-denial, to be temperate, to forego many comforts of which he might otherwise have partaken, and that the grandeur and glory of this object was enough to justify all his self denial, and to make all his sacrifices pleasant ; ver. 24—27.

Thus the whole chapter is an *incidental* discussion of the subject of his apostleship, in *illustration* of the sentiment advanced in chap. viii. 13, that he was willing to practise self-denial for the good of others ; and is one of the most elevated, heavenly, and beautiful discussions in the New Testament, and contains one of the most ennobling descriptions of the virtue of self-denial, and of the principles which should actuate the Christian ministry, any where to be found. All classic writings would be searched in vain, and all records of profane history, for an instance of such pure and elevated principle as is presented in this chapter.

1. *Am I not an apostle?* This was the point to be settled ; and it is probable that some at Corinth had denied that he *could* be an apostle, since it was requisite, in order to that, to have seen the Lord Jesus ; and since it was supposed that Paul had *not* been a witness of his life, doctrines, and death. ¶ *Am I not free?* Am I not a free man ; have I not the liberty which all Christians possess, and especially which all the apostles possess? The *liberty* referred to here is doubtless the privilege or right of abstaining from labour ; of enjoying as others did the domestic relations of life ; and of a support as a public minister and apostle. Probably some had objected to his claims of apostleship that he had not used this right, and that ho was conscious that he had no claim to it. By this mode of interrogation, he strongly *implies* that he *was* a freeman, and that he had this right. ¶ *Have I not seen Jesus Christ our Lord?* Here it is implied, and seems to be admitted by Paul, that in order to be an apostle it was necessary to have seen the Saviour. This is often declared expressly ; see Note on Acts i. 21, 22. The *reason* of this was, that the apostles were appointed to be WITNESSES of the life, doctrines, death, and resurrection of the Lord Jesus, and that in their *being witnesses* consisted the PECULIARITY of the apostolic office. That this was the case is abundantly manifest from Mat. xxviii. 18, 19 ; Luke xxiv. 48 Acts i. 21, 22 ; ii. 32 ; x. 39—41. Hence it was essential, in order that any one should be such a witness, and an apostle, that he should have *seen* the Lord Jesus. In the case of Paul, therefore, who was called to this office *after* the death and resurrection of the

2 If I be not an apostle unto others, yet doubtless I am to you ; for the seal of mine apostleship are ye in the Lord.

Saviour, and who had not therefore had an opportunity of seeing and hearing him when living, this was provided for by the fact that the Lord Jesus showed himself to him *after* his death and ascension, in order that he might have this qualification for the apostolic office, Acts ix. 3—5, 17. To the fact of his having been thus in a miraculous manner *qualified* for the apostolic office, Paul frequently appeals, and always with the same view that it was *necessary* to have *seen* the Lord Jesus to qualify one for this office, Acts xxii. 14, 15 ; xxvi. 16 ; 1 Cor. xv. 8. It follows from this, therefore, that no one was an *apostle* in the strict and proper sense who had not *seen* the Lord Jesus. And it follows, also, that the apostles could have no successors in that which constituted the PECULIARITY of their office ; and that the office must have commenced and ended with them. ¶ *Are not ye my work in the Lord?* Have you not been converted by my labours, or under my ministry ; and are you not a proof that the Lord, when I have been *claiming* to be an apostle, has owned me *as an apostle*, and blessed me in this work ? God would not give his sanction to an impostor, and a false pretender ; and as Paul had laboured there *as* an apostle, this was an argument that he had been truly commissioned of God. A minister *may* appeal to the blessing of God on his labours in proof that he is sent of Him. And one of the best of all arguments that a man is sent from God exists where multitudes of souls are converted from sin, and turned to holiness, by his labours. What better credentials than this can a man need that he is in the employ of God ? What more consoling to his own mind ? What more satisfactory to the world?

2. *If I be not an apostle unto others.* "If I have not given evidence to others of my apostolic mission ; of my being sent by the Lord Jesus, yet I have to you. Assuredly you, among whom I have laboured so long and so successfully, should not doubt that I am sent

from the Lord. You have been well acquainted with me ; you have witnessed my endowments, you have seen my success, and you have had abundant evidence that I have been sent on this great work. It is therefore strange in you to doubt my apostolic commission ; and it is unkind in you so to construe my declining to accept your contributions and aid for my support, as if I were conscious that I was not entitled to that." ¶ *For the seal of mine apostleship.* Your conversion is the demonstration that I am an apostle. Paul uses strong language. He does not mean to say that their conversion furnished *some* evidence that he was an apostle ; but that it was absolute proof, and irrefragable demonstration, that he was an apostle. A *seal* is that which is affixed to a deed, or other instrument, to make it firm, secure, and indisputable. It is the proof or demonstration of the validity of the conveyance, or of the writing ; Notes, John iii. 33 ; vi. 27. The sense here is, therefore, that the conversion of the Corinthians was a certain demonstration that he was an apostle, and should be so regarded by them, and treated by them. It was such a proof, (1.) Because Paul *claimed* to be an apostle while among them, and God blessed and owned this claim ; (2.) Their conversion could not have been accomplished by man. It was the work of God. It was the evidence then which God gave to Paul and to them, that he was with him, and had sent him. (3.) They knew him, had seen him, heard him, were acquainted with his doctrines and manner of life, and could bear testimony to what he was, and what he taught. We may remark, that the conversion of sinners is the best evidence to a minister that he is sent of God. The divine blessing on his labours should cheer his heart, and lead him to believe that God has sent and that he approves him. And every minister should so live and labour, should so deny himself, that he may be able *to appeal* to the people among

3 Mine answer to them that do examine me is this;

4 Have we not power to eat and to drink?

5 Have we not power to lead about a sister, a ¹ wife, as well as other apostles, and *as* the brethren of the Lord, and Cephas?

1 or, *woman.*

---

whom he labours that he is a minister of the Lord Jesus.

3. *Mine answer.* Gr. 'H ἐμὴ ἀπολο-γία. My *apology;* my defence. The same word occurs in Acts ʼxxii. 1; xxv. 16; 2 Cor. vii. 11; Phil. i. 7, 17; 2 Tim. iv. 16; 1 Pet. iii. 15; see Note, Acts xxii. 1. Here it means his answer, or defence against those who sat in judgment on his claims to be an apostle. ¶ *To them that do examine me.* To those who *inquire* of me; or who *censure* and condemn me as not having any claims to the apostolic office. The word used here (ἀνακρίνω) is properly a *forensic* term, and is usually applied to judges in courts; to those who sit in judgment, and investigate and decide in litigated cases brought before them; Luke xxiii. 14; Acts iv. 9; xii. 19; xxiv. 8. The apostle here may possibly allude to the *arrogance* and pride of those who presumed to sit as judges on *his* qualification for the apostolic office. It is not meant that this answer *had* been given by Paul before this, but that this was the defence which he had to offer. ¶ *Is this.* This which follows; the statements which are made in the following verses. In those statements (ver. 4, 5, 6, &c.) he seems to have designed to take up their objections to his apostolic claims one by one, and to show that they were of no force.

4. *Have we not power* (ἐξουσίαν). Have we not the *right.* The word *power* here is evidently used in the sense of *right* (comp. John i. 12, *margin);* and the apostle means to say that though they had not exercised this *right* by *demanding* a maintenance, yet it was not because they were conscious that they had no such right, but because they chose to forego it for wise and important purposes. ¶ *To eat and to drink.* To be maintained at the expense of those among whom we labour. Have we not a right to demand that they shall yield us a

proper support? By the interrogative form of the statement, Paul intends more strongly to *affirm* that they *had* such a right. The interrogative mode is often adopted to express the strongest affirmation. The *objection* here urged seems to have been this, "You, Paul and Barnabas, labour with your own hands. Acts xviii. 3. Other religious teachers lay claim to maintenance, and are supported without personal labour. This is the case with pagan and Jewish priests, and with Christian teachers among us. You must be *conscious,* therefore, that you are not apostles, and that you have no claim or right to support." To this the *answer* of Paul is, "We admit that we labour with our own hands. But your inference does not follow. It is not because we have not a *right* to such support, and it is not because we are *conscious* that we have no such claim, but it is for a higher purpose. It is because it will do good if we should not urge this right, and enforce this claim." That they *had* such a right, Paul proves at length in the subsequent part of the chapter.

5. *Have we not power?* Have we not a right? The objection here seems to have been, that Paul and Barnabas were unmarried, or at least that they travelled without wives. The objectors urged that others had wives, and that they took them with them, and expected provision to be made for them as well as for themselves. They therefore showed that they felt that they had a *claim* to support for their families, and that they were conscious that they were sent of God. But Paul and Barnabas had no families. And the objectors inferred that they were *conscious* that they had no claim to the apostleship, and no right to support. To this Paul replies as before, that they had a *right* to do as others did, but they chose *not* to do it for other rea-

sons than that they were conscious that they *had* no such right. ¶ *To lead about.* To have in attendance with us; to conduct from place to place; and to have them maintained at the expense of the churches amongst which we labour. ¶ *A sister, a wife.* Marg. "or *woman.*" This phrase has much perplexed commentators. But the simple meaning seems to be, "A wife who should be a Christian, and regarded as sustaining the relation of a Christian sister." Probably Paul meant to advert to the fact that the wives of the apostles *were* and *should be* Christians; and that it was a matter of course, that if an apostle led about a wife she would be a Christian; or that he would marry no other; comp. 1 Cor. iii. 11. ¶ *As well as other apostles.* It is evident from this that the apostles generally were married. The phrase used here is (οἱ λοιποὶ ἀπόστολοι (*the remaining apostles,* or the other apostles). And if *they* were married, it is right and proper for ministers to marry now, whatever the papist may say to the contrary. It is safer to follow the example of the apostles than the opinions of the papal church. The *reasons* why the apostles had wives with them on their journeys may have been various. They may have been either to give instruction and counsel to those of their own sex to whom the apostles could not have access, or to minister to the wants of their husbands as they travelled. It is to be remembered that they travelled among heathens; they had no acquaintance and no friends there; they therefore took with them their female friends and wives to minister to them, and sustain them in sickness, trial, &c. Paul says that he and Barnabas had a *right* to do this; but they had not used this right because they chose rather to make the gospel without charge (ver. 18), and that thus they judged they could do more good. It follows from this, (1.) That it is right for ministers to marry, and that the papal doctrine of the celibacy of the clergy is contrary to apostolic example. (2.) It is *right* for missionaries to marry, and to take their wives with them to heathen

lands. The apostles were missionaries, and spent their lives in heathen nations as missionaries do now, and there *may be* as good reasons for missionaries marrying now as there were then. (3.) Yet there are men, like Paul, who can do more good without being married. There *are* circumstances, like his, where it is not advisable that they should marry, and there can be no doubt that Paul regarded the unmarried state for a missionary as preferable and advisable. Probably the same is to be said of most missionaries at the present day, that they could do more good if unmarried, than they can if burdened with the cares of families. ¶ *And as the brethren of the Lord.* The brothers of the Lord Jesus,—James and Joses, and Simon and Judas, Mat. xiii. 55. It seems from this, that although at first they did not believe in him (John vii. 5), and had regarded him as disgraced (Mark iii. 21), yet that they had subsequently become converted, and were employed as ministers and evangelists. It is evident also from this statement that they were married, and were attended with their wives in their travels. ¶ *And Cephas.* Peter; Note, John i. 42. This proves, (1.) as well as the declaration in Mat. viii. 14, that Peter *had been* married. (2.) That he had a wife after he became an apostle, and while engaged in the work of the ministry. (3.) That his wife accompanied him in his travels. (4.) That it is right and proper for ministers and missionaries to be married now. Is it not strange that the *pretended* successor of Peter, the pope of Rome, should forbid marriage when Peter himself was married? Is it not a proof how little the papacy regards the Bible, and the example and authority of those from whom it pretends to derive its power? And is it not strange that this doctrine of the celibacy of the clergy, which has been the source of abomination, impurity, and licentiousness every where, should have been sustained and countenanced at all by the Christian world? And is it not strange that this, with all the other corrupt doctrines of the papacy,

6 Or I only and Barnabas, have not we ^a power to forbear working?

a 2 Thess.3.8,9.

should be attempted to be imposed on the enlightened people of the United States, or of Great Britain, as a part of the religion of Christ ?

6. *Or I only and Barnabas.* Paul and Barnabas had wrought, together as tent-makers at Corinth; Acts xviii. 3. From this fact it had been inferred that they *knew* that they had no claim to a support. ¶ *Power to forbear working.* To abstain from labour, and to receive support as others do. The question implies a strong affirmation that they *had* such power. The sense is, ' Why should *I* and Barnabas be regarded as having no right to support? Have we been less faithful than others? Have we done less? Have we given fewer evidences that we are sent by the Lord, or that God approves us in our work? Have we been less successful? Why then should *we* be singled out; and why should it be supposed that *we* are obliged to labour for our support? *Is there no other conceivable reason* why we should support ourselves than a consciousness that we have no right to support from the people with whom we labour ? " It is evident from ver. 12, that Barnabas as well as Paul relinquished his right to a support, and laboured to maintain himself. And it is manifest from the whole passage, that there was some peculiar " spleen " (*Doddridge*) against these two ministers of the gospel. What it was we know not. It might have arisen from the enmity and opposition of Judaizing teachers, who were offended at their zeal and success among the Gentiles, and who could find no other cause of complaint against them than that they chose to support themselves, and not live in idleness, or to tax the church for their support. That must have been a bad cause which was sustained by such an argument.

7. *Who goeth a warfare, &c.* Paul now proceeds to illustrate the RIGHT which he knew ministers had to a sup-

7 Who goeth a warfare ^b any time at his own charges? who planteth ^c a vineyard, and eateth

b 1 Tim.1.18.　　*c* Deut.20.6; Pr.27.18.

port (ver. 7—14), and then to show the REASON why he had not availed himself of that right ; ver. 15—23. The *right* he illustrates from the nature of the case (ver. 7. 11); from the authority of Scripture (ver. 8—10); from the example of the priests under the Jewish law (ver. 13); and from the authority of Jesus Christ; ver. 14. In this verse (7th) the right is enforced by the nature of the case, and by three illustrations. The first is, the right of a soldier or warrior to his wages. The Christian ministry is compared to a warfare, and the Christian minister to a soldier; comp. 1 Tim. i. 18. The soldier had a right to receive pay from him who employed him. He did not go at his own expense. This was a matter of common equity; and on this principle all acted who enlisted as soldiers. So Paul says it is but equitable also that the soldier of the Lord Jesus should be sustained, and should not be required to support himself. And why, we may ask, should he be, any more than the man who devotes his strength, and time, and talents to the defence of his country? The work of the ministry is as arduous, and as self-denying, and perhaps as dangerous, as the work of a soldier , and common justice, therefore, demands that he who devotes his youth, and health, and life to it, for the benefit of others should have a competent support. Why should he not receive a competent support who seeks to *save* men, as well as he who lives to *destroy* them? Why not he who endeavours to recover them to God, and make them pure and happy, as well as he who lives to destroy life, and pour out human blood, and to fill the air with the shrieks of new-made widows and orphans? Or why not he who seeks, though in another mode, to defend the great interests of his country, and to maintain the interests of justice, truth, and mercy, for the benefit of mankind, as well as he

not of the fruit thereof? or who feedeth *a* a flock, and eateth not of the milk of the flock?

a 1 Pet.5.2.

who is willing in the tented field to spend his time, or exhaust his health and life in protecting the rights of the nation? ¶ *At his own charges.* His own expense. On the meaning of the word "charges" (ὀψωνίοις) see Note, Luke iii. 14; comp. Rom. vi. 23; 2 Cor. xi. 8. The word does not occur elsewhere in the New Testament. ¶ *Who planteth a vineyard,* &c. This is the *second* illustration from the nature of the case, to show that ministers of the gospel have a right to support. The argument is this: 'It is reasonable that those who labour should have a fair compensation. A man who plants a vineyard does not expect to labour for nothing; he expects support from that labour, and looks for it *from* the vineyard. The vineyard owes its beauty, growth, and productiveness to him. It is reasonable, therefore, that *from* that vineyard he should receive a support, as a compensation for his toil. So *we* labour for your welfare. You derive advantage from our toil. We spend our time, and strength, and talent for your benefit; and it is reasonable that we should be supported while we thus labour for your good." The church of God is often compared to a *vineyard;* and this adds to the beauty of this illustration; see Isa. v. 1—4; Notes, Luke xx. 9—16. ¶ *Who feedeth a flock,* &c. This is the *third* illustration drawn from the nature of the case, to show that ministers have a right to support. The word "feedeth" (ποιμαίνει) denotes not only to *feed,* but to guard, protect, defend, as a shepherd does his flock; see Notes, John xxi. 15—17. "The wages of the shepherds in the East do not consist of ready money, but in a part of the milk of the flocks which they tend. Thus Spon says of the shepherds in modern Greece, "These shepherds are poor Albanians, who feed the cattle, and live in huts built of rushes: they have a tenth part of the milk and of the lambs which is

8 Say **I** these things as a man? or saith not the law the same also?

their whole wages: the cattle belong to the Turks." The shepherds in Ethiopia, also, according to Alvarez, have no pay except the milk and butter which they obtain from the cows, and on which they and their families subsist."—*Rosenmüller.* The church is often compared to a flock; see Note, John x. 1, &c. The argument here is this: "A shepherd spends his days and nights in guarding his folds. He leads his flock to green pastures, he conducts them to still waters (comp. Ps. xxiii. 2); he defends them from enemies; he guards the young, the sick, the feeble, &c. He spends his time in protecting it and providing for it. He expects support, when in the wilderness or in the pastures, mainly from the milk which the flock should furnish. He labours for their comfort; and it is proper that he should derive a maintenance from them, and he has a right to it. So the minister of the gospel watches for the good of souls. He devotes his time, strength, learning, talents, to their welfare. He instructs, guides, directs, defends; he endeavours to guard them against their spiritual enemies, and to lead them in the path of comfort and peace. He lives to instruct the ignorant; to warn and secure those who are in danger; to guide the perplexed; to reclaim the wandering; to comfort the afflicted; to bind up the broken in heart; to attend on the sick; to be an example and an instructor to the young; and to be a counsellor and a pattern to all. As he labours for their good, it is no more than equal and right that they should minister to his temporal wants, and compensate him for his efforts to promote their happiness and salvation. And can any man say that this is NOT right and just?

8. *Say I these things as a man?* Do I speak this on my own authority, or without the sanction of God? Is not this, which appears to be so rea-

9 For it is written *a* in the law of Moses, Thou shalt not muzzle the mouth of the ox that tread-

a Deut.25.4; 1 Tim.5.18.

eth out the corn. Doth God take care for oxen ?

10 Or saith he *it* altogether

---

sonable and equitable, also supported by the authority of God ? ¶ *Or saith not the law the same also ?* The law of Moses, to which the *Jewish* part of the church at Corinth—which probably had mainly urged these objections —professed to bow with deference. Paul was accustomed, especially in arguing with the Jews, to derive his proofs from the Old Testament. In the previous verse he had shown that it was *equitable* that ministers of the gospel should be supported. In this and the following verses he shows that the same *principle* was recognised and acted on under the Jewish dispensation. He does not mean to say, by this example of the ox treading out the corn, that the law as given by Moses referred to the Christian ministry; but that the *principle* there was settled that the labourer should have a support, and that a suitable provision should not be withheld even from an ox ; and if God so regarded the welfare of a brute when labouring, it was much more reasonable to suppose that he would require a suitable provision to be made for the ministers of religion.

9. *For it is written ;* Deut. xxv. 4. ¶ *In the law of Moses ;* see Note, Luke xxiv. 44. ¶ *Thou shalt not muzzle the mouth,* &c. To muzzle means, " to bind the mouth ; to fasten the mouth to prevent eating or biting." — *Webster.* This was done either by passing straps around the mouth, or by placing, as is now sometimes done, a small *basket* over the mouth, fastened by straps to the horns of the animal, so as to prevent its eating, but not to impede its breathing freely. This was an instance of the humanity of the laws of Moses. The idea is, that the ox should not be prevented from eating when it was in the midst of food ; and that as it laboured for its owner, it was *entitled* to support; and there was a propriety that it should be permitted to partake of the grain which it was threshing.

¶ *That treadeth,* &c. This was one of the common modes of threshing in the east, as it is with us; see Note and illustration on Mat. iii. 12. ¶ *The corn.* The *grain,* of any kind ; wheat, rye, barley, &c. Maize, to which we apply the word *corn,* was then unknown ; see Note, Mat. xii. 1. ¶ *Doth God take care for oxen?* Doth God take care for oxen ONLY ? Or is not this rather *a principle* which shows God's care for *all* that labour, and the humanity and equity of his laws? And if he is so solicitous about the welfare of brutes as to frame an express law in their behalf, is it not to be presumed that the same *principle* of humanity and equity will run through all his dealings and requirements ? The apostle does not mean to deny that God does take care for oxen, for the very law was proof that he did ; but he means to ask whether it is to be supposed that God would regard the comfort of oxen and not of men also? whether we are not to suppose that the same principle would apply also to those who labour in the service of God? He uses this passage, therefore, not as originally having reference to men, or to ministers of the gospel, which cannot be ; but as establishing a general *principle* in regard to the equity and humanity of the divine laws; and as thus showing that the *spirit* of the law of God would lead to the conclusion that God intended that the labourer everywhere should have a competent support.

10. *Or saith he it altogether for our sakes ?* The word "altogether" (πάντως) cannot mean that this was the *sole* and *only* design of the law, to teach that ministers of the gospel were entitled to support; for, (1.) This would be directly contrary to the law itself, which had *some* direct and undoubted reference to oxen; (2.) The scope of the argument here does not require this interpretation, since the whole object will be met by

for our sakes? For our sakes, no doubt, *this* is written; that he *a* that ploweth should plow in hope; and that he that thresheth

in hope should be partaker of his hope?

11 If *b* we have sown unto you spiritual things, *is it* a great

a 2 Tim.2 6.

b Rom. 15.27.

supposing that this settled a *principle* of humanity and equity in the divine law, according to which it was *proper* that ministers should have a support; and, (3.) The word "altogether" (πάντως) does not of necessity require this interpretation. It may be rendered *chiefly, mainly, principally*, or *doubtless;* Luke iv. 23, "Ye will *surely* (πάντως, certainly, surely, doubtless) say unto me this proverb," &c.; Acts xviii. 21, "I must *by all means* (πάντως, certainly, surely) keep this feast; Acts xxi. 22, "The multitude *must needs* (πάντως, will certainly, surely, inevitably) come together," &c.; Acts xxviii. 4, "*No doubt* (πάντως) this man is a murderer," &c. The word here, therefore, means that the *principle* stated in the law about the oxen was so broad and humane, that it might *certainly, surely, particularly* be regarded as applicable to the case under consideration. An important and material argument might be drawn from it; an argument from the less to the greater. The precept enjoined justice, equity, humanity; and that was *more* applicable to the case of the ministers of the gospel than to the case of oxen. ¶ *For our sakes*, &c. To show that the laws and requirements of God are humane, kind, and equitable: not that Moses had Paul or any other minister in his eye, but the *principle* was one that applied particularly to this case. ¶ *That he that ploweth*, &c. The Greek in this place would be more literally and more properly rendered, "For (ὅτι) he that ploweth ought (ὀφείλει) to plow in hope;" *i. e.* in hope of reaping a harvest, or of obtaining success in his labours: and the sense is, "The man who cultivates the earth, in order that he may be excited to industry and diligence, *ought* to have a reasonable prospect that he shall himself be permitted to enjoy

the fruit of his labours. This *is* the case with those who *do* plow: and if this should be the case with those who cultivate the earth, it is *as* certainly reasonable that those who labour in God's husbandry, and who devote their strength to his service, should be encouraged with a reasonable prospect of success and support." ¶ *And that he that thresheth*, &c. This sentence, in the Greek, is very elliptical and obscure; but the sense is, evidently, "He that thresheth *ought* to partake of his hope;" *i. e.* of the fruits of his hope, or of the result of his labour. It is fair and right that he should enjoy the fruits of his toil. So in God's husbandry; it is right and proper that they who toil for the advancement of his cause should be supported and rewarded." The same sentiment is expressed in 2 Tim. ii. 6, "The husbandman that laboureth must be first partaker of the fruits."

11. *If we have sown unto you spiritual things.* If we have been the means of imparting to you the gospel, and bestowing upon you its high hopes and privileges; see Note, Rom. xv. 27. The figure of *sowing*, to denote the preaching of the gospel, is not unfrequently employed in the Scriptures; see John iv. 37, and the parable of the sower, Mat. xiii. 3, &c. ¶ Is it *a great thing*, &c.; Note, Rom. xv. 27. Is it to be regarded as unequal, unjust, or burdensome? Is it to be supposed that we are receiving that for which we have not rendered a valuable consideration? The sense is, "We impart blessings of more value than we receive. We receive a supply of our temporal wants. We impart to you, under the divine blessing, the gospel, with all its hopes and consolations. We make you acquainted with God; with the plan of salvation; with the hope of heaven. We instruct your children; we guide you

thing if we shall reap your carnal things?

12 If others be partakers of *this* power over you, *are* not we

in the path of comfort and peace; we raise you from the degradations of idolatry and of sin; and we open before you the hope of the resurrection of the just, and of all the bliss of heaven: and to do this, we give ourselves to toil and peril by land and by sea. And can it be made a matter of question whether all these high and exalted hopes are of as much value to dying man as the small amount which shall be needful to minister to the wants of those who are the means of imparting these blessings?" Paul says this, therefore, from the reasonableness of the case. The propriety of support *might* be further urged, (1.) Because without it the ministry would be comparatively useless. Ministers, like physicians, lawyers, and farmers, should be allowed to attend mainly to the great business of their lives, and to their appropriate work. No physician, no farmer, no mechanic, could accomplish much, if his attention was constantly turned off from his appropriate business to engage in something else. And how can the minister of the gospel, if his time is nearly all taken up in labouring to provide for the wants of his family? (2.) The great mass of ministers spend their early days, and many of them all their property, in preparing to preach the gospel to others. And as the mechanic who has spent his early years in learning a trade, and the physician and lawyer in preparing for their profession, receive support *in* that calling, why should not the minister of the gospel? (3.) Men in other things cheerfully *pay* those who labour for them. They compensate the schoolmaster, the physician, the lawyer, the merchant, the mechanic; and they do it cheerfully, because they suppose they receive a valuable consideration for their money. But is it not so with regard to ministers of the gospel? Is not a man's family as *certainly* benefited by the labours of a faithful clergyman and pastor, as by the skill of a physician or a lawyer, or by the service of the schoolmaster? Are not the affairs

of the soul and of eternity as important to a man's family as those of time and the welfare of the body? So the music-master and the dancing master are paid, and paid cheerfully and liberally; and yet can there be any comparison between the value of their services and those of the minister of the gospel? (4.) It might be added, that society is benefited in a *pecuniary* way by the service of a faithful minister to a far greater extent than the amount of compensation which he receives. One drunkard, reformed under his labours, may earn and save to his family and to society as much as the whole salary of the pastor. The promotion of order, peace, sobriety, industry, education, and regularity in business, and honesty in contracting and in paying debts, saves much more to the community at large than the cost of the support of the gospel. In regard to this, any man may make the comparison at his leisure, between those places where the ministry is established, and where temperance, industry, and sober habits prevail, and those places where there is *no* ministry, and where gambling, idleness, and dissipation abound. It is always a matter of *economy* to a people, in the end, to support schoolmasters and ministers as they ought to be supported. ¶ *Reap your carnal things.* Partake of those things which relate to the present life; the support of the body, *i. e.* food and raiment.

12. *If others.* Other teachers living with you. There can be no doubt that the teachers in Corinth urged this right, and received a support. ¶ *Be partakers of* this *power.* Of this right to a support and maintenance. ¶ Are *not we rather.* We the apostles; we who have laboured for your conversion; who have founded your church; who have been the first, and the most laborious in instructing you, and imparting to you spiritual blessings? Have not we a better claim than they? ¶ *Nevertheless we have not used this power.* We have not urged this claim; we have chosen to forego this

rather? Nevertheless *a* we have not used this power; but suffer all things, lest we should hinder the gospel of Christ.

a 2 Cor.11.7—9; 12.14.

right, and to labour for our own support. The *reason* why they had done this, he states in the subsequent part of the chapter; see 2 Cor. xi. 7—9; xii. 14; comp. Acts xviii. 3; xx. 34, 35. ¶ *But suffer all things.* Endure all privations and hardships; we subject ourselves to poverty, want, hunger, thirst, nakedness, rather than urge a *claim* on you, and thus leave the suspicion that we are actuated by mercenary motives. The word used here (στέγομεν *suffer*) means properly *to cover*, to keep off, as rain, &c., and then to *contain*, to *sustain, tolerate, endure.* Here it means to bear, or endure all hardships; comp. Notes, chap. iv. 11 —13. ¶ *Lest we should hinder the gospel of Christ.* Paul here states the reason why he had not urged a claim to support in preaching the gospel. It was not because he was not entitled to a full support, but it was that by denying himself of this right he could do good, and avoid some evil consequences which would have resulted if he had strenuously urged it. His conduct therefore in this was just one illustration of the principle on which he said (ch. viii. 13) he would always act; a readiness to deny himself of things lawful, if by that he could promote the welfare of others. The *reasons* why his urging this claim might have hindered the gospel may have been many. (1.) It might have exposed him and the ministry generally to the charge of being mercenary. (2.) It would have prevented his presenting in bold relief the fact that he was bound to preach the gospel at all events, and that he was actuated in it by a simple conviction of its truth. (3.) It might have alienated many minds who might otherwise have been led to embrace it. (4.) It would have prevented the exercise of self-denial in him, and the benefits which resulted from that self-denial, &c., ver. 17, 18, 23, 27.

13 Do ye not know, that they which minister about holy things 1 live *of the things* of the temple? and they *b* which wait

1 or, *feed.*   b Num.18.8,&c.; Deut.18.1.

13. *Do ye not know*, &c. In this verse Paul illustrates the doctrine that the ministers of religion were, entitled to a support from the fact that those who were appointed to offer sacrifice receive a maintenance in their work. ¶ *They which minister about holy things.* Probably the *Levites.* Their office was to render assistance to the priests, to keep guard around the tabernacle, and subsequently around the temple. It was also their duty to see that the temple was kept clean, and to prepare supplies for the sanctuary, such as oil, wine, incense, &c. They had the care of the revenues, and after the time of David were required to sing in the temple, and to play upon instruments. Num. iii. 1—36; iv. 1, 30, 35, 42; viii. 5—22; 1 Chron. xxiii. 3—5, 24, 27; xxiv. 20—31. ¶ *Live of the things of the temple.* Marg., *Feed; i. e.*, are supported in their work by the offerings of the people, and by the provisions which were made for the temple service; see Num. xviii. 24— 32. ¶ *And they which wait at the altar.* Probably the *priests* who were employed in offering sacrifice. ¶ *Are partakers with the altar.* That is, a part of the animal offered in sacrifice is burned as an offering to God, and a part becomes the property of the priest for his support; and thus the altar and the priest become joint participators of the sacrifice. From these offerings the priest derived their maintenance; see Num. xviii. 8—19; Deut. xviii. 1, &c. The argument of the apostle here is this: "As the ministers of religion under the Jewish dispensation were entitled to support by the authority and the law of God, that fact settles a general principle which is applicable also to the gospel, that he intends that the ministers of religion should derive their support in their work. If it was reasonable then, it is reasonable now. If God com-

at the altar are partakers with the ultar?

14 Even so hath the Lord *a*

a Luke 10.7.

manded it then, it is to be presumed that he intends to require it now.

14. *Even so.* In the same manner, and for the same reasons. ¶ *Hath the Lord ordained.* Hath the Lord appointed, commanded, *arranged* that it should be so (διέταξε). The word here means that he has made this a law, or has required it. The word " Lord " here doubtless refers to the Lord Jesus, who has sent forth his ministers to labour in the great harvest of the world. ¶ *That they which preach the gospel.* They who are sent forth by him; who devote their lives to this work; who are called and employed by him in this service. This refers, therefore, not only to the apostles, but to all who are duly called to this work, and who are his ambassadors. ¶ *Should live of the gospel.* Should be supported and maintained in this work. Paul here probably refers to the appointment of the Lord Jesus, when he sent forth his disciples to preach, Mat. x. 10; Luke x. 8; comp. Gal. vi. 6. The man may be said to " live in the gospel " who is supported while he preaches it, or who derives his maintenance *in* that work. Here we may observe, (1.) That the command is that they shall *live* (ζῆν) of the gospel. It is not that they should grow rich, or lay up treasures, or speculate in it, or become merchants, farmers, teachers, or bookmakers for a living; but it is that they should have such a maintenance as to constitute a livelihood. They should be made comfortable; not rich. They should receive so much as to keep their minds from being harassed with cares, and their families from want; not so much as to lead them to forget their dependence on God, or on the people. Probably the true rule is, that they should be able to live as the *mass* of the people among whom they .abour live; that they should be able to receive and entertain the poor, and be willing to do it; and so that the rich also may not despise them, or

ordained, that they *b* which preach the gospel should live of the gospel.

15 But I *c* have used none of

b Gal.6.6.   *c* Acts 20.33; 2 Thess.3.8.

turn away from their dwelling. (2.) This is a *command* of the Lord Jesus; and if it is a *command*, it should be obeyed as much as any other law of the Redeemer. And if this is a command, then the minister is *entitled* to a support; and then also a people are not at liberty to withhold it. Further, there are as strong reasons why they should support him, as there are why they should pay a schoolmaster, a lawyer, a physician, or a day-labourer. The minister usually toils as hard as others ; expends as much in preparing for his work ; and does *as much* good. And there is even a higher claim in this case. God has given an *express* command in this case ; he has not in the others. (3.) The salary of a minister should not be regarded as a *gift* merely, any more than the pay of a congress man, a physician, or a lawyer. He has a claim to it; and God has commanded that it should be paid. It is, moreover, a matter of stipulation and of compact, by which a people agree to compensate him for his services. And yet, is there any thing in the shape of *debt* where there is so much looseness as in regard to this subject ? Are men usually as conscientious in this as they are in paying a physician or a merchant ? Are not ministers often in distress for that which has been promised them, and which they have a right to expect ? And is not their usefulness, and the happiness of the people, and the honour of religion intimately connected with obeying the rule of the Lord Jesus in this respect ?

15. *But I have used none of these things.* I have not urged and enforced this right. I have chosen to support myself by the labour of my own hands. This had been objected to him as a reason why he could not be an apostle. He here shows that *that* was not the reason why he had not urged this claim; but that it was because in this way he could do most to honour the gospel and save the souls

these things: neither have I written these things, that it should be so done unto me: for *a it were* better for me to die than that any man should make my glorying void.

a 2 Cor.11.10.

of men ; comp. Acts xx. 33 ; 2 Thess. iii. 8. The sense is, " Though my right to a support is established, in common with others, both by reason, the nature of the case, the examples in the law, and the command of the Lord Jesus, yet there are reasons why I have not chosen to avail myself of this right, and why I have not urged these claims." ¶ *Neither have I written these things,* &c. " I have not presented this argument now in order to induce you to provide for me. I do not intend now to ask or receive a support from you. I urge it to show that I *feel* that I have a right to it ; that my conduct is not an argument that I am conscious I am not an apostle ; and that I *might* urge it were there not strong reasons which determine me not to do it. I neither ask you to send me now a support, nor, if I visit you again, do I expect you will contribute to my maintenance." ¶ *For* it were *better for me to die,* &c. There are advantages growing out of my not urging this claim which are of more importance to me than life. Rather than forego these advantages, it would be better for me—it would be a thing which I would prefer—to pine in poverty and want ; to be exposed to peril, and cold, and storms, until life should close. I esteem my " glorying," the advantages of my course, to be of more value than life itself. ¶ *Than that any man should make my glorying void.* His glorying, or boasting, or joying, as it may be more properly rendered (τὸ καύχημά μου; comp. Phil. i. 26 ; Heb. iii. 6), was, (1.) That he had preached the gospel without expense to anybody, and had thus prevented the charge of avarice (ver. 18); and (2.) That he had been able to keep his body under, and pursue a course of self-denial that would result in his happiness and glory in heaven, ver.

16 For though I preach the gospel, I have nothing to glory of : for *b* necessity is laid upon me ; yea, woe is unto me if I preach not the gospel.

b Jer.50.17; 20.9.

23—27. " Any man" would have made that " void," if he had supported Paul ; had prevented the necessity of his labour, and had thus exposed him to the charge of having preached the gospel for the sake of gain.

16. *For though I preach the gospel,* &c. This, with the two following verses, is a very difficult passage, and has been very variously understood by interpreters. The general scope and purpose of the passage is to show what was the ground of his " glorying," or of his hope of " reward " in preaching the gospel. In ver. 15. he had intimated that he had cause of " glorying," and that that cause was one which he was determined no one should take away. In this passage (ver. 16—18.) he states what that was. He says, it was not simply that he preached ; for there was a necessity laid on him, and he could not help it : his call was such, the command was such, that his life would be miserable if he did not do it. *But* all idea of " glorying," or of " reward," must be connected with some *voluntary* service — something which would show the inclination, disposition, desire of the soul. And as that in his case could not be well shown where a " necessity " was laid on him, it could be shown only in his submitting *voluntarily* to trials ; in denying himself ; in being willing to forego comforts which he *might* lawfully enjoy ; and in thus furnishing a full and complete test of his readiness to do any thing to promote the gospel. The essential idea here is, therefore, that there was such a *necessity* laid on him in his call to preach the gospel, that his compliance with that call could not be regarded as appropriately connected with reward ; and that in his case the circumstance which showed that reward would be proper, was, his denying himself, and making the gospel without

charge. This would show that *his heart was in the thing ;* that he was was not urged on by necessity; that he loved the work; and that it would be consistent for the Lord to reward him for his self-denials and toils in his service. ¶ *I have nothing to glory of.* The force of this would be better seen by a more literal translation. "It is not to me glorying;" *i. e.* this is not the cause of my glorying, or rejoicing (*οὐκ ἔστι μοι καύχημα*). In ver. 15 he had said that he *had* a cause of glorying, or of joy (*καύχημα*). He here says that *that* joy or glorying did not consist in the simple fact that he *preached* the gospel; for necessity was laid on him; there was some *other* cause and source of his joy or glorying than that simple fact; ver. 18. Others preached the gospel also: in common with them, it might be a source of joy to him that he preached the gospel; but it was not the source of his *peculiar* joy, for *he* had been called into the apostleship in such a manner as to render it inevitable that he should preach the gospel. *His* glorying was of another kind. ¶ *For necessity is laid upon me.* My preaching is in a manner inevitable, and cannot therefore be regarded as that in which I peculiarly glory. I was called into the ministry in a miraculous manner; I was addressed personally by the Lord Jesus; I was arrested when I was a persecutor; I was commanded to go and preach ; I had a direct commission from heaven. There was no room for hesitancy or debate on the subject (Gal. i. 16), and I gave myself at once and entirely to the work; Acts ix. 6. I have been urged to this by a direct call from heaven; and to yield obedience to this call cannot be regarded as evincing such an inclination to give myself to this work as if the call had been in the usual mode, and with less decided manifestations. We are not to suppose that Paul was *compelled* to preach, or that he was not voluntary in his work, or that he did not prefer it to any other employment: but he speaks in a popular sense, as saying that he "could not help it;" or that the evidence of his call was irresistible, and left no room for hesitation. He was

free; but there was not the slightest room for debate on the subject. The evidence of his call was so strong that he could not but yield. Probably none now have evidences of their call to the ministry *as* strong as this. But there are many, very many, who feel that a kind of *necessity* is laid on them to preach. Their consciences urge them to it. They would be miserable in any other employment. The course of Providence has shut them up to it. Like Saul of Tarsus, they may have been persecutors, or revilers, or "injurious," or blasphemers (1 Tim. i. 13); or they may, like him, have commenced a career of ambition; or they may have been engaged in some scheme of money-making or of pleasure; and in an hour when they little expected it, they have been arrested by the truth of God, and their attention directed to the gospel ministry. Many a minister has, before entering the ministry, formed many other purposes of life; but the providence of God barred his way, hemmed in his goings, and constrained him to become an ambassador of the cross. ¶ *Yea, woe is unto me,* &c. I should be miserable and wretched if I did not preach. My preaching, therefore, in itself considered, cannot be a subject of glorying. I am shut up to it. I am urged to it in every way. I should be wretched were I not to do it, and were I to seek any other calling. My conscience would reproach me. My judgment would condemn me. My heart would pain me. I should have no comfort in any other calling; and God would frown upon me. Learn hence, (1. That Paul had been converted. Once he had no love for the ministry, but persecuted the Saviour. With the feelings which he *then* had, he would have been wretched *in* the ministry; with those which he *now* had, he would have been wretched *out* of it. His heart, therefore, had been wholly changed. (2.) All ministers who are duly called to the work can say the same thing. They would be wretched in any other calling. Their conscience would reproach them. They would have no interest in the plans of the world; in the schemes of wealth, and

17 For if I do this thing willingly, I have a reward : but if against my will, a dispensation *a of the gospel* is committed unto me.

a Col.1.25.

pleasure, and fame. Their heart is in *this* work, and in this alone. In this, though amidst circumstances of poverty, persecution, nakedness, cold, peril, sickness, they have comfort. In any other calling, though surrounded by affluence, friends, wealth, honours, pleasures, gayety, fashion, they would be miserable. (3.) A man whose heart is not in the ministry, and who would be *as* happy in any other calling, is not fit to be an ambassador of Jesus Christ. Unless his *heart* is there, and he *prefers* that to any other calling, he should never think of preaching the gospel. (4.) Men who *leave* the ministry, and voluntarily devote themselves to some other calling when they might preach, never had the proper spirit of an ambassador of Jesus. If for the sake of ease or gain; if to avoid the cares and anxieties of the life of a pastor; if to make money, or secure money when made; if to cultivate a farm, to teach a school, to write a book, to live upon an estate, or to *enjoy life*, they lay aside the ministry, it is proof that they never had a call to the work. So did not Paul; and so did not Paul's Master and ours. They loved the work, and they left it not till death. Neither for ease, honour, nor wealth; neither to avoid care, toil, pain, or poverty, did they cease in their work, until the one could say, " I have fought a good fight, *I have finished my course*, I have kept the faith" (2 Tim. iv. 7; and the other, "I have finished the work which thou gavest me to do;" John xvii. 4. (5.) We see the reason why men are sometimes *miserable* in other callings. They *should* have entered the ministry. God called them to it; and they became hopefully pious. But they chose the law, or the practice of medicine, or chose to be farmers, merchants, teachers, professors, or statesmen. And God withers their piety, blights their happiness, follows them with the reproaches of conscience, makes them sad, melancholy, wretched. They do no good; and they have no comfort in life. Every man should do the will of God, and then every man would be happy.

17. *For if I do this thing willingly.* If I preach so as to show that my heart is in it; that I am not compelled. If I pursue such a course as to show that I prefer it to all other employments. If Paul took a compensation for his services, he could not well do this ; if he did not, he showed that his heart was in it, and that he preferred the work to all others. Even though he had been in a manner *compelled* to engage in that work, yet he *so* acted *in* the work as to show that it had his hearty preference. This was done by his submitting to voluntary self-denials and sacrifices in order to spread the Saviour's name. ¶ *I have a reward.* I shall meet with the approbation of my Lord, and shall obtain the reward in the world to come, which is promised to those who engage heartily, and laboriously, and successfully in turning sinners to God ; Prov. xi. 30; Dan. xii. 3; Mat. xiii. 43; xxv. 21—23; James v. 20. ¶ *But if against my will* (ἄκων). If under a necessity (ver. 16); if by the command of another (*Grotius*); if I do it by the fear of punishment, or by any strong necessity which is laid on me. ¶ *A dispensation* of the gospel *is committed unto me.* I am intrusted with (πεπίστευμαι) this dispensation, office, economy (οἰκονομίαν) of the gospel. It has been laid upon me; I have been called to it; I *must* engage in this work; and if I do it from mere compulsion or in such a way that my will shall not acquiesce in it, and concur with it, I shall have no distinguished reward. The work *must* be done; I *must* preach the gospel; and it becomes me so to do it as to show that my heart and will entirely concur; that it is not a matter of compulsion, but of choice. This he proposed to do by so denying himself, and so foregoing comforts which he might lawfully enjoy, and so subjecting himself to perils and toils in preaching the gospel, as to show that his heart was *in* the work, and that he truly loved it.

18 What is my reward then? *Verily* that, when I preach the gospel, I may make the gospel of Christ without charge; that I abuse not my power in the gospel.

19 For though I be free from all *men*, yet have I made myself

---

18. *What is my reward then?* What is the source of my reward? or what is there in my conduct that will show that I am entitled to reward? What is there that will demonstrate that my heart is in the work of the ministry; that I am free and voluntary, and that I am not urged by mere necessity? Though I have been called by miracle, and though necessity is laid upon me, so that I cannot *but* preach the gospel, yet how shall I so do it as to make it proper for God to reward me as a voluntary agent? Paul immediately states the circumstance that showed that he was entitled to the reward, and that was, that he denied himself, and was willing to forego his lawful enjoyments, and even his rights, that he might make the gospel without charge. ¶ *I may make the gospel of Christ without charge.* Without expense to those who hear it. I will support myself by my own labour, and will thus show that I am not urged to preaching by mere "necessity," but that I love it. Observe here, (1.) That Paul did not give up a support because he was not entitled to it. (2.) He does not say that it would be well or advisable for others to do it. (3.) It is right, and well for a man, if he chooses, and can do it, to make the gospel without charge, and to support himself. (4.) All that *this* case proves is, that it would be proper only where a "necessity" was laid on a man, as it was on Paul; when he could not otherwise show that his heart was in the work, and that he was voluntary and loved it. (5.) This passage cannot be urged *by a people* to prove that ministers ought not to have a support. Paul says they have a *right* to it. A man may forego a right if he pleases. He may *choose* not to urge it; but no one can demand of him that he should not urge it; much less have they a *right* to demand that he should give up *his* rights. (6.) It is best in general that those who hear the gospel should con-

tribute to its support. It is not only equal and right, but it is best for them. We generally set very little value on that which costs us nothing; and the very way to make the gospel contemptible is, to have it preached by those who are supported by the state, or by their own labour in some other department: or by men who neither by their talents, their learning, nor their industry have any claim to a support. All ministers are not like Paul. They have neither been called as he was; nor have they his talent, his zeal, or his eloquence. Paul's example then should not be urged as an authority for a people to withhold from their pastor what is his due; nor, because Paul *chose* to forego his rights, should people now *demand* that a minister should devote his time, and health, and life to their welfare for naught. ¶ *That I abuse not my power in the gospel.* Paul had a right to a support. This power he might urge. But to urge it in his circumstances would be a hinderance of the gospel. And to do that would be to abuse his power, or to pervert it to purposes for which it was never designed.

19. *For though I be free.* I am a freeman. I am under obligation to none. I am not bound to give them my labours, and at the same time to toil for my own support. I have claims like others, and could urge them; and no man could demand that I should give myself to a life of servitude, and comply with their prejudices and wishes, as if I were *a slave*, in order to their conversion; comp. ver. 1; Notes, chap. vi. 12. ¶ *From all* men (ἐκ πάντων). This may either refer to all *persons* or to all *things.* The word *men* is not in the original. The connection, however, seems to fix the signification to *persons.* "I am a freeman. And although I have conducted like a slave, yet it has been done voluntarily." ¶ *I have made myself the servant of all.* Greek, "I

servant *a* unto all, that I might gain the more.

20 And unto the Jews *b* I became as a Jew, that I might gain

a Rom.1.14; Gal.5.13.

the Jews; to them that are under the law, as under the law, that I might gain them that are under the law;

b Acts 16.3; 21. 23—26.

have *enslaved myself* (ἐμαυτὸν ἐδούλωσα) unto all." That is, (1.) I *labour* for them, or in their service, and to promote their welfare. (2.) I do it, as the slave does, without reward or hire. I am not paid for it, but submit to the toil, and do it without receiving pay. (3.) Like the slave who wishes to gratify his master, or who is compelled from the necessity of the case, I comply with the prejudices, habits, customs, and opinions of others as far as I can with a good conscience. The *slave* is subject to the master's will. That will must be obeyed. The whims, prejudices, caprices of the master must be submitted to, even if they are *mere* caprice, and wholly unreasonable. So Paul says that he had voluntarily put himself into this condition, a condition making it necessary for him to suit himself to the opinions, prejudices, caprices, and feelings of all men, so far as he could do it with a good conscience, in order that he might save them. We are not to understand here that Paul embraced any opinions which were false in order to do this, or that he submitted to any thing which is morally wrong. But he complied with their customs, and habits, and feelings, as far as it could lawfully be done. He did not needlessly offend them, or run counter to their prejudices. ¶ *That I might gain the more.* That I might gain more to Christ; that I might be the means of saving more souls. What a noble instance of self-denial and true greatness is here! How worthy of religion! How elevated the conduct! How magnanimous, and how benevolent! No man would do this who had not a greatness of intellect that would rise above narrow prejudices; and who had not a nobleness of heart that would seek at personal sacrifice the happiness of all men. It is said that not a few early Christians, in illustration of this principle of conduct, actually sold themselves into slavery in order

that they might have access to and benefit slaves, an act to which nothing would prompt a man but the religion of the cross; comp. Note, Rom. i. 14.

20. *And unto the Jews.* In this verse, and the two following, Paul states more at length the conduct which he had exhibited, and to which he refers in ver. 19. He had shown this conduct to all classes of men. He had preached much to his own countrymen, and had evinced these principles there. ¶ *I became as a Jew.* I complied with their rites, customs, prejudices, as far as I could with a good conscience. I did not needlessly offend them. I did not attack and oppose their views, when there was no danger that my conduct should be mistaken. For a full illustration of Paul's conduct in this respect, and the principles which influenced him, see Notes on Acts xvi. 3; xviii. 18; xxi. 21 –27; xxiii. 1—6. ¶ *To those that are under the law.* This I understand as another form of saying that he conformed to the rites, customs, and even prejudices, of the Jews. The phrase "under the law" means undoubtedly the law of Moses; and probably he here refers particularly to those Jews who lived in the land of Judea, as being more *immediately* and *entirely* under the law of Moses, than those who lived among the Gentiles. ¶ *As under the law.* That is, I conformed to their rites and customs as far as I could do it. I did not violate them unnecessarily. I did not disregard them for the purpose of offending them; nor refuse to observe them when it could be done with a good conscience. There can be no doubt that Paul, when he was in Judea, submitted himself to the laws, and lived in conformity with them. ¶ *That I might gain.* That I might obtain their confidence and affection. That I might not outrage their feelings, excite their prejudices, and provoke them to anger; and that I might thus have access to their

21 To them that are without law, as without law, (being not *a* without law to God, but under the

law to Christ,) that I might gain them that are without law.

22 To the weak *b* became I as

a chap.7.22.

b Rom.15.1; 2Cor.11.29.

minds, and be the means of converting them to the Christian faith.

21. *To them that are without law* To the Gentiles, who have not the law of Moses ; see Note, Rom. ii. 12, 14. ¶ *As without law.* Not practising the peculiar rites and ceremonies enjoined in the law of Moses. Not insisting on them, or urging them : but showing that the *obligation* to those rites had been done away ; and that they were not binding, though when among the Jews I might still continue to observe them; see Notes, Acts xv. ; and the argument of Paul in Gal. ii. 11 18. I neglected the ceremonial precepts of the Mosaic law, when I was with those who had not *heard* of the law of Moses, or those who did not observe them, because I knew that the binding obligation of these ceremonial precepts had ceased. I did not, therefore, *press* them upon the Gentiles, nor did I superstitiously and publicly practise them. In all this, Paul has reference only to those things which he regarded as in themselves *indifferent*, and not a matter of conscience ; and his purpose was not needlessly to excite the prejudice or the opposition of the world. Nothing is ever gained by *provoking* opposition for the mere sake of opposition. Nothing tends more to hinder the gospel than that. In all things of *conscience* and *truth* a man should be firm, and should lose his life rather than abandon either ; in all things of indifference, of mere custom, of prejudice, he should yield, and accomodate himself to the modes of thinking among men, and adapt himself to their views, feelings, and habits of life, that he may win them to Christ. ¶ *Being not without law to God.* Not regarding myself as being *absolutely* without law, or as being freed from obligation to obey God. Even in all this, I endeavoured so to live as that it might be seen that I felt myself bound by law to God. I was not a despiser,

and contemner, and neglector of *law as such*, but only regarded myself as not bound by the peculiar ceremonial law of Moses. This is an instance of Paul's conscientiousness. He would not leave room to have it supposed for a moment that he disregarded all law. He was bound to God by law ; and in the conduct to which he was referring he felt that he was obeying *him.* He was bound by higher law than those ceremonial observances which were now to be done away. This passage would destroy all the refuges of the Antinomians. Whatever privileges the gospel has introduced, it has not set us free from the restraints and obligations of law. That is binding still ; and no man is at liberty to disregard the moral law of God. Christ came to magnify, strengthen, and to honour the law, not to destroy it. ¶ *But under the law to Christ.* Bound by the law enjoined by Christ ; under the law of affectionate gratitude and duty to him. I obeyed his commands ; followed his instructions , sought his honour ; yielded to his will. In this he would violate none of the rules of the moral law. And he here intimates, that his grand object was to yield obedience to the law of the Saviour, and that this was the governing purpose of his life. And this *would* guide a man right. In doing this, he would never violate any of the precepts of the moral law, for Christ obeyed them, and enjoined their observance. He would never feel that he was without law to God, for Christ obeyed God, and enjoined it on all. He would never feel that religion came to set him free from law, or to authorize licentiousness ; for its grand purpose and aim is to make men holy, and to bind them every where to the observance of the pure law of the Redeemer.

[Believers are "delivered from the law" as a covenant of works. They do not seek to us

weak, that I might gain the weak;
I *a* am made all things to all *men*, that
b I might by all means save some.

a chap.10.33.

justified by it, neither can it condemn them.
Still the authority of Christ binds them to re-
gard it as a rule of life, or directory of con-
duct. Thus they are "not without law to
God, being under the law to Christ" See the
Supplementary Notes on Rom. vii.]

22. *To the weak ;* see Note, Rom.
xv. 1. To those weak in faith; scrupulous in regard to certain observances ; whose consciences were tender
and unenlightened, and who would be
offended even by things which might
be in themselves lawful. He did not
lacerate their feelings, and run counter to their prejudices, for the mere
sake of doing it. ¶ *Became I as weak.*
I did not shock them. I complied
with their customs. I conformed to
them in my dress, habits, manner of
life, and even in the services of religion. I abstained from food which
they deemed it their duty to abstain
from ; and where, if I had partaken
of it, I should have offended them.
Paul did not do this to gratify himself, or them, but to do them good.
And Paul's example should teach us
not to make it the main business of
life to gratify ourselves : and it should
teach us not to lacerate the feelings
of others ; not to excite their prejudices needlessly ; not to offend them
where it will do no good. If truth
offends men, we cannot help it. But
in matters of ceremony, and dress,
and habits, and customs, and forms,
we should be willing to conform to
them, as far as can be done, and for
the sole purpose of saving their souls.
¶ *I am made all things to all* men. I
become all things ; that is, I accommodate myself to them in all things,
so far as can be done with a good conscience. ¶ *That I might by all means*
(πάντως). That I might use every possible endeavour that some at least might
be saved. It is implied here that the
opposition to the gospel was everywhere great; that men were reluctant
to embrace it ; that the great mass
were going to ruin, and that Paul was

23 And this I do for the gospel's
sake, that I might be partaker
thereof with *you.*

b Rom.11.14.

willing to make the highest possible
exertions, to deny himself, and practise every innocent art, that he might
save *a few at least* out of the innumerable multitudes that were going
to death and hell. It follows from
this, (1.) That men are in danger of
ruin. (2.) We should make an effort
to save men. We should deny ourselves, and give ourselves to toil and
privation, that we may save some at
least from ruin. (3.) The doctrine
of universal salvation is not true. If
it were, what use or propriety would
there have been in these efforts of
Paul? If *all* were to be saved, why
should he deny himself, and labour,
and toil, to save "some?" Why
should a man make a constant effort
to save *a few at least,* if he well knew
that *all* were to be saved? Assuredly
Paul did not *know* or believe that all
men would be saved ; but if the doctrine is true, he would have been
quite as likely to have known it as its
modern advocates and defenders.

23. *For the gospel's sake.* That it
may be advanced, and may be successful. ¶ *That I might be partaker
thereof with* you. You hope to be
saved. You regard yourselves as
Christians ; and I wish to give evidence also that *I* am a Christian, and
that I shall be admitted to heaven to
partake of the happiness of the redeemed. This he did, by so denying
himself as to give evidence that he
was truly actuated by Christian principles.

24. *Know ye not,* &c. In the remainder of this chapter, Paul illustrates the general sentiment on which
he had been dwelling—the duty of
practising self-denial for the salvation
of others—by a reference to the well
known games which were celebrated
near Corinth. Throughout the chapter, his object had been to show that
in declining to receive a support for
preaching, he had done it, not because
he was conscious that he had no claim

24 Know ye not that they which run in a race run all, but one receiveth a prize ? So run, *a* that ye may obtain.

*a*Phil.2 16; 3.14; 1Tim 6.12; 2Tim.2.5.

to it, but because by doing it he could better advance the salvation of men, the furtherance of the gospel, and in his peculiar case (ver. 16, 17) could obtain better evidence, and furnish to others better evidence that he was actuated by a sincere desire to honour God in the gospel. He had denied himself. He had voluntarily submitted to great privations. He had had a great object in view in doing it. And he now says, that in the well known athletic games at Corinth, the same thing was done by the *racers* (ver. 24), and by *wrestlers*, or *boxers;* ver. 25. If *they* had done it, for objects so comparatively unimportant as the attainment of an *earthly* garland, assuredly it was proper for him to do it to obtain a crown which should never fade away. This is one of the most beautiful, appropriate, vigorous, and bold illustrations that can anywhere be found ; and is a striking instance of the force with which the most vigorous and self-denying efforts of Christians can be vindicated, and can be *urged* by a reference to the conduct of men in the affairs of this life. By the phrase " know ye not," Paul intimates that those games to which he alludes were well known to them, and that they must be familiar with their design, and with the manner in which they were conducted. The games to which the apostle alludes were celebrated with extraordinary pomp and splendour, every fourth year, on the isthmus which joined the Peloponnesus to the main land, and on a part of which the city of Corinth stood. There were in Greece four species of games,—the Pythian, or Delphic; the Isthmian, or Corinthian ; the Nemean, and the Olympic. On these occasions persons were assembled from all parts of Greece, and the time during which they continued was devoted to extraordinary festivity and amusement. The Isthmian or Corinthian games were celebrated in the narrow part of the Isthmus of Corinth, to the north

of the city, and were doubtless the games to which the apostle more particularly alluded, though the games in each of the places were substantially of the same nature, and the same illustration would in the main apply to all. The Nemean games were celebrated at *Nemœa*, a town of Argolis, and were instituted by the Argives in honour of Archemorus, who died by the bite of a serpent, but were renewed by Hercules. They consisted of horse and foot races, of boxing, leaping, running, &c. The conqueror was at first rewarded with a crown of olive, afterwards of green parsley. They were celebrated every third, or, according to others, every fifth year. The *Pythian* games were celebrated every four years at Delphi, in Phocis, at the foot of mount Parnassus, where was the seat of the celebrated Delphic oracle. These games were of the same character substantially as those celebrated in other places, and attracted persons not only from other parts of Greece, but from distant countries; see Travels of Anacharsis, vol. ii. pp. 375—418. The *Olympic* games were celebrated in Olympia, a town of Elis, on the southern bank of the Alphias river, on the western part of the Peloponnesus. They were on many accounts the most celebrated of any in Greece. They were said to have been instituted by Hercules, who planted a grove called *Altis*, which he dedicated to Jupiter. They were attended not only from all parts of Greece, but from the most distant countries. These were celebrated every fourth year ; and hence, in Grecian chronology, a period of four years was called an Olympiad; see Anacharsis, vol. iii. 434, seq. It thus happened that in one or more of these places there were games celebrated every year, to which no small part of the inhabitants of Greece were attracted. Though the apostle probably had *particular* reference to the *Isthmian* games celebrated in the vicinity of Corinth, yet his illustration is applicable to them all ; for in all the exercises were nearly the same. They consisted chiefly in leaping, running, throwing the discus or quoit, boxing, wrestling, and were expressed in the following line :—

'Αλμά, ποδωκείην, δίσκον, ἀκοντα, πάλην,

leaping, running, throwing the quoit, darting, wrestling. Connected with these were also, sometimes, other exercises, as races of chariots, horses, &c. The apostle refers to but *two* of these exercises in his illustration. ¶ *They which run.* This was one of the principal exercises at the games. Fleetness or swiftness was regarded as an extraordinary virtue; and great pains were taken in order to excel in this. Indeed they regarded it so highly that those who prepared themselves for it thought it worth while to use means to burn their spleen, because it was believed to be a hinderance to them, and to retard them in the race. Rob. Cal. Homer tells us that swiftness was one of the most excellent endowments with which a man can be blessed.

"No greater honour e'er has been attain'd,
Than what strong hands or nimble feet have
    gain'd.''

One reason why this was deemed so valuable an attainment among the Greeks, was, that it fitted men eminently for war as it was then conducted. It enabled them to make a sudden and unexpected onset, or a rapid retreat. Hence the character which Homer constantly gives of Achilles is, that he was swift of foot. And thus David, in his poetical lamentations over Saul and Jonathan, takes special notice of this qualification of theirs, as fitting them for war.

"They were swifter than eagles,
Stronger than lions." 2 Sam. i. 23.

For these races they prepared themselves by a long course of previous discipline and exercise ; and nothing was left undone that might contribute to secure the victory. ¶ *In a race* (ἐν σταδίῳ). In the *stadium.* The *stadium,* or running ground, or place in which the boxers contended, and where races were run. At Olympia

the stadium was a causeway 604 feet in length, and of proportionable width. Herod. lib. 2. c. 149. It was surrounded by a terrace, and by the seats of the judges of the games. At one end was fixed the boundary or goal to which they ran. ¶ *Run all.* All run who have entered the lists. Usually there were many racers who contended for the prize. ¶ *But one receiveth the prize.* The victor, and he alone. The prize which was conferred was a wreath of olive at the Olympic games; a wreath of apple at Delphi ; of pine at the Isthmian ; and of parsley at the Nemean games.—*Addison.* Whatever the prize was, it was conferred on the successful champion on the last day of the games, and with great solemnity, pomp, congratulation, and rejoicing. " Every one thronged to see and congratulate them ; their relations, friends, and countrymen, shedding tears of tenderness and joy, lifted them on their shoulders to show them to the crowd, and held them up to the applauses of the whole assembly, who strewed handfuls of flowers over them." Anachar. iii. 448. Nay, at their return home, they rode in a triumphal chariot; the walls of the city were broken down to give them entrance ; and in many cities a subsistence was given them out of the public treasury, and they were exempted from taxes. Cicero says that a victory at the Olympic games was not much less honourable than a triumph at Rome : see Anachar. iii. 469, and Rob. Cal. art. *Race.* When Paul says that the one receives the prize, he does not mean to say that there will be the same small proportion among those who shall enter into heaven, and among Christians. But his idea is, that as *they* make an effort to obtain the prize, so should we; as many who strive for it then lose it, it is possible that we may; and that therefore we should strive for the crown, and make an effort for it, *as if* but one out of many could obtain it. This, he says, was the course which he pursued ; and it shows, in a most striking manner, the fact that an effort *may* be made, and *should* be made to enter into heaven. ¶ *So run, that ye may*

25 And every man that striveth for the mastery is temperate in all things.

a 2 Tim.4.8; James 1.12; 1 Pet.5.4; Rev.2.10;

Now they *do it* to obtain a corruptible crown ; but we an incorruptible.*a*

3.11.

obtain. So run in the Christian race, that you may obtain the prize of glory, the crown incorruptible. So live ; so deny yourselves ; so make constant exertion, that you may not fail of that prize, the crown of glory, which awaits the righteous in heaven ; comp. Heb. xii. 1. Christians may do this when (1.) They give themselves wholly to God, and make this the grand business of life ; (2.) " When they lay aside every weight" (Heb. xii. 1) ; and renounce all sin and all improper attachments ; (3.) When they do not allow themselves to be *diverted* from the object, but keep the goal constantly in view ; (4.) When they do not flag, or grow weary in their course; (5.) When they deny themselves ; and (6.) When they keep their eye fully fixed on Christ (Heb. xii. 2) as their example and their strength, and on heaven as the end of their race, and on the crown of glory as their reward.

25. *And every man that striveth for the mastery* (*ὁ ἀγωνιζόμενος*). That *agonizes* ; that is, that is engaged in the exercise of *wrestling, boxing*, or pitching the bar or quoit; comp. Note, Luke xiii. 24. The sense is, every one who endeavours to obtain a victory in these athletic exercises. ¶ *Is temperate in all things.* The word which is rendered " is temperate " (*ἐγκρατεύεται*) denotes *abstinence* from all that would excite, stimulate, and ultimately enfeeble ; from wine, from exciting and luxurious living, and from licentious indulgences. It means that they did all they could to make the body vigorous, active, and supple. They pursued a course of entire temperate living ; comp. Acts xxiv. 25 ; 1 Cor. vii. 9 ; Gal. v. 23 ; 2 Pet. i. 6. It relates not only to indulgences unlawful in themselves, but to abstinence from many things that were regarded as *lawful*, but which were believed to render the body weak and effeminate. The phrase " in all things " means that this course of temperance or

abstinence was not confined to one thing, or to one class of things, but to every kind of food and drink, and every indulgence that had a tendency to render the body weak and effeminate. The preparations which those who propose to contend in these games made is well known; and is often referred to by the classic writers. Epictetus, as quoted by Grotius (in loco), thus speaks of these preparations. " Do you wish to gain the prize at the Olympic games? consider the requisite preparations and the consequence You must observe a strict regimen : must live on food which is unpleasant; must abstain from all delicacies; must exercise yourself at the prescribed times in heat and in cold; you must drink nothing cool (*ψυχρὸν*); must take no wine as usual; you must put yourself under a *pugilist*, as you would under a physician, and afterwards enter the lists." Epict. chap. xxxv. Horace has described the preparations necessary in the same way.

Qui studet optatam cursu contingere metam
Multa tulit fecitque puer; sudavit, et alsit,
Abstinuit venere et Baccho.
                                  De Arte Poet. 412.

A youth who hopes the Olympic prize to gain,
All arts must try, and every toil sustain ;
The extremes of heat and cold must often prove,
And shun the weakening joys of wine and love.   *Francis.*

¶ *To obtain a corruptible crown.* A garland, diadem, or civic wreath, that must soon fade away. The garland bestowed on the victor was made of olive, pine, apple, laurel, or parsley. That would soon lose its beauty and fade; of course, it could be of little value. Yet we see how eagerly they sought it; how much self-denial those who entered the lists would practice to obtain it; how long they would deny themselves of the common pleasures of life that they might be successful. So much *temperance* would heathens practise to obtain a fading wreath of laurel, pine, or parsley

Learn hence, (1.) The duty of denying ourselves to obtain a far more valuable reward, the incorruptible crown of heaven. (2.) The duty of all Christians who strive for that crown to be temperate in all things. If the heathens practised temperance to obtain a fading laurel, should not we to obtain one that never fades? (3.) How much *their* conduct puts to shame the conduct of many professing Christians and Christian ministers. *They* set such a value on a civic wreath of pine or laurel, that they were willing to deny themselves, and practise the most rigid abstinence. *They* knew that indulgence in WINE and in luxurious living unfitted them for the struggle and for victory; *they* knew that it enfeebled their powers, and weakened their frame; and, like men intent on an object dear to them, they abstained wholly from these things, and embraced the principles of *total abstinence.* Yet how many professed Christians, and Christian ministers, though striving for the crown that fadeth not away, indulge in wine, and in the filthy, offensive, and disgusting use of tobacco; and in luxurious living, and in habits of indolence and sloth! How many there are that WILL not give up these habits, though they know that they are enfeebling, injurious, offensive, and destructive to religious comfort and usefulness. Can a man be truly in earnest in his professed religion; can he be a sincere Christian, who is not willing to abandon any thing and every thing that will tend to impair the vigour of his mind, and weaken his body, and make him a stumbling-block to others? (4.) The value of *temperance* is here presented in a very striking and impressive view. When even the heathens wished to accomplish any thing that demanded skill, strength, power, vigour of body, they saw the necessity of being temperate, and they were so. And this *proves* what all experiment has proved, that if men wish to *accomplish* much, they must be temperate. It *proves* that men can do *more* without intoxicating drink than they can with it. The example of these Grecian *Athletae*—their wrestlers, boxers, and

racers, is *against* all the farmers, and mechanics, and seamen, and day-labourers, and *gentlemen,*and *clergymen.* and *lawyers,* who plead that stimulating drink is necessary to enable them to bear cold and heat, and toil and exposure. A little *experience* from men like the Grecian wrestlers, who had something that they wished to do, is much better than a great deal of philosophy and sophistical reasoning from men who *wish* to drink, and to find some argument for drinking that shall be a *salvo* to their consciences. Perhaps the world has furnished no stronger argument in favour of *total abstinence* than the example of the Grecian *Athletae.* It is certain that their example, the example of men who wished to accomplish much by bodily vigour and health, is an effectual and irrefragable argument against all those who plead that stimulating drinks are desirable or necessary in order to increase the vigour of the bodily frame. ¶ *But we.* We Christians. ¶ *An incorruptible.* An incorruptible, an unfading crown. The blessings of heaven that shall be bestowed on the righteous are often represented under the image of a crown or diadem; a crown that is unfading, and eternal; 2 Tim. iv. 8; James i. 12; 1 Pet. v. 4. Rev. ii. 10; iii. 11; iv. 4. The doctrine here taught is, the necessity of making an effort to secure eternal life. The apostle never thought of entering heaven by indolence, or by inactivity. He urged, by every possible argument, the necessity of making an exertion to secure the rewards of the just. His *reasons* for this effort are many. Let a few be pondered. (1.) The work of salvation is difficult. The thousand obstacles arising, the love of sin, and the opposition of Satan and of the world, are in the way. (2.) The *danger* of losing the crown of glory is great. Every moment exposes it to hazard, for at any moment we may die. (3.) The danger is not only great, but it is *dreadful.* If any thing should arouse man, it should be the apprehension of eternal damnation and everlasting wrath. (4.) Men in this life, in the games of Greece, in the

26 I therefore so run, not as uncertainly ; so fight I, not as one that beateth the air :

27 But I [a] keep under my body,

a Rom. 8. 13.

and bring *it* into subjection ; lest that by any means, when I have preached to others, I myself should be a cast-away.

career of ambition, in the pursuit of pleasure and wealth, make immense efforts to obtain the fading and perishing object of their desires. Why should not a man be willing to make *as great* efforts at least to secure eternal glory? (5.) The value of the interest at stake. Eternal happiness is before those who will embrace the offers of life. If a man should be influenced by any thing to make an effort, should it not be by the prospect of eternal glory? What *should* influence him if this should not?

26. *I therefore so run.* In the Christian race ; in my effort to obtain the prize, the crown of immortality. I exert myself to the utmost, that I may not fail of securing the crown. ¶ *Not as uncertainly* (οὐκ ἀδήλως). This word occurs no where else in the New Testament. It usually means, in the classic writers, *obscurely.* Here it means that he did not run as not knowing to what object he aimed. " I do not run at hap-hazard; I do not exert myself for naught; I know at what I aim, and I keep my eye fixed on the object ; I have the goal and the crown in view." Probably also the apostle intended to convey this idea, " I so live and act that I am *sure* of obtaining the crown. I make it a great and grand point of my life *so* to live that there may be no room for doubt or hesitancy about this matter. I believe it *may* be obtained; and that by a proper course there may be a constant certainty of securing it ; and I so LIVE." O how happy and blessed would it be if all Christians thus lived! How much doubt, and hesitancy, and despondency would it remove from many a Christian's mind ! And yet it is morally certain that if every Christian were to be only *as* anxious and careful as were the ancient Grecian wrestlers and racers in the games, they would have the undoubted assurance of gaining the prize. Doddridge and Macknight, however, render

this " as not out of view ;" or as not distinguished ; meaning that the apostle was not *unseen,* but that he regarded himself as constantly in the view of the judge, the Lord Jesus Christ. I prefer the other interpretation, however, as best according with the connection and with the proper meaning of the word. ¶ *So fight I* (οὕτω πυκτεύω). This word is applied to the *boxers,* or the pugilists, in the Grecian games. The exercise of boxing, or *fighting* with the fist, was a part of the entertainment with which the *enlightened* nations of Greece delighted to amuse themselves. ¶ *Not as one that beateth the air.* The *phrase* here is taken from the habits of the pugilists or boxers, who were accustomed, before entering the lists, to exercise their limbs with the gauntlet, in order to acquire greater skill and dexterity. There was also, before the real contest commenced, a *play* with their fists and weapons, by way of show or bravado, which was called σκιαμαχία, a mock-battle, or a fighting the air. The phrase also is applicable to a *missing the aim,* when a blow was struck in a real struggle, and when the adversary would elude the blow, so that it would be spent in the empty air. This last is the idea which Paul means to present. He did not miss his aim ; he did not exert himself and spend his strength for naught. Every blow that he struck *told ;* and he did not waste his energies on that which would produce no result. He did not strive with rash, ill-advised, or uncertain blows ; but all his efforts were directed, with good account, to the grand purpose of subjugating his enemy—sin, and the corrupt desires of the flesh—and bringing every thing into captivity to God. Much may be learned from this. Many an effort of Christians is merely beating the air. The energy is expended for naught. There is a want of wisdom, or skill, or perseverance ;

there is a failure of plan; or there is a mistake in regard to what *is* to be done, and what should be done. There is often among Christians very little *aim* or object; there is no *plan;* and the efforts are wasted, scattered, inefficient efforts; so that, at the close of life, many a man may say that he has spent his ministry or his Christian course mainly, or entirely, *in beating the air.* Besides, many a one sets up a man of straw, and fights that. He *fancies* error and heresy in others, and opposes that. He becomes a *heresy-hunter;* or he opposes some irregularity in religion that, if left alone, would die of itself; or he fixes all his attention on some minor evil, and devotes his life to the destruction of that alone. When death comes, he may have never struck a blow at one of the *real* and dangerous enemies of the gospel; and the simple record on the tombstone of many a minister and many a private Christian might be, " Here lies one who spent his life in beating the air."

27. *But I keep under my body* (ὑπωπιάζω). This word occurs in the New Testament only here and in Luke xviii. 5, " Lest by her continual coming she *weary* me." The word is derived probably from ὑπώπιον, the part of the face *under the eye* (*Passow*), and means properly, to strike under the eye, either with the fist or the cestus, so as to render the part livid, or as we say, black and blue; or as is vulgarly termed, to give any one a black eye. The word is derived, of course, from the athletic exercises of the Greeks. It then comes to mean, *to treat any one with harshness, severity,* or *cruelty;* and thence also, so to treat any evil inclinations or dispositions; or to subject one's-self to mortification or self-denial, or to a severe and rigid discipline, that all the corrupt passions might be removed. The word here means, that Paul made use of all possible means to subdue his corrupt and carnal inclinations; to show that he was not under the dominion of evil passions, but was wholly under the dominion of the gospel. ¶ *And bring* it *into subjection.* (δουλαγωγῶ). This word properly means, to

reduce to servitude or slavery; and probably was usually applied to the act of subduing an enemy, and leading him captive from the field of battle; as the captives in war were regarded as slaves. It then means, effectually and totally to subdue, to conquer, to reduce to bondage and subjection. Paul means by it, the purpose to obtain a complete *victory* over his corrupt passions and propensities, and a design to gain the mastery over all his natural and evil inclinations. ¶ *Lest that by any means;* Note, ver. 22. Paul designed to make every possible effort to be saved. He did not *mean* to be lost, but he *meant* to be saved. He felt that there was danger of being deceived and lost; and he *meant* by some means to have evidence of piety that would abide the trial of the day of judgment. ¶ *When I have preached to others.* Doddridge renders this, "lest after having served as a herald to others, I should myself be disapproved;" and supposes that there was allusion in this to the Grecian *herald,* whose business it was to proclaim the conditions of the games, to display the prizes, &c. In this interpretation, also, Macknight, Rosenmüller, Koppe, and most of the modern interpreters agree. They suppose, therefore, that the allusion to the games is carried through all this description. But there is this difficulty in this interpretation, that it represents the apostle as *both* a herald and a contender in the games, and thus leads to an inextricable confusion of metaphor. Probably, therefore, this is to be taken in the usual sense of the word *preaching* in the New Testament; and the apostle here is to be understood as *dropping* the metaphor, and speaking in the usual manner. He had preached to others, to many others. He had proclaimed the gospel far and near. He had preached to many thousands, and had been the means of the conversion of thousands. The contest, the agony, the struggle in which he had been engaged, was that of preaching the gospel in the most effectual manner. And yet he felt that there was a *possibility* that even after all this he might be lost.

[The apostle's language seems not to imply any doubt in regard to his own final perseverance, a matter concerning which in numerous other places he expresses the most decided assurance; but points rather to the *means* by which that perseverance was secured, and without which it could not possibly be attained. " Whom God predestinates he calls, whom he calls he justifies, and whom he justifies he glorifies." Not a link in this golden chain can be broken. But God fulfils his purpose not *without* exertion and self-denial but *by means* of these. And the means are involved in the decree, as well as the end. Paul therefore, "ran, and fought, and kept his body under," *that* in the end he might not be disapproved. *It is certain*, that all who neglect the diligent use of means, under whatever doctrinal notions they may shield themselves, shall, in the day of trial, be rejected, as base and counterfeit metal. If Paul himself neglected these, *even he* should be "cast away!"]

¶ *I myself should be a cast-away.* This word (ἀδόκιμος) is taken from *bad metals*, and properly denotes those which will not bear the *test* that is applied to them; that are found to be base and worthless, and are therefore rejected and cast away. The apostle had subjected himself to trials. He had given himself to self-denial and toil; to persecution and want; to perils, and cold, and nakedness, and hunger. He had done this, among other things, to give his religion a fair trial, to see whether it would bear all these tests, as metal is cast into the fire to see whether it is genuine, or is base and worthless. In doing this, he had endeavoured to subdue his corrupt propensities, and bring everything into captivity to the Redeemer, that it might be found that he was a sincere, and humble, and devoted Christian. Many have supposed that the word "cast-away" here refers to those who had entered the lists, and had contended, and who had then been examined as to the manner in which they had conducted the contest, and had been found to have departed from the rules of the games, and who were then rejected. But this interpretation is too artificial and unnatural. The simple idea of Paul is, that he was afraid that he should be disapproved, rejected, cast off; that it would appear, after all, that he had no religion, and would

then be cast away as unfit to enter into heaven.

From the many remarks which might be made from this interesting chapter, we may select the following:

1st. We see the great anxiety which Paul had to save souls. This was his grand purpose; and for this he was willing to deny himself and to bear any trial.

2d. We should be kind to others; we should not needlessly offend them; we should conform to them, as far as it can be done consistently with Christian integrity.

3d. We should make an effort to be saved. O, if men made such exertions to obtain a corruptible crown, how much greater should we make to obtain one that fadeth not away!

4th. Ministers, like others, are in danger of losing their souls. If *Paul* felt this danger, who is there among the ministers of the cross who should not feel it? If Paul was not safe, who is? [See the Supplementary Note on ver. 27.]

5th. The fact that a man has preached to many is no certain evidence that he will be saved, ver. 27. Paul had preached to thousands, and yet he felt that after all this there was a possibility that he might be lost.

6th. The fact that a man has been very successful in the ministry is no certain evidence that he will be saved. God converts men; and he may sometimes do it by the instrumentality of those who themselves are deceived, or are deceivers. They may preach much truth; and God may bless that truth, and make *it* the means of saving the soul. There is no conclusive evidence that a man is a Christian simply because he is a successful and laborious preacher, any more than there is that a man is a Christian because he is a good farmer, and because God sends down the rain and the sunshine on his fields. Paul felt that even *his* success was no certain evidence that he would be saved. And if Paul felt thus, who should *not* feel that after the most distinguished success, he may himself be at last a cast-away?

7th. It will be a solemn and awful

CHAPTER X.

MOREOVER, brethren, I would not that ye should

a Ex.13.21,22; Num.9.18-22.

thing for a minister of the gospel, and a *successful* minister, to go down to hell. What more fearful doom can be conceived, than after having led others in the way to life; after having described to them the glories of heaven; after having conducted them to the "sweet fields beyond the swelling flood" of death, he should find himself shut out, rejected, and cast down to hell! What more terrible can be imagined in the world of perdition than the doom of one who was once a minister of God, and once esteemed as a light in the church and a guide of souls, now sentenced to inextinguishable fires, while multitudes saved by him shall have gone to heaven! How fearful is the condition and how solemn the vocation of a minister of the gospel!

8th. Ministers should be solicitous about their personal piety. Paul, one might suppose, might have rested contented with the remarkable manner of his conversion. He might have supposed that that put the matter beyond all possible doubt. But he did no such thing. He felt that it was necessary to have evidence day by day that he was *then* a Christian. Of all men, Paul was perhaps *least* disposed to live on past experience, and to trust to such experience. Of all men, he had perhaps most reason to trust to such experience; and yet how seldom does he refer to it, how little does he regard it! The great question with him was, " Am I *now* a Christian? am I living as a Christian should *now?* am I evincing to others, am I giving to myself daily, constant, growing evidence that I am actuated by the pure principles of the gospel, and that that gospel is the object of my highest preference, and my holiest and constant desire?' O how holy would be the ministry, if all should endeavour every day to live and act for Christ and for souls with as much steadiness and fidelity as did the apostle Paul!

be ignorant, how that all our fathers were under *a* the cloud, and *b* all passed through the sea;

b Ex.14.19-22,29.

CHAPTER X.

IN regard to the design of this chapter commentators have not been agreed. Some have supposed that there is no connection with the preceding, but that this is a digression. The ancient Greek expositors generally, and some of the moderns, as Grotius, supposed that the connection was this: Paul had in the previous chapter described himself as mortifying his flesh, and keeping his body under, that he might gain the prize. In this chapter they suppose that his object is to exhort the Corinthians to do the same ; and that in order to do this, he admonishes them not to be lulled into security by the idea of the many spiritual gifts which had been conferred upon them. This admonition he enforces by the example of the Jews, who had been highly favoured also, but who had nevertheless been led into idolatry. This is also the view of Doddridge, Calvin, and others. Macknight regards the chapter as an independent discussion of the three questions, which he supposes had been submitted to Paul : (1.) Whether they might innocently go with their friends into the heathen temples, and partake of the feasts which were there made in honour of the idol. (2.) Whether they might buy and eat meat sold in the markets which had been sacrificed to idols. (3.) Whether, when invited to the houses of the heathens, they might partake of the meat sacrificed to idols, and which was set before them as a common meal.—I regard this chapter as having a very close connection with chap. viii. In the close of chap. viii. (ver. 13), Paul had stated, when examining the question whether it was right to eat meat offered in sacrifice to idols, that the grand principle on which *he* acted, and on which *they* should act, was that of *self-denial*. To illustrate this he employs the ninth chapter, by showing how *he* acted on it in reference to a maintenance; showing that it was this principle that led him to decline a support to which he was really entitled. Having illustrated that, he *returns* in this chapter to the subject which he was discussing in chap. viii.; and the design of this chapter is further to explain and enforce the sentiments advanced there, and to settle some other inquiries pertaining to the same general subject. The *first* point, therefore, on which he insists is, *the danger of relapsing into idolatry*—a danger which would arise should they be in the habit of frequenting the temples of idols, and of partaking of the meats offered in sacrifice; ver. 1 —24. Against this he had cautioned them in general, in chap. viii. 7, 9 — 12. This danger he now sets forth by a variety of illustrations. He first shows them that the Jews had been highly favoured, had been solemnly consecrated to Moses and to God, and had been under the divine protection and guidance (ver. 1—4); yet that this had not kept them from the displeasure of God when they sinned; ver. 5. He shows that notwithstanding their privileges, they had indulged in inordinate desires (ver. 6); that they had become idolaters (ver. 7); that they had been guilty of licentiousness (ver. 8); that they had tempted their leader and guide (ver. 9); that they had murmured (ver. 10); and that, as a consequence of this, many of them had been destroyed. In view of all this, Paul cautions the Corinthians not to be self-confident, or to feel secure; and not to throw themselves in the way of temptation by partaking of the feasts of idolatry; ver. 12—14. This danger he further illustrates (ver. 15, 24) by showing that if they partook of those sacrifices, they in fact became identified with the worshippers of idols. This he proved by showing that in the Christian communion, those who partook of the Lord's supper were identified with Christians (ver. 16, 17); that in the Jewish sacrifices the same thing occurred, and that those who partook of them were regarded as Jews, and as worshippers of the same God with them (ver. 18); and that

the same thing must occur, in the nature of the case, by partaking of the sacrifices offered to idols. They were *really* partaking of that which had been offered to *devils;* and against any such participation Paul would solemnly admonish them; ver. 19—22. Going on the supposition, therefore, that there was nothing wrong in itself in partaking of the meat that had been thus killed in sacrifice, yet Paul says (ver. 23), that it was not expedient thus to expose themselves to danger; and that the grand principle should be to seek the comfort and edification of others; ver. 24. Paul thus strongly and decisively admonishes them *not* to enter the temples of idols to partake of those feasts; not to unite with idolaters in their celebration; not to endanger their piety by these temptations.

There were, however, two other questions on the subject which it was important to decide, and which had probably been submitted to him in the letter which they had sent for counsel and advice. The first was, whether it was right to purchase and eat the meat which had been sacrificed, and which was exposed indiscriminately with other meat in the market; ver. 25. To this Paul replies, that as no evil could result from this, as it could not be alleged that they purchased it *as* meat sacrificed to idols, and as all that the earth contained belonged to the Lord, it was not wrong to purchase and to use it. Yet if even this was pointed out to them as having been sacrificed to idols, he then cautioned them to abstain from it; ver. 28. The other question was, whether it was right for them to accept the invitation of a heathen, and to partake of meat then that had been offered in sacrifice; ver. 27. To this a similar answer was returned. The general principle was, that no questions were to be asked in regard to what was set before them; but if the food was expressly pointed out as having been offered in sacrifice, then to partake of it would be regarded as a public recognition of the idol; ver. 28—30. Paul then concludes the discussion by stating the noble rule that is to guide in all this : that every thing is to be done to the glory of God (ver. 31); and that the great effort of the Christian should be so to act in all things as to honour his religion, as not to lead others into sin; ver. 32, 33.

1. *Moreover, brethren.* But, or now (δὲ). This verse, with the following illustrations (ver. 1—4), is properly connected in Paul's argument with the statements which he had made in chap. viii. 8, &c., and is designed to show the danger which would result from their partaking of the feasts that were celebrated in honour of idols. It is not improbable, as Mr. Locke supposes, that the Corinthians might have urged that they were constantly solicited by their heathen friends to attend those feasts; that in their circumstances it was scarcely possible to avoid it; that there could be no danger of their relapsing into idolatry; and their doing so could not be offensive to God, since they were known to be Christians; since they had been baptized, and purified from sin : since they were devoted to his service; since they knew that an idol was nothing in the world; and since they had been so highly favoured, as the people of God, with so many extraordinary endowments, and were so strongly guarded against the possibility of becoming idolaters. To meet these considerations, Paul refers them to the example of the ancient Jews. They also were the people of God. They had been solemnly dedicated to Moses and to God. They had been peculiarly favoured with spiritual food from heaven, and with drink miraculously poured from the rock. Yet notwithstanding this, they had forgotten God, had become idolaters, and had been destroyed. By their example, therefore, Paul would warn the Corinthians against a similar danger. ¶ *I would not that ye should be ignorant.* A large part of the church at Corinth were Gentiles. It could hardly be supposed that they were well informed respecting the ancient history of the Jews. Probably they had read these things in the Old Testament; but they might not have them distinctly in their recollection. Paul brings them distinctly before their minds, as an illustration and an admonition. The sense is, "I would not have you unmindful or forgetful of these things; I would have you recollect this case, and suffer their example to influence your conduct. I would not have you suppose that even a solemn consecration to God and the possession of distinguished tokens of divine favour are a security against the danger of sin, and even apostasy; since the example of the favoured Jews shews that even in such circumstances there is danger." ¶ *How that all our fathers.* That is, the fathers of the Jewish community; the fathers of us who are Jews. Paul speaks here as being himself a Jew, and refers to his own ancestors as such. The word "all" here seems to be introduced to give emphasis to the fact that even those who were destroyed (ver. 5) also had this privilege. It could not be pretended that *they* had not been devoted to God, since *all* of them had been thus consecrated professedly to his service. The entire Jewish community which Moses led forth from Egypt had thus been devoted to him. ¶ *Were under the cloud.* The cloud—the *Shechinah* —the visible symbol of the divine presence and protection that attended them out of Egypt. This went before them by day as a cloud to guide them, and by night it became a pillar of fire to give them light; Ex. xiii. 21, 22. In the dangers of the Jews, when closely pressed by the Egyptians, it went *behind* them, and became dark to the Egyptians, but light to the Israelites, thus constituting a defence; Ex. xiv. 20. In the wilderness, when travelling through the burning desert, it seems to have been expanded over the camp as a covering, and a defence from the intense rays of a burning sun; Num. x. 34, "And the cloud of JEHOVAH was upon them by day;" Num. xiv. 14, "Thy cloud standeth over them." To this fact the apostle refers here. It was a symbol of the divine favour and protection; comp.

2 And were all baptized unto Moses in the cloud and in the sea;

3 And did all eat the same spiritual meat ; [a]

a Ex.16.15,35 ; Neb.9.15,20; Ps.78,24,25.

Isa. iv. 5. It was a guide, a shelter, and a defence. The Jewish Rabbins say that " the cloud *encompassed* the camp of the Israelites as a wall encompasses a city, nor could the enemy come near them." Pirke Eleazer, chap. 44, as quoted by Gill. The probability is, that the cloud extended over the whole camp of Israel, and that to those at a distance it appeared as *a pillar.* ¶ *And all passed through the sea.* The Red sea, under the guidance of Moses, and by the miraculous interposition of God; Ex. xiv. 21, 22. This was also a proof of the divine protection and favour, and is so adduced by the apostle. His object is to *accumulate* the evidences of the divine favour to them, and to show that they had as many securities against apostasy as the Corinthians had, on which they so much relied.

2. *And were all baptized.* In regard to the meaning of the word *baptized,* see Note on Mat. iii. 6. We are not to suppose that the rite of baptism, as we understand it, was formally administered by Moses, or by any other person, to the Jews, for there is not the least evidence that any such rite was then known, and the very circumstances here referred to forbid such an interpretation. They were baptized " in the cloud and " in the sea," and this cannot be understood as a religious rite administered by the hand of man. It is to be remembered that the word *baptism* has two senses—the one referring to the application of water as a religious rite, in whatever mode it is done ; and the other in the sense of *dedicating, consecrating, initiating into,* or bringing under obligation to. And it is evidently in this latter sense that the word is used here, as denoting that they were *devoted* to Moses as a leader, they were brought under his laws, they became bound to obey him, they were placed under his protection and guidance by the miraculous interposition of God. This was done by

the fact that their passing through the sea, and under the cloud, in this manner, brought them under the author·ity and direction of Moses as a leader, and was a public recognition of their being his followers, and being bound to obey his laws. ¶ *Unto Moses* (εἰς). This is the same preposition which is used in the form of baptism prescribed in Mat. xxviii. 19. See Note on that place. It means that they were thus devoted or dedicated to Moses; they received and acknowledged him as their ruler and guide; they professed subjection to his laws, and were brought under his authority. They were thus *initiated into* his religion, and thus recognised his divine mission, and bound themselves to obey his injunctions.—*Bloomfield.* ¶ *In the cloud.* This cannot be proved to mean that they were enveloped and, as it were, *immersed* in the cloud, for there is no evidence that the cloud thus enveloped them, or that they were immersed in it as a person is in water. The whole account in the Old Testament leads us to suppose that the cloud either passed before them as a pillar, or that it had the same form in the rear of their camp, or that it was suspended over them, and was thus the symbol of the divine protection. It would be altogether improbable that the dark cloud would *pervade* the camp. It would thus embarrass their movements, and there is not the slightest intimation in the Old Testament that it did. Nor is there any probability in the supposition of Dr. Gill and others, that the cloud, as it passed from the rear to the front of the camp, "let down a plentiful rain upon them, whereby they were in such a condition as if they had been all over dipped in water." For, (1.) There is not the slightest intimation of this in the Old Testament. (2.) The supposition is contrary to the very design of the cloud. It was not a natural cloud, but was a symbol of the divine presence and protection. It was not to give rain on the Israelites, or on the land, but it was to guide, and to be an emblem of the care of God. (3.) It is doing violence to the Scriptures to introduce suppositions in this manner without the slightest authority. It is further to be observed, that this supposition does by no means give any aid to the cause of the Baptist after all. In what conceivable sense were they, even on this supposition, *immersed?* Is it *immersion in water* when one is exposed to a shower of rain? We speak of being *sprinkled* or *drenched* by rain, but is it not a violation of all propriety of language to say that a man is *immersed* in a shower? If the supposition, therefore, is to be admitted, that rain fell from the cloud as it passed over the Jews, and that this is meant here by "baptism unto Moses," then it would follow that *sprinkling* would be the mode referred to, since this is the only form that has resemblance to a falling shower. But the supposition is not necessary. Nor is it needful to suppose that water was applied to them at all. The thing itself is improbable; and the whole case is met by the simple supposition that the apostle means that they were initiated in this way into the religion of Moses, recognised his divine mission, and under the cloud became his followers and subject to his laws. And if this interpretation is correct, then it follows that the word *baptize* does not of necessity mean to *immerse.* ¶ *And in the sea.* This is another expression that goes to determine the sense of the word *baptize.* The sea referred to here is the Red sea, and the event was the passage through that sea. The fact in the case was, that the Lord caused a strong east wind to blow all night, and made the sea dry land, and the waters were divided (Ex. xiv. 21), and the waters were a wall unto them on the right hand and on the left, Ex. xiv. 22. From this whole narrative it is evident that they passed through the sea without being *immersed* in it. The waters were driven into high adjacent walls for the very purpose that they might pass between them dry and safe.

There is the fullest proof that they were not submerged in the water. Dr. Gill supposes that the water stood up above their heads, and that "they seemed to be immersed in it." This might be true; but this is to give up the idea that the word baptize means always to immerse in water, since it is a fact, according to this supposition, that they were *not* thus immersed, but only seemed to be. And all that can be meant, therefore, is, that they were in this manner initiated into the religion of Moses, convinced of his divine mission, and brought under subjection to him as their leader, lawgiver, and guide. This passage is a very important one to prove that the word baptism does not necessarily mean entire immersion in water. It is perfectly clear that neither the cloud nor the waters touched them. "They went through the midst of the sea on *dry* ground." It remains only to be asked whether, if immersion was the only mode of baptism known in the New Testament, the apostle Paul would have used the word not only so as not necessarily to imply that, but as *necessarily* to mean something else?

2. *And did all eat the same spiritual meat.* That is, *manna.* Ex. xvi. 15, 35; Neh. ix. 15, 20. The word *meat* here is used in the old English sense of the word, to denote *food* in general. They lived on *manna.* The word *spiritual* here is evidently used to denote that which was given by the Spirit, or by God; that which was the result of his miraculous gift, and which was not produced in the ordinary way, and which was not the gross food on which men are usually supported. It had an excellency and value from the fact that it was the immediate gift of God, and is thus called "angel's food." Ps. lxxviii. 25. It is called by Josephus "divine and extraordinary food." Ant. iii. 1. In the language of the Scriptures, that which is distinguished for excellence, which is the immediate gift of God, which is unlike that which is gross and of earthly origin, is called *spiritual,* to denote its purity, value, and excellence. Comp. Rom. vii. 14; 1 Cor. iii. 1; xv. 44, 46; Eph. i. 3.

4 And did all drink the same spiritual drink ; *a* for they drank of that spiritual Rock that [1] followed them : and that Rock was Christ.

a Ex.17.6 ; Num.20.11.

1 or, *went with*.

The idea of Paul here is, that *all* the Israelites were nourished and supported in this remarkable manner by food given directly by God ; that they all had thus the evidence of the divine protection and favour, and were all under his care.

4. *And did all drink the same spiritual drink.* The idea here is essentially the same as in the previous verse, that they had been highly favoured of God, and enjoyed tokens of the divine care and guardianship. That was manifested in the miraculous supply of water in the desert, thus showing that they were under the divine protection, and were objects of the divine favour. There can be no doubt that by "spiritual drink" here, the apostle refers to the water that was made to gush from the rock that was smitten by Moses. Ex. xvii. 6 ; Num. xx. 11. Why this is called "spiritual" has been a subject on which there has been much difference of opinion. It cannot be because there was any thing peculiar in the nature of the water, for it was evidently real water, fitted to allay their thirst. There is no evidence, as many have supposed, that there was a reference in this to the drink used in the Lord's supper. But it must mean that it was bestowed in a miraculous and supernatural manner ; and the word "spiritual" must be used in the sense of supernatural, or that which is immediately given by God. Spiritual blessings thus stand opposed to natural and temporal blessings, and the former denote those which are immediately given by God as an evidence of the divine favour. That the Jews used the word "spiritual" in this manner is evident from the writings of the Rabbins. Thus they called the manna "spiritual food" (Yade Mose in Shemor Rabba, fol. 109. 3) ; and their sacrifices they called "spiritual bread" (Tzeror Hammor, fol. 93. 2).—*Gill.* The drink, therefore, here referred to was that bestowed in a supernatural manner and as a proof of the divine favour. ¶ *For they drank of that spiritual Rock.* Of the waters which flowed from that Rock. The Rock here is called "spiritual," not from any thing peculiar in the nature of the rock, but because it was the source to them of supernatural mercies, and became thus the emblem and demonstration of the divine favour, and of spiritual mercies conferred upon them by God. ¶ *That followed them.* Margin. *Went with* (ἀκολουθούσης). This evidently cannot mean that the rock itself literally followed them, any more than that they literally drank the rock, for one is as expressly affirmed, if it be taken literally, as the other. But as when it is said they "drank of the rock," it must mean that they drank of the *water* that flowed from the rock ; so when it is said that the "rock followed" or accompanied them, it must mean that the *water* that flowed from the rock accompanied them. This figure of speech is common everywhere. Thus the Saviour said (1 Cor. xi. 25), "This cup is the new testament," that is, the *wine* in this cup represents my blood, &c. ; and Paul says (1 Cor. xi. 25, 27), "whosoever shall drink this *cup* of the Lord unworthily," that is, the *wine* in the cup, &c., and "as often as ye drink this cup," &c., that is, the wine contained in the cup. It would be absurd to suppose that the rock that was smitten by Moses literally followed them in the wilderness ; and there is not the slightest evidence in the Old Testament that it did. Water was twice brought out of a rock to supply the wants of the children of Israel. Once at mount Horeb, as recorded in Ex. xvii. 6, in the wilderness of Sin, in the first year of their departure from Egypt. The second time water was brought from a rock about the time of the death of Miriam at Kadesh, and probably in the fortieth year of their departure from Egypt, Num. xx. 1. It was to the former of these occasions that the apostle evidently refers. In regard

to this we may observe, (1.) That there must have been furnished a large quantity of water to have supplied the wants of more than two millions of people. (2.) It is expressly stated Deut. ix. 21), that "the brook (הנחל, stream, torrent, or river, see Num. xxxiv. 5; Josh. xv. 4, 47; 1 Kings viii. 65; 2 Kings xxiv. 7) descended out of the mount," and was evidently a stream of considerable size. (3.) Mount Horeb was higher than the adjacent country, and the water that thus gushed from the rock, instead of collecting into a pool and becoming stagnant, would flow off in the direction of the sea. (4.) The sea to which it would naturally flow would be the Red sea, in the direction of the Eastern or Elanitic branch of that sea. (5.) The Israelites would doubtless, in their journeyings, be influenced by the natural direction of the water, or would not wander far from it, as it was daily needful for the supply of their wants. (6.) At the end of thirty-seven years we find the Israelites at Ezion-geber, a sea-port on the eastern branch of the Red sea, where the waters probably flowed into the sea; Num. xxxiii. 36. In the fortieth year of their departure from Egypt, they left this place to go into Canaan by the country of Edom, and were immediately in distress again by the want of water. It is thus *pro-bable* that the water from the rock continued to flow, and that it consti-tuted a stream, or river; that it was near their camp all the time till they came to Ezion-geber; and that thus, together with the daily supply of manna, it was a proof of the protec-tion of God, and an emblem of their dependence. If it be said that there is *now* no such stream to be found there, it is to be observed that it is represented as miraculous, and that it would be just as reasonable to look for the daily descent of manna there in quantities sufficient to supply more than two millions of men, as to expect to find the gushing and running river of water. The only question is, whe-ther God *can* work a miracle, and whether there is evidence that he has done it. This is not the place to exa-

mine that question. But the evi-dence is as strong that he wrought this miracle as that he gave the manna, and neither of them is incon-sistent with the power, the wisdom, or the benevolence of God. ¶ *And that Rock was Christ.* This cannot be intended to be understood *literally*, for it was not literally true. The rock from which the water flowed was evidently an ordinary rock, a part of mount Horeb; and all that this can mean is, that that rock, with the stream of water thus gushing from it, was a *representation* of the Messiah. The word *was* is thus often used to denote similarity or representation, and is not to be taken literally. Thus, in the institution of the Lord's supper, the Saviour says of the bread, " This *is* my body," that is, it *represents* my body. Thus also of the cup, " This cup *is* the new testament in my blood," that is, it represents my blood, 1 Cor. xi. 24, 25. Thus the gushing fountain of water might be regarded as a representation of the Messiah, and of the blessings which result from him. The apostle does not say that the Israelites knew that this was designed to be a representation of the Messiah, and of the blessings which flow from him, though there is nothing improbable in the supposition that they so understood and regarded it, since all their institutions were pro-bably regarded as typical. But he evidently *does* mean to say that the rock was a vivid and affecting repre-sentation of the Messiah; that the Jews *did* partake of the mercies that flow from him; and that even in the desert they were under his care, and had in fact among them a vivid repre-sentation of him in some sense corres-ponding with the emblematic repre-sentation of the same favours which the Corinthian and other Christians had in the Lord's supper. This repre-sentation of the Messiah, *perhaps*, was understood by Paul to consist in the following things: (1.) Christians, like the children of Israel, are passing through the world as pilgrims, and to them that world is a wilderness—a desert. (2.) They need continued supplies, as the Israelites did, in their

5 But with many of them God was not well pleased ; for they were overthrown *a* in the wilderness.

6 Now these things were [1] our

a Num.14.29-35 ; 26.64,65; Heb.3.17; Jude 5.

examples, to the intent we should not lust after evil things, as they *b* also lusted.

7 Neither be ye idolaters, as *we* some of them ; as it is writ-

1 *the figures.*   *b* Num.11.4,33,34.

journey. The world, like that wilderness, does not meet their necessities, or supply their wants. (3.) That rock was a striking representation of the fulness of the Messiah, of the abundant grace which he imparts to his people. (4.) It was an illustration of their continued and constant dependence on him for the daily supply of their wants. It should be observed that many expositors understand this literally. Bloomfield translates it, "and they were supplied with drink from the spiritual Rock which followed them, even Christ." So Rosenmuller, Calvin, Glass, &c. In defence of this interpretation, it is said, that the Messiah is often called " a rock" in the Scriptures ; that the Jews believe that the "angel of JEHOVAH" who who attended them (Ex. iii. 2, and other places) was the Messiah ; and that the design of the apostle was, to show that this *attending Rock*, the Messiah, was the source of all their blessings, and particularly of the water that gushed from the rock. But the interpretation suggested above seems to me to be most natural. The *design* of the apostle is apparent. It is to show to the Corinthians, who relied so much on their privileges, and felt themselves so secure, that the Jews *had the very same privileges*—had the highest tokens of the divine favour and protection, were under the guidance and grace of God, and were partakers constantly of that which adumbrated or typified the Messiah, in a manner as real, and in a form as much fitted to keep up the remembrance of their dependence, as even the bread and wine in the Lord's supper.

5. *But with many of them*, &c. That is, with their conduct. They rebelled and sinned, and were destroyed. The design of the apostle here is, to remind them that although they enjoyed so many privileges, yet they were destroyed ; and thus to admonish

the Corinthians that *their* privileges did not constitute an absolute security from danger, and that *they* should be cautious against the indulgence of sin. The phrase rendered here "with many" (ἐν τοῖς πλείοσιν) should have been rendered "with the many," literally " with *the* many ; and it means that with the greater part of them God was not well pleased ; that is, he was pleased with but few of them. ¶ *Was not well pleased.* Was offended with their ingratitude and rebellion. ¶ *For they were overthrown*, &c. That is, by the pestilence, by wars, or died by natural and usual diseases, so that they did not reach the land of Canaan. But two men of that generation, Caleb and Joshua, were permitted to enter the land of promise ; Num. xiv. 29, 30.

6. *Now these things.* The judgments inflicted on them by God for their sins. ¶ *Were our examples.* Greek, *Types* (τύποι). Margin, *Figures.* They were not *designed* to be types of us, but they are to be held up as furnishing an admonition to us, or a warning that we do not sin in the same way. The same God directs our affairs that ordered theirs ; and if we sin as they did, we also must expect to be punished, and excluded from the favour of God, and from heaven. ¶ *Lust after evil things.* Desire those things which are forbidden, and which would be injurious. They lusted after flesh, and God granted them their desires, and the consequence was a plague, and the destruction of multitudes ; Ex. xi. 4, 31—34. So Paul infers that the Corinthian Christians should not lust after, or desire the meat offered in sacrifice to idols, lest it should lead them also to sin and ruin.

7. *Neither be ye idolaters.* This caution is evidently given in view of the danger to which they would be exposed if they partook of the feasts that were celebrated in honour of idols in their temples. The particular idol-

ten, *a* The people sat down to eat and drink, and rose up to play.

8 Neither let us commit fornica-

a Ex.32.6.

atry which is referred to here is, the worship of the golden calf that was made by Aaron; Ex. xxxii. 1—5. ¶ *As it is written;* Ex. xxxii. 6. ¶ *The people sat down to eat and to drink.* To worship the golden calf. They partook of a feast in honour of that idol. I have already observed that it was common to keep a feast in honour of an idol, and that the food which was eaten on such an occasion was mainly the meat which had been offered in sacrifice to it. This instance was particularly to the apostle's purpose, as he was cautioning the Corinthians against the danger of participating in the feasts celebrated in the heathen temples. ¶ *And rose up to play* (παίζειν). The Hebrew word used in Ex. xxxii. 7 (לְצַחֵק) means to laugh, to sport, to jest, to mock, to insult (Gen. xxi. 9); and then to engage in dances accompanied with music, in honour of an idol. This was often practised, as the worship of idols was celebrated with songs and dances. This is particularly affirmed of this instance of idol worship (Ex. xxxii. 19); and this was common among ancient idolaters; and this mode of worship was even adopted by David before the ark of the Lord; 2 Sam. vi. 5; 1 Chron. xiii. 8; xv. 29. All that the word "to play" here necessarily implies, is, that of choral songs and dances, accompanied with revelry in honour of the idol. It was, however, the fact that such worship was usually accompanied with much licentiousness; but that is not necessarily implied in the use of the word. Most of the oriental dances were grossly indecent and licentious, and the word here *may* be designed to include such indelicacy and licentiousness.

8. *Neither let us commit fornication,* &c. The case referred to here was that of the licentious intercourse with the daughters of Moab, referred to in Num. xxv. 1—9. ¶ *And fell in one*

tion, as some *b* of them committed, and fell in one day three and twenty thousand.

9 Neither let us tempt *c* Christ,

b Num.25.1—9. *c* Ex.17.2,7.

day. Were slain for their sin by the plague that prevailed. ¶ *Three and twenty thousand.* The Hebrew text in Num. xxv. 9, is twenty-four thousand. In order to reconcile these statements, it may be observed that perhaps twenty-three thousand fell directly by the plague, and one thousand were slain by Phinehas and his companions (*Grotius*); or it may be that the number was between twenty-three and twenty-four thousand, and it might be expressed in round numbers by either.—*Macknight.* At all events, Paul has not exceeded the truth. There were *at least* twenty-three thousand that fell, though there might have been more. The *probable* supposition is, that the three and twenty thousand fell immediately by the hand of God in the plague, and the other thousand by the judges; and as Paul's design was particularly to mention the proofs of the immediate divine displeasure, he refers only to those who fell by that, in illustration of his subject.—There was a particular reason for this caution in respect to licentiousness. (1.) It was *common* among all idolaters; and Paul in cautioning them against idolatry, would naturally warn them of this danger. (2.) It was common at Corinth. It was the prevalent vice there. To *Corinthianize* was a term synonymous among the ancients with licentiousness. (3.) So common was this at Corinth, that, as we have seen (see the Introduction), not less than a thousand prostitutes were supported in a single temple there; and the city was visited by vast multitudes of foreigners, among other reasons on account of its facilities for this sin. Christians, therefore, were in a peculiar manner exposed to it; and hence the anxiety of the apostle to warn them against it.

9. *Neither let us tempt Christ,* &c. The word *tempt,* when applied to man, means to present motives or induce-

as some of them also tempted, and were destroyed of serpents. *a*

10 Neither murmur ye, as some

a Num.21.6.

ments to sin : when used with reference to God, it means to try his patience, to provoke his anger, or to act in such a way as to see how much he will bear, and how long he will endure the wickedness and perverseness of men. The Israelites tempted him, or *tried his patience and forbearance*, by rebellion, murmuring, impatience, and dissatisfaction with his dealings. In what way the Corinthians were in danger of tempting Christ is not known, and can only be conjectured. It may be that the apostle cautions them against exposing themselves to temptation in the idol temples—placing themselves, as it were, under the unhappy influence of idolatry, and thus needlessly *trying* the strength of their religion, and making an experiment on the grace of Christ, as if he were bound to keep them even in the midst of dangers into which they needlessly ran. They would have the promise of grace to keep them only when they were in the way of their duty, and using all proper precautions. To go beyond this, to place themselves in needless danger, to *presume* on the grace of Christ to keep them in all circumstances, would be to *tempt* him, and provoke him to leave them; see Note on Mat. iv. 7. ¶ *As some of them also tempted.* There is evidently here a word to be understood, and it may be either " Christ" or " God." The construction would naturally require the former; but it is not certain that the apostle meant to say that the Israelites tempted *Christ.* The main idea is that of *temptation*, whether it be of Christ or of God; and the purpose of the apostle is to caution them against the danger of tempting Christ, from the fact that the Israelites were guilty of the sin of tempting their leader and protector, and thus exposing themselves to his anger. It cannot be denied, however, that the more natural construction of this place is that which supposes that the word " Christ" is understood here rather than "God." In order to relieve this interpretation

of them also murmured, *b* and were destroyed of the destroyer. *c*

11 Now all these things hap-

b Num.14.2, 29.   *c* 2 Sam.24.16.

from the difficulty that the Israelites could not be said with any propriety to have tempted " *Christ*," since he had not then come in the flesh, two remarks may be made. First, by the " angel of the covenant," and the " angel of his presence" (Ex. xxiii. 20, 23 ; xxxii. 36; xxxiii. 2 ; Num. xx. 16 ; Isa. lxiii. 9; Heb. xi. 26), that went with them, and delivered them from Egypt, there is reason to think the sacred writers understood the Messiah to be intended : and that he who subsequently became incarnate was he whom they tempted. And secondly, We are to bear in mind that the term *Christ* has acquired with us a signification somewhat different from that which it originally had in the New Testament. *We* use it as *a proper name*, applied to Jesus of Nazareth. But it is to be remembered that it is the mere Greek word for the Hebrew " Anointed," or the " Messiah;" and by retaining this signification of the word here, no small part of the difficulty will be avoided ; and the expression then will mean simply that the Israelites "tempted *the Messiah*;" and the idea will be that he who conducted them, and against whom they sinned, and whom they tempted, was *the Messiah*, who afterwards became incarnate ; an idea that is in accordance with the ancient ideas of the Jews respecting this personage, and which is not forbidden, certainly, in any part of the Bible. ¶ *And were destroyed of serpents.* Fiery serpents; see Num. xxi. 6.

10. *Neither murmur ye.* Do not repine at the allotments of Providence, or complain of his dealings. ¶ *As some of them also murmured ;* Num. xiv. 2. The ground of their murmuring was, that they had been disappointed; that they had been brought out of a land of plenty into a wilderness of want; and that instead of being conducted at once to the land of promise, they were left to perish in the desert. They therefore complained of their leaders,

pened unto them for ¹ ensamples : and they are written for our admonition, upon whom the ends of the world are come.

¹ or, *types.*

and proposed to return again into Egypt. ¶ *And were destroyed of the destroyer.* That is, they were doomed to die in the wilderness without seeing the land of Canaan; Ex. xiv. 29. The "destroyer" here is understood by many to mean *the angel of death,* so often referred to in the Old Testament, and usually called by the Jews *Sammael.* The work of death, however, is attributed to an angel in Ex. xii. 23; comp. Heb. xi. 28. It was customary for the Hebrews to regard most human events as under the direction of angels. In Heb. ii. 14, he is described as he "that had the power of death;" comp. the book of Wisdom xviii. 22, 25. The simple idea here, however, is, that they *died* for their sin, and were not permitted to enter the promised land.

11. *For ensamples.* Greek, *Types* (τύπα). The same word which is used in ver. 6. This verse is a repetition of the admonition contained in that verse, in order to impress it more deeply on the memory; see Note on verse 6. The sense is, not that these things took place simply and solely *to be* examples, or admonitions, but that their occurrence illustrated great principles of human nature and of the divine government; they showed the weakness of men, and their liability to fall into sin, and their need of the divine protection, and they might thus be used for the admonition of succeeding generations. ¶ *They are written for our admonition.* They are recorded in the writings of Moses, in order that we and all others might be admonished not to confide in our own strength. The admonition did not pertain merely to the Corinthians, but had an equal applicability to Christians in all ages of the world. ¶ *Upon whom the ends of the world are come.* This expression is equivalent to that which so often occurs in the Scriptures, as, "the last time," "the latter day," &c.; see it fully explained in Notes

12 Wherefore *ᵃ* let him that thinketh he standeth take heed lest he fall.

13 There hath no temptation

a Prov. 28. 14; Rom. 11. 20.

on Acts ii. 17. It means the last dispensation; or, that period and mode of the divine administration under which the affairs of the world would be wound up. There would be no mode of administration *beyond* that of the gospel. But it by no means denotes necessarily that the continuance of this period called "the last times," and "the ends of the world" would be brief, or that the apostle believed that the world would soon come to an end. It might be the *last* period, and yet be longer than any one previous period, or than all the previous periods put together. There may be a last dynasty in an empire, and yet it may be longer than any previous dynasty, or than all the previous dynasties put together. The apostle Paul was at special pains in 2 Thess. ii. to show, that by affirming that the last time had come, he did not mean that the world would soon come to an end.

12. *Wherefore.* As the result of all these admonitions. Let this be the effect of all that we learn from the unhappy self-confidence of the Jews, to admonish us not to put reliance on our own strength. ¶ *That thinketh he standeth.* That supposes himself to be firm in the love of God, and in the knowledge of his truth; that regards himself as secure, and that will be therefore disposed to rely on his own strength. ¶ *Take heed lest he fall.* Into sin, idolatry, or any other form of iniquity. We learn here, (1.) That a confidence in our own security is no evidence that we are safe. (2.) Such a confidence may be one of the strongest evidences that we are in danger. Those are most safe who feel that they are weak and feeble, and who feel their need of divine aid and strength. They will then rely on the true source of strength; and they will be secure. (3.) All professed Christians should be admonished. All are in danger of falling into sin, and of dishonouring

taken you but [1] such as is common to man : but God *is* faithful,

who *a* will not suffer you to be tempted above that ye are able ; *b*

a Dan.3.17; 2Pet.2.9.　　b James 5.11.

their profession ; and the exhortation cannot be too often or too urgently pressed, that they should take heed lest they fall into sin. The leading and special idea of the apostle here should not be forgotten or disregarded. It is, that Christians *in their favoured moments*, when they are permitted to approach near to God, and when the joys of salvation fill their hearts, should exercise peculiar caution. For *a)* Then the adversary will be peculiarly desirous to draw away their thoughts from God, and to lead them into sin, as *their* fall would most signally dishonour religion ; *(b)* Then they will be less likely to be on their guard, and more likely to feel themselves strong, and not to need caution and solicitude. Accordingly, it often happens that Christians, after they have been peculiarly favoured with the tokens of the divine favour, soon relapse into their former state, or fall into some sin that grieves the hearts of their brethron, or wounds the cause of religion. So it is in revivals ; so it is in individuals. Churches that are thus favoured are filled with joy, and love, and peace. Yet they become self-confident and elated ; they lose their humility and their sense of their dependence ; they cease to be watchful and prayerful, supposing that all is safe ; and the result often is, that a season of revival is succeeded by a time of coldness and declension. And thus, too, it is with individuals. Just the opposite effect is produced from what should be, and from what need be. Christians should *then* be peculiarly on their guard ; and if they then availed themselves of their elevated advantages, churches *might* be favoured with continued revivals and ever-growing piety ; and individuals *might* be filled with joy, and peace, and holiness, and ever-expanding and increasing love.

13. *There hath no temptation taken you.* What temptation the apostle refers to here is not quite certain.

It is probable, however, that he refers to such as would, in their circumstances, have a tendency to induce them to forsake their allegiance to their Lord, and to lead them into idolatry and sin. These might be either open persecutions, or afflictions on account of their religion ; or they might be the various allurements which were spread around them from the prevalence of idolatry. They might be the open attacks of their enemies, or the sneers and the derision of the gay and the great. The design of the apostle evidently is, to show them that, if they were faithful, they had nothing to fear from any such forms of temptation, but that God was able to bring them through them all. The sentiment in the verse is a very important one, since the general principle here stated is as applicable to Christians now as it was to the Corinthians. ¶ *Taken you.* Seized upon you, or assailed you. As when an enemy *grasps* us, and attempts to hold us fast. ¶ *But such as is common to man* (εἰ μὴ ἀνθρώπινος). Such as is *human.* Margin, *Moderate.* The sense is evident. It means such as human nature is liable to, and has been often subjected to ; such as the human powers, under the divine aid, may be able to resist and repel. The temptations which they had been subjected to were not such as would be fitted to angelic powers, and such as would require angelic strength to resist ; but they were such as human nature had been often subjected to, and such as man had often contended with successfully. There is, therefore, here a recognition of the doctrine that man has natural ability to resist all the temptations to which he is subject ; and that consequently, if he yields, he is answerable for it. The *design* of the apostle is to comfort the Corinthians, and to keep their minds from despondency. He had portrayed their danger ; he had shown them how others had fallen ; and they might be led to suppose that in such circumstances they could not be secure. He therefore tells them that they might still be safe, for their temptations were such as human nature had often been subject to, and God was able to keep them from falling. ¶ *But God is faithful.* This was the only source of security ; and this was enough. If they looked only to themselves, they would fall. If they depended on the faithfulness of God, they would be secure. The sense is, not that God would keep them without any effort of their own ; not that he would secure them if they plunged into temptation ; but that if they used the proper means, if they resisted temptation, and sought his aid, and depended on his promises, then he would be faithful. This is everywhere implied in the Scriptures ; and to depend on the faithfulness of God, otherwise than in the proper use of means and in avoiding the places of temptation, is to *tempt him,* and provoke him to wrath ; see Notes on Mat. iv. ¶ *Who will not suffer you to be tempted,* &c. This is a general promise, just as applicable to all Christians as it was to the Corinthians. It implies, (1.) That all the circumstances, causes, and agents that lead to temptation are under the control of God. Every man that tempts another ; every fallen spirit that is engaged in this; every book, picture, place of amusement ; every charm of music, and of song ; every piece of indecent statuary ; and every plan of business, of gain or ambition, are all under the control of God. He can check them ; he can control them ; he can paralyze their influence ; he can destroy them ; comp. Mat. vi. 13. (2.) When men are *tempted,* it is because God *suffers* or permits it. He does not himself tempt men (James i. 13) ; he does not infuse evil thoughts into the mind; he does not *create* an object of temptation to place in our way, but he suffers it to be placed there by others. When we are tempted, therefore, we are to remember that it is because he *suffers* or *permits* it ; not because he *does* it. His agency is that of sufferance, not of creation. We are to re-

member, too, that there is some good reason why it is thus permitted ; and that it *may* be turned in some way to his glory, and to our advancement in virtue. (3.) There is a certain extent to which we are *able* to resist temptation. There is a *limit* to our power. There is a point beyond which we are not *able* to resist it. We have not the strength of angels. (4.) That limit will, in all cases, be beyond the point to which we are tempted. If not, there would be no sin in falling, any more than there is sin in the oak when it is prostrated before the tempest. (5.) If men fall into sin, under the power of temptation, they only are to blame. They have strength to resist all the temptations that assail them, and God has given the assurance that no temptation shall occur which they shall not be able, by his aid, to resist. In all instances, therefore, where men fall into sin ; in all the yielding to passion, to allurement, and to vice, man is to blame, and must be responsible to God. And this is especially true of Christians, who, whatever may be said of others, cannot plead that there was not power sufficient to meet the temptation, or to turn aside its power. ¶ *But will with the temptation,* &c. He will, at the same time that he suffers the trial or temptation to befall us, make a way of deliverance ; he will save us from being entirely overcome by it. ¶ *That ye may be able to bear* it. Or that you may be able to bear up under it, or endure it. God knows what his people are *able* to endure, and as he has entire control of all that can affect them, he will adapt all trials to their strength, and will enable them to bear all that is appointed to them. This is a general promise, and is as applicable to other Christians as it was to the Corinthians. It was to them a positive promise, and to all in the same circumstances it may be regarded as such now. It may be used, therefore, (1.) As a ground of *encouragement* to those who are in temptation and trial. God knows what they are able to endure; and he will sustain them in their temptations. It matters not how severe the trial ;

but will with the temptation also make a way to escape, that ye may be able to bear *it*.

14 Wherefore, my dearly beloved, *a* flee from idolatry.

a 1John 5.21.

15 I speak as to wise men; judge ye what I say.

16 The cup of blessing which we bless, is it not the communion of the blood of Christ? the bread

---

or how long it may be continued ; or how much they may feel their own feebleness; yet He who has appointed the trial is abundantly able to uphold them. They may, therefore, repose their all upon him, and trust to his sustaining grace. (2.) It may be used as an *argument*, that none who are true Christians, and who are thus tried, shall ever fall away, and be lost. The promise is positive and certain, that a way shall be made for their escape, and they shall be able to bear it. God is faithful to them , and though he *might* suffer them to be tempted beyond what they are able to bear, yet he will not, but will secure an egress from all their trials. With this promise in view, how can it be believed that any true Christians who are tempted will be suffered to fall away and perish? If they do, it must be from one of the following causes ; either because God is *not* faithful; or because he *will* suffer them to be tempted above what they are able to bear ; or because he will *not* make a way for their escape. As no Christian can believe either of these, it follows that they who are converted shall be kept unto salvation.

14. *Wherefore.* In view of the dangers and temptations that beset you ; in view of your own feebleness, and the perils to which you would be exposed in the idol temples, &c. ¶ *Flee from idolatry.* Escape from the service of idols ; from the feasts celebrated in honour of them ; from the temples where they are worshipped. This was one of the dangers to which they were peculiarly exposed ; and Paul therefore exhorts them to escape from every thing that would have a tendency to lead them into this sin. He had told them, indeed, that God was faithful; and yet he did not expect God would keep them without any effort of their own. He therefore

exhorts them to flee from all approaches to it, and from all the customs which would have a tendency to lead them into idolatrous practices. He returns, therefore, in this verse, to the particular subject discussed in chap. viii—the propriety of partaking of the feasts in honour of idols ; and shows the danger which would follow such a practice. That danger he sets forth in view of the admonitions contained in this chapter, from ver. 1 to ver. 12. The remainder of the chapter is occupied with a discussion of the question stated in chap. viii., whether it was right for them to partake of the meat which was used in the feasts of idolaters.

15. *I speak as to wise men, &c.* I speak to men qualified to understand the subject; and present *reasons* which will commend themselves to you. The reasons referred to are those which occupy the remainder of the chapter.

16. *The cup of blessing which we bless.* The *design* of this verse and the following verses seems to be, to prove that Christians, by partaking of the Lord's supper, are solemnly set apart to the service of the Lord Jesus; that they acknowledge *him* as their Lord, and dedicate themselves to him, and that as they could not and ought not to be devoted to idols and to the Lord Jesus at the same time, so they ought not to participate in the feasts in honour of idols, or in the celebrations in which idolaters would be engaged; see ver. 21. He states, therefore, (1.) That Christians are *united* and dedicated to Christ in the communion ; ver. 16, 17. (2.) That this was true of the Israelites, that they were one people, devoted by the service of the altar to the same God ; ver. 18. (3.) That though an idol was nothing, yet the heathen actually sacrificed to devils, and Christians ought not to partake with them ; ver.

which we break, is it not the communion of the body of Christ?

17 For we, *being* many are one bread, *and* one body; for

19—21. The phrase "cup of blessing" evidently refers to the wine used in the celebration of the Lord's supper. It is called "the cup of blessing" because over it Christians praise or bless God for his mercy in providing redemption. It is not because it is the means of conveying a blessing to the souls of those who partake of it—though that is true—but because thanksgiving, blessing, and praise were rendered to God in the celebration, for the benefits of redemption; see Note, Mat. xxvi. 26. Or it may mean, in accordance with a well known Hebraism, *the blessed cup;* the cup that is blessed. This is the more literal interpretation; and it is adopted by Calvin, Beza, Doddridge, and others. ¶ *Which we bless.* Grotius, Macknight, Vatablus, Bloomfield, and many of the Fathers suppose that this means, "over which we bless God;" or, "for which we bless God." But this is to do violence to the passage. The more obvious signification is, that there is a sense in which it may be said that the cup is blessed, and that by prayer and praise it is set apart and rendered in some sense sacred to the purposes of religion. It cannot mean that the cup has undergone any physical change, or that the wine is any thing but wine; but that it has been solemnly set apart to the service of religion, and by prayer and praise designated to be used for the purpose of commemorating the Saviour's love. That may be said to be blessed which is set apart to a sacred use (Gen. ii. 3; Ex. xx. 11); and in this sense the cup may be said to be blessed; see Luke ix. 16, "And he took the five loaves and the two fishes, and looking up to heaven, he blessed THEM," &c; comp. Gen. xiv. 9; xxvii. 23, 33, 41; xxviii. 1; Lev. ix. 22, 23; 2 Sam. vi. 18; 1 Kings viii. 41. ¶ *Is it not the communion of the blood of Christ?* Is it not the emblem by which the blood of Christ is exhibited, and the means by which our union through that blood is exhibited? Is it not the means by

which we express our attachment to him as Christians; showing our union to him and to each other; and showing that we partake in common of the benefits of his blood? The main idea is, that by partaking of this cup they showed that they were united to him and to each other; and that they should regard themselves as set apart to him. We have communion with one (*κοινωνία,*) that which is in *common,* that which pertains to all, that which evinces fellowship) when we partake together; when all have an equal right, and all share alike; when the same benefits or the same obligations are extended to all. And the sense here is, that Christians *partake alike* in the benefits of the blood of Christ; they share the same blessings; and they *express* this together, and in common, when they partake of the communion. ¶ *The bread,* &c. In the communion. It shows, since we all partake of it, that we share alike in the benefits which are imparted by means of the broken body of the Redeemer. In like manner it is implied that if Christians should partake with idolaters in the feasts offered in honour of idols, that they would be regarded as *partaking* with them in the services of idols, or as united to them, and therefore such participation was improper.

17. *For we.* We Christians. ¶ *Being many.* Gr. *The many* (*οἱ πολλοί*). This idea is not, as our translation would seem to indicate, that Christians were numerous, but that all (for *οἱ πολλοί* is here evidently used in the sense of *πάντες, all*) were united, and constituted one society. ¶ *Are one bread.* One loaf; one cake. That is, we are united, or are one. There is evident allusion here to the fact that the loaf or cake was composed of many separate grains of wheat, or portions of flour united in one; or, that as one loaf was broken and partaken by all, it was implied that they were all one. We are all one society; united as one, and for the same object. Our partaking of

we are all partakers of that one bread.

18 Behold Israel after ^a the flesh: ^b are not they which eat of the sacrifices partakers of the altar?

a Rom.4.1,12.　　b chap.9.13.

the same bread is an emblem of the fact that we are one. In almost all nations the act of eating together has been regarded as a symbol of unity or friendship. ¶ And *one body.* One society; united together. ¶ *For we are all partakers,* &c. And we thus show publicly that we are united, and belong to the same great family. The argument is, that if we partake of the feasts in honour of idols with their worshippers, we shall thus show that we are a part of their society.

18. *Behold Israel.* Look at the Jews. The design here is to illustrate the sentiment which he was establishing, by a reference to the fact that among the Jews those who partook of the same sacrifices were regarded as being one people, and as worshipping one God. So, if they partook of the sacrifices offered to idols, they would be regarded also as being fellow-worshippers of idols with them. ¶ *After the flesh;* see Rom. iv. 1. The phrase "after the flesh" is designed to denote the Jews who were not converted to Christianity; the natural descendants of Israel, or Jacob. ¶ *Are not they which eat of the sacrifices.* A portion of the sacrifices offered to God was eaten by the offerer, and another portion by the priests. Some portions of the animal, as the fat, were burnt; and the remainder, unless it was a holocaust, or whole burnt-offering, was then the property of the priests who had officiated, or of the persons who had brought it; Ex. xxix. 13, 22; Lev. iii. 4, 10, 15; iv. 9; vii. 3, 4; viii. 26. The right shoulder and the breast was the part which was assigned to the priests; the remainder belonged to the offerer. ¶ *Partakers of the altar.* Worshippers of the same God. They are united in their worship, and are so regarded. And in like manner, if you partake of the sacrifices offered to idols, and join with their worship-

19 What say I then? that the idol ^c is any thing? or that which is offered in sacrifice to idols is any thing

20 But *I say,* that the things

c chap.8.4.

pers in their temples, you will be justly regarded as *united* with them in their worship, and partaking with them in their abominations.

19. *What say I then?* This is in the present tense; τί οὖν φημι, what *do* I say? What is my meaning? What follows from this? Do I mean to say that an idol is anything; that it has a real existence? Does my reasoning lead to that conclusion; and am I to be understood as affirming that an idol is of itself of any consequence? It must be recollected that the Corinthian Christians are introduced by Paul (chap. viii. 4) as saying that they knew that an idol was nothing in the world. Paul did not *directly* contradict that; but his reasoning had led him to the necessity of calling the propriety of their attending on the feasts of idols in question; and he introduces the matter now by asking these questions, thus leading the mind *to* it rather than directly affirming it at once. " Am I in this reasoning to be understood as affirming that an idol is any thing, or that the meat there offered differs from other meat? No; you know, says Paul, that this is not my meaning. I admit that an idol in itself is nothing; but I do *not* admit, therefore, that it is right for you to attend in their temples; for though the *idol* itself—the block of wood or stone—is nothing, yet the offerings are really made to devils; and I would not have you engage in such a service;" ver. 20, 21. ¶ *That the idol is any thing?* That the block of wood or stone is a real living object of worship, to be dreaded or loved? See Note, chap. viii. 4. ¶ *Or that which is offered in sacrifice to idols is any thing?* Or that the meat which is offered *differs* from that which is not offered; that the mere act of offering it changes its qualities? I do not admit or suppose this.

which the Gentiles sacrifice, they sacrifice to devils, *a* and not to God: and I would not that ye should have fellowship with devils.

a Lev.17.7; Deut.32.17; Ps.106.37.

20. *But.* The negative here is omitted, but is understood. The ellipsis of a negative after an interrogative sentence is common in the classical writers as well as in the Scriptures. *Bloomfield.* The sense is, "No; I do not say *this*, but I say that there are reasons why you should not partake of those sacrifices; and one of those reasons is, that they have been really offered to devils." ¶ *They sacrifice to devils* (δαιμονίοις, *demons*). The heathens used the word *demon* either in a good or a bad sense. They applied it commonly to spirits that were supposed to be inferior to the supreme God; genii; attending spirits; or, as they called them, divinities, or gods. A part were in their view good, and a part evil. Socrates supposed that such a *demon* or genius attended him, who suggested good thoughts to him, and who was his protector. As these beings were good and well disposed, it was not supposed to be necessary to offer any sacrifices in order to appease them. But a large portion of those genii were supposed to be evil and wicked, and hence the necessity of attempting to appease their wrath by sacrifices and bloody offerings. It was therefore true, as the apostle says, that the sacrifices of the heathen were made, usually at least, to devils or to evil spirits. Many of these spirits were supposed to be the souls of departed men, who were entitled to worship after death, having been enrolled among the gods. The word "demons," among the Jews, was employed only to designate evil beings. It is not implied in their writings to good angels or to blessed spirits, but to evil angels, to idols, to false gods. Thus in the LXX. the word is used to translate אֱלִילִים, *Elilim, idols* (Ps. xcv. 5; Isa. lxv. 10); and שֵׁד, *Shaid*, as in Deut. xxxii. 17, in a passage which Paul has here almost literally used, "They sacrificed unto devils, not to God." No where in the Septuagint is it used

in a good sense. In the New Testament the word is uniformly used also to denote *evil spirits*, and those usually which had taken possession of men in the time of the Saviour; Mat. vii. 22; ix. 33, 34; x. 8; xi. 18; Mark i. 34, 39, et alii. See also Campbell on the Gospels, Pre. Diss. vi. part i. § 14—16. The precise force of the original is not, however, conveyed by our translation. It is not true that the heathens sacrificed to *devils*, in the common and popular sense of that word, meaning thereby the apostate angel and the spirits under his direction; for the heathens were as ignorant of their existence as they were of the true God; and it is not *true* that they *designed* to worship such beings. But it is true, (1.) That they did not worship the supreme and the true God. They were not acquainted with his existence; and they did not profess to adore him. (2.) They worshipped *demons;* beings that they regarded as inferior to the true God; created spirits, or the spirits of men that had been enrolled among the number of the gods. (3.) It was true that many of these beings were supposed to be malign and evil in their nature, and that their worship was designed to deprecate their wrath. So that, although an idol was nothing in itself, the gold or wood of which it was made was inanimate, and incapable of aiding or injuring them; and although there *were* no real beings such as the heathens supposed —no *genii* or inferior gods; yet they *designed* to offer sacrifice to such beings, and to deprecate their wrath. To join them in this, therefore, would be to express the belief that there were such beings, and that they ought to be worshipped, and that their wrath should be deprecated. ¶ *I would not that ye should have fellowship with devils.* I would not that you should have communion with demons. I would not have you express a belief of their existence; or join in worship to them; or par-

21 Ye cannot drink the cup of the Lord, and the cup *a* of devils: ye cannot be partakers of the

a Deut.32.38.

take of the spirit by which they are supposed to be actuated—a spirit that would be promoted by attendance on their worship. I would not have you, therefore, join in a mode of worship where such beings are acknowledged. You are solemnly dedicated to Christ; and the homage due to him should not be divided with homage offered to devils, or to imaginary beings.

21. *Ye cannot drink the cup of the Lord,* &c. This does not mean that they had no physical ability to do this, or that it was a natural impossibility; for they certainly had power to do it. But it must mean that they could not *consistently* do it. It was not fit, proper, decent. They were solemnly bound to serve and obey Christ: they had devoted themselves to him: and they could not, consistently with these obligations, join in the worship of demons. This is a striking instance in which the word *cannot* is used to denote not natural but moral inability. ¶ *And the cup of devils.* Demons; ver. 20. In the feasts in honour of the gods, wine was poured out as a libation, or drank by the worshippers; see Virg. Æn. viii. 273. The custom of drinking *toasts* at feasts and celebrations arose from this practice of pouring out wine, or drinking in honour of the heathen gods; and is a practice that partakes still of the nature of heathenism. It was one of the abominations of heathenism to suppose that their gods would be pleased with the intoxicating draught. Such a pouring out of a libation was usually accompanied with a *prayer* to the idol god, that he would accept the offering; that he would be propitious; and that he would grant the desire of the worshipper. From that custom the habit of expressing a sentiment, or proposing a toast, uttered in drinking wine, has been derived. The toast or sentiment which now usually accompanies the drinking of a glass in this manner, if

Lord's table, and of the table of devils.

22 Do we *b* provoke the Lord

b Deut.32.21; Job 9.4; Ezek.22.14.

it mean anything, is now also *a prayer:* but to whom? to the god of wine? to a heathen deity? Can it be supposed that it is a prayer offered to the true God; the God of purity? Has Jehovah directed that *prayer* should be offered to him in such a manner? Can it be acceptable to him? Either the sentiment is unmeaning, or it is a prayer offered to a heathen god, or it is mockery of JEHOVAH; and in either case it is improper and wicked. And it may as truly be said now of Christians as in the time of Paul. "Ye cannot consistently drink the cup of the Lord at the communion table, and the cup where a PRAYER is offered to a false god, or to the dead, or to the air; or when, if it means any thing, it is a mockery of JEHOVAH." Now can a Christian with any more consistency or propriety join in such celebrations, and in such unmeaning or profane libations, than he could go into the temple of an idol, and partake of the idolatrous celebrations there? ¶ *And of the table of devils.* Demons. It is not needful to the force of this that we should suppose that the word means necessarily evil spirits. They were not God; and to worship them was idolatry. The apostle means that Christians could not consistently join in the worship that was offered to them, or in the feasts celebrated in honour of them.

22. *Do we provoke the Lord to jealousy?* That is, shall we, by joining in the worship of idols, *provoke* or *irritate* God, or excite him to anger? This is evidently the meaning of the word παραζηλοῦμεν, rendered "provoke to jealousy." The word קנא, usually rendered by this word by the LXX., has this sense in Deut. xxxii. 21; 1 Kings xiv. 22; Ezra viii. 3; Ps. lxxviii. 58. There is a reference here, doubtless, to the truth recorded in Ex. xx. 5, that God "is a jealous God," and that he regards the worship of idols as a direct

to jealousy? are we stronger than he?

23 All *a* things are lawful for me, but all things are not expe-

a chap.6.12.

dient : all things are lawful for me, but all things edify not.

24 Let *b* no man seek his own, but every man another's *wealth.*

b Phil.2.4,21

affront to himself. The sentiment of Paul is, that to join in the worship of idols, or in the observance of their feasts, would be to participate in that which had ever been regarded by God with peculiar abhorrence, and which more than any thing else tended to provoke his wrath. We may observe, that any course of life that tends to alienate the affections from God, and to fix them on other beings or objects, is a sin of the same kind as that referred to here. Any inordinate love of friends, of property, of honour, has substantially the same idolatrous nature, and will tend to provoke him to anger. And it may be asked of Christians now, whether they will by such inordinate attachments provoke the Lord to wrath? whether they will thus excite his displeasure, and expose themselves to his indignation? Very often Christians *do* thus provoke him. They become unduly attached to a friend, or to wealth, and God in anger takes away that friend by death, or that property by the flames: or they conform to the world, and mingle in its scenes of fashion and gayety, and forget God; and in displeasure he visits them with judgments, humbles them, and recalls them to himself. ¶ *Are we stronger than he?* This is given as a reason why we should not provoke his displeasure. We cannot contend successfully with him; and it is therefore madness and folly to contend with God, or to expose ourselves to the effects of his indignation.

23. *All things are lawful for me.* See Note, chap. vi. 12. This is a repetition of what he had said before; and it is here applied to the subject of eating the meat that had been offered to idols. The sense is, " Though it may be admitted that it was strictly *lawful* to partake of that meat, yet there were strong reasons why it was inexpedient; and those reasons ought to have the binding force of law."

¶ *All things edify not.* All things do not tend to build up the church, and to advance the interests of religion; and when they do *not* have this effect, they are not expedient, and are improper. Paul acted for the welfare of the church. His object was to save souls. Any thing that would promote that object was proper; any thing which would hinder it, though in itself it might not be strictly unlawful, was in his view improper. This is a simple rule, and might be easily applied by all. If a man has his heart on the conversion of men and the salvation of the world, it will go far to regulate his conduct in reference to many things concerning which there may be no exact and positive law. It will do much to regulate his dress; his style of living; his expenses; his entertainments; his mode of intercourse with the world. He may not be able to fix his finger on any positive law, and to say that this or that article of dress is improper; that this or that piece of furniture is absolutely forbidden; or that this or that manner of life is contrary to any explicit law of JEHOVAH; but he *may* see that it will interfere with his great and main purpose, *to do good on the widest scale possible ;* and THEREFORE to him it will be inexpedient and improper. Such a grand leading purpose is a much better guide to direct a man's life than would be exact positive statutes to regulate every thing, even if such minute statutes were possible.

24. *Let no man seek his own.* This should be properly interpreted of the matter under discussion, though the direction assumes the form of a general principle. Originally it meant, " Let no man, in regard to the question about partaking of the meat offered in sacrifice to idols, consult his own pleasure, happiness, or convenience; but let him, as the leading rule on the subject, ask what will be for the welfare of others. Let him not

25 Whatsoever *a* is sold in the shambles, *that* eat, asking no question for conscience' sake.

a 1 Tim.4.4.

26 For *b* the earth *is* the Lord's and the fulness thereof.

27 If any of them that believe

b Deut.10.14; Ps.24.1; 50.12.

gratify his own taste and inclinations, regardless of their feelings, comfort, and salvation; but let him in these things have a primary reference to their welfare." He may dispense with these things without danger or injury; he cannot indulge in them without endangering the happiness or purity of others. His duty therefore requires him to abstain. The injunction, however, has a general form, and is applicable to all Christians, and to all cases *of a similar kind.* It does not mean that a man is not in any instance to regard his own welfare, happiness, or salvation; it does not mean that a man owes no duty to himself or family; or that he should neglect all these to advance the welfare of others: but the precept means, that *in cases like that under consideration,* when there is no positive law, and when a man's example would have a great influence, he should be guided in his conduct, not by a reference to his own ease, comfort or gratification, but by a reference to the purity and salvation of others. And the observance of this simple rule would make a prodigious change in the church and the world. ¶ *But every man another's* wealth. The word *wealth* is not in the Greek. Literally, "that which is of another;" the word το referring to any thing and every thing that pertains to his comfort, usefulness, happiness, or salvation.—The sentiment of the whole is, *when a man is bound and directed by no positive law, his grand rule should be the comfort and salvation of others.* This is a simple rule; it might be easily applied; and this would be a sort of balance-wheel in the various actions and plans of the world. If every man would adopt this rule, he could not be in much danger of going wrong; he would be certain that he would not live in vain.

25. *Whatsoever is sold in the shambles.* In the market. The meat of animals offered in sacrifice would be exposed there to sale as well as other meat. The apostle says that it might be purchased, since the mere fact that it had been offered in sacrifice could not change its quality, or render it unfit for use. They were to abstain from attending on the feasts of the idols in the temple, from partaking of meat that had been offered them, and from celebrations observed expressly in honour of idols; but lest they should become too scrupulous, the apostle tells them that if the meat was offered indiscriminately in the market with other meat, they were not to hesitate to purchase it, or eat it. ¶ *Asking no question for conscience' sake.* Not hesitating or doubting, as if it might *possibly* have been offered in sacrifice. Not being scrupulous, as if it were *possible* that the conscience should be defiled. This is a good rule still, and may be applied to a great many things. But, (1.) That which is purchased should be in itself lawful and right. It would not be proper for a man to use ardent spirits or any other intoxicating drinks because they were offered for sale, any more than it would be to commit suicide because men offered pistols, and bowie-knives, and halters to sell. (2.) There are many things now concerning which similar questions may be asked; as, *e. g.* is it right to use the productions of slave-labour, the sugar, cotton, &c., that are the price of blood? Is it right to use that which is known to be made on the Sabbath; or that which it is known a man has made by a life of dishonesty and crime? The consciences of many persons are tender on all such questions; and the questions are not of easy solution. Some rules may perhaps be suggested arising from the case before us. (*a*) If the article is exposed indiscriminately with others in the market, if it be in itself lawful, if there is no ready mark of distinction, then the apostle would direct us not to hesitate. (*b*) If the use and purchase of the article would go directly and knowingly to countenance

not bid you *to a feast*, and ye be disposed to go ; whatsoever *a* is set before you, eat, asking no question for conscience' sake.

a Luke 10.7.

the existence of slavery, to encourage a breach of the Sabbath, or to the continuance of a course of dishonest living, then it would seem equally clear that it is not right to purchase or to use it. If a man abhors slavery, and Sabbath-breaking, and dishonesty, then how can he knowingly partake of that which goes to patronise and extend these abominations? (c) If the article is expressly pointed out to him as an article that has been made in this manner, and his partaking of it will be *construed* into a participation of the crime, then he ought to abstain ; see ver. 28. No man is at liberty to patronise slavery, Sabbath-breaking, dishonesty, or licentiousness, in any form. Every man *can* live without doing it ; and where it can be done it should be done. And perhaps there will be no other way of breaking up many of the crimes and cruelties of the earth than for good men to act conscientiously, and to refuse to partake of the avails of sin, and of gain that results from oppression and fraud.

26. *For the earth* is *the Lord's.* This is quoted from Ps. xxiv. 1. The same sentiment is also found in Ps. l. 11, and in Deut. x. 14. It is here urged as a reason why it is right to partake of the meat offered in the market. It all belongs to the Lord. It does not *really* belong to the idol, even though it has been offered to it. It may, therefore, be partaken of as his gift, and should be received with gratitude. ¶ *And the fulness thereof.* All that the earth produces belongs to him. *He* causes it to grow ; and he has given it to be food for man ; and though it may have been devoted to an idol, yet its nature is not changed. It is still the gift of God ; still the production of his hand ; still the fruit of his goodness and love.

27. *If any of them that believe not.* That are not Christians; that are still heathens. ¶ *Bid you* to a feast.

28 But if any man say unto you, This is offered in sacrifice unto idols, eat not, *b* for his sake that showed it, and for conscience' sake:

b chap.8.10,12.

Evidently not a feast in the temple of an idol, but at his own house. If he *ask* you to partake of his hospitality. ¶ *And ye be disposed to go.* Greek, " And you will to go." It is evidently implied here that it would be not improper to go. The Saviour accepted such invitations to dine with the Pharisees (see Note, Luke xi. 37) ; and Christianity is not designed to abolish the courtesies of social life ; or to break the bonds of intercourse ; or to make men misanthropes or hermits. It allows and cultivates, under proper Christian restraints, the intercourse in society which will promote the comfort of men, and especially that which may extend the usefulness of Christians. It does not require, therefore, that we should withdraw from social life, or regard as improper the courtesies of society ; see Note on chap. v. 10. ¶ *Whatever is set before you,* &c. Whether it has been offered in sacrifice or not ; for so the connection requires us to understand it. ¶ *Eat.* This should be interpreted strictly. The apostle says " *eat,*" not "*drink ;*" and the principle will not authorize us to *drink* whatever is set before us, asking no questions for conscience' sake ; for while it was a matter of indifference in regard to eating, whether the meat had been sacrificed to idols or not, it is *not* a matter of indifference whether a man may drink intoxicating liquor. *That* is a point on which the *conscience* should have much to do ; and on which its honest decisions, and the will of the Lord, should be faithfully and honestly regarded.

28. *But if any man.* If any fellow guest; any scrupulous fellow Christian who may be present. That the word " any" (τις) refers to a fellow guest seems evident ; for it is not probable that the *host* would point out any part of the food on his own table, of the lawfulness of eating which he would suppose there was any doubt.

for [a] the earth *is* the Lord's, and the fulness thereof :

29 Conscience, I say, not thine own, but of the other : for why is my liberty judged of another *man's* conscience ?

a ver.26.   1 or, *thanksgiving.*

Yet there might be present some scrupulous fellow Christian who would have strong doubts of the propriety of partaking of the food, and who would indicate it to the other guests. ¶ *For his sake that showed it.* Do not offend him; do not lead him into sin; do not pain and wound his feelings. ¶ *And for conscience' sake.* Eat not, out of respect to the conscientious scruples of him that told thee that it had been offered to idols. The word *conscience* refers to the conscience of the informer (ver. 29); still *he* should make it a matter of conscience not to wound his weak brethren, or lead them into sin. ¶ *For the earth is the Lord's,* &c. ; see ver. 26. These words are wanting in many MSS. (see Mill's Gr. Tes.), and in the Vulgate, Syriac, Coptic, and Arabic versions; and are omitted by Griesbach. Grotius says that they should be omitted. There might easily have been a mistake in transcribing them from ver. 26. The authority of the MSS., however, is in favour of retaining them; and they are quoted by the Greek fathers and commentators. If they are to be retained, they are to be interpreted, probably, in this sense; " There is no *necessity* that you should partake of this food. All things belong to God; and he has made ample provision for your wants without subjecting you to the necessity of eating this. Since this is the case, it is best to regard the scruples of those who have doubts of the propriety of eating *this* food, and to abstain."

29. *Conscience, I say, not thine own.* I know that you may have no scruples on the subject. I do not mean that with you this need be a matter of conscience. I do not put it on that ground, as if an idol were any thing, or as if it were in itself wrong, or as if the quality of the meat so offered had been changed; but I

30 For if I by [1] grace be a partaker, why am I evil spoken of for that for which I give thanks ? [b]

31 Whether [c] therefore ye eat or drink, or whatsoever ye do, do all to the glory of God.

b Rom.14.6.   *c* Col.3.17; 1 Pet.4.11.

put it on the ground of not wounding the feelings of those who are scrupulous, or of leading them into sin. ¶ *For why is my liberty,* &c. There is much difficulty in this clause; for as it now stands, it seems to be entirely contradictory to what the apostle had been saying. He had been urging them to *have* respect to other men's consciences, and in some sense to give up their liberty *to* their opinions and feelings. Macknight and some others understand it as an objection : " Perhaps you will say, But why is my liberty to be ruled by another man's conscience ? " Doddridge supposes that this and ver. 30 come in as a kind of parenthesis, to prevent their extending his former caution beyond what he designed. " I speak only of acts obvious to human observation ; for as to what immediately lies between God and my own soul, why is my liberty to be judged, arraigned, condemned at the bar of another man's conscience? " But it is probable that this is not an objection. The sense may be thus expressed : " I am free ; I have *liberty* to partake of that food, if I please; there is no *law* against it, and it is not morally wrong : but if I do, when it is pointed out to me as having been sacrificed to idols, my liberty—the right which I exercise— will be *misconstrued, misjudged, condemned* (for so the word *κρινεται* seems to be used here) by others. The weak and scrupulous believer will censure, judge, condemn me as regardless of what is proper, and as disposed to fall in with the customs of idolaters; and will suppose that I cannot have a good conscience. Under these circumstances, why should I act so as to expose myself to this censure and condemnation? It is better for me to abstain, and not to use this liberty in the case, but to deny myself for the sake of others."

30. *For if I by grace be a partaker.*

Or rather, " If I *partake* by grace; if by the grace and mercy of God, I have a *right* to partake of this; yet why should I so conduct as to expose myself to the reproaches and evil surmises of others? Why should I lay myself open to be blamed on the subject of eating, when there are so many bounties of Providence for which I may be thankful, and which I may partake of without doing injury, or exposing myself in any manner to be blamed?" ¶ *Why am I evil spoken of.* Why should I pursue such a course as to expose myself to blame or censure? ¶ *For that for which I give thanks.* For my food. The phrase "for which I give thanks" seems to be a periphrasis for *food*, or for that of which he partook to nourish life. It is implied that he always gave thanks for his food; and that this was with him such a universal custom, that the phrase "for which I give thanks" might be used as convenient and appropriate phraseology to denote his ordinary food. The idea in the verse, then, is this: "By the favour of God, I have a *right* to partake of this food. But if I did, I should be evil spoken of, and do injury. And it is unnecessary. God has made ample provision elsewhere for my support, for which I may be thankful. I will not therefore expose myself to calumny and reproach, or be the occasion of injury to others by partaking of the food offered in sacrifice to idols."

31. *Whether therefore ye eat or drink.* This direction should be strictly and properly applied to the case in hand; that is, to the question about eating and drinking the things that had been offered in sacrifice to idols. Still, however, it contains a general direction that is applicable to eating and drinking at all times; and the phrase "whatsoever ye do" is evidently designed by the apostle to make the direction universal. ¶ *Or whatsoever ye do.* In all the actions and plans of life; whatever be your schemes, your desires, your doings, let all be done to the glory of God. ¶ *Do all to the glory of God.* The phrase "the glory of God" is equivalent to the *honour* of God; and the direction

is, that we should *so* act in all things as to *honour* him as our Lawgiver, our Creator, our Redeemer; and so as to lead others by our example to praise him and to embrace his gospel. A child acts so as to honour a father when he always cherishes reverential and proper thoughts of him; when he is thankful for his favours; when he keeps his laws; when he endeavours to advance his plans and his interests; and when he so acts as to lead all around him to cherish elevated opinions of the character of a father. He *dishonours* him when he has no respect to his authority; when he breaks his laws; when he leads others to treat him with disrespect. In like manner, we live to the glory of God when we honour him in all the relations which he sustains to us; when we keep his laws; when we partake of his favours with thankfulness, and with a deep sense of our dependence; when we pray unto him; and when we so live as to lead those around us to cherish elevated conceptions of his goodness, and mercy, and holiness. Whatever plan or purpose will tend to advance his kingdom, and to make him better known and loved, will be to his glory. We may observe in regard to this, (1.) That the rule is *universal*. It extends to every thing. If in so small matters as eating and drinking we should seek to honour God, assuredly we should in all other things. (2.) It is designed that this should be the constant rule of conduct, and that we should be often reminded of it. The acts of eating and drinking must be performed often; and the command is attached to that which *must* often occur, that we may be often reminded of it, and that we may be kept from forgetting it. (3.) It is intended that we should honour God in our families and among our friends. We eat with them; we share together the bounties of Providence; and God designs that we should honour him when we partake of his mercies, and that thus our daily enjoyments should be sanctified by a constant effort to glorify him. (4.) We should devote the strength which we derive from the bounties of his hand to his honour and in his ser-

32 Give ^a none offence, neither to the Jews, nor to the [1] Gentiles, nor to the church of God:

a Rom.14.13; 2 Cor.6.3.

33 Even as I please all *men* in all *things,* not seeking mine own profit, but the *profit* of many, that they may be saved.

[1] *Greeks.*

vice. He gives us food ; he makes it nourishing; he invigorates our frame; and that strength should *not* be devoted to purposes of sin, and profligacy, and corruption. It is an act of high dishonour to God, when HE gives us strength, that WE should at once devote that strength to pollution and to sin. (5.) This rule is designed to be one of the chief directors of our lives. It is to guide all our conduct, and to constitute a *test* by which to try our actions. Whatever can be done to advance the honour of God is right; whatever cannot be done with that end is wrong. Whatever plan a man can form that will have this end is a good plan; whatever cannot be made to have this tendency, and that cannot be commenced, continued, and ended with a distinct and definite desire to promote his honour, is wrong, and should be forthwith abandoned. (6.) What a change would it make in the world if this rule were every where followed ! How differently would even professing Christians live ! How many of their plans would they be constrained at once to abandon ! And what a mighty revolution would it at once make on earth should all the actions of men begin to be performed to promote the glory of God ! (7.) It may be added that sentiments like that of the apostle were found among the Jews, and even among heathens. Thus Maimonides, as cited by Grotius, says, " Let every thing be in the name of-Heaven," *i. e.* in the name of God. Capellus cites several of the rabbinical writers who say that all actions, even eating and drinking, should be done *in the name of God.* See the *Critici Sacri.* Even the heathen writers have something that resembles this. Thus Arrian (Ep. i. 19) says, " Looking unto God in all things small and great.' Epictetus, too, on being asked how any one may eat so as to please God, answered,

" By eating justly, temperately, and thankfully."

32. *Give none offence.* Be inoffensive ; that is, do not act so as to lead others into sin ; see Note, Rom. xiv. 13. ¶ *Neither to the Jews, &c.* To no one, though they are the foes of God or strangers to him. To the Jews be inoffensive, because they think that the least approach to idol worship is to be abhorred. Do not *so* act as to lead them to think that you connive at or approve idol worship, and so as to prejudice them the more against the Christian religion, and lead them more and more to oppose it. In other words, do not attend the feasts in honour of idols. ¶ *Nor to the Gentiles.* Gr. *Greeks.* To the pagans who are unconverted. They are attached to idol worship. They seek every way to justify themselves in it. Do not countenance them in it, and thus lead them into the sin of idolatry. ¶ *Nor to the church of God.* To Christians. Many of them are weak. They may not be as fully instructed as you are. Your example would lead them into sin. Abstain, therefore, from things which, though they are in themselves strictly *lawful,* may yet be the occasion of leading others into sin, and endangering their salvation.

33. *Even as I, &c.* Paul here proposes his own example as their guide. The example which he refers to is that which he had exhibited as described in this and the preceding chapters. *His* main object had been to please all men ; *i. e.* not to alarm their prejudices, or needlessly to excite their opposition (see Note on chap. ix. 19—23), while he made known to them the truth, and sought their salvation.—It is well when a minister can without ostentation appeal to his own example, and urge others to a life of self-denial and holiness, by his own manner of living, and by what he

CHAPTER XI.

BE ye followers *a* of me, even as I also *am* of Christ.

2 Now I praise you, brethren,

a Eph.5.1; 1 Thess.1.6.   *b* chap.4.17.

is himself in his daily walk and conversation.

CHAPTER XI.

THE first verse in this chapter properly belongs to the preceding, and is the conclusion of the discussion which the apostle had been carrying on in that and the previous chapters. It has been improperly separated from that chapter, and in reading should be read in connection with it. The remainder of the chapter is properly divided into two parts : I. A discussion respecting the impropriety of a woman's praying or prophesying with her head uncovered (ver. 2—16); and, II. A reproof of their irregularities in the observance of the Lord's supper, ver. 17—36.

I. In regard to the first, it seems probable that some of the women who, on pretence of being inspired, had prayed or prophesied in the Corinthian church, had cast off their veils after the manner of the heathen priestesses. This indecent and improper custom the apostle reproves. He observes, therefore, that the pre-eminence belongs to man over the woman, even as pre-eminence belonged to Christ over the man ; that it was a dishonour to Christ when a man prayed or prophesied with his head covered, and in like manner it was regarded every where as dishonourable and improper for a woman to lay aside the appropriate symbol of her sex, and the emblem of subordination, and to be uncovered in the presence of the man (ver. 3—5 ;) that if a woman was not veiled, if she laid aside the appropriate emblem of her sex and of her subordinate condition, she might as well part with her hair, which all knew would be dishonourable and improper (ver. 6); that the woman had been created for a subordinate station, and should observe it (ver. 7 —9); that she should have power on her head because of the angels (ver. 10) ; and yet, lest this should *depress*

that *o* ye remember me in all things, and keep *c* the ordinances, [1] as I delivered *them* to you.

3 But I would have you know,

c Luke 1.6.   [1] *traditions.*

her, and seem to convey the idea of her utter inferiority and unimportance, he adds, that in the plan of salvation they are in many respects on an equality with the man, that the same plan was adapted to both, that the same blessings are appointed for both sexes, and the same high hopes are held out to both (ver. 11, 12); and that nature on this subject was a good instructor, and showed that it was uncomely for a woman to pray with her head uncovered, that her hair had been given her for an ornament and for beauty, and that, as it would be *as* improper for her to remove her veil as to cut off her hair, nature itself required that this symbol of her subordination should be laid aside in public, ver. 13—16.

II. Next, as to the irregularities in the observance of the Lord's supper, the apostle observes (ver. 17), that he could not commend them for what he was about to say. There had been and there were irregularities among them, which it was his duty to reprove. In ver. 18—22, he states what those irregularities were. He then (ver. 23—26) states the true nature and design of the Lord's supper, as it was very evident that they had not understood it, but supposed it was a common feast, such as they had been accustomed to observe in honour of idols. In ver. 27—29, he states the consequences of observing this ordinance in an improper manner, and the proper way of approaching it.; and in ver. 30—32, observes that their improper mode of observing it was the cause of the punishment which many of them had experienced. He then concludes by directing them to celebrate the Lord's supper *together ;* to eat at home when they were hungry; and not to abuse the Lord's supper by making it an occasion of feasting; and assures them that the other matters of irregularity he would set in order when he should come among them.

that the head ^a of every man is Christ; ^b and the head of the woman

a Eph.5.23.　　　b Gen.3.16; 1 Pet.3.1,5,6.

1. *Be ye followers of me.* Imitate my example in the matter now under discussion. As I deny myself; as I seek to give no offence to any one; as I endeavour not to alarm the prejudices of others, but in all things to seek their salvation, so do you. This verse belongs to the previous chapter, and should not have been separated from it. It is the close of the discussion there. ¶ *Even as I also am of Christ.* I make Christ my example. He is my model in all things; and if you follow him, and follow me as far as *I* follow him, you will not err. This is the only safe example; and if we follow this, we can never go astray.

2. *Now I praise you, brethren.* Paul always chose to commend Christians when it could be done, and never seemed to suppose that such praise would be injurious to them. Note, chap. i. 4, 5. On this occasion he was the more ready to praise them as far as it could be done, because there were some things in regard to them in which he would have occasion to reprove them. ¶ *That ye remember me in all things.* That you are disposed to regard my authority and seek my direction in all matters pertaining to the good order of the church. There can be little doubt that they had consulted him in their letter (chap. vii. 1) about the proper manner in which a woman ought to demean herself if she was called upon, under the influence of divine inspiration, to utter any thing in public. The question seems to have been, whether, since she was inspired, it was proper for her to retain the marks of her inferiority of rank, and remain covered; or whether the fact of her inspiration did not release her from that obligation, anr make it proper that she should lay aside her veil, and appear as public speakers did among men. To this the apostle refers, probably, in the phrase "all things," that even in matters of this kind, pertaining to the good order of the church, they were disposed to regard his authority.

is the man; ^c and the head of Christ *is* God.

c John 14.28; chap.15.27,28.

¶ *And keep the ordinances.* Margin, *Traditions* (τὰς παραδώσεις). The word does not refer to any thing that had been delivered down from a former generation, or from former times, as the word *tradition* now usually signifies; but it means that which had been *delivered to them* (παραδίδωμι); *i. e.* by *the apostles.* The apostles had *delivered* to them certain doctrines, or rules, respecting the good order and the government of the church; and they had in general observed them, and were disposed still to do it. For this disposition to regard his authority, and to keep what he had enjoined, he commends them. He proceeds to specify what would be proper in regard to the particular subject on which they had made inquiry.

3. *But I would have you know.* "I invite your attention particularly to the following considerations, in order to form a correct opinion on this subject." Paul does not *at once* answer the inquiry, and determine what ought to be done; but he invites their attention to a series of remarks on the subject, which led *them* to draw the conclusion which he wished to establish. The phrase here is designed to call the attention to the subject, like that used so often in the New Testament, "he that hath ears to hear, let him hear." ¶ *That the head, &c.* The word *head*, in the Scriptures, is designed often to denote *master, ruler, chief.* The word שׂן is often thus used in the Old Testament; see Num. xvii. 3; xxv. 15; Deut. xxviii. 13, 44; Judg. x. 18; xi. 8, 11; 1 Sam. xv. 17; 2 Sam. xxii. 44. In the New Testament the word is used in the sense of Lord, ruler, chief, in Eph. i. 22; iv. 15; v. 23; Col. ii. 10. Here it means that Christ is the ruler, director, or Lord of the Christian man. This truth was to be regarded in all their feelings and arrangements, and was never to be forgotten. Every Christian should recollect the relation in which he stands to him, as one that is fitted to produce the strictest

4 Every man praying or prophesying, having *his* head covered, dishonoureth his head.

5 But every woman *a* that pray-

eth or prophesieth with *her* head
uncovered, dishonoureth her head:
for that is even all one as if she
were shaven.

decorum, and a steady sense of subordination. ¶ *Of every man.* Every
Christian. All acknowledge Christ
as their Ruler and Master. They are
subject to him; and in all proper ways
recognise their subordination to him.
¶ *And the head of the woman is the
man.* The sense is, she is subordinate to him ; and in all circumstances
—in her demeanour, her dress, her
conversation, in public and in the
family circle—should recognise her
subordination to him. The particular
thing here referred to is, that if the
woman is inspired, and speaks or prays
in public, she should by no means lay
aside the usual and proper symbols of
her subordination. The danger was,
that those who were under the influence of inspiration would regard themselves as freed from the necessity of
recognising that, and would lay aside
the *veil*, the usual and appropriate
symbol of their occupying a rank
inferior to the man. This was often
done in the temples of the heathen
deities by the priestesses, and it would
appear also that it had been done by
Christian females in the churches.
¶ *And the head of Christ is God.*
Christ, as Mediator, has consented to
assume a subordinate rank, and to
recognise God the Father as superior
in office. Hence he was obedient in
all things as a Son; he submitted to
the arrangement required in redemption ; he always recognised his subordinate rank as Mediator, and always
regarded God as the supreme Ruler,
even in the matter of redemption.
The sense is, that Christ, throughout
his entire work, regarded himself as
occupying a subordinate station to the
Father; and that it was proper from
his example to recognise the propriety
of rank and station every where.

4. *Every man praying or prophesying.* The word *prophesying* here
means, evidently, *teaching ;* or publicly speaking to the people on the sub-

ject of religion ; see Note on Acts ii.
17. See also the subject considered
more at length in the Notes on chap.
xiv. Whether these persons who are
here said to prophesy were all inspired,
or claimed to be inspired, may admit
of a question. The simple idea here
is, that they spoke in the public
assemblies, and professed to be the
expounders of the divine will. ¶ *Having* his *head covered.* With a veil,
or turban, or cap, or whatever else is
worn on the head. To remove the
hat, the turban, or the covering of
the head, is a mark of respect for a
superior when in his presence. ¶ *Dishonoureth his head.* Does dishonour
to Christ as his head (ver. 2): that
is, he does not, in his presence and in
his service, observe the usual and
proper custom by which a subordinate
station is recognised, and which indicates respect for a superior. In the
presence of a prince or a nobleman, it
would be considered as a mark of disrespect should the head be covered.
So in the presence of Christ, in whose
name he ministers, it is a mark of disrespect if the head is covered. This
illustration is drawn from the customs
of all times and countries by which
respect for a superior is indicated by
removing the covering from the head.
This is *one* reason why a man should
not cover his head in public worship.
Another is given in ver. 7. Other
interpretations of the passage may be
seen in Bloomfield's Critical Digest.

5. *But every woman that prayeth
or prophesieth.* In the Old Testament prophetesses are not unfrequently mentioned. Thus Miriam is
mentioned (Ex. xv. 20); Deborah
(Judg. iv. 4); Huldah (2 Kings xxii.
14); Noadiah (Neh. vi. 14). So also
in the New Testament Anna is mentioned as a prophetess; Luke ii. 36.
That there were females in the early
Christian church who corresponded
to those known among the Jews in

some measure as endowed with the inspiration of the Holy Spirit, cannot be doubted. What was their precise office, and what was the nature of the public services in which they were engaged, is not however known. That they prayed is clear; and that they publicly expounded the will of God is apparent also; see Note on Acts ii. 17. As the presumption is, however, that they were inspired, their example is no warrant now for females to take part in the public services of worship, unless they also give evidence that they are under the influence of inspiration, and the more especially as the apostle Paul has expressly forbidden their becoming public teachers; 1 Tim. ii. 12. If it is now pled, from this example, that women should speak and pray in public, yet it should be just so far only *as this example goes*, and it should be *only* when they have the qualifications that the early *prophetesses* had in the Christian church. If there are any such; if any are directly inspired by God, there then will be an evident propriety that they should publicly proclaim his will, and not till then. It may be further observed, however, that the fact that Paul here mentions the custom of women praying or speaking publicly in the church, does not prove that it was right or proper. His immediate object now was not to consider whether the practice was itself right, but to condemn the manner of its performance as a violation of all the proper rules of modesty and of subordination. On another occasion, in this very epistle, he fully condemns the practice in any form, and enjoins silence on the female members of the church in public; chap. xiv. 34. ¶ *With* her *head uncovered*. That is, with the veil removed which she usually wore. It would seem from this that the women removed their veils, and wore their hair dishevelled, when they pretended to be under the influence of divine inspiration. This was the case with the heathen priestesses; and in so doing, the Christian women imitated them. On this account, if on no other, Paul declares the impropriety of this conduct. It

was, besides, a custom among ancient females, and one that was strictly enjoined by the traditional laws of the Jews, that a woman should not appear in public unless she were veiled. See this proved by Lightfoot *in loco*. ¶ *Dishonoureth her head.* Shows a want of proper respect to man,—to her husband, to her father, to the sex in general. The veil is a token of modesty and of subordination. It is regarded among Jews, and everywhere, as an emblem of her sense of inferiority of rank and station. It is the customary mark of her sex, and that by which she evinces her modesty and sense of subordination. To remove that, is to remove the appropriate mark of such subordination, and is a public act by which she thus shows dishonour to the man. And as it is proper that the grades and ranks of life should be recognised in a suitable manner, so it is improper that, even on pretence of religion, and of being engaged in the service of God, these marks should be laid aside. ¶ *For that is even all one as if she were shaven.* As if her long hair, which nature teaches her she should wear for a veil (ver. 15, *margin*,) should be cut off. Long hair is, by the custom of the times, and of nearly all countries, a mark of the sex, an ornament of the female, and judged to be beautiful and comely. To remove that is to appear, in this respect, like the other sex, and to lay aside the badge of her own. This, says Paul, all would judge to be improper. You yourselves would not allow it. And yet to lay aside the veil—the appropriate badge of the sex, and of her sense of subordination—would be an act of the same kind. It would indicate the same feeling, the same forgetfulness of the proper sense of subordination; and if that is laid aside, ALL the usual indications of modesty and subordination might be removed also. Not even under religious pretences, therefore, are the usual marks of sex, and of propriety of place and rank, to be laid aside. Due respect is to be shown, in dress, and speech, and deportment, to those whom God has placed above us; and

6 For if the woman be not covered, let her also be shorn: *a* but if it be a shame for a woman to be shorn or shaven, let her be covered.

7 For a man indeed ought not to cover *his* head, forasmuch as he is the image *b* and glory of God: but the woman is the glory of the man.

a Num.5.18; Deut.21.12.

b Gen.5.1.

neither in language, in attire, nor in habit are we to depart from what all judge to be proprieties of life, or from what God has judged and ordained to be the proper indications of the regular gradations in society.

6. *For if the woman be not covered.* If her head be not covered with a veil. ¶ *Let her also be shorn.* Let her long hair be cut off. Let her lay aside all the usual and proper indications of her sex and rank in life. If it is done in one respect, it may with the same propriety be done in all; see Note above. ¶ *But if it be a shame,* &c. If custom, nature, and habit; if the common and usual feelings and views among men would pronounce this to be a shame, the other would be pronounced to be a shame also by the same custom and common sense of men. ¶ *Let her be covered.* With a veil. Let her wear the customary attire indicative of modesty and a sense of subordination. Let her not lay this aside even on any pretence of religion.

7. *For a man indeed ought not to cover* his *head.* That is, with a veil; or in public worship; when he approaches God, or when in His name he addresses his fellow men. It is not fit and proper that he should be covered. The reason why it is not proper, the apostle immediately states. ¶ *Forasmuch as he is the image and glory of God.* The phrase "the image of God" refers to the fact that man was made in the likeness of his Maker (Gen. i. 27): and proves that, though fallen, there is a sense in which he is still the image of God. It is not because man is holy or pure, and thus resembles his Creator; but it evidently is because he was invested by his Maker with authority and dominion; he was superior to all other creatures; Gen. i. 28. This is still retained; and this the apostle

evidently refers to in the passage before us, and this he says should be recognised and regarded. If he wore a veil or turban, it would be a mark of servitude or inferiority. It was therefore improper that he should appear in this manner; but he should be so clad as not to obscure or hide the great truth that he was the direct representative of God on the earth, and had a superiority to all other creatures. ¶ *And glory of God.* The word *glory* in the classic writers means, (1.) Opinion, sentiment, &c.; (2.) Fame, reputation. Here it means, as it often does, splendour, brightness, or that which stands forth to *represent* God, or by which the glory of God is known. Man was created first; he had dominion given him; by him, therefore, the divine authority and wisdom first shone forth; and this fact should be recognised in the due subordination of rank, and even in the apparel and attire which shall be worn. The impression of his rank and superiority should be everywhere retained. ¶ *But the woman is the glory of the man.* The honour, the ornament, &c. She was made *for* him; she was made after he was; she was taken from him, and was "bone of his bone, and flesh of his flesh." All her comeliness, loveliness, and purity are therefore an expression of his honour and dignity, since all that comeliness and loveliness were made of him and for him. This, therefore, ought to be acknowledged by a suitable manner of attire; and in his presence this sense of her inferiority of rank and subordination should be acknowledged by the customary use of the veil. She should appear with the symbol of modesty and subjection, which are implied by the head being covered. This sense is distinctly expressed in the following verse.

8 For *a* the man is not of the woman; but the woman of the man;
9 Neither was the man created

a Gen.2.18,22,23.

for the woman, but the woman for
the man.
10 For this cause ought the

---

8. *For the man is not of the woman.*
The man was not formed *from* the
woman.   ¶ *But the woman of the
man.*   From his side; Gen. ii. 18.
22, 23.

9 *Neither was the man created for
the woman,* &c.   This is a simple
statement of what is expressed in
Genesis.   The woman was made for
the comfort and happiness of the man.
Not to be a slave, but a help-meet;
not to be the minister of his pleasures, but to be his aid and comforter
in life; not to be regarded as of
inferior nature and rank, but to be
his friend, to divide his sorrows, and
to multiply and extend his joys, yet
still to be in a station subordinate to
him.   He is to be the head; the
ruler; the presider in the family
circle; and she was created to aid
him in his duties, to comfort him in
his afflictions, to partake with him of
his pleasures.   Her rank is therefore
honourable, though it is subordinate.
It is, in some respects, the more honourable because it is subordinate;
and as her happiness is dependent on
him, she has the higher claim to his
protection and his tender care.   The
whole of Paul's idea here is, that her
situation and rank as subordinate
should be recognised by her at all
times, and that in his presence it was
proper that she should wear the usual
symbol of modesty and subordination,
the veil.

10. *For this cause,* &c.   There is
scarcely any passage in the Scriptures
which has more exercised the ingenuity of commentators than this
verse.   The various attempts which
have been made to explain it may be
seen in Pool, Rosenmüller, Bloomfield, &c.   After all the explanations
which have been given of it, I confess, I do not understand it.   It is
not difficult to see what the connection
requires us to suppose in the explanation.   The obvious interpretation
would be, that a woman should have
a veil on her head because of the

angels who were supposed to be present, observing them in their public
worship; and it is generally agreed
that the word *power* (ἐξουσίαν) denotes
a veil, or a covering for the head.
But the word *power* does not occur
in this sense in any classic writer.
Bretschneider understands it of a
veil, as being a defence or guard to
the face, lest it should be seen by
others.   Some have supposed that it
was the name of a female ornament
that was worn on the head, formed
of braids of hair set with jewels.
Most commentators agree that it
means a *veil*, though some think (see
Bloomfield) that it is called *power* to
denote the veil which was worn by
married women, which indicated the
superiority of the married woman
to the maiden.   But it is sufficient to
say in reply to this, that the apostle
is not referring to married women in
contradistinction from those who are
unmarried, but is showing that *all*
women who prophecy or pray in public
should be veiled.   There can, perhaps, be no doubt that the word
"power" has reference to a veil, or
to a covering for the head; but why
it is called *power* I confess I do not
understand; and most of the com-
ments on the word are, in my view,
egregious trifling   ¶ *Because of the
angels.*   Some have explained this of
good angels, who were supposed to be
present in their assemblies (see Doddridge); others refer it to evil angels;
and others to messengers or spies
who, it has been supposed, were present in their public assemblies, and
who would report greatly to the disadvantage of the Christian assemblies
if the women were seen to be unveiled.
I do not know what it means; and I
regard it as one of the very few passages in the Bible whose meaning as
yet is wholly inexplicable.   The most
natural interpretation seems to me to
be this: "A woman in the public
assemblies, and in speaking in the
presence of men, should wear a veil—

woman to have power [1] on *her* head, because of the angels.

11 Nevertheless, neither is the man without the woman, neither

[1] i. e. *a covering, in sign that she is under*

the honour of her husband, Gen. 24. 65.

the usual symbol of modesty and subordination—because the angels of God are witnesses of your public worship (Heb. i. 13), and because they know and appreciate the propriety of subordination and order in public assemblies." According to this, it would mean that the simple reason would be that the angels were witnesses of their worship; and that they were the friends of propriety, due subordination, and order; and that they ought to observe these in all assemblies convened for the worship of God.—I do not know that this sense has been proposed by any commentator; but it is one which strikes me as the most obvious and natural, and consistent with the context. The following remarks respecting the ladies of Persia may throw some light on this subject:—" The head-dress of the women is simple; their hair is drawn behind the head, and divided into several tresses: the beauty of this head-dress consists in the thickness and length of these tresses, which should fall even down to the heels, in default of which, they lengthen them with tresses of silk. The ends of these tresses they decorate with pearls and jewels, or ornaments of gold or silver. The head is covered, *under* the veil or kerchief (*course chef*), only by the end of a small *bandeau,* shaped into a triangle; this *bandeau,* which is of various colours, is thin and light. The *bandalette* is embroidered by the needle, or covered with jewellery, according to the quality of the wearer. This is, in my opinion, the ancient *tiara,* or *diadem,* of the queens of Persia: only married women wear it; and it is the mark by which it is known that they are under subjection (*c'est là la marque à laquelle on reconnoit qu'elles sont sous* PUISSANCE—*power*). The girls have little *caps,* instead of this kerchief or tiara; they wear no veil at home, but let two tresses of their hair fall under their cheeks. The

caps of girls of superior rank are tied with a row of pearls. Girls are not shut up in Persia till they attain the age of six or seven years; before that age they go out of the seraglio, sometimes with their father, so that they may then be seen. I have seen some wonderfully pretty. They show the neck and bosom; and more beautiful cannot be seen."—*Chardin.* "The wearing of a veil by a married woman was a token of her being under power The Hebrew name of the veil signifies dependence. Great importance was attached to this part of the dress in the East. All the women of Persia are pleasantly apparelled. When they are abroad in the streets, all, both rich and poor, are covered with a great veil, or sheet of very fine white cloth, of which one half, like a forehead cloth, comes down to the eyes, and, going over the head, reaches down to the heels; and the other half muffles up the face below the eyes, and being fastened with a pin to the left side of the head, falls down to their very shoes, even covering their hands, with which they hold that cloth by the two sides, so that, except the eyes, they are covered all over with it. Within doors they have their faces and breasts uncovered; but the Armenian women in their houses have always one half of their faces covered with a cloth, that goes athwart their noses, and hangs over their chin and breasts, except the maids of that nation, who, within doors, cover only the chin until they are married." — *Thevenot.*

11. *Nevertheless.* Lest the man should assume to himself too much superiority, and lest he should regard the woman as made solely for his pleasure, and should treat her as in all respects inferior, and withhold the respect that is due to her. The design of this verse and the following is to show, that the man and woman are united in the most tender interests; that the one cannot live comfortably

the woman without the man in the Lord.

12 For as the woman *is* of the man, even so *is* the man also by the woman : but all *a* things of God.

a Rom.11.36.

without the other; that one is necessary to the happiness of the other; and that though the woman was formed from the man, yet it is also to be remembered that the man is descended from the woman. She should therefore be treated with proper respect, tenderness, and regard. ¶ *Neither is the man without the woman*, &c. The man and the woman were formed for union and society. They are not in any respect independent of each other. One is necessary to the comfort of the other; and this fact should be recognised in all their intercourse. ¶ *In the Lord*. By the arrangements or direction of the Lord. It is the appointment and command of the Lord that they should be mutual helps, and should each regard and promote the welfare of the other.

12. *As the woman* is *of the man*. In the original creation, she was formed from the man. ¶ *So is the man also by the woman*. Is born of the woman, or descended from her. The sexes are dependent on each other, and should therefore cultivate an indissoluble union. ¶ *But all things of God* All things were created and arranged by him. This expression seems designed to suppress any spirit of complaint or dissatisfaction with this arrangement; to make the woman contented in her subordinate station, and to make the man humble by the consideration that it is all owing to the appointment of God. The woman should therefore be contented, and the man should not assume any improper superiority, since the whole arrangement and appointment is of God.

13. *Judge in yourselves*. Or, "Judge among yourselves." I appeal to you. I appeal to your natural sense of what is proper and right. Paul had used various arguments to show them the impropriety of their females speaking

13 Judge in yourselves : is it comely that a woman pray unto God uncovered ?

14 Doth not even nature itself teach you, that if a man have long hair, it is a shame unto him ?

unveiled in public. He now appeals to their natural sense of what was decent and right, according to established and acknowledged customs and habits. ¶ *Is it comely*, &c. Is it decent, or becoming ? The Grecian women, except their priestesses, were accustomed to appear in public with a veil.—*Doddridge*. Paul alludes to that established and proper habit, and asks whether it does not accord with their own views of propriety that women in Christian assemblies should also wear the same symbol of modesty.

14. *Doth not even nature itself*. The word *nature* (φύσις) denotes evidently that sense of propriety which all men have, and which is expressed in any prevailing or universal custom. That which is universal we say is according to nature. It is such as is demanded by the natural sense of fitness among men. Thus we may say that nature demands that the sexes should wear different kinds of dress ; that nature demands that the female should be modest and retiring ; that nature demands that the toils of the chase, of the field, of war—the duties of office, of government, and of professional life, should be discharged by men. Such are in general the customs the world over; and if any reason is asked for numerous habits that exist in society, no better answer can be given than that *nature*, as arranged by God, has demanded it. The word in this place, therefore, does not mean the constitution of the sexes, as Locke, Whitby, and Pierce maintain ; nor reason and experience, as Macknight supposes ; nor simple use and custom, as Grotius, Rosenmüller, and most recent expositors suppose ; but it refers to a deep internal sense of what is proper and right; a sense which is expressed extensively in all nations, showing what that sense is. No *reason* can be given, in the nature **of**

15 But if a woman have long hair it is a glory to her: for *her* hair is given her for a [1] covering.

[1] or, *veil.*

16 But *a* if any man seem to be contentious, we have no such custom, neither the churches of God.

a 1 Tim.6.4.

things, why the woman should wear long hair and the man not; but the custom prevails extensively everywhere, and nature, in all nations, has prompted to the same course. " Use is second nature;" but the usage in this case is not arbitrary, but is founded in an anterior universal sense of what is proper and right. A few, and only a few, have regarded it as comely for a man to wear his hair long. Aristotle tells us, indeed (Rhet. i.—see Rosenmüller), that among the Lacedemonians, freemen wore their hair long. In the time of Homer, also, the Greeks were called by him καρηκομόωντες 'Αχαιοι, long - haired Greeks; and some of the Asiatic nations adopted the same custom. But the general habit among men has been different. Among the Hebrews, it was regarded as disgraceful to a man to wear his hair long, except he had a vow as a Nazarite, Num. vi. 1 —5; Judg. xiii. 5; xvi. 17; 1 Sam. i. 11. Occasionally, for affectation or singularity, the hair was suffered to grow, as was the case with Absalom (2 Sam. xiv. 26); but the traditional law of the Jews on the subject was strict. The same *rule* existed among the Greeks; and it was regarded as disgraceful to wear long hair in the time of Ælian; Hist. lib. ix. c. 14. Eustath. on Hom. ii. v. ¶ *It is a shame unto him.* It is improper and disgraceful. It is doing that which almost universal custom has said appropriately belongs to the female sex.

15. *It is a glory unto her.* It is an ornament, and adorning. The same instinctive promptings of nature which make it proper for a man to wear short hair, make it proper that the woman should suffer hers to grow long. ¶ *For a covering.* Marg. *Veil.* It is given to her as a sort of natural veil, and to indicate the propriety of her wearing a veil. It answered the purposes of a veil when it was suffered to grow long, and to spread over the

shoulders and over parts of the face, before the arts of dress were invented or needed. There may also be an allusion here to the fact that the hair of women naturally grows longer than that of men. See Rosenmüller. The value which eastern females put on their long hair may be learned from the fact that when Ptolemy Euergetes, king of Egypt, was about to march against Seleucus Callinicus, his queen Berenice vowed, as the most precious sacrifice which she could make, to cut off and consecrate her hair if he returned in safety. " The eastern ladies," says Harmer, " are remarkable for the length and the great number of the tresses of their hair. The men there, on the contrary, wear very little hair on their heads." Lady M. W. Montague thus speaks concerning the hair of the women : " Their hair hangs at full length behind, divided into tresses, braided with pearl or riband, which is always in great quantity. I never saw in my life so many fine heads of hair. In one lady's I have counted one hundred and ten of these tresses, all natural; but it must be owned that every kind of beauty is more common here than with us." The men there, on the contrary, shave all the hair off their heads, excepting one lock ; and those that wear hair are thought effeminate. Both these particulars are mentioned by Chardin, who says they are agreeable to the custom of the East : "the men are shaved ; the women nourish their hair with great fondness, which they lengthen, by tresses and tufts of silk, down to the heels. The young men who wear their hair in the East are looked upon as effeminate and infamous."

16. *But if any man seem to be contentious.* The sense of this passage is probably this : " If any man, any teacher, or others, *is disposed* to be strenuous about this, or to make it a matter of difficulty; if he is disposed

17 Now in this that I declare *unto you* I práise *you* not, that ye come together not for the better, but for the worse.

a chap.1.11,12.

18 For first of all, when ye come together in the church, I hear *a* that there be divisions [1] among you ; and I partly believe it.

1 or, *schisms.*

to call in question my reasoning, and to dispute my premises and the considerations which I have advanced, and to maintain still that it is proper for women to appear unveiled in public, I would add that in Judea we have no such custom, neither does it prevail among any of the churches. This, therefore, would be a sufficient reason why it should not be done in Corinth, even if the abstract reasoning should not convince them of the impropriety. It would be singular ; would be contrary to the usual custom; would offend the prejudices of many and should, therefore, be avoided." ¶ *We have no such custom.* We the apostles in the churches which we have elsewhere founded ; or we have no such custom in Judea. The sense is, that it is contrary to custom there for women to appear in public unveiled. This custom, the apostle argues, ought to be allowed to have some influence on the church of Corinth, even though they should not be convinced by his reasoning. ¶ *Neither the churches of God.* The churches elsewhere. It is customary there for the woman to appear veiled. If at Corinth this custom is not observed, it will be a departure from what has elsewhere been regarded as proper; and will offend these churches. Even, therefore, if the *reasoning* is not sufficient to silence all cavils and doubts, yet the propriety of uniformity in the habits of the churches, the fear of giving offence should lead you to discountenance and disapprove the custom of your females appearing in public without their veil.

17. *Now in this that I declare.* In this that I am about to state to you ; to wit, your conduct in regard to the Lord's supper. Why this subject is introduced here is not very apparent. The connection may be this. In the subjects immediately preceding he had seen much to commend, and he was

desirous of commending them as far as it could be done. In ver. 2 of this chapter he commends them *in general* for their regard to the ordinances which he had appointed when he was with them. But while he thus commended them, he takes occasion to observe that there was *one* subject on which he could not employ the language of approval or praise. Of their irregularities in regard to the Lord's supper he had probably heard by rumour, and as the subject was of great importance, and their irregularities gross and deplorable, he takes occasion to state to them again more fully the nature of that ordinance, and to reprove them for the manner in which they had celebrated it. ¶ *That ye come together.* You assemble for public worship. ¶ *Not for the better, but for the worse.* Your meetings, and your observance of the ordinances of the gospel, do not promote your edification, your piety, spirituality, and harmony; but tend to division, alienation, and disorder. You *should* assemble to worship God, and promote harmony, love, and piety; the actual effect of your assembling is just the reverse. In what way this was done he states in the following verses. These evil consequences were chiefly two,—first, divisions and contentions; and, secondly, the abuse and profanation of the Lord's supper.

18. *For first of all.* That is, I mention as the first thing to be reproved. ¶ *When ye come together in the church.* When you come together in a religious assembly ; when you convene for public worship. The word *church* here does not mean, as it frequently does with us, a *building*. No instance of such a use of the word occurs in the New Testament; but it means when they came together as a Christian assembly; when they convened for the worship of God. These divisions took place *then ;* and from some cause which

19 For there must [a] be also [1] heresies among you, that [b] they

d Mat.18.7 ; 2 Pet.2.1,2.   1 or, *sects.*   b Luke 2.35.

it seems *then* operated to produce alienations and strifes. ¶ *I hear.* I have learned through some members of the family of Chloe; chap. i. 11. ¶ *That there be divisions among you.* Greek, as in the margin, *Schisms.* The word properly means *a rent,* such as is made in cloth (Mat. ix. 16 ; Mark ii. 21), and then a division, a split, a faction among men ; John vii. 43 ; ix. 16 ; x. 19. It does not mean here that they had proceeded so far as to form separate churches, but that there was discord and division in the church itself ; see Notes on chap. i. 10, 11. ¶ *And I partly believe it.* I credit a part of the reports ; I have reason to think, that, though the evil may have been exaggerated, yet that it is true at least in part. I believe that there *are* dissensions in the church that should be reproved.

19. *For there must be.* It is necessary (δεῖ); it is to be expected ; there are reasons why there should be. What these reasons are he states in the close of the verse ; comp. Mat. xviii. 7 ; 2 Pet. ii. 1, 2. The meaning is, not that divisions are inseparable from the nature of the Christian religion, not that it is the design and wish of the Author of Christianity that they should exist, and not that they are physically impossible, for then they could not be the subject of blame ; but that such is human nature, such are the corrupt passions of men, the propensity to ambition and strifes, that they are to be expected, and they serve the purpose of showing who are, and who are not, the true friends of God. ¶ *Heresies.* Margin, *Sects.* Gr. Ἁιρεσεις ; see Note, Acts xxiv. 14. The words *heresy* and *heresies* occur only in these places, and in Gal. v. 20 ; 2 Pet. ii. 1. The Greek word occurs also in Acts v. 17 (translated *sect*); xv. 5 ; xxiv. 5 ; xxvi. 5 ; xxviii. 22, in all which places it denotes, and is translated, *sect.* We now attach to the word usually the idea of a fundamental error in religion, or some *doctrine* the holding of which will exclude from salvation. But there is no evidence that the word is used in this signification in the New Testament. The only place where it can be supposed to be so used, unless this is one, is in Gal. v. 20, where, however, the word *contentions* or *divisions,* would be quite as much in accordance with the connection. That the word here does not denote error in doctrine, but schism, division, or *sects,* as it is translated in the margin, is evident from two considerations. (1.) It is the proper philological meaning of the word, and its established and common signification in the Bible. (2.) It is the sense which the connection here demands. The apostle had made no reference to error of doctrine, but is discoursing solely of *irregularity in conduct ;* and the first thing which he mentions, is, that there were schisms, divisions, strifes. The idea that the word here refers to *doctrines* would by no means suit the connection, and would indeed make nonsense. It would then read, " I hear that there are divisions or parties among you, and this I cannot commend you for. For it must be expected that there would be *fundamental errors of doctrine* in the church.," But *Paul* did not reason in this manner. The sense is, " There are divisions among you. It is to be expected : there are causes for it ; and it cannot be avoided that there should be, in the present state of human nature, divisions and sects formed in the church ; and this is to be expected in order that those who are true Christians should be separated from those who are not." The *foundation* of this necessity is not in the Christian religion itself, for that is pure, and contemplates and requires union ; but the existence of sects, and denominations, and contentions may be traced to the following causes. (1.) The love of power and popularity. Religion may be made the means of power ; and they who have the control of the consciences of men, and of their religious feelings and opinions, can control them altogether. (2.) Showing more respect to a religious teacher than to Christ ; see Notes on chap. i. 12. (3.) The

which are approved may be made manifest among you.

20 When ye come together

therefore into one place, [1] *this* is not to eat the Lord's supper.

1 or, *ye cannot eat.*

---

multiplication of tests, and the enlargement of creeds and confessions of faith. The consequence is, that every new doctrine that is incorporated into a creed gives occasion for those to separate who cannot accord with it. (4.) The passions of men—their pride, and ambition, and bigotry, and unenlightened zeal. Christ evidently meant that his church should be one; and that all who were his true followers should be admitted to her communion, and acknowledged everywhere as his own friends. And the time may yet come when this union shall be restored to his long distracted church, and that while there may be an honest difference of opinion maintained and allowed, still the bonds of Christian love shall secure union of *heart* in all who love the Lord Jesus, and union of *effort* in the grand enterprise in which ALL can unite—that of making war upon sin, and securing the conversion of the whole world to God. ¶ *That they which are approved.* That they who are approved of God, or who are his true friends, and who are disposed to abide by his laws. ¶ *May be made manifest.* May be known; recognised; seen. The effect of divisions and separations would be to show who were the friends of order, and peace, and truth. It seems to have been assumed by Paul, that they who made divisions *could* not be regarded as the friends of order and truth; or that their course could not be approved by God. The effect of these divisions would be to show who they were. So in all divisions, and all splitting into factions, where the great truths of Christianity are held, and where the corruption of the mass does not require separation, such divisions show who are the restless, ambitious, and dissatisfied spirits; who they are that are *indisposed* to follow the things that make for peace, and the laws of Christ enjoining union; and who they are who are gentle and peaceful, and disposed to pursue the way of truth, and

love, and order, without contentions and strifes. This is the effect of schisms in the church; and the whole strain of the argument of Paul is to reprove and condemn such schisms, and to hold up the authors of them to reproof and condemnation; see Rom. xvi. 17, " Mark them which cause divisions, and AVOID THEM."

20. *When ye come together therefore, &c.* When you are assembled as a church; comp. Heb. x. 25, and Note on Acts ii. 1. Christians were constantly in the habit of *assembling* for public worship. It is probable that at this early period all the Christians in Corinth were accustomed to meet in the same place. The apostle here particularly refers to their assembling to observe the ordinance of the Lord's supper. At that early period it is probable that this was done on every Lord's day. ¶ This *is not, &c.* Margin, " Ye cannot eat." The meaning of this expression seems to be this. " Though you come together professedly to worship God, and to partake of the Lord's supper, yet this cannot be the *real design* which you have in view. It *cannot be* that such practices as are allowed among you can be a part of the celebration of that supper, or consistent with it. Your greediness (ver. 21), your intemperance (ver. 21), your partaking of the food separately and not in common, *cannot* be a celebration of the Lord's supper. Whatever, therefore, you may profess to be engaged in, yet really and truly you are *not* celebrating the Lord's supper." ¶ *The Lord's supper.* That which the Lord Jesus instituted to commemorate his death. It is called "the Lord's," because it is his appointment, and is in honour of him; it is called "supper" (δεῖπνον), because the word denotes the evening repast; it was instituted in the evening; and it is evidently most proper that it should be observed in the after part of the day. With most churches the time is improperly changed to the morning—

21 For in eating, every one taketh before *other* his own supper : and one is hungry and [a] another is drunken.

a 2 Pet.2.13 ; Jude 12.

a custom which has no sanction in the New Testament ; and which is a departure from the very idea of a supper. 21. *For in eating.* When you eat, having professedly come together to observe this ordinance. In order to understand this, it seems necessary to suppose that they had in some way made the Lord's supper either connected with a common feast, or that they regarded it as a mere common festival to be observed in a way similar to the festivals among the Greeks. Many have supposed that this was done by making the observance of the supper follow a festival, or what were afterwards called *love feasts* ('Αγαπαι —*Agapae*). Many have supposed that that custom was derived from the fact that the Saviour instituted the supper *after* a festival, a feast in which he had been engaged with his disciples, and that thence the early Christians derived the custom of observing such a festival, or common meal, before they celebrated the Lord's supper. But it may be observed, that the passover was not a mere preliminary festival, or feast. It had no resemblance to the so called love feasts. It was itself a religious ordinance ; a direct appointment of God ; and was never regarded as designed to be *preliminary* to the observance of the Lord's supper, but was always understood as designed to be *superseded* by that. Besides, I know not that there is the slightest evidence, as has been often supposed, that the observance of the Lord's supper was *preceded,* in the times of the apostles, by such a festival as a love feast. There is no evidence in the passage before us ; nor is any adduced from any other part of the New Testament. To my mind it seems altogether improbable that the disorders in Corinth would assume this form—that they would *first* observe a common feast, and *then* the Lord's supper in the regular manner. The statement before us leads to the belief that *all* was irregular and improper ; that they had entirely mistaken the nature of the

ordinance, and had converted it into an occasion of ordinary festivity, and even intemperance ; that they had come to regard it as a feast in honour of the Saviour on some such principles as they observed feasts in honour of idols, and that they observed it in some such manner ; and that all that was supposed to make it *unlike* those festivals was, that it was in honour of Jesus rather than an idol, and was to be observed with some reference to his authority and name. ¶ *Every one taketh before* other *his own supper.* That is, each one is regardless of the wants of the others ; instead of making even a meal in common, and when all could partake together, each one ate by himself, and ate that which he had himself brought. They had not only erred, therefore, by misunderstanding altogether the nature of the Lord's supper, and by supposing that it was a common festival like those which they had been accustomed to celebrate ; but they had also entirely departed from the idea that it was a festival to be partaken of in common, and at a common table. It had become a scene where every man ate by himself ; and where the very idea that there was any thing like a *common* celebration, or a celebration *together*, was abandoned. There is allusion here, doubtless, to what was a custom among the Greeks, that when a festival was celebrated, or a feast made, it was common for each person to provide, and carry a part of the things necessary for the entertainment. These were usually placed in common, and were partaken of alike by all the company. Thus Xenophon (Mem. lib. iii. cap. xiv.) says of Socrates, that he was much offended with the Athenians for their conduct at their common suppers, where some prepared for themselves in a delicate and sumptuous manner, while others were poorly provided for. Socrates endeavoured, he adds, to shame them out of this indecent custom by offering his provisions to all the company. ¶ *And one is hungry.* Is

22 What! have ye not houses to eat and to drink in? or despise ye the church of God, and

shame them that [1] have not? What shall I say to you? shall I praise you in this? I praise *you* not.

1 *are poor.*

deprived of food. It is all monopolized by others. ¶ *And another is drunken.* The word here used (μεθύω) means properly to become inebriated, or intoxicated; and there is no reason for understanding it here in any other sense. There can be no doubt that the apostle meant to say, that they ate and drank to excess; and that their professed celebration of the Lord's supper became a mere revel. It may seem remarkable that such scenes should ever have occurred in a Christian church, or that there could have been such an entire perversion of the nature and design of the Lord's supper. But we are to remember the following things: (1.) These persons had recently been heathens, and were grossly ignorant of the nature of true religion when the gospel was first preached among them. (2.) They had been accustomed to such revels in honour of idols under their former modes of worship, and it is the less surprising that they transferred their views to Christianity. (3.) When they had once so far misunderstood the nature of Christianity as to suppose the Lord's supper to be like the feasts which they had formerly celebrated, all the rest followed as a matter of course. The festival would be observed in the same manner as the festivals in honour of idolaters; and similar scenes of gluttony and intemperance would naturally follow. (4.) We are to bear in mind, also, that they do not seem to have been favoured with pious, wise, and prudent teachers. There were false teachers; and there were those who prided themselves on their wisdom, and who were self-confident, and who doubtless endeavoured to model the Christian institutions according to their own views; and they thus brought them, as far as they could, to a conformity with pagan customs and idolatrous rites. We may remark here, (1.) We are not to expect perfection at once among a people recently converted from paganism. (2.) We see

how prone men are to abuse even the most holy rites of religion, and hence how corrupt is human nature. (3.) We see that even Christians, recently converted, need constant guidance and superintendence; and that if left to themselves they soon, like others, fall into gross and scandalous offences.

22. *What!* This whole verse is designed to convey the language of severe rebuke for their having so grossly perverted the design of the Lord's supper. ¶ *Have ye not houses,* &c. Do you not know that the church of God is not designed to be a place of feasting and revelry; nor even a place where to partake of your ordinary meals? Can it be, that you will come to the places of public worship, and make them the scenes of feasting and riot? Even on the supposition that there had been no disorder; no revelry; no intemperance; yet on every account it was grossly irregular and disorderly to make the place of public worship a place for a festival entertainment. ¶ *Or despise ye the church of God.* The phrase "church of God" Grotius understands of the place. But the word *church* (ἐκκλησία) is believed not to be used in that sense in the New Testament; and it is not necessary to suppose it here. The sense is, that their conduct was such as if they had held in contempt the whole church of God, in all places, with all their views of the sacredness and purity of the Lord's supper. ¶ *And shame them that have not.* Margin, *Are poor.* Something must here be understood in order to make out the sense. Probably it meant something like *possessions, property, conveniences, accommodations.* The connection would make it most natural to understand "houses to eat and drink in;" and the sense then would be, "Do you thus expose to public shame those who have no accommodations at home; who are destitute and poor? You thus reflect publicly

23 For *a* I have received of the | Lord that which also I delivered
a chap.15.3.

upon their poverty and want, while you bring your own provisions and fare sumptuously, and while those who are thus unable to provide for themselves are thus seen to be poor and needy." It is hard enough, the idea is, to be poor, and to be destitute of a home. But it greatly aggravates the matter to be *publicly treated* in that manner; to be exposed publicly to the contempt which such a situation implies. Their treatment of the poor in this manner would be a public exposing them to shame; and the apostle regarded this as particularly dishonourable, and especially in a Christian church, where all were professedly on an equality. ¶ *What shall I say to you?* &c. How shall I sufficiently express my surprise at this, and my disapprobation at this course? It cannot be possible that this is right. It is not possible to conceal surprise and amazement that this custom exists, and is tolerated in a Christian church.

23. *For*, &c. In order most effectually to check the evils which existed, and to bring them to a proper mode of observing the Lord's supper, the apostle proceeds to state distinctly and particularly its design. They had mistaken its nature. They supposed it might be a common festival. They had made it the occasion of great disorder. He therefore adverts to the solemn circumstances in which it was instituted; the particular object which it had in view—the commemoration of the death of the Redeemer, and the purpose which it was designed to subserve, which was not that of a festival, but to keep before the church and the world a constant remembrance of the Lord Jesus until he should again return, ver. 26. By this means the apostle evidently hoped to recall them from their irregularities, and to bring them to a just mode of celebrating this holy ordinance. He did not, therefore, denounce them even for their irregularity and gross disorder: he did not use harsh, violent, vituperative language, but he expected to reform the evil by a mild and tender

statement of the truth, and by an appeal to their consciences as the followers of the Lord Jesus. ¶ *I have received of the Lord.* This cannot refer to tradition, or mean that it had been communicated to him through the medium of the other apostles; but the whole spirit and scope of the passage seems to mean that he had derived the knowledge of the institution of the Lord's supper *directly* from the Lord himself. This might have been when on the road to Damascus, though that does not seem probable, or it may have been among the numerous revelations which at various times had been made to him; comp. 2 Cor. xii. 7. The *reason* why he here says that he had received it directly from the Lord is, doubtless, that he might show them that it was of divine authority. " The institution to which I refer is what I myself received an account of *from personal and direct communication with the Lord Jesus himself, who appointed it.* It is not, therefore, of human authority. It is not of my devising, but is of divine warrant, and is holy in its nature, and is to be observed in the exact manner prescribed by the Lord himself." ¶ *That which also I delivered*, &c. Paul founded the church at Corinth; and of course he first instituted the observance of the Lord's supper there. ¶ *The* same *night in which he was betrayed.* By Judas; see Mat. xxvi. 23—25, 48—50. Paul seems to have mentioned the fact that it was on the very night on which he was betrayed, in order to throw around it the idea of greater solemnity. He wished evidently to bring before their minds the deeply affecting circumstances of his death; and thus to show them the utter impropriety of their celebrating the ordinance with riot and disorder. The idea is, that in order to celebrate it in a proper manner, it was needful *to throw themselves as much as possible into the very circumstances in which it was instituted;* and one of these circumstances most fitted to affect the mind deeply was the fact that he was

unto you, That the Lord Jesus, *a* the *same* night in which he was betrayed, took bread :

24 And when he had given thanks, he brake *it*, and said, Take,

eat ; this is my body, which is broken for you : this do in [1] remembrance of me.

25 After the same manner also *he took* the cup, when he had sup-

---

a Mat.26.26.

[1] or, *for a.*

---

betrayed by a professed friend and follower. It is also a circumstance the memory of which is eminently fitted to prepare the mind for a proper celebration of the ordinance now. ¶ *Took bread.* Evidently the bread which was used at the celebration of the paschal supper. He took the bread which happened to be before him—such as was commonly used. It was not *a wafer* such as the papists now use ; but was the ordinary bread which was eaten on such occasions ; see Note on Mat. xxvi. 26.

24. *And when he had given thanks ;* see Note on Matt. xxvi. 26. Matthew reads it, "and blessed it." The words here used are, however, substantially the same as there ; and this fact shows that since this was communicated to Paul *directly* by the Saviour, and in a manner distinct from that by which Matthew learned the mode of the institution, the Saviour designed that the exact form of the words should be used in its observance, and should thus be constantly borne in mind by his people. ¶ *Take eat,* &c.; see Note on Mat. xxvi. 26.

25. *After the same manner.* In like manner; likewise. With the same circumstances, and ceremonies, and designs. The purpose was the same. ¶ *When he had supped.* That is, all this occurred *after* the observance of the usual paschal supper. It could not, therefore, be a part of it, nor could it have been designed to be a festival or feast merely. The apostle introduces this evidently in order to show them that it could not be, as they seemed to have supposed, an occasion of feasting. It was *after* the supper, and was therefore to be observed in a distinct manner. ¶ *Saying, This cup,* &c.; see Note, Mat. xxvi. 27, 28. ¶ *Is the New Testament.* The new covenant which God is about to establish with men. The

word "testament" with us properly denotes *a will*—an instrument by which a man disposes of his property after his death. This is also the proper classic meaning of the Greek word here used, διαθηκη (*diatheke*). But this is evidently not the sense in which the word is designed to be used in the New Testament. The idea of a *will* or *testament,* strictly so called, is not that which the sacred writers intend to convey by the word. The idea is evidently that of a compact, agreement, COVENANT, to which there is so frequent reference in the Old Testament, and which is expressed by the word ברית (*Berith*), a compact, a covenant. Of that word the proper translation in Greek would have been συνθηκη, a covenant, agreement. But it is remarkable that that word never is used by the LXX. to denote the covenant made between God and man. That translation uniformly employs for this purpose the word διαθηκη, a *will,* or *a testament,* as a translation of the Hebrew word, where there is a reference to the covenant which God is represented as making with men. The word συνθηκη is used by them but three times (Isa. xxviii. 15; xxx. 1; Dan. xi. 6), and in neither instance with any reference to the *covenant* which God is represented as making with man. The word διαθηκη, as the translation of ברית (*Berith*), occurs more than two hundred times. (See *Trommius' Concord.*) Now this must have evidently been of design. What the reason was which induced them to adopt this can only be conjectured. It may have been that as the translation was to be seen by the Gentiles as well as by the Jews (if it were not expressly made, as has been affirmed by Josephus and others, for the use of Ptolemy), they were unwilling to represent the eternal and infinite JEHOVAH as entering

ped, saying, This is the new testament in my blood: this do ye, as oft as ye drink *it*, in remembrance of me.

1 or *shew ye.*

into a *compact, an agreement* with his creature man. They, therefore, adopted a word which would represent him as expressing *his will* to them in a book of revelation. The version by the LXX. was evidently in use by the apostles, and by the Jews everywhere. The writers of the New Testament, therefore, adopted the word as they found it; and spoke of the new dispensation as a new *testament* which God made with man. The meaning is, that this was the new compact or covenant which God was to make with man in contradistinction from that made through Moses. ¶ *In my blood.* Through my blood; that is, this new compact is to be sealed with my blood, in illusion to the ancient custom of sealing an agreement by a sacrifice; see Note, Mat. xxvi. 28. ¶ *This do ye.* Partake of this bread and wine; that is, celebrate this ordinance. ¶ *As oft as ye drink it.* Not prescribing any time; and not even specifying the frequency with which it was to be done; but leaving it to themselves to determine how often they would partake of it. The time of the passover had been fixed by positive statute; the more mild and gentle system of Christianity left it to the followers of the Redeemer themselves to determine how often they would celebrate his death. It was commanded them to do it; it was presumed that their love to him would be so strong as to secure a frequent observance; it was permitted to them, as in prayer, to celebrate it on any occasion of affliction, trial, or deep interest when they would feel their need of it, and when they would suppose that its observance would be for the edification of the Church. ¶ *In remembrance of me.* This expresses the whole design of the ordinance. It is a simple memorial, or remembrancer; designed to recall in a striking and impressive manner the memory of the Redeemer. It does this by a tender

26 For as often as ye eat this bread, and drink this cup, [1] ye do shew the Lord's death till he come.[a]

27 Wherefore, whosoever shall

a Rev.22.20.

appeal to the senses—by the exhibition of the broken bread, and by the wine. The Saviour knew how prone men would be to forget him; and he, therefore, appointed this ordinance as a means by which his memory should be kept up in the world. The ordinance is rightly observed when it recalls the memory of the Saviour; and when its observance is the means of producing a deep, and lively, and vivid impression on the mind, of his death for sin. This expression, at the institution of the supper, is used by Luke (chap. xxii. 19); though it does not occur in Matthew, Mark, or John.

26. *For as often.* Whenever you do this. ¶ *Ye eat this bread.* This is a direct and positive refutation of the doctrine of the papists that the *bread* is changed into the real body of the Lord Jesus. Here it is expressly called *bread*—bread still—bread after the consecration. Before the Saviour instituted the ordinance he took "bread"—it was bread then; it was "bread" which he "blessed" and "brake;" and it was bread when it was given to them; and it was bread when Paul here says they *ate.* How then can it be pretended that it is any thing else but bread? And what an amazing and astonishing absurdity it is to believe that that bread is changed into the flesh and blood of Jesus Christ! ¶ *Ye do show the Lord's death.* You set forth, or exhibit in an impressive manner, the fact that he was put to death; you exhibit the emblems of his broken body and shed blood, and your belief of the fact that he died. This shows that the ordinance was to be so far *public* as to be a proper showing forth of their belief in the death of the Saviour. It *should be* public. It is one mode of professing attachment to the Redeemer; and its public observance often has a most impressive effect on those who witness its observance. ¶ *Till he come.* Till he re-

eat this bread, and drink *this* cup of the Lord, unworthily,*a* shall be

guilty of the body and blood of the Lord.

a John 6.63,64; chap.10.21.

turn to judge the world. This demonstrates, (1.) That it was the steady belief of the primitive church that the Lord Jesus would return to judge the world; and (2.) That it was designed that this ordinance should be perpetuated, and observed to the end of time. In every generation, therefore, and in every place where there are Christians, it is to be observed, until the Son of God shall return; and the necessity of its observance shall cease only when the whole body of the redeemed shall be permitted to see their Lord, and there shall be no need of those emblems to remind them of him, for all shall see him as he is.

27. *Wherefore* (ὥστε). So that, or it follows from what has been said. If this be the origin and intention of the Lord's supper, then it follows that whoever partakes of it in an improper manner is guilty of his body and blood. The design of Paul is to correct their improper mode of observing this ordinance; and having showed them the true nature and design of the institution, he now states the consequences of partaking of it in an improper manner. ¶ *Shall eat this bread;* see ver. 26. Paul still calls it *bread,* and shows thus that he was a stranger to the doctrine that the bread was changed into the very body of the Lord Jesus. Had the papal doctrine of transubstantiation been true, Paul could not have called it bread. The Romanists do not believe that it is bread, nor would they call it such; and this shows how needful it is for them to keep the Scriptures from the people, and how impossible to express their dogmas in the language of the Bible. Let Christians adhere to the simple language of the Bible, and there is no danger of their falling into the errors of the papists. ¶ *Unworthily.* Perhaps there is no expression in the Bible that has given more trouble to weak and feeble Christians than this. It is certain that there is no one that

has operated to deter so many from the communion; or that is so often made use of as an excuse for not making a profession of religion. The excuse is, "I am unworthy to partake of this holy ordinance. I shall only expose myself to condemnation. I must therefore wait until I become more worthy, and better prepared to celebrate it." It is important, therefore, that there should be a correct understanding of this passage. Most persons interpret it as if it were *unworthy,* and not *unworthily,* and seem to suppose that it refers to their personal qualifications, to their *unfitness* to partake of it, rather than to the *manner* in which it is done. It is to be remembered, therefore, that the word here used is an *adverb,* and not an *adjective,* and has reference to the *manner* of observing the ordinance, and not to their personal qualifications or fitness. It is true that in ourselves we are all *unworthy* of an approach to the table of the Lord; *unworthy* to be regarded as his followers; *unworthy* of a title to everlasting life: but it does not follow that we may not partake of this ordinance in a worthy, *i. e.* a proper manner, with a deep sense of our sinfulness, our need of a Saviour, and with some just views of the Lord Jesus as our Redeemer. Whatever may be our consciousness of personal unworthiness and unfitness—and that consciousness cannot be too deep—yet we may have such love to Christ, and such a desire to be saved by him, and such a sense of *his* worthiness, as to make it proper for us to approach and partake of this ordinance. The term *unworthily* (ἀναξίως) means properly *in an unworthy or improper* MANNER, *in a manner unsuitable to the purposes for which it was designed or instituted;* and may include the following things, viz. (1.) Such an irregular and indecent observance as existed in the church of Corinth, where even gluttony and intemperance prevailed under the professed design of celebrating the supper. (2.) An observance of the ordinance where there should be no distinction between it and common meals (Note on ver. 29); where they did not regard it as designed to show forth the death of the Lord Jesus. It is evident that where *such* views prevailed, there could be no proper qualification for this observance; and it is equally clear that such ignorance can hardly be supposed to prevail now in those lands which are illuminated by Christian truth. (3.) When it is done for the sake of mockery, and when the purpose is to deride religion, and to show a marked contempt for the ordinances of the gospel. It is a remarkable fact that many infidels have been so full of malignity and bitterness against the Christian religion as to observe a mock celebration of the Lord's supper. There is no profounder depth of depravity than this; there is nothing that can more conclusively or painfully show the hostility of man to the gospel of God. It is a remarkable fact, also, that not a few such persons have died a most miserable death. Under the horrors of an accusing conscience, and the anticipated destiny of final damnation, they have left the world as frightful monuments of the justice of God. It is *also* a fact that not a few infidels who have been engaged in such unholy celebrations have been converted to that very gospel which they were thus turning into ridicule and scorn. Their consciences have been alarmed; they have shuddered at the remembrance of the crime; they have been overwhelmed with the consciousness of guilt, and have found no peace until they have found it in that blood whose shedding they were thus profanely celebrating. ¶ *Shall be guilty* (ἔνο-χος). This word properly means obnoxious to punishment for personal crime. It always includes the idea of ill-desert, and of exposure to punishment on account of crime or ill-desert; Mat. v. 22; comp. Exod. xxii. 3; xxxiv. 7; Num. xiv. 18; xxxv. 27; Lev. xx. 9; see also Deut. xix. 10; Mat. xxvi. 66. ¶ *Of the body and blood of the Lord.* Com-

mentators have not been agreed in regard to the meaning of this expression. Doddridge renders it, " Shall be counted guilty of profaning and affronting in some measure that which is intended to represent the body and blood of the Lord." Grotius renders it, " He does the same thing as if he should slay Christ." Bretschneider (Lex.) renders it, " Injuring by crime the body of the Lord." Locke renders it, " Shall be guilty of a misuse of the body and blood of the Lord;" and supposes it means that they should be liable to the punishment due to one who made a wrong use of the sacramental body and blood of Christ in the Lord's supper. Rosenmüller renders it, " He shall be punished for such a deed as if he had affected Christ himself with ignominy." Bloomfield renders it, " He shall be guilty respecting the body, *i. e.* guilty of profaning the symbols of the body and blood of Christ, and consequently shall be amenable to the punishment due to such an abuse of the highest means of grace." But it seems to me that this does not convey the fulness of the meaning of the passage. The obvious and literal sense is evidently that they should by such conduct be involved in the sin of putting the Lord Jesus to death. The phrase " the body and blood of the Lord," in this connection, obviously, I think, refers to his death,—to the fact that his body was broken, and his blood shed, of which the bread and wine were symbols; and to be *guilty* of that, means to be guilty of putting him to death; that is, to be involved in the crime, or to do a thing which should involve the same criminality as that. To see this, we are to remember, (1.) That the bread and wine were symbols or emblems of that event, and designed to set it forth. (2.) To treat with irreverence and profaneness the bread which was an emblem of his broken body, was to treat with irreverence and profaneness the body itself; and in like manner the wine, the symbol of his blood. (3.) Those, therefore who treated the symbols of his body and blood with profaneness and contempt were *united*

28 But let a man examine ^a him-

self, and so let him eat of *that* bread, and drink of *that* cup.

in spirit with those who put him to death. They evinced the same feelings towards the Lord Jesus that his murderers did. They treated him with scorn, profaneness, and derision; and showed that with the same spirit they would have joined in the act of murdering the Son of God. They would evince their hostility to the Saviour himself as far as they could do, by showing contempt for the memorials of his body and blood. The apostle does by no means, however, as I understand him, mean to say that any of the Corinthians *had* been thus guilty of his body and blood. He does not charge on them this murderous intention. But he states what is the fair and obvious construction which is to be put on a wanton disrespect for the Lord's supper. And the design is to guard them, and all others, against this sin. There can be no doubt that those who celebrate his death in mockery and derision *are* held guilty of his body and blood. They show that they have the spirit of his murderers; they evince it in the most awful way possible; and they who would thus join in a profane celebration of the Lord's supper would have joined in the cry, " Crucify him, crucify him," For it is a most fearful and solemn act to trifle with sacred things; and especially to hold up to derision and scorn, the bitter sorrows by which the Son of God accomplished the redemption of the world.

28. *But let a man examine himself.* Let him search and see if he have the proper qualifications—if he has knowledge to discern the Lord's body (Note, ver. 29); if he has true repentance for his sins; true faith in the Lord Jesus; and a sincere desire to live the life of a Christian, and to be like the Son of God, and be saved by the merits of his blood. Let him examine himself, and see whether he have the right feelings of a communicant, and can approach the table in a proper manner. In regard to this we may observe, (1.) That this examination should include the great question

about his personal piety, and about his particular and special fitness for this observance. It should go back into the great inquiry whether he has ever been born again; and it should also have special reference to his immediate and direct preparation for the ordinance. He should not only be able to say *in general* that he is a Christian, but he should be able to say that he has *then* a particular preparation for it. He should be in a suitable frame of mind for it. He should have *personal* evidence that he is a penitent; that he has true faith in the Lord Jesus; that he is depending on him, and is desirous of being saved by him. (2.) This examination should be minute and particular. It should extend to the words, the thoughts, the feelings, the conduct. We should inquire whether in our family and in our business; whether among Christians, and with the world, we have lived the life of a Christian. We should examine our private thoughts; our habits of secret prayer and of searching the Scriptures. Our examination should be directed to the inquiry whether we are gaining the victory over our easily besetting sins and becoming more and more conformed to the Saviour. It should, in short, extend to all our Christian character; and every thing which goes to make up or to mar that character should be the subject of faithful and honest examination. (3.) It should be done because, (*a*) It is well to pause occasionally in life, and take an account of our standing in the sight of God. Men make advances in business and in property only when they often *examine* their accounts, and know just how they stand. (*b*) Because the observance of the Lord's supper is a solemn act, and there will be fearful results if it is celebrated in an improper manner. (*c*) Because self-examination supposes seriousness and calmness, and prevents precipitation and rashness—states of mind entirely unfavourable to a proper observance of the Lord's supper. (*d*)

29 For he that eateth and drinketh unworthily, eateth and drinketh ¹ damnation to himself, not discerning the Lord's body.

1 *judgment*, Rom.13.2.

Because by self-examination one may search out and remove those things that are offensive to God, and the sins which so easily beset us may be known and abandoned. (*e*) Because the approach to the table of the Lord is a solemn approach to the Lord himself; is a solemn profession of attachment to him; is an act of consecration to his service in the presence of angels and of men; and this should be done in a calm, deliberate and sincere manner; such a manner as may be the result of a prayerful and honest self-examination. ¶ *And so let him eat*, &c. And as the result of such examination, or *after* such an examination; that is, let the act of eating that bread be *always* preceded by a solemn self-examination. Bloomfield renders it, "and then," "then only." The sense is plain, that the communion should *always* be preceded by an honest and prayerful self-examination.

29. *For he that eateth*, &c. In order to excite them to a deeper reverence for this ordinance, and to a more solemn mode of observing it, Paul in this verse states another consequence of partaking of it in an improper and irreverent manner; comp. ver. 27. ¶ *Eateth and drinketh damnation.* This is evidently a figurative expression, meaning that by eating and drinking improperly he incurs condemnation; which is here expressed by eating and drinking condemnation itself. The word *damnation* we now apply, in common language, exclusively to the future and final punishment of the wicked in hell. But the word here used does not of necessity refer to that; and according to our use of the word now, there is a harshness and severity in our translation which the Greek does not require, and which probably was not conveyed by the word 'damnation" when the translation was made. In the margin it is correctly rendered "judgment." The word here used (*κρῖμα*) properly denotes *judgment;* the result of judg-

ing, that is, a sentence; then a sentence by which one is condemned, or condemnation; and then punishment; see Rom. iii. 8; xiii. 2. It has evidently the sense of judgment here; and means, that by their improper manner of observing this ordinance, they would expose themselves to the divine displeasure, and to punishment. And it refers, I think, to the punishment or judgment which the apostle immediately specifies, ver. 30, 32. It means a manifestation of the divine displeasure which might be evinced in this life; and which, in the case of the Corinthians, was manifested in the judgments which God had brought upon them. It cannot be denied, however, that a profane and intentionally irreverent manner of observing the Lord's supper will meet with the divine displeasure in the eternal world, and aggravate the doom of those who are guilty of it. But it is clear that this was not the punishment which the apostle had here in his eye. This is apparent, (1.) Because the Corinthians *did* eat unworthily, and yet the judgments inflicted on them were only temporal, that is, weakness, sickness, and temporal death (ver. 30); and, (2.) Because the reason assigned for these judgments is, that they might *not* be condemned with the wicked; *i. e.* as the wicked are in hell, ver. 32. *Whitby.* Comp. 1 Pet. iv. 17. ¶ *Not discerning the Lord's body.* Not *discriminating* (*μὴ διακρίνων*) between the bread which is used on this occasion and common and ordinary food. Not making the proper difference and distinction between this and common meals. It is evident that this was the leading offence of the Corinthians (see Notes, ver. 20, 21), and this is the proper idea which the original conveys. It does not refer to any intellectual or physical power to *perceive* that that bread represented the body of the Lord; not to any spiritual perception which it is often supposed that piety has to distinguish this; not to any view which faith may

30 For this cause many *are* weak and sickly among you, and many sleep.

31 For if *a* we would judge ourselves, we should not be judged.

a Ps.32.5; 1 John 1.9.

be supposed to have to discern the body of the Lord through the elements; but to the fact that they did not *distinguish* or *discriminate* between this and common meals. They did not regard it in a proper manner, but supposed it to be simply an historical commemoration of an event, such as they were in the habit of observing in honour of an idol or a hero by a public celebration. They, therefore, are able to "discern the Lord's body" in the sense intended here, who with a serious mind, *regard* it as an institution appointed by the Lord Jesus to commemorate his death; and who *did distinguish* thus between this and ordinary meals and all festivals and feasts designed to commemorate other events. In other words, who deem it to be designed to show forth the fact that his body was broken for sin, and who desire to observe it as such. It is evident that all true Christians may have ability of this kind, and need not incur condemnation by any error in regard to this. The humblest and obscurest follower of the Saviour, with the feeblest faith and love, may regard it as designed to set forth the death of his Redeemer; and observing it thus, will meet with the divine approbation.

30. *For this cause.* On account of the improper manner of celebrating the Lord's supper; see ver. 21. ¶ *Many are weak* (ἀσθενεῖς). Evidently referring to prevailing bodily sickness and disease. This is the natural and obvious interpretation of this passage. The sense clearly is, that God had sent among them bodily distempers as an expression of the divine displeasure and judgment for their improper mode of celebrating the Lord's supper. That it was not uncommon in those times for God in an extraordinary manner to visit men with calamity, sickness, or death for their sins, is evident from the New Testament; see Note, chap. v. 5; Acts v. 1—10; xiii. 11; 1 Tim. i. 20; and

perhaps 1 John v. 16; and James v. 14, 15. It may possibly have been the case that the intemperance and gluttony which prevailed on these occasions was the direct cause of no small part of the bodily disease which prevailed, and which in some cases terminated in death. ¶ *And many sleep.* Have died. The death of Christians in the Scriptures is commonly represented under the image of *sleep*; Dan. xii. 2; John xi. 11, 12; 1 Cor. xv. 51; 1 Thess. iv. 14; v. 10. *Perhaps* it may be implied by the use of this mild term here, instead of the harsher word *death*, that these were true Christians. This sentiment is in accordance with all that Paul states in regard to the church at Corinth. Notwithstanding all their irregularities, he does not deny that they were sincere Christians, and all his appeals and reasonings proceed on that supposition, though there was among them much ignorance and irregularity. God often visits his own people with trial; and though they are his children, yet this does not exempt them from affliction and discipline on account of their imperfections, errors, and sins. The *practical lesson* taught by this is, that Christians should serve God with purity; that they should avoid sin in every form; and that the commission of sin will expose them, as well as others, to the divine displeasure. The *reason* why this judgment was inflicted on the Corinthians was, that there might be a suitable impression made of the holy nature of that ordinance, and that Christians might be led to observe it in a proper manner. If it be asked whether God ever visits his people *now* with his displeasure for their improper manner of observing this ordinance, we may reply, (1.) That we have no reason to suppose that he inflicts *bodily* diseases and corporeal punishments on account of it. But, (2.) There is no reason to doubt that the improper observance of the Lord's supper, like the impro-

32 But when we are judged, we [a] are chastened of the Lord, that we should not be condemned with the world.

a Ps.94.12,13; Heb.12.5—11.

per observance of any other religious duty, will be followed with the expression of God's displeasure, and with a spiritual blighting on the soul. This may be evinced in the following modes. (a) In hardening the heart by an improper familiarity with the most sacred and solemn ordinances of religion. (b) Increased coldness and deadness in the service of God. If the ordinances of the gospel are not the means of making us better, they are the means of making us worse. (c) The loss of the favour of God, or of those pure, and spiritual, and elevated joys which we might have obtained by a proper observance of the ordinance. There is no reason to doubt that God may make it the occasion of *manifesting* his displeasure. It may be followed by a want of spiritual comfort and peace; by a loss of communion with God; and by a withholding of those comforts from the soul which *might* have been enjoyed, and which *are* imparted to those who observe it in a proper manner. The general principle is, that an improper discharge of any duty will expose us to his displeasure, and to the certain loss of all those favours which might have resulted from a proper discharge of the duty, and to the tokens of the divine displeasure. And this is as true of prayer, or of any other religious duty, as of an improper observance of the Lord's supper.

31. *For if we would judge ourselves.* If we would examine ourselves, (ver. 28); if we would exercise a strict scrutiny over our hearts and feelings, and conduct, and come to the Lord's table with a proper spirit, we should escape the condemnation to which they are exposed who observe it in an improper manner. If we would exercise proper *severity* and *honesty* in determining our own character and fitness for the ordinance, we should not expose ourselves to the divine displeasure. ¶ *We should not be judged.* We should not be exposed to the expression of God's disapprobation. He refers here to the punishment which had come upon the Corinthians for their improper manner of observing the ordinance; and he says that if they had properly examined themselves, and had understood the nature of the ordinance, that they would have escaped the judgments that had come upon them. This is as true now as it was then. If we wish to escape the divine displeasure; if we wish the communion *to be followed* with joy, and peace, and growth in grace, and not with blighting and spiritual barrenness, we should exercise a severe judgment on our character, and feelings, and motives; and should come to it with a sincere desire to honour Christ, and to advance in the divine life.

32. *But when we are judged.* This is added, evidently, to console those who had been afflicted on account of their improper manner of observing the Lord's supper. The sense is, that though they were thus afflicted by God; though he had manifested his displeasure at the manner in which they had observed the ordinance, yet the divine judgment in the case was not inexorable. They were not regarded by God as wholly strangers to piety, and would not be lost for ever. They should not be alarmed, therefore, as if there was no mercy for them; but they should rather regard their calamities as the chastening of the Lord on his own children, and as designed for their salvation. ¶ *We are chastened of the Lord.* It is *his* act; and it is not vengeance and wrath; but it is to be regarded as the chastisement of a father's hand, *in order* that we should not be condemned with the wicked. We are *under the discipline* (παιδευόμεθα) of the Lord; we are dealt with as children, and are corrected as by the hand of a father; comp. Heb. xii. 5—10, and 2 Cor. vi. 9. The *design* of God's correcting his children is, that they should

33 Wherefore, my brethren, when ye come together to eat, tarry one for another.

34 And if any man hunger, let him eat at home; that ye come not together unto condemnation. [1]

[1] *judgment.*

be *reclaimed,* and not *destroyed.* ¶ *That we should not be condemned with the world.* It is implied here, (1.) That the world—those who were not Christians, would be condemned; (2.) That Paul regarded the Corinthians, whom he addressed, and who had even been guilty of this improper manner of observing the Lord's supper, and who had been punished for it, as true Christians; and, (3.) That the purpose which God had in view in inflicting these judgments on them was, that they might be purified, and enlightened, and recovered from their errors, and saved. This is the design of God in the calamities and judgments which he brings on his own children.—And so now, if he afflicts us, or leaves us to darkness, or follows the communion with the tokens of his displeasure, it is, that we may be recovered to a deeper sense of our need of him; to juster views of the ordinance; and to a more earnest wish to obtain his favour.

33. *When ye come together to eat.* Professedly to eat the Lord's supper. ¶ *Tarry one for another.* Do not be guilty of disorder, intemperance, and gluttony; see Note, ver. 21. Doddridge understands this of the feast that he supposes to have preceded the Lord's supper. But the more obvious interpretation is, to refer it to the Lord's supper itself; and to enjoin perfect order, respect, and sobriety. The idea is, that the table was common for the rich and the poor; and that the rich should claim no priority or precedence over the poor.

34. *And if any man hunger,* &c. The Lord's supper is not a common feast; it is not designed as a place where a man may gratify his appetite. It is designed as a simple *commemoration,* and not as a *feast.* This remark was designed to correct their views of the supper, and to show them that it

And the rest will I set in order when I come.

CHAPTER XII.

NOW concerning spiritual *gifts,* brethren, I would not have you ignorant.

was to be distinguished from the ordinary idea of a feast or festival. ¶ *That ye come not together unto condemnation.* That the effect of your coming together for the observance of the Lord's supper be not to produce condemnation; see Note, ver. 29. ¶ *And the rest will I set in order,* &c. Probably he refers here to other matters on which he had been consulted; or other things which he knew required to be adjusted. The *other matters* pertaining to the order and discipline of the church I will defer until I can come among you, and personally arrange them. It is evident from this, that Paul at this time purposed soon to go to Corinth; see 2 Cor. 1. 15, 16. It was doubtless true that there might be many things which it was desirable to adjust in the church there, which could not be so well done by letter. The main things, therefore, which it was needful to correct immediately, he had discussed in this letter; the other matters he reserved to be arranged by himself when he should go among them. Paul was disappointed in his expectations of returning among them as soon as he had intended (see 2 Cor. i. 17), and under this disappointment he forwarded to them another epistle. If all Christians would follow implicitly his directions here in regard to the Lord's supper, it would be an ordinance full of comfort. May all so understand its nature, and so partake of it, that they shall meet the approbation of their Lord, and so that it may be the means of saving grace to their souls.

CHAPTER XII.

THIS chapter commences a new subject, the discussion of which continues to the close of the fourteenth chapter. The general subject is that of spiritual endowments, or the right mode of exercising their spiritual gifts, and the degree of honour which was due to those who had been distinguished by God by the special influences of his Spirit. It is evident that many in the church at Corinth had been thus favoured; and it is evident that they had greatly abused these endowments, and that those who were thus favoured had claimed a precedency of honour above those who had been less distinguished. It is not improbable that they had in their letter to Paul (see Note, chap. vii. 1), requested his counsel on this subject, and asked him to teach them what measure of honour should be given to those who had been thus endowed. This subject, as it was of importance not only for them, but for the church at large in all future times, he proceeds to discuss in this, and the two following chapters; and this discussion closes the *second* part of the epistle; see the Introduction. The general scope of these chapters is this. (1.) He shows that all those endowments were conferred by the Holy Ghost, and were all for the use of the church; that the church was one, but that there was a necessity for diversified operations in that church; and that, therefore, no one should value himself on that gift above his brother, and no one should feel himself dishonoured because he had not been thus favoured. All filled important places in the church, just as the various members and parts of the human system were necessary for its symmetry, action and health; and all therefore, should be willing to occupy the place which God had assigned them, chap. xii. (2.) In chapter xiii. he recommends *love*, or charity, as of more value than all other spiritual gifts put together, and therefore recommends that *that* should be especially the object of their desire. (3.) In chapter xiv. he gives particular rules about the proper exercise of spiritual gifts in their public assemblies. This chapter, therefore, is occupied in stating and illustrating the position that all spiritual gifts are conferred by the Holy Ghost, and that no one should so value himself on this gift as to despise those who had not been thus endowed: and that no

one who had not thus been favoured should be dejected, or regard himself as dishonoured. This statement is illustrated in the following manner.

(1.) Paul states the importance of the subject, ver. 1.

(2.) He reminds them that they were formerly in a state of ignorance, sin, and idolatry, ver. 2.

(3.) He states *one* mark of being under the influence of the Spirit of God—that is, that it would lead them to acknowledge and honour Jesus Christ. If the Spirit by which they were influenced led them to this, it was proof that it was the Holy Ghost, ver. 3. If any *pretenders* to inspiration were in the habit of speaking disrespectfully of Jesus Christ, or of calling him " *accursed*, " it proved that they were not under the influence of the Holy Ghost.

(4.) There were *diversities* in the operations of the Spirit, but however various were these operations, they all proceeded from the same agent, ver. 4—11. All were not, therefore, to expect precisely the same influences or operations; nor were they to suppose that because there were various operations, that therefore they were not influenced by the Spirit of God.

(5.) Paul states and illustrates the truth that the church is one, ver. 12 —27. As the body is one, yet has many members, so is it with the church, ver. 12. The body has many members, and no members in the body are useless, but all perform important parts, however unimportant they may seem to be; and no one member can say that it has no need of the others. So it is in the church, ver. 13—27.

(6.) This beautiful allegory, drawn from the functions of the various parts of the human body, Paul applies now to the church, and shows (ver. 28—30) that the same thing should be expected in the church of Christ. It followed, therefore, that those who were not as highly favoured as others should not regard themselves as useless, and decline their station in the church. It followed also, that those who were in inferior stations should

2 Ye know that ye were Gentiles, carried away unto these

dumb *a* idols, even as ye were led.

a 1 Thess.1.9.

not envy those who had been more highly favoured; and that those who were in more elevated stations, and who had been more signally favoured, should not look down on those beneath them with contempt. It followed also, that they should regard themselves as one body; and love and cherish each other with constant Christian affection.

(7.) Paul tells them that it was not improper to desire the highest endowments, but says that he will propose an object of desire to be preferred to these gifts—and that is LOVE, ver. 31.

1. *Now concerning.* It is now time that I should speak of spiritual endowments. He had no doubt been consulted in regard to them, and probably various questions had been proposed, which he now proceeded to answer. ¶ *Spiritual* gifts. The word "gifts" is not in the original. The Greek refers to "spiritual" things in general, or to any thing that is of a spiritual nature. The whole discussion, however, shows that he refers to the various endowments, gifts, or graces that had been bestowed in different degrees on the members of the church—including the distinctions in graces, and in degrees of office and rank, which had been made in the Christian church in general (chap. xii.), as well as the extraordinary endowments of the gift of tongues which had been bestowed upon many, chap. xiv. ¶ *I would not have you ignorant.* The subject is of so much importance that it demands particular attention and special care ; comp. Note, chap. x. 1. I would not have you ignorant in regard to the nature of those endowments; the spirit with which they should be received; the rules to which they who are thus favoured should be subjected; and the feelings and views which should be cherished in all the members of the church in regard to them. Nothing is of more importance in the church than the doctrine respecting the influences and endowments of the Holy Spirit.

2. *Ye know,* &c. This verse is regarded by many as a parenthesis. But it is not necessary to suppose that it is so, or that it does not cohere with that which follows. The design seems to be to remind them of their former miserable condition as idolaters, in order to make them more sensible of their advantages as Christians, and that they might be led more highly to appreciate their present condition. Paul often refers Christians to their former condition, to excite in them gratitude for the mercies that God has conferred on them in the gospel ; see Note, chap. vi. 11, comp. Rom. vi. 17. Eph. ii. 11, 12; Titus iii. 3. ¶ *That ye were Gentiles.* Heathen ; worshippers of idols. The idea is, that they were pagans ; that they had no knowledge of the true God, but were sunk in miserable superstition and idolatry. ¶ *Carried away.* Led along; that is, deluded by your passions, deluded by your priests, deluded by your vain and splendid rites of worship. The whole system made an appeal to the senses, and *bore along* its votaries as if by a foreign and irresistible impulse. The word which is used ($\dot{a}\pi a\gamma \acute{o}\mu s\nu o\iota$) conveys properly the idea of being carried into bondage, or being led to punishment, and refers here doubtless to the strong means which had been used by crafty politicians and priests in their former state to delude and deceive them. ¶ *Unto these dumb idols.* These idols which could not speak—an attribute which is often given to them, to show the folly of worshipping them ; Ps. cxv. 5 ; cxxxv. 15 ; Hab. ii. 18, 19. The ancient priests and politicians deluded the people with the notion that oracles were uttered by the idols whom they worshipped, and thus they maintained the belief in their divinity. The idea of Paul here seems to be, (1.) That their idols never could have uttered the oracles which were ascribed to them, and consequently that they had been deluded. (2.) That these idols could never have endowed them with such

3 Wherefore I give you to understand, that no man *a* speaking by

a Mark 9.39; 1 John 4,2,3.

the Spirit of God calleth Jesus [1] accursed: and *b that* no man can

1 or, *anathema.*   b Mat.16.17.

spiritual privileges as they now had, and consequently that their present state was far preferable to their former condition. ¶ *Even as ye were led.* Were led by the priests in the temples of the idols. They were under strong delusions and the arts of cunning and unprincipled men. The idea is, that they had been under a strong infatuation, and were entirely at the control of their spiritual leaders—a description remarkably applicable now to all forms of imposture in the world. No system of paganism consults the freedom and independence of the mind of man ; but it is everywhere characterized as a system of *power,* and not of *thought ;* and all its arrangements are made to secure that power without an intelligent assent of the understanding and the heart.

3. *Wherefore I give you to understand.* I make known to you. The force of this expression is, *I give you this rule to distinguish,* or by which you may know what influences and operations are from God. The design of the passage is, to give them some simple general guide by which they could at once recognise the operations of the Spirit of God, and determine whether they who claimed to be under that operation were really so. That rule was, that all who were truly influenced by the Holy Ghost would be disposed to acknowledge and to know Jesus Christ; and where this disposition existed, it was of itself a clear demonstration that it was the operation of the Spirit of God. The same rule substantially is given by John (1 John iv. 2), by which to test the nature of the spirit by which men profess to be influenced. " Hereby know ye the Spirit of God: Every spirit that confesses that Jesus Christ is come in the flesh is of God," comp. also Note to Mat. xvi. 17. ¶ *That no man.* No one (οὐδεὶς). It may refer to a man, or to demons, or to those who pretended to be under inspiration of any kind. And it may refer to

the Jews who may have pretended to be under the influence of God's Spirit, and who yet anathematized and cursed the name of Jesus. Or it may be intended simply as a general rule ; meaning that *if any one,* whoever he might be, should blaspheme the name of Jesus, whatever were his pretensions, whether professing to be under the influence of the Holy Spirit among the Jews, or to be inspired among the Gentiles, it was full proof that he was an impostor. The argument is, *that the Holy Spirit in all instances would do honour to Jesus Christ, and would prompt all who were under his influence to love and reverence his name.* ¶ *Speaking by the Spirit of God.* Under the influence of inspiration. ¶ *Calleth.* Says, or would say; that is, no such one would use the language of anathema in regard to him. ¶ *Accursed.* Marg. *Anathema* (ἀνάθεμα) ; see Note, Acts xxiii. 14 ; Rom. ix. 3 ; comp. 1 Cor. xvi. 22 ; Gal. i. 8, 9. The word is one of execration, or cursing ; and means, that no one under the influence of the Holy Spirit could curse the name of Jesus, or denounce him as execrable and as an impostor. The effect of the influences of the Spirit would be in all instances to inspire reverence for his name and work. It is probable that the *Jews* were here principally intended, since there is a bitterness and severity in the language which accords with all their expressions of feeling towards Jesus of Nazareth. It is possible, also, and indeed probable, that the priests and priestesses of the pagan gods who pretended to be under the influence of inspiration might denounce the name of Jesus, because they would all be opposed to the purity of his religion. ¶ *And that no man can say,&c.* That is, that it cannot occur, or even happen, that any one will acknowledge Jesus as the Messiah who is not influenced by the Holy Ghost. The meaning is, not that no one has physical ability *to say* that Jesus is

say that Jesus is the Lord, but by the Holy Ghost.

4 Now there are diversities *a* of gifts, but the same Spirit.

a Heb.2.4; 1 Pet.1.10.

Lord unless aided by the Holy Ghost, since all men can *say* this ; but that no one will be disposed heartily to say it; no one will acknowledge him as their Lord; it can never happen that any one will confess him as the true Messiah who has not been brought to this state by the agency of the Holy Ghost. ¶ *Is the Lord.* Is the Messiah ; or shall acknowledge him as their Lord. ¶ *But by the Holy Ghost.* Unless he is influenced by the Holy Spirit. This is a very important verse, not only in regard to the particular subject under consideration in the time of Paul, but also in its practical bearing at present. We may learn from it, (1.) That it is a proof that any man is under the influence of the Holy Spirit who is heartily disposed to honour the name and work of Jesus Christ. (2.) Those forms and modes of religion ; those religious opinions and practices, will be most in accordance with the designs of the Spirit of God, which do most to honour the name and work of Jesus Christ. (3.) It is true that no man will ever cherish a proper regard for Jesus Christ, nor love his name and work, unless he is influenced by the Holy Ghost. No man loves the name and work of the Redeemer by following simply the inclinations of his own corrupt heart. In all instances of those who have been brought to a willingness to honour him, it has been by the agency of the Holy Ghost. (4.) If any man, in any way, is disposed to disparage the work of Christ, to speak lightly of his person or his name ; or holds doctrines that infringe on the fulness of the truth respecting his divine nature, his purity, his atonement, it is proof that he is not under the influence of the Spirit of God. Just in proportion as he shall disparage that work or name, just in that proportion does he give evidence that he is not influenced by the Divine Spirit ; but by proud reason, or by imagination, or by a heart that is not reconciled to

God. (5.) All true religion is the production of the Holy Spirit. For religion consists essentially in a willingness to honour, and love, and serve the Lord Jesus Christ; and where *that* exists, it is produced by the Holy Spirit. (6.) The influence of the Holy Spirit should be cherished. To grieve away that Spirit is to drive all proper knowledge of the Redeemer from the soul ; to do this is to leave the heart to coldness, and darkness, and barrenness, and spiritual death.

4. *Now there are diversities of gifts.* There are different endowments conferred on Christians. For the meaning of the word *gifts*, see Note, Rom. i. 11; comp. Rom. v. 15, 16; vi. 23; xi. 29; xii. 6; 1 Cor. i. 7; vii. 7. ¶ *But the same Spirit.* Produced by the same Spirit—the Holy Ghost. What those diversities of gifts are, the apostle enumerates in ver. 8—11. The design for which he refers to these various endowments is evidently to show those whom he addressed, that since they are all produced by the same Holy Spirit, have all the same divine origin, and are all intended to answer some important purpose and end in the Christian church, that, therefore, none are to be despised; nor is one man to regard himself as authorized to treat another with contempt. The Spirit has divided and conferred those gifts according to his sovereign will; and his arrangements should be regarded with submission, and the favours which he confers should be received with thankfulness. That the Holy Spirit—the third person of the adorable Trinity—is here intended by the word "Spirit," seems to be manifest on the face of the passage, and has been the received interpretation of the church until it was called in question by some recent German commentators, at the head of whom was Eichhorn. It is not the design of these Notes to go into an examination of questions of criticism, such as an inquiry like this would involve.

5 And there are differences of ¹ administrations, but the same Lord.

6 And there are diversities *a* of operations; but it is the same God which worketh all in all.

1 or *ministries.*

a Rom.12.6,&c.

Nor is it necessary. Some of the arguments by which the common interpretation is defended are the following. (1.) It is the obvious interpretation. It is that which occurs to the great mass of readers, as the true and correct exposition. (2.) It accords with the usual meaning of the word Spirit. No other intelligible sense can be given to the word here. To say, with Eichhorn, that it means "nature," that there are the same natural endowments, though cultivated in various measures by art and education, makes manifest nonsense, and is contrary to the whole structure and scope of the passage. (3.) It accords with all the other statements in the New Testament, where the endowments here referred to "wisdom," "knowledge," "faith," "working of miracles," &c., are traced to the Holy Spirit, and are regarded as his gift. (4.) The harmony, the concinnity of the passage is destroyed by supposing that it refers to any thing else than the Holy Spirit. In this verse the agency of the Spirit is recognised, and *his* operations on the mind referred to; in the next verse the agency of the Son of God (see Note on the verse) is referred to; and in the following verse, the agency of God—evidently the Father —is brought into view; and thus the entire passage (ver. 4—6) presents a connected view of the operations performed by the Father, Son, and Holy Ghost in the work of redemption. To deny that this verse refers to the Holy Spirit is to break up the harmony of the whole passage, and to render it in no small degree unmeaning. But if this refers to the Holy Spirit, then it is an unanswerable argument for his personality, and for his be'ng on an equality with the Father and the Son.

5. *Of administrations.* Marg. *Ministries.* The word properly denotes *ministries;* so that there are

different ranks and grades in the ministries which Christ has appointed, to wit, those specified in ver. 9, 10, 28. ¶ *But the same Lord.* This refers evidently to the Lord Jesus, by whom these various orders of ministers were appointed, and under whose control they are; see Note, Acts i. 24; comp. Eph. iv. 5. The term *Lord,* when it stands by itself in the New Testament, usually refers to the Lord Jesus, the name by which he was commonly known by the disciples; see John xx. 25. The fact also that this stands between the mention of the work of the Spirit (ver. 4) and the work of God (ver. 6), and the fact that to the Lord Jesus appertained the appointment of these various grades of officers in the church (comp. Mat. x. 1, seq., and Luke x. 1, seq.), is further proof that this refers to him. The design of the verse is, to show that all these offices had their appointment from him; and that since all were his appointment, and all were necessary, no one should be proud of an elevated station; no one should be depressed, or feel himself degraded, because he had been designated to a more humble office.

6. *Of operations.* Of works; to wit, of miracles, such as God produces in the church, in the establishment and defence of his religion. There are different operations on the mind and heart; and different powers given to man, or different qualifications in building up and defending his cause. Or it may be, possibly, that Paul here refers to the works of God mainly for mere *illustration,* and by the word "operations" means the works which God has performed in creation and providence. His works are various. They are not all alike, though they come from the same hand. The sun, the moon, the stars, the earth are different; the trees of the forest, the beasts of the field, the fowls of the air, the inhabitants of the

7 But the manifestation of the Spirit is given to every man to profit *a* withal.

8 For to one is given, by the Spirit, *b* the word of wisdom; *c* to another the word of knowledge, *d* by the same Spirit;

9 To another faith *e* by the

a Eph.4.7.   b Isa.11.2,3.   c chap.2.6,7.   d chap. 13.2.   e Eph.2.8.

deep are different; the flowers, and shrubs, and herbs are different from each other; yet, however much they may vary, they are formed by the same hand, are the productions of the same God, are to be regarded as proofs of the same wisdom and power. The same thing should be expected in his church; and we should anticipate that the endowments of its members would be various. ¶ *But it is the same God.* The same Father; all these operations are produced by the same God. They should not, there-fore, be undervalued or despised; nor should any one be unduly elated, or pride himself on what has been con-ferred by God alone. ¶ *All in all.* All these operations are to be traced to him. His agency is everywhere. It is as really seen in the insect's wing as in the limbs of the mammoth; as really in the humblest violet as in the loftiest oak of the forest. All, therefore, should regard themselves as under his direction, and should submit to his arrangements. If men regard their endowments as the gift of God, they will be thankful for them, and they will not be disposed to des-pise or undervalue others who have been placed in a more humble condi-tion and rank in the church.

7. *But the manifestation of the Spirit.* The word "manifestation" (φανέρωσις;) means properly that which makes manifest, conspicuous, or plain; that which illustrates, or makes any thing seen or known. Thus conduct manifests the state of the heart; and the actions are a manifestation, or *showing forth* of the real feelings. The idea here is, that there is given to those referred to, such gifts, endow-ments, or graces as shall *manifest* the work and nature of the Spirit's opera-tions on the mind; such endowments as the Spirit makes himself known by to men. All that he produces in the mind is a manifestation of his charac-

ter and work, in the same way as the works of God in the visible creation are a manifestation of his perfections ¶ *Is given to every man.* To every man whose case is here under consi-deration. The idea is not at all that the manifestation of the Spirit is given to *all* men indiscriminately, to pagans, and infidels, and scoffers as well as to Christians. The apostle is discoursing only of those who are Christians, and his declaration should be confined to them alone. What-ever may be true of other men, this statement should be confined wholly to Christians, and means simply that the Spirit of God gives to each Chris-tian such graces and endowments as he pleases; that he distributes his gifts to all, not equally, but in a man-ner which he shall choose; and that the design of this is, that all Chris-tians should use his endowments for the common good. This passage, therefore, is very improperly adduced to prove that the gifts and graces of the Holy Spirit are conferred alike on all men, and that pagans, and blasphemers, and sinners in general are under his enlightening influences. It has no reference to any such doc-trine, but should be interpreted as referring solely to Christians, and the various endowments which are con-ferred on them. ¶ *To profit withal* (πρὸς τὸ συμφέρον). Unto profit; *i. e.* for utility, or use; or to be an advan-tage to the church; for the common good of all. This does not mean that each one must cultivate and improve his graces and gifts, however true that may be, but that they are to be used for the common good of the church; they are bestowed *for utility*, or *pro-fit*; they are conferred in such mea-sures and in such a manner as are best adapted to be useful, and to do good. They are bestowed not on all equally, but in such a manner as shall best subserve the interests of piety and the church, and as shall tend harmoniously to carry on the great interests of religion, and further the welfare of the whole Christian body. The doctrine of this verse is, therefore, (1.) That the Holy Spirit bestows such endowments on all Christians as he pleases; and, (2.) That the design is, in the best manner to promote the common welfare—the peace and edification of the whole church. It follows from this, (1.) That no Christian should be unduly elated, as if he were more worthy than others, since *his* endowments are the simple gift of God; (2.) That no Christian should be depressed and disheartened, as if he occupied an inferior or unimportant station, since *his* place has also been assigned him by God; (3.) That all should be contented, and satisfied with their allotments in the church, and should strive only to make the best use of their talents and endowments; and, (4.) That all should employ their time and talents for the common utility; for the furtherance of the common welfare, and the advancement of the kingdom of Christ on earth.

8. *For to one is given.* In order to show what endowments he refers to, the apostle here particularizes the various gifts which the Holy Spirit imparts in the church. ¶ *By the Spirit.* By the Holy Ghost; by his agency on the mind and heart. ¶ *The word of wisdom.* One he has endowed with *wisdom,* or has made distinguished for wise, and prudent, and comprehensive views of the scheme of redemption, and with a faculty of clearly explaining it to the apprehension of men. It is not certain that the apostle meant to say that this was the most important or most elevated endowment because he places it first in order. His design does not seem to be to observe the order of importance and value, but to state, as it occurred to him, the fact that these various endowments *had* been conferred on different men in the church. The sense is, that one man would be prominent and distinguished as a *wise* man—a prudent

counsellor, instructer, and adviser. ¶ *To another the word of knowledge.* Another would be distinguished for knowledge. He would be learned; would have a clear view of the plan of salvation, and of the doctrines and duties of religion. The same variety is observed in the ministry at all times. One man is eminent as a wise man; another as a man of intelligence and knowledge; and both may be equally useful in their place in the church. ¶ *By the same Spirit.* All is to be traced to the same Spirit; all, therefore, may be really useful and necessary; and the one should not pride himself in his endowments above the other.

9. *To another faith.* Another shall be distinguished for simple confidence in God; and *his* endowment is also given by the same Spirit. Many of the most useful men in the church are distinguished mainly for their simple confidence in the promises of God; and often accomplish more by prayer and by their faith in God than others do who are distinguished for their wisdom and learning. Humble piety and reliance in the divine promises, and that measure of ardour, fearlessness, and zeal which result from such confidence; that belief that all obstacles *must* be and *will* be overcome that oppose the gospel; and that God *will* secure the advancement of his cause, will often do infinitely more in the promotion of his kingdom than the most splendid endowments of learning and talent. Indeed, if a man were disposed to do good on the widest scale possible, to do the utmost that he possibly could in saving men, he would best accomplish it by seeking simple *faith* in God's aid and promises, and then under the influence of this, engage with ardour in doing what he could. Faith is one of the highest endowments of the Christian life; and yet, though all may obtain it, it is one of the rarest endowments. Perhaps by many it is despised, *because* it may be obtained by all; because it is a grace in which the poor and the humble may be as much distinguished as the man of splendid talents and profound learning. ¶ *To*

same Spirit; to another the gifts of healing, *a* by the same Spirit; 10 To another the working of

miracles; to another prophecy, to another discerning of spirits; *b* to another *divers* kinds of tongues;*c*

a Mark 16.18; James 5.14.   *b* 1 John 4.1.   *c* Acts 2.4,7—11.

---

another the gifts of healing; see Mark xvi. 18. This was promised to the disciples of the Saviour; and in the early church was conferred on many; comp. Acts v. 12, 15, 16; xix. 12. It would seem from this passage that the gift of healing was conferred on some in a more eminent degree than on others.

10. *To another the working of miracles.* Commentators have felt some perplexity in distinguishing this from what is mentioned in ver. 9, of the gift of healing. It is evident that the apostle there refers to the power of working miracles in healing inveterate and violent diseases. The expression here used, "working of miracles" (ἐνεργήματα δυνάμεων,) refers probably to the more *extraordinary* and *unusual* kinds of miracles; to those which were regarded as in advance of the power of healing diseases. It is possible that it may denote what the Saviour had reference to in Mark xvi. 18, where he said they should take up serpents, and if they drank any deadly thing it should not hurt them; and possibly also to the power of raising up the dead. That this power was possessed by the apostles is well known; and it is possible that it was possessed by others also of the early Christians. It is clear from all this that there was a *difference* even among those who had the power of working miracles, and that this power was conferred in a more eminent degree on some than on others. Indeed, the *extraordinary* endowments conferred on the apostles and the early Christians, seem to have been regulated to a remarkable degree in accordance with the rule by which *ordinary* endowments are conferred on men. Though all men have understanding, memory, imagination, bodily strength, &c., yet one has these in a more eminent degree than others; and one is characterized for the possession of one of those qualities more than for another. Yet all are bestowed by

the same God. So it was in regard to the extraordinary endowments conferred on the early Christians; comp. chap. xiv., especially ver. 32.

10. *To another prophecy;* see Note, Rom. xii. 6. ¶ *To another discerning of spirits;* comp. 1 John iv. 1. This must refer to some power of searching into the secrets of the heart; of knowing what were a man's purposes, views, and feelings. It may relate either to the power of determining by what spirit a man spoke who pretended to be inspired, whether he was truly inspired or whether he was an impostor; or it may refer to the power of seeing whether a man was sincere or not in his Christian profession. That the apostles had this power, is apparent from the case of Ananias and Sapphira, (Acts v. 1—10), and from the case of Elymas, Acts xiii. 9—11. It is evident that where the gift of prophecy and inspiration was possessed, and where it would confer such advantages on those who possessed it, there would be many pretenders to it; and that it would be of vast importance to the infant church, in order to prevent imposition, that there should be a power in the church of detecting the imposture. ¶ *To another* divers *kinds of tongues.* The power of speaking various languages; see Acts ii. 4, 7—11. This passage also seems to imply that the extraordinary endowments of the Holy Spirit were not conferred on all alike. ¶ *To another the interpretation of tongues.* The power of interpreting foreign languages; or of interpreting the language which might be used by the "prophets" in their communications; see Note, chap. xiv. 27. This was evidently a faculty different from the power of speaking a foreign language; and yet it might be equally useful. It would appear possible that some might have had the power of speaking foreign languages who were not themselves apprized of the meaning, and

to another the interpretation of tongues:

11 But all these worketh that one and the self-same Spirit, divid-ing *a* to every man severally as he will.

12 For as the body is one, and hath many members, and all the

---

that interpreters were needful in order to express the sense to the hearers. Or it may have been that in a promiscuous assembly, or in an assembly made up of those who spoke different languages, a part might have understood what was uttered, and it was needful that an interpreter should explain it to the other portion; see Notes on chap. xiv. 28.

11. *But all these.* All these various endowments. ¶ *Worketh.* Produces. All these are to be traced to him. ¶ *That one and the self-same Spirit.* The Holy Spirit, Acts ii. They were all, though so different in themselves, to be traced to the Holy Ghost, just as all the natural endowments of men —their strength, memory, judgment, &c.—though so various in themselves, are to be traced to the same God. ¶ *Dividing to every man severally.* Conferring on each one as he pleases. He confers on each one that which he sees to be best, and most wise, and proper. ¶ *As he will.* As he chooses; or as in his view seems best. Dr. Doddridge remarks, that this word does " not so much express arbitrary pleasure, as a determination founded on *wise* counsel." It implies, however, that he does it as a sovereign; as he sees to be right and best. He distributes these favours as to him seems best adapted to promote the welfare of the whole church and to advance his cause. Some of the doctrines which are taught by this verse are the following: (1.) The Holy Ghost is *a person.* For, he acts as a person; distributes favours, confers endowments and special mercies " as he will." This proves that he is, in some respects, distinguished from the Father and the Son. It would be absurd to say of an *attribute* of God, that it confers favours, and distributes the various endowments of speaking with tongues, and raising the dead. And if so, then the Holy Ghost is *not*

an attribute of God. (2.) He is a sovereign. He gives to all as he pleases. In regard to spiritual endowments of the highest order, he deals with men as he does in the common endowments bestowed on men, and as he does in temporal blessings. He does not bestow the same blessings on all, nor make all alike. He dispenses his favours by a rule which he has not made known, but which, we may be assured, is in accordance with wisdom and goodness. He wrongs no one; and he gives to all the favours which *might* be connected with eternal life. (3.) No man should be proud of his endowments. Whatever they may be, they are the gifts of God, bestowed by his sovereign will and mercy. But assuredly we should not be proud of that which is the mere *gift* of another; and which has been bestowed, not in consequence of any merit of ours, but according to his mere sovereign will. (4.) No man should be depressed, or should despise his own gifts, however humble they may be. In their own place, they may be as important as the higher endowments of others. That God has placed him where he is, or has given less splendid endowments than he has to others, is no fault of his. There is no crime in it; and he should, therefore, strive to improve his " one talent," and to make himself useful in the rank where he is placed. And, (5.) No man should despise another because he is in a more humble rank, or is less favoured than himself. God has made the difference, and we should *respect* and *honour* his arrangements, and should show that respect and honour by regarding with kindness, and treating as fellow labourers with us, all who occupy a more humble rank than we do.

12. *For as the body is one.* The general sentiment which the apostle had been illustrating and enforcing was, that all the endowments which

members of that one body : being many, are one body ; so *a* also *is* Christ.

13 For by one Spirit are we all

a ver. 27.   *b* John 1.16; Eph 4 5.

were possessed in the church were the work of the same Holy Spirit, and that they ought to be appropriately cherished and prized, as being all useful and valuable in their places. This sentiment he now illustrates (ver. 12—27) by a beautiful similitude taken from the mutual dependence of the various parts of the human body. The human body is one, and yet is composed of various members and parts that all unite harmoniously in one whole. ¶ *Being many.* Or, although they are many ; or while they are in some respects separate, and perform distinct and different functions, yet they all unite in one harmonious whole. ¶ *So also is Christ.* The church is represented as the body of Christ (ver. 27), meaning that it is one, and that he sustains to it the relation of Head ; comp. Eph. i. 22, 23. As the *head* is the most important part of the body, it may be put for the whole body; and the name *Christ* here, the head of the church, is put for the whole body of which he is the head ; and means here the Christian society, or the church. This figure, of a part for the whole, is one that is common in all languages; see Note, Rom. xii. 4, 5.

13. *For by one Spirit.* That is, by the agency or operation of the same Spirit, the Holy Ghost, we have been united into one body. The idea here is the same as that presented above (ver. 7. 11), by which all the endowments of Christians are traced to the same Spirit. Paul here says, that that Spirit had *so* endowed them as to fit them to constitute one body, or to be united in one, and to perform the various duties which resulted from their union in the same Christian church. The idea of its having been done by one and the same Spirit is kept up and often presented, in order that the endowments conferred on them might be duly appreciated. ¶ *Are we all.* Every member of the

b baptized into one body, whether *we be* Jews or Gentiles, [1] whether *we be* bond or free ; and have been all made to drink *c* into one Spirit.

1 *Greeks.*   *c* John 7.37 - 39.

church, whatever may be his rank or talents, has received his endowments from the same Spirit. ¶ *Baptized into one body.* Many suppose that there is reference here to the ordinance of baptism by water. But the connection seems rather to require us to understand it of the baptism of the Holy Ghost (Mat. iii. 11); and if so, it means, that by the agency of the Holy Spirit, they had all been fitted, each to his appropriate place, to constitute the body of Christ—the church. If, however, it refers to the ordinance of baptism, as Bloomfield, Calvin, Doddridge, &c. suppose, then it means, that by the very profession of religion as made at baptism, by there being but one baptism (Eph. iv. 5), they had all professedly become members of one and the same body. The former interpretation, however, seems to me best to suit the connection. ¶ *Whether we be Jews or Gentiles.* There is no difference. All are on a level. In regard to the grand point, no distinction is made, whatever may have been our former condition of life. ¶ *Bond or free.* It is evident that many who were slaves were converted to the Christian faith. Religion, however, regarded all as on a level ; and conferred no favours on the free which it did not on the slave. It was one of the happy lessons of Christianity, that it taught men that in the great matters pertaining to their eternal interests they were on the same level. This doctrine would tend to secure, more than any thing else could, the proper treatment of those who were in bondage, and of those who were in humble ranks of life. At the same time it would not diminish, but would increase *their* real respect for their masters, and for those who were above them, if they regarded them as fellow Christians, and destined to the same heaven ; see Note, chap. vii. 22. ¶ *And have been all made to drink*, &c, This probably

14 For the body is not one member, but many.

15 If the foot shall say, Because I am not the hand, I am not of the body; is it therefore not of the body?

16 And if the ear shall say, Because I am not the eye, I am not of the body ; is it therefore not of the body ?

17 If the whole body *were* an

a ver.28.

eye, where *were* the hearing? If the whole *were* hearing, where *were* the smelling ?

18 But now hath God set *a* the members every one of them in the body as *b* it hath pleased him.

19 And if they were all one member, where *were* the body ?

20 But now *are they* many members, yet but one body.

b Rom.12.3;ver.11.

refers to their partaking together of the cup in the Lord's supper. The sense is, that by their drinking of the same cup commemorating the death of Christ, they had partaken of the same influences of the Holy Ghost, which descend alike on all who observe that ordinance in a proper manner. They had shown also, that they belonged to the same body, and were all united together ; and that however various might be their graces and endowments, yet they all belonged to the same great family.

14. *For the body,* &c. The body is made up of many members, which have various offices. So it is in the church. We are to expect the same variety there; and we are not to presume either that all will be alike, or that any member that God has placed there will be useless.

15. *If the foot shall say,* &c. The same figure and illustration which Paul here uses occurs also in heathen writers. It occurs in the apologue which was used by Menenius Agrippa, as related by Livy (lib. ii. cap. 32), in which he attempted to repress a rebellion which had been excited against the nobles and senators, as useless and cumbersome to the state. Menenius, in order to show the folly of this, represents the different members of the body as conspiring against the stomach, as being inactive, and as refusing to labour, and consuming every thing. The consequence of the conspiracy which the feet, and hands, and mouth entered into, was a universal wasting away of the whole frame for want of the nutriment which would have been supplied from the stomach. Thus he argued it would be by the conspiracy

against the nobles, as being inactive, and as consuming all things. The representation had the desired effect, and quelled the rebellion. The same figure is used also by Æsop. The idea here is, that as the foot and the ear could not pretend that they were not parts of the body, and even not important, because they were not the eye, &c.; that is, were not more honourable parts of the body; so no Christian, however humble his endowments, could pretend that he was useless because he was not more highly gifted, and did not occupy a more elevated rank.

17. *If the whole body,* &c. The idea in this verse is, that all the parts of the body are useful in their proper place, and that it would be as absurd to require or expect that all the members of the church should have the same endowments, as it would be to attempt to make the body *all eye.* If all were the same; if all had the same endowments, important offices which are now secured by the other members would be unknown. All, therefore, are to be satisfied with their allotment; all are to be honoured in their appropriate place.

18. *Hath God set the members,* &c. God has formed the body, with its various members, as he saw would best conduce to the harmony and usefulness of all.

19. *And if all were one member.* If there were nothing but an eye, an ear, or a limb, there would be no body The idea which this seems intended to illustrate is, that if there was not variety of talent and endowment in the church, the church could not itself exist. If, for example, there

21 And the eye cannot say unto the hand, I have no need of thee : nor again, the head to the feet, I have no need of you.

22 Nay much more, those *a* members of the body, which seem to be more feeble, are necessary :

23 And those *members* of the body which we think to be less honourable, upon these we [1] bestow more abundant honour ; and our uncomely *parts* have more abundant comeliness.

24 For our comely *parts* have

1 or, *put on.*

were nothing *but* apostles, or prophets, or teachers ; if there were none but those who spoke with tongues or could interpret them, the church could not exist. A variety of talents and attainments in their proper places is as useful as are the various members of the human body.

21: *And the eye cannot say to the hand, &c.* The hand in its place is as needful as the eye ; and the feet as the head. Nay, the eye and the head could not perform their appropriate functions, or would be in a great measure useless but for the aid of the hands and feet. Each is useful in its proper place. So in the church. Those that are most talented, and most richly endowed with gifts, cannot say to those less so, that there is no need of their aid. All are useful in their place. Nay, those who are most richly endowed could very imperfectly perform their duties without the aid and co-operation of those of more humble attainments.

22. *Which seem to be more feeble.* Weaker than the rest ; which seem less able to bear fatigue and to encounter difficulties, which are more easily injured, and which become more easily affected with disease. It is possible that Paul may here refer to the brain, the lungs, the heart, &c., as more feeble in their structure, and more liable to disease than the hands and the feet, &c., and in reference to which disease is more dangerous and fatal. ¶ *Are more necessary.* The sense seems to be this. A man can live though the parts and members of his body which are more strong were removed ; but not if those parts which are more feeble. A man can live if his arm or his leg be amputated; but not if his brain, his lungs or his heart be removed. So that, although these parts are more feeble, and more

easily injured, they are really more necessary to life, and therefore more useful than the more vigorous portions of the frame. Perhaps the idea is—and it is a beautiful thought—that those members of the church which are most retiring and feeble apparently : which are concealed from public view, unnoticed and unknown—the humble, the meek, the peaceful, and the prayerful—are often more necessary to the true welfare of the church than those who are eminent for their talent and learning. And it is so. The church can better spare many a man, even in the ministry, who is learned, and eloquent, and popular, than some obscure and humble Christian, that is to the church what the heart and the lungs are to the life. The one is strong, vigorous, active, like the hands or the feet, and the church often depends on them ; the other is feeble, concealed, yet vital, like the heart or the lungs. The vitality of the church could be continued though the man of talent and learning should be removed ; as the body may live when the arm or the leg is amputated ;—but that vitality could not continue if the saint of humble and retiring piety, and of fervent prayerfulness, were removed, any more than the body can live when there is no heart and no lungs.

23. *We bestow more abundant honour.* Marg. "Put on." The words rendered "abundant honour" here, refer to clothing. We bestow upon them more attention and honour than we do on the face that is deemed comely, and that is not covered and adorned as the other parts of the body are. ¶ *More abundant comeliness.* We adorn and decorate the body with gay apparel. Those parts which decency requires us to conceal we not only cover, but we endeavour as

no need ; but God hath tempered the body together, having given more abundant honour to that *part* which lacked :

25 That there should be no [1]

1 *or, division.*

---

far as we can to adorn them. The face in the mean time we leave uncovered. The idea is, that, in like manner, we should not despise or disregard those members of the church who are of lower rank, or who are less favoured than others with spiritual endowments.

24. *For our comely parts.* The face, &c. ¶ *Have no need.* No need of clothing or ornament. ¶ *But God hath tempered the body together.* Literally *mingled* or mixed ; that is, has made to coalesce, or strictly and closely joined. He has formed a strict union ; he has made one part dependent on another, and necessary to the harmony and proper action of another. Every part is useful, and all are fitted to the harmonious action of the whole. God has so arranged it, in order to produce harmony and equality in the body, that those parts which are less comely by nature should be more adorned and guarded by apparel. ¶ *Having given more abundant honour, &c.* By making it necessary that we should labour in order to procure for it the needful clothing ; thus making it more the object of our attention and care. We thus bestow more abundant honour upon those parts of the body which a suitable protection from cold, and heat, and storms, and the sense of comeliness, requires us to clothe and conceal. The "more abundant honour," therefore, refers to the greater attention, labour, and care which we bestow on those parts of the body.

25. *That there should be no schism.* Marg. *Division ;* see Note on chap. xi. 18. The sense here is, that the body might be united, and be one harmonious whole ; that there should be no separate interests; and that all the parts should be equally necessary, and truly dependent on each other ; and that no member should be regarded as separated from the others, or as

schism in the body ; but *that* the members should have the same care one for another.

26 And whether one member suffer, all the members suffer with

needless to the welfare of all. The sense to be illustrated by this is, that no member of the church, however feeble, or illiterate, or obscure, should be despised or regarded as unnecessary or valueless ; that all are needful in their places; and that it should not be supposed that they belonged to different bodies, or that they could not associate together, any more than the less honourable and comely parts of the body should be regarded as unworthy or unfit to be united to the parts that were deemed to be more beautiful or honourable. ¶ *Should have the same care.* Should care for the same thing; should equally regard the interests of all, as we feel an equal interest in all the members and parts of the body, and desire the preservation, the healthy action, and the harmonious and regular movement of the whole. Whatever part of the body is affected with disease or pain, we feel a deep interest in its preservation and cure. The idea is, that no member of the church should be overlooked or despised ; but that the whole church should feel a deep interest for, and exercise a constant solicitude over, all its members.

26. *And whether one member suffer.* One member, or part of the body. ¶ *All the members suffer with it.* This, we all know, is the case with the body. A pain in the foot, the hand, or the head excites deep solicitude. The interest is not confined to the part affected; but we feel that we ourselves are affected, and that our body, as a whole, demands our care. The word " suffer " here refers to disease, or sickness. It is true also that not only we feel an *interest* in the part that is affected, but that disease in any one part tends to diffuse itself through, and to affect the whole frame. If not arrested, it is conveyed by the blood through all the members until life itself is destroyed. It is not by

it; or one member be honoured, all the members rejoice with it.

27 Now ye are the body of Christ, and members*a* in particular.

a Eph.5.30.   b Luke 6.13.

mere interest, then, or sympathy, but it is by the natural connection and the inevitable result that a diseased member tends to affect the whole frame. There is not, indeed, in the church the same *physical* connection and *physical* effect, but the union is really not less close and important, nor is it the less certain that the conduct of one member will affect all. It is implied here also, that we *should* feel a deep interest in the welfare of all the members of the body of Christ. If one is tempted or afflicted, the other members of the church should feel it, and " bear one another's burdens, and so fulfil his law." If one is poor, the others should aid him, and supply his wants ; if one is persecuted and opposed for righteousness'- sake, the others should sympathize with him, and make common cause with him. In all things pertaining to religion and to their mutual welfare, they should feel that they have a common cause, and regard it as a privilege to aid one another. Nor should a man regard it as any more a burden and hardship to aid a poor or afflicted brother in the church, than it should be deemed a hardship that the head, and the heart, and the hands should sympathize when any other member of the body is diseased. ¶ *Or one member be honoured.* If applied to the body, this means, if one member or part be regarded and treated with special care ; be deemed honourable ; or be in a sound, healthy, and vigorous condition. If applied to the church, it means, if one of its members should be favoured with extraordinary endowments ; or be raised to a station of honour and influence above his brethren. ¶ *All the members rejoice with it.* That is, in the body, all the other members partake of the benefit and honour. If one member be sound and healthy, the benefit extends to all. If the hands, the feet, the heart, the lungs, the brain be in a

28 And God hath set some in the church ; first, apostles ; *b* secondarily, prophets ; *c* thirdly, teachers ; after that, miracles ; *d*

c Acts 13.1.   d ver.10.

healthy condition, the advantage is felt by all the members, and all derive advantage from it. So in the church. If one member is favoured with remarkable talent, or is raised to a station of influence, and exerts his influence in the cause of Christ, all the members of the church partake of the benefit. It is for the common good ; and all should rejoice in it. This consideration should repress envy at the elevation of others, and should lead all the members of a church to rejoice when God, by his direct agency, or by the arrangements of his providence, confers extraordinary endowments, or gives opportunity for extended usefulness to others.

27. *Now ye.* Ye Christians of Corinth, as a part of the whole church that has been redeemed. ¶ *Are the body of Christ.* The allusion to the human body is here kept up. As all the members of the human body compose one body, having a common head, so it is with all the members and parts of the Christian church. The specific idea is, that Christ is the Head of the whole church ; that he presides over all ; and that all its members sustain to each other the relation of fellow members in the same body, and are subject to the same head ; comp. Note, chap. xi. 3. The church is often called the body of Christ ; Eph. i. 23 ; Col. i. 18, 24. ¶ *And members in particular.* You are, as individuals, members of the body of Christ ; or each individual is a member of that body.

28. *And God hath set.* That is, has appointed, constituted, ordained. He has established these various orders or ranks in the church. The apostle, having illustrated the main idea that God had conferred various endowments on the members of the church, proceeds here to specify particularly what he meant, and to refer more directly to the various ranks

then gifts of healing, [a] helps, [b] governments, [c] [1] diversities of tongues. [d]

a ver.9.　　b Num.11.17.　　c Heb.13.17,24.

which existed in the church. ¶ *Some in the church.* The word "some," in this place (*ους*), seems to mean rather *whom*, "and whom God hath placed in the church," or, they whom God hath constituted in the church in the manner above mentioned are, first, apostles, &c. ¶ *First, apostles.* In the first rank or order ; or as superior in honour and in office. He has given them the highest authority in the church; he has more signally endowed them and qualified them than he has others. ¶ *Secondarily, prophets.* As second in regard to endowments and importance. For the meaning of the word "prophets," see Note on Rom. xii. 6. ¶ *Thirdly, teachers.* As occupying the third station in point of importance and valuable endowments. On the meaning of this word, and the nature of this office, see Note on Rom. xii. 7. ¶ *After that, miracles.* Power. (*δυναμις*). Those who had the power of working miracles ; referred to in ver. 10. ¶ *Then gifts of healings.* The power of healing those who were sick ; see Note on ver. 9 ; comp. James v. 14, 15. ¶ *Helps* (*αντιληψεις*). This word occurs no where else in the New Testament. It is derived from *αντιλαμβανω*, and denotes properly, *aid, assistance, help;* and then those who render aid, assistance, or help ; helpers. *Who* they were is not known. They might have been those to whom was intrusted the care of the poor, and the sick, and strangers, widows, and orphans, &c. ; *i. e.* those who performed the office of deacons. Or they may have been those who attended on the apostles to aid them in their work, such as Paul refers to in Rom. xvi. 3. "Greet Priscilla, and Aquilla, my *helpers* in Christ Jesus;" and in ver. 9, "Salute Urbane our *helper* in Christ ;" see Note on Rom. xvi. 3. It is not possible, perhaps, to determine the precise meaning of the word, or the nature of the office which they discharged ; but

29 *Are* all apostles? *are* all prophets? *are* all teachers? *are* all [1] workers of miracles?

1 or, *kinds.*　　d Acts 2.8-11.　　1 or, *powers.*

the word means, in general, those who in any way aided or rendered assistance in the church, and may refer to the temporal affairs of the church, to the care of the poor, the distribution of charity and alms, or to the instruction of the ignorant, or to aid rendered directly to the apostles. There is no evidence that it refers to a distinct and permanent *office* in the church; but may refer to aid rendered by any class in any way. Probably many persons were profitably and usefully employed in various ways as aids in promoting the temporal or spiritual welfare of the church. ¶ *Governments* (*κυβερνησεις*). This word is derived from *κυβεραω, to govern;* and is usually applied to the government or *steering* of a ship. The word occurs no where else in the New Testament, though the word *κυβερνητης* (governor) occurs in Acts xxvii. 11, rendered "master," and in Rev. xviii. 17, rendered "shipmaster." It is not easy to determine what particular office or function is here intended. Doddridge, in accordance with Amyraut, supposes that distinct offices may not be here referred to, but that the same persons may be denoted in these expressions as being distinguished in various ways ; that is, that the same persons were called helpers in reference to their skill in aiding those who were in distress, and governments in regard to their talent for doing business, and their ability in presiding in councils for deliberation, and in directing the affairs of the church. There is no reason to think that the terms here used referred to permanent and established ranks and orders in the ministry and in the church ; or in permanent offices which were to continue to all times as an essential part of its organization. It is certain that the "order" of *apostles* has ceased, and also the "order" of *miracles,* and the order of *healings,* and of *diversity of tongues.* And it is certain that in the use of these terms of office, the apostle does not affirm that they *would* be permanent, and essential to the very existence of the church; and from the passage before us, therefore, it cannot be argued that there was to be an order of men in the church who were to be called *helps*, or *governments*. The truth probably was, that the circumstances of the primitive churches required the aid of many persons in various capacities which might not be needful or proper in other times and circumstances. Whether, therefore, this is to be regarded as a permanent arrangement that there should be " governments" in the church, or an order of men intrusted with the sole office of governing, is to be learned not from this passage, but from other parts of the New Testament. Lightfoot contends that the word which is here used and translated " governments " does not refer to the power of *ruling*, but to a person endued with a deep and comprehensive mind, one who is wise and prudent; and in this view Mosheim, Macknight, and bishop Horsley coincide. Calvin refers it to the elders to whom the exercise of discipline was intrusted. Grotius understands it ot the pastors (Eph. iv. 1), or of the elders who presided over particular churches; Rom. xii. 8. Locke supposes that they were the same as those who had the power of discerning spirits. The simple idea, however, is that of *ruling*, or exercising government; but whether this refers to a permanent office, or to the fact that some were specially qualified by their wisdom and prudence, and in virtue of this usually regulated or directed the affairs of the church by giving counsel, &c., or whether they were *selected* and appointed for this purpose for a time; or whether it refers to the same persons who might also have exercised other functions, and this in addition, cannot be determined from the passage before us. All that is clear is, that there were those who administered government in the church. But the passage does not determine the form, or manner; nor does it *prove*—whatever may be true—that such an office was to be permanent in the church.

[There can be little doubt that the κυβερνήσεις, or governments, refer to offices of rule and authority in the church. Two things, therefore, are plain from this text: 1. That in the primitive church there were rulers distinct from the people or church members, to whom these were bound to yield obedience. 2. That these rulers were appointed of God. "God set them in the church." As to the question of *permanence*, on which our author thinks this passage affirms nothing: a distinction must be made between those offices which were obviously of an extraordinary kind, and which therefore must cease; and those of an ordinary kind, which are essential to the edification of the church in all ages. " The universal commission which the apostles received from their Master to make disciples of all nations, could not be permanent as to the extent of it, because it was their practice to ordain elders in every city, and because the course of human affairs required, that after Christianity was established, the teachers of it should officiate in particular places. The infallible guidance of the Spirit was not promised in the same measure to succeeding teachers. But being, in their case, vouched by the power of working miracles, it directed the Christians of their day, to submit implicitly to their injunctions and directions; and it warrants the Christian world, in all ages, to receive with entire confidence, that system of faith and morality which they were authorised to deliver in the name of Christ. But as all protestants hold that this system was completed when the canon of scripture was closed—it is admitted by them, that a great part of the apostolical powers ceased with those to whom Jesus first committed them. Amongst the ordinary functions belonging to their office as teachers, are to be ranked not only preaching the word, and dispensing the sacraments, but also that rule and government over Christians as such, which is implied in the idea of the church as a society:"—*Hill's Lectures*, vol. ii. p. 479. Now, though these extraordinary offices and functions have ceased with the age of the apostles, and of miraculous influence; it by no means follows, that the ordinary offices of teaching and ruling have ceased also. What was plainly of a *peculiar* kind, and could not possibly be *imitated* after the withdrawment of miraculous power, is quite distinct from that which, not depending on such power, is suited to the condition of the church always. Proceeding on any other principle, we should find it impossible to argue at all on what ought to be the constitution of the church, from any hints we find in the New Testament. What is extraordinary cannot be permanent, but what is ordinary must be so. See the Supplementary Note on ch. v. 4.]

30 Have all the gifts of healing? do all speak with tongues? do all interpret?

a chap.14.39.

¶ *Diversities of tongues.* Those endowed with the power of speaking various languages; see Note on ver. 10.

29, 30. Are *all apostles?* &c. These questions imply, with strong emphasis, that it could not be, and ought not to be, that there should be perfect equality of endowment. It was not a matter of fact that all were equal, or that all were qualified for the offices which others sustained. Whether the arrangement was approved of or not, it was a simple matter of fact that some were qualified to perform offices which others were not; that some were endowed with the abilities requisite to the apostolic office, and others not; that some were endowed with prophetic gifts, and others were not; that some had the gift of healing, or the talent of speaking different languages, or of interpreting and that others had not.

31. *But covet earnestly.* Gr. "Be zealous for" (Ζηλοῦτε). This word, however, may be either in the indicative mood (ye do covet earnestly), or in the imperative, as in our translation. Doddridge contends that it should be rendered in the indicative mood, for he says it seems to be a contradiction that after the apostle had been showing that these gifts were not at their own option, and that they ought not to emulate the gifts of another, or aspire to superiority, to undo all again, and give them such contrary advice. The same view is given by Locke, and so Macknight. The Syriac renders it, "Because you are zealous of the best gifts, I will show to you a more excellent way." But there is no valid objection to the common translation in the imperative, and indeed the connection seems to demand it. Grotius renders it, "Pray to God that you may receive from him the best, that is, the most useful endowments." The sense seems to be this, " I have proved that *all* endowments in the church are produced by

31 But covet *a* earnestly the best *b* gifts: and yet shew I unto you a more excellent way.

b Mat.5.6; Luke 10.42.

the Holy Spirit; and that he confers them as he pleases. I have been showing that no one should be proud or elated on account of extraordinary endowments; and that, on the other hand, no one should be depressed, or sad, or discontented, because he has a more humble rank. I have been endeavouring to repress and subdue the spirit of discontent, jealousy, and ambition; and to produce a willingness in all to occupy the station where God has placed you. But, I do not intend to deny that it is *proper* to desire the most useful endowments; that a man should wish to be brought under the influence of the Spirit, and qualified for eminent usefulness. I do not mean to say that it is wrong for a man to regard the higher gifts of the Spirit as valuable and desirable, if they may be obtained; nor that the spirit which seeks to excel in spiritual endowments and in usefulness, is improper. Yet all cannot be apostles; all cannot be prophets. I would not have you, therefore, seek *such* offices, and manifest a spirit of ambition. I would seek to regulate the desire which I would not repress as improper; and in order to that, I would show you that, instead of aspiring to offices and extraordinary endowments which are beyond your grasp, there *is* a way, more truly valuable, that is open to you all, and where all may excel." Paul thus endeavours to give a practicable and feasible turn to the whole subject, and further to repress the longings of ambition and the contentions of strife, by exciting emulation to obtain that which was accessible to them all, and *which, just in the proportion in which it was obtained,* would repress discontent, and strife, and ambition, and produce order, and peace, and contentedness with their endowments and their lot,—the main thing which he was desirous of producing in this chapter. This, therefore, is one of the *happy turns* in

CHAPTER XIII.

THOUGH I speak with the
tongues of men and of angels,

a 2 Cor. 12. 4.

and have not charity, *b* I am become *as* sounding brass, or a tink
ling cymbal.

b 1 Pet 4. 8.

which the writings of Paul abounds.
He did not denounce their zeal as
wicked. He did not attempt at once
to repress it. He did not say that it
was wrong to desire high endowments.
But he showed them an endowment
which was more valuable than all the
others ; which was accessible to all ;
and which, if possessed, would make
them contented, and produce the harmonious operation of all the parts of
the church. That endowment was LOVE.
¶ *A more excellent way;* see the next
chapter. " I will show you a more
excellent way of evincing your *zeal*
than by aspiring to the place of apostles, prophets, or rulers, and that is
by cultivating universal charity or
love."

CHAPTER XIII.

THIS chapter is a continuation of
the subject commenced in chap. xii.
In that chapter Paul had introduced
the subject of the various endowments
which the Holy Spirit confers on
Christians, and had shown that these
endowments, however various they
were, were conferred in such a manner as best to promote the edification
and welfare of the church. In the
close of that chapter (ver. 31) he had
said that it was lawful for them to
desire the most eminent of the gifts
conferred by the Spirit; and yet says
that there was *one* endowment that
was more valuable than all others, and
that might be obtained by all, and that
he proposed to recommend to them.
That was LOVE; and to illustrate its
nature, excellency, and power, is the
design of this exquisitely beautiful
and tender chapter. In doing this, he
dwells particularly on three points or
views of the excellency of love; and
the chapter may be regarded as consisting of three portions.

I. The excellency of love above the
power of speaking the languages of
men and of angels; above the power
of understanding all mysteries; above
all faith, even of the highest kind ;
and above the virtue of giving all one's

goods to feed the poor, or one's body
to be burned. All these endowments
would be valueless without love, ver.
1—3.

II. A statement of the characteristics of love ; or its happy influences
on the mind and heart, ver. 4—7.

III. A comparison of love with the
gift of prophecy, and with the power
of speaking foreign languages, and
with knowledge, ver. 8—13. In this
portion of the chapter, Paul shows
that love is superior to them all. It
will live in heaven ; and will constitute the chief glory of that world of
bliss.

1. *Though I speak with the tongues
of men.* Though I should be able to
speak all the languages which are
spoken by men. To speak foreign
languages was regarded then, as it is
now, as a rare and valuable endowment ; comp. Virg. Æn. vi. 625, seq.
The word *I* here is used in a popular
sense, and the apostle designs to illustrate, as he often does, his idea by a
reference to himself, which, it is evident, he wishes to be understood as
applying to those whom he addressed.
It is evident that among the Corinthians the power of speaking a foreign
language was regarded as a signally
valuable endowment; and there can
be no doubt that some of the leaders
in that church valued themselves especially on it; see chap. xiv. To correct this, and to show them that all
this would be vain without love, and
to induce them, therefore, to seek for
love as a more valuable endowment,
was the design of the apostle in this
passage. Of this verse Dr. Bloomfield, than whom, perhaps, there is no
living man better qualified to give
such an opinion, remarks, that " it
would be difficult to find a finer passage than this in the writings of Demosthenes himself." ¶ *And of angels.*
The language of angels ; such as they
speak. Were I endowed with the
faculty of eloquence and persuasion
which we attribute to them ; and the

power of speaking to any of the human family with the power which they have. The language of angels here seems to be used to denote the highest power of using language, or of the most elevated faculty of eloquence and speech. It is evidently derived from the idea that the angels are *superior* in all respects to men; that they must have endowments in advance of all which man can have. It may possibly have reference to the idea that they must have some mode of communicating their ideas one to another, and that this dialect or mode must be far superior to that which is employed by man. Man is imperfect. All his modes of communication are defective. We attribute to the angels the idea of perfection; and the idea here is, that even though a man had a far higher faculty of speaking languages than would be included in the endowment of speaking all the languages of men as men speak them, and even had the higher and more perfect mode of utterance which the angels have, and yet were destitute of love, all would be nothing. It is possible that Paul may have some allusion here to what he refers to in 2 Cor. xii. 4, where he says that when he was caught up into paradise, he heard unspeakable words which it was not possible for a man to utter. To this higher, purer language of heaven he may refer here by the language of the angels. It was not with him mere *conjecture* of what that language might be; it was language which he had been permitted himself to hear. Of that scene he would retain a most deep and tender recollection; and to that language he now refers, by saying that even *that* elevated language would be valueless to a creature if there were not love. ¶ *And have not charity* (ἀγάπην δὲ μὴ ἴχω). And have not LOVE. This is the proper and usual meaning of the Greek word. The English word *charity* is used in a great variety of senses; and some of them cannot be included in the meaning of the word here. It means, (1.) In a general sense, love, benevolence, good-will; (2.) In theology, it includes supreme love to God and universal good-will

to men; (3.) In a more particular sense, it denotes the love and kindness which springs from the natural relations, as the *charities* of father, son, brother; (4.) Liberality to the poor, to the needy, and to objects of beneficence, as we speak commonly of *charity*, meaning almsgiving, and of charitable societies; (5.) *Candour* liberality in judging of men's actions indulgence to their opinions; attributing to them good motives and intentions; a disposition to judge of them favourably, and to put on their words and actions the best construction. This is a very common signification of the word in our language now, and this is one modification of the word *love*, as all such charity is supposed to proceed from *love* to our neighbour, and a desire that he should have a right to *his* opinions as well as we to ours. The Greek word ἀγάπη means properly *love*, affection, regard, good-will, benevolence. It is applied, (*a*) To love in general; (*b*) To the love of God and of Christ; (*c*) The love which God or Christ exercises towards Christians, (Rom. v. 5; Eph. ii. 4; 2 Thess. iii. 5); (*d*) The effect, or proof of beneficence, favour conferred; Eph. i. 15; 2 Thess. ii. 10; 1 John iii. 1. *Robinson, Lex.* In the English word *charity*, therefore, there are now some ideas which are not found in the Greek word, and especially the idea of *almsgiving*, and the common use of the word among us in the sense of *candour*, or *liberality in judging*. Neither of these ideas, perhaps, are to be found in the use of the word in the chapter before us; and the more proper translation would have been, in accordance with the usual mode of translation in the New Testament, LOVE. Tindal in his translation, renders it by the word *love*. The *love* which is referred to in this chapter, and illustrated, is mainly *love to man* (ver. 4—7); though there is no reason to doubt that the apostle meant also to include in the general term love to God, or love in general. His *illustrations*, however, are chiefly drawn from the effects of love towards men. It properly means love to the whole church, love to the whole world; love

2 And though I have *the gift of* prophecy, [a] and understand all

a chap. 14. 1.

mysteries, and all knowledge; and though I have all faith, so

---

to all creatures which arises from true piety, and which centres ultimately in God.—*Doddridge.* It is this love whose importance Paul, in this beautiful chapter, illustrates as being more valuable than the highest possible endowments without it. It is not necessary to suppose that any one *had* these endowments, or had the power of speaking with the tongues of men and angels; or had the gift of prophecy, or had the highest degree of faith, who had no love. The apostle *supposes* a case; and says that if it *were* so, if all these *were* possessed without love, they would be comparatively valueless; or that love was a more valuable endowment than all the others would be without it. ¶ *I am become.* I am. I shall be. ¶ *As sounding brass.* Probably a *trumpet.* The word properly means *brass;* then that which is made of brass; a trumpet, or wind instrument of any kind made of brass or copper. The sense is that of a sounding or resounding instrument, making a great noise, apparently of great importance, and yet without vitality; a mere instrument; a base metal that merely makes a sound. Thus noisy, valueless, empty, and without vitality would be the power of speaking all languages without love. ¶ *Or a tinkling cymbal.* A cymbal giving a clanging, clattering sound. The word rendered "tinkling" (ἀλαλάζον, from ἀλαλή or ἀλαλα, a *war-cry*) properly denotes a loud cry, or shout, such as is used in battle; and then also a loud cry or mourning, cries of lamentation or grief; the loud *shriek* of sorrow, Mark v. 38, "Them that wept and *wailed* greatly." It then means a clanging or clattering sound, such as was made on a cymbal. The cymbal is a well-known instrument, made of two pieces of brass or other metal, which, being struck together, gives a tinkling or clattering sound. Cymbals are commonly used in connection with other music. They make a tinkling, or clanging, with very little variety of sound. The music is

little adapted to produce emotion, or to excite feeling. There is no melody and no harmony. They were, therefore, well adapted to express the idea which the apostle wished to convey. The sense is, " If I could speak all languages, yet if I had not love, the faculty would be like the clattering, clanging sound of the cymbal, that contributes nothing to the welfare of others. It would all be hollow, vain, useless. It could neither save me nor others, any more than the notes of the trumpet, or the jingling of the cymbal, would promote salvation. *Love* is the vital principle; it is that without which all other endowments are useless and vain."

2. *And though I have* the gift of *prophecy;* see Note, chap. xii. 10; xiv. 1. ¶ *And understand all mysteries.* On the meaning of the word *mystery,* see Note, chap. ii. 7. This passage proves that it was one part of the prophetic office, as referred to here, to be able to understand and explain the *mysteries* of religion; that is, the things that were before unknown, or unrevealed. It does not refer to the prediction of future events, but to the great and deep truths connected with religion; the things that were unexplained in the old economy, the meaning of types and emblems, and the obscure portions of the plan of redemption. All these might be *plain* enough if they were revealed; but there were many things connected with religion which God had not chosen to reveal to men. ¶ *And all knowledge;* Note, chap. xii. 8. Though I knew every thing. Though I were acquainted fully with all the doctrines of religion; and were with all sciences and arts. ¶ *And though I have all faith, so that I could remove mountains.* Thould I should have the highest kind of faith. This is referred to by the Saviour (Mat. xvii. 20,) as the highest kind of faith; and Paul here had this fact doubtless in his eye. ¶ *I am nothing.* All would be of no value. It would not save me.]

that I could remove ^a mountains, and have not charity, I am nothing. ^b

a Mat.17.20.   b Mat.21.19.

3 And though ^c I bestow all my goods to feed *the poor,* and though ^d I give my body to be

c Mat.6.1,2.   d Mat.7.22,23; James 2.14.

should still be an unredeemed, unpardoned sinner. I should do good to no one; I should answer none of the great purposes which God has designed; I should not by all this secure my salvation. All would be in vain in regard to the great purpose of my existence. None of these things could be placed before God as a ground of acceptance in the day of judgment. Unless I should have *love,* I should still be lost. A somewhat similar idea is expressed by the Saviour, in regard to the day of judgment, in Mat. vii. 22, 23, "Many will say unto me in that day, Lord, Lord, have we not prophesied in thy name? and in thy name have cast out devils? and in thy name done many wonderful works? And then will I profess unto them, I never knew you: depart from me, ve that work iniquity."

3. *And though I bestow.* The Greek word here used (ψωμίσω, from ψάω, to break off) meant properly to break off, and distribute in small portions; to feed by morsels; and may be applicable here to distributing one's property in small portions. Charity or alms to the poor, was usually distributed at one's gate (Luke xvi. 20,) or in some public place. Of course, if property was distributed in this manner, many more would be benefitted than if all were given to one person. There would be many more to be thankful, and to celebrate one's praises. This was regarded as a great virtue; and was often performed in a most ostentatious manner. It was a gratification to wealthy men who desired the praise of being benevolent, that *many* of the poor flocked daily to their houses to be fed; and against this desire of distinction, the Saviour directed some of his severest reproofs; see Mat. vi. 1—4. To make the case as strong as possible, Paul says that if ALL that a man had were dealt out in this way, in small portions, so as to benefit as many as possible, and yet

were not attended *with true love towards God and towards man,* it would be all false, hollow, hypocritical, and really of no value in regard to his own salvation. It would profit nothing. It would not be such an act as God would approve; it would be no evidence that the soul would be saved. Though good might be done to others, yet where the *motive* was wrong, it could not meet with the divine approbation, or be connected with his favour. ¶ *And though I give my body to be burned.* Evidently as a martyr, or a witness to the truth of religion. Though I should be willing to lay down my life in the most painful manner, and have not charity, it would profit me nothing. Many of the ancient prophets were called to suffer martyrdom, though there is no evidence that any of them were burned to death as martyrs. Shadrach, Meshech, and Abednego were indeed thrown into a fiery furnace, because they were worshippers of the true God; but they were not consumed in the flame, Dan. iii. 19—26; comp. Heb. xi. 34. Though Christians were early persecuted, yet there is no evidence that they were burned as martyrs as early as this epistle was written. Nero is the first who is believed to have committed this horrible act; and under his reign, and during the persecution which he excited, Christians were covered with pitch, and set on fire to illuminate his gardens. It is possible that some Christians had been put to death in this manner when Paul wrote this epistle; but it is more probable that he refers to this as *the most awful kind of death,* rather than as any thing which had really happened. Subsequently, however, as all know, this was often done, and thousands, and perhaps tens of thousands, of Christians have been called to evince their attachment to religion in the flames. ¶ *And have not charity.* Have no love to God, or to men; have no true piety. If I do it from any selfish or

burned, and have not charity, it profiteth me nothing.

a Prov.10.12.

sinister motive; if I do it from fanaticism, obstinacy, or vain-glory; if I am deceived in regard to my character, and have never been born again. It is not *necessary* to an explanation of this passage to suppose that this ever *had* been done, for the apostle only puts a supposable case. There is reason, however, to think that it *has* been done frequently; and that when the desire of martyrdom became the *popular passion*, and was believed to be connected infallibly with heaven, not a few have been willing to give themselves to the flames who never knew any thing of love to God or true piety. Grotius mentions the instance of Calanus, and of Peregrinus the philosopher, who did it. Although this was not the common mode of martyrdom in the time of Paul, and although it was then perhaps unknown, it is remarkable that he should have referred to that which in subsequent times became the common mode of death on account of religion. In his time, and before, the common mode was by stoning, by the sword, or by crucifixion. Subsequently, however, all these were laid aside, and *burning* became the common way in which martyrs suffered. So it was, extensively, under Nero : and so it was, exclusively, under the Inquisition ; and so it was in the persecutions in England in the time of Mary. Paul seems to have been *directed* to specify this rather than stoning, the sword, or crucifixion, in order that, in subsequent times, martyrs might be led to examine themselves, and to see whether they were actuated by true love to God in being willing to be consumed in the flames. ¶ *It profiteth me nothing.* If there is no true piety, there can be no benefit in this to my soul. It will not save me. If I have no true love to God, I must perish, after all. *Love,* therefore, is more valuable and precious than all these endowments. Nothing can supply its place ; nothing can be connected with salvation without it.

4 Charity suffereth *a* long, *and* is kind; charity envieth *b* not;

b James 3.16.

4. *Charity suffereth long.* Paul now proceeds to illustrate the *nature* of love, or to show how it is exemplified. His illustrations are all drawn from its effect in regulating our conduct towards others, or our intercourse with them. The *reason* why he made use of this illustration, rather than its nature as evinced towards *God,* was, probably, because it was especially necessary for them to understand in what way it should be manifested towards each other. There were contentions and strifes among them ; there were of course suspicions, and jealousies, and heart-burnings ; there would be unkind judging, the imputation of improper motives, and selfishness; there were envy, and pride, and boasting, all of which were inconsistent with love ; and Paul therefore evidently designed to correct these evils, and to produce a different state of things by showing them what would be produced by the exercise of love. The word here used($\mu\alpha\kappa\rho\varrho\vartheta\upsilon\mu\varepsilon\tilde{\iota}$) denotes *longanimity,* slowness to anger or passion ; longsuffering, patient endurance, forbearance. It is opposed to *haste;* to passionate expressions and thoughts, and to irritability. It denotes the state of mind which can BEAR LONG when oppressed, provoked, calumniated, and when one seeks to injure us; comp. Rom. ii. 4; ix. 22 ; 2 Cor. vi. 6; Gal. v. 22 ; Eph. iv. 2 ; Col. iii. 12 ; 1 Tim. i. 16 ; 2 Tim. iii. 10 ; iv. 2 ; 1 Pet. iii. 20 ; 2 Pet. iii. 15. ¶ *And is kind.* The word here used denotes to be goodnatured, gentle, tender, affectionate. Love is benignant. It wishes well. It is not harsh, sour, morose, illnatured. Tindal renders it, "is courteous." The idea is, that under all provocations and ill-usage it is gentle and mild. *Hatred* prompts to harshness, severity, unkindness of expression, anger, and a desire of revenge. But love is the reverse of all these. A man who truly loves another will be *kind* to him, desirous of doing him good; will be *gentle,* not severe and harsh ;

charity ¹ vaunteth not itself, is not puffed *a* up.

5 Doth not behave itself unseemly, seeketh not *b* her own, is

1 or, *is not rash.*   *a* Col.2.18.

b chap.10.24.

will be *courteous* because he desires his happiness, and would not pain his feelings. And as religion is love, and prompts to love, so it follows that it requires courtesy or true politeness, and will secure it; see 1 Pet. iii. 8. If all men were under the influence of true religion, they would always be *truly* polite and courteous; for true politeness is nothing more than an expression of benignity, or a desire to promote the happiness of all around us. ¶ *Envieth not (οὐ ζηλοῖ).* This word properly means to be *zealous* for or against any person or thing; *i. e.* to be eager for, or anxious for or against any one. It is used often in a good sense (1 Cor. xii. 31; Note, xiv. 1, 39; 2 Cor. xi. 2, &c); but it may be used in a bad sense—to be zealous *against* a person; to be jealous of; to envy. Acts vii. 9; xvii. 5; James iv. 2, " Ye kill and *envy*." It is in this sense, evidently, that it is used here, —as denoting zeal, or ardent desire *against* any person. The sense is, love does not envy others the happiness which they enjoy; it delights in their welfare; and as their happiness is increased by their endowments, their rank, their reputation, their wealth, their health, their domestic comforts, their learning &c., those who are influenced by love *rejoice* in all this. They would not diminish it; they would not embarrass them in the possession; they would not detract from that happiness; they would not murmur or repine that they themselves are not so highly favoured.—To envy is to feel uneasiness, mortification, or discontent at the sight of superior happiness, excellence or reputation enjoyed by another; to repine at another's prosperity; and to fret oneself on account of his real or fancied superiority. Of course, it may be excited by *any thing* in which another excels, or in which he is more favoured than we are. It may be excited by superior wealth, beauty, learning, accomplishment, reputation, success. It

may extend to any employment, or any rank in life. A man may be envied because he is happy while we are miserable; well, while we are sick; caressed, while we are neglected or overlooked; successful, while we meet with disappointment; handsome, while we are ill-formed; honoured with office, while we are overlooked. He may be envied because he has a better farm than we have, or is a more skilful mechanic, or a more successful physician, lawyer, or clergyman. *Envy commonly lies in the same line of business, occupation, or rank.* We do not usually envy a monarch, a conqueror, or a nobleman, unless we are *aspiring* to the same rank. The farmer does not usually envy the blacksmith, but another farmer; the blacksmith does not usually envy the schoolmaster, or the lawyer, but another man in the same line of business with himself. The physician envies another physician more learned or more successful; the lawyer, another lawyer; the clergyman, another clergyman. The fashionable female, who seeks admiration or flattery on account of accomplishment or beauty, envies another who is more distinguished and more successful in those things. And so the poet envies a rival poet; and the orator, a rival orator; and the statesman, a rival statesman. The correction of all these things is *love*. If we loved others; if we rejoiced in their happiness, we should not envy them. *They are not to blame* for these superior endowments; but if those endowments are the direct gift of God, *we* should be thankful that he has made others happy; if they are the fruit of their own industry, and virtue, and skill and application, we should esteem them the more, and value them the more highly. They have not injured *us;* and *we* should not be unhappy, or seek to injure them, because God has blessed them, or because they have been more industrious, virtuous, and successful than we have. Every man should have his own level in society, and we should rejoice in the happiness of all.—Love will produce another effect. We should not *envy* them, because he that is under the influence of Christian love is more happy than those in the world who are usually the objects of envy. There is often much wretchedness under a clothing "of purple and fine linen." There is not *always* happiness in a splendid mansion; in the caresses of the great; in a post of honour; in a palace, or on a throne. Alexander the Great wept on the throne of the world. Happiness is in the heart; and contentment, and the love of God, and the hope of heaven produce happiness which rank, and wealth, and fashion, and earthly honour cannot purchase. And could the sad and heavy hearts of those in elevated ranks of life be always seen; and especially could their end be seen, there would be no occasion or disposition to envy them.

Lord, what a thoughtless wretch was I,
To mourn, and murmur, and repine,
To see the wicked placed on high,
In pride and robes of honour shine!

But oh! their end, their dreadful end!
Thy sanctuary taught me so;
On slipp'ry rocks I see them stand,
And fiery billows roll below.

Now let them boast how tall they ri-e,
I'll never envy them again;
There they may stand with haughty eyes,
Till they plunge deep in endless pain.

Their fancied joys how fast they flee,
Like dreams as fleeting and as vain;
Their songs of softest harmony
Are but a prelude to their pain.

Now I esteem their mirth and wine
Too dear to purchase with my blood;
Lord, 'tis enough that thou art mine,
My life, my portion, and my God.

¶ *Vaunteth not itself* (περπερευεται, from περπερος, a boaster, braggart. *Robinson*.) The idea is that of boasting, bragging, vaunting. The word occurs nowhere else in the New Testament. Bloomfield supposes that it has the idea of acting precipitously, inconsiderately, incautiously; and this idea our translators have placed in the margin, " *he is not rash.*" But most expositors suppose that it has the notion of boasting, or vaunting of one's own excellencies or endowments. This spirit proceeds from the idea of *superiority* over others; and is connected with a feeling of contempt or disregard for them. Love would correct this, because it would produce a desire that they should be happy—and to treat a man with contempt is not the way to make him happy; love would regard others with esteem—and to boast over them is not to treat them with esteem; it would teach us to treat them with affectionate regard—and no man who has affectionate regard for others is disposed to boast of his own qualities over them. Besides, love produces a state of mind just the opposite of a disposition to boast. It receives its endowments with gratitude; regards them as the gift of God; and is disposed to employ them not in vain boasting, but in purposes of utility, in doing good to all others on as wide a scale as possible. The boaster is not a man who does good. To *boast* of talents is not to employ them to advantage to others. It will be of no account in feeding the hungry, clothing the naked, comforting the sick and afflicted, or in saving the world. Accordingly, the man who does the most good is the least accustomed to boast; the man who boasts may be regarded as doing nothing else. ¶ *Is not puffed up* (φυσιουται). This word means to blow, to puff, to pant; then to inflate with pride, and vanity, and self-esteem. See the word explained in the Note on chap. viii. 1. It perhaps differs from the preceding word, inasmuch as that word denotes the *expression* of the feelings of pride, vanity, &c., and this word the feeling itself. A man may be very proud and vain, and not express it in the form of boasting. That state is indicated by this word. If he gives expression to this feeling, and boasts of his endowments, that is indicated by the previous word. Love would prevent this, as it would the former. It would destroy the *feeling*, as well as the *expression* of it. It would teach a man that others had good qualities as well as he; that they had high endowments as well as he; and would *dispose* him to concede to them full credit for all that they have, and not to be vain-glorious of his

not *a* easily provoked, thinketh no evil ;

a Prov.14.17.

6 Rejoiceth *b* not in iniquity, but rejoiceth 1 in the truth ;

b Rom.1.32   1 or, *with.*

own. Besides, it is not the *nature* of love to fill the mind in this manner. Pride, vanity, and even knowledge (chap. viii. 1), may swell the mind with the conviction of self-importance ; but love is humble, meek, modest, unobtrusive. A brother that loves a sister is not filled with pride or vanity on account of it ; a man that loves the whole world, and desires its salvation, is not filled with pride and vanity on account of it. Hence the Saviour, who had *most* love for the human race, was at the farthest possible remove from pride and vanity.

5. *Doth not behave itself unseemly* (οὐκ ἀσχημονεῖ). This word occurs in chap. vii. 36. See Note on that verse. It means to conduct improperly, or disgracefully, or in a manner to deserve reproach. Love seeks that which is proper or becoming in the circumstances and relations of life in which we are placed. It prompts to the due respect for superiors, producing veneration and respect for their opinions ; and it prompts to a proper regard for inferiors, not despising their rank, their poverty, their dress, their dwellings, their pleasures, their views of happiness ; it prompts to the due observance of all the *relations* of life, as those of a husband, wife, parent, child, brother, sister, son, daughter, and produces a proper conduct and deportment in all these relations. The proper idea of the phrase is, that it prompts to all that is fit and becoming in life ; and would save from all that is unfit and unbecoming. There may be included in the word also the idea that it would prevent any thing that would be a violation of decency or delicacy. It is well known that the Cynics were in the habit of setting at defiance all the usual ideas of decency ; and indeed this was, and is, commonly done in the temples of idolatry and pollution every where. Love would prevent this, because it teaches to promote the *happiness* of

all, and of course to avoid every thing that would offend purity of taste and mar enjoyment. In the same way it prompts to the fit discharge of all the relative duties, because it leads to the desire to promote the happiness of all. And in the same manner it would lead a man to avoid profane and indecent language, improper allusions, double meanings and inuendoes, coarse and vulgar expressions, because such things pain the ear, and offend the heart of purity and delicacy. There is much that is indecent and unseemly still in society that would be corrected by Christian love. What a change would be produced if, under the influence of that love, nothing should be said or done in the various relations of life but what would be *seemly, fit, and decent!* And what a happy influence would the prevalence of this love have on the intercourse of mankind ! ¶ *Seeketh not her own.* There is, perhaps, not a more striking or important expression in the New Testament than this ; or one that more beautifully sets forth the nature and power of that love which is produced by true religion. Its evident meaning is, that it is not selfish ; it does not seek its own happiness exclusively or mainly ; it does not seek its own happiness to the injury of others. This expression is not, however, to be pressed as if Paul meant to teach that a man should not regard his own welfare at all ; or have no respect to his health, his property, his happiness, or his salvation. Every man is bound to pursue such a course of life as will ultimately secure his own salvation. But it is not simply or mainly that he may be happy that he is to seek it. It is, that he may thus glorify God his Saviour ; and accomplish the great design which his Maker has had in view in his creation and redemption. If his happiness is the main or leading thing, it proves that he is supremely selfish ; and selfishness is not religion. The expression here used is *comparative*, and denotes that this is not the main, the chief, the only thing which one who is under the influence of love or true religion will seek. True religion, or love to others, will prompt us to seek their welfare with self-denial, and personal sacrifice and toil. Similar expressions, to denote comparison, occur frequently in the sacred Scriptures. Thus, where it is said (Hos. vii. 6; comp. Micah vi. 8; Mat. ix. 13), " I desired mercy, and not sacrifice ;" it is meant, " I desired mercy *more* than I desired sacrifice ; I did not wish that mercy should be forgotten or excluded in the attention to the mere ceremonies of religion." The sense here is, therefore, that a man under the influence of true love or religion does not make his own happiness or salvation the main or leading thing ; he does not make all other things subservient to this ; he seeks the welfare of others, and desires to promote their happiness and salvation, even at great personal sacrifice and self-denial. It is the *characteristic* of the man, not that he promotes his own worth, health, happiness, or salvation, but that he lives to do good to others. Love to others will prompt to that, and that alone. There is not a particle of selfishness in true love. It seeks the welfare of others, and of all others. That true religion will produce this, is evident every where in the New Testament ; and especially in the life of the Lord Jesus, whose whole biography is comprehended in one expressive declaration, " who went about DOING GOOD :" Acts x. 38. It follows from this statement, (1.) That no man is a Christian who lives for himself alone ; or who makes it his main business to promote his own happiness and salvation. (2.) No man is a Christian who does not deny himself ; or no one who is not willing to sacrifice his own comfort, time, wealth, and ease, to advance the welfare of mankind. (3.) It is this principle which is yet to convert the world. Long since the whole world would have been converted, had all Christians been under its influence. And when ALL Christians make it their

grand object *not* to seek their own, but the good of others ; when true charity shall occupy its appropriate place in the heart of every professed child of God, then this world will be speedily converted to the Saviour. Then there will be no want of funds to spread Bibles and tracts ; to sustain missionaries, or to establish colleges and schools ; then there will be no want of men who shall be willing to go to any part of the earth to preach the gospel ; and then there will be no want of prayer to implore the divine mercy on a ruined and perishing world. O may the time soon come when all the selfishness in the human heart shall be dissolved, and when the whole world shall be embraced in the benevolence of Christians, and the time, and talent, and wealth of the whole church shall be regarded as consecrated to God, and employed and expended under the influence of Christian love ! Comp. Note, chap. x. 24. ¶ *Is not easily provoked* (παρ-οξύνεται). This word occurs in the New Testament only in one other place. Acts xvii. 16, " His spirit *was stirred* within him when he saw the city wholly given to idolatry." See Note on that place. The word properly means to sharpen by, or with, or on any thing (from ὀξύς, *sharp*), and may be applied to the act of sharpening a knife or sword ; then it means to sharpen the mind, temper, courage of any one ; to excite, impel, &c. Here it means evidently to rouse to anger ; to excite to indignation or wrath. Tindal renders it, " is not provoked to anger." Our translation does not exactly convey the sense. The word " easily" is not expressed in the original. The translators have inserted it to convey the idea that he who is under the influence of love, though he may be provoked, that is, injured, or though there might be incitements to anger, yet that he would not be roused, or readily give way to it. The meaning of the phrase in the Greek is, that a man who is under the influence of love or religion is not *prone* to violent anger or exasperation ; it is not his character to be hasty, excited, or passionate. He is calm, serious, patient. He looks soberly at things; and though he may be injured, yet he governs his passions, restrains his temper, subdues his feelings. This, Paul says, would be produced by love. And this is apparent. If we are under the influence of benevolence, or love to any one, we shall not give way to sudden bursts of feeling. We shall look kindly on his actions; put the best construction on his motives; deem it possible that we have mistaken the nature or the reasons of his conduct; seek or desire explanation (Mat. v. 23, 24); wait till we can look at the case in all its bearings; and suppose it possible that he may be influenced by good motives, and that his conduct will admit a satisfactory explanation. That true religion is designed to produce this, is apparent every where in the New Testament, and especially from the example of the Lord Jesus; that it actually does produce it, is apparent from all who come under its influence in any proper manner. The effect of religion is no where else more striking and apparent than in changing a temper naturally quick, excitable, and irritable, to one that is calm, and gentle, and subdued. A consciousness of the presence of God will do much to produce this state of mind; and if we truly loved all men, we should be soon angry with none. ¶ *Thinketh no evil.* That is, puts the best possible construction on the motives and the conduct of others. This expression also is *comparative.* It means that love, or that a person under the influence of love, is not malicious, censorious, disposed to find fault, or to impute improper motives to others. It is not only "not easily provoked," not soon excited, but it is not disposed to *think* that there was any evil intention even in cases which might tend to irritate or exasperate us. It is not disposed to think that there was any evil in the case; or that what was done was with any improper intention or design; that is, it puts the best possible construction on the conduct of others, and supposes, as far as can be done, that it was in consistency with honesty, truth, friendship, and love. The Greek

word (λογίζεται) is that which is commonly rendered *impute,* and is correctly rendered here *thinketh.* It means, does not reckon, charge, or impute to a man any evil intention or design. We desire to think well of the man whom we love; nor will we think ill of his motives, opinions, or conduct until we are compelled to do so by the most irrefragable evidence. True religion, therefore, will prompt to charitable judging; nor is there a more striking evidence of the destitution of true religion than a disposition to impute the worst motives and opinions to a man.

6. *Rejoiceth not in iniquity.* Does not rejoice over the *vices* of other men; does not take delight when they are guilty of crime, or when, in any manner, they fall into sin. It does not find pleasure in hearing others accused of sin, and in having it proved that they committed it. It does not find a malicious pleasure in the *report* that they have done wrong; or in following up that report, and finding it established. Wicked men often find pleasure in this (Rom. i. 32), and rejoice when others have fallen into sin, and have disgraced and ruined themselves. Men of the world often find a malignant pleasure in the report, and in the evidence that a member of the Church has brought dishonour on his profession. A man often rejoices when an enemy, a persecutor, or a slanderer has committed some crime, and when he has shown an improper spirit, uttered a rash expression, or taken some step which shall involve him in ignominy. But love does none of these things. It does not desire that an enemy, a persecutor, or a slanderer should do evil, or should disgrace and ruin himself It does not rejoice, but grieves, when a professor of religion, or an enemy of religion—when a personal friend or foe has done any thing wrong. It neither loves the wrong, nor the fact that it has been done. And perhaps there is no greater triumph of the gospel than in its enabling a man to rejoice that even his enemy and persecutor in any respect does well; or to rejoice that he is in any way honoured and respected among men. Human nature, without the gospel, manifests a dif-

7 Beareth *a* all things, believeth *b* all things, hopeth *c* all things, endureth *d* all things.

a Rom.15.1.　　b Ps.119.66.　　c Rom.8.24.

8 Charity never faileth : but whether *there be* prophecies, they shall fail; but whether *there be*

d Job 13.15.

ferent feeling; and it is only as the heart is subdued by the gospel, and filled with universal benevolence, that it is brought to rejoice when all men do well. ¶ *Rejoiceth in the truth.* The word *truth* here stands opposed to *iniquity*, and means virtue, piety, goodness. It does not rejoice in the *vices*, but in the *virtues* of others. It is pleased, it rejoices when they *do well.* It is pleased when those who differ from us conduct themselves in any manner in such a way as to please God, and to advance their own reputation and happiness. They who are under the influence of that love rejoice that good is done, and the truth defended and advanced, whoever may be the instrument; rejoice that others are successful in their plans of doing good, though they do not act with us; rejoice that other men have a reputation well earned for virtue and purity of life, though they may differ from us in opinion, and may be connected with a different denomination. They do not rejoice when other denominations of Christians fall into error ; or when their plans are blasted ; or when they are calumniated, and oppressed, and reviled. By whomsoever good is done, or wheresoever, it is to them a matter of rejoicing ; and by whomsoever evil is done, or wheresoever, it is to them a matter of grief; see Phil. i. 14—18. The *reason* of this is, that all sin, error, and vice will ultimately ruin the happiness of any one; and as *love* desires their happiness, it desires that they should walk in the ways of virtue, and is grieved when they do not. What a change would the prevalence of this feeling produce in the conduct and happiness of mankind! How much ill-natured joy would it repress at the faults of others ? How much would it do to repress the pains which a man often takes to circulate reports disadvantageous to his adversary ; to find out and establish some flaw in his character ; to prove that he has said or done something disgraceful and

evil ! And how much would it do even among Christians, in restraining them from rejoicing at the errors, mistakes, and improprieties of the friends of revivals of religion, and in leading them to mourn over their errors in secret, instead of taking a malicious pleasure in promulgating them to the world ! This would be a very different world if there were none to rejoice in iniquity ; and the church would be a different church if there were none in its bosom but those who rejoiced in the truth, and in the efforts of humble and self-denying piety.

7. *Beareth all things.* Comp. Note, chap. ix. 12. Doddridge renders this, " covers all things." The word here used ($\sigma\tau\epsilon\gamma\epsilon\iota$) properly means *to cover* (from $\sigma\tau\epsilon\gamma\eta$, a covering, roof; Mat. viii. 8 ; Luke vii. 6) ; and then to hide, conceal, not to make known. If this be the sense here, then it means that love is disposed to *hide* or *conceal* the faults and imperfections of others; not to promulgate or blazon them abroad, or to give any undue publicity to them. Benevolence to the individual or to the public would require that these faults and errors should be concealed. If this is the sense, then it accords nearly with what is said in the previous verse. The word may also mean, to forbear, bear with, endure. Thus it is used in 1 Thess. iii. 1, 5. And so our translators understand it here, as meaning that love is patient, long-suffering, not soon angry not disposed to revenge. And if this is the sense, it accords with the expression in ver. 4, " love suffers long." The more usual classic meaning is the former ; the usage in the New Testament seems to demand the latter. Rosenmüller renders it, "*bears* all things ;" Bloomfield prefers the other interpretation. Locke and Macknight render it " cover." The *real* sense of the passage is not materially varied, whichever interpretation is adopted. It means, that in regard to the errors and faults of others, there is a disposi-

tion *not* to notice or to revenge them. There is a willingness to conceal, or to bear with them patiently. ¶ *All things.* This is evidently to be taken in a popular sense, and to be interpreted in accordance with the connection. All universal expressions of this kind demand to be thus limited. The meaning must be, "as far as it can consistently or lawfully be done." There are offences which it is not proper or right for a man to conceal, or to suffer to pass unnoticed. Such are those where the laws of the land are violated, and a man is called on to testify, &c. But the phrase here refers to private matters; and indicates a disposition *not* to make public or to avenge the faults committed by others. ¶ *Believeth all things.* The whole scope of the connection and the argument here requires us to understand this of the conduct of others. It cannot mean, that the man who is under the influence of love is a man of *universal credulity;* that he makes no discrimination in regard to things to be believed; and is as prone to believe a falsehood as the truth; or that he is at no pains to inquire what is true and what is false, what is right and what is wrong. But it must mean, that in regard to the conduct of others, there is a disposition to put the best construction on it; to believe that they may be actuated by good motives, and that they intend no injury; and that there is a willingness to suppose, as far as can be, that what is done is done consistently with friendship, good feeling, and virtue. Love produces this, because it rejoices in the happiness and virtue of others, and will not believe the contrary except on irrefragable evidence. ¶ *Hopeth all things.* Hopes that all will turn out well. This must also refer to the conduct of others; and it means, that however dark may be appearances; how much soever there may be to produce the fear that others are actuated by improper motives or are bad men, yet that there is a *hope* that matters may be explained and made clear; that the difficulties may be made to vanish; and that the conduct of others may be made to *appear* to be fair and pure.

Love will *hold on to this hope* until all possibility of such a result has vanished and it is compelled to believe that the conduct is not susceptible of a fair explanation. This hope will extend to *all things*—to words and actions, and plans; to public and to private intercourse; to what is said and done in our own presence, and to what is said and done in our absence. Love will do this, because it delights in the virtue and happiness of others, and will not credit any thing to the contrary unless compelled to do so. ¶ *Endureth all things.* Bears up under, sustains, and does not murmur. Bears up under all persecutions at the hand of man; all efforts to injure the person, property, or reputation; and bears all that may be laid upon us in the providence and by the direct agency of God; comp. Job xiii. 15. The connection requires us to understand it principally of our treatment at the hands of our fellow-men.

8. *Charity never faileth.* Paul here proceeds to illustrate the value of love, from its *permanency* as compared with other valued endowments. It is valuable, and is to be sought because it will always abide; may be always exercised; is adapted to all circumstances, and to all worlds in which we may be placed, or in which we may dwell. The word rendered *faileth* (ἐκπίπτει) denotes properly to fall out of, to fall from or off; and may be applied to the stars of heaven falling (Mark xiii. 25), or to flowers that fall or fade (James i. 11; 1 Pet. i. 24), or to chains falling from the hands, &c.; Acts xii. 7. Here it means to fall away, to fail; to be without effect, to cease to be in existence. The expression *may* mean that it will be adapted to all the situations of life, and is of a nature to be always exercised; or it may mean that it will continue to all eternity, and be exercised in heaven for ever. The connection demands that the latter should be regarded as the true interpretation; see ver. 13. The sense is, that while other endowments of the Holy Spirit must soon cease and be valueless, LOVE would abide, and would always exist. The *argu-*

ment is, that we ought to seek that which is of enduring value ; and that, therefore, love should be preferred to those endowments of the Spirit on which so high a value had been set by the Corinthians. ¶ *But whether* there be *prophecies.* That is, the *gift* of prophecy, or the power of speaking as a prophet; that is, of delivering the truth of God in an intelligible manner under the influence of inspiration: the gift of being a public speaker, of instructing and edifying the church, and foretelling future events; see Note, chap. xiv. 1. ¶ *They shall fail.* The gift shall cease to be exercised; shall be abolished, come to naught. There shall be no further use for this gift in the light and glory of the world above, and it shall cease. God shall be the teacher there. And as there will be no need of confirming the truth of religion by the prediction of future events, and no need of warning against impending dangers there, the gift of foretelling future events will be of course unknown. In heaven, also, there will be no need that the faith of God's people shall be encouraged, or their devotions excited, by such exhortations and instructions as are needful now; and the endowment of prophecy will be, therefore, unknown. ¶ *There be tongues.* The power of speaking foreign languages. ¶ *They shall cease.* Macknight supposes this means that they shall cease in the church after the gospel shall have been preached to all nations. But the more natural interpretation is, to refer it to the future life; since the main idea which Paul is urging here is the value of love above all other endowments, from the fact that it would be *abiding,* or permanent—an idea which is more certainly and fully met by a reference to the future world than by a reference to the state of things in the church on earth. If it refers to heaven, it means that the power of communicating thoughts there will not be by the medium of learned and foreign tongues. What *will* be the mode is unknown. But as the diversity of tongues is one of the fruits of sin (Gen. xi.), it is evi-

dent that in those who are saved there will be deliverance from all the disadvantages which have resulted from the confusion of tongues. Yet LOVE will not cease to be necessary; and LOVE will live for ever. ¶ *Whether* there be *knowledge ;* see Note, chap. xiv. 8. This refers, I think, to knowledge as *we now possess it.* It cannot mean that there will be no knowledge in heaven; for there must be a vast increase of knowledge in that world among all its inhabitants. The idea in the passage here, I think, is, " All the knowledge which we now possess, valuable as it is, will be obscured and lost, and rendered comparatively valueless, in the fuller splendours of the eternal world; as the feeble light of the stars, beautiful and valuable as it is, *vanishes,* or is lost in the splendours of the rising sun. The knowledge which we now have is valuable, as the gift of prophecy and the power of speaking foreign languages is valuable, but it will be lost in the brighter visions of the world above." That this is the sense is evident from what Paul says in illustration of the sentiment in ver. 9, 10. *Now* we know in part. What we deem ourselves acquainted with, we imperfectly understand. There are many obscurities and many difficulties. But in that future world we shall know distinctly and clearly (ver. 12); and then the knowledge which we now possess will appear so dim and obscure, that it will seem to have vanished away and disappeared,

" As a dim candle dies at noon."

Macknight and others understand this of the knowledge of the mysteries of the Old Testament, or " the inspired knowledge of the ancient revelations, which should be abolished when the church should have attained its mature state ;" a most meagre, jejune, and frigid interpretation. It is true, also, that not only shall our imperfect knowledge seem to have vanished in the superior light and glory of the eternal world but that much of that which here *passes* for knowledge shall be then unknown. Much of that which is called *science*

tongues, they shall cease; whether *there be* knowledge, it shall vanish away.

9 For we know in part, *a* and we prophesy in part;

a chap.8.2.

10 But *b* when that which is perfect is come, then that which is in part shall be done away.

11 When I was a child, I spake as a child, I understood as a child,

b 1 John 3.2.

is "falsely so called;" and much that is connected with literature that has attracted so much attention, will be unknown in the eternal world. It is evident that much that is connected with criticism, and the knowledge of language, with the different systems of mental philosophy which are erroneous; perhaps much that is connected with anatomy, physiology, and geology; and much of the science which now is connected with the arts, and which is of use only as tributary to the arts, will be then unknown. Other subjects may rise into importance which are now unknown; and possibly things connected with science which are now regarded as of the least importance will then become objects of great moment, and ripen and expand into sciences that shall contribute much to the eternal happiness of heaven. The essential idea in this passage is, that all the knowledge which we now possess shall lose its effulgence, be dimmed and lost in the superior light of heaven. But LOVE shall live there; and we should, therefore, seek that which is permanent and eternal.

9. *For we know in part.* Comp. Note on chap. xii. 27. This expression means "*only* in part;" that is, *imperfectly.* Our knowledge here is imperfect and obscure. It may, therefore, all vanish in the eternal world amidst its superior brightness; and we should not regard that as of such vast value which is imperfect and obscure; comp. Note chap. viii. 2. This idea of the obscurity and imperfection of our knowledge, as compared with heaven, the apostle illustrates (ver. 11) by comparing it with the knowledge which a child has, compared with that in maturer years; and (ver. 12) by the knowledge which we have in looking through a glass— an imperfect medium—compared with

that which we have in looking closely and directly at an object without any medium. ¶ *And we prophesy in part.* This does not mean that we partly *know* the truths of religion, and partly *conjecture* or *guess* at them; or that we know only a part of them, and *conjecture* the remainder. But the apostle is showing the imperfection of the prophetic gift; and he observes, that there is the same imperfection which attends knowledge. It is only in part; it is imperfect; it is indistinct, compared with the full view of truth in heaven; it is obscure, and all that is imparted by that gift will soon become dim and lost in the superior brightness and glory of the heavenly world. The *argument* is, that we ought not to seek so anxiously that which is so imperfect and obscure, and which must soon vanish away; but we should rather seek that love which is permanent, expanding, and eternal.

10. *But when that which is perfect is come.* Does come; or shall come. This proposition is couched in a general form. It means that when *any* thing which is perfect is seen or enjoyed, then that which is imperfect is forgotten, laid aside, or vanishes. Thus, in the full and perfect light of day, the imperfect and feeble light of the stars vanishes. The sense here is, that *in heaven*—a state of absolute perfection—that which is "in part," or which is imperfect, shall be lost in superior brightness. All imperfection will vanish. And all that we here possess that is obscure shall be lost in the superior and perfect glory of that eternal world. All our present unsatisfactory modes of obtaining knowledge shall be unknown. All shall be clear, bright, and eternal.

11. *When I was a child.* The idea here is, that the knowledge which we now have, compared with that which

I ¹ thought as a child; but when I became a man, I put away childish things.

12 For now we see through a

1 or, *reasoned*.

glass, *a* darkly; ¹ but then face to face : now I know in part; but then shall I know even as also I am known.

a 2 Cor.3.18.   1 or, *in a riddle*.

we shall have in heaven, is like that which is possessed in infancy compared with that we have in manhood; and that as, when we advance in years, we lay aside, as unworthy of our attention, the views, feelings, and plans which we had in boyhood, and which we then esteemed to be of so great importance, so, when we reach heaven, we shall lay aside the views, feelings, and plans which we have in this life, and which we now esteem so wise and so valuable. The word *child* here (νήπιος) denotes properly a babe, an infant, though without any definable limitation of age. It refers to the first periods of existence; before the period which we denominate boyhood, or youth. Paul here refers to a period when he could *speak*, though evidently a period when his speech was scarcely intelligible—when he first began to articulate. ¶ *I spake as a child.* Just beginning to articulate, in a broken and most imperfect manner. The idea here is, that our knowledge at present, compared with the knowledge of heaven, is like the broken and scarcely intelligible efforts of a child to speak compared with the power of utterance in manhood ¶ *I understood as a child.* My understanding was feeble and imperfect. I had narrow and imperfect views of things. I knew little. I fixed my attention on objects which I now see to be of little value. I acquired knowledge which has vanished, or which has sunk in the superior intelligence of riper years. " I was affected as a child. I was thrown into a transport of joy or grief on the slightest occasions, which manly reason taught me to despise." —*Doddridge*. ¶ *I thought as a child.* Marg. *Reasoned.* The word may mean either. I thought, argued, reasoned in a weak and inconclusive manner. My thoughts, and plans, and argumentations were puerile, and

such as I now see to be short-sighted and erroneous. Thus it will be with our thoughts compared to heaven. There will be, doubtless, *as much* difference between our present knowledge, and plans, and views, and those which we shall have in heaven, as there is between the plans and views of a child and those of a man. Just before his death, Sir Isaac Newton made this remark : " I do not know what I may appear to the world; but to myself I seem to have been only like a boy playing on the sea-shore, and diverting myself by now and then finding a smoother pebble or a prettier shell than ordinary, while the great ocean of truth lay all undiscovered before me."—*Brewster's Life of Newton*, pp. 300, 301. Ed. New York, 1832.

12. *For now we see through a glass.* Paul here makes use of another illustration to show the imperfection of our knowledge here. Compared with what it will be in the future world, it is like the imperfect view of an object which we have in looking through an obscure and opaque medium compared with the view which we have when we look at it "face to face." The word *glass* here (ἔσοπτρον) means properly a mirror, a looking glass. The mirrors of the ancients were usually made of polished metal; Ex. xxxviii. 8; Job xxxvii. 18. Many have supposed (see Doddridge, in loc. and Robinson's Lexicon) that the idea here is that of seeing objects by reflection from a mirror, which reflects only their imperfect forms. But this interpretation does not well accord with the apostle's idea of seeing things obscurely. The most natural idea is that of seeing objects by an imperfect medium, by looking *through* something in contemplating them. It is, therefore, probable that he refers to those transparent substances which the ancients had, and which they used in their windows occasionally; such

as thin plates of horn, transparent stone, &c. Windows were often made of the *lapis specularis* described by Pliny (xxxvi. 22), which was pellucid, and which admitted of being split into thin *laminæ* or scales, probably the same as mica. Humboldt mentions such kinds of stone as being used in South America in church windows.— *Bloomfield.* It is not improbable, I think, that even in the time of Paul the ancients had the knowledge of glass, though it was probably at first very imperfect and obscure. There is some reason to believe that glass was known to the Phenicians, the Tyrians, and the Egyptians. Pliny says that it was first discovered by accident. A merchant vessel, laden with nitre or fossil alkali, having been driven on shore on the coast of Palestine near the river Belus, the crew went in search of provisions, and accidentally supported the kettles on which they dressed their food upon pieces of fossil alkali. The river sand above which this operation was performed was vitrified by its union with the alkali, and thus produced glass. —See Edin. Ency., art. *Glass.* It is known that glass was in quite common use about the commencement of the Christian era. In the reign of Tiberius an artist had his house demolished for making glass malleable. About this time drinking vessels were made commonly of glass; and glass bottles for holding wine and flowers were in common use. That glass was in quite common use has been proved by the remains that have been discovered in the ruins of Herculaneum and Pompeii. There is, therefore, no impropriety in supposing that Paul here may have alluded to the imperfect and discoloured glass which was then in extensive use; for we have no reason to suppose that it was then as transparent as that which is now made. It was, doubtless, an imperfect and obscure medium, and, therefore, well adapted to illustrate the nature of our knowledge here compared with what it will be in heaven. ¶ *Darkly.* Marg. *In a riddle* (ἐν αἰνίγματι). The word means a riddle; an enigma; then an

obscure intimation. In a riddle a statement is made with some resemblance to the truth; a puzzling question is proposed, and the solution is left to conjecture. Hence it means, as here, obscurely, darkly, imperfectly. Little is known; much is left to conjecture;—a very accurate account of most of that which passes for knowledge. Compared with heaven, our knowledge here much resembles the obscure intimations in an enigma compared with clear statement and manifest truth. ¶ *But then.* In the fuller revelations in heaven. ¶ *Face to face.* As when one looks upon an object openly, and not through an obscure and dark medium. It here means, therefore, *clearly, without obscurity.* ¶ *I know in part;* ver. 9. ¶ *But then shall I know.* My knowledge shall be clear and distinct. I shall have a clear view of those objects which are now so indistinct and obscure. I shall be in the presence of those objects about which I now inquire; I shall *see* them; I shall have a clear acquaintance with the divine perfections, plans, and character. This does not mean that he would know *every thing*, or that he would be omniscient; but that in regard to those points of inquiry in which he was then interested, he would have a view that would be distinct and clear—a view that would be clear, arising from the fact that he would be present with them, and permitted to see them, instead of surveying them at a distance, and by imperfect mediums. ¶ *Even as also I am known. In the same manner* (καθὼς), not *to the same extent.* It does not mean that he would know God as clearly and as fully as God would know him; for his remark does not relate to the *extent*, but to the *manner* and the comparative *clearness* of his knowledge. He would see things as he was now seen and would be seen there. It would be face to face. He would be in their presence. It would not be where *he* would be seen clearly and distinctly, and himself compelled to look upon all objects confusedly and obscurely, and through an imperfect medium. But he would be with

13 And now abideth faith, ᵃ hope, charity, these three ; but the greatest of these *is* charity.

a Heb.10.35, 39 ; 1 Pet.1.21.

them ; would see them face to face ; would see them without any medium ; would see them *in the same manner* as they would see him. Disembodied spirits, and the inhabitants of the heavenly world, have this knowledge : and when we are there, we shall see the truths, not at a distance and obscurely, but plainly and openly.

13. *And now abideth. Remains* (μίνυ). The word means properly to remain, continue, abide ; and is applied to persons remaining in a place, in a state or condition, in contradistinction from removing or changing their place, or passing away. Here it must be understood to be used to denote *permanency,* when the other things of which he had spoken had passed away ; and the sense is, that faith, hope, and love would *remain* when the gift of tongues should cease, and the need of prophecy, &c. ; that is, these should survive them all And the connection certainly requires us to understand him as saying that faith, hope, and love would survive *all* those things of which he had been speaking, and must, therefore, include knowledge (ver. 8, 9,), as well as miracles and the other endowments of the Holy Spirit. They would survive them all ; would be valuable when they should cease ; and should, therefore, be mainly sought ; and of these the greatest and most important is love. Most commentators have supposed that Paul is speaking here only of this life, and that he means to say that in this life these three exist ; that "faith, hope, and charity exist in this scene *only,* but that in the future world faith and hope will be done away, and therefore the greatest of these is charity."—*Bloomfield.* See also Doddridge, Macknight, Rosenmüller, Clarke, &c. But to me it seems evident that Paul means to say that faith, hope, and love will survive *all* those other things of which he had been speaking ; that *they* would vanish away, or be lost in superior attainments and endowments ; that the time would come when they would be useless ; but that faith, hope, and love

would then remain ; but of *these,* for important reasons, love was the most valuable. Not because it would *endure* the longest, for the apostle does not intimate that, but because it is more important to the welfare of others, and is a more eminent virtue than they are. As the strain of the argument requires us to look to another state, to a world where prophecy shall cease and knowledge shall vanish away, so the same strain of argumentation requires us to understand him as saying that faith, and hope, and love will subsist there ; and that there, as here, LOVE will be of more importance than faith and hope. It cannot be objected to this view that there will be no occasion for faith and hope in heaven. That is assumed without evidence, and is not affirmed by Paul. He gives no such intimation. Faith is *confidence* in God and in Christ ; and there will be as much necessity of *confidence* in heaven as on earth. Indeed, the great design of the plan of salvation is to restore *confidence* in God among alienated creatures ; and heaven could not subsist a moment without *confidence ;* and faith, therefore, must be eternal. No society—be it a family, a neighbourhood, a church, or a nation ; be it mercantile, professional, or a mere association of friendship—can subsist a moment without mutual *confidence* or faith, and in heaven such confidence in God MUST subsist for ever. And so of hope. It is true that many of the objects of hope will then be realized, and will be succeeded by possession. But will the Christian have nothing to hope for in heaven ? Will it be nothing to expect and desire greatly augmented knowledge, eternal enjoyment ; perfect peace in all coming ages, and the happy society of the blessed for ever ? All heaven cannot be enjoyed at once ; and if there is any thing *future* that is an object of desire, there will be hope. *Hope* is a compound emotion, made up of a *desire* for an object and an *expectation* of obtaining it. But both these will exist in heaven. It is folly to say that a redeemed saint will

CHAPTER XIV.

FOLLOW after charity, and desire spiritual *a* *gifts;*

but rather that ye may prophesy.

a Eph.1,3.

not *desire* there eternal happiness; it is equal folly to say that there will be no strong expectation of obtaining it. All that is said, therefore, about faith as about to cease, and hope as not having an existence in heaven, is said without the authority of the Bible, and in violation of what must be the truth, and is contrary to the whole scope of the reasoning of Paul here. ¶ *But the greatest of these* is *charity.* Not because it is to *endure* the longest, but because it is the more important virtue; it exerts a wider influence; it is more necessary to the happiness of society; it overcomes more evils. It is *the* great principle which is to bind the universe in harmony, which unites God to his creatures, and his creatures to himself, and which binds and confederates all holy beings with each other. It is therefore more important, because it pertains to *society* to the great kingdom of which God is the head, and because it enters into the very conception of a holy and happy organization. Faith and hope rather pertain to individuals; love pertains to society, and is that without which the kingdom of God cannot stand. Individuals may be saved by faith and hope; but the whole immense kingdom of God depends on LOVE. It is, therefore, of more importance than all other graces and endowments; more important than prophecy and miracles, and the gift of tongues and knowledge, because it will SURVIVE them all; more important than faith and hope, because, although it may co-exist with them, and though they all shall live for ever, yet LOVE enters into the very nature of the kingdom of God; binds society together; unites the Creator and the creature; and blends the interests of all the redeemed, and of the angels, and of God, INTO ONE.

CHAPTER XIV.

THIS chapter is a continuation of the subject commenced in chap. xii. and pursued through chap. xiii. In chap. xii. Paul had entered on the discussion of the various endowments which the Holy Spirit confers on Christians, and had shown that these endowments were bestowed in a different degree on different individuals, and yet so as to promote in the best way the edification of the church. It was proper, he said (chap. xii. 31), to desire the more eminent of these endowments, and yet there was one gift of the Spirit of more value than all others, which might be obtained by all, and which should be an object of desire to all. That was LOVE; and to show the nature, power, and value of this, was the design of the thirteenth chapter, —certainly one of the most tender and beautiful portions of the Bible. In this chapter the subject is continued with special reference to the subject of *prophecy,* as being the most valuable of the miraculous endowments, or the extraordinary gifts of the Spirit.

In doing this, it was necessary to correct an erroneous estimate which they had placed on the power of speaking foreign languages. They had prized this, perhaps, because it gave them importance in the eyes of the heathen. And in proportion as they valued this, they undervalued the gift of being able to edify the church by speaking in a known and intelligible language. To correct this misapprehension; to show the relative value of these endowments, and especially to recommend the gift of " prophecy" as the more useful and desirable of the gifts of the Spirit, was the leading design of this chapter. In doing this, Paul first directs them to seek for charity. He also recommends to them, as in chap. xii. 31, to desire spiritual endowments, and of these endowments especially to desire prophecy; ver. 1. He then proceeds to set forth the advantage of speaking in intelligible language, or of speaking so that the church may be edified, by the following considerations, which comprise the chapter :—

1. The advantage of being understood, and of speaking for the edification of the church; ver. 2—5.

2. No man could be useful to the

church except he delivered that which was understood, any more than the sound of a trumpet in times of war would be useful, unless it were so sounded as to be understood by the army; ver. 6—11.

3. It was the duty of all to seek to edify the church; and *if* a man could speak in an unknown tongue, it was his duty also to seek to be able to interpret what he said; ver. 12—15.

4. The use of tongues would produce embarrassment and confusion, since those who heard them speak would be ignorant of what was said, and be unable to join in the devotions; ver. 16, 17.

5. Though Paul himself was more signally endowed than any of them, yet he prized far more highly the power of promoting the edification of the church, though he uttered but five words, if they were understood, than all the power which he possessed of speaking foreign languages; ver. 18, 19.

6. This sentiment illustrated from the Old Testament; ver. 20, 21.

7. The real use of the power of speaking foreign languages was to be a sign to unbelievers,—an evidence that the religion was from God, and not to be used among those who were already Christians; ver. 22.

8. The effect of their all speaking with tongues would be to produce confusion and disorder, and disgust among observers, and the conviction that they were deranged; but the effect of order, and of speaking intelligibly, would be to convince and convert them; ver. 23—25.

9. The apostle then gives *rules* in regard to the proper conduct of those who were able to speak foreign languages; ver. 26—32.

10. The great rule was, that order was to be observed, and that God was the author of peace; ver. 33.

11. The apostle then gives a positive direction that on no pretence are women to be allowed to speak in the church, even though they should claim to be inspired; ver. 34, 35.

12. He then required all to submit to his authority, and to admit that what he had spoken was from the Lord; ver. 36, 37.   And then,

13. Concludes with directing them to desire to prophesy, and not to forbid speaking with tongues on proper occasions, but to do all things in decency and order; ver. 38—40.

1. *Follow after charity.* Pursue love (chap. xiii. 1); that is, earnestly desire it; strive to possess it; make it the object of your anxious and constant solicitude to obtain it, and to be influenced by it always. Cultivate it in your own hearts, as the richest and best endowment of the Holy Spirit, and endeavour to diffuse its happy influence on all around you. ¶ *And desire spiritual* gifts. I do not forbid you, while you make the possession of love your great object, and while you do not make the desire of spiritual gifts the occasion of envy or strife, to desire the miraculous endowments of the Spirit and to seek to excel in those endowments which he imparts; see Note, chap. xii. 31. The main thing was to cultivate a spirit of love. Yet it was not improper also to desire to be so endowed as to promote their highest usefulness in the church. On the phrase " spiritual gifts," see Note, chap. xii. 1. ¶ *But rather that ye may prophesy.* But especially, or particularly desire to be qualified for the office of prophesying The apostle does not mean to say that prophecy is to be preferred to love or charity; but that, of the spiritual gifts which it was proper for them to desire and seek, *prophecy* was the most valuable. That is, they were not most earnestly and especially to desire to be able to speak foreign languages or to work miracles; but they were to desire to be qualified to speak in a manner that would be edifying to the church. They would naturally, perhaps, most highly prize the power of working miracles and of speaking foreign languages. The object of this chapter is to show them that the ability to speak in a plain, clear, instructive manner, so as to edify the church and convince sinners, was a more valuable endowment than the power of working miracles, or the power of speaking foreign languages. On the meaning of the word *prophesy*, see Note, Rom. xi. 6. To what is said there on the nature of this office, it

2 For he that speaketh in an *unknown* tongue, *a* speaketh not

a Acts 10.46.

seems necessary only to add an idea suggested by Prof. Robinson (Gr. and Eng. Lexicon, Art. Προφήτης), that the prophets were distinguished from the teachers (διδάσκαλοι), "in that, while the latter spoke in a calm, connected, didactic discourse adapted to instruct and enlighten the hearers, the prophet spoke more from the impulse of sudden inspiration, from the light of a sudden revelation at the moment (1 Cor. xiv. 30, ἀποκάλυφθη), and his discourse was probably more adapted, by means of powerful exhortation, to awaken the feelings and conscience of the hearers." The idea of speaking from *revelation*, he adds, seems to be fundamental to the correct idea of the nature of the prophecy here referred to. Yet the communications of the prophets were always in the vernacular tongue, and were always in intelligible language, and in this respect different from the endowments of those who spoke foreign languages. The same truth might be spoken by both; the influence of the Spirit was equally necessary in both; both were inspired; and both answered important ends in the establishment and edification of the church. The gift of tongues, however, as it was the most striking and remarkable, and probably the most rare, was most highly prized and coveted. The object of Paul here is, to show that it was really an endowment of less value, and should be less desired by Christians than the gift of prophetic instruction, or the ability to edify the church in language intelligible and understood by all, under the immediate influences of the Holy Spirit.

2. *For he that speaketh in an* unknown *tongue.* This verse is designed to show that the faculty of speaking intelligibly, and to the edification of the church, is of more value than the power of speaking a foreign language. The reason is, that however valuable may be the endowment in itself, and however important the truth which he may utter, yet it is as if he spoke to God only. No one could understand

unto men, but unto God : for *b* no man 1 understandeth *him ;* how-

b Acts 22.9.   1 heareth.

him. ¶ *Speaketh not unto men.* Does not speak so that men can understand him. His address is really not made to men, that is, to the church. He might have this faculty without being able to speak to the edification of the church. It is possible that the power of speaking foreign languages and of prophesying were sometimes united in the same person; but it is evident that the apostle speaks of them as different endowments, and they probably were found usually in different individuals. ¶ *But unto God.* It is as if he spoke to God. No one could understand him but God. This must evidently refer to the addresses *in the church,* when Christians only were present, or when those only were present who spoke the same language, and who were unacquainted with foreign tongues. Paul says that *there* that faculty would be valueless compared with the power of speaking in a manner that should edify the church. He did not undervalue the power of speaking foreign languages when foreigners were present, or when they went to preach to foreigners; see ver. 22. It was only when it was needless, when all present spoke one language, that he speaks of it as of comparatively little value. ¶ *For no man* understandeth *him.* That is, no man in the church, since they all spoke the same language, and that language was different from what was spoken by him who was endowed with the gift of tongues. As God only could know the import of what he said, it would be lost upon the church, and would be useless. ¶ *Howbeit in the Spirit.* Although, by the aid of the Spirit, he should, in fact, deliver the most important and sublime truths. This would doubtless be the case, that those who were thus endowed *would* deliver most important truths, but they would be *lost* upon those who heard them, because they could not understand them. The phrase "in the Spirit," evidently means "by the Holy Spirit," *i. e.,* by his aid and influence. Though

beit in the spirit he speaketh mysteries.

3 But he that prophesieth speaketh unto men *to* edification, and exhortation, and comfort.

4 He that speaketh in an *unknown* tongue edifieth himself;

but he that prophesieth edifieth the church.

5 I would that ye all spake with tongues, but rather that ye prophesied : for greater *is* he that prophesieth than he that speaketh with tongues, except he interpret,

---

he should be *really* under the influence of the Holy Spirit, and though the important truth which he delivers should be imparted by his aid, yet all would be valueless unless it were understood by the church. ¶ *He speaketh mysteries.* For the meaning of the word *mystery*, see Note, chap. ii. 7. The word here seems to be synonymous with sublime and elevated truth ; truth that was not before known, and that might be of the utmost importance.

3. *But he that prophesieth ;* Note, ver. 1. He that speaks under the influence of inspiration in the common language of his hearers. This seems to be the difference between those who spoke in foreign languages and those who prophesied. Both were under the influence of the Holy Spirit ; both might speak the same truths ; both might occupy an equally important and necessary place in the church ; but the language of the one was intelligible to the church, the other not ; the one was designed to edify the church, the other to address those who spoke foreign tongues, or to give demonstration, by the power of speaking foreign languages, that the religion was from God. ¶ *Speaketh unto men.* So as to be understood by those who were present. ¶ *To edification ;* Note, chap. x. 8, 23. Speaks so as to enlighten and strengthen the church. ¶ *And exhortation ;* see Note, Rom. xii. 8. He applies and enforces the practical duties of religion, and urges motives for a holy life. ¶ *And comfort.* Encouragement. That is, he presents the *promises* and the *hopes* of the gospel; the various considerations adapted to administer comfort in the time of trial. The other might do this, but it would be in a foreign language, and would be useless to the church.

4. *Edifieth himself.* That is, the truths which are communicated to him by the Spirit, and which he utters in an unknown language, may be valuable, and may be the means of strengthening his faith, and building him up in the hopes of the gospel, but they can be of no use to others. His own holy affections might be excited by the truths which he would deliver, and the consciousness of possessing miraculous powers might excite his gratitude. And yet, as Doddridge has well remarked, there might be danger that a man might be injured by this gift when exercised in this ostentatious manner.

5. *I would that ye all spake with tongues.* "It is an important endowment, and is not, in its place, to be undervalued. It may be of great service in the cause of truth, and if properly regulated, and not abused, I would rejoice if these extraordinary endowments were conferred on all. I have no envy against any one who possesses it ; no opposition to the endowment ; but I wish that it should not be overvalued; and would wish to exalt into proper estimation the more useful but humble gift of speaking for the edification of the church." ¶ *Greater is he that prophesieth.* This gift is of more value, and he really occupies a more elevated rank in the church. He is more *useful.* The idea here is, that talents are not to be estimated by their *brilliancy*, but by their *usefulness.* The power of speaking in an unknown tongue was certainly a more striking endowment than that of speaking so as simply to be *useful*, and yet the apostle tells us that the latter is the more valuable. So it is always. A man who is useful, however humble and unknown he may be, really occupies a more elevated and venerable rank than the man of most splendid talents and dazzling eloquence, who

that the church may receive edifying.*a*

6 Now, brethren, if I come unto you speaking with tongues, what

accomplishes nothing in saving the souls of men. ¶ *Except he interpret.* However important and valuable the truth might be which he uttered, it would be useless to the church, unless he should explain it in language which they could understand. In that case, the apostle does not deny that the power of speaking foreign languages was a higher endowment and more valuable than the gift of prophecy. That the man who spoke foreign languages had the power of interpreting, is evident from this verse. From ver. 27, it appears that the office of interpreting was sometimes performed by others.

6. *Now, brethren, if I come unto you,* &c. The truth which the apostle had been illustrating in an abstract manner, he proceeds to illustrate by applying it to himself. If he should come among them speaking foreign languages, it could be of no use unless it were interpreted to them. ¶ *Speaking with tongues.* Speaking foreign languages; that is, speaking them *only,* without any interpreter. Paul had the power of speaking foreign languages (ver. 18); but he did not use this power for ostentation or display, but merely to communicate the gospel to those who did not understand his native tongue. ¶ *Either by revelation.* Macknight renders this, "speak INTELLIGIBLY;" that is, as he explains it, "by the revelation peculiar to an apostle." Doddridge, "by the revelation of some gospel doctrine and mystery." Locke interprets it, that you might understand the revelation, or knowledge," &c.; but says in a note, that we cannot now certainly understand the difference between the meaning of the four words here used. "It is sufficient," says he, "to know that these terms stand for some intelligible discourse tending to the edification of the church." Rosenmüller supposes the word *revelation* stands for some "clear and open knowledge of any truth arising from meditation."

shall I profit you, except I shall speak to you either by revelation,*b* or by knowledge, or by prophesying, or by doctrine?

It is probable that the word here does not refer to divine inspiration, as it usually does, but that it stands opposed to that which is unknown and unintelligible, as that which is *revealed* (ἀποκαλύψις) stands opposed to what is unknown, concealed, *hidden,* obscure. Here, therefore, it is synonymous, perhaps, with *explained.* "What shall it profit, unless that which I speak be brought out of the obscurity and darkness of a foreign language, and *uncovered* or explained!" The original sense of the word *revelation* here is, I suppose, intended (ἀποκαλύψις, from ἀποκαλύπτω, *to uncover*), and means that the sense should be uncovered, *i. e.* explained or what was spoken could not be of value. ¶ *Or by knowledge.* By making it intelligible. By so explaining it as to make it understood. Knowledge here stands opposed to the *ignorance* and *obscurity* which would attend a communication in a foreign language. ¶ *Or by prophesying;* Note, ver. 1. That is, unless it be communicated, through interpretation, in the manner in which the prophetic teachers spoke; that is, made intelligible, and explained, and actually brought down to the usual characteristics of communications made in their own language. ¶ *Or by doctrine.* By teaching (διδαχῇ). By instruction; in the usual mode of plain and familiar instruction. The sense of this passage, therefore, is clear. Though Paul should utter among them, as he had abundant ability to do, the most weighty and important truths, yet, unless he interpreted what he said in a manner clear from obscurity, like *revelation;* or intelligibly, and so as to constitute *knowledge;* or in the manner that the prophets spoke, in a plain and intelligible manner; or in the manner usual in simple and plain *instruction,* it would be useless to them. The perplexities of commentators may be seen stated in Locke, Bloomfield, and Doddridge.

7 And even things without life giving sound, whether pipe or harp, except they give a distinction in the [1] sounds, how shall it be known what is piped or harped?

1 or, *tunes.*

8 For if the trumpet *a* give an uncertain sound, who shall prepare himself to the battle?

9 So likewise ye, except ye utter by the tongue words [1] easy to be

a Num.10.9 1 *significant.*

---

7. *Things without life.* Instruments of music. ¶ *Whether pipe.* This instrument (αὐλὸς) was usually made of reeds, and probably had a resemblance to a flageolet. ¶ *Or harp.* This instrument (κιθάρα) was a stringed instrument, and was made in the same way as a modern harp. It usually had ten strings, and was struck with the plectrum, or with a key. It was commonly employed in praise. ¶ *Except they give a distinction in the sounds.* Unless they give a difference in the *tones,* such as are indicated in the gamut for music. ¶ *How shall it be known,* &c. That is, there would be no time, no music. Nothing would be indicated by it. It would not be fitted to excite the emotions of sorrow or of joy. All music is designed to excite emotions; but if there be no difference in the tones, no emotion would be produced. So it would be in words uttered. Unless there was something that was fitted to excite thought or emotion; unless what was spoken was made *intelligible,* no matter how important in itself it might be, yet it would be useless.

8. *For if the trumpet give an uncertain sound.* The trumpet was used commonly in war. It is a well-known wind instrument, and was made of brass, silver, &c. It was used for various purposes in war—to summon the soldiers; to animate them in their march; to call them forth to battle ; to sound a retreat ; and to signify to them what they were to do in battle, whether to charge, advance, or retreat, &c. It therefore employed a *language* which was intelligible to an army. An uncertain sound was one in which none of these things were indicated, or in which it could not be determined what was required. ¶ *Who shall prepare himself,* &c. The apostle selects a single instance of what was indicated by the trumpet, as an illustration of what he meant. The

idea is, that foreign tongues spoken in their assembly would be just as useless in regard to their duty, their comfort, and edification, as would be the sound of a trumpet when it gave one of the usual and intelligible sounds by which it was known what the soldiers were required to do. Just as we would say, that the mere beating on a drum would be useless, unless some tune was played by which it was known that the soldiers were summoned to the parade, to advance, or to retreat.

9. *So likewise ye,* &c. To apply the case. If you use a foreign language, how shall it be known what is said, or of what use will it be, unless it is made intelligible by interpretation? ¶ *Utter by the tongue.* Unless you speak. ¶ *Words easy to be understood.* Significant words (margin), words to which your auditors are accustomed. ¶ *For ye shall speak into the air.* You will not speak so as to be understood; and it will be just the same as if no one was present, and you spoke to the air. We have a proverb that resembles this: "You may as well speak to the winds ;" that is, you speak where it would not be understood, or where the words would have no effect. It may be observed here, that the practice of the papists accords with what the apostle here condemns, where worship is conducted in a language not understood by the people; and that there is much of this same kind of speaking now, where unintelligible terms are used, or words are employed that are above the comprehension of the people ; or where doctrines are discussed which are unintelligible, and which are regarded by them without interest. All preaching should be plain, simple, perspicuous, and adapted to the capacity of the hearers.

10. *There are it may be,* &c. There has been considerable variety in the

understood, how shall it be known what is spoken? for ye shall speak into the air.

10 There are, it may be, so many kinds of voices in the world, and none of them is without signification.

11 Therefore if I know not the meaning of the voice, I shall be unto him that speaketh a bar-

a Rom.1.1.

barian; *a* and he that speaketh *shall be* a barbarian unto me.

12 Even so ye, forasmuch as ye are zealous of ¹ spiritual *gifts*, seek that ye may excel to the edifying of the church.

13 Wherefore let him that speak-eth in an *unknown* tongue, pray that he may interpret.

1 *spirits.*

interpretation of this expression. Rosenmüller renders it, " for the sake of example." Grotius supposes that Paul meant to indicate that there were, perhaps, or might be, as many languages as the Jews supposed, to wit, seventy. Beza and others suppose it means, that there may be as many languages as there are nations of men. Bloomfield renders it, " Let there be as many kinds of languages as you choose." Macknight, " There are, no doubt, as many kinds of languages in the world as ye speak." Robinson (Lex.) renders it, " If so happen, it may be; perchance, perhaps;" and says the phrase is equivalent to "for example." The sense is, " There are perhaps, or for example, very many kinds of voices in the world; and all are significant. None are used by those who speak them without mean-ing; none speak them without design-ing to convey some intelligible idea to their hearers." The *argument* is, that as *all* the languages that are in the world, however numerous they are, are for *utility*, and as none are used for the sake of mere display, so it should be with those who had the power of speaking them in the Chris-tian church. They should speak them only when and where they would be understood. ¶ *Voices.* Lan-guages.

11. *The meaning of the voice.* Of the language that is uttered, or the sounds that are made. ¶ *I shall be unto him,* &c. What I say will be unintelligible to him, and what he says will be unintelligible to me. We cannot understand one another any more than people can who speak dif-ferent languages. ¶ *A barbarian;* see Note, Rom. i. 14. The word

means one who speaks a different, or a foreign language.

12. *Even so ye.* Since you desire spiritual gifts, I may urge it upon you to seek to be able to speak in a clear and intelligible manner, that you may edify the church. This is one of the most valuable endowments of the Spirit; and this should be earnestly desired. ¶ *Forasmuch as ye are zealous.* Since you earnestly desire; Note, chap. xii. 31. ¶ *Spiritual* gifts. The endowments conferred by the Holy Spirit ; Note, chap. xii. 1. ¶ *Seek that ye may excel,* &c. Seek that you may be able to convey truth in a clear and plain manner ; seek to be distinguished for that. It is one of the most rare and valuable endow-ments of the Holy Spirit.

13. *Pray that he may interpret.* Let him ask of God ability that he may explain it clearly to the church. It would seem probable that the power of speaking foreign languages, and the power of conveying truth in a clear and distinct manner, were not always found in the same person, and that the one did not of necessity im-ply the other. The truth seems to have been, that these extraordinary endowments of the Holy Spirit were bestowed on men in some such way as *ordinary* talents and mental powers are now conferred; and that they became in a similar sense *the charac-teristic mental endowments of the in-dividual,* and of course were subject to the same laws, and liable to the same kinds of abuse, as mental en-dowments are now. And as it *now* happens that one man may have a peculiar faculty for acquiring and ex-pressing himself in a foreign lan-guage who may not be by any means

14 For if I pray in an *unknown* tongue, my spirit prayeth; but my understanding is unfruitful.

15 What is it then? I will pray with the spirit, *a* and I will pray with the understanding also:

a John 4,24.

distinguished for clear enunciation, or capable of conveying his ideas in an interesting manner to a congregation, so it was then. The apostle, therefore, directs such, if any there were, instead of priding themselves on their endowments, and instead of always speaking in an unknown tongue, which would be useless to the church, to *pray* for the more useful gift of being able to convey their thoughts in a clear and intelligible manner in their vernacular tongue. This would be useful. The truths, therefore, that they had the power of speaking with eminent ability in a foreign language, they ought to desire to be able to *interpret* so that they would be intelligible to the people whom they addressed in the church. This seems to me to be the plain meaning of this passage, which has given so much perplexity to commentators. Macknight renders it, however, " Let him who prayeth in a foreign language, pray so as SOME ONE may interpret ;" meaning that he who prayed in a foreign language was to do it by two or three sentences at a time, so that he might be followed by an interpreter. But this is evidently forced. In order to this, it is needful to suppose that the phrase ὁ λαλῶν, " that speaketh," should be rendered, contrary to its obvious and usual meaning, " who prays," and to supply τις, *some one*, in the close of the verse. The obvious interpretation is that which is given above ; and this proceeds only on the supposition that the power of speaking foreign languages and the power of interpreting were not always united in the same person—a supposition that is evidently true, as appears from chap. xii. 10.

14. *For if I pray*, &c. The reference to prayer here, and to singing in ver. 15, is designed to illustrate the propriety of the general sentiment which he is defending, that public worship should be conducted in a language that would be intelligible to the people. However well meant it might be, or however the *heart* might be engaged in it, yet unless it was intelligible, and the understanding could join in it, it would be vain and profitless. ¶ *My spirit prayeth.* The word *spirit* here (πνεῦμα) has been variously understood. Some have understood it of the Holy Spirit—the Spirit by which Paul says he was actuated. Others of the *spiritual gift*, or that spiritual influence by which he was endowed. Others of the mind itself. But it is probable that the word " spirit" refers to the *will;* or to the mind, as the seat of the affections and emotions; *i. e.* to the heart, desires, or intentions. The word *spirit* is often used in the Scriptures as the seat of the affections, and emotions, and passions of various kinds; see Mat. v. 3, " Blessed are the poor in spirit ;" Luke x. 21, " Jesus rejoiced in spirit." So it is the seat of ardour or fervour (Luke i. 17 ; Acts xviii. 25 ; Rom. xii. 11) ; of grief or indignation; Mark iii. 12 ; John xi. 33 ; xiii. 21 ; Acts xvii. 16. It refers also to feelings, disposition, or temper of mind, in Luke ix. 55 ; Rom. viii. 15. Here it refers, it seems to me, to the heart, the will, the disposition, the feelings, as contradistinguished from the understanding; and the sense is, " My feelings find utterance in prayer ; my heart is engaged in devotion ; my prayer will be acceptable to God, who looks upon the feelings of the heart, and I may have true enjoyment; but my understanding will be unfruitful, that is, will not profit others. What I say will not be understood by them ; and of course, however much benefit *I* might derive from my devotions, yet they would be useless to others." ¶ *But my understanding* (ὁ δὲ νοῦς μου). My intellect, my mind ; my mental efforts and operations. ¶ *Is unfruitful.* Produces nothing that will be of advantage to them. It is like a barren tree ; a tree that bears nothing that can be of

I will sing [a] with the spirit, and I will sing with the understanding [b] also.

a Eph.5.19; Col.3.16.

16 Else, when thou shalt bless with the spirit, how shall he that occupieth the room of the unlearn-

b Ps. 47.7.

benefit to others. They cannot understand what I say, and of course, they cannot be profited by what I utter. 15. *What is it then?* What shall I do? What is the proper course for me to pursue? What is my practice and my desire; see the same form of expression in Rom. iii. 9, and vi. 15. It indicates the *conclusion* to which the reasoning had conducted him, or the course which he would pursue in view of all the circumstances of the case. ¶ *I will pray with the spirit,* &c. I will endeavour to *blend* all the advantages which can be derived from prayer; I will *unite* all the benefits which *can* result to myself and to others. I deem it of vast importance to pray with the spirit in such a way that the *heart* and the *affections* may be engaged, so that I may myself derive benefit from it; but I will also unite with that, utility to others; I will use such language that they may understand it, and be profited. ¶ *And I will pray with the understanding also.* So that others may understand me. I will make the appropriate use of the intellect, so that it may convey ideas, and make suitable impressions on the minds of others. ¶ *I will sing with the spirit.* It is evident that the same thing might take place in singing which occurred in prayer. It might be in a foreign language, and might be unintelligible to others. The affections of the man himself might be excited, and his heart engaged in the duty, but it would be profitless to others. Paul, therefore, says that he would so celebrate the praises of God as to excite the proper affections in his own mind, and so as to be intelligible and profitable to others. This passage proves, (1.) That the praises of God are to be celebrated among Christians, and that it is an important part of worship; (2.) That the *heart* should be engaged in it, and that it should be so performed as to excite proper affec-

tions in the hearts of those who are engaged in it; and, (3.) That it should be so done as to be *intelligible* and edifying to others. The *words* should be so uttered as to be distinct and understood. There should be clear enunciation as well as in prayer and preaching, since the design of sacred music in the worship of God is not only to utter praise, but it is to impress the sentiments which are sung on the heart by the aid of musical sounds and expression more deeply than could otherwise be done. If this is not done, the singing might as well be in a foreign language. Perhaps there is no part of public worship in which there is greater imperfection than in the mode of its psalmody. At the same time, there is scarcely any part of the devotions of the sanctuary that may be made more edifying or impressive. It has the *advantage*—an advantage which preaching and praying have not—of using the sweet tones of melody and harmony to *impress* sentiment on the heart : and it should be done. 16. *Else* (Ἐπεί). Since; if this is not done; if what is said is not intelligible, how shall the unlearned be able appropriately to express his assent, and join in your devotions? ¶ *When thou shalt bless.* When thou shalt bless God, or give thanks to him. If thou shalt lead the devotions of the people in expressing thanksgiving for mercies and favours. This may refer to a part of public worship, or to the thanks which should be expressed at table, and the invocation of the divine blessing to attend the bounties of his providence. Paul had illustrated his subject by prayer and by singing; he now does it by a reference to the important part of public worship expressed in giving thanks. ¶ *With the spirit.* In the manner referred to above ; that is, in an unknown tongue, in such a way that your own *heart* may be engaged in it, but which would be unintelligible to

ed say Amen at thy giving *a* of thanks? seeing he understandeth not what thou sayest.

17 For thou verily givest thanks well, but the other is not edified.

18 I thank my God, I speak with tongues more than ye all.

a chap 11.24.

19 Yet in the church I had rather speak five words with my understanding, that *by my voice* I might teach others also, than ten thousand words in an *unknown* tongue.

20 Brethren, be not *b* children in

b Eph.4.14,15; Heb.6.1—3; 2.Pet.3.18.

others. ¶ *He that occupieth the room.* Is in the place, or the seat of the unlearned; that is, he who *is* unlearned. On the meaning of the word *room*, see Note, Luke xiv. 8. To *fill a place* means to occupy a station, or to be found in a state or condition. ¶ *Of the unlearned (τοῦ ἰδιώτου).* On the meaning of this word, see Note, Acts iv. 13. Here it means one who was unacquainted with the foreign language spoken by him who gave thanks. It properly denotes a man in *private*, in contradistinction from a man in *public* life; and hence a man who is ignorant and unlettered, as such men generally were. ¶ *Say Amen.* This word means *truly, verily;* and is an expression of affirmation (John iii. 5) or of assent. Here it means *assent.* How can he pronounce *the* AMEN; how can he express his assent; how can he join in the act of devotion? This *might* have been, and probably *was*, expressed aloud; and there is no impropriety in it. It *may*, however, be *mental*—a silent assent to what is said, and a silent uniting in the act of thanksgiving. In one way or the other, or in both, the assent should always be expressed by those who join in acts of public worship.

17. *For thou verily givest thanks well.* That is, even if you use a foreign language. You do it with the heart; and it is accepted by God as *your* offering; but the other, who cannot understand it, cannot be benefited by it.

18. *I thank my God.* Paul here shows that he did not undervalue or despise the power of speaking foreign languages. It was with him a subject of thanksgiving that he could speak so many; but he felt that there were more valuable endowments than this; see the next verse. ¶ *With tongues more than ye all.* I am able

to speak more foreign languages than all of you. *How many* languages Paul could speak, he has no where told us. It is reasonable, however, to presume that he was able to speak the language of any people to whom God in his providence, and by his Spirit, called him to preach. He had been commissioned to preach to the *Gentiles*, and it is probable that he was able to speak the languages of all the nations among whom he ever travelled. There is no account of his being under a necessity of employing an interpreter wherever he preached.

19. *Yet in the church.* In the Christian assembly. The word *church* does not refer to the *edifice* where Christians worshipped, but to the organized body of Christians. ¶ *I had rather*, &c. It is probable that in the Christian assembly, usually, there were few who understood foreign languages. Paul, therefore, would not speak in a foreign language when its only use would be mere display. ¶ *With my understanding.* So as to be intelligible to others; so that *I* might understand it, and so that at the same time others might be bene fitted.

20. *Brethren, be not children in understanding.* Be not childish; do not behave like little children. They admire, and are astonished at what is striking, novel, and what may be of no real utility. They are pleased with any thing that will amuse them, and at little things that afford them play and pastime. So your admiration of a foreign language, and of the ability to speak it, is of as little solid value as the common sports and plays of boys. This, says Doddridge, is an admirable stroke of oratory, and adapted to bring down their pride by showing them that those things on which they were disposed to value

understanding : howbeit in malice
be *a* ye children, but in understanding be [1] men. *b*

a Ps.131.2; Mat.18 3; Rom.16.19; 1Pet.2 2.
1 *perfect*, or *of a riper age*.   b Ps.114.99.

themselves were *childish*. It is sometimes well to appeal to Christians in
this manner, and to show them that
what they are engaged in is *unworthy*
the dignity of the understanding—
unfit to occupy the time and attention
of an immortal mind. Much, alas !
very much of that which engages the
attention of Christians is just as unworthy of the dignity of the mind, and
of their immortal nature, as were the
aims and desires which the apostle rebuked among the Christians at Corinth.
Much that pertains to dress, to accomplishment, to living, to employment,
to amusement, to conversation, will
appear, when we come to die, to have
been like the playthings of *children ;*
and we shall feel that the immortal
mind has been employed, and the time
wasted, and the strength exhausted
in that which was foolish and puerile.
¶ *Howbeit in malice be ye children.*
This is one of Paul's most happy
turns of expression and of sentiment.
He had just told them that in one
respect they ought not to be children.
Yet, as if this would appear to be
speaking lightly of children—and
Paul would not speak lightly of any
one, even of a child—he adds, that in
another respect it would be well to be
like them—nay, not only like children,
but like infants. The phrase " be ye
children," here, does not express the
force of the original *νηπιάζετε*. It
means, "be *infants*," and is emphatic,
and was used, evidently, by the apostle
of design. The meaning may be thus
expressed. " Your admiration of
foreign languages is like the sports
and plays of *childhood*. In this respect be not children (*παιδία*) ; be
men. Lay aside such childish things.
Act worthy of the *understanding*
which God has given you. I have
mentioned children. Yet I would not
speak unkindly or with contempt even
of them. *In one respect* you may imitate them. Nay, you should not only
be like *children*, that are somewhat

21 In the law *c* it is written, *d*
With *men of* other tongues and
other lips will I speak unto this

c John 10.34.   d Isa.28.11,12.

advanced in years, but like *infants*.
Be as free from malice, from any ill-
will toward others, from envy, and
every improper passion, as they are."
This passage, therefore, accords with
the repeated declaration of the Saviour, that in order to enter into heaven, it was needful that we should
become as little children; Mat. xviii.
3. ¶ *Be men*. Margin, "*Perfect*, or
of a riper age" (*τέλειοι*). The word
means *full grown men*. Act like
them whose understandings are mature
and ripe.
   21. *In the law it is written*. This
passage is found in Isa. xxviii. 11, 12.
The word *law* here seems to mean the
same as revelation ; or is used to denote the Old Testament in general.
A similar use occurs in John x. 34,
and John xv. 25. ¶ *With* men of
other tongues, &c. This passage,
where it occurs in Isaiah, means, that
God would teach the rebellious and
refractory Jews submission to himself,
by punishing them amidst a people of
another language, by removing them
to a land—the land of Chaldea—
where they would hear only a language
that to them would be unintelligible
and barbarous. Yet, notwithstanding
this discipline, they would be still, to
some extent, a rebellious people.
The passage in Isaiah has no reference to the miraculous gift of tongues.
and cannot have been used by the
apostle as containing any intimation
that such miraculous gifts would be
imparted. It seems to have been
used by Paul, because the *words*
which occurred in Isaiah would *appropriately express* the idea which he
wished to convey (see Note, Mat. i.
23), that God would make use of foreign languages for *some valuable
purpose*. But he by no means intimates that Isaiah had any such reference ; nor does he quote this as a
fulfilment of the prophecy ; nor does
he mean to say, that God would accomplish *the same purpose* by the use

people ; and yet for all that will they not hear me, saith the Lord.

22 Wherefore tongues are for a sign, *a* not to them *b* that believe, but to them that believe not : but

a Mark 16.17; Acts 2.6,&c.

prophesying *serveth* not for them that believe not, but for them which believe.

23 If therefore the whole church be come together into one place,

b 1 Tim.1.9.

of foreign languages, which was contemplated in the passage in Isaiah. The sense is, as God accomplished an important purpose by the use of a foreign language in regard to his ancient people, as recorded in Isaiah, so he will make use of foreign languages to accomplish important purposes still. They shall be used in the Christian church to effect important objects, though not in the same manner, nor for the same end, as in the time of the captivity. What tho design of making use of foreign languages was, in the Christian church, the apostle immediately states; ver. 22, 23. ¶ *Yet for all that,* &c. Notwithstanding all this chastisement that shall be inflicted on the Jews in a distant land, and among a people of a different language, they will still be a rebellious people. This is the sense of the passage, as it is used by Isaiah ; see Isa. xxviii. 12. It is not quoted literally by the apostle, but the main idea is retained. He does not appear to design to apply this to the Corinthians, unless it may be to intimate that the power of speaking foreign languages did not of necessity secure obedience. It might be that this power might be possessed, and yet they be a sinful people ; just as the Jews were admonished by the judgments of God, inflicted by means of a people speaking a foreign language, and yet were not reformed or made holy.

22. *Wherefore.* Thus ("Ωστε), or wherefore. The apostle does not mean to say that what he was about to state was a direct conclusion from the passage of Scripture which he had quoted, but that it followed from all that he had said, and from the whole view of the subject. " The true statement or doctrine is, that tongues are for a sign," &c. ¶ *Tongues.* The power of speaking foreign languages. ¶ *Are for a sign.* An indication, an evi-

dence, or a proof that God has imparted this power, and that he attends the preaching of the gospel with his approbation. It is a *sign,* or a *miracle,* which, like all other miracles, may be designed to convince the unbelieving world that the religion is from God. ¶ *Not to them that believe.* Not to Christians. They are already convinced of the truth of religion, and they would not be benefited by that which was spoken in a language which they could not understand. ¶ *But to them that believe not.* It is a miracle designed to convince them of the truth of the Christian religion. God alone could confer the power of thus speaking ; and as it was conferred expressly to aid in the propagation of the gospel, it proved that it was from God ; see Note on Acts ii. 1—15. ¶ *But prophesying.* Speaking in a calm, connected, didactic manner, in language intelligible to all under the influence of inspiration ; see Notes on ver. 1. ¶ *For them that believe not.* Is not particularly intended for them; but is intended mainly for the edifying of the church. It is not so striking, so replete with proofs of the divine presence and power as the gift of tongues. Though it may be really under the influence of the Holy Spirit, and may be really by inspiration, yet it is not so evidently such as is the power of speaking foreign languages. It was, therefore, better adapted to edify the church than to convince gainsayers. At the same time the *truths* conveyed by it, and the consolations administered by it, might be as clear evidence to the church of the attending power, and presence, and goodness of God, as the power of speaking foreign languages might be to infidels.

23. *Be come together into one place.* For public worship. ¶ *And all speak with tongues.* All speak with a variety

and all speak with tongues, and there come in *those that are* unlearned or unbelievers, will they not say that ye are mad ? *a*

24 But if all prophesy, and there

a Acts 2.13.

come in one that believeth not, or *one* unlearned, he is convinced of all, he is judged of all :

25 And thus are the secrets of his heart made manifest ; and so, fall-

---

of unknown tongues; all speak foreign languages. The idea is, that the church would usually speak the same language with the people among whom they dwelt; and if they made use of foreign languages which were unintelligible to their visitors, it would leave the impression that the church was a bedlam. ¶ *And there come in* those that are *unlearned*. Those that are unacquainted with foreign languages, and to whom, therefore, what was said would be unintelligible. ¶ *Or unbelievers*. Heathen, or Jews, who did not believe in Christ. It is evident from this that such persons often attended on the worship of Christians. Curiosity might have led them to it ; or the fact that they had relatives among Christians might have caused it. ¶ *That ye are mad*. They will not understand what is said ; it will be a confused jargon : and they will infer that it is the effect of insanity. Even though it might not, therefore, be in itself improper, yet a regard to the honour of Christianity should have led them to abstain from the use of such languages in their worship when it was needless. The apostles were charged, from a similar cause, with being intoxicated ; see Acts ii. 13.

24. *But if all prophesy*. Note, ver. 1. If all, in proper order and time, shall utter the truths of religion in a language intelligible to all. ¶ *Or one unlearned*. One unacquainted with the nature of Christianity, or the truths of the gospel. ¶ *He is convinced of all*. He will be convinced by all that speak. He will understand what is said ; he will see its truth and force, and he will be satisfied of the truth of Christianity. The word here rendered *convinced* (ἐλίγχεται) is rendered *reprove* in John xvi. 8, " And when he is come, he will reprove the world of sin," &c. Its proper meaning is to *convict*, to show one

to be wrong ; and then to rebuke, reprove, admonish, &c. Here it means, evidently, that the man would be convicted, or convinced of his error and of his sin ; he would see that his former opinions and practice had been wrong; he would see and acknowledge the force and truth of the Christian sentiments which should be uttered, and would acknowledge the error of his former opinions and life. The following verse shows that the apostle means something more than a mere convincing of the understanding, or a mere conviction that his opinions had been erroneous. He evidently refers to what is now known also as *conviction* for sin ; that is, a deep sense of the depravity of the heart, of the errors and follies of the past life, accompanied with mental anxiety, distress, and alarm. The force of truth, and the appeals which should be made, and the observation of the happy effects of religion, would convince him that he was a sinner, and show him also his need of a Saviour. ¶ *He is judged by all*. By all that speak ; by all that they say. The *effect* of what they say shall be, as it were, to pass a *judgment* on his former life; or to condemn him. What is said will be approved by his own conscience, and will have the effect to condemn him in his own view as a lost sinner. This is now the effect of faithful preaching, to produce deep self-condemnation in the minds of sinners.

25. *And thus are the secrets of his heart made manifest*. Made manifest to himself in a surprising and remarkable manner. He shall be led to see the *real* designs and motives of his heart. His conscience would be awakened ; he would recall his former course of life; he would see that it was evil ; and the present state of his heart would be made known to himself. It is possible that he would *sup-*

ing down on *his* face, he will worship God, and report that God is *a*
in you of a truth.

a Isa.45.14; Zech.8.23.

pose that the speaker was aiming directly at him, and *revealing* his feelings
to others ; for such an effect is often
produced. The convicted sinner often
supposes that the preacher particularly intends *him*, and wonders that he
has such an acquaintance with his
feelings and his life; and often supposes that he is designing to disclose
his feelings to the congregation. It
is *possible* that Paul here may mean
that the prophets, by inspiration,
would bo ablo to roveal oomo oooret
facts in regard to the stranger; or to
state the ill design which he might
have had in coming into the assembly;
or to state some things in regard to
him which could be known only to
himself; as was the case with Ananias
and Sapphira (Acts v. 1, seq.) ; but
perhaps it is better to understand this
in a more gcncral oenoe, ao deooribing
the proper and more common effect
of truth, when it is applied by a man's
own conscience. Such effects are
often witnessed now ; and such effects
ahow the truth of religion ; its adapt-
edness to men ; the omniscience and
the power of God; the design of the
conscience, and its use in the conversion of sinners. ¶ *And so falling
down on* his *face.* The usual posture
of worship or reverence in eastern
countrles. It was performed by sinking on the knees and hands, and then
placing the face on the ground. This
might be done publicly; or the apostle
may mean to say that it would lead
him to do it in private. ¶ *He will
worship God.* He will be converted,
and become a Christian. ¶ *And report that God,* &c. Will become your
friend, and an advocate for the Christian religion. An enemy will be
turned to a friend. Doubtless this
was often done. It is now often done.
Paul's argument is, that they should
so conduct their public devotions as
that they should be adapted to produce
this result.

26. *How is it then, brethren?* Note,
ver. 15. What is the fact? What

26 How is it then, brethren ?
when ye come together, every one
of you hath a psalm, hath a doc-

actually occurs among you? Does
that state of things exist which I
have described? Is there that order
in your public worship which is demanded and proper? It is implied
in his asking this question that **there**
might be some things among them
which were improper, and which deserved reproof. ¶ *When ye come together.* For worship. ¶ *Every one
of you,* &c. That is, all the things
which are specified would be found
among them. It io, ovidontly, not
meant that all these things would be
found in the same person, but would
all exist at the same time ; and thus
confusion and disorder would be inevitable. Instead of waiting for an
intimation from the presiding officer
in the assembly, or spcaking in succession and in order, each one probably
regarded himoolf ao under tho influence of the Holy Spirit ; as having
an important message to communicate, or as being called on to celebrate
the praises of God ; and thus confusion and disorder would prevail. Many
would be speaking at the same time,
and a most unfavourable impression
would be made on the minds of the
strangers who should be present, ver.
23. This implied reproof of the Corinthians is certainly a reproof of those
publlc assemblles where many speak
at the same time; or where a portion
are engaged in praying, and others
in exhortation. Nor can it be urged
that in such cases those who engage
in these exercises are under the influence of the Holy Spirit ; for, however
true that may be, yet it is no more
true than it was in Corinth, and yet
the apostle reproved the practice
there. The Holy Spirit is the author
of order, and not of confusion (ver.
33) ; and true religion prompts to
peace and regularity, and not to discord and tumult. ¶ *Hath a psalm.* Is
disposed to sing ; is inclined to praise;
and, however irregular or improper,
expresses his thanks in a public manner, Note, ver. 15. ¶ *Hath a doc.*

trine, *a* hath a tongue, hath a revelation, hath an interpretation   Let
b all things be done unto edifying.

27 If any man speak in an *unknown* tongue, *let it be* by two, or
at the most *by* three, and *that* by
course ; and let one interpret.

a ver.6.   *b* ver.40.

28 But if there be no interpreter,
let him keep silence in the church;
and let him speak to himself and to
God.

29 Let *c* the prophets speak two
or three, and let the other judge.

30 If *any thing* be revealed to

c ver.39; 1 Thess.5.19.20.

trine. Has some religious truth on
his mind which he deems it of special
importance to inculcate, Note, ver. 6.
¶ *Hath a tongue.* Has something
made known to him in a foreign
language, or has a power of speaking a
foreign language, and exercises it,
though it produces great confusion.
¶ *Hath a revelation.* Some truth
which has been particularly revealed
to him; perhaps an explanation of some
mystery (*Doddridge*) ; or a revelation of some future event (*Macknight*) ; or a prophecy (*Bloomfield*);
or a power of explaining some of the
truths couched in the types and figures of the Old Testament. *Grotius.*
¶ *Hath an interpretation.* An explanation of something that has been
uttered by another in a foreign
language ; Note, chap. xii. 10. ¶ *Let
all things,* &c. Let this be the great
principle, to promote the edification
of the church ; Note, ver. 12. If this
rule were followed, it would prevent
confusion and disorder.

27. Let it be *by two, or at the most*
by *three.* That is, two, or at most
three in one day, or in one meeting.
So Grotius, Rosenmüller, Doddridge,
Bloomfield, and Locke, understand it.
It is probable that many were endowed
with the gift of tongues ; and it is
certain that they were disposed to exercise the gift even when it could be
of no real advantage, and when it was
done only for ostentation. Paul had
shown to them (ver. 22), that the
main design of the gift of tongues
was to convince unbelievers ; he here
shows them that if that gift *was* exercised in the church, it should be in
such a way as to promote edification.
They should not speak at the same
time ; nor should they regard it as
necessary that all should speak at the
same meeting. It should not be so

as to produce disorder and confusion ;
nor should it be so as to detain the
people beyond a reasonable time. The
speakers, therefore, in any one assembly should not exceed two or three.
¶ *And* that *by course.* Separately ;
one after another. They should not
all speak at the same time. ¶ *And
let one interpret.* One who has the
gift of interpreting foreign languages,
(Note, chap. xii. 10), so that they may
be understood,and the church be edified.

28. *But if there be no interpreter.*
If there be no one present who has the
gift of interpretation. ¶ *And let him
speak to himself and to God ;* see
Note, ver. 2, 4. Let him commune
with himself, and with God ; let him
meditate on the truths which are revealed to him, and let him in secret
express his desires to God.

29. *Let the prophets,* Note, ver. 1.
¶ *Speak two or three.* On the same
days, or at the same meeting ; Note,
ver. 27. ¶ *And let the other judge.*
The word "other" (*οἱ ἄλλοι, the others*),
Bloomfield supposes refers to the other
prophets ; and that the meaning is,
that they should decide whether what
was said was dictated by the Holy
Spirit, or not. But the more probable
sense, I think, is that which refers it
to the rest of the congregation, and
which supposes that they were to compare one doctrine with another, and
deliberate on what was spoken, and
determine whether it had evidence of
being in accordance with the truth.
It may be that the apostle here refers
to those who had the gift of discerning spirits, and that he meant to say
that they were to determine by what
spirit the prophets who spoke were
actuated. It was possible that those
who claimed to be prophets might err,
and it was the duty of all to examine
whether that which was uttered was

another that sitteth by, let the *a* first hold his peace.

31 For ye may all prophecy one by one, that all may learn, and all may be comforted.

a Job 32.11.   b 1 John 4.1.

32 And the spirits *b* of the prophets are subject to the prophets.

33 For God is not *the author* of [1] confusion, but of peace, as *c* in all churches of the saints.

1 tumult, or *unquietness*.   a chap.11.16.

in accordance with truth. And if this was a duty then, it is a duty now; if it was proper even when the teachers claimed to be under divine inspiration, it is much more the duty of the people now. No minister of religion has a right to demand that all that he speaks shall be regarded as truth, unless he can give good reasons for it: no man is to be debarred from the right of canvassing freely, and comparing with the bible, and with sound reason, all that the minister of the gospel advances. No minister who has just views of his office, and a proper acquaintance with the truth, and confidence in it, would desire to prohibit the people from the most full and free examination of all that he utters. It may be added, that the Scripture everywhere encourages the most full and free examination of all doctrines that are advanced; and that true religion advances just in proportion as this spirit of candid, and earnest, and prayerful examination prevails among a people; see Note, Acts xvii. 11; comp. 1 Thess. v. 21.

30. *If* any thing *be revealed to another.* If, while one is speaking, an important truth is revealed to another, or is suggested to his mind by the Holy Spirit, which he feels it to be important to communicate. ¶ *Let the first hold his peace.* That is, let him that was speaking conclude his discourse, and let there not be the confusion arising from two persons speaking at the same time. Doddridge understands this as meaning, that he to whom the revelation was made should sit still, until the other was done speaking, and not rise and rudely interrupt him. But this is to do violence to the language. So Macknight understands it, that the one who was speaking was *first* to finish his discourse, and be silent, before the other began to speak. But

this is evidently a forced construction. Locke understands it as meaning, that if, while one was speaking, the meaning of what he said was revealed to another, the first was to cease speaking until the other had interpreted or explained it. But the obvious meaning of the passage is, that the man that was speaking was to close his discourse and be silent. It does not follow, however, that he was to be rudely interrupted. He might close his discourse deliberately, or perhaps by an intimation from the person to whom the revelation was made. At any rate, two were not to speak at the same time, but the one who was speaking was to conclude before the other addressed the assembly.

31. *For ye may all prophecy, &c.* There is time enough for all: there is no need of speaking in confusion and disorder. Every person may have an opportunity of expressing his sentiments at the proper time. ¶ *That all may learn.* In such a manner that there may be edification. This might be done if they would speak one at a time in their proper order.

32. *And the spirits of the prophets.* See in ver. 1 for the meaning of the word prophets. The evident meaning of this is, that they were able to *control* their inclination to speak; they were not under a *necessity* of speaking, even though they might be inspired. There was no need of disorder. This verse gives confirmation to the supposition, that the extraordinary endowments of the Holy Spirit were subjected to substantially the same laws as a man's natural endowments. They were conferred by the Holy Ghost; but they were conferred on free agents, and did not interfere with their free agency. And as a man, though of the most splendid talents and commanding eloquence, has *control* over his own mind, and is not com-

34 Let *a* your women keep silence in the churches; for it is not permitted unto them to speak ;

a 1Tim.2.11,12.   *b* Eph.5.22; Tit.2.5; 1Pet.3.1.

but *they are commanded* to be *b* under obedience, as also saith *c* the law.

c Gen.3.16; Num.30.3—12; Esth.1.20.

pelled to speak, so it was with those who are here called prophets. The immediate reference of the passage is to those who are called *prophets* in the New Testament : and the interpretation should be confined to them. It is not improbable, however, that the same thing was true of the prophets of the Old Testament ; and that it is really true as a general declaration of *all* the prophets whom God has inspired, that they *had* control over their own minds, and could speak or be silent at pleasure.   In this the spirit of true inspiration differed essentially from the views of the heathen, who regarded themselves as driven on by a wild, controlling influence, that *compelled* them to speak even when they were unconscious of what they said.   Universally, in the heathen world, the priests and priestesses supposed or feigned that they were under an influence which was incontrollable ; which took away their powers of self-command, and which made them the mere organs or unconscious instruments of communicating the will of the gods.   The Scripture account of inspiration is, however, a very different thing.   In whatever way the mind was influenced, or whatever was the mode in which the truth was conveyed, yet it was not such as to destroy the conscious powers of free agency, nor such as to destroy 'the individuality of the inspired person, or to annihilate what was peculiar in his mode of thinking, his style, or his customary manner of expression.

33. *God is not* the author *of confusion.*   Marg. *Tumult,* or *unquietness.* His religion cannot tend to produce disorder.   He is the God of peace ; and his religion will tend to promote order.   It is calm, peaceful, thoughtful.   It is not boisterous and disorderly.   ¶ *As in all churches of the saints.*   As was everywhere apparent in the churches.   Paul here appeals to them, and says that this was the

fact wherever the true religion was spread, that it tended to produce peace and order.   This is as true now as it was then.   And we may learn, therefore, (1.) That where there is disorder, there is little religion.   Religion does not *produce* it ; and the tendency of tumult and confusion is to drive religion away.   (2.) True religion will not lead to tumult, to outcries, or to irregularity.   It will not prompt many to speak or pray at once ; nor will it justify tumultuous and noisy assemblages.   (3.) Christians should regard God as the author of peace.   They should always in the sanctuary demean themselves in a reverent manner, and with such decorum as becomes men when they are in the presence of a holy and pure God, and engaged in his worship. (4.) All those pretended conversions, however sudden and striking they may be, which are attended with disorder, and confusion, and public outcries, are to be suspected.   Such excitement may be *connected with* genuine piety, but it is no part of pure religion.   That is calm, serious, orderly, heavenly. No man who is under its influence is disposed to engage in scenes of confusion and disorder.   Grateful he may be, and he may and will express his gratitude ; prayerful he will be, and he will pray ; anxious for others he will be, and he will express that anxiety ; but it will be with seriousness, tenderness, love ; with a desire for the order of God's house, and not with a desire to break in upon and disturb all the solemnities of public worship.

34. *Let your women keep silence,* &c.   This rule is positive, explicit, and universal.   There is no ambiguity in the expressions ; and there can be no difference of opinion, one would suppose, in regard to their meaning. The sense evidently is, that in all those things which he had specified, the women were to keep silence ; they were to take no part.   He had dis-

35 And if they will learn any thing, let them ask their husbands at home: for it is a shame for women to speak in the church.

coursed of speaking foreign languages, and of prophecy; and the evident sense is, that in regard to all these they were to keep silence, or were not to engage in them. These pertained solely to the male portion of the congregation. These things constituted the business of the public teaching; and in this the female part of the congregation were to be silent. " They were not to teach the people, nor were they to interrupt those who were speaking."—*Rosenmüller*. It is probable that, on pretence of being inspired, the women had assumed the office of public teachers. In chap. xi. Paul had argued against their doing this in a certain manner without their veils (chap. xi. 4), and he had shown, that *on that account*, and *in that manner*, it was improper for them to assume the office of public teachers, and to conduct the devotions of the church. The force of the argument in chap. xi. is, that what he there states would be a sufficient reason against the practice, even if there were no other. It was contrary to all decency and propriety that they should appear *in that manner* in public. He *here* argues against the practice on EVERY GROUND; forbids it altogether; and shows that on every consideration it was to be regarded as improper for them even so much as *to ask a question* in time of public service. There is, therefore, no inconsistency between the argument in chap. xi. and the statement here; and the force of the whole is, that *on every consideration* it was improper, and to be expressly prohibited, for women to conduct the devotions of the church. It does not refer to those only who claimed to be inspired, but to all; it does not refer merely to acts of public preaching, but to all acts of speaking, or even asking questions, when the church is assembled for public worship. No rule in the New Testament is more positive than this; and however plausible may be the reasons which may be urged for disregarding it, and for suffering women to take part in conducting public worship, yet the authority of the apostle Paul is positive, and his meaning cannot be mistaken; comp. 1 Tim. ii. 11, 12. ¶ *To be under obedience.* To be subject to their husbands; to acknowledge the superior authority of the man; Note, chap. xi. 3. ¶ *As also saith the law;* Gen. iii. 16, " And thy desire shall be to thy husband, and he shall rule over thee."

35. *And if they will learn any thing.* If any thing has been spoken which they do not understand; or if on any particular subject they desire more full information, let them inquire of their husbands in their own dwelling. They may there converse freely; and their inquiries will not be attended with the irregularity and disorder which would occur should they interrupt the order and solemnity of public worship. ¶ *For it is a shame.* It is disreputable and shameful; it is a breach of propriety. Their station in life demands modesty, humility, and they should be free from the ostentation of appearing so much in public as to take part in the public services of teaching and praying. It does not become their rank in life; it is not fulfilling the object which God evidently intended them to fill. He has appointed *men* to rule; to hold offices; to instruct and govern the church; and it is improper that women should assume that office upon themselves. This evidently and obviously refers to the church assembled for public worship, in the ordinary and regular acts of devotion. There the assembly is made up of males and females, of old and young, and there it is improper for them to take part in conducting the exercises. But this cannot be interpreted as meaning that it is improper for females to speak or to pray in meetings of their own sex, assembled for prayer or for benevolence; nor that it is improper for a female to speak or to pray in a Sabbath-school. Neither of these come under the apostle's idea of a church. And in such meetings, no rule of propriety or of the Scrip-

36 What! came the word of God out from you? or ^a came it unto you only?

37 If ^b any man think himself

a chap.4.7.   b 2Cor.10.7; 1John 4.6.

to be a prophet, or spiritual, let him acknowledge that the things that I write unto you are the commandments of the Lord.

---

tures is violated in their speaking for the edification of each other, or in leading in social prayer. It may be added here, that on this subject the Jews were very strenuous, and their laws were very strict. The Rabbins taught that a woman should know nothing but the use of the distaff, and they were specially prohibited from asking questions in the synagogue, or even from reading. See *Lightfoot*. The same rule is still observed by the Jews in the synagogues.

36. *What! came the word of God out from you?* The meaning of this is, " Is the church at Corinth the *mother church?* Was it first established; or has it been alone in sending forth the word of God? You have adopted customs which are unusual. You have permitted women to speak in a manner unknown to other churches; see chap. xi. 16. You have admitted irregularity and confusion unknown in all the others. You have allowed many to speak at the same time, and have tolerated confusion and disorder. Have you any *right* thus to differ from others? Have you any authority, as it were, to dictate to them, to teach them, contrary to their uniform custom, to allow these disorders? Should you not rather be conformed to them, and observe the rules of the churches which are older than yours?" The *argument* here is, that the church at Corinth was *not* the first that was established; that it was one of the *last* that had been founded; and that it could, therefore, claim no right to differ from others, or to prescribe to them. The same argument is employed in chap. xi. 16; see Note. ¶ *Or came it unto you only?* As you are not the first of those who believed, neither are you the only ones. God has sent the same gospel to others, and it is travelling over the world. Others, therefore, have the same right as you to originate customs and peculiar habits; and as this would be attended with

confusion and disorder, you should all follow the same rule, and the customs which do not prevail in other churches should not be allowed in yours.

37. *If any man think himself to be a prophet;* Note, ver. 1. If any man claim to be divinely endowed. Macknight renders it, " be really a prophet." But the more correct meaning here is, doubtless, " If any man *profess* to be a prophet ; or is *reputed* to be a prophet." *Bloomfield.* The proper meaning of the word δοχέω is to seem to one's self; to be of opinion, to suppose, believe, &c.; and the reference here is to one who should *regard himself*, or who should believe and profess to be thus endowed. ¶ *Or spiritual.* Regarding himself as under the extraordinary influence of the Spirit. ¶ *Let him acknowledge, &c.* He will show that he is truly under the influence of the Holy Spirit, by acknowledging my authority, and by yielding obedience to the commands which I utter in the name and by the authority of the Lord. All would probably be disposed to acknowledge the right of Paul to speak to them; all would regard him as an apostle ; and all would show that God had influenced their hearts, if they listened to his commands, and obeyed his injunctions. I do not speak by my own authority, or in my own name, says Paul. I speak in the name of the Lord; and to obey the commands of the Lord is a proof of being influenced by his Spirit. True religion everywhere, and the most ardent and enthusiastic zeal that is prompted by true religion, will show their genuineness and purity by a sacred and constant regard for the commands of the Lord. And that zeal which disregards those commands, and which tramples down the authority of the Scriptures and the peace and order of the church, gives demonstration that it is not genuine. It is false zeal, and, however ardent, will not ultimately do good to the cause.

38 But if any be ignorant, let him be ignorant.

39 Wherefore, brethren, covet

a ver.26,33.

to prophesy, and forbid not to speak with tongues.

40 Let *a* all things be done decently and in order.

---

38. *But if any be ignorant*, &c. If any one *affects* to be ignorant of my authority, or whether I have a right to command. If he affects to *doubt* whether I am inspired, and whether what I utter is in accordance with the will of God. ¶ *Let him be ignorant,* At his own peril, let him remain so, and abide the consequences. I shall not take any further trouble to debate with him. I have stated my authority. I have delivered the commands of God. And now, if he disregards them, and still doubts whether all this is said by divine authority, let him abide the consequences of rejecting the law of God. I have given full proof of my divine commission. I have nothing more to say on that head. And now, if he chooses to remain in ignorance or incredulity, the fault is his own, and he must answer for it to God.

39. *Covet to prophesy;* Note, ver. 1. This is the *summing up* of all that he had said. It was *desirable* that a man should wish to be able to speak, under the teaching of the Holy Spirit, in such a manner as to edify the church. ¶ *And forbid not,* &c. Do not suppose that the power of speaking foreign languages is useless, or is to be despised, or that it is to be prohibited. *In its own place* it is a valuable endowment; and on proper occasions the talent should be exercised; see in ver. 22.

40. *Let all things be done decently and in order.* Let all things be done in an *appropriate* and *becoming* manner; *decorously*, as becomes the worship of God. Let all be done *in order*, *regularly*, without confusion, discord, tumult. The word used here (κατὰ τάξιν) is properly a military term, and denotes the order and regularity with which an army is drawn up. This is a general rule, which was to guide them. It was simple, and easily applied. There might be a thousand questions started about the modes and forms of worship, and the customs in the churches, and much difficulty

might occur in many of these questions; but here was a simple and plain rule, which might be easily applied. Their good sense would tell them what became the worship of God; and their pious feelings would restrain them from excesses and disorders. This rule is still applicable, and is safe in guiding us in many things in regard to the worship of God. There are many things which cannot be subjected to *rule*, or exactly prescribed; there are many things which may and must be left to pious feeling, to good sense, and to the views of Christians themselves, about what will promote their edification and the conversion of sinners. The rule in such questions is plain. Let all be done *decorously, as* becomes the worship of the great and holy God; let all be without confusion, noise, and disorder.

In view of this chapter, we may remark:—

(1.) That public worship should be in a language understood by the people; the language which they commonly employ. Nothing can be clearer than the sentiments of Paul on this. The whole strain of the chapter is to demonstrate this, in opposition to making use of a foreign and unintelligible language in any part of public worship. Paul specifies in the course of the discussion every part of public worship; *public preaching* (ver. 2, 3, 5, 13,. 19); *prayer* (ver. 14, 15); *singing* (ver. 15); and insists that all should be in a language that should be understood by the people. It would almost seem that he had anticipated the sentiments and practice of the Roman Catholic denomination. It is remarkable that a practice should have grown up, and have been defended, in a church professedly Christian, so directly in opposition to the explicit meaning of the New Testament. Perhaps there is not even in the Roman Catholic denomination, a more striking instance of a custom or doctrine in direct contradiction to the Bible. If any thing is plain and obvious, it is that worship, in order to be edifying, should be in a language that is understood by the people. Nor can that service be acceptable to God which is not understood by those who offer it; which conveys no idea to their minds, and which cannot, therefore, be the homage of the heart. Assuredly, God does not require the offering of unmeaning words. Yet, this has been a grand device of the great enemy of man. It has contributed to keep the people in ignorance and superstition; it has prevented the mass of the people from seeing how utterly unlike the New Testament are the sentiments of the papists; and it has, in connection with the kindred doctrine that the Scripture should be withheld from the people, contributed to perpetuate that dark system, and to bind the human mind in chains. Well do the Roman Catholics know, that if the Bible were given to the people, and public worship conducted in a language which they could understand, the system would soon fall. It could not live in the midst of light. It is a system which lives and thrives only in darkness.

(2.) Preaching should be simple and intelligible. There is a great deal of preaching which might as well be in a foreign tongue as in the language which is actually employed. It is dry, abstruse, metaphysical, remote from the common manner of expression, and the common habits of thought among men. It may be suited to schools of philosophy, but it cannot be suited to the pulpit. The preaching of the Lord Jesus was simple, and intelligible even to a child. And nothing can be a greater error, than for the ministers of the gospel to adopt a dry and metaphysical manner of preaching. The most successful preachers have been those who have been most remarkable for their simplicity and clearness. Nor is simplicity and intelligibleness of manner inconsistent with bright thought and profound sentiments. A diamond is the most pure of all minerals; a river

may be deep, and yet its water so pure that the bottom may be seen at a great depth; and glass in the window is most valuable the clearer and purer it is, when it is itself least seen, and when it gives no obstruction to the light. If the purpose is that the glass may be *itself* an ornament, it may be well to stain it; if to give light, it should be pure. A very shallow stream may be very muddy; and because the bottom cannot be seen, it is no evidence that it is deep. So it is with style. If the purpose is to convey thought, to enlighten and save the soul, the style should be plain, simple, pure. If it be to bewilder and confound, or to be admired as unintelligible, or perhaps as profound, then an abstruse and metaphysical, or a flowery manner may be adopted in the pulpit.

(3.) We should learn to value *useful* talent more than that which is splendid and showy; ver. 3. The whole scope of this chapter goes to demonstrate that we should more highly prize and desire that talent which may be *useful* to the church, or which may be useful in convincing unbelievers (ver. 24, 25), than that which merely dazzles, or excites admiration. Ministers of the gospel who preach as they should do, engage in their work to win souls to Christ, not to induce them to admire eloquence; they come to teach men to adore the great and dreadful God, not to be loud in their praises of a mortal man.

(4.) Ministers of the gospel should not aim to be admired. They should seek to be useful. Their aim should not be to excite admiration of their acute and profound talent for reasoning; of their clear and striking power of observation; of their graceful manner; of their glowing and fervid eloquence; of the beauty of their words, or the eloquence of their well-turned periods. They should seek to build up the people of God in holy faith, and so to present truth as that it shall make a deep impression on mankind. No work is so important, and so serious in its nature and results, as the ministry of the gospel; and in no

CHAPTER XV.

MOREOVER, brethren, I ^a declare unto you the gospel which I preached unto you, which ^b also ye have received, and wherein ^c ye stand:

a Gal.1.11.   b chap. 1.4-8.   c 1 Pet.5.12.

work on earth should there be more seriousness, simplicity, exactness, and correctness of statement, and invincible and unvarying adherence to simple and unvarnished truth. Of all places, the pulpit is the last, in which to seek to excite admiration, or where to display profound learning, or the powers of an abstract and subtle argumentation, *for the sake* of securing a reputation. Cowper has drawn the character of what a minister of the gospel should be, in the well-known and most beautiful passage in the " Task."

Would I describe a preacher, such as Paul
Were he on earth, would hear, approve, and
    own,
Paul should himself direct me. I would trace
His master-strokes, and draw from his design.
I would express him simple, grave, sincere;
In doctrine uncorrupt; in language plain;
And plain in manner; decent, solemn, chaste,
And natural in gesture; much impress'd
Himself, as conscious of his awful charge,
And anxious mainly that the flock he feeds
May feel it too; affectionate in look,
And tender in address, as well becomes
A messenger of grace to guilty men.

He stablishes the strong, restores the weak,
Reclaims the wanderer, binds the broken
    heart,
And, arm'd himself in panoply complete
Of heavenly temper, furnishes with arms,
Bright as his own, and trains, by every rule
Of holy discipline, to glorious war,
The sacramental host of God's elect.

CHAPTER XV.

THIS important and deeply interesting chapter, I have spoken of as the *third* part of the epistle. See the Introduction. It is more important than any other portion of the epistle, as it contains a connected, and laboured, and unanswerable argument for the main truth of Christianity, and, consequently, of Christianity itself; and it is more interesting to us as *mortal* beings, and as having an instinctive dread of death, than any other portion of the epistle. It has always, therefore, been regarded with deep interest by expositors, and it is worthy of the deepest attention of all. If the argument in this chapter is solid, then Christianity is true; and if true, then this chapter unfolds to us the most elevated and glorious prospect which can be exhibited to dying, yet immortal man.

There were, probably, two reasons why the apostle introduced here this discussion about the resurrection. *First*, it was desirable to introduce a condensed and connected statement of the main argument for the truth of Christianity. The Corinthians had been perplexed with subtle questions, and torn by sects and parties, and it was possible that in their zeal for sect and party, they would lose their hold on this great and vital argument for the truth of religion itself. It might be further apprehended, that the enemies of the gospel, from seeing the divisions and strifes which existed there, would take advantage of these contentions, and say that a religion which produced *such* fruits could not be from God. It was important, therefore, that they should have access to an argument plain, clear, and unanswerable, for the truth of Christianity; and that thus the evil effects of their divisions and strifes might be counteracted. *Secondly.* It is evident from ver. 12, that the important doctrine of the resurrection of the dead had been denied at Corinth, and that this error had obtained a footing in the church itself. On what grounds, or by what portion or party it was denied, is unknown. It may have been that the influence of some Sadducean teacher may have led to the rejection of the doctrine; or it may have been the effect of philosophy. From Acts xvii. 32, we know that among some of the Greeks, the doctrine of the resurrection was regarded as ridiculous; and from 2 Tim. ii. 18, we learn that it was held by some that the resurrection was passed already, and consequently that there was nothing but a spiritual resurrection. To counteract these errors, and to put the doctrine of the resurrection of the dead on a firm foundation, and thus to furnish a demonstration of the truth of Christianity, was the design of this chapter.

The chapter may be regarded as divided into four parts, and four questions in regard to the resurrection are solved. 1. Whether there is any resurrection of the dead? ver. 1—34. 2. With what body will the dead rise? ver. 35—51. 3. What will become of those who shall be alive when the Lord Jesus shall come to judge the world? ver. 51—54. 4. What are the practical bearings of this doctrine? ver. 55—58.

I. The dead will be raised; ver. 1—34. This Paul proves by the following arguments, and illustrates in the following manner.

(1.) By adducing *reasons* to show that Christ rose from the dead ; ver. 1—11.

(*a*) From the Scripture ; ver. 1—4.

(*b*) From the testimony of eyewitnesses; ver. 5—11.

(2.) By showing the absurdity of the contrary doctrine; ver. 12—34.

(*a*) If the dead do not rise, it would follow that Christ has not risen; ver. 13.

(*b*) If Christ is not risen, he is preached in vain, and faith is reposed in him for naught; ver. 14.

(*c*) It would follow that the apostles would be false witnesses and wicked men ; whereas, the Corinthians had abundant reason to know the contrary ; ver. 15.

(*d*) The faith of the Corinthians must be vain if he was not risen, and they must regard themselves as still unpardoned sinners, since all their hope of pardon must arise from the fact that his work was accepted, and that he was raised up; ver. 16, 17.

(*e*) If Christ was not risen, then all their pious friends who had believed in him must be regarded as lost; ver. 18.

(*f*) It would follow that believers in Christ would be in a more misera-

ble condition than any others, if there was no resurrection; ver. 19.

(*g*) Baptism for the resurrection of the dead would be absurd and in vain, unless the dead arose; it would be vain to be baptized with the belief, and on the ground of the belief that Christ rose, and on the ground of the hope that they would rise; ver. 29.

(*h*) It would be in vain that the apostles and others had suffered so many toils and persecutions, unless the dead should rise; ver. 30—32.

In the course of this part of his argument (ver. 20—28) Paul introduces an *illustration* of the doctrine, or a statement of an important *fact* in regard to it, thus *separating* the argument in ver. 19 from the next, which occurs in ver. 29. Such interruptions of a train of thinking are not uncommon in the writings of Paul, and indicate the *fulness* and *richness* of his conceptions, when some striking thought occurs, or some plausible objection is to be met, and when he suspends his argument in order to state it. This interjected portion consists of the following items. (1.) A triumphant and joyful assurance that Christ *had in fact* risen; as if his mind was full, and he was impatient of the delay caused by the necessity of slow argumentation ; ver. 19, 20. (2.) He *illustrates* the doctrine, or shows that it is *reasonable* that the certainty of the resurrection should be demonstrated by one in human nature, since death had been introduced by man; ver. 21, 22. This is an argument from *analogy*, drawn from the obvious propriety of the doctrine that man should be raised up in a manner somewhat similar to the mode in which he had been involved in ruin. (3.) He states the *order* in which all this should be done; ver. 23—28. It is possible that some may have held that the resurrection must have been already passed, since it depended so entirely and so closely on the resurrection of Christ; comp. 2 Tim. ii. 18. Paul, therefore, meets this objection; and shows that it must take place in a regular order; that Christ rose first, and that they who were his friends should rise at his coming. He then states what would take place at that time, when the work of redemption should have been consummated by the resurrection of the dead, and the entire recovery of all the redeemed to God, and the subjection of every foe.

II. What will be the nature of the bodies that shall be raised up? ver. 35—51.

This inquiry is illustrated,

(1.) By a reference to grain that is sown; ver. 36—38.

(2.) By a reference to the fact that there are different kinds of flesh; ver. 39.

(3.) By a reference to the fact that there are celestial bodies and earthly bodies; ver. 40.

(4.) By the fact that there is a difference between the sun, and moon, and stars; ver. 41.

(5.) By a direct statement, for which the mind is prepared by these illustrations, of the important changes which the body of man must undergo, and of the nature of that body which he will have in heaven; ver. 42—50. It is,

(a) Incorruptible; ver. 42.

(b) Glorious; ver. 43.

(c) Powerful; ver. 43.

(d) A spiritual body; ver. 44.

(e) It is like the body of the second man, the Lord from heaven; ver. 45—50.

III. What will become of those who shall be alive when the Lord Jesus shall return to raise the dead?

Ans. They shall be changed instantly, and fitted for heaven, and made like the glorified saints that shall be raised from the dead; ver. 51—54.

IV. The practical consequences or influences of this doctrine; ver. 55—58.

(1.) The doctrine is glorious and triumphant; it overcame all the evils of sin, and should fill the mind with joy; ver. 55—57.

(2.) It should lead Christians to diligence, and firmness of faith, and patience, since their labour was not to be in vain; ver. 58.

1. Moreover. But (δὲ). In addition to what I have said, or in that

which I am now about to say, I make known the main and leading truth of the gospel. The particle δὲ is "strictly adversative, but more frequently denotes transition and conversion, and serves to introduce something else, whether opposite to what precedes, or simply continuative or explanatory."—Robinson. Here it serves to introduce another topic that was not properly a continuation of what he had said, but which pertained to the same general subject, and which was deemed of great importance. ¶ I declare unto you (Γνωρίζω). This word properly means to make known, to declare, to reveal (Luke ii. 15; Rom. ix. 22, 23); then to tell, narrate, inform (Eph. vi. 21; Col. iv. 7, 9); and also to put in mind of, to impress, to confirm; see Note, chap. xii. 3. Here it does not mean that he was communicating to them any new truth, but he wished to remind them of it; to state the arguments for it, and to impress it deeply on their memories. There is an abruptness in our translation which does not exist in the original. Bloomfield. ¶ The gospel; Note, Mark i. 1. The word here means the glad announcement, or the good news about the coming of the Messiah, his life, and sufferings, and death, and especially his resurrection. The main subject to which Paul refers in this chapter is the resurrection; but he includes in the word gospel, here, the doctrine that he died for sins, and was buried, as well as the doctrine of his resurrection; see ver. 3, 4. ¶ Which I preached unto you. Paul founded the church at Corinth; Acts xviii. 1, seq. It was proper that he should remind them of what he had taught them at first; of the great elementary truths on which the church had been established, but from which their minds had been diverted by the other subjects that had been introduced as matters of debate and strife. It was fair to presume that they would regard with respect the doctrines which the founder of their church had first proclaimed, if they were reminded of them; and Paul, therefore, calls their attention to the great and vital truths

2 By which also ye are saved, if *a* ye keep ¹ in memory ² what I preached unto you, unless *b* ye have believed in vain.

a Heb.3.6.   1 or, *hold fast.*
2 *by what speech.*   b Gal.3.4.

3 For I delivered unto you first of all that which I also received, how that Christ died for our sins according *c* to the Scriptures ;

c Gen.3.15; Ps.xxii; Isa.liii; Dan.9.26; Zech. 13.7; Luke 24.26,46.

by which they had been converted, and by which the church had thus far prospered. It is well, often, to remind Christians of the truths which were preached to them *when* they were converted, and which were instrumental in their conversion. When they have gone off from these doctrines, when they had given their minds to speculation and philosophy, it has a good effect to *remind* them that they were converted by the simple truths, that Christ died, and was buried, and rose again from the dead. The argument of Paul here is, that they owed all the piety and comfort which they had to these doctrines; and that, therefore, they should still adhere to them as the foundation of all their hopes. ¶ *Which also ye have received.* Which you embraced; which you all admitted as true ; which were the means of your conversion. I would remind you, that, however that truth may *now* be denied by you, it was once received by you, and you professed to believe in the fact that Christ rose from the dead, and that the saints would rise. ¶ *And wherein ye stand.* By which your church was founded, and by which all your piety and hope has been produced, and which is at the foundation of all your religion. You were built up *by* this, and by this only can you stand as a Christian church. This doctrine was vital and fundamental. This demonstrates that the doctrines that Christ died "for sins," and rose from the dead, are fundamental truths of Christianity. They enter into its very nature ; and without them there can be no true religion.

2. *By which also ye are saved.* On which your salvation depends ; the belief of which is indispensable to your salvation ; see Note on Mark xvi. 16. The apostle thus shows the *importance* of the doctrine. In every

respect it demanded their attention. It was that which was first preached among them ; that which they had solemnly professed ; that by which they had been built up ; and that which was connected with their salvation. It does not mean simply that by this they were brought into a salvable state (Clarke, Macknight, Whitby, Bloomfield, &c.), but it means that their hopes of eternal life rested on this ; and by this they were then *in fact* saved from the condemnation of sin, and were in the possession of the hope of eternal life. ¶ *If ye keep in memory.* Margin, as in the Greek, *if ye hold fast.* The idea is, that they were saved by this, or would be, if they faithfully retained or held the doctrine as he delivered it ; if they observed it, and still believed it, notwithstanding all the efforts of their enemies, and all the arts of false teaching to wrest it from them. There is a doubt delicately suggested here, whether they did in fact still adhere to his doctrine, or whether they had not abandoned it in part for the opposite. ¶ *Unless ye have believed in vain.* You will be saved by it, if you adhere to it, unless it shall turn out that it was vain to believe, and that the doctrine was false. That it was *not* false, he proceeds to demonstrate. Unless all your trials, discouragements, and hopes were to no purpose, and all have been the result of imposture ; and unless all your profession is false and hollow, you will be saved by this great doctrine which I first preached to you.

3. *For I delivered unto you ;* Note, chap. xi. 23. ¶ *First of all.* Among the first doctrines which I preached. As the leading and primary doctrines of Christianity. ¶ *That which I also received.* Which had been communicated to me. Not doctrines of which I was the author, or which were to be

4 And that he was buried, and that he rose again the third day according *a* to the Scriptures;

a Ps.16.10; Hos.6.2.

5 And that he was seen of *b* Cephas, then of the twelve.

6 After that, he was seen of

b Luke 23.34,&c.

regarded as my own. Paul here refers to the fact that he had received these doctrines from the Lord Jesus by inspiration; comp. Note, chap. x. 23 ; Gal. i. 2. This is one instance in which he claims to be under the divine guidance, and to have received his doctrines from God. ¶ *How that Christ died for our sins.* The Messiah, The Lord Jesus, died as an expiatory offering on account of our sins. They caused his death; for them he shed his blood ; to make expiation for them, and to wipe them away, he expired on the cross. This passage is full proof that Christ did not die merely as a martyr, but that his death was to make atonement for sin. That he died as an atoning sacrifice, or as a vicarious offering, is here declared by Paul to be among the *first* things that he taught ; and the grand fundamental truth on which the church at Corinth had been founded, and by which it had been established, and by which they would be saved. It follows that there can be no true church, and no wellfounded hope of salvation, where the doctrine is not held that Christ died for sin. ¶ *According to the Scriptures.* The writings of the Old Testament ; Note, John v. 39. It is, of course, not certain to what parts of the Old Testament Paul here refers. He teaches simply that the doctrine is contained there that the Messiah would die for sin; and, in his preaching, he doubtless adduced and dwelt upon the particular places. *Some* of the places where this is taught are the following: Psa. xxii: Isa. liii; Dan. ix. 26; Zech. xii. 10; comp. Luke xxiv. 26, 46. See also Hengstenberg's Christology of the O. T. vol. i. pp. 187, 216, translated by Keith.

4. *And that he was buried.* That is, evidently according to the Scriptures; see Isa. liii. 9. ¶ *And that he rose again the third day,* &c. That is, that he should rise from the dead was foretold in the Scriptures. It is not of necessity implied that it was

predicted that he should rise *on the third day,* but that he should rise from the dead. See the argument for this stated in the discourse of Peter, in Acts ii. 24—32. The particular passage which is there urged in proof of his resurrection is derived from Ps. xvi.

5. *And that he was seen of Cephas.* Peter; Note, John i. 42. The resurrection of Christ was *a fact* to be proved, like all other facts, by competent and credible witnesses. Paul, therefore, appeals to the witnesses who had attested, or who yet lived to attest, the truth of the resurrection of the Lord Jesus ; and shows that it was not possible that so many witnesses should have been deceived. As this was not the first time in which the evidence had been stated to them, and as his purpose was merely to *remind* them of what they had heard and believed, he does not adduce *all* the witnesses to the event, but refers only to the more important ones. He does not, therefore, mention the woman to whom the Saviour first appeared, nor does he refer to *all* the times when the Lord Jesus manifested himself to his disciples. But he does not refer to them in *general* merely, but mentions *names,* and refers to persons who *were then alive,* who could attest the truth of the resurrection. It may be observed, also, that Paul observes probably the exact *order* in which the Lord Jesus appeared to the disciples, though he does not mention *all* the instances. For an account of the persons to whom the Lord Jesus appeared after his resurrection, and the order in which it was done, see Notes on the Gospels, vol. i. pp. 333—336. ¶ *Then of the twelve.* The apostles ; still called " the twelve," though Judas was not one of them. It was common to call the apostles " the twelve." Jesus appeared to the apostles at one time in the absence of Thomas (John xx. 19, 24); and also to them when Thomas was present, John xx. 24—29

above five hundred brethren at once; of whom the greater part remain unto this present, but some are fallen asleep.

Probably Paul here refers to the latter occasion, when all the surviving apostles were present.

6. *Above five hundred brethren at once.* More than five hundred Christians or followers of Jesus at one time. This was *probably* in Galilee, where the Lord Jesus had spent the greater part of his public ministry, and where he had made most disciples. The place, however, is not designated, and, of course, cannot be known. It is remarkable that this fact is omitted by all the evangelists; but why they should have omitted so remarkable a proof of the resurrection of the Lord Jesus, is unknown. There is a slight circumstance hinted at in Mat. xxviii. 10, which may throw some light on this passage. After his resurrection, Jesus said to the women who were at the sepulchre, " Go tell my brethren that they go into Galilee, and there shall they see me." And in ver. 16 it is said, " The eleven disciples went away into Galilee, into a mountain where Jesus had appointed them." Jesus had spent most of his public life in Galilee. He had made most of his disciples there. It was proper, therefore, that those disciples, who would, of course, hear of his death, should have some public confirmation of the fact that he had risen. It is very probable, also, that the eleven who went down into Galilee after he rose would apprize the brethren there of what had been said to them, that Jesus would meet them on a certain mountain; and it is morally certain that they who had followed him in so great numbers in Galilee would be drawn together by the report that the Lord Jesus, who had been put to death, was about to be seen there again alive. Such is human nature, and such was the attachment of these disciples to the Lord Jesus, that it is morally certain a large concourse would assemble on the slightest rumour that such an occurrence was to happen. Nothing more would be necessary anywhere to draw a concourse of people than a rumour that one who was dead would appear again; and in this instance, where they ardently loved him, and when, perhaps, many believed that he would rise, they would naturally assemble in great numbers to see him once more. One thing is proved by this, that the Lord Jesus had many more disciples than is generally supposed. If there were five hundred who could be assembled at once in a single part of the land where he had preached, there is every reason to suppose that there were many more in other parts of Judea. ¶ *The greater part remain unto this present.* Are now alive, and can be appealed to, in proof that they saw him. What more conclusive argument for the truth of his resurrection *could* there be than that five hundred persons had seen him, who had been intimately acquainted with him in his life, and who had become his followers? If the testimony of five hundred could not avail to prove his resurrection, no number of witnesses could. And if five hundred men could thus be deceived, any number could; and it would be impossible to substantiate *any* simple matter of fact by the testimony of eye-witnesses. ¶ *But some are fallen asleep.* Have died. This is the usual expression employed in the Scripture to describe the death of saints. It denotes, (1.) The calmness and peace with which they die, like sinking into a gentle sleep; (2.) The hope of a resurrection, as we sink to sleep with the expectation of again awaking: see Note, John xi. 11; 1 Cor. 11. 30.

7. *After that, he was seen of James.* This appearance is not recorded by the evangelists. It is mentioned in the fragment of the apocryphal gospel according to the Hebrews, which is, however, of no authority. It is probable that the Lord Jesus appeared often to the disciples, as he was forty days on earth after his resurrection, and the evangelists have only mentioned the more prominent instances, and enough to substantiate the fact of his resurrection. This

7 After that, he was seen of James ; then of all the apostles.

8 And last *a* of all, he was seen

a Acts 9.17.

of me also, as of [1] one born out of due time.

9 For I am the least *b* of the

1 or, *an abortive.* *b* Eph.3.7,8.

James, the fathers say, was James the Less, the brother or cousin-german of the Lord Jesus. The other James was dead (see Acts xii. 1) when this epistle was written. This James, the author of the epistle that bears his name, was stationed in Jerusalem. When Paul went there, after his return from Arabia, he had an interview with James (see Gal. i. 19, "But other of the apostles saw I none, save James the Lord's brother"), and it is highly probable that Paul would state to him the vision which he had of the Lord Jesus on his way to Damascus, and that James also would state to Paul the fact that *he* had seen him after he rose. This may be the reason why Paul here mentions the fact, because he had it from the lips of James himself. ¶ *Then of all the apostles.* By all the apostles. Perhaps the occasion at the sea of Galilee, recorded in John xxi. 14. Or it is possible that he frequently met the apostles assembled together, and that Paul means to say, that during the forty days after his resurrection he was often seen by them.

8. *And last of all.* After all the other times in which he appeared to men ; after he had ascended to heaven. This passage proves that the apostle Paul saw the same Lord Jesus, the same *body* which had been seen by the others, or else his assertion would be no proof that he was risen from the dead. It was not a fancy, therefore, that he had seen him ; it was not the work of imagination ; it was not even a *revelation* that he had risen ; it was a real *vision* of the ascended Redeemer. ¶ *He was seen of me also.* On the way to Damascus, see Acts ix. 3—6, 17. ¶ *As of one born out of due time.* Marg. Or, *an abortive.* Our translation, to most readers, probably, would not convey the real meaning of this place. The expression, "as of one born out of due time," would seem to imply that Paul meant

to say that there was some unfitness *as to the time* when he saw the Lord Jesus ; or that it was *too late* to have as clear and satisfactory a view of him as those had who saw him before his ascension. But this is by no means the idea in the passage. The word here used (ἔκτρωμα) properly means an abortion, one born prematurely. It is found no where else in the New Testament ; and here it means, as the following verse shows, one that was *exceedingly unworthy;* that was not worth regard ; that was unfit to be employed in the service of the Lord Jesus ; that had the same relation to that which was worthy of the apostolic office which an abortion has to a living child. The word occurs (in the Septuagint) in Job iii. 16 ; Eccl. vi. 3, as the translation of נֶפֶל, *nephel,* an abortion, or untimely birth. The expression seems to be proverbial, and to denote any thing that is vile, offensive, loathsome, unworthy, see Num. xii. 11. The word, I think, has no reference to the mode of *training* of the apostle, as if he had not had the same opportunity as the others had, and was therefore, compared with their advantages, like an untimely child compared with one that had come to maturity before its birth, as Bloomfield supposes ; nor does it refer to his diminutive stature, as Wetstein supposes ; but it means that he felt himself *vile,* guilty, unworthy, abominable as a persecutor, and as unworthy to be an apostle. The verse following shows that this is the sense in which the word is used.

9. *For.* A reason for the appellation which he had given to himself in ver. 8. ¶ *I am the least of the apostles.* Not on account of any defect in his commission, or any want of qualification to bear witness in what he saw, but on account of *the* great crime of his life, the fact that he had been a persecutor. Paul could never forget that ; as a man who has been profane

apostles, that am not meet to be called an apostle, because I persecuted the church of God.

10 But by the grace of God I am what I am: and his grace which *was bestowed* upon me was not in vain; but I laboured more abundantly than they all: yet not I, *a* but the grace of God which was with me.

a Matt.10.20.

and a scoffer, when he becomes converted, can never forget the deep guilt of his former life. The effect will be to produce humility, and a deep sense of unworthiness, ever onward. ¶ *Am not meet to be called an apostle.* Am not fit to be regarded as a follower of the Lord Jesus, and as appointed to defend his cause, and to bear his name among the Gentiles. Paul had a deep sense of his unworthiness; and the memory of his former life tended ever to keep him humble. Such should be, and such will be, the effect of the remembrance of a life of sin on those who become converted to the gospel, and especially if they are intrusted with the high office of the ministry, and occupy a station of importance in the church of God. ¶ *Because I persecuted the church of God;* see Acts ix. It is evident, however, that deeply as Paul might feel his unworthiness, and his unfitness to be called an apostle, yet that this did not render him an incompetent *witness* of what he had seen. He was unworthy; but he had no doubt that he had seen the Lord Jesus; and amidst all the expressions of his deep sense of his unfitness for his office, he never once intimates the slightest doubt that he had seen the Saviour. He felt himself fully qualified to testify to that; and with unwavering firmness he *did* testify to it to the end of life. A man may be deeply sensible that he is unworthy of an elevated station or office, and yet not the *less* qualified to be a witness. Humility does not disqualify a man to give testimony, but rather furnishes an additional qualification. There is no man to whom we listen more attentively, or whose words we more readily believe, than the modest and humble man,—the man who has had abundant opportunities to observe that of which he testifies, and yet who is deeply humble. Such a man was the apostle Paul; and

he evidently felt that, much as he felt his unworthiness, and ready as he was to confess it, yet his testimony on the subject of the resurrection of the Lord Jesus ought to have, and would have, great weight in the church at Corinth; comp. Note on Acts ix. 19.

10. *But by the grace of God I am what I am.* By the *favour* or mercy of God. What I have is to be traced to him, and not to any native tendency to goodness, or any native inclination to his service, or to any merit of my own. All my hopes of heaven; all my zeal; all my success; all my piety; all my apostolic endowments, are to be traced to him. Nothing is more common in the writings of Paul, than a disposition to trace all that he had to the *mere* mercy and grace of God. And nothing is a more certain indication of true piety than such a disposition. The reason why Paul *here* introduces the subject seems to be this. He had incidentally, and undesignedly, introduced a comparison *in one respect* between himself and the other apostles. He had not had the advantages which they had. Most of all, he was overwhelmed with the recollection that he had been a persecutor. He felt, therefore, that there was a peculiar obligation resting on him to make up by diligence for the want of their advantages of an early personal conversation with the Lord Jesus, and to express his gratitude that so great a sinner had been made an apostle. He, therefore, says, that he had not been idle. He had been enabled by the grace of God, to labour more than all the rest, and he had thus shown that he had not been insensible of his obligations. ¶ *But I laboured more abundantly,* &c. I was more diligent in preaching; I encountered more perils; I have exerted myself more. The records of his life, compared with the records of the other apostles, fully show this. ¶ *Yet*

11 Therefore whether *it were* I or they, so we preach, and so ye believed.

12 Now if Christ be preached

a Acts 26.8.

that he rose from the dead, how *a* say some among you that there is no resurrection of the dead?

13 But if *b* there be no resurrec-

b 1 Thess.4.14.

not I. I do not attribute it to myself. I would not boast of it. The *fact* is plain, and undeniable, that I *have* so laboured. But I would not attribute it to myself. I would not be proud or vain. I would remember my former state; would remember that I was a persecutor; would remember that all my disposition to labour, and all my ability, and all my success, are to be traced to the mere favour and mercy of God. So every man who has just views feels who has been favoured with success in the ministry. If a man has been successful as a preacher; if he has been self-denying, laborious, and the instrument of good, he cannot be insensible to the fact, and it would be foolish affectation to pretend ignorance of it. But he may feel that it is all owing to the mere mercy of God; and the effect will be to produce humility and gratitude, not pride and self-complacency.

11. *Therefore, whether* it were *I or they.* I or the other apostles. It is comparatively immaterial by whom it was done. The establishment of the truth is the great matter; and the question by whom it is done is one of secondary importance. ¶ *So we preach.* So we all preach. We all defend the same great doctrines; we all insist on the fact that the Lord Jesus died and rose; and this doctrine you all have believed. This doctrine is confirmed by *all* who preach; and this enters into the faith of *all* who believe. The design of Paul is to affirm that the doctrines which he here refers to were great, undeniable, and fundamental doctrines of Christianity; that they were proclaimed by *all* the ministers of the gospel, and believed by *all* Christians. They were, therefore, immensely important to all; and they must enter essentially into the hopes of all.

12. *Now if Christ,* &c. Paul, having (ver. 1—11) stated the *direct* evidence for the resurrection of the Lord Jesus, proceeds here to demonstrate that the dead would rise, by showing how it followed from the fact that the Lord Jesus had risen, and by showing what consequences would follow from denying it. The whole argument is based on the fact that the Lord Jesus had risen. If *that* was admitted, he shows that it *must* follow that his people would also rise. ¶ *Be preached.* The word *preached* here seems to include the idea of *so* preaching as to be believed; or so as to *demonstrate* that he did rise. If this was the doctrine on which the church was based, that the Lord Jesus rose from the dead, how could the resurrection of the dead be denied? ¶ *How say.* How can any say; how can it be maintained? ¶ *Some among you.* See the introduction to the chapter. Who these were is unknown. They may have been some of the philosophic Greeks, who spurned the doctrine of the resurrection (see Acts xvii. 32); or they may have been some followers of Sadducean teachers; or it may be that the Gnostic philosophy had corrupted them. It is most probable, I think, that the denial of the resurrection was the result of reasoning after the manner of the Greeks, and the effect of the introduction of philosophy into the church. This has been the fruitful source of most of the errors which have been introduced into the church. ¶ *That there is no resurrection of the dead.* That the dead cannot rise. How can it be held that there *can* be no resurrection, while yet it is admitted that Christ rose? The argument here is twofold. (1.) That Christ rose was one *instance* of a fact which demonstrated that there *had been* a resurrection, and of course that it was possible. (2.) That such was the connection between Christ and his people that the admission of this fact involved also the doc-

tion of the dead, then is Christ not risen.

14 And if *a* Christ be not risen,

a Acts 17.31.

then *is* our preaching vain, and your faith *is* also vain.

15 Yea, and we are found false

---

trine that all his people would also rise. This argument Paul states at length in the following verses. It was probably held by them that the resurrection was *impossible*. To all this, Paul answers in accordance with the principles of inductive philosophy as now understood, by demonstrating *a fact*, and showing that such an event *had* occurred, and that consequently all the difficulties were met. Facts are unanswerable demonstrations; and when a fact is established, all the obstacles and difficulties in the way must be admitted to be overcome. So philosophers now reason; and Paul, in accordance with these just principles, laboured simply to establish *the fact* that one had been raised, and thus met at once all the objections which could be urged against the doctrine. It would have been most in accordance with the philosophy of the Greeks to have gone into a metaphysical discussion to show that it was not impossible or absurd, and this might have been done. It was most in accordance with the principles of true philosophy, however, to establish *the fact* at once, and to argue *from* that, and thus to meet all the difficulties at once. The doctrine of the resurrection, therefore, does not rest on a metaphysical subtilty ; it does not depend on human reasoning ; it does not depend on analogy ; it rests just as the sciences of astronomy, chemistry, anatomy, botany, and natural philosophy do, *on well ascertained facts;* and it is now a well understood principle of all true science that no difficulty, no obstacle, no metaphysical subtilty; no embarrassment about being able to see HOW it is, is to be allowed to destroy the conviction in the mind which the facts are fitted to produce.

13. *But if there be no resurrection of the dead.* If the whole subject is held to be impossible and absurd, then it must follow that Christ is not risen, since there were the same difficulties in the way of raising him up which

will exist in any case. He was dead and was buried. He had lain in the grave three days. His human soul had left the body. His frame had become cold and stiff. The blood had ceased to circulate, and the lungs to heave. In his case there was the same difficulty in raising him up to life that there is in any other ; and if it is held to be impossible and absurd that the dead should rise, then it must follow that Christ has not been raised. This is the first consequence which Paul states as resulting from the denial of this doctrine, and this is inevitable. Paul thus shows them that the denial of the doctrine, or the maintaining the general proposition " that the dead would not rise," led also to the denial of the *fact* that the Lord Jesus had risen, and consequently to the denial of Christianity altogether, and the annihilation of all their hopes. There was, moreover, such a close connection between Christ and his people, that the resurrection of the Lord Jesus made their resurrection certain. See 1 Thess. iv. 14 ; see Note, John xiv. 19.

14. *And if Christ is not risen, then is our preaching vain.* Another consequence which must follow if it be held that there was no resurrection, and consequently that Christ was not risen. It would be vain and useless to preach. The substance of their preaching was that Christ was raised up ; and all their preaching was based on that. If that were not true, the whole system was false, and Christianity was an imposition. The word *vain* here seems to include the idea of useless, idle, false. It would be *false* to affirm that the Christian system was from heaven ; it would be useless to proclaim such a system, as it could save no one. ¶ *And your faith is also vain.* It is useless to believe. It can be of no advantage. If Christ was not raised, he was an impostor, since he repeatedly declared that he would rise (Mat. xvi. 21;

witnesses of God ; because we have testified of God that he raised up Christ: whom he raised not up, if so be that the dead rise not.

16 For if the dead rise not, then is not Christ raised:

17 And if Christ be not raised, your faith *a is* vain ; ye are yet in your sins.

18 Then they also which are fallen asleep in Christ are perished.

xviii. 22, 23 ; Luke ix. 22), and since the whole of his religion depended on that. The system could not be true unless Christ had been raised, as he said he would be ; and to believe a false system could be of no use to any man. The argument here is one addressed to all their feelings, their hopes, and their belief. It is drawn from all their convictions that the system was true. Were they, could they be prepared to admit a doctrine which involved the consequence that all the evidences which they had that the apostles preached the truth were delusive, and that all the evidences of the truth of Christianity which had affected their minds and won their hearts were false and deceptive? If they were not prepared for this, then it followed that they should not abandon or doubt the doctrine of the resurrection of the dead.

15. *Yea, and we are found.* We are ; or we shall be proved to be. It will follow, if the Lord Jesus was not raised up, that we have been false witnesses. ¶ *Of God.* Respecting God. It will be found that we have affirmed that which is not true of God ; or have said that he has done that which he has not done. Nothing could be regarded as a greater crime than this, whatever might be the immediate subject under consideration. To bear false witness of a man, or to say that a man has done what he has not done, is regarded as a grievous crime. How much more so to bear false testimony of God! ¶ *Because we have testified of God.* Or rather *against* God (κάτα τοῦ Θεοῦ). Our evidence has been *against* him. We have affirmed that which is not true ; and this is *against* God. It is implied here that it would be a *crime* to testify that God had raised up the Lord Jesus if he had not done it ; or that it

would be affirming that of God which would be *against* his character, or which it would be improper for him to do. This would be so, (1.) Because it would be wrong to bear *any* false witness of God, or to affirm that he had done what he had not done ; (2.) Because *if* the Lord Jesus had not been raised up, it would prove that he was an *impostor*, since he had declared that he would be raised up ; and to affirm of God that he had raised up an impostor would be *against* him, and would be highly dishonourable to him. ¶ *If the dead rise not.* If there is, and can be no resurrection. If this general proposition is true that there can be no resurrection, then it will apply to Christ as well as any others, and must prove that he did not rise. The *argument* in this verse is this. (1.) If it was denied that Christ was raised, it would prove that all the apostles were false witnesses of the worst character ; false witnesses against God. (2.) This the apostle seems to have presumed they *could not* believe. They had had too many evidences that they spoke the truth, they had seen their uniform respect *for* God, and desire to bear witness of him and in his favour ; they had had too conclusive evidence that they were inspired by him, and had the power of working miracles ; they were too fully convinced of their honesty, truth, and piety, ever to believe that they could be false witnesses against God. They had had ample opportunity to know whether God did raise up the Lord Jesus ; and they were witnesses who had no inducement to bear a false witness in the case.

16. *For if the dead rise not, &c.* This is a repetition of what is said in ver. 13. It is repeated here, evidently, because of its importance. It was a

great and momentous truth which would *bear* repetition, that if there was no resurrection, as some held, then it would follow that the Lord Jesus was not raised up.

17. *Your faith is vain,* ver. 14. The meaning of this passage here is, that their faith was vain, *because,* if Christ was not raised up, they were yet unpardoned sinners. The pardon of sin was connected with the belief of the resurrection of the Lord Jesus, and, if he was not raised, they were still in a state of sin. ¶ *Ye are yet in your sins.* Your sins are yet unpardoned. They can be forgiven only by faith in him, and by the efficacy of his blood. But if he was not raised, he was an impostor; and, of course, all your hopes of pardon by him, and through him, must be vain. The argument in this verse consists in an appeal to their Christian experience and their hopes. It may be thus expressed : (1.) You have reason to believe that your sins are forgiven. You cherish that belief on evidence that is satisfactory to you. But if Christ is not raised, that cannot be true. He was an impostor, and sins cannot be forgiven by him. As you are not, and cannot be prepared to admit that your sins are not forgiven, you cannot admit a doctrine which involves that. (2.) You have evidence that you are not under the dominion of sin. You have repented of it; have forsaken it ; and are leading a holy life. You know that, and cannot be induced to doubt this fact. But all that is to be traced to the doctrine that the Lord Jesus rose from the dead. It is only by believing that, and the doctrines which are connected with it, that the power of sin in the heart has been destroyed. And as you *cannot* doubt that under the influence of *that truth* you have been enabled to break off from your sins, so you cannot admit a doctrine which would involve it as a consequence that you are yet under the condemnation and the dominion of sin. You *must* believe, therefore, that the Lord Jesus rose ; and that, if he rose, others will also. This argument is good also now, just so far as there is

evidence that, through the belief of a risen Saviour, the dominion of sin has been broken ; and every Christian is, therefore, in an important sense, a witness of the resurrection of the Lord Jesus,—a living proof that a system which can work so great changes, and produce such evidence that sins are forgiven as are furnished in the conversion of sinners, must be from God ; and, of course, that the work of the Lord Jesus was accepted, and that he was raised up from the dead.

18. *Then they also,* &c. This verse contains a statement of another consequence which must follow from the denial of the resurrection—that all Christians who had died had failed of salvation, and were destroyed. ¶ *Which are fallen asleep in Christ.* Which have died as Christians ; Note, ver. 6 ; 1 Thess. iv. 15. ¶ *Are perished.* Are destroyed ; are not saved. They hoped to have been saved by the merits of the Lord Jesus ; they trusted to a risen Saviour, and fixed all their hopes of heaven there ; but if he did not rise, of course the whole system was delusion, and they have failed of heaven, and been destroyed. Their bodies lie in the grave, and return to their native dust without the prospect of a resurrection, and their souls are destroyed. The *argument* here is mainly an appeal to their feelings : " Can you believe it possible that the good men who have believed in the Lord Jesus are destroyed ? Can you believe that your best friends, your kindred, and your fellow Christians who have died, have gone down to perdition ? Can you believe that they will sink to woe with the impenitent, and the polluted, and abandoned ? If you *cannot,* then it must follow that they are saved. And then it will follow that you *cannot* embrace a doctrine which involves this consequence." And this argument is a sound one still. There are multitudes who are made good men by the gospel. They are holy, humble, self-denying, and prayerful friends of God. *They have become such by the belief of the death and resurrection of the Lord Jesus.* Can it be believed that they

19 If in this life only we have hope in Christ, we *a* are of all men most miserable.

a John 16.2; chap.4.13; 2 Tim.3.12.

20 But now is *b* Christ risen from the dead, *and* become the first-fruits *c* of them that slept.

b 1 Pet.1.3.	*c* Acts 26.23; Col.1.18; Rev.1.5.

will be destroyed? That they will perish with the profane, and licentious, and unprincipled? That they will go down to dwell with the polluted and the wicked? " Shall not the Judge of all the earth do right?" Gen. viii. 25. If it *cannot* be so believed, then they will be saved; and *if* saved it follows that the system is true which saves them, and, of course, that the Lord Jesus rose from the dead. We may remark here, that a denial of the truth of Christianity involves the belief that its friends will perish with others; that all their hopes are vain; and that their expectations are delusive. He, therefore, who becomes an infidel *believes* that his pious friends —his sainted father, his holy mother, his lovely Christian sister or child, is deluded and deceived; that they will sink down to the grave to rise no more; that their hopes of heaven will all vanish, and that they will be destroyed with the profane, the impure, and the sensual. And if infidelity demands *this* faith of its votaries, it is a system which strikes at the very happiness of social life, and at all our convictions of what is true and right. It is a system that is withering and blighting to the best hopes of men. *Can* it be believed that God will destroy those who are living to his honour; who are pure in heart, and lovely in life, *and who have been made such by the Christian religion?* If it cannot, then every man knows that Christianity *is not false,* and that infidelity IS NOT TRUE.

19. *If in this life only we have hope in Christ.* If our hope in Christ shall not be followed by the resurrection of the dead and future glory, and if all our hopes shall be disappointed. ¶ *We are,* &c. Doddridge, Macknight, Grotius, and some others, suppose that this refers to the apostles only, and that the sense is, that if there was no resurrection, they, of all men, would be most to be pitied, since they had exposed themselves to such a variety of dangers and trials, in which

nothing could sustain them but the hope of immortality. If they failed in that they failed in every thing. They were regarded as the most vile of the human family; they suffered more from persecution, poverty, and perils than other men; and if, after all, they were to be deprived of all their hopes, and disappointed in their expectation of the resurrection, their condition would be more deplorable than that of any other men. But there is no good reason for supposing that the word "we," here, is to be limited to the apostles. For, (1.) Paul had not mentioned the apostles particularly in the previous verses; and, (2.) The argument demands that it should be understood of all Christians, and the declaration is as true, substantially, of all Christians as it was of the apostles. ¶ *Of all men most miserable* More to be pitied or commiserated than any other class of men. The word here used (ἐλεεινότεροι) means, properly, more deserving of pity, more pitiable. It *may* mean sometimes, more wretched or unhappy; but this is not necessarily its meaning, nor is it its meaning here. It refers rather to their condition and hopes than to their personal feeling; and does not mean that Christians are unhappy, or that their religion does not produce comfort, but that their condition would be most deplorable; they would be more deserving of pity than any other class of men. This would be, (1.) Because no other men had so elevated hopes, and, of course, no others could experience so great disappointment. (2.) They were subjected to more trials than any other class of men. They were persecuted and reviled, and subjected to toil, and privation, and want, on account of their religion; and if, after all, they were to be disappointed, their condition was truly deplorable. (3.) They do not indulge in the pleasures of this life; they do not give themselves, as others do, to the enjoyments of this world. They voluntarily subject themselves to trial and self-denial; and if they are not admitted to eternal life, they are not only disappointed in this but they are cut off from the sources of happiness which their fellow-men enjoy in this world.—*Calvin.* (4.) On the whole, therefore, there would be disappointed hopes, and trials, and poverty, and want, and all for naught; and no condition could be conceived to be more deplorable than where a man was looking for eternal life, and for it subjecting himself to a life of want, and poverty, persecution, and tears, and should be finally disappointed. This passage, therefore, does not mean that virtue and piety are not attended with happiness; it does not mean that, even if there were no future state, a man would not be more happy if he walked in the paths of virtue than if he lived a life of sin; it does not mean that the Christian has no happiness in *religion itself*—in the love of God, and in prayer, and praise, and in purity of life. In all this he has enjoyment; and even if there were *no* heaven, a life of virtue and piety would be more happy than a life of sin. But it means that the condition of the Christian would be more *deplorable* than that of other men; he would be more to be pitied. All his high hopes would be disappointed. Other men have no such hopes to be dashed to the ground; and, of course, no other men would be such objects of pity and compassion. The *argument* in this verse is derived from the high hopes of the Christian. "Could they believe that all their hopes were to be frustrated? Could they subject themselves to all these trials and privations, without believing that they would rise from the dead? Were they prepared, by the denial of the doctrine of the resurrection, to put themselves in the condition of the most miserable and wretched of the human family—to *admit* that they were in a condition most to be deplored?

20. *But now is Christ risen,* &c. This language is the bursting forth of a full heart and of overpowering conviction. It would seem as if Paul were *impatient* of the slow process of argument; weary of meeting objec-

tions, and of stating the consequences of a denial of the doctrine; and longing to give utterance *to what he knew*, that Christ was risen from the dead. That was a point on which he was certain. He had seen him after he was risen; and he could no more doubt this fact than he could any other which he had witnessed with his own eyes. He makes, therefore, this strong affirmation; and in doing it, he at the same time affirms that the dead will also rise, since he had shown (ver. 12—18) that all the objection to the doctrine of the resurrection was removed by the *fact* that Christ had risen, and had shown that *his* resurrection involved the certainty that his people also would rise. There is peculiar force in the word " *now* " in this verse. The meaning may be thus expressed : " I have showed the consequences which would follow from the supposition that Christ was not raised up. I have shown how it would destroy all our hopes, plunge us into grief, annihilate our faith, make our preaching vain, and involve us in the belief that our pious friends have perished, and that we are yet in our sins. I have shown how it would produce the deepest disappointment and misery. *But* all this was mere supposition. There is no reason to apprehend any such consequences, or to be thus alarmed. *Christ* is *risen.* Of that there is no doubt. That is not to be called in question. It is established by irrefragable testimony; and *consequently* our hopes are not vain, our faith is not useless, our pious friends have not perished, and we shall not be disappointed." ¶ *And become the first-fruits.* The word rendered *first-fruits* (ἀπαρχὴ) occurs in the New Testament in the following places; Rom. viii. 23. (see Note on this place); xi. 16; xvi. 5; 1 Cor. xv. 20, 23; xvi. 15; James i. 18; Rev. xiv. 4. It occurs often in the LXX. as the translation of הלב‎, *ehlab, fat,* or fatness (Num. xviii. 12, 29, 30, 32); as the translation of מעשר‎, *moshar,* the tenth or tithe (Deut. xii. 6); of עון‎, *shoon,* iniquity (Num. xviii. 1); of ראשית‎, *rashith,* the beginning, the commencement, the first (Ex. xxiii. 19; Lev. xxiii. 10; Num. xv. 18, 19, &c.);

21 For *a* since by man *came* death, *b* by man *came* also the resurrection of the dead.

a Rom.5.12,17.   *b* John 11.25.

of תְּרוּמָה, *tharoomeh*, oblation, offering ; lifting up ; of that which is lifted up or waved as the first sheaf of the harvest, &c. Ex. xxv. 2, 3 ; xxxv. 5 ; Num. v. 9 ; xviii. 8, &c. The first-fruits, or the first sheaf of ripe grain, was required to be offered to the Lord, and was waved before him by the priest, as expressing the sense of gratitude by the husbandman, and his recognition of the fact that God had a right to all that he had ; Lev. xxiii. 10—14. The word, therefore, comes to have two senses, or to involve two ideas : (1.) That which is first, the beginning, or that which has the priority of time ; and, (2.) That which is a part and portion of the whole which is to follow, and which is the earnest or pledge of that ; as the first sheaf of ripe grain was not only *the first* in order of time, but was the earnest or pledge of the entire harvest which was soon to succeed. In allusion to this, Paul uses the word here. It was not merely or mainly that Christ was the first in order of time that rose from the dead, for Lazarus and the widow's son had been raised before him, but it was that he was chief in regard to the dignity, value, and importance of his rising ; he was connected with all that should rise, as the first sheaf of the harvest was with the crop ; he was *a part* of the mighty harvest of the resurrection, and his rising was *a portion* of that great rising, as the sheaf was a portion of the harvest itself; and he was so connected with them all, and their rising so depended on his, that his resurrection was a demonstration that they would rise. It may also be implied here, as Grotius and Schoettgen have remarked, that he is the first of those who were raised *so* as not to die again; and that, therefore, those raised by Elisha and by the Saviour himself do not come into the account. They all died again ; but the Saviour will not die, nor will those whom he will raise up in the resurrection die any more.

22 For as in Adam all die, even so in Christ shall all be made alive.

He is, therefore, the first of those that thus rise, and a portion of that great host which shall be raised to die no more. *May* there not be another idea? The first sheaf of the harvest was consecrated to God, and *then* all the harvest was regarded as consecrated to him. May it not be implied that, by the resurrection of the Lord Jesus, *all* those of whom he speaks are regarded as sacred to God, and as consecrated and accepted by the resurrection and acceptance of him who was the first-fruits? ¶ *Of them that slept.* Of the pious dead ; Note, ver. 6.

21, *For since by man came death.* By Adam, or by means of his transgression; see ver. 22. The sense is, evidently, that in consequence of the sin of Adam all men die, or are subjected to temporal death. Or, in other words, man would not have died had it not been for the crime of the first man ; see Note on Rom. v. 12. This passage may be regarded as proof that death would not have entered the world had it not been for transgression ; or, in other words, if man had not sinned, he would have remained immortal on the earth, or would have been translated to heaven, as Enoch and Elijah were, without seeing death. The apostle here, by "man," undoubtedly refers to Adam; but the particular and specific idea which he intends to insist on is, that, as death came by human nature, or by a human being, by a man, so it was important and proper that immortality, or freedom from death, should come in the same way, by one who was a man. Man introduced death ; man also would recover from death. The evil was introduced by one man ; the recovery would be by another. ¶ *By man* came *also.* By the Lord Jesus, the Son of God in human nature. The resurrection came by him, because he first rose—first of those who should not again die ; because he proclaimed the doctrine, and placed it on a firm foundation ; and because by his power the dead will be raised up. Thus he came to counteract the evils of the fall, and to restore man to more than his primeval dignity and honour. The resurrection through Christ will be with the assurance that all who are raised up by him shall never die again.

22. *For as in Adam* (ἐν τῷ 'Αδαμ). By Adam ; by the act, or by means of Adam; as a consequence of his act. His deed was the procuring cause, or the reason, why all are subjected to temporal death; see Gen. iii. 19. It does not mean that all men became actually dead when he sinned, for they had not then an existence; but it must mean that the death of all can be traced to him as the procuring cause, and that his act made it certain that all that came into the world would be mortal. The sentence which went forth against him (Gen. iii. 19) went forth against all; affected all; involved all in the certainty of death; as the sentence that was passed on the serpent (Gen. iii. 14) made it certain that all serpents would be " cursed above all cattle," and be prone upon the earth; the sentence that was passed upon the woman (Gen. iii. 16) made it certain that all women would be subjected to the same condition of suffering to which Eve was subjected; and the sentence that was passed on man (Gen. iii. 17) that he should cultivate the ground in sorrow all the days of his life, that it should bring forth thistles and thorns to him (ver. 18), that he should eat bread in the sweat of his brow (ver. 19), made it certain that this would be the condition of all men as well as of Adam. It was a blow at the head of the human family, and they were subjected to the same train of evils as he was himself. In like manner they were subjected to death. It was done in Adam, or *by* Adam, in the same way as it was in him, or by him, that they were subjected to toil and to the necessity of procuring food by the sweat of the brow; see Notes, Rom. v. 12—19; see ver. 47, 48. ¶ *All die.* All mankind are subjected to temporal death; or are mortal. This passage has been often adduced to prove that all mankind became sinful in Adam, or in

virtue of a covenant transaction with him; and that they are subjected to spiritual death as a punishment for his sins. But, whatever may be the truth on that subject, it is clear that *this* passage does not relate to it, and should not be adduced as a proof text. For, (1.) The words *die* and *dieth* obviously and usually refer to temporal death ; and they should be so understood, unless there is something in the connection which requires us to understand them in a figurative and metaphorical sense. But there is, evidently, no such necessity here. (2.) The context requires us to understand this as relating to temporal death. There is not here, as there is in Rom. v., any intimation that men became sinners in consequence of the transgression of Adam, nor does the course of the apostle's argument require him to make any statement on that subject. His argument has reference to the subject of temporal death, and the resurrection of the dead ; and not to the question in what way men became sinners. (3.) The whole of this argument relates to the *resurrection of the dead.* That is the main, the leading, the exclusive point. He is demonstrating that the dead would rise. He is showing how this would be done. It became, therefore, important for him to show in what way men were subjected to temporal death. His argument, therefore, requires him to make a statement *on that point,* and that only ; and to show that the resurrection by Christ was adapted to meet and overcome the evils of the death to which men were subjected by the sin of the first man. In Rom. v. the design of Paul is to prove that the effects of the work of Christ were more than sufficient to meet ALL the evils introduced by the sin of Adam. This leads him to an examination *there* of the question in what way men became sinners. *Here* the design is to show that the work of Christ is adapted to overcome the evils of the sin of Adam *in one specific matter—the matter under discussion, i. e.* on the point of the resurrection ; and his argument therefore requires him to show *only* that temporal death, or mortality, was introduced by the first man, and that this has been counteracted by the second; and to this specific point the interpretation of this passage should be confined. Nothing is more important in interpreting the Bible than to ascertain the specific point in the argument of a writer to be defended or illustrated, and *then* to confine the interpretation to that. The argument of the apostle here is ample to prove that all men are subjected to temporal death by the sin of Adam; and that this evil is counteracted fully by the resurrection of Christ, and the resurrection through him. And to this point the passage should be limited. (4.) If this passage means, that in Adam, or by him, all men became sinners, then the correspondent declaration " all shall be made alive" must mean that all men shall become righteous, or that all shall be saved. This would be the natural and obvious interpretation; since the words " be made alive" must have reference to the words " all die," and must affirm the co-relative and opposite fact. If the phrase " all die" there means all become sinners, then the phrase " all be made alive" must mean all shall be made holy, or be recovered from their spiritual death; and thus an *obvious* argument is furnished for the doctrine of universal salvation, which it is difficult, if not impossible, to meet. It is not a sufficient answer to this to say, that the word " all," in the latter part of the sentence, means all the elect, or all the righteous; for its most natural and obvious meaning is, that it is co-extensive with the word "all" in the former part of the verse. And although it has been held by many who suppose that the passage refers only to the resurrection of the dead, that it means that all the righteous shall be raised up, or all who are given to Christ, yet that interpretation is not the obvious one, nor is it yet sufficiently clear to make it the basis of an argument, or to meet the strong argument which the advocate of universal salvation will derive from the former interpretation of the passage. It *is* true *literally* that ALL the dead will rise; it is *not* true literally that

all who became mortal, or became sinners by means of Adam, will be saved. And it must be held as a great principle, that this passage is *not* to be so interpreted as to teach the doctrine of the salvation of all men. At least, this may be adopted as a principle in the argument with those who adduce it to prove that all men became sinners by the transgression of Adam. This passage, therefore, should not be adduced in proof of the doctrine of imputation, or as relating to the question how men became sinners, but should be limited to the subject that was immediately under discussion in the argument of the apostle. *That object was, to show that the doctrine of the resurrection by Christ was such as to meet the obvious doctrine that men became mortal by Adam; or that the one was adapted to counteract the other.* ¶ *Even so* (οὕτω.) In this manner; referring not merely to the certainty of the event, but to the mode or manner. As the death of all was occasioned by the sin of one, even so, in like manner, the resurrection of all shall be produced by one. His resurrection shall meet and counteract the evils introduced by the other, so far as the subject under discussion is concerned; that is, so far as relates to temporal death. ¶ *In Christ.* By Christ; in virtue of him; or as the result of his death and resurrection. Many commentators have supposed that the word " all" here refers only to believers, meaning all who were united to Christ, or all who were his friends; all included in a covenant with him; as the word " all" in the former member of the sentence means all who were included in the covenant with Adam; that is, all mankind. But to this view there are manifest objections. (1.) It is not the *obvious* sense; it is not that which will occur to the great mass of men who interpret the Scriptures on the principles of common sense; it is an interpretation which is to be *made out* by reasoning and by theology—always a suspicious circumstance in interpreting the Bible. (2.) It is not necessary. All the wicked will be raised up from the dead as well as all the righteous. Dan. xii.

23 But *a* every man in his own order; Christ the first-fruits; after-

ward they that are Christ's at his coming.

a 1 Thess.4.15—17.

2; John v. 28, 29. (3.) The form of the passage requires us to understand the word "all" in the same sense in both members, unless there be some indispensable necessity for limiting the one or the other. (4.) The argument of the apostle requires this. For his object is to show that the effect of the sin of Adam, by introducing *temporal* death, will be counteracted by Christ in raising up all who die; which would not be shown if the apostle meant to say that only *a part* of those who had died in consequence of the sin of Adam would be raised up. The argument would then be inconclusive. But now it is complete if it be shown that *all* shall be raised up, whatever may become of them afterwards. The sceptre of death shall be broken, and his dominion destroyed, by the fact that ALL shall be raised up from the dead. ¶ *Be made alive.* Be raised from the dead; be made alive, in a sense contradistinguished from that in which he here says they were subjected to death, by Adam. If it should be held that *that* means that all were made sinners by him, then this means, as has been observed, that all shall be made righteous, and the doctrine of universal salvation has an unanswerable argument; if it means, as it obviously does, that all were subjected to temporal death by him, then it means that all shall be raised from the dead by Christ.

[That the whole human family, in consequence of the sin of Adam, are subjected not only to temporal but to spiritual and eternal death, is without doubt a doctrine of scripture. As much is comprehended in the original sentence, Gen. ii. 17, which involved not Adam only but his posterity also. See the Supplementary Notes on Rom. v. 12. In this place, however, the apostle certainly *does* speak *especially*, if not *exclusively*, of temporal death. The scope of the passage demands this admission. Yet it by no means follows, that the text "ought not to be adduced in proof of the doctrine of imputation." Of that doctrine it is strong proof; "In Adam all die," or are subjected to natural death. Now, if all are visited with penal evil—with death through Adam, does not this involve the imputation of

his guilt? It will not do to say that each sins *personally*, and therefore dies; for infants die, and all men come into the world under the necessity of dying. The infliction of the punishment *prior* to all personal guilt, proves, that the cause of it must be sought higher, viz. in the imputation of Adam's guilt. See the Supplementary Notes on Rom. v.

As to the question, whether the "all" in the latter clause of the verse be co-extensive with the "all" in the former: although the author has very ingeniously argued that it must be so regarded, there is this insuperable objection to his whole theory, that the apostle *does not once speak of the resurrection of the wicked* in this chapter. In the very next verse he speaks of "them *that are Christ's* at his coming," and then goes on to show the glory of the *saints'* resurrection body, and concludes in such a strain of triumph as plainly confines the whole discourse to the case of the righteous. *Their* resurrection is the specific point of which the apostle is treating, and the author should have remembered his own excellent canon, that *to this* the interpretation of a passage should be confined. Besides it will occur to any one on reading the passage, that the resurrection here referred to is throughout spoken of as a *vast benefit*, secured by the mediation of Christ. "The design," says the commentator, "is to show that the work of Christ is adapted to overcome the evils of the sin of Adam in one specific matter, *i. e.* on the point of the resurrection. His argument, therefore, requires the apostle to show *only* that temporal death introduced by the first man has been counteracted by the second." But where is the *benefit* to them who rise "to shame and everlasting contempt?" And what kind of counteraction of evil is this? The *evils of the sin of Adam* would be *mitigated* to the wicked, if rather they were allowed to slumber in the grave for ever. To them annihilation would comparatively be a benefit. Their resurrection on the other hand *would counteract no evil* but inconceivably increase, and eternally perpetuate whatever comes under that name. The "all" in the last clause, therefore, must be taken in a restricted sense, embracing the righteous only. The verse is to be explained on the principle of representation. Adam and Christ are the heads of their respective covenants. All represented by the one die in him, and all represented by the other live in him. It is on the same principle that Rom. v. 15, is to be interpreted. See the Supplementary Note there. Finally, it is obvious, that the text thus explained can give no encouragement to the doctrine of universal salvation whatever.

24 Then *cometh* the end, when he shall have delivered up the kingdom *a* to God, even the Fa-

a Dan.7.14,27.

Bulroth has this excellent Note on the verse: "The previous comparison ὥσπερ ἐν τῷ Ἀδαμ παντες ἀποθνησκουσιν forbids the supposition. (*i. e.* that the παντες includes also unbelievers). In Adam all die, ἐφ ᾧ παντες ἡμαρτον. Rom. v. 12; but in Christ only those can live and rise who are justified through him, and this none are without faith in him. That Paul taught also a resurrection of the ἀδιϰοι to judgment, is clear from other parts of scripture, Acts xxiv. 15, but it is not to that he is referring here."

23. *But every man.* Every one, including Christ as well as others. ¶ *In his own order.* In his proper order, rank, place, time. The word τάγμα usually relates to military order or array; to the arrangement of a cohort, or band of troops; to their being properly marshalled with the officers at the head, and every man in his proper place in the ranks. Here it means that there was a proper *order* to be observed in the resurrection of the dead. And the design of the apostle is, probably, to counteract the idea that the resurrection was passed already, or that there was no future resurrection to be expected. The *order* which is here referred to is, doubtless, mainly that of *time:* meaning that Christ would be first, and then that the others would follow. But it also means that Christ would be first, because it was *proper* that he should be first. He was first in rank, in dignity, and in honour; he was the leader of all others, and their resurrection depended on his. And as it was proper that a leader or commander should have the first place in a march, or in an enterprise involving peril or glory, so it was proper that Christ should be first in the resurrection, and that the others should follow on in due order and time. ¶ *Christ the first-fruits.* Christ first in time, and the pledge that they should rise; see Note on ver. 20. ¶ *Afterward.* After he has risen. Not before, because their resurrection depended on him. ¶ *They that are Christ's.* They who are Chris-

ther; when he shall have put down all rule and all authority and power.

tians. The apostle, though in ver. 22 he had stated the truth that *all* the dead would rise, yet here only mentions Christians, because to them only would the doctrine be of any consolation, and because it was to them particularly that this whole argument was directed. ¶ *At his coming.* When he shall come to judge the world, and to receive his people to himself. This proves that the dead will not be raised until Christ shall re-appear. He shall come for that purpose; and he shall assemble all the dead, and shall take his people to himself; see Matt. xxv. And this declaration fully met the opinion of those who held that the resurrection was past already; see 2 Tim. ii. 18.

24. *Then* cometh *the end.* Then is the end; or then is the consummation. It does not mean that the end, or consummation is to *follow* that event; but that this *will be* the ending, the winding up, the consummation of the affairs under the mediatorial reign of Christ. The word *end* (τέλος) denotes properly a limit, termination, completion of any thing. The proper and obvious meaning of the word here is, that then shall be the end or completion of the work of redemption. That shall have been done which was intended to be done by the incarnation and the work of the atonement; the race shall be redeemed; the friends of God shall be completely recovered; and the administration of the affairs of the universe shall be conducted as they were before the incarnation of the Redeemer. Some understand the word "end" here, however, as a metaphor, meaning "the *last,* or the rest of the dead;" but this is a forced and improbable interpretation. The word *end* here may refer to the end of human affairs, or the end of the kingdoms of this world, or it may refer to the ends of the mediatorial kingdom of the Redeemer; the consummation of his peculiar reign and work result-

ing in the surrender of the kingdom to the Father. The connection demands the *last* interpretation, though this involves also the former. ¶ *When he shall have delivered up* (παραδῷ). This word means properly to give *near*, *with*, or *to* any one; to give over, to deliver up.—*Robinson*. It is applied to the act of delivering up *persons* to the power or authority of others, as *e. g.* to magistrates for trial, and condemnation, (Mat. v. 25; Mark xv. 1; Luke xx. 20); to lictors, or soldiers, for punishment (Mat. xviii. 24); or to one's enemies, Mat. xxvi. 15. It is applied also to persons or things delivered over or surrendered to do or suffer any thing, Acts xv. 26; 1 Cor. xiii. 3; Eph. iv. 19. It is also applied to persons or things delivered over to the care, charge, or supervision of any one, in the sense of giving up, intrusting, committing, Mat. xi. 27; xxv. 14; Luke iv. 6, 10, 22. Here the obvious sense is that of surrendering, giving back, delivering up, rendering up that which had been received, implying that an important trust had been received, which was now to be rendered back. And according to this interpretation, it means, (1.) That the Lord Jesus had received or been intrusted with an important power or office as mediator : comp. Note, Mat. xviii. 18. (2.) That he had executed the purpose implied in that trust or commission; and, (3.) That he was now rendering back to God that office or authority which he had received at his hands. As the work had been accomplished which had been contemplated in his design; as there would be no further necessity for mediation when redemption should have been made, and his church recovered from sin and brought to glory; there would be no further need of that *peculiar* arrangement which had been implied in the work of redemption, and, of course, all the intrustment of power involved in that would be again restored to the hands of God. The idea, says Grotius, is, that he would deliver up the kingdom as the governors of provinces render again or deliver up their commission and authority to the Cæsars who appointed

them. There is no absurdity in this view. For *if* the world was to be redeemed, it was necessary that the Redeemer should be intrusted with power sufficient for his work. When that work was done, and there was no further need of that peculiar exercise of power, then it would be proper that it should be restored, or that the government of God should be administered as it was before the work of redemption was undertaken; that the Divinity, or the Godhead, as *such*, should preside over the destinies of the universe. Of course, it will not follow that the Second Person of the Trinity will surrender *all* power, or *cease* to exercise government. It will be that power only which he had *as* Mediator; and whatever part in the administration of the government of the universe he shared as Divine before the incarnation, he will *still* share, with the additional *glory* and *honour* of having redeemed a world by his death. ¶ *The kingdom.* This word means properly dominion, reign, the exercise of kingly power. In the New Testament it means commonly the reign of the Messiah, or the dominion which God would exercise through the Messiah; the reign of God over men by the laws and institutions of the Messiah; see Note, Mat. iii. 2. Here it means, I think, evidently, dominion in general. It cannot denote the peculiar administration over the world involved in the work of mediation, for that will be ended; but it means that the empire, the sovereignty, shall have been delivered up to God. His enemies shall have been subdued. His power shall have been asserted. The authority of God shall have been established, and the kingdom, or the dominion, shall be in the hands of God himself; and he shall reign, not in the peculiar form which existed in the work of mediation, but absolutely, and as he did over obedient minds before the incarnation. ¶ *To God.* To God *as* God; to the Divinity. The Mediator shall have given up the peculiar power and rule as Mediator, and it shall be exercised by God as God. ¶ *Even the Father.* And (καὶ) the Father. The word *Father*, as applied to God in the Scriptures, is used in two senses—to designate *the* Father, the first person of the Trinity as distinguished from the Son; and in a broader, wider sense, to denote God as sustaining the relation of a Father to his creatures; as the Father of all. Instances of this use are too numerous to be here particularly referred to. It is in this latter sense, perhaps, that the word is used here—not to denote that the second person of the Trinity is to surrender all power into the hands of the first, or that he is to cease to exercise dominion and control; but that the power is to be yielded into the hands of God *as* God, *i. e.* as the universal Father, as the Divinity, without being exercised in any peculiar and special manner by the different persons of the Godhead, as had been done in the work of redemption. At the close of the work of redemption this *peculiar* arrangement would cease; and God, *as* the universal Father and Ruler of all, would exercise the government of the world; see, however, Note on ver. 28. ¶ *When he shall have put down.* When he shall have *abolished*, or brought to naught, all that opposed the reign of God. ¶ *All rule,* &c. All those mighty powers that opposed God and resisted his reign. The words here used do not seem intended to denote the several departments or forms of opposition, but to be general terms, meaning that whatever opposed God should be subdued. They include, of course, the kingdoms of this world; the sins, pride, and corruption of the human heart; the powers of darkness—the spiritual dominions that oppose God on earth, and in hell; and death and the grave. All shall be completely subdued, and cease to interpose any obstacles to the advancement of his kingdom and to his universal reign. A monarch reigns when all his enemies are subdued or destroyed; or when they are prevented from opposing his will, even though all should not voluntarily submit to his will. The following remarks of Prof. Bush present a plausible and ingenious view of this difficult passage, and they are, therefore, subjoined here. "If the opinion of the eminent critic, Storr, may be admitted, that the kingdom here said to be delivered up to the Father is *not* the kingdom of Christ, but the rule and dominion of all adverse powers—an opinion rendered very probable by the following words: "when he shall have *put down* (Gr. done away, abolished) all rule, and all authority and power,"—and ver. 25, "till he hath put all *enemies* under his feet" —then is the passage of identical import with Rev. xi. 15, referring to precisely the same period: " And the seventh angel sounded; and there were great voices in heaven, saying, The kingdoms of the world are become the kingdoms of our Lord and of his Christ; and he shall reign for ever and ever. It is, therefore, we conceive, but a peculiar mode of denoting the *transfer,* the *making over* of the kingdoms of this world from their former despotic and antichristian rulers to the sovereignty of Jesus Christ, the appointed heir and head of all things, whose kingdom is to be everlasting. If this interpretation be correct, we are prepared to advance a step farther, and suggest that the phrase, *he shall have delivered up* (Greek, παραδῷ), be understood as an instance of the idiom in which the verb is used without any personal nominative, but has reference to the *purpose of God as expressed in the Scriptures;* so that the passage may be read, " Then cometh the end (*i. e.* not the close, the final winding up, but the perfect developement, expansion, completion, consummation of the divine plans in regard to this world), when the prophetic announcements of the Scriptures require the delivering up (*i. e.* the making over) of all adverse dominion into the hands of the Messiah, to whose supremacy we are taught to expect that every thing will finally be made subject." — *Illustrations of Scripture.* A more extended examination of this difficult passage may be seen in Storr's Opuscula, vol. i, pp. 274—282. See also Biblical Repository, vol. iii. pp. 748—755.

25 For he *a* must reign, till he hath put all enemies under his feet.

26 The last enemy *that* shall be destroyed *b* *is* death.

27 For he *c* hath put all things

a Ps.2.6-10; 45.3-6; 110.1; Eph.1.22; Heb.1.13.

b Hos.13.14; 2 Tim.1.10; Rev.20.14.   *c* Ps.8.6.

25. *For he must reign.* It is fit, or proper (δεῖ), that he should reign till this is accomplished. It is proper that the mediatorial kingdom should continue till this great work is effected. The word "must" here refers to the propriety of this continuance of his reign, and to the fact that this was contemplated and predicted as the work which he would accomplish. He came to subdue all his enemies; see Ps. ii. 6—10; or Ps. cx. 1, "The Lord said unto my Lord, Sit thou at my right hand until I make thine enemies thy footstool." Paul, doubtless, had this passage in his eye as affirming the necessity that he should reign until all his foes should be subdued. That this refers to the Messiah is abundantly clear from Mat. xxii. 44, 45.

26. *The last enemy* that *shall be destroyed* is *death.* The other foes of God should be subdued *before* the final resurrection. The enmity of the human heart should be subdued by the triumphs of the gospel. The sceptre of Satan should be broken and wrested from him. The false systems of religion that had tyrannized over men should be destroyed. The gospel should have spread everywhere, and the world be converted to God. And nothing should remain but to *subdue* or destroy death, and that would be by the resurrection. It would be, (1.) Because the resurrection would be a *triumph* over death, showing that there was one of greater power, and that the sceptre would be wrested from the hands of death. (2.) Because death would cease to reign. No more would ever die. All that should be raised up would live for ever; and the effects of sin and rebellion in this world would be thus for ever ended, and the kingdom of God restored. Death is here personified as a tyrant, exercising despotic power over the human race; and *he* is to be subdued.

27. *For he hath put.* God has put by promise, purpose, or decree. ¶ *All things under his feet.* He has made all things subject to him; or has appointed him to be head over all things; comp. Mat. xxviii. 18; John xvii. 2; Eph. i. 20—22. It is evident that Paul here refers to some promise or prediction respecting the Messiah, though he does not expressly quote any passage, or make it certain to what he refers. The *words* "hath put all things under his feet" are found in Ps. viii. 6, as applicable to *man,* and as designed to show the dignity and dominion of man. Whether the psalm has any reference to the Messiah, has been made a question. Those who are disposed to see an examination of this question, may find it in Stuart on the Hebrews, on chap. ii. 6—8; and in Excurses ix. of the same work, pp. 568—570. Ed. 1833. In the passage before us, it is not *necessary* to suppose that Paul meant to say that the psalm had a particular reference to the Messiah. All that is implied is, that it was the intention of God to subdue all things to him; this was the general strain of the prophecies in regard to him; this was the purpose of God; and this idea is accurately expressed in the words of the psalm; or these words will convey the *general sense* of the prophetic writings in regard to the Messiah. It may be true, also, that although the passage in Ps. viii. has no immediate and direct reference to the Messiah, yet it *includes* him as one who possessed human nature. The psalm may be understood as affirming that all things were subjected to *human nature; i. e.* human nature had dominion and control over all. But this was more particularly and eminently true of the Messiah than of any other man. In all other cases, great as was the dignity of man, yet his control over "all things" was limited and partial. In the Messiah

under his feet. But when he saith, All things are put under *him ; it is* manifest that he is excepted which did put all things under him.

28 And when all things shall be

---

it was to be complete and entire. His dominion, therefore, was a complete *fulfilment, i. e. filling up* (πλή-ρωμα) of the words in the psalm. Under him alone was there to be an entire accomplishment of what is there said; and as that psalm was to be fulfilled, as it was to be true that it might be said of man that all things were subject to him, it was to be fulfilled mainly in the person of the Messiah, whose human nature was to be exalted above all things; comp. Heb. ii. 6—9. ¶ *But when he saith.* When God says, or when it is said; when that promise is made respecting the Messiah. ¶ *It is manifest.* It must be so; it must be so understood and interpreted. ¶ *That he is excepted,* &c. That God is excepted; that it cannot mean that the appointing power is to be subject to him. Paul may have made this remark for several reasons. Perhaps, (1.) To avoid the possibility of cavil, or misconstruction of the phrase, "all things," as if it meant that God would be included, and would be subdued to him; as among the heathen, Jupiter is fabled to have expelled his father Saturn from his throne and from heaven. (2.) It might be to prevent the supposition, from what Paul had said of the extent of the Son's dominion, that he was in any respect superior to the Father. It is implied by this exception here, that when the necessity for the peculiar mediatorial kingdom of the Son should cease, there would be a resuming of the authority and dominion of the Father, in the manner in which it subsisted before the incarnation. (3.) The expression may also be regarded as intensive or emphatic; as denoting, in the most absolute sense, that there was *nothing* in the universe, but God, which was not subject to him. God was the *only* exception; and his dominion, therefore, was absolute over all other beings and things.

28. *And when,* &c. In this future time, when this shall be accomplished. This implies that the time has not yet arrived, and that his dominion is now exercised, and that he is carrying forward his plans for the subjugation of all things to God. ¶ *Shall be subdued unto him.* Shall be brought under subjection. When all his enemies shall be overcome and destroyed; or when the hearts of the redeemed shall be entirely subject to God. When God's kingdom shall be fully established over the universe. It shall then be seen that he is Lord of all. In the previous verses he had spoken of the promise that all things should be subjected to God; in this, he speaks of its being actually done. ¶ *Then shall the Son also himself be subject,* &c. It has been proposed to render this, "*even then* shall the Son," &c.; implying that he *had* been all along subject to God; had acted under his authority; and that this subjection would continue *even then* in a sense similar to that in which it had existed; and that Christ would *then* continue to exercise a delegated authority over his people and kingdom. See an article "on the duration of Christ's kingdom," by Prof. Mills, in Bib. Rep. vol. iii. p. 748, seq. But to this interpretation there are objections. (1.) It is not the obvious interpretation. (2.) It does not seem to comport with the design and scope of the passage, which most evidently refers to some change, or rendering back of the authority of the Messiah; or to some resumption of authority by the Divinity, or by God as God, in a different sense from what existed under the Messiah. (3.) Such a statement would be unnecessary and vain. Who could reasonably doubt that the Son would be as much subject to God when all things had been subdued to him as he was before? (4.) It is not necessary to suppose this in order to reconcile the passage with what is said of the perpetuity of

subdued *a* unto him, then shall the
Son also himself be subject unto

him *b* that put all things under
him, that God may be all in all.

a Phil.3.21.

b chap.11.3.

Christ's kingdom and his eternal
reign. That he would reign; that
his kingdom would be perpetual, and
that it would be unending, was indeed
clearly predicted; see 2 Sam. vii. 16;
Ps. xlv. 6; Isa. ix. 6, 7; Dan. ii. 44;
vii. 14; Luke i. 22, 23; Heb. i. 8.
But these predictions may be all
accomplished on the supposition that
the peculiar mediatorial kingdom of
the Messiah shall be given up to God,
and that he shall be subject to him.
For, (*a*) His kingdom will be perpetual, in contradistinction from the
kingdoms of this world. They are
fluctuating, changing, short in their
duration. His shall not cease, and
shall continue to the end of time.
(*b*) His kingdom shall be perpetual,
because those who are brought under
the laws of God by him shall remain
subject to those laws for ever. The
sceptre never shall be broken, and the
kingdom shall abide to all eternity.
(*c*) Christ, the Son of God, in his
divine nature, *as God*, shall never
cease to reign. As Mediator, he may
resign his commission and his *peculiar*
office, having made an atonement,
having recovered his people, having
protected and guided them to heaven.
Yet as one with the Father; as the
"Father of the everlasting age" (Isa.
ix. 6), he shall not cease to reign.
The functions of a peculiar office may
have been discharged, and delegated
power laid down, and that which
appropriately belongs to him in virtue
of his own nature and relations may
be resumed and executed for ever;
and it shall still be true that the reign
of the Son of God, in union, or in
oneness with the Father, shall continue for ever. (5.) The interpretation which affirms that the Son shall
then be subject to the Father in the
sense of laying down his delegated
authority, and ceasing to exercise his
mediatorial reign, has been the common interpretation of all times. This
remark is of value only, because, in
the interpretation of plain words, it

is not probable that men of all classes
and ranks in different ages would err.
¶ *The Son also himself.* The term
" Son of God" is applied to the Lord
Jesus with reference to his human
nature, his incarnation by the Holy
Ghost, and his resurrection from the
dead; see Note on Rom. i. 4. [For
the evidence of the eternal sonship,
see the supplementary Note on the
same passage.] It refers, I apprehend, to that in this place. It does
not mean that the second person in
the Trinity, as such, should be subject to the first; but it means the
Incarnate Son, the Mediator,—the
man that was born and that was
raised from the dead, and to whom
this wide dominion had been given,—
should resign that dominion, and that
the government should be re-assumed
by the Divinity *as* God. As man,
he shall cease to exercise any distinct
dominion. This does not mean, evidently, that the union of the divine and
human nature will be dissolved; nor
that important purposes may not be
answered by that continued union for
ever; nor that the divine perfections
may not shine forth in some glorious
way through the man Christ Jesus;
but that *the purpose of government*
shall no longer be exercised in that
way; the mediatorial kingdom, as
such, shall no longer be continued,
and power shall be exercised by God
as God. The redeemed will still
adore their Redeemer as their incarnate God, and dwell upon the remembrance of his work and upon his perfections (Rev. i. 5, 6; v. 12; xi. 15);
but not as exercising the peculiar
power which he now has, and which
was needful to effect their redemption.
¶ *That God may be all in all.* That
God may be SUPREME; that the Divinity, the Godhead, may rule; and
that it may be seen that he is the
Sovereign over all the universe. By
the word " God" (*ὁ Θεὸς*), Whitby and
Hammond, I think correctly, understand the Godhead, the Divine Na-

29 Else what shall they do which | *a* are baptized for the dead, if the

a Rom.6 3,4.

ture, the Divinity, consisting of the three persons, without respect to any peculiar office or kingdom.

29. *Else what shall they do, &c.* The apostle here resumes the argument for the resurrection which was interrupted at ver. 19. He goes on to state further consequences which must follow from the denial of this doctrine, and thence infers that the doctrine must be true. There is, perhaps, no passage of the New Testament in respect to which there has been a greater variety of interpretation than this ; and the views of expositors now by no means harmonize in regard to its meaning. It is possible that Paul may here refer to some practice or custom which existed in his time respecting baptism, the knowledge of which is now lost. The various opinions which have been entertained in regard to this passage, together with an examination of them, may be seen in Pool's Synopsis, Rosenmüller, and Bloomfield. It may be not useless just to refer to some of them, that the perplexity of commentators may be seen. (1.) It has been held by some that by "the dead" here is meant the Messiah who was put to death, the plural being used for the singular, meaning "the dead one." (2.) By others, that the word baptized here is taken in the sense of washing, cleansing, purifying, as in Mat. viii. 4 ; Heb. ix. 10; and that the sense is, that the dead were carefully washed and purified when buried, with the hope of the resurrection, and, as it were, preparatory to that. (3.) By others, that to be baptized for the dead means to be baptised *as* dead, being baptized into Christ, and buried with him in baptism, and that by their immersion they were regarded *as* dead. (4.) By others, that the apostle refers to a custom of vicarious baptism, or being baptized for those who were dead, referring to the practice of having some person baptized in the place of one who had died without baptism. This was the opinion of

Grotius, Michaelis, Tertullian, and Ambrose. Such was the estimate which was formed, it is supposed, of the importance of baptism, that when one had died without being baptized, some other person was baptized over his dead body in his place. That this custom prevailed in the church *after* the time of Paul, has been abundantly proved by Grotius, and is generally admitted. But the objections to this interpretation are obvious. (*a*) There is *no* evidence that such a custom prevailed in the time of Paul. (*b*) It cannot be believed that Paul would give countenance to a custom so senseless and so contrary to the Scripture, or that he would make it the foundation of a solemn argument. (*c*) It does not accord with the strain and purpose of his argument. If *this* custom had been referred to, his design would have led him to say, " What will become of them *for whom* others have been baptized ? Are we to believe that they have perished?" (*d*) It is far more probable that the custom referred to in this opinion arose from an erroneous interpretation of this passage of Scripture, than that it existed in the time of Paul. (5.) There remain two other opinions, both of which are plausible, and one of which is probably the true one. One is, that the word *baptized* is used here as it is in Mat. xx. 22, 23 ; Mark x. 39; Luke xii. 50, in the sense of being overwhelmed with calamities, trials, and sufferings ; and as meaning that the apostles and others were subjected to great trials on account of the dead, *i. e.* in the hope of the resurrection ; or with the expectation that the dead would rise. This is the opinion of Lightfoot, Rosenmüller, Pearce, Homberg, Krause, and of Prof. Robinson (Lex. art. Βαπτίζω), and has much that is plausible. That the word is thus used to denote a deep sinking into calamities, there can be no doubt. And that the apostles and early Christians subjected themselves, or were subjected to great and overwhelming

dead rise not at all? why are they then baptized for the dead?

30 And why stand we in *a* jeopardy every hour?

calamities on account of the hope of the resurrection, is equally clear. This interpretation, also, agrees with the general tenor of the argument; and *is* an argument for the resurrection. And it implies that this was the full and constant belief of all who endured these trials, that there would be a resurrection of the dead. The *argument* would be, that they should be slow to adopt an opinion which would imply that all their sufferings were endured for naught, and that God had supported them in this in vain; that God had plunged them into all these sorrows, and had sustained them in them only to disappoint them. That this view is plausible, and that it suits the strain of remark in the *following* verses, is evident. But there are objections to it. (*a*) It is not the usual and natural meaning of the word baptize. (*b*) A metaphorical use of a word should not be resorted to unless necessary. (*c*) The literal meaning of the word here will as well meet the design of the apostle as the metaphorical. (*d*) This interpretation does not relieve us from any of the difficulties in regard to the phrase "for the dead;" and, (*e*) It is altogether more natural to suppose that the apostle would derive his argument from the baptism of *all* who were Christians, than from the figurative baptism of a few who went into the perils of martyrdom.—The other opinion, therefore, is, that the apostle here refers to *baptism* as administered to all believers. This is the most correct opinion; is the most simple, and best meets the design of the argument. According to this, it means that they had been baptized with the hope and expectation of a resurrection of the dead. They had received this as one of the leading doctrines of the gospel when they were baptized. It was a part of their full and firm belief that the dead would rise. The *argument* according to this interpretation is, that this was an essential article of the faith of a Christian; that it was

embraced by all; that it constituted a part of their very profession; and that for any one to deny it was to deny that which entered into the very foundation of the Christian faith. If they embraced a different doctrine, if they denied the doctrine of the resurrection, they struck a blow at the very nature of Christianity, and dashed all the hopes which had been cherished and expressed at their baptism. And what could they do? What would become of them! What would be the destiny of all who were thus baptized? Was it to be believed that all their hopes at baptism were vain and that they would all perish? As such a belief could not be entertained, the apostle infers that, if they held to Christianity at all, they must hold to *this* doctrine as a part of their very profession. According to this view, the phrase "for the dead" means, with reference to the dead; with direct allusion to the condition of the dead, and their hopes; with a belief that the dead will rise. It is evident that the passage is elliptical, and this seems to be as probable as any interpretation which has been suggested. Mr. Locke says, frankly, "What this baptizing for the dead was, I know not; but it seems, by the following verses, to be something wherein they exposed themselves to the danger of death." Tindal translates it, "*over* the dead." Doddridge renders it, "*in the room of the dead*, who are just fallen in the cause of Christ, but are yet supported by a succession of new converts, who immediately offer themselves to fill up their places, as ranks of soldiers that advance to the combat in the room of their companions who have just been slain in their sight."

30. *And why stand we in jeopardy.* Why do we constantly risk our lives, and encounter danger of every kind? This refers particularly to Paul himself and the other apostles, who were constantly exposed to peril by land or by sea in the arduous work of making known the gospel. The argument

31 I protest by ¹your rejoicing ᵃ which I have in Christ Jesus our Lord, I ᵇ die daily.

32 If ² after the manner of men

1 some read, *our*.   a Phil. 3.3.   b Rom.8.36.

I have fought with beasts at Ephesus, what advantageth it me. if the dead rise not? Let us ᶜ eat and drink, for to-morrow we die.

2 or, *to speak after*.   c Eccl.2.24; Isa.22.13.

here is plain. It is, that such efforts would be vain, useless, foolish, unless there was to be a glorious resurrection. They had no other object in encountering these dangers than to make known the truths connected with that glorious future state; and if there were no such future state, it would be wise for them to avoid these dangers. " It would not be supposed that we would encounter these perils constantly, unless we were sustained with the hope of the resurrection, and unless we had evidence which convinced our own minds that there would be such a resurrection." ¶ *Every hour.* Constantly; comp. 2 Cor. xv. 26. So numerous were their dangers, that they might be said to occur every hour. This was particularly the case in the instance to which he refers in Ephesus, ver. 32.

31. *I protest* (νὴ). This is a particle of swearing, and denotes a strong asseveration. The subject was important; it deeply interested his feelings; and he makes in regard to it a strong protestation; comp. John iii. 5. " I solemnly affirm, or declare." ¶ *By your rejoicing.* Many MSS. here read "by *our* rejoicing," but the correct reading is doubtless that which is in the present Greek text, by your rejoicing. The meaning of the phrase, which is admitted by all to be obscure, is probably, " I protest, or solemnly declare by the glorying or exultation which I have on your account; by all my ground of glorying in you; by all the confident boasting and expectation which I have of your salvation." He hoped for their salvation. He had laboured for that. He had boasted of it, and confidently believed that they would be saved. Regarding that as safe and certain, he says it was *just as certain* that he died daily on account of the hope and belief of the resurrection. " By our hopes and joys as Christians; by our dearest expectations and grounds of confidence,

I swear, or solemnly declare, that I die daily." Men swear or affirm by their objects of dearest affection and desire; and the meaning here is, " So certainly as I confidently expect your salvation, and so certainly as we look to eternal life, so certain is it that I am constantly exposed to die, and suffer that which may be called a daily death." ¶ *Which I have in Christ Jesus.* The rejoicing, boasting, glorying in regard to you which I am permitted to cherish through the grace and favour of the Saviour. His boasting, or confident expectation in regard to the Corinthians, he enjoyed only by the mercy of the Lord Jesus, and he delighted to trace it to him. ¶ *I die daily;* comp. Rom. viii. 36. I endure so many sufferings and persecutions, that it may be said to be a daily dying. I am constantly in danger of my life; and my sufferings each day are equal to the pains of death. Probably Paul here referred particularly to the perils and trials which he then endured at Ephesus; and his object was to impress their minds with the firmness of *his* belief in the certainty of the resurrection, on account of which he suffered so much, and to show them that all their hopes rested also on this doctrine.

32. *If after the manner of men.* Marg. *To speak after the manner of men* (κατὰ ἄνθρωπον). There has been a great difference of opinion in regard to the meaning of these words. The following are some of the interpretations proposed. (1.) If I have fought after the manner of men, who act only with reference to this life, and on the ordinary principles of human conduct, as men fought with wild beasts in the amphitheatre. (2.) Or if, humanly speaking, or speaking after the manner of men, I have fought, referring to the fact that he had contended with *men* who should be regarded as wild beasts. (3.) Or, that I may speak of myself as men

speak, that I may freely record the events of my life, and speak of what has occurred. (4.) Or, I have fought with wild beasts as far as it was possible for man to do it while life survived. (5.) Or, as much as was in the power of man, who had destined me to this; if, so far as depended on man's will, I fought, supposing that the infuriated multitude demanded that I should be thus punished. So Chrysostom understands it. (6.) Or, that Paul actually fought with wild beasts at Ephesus. (7.) Others regard this as a *supposable* case; on the supposition that I *had* fought with wild beasts at Ephesus. Amidst this variety of interpretation, it is not easy to determine the true sense of this difficult passage. The following thoughts, however, may perhaps make it clear.

(1.) Paul refers to some *real* occurrence at Ephesus. This is manifest from the whole passage. It is not a supposable case.

(2.) It was some *one* case when his life was endangered, and when it was regarded as remarkable that he escaped and survived; comp. 2 Cor. i. 8—10.

(3.) It was *common* among the Romans, and the ancients generally, to expose criminals to fight with wild beasts in the amphitheatre for the amusement of the populace. In such cases it was but another form of dooming them to certain death, since there was no human possibility of escape; see Adam's Rom. Ant., p. 344. That this custom prevailed at the East, is apparent from the following extract from Rosenmüller; and there is no improbability in the supposition that Paul was exposed to this:—"The barbarous custom of making men combat with wild beasts has prevailed in the East down to the most modern times. Jurgen Andersen, who visited the states of the Great Mogul in 1646, gives an account in his Travels of such a combat with animals, which he witnessed at Agra, the residence of the Great Mogul. His description affords a lively image of those bloody spectacles in which ancient Rome took so much pleasure, and to which the above words of the apostle refer. Alamardan-chan, the governor of Cashmire,

who sat among the chans, stood up, and exclaimed, 'It is the will and desire of the great mogul, Schah Choram, that if there are any valiant heroes who will show their bravery by combating with wild beasts, armed with shield and sword, let them come forward; if they conquer, the mogul will load them with great favour, and clothe their countenance with gladness.' Upon this three persons advanced, and offered to undertake the combat. Alamardan-chan again cried aloud, 'None should have any other weapon than a shield and a sword; and whosoever has any breastplate under his clothes should lay it aside, and fight honourably.' Hereupon a powerful lion was let into the garden, and one of the three men above mentioned advanced against him; the lion, on seeing his enemy, ran violently up to him; the man, however, defended himself bravely, and kept off the lion for a good while, till his arms grew tired; the lion then seized the shield with one paw, and with the other his antagonist's right arm, so that he was not able to use his weapon; the latter, seeing his life in danger, took with his left hand his Indian dagger, which he had sticking in his girdle, and thrust it as far as possible into the lion's mouth; the lion then let him go; the man, however, was not idle, but cut the lion almost through with one stroke, and after that entirely to pieces. Upon this victory the common people began to shout, and call out, 'Thank God, he has conquered.' But the mogul said, smiling, to this conqueror, 'Thou art a brave warrior, and hast fought admirably! But did I not command to fight honourably only with shield and sword? But, like a thief, thou hast stolen the life of the lion with thy dagger.' And immediately he ordered two men to rip up his belly, and to place him upon an elephant, and, as an example to others, to lead him about, which was done on the spot. Soon after a tiger was set loose; against which a tall, powerful man advanced with an air of defiance, as if he would cut the tiger up. The tiger, however, was far too sagacious and active, for, in the first attack, he seized the combatant by the neck, tore his throat, and then his whole body in pieces. This enraged another good fellow, but little, and of mean appearance, from whom one would not have expected it: he rushed forward like one mad, and the tiger on his part undauntedly flew at his enemy; but the man at the first attack cut off his two fore paws, so that he fell, and the man cut his body to pieces. Upon this the king cried, 'What is your name?' He answered, 'My name is Geyby.' Soon after one of the king's servants came and brought him a piece of gold brocade, and said, 'Geyby, receive the robe of honour with which the mogul presents you.' He took the garment with great reverence, kissed it three times, pressing it each time to his eyes and breast, then held it up, and in silence put up a prayer for the health of the mogul; and when he concluded it, he cried, 'May God let him become as great as Tamerlane, from whom he is descended. May he live seven hundred years, and his house continue to eternity!' Upon this he was summoned by a chamberlain to go from the garden up to the king; and when he came to the entrance, he was received by two chans, who conducted him between them to kiss the mogul's feet. And when he was going to retire, the king said to him, 'Praised be thou, Geyby-chan, for thy valiant deeds, and this name shalt thou keep to eternity. I am your gracious master, and thou art my slave.' "—*Bush's Illustrations.*

(4.) It is the most *natural* interpretation to suppose that Paul, on some occasion, had such a contest with a wild beast at Ephesus. It is that which would occur to the great mass of the readers of the New Testament as the obvious meaning of the passage.

(5.) The state of things in Ephesus when Paul was there (Acts xix.) was such as to make it nowise improbable that he would be subjected to such a trial.

(6.) It is no objection to this supposition that Luke has not recorded this occurrence in the Acts of the Apostles. No conclusion adverse to this supposition can be drawn from the mere *silence* of the historian. Mere

silence is not a contradiction. There is no reason to suppose that Luke designed to record *all* the perils which Paul endured. Indeed, we know from 2 Cor. xi. 24—27, that there must have been *many* dangers which Paul encountered which are not referred to by Luke. It must have happened, also, that many important events must have taken place during Paul's abode at Ephesus which are not recorded by Luke; Acts xix. Nor is it any objection to this supposition that Paul does not, in 2 Cor. xi. 24—27, mention particularly this contest with a wild beast at Ephesus. His statement there is *general.* He does not descend into particulars. Yet, in 2 Cor. xi. 23, he says that he was " in deaths oft,"—a statement which is in accordance with the supposition that in Ephesus he may have been exposed to death in some cruel manner.

(7.) The phrase κατὰ ἄνθρωπον, *as a man,* may mean, that, *to human appearance,* or so far as man was concerned, had it not been for some divine interposition, he would have been a prey to the wild beasts. Had not God interposed and kept him from harm, as in the case of the viper at Melita (Acts xxviii. 5), he would have been put to death. He was sentenced to this; was thrown to the wild beast; had every *human* prospect of dying; it was done on account of his religion; and but for the interposition of God, he would have died. This I take to be the fair and obvious meaning of this passage, demanded alike by the language which is used and by the tenor of the argument in which it is found. ¶ *What advantageth it me?* What benefit shall I have? Why should I risk my life in this manner? see Note on ver. 19. ¶ *Let us eat and drink.* These words are taken from Isa. xxii. 13. In their original application they refer to the Jews when besieged by Sennacherib and the army of the Assyrians. The prophet says, that instead of weeping, and fasting, and humiliation, as became them in such circumstances, they had given themselves up to feasting and revelry, and that their language was, " Let us eat and drink, for to-morrow

33 Be not deceived : evil *a* | communications corrupt good manners.

we shall die ;" that is, there is no use in offering resistance, or in calling upon God. We must die; and we may as well enjoy life as long as it lasts, and give ourselves up to unrestrained indulgence. Paul does not quote these words as having any original reference to the subject of the resurrection, but as language appropriately expressing the idea, that if there is no future state; if no resurrection of the dead : if no happy result of toils and sufferings in the future world, it is vain and foolish to subject ourselves to trials and privations here. We should rather make the most of this life; enjoy all the comfort we can; and make pleasure our chief good, rather than look for happiness in a future state. This *seems* to be the language of the great mass of the world. They look to no future state. They have no prospect, no desire of heaven ; and they, therefore, seek for happiness here, and give themselves up to unrestrained enjoyment in this life. ¶ *To-morrow.* Very soon. We have no security of life ; and death is so near that it may be said we must die to-morrow. ¶ *We die.* We *must* die. The idea here is, " We must die, without the prospect of living again, unless the doctrine of the resurrection be true."

33. *Be not deceived.* By your false teachers, and by their smooth and plausible arguments. This is an *exhortation.* He had thus far been engaged in an *argument* on the subject. He now entreats them to beware lest they be deceived—a danger to which they were very liable from their circumstances. There was, doubtless, much that was plausible in the objections to the doctrine of the resurrection; there was much subtilty and art in their teachers, who denied this doctrine; perhaps, there was something in the character of their own minds, accustomed to subtle and abstruse inquiry rather than to an examination of simple facts, that exposed them to this danger. ¶ *Evil communications.* The word rendered "communications" means, properly, a being together;

companionship; close intercourse; converse. It refers not to *discourse* only, but to intercourse, or companionship. Paul quotes these words from Menander (in Sentent. Comicor. Gr. p. 248, ed. Steph.), a Greek poet. He thus shows that he was, in some degree at least, familiar with the Greek writers; comp. Note, Acts xvii. 28. Menander was a celebrated comic poet of Athens, educated under Theophrastus. His writings were replete with elegance, refined wit, and judicious observations. Of one hundred and eight comedies which he wrote, nothing remains but a few fragments. He is said to have drowned himself, in the 52d year of his age, B. C. 293, because the compositions of his rival Philemon obtained more applause than his own. Paul quoted this sentiment from a Greek poet, perhaps, because it might be supposed to have weight with the Greeks. It was a sentiment of one of their own writers, and here was an occasion in which it was exactly applicable. It is implied in this, that there were some persons who were endeavouring to corrupt their minds from the simplicity of the gospel. The sentiment of the passage is, that the intercourse of evil-minded men, or that the close friendship and conversation of those who hold erroneous opinions, or who are impure in their lives, tends to corrupt the morals, the heart, the sentiments of others. The particular thing to which Paul here applies it is the subject of the resurrection. Such intercourse would tend to corrupt the simplicity of their faith, and pervert their views of the truth of the gospel, and *thus* corrupt their lives. It is *always* true that such intercourse has a pernicious effect on the mind and the heart. It is done, (4.) By their direct effort to corrupt the opinions, and to lead others into sin. (2.) By the secret, silent influence of their words, and conversation, and example. We have less horror at vice by becoming familiar with it ; we look with less alarm on error when we hear it often expressed; we become less watchful

34 Awake *a* to righteousness, and sin not; for some have not the knowledge of God: I *b* speak *this* to your shame.

a Rom.13.11; Eph.5.14.   *b* chap.6.5.

35 But some *man* will say, How *c* are the dead raised up? and with what body do they come?

c Ezek.37.3.

and cautious when we are constantly with the gay, the worldly, the unprincipled, and the vicious. Hence Christ sought that there should be a pure society, and that his people should principally seek the friendship and conversation of each other, and withdraw from the world. It is in the way that Paul here refers to, that Christians embrace false doctrines; that they lose their spirituality, love of prayer, fervour of piety, and devotion to God. It is in this way that the simple are beguiled, the young corrupted, and that vice, and crime, and infidelity spread over the world.

34. *Awake to righteousness;* see Note, Rom. xiii. 11. The word here translated "awake" denotes, properly, to awake up from a deep sleep or torpor; and is usually applied to those who awake, or become sober after drunkenness. The phrase "to righteousness" (δικαίως) may mean either "rouse to the ways of righteousness; to a holy life; to sound doctrine," &c.; or it may mean "as it is right and just that you should do." Probably the latter is the correct idea, and then the sense will be, "Arouse from stupidity on this subject; awake from your conscious security; be alarmed, as it is *right* and *proper* that you should do, for you are surrounded by dangers, and by those who would lead you into error and vice; rouse from such wild and delusive opinions as these persons have, and exercise a constant vigilance as becomes those who are the friends of God and the expectants of a blessed resurrection." ¶ *And sin not.* Do not err; do not depart from the truth and from holiness; do not embrace a doctrine which is not only erroneous, but the tendency of which is to lead into sin. It is implied here, that if they suffered themselves to embrace a doctrine which was a denial of the resurrection, the effect would be that they would fall into sin; or that a denial of that doctrine led to

a life of self-indulgence and transgression. This truth is everywhere seen and against this effect Paul sought to guard them. He did not regard the denial of the doctrine of the resurrection as a harmless speculation, but as leading to most dangerous consequences in regard to their manner of life or their conduct. ¶ *For some have not.* Some among you. You are surrounded by strangers to God; you have those among you who would lead you into error and sin. ¶ *I speak this to your shame.* To your shame as a church; because you have had abundant opportunities to know the truth, and because it is a subject of deep disgrace that there are any in your bosom who deny the doctrine of the resurrection of the dead, and who are strangers to the grace of God.

35. *But some* man *will say.* An objection will be made to the statement that the dead will be raised. This verse commences the *second* part of the chapter, in which the apostle meets the objections to the argument, and shows in what manner the dead will be raised. See the Analysis. That objections were made to the doctrine is apparent from ver. 12. ¶ *How are the dead raised up?* (Πῶς.) In what way or manner; by what means. This I regard as the *first* objection which would be made, or the first inquiry on the subject which the apostle answers. The question is one which would be likely to be made by the subtle and doubting Greeks. The apostle, indeed, does not draw it out at length, or state it fully, but it may be regarded probably as substantially the same as that which has been made in all ages. "How is it possible that the dead should be raised? They return to their native dust. They become entirely disorganized. Their dust may be scattered; how shall it be re-collected? Or they may be burned at the stake, and how shall the particles

36 *Thou* fool! that *a* which thou sowest is not quickened, except it die.

a John 12.24.

37 And that which thou sowest, thou sowest not that body that shall be, but bare grain, it may

which composed their bodies be re-collected and re-organized? Or they may be devoured by the beasts of the field, the fowls of heaven, or the fishes of the sea, and their flesh may have served to constitute the food of other animals, and to form *their* bodies; how can it be re-collected and re-or-ganized? Or it may have been the food of plants, and like other dust have been used to constitute the leaves or the flowers of plants, and the trunks of trees; and *how* can it be remoulded into a human frame?" This objection the apostle answers in ver. 36—38. ¶ *And with what body do they come?* This is the *second* objection or inquiry which he answers. It may be understood as meaning, "What will be the form, the shape, the size, the organization of the new body? Are we to suppose that *all* the matter which at any time entered into its composition here is to be re-collected, and to constitute a colossal frame? Are we to suppose that it will be the same as it is here, with the same organization, the same necessi-ties, the same wants? Are we to suppose that the aged will be raised *as* aged, and the young *as* young, and that infancy will be raised in the same state, and remain such for ever? Are we to suppose that the bodies will be gross, material, and needing support and nourishment, or, that there will be a new organization?" All these and numerous other questions have been asked, in regard to the bodies at the resurrection; and it is by no means improbable that they were asked by the subtle and philosophiz-ing Greeks, and that they constituted a part of the reasoning of those who denied the doctrine of the resurrec-tion. This question, or objection, the apostle answers ver. 39—50. It has been doubted, indeed, whether he refers in this verse to *two* inquiries— to the *possibility* of the resurrection, and to the *kind* of bodies that should be raised; but it is the most obvious

interpretation of the verse, and it is certain that in his argument he dis-cusses both these points.

36. Thou *fool*. Foolish, inconsider-ate man! The meaning is, that it was foolish to make this objection, when the same difficulty existed in an undeniable *fact* which fell under daily observation. A man was a fool to urge that as an objection to religion which *must* exist in the undeniable and every-day facts which they wit-nessed. The idea is, "The same dif-ficulty may be started about the growth of grain. Suppose a man who had never seen it, were to be told that it was to be put into the earth; that it was to die; to be decomposed; and that from the decayed kernel there should be seen to start up first a slen-der, green, and tender spire of grass, and that this was to send up a strong stalk, and was to produce hundreds of similar kernels at some distant period. These facts would be as *improbable* to him as the doctrine of the resurrec-tion of the dead. When he saw the kernel laid in the ground; when he saw it decay; when apparently it was returning to dust, he would ask, How CAN these be connected with the pro-duction of similar grain? Are not all the indications that it will be totally corrupted and destroyed?" Yet, says Paul, this is connected with the hope of the harvest, and this fact should remove all the objection which is de-rived from the fact that the body re-turns to its native dust. The idea is, that there is an analogy, and that the *main* objection in the one case would lie equally well against the acknow-ledged and indisputable fact in the other. It is evident, however, that this argument is of a popular charac-ter, and is not to be pressed to the quick; nor are we to suppose that the resemblance will be in all respects the same. It is to be used as Paul used it. The objection was, that the body died, and returned to dust, and could not, therefore, rise again. The reply

chance of wheat, or of some other *grain:*

38 But God *a* giveth it a body

a Gen.1.11,12.

of Paul is, " You may make the same objection to grain that is sown. That dies also. The main body of the kernel decays. *In itself* there is no prospect that it will spring up. Should *it stop here*, and had you *never seen* a grain of wheat grow; had you only seen it in the earth, as you have seen the body in the grave, there would be the same difficulty as to now it would produce other grains, which there is about the resurrection of the body." ¶ *Is not quickened.* Does not become alive ; does not grow. ¶ *Except it die;* see Note, John xii. 24. The main body of the grain decays that it may beoome food and nourishment to the tender germ. *Perhaps* it is implied here also that there was a *fitness* that men should die in order to obtain the glorious body of the resurrection, in the same way as it is *fit* that the kernel should die, in order that there may be a new and beautiful harvest.

37. *And that which thou sowest.* The seed which is sown. ¶ *Not that body that shall be.* You sow one kernel which is to produce many others. They shall not be the same that is sown. They will be *new* kernels raised from that ; of the same kind, indeed, and showing their intimate and necessary connection with that which is sown. It is implied here that the body which will be raised will not be the same in the sense that the same particles of matter shall compose it, but the same only in the sense that it will have sprung up from that ; will constitute the same order, rank, species of being, and be subject to the same laws, and deserve the same course of treatment as that which died ; as the grain *produced* is subject to the same laws, and belongs to the same rank, order, and species as that which is sown. And as the same particles of matter which are sown do not enter into that which shall be in the harvest, so it is taught that the same particles of matter which constitute the body when it dies, do not

as it hath pleased him, and to every seed his own body.

39 All flesh *is* not the same flesh :

constitute the new body at the resurrection. ¶ *But bare grain.* Mere grain ; a mere kernel, without any husk, leaf, blade, or covering of any kind. Those are added in the process of reproduction. The design of this is to make it appear more remarkable, and to destroy the force of the objection. It was not only *not* the grain that should be produced, but it was without the appendages and ornaments of blade, and flower, and beard of the new grain. How could any one tell but what it would be so in the resurrection? How could any know but what there might be appendages and ornaments there, which were not connected with the body that died? ¶ *It may chance of wheat*, &c. For example ; or suppose it be wheat or any other grain. The apostle adduces this merely for an *example;* not to intimate that there is any *chance* about it.

38. *But God giveth it a body*, &c. God gives to the seed sown its own proper body, formation, and growth. The word *body* here, as applied to grain, seems to mean the whole *system*, or arrangement of roots, stalks, leaves, flowers, and kernels that start out of the seed that is sown The meaning is, that such a form is produced from the seed sown as God pleases. Paul here traces the result to God, to show that there is no chance, and that it did not depend on the nature of things, but was dependent on the wise arrangement of God. There was nothing in the decaying kernel itself that would produce this result ; but God chose that it should be so. There is nothing in the decaying body of the dead which in itself should lead to the resurrection; but God chose it should be so. ¶ *As it hath pleased him.* As he chose. It is by his arrangement and agency. Though it is by regular laws, yet it is as God pleases. He acts according to his own pleasure, in the formation of each root, and stalk, and kernel of

but *there is* one *kind of* flesh of men, another flesh of beasts, an-

grain. It is, probably, here intimated that God would give to each one of the dead at the resurrection such a body as he should choose, though it will be, doubtless, in accordance with general laws. ¶ *And to every seed his own body.* That which appropriately belongs to it; which it is fitted to produce; which is of the same kind. He does not cause a stalk of rye to grow from a kernel of wheat; nor of maize from barley; nor of hemp from lentiles. He has fixed proper laws, and he takes care that they shall be observed. So it will be in the resurrection. Every one shall have his own, *i. e.* his proper body—a body which shall belong to him, and be fitted to him. The wicked shall not rise with the body of the just, or with a body adapted to heaven; nor shall the saint rise with a body adapted to perdition. There shall be a fitness or appropriateness in the new body to the character of him who is raised. The *argument* here is designed to meet the inquiry ʜow should the body be raised, and it is that there is nothing more remarkable and impossible in the doctrine of the resurrection, than in the fact constantly before us, that grain that seems to rot sends up a shoot or stalk, and is reproduced in a wonderful and beautiful manner. In a manner similar to this, the body will be raised; and the illustration of Paul meets all the difficulties about the *fact* of the resurrection. It cannot be shown that one is more difficult than the other; and as the facts of vegetation are constantly passing before our eyes, we ought not to deem it strange if *similar* facts shall take place hereafter in regard to the resurrection of the dead.

39. *All flesh is not the same flesh.* This verse and the following are designed to answer the question (ver. 35), "with what bodies do they come?" And the argument here is, that there are *many kinds* of bodies; that all are not alike; that while they are *bodies*, yet they partake of different qualities, forms, and properties; and

other of fishes, *and* another of birds.

that, *therefore*, it is not absurd to suppose that God may transform the human body into a different form, and cause it to be raised up with somewhat different properties in the future world. Why, the argument is, why should it be regarded as impossible? Why is it to be held that the human body may not undergo a transformation, or that it will be absurd to suppose that it may be different in some respects from what it is now? Is it not a matter of fact that there is a great variety of bodies even on the earth? The word *flesh* here is used to denote *body*, as it often is. 1 Cor. v. 5; 2 Cor. iv. 11; vii. 1; Phil. i. 22, 24; Col. ii. 5; 1 Pet. iv. 6. The idea here is, that although all the bodies of animals may be composed essentially of the same elements, yet God has produced a wonderful variety in their organization, strength, beauty, colour, and places of abode, as the air, earth, and water. It is not *necessary*, therefore, to suppose that the body that shall be raised shall be precisely like that which we have here. It is certainly *possible* that there may be *as great* a difference between that and our present body, as between the most perfect form of the human frame here and the lowest reptile. It would still be *a body*, and there would be no absurdity in the transformation. The body of the worm, the chrysalis, and the butterfly is the same. It is the same animal still. Yet how different the gaudy and gay butterfly from the creeping and offensive caterpillar! So there *may* be a similar change in the body of the believer, and yet be still the same. Of a sceptic on this subject we would ask, whether, if there had been a *revelation* of the changes which a caterpillar might undergo before it became a butterfly —a new species of existence adapted to a new element, requiring new food, and associated with new and other beings—if he had never *seen* such a transformation, would it not be attended with all the difficulty which now encompasses the doctrine of the

40 *There* *a* *are* also celestial bodies, and bodies terrestrial : but the glory of the celestial *is* one, and the *glory* of the terrestrial *is* another.

41 *There is* one glory of the sun, *b* and another glory of the

a Gen.1.16.

resurrection ? The sceptic would no more have believed it *on the authority of revelation* than he will believe the doctrine of the resurrection of the dead. And no infidel can prove that the one is attended with any more difficulty or absurdity than the other.

40. There are *also celestial bodies.* The planets ; the stars ; the host of heaven; see ver. 41. ¶ *And bodies terrestrial.* On earth; earthly. He refers here to the bodies of men, beasts, birds, &c.; perhaps, also, of trees and vegetables. The sense is, " There is a great variety of bodies. Look upon the heavens, and see the splendour of the sun, the moon, and the stars. And then look upon the earth, and see the bodies there—the bodies of men, and brutes, and insects. You see here two entire *classes* of bodies. You see how they differ. Can it be deemed strange if there should be a difference between our bodies when on earth and when in heaven ? Do we not, *in fact,* see a vast difference between what strikes our eye here on earth and in the sky ? And why should we deem it strange that between bodies adapted to live *here* and bodies adapted to live *in heaven,* there should be a difference, *like* that which is seen between the objects which appear on earth and those which appear in the sky ?" The argument is a popular one; but it is striking, and meets the object which he has in view. ¶ *The glory of the celestial* is *one.* The splendour, beauty, dignity, magnificence of the heavenly bodies differs much from those on earth. That is *one thing;* the beauty of earthly objects is *another* and *a different thing.* Beautiful as may be the human frame; beautiful as may be the plumage of birds; beautiful as may be the flower, the fossil, the mineral, the topaz, or the diamond; yet

moon, and another glory of the stars: for *one* star differeth from *another* star in glory.

42 So also *is* the resurrection of the dead. It is sown in corruption ; it is raised in incorruption.

b Ps. 19.4,5

they *differ* from the heavenly bodies, and are not to be compared with them. Why should we deem it strange that there may be a similar difference between the body as adapted to its residence here and as adapted to its residence in heaven ?

41. There is *one glory of the sun,* &c. The sun has one degree of splendour, and the moon another, and so also the stars. They differ from each other in magnitude, in brightness, in beauty. The idea in this verse differs from that in the former. In that (ver. 40) Paul says, that there was a difference between the different *classes* of bodies ; between those in heaven and those on earth. He here says, that in the former *class,* in the heavenly bodies themselves, there was a difference. They not only differed from those on earth, but they differed from each other. The sun was more splendid than the moon, and one star more beautiful than another. The idea here is, therefore, not only that the bodies of the saints in heaven shall differ from those on earth, but that they shall differ among themselves, in a sense somewhat like the difference of the splendour of the sun, the moon, and the different stars. Though *all* shall be unlike what they were on earth, and all shall be glorious, yet there may be a difference in thas splendour and glory. The *argument* is, since we see so great differences *in fact* in the works of God, why should we doubt that he is able to make the human body different from what it is now, and to endow it with immortal and eternal perfection ?

42. *So also is the resurrection.* In a manner similar to the grain that is sown, and to the different degrees of splendour and magnificence in the bodies in the sky and on the earth. The

43 It *a* is sown in dishonour; it is raised in glory: it is sown

in weakness; it is raised in power:

a Dan.12.3; Mat.13.43; Phil.3.21.

dead shall be raised in a manner analogous to the springing up of grain; and there shall be a difference between the body here and the body in the resurrection. ¶ *It is sown.* In death. As we sow or plant the kernel in the earth. ¶ *In corruption.* In the grave; in a place where it shall be corrupt; in a form tending to putrefaction, disorganization, and dust. ¶ *It is raised in incorruption.* It will be so raised. In the previous verses (36—41) he had reasoned from analogy, and had demonstrated that it was *possible* that the dead should rise, or that there was no greater difficulty attending it than actually occurred in the events which were in fact constantly taking place. He here states positively what would be, and affirms that it was not only possible, but that such a resurrection would actually occur. They body would be raised "in incorruption," "uncorruptible" (ver. 52); that is, no more liable to decay, sickness, disorganization, and putrefaction. This is *one* characteristic of the body that shall be raised, that it shall be no more liable, as here, to wasting sickness, to disease, and to the loathsome corruption of the grave. That God *can* form a body of that kind, no one can doubt; that he actually will, the apostle positively affirms. That such *will* be the bodies of the saints is one of the most cheering prospects that can be presented to those who are here wasted away by sickness, and who look with dread and horror on the loathsome putrefaction of the tomb.

43. *It is sown in dishonour.* In the grave, where it is shut out from human view; hurried away from the sight of friends; loathsome and offensive as a mass turning to decay. There is, moreover, a kind of disgrace and ignominy attending it here, as under the curse of God, and, on account of sin, sentenced to the offensiveness of the grave. ¶ *It is raised in glory.* In honour; in beauty; honoured by God by the removal of the curse, and

in a form and manner that shall be glorious. This refers to the fact that every thing like dishonour, vileness, ignominy, which attends it here shall be removed there, and that the body shall bear a resemblance to the glorified body of Jesus Christ, Eph. iii. 21. It shall be adapted to a world of glory; and every thing which here rendered it vile, valueless, cumbersome, offensive, or degraded, shall be there removed. Of course, every idea which we can get from this is chiefly negative, and consists in denying that the body will have there the qualities which here render it vile or loathsome. The word glory (δόξα) means dignity, splendour, honour, excellence, perfection; and is here used as denoting the *combination* of all those things which shall rescue it from ignominy and disgrace. ¶ *It is sown in weakness.* Weak, feeble, liable to decay. Here disease prostrates the strength, takes away its power, consigns it to the dust. It denotes the many weaknesses, frailties, and liabilities to sickness, to which we are here exposed. Its feeble powers are soon prostrate; its vital functions soon cease in death. ¶ *It is raised in power.* This does not denote power like that of God, nor like the angels. It does not affirm that it shall be endued with remarkable and enormous physical strength, or that it shall have the power of performing what would now be regarded as miraculous. It is to be regarded as the opposite of the word "weakness," and means that it shall be no longer liable to disease; no more overcome by the attacks of sickness; no more subject to the infirmities and weaknesses which it here experiences. It shall not be prostrate by sickness, nor overcome by fatigue. It shall be capable of the service of God without weariness and languor; it shall need no rest as it does here (see Rev. vii. 15; comp. xxii. 5); but it shall be in a world where there shall be no fatigue, lassitude, disease; but where there shall be ample power to engage in the service of God for ever.

44 It is sown a natural body; it is raised a spiritual body. There is a natural body, and there is a spiritual [a] body.

a Luke 24.31; John 20.19,26.

There is, however, no improbability in supposing that the physical powers of man, as well as his intellectual, *may be* greatly augmented in heaven. But on this point there is no revelation.

44. *It is sown a natural body* (σῶμα ψυχικόν). This word, "natural," denotes properly that which is endowed with *animal* life, having breath, or vitality. The word from which it is derived (ψυχή) denotes properly the breath; vital breath; the soul, as the vital principle; the animal soul, or the vital spirit; the soul, as the seat of the sentient desires, passions, and propensities; and then a living thing, an animal. It may be applied to *any* animal, or any living thing, whether brutes or men. It is distinguished from the soul or spirit (πνεῦμα), inasmuch as that more commonly denotes the *rational* spirit, the immortal soul, that which thinks, reasons, reflects, &c. The word "natural" here, therefore, means that which has *animal* life; which breathes and acts by the laws of the animal economy; that which draws in the breath of life; which is endowed with senses, and which has need of the *supports* of animal life, and of the refreshments derived from food, exercise, sleep, &c. The apostle here, by affirming that the body will be spiritual, intends to deny that it will need that which is now necessary to the support of the animal functions; it will not be sustained in that way; it will lay aside these peculiar animal organizations, and will cease to convey the idea which we now attach to the word *animal*, or to possess that which we now include under the name of *vital functions*. Here the body of man is endowed simply with *animal* functions. It is the dwelling-place indeed of an immortal mind; but *as* a body it has the properties of *animal* life, and is subject to the same laws and inconveniences as the bodies of other animals. It is sustained by breath, and food, and sleep; it is endowed with the organs of sense, the eye, the ear, the smell, the touch, by which alone the soul can hold communication with the external world; it is liable to disease, languor, decay, death. These *animal* or *vital* functions will cease in heaven, and the body be raised in a different mode of being, and where all the inconveniences of this mere animal life shall be laid aside. ¶ *It is raised a spiritual body.* Not a mere spirit, for then it would not be a body. The word *spiritual* (πνευματικόν) here stands opposed to the word *natural*, or *animal*. It will *not* be a body that is subject to the laws of the vital functions, or organized or sustained in that way. It will still be a "body" (σῶμα), but it will have *so far* the nature of spirit as to be *without* the vital functions which here control the body. This is all that the word here means. It does not mean refined, sublimated, or transcendental; it does not mean that it will be without shape or form; it does not mean that it will not be properly *a body*. The idea of Paul seems to be this: "We conceive of soul or spirit as not subject to the laws of vital or animal agency. It is independent of them. It is not sustained or nourished by the functions of the animal organization. It has an economy of its own; living without nourishment; not subject to decay; not liable to sickness, pain, or death. So will be the body in the resurrection. It will not be subject to the laws of the vital organization. It will be so much LIKE a spirit as to be continued without food or nutriment; to be destitute of the peculiar physical organization of flesh, and blood, and bones; of veins, and arteries, and nerves, as here (ver. 50.); and it will live in the manner in which we conceive spirits to live; sustained, and exercising its powers, without waste, weariness, decay, or the necessity of having its powers recruited by food and sleep." All, therefore, that has been said about a refined body, a body that shall be spirit, a body that shall be pure, &c., whatever may be its truth, is not

45 And so it is written, ^a The first man Adam was made a living

a Gen.2.7.

soul; the ^b last Adam *was made* a quickening spirit.

b John 5.21; 6.33,40.

sustained by this passage. It will be a body without the vital functions of the animal economy; a body sustained in the manner in which we conceive the spirit to be. ¶ *There is a natural body.* This seems to be added by Paul in the way of strong affirmation arising from earnestness, and from a desire to prevent misconception. The affirmation is, that there *is* a natural body; that is apparent: it is everywhere seen. No one can doubt it. So, with equal certainty, says Paul, there *is* a spiritual body. It is just as certain and indisputable. This assertion is made, not because the evidence of both is the same, but is made on his apostolic authority, and is to be received on that authority. That there was an animal body was apparent to all; that there was a spiritual body was a position which he affirmed to be as certain as the other. The only proof which he alleges is in ver. 45, which is the proof arising from revelation.

45. *And so it is written,* Gen. ii. 7. It is only the first part of the verse which is quoted. ¶ *The first man Adam was made a living soul.* This is quoted exactly from the translation by the LXX., except that the apostle has added the words "first" and "Adam." This is done to designate whom he meant. The meaning of the phrase "was made a living soul" (ἐγένετο εἰς ψυχὴν ζῶσαν—in Hebrew, לנפש היה) is, became a living, animated being; a being endowed with life. The use of the word "soul" in our translation, for ψυχή and נפש (*nephesh*), does not quite convey the idea. We apply the word *soul,* usually, to the intelligent and the immortal part of man; that which reasons, thinks, remembers, is conscious, is responsible, &c. The Greek and Hebrew words, however, more properly denote that which is alive, which is animated, which breathes, which has an animal nature, Note on ver. 44. And this is precisely the idea which Paul uses here, that the first man was

made an animated being by having breathed into him the breath of life (Gen. ii. 7), and that it is the image of this animated or vital being which we bear, ver. 48. Neither Moses nor Paul deny that in addition to this, man was endowed with a rational soul, an immortal nature; but that is not the idea which they present in the passage in Genesis which Paul quotes. ¶ *The last Adam.* The second Adam, or the "second man," ver. 47. That Christ is here intended is apparent, and has been usually admitted by commentators. Christ here seems to be called *Adam* because he stands in contradistinction from the first Adam; or because, as we derive our animal and dying nature from the one, so we derive our immortal and undying bodies from the other. From the one we derive an animal or vital existence; from the other we derive our immortal existence, and resurrection from the grave. The one stands at the head of all those who have an existence represented by the words, "a living soul;" the other of all those who shall have a spiritual body in heaven. He is called "the *last* Adam;" meaning that there shall be no other after him who shall affect the destiny of man in the same way, or who shall stand at the head of the race in a manner similar to what had been done by him and the first father of the human family. They sustain peculiar relations to the race; and in this respect they were "the first" and "the last" in the peculiar economy. The name "Adam" is not elsewhere given to the Messiah, though a comparison is several times instituted between him and Adam. [See the supplementary Note on ver. 22; also on Rom. v. 12.] ¶ *A quickening spirit* (εἰς πνεῦμα ζωοποιοῦν). A vivifying spirit; a spirit giving or imparting life. Not a being having mere vital functions, or an animated nature, but a being who has the power of imparting life. This is not a quotation from any part of the Scriptures, but seems to be used by Paul

46 Howbeit that *was* not first which is spiritual, but that which is natural ; and afterward that which is spiritual.

47 The *a* first man *is* of the earth, earthy : the second man *is* the Lord from heaven.

48 As *is* the earthy, such *are*

a John 3.13,31.

either as affirming what was true on his own apostolic authority, or as conveying the *substance* of what was revealed respecting the Messiah in the Old Testament. There may be also reference to what the Saviour himself taught, that he was the source of life; that he had the power of imparting life, and that he gave life to all whom he pleased ; see Note, John i. 4 ; v. 26, " For as the Father hath life in himself, so hath he given to the Son to have life in himself." ver. 21, " For as the Father raiseth up the dead, and quickeneth them, even so the Son quickeneth whom he will." The word "spirit," here applied to Christ, is in contradistinction from " a living being," as applied to Adam, and seems to be used in the sense of spirit of life, as raising the bodies of his people from the dead, and imparting life to them. He was constituted not as having life merely, but as endowed with the power of imparting life ; as endowed with that spiritual or vital energy which was needful to impart life. All life is the creation or production of *spirit* (Πνεῦμα) ; as applied to God the Father, or the Son, or the Holy Spirit. *Spirit* is the source of all vitality. God is a spirit, and God is the source of all life. And the idea here is, that Christ had such a spiritual existence, such power as a spirit ; that he was the source of all life to his people. The word spirit is applied to his exalted spiritual nature, in distinction from his human nature, in Rom. i. 4 ; 1 Tim. iii. 16 ; 1 Pet. iii. 18. The apostle does not here affirm that he had not a human nature, or a vital existence as a man ; but that his *main* characteristic in contradistinction from Adam was, that he was endowed with an elevated spiritual nature, which was capable of imparting vital existence to the dead.

46. *Howbeit.* There is a due order observed, ver. 23. The decaying, the dying, the weak, the corruptible, in the

proper order of events, was first. This order was necessary, and this is observed everywhere. It is seen in the grain that dies in the ground, and in the resurrection of man. The imperfect is succeeded by the perfect ; the impure by the pure ; the vile and degraded by the precious and the glorious. The idea is, that there is a tendency towards perfection, and that God observes the proper order by which that which is most glorious shall be secured. It was not his plan that all things in the beginning should be perfect, but that perfection should be the work of time, and should be secured in an appropriate *order* of events. The design of Paul in this verse seems to be to vindicate the statement which he had made, by showing that it was in accordance with what was everywhere observed, that the proper *order* should be maintained. This idea is carried through the following verses.

47. *The first man.* Adam. ¶ Is *of the earth.* Was made of the dust ; see Gen. ii. 7. ¶ *Earthy.* Partaking of the earth : he was a mass of animated clay, and could be appropriately called "DUST ;" Gen. iii. 19. Of course, he must partake of a nature that was low, mean, mortal, and corruptible. ¶ *The second man.* Christ ; see Note on ver. 45. He is called the *second* man, as being the second who sustained a relation to men that was materially to affect their conduct and destiny ; the second and the last (ver. 45), who should sustain a peculiar headship to the race. ¶ *The Lord from heaven.* Called in chap. ii. 8, the "Lord of glory ;" see Note on that place. This expression refers to the fact that the Lord Jesus had a heavenly origin, in contradistinction from Adam, who was formed from the earth. The Latin Vulgate renders this, "the second man from heaven is heavenly ;" and this idea seems to accord with the meaning in the former member of the

they also that are earthy : and as *is* the heavenly, such *are* they also that are heavenly.

49 And as we have borne the image of the earthy, we shall also [a] bear the image of the heavenly.

50 Now this I say, brethren,

a Rom.8.29.

verse. The sense is, evidently, that as the first man had an earthly origin, and was, therefore, earthy, so the second man being from heaven, as his proper home, would have a body adapted to that abode; unlike that which was earthy, and which would be fitted to his exalted nature, and to the world where he would dwell. And while, therefore, the phrase "from heaven" refers to his heavenly origin, the essential idea is, that he would have a body that was adapted to such an origin and such a world— a body unlike that which was earthy. That is, Christ had a glorified body to which the bodies of the saints must yet be made like.

48. *As is the earthy.* Such as Adam was. ¶ *Such* are *they also,* &c. Such are all his descendants; all who derive their nature from him. That is, they are frail, corruptible, mortal; they live in an animal body as he did, and like him, they are subject to corruption and decay. ¶ *And as is the heavenly.* As is he who was from heaven; as is the Lord Jesus now in his glorified body. ¶ *Such* are *they also,* &c. Such will they be also. They will be like him; they will have a body like his. This idea is more fully expressed in Phil. iii. 21, "Who shall change our vile body, that it may be fashioned like unto his glorious body."

49. *And as we have borne the image of the earthy.* As like our first father, we are frail, decaying, dying; as we are so closely connected with him as to be like him. This does not refer, mainly, to one bearing his moral character, but to the fact that we are, like him, subject to sickness, frailty, sorrow, and death. ¶ *We shall also bear the image of the heavenly.* The Lord Jesus Christ, who was from heaven, and who is in heaven. As we are so closely connected with Adam as to resemble him. so by the divine arrangement, and by faith in the Lord Jesus, we are so closely connected with him that we shall resemble him in heaven. And as he is now free from frailty, sickness, pain, sorrow, and death, and as he has a pure and spiritual body, adapted to a residence in heaven, so shall we be in that future world. The *argument* here is, that the connection which is formed between the believer and the Saviour is as close as that which subsisted between him and Adam; and as that connection with Adam involved the certainty that he would be subjected to pain, sin, sickness, and death, so the connection with Christ involves the certainty that he will like him be free from sin, sickness, pain, and death, and like him will have a body that is pure, incorruptible, and immortal.

50. *Now this I say, brethren.* " I make this affirmation in regard to this whole subject. I do it as containing the substance of all that I have said. I do it in order to prevent all mistake in regard to the nature of the bodies which shall be raised up." This affirmation is made respecting all the dead and all the living, that there must be a material and important change in regard to them before they can be prepared for heaven. Paul had proved in the previous verses that it was *possible* for God to give us bodies different from those which we now possess; he here affirms, in the most positive manner, that it was indispensable that we should have bodies different from what we now have. ¶ *Flesh and blood.* Bodies organized as ours now are. " Flesh and blood" denotes such bodies as we have here,—bodies that are fragile, weak, liable to disease, subject to pain and death. They are composed of changing particles; to be repaired and strengthened daily; they are subject to decay, and are wasted away by sickness, and of course they cannot be fitted to a world where there shall

that *a* flesh and blood cannot inherit the kingdom of God ; neither doth corruption inherit incorruption.

a John 3.2,5.

51 Behold, I show you a mystery : We *b* shall not all sleep, but we shall all be changed.

b 1 Thess.4.15-17.

be no decay and and no death. ¶ *Cannot inherit.* Cannot be admitted as heir to the kingdom of God. The future world of glory is often represented as an heirship; see Note on Rom. viii. 17. ¶ *The kingdom of God.* Heaven; appropriately called his kingdom, because he shall reign there in undivided and perfect glory for ever. ¶ *Neither doth corruption,* &c. Neither can that which is in its nature corruptible, and liable to decay, be adapted to a world where all is incorruptible. The apostle here simply states the fact. He does not tell us *why* it is impossible. It *may be* because the mode of communication there is not by the bodily senses; it may be because such bodies as ours would not be fitted to relish the pure and exalted pleasures of an incorruptible world; it may be because they would interfere with the exalted worship, the active service, and the sleepless employments of the heavenly world; it may be because *such* a body is constituted to derive pleasure from objects which shall not be found in heaven. It is adapted to enjoyment in eating and drinking, and the pleasures of the eye, the ear, the taste, the touch; in heaven the soul shall be awake to more elevated and pure enjoyments than these, and, of course, such bodies as we here have would impede our progress and destroy our comforts, and be ill adapted to all the employments and enjoyments of that heavenly world.

51. *Behold I show you.* This commences the *third* subject of inquiry in the chapter,—the question, what will become of those who are alive when the Lord Jesus shall return to raise the dead? This was an *obvious* inquiry, and the answer was, perhaps, supposed to be difficult. Paul answers it directly, and says that they will undergo an instantaneous change, which will make them like the dead

that shall be raised. ¶ *A mystery.* On the meaning of this word, see Note, chap. ii. 7. The word here does not mean any thing which was in its nature unintelligible, but that which to them had been hitherto unknown. "I now communicate to you a truth which has not been brought into the discussion, and in regard to which no communication has been made to you." On this subject there had been no revelation. Though the Pharisees held that the dead would rise, yet they do not seem to have made any statement in regard to the living who should remain when the dead should rise. Nor, perhaps, had the subject occupied the attention of the apostles; nor had there been any direct communication on it from the Lord Jesus himself. Paul then here says, that he was about to communicate a great truth which till then had been unknown, and to resolve a great inquiry on which there had as yet been no revelation. ¶ *We shall not all sleep.* We Christians; grouping all together who then lived and should live afterwards, for his discussion has relation to them all. The following remarks may, perhaps, remove some of the difficulty which attends the interpretation of this passage. The *objection* which is made to it is, that Paul expected to live until the Lord Jesus should return; that he, therefore, expected that the world would soon end, and that in this he was mistaken, and could not be inspired. To this, we may reply, (1.) He is speaking of Christians as such—of the whole church that had been redeemed—of the entire mass that should enter heaven; and he groups them all together, and connects himself with them, and says, "*We* shall not die; we Christians, including the whole church, shall not *all* die," &c. That he did not refer only to those whom he was then addressing, is apparent from the whole discussion. The argument relates to Christians—to the church at large; and the affirmation here has reference to that church considered as one church that was to be raised up on the last day. (2.) That Paul did not expect that the Lord Jesus would *soon* come, and that the world would *soon* come to an end, is apparent from a similar place in the epistle to the Thessalonians. In 1 Thess. iv. 15, he uses language remarkably similar to that which is here used: " *We* which are alive, and remain unto the coming of the Lord," &c. This language was interpreted by the Thessalonians as teaching that the world would soon come to an end, and the effect had been to produce a state of alarm. Paul was, therefore, at special pains to show in his second epistle to them, that he did not mean any such thing. He showed them (2 Thess. ii.) that the end of the world was *not* near; that very important events were to occur before the world would come to an end; and that his language did not imply any expectation on his part that the world would soon terminate, or that the Lord Jesus would soon come. (3.) Parallel expressions occur in the other writers of the New Testament, and with a similar signification. Thus, John (1 Epis. ii. 18) says, "It is the last time;" comp. Heb. i. 2. But the meaning of this is not that the world would soon come to an end. The prophets spoke of a period which they called " the last days" (Isa. ii. 2; Micah iv. 1; in Hebrew, "the after days"), as the period in which the Messiah would live and reign. By it they meant the dispensation which should be *the last;* that under which the world would close; the reign of the Messiah, which would be the *last* economy of human things. But it did not follow that this was to be a *short* period; or that it might not be longer than any one of the former, or than *all* the former put together. This was that which John spoke of as the last time. (4.) I do not know that the proper doctrine of inspiration suffers, if we admit that

the apostles *were* ignorant of the exact time when the world would close ; or even that in regard to the precise period when that would take place, they might be in error. The following considerations may be suggested on this subject, showing that the claim to inspiration did not extend to the knowledge of this fact. (*a*) That they were not omniscient, and there is no more absurdity in supposing that they were ignorant on *this* subject than in regard to any other. (*b*) Inspiration extended to the *order* of future events, and not to the *times.* There is in the Scriptures *no* statement of the *time* when the world would close. Future events were made to pass before the minds of the prophets, as *in a landscape.* The *order* of the images may be distinctly marked, but the *times* may not be designated. And even events which may occur in fact at distant periods, may in vision appear to be near each other ; as in a landscape, objects which are in fact separated by distant intervals, like the ridges of a mountain, may appear to lie close to each other. (*c*) The Saviour expressly said, that it was not designed that they should *know* when future events would occur. Thus, after his ascension, in answer to an inquiry whether he then would restore the kingdom to Israel, he said (Acts i. 7), "It is not *for you* to know the times or the seasons which the Father hath put in his own power." See Note on that verse. (*d*) The Saviour said that even he himself, as man, was ignorant in regard to the exact time in which future events would occur. " But of that day, and that hour, knoweth no man, no, not the angels which are in heaven, neither the Son, but the Father;" Mark xiii. 32. (*e*) The apostles *were in fact* ignorant, and mistaken in regard to, at least, the time of the occurrence of *one* future event, the death of John; xxi. 23. There is, therefore, no departure from the proper doctrine of inspiration, in supposing that the apostles were not inspired on these subjects, and that they might be ignorant like others. The proper *order* of events they state truly and exactly; the

52 In a moment, ^a in the twinkling of an eye, at the last trump : for the ^b trumpet shall sound, and the dead ^c shall be raised incorruptible, and we shall be changed.

a 2Pet.3.10.　　　b Zech.9.14; Mat.24.31.

53 For this corruptible must put on incorruption, and this mortal ^d must put on immortality.

54 So when this corruptible shall have put on incorruption,

c John 5.25.　　　d 2Cor.5.4; 1John 3.2.

exact *time* God did not, for wise reasons, intend to make known. ¶ *Shall not all sleep.* Shall not all die; see Note, chap. xi. 30. ¶ *But we shall all be changed.* There is considerable variety in the reading of this passage. The Vulgate reads it, "We shall all indeed rise, but we shall not all be changed." Some Greek MSS. read it, " We shall all sleep, but we shall not all be changed." Others, as the Vulgate, " We shall all rise, but we shall not all be changed." But the present Greek text contains, doubtless, the true reading; and the sense is, that all who are alive at the coming of the Lord Jesus shall undergo such a change as to fit them for their new abode in heaven; or such as shall make them like those who shall be raised from the dead. This change will be instantaneous (ver. 52), for it is evident that God can as easily change the living as he can raise the dead ; and as the affairs of the world will then have come to an end, there will be no necessity that those who are then alive should be removed by death ; nor would it be proper that they should go down to lie any time in the grave. The ordinary laws, therefore, by which men are removed to eternity, will not operate in regard to them, and they will be removed at once to their new abode.

52. *In a moment* (ἐν ἀτόμῳ). In an *atom,* scil. of time ; a point of time which cannot be cut or divided (α priv. and τομη, from τέμνω, to cut). A single instant ; immediately. ¶ *In will be done instantaneously.* ¶ *In the twinkling of an eye.* This is an expression also denoting the least conceivable duration of time. The *suddenness* of the coming of the Lord Jesus is elsewhere compared to the coming of a thief in the night; 2 Pet.

iii. 10. The word rendered " twinkling" (ῥιπῆ, from ῥίπτω, to throw, cast) means a throw, cast, jerk, as of a stone ; and then a *jerk* of the eye, *i. e.* a wink.—*Robinson.* ¶ *At the last trump.* When the trumpet shall sound to raise the dead. The word " last" here does not imply that any trumpet shall have been *before* sounded at the resurrection, but is a word denoting that this is the consummation or close of things; it will end the economy of this world; it will be connected with the *last* state of things. ¶ *For the trumpet shall sound ;* see Note, Mat. xxiv. 31. ¶ *And the dead shall be raised ;* Note, John v. 25.

53. *For this corruptible, &c.* It is necessary that a change should take place, either by dying and then being raised, or by being changed without seeing death ; for we cannot enter heaven as we are now. ¶ *Must put on.* The word here used (ἐνδύνω) properly means to go in, to envelope, to put on as a garment ; and then to put on any thing; as the soul is, as it were, clothed with, or invested with a body; and here it means, must be endued with, or furnished with. It is equivalent to saying that this corruptible must become incorruptible, and this mortal must become immortal. We must cease to be corruptible and mortal, and must become incorruptible and immortal. The righteous who remain till the coming of Christ shall be at once changed, and invested, as Enoch and Elijah were, with incorruption and immortality.

54. *So when, &c.* In that future glorious world, when all this shall have been accomplished. ¶ *Then shall be brought to pass.* Then shall be fully accomplished ; these words shall then receive their entire fulfilment ; or this event shall meet all that is implied in these words. ¶ *The*

and this mortal shall have put on immortality, then shall be brought to pass the saying that

a Isa. 25.8.

is written, Death *a* is swallowed up in victory.

55 O *b* death, where *is* thy

b Hos. 13.14.

saying that is written. What is written, or the record which is made. These words are quoted from Isa. xxv. 8; and the fact that Paul thus quotes them, and the connection in which they stand, prove that they had reference to the times of the gospel, and to the resurrection of the dead. Paul does not quote directly from the Hebrew, or from the LXX., but gives the substance of the passage. ¶ *Death.* Referring here, undoubtedly, to death in the proper sense; death as prostrating the living, and consigning them to the grave. ¶ *Is swallowed up.* Κατεπόθη (from καταπίνω, to drink down, to swallow down) means to absorb (Rev. xii. 16); to overwhelm, to drown (Heb. xi. 29); and then to destroy or remove. The idea may be taken from a whirlpool, or Maelstrom, that absorbs all that comes near it; and the sense is, that he will abolish or remove death; that is, cause it to cease from its ravages and triumphs. ¶ *In victory* (εἰς νῖκος). Unto victory; so as to obtain a complete victory. The Hebrew (Isa. xxv. 8) is לנצח, The LXX. often render the word נצח, which properly means splendour, purity, trust, perpetuity, eternity, perfection, by νῖκος, victory; 2 Kings ii. 26; Job xxxvi. 7; Lam. iii. 18; v. 20; Amos i.; ii.; viii. 7. The Hebrew word here may be rendered either *unto the end, i. e.* to completeness or perfection, or unto victory, with triumph. It matters little which is the meaning, for they both come to the same thing. The idea is, that the power and dominion of death shall be entirely destroyed, or brought to an end.

55. *O death.* This triumphant exclamation is the commencement of the *fourth* division of the chapter,—the practical consequences of the doctrine. It is such an exclamation as every man with right feelings will be disposed to make, who contemplates the ravages of death; who looks upon a world where in all forms he has

reigned, and who then contemplates the glorious truth, that a complete and final triumph has been obtained over this great enemy of the happiness of man, and that man would die no more. It is a triumphant view which bursts upon the soul as it contemplates the fact that the work of the second Adam has repaired the ruins of the first, and that man is redeemed; his body will be raised; not another human being should die, and the work of death should be ended. Nay, it is more. Death is not only at an end; it shall not only cease, but its evils shall be repaired; and a glory and honour shall encompass the body of man, such as would have been unknown had there been no death. No commentary can add to the beauty and force of the language in this verse; and the best way to see its beauty, and to enjoy it, is to sit down and think of DEATH; of what death has been, and has done; of the millions and millions that have died; of the earth strewed with the dead, and "arched with graves;" *of our own death;* the certainty that *we* must die, and our parents, and brothers, and sisters, and children, and friends; that all, *all* must die;—and *then* to suffer the truth, in its full-orbed splendour, to rise upon us, that the time will come when DEATH SHALL BE AT AN END. Who, in such contemplation, can refrain from the language of triumph, and from hymns of praise? ¶ *Where* is *thy sting?* The word which is here rendered *sting* (κέντρον) denotes properly a prick, a point, hence a goad or stimulus; *i. e.* a rod or staff with an iron point, for goading oxen; (see Note, Acts ix. 5); and then a *sting* properly, as of scorpions, bees, &c. It denotes here a venomous thing, or weapon, applied to death personified, as if death employed it to destroy life, as the sting of a bee or a scorpion is used. The idea is derived from the venomous sting of serpents, or other reptiles, as being destructive

sting? O grave, [1] where *is* thy victory?

56 The [a] sting of death *is* sin; and [b] the strength of sin *is* the law.

a Rom.6.23.　　　　b Rom.4.15

and painful. The language here is the language of exultation, as if that was taken away or destroyed. ¶ *O grave* (ᾅδη). Hades, the place of the dead. It is not improperly rendered, however, *grave.* The word properly denotes a place of darkness; then the world, or abodes of the dead. According to the Hebrews, Hades, or Sheol, was a vast subterranean receptacle, or abode, where the souls of the dead existed. It was dark, deep, still, awful. The descent to it was through the grave; and the spirits of all the dead were supposed to be assembled there; the righteous occupying the upper regions, and the wicked the lower; see Note on Isa. xiv. 9; comp. Lowth, Lect. on Heb. Poet. vii. Campbell, Prel. Diss. vi. part 2, § 2, It refers here to the dead; and means that the grave, or Hades, should no longer have a victory. ¶ *Thy victory.* Since the dead are to rise; since all the graves are to give up all that dwell in them; since no man will die after that, where is its victory? It is taken away. It is despoiled. The power of death and the grave is vanquished, and Christ is triumphant over all. It has been well remarked here, that the words in this verse rise above the plain and simple language of prose, and resemble a hymn, into which the apostle breaks out in view of the glorious truth which is here presented to the mind. The whole verse is indeed a somewhat loose quotation from Hos. xiii. 14, which we translate,

"O death, I will be thy plagues;
O grave, I will be thy destruction."

But which the LXX. render,

"O death, where is thy punishment?
O grave, where is thy sting?"

Probably Paul did not intend this as a direct quotation; but he spoke as a man naturally does who is familiar with the language of the Scriptures, and used it to express the sense which he intended, without meaning to make a direct and literal quotation. The form which Paul uses is so poetic in its structure that Pope has adopted it, with only a change in the location of the members, in the "Dying Christian:"

"O grave, where is thy victory?
O death, where is thy sting?"

56. *The sting of death.* The sting which death bears; that with which he effects his purpose; that which is made use of to inflict death; or that which is the cause of death. There would be no death without sin. The apostle here *personifies* death, as if it were a living being, and as making use of sin to inflict death, or as being the sting, or envenomed instrument, with which he inflicts the mortal agony. The idea is, that sin is the cause of death. It introduced it; it makes it certain; it is the cause of the pain, distress, agony, and horror which attends it. Had there been no sin, men would not have died. If there were no sin, death would not be attended with horror or alarm. For why should innocence be afraid to die? What has innocence to fear anywhere in the universe of a just God? The fact, therefore, that men die, is proof that they are sinners; the fact that they feel horror and alarm, is proof that they feel themselves to be guilty, and that they are afraid to go into the presence of a holy God. If *this* be taken away, if sin be removed, of course the horror, and remorse, and alarm which it is fitted to produce will be removed also. ¶ *Is sin.* Sin is the cause of it; see Note, Rom. v. 12. ¶ *The strength of sin.* Its power over the mind; its terrific and dreadful energy; and *especially* its power to produce alarm in the hour of death. ¶ *Is the law.* The pure and holy law of God. This idea Paul has illustrated at length in Rom. vii. 9—13; see Notes on that passage. He probably made the statement here in order to meet the Jews, and to show that the law of God had no power to take away the fear of death; and that,

57 But thanks *a be* to God, which giveth us the victory *b* through our Lord Jesus Christ.

a Rom.7.25.   b Rom.8.37; 1John 5.4,5.

therefore, there was need of the gospel, and that this alone could do it. The Jews maintained that a man might be justified and saved by obedience to the law. Paul here shows that it is the law which gives its chief vigour to sin, and that it does not tend to subdue or destroy it ; and that power is seen most strikingly in the pangs and horrors of a guilty conscience on the bed of death. There was need, therefore, of the gospel, which alone could remove the *cause* of these horrors, by taking away sin, and thus leaving the pardoned man to die in peace ; comp. Note, Rom. iv. 15.

57. *But thanks* be *to God;* see Note, Rom. vii. 25. ¶ *Which giveth us the victory.* Us who are Christians ; all Christians. The victory over sin, death, and the grave. *God* alone is the author of this victory. He formed the plan ; he executed it in the gift of his Son ; and he gives it to us *personally* when we come to die. ¶ *Through our Lord Jesus Christ.* By his death, thus destroying the power of death ; by his resurrection and triumph over the grave ; and by his grace imparted to us to enable us to sustain the pains of death, and giving to us the hope of a glorious resurrection ; comp. Note, Rom. vii. 25 ; viii. 37.

58. *Therefore, my beloved brethren.* In view of the great and glorious truths which have been revealed to us respecting the resurrection, Paul closes the whole of this important discussion with an exhortation to that firmness in the faith which ought to result from truths so glorious, and from hopes so elevated as these truths are fitted to impart. The exhortation is so plain, that it needs little explanation ; it so obviously follows from the argument which Paul had pursued, that there is little need to attempt to enforce it. ¶ *Be ye steadfast* (ἑδραῖοι, from ἕδρα). Seated, sedentary (Robinson) ; perhaps with an

58 Therefore, my beloved brethren, *a* be ye steadfast, unmovable, always abounding in the work of the Lord,

a 2Pet.3.14.

allusion to a *statue* (Bloomfield) ; or perhaps to wrestling, and to standing one's ground (Wolf). Whatever may be the allusion, the sense is clear. Be firm, strong, confident in the faith, in view of the truth that you will be raised up. Be not shaken or agitated with the strifes, the temptations, and the cares of life. Be fixed in the faith, and let not the power of sin, or the sophistry of pretended philosophy, or the arts of the enemy of the soul seduce you from the faith of the gospel. ¶ *Unmovable.* Firm, fixed, stable, unmoved. This is probably a stronger expression than the former, though meaning substantially the same thing—that we are to be firm and unshaken in our Christian hopes, and in our faith in the gospel. ¶ *Always abounding in the work of the Lord.* Always engaged in doing the will of God ; in promoting his glory, and advancing his kingdom. The phrase means not only to be engaged in this, but to be engaged diligently, laboriously ; excelling in this. The "work of the Lord" here means that which the Lord requires ; all the appropriate duties of Christians. Paul exhorts them to practise every Christian virtue, and to do all that they could do to further the gospel among men. ¶ *Forasmuch as ye know.* Gr. *Knowing.* You know it by the arguments which have been urged for the truth of the gospel ; by your deep conviction that that gospel is true. ¶ *Your labour is not in vain.* It will be rewarded. It is not as if you were to die and never live again. There will be a resurrection, and you will be suitably recompensed then What you do for the honour of God will not only be attended with an approving conscience, and with happiness here, but will be met with the glorious and eternal rewards of heaven. ¶ *In the Lord.* This probably means, " Your labour or work in the Lord, *i. e.* in the cause of the Lord, will not be in vain." And the senti-

forasmuch as ye know that your labour is not in vain in the Lord.

ment of the whole verse is, that the hope of the resurrection and of future glory should stimulate us to great and self-denying efforts in honour of Him who has revealed that doctrine, and who purposes graciously to reward us there. Other men are influenced and excited to great efforts by the hope of honour, pleasure, or wealth. Christians should be excited to toil and self-denial by the prospect of immortal glory; and by the assurance that their hopes are not in vain, and will not deceive them.

Thus closes this chapter of inimitable beauty, and of unequalled power of argumentation. Such is the prospect which is before the Christian. He shall indeed die like other men. But his death is *a sleep*—a calm, gentle, undisturbed sleep, in the expectation of being again awaked to a brighter day, ver. 6. He has the assurance that his Saviour rose, and that his people shall *therefore* also rise, ver. 12—20. He encounters peril, and privation, and persecution; he may be ridiculed and despised; he may be subjected to danger, or doomed to fight with wild beasts, or to contend with men who resemble wild beasts; he may be doomed to the pains and terrors of a martyrdom at the stake, but he has the assurance that all these are of short continuance, and that before him there is a world of eternal glory; ver. 29—32. He may be poor, unhonoured, and apparently without an earthly friend or protector; but his Saviour and Redeemer reigns; ver. 25. He may be opposed by wicked men, and his name slandered, and body tortured, and his peace marred, but his enemies shall all be subdued; ver. 26, 27. He will himself die, and sleep in his grave, but he shall live again; ver. 22, 23. He has painful proof that his body is corruptible, but it will be incorruptible; that it is now vile, but it will be glorious; that it is weak, frail, feeble, but it will yet be strong, and no more subject to disease or decay; ver. 42, 43. And he will be brought under the power of death, but death shall

be robbed of its honours, and despoiled of its triumph. Its sting from the saint is taken away, and it is changed to a blessing. It is now not the dreaded monster, the king of terrors it is a friend that comes to remove him from a world of toil to a world of rest; from a life of sin to a life of glory. The grave is not to him the gloomy *abode*, the permanent resting-place of his body; it is a place of rest for a little time; grateful like the bed of down to a wearied frame, where he may lie down and repose after the fatigues of the day, and gently wait for the morning. He has nothing to fear in death; nothing to fear in the dying pang, the gloom, the chill, the sweat, the paleness, the tiredness of death; nothing to fear in the chilliness, the darkness, the silence, the corruption of the grave. All this is in the way to immortality, and is closely and indissolubly connected with immortality; ver. 55—57. And in view of all this, we should be patient, faithful, laborious, self-denying; we should engage with zeal in the work of the Lord; we should calmly wait till our change come; ver. 58. No other system of religion has any such hopes as this; no other system does *any* thing to dispel the gloom, or drive away the horrors of the grave. How foolish is the man who rejects the gospel—the only system which brings life and immortality to light! How foolish to reject the doctrine of the resurrection, and to lie down in the grave without peace, without hope, without any belief that there will be a world of glory; living without God, and dying like the brute. And yet infidelity seeks and claims its chief triumphs in the attempt to convince poor dying man that he has no solid ground of hope; that the universe is "without a Father and without a God;" that the grave terminates the career of man for ever; and that in the grave he sinks away to eternal annihilation. Strange that man should seek such degradation! Strange that *all* men, conscious that they must die, do not at once greet

CHAPTER XVI.

NOW concerning the collection for the saints, as *a* I have given order to the churches of Galatia, even so do ye.

a Gal.2.10.

Christianity as their best friend, and hail the doctrine of the future state, and of the resurrection, as that which is adapted to meet the deeply-felt evils of this world; to fill the desponding mind with peace; and to sustain the soul in the temptations and trials of life, and in the gloom and agony of death !

CHAPTER XVI.

THE *doctrinal* part of this epistle was closed at the end of the fifteenth chapter; see the Introduction. Before closing the epistle, Paul adverts to some subjects of a miscellaneous nature, and particularly to the subject of a collection for the poor and persecuted Christians in Judea, on which his heart was much set, and to which he several times adverts in his epistles; see Note on ver. 1. This subject he had suggested to them when he was with them, and they had expressed, some time before, the utmost readiness to make the collection, and Paul had commended their readiness when he was urging the same subject in Macedonia; see 2 Cor. ix. It is evident, however, that for some cause, perhaps owing to the divisions and contentions in the church, this collection had not yet been made. Paul, therefore, calls their attention to it, and urges them to make it, and to forward it either by him alone, or with others, whom they might designate, to Judea; ver. 1—4. In connection with this, he expresses his intention of coming to Corinth, and perhaps of passing the winter with them. He was then in Ephesus. He was expecting to go to Macedonia, probably on the business of the collection. He purposed *not* to visit them on his way *to* Macedonia, but on his return. He had formerly intended to pass through Corinth on his way to Macedonia, and had perhaps given them such an intimation of his purpose; 2 Cor. i. 16, 17. But from some cause (see Notes on 2 Cor. i. 15—23), he tells the Corinthians that he had abandoned the purpose of seeing them on the way to Macedonia, though he still intended to go to Macedonia,

and would see them on his return; ver. 5—7. At that time there was a state of things in Ephesus which required his presence. His labours were greatly blessed; and, as a consequence which often attends the successful preaching of the gospel, there was much opposition. He had resolved, therefore, to remain in Ephesus until Pentecost; ver. 8, 9. In the mean time, to show them his deep interest in them, he informed them that Timothy was coming among them, for whom he asked a kind and cordial reception, and assured them that he had endeavoured to persuade Apollos to visit them, but was not able; ver. 10—12. Paul then urges them to watch, and be firm, and live in love (ver. 13, 14); and then besought them to show particular attention to the family of Stephanas, the first-fruits of Achaia (ver. 15, 16); and expresses his gratitude that Stephanas, and Fortunatus, and Achaicus had come to him at Ephesus; ver. 17, 18. They were probably the persons by whom the Corinthians had sent their letter (chap. viii. 1), and by whom Paul sent this epistle. He then closes the whole epistle with Christian salutations; with an expression of regard in his own handwriting; with a solemn charge to love the Lord Jesus Christ, as the great thing to be done, and with the assurance that, if not done, it would expose the soul to a dreadful curse when the Lord should come; with an invocation of the grace of the Lord Jesus to be with them; and with a tender expression of his own love to them all; ver. 19—24.

1. *Now concerning the collection for the saints*. The use of the article here shows that he had mentioned it to them before, and that it was a subject which they would readily understand. It was not new to them, but it was needful only to give some instructions in regard to the *manner* in which it should be done, and not in regard to the occasion for the collection, or the duty of making it. Accordingly, all his instructions relate simply to the *manner* in which

2 Upon the first *a day* of the week let every one of you lay by

a Acts 20.7; Rev.1.10.

him in store, as *God* hath prospered him, that there be no gatherings when I come.

the collection should be made. The word rendered *collection* (λογία) does not occur anywhere else in the New Testament, and is not found in the classic writers. It is from λέγω, to collect, and, undoubtedly, here refers to a contribution, or collection of money for a charitable purpose. The word *saints* (ἁγίους) here refers, doubtless, to *Christians;* to the persecuted Christians in Judea. There were many there; and they were generally poor, and exposed to various trials. In regard to the meaning of this word, and the circumstances and occasion of this collection; see Notes on Rom. xv. 25, 26. ¶ *As I have given order* (διέταξα). As I have directed, enjoined, commanded, arranged. It does not mean that he had assumed the authority to tax them, or that he had *commanded* them to make a collection, but that he had left directions as to the best *manner* and *time* in which it should be done. The collection was voluntary and cheerful in all the churches (Rom. xv. 26, 27; 2 Cor. ix. 2); and Paul did not assume authority to impose it on them as a tax. Nor was it necessary. Self-denial and liberality were among the distinguishing virtues of the early Christians; and to be a Christian *then* implied that a man would freely impart of his property to aid the poor and the needy. The order related solely to the manner of making the collection; and as Paul had suggested one mode to the churches in Galatia, he recommended the same now to the Corinthians. ¶ *To the churches of Galatia.* Galatia was a province in Asia Minor. On its situation, see Note, Acts xvi. 6. There were evidently several churches planted in that region; see Gal. i. 2. At what time he gave this order to the churches there is not mentioned; though it was doubtless on occasion of a visit to the churches there; see Acts xvi. 6.

2. *Upon the first* day *of the week.* Greek, "On one of the Sabbaths." The Jews, however, used the word

Sabbath to denote the week; the period of seven days; Mat. xxviii. 1; Mark xvi. 9; Luke xviii. 12; xxiv. 1; John xx. 1, 19; comp. Lev. xxiii. 15; Deut. xvi. 9. It is universally agreed that this here denotes the first day of the week, or the Lord's day. ¶ *Let every one of you.* Let the collection be universal. Let each one esteem it his duty and his privilege to give to this object. It was not to be confined to the rich only, but was the common duty of all. The poor, as well as the rich, were expected to contribute according to their ability. ¶ *Lay by him in store* (παρ᾽ ἑαυτῷ τιθέτω θησαυρίζων). Let him lay up at home, treasuring up as he has been prospered. The Greek phrase, "by himself," means, probably, the same as at home. Let him set it apart; let him designate a certain portion; let him do this *by himself,* when he is at home, when he can calmly look at the evidence of his prosperity. Let him do it not under the influence of pathetic appeals, or for the sake of display when he is with others; but let him do it as a matter of principle, and when he is by himself. The phrase in Greek, "treasuring up," may mean that each one was to put the part which he had designated into the common *treasury.* This interpretation seems to be demanded by the latter part of the verse. They were to lay it by, and to put it into the common treasury, that there might be no trouble of collecting when he should come. Or it may, perhaps, mean that they were individually to *treasure it up,* having designated in their own mind the sum which they could give, and have it in readiness when he should come. This was evidently to be done not on one Sabbath only, but was to be done on each Lord's-day until he should come. ¶ *As God hath prospered him.* The word "God" is not in the original, but it is evidently understood, and necessary to the sense. The word rendered "hath prospered" (εὐοδῶται) means, properly, to set forward on one's way; to prosper one's

3 And when I come, whomsoever *a* ye shall approve by *your*

letters, them will I send to bring your [1] liberality unto Jerusalem.

1 *gift.*

journey; and then to prosper, or be prospered. This is the rule which Paul lays down here to guide the Christians at Corinth in giving alms,—a rule that is as applicable now, and as valuable now, as it was then. ¶ *That there be no gatherings when I come.* No collections (λογίαι, ver. 1). The apostle means that there should be no trouble in collecting the small sums; that it should all be prepared; that each one might have laid by what he could give; and that all might be ready to be handed over to him, or to whomsoever they might choose to send with it to Jerusalem; ver. 3.—In view of this important verse, we may remark, (1.) That there is here clear proof that the first day of the week was observed by the church at Corinth as holy time. If it was not, there can have been no propriety in selecting that day in preference to any other in which to make the collection. It was the day which was set apart to the duties of religion, and therefore an appropriate day for the exercise of charity and the bestowment of alms. There can have been no reason why this day should have been designated except that it was a day set apart to religion, and therefore deemed a proper day for the exercise of benevolence towards others. (2.) This order extended also to the churches in Galatia, proving also that the first day of the week was observed by them, and was regarded as a day proper for the exercise of charity towards the poor and the afflicted. And if the first day of the week was observed, by apostolic authority, in those churches, it is morally certain that it was observed by others. This consideration, therefore, demonstrates that it was the custom to observe this day, and that it was observed by the authority of the early founders of Christianity. (3.) Paul intended that they should be *systematic* in their giving, and that they should give from *principle*, and not merely under the impulse of feeling. (4.) Paul designed that the habit of doing good with their money should be *constant.*

He, therefore, directed that it should be on the return of each Lord's-day, and that the subject should be constantly before their minds. (5.) It was evident that Paul in this way would obtain *more* for his object than he would if he waited that they should give all at once. He therefore directed them honestly to lay by each week what they could *then* give, and to regard it as a sacred *treasure.* How much would the amount of charities in the Christian churches be swelled if this were the practice now, and if *all* Christians would lay by *in store* each week what they could then devote to sacred purposes. (6.) The true rule of giving is, "as the Lord hath prospered us." If he has prospered us, we owe it to him as a debt of gratitude. And according to our prosperity and success, we should honestly devote our property to God. (7.) It is right and proper to lay by of our wealth for the purposes of benevolence on the Sabbath-day. It is right to do good then (Mat. xii. 12); and one of the appropriate exercises of religion is to look at the evidence of our prosperity with a view to know what we may be permitted to give to advance the kingdom of the Lord Jesus. (8.) If every Christian would honestly do this every week, it would do much to keep down the spirit of worldliness that now prevails everywhere in the Christian church; and if every Christian would conscientiously follow the direction of Paul here, there would be no want of funds for any well-directed plan for the conversion of the world.

3. *Whomsoever ye shall approve by your letters.* There has been great variety of opinion in regard to the proper construction of this verse. Macknight supposes that the "letters" here referred to were not letters either to or from the apostle, but letters signed and sent by the church at Corinth, designating their appointment and their authority. With this interpretation Doddridge coincides; and this is required by the usual point-

4 And if it be meet that I go also, they shall go with me.

5 Now I will come unto you, ^a when I shall pass through Macedonia: for I do pass through Macedonia.

6 And it may be that I will

a 2 Cor.1.15.

abide, yea, and winter with you, that ye may bring me on my journey whithersoever I go.

7 For I will not see you now by the way; but I trust to tarry a while with you, if the Lord permit.

---

ing of the Greek text, where the comma is inserted after the word letters, as in our translation. But a different interpretation has been proposed by inserting the comma after the word "approve," so that it shall read, " Whom you approve, or designate, them I will send *with letters* to convey your charity to Jerusalem." This is followed by Griesbach, Locke, Rosenmüller, Bloomfield, Beza, Hammond, Grotius, Whitby, &c. Certainly this accords better with the design of the passage. For it is evident (see ver. 4) that, though Paul was willing to go, yet he was not expecting to go. If he did not go, what was more natural than that he should offer to give them letters of commendation to his brethren in Judea? Mill has doubted whether this construction is in accordance with Greek usage, but the names above cited are sufficient authority on that subject. The proper construction, therefore, is, that Paul would give them letters to his friends in Jerusalem, and certify their appointment to dispense the charity, and commend the persons sent to the favour and hospitality of the church there. ¶ *Your liberality.* Marg. *Gift.* Your donation; your alms. The Greek word χάριν usually signifies grace, or favour. Here it means an act of grace or favour; kindness; a favour conferred; benefaction: comp. 2 Cor. viii. 4, 6, 7, 19.

4. *And if it be meet,* &c. If it be judged desirable and best. If my presence can further the object; or will satisfy you better; or will be deemed necessary to guide and aid those who may be sent, I will be willing to go also. For some appropriate and valuable remarks in regard to the apostle Paul's management of pecuniary matters, so as not to excite suspicion, and to preserve a blameless

reputation, see Paley's Horæ Paulinæ, chap. iv. No. 1, 3. Note.

5. *Now I will come unto you.* I purpose to come unto you. He had expected to see them on his way to Macedonia, but, on some account, had been induced to abandon that design. See Notes, 2 Cor. i. 15—17. ¶ *When I shall pass through Macedonia.* When I shall have passed through Macedonia. He proposed to go to Macedonia first, and, having passed through that country, visiting the churches, to go to Corinth. For the situation of Macedonia, see Note, Acts xvi. 9. ¶ *For I do pass through Macedonia.* I design to do it. It is my present intention. Though he had abandoned, from some cause, the design of passing through Corinth on his way to Macedonia, yet he had not given up the design itself. It was still his intention to go there.

6. *That ye may bring me on my journey.* That you may accompany me, or aid me, and furnish me the means of going on my journey. It was customary for the apostles to be attended by some members of the churches and friends in their travels. See Note, Acts x. 23. ¶ *On my journey,* &c. Probably to Judea. This was evidently his intention. But wherever he should go, it would be gratifying to him to have their aid and companionship.

7. *For I will not see you now by the way.* On the way to Macedonia. Something had occurred to change his mind, and to induce him to go to Macedonia by another way. ¶ *But I trust to tarry a while with you.* That is, on my return from Macedonia, ver. 5. Greek, " I *hope* to remain with you a little while. ¶ *If the Lord permit.* The apostle did not use the language of certainty and of confidence. He felt his dependence on

8 But I will tarry at Ephesus until Pentecost.

9 For a great door *a* and effec-

tual is opened unto me, and *there are* many adversaries.*b*

10 Now if Timotheus *c* come,

---

a 2 Cor.2.12; Rev.3.8.

b Phil.3.18.   *c* Acts 19.22.

God, and regarded all as under his direction ; see the same form of expression in 1 Cor. iv. 19, and the Note on that place.

8. *But I will tarry at Ephesus.* This passage proves that this letter was written from Ephesus. It is by such indications as this usually that we are able to determine the place where the epistles were written. In regard to the situation of Ephesus, see Note on Acts xviii. 19. ¶ *Until Pentecost.* This was a Jewish festival occurring fifty days after the Passover, and hence called the *Pentecost.* See Note, Acts ii. 1. As there were Jews at Corinth, and doubtless in the church, they would understand the time which Paul referred to ; and as he was a Jew, he naturally used their mode of reckoning time where it would be understood. Doubtless the great festivals of the Jews were well known among most of the cities of Greece, as there were Jews in them all who were scrupulous in their observances. It is no improbable supposition, also, that *Christians* every where regarded this day with deep interest, as being the day on which the Holy Spirit descended on the apostles and on the people of Jerusalem, Acts ii.

9. *For a great door.* There is abundant opportunity for usefulness. The word *door* is used evidently to denote an occasion or an opportunity for doing any thing. It is the means by which we have entrance or access ; and hence denotes facility in doing any thing when there is no obstruction ; see Acts xiv. 27; 2 Cor. ii. 12 ; Col. iv. 3. ¶ *And effectual.* That is, *effective,* or adapted to success ; presenting opportunity for great effects. There is abundant opportunity to preach the gospel ; there is attention to what is spoken, and great interest in it ; there is great encouragement to labour. It is possible that this was one of the reasons why Paul had changed his mind about

passing through Corinth on his way to Macedonia. It would require *time* to visit Corinth, as he would wish to remain there ; and an unexpected opportunity having arisen for doing good, he judged it best to remain at Ephesus as long as practicable, and then to go at once to Macedonia. ¶ *And* there are *many adversaries.* Many opposers ; many who resist the gospel. These were doubtless in part Jews who excited opposition to him, and in part the friends of Demetrius ; see Acts xix. That Paul had great success in Ephesus, and that his labours were attended with a great revival of religion there, is manifest from that chapter. We may remark here, (1.) That such a work of grace, such a setting open a great and effectual door, is often the occasion of increased opposition to the gospel. It is no uncommon thing that the adversaries of Christ should be excited at such times ; and we are not to be surprised if the same thing should occur now which occured in the time of Paul. (2.) This was regarded by Paul as no reason why he should leave Ephesus, but rather as a reason why he should remain there. It was regarded by him as an evidence that the Holy Spirit was there. It was proof that the enemies of God were alarmed, and that the kingdom of Christ was advancing. His presence, also, would be needed there, to encourage and strengthen the young converts who would be attacked and opposed ; and he deemed it his duty to remain. A minister should never wish to make enemies to the gospel, nor seek to excite them to make opposition ; but such opposition is often evidence that the Spirit of God is among a people ; that the consciences of sinners are aroused and alarmed ; and that the great enemy of God and man is making, as he was at Ephesus, a desperate effort to preserve his kingdom from being destroyed. (3.) A minister should regard it as his duty in a

see that he may be with you without fear : for he worketh *a* the work of the Lord, as I also *do*.

11 Let no man therefore despise *b* him : but conduct *c* him forth in peace, that he may come unto

a Phil.2.19-22.   *b* 1 Tim.4.12.

me : for I look for him with the brethren.

12 As touching *our* brother Apollos, *d* I greatly desired him to come unto you with the brethren : but his will was not at all to come

c 3 John 6.   *d* chap.1.12.

special manner to be among his people when there is such opposition excited. His presence is needed to comfort and encourage the church ; and when the minds of men are excited, it is often the best time to present truth, and to defend successfully the great doctrines of the Bible. (4.) Ministers should not be *discouraged* because there is opposition to the gospel. It is one ground of encouragement. It is an indication of the presence of God in awakening the conscience. And it is far more favourable as a season to do good than a dead calm, and when there is universal stagnation and unconcern.

10. *Now if Timotheus come.* Paul had sent Timothy to them (see Note, chap. iv. 17, 18), but as he had many churches to visit, it was not absolutely certain that he would go to Corinth. ¶ *May be with you without fear.* Let him be received kindly and affection ately. Timothy was then a young man ; Acts xvi. 1 ; 3 ; 1 Tim. iv. 12. There might be some danger that he might feel himself embarrassed among the rich, the gay, and the great. Paul, therefore, asks them to encourage him, to receive him kindly, and not to embarrass him. Perhaps, also, there may be some reference to the false teachers whom Timothy might be called on to oppose. They were powerful, and they might endeavour to intimidate and alarm him. Paul, therefore, asks the church to sustain him in his efforts to defend the truth. ¶ *For he worketh the work of the Lord.* He is engaged in the service of the Lord ; and he is worthy of your confidence, and worthy to be sustained by you.

11. *Let no man, therefore, despise him.* Let no one despise him on account of his youth and inexperience. It is probable that some of the more

wealthy and proud, some who valued themselves on their wisdom and experience, would be disposed to look upon him with contempt. On another occasion, he directed Timothy so to live as that no one should have occasion to despise him on account of his youth (1 Tim. iv. 12) ; and he here urges on the Corinthians, that they should not despise him because he was a young man, and comparatively inexperienced. A minister of the gospel, though young, should receive the respect that is due to his office ; and if he conducts himself in accordance with his high calling, his youth should be no barrier to the confidence and affection of even aged and experienced Christians. It should be rather a reason why they should treat him with affection, and encourage him in his work. ¶ *But conduct him forth in peace.* That is, when he leaves you. Attend him on his way, and help him forward on his journey to me ; see Note on ver. 6. ¶ *For I look for him with the brethren.* Erastus accompanied Timothy in this journey (Acts xix. 22), and probably there were others with him. Titus also had been sent to Corinth (2 Cor. xii. 17, 18), and it is not improbable that Paul had desired Titus to bring with him to Ephesus some of the Corinthian brethren, as he might need their assistance there.—*Grotius.*

12. *As touching* our *brother Apollos.* Tindal renders this, "To speak of brother Apollo." In regard to Apollos, see Note, chap. i. 12. ¶ *His will was not at all to come at this time.* It is probable that there were matters which detained him, or which required his presence in Ephesus. It is not known why Apollos had left Corinth, but it has been supposed that it was on account of the dissensions which existed there. For the same

at this time ; but he will come when he shall have convenient time.

13 Watch *a* ye, stand *b* fast. in

the faith, quit you like men, *c* be strong. *d*

14 Let *e* all your things be done with charity.

a 1 Pet.5.8.   *b* 2 Thess.2.15.   *c* chap.14.20.   *d* Eph.6.10.   *e* 1 Pet.4.8.

reason he might not be induced to return there while those dissensions lasted and there might be employment which he had where he then was which rendered his presence there important. The Latin fathers say that Apollos did after this return to Corinth, when the religious differences had been settled.—*Bloomfield.* It is probable that the Corinthians had requested, by the messengers who carried their letter to Paul, that either he or Apollos would come and visit them. Paul states, in reply, that he had endeavoured to prevail on Apollos to go, but had not succeeded. ¶ *He will come when he shall have convenient time.* The Greek word means, when he should have leisure, or a good opportunity. He might then be engaged; or he might be unwilling to go while their contentions lasted. They had probably (chap. i. 12) endeavoured to make him the head of a party, and on that account he might have been unwilling to return at present among them. But Paul assures them that he designed to come among them at some future time. This was said probably to show them that he still retained his affection for them, and had a tender solicitude for their peace and prosperity. Had this not been said, they might, perhaps, have inferred that he was offended, and had no desire to come among them.

13. *Watch ye.* The exhortation in this and the following verse is given evidently in view of the peculiar dangers and temptations which surrounded them. The word here used (Γρηγορεῖτε) means, to keep awake, to be vigilant, &c.; and this may, perhaps, be a military metaphor derived from the duty of those who are stationed as sentinels to guard a camp, or to observe the motions of an enemy. The term is frequently used in the New Testament, and the duty fre-

quently enjoined; Mat. xxiv. 41, 42; xxv. 13; Mark xiii. 35; Luke xxi. 36; Acts xx. 31; 1 Thess. v. 6; 2 Tim. iv. 5. The sense here is, that they were to watch, or be vigilant, against all the evils of which he had admonished them,—the evils of dissension, or erroneous doctrines, of disorder, of false teachers, &c. They were to watch lest their souls should be ruined, and their salvation endangered; lest the enemies of the truth and of holiness should steal silently upon them, and surprise them. They were to watch with the same vigilance that is required of a sentinel who guards a camp, lest an enemy should come suddenly upon them, and surprise the camp when the army was locked in sleep. ¶ *Stand fast in the faith.* Be firm in holding and defending the truths of the gospel. Do not yield to any foe, but maintain the truth, and adhere to your confidence in God and to the doctrines of the gospel with unwavering constancy; see Note, chap. xv. 1. Be firm in maintaining what you believe to be true, and in holding on to your personal confidence in God, notwithstanding all the arts, insinuations, and teachings of seducers and the friends of false doctrine. ¶ *Quit you like men* (ἀνδρίζεσθε, from ἀνήρ, a man). The word occurs no where else in the New Testament. In the LXX. it occurs in Josh. i. 6, 7, 9, 18; 1 Chron. xxviii. 20; 2 Chron. xxxii. 7; Neh. ii. 1; and in eighteen other places. See Trommius' Concordance. It occurs also in the classic authors; see Xen. Oec. v. 4. It means, to render one manly or brave ; to show one's-self a man ; that is, not to be a coward, or timid, or alarmed at enemies, but to be bold and brave. We have a similar phrase in common use : "Be a man," or "Show yourself a man ;" that is, be not mean, or be not cowardly. ¶ *Be strong.* Be firm,

15 I beseech you, brethren, (ye know the house of Stephanas, that it is the *a* first-fruits of Achaia, and *that* they have addicted themselves to the ministry of the saints,)

16 That ye submit *b* yourselves

a Rom.16.5.   *b* Heb.13.17.

unto such, and to every one that helpeth with *us*, and laboureth.

17 I am glad of the coming of Stephanas and Fortunatus and Achaicus: for that which was lacking *c* on your part they have supplied.

c Phil 2.30.

fixed, steadfast; comp. Eph. vi. 10, "Be strong in the Lord, and in the power of his might."

14. *Let all your things,* &c. All that you do. This direction is repeated on account of its great importance, and because it is a *summing up* of all that he had said in this epistle; see chap. xiii; xiv. 1. Here he says, that charity, or love, was to regulate all that they did. This was a simple rule, and if this was observed, every thing would be done well.

15. *I beseech you, brethren.* The construction here is somewhat involved, but the sense is plain. The words, "I beseech you," in this verse, are evidently to be taken in connection with ver. 16, "I beseech you that ye submit yourselves unto such," &c. The design is to exhort them to pay proper deference to Stephanas, and to all who sustained the same rank and character; and the remainder of ver. 15 is designed to state the reason why they should show respect and kindness to the household of Stephanas ¶ *Ye know the house.* You are acquainted with the household, or family. Probably a considerable portion, or all, of the family of Stephanas had been converted to the Christian faith. ¶ *Of Stephanas;* see Note, chap. i. 16. Paul there says that he had baptized his family. ¶ *That it is the first-fruits of Achaia.* They were the first converted to the Christian religion in Achaia; see Note, Rom. xvi. 5. Respecting Achaia, see Note, Acts xviii. 12. ¶ *That they have addicted themselves,* &c. That they have devoted themselves to the service of Christians. That is, by aiding the ministry; by showing hospitality; by providing for their wants; by attending and aiding the apostles in their journeys, &c.

16. *That ye submit yourselves,* &c. The word used here means evidently that you would show them proper deference and regard; that you would treat them with distinguished respect and honour for what they have done. ¶ *And to every one that helpeth with us,* &c. Every one that aids us in the ministry, or provides for our wants, &c. It is possible that Stephanas lived among them at this time (Note, chap. i. 16), though he had been converted in Achaia; and it is probable that, as Corinth was a central place and a thoroughfare, others might come among them who were the personal friends of Paul, and who had aided him in the ministry. Towards all such he bespeaks their kind, and tender, and respectful regards.

17. *I am glad of the coming.* That is, I am glad that they have come to me at Ephesus. I rejoice that he who was converted by my ministry in Achaia, and who has so long shown himself to be a personal friend to me, and an aid in my work, came where I am. ¶ *Stephanas.* The same person evidently mentioned in the previous verses. Probably he, as one of the oldest and most respected members of the church, had been selected to carry the letter of the Corinthians (chap. vii. 1) to Paul, and to consult with him respecting the affairs of the church there. ¶ *Fortunatus and Achaicus.* These persons are not referred to anywhere else in the New Testament. It appears that Fortunatus survived Paul, for he was subsequently the messenger of the church at Corinth to that at Rome, and bore back to the Corinthians the epistle which Clement of Rome sent to them. See that epistle, § 59. ¶ *For that which was lacking,* &c. The word which is here used, and rendered

18 For they have refreshed my spirit and yours: therefore acknowledge *a* ye them that are such.

19 The churches of Asia salute you. Aquila *b* and Priscilla

salute you much in the Lord, with the church *c* that is in their house.

20 All the brethren greet you. Greet ye one another with a holy kiss.

a 1 Thess.5.12.   *b* Acts 18.26.

c Rom.16.5.15.

"that which was lacking" (ὑστέρηνα), does not occur in the classic writers. It means properly that which is wanting, want, lack.—*Robinson.* It may be used to denote a want or lack of any kind, whether of support, sustenance, aid, consolation, information, or counsel; see Luke xxi. 4; Phil. ii. 30; 1 Thess. iii. 10. What this was which the Corinthians had neglected or failed to furnish Paul, and which had been supplied by the presence of these persons, can be only a matter of conjecture; and different commentators have supposed different things. It might be a neglect to provide for his wants, or a defect of informing him about their affairs in the letter which they had sent him; or it might be that these persons had furnished, by their presence and conversation, those consolations and friendly offices which the church at Corinth would have rendered had they been all present; and Paul may mean to say, that he had enjoyed with them that friendly intercourse and Christian communion which he had desired with them, but which was lacking, *i. e.* which he had not been permitted to enjoy by reason of his absence. This is the view which is given by Rosenmüller, Doddridge, Bloomfield; and as Paul does not seem here inclined to blame them, this view is most in accordance with the general strain of the passage.

18. *For they have refreshed my spirit.* By their presence and conversation. They have given me information respecting the state of things in the church; and their society has been with me of the most gratifying and cheering kind. ¶ *And yours.* "By removing," says Locke, "those suspicions and fears that were on both sides." "By thus supplying your absence, they have benefited us both."

For Paul gained information of those absent, and they gained in the counsel afforded to them by the apostle."— *Bloomfield.* "For they refreshed my spirit by their obliging behaviour and edifying conversation, as, I doubt not, they have often refreshed yours by their ministrations among you."— *Doddridge.* The sense seems to be, that their visit to him would be a benefit to both; would result in imparting comfort, a good understanding, an increase of their mutual attachment, and ultimately a large accession to their mutual joy when they should again meet. ¶ *Therefore acknowledge ye them that are such.* Receive affectionately; recognise as brethren; cherish, treat kindly all that evince such a spirit; see Notes on ver. 15, 16. The apostle here designs, evidently, that the Corinthians should receive them kindly on their return, and regard with deference and respect the counsel which they might offer, and the message which they might bear from him.

19. *The churches of Asia.* The word "Asia" in the New Testament usually denotes Asia Minor in general; see Note on Acts ii. 9. It was sometimes used in a more limited sense, to denote the region around Ephesus, and of which Ephesus was the centre and capital; see Note, Acts xvi. 6. This is the region undoubtedly which is intended here. ¶ *Salute you.* Greet you; send respectful and affectionate Christian regards; see Note, Rom. xvi. 3. ¶ *Aquila and Priscilla;* see Note on Acts xviii. 26. ¶ *Much in the Lord.* With affectionate Christian salutations; or as Christians. Wishing the blessing and favour of the Lord. ¶ *With the church that is in their house;* Note, Rom. xvi. 5.

20. *All the brethren,* &c. All the Christians with whom Paul was con-

21 The salutation of *me* Paul with mine own hand.

22 If any man love *a* not the Lord Jesus Christ, let him be anathema *b* maran-atha.*c*

---

a Eph.6.24.   *b* Gal.1.8,9.   *c* Jude 14,15.

---

nected in Ephesus. They felt a deep interest in the church at Corinth, and sent to them Christian salutations. ¶ *With a holy kiss;* see the Note on Rom. xvi. 16.

21. *The salutation of me, Paul, with mine own hand.* It is evident that Paul was accustomed to employ an amanuensis in penning his epistles (see Note on Rom. xvi. 22), though he signed his own name, and expressed his Christian salutation in every epistle, 2 Thess. iii. 17; comp. Col. iv. 18. This gave a sanction to what was written; was a proof that it was his own, and was a valuable token of affectionate regard. It was a proof that there was no fraud or imposition. *Why* he employed an amanuensis is not known.

22. *If any man love not the Lord Jesus Christ.* This is a most solemn and affecting close of the whole epistle. It was designed to direct them to the great and essential matter of religion, the love of the Lord Jesus; and was intended, doubtless, to turn away their minds from the subjects which had agitated them, the disputes and dissensions which had rent the church into factions, to the great inquiry whether they truly loved the Saviour. It is implied that there was danger, in their disputes and strifes about minor matters, of neglecting the love of the Lord Jesus, or of substituting attachment to a party in the place of that love to the Saviour which alone could be connected with eternal life. ¶ *Let him be anathema.* On the meaning of the word *anathema*, see Note, chap. xii. 3. The word properly means accursed, or devoted to destruction; and the idea here is, that he who did not believe in the Lord Jesus, and love him, would be, and ought to be. devoted to destruction, or accursed of God. It expresses what *ought* to be done; it expresses *a truth* in regard to God's dealings, not the *desire* of the apostle. No matter what any man's endow-

ments might be; no matter what might be his wealth, his standing, or his talent; no matter if he were regarded as a ruler in the church, or at the head of a party; yet if he had not true love to the Lord Jesus, he could not be saved. This sentiment is in accordance with the declaration of the Scripture everywhere. See particularly, John iii. 31; Micah xvi. 16, and the Note on the latter place. ¶ *Maran-atha.* These are Syriac words, *Moran Etho* — " the Lord comes;" *i. e.* will come. The reason why this expression is added may be. (1.) To give the greater *solemnity* to the declaration of the apostle; *i. e.* to give it an emphatic form. (2.) To intimate that, though there were no earthly power to punish a want of love to the Saviour; though the state could not, and ought not to punish it; and though the church could not exclude all who did not love the Lord Jesus from its bosom, yet they could not escape. For, the Lord would himself come to take vengeance on his enemies; and no one could escape. Though, therefore, those who did not love the Lord Jesus could not be punished by men, yet they could not escape divine condemnation. The Lord would come to execute vengeance himself, and they could not escape. It is probable (see Lightfoot in loco) that the Jews were accustomed to use such a form in their greater excommunication, and that they meant by it, that the person who was thus devoted to destruction, and excommunicated, *must* be destroyed; for the Lord would come to take vengeance on all his enemies. " It certainly was not now, for the first time, used as a new kind of cursing by the apostle; but was the application of a current mode of speech to the purpose he had in contemplation. Perhaps, therefore, by inspecting the manners of the East, we may illustrate the import of this singular passage. The nearest approach to it that I have

23 The grace *a* of our Lord Jesus Christ *be* with you.

24 My love *be* with you all in Christ Jesus.   Amen.

a Rom.16.20.

been able to discover is in the following extract from Mr. Bruce; and though, perhaps, this does not come up to the full power of the apostle's meaning, yet, probably, it gives the idea which was commonly attached to the phrase among the public.   Mr. Bruce had been forced by a pretended saint, in Egypt, to take him on board his vessel, as if to carry him to a certain place—whereas, Mr. Bruce meant no such thing ; but, having set him on shore at some little distance from whence he came, 'we slacked our vessel down the stream a few yards, filling our sails, and stretching away. On seeing this, our saint fell into a desperate passion, cursing, blaspheming, and stamping with his feet ; at every word crying "*Shar Ullah!*" *i. e.* "*May God send and do justice!*" This appears to be the strongest execration this passionate Arab could use, *i. e.* ' To punish you adequately is out of my power: I remit you to the vengeance of God.'   Is not this the import of *anathema maranatha?*"—*Taylor* in Calmet.   This solemn declaration, or denunciation, the apostle wrote with his own hand, as the summary of all that he had said, in order that it might be attentively regarded.   There is not a more solemn declaration in the Bible ; there is not a more fearful denunciation ; there is no one that will be more certainly executed.   No matter *what* we may have —be it wealth, or beauty, or vigour, or accomplishment, or adorning, or the praise and flattery of the world ; no matter if we are elevated high in office and in rank ; no matter if we are honoured by the present age, or gain a reputation to be transmitted to future times ; yet if we have not love to the Saviour, we cannot be saved. We must be devoted to the curse ; and the Lord Jesus will soon return to execute the tremendous sentence on a guilty world.   How important then to ask whether we have that love? Whether we are attached to the Lord

Jesus in such a manner as to secure his approbation ?   Whether we so love him as to be prepared to hail his coming with joy, and to be received into his everlasting kingdom.—In the close of the Notes on this epistle, I may ask any one who shall read these pages whether he has this love ?   And I may press it upon the attention of each one, though I may never see their faces in the flesh, as *the* great inquiry which is to determine their everlasting destiny.   The solemn declaration stands here, that if they do *not* love the Lord Jesus, they will be, and they ought to be, devoted to destruction. The Lord Jesus will soon return to make investigation, and to judge the world.   There will be no escape ; and no tongue can express the awful horrors of an ETERNAL CURSE PRONOUNCED BY THE LIPS OF THE SON OF GOD.

23. *The grace,* &c.   Note, Rom. xvi. 20.

24. *In Christ Jesus.*   Through Christ Jesus ; or in connection with your love to him ; *i. e.* as Christians. This is an expression of tender regard to them as Christian brethren ; of his love for the church ; and his earnest desire for their welfare.   It is in accordance with the usual manner in which he closes his epistles ; and it is peculiarly tender, affectionate, and beautiful here, when we consider the manner in which he had been treated by many of the Corinthians ; and as following the solemn declaration in ver. 22.   Paul loved them ; loved them intensely, and was ever ready to express his affectionate regard for them *all*, and his earnest desire for their salvation.

The subscription to the epistle, "The first epistle to the Corinthians," &c., was evidently written by some other hand than that of Paul, and has no claim to be regarded as inspired. Probably these subscriptions were added a considerable time after the epistles were first written ; and in some instances evidently by some person who was not well informed on the subject ; see the Note at the end of the Epistle to the Romans. In this instance, the subscription is evidently in its main statement false. The epistle bears internal marks that it was written from Ephesus, though there is every probability that it was sent by three of the persons who are here mentioned. It is absurd, however, to suppose that *Timothy* was concerned in bearing the epistle to them, since it is evident that when it was written he was already on a visit to the churches, and on his way to Corinth ; see Notes on chap. xvi. 10, 11 ; iv. 17.   There is not the slightest internal evidence that it was written from Philippi : but every thing in the epistle concurs in the supposition that it was sent from Ephesus. See the Introduction to the epistle.   There is, however, a considerable variety among the MSS. in regard to the subscription ; and they are evidently none of them of any authority, and as these subscriptions generally mislead the reader of the Bible, it would have been better had they been omitted.

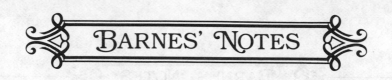

Notes
on the
New Testament

Albert Barnes

Edited by
Robert Frew

II CORINTHIANS
AND GALATIANS

BAKER BOOK HOUSE
Grand Rapids, Michigan 49506

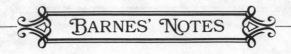

Heritage Edition

Fourteen Volumes 0834-4

When ordering by ISBN (International Standard Book Number), numbers listed above should be preceded by 0-8010-.

Reprinted from the 1884-85 edition published by Blackie & Son,
London, edited by Robert Frew

Reprinted 1983 by Baker Book House Company

ISBN: 0-8010-0846-8

Printed and bound in the United States of America

INTRODUCTION

§ i. *The Design of the Second Epistle to the Corinthians.*

In the Introduction to the first Epistle to the Corinthians, the situation and character of the city of Corinth, the history of the church there, and the design which Paul had in view in writing to them at first, have been fully stated. In order to a full understanding of the design of this epistle, those facts should be borne in distinct remembrance, and the reader is referred to the statement there made as material to a correct understanding of this epistle. It was shown there that an important part of Paul's design at that time was to reprove the irregularities which existed in the church at Corinth. This he had done with great fidelity. He had not only answered the inquiries which they proposed to him, but he had gone with great particularity into an examination of the gross disorders of which he had learned by some members of the family of Chloe. A large part of the epistle, therefore, was the language of severe reproof. Paul felt its necessity; and he had employed that language with unwavering fidelity to his Master.

Yet it was natural that he should feel great solicitude in regard to the reception of that letter, and to its influence in accomplishing what he wished. That letter had been sent from Ephesus, where Paul proposed to remain until after the succeeding Pentecost (1 Cor. xvi. 8); evidently hoping by that time to hear from them, and to learn what had been the manner of the reception of his epistle. He proposed then to go to Macedonia, and from that place to go again to Corinth (1 Cor. xvi. 5—7); but he was evidently desirous to learn in what manner his first epistle had been received, and what was its effect, before he visited them. He sent Timothy and Erastus before him to Macedonia and Achaia (Acts xix. 22; 1 Cor. xvi. 10), intending that they should visit Corinth, and commissioned Timothy to regulate the disordered affairs in the church there. It would appear also that he sent Titus to the church there in order to observe the effect which his epistle would produce, and to return and report to him, 2 Cor. ii. 13; vii. 6—16. Evidently Paul felt much solicitude on the subject; and the manner in which they received his admonitions would do much to regulate his own future movements. An important case of discipline; his authority as an apostle; and the interests of religion in an important city, and in a church which he had himself founded, were all at stake. In this state of mind he himself left Ephesus, and went to Troas on his way to Macedonia, where it appears he had appointed Titus to meet him, and to report to him the manner in which his first epistle had been received; see Note on chap. ii. 13. Then his mind was greatly agitated and distressed because he did not meet Titus as he had expected, and in this state of mind he went forward to Macedonia. There he had a direct interview with Titus (chap. vii. 5, 6), and learned from him that his first epistle had accomplished all which he had desired, chap. vii. 7—16. The act of discipline which he had directed had been performed; the abuses had been in a great measure corrected, and the Corinthians had been brought to a state of true repentance for their former irregularities and disorders. The heart of Paul was greatly comforted by this intelligence, and by the signal success which had attended this effort to produce reform. In this state of mind he wrote to them this second letter.

Titus had spent some time in Corinth. He had had an opportunity of learning the views of the parties, and of ascertaining the true condition of the church. This epistle is designed to meet some of the prevailing views of the party which was opposed to him there, and to refute some of the prevailing slanders in regard to himself. The epistle, therefore, is occupied to a considerable extent in refuting the slanders which had been heaped upon him, and in vindicating his own character. This letter also he sent by the hands of Titus, by whom the former had been sent, and he designed doubtless that the presence of Titus should aid in accomplishing the objects which he had in view in the epistle; see 2 Cor. viii. 17, 18.

§ 2. *The Subjects treated of in this Epistle.*

It has been generally admitted that this epistle is written without much definite arrangement or plan. It treats on a variety of topics mainly as they occurred to the mind of the apostle at the time, and perhaps without having formed any definite arrangement before he commenced writing it. Those subjects are all important, and are all treated in the usual manner of Paul, and are all useful and interesting to the church at large; but we shall not find in this epistle the same systematic arrangement which is apparent in the epistle to the Romans, or which occurs in the first epistle to the Corinthians. Some of the subjects of which it treats are the following.

(1.) He mentions his own sufferings, and particularly his late trials in Asia. For deliverance from these trials, he expresses his gratitude to God; and states the design for which God called him to endure such trials to have been, that he might be better qualified to comfort others who might be afflicted in a similar manner. chap. i. 1—12.

(2.) He vindicates himself from one of the accusations which his enemies had brought against him, that he was unstable and fickle-minded. He had promised to visit them; and he had not yet fulfilled his promise. They took occasion, therefore, to say that he was unstable, and that he was afraid to visit them. He shows to them, in reply, the true reason why he had not come to them, and that his real object in not doing it, had been "to spare"; them, chap. i. 13—24.

(3.) The case of the unhappy individual who had been guilty of incest, had deeply affected his mind. In the first epistle, he had treated of this case at large, and had directed that discipline should be exercised. He had felt deep solicitude in regard to the manner in which his commands on that subject should be received, and had judged it best not to visit them until he should be informed of the manner in which they had complied with his directions. Since they had obeyed him, and had inflicted discipline on him, he now exhorts them to forgive the unhappy man, and to receive him again to their fellowship, chap. ii. 1—11.

(4.) He mentions the deep solicitude which he had on this subject, and his disappointment when he came to Troas and did not meet with Titus as he had expected, and had not been informed as he hoped to have been of the manner in which his former epistle had been received, chap. ii. 12—17. In view of the manner in which they had received his former epistle, and of the success of his efforts, which he learned when he reached Macedonia, he gives thanks to God that all his efforts to promote the welfare of the church had been successful, chap. ii. 14—17.

(5.) Paul vindicates his character, and his claims to be regarded as an apostle. He assures them that he does not need letters of commendation to them, since they were fully acquainted with his character, chap. iii. 1—6. This subject leads him into an examination of the nature of the ministry and its importance, which he illustrates by showing the comparative obscurity of the Mosaic ministrations, and the greater dignity, and permanency of the gospel, chap. iii. 7—18.

(6.) In chaps. iv. v. he states the principles by which he was actuated in the ministry. He and the other apostles were greatly afflicted, and were subjected to great and peculiar trials, but they had also great and peculiar consolations. They were sustained with the hope of heaven, and with the assurance that there was a world of glory. They acted in view of that world, and had gone forth in view of it to entreat men to be reconciled to God.

(7.) Having referred in chap. v. to the nature and objects of the Christian ministry, he expatiates with great beauty on the temper with which he and his brethren, in the midst of great trials and afflictions, executed this import-ant work; chap. vi. 1—10.

(8.) Having in this manner pursued a course of remark that was calculated to conciliate their regard, and to show his affection for them, he exhorts them (chap. vi. 11—10), to avoid those connections which would injure their piety, and which were inconsistent with the gospel which they professed to love. The connections to which he particularly referred were, improper marriages and ruinous alliances with idolaters, to which they were particularly exposed.

(9.) In chap. vii. he again makes a transition to Titus, and to the joy which he had brought him in the intelligence which he gave of the manner in which the commands of Paul in the first epistle had been received, and of its happy effect on the minds of the Corinthians.

(10.) In chaps. viii. and ix. Paul refers to, and discusses the subject on which his heart was so much set—the collection for the poor and afflicted Christians in Judea. He had commenced the collection in Macedonia, and had boasted to them that the Corinthians would aid largely in that benevo-lent work, and he now sent Titus to complete it in Corinth.

(11.) In chap. x. he enters upon a vindication of himself, and of his apos-tolic authority against the accusation of his enemies; and pursues the subject through chap. xi. by a comparison of himself with others, and in chap. xii. by an argument directly in favour of his apostolic authority from the favours which God had bestowed on him, and the evidence which he had given of his having been commissioned by God. This subject he pursues also in various illustrations to the end of the epistle.

The *objects* of this epistle, therefore, and subjects discussed, are various. They are, to show his deep interest in their welfare—to express his gratitude that his former letter had been so well received, and had so effectually ac-complished what he wished to accomplish—to carry forward the work of reformation among them which had been so auspiciously commenced—to vin-dicate his authority as an apostle from the objections which he had learned through Titus they had continued to make—to secure the collection for the poor saints in Judea, on which his heart had been so much set—and to assure them of his intention to come and visit them according to his repeated pro-mises. The epistle is substantially of the same character as the first. It was written to a church where great dissensions and other evils prevailed; it was designed to promote a reformation; and is a model of the manner in which evils are to be corrected in a church. In connection with the first epistle, it shows the manner in which offenders in the church are to be dealt with, and the spirit and design with which the work of discipline should be entered on and pursued. Though these were local evils, yet great principles are involved here, of use to the church in all ages; and to these epistles the church must refer at all times, as an illustration of the proper manner of administering discipline, and of silencing the calumnies of enemies.

§ 3. *The time and place in which the Epistle was written.*

It is manifest that this epistle was written from Macedonia (see chap. viii. 1—14, and ix. 2), and was sent by Titus to the church at Corinth. If so, it was written probably about a year after the former epistle. Paul was on his way to Corinth, and was expecting to go there soon. He had left Ephesus, where he was when he wrote the first epistle, and had gone to Troas, and from thence to Macedonia, where he had met with Titus, and had from him learned what was the effect of his first epistle. In the overflowing of his heart with gratitude for the success of that letter, and with a desire to carry forward the work of reformation in the church, and completely to remove all the objections which had been made to his apostolic authority, and to prepare for his own welcome reception when he went there, he wrote this letter—a letter which we cannot doubt was as kindly received as the former, and which like that accomplished the objects which he had in view.

EPISTLE TO THE CORINTHIANS

CHAPTER I.

PAUL, an apostle *a* of Jesus Christ by the will of God, and Timothy *our* brother, untc the church of God which is at

CHAPTER I.

This chapter consists of the following parts, or subjects :

1. The usual salutation and benediction in the introduction of the epistle, ver. 1. 2. This is found in all the epistles of Paul, and was at once an affectionate salutation and an appropriate expression of his interest in their welfare, and also an appropriate mode of commencing an address to them by one who claimed to be inspired and sent from God.

2. He refers to the consolation which he had had in his heavy trials, and praises God for that consolation, and declares that the reason for which he was comforted was, that he might be qualified to administer consolation to others in the same or in similar circumstances, ver. 3—7.

3. He informs them of the heavy trials which he was called to experience when he was in Ephesus, and of his merciful deliverance from those trials, ver. 8—19. He had been exposed to death, and had despaired of life, (ver. 8, 9); yet he had been delivered (ver. 10); he desired them to unite with him in thanksgiving on account of it (ver. 11); and in all this he had endeavoured to keep a good conscience, and *had* that testimony that he had endeavoured to maintain such a conscience toward all, and especially toward them, ver. 12.

4. He refers to the design which he had in writing the former letter to them, ver. 13. 14. He had written to them only such things as they admitted to be true and proper; and such as he was persuaded they would always admit. They had always re-

ceived his instructions favourably and kindly ; and he had always sought their welfare.

5. In this state of mind, Paul had designed to have paid them a second visit, ver. 15, 16. But he had not done it yet, and it appears that his enemies had taken occasion from this to say that he was inconstant and fickle-minded. He, therefore, takes occasion to vindicate himself, and to convince them that he was not faithless to his word and purposes, and to show them the true reason why he had not visited them, ver. 17—24. He states, therefore, that his real intentions had been to visit them (ver. 15, 16); that his failure to do so had not proceeded from either levity or falsehood (ver. 17); as they might have known from the uniform doctrine which he had taught them, in which he had inculcated the necessity of a strict adherence to promises, from the veracity of Jesus Christ his great example (ver. 18—20), and from the fact that God had given to him the Holy Spirit, and anointed him (ver. 21, 22); and he states, therefore, that the true reason why he had not come to them was, that he wished to spare them (ver. 23, 24); he was willing to remain away from them until they should have time to correct the evils which existed in their church, and prevent the necessity of severe discipline when he should come.

1. *Paul an apostle*, &c.; see Notes on Rom. i. 1, and 1 Cor. i. 1. ¶ *By the will of God.* Through, or agreeably to the will of God; Note, 1 Cor. i. 1. ¶ *And Timothy* our *brother.* Paul was accustomed to associate some other person or persons with

Corinth, with all the saints *a* which are in all Achaia :

2 Grace *b be* to you, and peace, from God our Father, and *from* the Lord Jesus Christ.

3 Blessed *c be* God, even the Father of our Lord Jesus Christ, the Father of mercies, and the God of all comfort ;

a Ph.1.1   *b* Rom.1.7.   *c* Ep.1.3.

him in writing his epistles. Thus in the first epistle to the Corinthians, Sosthenes was associated with him. For the reasons of this, see Note on 1 Cor. i. 1. The name of Timothy *is* associated with his in the epistles to the Philippians and Colossians. From the former epistle to the Corinthians (chap. xvi. 10), we learn that Paul had sent Timothy to the church at Corinth, or that he expected that he would visit them. Paul had sent him into Macedonia in company with Erastus (Acts xix. 21, 22), intending himself to follow them, and expecting that they would visit Achaia. From the passage before us, it appears that Timothy had returned from this expedition, and was now with Paul. The reason why Paul joined Timothy with him in writing this epistle may have been the following : (1.) Timothy had been recently with them, and they had become acquainted with him, and it was not only natural that he should express his friendly salutations, but his name and influence among them might serve in some degree to confirm what Paul wished to say to them ; comp. Note, 1 Cor. i. 1. (2.) Paul may have wished to give as much influence as possible to Timothy. He designed that he should be his fellow-labourer ; and as Timothy was much younger than himself, he doubtless expected that he would survive him, and that he would in some sense succeed him in the care of the churches. He was desirous, therefore, of securing for him all the authority which he could, and of letting it be known that he regarded him as abundantly qualified for the great work with which he was intrusted. (3.) The influence and name of Timothy might be supposed to have weight with the party in the church that had slandered Paul, by accusing him of insincerity or instability in regard to his purposed visit to them. Paul had

designed to go to them directly from Ephesus, but he had changed his mind, and the testimony of Timothy might be important to prove that it was done from motives purely conscientious. Timothy was doubtless acquainted with the reasons ; and his testimony might meet and rebut a part of the charges against him ; see chap. i. ver. 13—16. ¶ *Unto the church of God,* &c.; see Note 1 Cor. i. 2. ¶ *With all the saints which are in all Achaia.* Achaia, in the largest sense, included the whole of Greece. Achaia proper, however, was the district or province of which Corinth was the capital. It comprehended the part of Greece lying between Thessaly and the southern part of the Peloponnesus, embracing the whole western part of the Peloponnesus. It is probable that there were not a few Christians scattered in Achaia, and not improbably some small churches that had been established by the labours of Paul or of others. From Rom. xvi. 1, we know that there was a church at Cenchrea, the eastern port of Corinth, and it is by no means improbable that there were other churches in that region. Paul doubtless designed that copies of this epistle should be circulated among them.

2. *Grace* be *to you,* &c. This is the usual Christian salutation ; see Note, Rom. i. 7 ; 1 Cor. i. 3.

3. *Blessed* be *God.* This is the commencement properly of the epistle, and it is the language of a heart that is full of joy, and that bursts forth with gratitude in view of mercy. It may have been excited by the recollection that he had formerly written to them, and that during the interval which had elapsed between the time when the former epistle was written and when this was penned, he had been called to a most severe trial, and that from that trial he had been

4 Who comforteth us in all our tribulation, that we may be able to comfort them which are in any trouble, by the comfort

mercifully delivered. With a heart full of gratitude and joy for this merciful interposition, he commences this epistle. It is remarked by Doddridge, that eleven out of the thirteen epistles of Paul, begin with exclamations of praise, joy, and thanksgiving. Paul had been afflicted, but he had also been favoured with remarkable consolations, and it was not unnatural that he should allow himself to give expression to his joy and praise in view of all the mercies which God had conferred on him. This entire passage is one that is exceedingly valuable, as showing that there may be elevated joy in the midst of deep affliction, and as showing what is the reason why God visits his servants with trials. The phrase "blessed be God," is equivalent to "praised be God," or is an expression of thanksgiving. It is the usual formula of praise (comp. Eph. i. 3); and shows his entire confidence in God, and his joy in him, and his gratitude for his mercies. It is *one* of innumerable instances which show that it is possible and proper to bless God in view of the trials with which he visits his people, and of the consolations which he causes to abound. ¶ *The Father of our Lord Jesus Christ.* God is mentioned here in the relation of the "Father of the Lord Jesus," doubtless because it was through the Lord Jesus, and him alone, that He had imparted the consolation which he had experienced, ver. 5. Paul knew no other God than the "Father of the Lord Jesus;" he knew no other source of consolation than the gospel; he knew of no way in which God imparted comfort except through his Son. That is genuine Christian consolation which acknowledges the Lord Jesus as the medium by whom it is imparted; that is proper thanksgiving to God which is offered through the Redeemer; that only is the proper acknowledgment of God which recognises him as the "Father of the Lord Jesus." ¶ *The Father of mercies.* This is a Hebrew mode of expression, where a noun performs the place of an adjective, and the phrase is synonymous nearly with "merciful Father." The expression has however somewhat more energy and spirit than the simple phrase "merciful Father." The Hebrews used the word *father* often to denote the author, or source of any thing; and the idea in phraseology like this is, that mercy proceeds from God, that he is the source of it, and that it is his nature to impart mercy and compassion, as if he *originated* it; or was the source and fountain of it—sustaining a relation to all true consolation analogous to that which a father sustains to his offspring. God has the *paternity* of all true joy. It is one of his peculiar and glorious attributes that he thus *produces* consolation and mercy. ¶ *And the God of all comfort.* The source of all consolation. Paul delighted, as all should do, to trace *all* his comforts to God; and Paul, as all Christians have, had sufficient reason to regard God as the source of true consolation. There is no other real source of happiness but God; and he is able abundantly, and willing to impart consolation to his people.

4 *Who comforteth us.* Paul here doubtless refers primarily to himself and his fellow apostles as having been filled with comfort in their trials; to the support which the promises of God gave; to the influences of the Holy Spirit, the Comforter; and to the hopes of eternal life through the gospel of the Redeemer. ¶ *That we may be able to comfort,* &c. Paul does not say that this was the *only* design which God had in comforting them that they might be able to impart comfort to others; but he does say that this is an important and main purpose. It is an object which he seeks, that his people in their afflictions should be supported and comforted; and for this purpose he fills the hearts of his ministers with consolation; gives them personal experience of the sustaining power of grace in their trials; and enables them to

wherewith we ourselves are comforted of God.

5 For as the sufferings *a* of Christ abound in us, so our consolation also aboundeth by Christ.

6 And whether we be afflicted, *it is* for *b* your consolation and salvation, which is [1] effectual in the enduring of the same sufferings, which we also suffer; or whether we be comforted, *it is*

speak of what they have felt in regard to the consolations of the gospel of the Lord Jesus. ¶ *By the comfort,* &c. By the same topics of consolation; by the same sources of joy which have sustained us. They would have experience; and by that experience they would be able to minister consolation to those who were in any manner afflicted. It is only by personal experience that we are able to impart consolation to others. Paul refers here undoubtedly to the consolations which are produced by the evidence of the pardon of sin, and of acceptance with God, and the hope of eternal life. These consolations abounded in him and his fellow apostles richly; and sustained by them he was able also to impart like consolation to others who were in similar circumstances of trial.

5. *For as the sufferings of Christ abound in us.* As we are called to experience the same sufferings which Christ endured; as we are called to suffer in his cause, and in the promotion of the same object. The sufferings which they endured were in the cause of Christ and his gospel; were endured in endeavouring to advance the same object which Christ sought to promote; and were substantially of the same nature. They arose from opposition, contempt, persecution, trial, and want, and were the same as the Lord Jesus was himself subjected to during the whole of his public life; comp. Col. i. 24. Thus Peter says (1 Pet. iv. 13) of Christians that they were "partakers of Christ's sufferings." ¶ *So our consolation also aboundeth by Christ.* By means of Christ, or through Christ, consolation is abundantly imparted to us. Paul regarded the Lord Jesus as the source of consolation, and felt that the comfort which *he* imparted, or which was

imparted through him, was more than sufficient to overbalance all the trials which he endured in his cause. The comforts which he derived from Christ were those, doubtless, which arose from his presence, his supporting grace, from his love shed abroad in the heart; from the success which he gave to his gospel, and from the hope of reward which was held out to him by the Redeemer, as the result of all his sufferings. And it may be observed as an universal truth, that if we suffer in the cause of Christ, if we are persecuted, oppressed, and calumniated on his account, he will take care that our hearts shall be filled with consolation.

6. *And whether we be afflicted.* If we are afflicted; or, our affliction is for this purpose. This verse is designed to show one of the reasons of the sufferings which the apostles had endured; and it is a happy specimen of Paul's skill in his epistles. He shows that all his trials were for their welfare and would turn to their benefit. He suffered that they might be comforted; he was afflicted for their advantage. This assurance would tend to conciliate their favour, and strengthen their affection for him, as it would show them that he was disinterested. We are under the deepest obligations of gratitude to one who suffers for us; and there is nothing that will bind us more tenderly to any one than the fact that he has been subjected to great calamity and trial on our account. This is *one* of the reasons why the Christian feels so tenderly his obligation to the Lord Jesus Christ. ¶ It is *for your consolation and salvation.* It will be *useful* for your consolation; or it is endured in order to secure your comfort, and promote your salvation Paul had suffered in Ephesus, and it

for your consolation and salvation.

7 And our hope of you *is* steadfast, knowing that as *a* ye

a Rom 8.17.

are partakers of the sufferings so *shall ye be* also of the consolation.

8 For we would not, brethren, have you ignorant of our trouble *b*

b Acts 19 23.

is to this that he here particularly refers. He does not mean to say that his sufferings there were particularly for the comfort of the Corinthians; but that they had been endured in the general purpose of promoting the salvation of men, and that they, together with others, would reap the benefit of his trials. He endured them in order to spread the true religion, and they would be benefitted by that, and besides, he would be the better able by his trials to administer to them the true consolations of the gospel in their sufferings; and his example, and experience, and counsel, would enable them to bear up under their own trials in a proper manner. ¶ *Which is effectual*, &c. Margin, *wrought*. The Greek word ἐνεργουμένη denotes here *efficacious, operating to, producing;* and the phrase denotes that their salvation would be effected, wrought out, or secured by the patient endurance of such sufferings. Those sufferings were necessary; and a patient endurance of them would tend to promote their salvation. The doctrine that the patient endurance of affliction tends to promote salvation, is everywhere taught in the Bible; see Notes on Rom. v, 3—5. ¶ *In the enduring*. By your enduring; or by your patience in such sufferings. You are called to endure the same kind of sufferings; and patience in such trials will tend to promote your salvation. ¶ *Or whether we be comforted*, &c. One design of our being comforted is, that we may be able to impart consolation to you in the times of similar trial and calamity; see ver. 4. The sentiment of the whole passage is, that their eternal welfare would be promoted by the example of the apostles in their trials, and by the consolations which they would be able to impart as the result of their afflictions.

7. *And our hope of you* is *steadfast*. We have a firm and unshaken hope in

regard to you; we have a confident expectation that you will be saved. We believe that you will be enabled so to bear trial as to show that you are sustained by the Christian hope; and so as to advance your own piety, and confirm your prospect of heaven. ¶ *As ye are partakers of the sufferings*. It is evident from this, that the Corinthians had been subjected to trials similar to those which the apostle had endured. It is not known to what afflictions they were then subjected; but it is not improbable that they were exposed to some kind of persecution and opposition. Such trials were common in all the early churches; and they served to unite all the friends of the Redeemer in common bonds, and to make them feel that they were one. They had united sorrows; and they had united joys; and they felt they were tending to the same heaven of glory. United sorrows and united consolations tend more than any thing else to bind people together. We always have a *brotherly* feeling for one who suffers as we do, or who has the same kind of joy which we have.

8. *For we would not have you ignorant*. We wish you to be fully informed; see Note, 1 Cor. x. 1; xii. 1. The object of Paul here is, to give a full explanation of the nature of his trials, to which he had referred in ver. 4. He presumed that the Corinthians would feel a deep interest in him and in his trials; that they would sympathize with him, and would pray that those sufferings, and that this deliverance might be attended with a blessing (ver. 11); and perhaps he wished also to conciliate their kindness towards himself by mentioning more at length the nature of the trials which he had been called to endure on account of the Christian religion, of which they were reaping so material benefits. ¶ *Of our trouble*

which came to us in Asia, that we were pressed out of measure, above

strength, insomuch that we despaired even of life:

---

which came to us in Asia. The term *Asia* is often used to denote that part of Asia Minor of which Ephesus was the capital; see Note, Acts ii. 9. There has been considerable diversity of opinion as to the "troubles" to which Paul here refers. Some have supposed that he refers to the persecutions at Lystra (Acts xiv. 6, 19, 20), from which he had been recovered as it were by miracle; but as that happened so long before this, it seems improbable that he should here refer to it. There is every mark of *freshness* and *recentness* about this event; and Paul evidently referred to some danger from which he had been *lately* delivered, and which made a deep impression on his mind when he wrote this epistle. Semler supposes that he refers to the lying in wait of the Jews for him when he was about to go to Macedonia, mentioned in Acts xx. 3. Most commentators have supposed that he refers to the disturbances which were made at Ephesus by Demetrius and his friends, mentioned in Acts xix., and by reason of which he was compelled to leave the city. The only objection to this is, that which is mentioned by Whitby and Macknight, that as Paul did not go *into* the theatre there (Acts xix. 31), he incurred no such risk of his life as to justify the strong expressions mentioned in ver. 9 and 10. They suppose, therefore, that he refers to the danger to which he was exposed in Ephesus on another occasion, when he was compelled to fight there with wild beasts; see 1 Cor. xv. 32. But nearly all these opinions may be reconciled, perhaps, by supposing that he refers to the *group* of calamities to which he had been exposed in Asia, and from which he had just escaped by going to Macedonia—referring perhaps more particularly to the conflict which he had been compelled to have with the wild beasts there. There was the riot excited by Demetrius (Acts xix.), in which his life had been endangered, and from which he had just escaped; and there had been the

conflict with the wild beasts at Ephesus (see Note 1 Cor. xv. 32), which perhaps had occurred but just before; and there were the plots of the Jews against him (Acts xx. 3), from which, also, he had just been delivered. By these trials, his life had been endangered, perhaps, more than once, and he had been called to look death calmly in the face, and to anticipate the probability that he might soon die. Of these trials; of *all* these trials, he would not have the Corinthians ignorant; but desired that they should be fully apprized of them, that they might sympathize with him, and that through their prayers they might be turned to his benefit. ¶ *That we were pressed out of measure;* see Acts xix. We were borne down, or weighed down by calamity (ἐβαρηθμεν) exceedingly (καθ' ὑπερβολην), supereminently. The expression denotes excess, eminence, or intensity. It is one of Paul's common and very strong expressions to denote any thing that is intensive or great; see Rom. vii. 13; Gal. i. 13; 2 Cor. iv. 17. ¶ *Above strength.* Beyond our strength. More than in ourselves we were able to bear ¶ *Insomuch that we despaired even of life.* Either expecting to be destroyed by the wild beasts with which he had to contend, or to be destroyed by the people. This was one of the instances undoubtedly to which he refers in chap. xi. 23, where he says he had been "in death oft." And this was one of the many cases in which Paul was called on to contemplate death as near. It was doubtless one cause of his fidelity, and of his great success in his work, that he was thus called to regard death as near at hand, and that, to use the somewhat unpoetical, but deeply affecting lines of Baxter, expressing a sentiment which guided all *his* ministry, and which was one source of his eminent success,

He preach'd as though he ne'er would preach again,
As a dying man to dying men.

9. *But we had the sentence of death*

9 But we had the [1] sentence of death in ourselves, that we should not trust [a] in ourselves,

1 Or, *answer.*	a Jer.17.5,7.

in ourselves. Marg. "answer." The word rendered "sentence" (απόκρι-σα) means properly an answer, judicial response, or sentence; and is here synonymous with *verdict.* It means that Paul felt that he was condemned to die; that he felt as if he were under sentence of death and with no hope of acquittal; he was called to contemplate the hour of death as just before him. The words "in ourselves," mean, against ourselves; or, we expected certainly to die. This seems as if he had been condemned to die, and may either refer to some instance when the popular fury was so great that he felt it was determined he should die; or more probably to a judicial sentence that he should be cast to the wild beasts, with the certain expectation that he would be destroyed, as was always the case with those who were subjected to the execution of such a sentence. ¶ *That we should not trust in ourselves.* This is an exceedingly beautiful and important sentiment. It teaches that in the time to which Paul refers, he was in so great danger, and had so certain a prospect of death, that he could put no reliance on himself. He felt that he must die; and that human aid was vain. According to every probability he would die, and all that he could do was to cast himself on the protection of that God who had power to save him even then, if he chose, and who, if he did it, would exert power similar to that which is put forth when the dead are raised. The *effect,* therefore, of the near prospect of death was to lead him to put increased confidence in God. He felt that God only could save him; or that God only could sustain him if he should die. Perhaps also he means to say that the effect of this was to lead him to put increased confidence in God *after* his deliverance; not to trust in his own plans, or to confide in his own strength; but to feel that all that he had was entirely in the hands of God.

but in God which raiseth the dead:
10 Who delivered [b] us from so

b 2 Pet.2.9.

This is a common, and a happy effect of the near prospect of death to a Christian; and it is well to contemplate the effect on such a mind as that of Paul in the near prospect of dying, and to see how instinctively then it clings to God. A true Christian in such circumstances will rush to *His* arms and feel that there he is safe. ¶ *But in God which raiseth the dead.* Intimating that a rescue in such circumstances would be like raising the dead. It is probable that on this occasion Paul was near dying; that he had given up all hope of life — perhaps, as at Lystra (Acts xiv. 19), he was supposed to be dead. He felt, therefore, that he was raised up by the immediate power of God, and regarded it as an exertion of the same power by which the dead are raised. Paul means to intimate that so far as depended on any power of his own, he was dead. He had no power to recover himself, and but for the gracious interposition of God he would have died.

10. *Who delivered us from so great a death.* From a death so terrible, and from a prospect so alarming. It is intimated here by the word which Paul uses, that the death which he apprehended was one of a character peculiarly terrific—probably a death by wild beasts; Note, ver. 8. He was near to death; he had no hope of rescue; and the manner of the death which was threatened was peculiarly frightful. Paul regarded rescue from such a death as a kind of *resurrection;* and felt that he owed his life to God *as if* he had raised him from the dead. All deliverance from imminent peril, and from dangerous sickness, whether of ourselves or our friends, should be regarded as a kind of resurrection from the dead. God could with infinite ease have taken away our breath, and it is only by his merciful interposition that we live. ¶ *And doth deliver.* Continues yet to deliver us; or preserve us—intimating perhaps that danger had continued to follow him

great a death, and doth deliver: in whom we trust that he will yet deliver us;

11 Ye also helping *a* together by prayer for us, that for the gift *bestowed* upon us by the

a Rom.15.30; Phil.1.19; James 5.16—18.

after the signal deliverance to which he particularly refers, and that he had continued to be in similar peril of his life. Paul was daily exposed to danger; and was constantly preserved by the good providence of God. In what manner he was rescued from the peril to which he was exposed he has no where intimated. It is implied, however, that it was by a remarkable divine interposition; but whether by miracle, or by the ordinary course of providence, he no where intimates. Whatever was the mode, however, Paul regarded *God* as the source of the deliverance, and felt that his obligations were due to him as his kind Preserver. ¶ *In whom we trust that he will yet deliver* us. That he will continue to preserve us. We hope; we are accustomed to cherish the expectation that he will continue to defend us in the perils which we shall yet encounter. Paul felt that he was still exposed to danger. Everywhere he was liable to be persecuted (comp. Note, Acts xx. 23), and everywhere he felt that his life was in peril. Yet he had been thus far preserved in a most remarkable manner; and he felt assured that God would continue to interpose in his behalf, until his great purpose in regard to him should be fully accomplished, so that at the close of life he could look to God as his Deliverer, and feel that all along his perilous journey he had been his great Protector.

11. *Ye also helping together by prayer for us.* Tindal renders this in connection with the close of the previous verse; "we trust that yet hereafter he will deliver us, by the help of your prayer for us." The word rendered "helping together," means co-operating, aiding, assisting; and the idea is, that Paul felt that his trials might be turned to good account, and give occasion for thanksgiving; and that this was to be accomplished by the aid of the prayers of his fellow Christians. He felt that the church

was one, and that Christians should sympathize with one another. He evinced deep humility and tender regard for the Corinthians when he called on them to aid him by their prayers. Nothing would be better calculated to excite their tender affection and regard than thus to call on them to sympathize with him in his trials, and to pray that those trials might result in thanksgiving throughout the churches. ¶ *That for the gift* bestowed *upon us.* The sentence which occurs here is very perplexing in the original, and the construction is difficult. But the main idea is not difficult to be seen. The "gift" here referred to (τὸ χάρισμα) means doubtless the *favour* shown to him in his rescue from so imminent a peril; and he felt that this was owing to the prayers of many persons on his behalf. He believed that he had been remembered in the petitions of his friends and fellow Christians, and that his deliverance was owing to their supplications. ¶ *By the means of many persons.* Probably meaning that the favour referred to had been imparted by means of the prayers of many individuals who had taken a deep interest in his welfare. But it may also imply perhaps that he had been directly assisted, and had been rescued from the impending danger by the interposition of many friends who had come to his relief. The usual interpretation is, however, that it was by the prayers of many in his behalf. ¶ *Thanks may be given by many on our behalf.* Many may be induced also to render thanks for my deliverance. The idea is, that as he had been delivered from great peril by the prayers of many persons, it was proper also that thanksgiving should be offered by as many in his behalf, or on account of his deliverance. "Mercies that have been obtained by prayer should be acknowledged by praise." —*Doddridge.* God had mercifully interposed in answer to the prayers of

means of many persons, thanks may be given by many on our behalf.

his people; and it was proper that his mercy should be as extensively acknowledged. Paul was desirous that God should not be forgotten: and that those who had sought his deliverance should render praise to God: perhaps intimating here that those who had obtained mercies by prayer are prone to forget their obligation to return thanks to God for his gracious and merciful interposition.

12. *For our rejoicing is this.* The source or cause of our rejoicing. " I have a just cause of rejoicing, and it is, that I have endeavoured to live a life of simplicity and godly sincerity, and have not been actuated by the principles of worldly wisdom." The connection here is not very obvious, and it is not quite easy to trace it. Most expositors, as Doddridge, Locke, Macknight, Bloomfield, &c., suppose that he mentions the purity of his life as a reason why he had a right to expect their prayers, as he had requested in ver. 11. They would not doubt, it is supposed, that his life had been characterized by great simplicity and sincerity, and would feel, therefore, a deep interest in his welfare, and be disposed to render thanks that he had been preserved in the day of peril. But the whole context and the scope of the passage is rather to be taken into view. Paul had been exposed to death. He had no hope of life. *Then* the ground of his rejoicing, and of his confidence, was that he had lived a holy life. He had not been actuated by "fleshly wisdom," but he had been animated and guided by "the grace of God." His aim had been simple, his purpose holy, and he had the testimony of his conscience that his motives had been right, and he had, therefore, no concern about the result. A good conscience, a holy life through Jesus Christ, will enable a man always to look calmly on death. What has a Christian to fear in death? Paul had kept a good conscience towards all; but he says that he had special and peculiar joy

12 For our rejoicing is this, the testimony of our conscience, that in simplicity and godly sin-

that he had done it towards the Corinthians. This he says, because many there had accused him of fickleness, and of disregard for their interests. He declares, therefore, that even in the prospect of death he had a consciousness of rectitude towards them, and proceeds to show (ver. 13—23) that the charge against him was not well founded. I regard this passage, therefore, as designed to express the fact that Paul, in view of sudden death, had a consciousness of a life of piety, and was comforted with the reflection that he had not been actuated by the "fleshly wisdom" of the world. ¶ *The testimony of our conscience.* An approving conscience. It does not condemn me on the subject. Though others might accuse him, though his name might be calumniated, yet he had comfort in the approval which his own conscience gave to his course. Paul's conscience was enlightened, and its decisions were correct. Whatever others might charge him with, he *knew* what had been the aim and purpose of his life; and the consciousness of upright aims, and of such plans as the "grace of God" would prompt to, sustained him. An approving conscience is of inestimable value when we are calumniated;— *and when we draw near to death.* ¶ *That in simplicity* (ἐν ἁπλότητι.) Tindal renders this forcibly " without doubleness." The word means sincerity, candour, probity, plain-heartedness, Christian simplicity, frankness, integrity; see 2 Cor. xi. 3. It stands opposed to double-dealings and purposes; to deceitful appearances, and crafty plans; to mere policy, and craftiness in accomplishing an object. A man under the influence of this, is straight-forward, candid, open, frank; and he expects to accomplish his purpose by integrity and fair-dealing, and not by stratagem and cunning. Policy, craft, artful plans, and deep-laid schemes of deceit belong to the world; simplicity of aim and purpose are the true characteristics of a real Chris-

cerity, not *a* with fleshly wisdom, but by the grace of *b* God,

a 1 Cor.2.4,13.   *b* 1 Cor.15.10.

tian. ¶ *And godly sincerity.* Gr. "sincerity of God." This may be a Hebrew idiom, by which the superlative degree is indicated, when, in order to express the highest degree, they added the name of God, as in the phrases "mountains of God," signifying the highest mountains, or "cedars of God," denoting lofty cedars. Or it may mean such sincerity as God manifests and approves such as he, by his grace, would produce in the heart; such as the religion of the gospel is fitted to produce. The word used here, εἰλικρινεία, and rendered *sincerity*, denotes, properly, *clearness*, such as is judged of or discerned in sunshine (from εἴλη and κρίνω), and thence pureness, integrity. It is most probable that the *phrase* here denotes that sincerity which God produces and approves; and the sentiment is, that pure religion, the religion of God, produces entire sincerity in the heart. Its purposes and aims are open and manifest, *as if seen in the sunshine.* The plans of the world are obscure, deceitful, and dark, *as if in the night.* ¶ *Not with fleshly wisdom.* Not with the wisdom which is manifested by the men of this world; not by the principles of cunning, and mere policy, and expediency, which often characterize them. The phrase here stands opposed to simplicity and sincerity, to openness and straight-forwardness. And Paul means to disclaim for himself, and for his fellow-labourers, all that carnal policy which distinguishes the mere men of the world. And if Paul deemed such policy improper for him, we should deem it improper for us; if he had no plans which he wished to advance by it, we should have none; if he would not employ it in the promotion of good plans, neither should we. It has been the curse of the church and the bane of religion; and it is to this day exerting a withering and blighting influence on the church. The moment that such plans are resorted to, it is proof that the vitality of re-

we have had our conversation in the world, and more abundantly to you-ward.

ligion is gone, and any man who feels that his purposes cannot be accomplished *but* by such carnal policy, should set it down as full demonstration that his plans are wrong, and that his purpose should be abandoned. ¶ *But by the grace of God.* This phrase stands opposed, evidently, to "fleshly wisdom." It means that Paul had been influenced by such sentiments and principles as would be suggested or prompted by the influence of his grace. Locke renders it, "by the favour of God directing me." God had shown him *favour;* God had directed him; and he had kept him from the crooked and devious ways of mere worldly policy. The idea seems to be not merely that he had pursued a correct and upright course of life, but that he was indebted for this to the mere grace and favour of God, an idea which Paul omitted no opportunity of acknowledging. ¶ *We have had our conversation.* We have conducted ourselves (ἀναστρά-φημεν). The word here used means literally, to turn up, to overturn; then to turn back, to return, and in the middle voice, to turn one's self around, to turn one's self to any thing, and, also, to move about in, to live in, to be conversant with, to conduct one's self. In this sense it seems to be used here; comp. Heb. x. 33; xiii. 18; 1 Tim. iii. 15; 1 Pet. i. 17. The word *conversation*, we usually apply to oral discourse, but in the Scriptures, it means *conduct*, and the sense of the passage is, that Paul had conducted himself in accordance with the principles of the grace of God, and had been influenced by that. ¶ *In the world.* Everywhere; wherever I have been. This does not mean in the world as contradistinguished from the church, but in the world at large, or wherever he had been, as contradistinguished from the church at Corinth. It had been his common and universal practice. ¶ *And more abundantly to you-ward.* Especially towards you. This was added doubt-

13 For we write none other things unto you than what ye read

or acknowledge; and I trust ye shall acknowledge even to the end;

less because there had been charges against him in Corinth, that he had been crafty, cunning, deceitful, and especially that he had deceived them (see ver. 17), in not visiting them as he had promised. He affirms, therefore, that in all things he had acted in the manner to which the grace of God prompted, and that his conduct, in all respects, had been that of entire simplicity and sincerity.

13. *For we write none other things,* &c. There has been much variety in the interpretation of this passage; and much difficulty felt in determining what it means. The sense seems to me to be this. Paul had just declared that he had been actuated by pure intentions and by entire sincerity, and had in all things been influenced by the grace of God. This he had shown everywhere, but more particularly among them at Corinth. That they fully knew. In making this affirmation they had full evidence from what they had known of him in former times that such had been his course of life; and he trusted that they would be able to acknowledge the same thing to the end, and that they would never have any occasion to form a different opinion of him. It will be recollected that it is probable that some at Corinth had charged him with insincerity; and some had accused him of fickleness in having promised to come to Corinth and then changing his mind, or had charged him with never having intended to come to them. His object in this verse is to refute such slanders, and he says, therefore, that all that he affirmed in his writings about the sincerity and simplicity of his aims, were such as they *knew* from their past acquaintance with him to be true; and that they *knew* that he was a man who would keep his promises. It is an instance of a minister who was able to appeal to the people among whom he had lived and laboured in regard to the general sincerity and uprightness of his character—such an appeal as every minister *ought* to be able to

make to refute all slanders; and such as he *will* be able to make successfully, if his life, like that of Paul, is such as to warrant it. Such seems to me to be the sense of the passage. Beza, however, renders it, " I write no other things than what ye read, or may understand," and so Rosenmüller, Wetstein, Macknight, and some others interpret it; and they explain it as meaning, " I write nothing secretly, nothing ambiguously, but I express myself clearly, openly, plainly, so that I may be read and understood by all." Macknight supposes that they had charged him with using ambiguous language, that he might afterwards interpret it to suit his own purpose. The objection to this is, that Paul never adverts to the obscurity or perspicuity of his own language. It was his *conduct* that was the main subject on which he was writing, and the connection seems to demand that we understand him as affirming that they had abundant evidence that what he affirmed of his simplicity of aim, and integrity of life, was true. ¶ *Than what ye read* (ἀναγινώσκετε). This word properly means to *know accurately;* to distinguish; and in the New Testament usually to know by reading. Doddridge remarks, that the word is ambiguous, and may signify either to acknowledge, to know, or to read. He regards it as here used in the sense of *knowing.* It is probably used here in the sense of knowing accurately, or surely; of *recognising* from their former acquaintance with him. They would *see* that the sentiments which he now expressed were such as accorded with his character and uniform course of life. ¶ *Or acknowledge* (ἐπιγινώσκετε). The preposition ἐπι in composition here is *intensive,* and the word denotes to know fully; to receive full knowledge of; to know well; or to recognise. It here means that they would fully recognise, or know entirely to their satisfaction, that the sentiments which he here expressed were such as accorded with his general manner of life. From

14 As also ye have acknowledged us in part, that *a* we are
your rejoicing, even as ye also

a Phil.4.1.

are ours in the day of the Lord
Jesus.

15 And in this confidence I

---

what they knew of him, they could
not but admit that he had been influenced by the principles stated. ¶ *And
I trust ye shall acknowledge.* I trust
that my conduct will be such as to
convince you always that I am actuated by such principles. I trust you
will never witness any departure from
them—the language of a man of settled principle, and of fixed aims and
honesty of life. An honest man can
always use such language respecting
himself. ¶ *Even to the end.* To the
end of life; always. "We trust that
you will never have occasion to think
dishonourably of us; or to reflect on
any inconsistency in our behaviour."
—*Doddridge.*

14. *As also ye have acknowledged
us.* You have had occasion to admit
my singleness of aim, and purity of
intention and of life by your former
acquaintance with me; and you have
cheerfully done it. ¶ *In part* (ἀπὸ
μέρους). Tindal renders this, "as ye
have found us partly." The sense
seems to be, "as part of you acknowledge;" meaning that *a portion* of
the church was ready to concede to
him the praise of consistency and uprightness, though there was a faction,
or a part that denied it. ¶ *That we
are your rejoicing.* That we are your
joy, and your boasting. That is, you
admit me to be an apostle. You regard me as your teacher, and guide.
You recognise my authority, and acknowledge the benefits which you have
received through me. ¶ *Even as ye
also* are *ours.* Or, as you will be our
rejoicing in the day when the Lord
Jesus shall come to gather his people
to himself. Then it will be seen that
you were saved by our ministry; and
then it will be an occasion of abundant and eternal thanksgiving to God
that you were converted by our labours. And as you now regard it as
a matter of congratulation and thanksgiving that you have such teachers as
we are, so shall *we* regard it as a
matter of congratulation and thanks-

giving—as our chief joy—that we
were the instruments of saving *such* a
people. The expression implies that
there was mutual confidence, mutual
love, and mutual cause of rejoicing.
It is well when ministers and people
have such confidence in each other,
and have occasion to regard their
connection as a mutual cause of rejoicing and of καύχημα or *boasting.*

15. *And in this confidence.* In this
confidence of my integrity, and that
you had this favourable opinion of me,
and appreciated the principles of my
conduct. I did not doubt that you
would receive me kindly, and would
give me again the tokens of your affection and regard. In this Paul
shows that however *some* of them
might regard him, yet that he had no
doubt tnat the majority of the church
there would receive him kindly. ¶ *I
was minded.* I willed (ἐβουλόμην); it
was my intention. ¶ *To come unto
you before.* Tindal renders this, "the
other time." Paul refers doubtless
to the time when he wrote his former
epistle, and when it was his serious
purpose, as it was his earnest wish, to
visit them again; see 1 Cor. xvi. 5.
In this purpose he had been disappointed, and he now proceeds to state
the reasons why he had not visited
them as he had purposed, and to show
that it did not arise from any fickleness of mind. His purpose *had* been
at first to pass through Corinth on
his way to Macedonia, and to remain
some time with them; see ver. 16.
comp. 1 Cor. xvi. 5, 6. This purpose
he had now changed; and instead of
passing *through* Corinth on his way
to Macedonia, he had gone *to* Macedonia by the way of Troas (chap. ii.
12); and the Corinthians having, as
it would seem, become acquainted
with this fact, had charged him with
insincerity in the promise, or fickleness in regard to his plans. Probably
it had been said by some of his enemies that he had never intended to
visit them. ¶ *That ye might have a*

was minded to come unto you before, that ye might have a second [1] benefit ;

16 And to pass by you into Macedonia, and to come again out

1 Or, *grace.*

of Macedonia unto you, and of you to be brought on my [a] way toward Judea.

17 When I therefore was thus minded, did I use lightness ? or

a Acts 21. 5.

---

second benefit. Marg. *grace.* The word here used ($\chi \acute{\alpha} \rho_{is}$) is that which is commonly rendered *grace,* and means probably favour, kindness, good-will, beneficence; and especially favour to the undeserving. Here it is evidently used in the sense of gratification, or pleasure. And the idea is, that they had been formerly gratified and benefitted by his residence among them ; he had been the means of conferring important favours on them, and he was desirous of being again with them, in order to gratify them by his presence, and that he might be the means of imparting to them other favours. Paul presumed that his presence with them would be to them a source of pleasure, and that his coming would do them good. It is the language of a man who felt assured that he enjoyed, after all, the confidence of the mass of the church there, and that they would regard his being with them as a favour. He had been with them formerly almost two years. His residence there had been pleasant to them and to him ; and had been the occasion of important benefits to them. He did not doubt that it would be so again. Tindal renders this, "that ye might have had a double pleasure." It may be remarked here that several MSS. instead of $\chi \acute{\alpha} \rho_{i\nu}$, *grace,* read $\chi \alpha \rho \acute{\alpha} \nu$, *joy.*

16. *And to pass by you.* Through (δ_i) you ; that is, through your city, or province ; or to take them, as we say, in his way. His design was to pass through Corinth and Achaia on his journey. This was not the direct way from Ephesus to Macedonia. An inspection of a map (see the map of Asia Minor prefixed to the Notes on the Acts of the Apostles) will show at one view that the direct way was that which he concluded finally to take— that by Troas. Yet he had designed to go out of his way in order to make them a visit ; and intended also, per-

haps, to make them also a longer visit on his return. The former part of the plan he had been induced to abandon. ¶ *Into Macedonia.* A part of Greece having Thrace on the north, Thessaly south, Epirus west and the Ægean Sea east ; see Note, Acts xvi. 9. ¶ *And of you to be brought on my way.* By you ; see Note, 1 Cor. xvi. 6. ¶ *Toward Judea.* His object in going to Judea was to convey the collection for the poor saints which he had been at so much pains to collect throughout the churches of the Gentiles ; see Notes, Rom. xv. 25, 26 ; comp. 1 Cor. xvi. 3, 4.

17. *When I therefore was thus minded.* When I formed this purpose ; when I willed this, and expressed this intention. ¶ *Did I use lightness ?* The word $\mathring{\epsilon} \lambda \alpha \phi \rho \acute{\epsilon} \alpha$ (from $\mathring{\epsilon} \lambda \alpha \phi \rho \acute{o}s$) means properly *lightness* in weight. Here it is used in reference to the mind, and in a sense similar to our word *levity,* as denoting lightness of temper or conduct ; inconstancy, changeableness, or fickleness. This charge had been probably made that he had made the promise without any due consideration, or without any real purpose of performing it, or that he had made it in a trifling and thoughtless manner. By the interrogative form here, he sharply denies that it was a purpose formed in a light and trifling manner. ¶ *Do I purpose according to the flesh.* In such a manner, as may suit my own convenience and carnal interest. Do I form plans adapted only to promote my own ease and gratification, and to be abandoned when they are attended with inconvenience ? The phrase " according to the flesh" here seems to mean "in such a way as to promote my own ease and gratification ; in a manner such as the men of the world form ; such as would be formed under the influence of earthly passions and

the things that I purpose, do I purpose according *a* to the flesh, that with me there should be yea, yea, and nay, nay?

a chap.10.2.   1 Or, *preaching*.

18 But *as* God *is* true, our ¹ word toward you was not yea *b* and nay.

19 For the Son *c* of God, Jesus

b Mat.5.37.   c Mark 1.1.

desires, and to be forsaken when those plans would interfere with such gratifications." Paul denies in a positive manner that he formed *such* plans; and they should have known enough of his manner of life to be assured that that was not the nature of the schemes which he had devised? Probably no man ever lived who formed his plans of life *less* for the gratification of the flesh than Paul. ¶ *That with me there should be yea, yea, and nay, nay?* There has been a great variety in the interpretation of this passage; see Bloomfield, Crit. Dig. *in loco.* The meaning seems to be, "that there should be such inconstancy and uncertainty in my counsels and actions, that no one could depend on me, or know what they had to expect from me." Bloomfield supposes that the phrase is a proverbial one, and denotes a headstrong, self-willed spirit which will either do things, or not do them as pleases, without giving any reasons. He supposes that the *repetition* of the words "yea and nay" is designed to denote *positiveness* of assertion—such positiveness as is commonly shown by such persons, as in the phrases, "what I have written I have written," "what I have done I have done." It seems more probable, however, that the phrase is designed to denote the *ready compliance* which an inconstant and unsettled man is accustomed to make with the wishes of others; his expressing a ready assent to what they propose; falling in with their views; readily making promises; and instantly, through some whim, or caprice, or wish of others, saying "yea, nay," to the same thing; that is, changing his mind, and altering his purpose without any good reason, or in accordance with any fixed principle or settled rule of action. Paul says that this was not his character. He did not affirm a thing at one time and deny it at another; he did not pro-

mise to do a thing one moment and refuse to do it the next.

18. *But* as *God* is *true.* Tindal renders this, in accordance more literally with the Greek, "God is faithful; for our preaching unto you was not yea and nay." The phrase seems to have the form of an oath, or to be a solemn appeal to God as a witness, and to be equivalent to the expression "the Lord liveth," or "as the Lord liveth." The idea is, "God is faithful and true. He never deceives; never promises that which he does not perform. *So true* is it that I am not fickle and changing in my purposes." This idea of the faithfulness of God is the argument which Paul urges why he felt himself bound to be faithful also. That faithful God he regarded as a witness, and to that God he could appeal on the occasion. ¶ *Our word.* Marg. *preaching* (ὁ λόγος). This may refer either to his preaching, to his promises of visiting them, or his declarations to them in general on any subject. The particular subject under discussion was the promise which he had made to visit them. But he here seems to make his affirmation general, and to say universally of his promises, and his teaching, and of *all* his communications to them, whether orally or in writing, that they were not characterized by inconstancy and changeableness. It was not his character to be fickle, unsettled, and vacillating.

19. *For the Son of God.* In this verse, and the following, Paul states that he felt himself bound to maintain the strictest veracity for two reasons; the one, that Jesus Christ always evinced the strictest veracity (ver. 19); the other, God was always true to all the promises that he made (ver. 20); and as he felt himself to be the servant of the Saviour and of God, he was bound by the most sacred obligations also to maintain a character irreproachable in regard to veracity

Christ who was preached among you by us, *even* by me and Silvanus and Timotheus, was not yea and nay, but in him was yea.

20 For all the promises of God in *a* him *are* yea, and in him amen, unto the glory of God by us.

a Rom.15.8,9; Heb.13.8.

On the meaning of the phrase " Son of God," see Note, Rom. i. 4. ¶ *Jesus Christ.* It is agreed, says Bloomfield, by the best commentators, ancient and modern, that by Jesus Christ is here meant his doctrine. The sense is, that the preaching respecting Jesus Christ, did not represent him as fickle, and changeable ; as unsettled, and as unfaithful; but as TRUE, consistent, and faithful. As that had been the regular and constant representation of Paul and his fellow labourers in regard to the Master whom they served, it was to be inferred that they felt themselves bound sacredly to observe the strictest constancy and veracity. ¶ *By us,* &c. Silvanus, here mentioned, is the same person who in the Acts of the Apostles is called *Silas.* He was with Paul at Philippi, and was imprisoned there with him (Acts xvi.), and was afterwards with Paul and Timothy at Corinth when he first visited that city; Acts xviii. 5. Paul was so much attached to him, and had so much confidence in him, that he joined his name with his own in several of his epistles ; 1 Thess. i. 1 ; 2 Thess. i. 1. ¶ *Was not yea and nay.* Our representation of him was not that he was fickle and changeable. ¶ *But in him was yea.* Was not one thing at one time, and another at another. He is the same, yesterday, to-day, and forever. All that he says is true; all the promises that he makes are firm ; all his declarations are faithful. Paul may refer to the fact that the Lord Jesus when on earth was eminently characterized by TRUTH. Nothing was more striking than his veracity. He called himself " the truth," as being eminently true in all his declarations. " I am the way, and THE TRUTH, and the life ;" John xiv. 6 ; comp. Rev. iii. 7. And thus (Rev. iii. 14) he is called " the faithful and true witness." In all his life he was eminently distinguished for

that. His declarations were simple truth ; his narratives were simple, unvarnished, uncoloured, unexaggerated statements of what actually occurred. He never disguised the truth; never prevaricated ; never had any mental reservation ; never deceived ; never used any word, or threw in any circumstance, that was fitted to lead the mind astray. He himself said that this was the great object which he had in view in coming into the world. " To this end was I born and for this cause came I into the world, that I should bear witness unto the truth ;" John xviii. 37. As Jesus Christ was thus distinguished for simple truth, Paul felt that he was under sacred obligations to imitate him, and always to evince the same inviolable fidelity. The most deeply felt obligation on earth is that which the Christian feels to imitate the Redeemer.

20. *For all the promises of God in him.* All the promises which God has made through him. This is *another* reason why Paul felt himself bound to maintain a character of the strictest veracity. The reason was, that *God* always evinced that ; and that as none of *his* promises failed, he felt himself sacredly bound to imitate him, and to adhere to all his. The promises of God which are made through Christ, relate to the pardon of sin to the penitent ; the sanctification of his people ; support in temptation and trial ; guidance in perplexity; peace in death, and eternal glory beyond the grave. All of these are made through a Redeemer, and none of these shall fail. ¶ *Are yea.* Shall all be certainly fulfilled. There shall be no vacillation on the part of God; no fickleness ; no abandoning of his gracious intention. ¶ *And in him amen.* In Rev. iii. 14, the Lord Jesus is called the " Amen." The word means true, faithful, certain. And the expression here means that all the promises which are made to men

21 Now he which stablisheth *a* us with you in Christ, and hath anointed *b* us, *is* God ;

a 2 Th.2.8; 1 Pet.5.10.
b 1 John 2.20,27; Rev.3.18.

22 Who hath also sealed *c* us, and given the earnest of the Spirit *d* in our hearts.

c Ep.1.13,14; 4.30; 2Ti.2.19.
d Rom.8.9,14—16.

through a Redeemer shall be certainly fulfilled. They are promises which are confirmed and established, and which shall by no means fail. ¶ *Unto the glory of God by us.* Either by us ministers and apostles; or by us who are Christians. The latter, I think, is the meaning; and Paul means to say, that the fulfilment of all the promises which God has made to his people shall result in his glory and praise as a God of condescension and veracity. The fact that he has made such promises is an act that tends to his own glory—since it was of his mere grace that they were made; and the fulfilment of these promises in and through the church, shall also tend to produce elevated views of his fidelity and goodness.

21. *Now he which stablisheth us.* He who makes us *firm* (ὁ βεβαιῶν ἡμᾶς); that is, he who has confirmed us in the hopes of the gospel, and who gives us grace to be faithful, and firm in our promises. The *object* of this is to trace all to God, and to prevent the appearance of self-confidence, or of boasting. Paul had dwelt at length on his own fidelity and veracity. He had taken pains to prove that he was not inconstant and fickle-minded. He here says, that this was not to be traced to himself, or to any native goodness, but was all to be traced to God. It was God who had given them all confident hope in Christ ; and it was God who had given him grace to adhere to his promises, and to maintain a character for veracity. The first "us," in this verse refers probably to Paul himself ; the second includes also the Corinthians, as being also anointed and sealed. ¶ *And hath anointed us.* Us who are Christians. It was customary to *anoint* kings, prophets, and priests on their entering on their office as a part of the ceremony of inauguration. The word *anoint* is applied to a priest, Ex. xxviii. 41 ; xl. 15 ; to a prophet, 1

Kings xix. 16 ; Isa. lxi. 1 ; to a king, 1 Sam. x. 1 ; xv. 1 ; 2 Sam. ii. 4 ; 1 Kings i. 34. It is applied often to the Messiah as being set apart, or consecrated to his office as prophet, priest, and king—*i. e.* as appointed by God to the highest office ever held in the world. It is applied also to Christians as being consecrated, or set apart to the service of God by the Holy Spirit—a use of the word which is derived from the sense of *consecrating*, or setting apart to the service of God. Thus in 1 John ii. 20, it is said, " But ye have an unction from the Holy One and know all things." So in ver. 27, " But the anointing which ye have received abideth in you," &c. The anointing which was used in the consecration of prophets, priests, and kings, seems to have been designed to be emblematic of the influences of the Holy Spirit, who is often represented as *poured* upon those who are under his influence (Prov. i. 23 ; Isa. xliii. 4 ; Joel ii. 28, 29 ; Zech. xii. 10 ; Acts x. 45), in the same way as water or oil is poured out. And as Christians are everywhere represented as being under the influence of the Holy Spirit, as being those on whom the Holy Spirit is *poured*, they are represented as " anointed." They are in this manner solemnly set apart, and consecrated to the service of God. ¶ Is *God*. God has done it. All is to be traced to him. It is not by any native goodness which we have, or any inclination which we have by nature to his service. This is one of the instances which abound so much in the writings of Paul, where he delights to trace all good influences to God.

22. *Who hath also sealed us.* The word used here (from σφραγίζω) means to seal up ; to close and make fast with a seal, or signet; as, *e. g.*, books, letters, &c. that they may not be read. It is also used in the sense of setting a mark on any thing, or a seal, to

23 Moreover I call God for a record upon my soul, that, to spare you, I came not as yet unto Corinth.

---

denote that it is genuine, authentic, confirmed, or approved, as when a deed, compact, or agreement is sealed. It is thus made sure ; and is confirmed or established. Hence it is applied to *persons*, as denoting that they are approved, as in Rev. vii. 3 : "Hurt not the earth, neither the sea, nor the trees, till we have sealed the servants of our God in their foreheads;" comp. Ezek. ix. 4 ; see Note, John vi. 27, were it is said of the Saviour, "for him hath God the Father *sealed*;" comp. John iii. 33. In a similar manner Christians are said to be sealed ; to be sealed by the Holy Spirit (Eph. i. 13 ; iv. 30) ; that is, the Holy Spirit is given to them to confirm them as belonging to God. He grants them his Spirit. He renews and sanctifies them. He produces in their hearts those feelings, hopes, and desires which are an *evidence* that they are approved by God ; that they are regarded as his adopted children ; that their hope is genuine, and that their redemption and salvation are sure—in the same way as a seal makes a will or an agreement sure. God grants to them his Holy Spirit as the certain pledge that they are his, and shall be approved and saved in the last day. In this there is no thing miraculous, or in the nature of direct revelation. It consists of the ordinary operations of the Spirit on the heart, producing repentance, faith, hope, joy, conformity to God, the love of prayer and praise, and the Christian virtues generally ; and *these things* are the evidences that the Holy Spirit has renewed the heart, and that the Christian is sealed for the day of redemption. ¶ *And given the earnest of the Spirit.* The word here used (ἀῤῥαβών from the Heb. ערבון) means properly a pledge given to ratify a contract ; a part of the price, or purchase money; a first payment ; that which confirms the bargain, and which is regarded as a pledge that all the price will be paid. The word occurs in the Septuagint and Hebrew, in Gen. xxxviii. 17, 18 ; xxxviii. 20. In the New Testament it occurs only in this place, and in chap. v. 5, and Eph. i. 14, in each place in the same connection as applied to the Holy Spirit, and his influences on the heart. It refers to those influences as a *pledge* of the future glories which await Christians in heaven. In regard to the "earnest," or the part of a price which was paid in a contract, it may be remarked, (1.) That it was of the same *nature* as the full price, being regarded as a *part* of it ; (2.) It was regarded as a pledge or assurance that the full price would be paid. So the "earnest of the Spirit, " denotes that God gives to his people the influences of his Spirit : his operation on the heart as a part or pledge that all the blessings of the covenant of redemption shall be given to them. And it implies, (1.) That the comforts of the Christian here are of the same *nature* as they will be in heaven. Heaven will consist of *like* comforts ; of love, and peace, and joy, and purity begun here, and simply *expanded* there to complete and eternal perfection. The joys of heaven differ only in *degree*, not in *kind*, from those of the Christian on earth. That which is begun here is perfected there ; and the feelings and views which the Christian has here, if expanded and carried out, would constitute heaven. (2.) These comforts, these influences of the Spirit, are a *pledge* of heaven. They are the security which God gives us that we shall be saved. If we are brought under the renewing influences of the Spirit here ; if we are made meek, and humble, and prayerful by his agency ; if we are made to partake of the joys which result from pardoned sin ; if we are filled with the hope of heaven, it is all produced by the Holy Spirit, and is a *pledge*, or earnest of our future inheritance ; —as the first sheaves of a harvest are a pledge of a harvest ; or the first payment under a contract a pledge that all will be payed. God thus gives to his people the assurance that

24 Not for that we have *a* dominion over your faith, but are
a 1Cor.3 5; 1Pet.5.3.

helpers of your joy: for by *b* faith
ye stand.
b Rom.11.20; 1Cor.15.1.

they shall be saved; and by this
"pledge" makes their title to eternal
life sure.

23. *Moreover, I call God for a record upon my soul.* It is well remarked by Rosenmüller, that the
second chapter should have commenced here, since there is here a
transition in the subject more distinct
than where the second chapter is
actually made to begin. Here Tindal
commences the second chapter. This
verse, with the subsequent statements,
is designed to show them the true
reason why he had changed his purpose, and had not visited them according to his first proposal. And that
reason was not that he was fickle and
inconstant; but it was that he apprehended that if he should go to them
in their irregular and disorderly state,
he would be under a necessity of resorting to harsh measures, and to a
severity of discipline that would be
alike painful to them and to him. Dr.
Paley has shown with great plausibi-
ity, if not with moral certainty, that
Paul's change of purpose about visiting them was made *before* he wrote
his first epistle; that he had at first
resolved to visit them, but that on
subsequent reflection, he thought it
would be better to try the effect of *a
faithful letter to them,* admonishing
them of their errors, and entreating
them to exercise proper discipline
themselves on the principal offender;
that with this feeling he wrote his
first epistle, in which he does not
state to them *as yet* his change of
purpose, or the reason of it; but that
now after he had written that letter,
and after it had had all the effect
which he desired, he states the true
reason why he had not visited them.
It was now proper to do it; and that
reason was, that he desired to spare
them the severity of discipline, and
had resorted to the more mild and
affectionate measure of sending them
a letter, and thus not making it
necessary personally to administer
discipline; see Paley's Horæ Paulinæ,

on 2 Cor. Nos. iv. and v. The phrase,
" I call God for a record upon my
soul," is in the Greek, " I call God
for a witness against my soul." It is
a solemn oath, or appeal to God; and
implies, that if he did not in that case
declare the truth, he desired that God
would be a witness *against* him, and
would punish him accordingly. The
reason why he made this solemn appeal to God was, the importance of
his vindicating his own character
before the church, from the charges
which had been brought against him.
¶ *That to spare you.* To avoid the
necessity of inflicting punishment on
you; of exercising severe and painful
discipline. If he went among them
in the state of irregularity and disorder which prevailed there, he would
feel it to be necessary to exert his
authority as an apostle, and remove
at once the offending members from
the church. He expected to avoid
the necessity of these painful acts of
discipline, by sending to them a faithful and affectionate epistle, and thus
inducing them to reform, and to avoid
the necessity of a resort to that which
would have been so trying to him and
to them. It was not, then, a disregard for them, or a want of attachment to them, which had led him to
change his purpose, but it was the
result of tender affection. This cause
of the change of his purpose, of course,
he would not make known to them in
his first epistle, but now that that
letter had accomplished all he had
desired, it was proper that they should
be apprized of the reason why he had
resorted to this instead of visiting
them personally.

24. *Not for that we have dominion,*
&c. The sense of this passage I take
to be this: " The course which we
have pursued has been chosen not
because we wish to lord it over your
faith, to control your belief, but because we desired to promote your
happiness. Had the former been our
object, had we wished to set up a
lordship or dominion over you, we

should have come to you with our apostolical authority, and in the severity of apostolic discipline. We had power to command obedience, and to control your faith. But we chose not to do it. Our object was to promote your highest happiness. We, therefore, chose the mildest and gentlest manner possible ; we did not exercise authority in discipline, we sent an affectionate and tender letter." While the apostles had the right to prescribe the articles of belief, and to propound the doctrines of God, yet they would not do even that in such a manner as to seem to "lord it over God's heritage" (οὐκ κυριευομεν); they did not set up absolute authority, or prescribe the things to be believed in a lordly and imperative manner ; nor would they make use of the severity of power to enforce what they taught. They appealed to reason ; they employed persuasion ; they made use of light and love to accomplish their desires. ¶ *Are helpers of your joy.* This is our main object, to promote your joy. This object we have pursued in our plans, and in order to secure this, we forbore to come to you, when, if we *did* come at that time, we should have given occasion perhaps to the charge that we sought to lord it over your faith. ¶ *For by faith ye stand ;* see Note, 1 Cor. xv 1. This seems to be a kind of proverbial expression, stating a general truth, that it was by faith that Christians were to be established or confirmed. The connection here requires us to understand this as a reason why he would not attempt to lord it over their faith ; or to exercise dominion over them. That reason was, that thus far they *had* stood firm, in the main, in the faith (1 Cor. xv. 1); they had adhered to the truths of the gospel, and *in a special manner now, in yielding obedience to the commands and entreaties of Paul in the first epistle*, they had showed that they *were* in the faith, and firm in faith. It was not necessary or proper, therefore, for him to attempt to exercise lordship over their belief, but all that was needful was to help forward their joy, for they *were* firm in the faith.

We may observe, (1.) That it is a part of the duty of ministers to help forward the joy of Christians. (2.) This should be the object even in administering discipline and reproof. (3.) If even Paul would not attempt to lord it over the faith of Christians, to establish a domination over their belief, how absurd and wicked is it for uninspired ministers now, for individual ministers, for conferences, conventions, presbyteries, synods, councils, or for the pope, to attempt to establish a spiritual dominion in *controlling* the faith of men. The great evils in the church have arisen from their attempting to do what Paul *would* not do ; from attempting to establish a dominion which Paul never sought, and which Paul would have abhorred. Faith must be free, and religion must be free, or they cannot exist at all.

REMARKS.

In view of this chapter we may remark,

1st. God is the only true and real source of comfort in times of trial, ver. 3. It is from him that all real consolation must come, and he only can meet and sustain the soul when it is borne down with calamity. All persons are subjected to trial, and at some periods of their lives, to severe trial. Sickness is a trial ; the death of a friend is a trial ; the loss of property or health, disappointment, and reproach, and slander, and poverty, and want, are trials to which we are all more or less exposed. In these trials, it is natural to look to *some* source of consolation ; some way in which they may be borne. Some seek consolation in philosophy, and endeavour to blunt their feelings and destroy their sensibilities, as the ancient stoics did. But " to destroy sensibility is not to produce comfort."—*Dr. Mason.* Some plunge deep into pleasures, and endeavour to drown their sorrows in the intoxicating draught ; but this is not to produce *comfort* to the soul, even were it possible in such pleasures to forget their sorrows. Such were the ancient epicureans. Some seek consolation in their surviving friends, and look to them to comfort and sustain the sinking heart. But the arm of an earthly friend is feeble, when *God* lays his hand upon us. It is only the hand that smites that can heal; only the God that sends the affliction, that can bind up the broken spirit. He is the "Father of mercies," and he "the God of ALL consolation;" and in affliction there is no true comfort but in him.

(2.) This consolation in God is derived from many sources. (*a*) He is the "Father of mercies," and we may be assured, therefore, that he does nothing inconsistent with MERCY. (*b*) We may be assured that he is right—always right, and that he does nothing *but* right. We may not be able to see the *reason* of his doings, but we may have the assurance that it *is* all right, and will yet be seen to be right. (*c*) There is comfort in the fact, that our afflictions are ordered by an *intelligent* Being, by one who is all-wise, and all-knowing. They are not the result of blind chance; but they are ordered by one who is wise to *know* what *ought* to be done; and who is so just that he will do nothing wrong. There could be no consolation in the feeling that mere *chance* directed our trials; nor can there be consolation except in the feeling that a being of intelligence and goodness directs and orders all. The true comfort, therefore, is to be found in *religion*, not in atheism and philosophy.

(3.) It is possible to bless God in the midst of trials, and as the result of trial. It is possible so clearly to see his hand, and to be so fully satisfied with the wisdom and goodness of his dealings, even when we are severely afflicted, as to see that he is worthy of our highest confidence and most exalted praise, ver. 3. God may be seen, then, to be the "Father of mercies;" and he may impart, even then, a consolation which we never experience in the days of prosperity. Some of the purest and most elevated joys known upon earth, are experienced in the very midst of outward calamities, and the most sincere and elevated thanksgivings which are offered to God, are often those which are the result of sanctified afflictions. It is when we are brought out from such trials, where we have experienced the rich consolations and the sustaining power of the gospel, that we are most disposed to say with Paul, "Blessed be God;" and can most clearly see that he is the "Father of mercies." No Christian will ever have occasion to regret the trials through which God has brought him. I never knew a sincere Christian who was not finally benefitted by trials.

(4.) Christian joy is not *apathy*, it is *comfort*; ver. 4, 5. It is not insensibility to suffering; it is not stoical indifference. The Christian *feels* his sufferings as keenly as others. The Lord Jesus was *as* sensitive to suffering as any one of the human family ever was; he was as susceptible of emotion from reproach, contempt, and scorn, and he *as* keenly felt the pain of the scourge, the nails, and the cross, as any one could. But there is *positive* joy, there is true and solid comfort. There is substantial, pure, and elevated happiness. Religion does not blunt the feelings, or destroy the sensibility, but it brings in consolations which enable us to bear our pains, and to endure persecution without murmuring. In this, religion differs from all systems of philosophy. The one attempts to *blunt* and destroy our sensibilities to suffering; the other, while it makes us more delicate and tender in our feelings, gives consolation *adapted* to that delicate sensibility, and fitted to sustain the soul, *notwithstanding* the acuteness of its sufferings.

(5.) Ministers of the gospel may expect to be *peculiarly* tried and afflicted; ver. 5. So it was with Paul and his fellow-apostles; and so it has been since. They are the special objects of the hatred of sinners, as they stand in the way of the sinful pursuits and pleasures of the world; and they are, like their Master, especially hated by the enemy of souls. Besides, they are, by their office, required to minister consolation to others who are afflicted; and it is so ordered in the providence of God, that they are subjected to peculiar trials often, *in order* that they may be able to impart peculiar consolations. They are to be the examples and the guides of the church of God; and God takes care that they shall be permitted to show by their example, as well as by their preaching, the supporting power of the gospel in times of trial.

(6.) If we suffer much in the cause of the Redeemer, we may also expect much consolation; ver. 5. Christ will take care that our hearts shall be filled with joy and peace. As our trials in his cause are, so shall our consolations be. If we suffer much, we shall enjoy much; if we are persecuted much, we shall have much support; if our names are cast out among men for his sake, we shall have increasing evidence that they are written in his book of life. There *are* things in the Christian religion which can be learned only in the furnace of affliction; and he who has never been afflicted on account of his attachment to Christ, is a stranger yet to *much, very much* of the fulness and beauty of that system of religion which has been appointed by the Redeemer, and to much, very much, of the beauty and power of the promises of the Bible. No man will ever understand *all* the Bible who is not *favoured* with much persecution and many trials.

(7.) We should be willing to suffer; ver. 3 5. If we are willing *to be happy*, we should also be willing to suffer. If we *desire* to be happy in religion, we should be willing to suffer. If we *expect* to be happy, we should also be willing to endure much. Trials fit us for enjoyment here, as well as for heaven hereafter.

(8.) One great design of the consolation which is imparted to Christians in the time of affliction is, that they may be able to impart consolation also to others; ver. 4, 6, 7. God designs that we should thus be mutual aids. And he comforts a pastor in his trials, that he may, by his own experience, be able to minister consolation to the people of his charge; he comforts a parent, that he may administer consolation to his children;

a friend, that he may comfort a friend. He who attempts to administer consolation should be able to speak from experience: and God, therefore, afflicts and comforts all his people, that they may know how to administer consolation to those with whom they are connected.

(9.) If we have experienced peculiar consolations ourselves in times of trial, we are under obligations to seek out and comfort others who are afflicted. So Paul felt. We should feel that God has qualified us for this work; and having qualified us for it, that he calls on us to do it. The consolation which God gives in affliction is a rich treasure which we are bound to impart to others; the experience which we have of the true sources of consolation is an inestimable talent which we are to use for the promotion of his glory. No man has a talent for doing more direct good than he who can go to the afflicted, and bear testimony, from his own experience, to the goodness of God. And every man who *can* testify that God is good, and is able to support the soul in times of trial,—and what Christian cannot do it who has ever been afflicted?—should regard himself as favoured with a peculiar talent for doing good, and should rejoice in the privilege of using it to the glory of God. For there is no talent more honourable than that of being able to promote the divine glory, to comfort the afflicted, or to be able, from personal experience, to testify that God is good—always good. "The *power* of doing good, always implies an *obligation* to do it."—*Cotton Mather*.

(10.) In this chapter, we have a case of a near contemplation of death ver. 8, 9. Paul expected soon to die. He had the sentence of death in himself. He saw no human probability of escape. He was called, therefore, calmly to look death in the face, and to contemplate it as an event certain and near. Such a condition is deeply interesting, it is *the* important crisis of life. And yet it is an event which all must soon contemplate. We all, in a short period, each one for himself, *must* look upon death as certain, and as near to us; as an event in which we are personally interested, and from which we cannot escape. Much as we may turn away from it in health, and unanxious as we may be then in regard to it, yet by no possibility can we long avert our minds from the subject. It is interesting, then, to inquire how Paul felt when he looked at death; how we *should* feel ; and how we actually *shall* feel when we come to die.

(11.) A contemplation of death as near and certain, is fitted to lead us to trust in God. This was the effect in the case of Paul; ver. 9. He had learned in health to put his trust in him, and now, when the trial was apparently near, he had no where else to go, and he confided in him alone. He felt that if he was rescued, it could be only by the interposition of God; and that there was none but God who could sustain him if he should die. And what event *can* there be that is so well fitted to lead us to trust in God as death? And where else can we go in view of that dark hour? For, (*a*) We know not what death is. We have not tried it; nor do we know what grace may be necessary for us in those unknown pangs and sufferings ; in that deep darkness, and that sad gloom. (*b*) Our friends *cannot* aid us then. They will, they *must*, then, give us the parting hand; and as we *enter* the shades of the dark valley, they must bid us farewell. The skill of the physician then will fail. Our worldly friends will forsake us when we come to die. They do not love to be in the room of death, and they can give us no consolation if they are there. Our pious friends cannot attend us far in the dark valley. They may pray, and commend us to God, but even they must leave us to die alone. Who but God *can* attend us? Who but he can support us then? (*c*) God only knows what is *beyond* death. How do we know the way to his bar, to his presence, to his heaven? How can we direct our own steps in that dark and unknown world? None but God our Saviour can guide us there; none else can conduct us to his abode. (*d*) None but God can sus-

tain us in the pain, the anguish, the feebleness, the sinking of the powers of body and of mind in that distressing hour. He *can* uphold us then; and it is an unspeakable privilege to be permitted then, "when heart and flesh faint," to say of him, "God is the strength of" our "heart, and" our "portion for ever ;" Ps. lxxiii. 26.

(12.) We should regard a restoration from dangerous sickness, and from imminent peril of death as a kind of resurrection. So Paul regarded it; ver. 9. We should remember how easy it would have been for God to have removed us ; how rapidly we were tending to the grave; how certainly we should have descended there but for his interposition. We should feel, therefore, that we owe our lives to him as really and entirely as though we had been raised up from the dead; and that the same kind of power and goodness have been evinced as would have been had God given us life anew. Life is God's gift; and every instance of recovery from peril, or from dangerous illness, is as really an interposition of his mercy as though we had been raised up from the dead.

(13.) We should, in like manner, regard a restoration of our friends from dangerous sickness, or peril of any kind, as a species of resurrection from the dead. When a parent, a husband, a wife or a child has been dangerously ill, or exposed to some imminent danger, and has been recovered, we cannot but feel that the recovery is entirely owing to the interposition of God. With infinite ease he could have consigned them to the grave; and had he not mercifully interposed, they would have died. As they were originally his gift to us, so we should regard each interposition of that kind as a *new gift*, and receive the recovered and restored friend as a fresh gift from his hand.

(14.) We should feel that lives thus preserved and thus recovered from danger, belong to God. He has preserved them. In the most absolute sense they belong to him, and to him they should be consecrated. So Paul felt; and **his** whole life shows how entirely he regarded himself as bound to devote a life often preserved in the midst of peril, to the service of his kind Benefactor. There is no claim more absolute than that which God has on those whom he has preserved from dangerous situations, or whom he has raised up from the borders of the grave. All the strength which he has imparted, all the talent, learning, skill, which he has thus preserved, should be regarded in the most absolute sense as his, and should be honestly and entirely consecrated to him. *But* for him we should have died; and he has a right to our services and obedience which is entire, and which should be felt to be perpetual. And it may be added, that the right is not less clear and strong to the service of those whom he keeps without their being exposed to such peril, or raised up from such beds of sickness. A very few only of the interpositions of God in our behalf are seen by us. A small part of the perils to which we may be really exposed are seen. And it is no less owing to his preserving care that we are *kept in* health, and strength, and in the enjoyment of reason, than it is that we are *raised up* from dangerous sickness. Man is as much bound to devote himself to God for preserving him *from* sickness and danger, as he is for raising him up *when* he has been sick, and defending him in danger.

(15.) We have here an instance of the *principle* on which Paul acted, ver. 12. In his *aims*, and in the *manner* of accomplishing his aims, he was guided only by the principles of simplicity and sincerity, and by the grace of God. He had no sinister and worldly purpose; he had no crooked and subtle policy by which to accomplish his purposes. He sought simply the glory of God and the salvation of man ; and he sought this in a manner plain, direct, honest, and straight-forward. He admitted none of the principles of worldly policy which have been so often acted on since in the church; he knew nothing of "pious frauds," which have so often disgraced the *professed* friends of the Redeemer ; he admitted no form of deception and delusion, even for the promotion of objects which were great, and good, and desirable. He knew that all that *ought* to be done could be accomplished by straightforward and simple-hearted purposes; and that a cause which depended on the carnal and crooked policy of the world was a bad cause ; and that *such* policy would ultimately ruin the best of causes. How happy would it have been if these views had always prevailed in the church !

(16.) We see the value of a good conscience, ver. 12. Paul had the testimony of an enlightened conscience to the correctness and uprightness of his course of life everywhere. He felt assured that his aims had been right ; and that he had endeavoured in all simplicity and sincerity to pursue a course of life which such a conscience would approve. Such a testimony, such an approving conscience is of inestimable value. It is worth more than gold, and crowns, and all that the earth can give. When like Paul we are exposed to peril, or trial, or calamity, it matters little, if we have an approving conscience. When like him we are persecuted, it matters little if we have the testimony of our own minds that we have pursued an upright and an honest course of life. When like him we look death in the face, and feel that we "have the sentence of death in ourselves," of what inestimable value then will be an approving conscience ! How unspeakable the consolation if we can look back then on a life spent in conscious integrity; a life spent in endeavouring to promote the glory of God and the salvation of the world !

(17.) Every Christian should feel himself sacredly bound to maintain a character of veracity, ver. 19, 20. Christ was always true to his word ; and all that God has promised shall be certainly fulfilled. And as a Christian is a professed follower of him who was 'the Amen and the true witness," he should feel himself bound by the most sacred obligations to adhere to all his promises, and to fulfil all his word. No man can do any good who is not a man of truth; and in no way can Christians more dishonour their profession, and injure the cause of the Redeemer, than by a want of character for unimpeachable veracity. If they make promises which are never fulfilled; if they state that as true which is not true; if they overload their narratives with circumstances which had no existence; if they deceive, and defraud others; and if they are so loose in their statements that no one believes them, it is impossible for them to do good in their Christian profession. Every Christian *should* have—as he easily *may* have—such a character for veracity that every man shall put implicit confidence in all his promises and statements; *so* implicit that they shall deem his word as good as an oath; and his promise as certain as though it were secured by notes and bonds in the most solemn manner. The word of a Christian should *need* no strengthening by oaths and bonds; it should be such that it could really *not* be strengthened by any thing that notes and bonds could add to it.

(18.) All Christians should regard themselves as consecrated to God, ver. 21. They have been anointed, or set apart to his service. They should feel that they are as really set apart to his service as the ancient prophets, priests, and kings were to their appropriate offices by the ceremony of anointing. They belong to God, and are under every sacred and solemn obligation to live to him, and him alone.

(19.) It is an inestimable *privilege* to be a Christian, ver. 21, 22. It is regarded as a privilege to be an heir to an estate, and to have an assurance that it will be ours. But the Christian has an " earnest," a pledge that heaven is his. He is anointed of God; he is sealed for heaven. Heaven is his home; and God is giving to him daily evidence in his own experience that he will soon be admitted to its pure and blissful abodes.

(20.) The joys of the Christian on earth are of the same *nature* as the joys of heaven. These comforts are an " earnest ' of the future inherit-

ance; a *part* of that which the Christian is to enjoy forever. His joys on earth are " heaven begun;" and all that is needful to constitute *heaven* is that these joys should be expanded and perpetuated. There will be no other heaven than that which would be constituted by the expanded joys of a Christian.

(21.) No one is a Christian, no one is fitted for heaven, who has not such principles and joys as being fully expanded and developed would constitute heaven. The joys of heaven are not to be *created* for us as some new thing; they are not to be such as we have had no foretaste, no conception of; but they are to be such as will be produced of necessity by removing imperfection from the joys and feelings of the believer, and carrying them out without alloy, and without interruption, and without end. The man, therefore, who has such a character, that if fairly developed would not constitute the joys of heaven, is not a Christian. He has no evidence that he has been born again; and all his joys are fancied and delusive.

(22.) Christians should be careful not to grieve the Holy Spirit; comp. Eph. iv. 30. It is by that Spirit that they are " anointed" and " sealed," and it is by his influences that they have the earnest of their future inheritance. All good influences on their minds proceed from that Spirit; and it should be their high and constant aim not to grieve him. By no course of conduct, by no conversation, by no impure thought, should they drive that Spirit from their minds. All their peace and joy is dependent on their cherishing his sacred influences; and by all the means in their power they should strive to secure his constant agency on their souls.

CHAPTER II.

In this chapter Paul continues the discussion of the subject which had been introduced in the previous chapter. At the close of that chapter, he had stated the reasons why he had not visited the church at Corinth; see Notes on chap. i. 23, 24. The main reason was, that instead of com-

CHAPTER II.

BUT I determined this with myself, that I would not come again to you in heaviness. *a*

a chap.1,23; 12.20,21; 13.10.

ing to them in that disordered, and irregular state, he had preferred to send them an affectionate letter. Had he come to them personally he would have felt himself called on to exercise the severity of discipline. He chose, therefore, to try what the effect would be of a faithful and kind epistle. In this chapter, he prosecutes the same subject. He states, therefore, more at length, the reason why he had not come to them, ver. 1 —5. The reason was, that he resolved not to come to them, if he could avoid it, with severity; that his heart was pained even with the necessity of sending such a letter; that he wrote it with much anguish of spirit; yet that he cherished towards them the most tender love. In his former epistle (chap. v.) he had directed them to exercise discipline on the offending person in the church. This had been done according to his direction; and the offender had been suitably punished for his offence. He had been excommunicated; and it would seem that the effect on him had been to induce him to forsake his sin, and probably to put away his father's wife, and he had become a sincere penitent. Paul, therefore, in the next place (ver. 6—11), exhorts them to receive him again into fellowship with the church. The punishment he says had been sufficient (ver. 6); they ought now to be kind and forgiving to him lest he should be overwhelmed with his sorrow (ver. 7); he says, that *he* had forgiven him, so far as he was concerned, and he entreated them to do the same (ver. 10); and says that they ought, by all means, to pursue such a course that Satan could get no advantage of them, ver. 11. Paul then states the disappointment which he had had at Troas in not seeing Titus, from whom he had expected to learn what was the state of the church at Corinth, and what was the reception of his letter there; but that not

2 For if I make you sorry, who is he then that maketh me glad, but the same which is made sorry by me?

seeing him there, he had gone on to Macedonia, ver. 12, 13. There, it would seem, he met Titus, and learned that his letter had had all the success which he could have desired. It had been kindly received; and all that he had wished in regard to discipline had been performed, ver. 14. The hearing of this success gives him occasion to thank God for it, as one among many instances in which his efforts to advance his cause had been crowned with success. God had made him everywhere successful; and had made him triumph in Christ in every place. This fact gives him occasion (ver. 15, 16) to state the general effect of his preaching and his labours. His efforts, he says, were always acceptable to God—though he could not be ignorant that in some cases the gospel which he preached was the occasion of the aggravated condemnation of those who heard and rejected it. Yet he had the consolation of reflecting that it was by no fault of his, ver. 17. It was not because he had corrupted the word of God; it was not because he was unfaithful; it was not because he was not sincere. He had a good conscience—a conscience which assured him that he spoke in sincerity and as in the sight of God—though the unhappy effect might be that many would perish from under his ministry.

1. *But I determined this with myself.* I made up my mind on this point; I formed this resolution in regard to my course. ¶ *That I would not come again to you with heaviness.* In grief (ἐν λύπ). "I would not come, if I could avoid it, in circumstances which must have grieved both me and you. I would not come while there existed among you such irregularities as must have pained my heart, and as must have compelled me to resort to such acts of discipline as would be painful to you. I resolved, therefore, to endeavour to remove these evils

3 And I wrote this same unto you, lest, when I came, I should have sorrow from them of whom

I ought to rejoice; having confidence in you all, that my joy is *the joy* of you all.

before I came, that when I did come, my visit might be mutually agreeable to us both. For that reason I changed my purpose about visiting you, when I heard of those disorders, and resolved to send an epistle. If *that* should be successful, then the way would be open for an agreeable visit to you." This verse, therefore, contains the statement of the principal reason why he had not come to them as he had at first proposed. It was really from no fickleness, but it was from love to them, and a desire that his visit should be mutually agreeable, comp. Notes, chap. i. 23.

2. *For if I made you sorry.* "If when I should come among you, I should be called on to inflict sorrow by punishing your offending brethren by an act of severe discipline as soon as I came, who would there be to give me comfort but those very persons whom I had affected with grief? How little prepared would they be to make me happy, and to comfort me, amidst the deep sorrow which I should have caused by an act of severe discipline. After such an act—an act that would spread sorrow through the whole church, how could I expect that comfort which I should desire to find among you. The whole church would be affected with grief; and though I might be sustained by the sound part of the church, yet my visit would be attended with painful circumstances. I resolved, therefore, to remove all cause of difficulty, if possible, before I came, that my visit might be pleasant to us all." The idea is, that there was such a sympathy between him and them; that he was so attached to them, that he could not expect to be happy unless they were happy; that though he might be conscious he was only discharging a duty, and that God would sustain him in it, yet that it would mar the pleasure of his visit, and destroy all his anticipated happiness by the general grief.

3. *And I wrote this same unto you.* The words "this same" (τοῦτο αὐτὸ)

refer to what he had written to them in the former epistle, particularly to what he had written in regard to the incestuous person, requiring them to excommunicate him. Probably the expression also includes the commands in his former epistle to reform their conduct in general, and to put away the abuses and evil practices which prevailed in the church there. ¶ *Lest when I come,* &c. Lest I should be obliged if I came personally to exercise the severity of discipline, and thus to diffuse sorrow throughout the entire church. ¶ *I should have sorrow from them of whom I ought to rejoice.* Lest I should have grief in the church. Lest the conduct of the church, and the abuses which prevail in it should give me sorrow. I should be grieved with the existence of these evils; and I should be obliged to resort to measures which would be painful to me, and to the whole church. Paul sought to avoid this by persuading them before he came to exercise the discipline themselves, and to put away the evil practices which prevailed among them. ¶ *Having confidence in you all.* Having confidence that this is your general character, that whatever adds to my joy, or promotes my happiness, would give joy to you all. Paul had enemies in Corinth; he knew that there were some there whose minds were alienated from him, and who were endeavouring to do him injury. Yet he did not doubt that it was the general character of the church that they wished him well, and would desire to make him happy; that what would tend to promote his happiness would also promote theirs; and therefore, that they would be willing to do any thing that would make his visit agreeable to him when he came among them. He was, therefore, persuaded that if he wrote them an affectionate letter, they would listen to his injunctions, that thus all that was painful might be avoided when he came among them.

4. *For out of much affliction.* Pos-

4 For out of much affliction and anguish of heart I wrote unto you with many tears ; not that ye should be grieved, but that ye

a chap.11.2.

might know the love *a* which I have more abundantly unto you.

5 But if *b* any have caused

b Gal.5.10.

sibly Paul's enemies had charged him with being harsh and overbearing. They may have said that there was much needless severity in his letter. He here meets that, and says, that it was with much pain and many tears that he was constrained to write as he did. He was pained at their conduct, and at the necessity which existed for such an epistle. This is an eminently beautiful instance of Paul's kindness of heart, and his susceptibility to tender impressions. The evil conduct of others gives pain to a good man ; and the necessity of administering reproof and discipline is often as painful to him who does it, as it is to those who are the subjects of it. ¶ *And anguish of heart.* The word rendered " anguish" (συνοχή) means, properly, a holding together or shutting up ; and then, pressure, distress, anguish—an affliction of the heart by which one feels tightened or constrained ; such a pressure as great grief causes at the heart. ¶ *I wrote unto you with many tears.* With much weeping and grief that I was constrained to write such a letter. This was an instance of Paul's great tenderness of heart—a trait of character which he uniformly evinced. With all his strength of mind, and all his courage and readiness to face danger, Paul was not ashamed to weep ; and especially if he had any occasion of censuring his Christian brethren, or administering discipline; comp. Phil. iii. 88 ; Acts xx. 31. This is also a specimen of the manner in which Paul met the faults of his Christian brethren. It was not with bitter denunciation. It was not with sarcasm and ridicule. It was not by blazoning those faults abroad to others. It was not with the spirit of rejoicing that they had committed errors, and had been guilty of sin. It was not as if he was glad of the opportunity of administering rebuke, and took pleasure in denunciation and

in the language of reproof. All this is often done by others ; but Paul pursued a different course. He sent an affectionate letter to the offenders themselves ; and he did it with many tears. It was done weeping. Admonition would always be done right if it was done with tears. Discipline would always be right, and would be effectual, if it were administered with tears. Any man will receive an admonition kindly, if he who administers it does it weeping ; and the heart of an offender will be melted, if he who attempts to reprove him comes to him with tears. How happy would it be if all who attempt to reprove should do it with Paul's spirit. How happy, if all discipline should be administered in the church in his manner. But, we may add, how seldom is this done! How few are there who feel themselves called on to reprove an offending brother, or to charge a brother with heresy or crime, that do it with tears ! ¶ *Not that ye should be grieved.* It was not my object to give you pain. ¶ *But that ye might know the love,* &c. This was one of the best evidences of his great love to them which he could possibly give. It is proof of genuine friendship for another, when we faithfully and affectionately admonish him of the error of his course ; it is the highest proof of affection when we do it with tears. It is cruelty to suffer a brother to remain in sin unadmonished ; it is cruel to admonish him of it in a harsh, severe, and authoritative tone ; but it is proof of tender attachment when we go to him with tears, and entreat him to repent and reform. No man gives higher proof of attachment to another than he who affectionately admonishes him of his sin and danger.

5. *If any have caused grief.* There is doubtless here an allusion to the incestuous person. But it is very delicately done. He does not mention him by *name.* There is not *any*-

grief, he hath not grieved me, [a] but in part : that I may not over-charge you all.

a Gal.4.12.

where an allusion to his name ; nor is it possible now to know it. Is this not a proof that the *names* of the offending brethren in a church should not be put on the records of sessions, and churches, and presbyteries, to be handed down to posterity? Paul does not here either *expressly* refer to such a person. He makes his remark *general*, that it might be *as* tender and kind to the offending brother as possible. They would know whom he meant, but they had already punished him, as Paul supposed, enough, and *now* all that he said in regard to him was as tender as possible, and fitted, as much as possible, to concili-ate his feelings and allay his grief. He did not harshly charge him with sin ; he did not use any abusive or severe epithets ; but he gently insin-uates that he " had caused grief;" he had pained the hearts of his brethren. ¶ *He hath not grieved me, but in part.* He has not particularly offended or grieved ME. He has grieved me only in common with others, and as a part of the church of Christ. All have common cause of grief ; and I have no interest in it which is not common to you all. I am but one of a great number who have felt the deepest concern on account of his conduct. ¶ *That I may not overcharge you all.* That I may not *bear hard* (ἐπιβαρῶ) on you all; that I may not accuse you all of having caused me grief. The sense is, " Grief has been produced. I, in common with the church, have been pained, and deeply pained, with the conduct of the individual referred to ; and with that of his abettors and friends. But I would not charge the whole church with it; or seem to bear hard on them, or overcharge them with want of zeal for their purity, or unwillingness to remove the evil." They had shown their willingness to correct the evil by promptly removing the offender when he had directed it. The *sense* of this verse should be con-nected with the verse that follows ;

6 Sufficient to such a man *is* this [1] punishment, which *was inflicted* [b] of many.

1 or, *censure*.   b 1 Cor.5.4,5; 1 Tim.5.20.

and the idea is, that they had promptly administered sufficient dis-cipline, and that they were not now to be charged severely with having neglected it. Even while Paul said he had been pained and grieved, he had seen occasion not to bear hard on the whole church, but to be ready to commend them for their prompt-ness in removing the cause of the offence.

6. *Sufficient to such a man.* The incestuous person that had been by Paul's direction removed from the church. The object of Paul here is to have him again restored. For that purpose he says that the punishment which they had inflicted on him was " sufficient." It was, (1.) A suffi-cient expresion of the evil of the offence, and of the readiness of the church to preserve itself pure ; and, (2.) It was a sufficient punish-ment to the offender. It had accom-plished all that he had desired. It had humbled him, and brought him to repentance ; and doubtless led him to put away his wife ; comp. Note, 1 Cor. v. 1. As that had been done, it was proper now that he should be again restored to the privileges of the church. No evil would result from such a restoration, and their duty to their penitent brother demanded it. Mr. Locke has remarked that Paul conducts this subject here with very great tenderness and delicacy. The entire passage from ver. 5 to ver. 10 relates solely to this offending brother, yet he never once mentions his *name*, nor does he mention his *crime*. He speaks of him only in the soft terms of "such a one" and "any one :" nor does he use an epithet which would be calculated to wound his feel-ings, or to transmit his name to pos-terity, or to communicate it to other churches. So that though this epistle should be read, as Paul doubtless in-tended, by other churches, and be transmitted to future times, yet no one would ever be acquainted with

7 So *a* that contrariwise ye | *ought* rather to forgive *him*, and

a Gal. 6. 1.

---

the name of the individual. How different this from the temper of those who would blazon abroad the names of offenders, or make a permanent record to carry them down with dishonour to posterity? ¶ *Which* was inflicted *of many.* By the church in its collective capacity; see Note on 1 Cor. v. 4. Paul had required the church to administer this act of discipline, and they had promptly done it. It is evident that the *whole* church was concerned in the administration of the act of discipline; as the words " of many" (ἀπὸ τῶν πλειόνων) are not applicable either to a single "bishop," or a single minister, or a presbytery, or a bench of elders; nor can they be so regarded, except by a forced and unnatural construction. Paul had directed it to be done by the assembled church (1 Cor. v. 4), and this phrase shows that they had followed his instructions. Locke supposes that the phrase means, "by the majority;" Macknight renders it, "by the greater number;" Bloomfield supposes that it means that the "punishment was carried into effect by all." Doddridge paraphrases it, "by the whole body of your society." The expression proves beyond a doubt that the whole body of the society was concerned in the act of the excommunication, and that is a proper way of administering discipline. Whether it proves, however, that that is the mode which is to be observed in all instances, may admit of a doubt, as the *example* of the early churches, in a particular case, does not prove that that mode has the force of a binding rule on all.

[It cannot fairly be argued from this verse, that the "many" or the whole congregation, were *judicially* concerned in the act of excommunication; yet as their concurrence was essential, in order to carry the sentence into effect, it was "inflicted of many" in a most emphatic sense. The refusal, on the part of the members of the church, to hold intercourse with the incestuous man, *carried into effect* what the apostle had *judicially pronounced.* See the Supplementary Note on 1 Cor. v. 4.]

7. *So that contrariwise.* On the other hand: on the contrary. That is, instead of continuing the punishment. Since the punishment was sufficient, and has answered all the purpose of bearing your testimony against the offence, and of bringing him to repentance, you ought again to admit him to your communion. ¶ *Ye* ought *rather to forgive* him. Rather than continue the pain and disgrace of excommunication. It follows from this, (1.) That the proper time for restoring an offender is only when the punishment has answered the purpose for which it was designed; *i. e.* has shown the just abhorrence of the church against the sin, and has reformed the offender; and, (2.) That *when* that is done the church ought to forgive the offending brother, and admit him again to their fellowship. *When* it can be ascertained that the punishment has been effectual in reforming him, may depend somewhat on the nature of the offence. In this case, it was sufficiently shown by his putting away his wife, and by the manifestations of sorrow. So in other cases, it may be shown by a man's abandoning a course of sin, and reforming his life. If he has been unjust, by his repairing the evil; if he has been pursuing an unlawful business, by abandoning it; if he has pursued a course of vice; by his forsaking it, and by giving satisfactory evidences of sorrow and of reformation, for a period sufficiently long to show his sincerity. The *time* which will be required in each case, must depend, of course, somewhat on the nature of the offence, the previous character of the individual, the temptations to which he may be exposed, and the disgrace which he may have brought on his Christian calling. It is to be observed, also, that *then* his restoration is to be regarded as an act of *forgiveness,* a favour (χαρίσασθαι, *i. e.* χαρις, favour, grace) on the part of the church. It is not a matter of justice, or of claim on his part, for having once dishonoured his call-

comfort *him*, lest perhaps such a one should be swallowed up with overmuch sorrow.

8 Wherefore I beseech you that

ing, he has forfeited his right to a good standing among Christians; but it is a matter of favour, and he should be willing to humble himself before the church, and make suitable acknowledgment for his offences. ¶ *And comfort* him. There is every reason to think that this man became a sincere penitent. If so, he must have been deeply pained at the remembrance of his sin, and the dishonour which he had brought on his profession, as well as at the consequences in which he had been involved. In this deep distress, Paul tells them that they ought to comfort him. They should receive him kindly, as God receives to his favour a penitent sinner. They should not cast out his name as evil; they should not reproach him for his sins; they should not harrow up his recollection of the offence by often referring to it; they should be willing to bury it in lasting forgetfulness, and treat him now as a brother. It is a duty of a church to treat with kindness a true penitent, and receive him to their affectionate embrace. The offence should be forgiven and forgotten. The consolations of the gospel, adapted to the condition of penitents, should be freely administered; and all should be done that can be, to make the offender, when penitent, happy and useful in the community. ¶ *Lest perhaps such a one.* Still forbearing to mention his name; still showing towards him the utmost tenderness and delicacy. ¶ *Should be swallowed up*, &c. Should be overcome with grief, and should be rendered incapable of usefulness by his excessive sorrow. This is a strong expression, denoting intensity of grief. We speak of a man's being drowned in sorrow; or overwhelmed with grief; of grief preying upon him. The figure here is probably taken from deep waters, or from a whirlpool which seems to swallow up any thing that comes within reach. Excessive grief or ca-

ye would confirm *your* love toward him.

9 For to this end also did I write, that I might know the proof

lamity, in the Scriptures, is often compared to such waters; see Ps. cxxiv. 2—5. " If it had not been the Lord who was on our side when men rose up against us, then they had swallowed us up quick, when their wrath was kindled against us; then the waters had overwhelmed us, the stream had gone over our soul; then the proud waters had gone over our soul;" see Ps. lxix. 1. " Save me, O God, for the waters are come into my soul." Paul apprehended that by excessive grief, the offending brother would be destroyed. His life would waste away under the effect of his excommunication and disgrace, and the remembrance of his offence would prey upon him, and sink him to the grave.

8. *Wherefore I beseech you that ye would confirm your love toward him.* The word here rendered confirm (κυρῶσαι) occurs in the New Testament only here and in Gal. iii. 15. It means to give authority, to establish as valid, to confirm; and here means that they should give strong expressions and assurances of their love to him; that they should pursue such a course as would leave no room for doubt in regard to it. Tindal has well rendered it, "Wherefore I exhort you that love may have strength over him." Paul referred, doubtless, here to some public act of the church by which the sentence of excommunication might be removed, and by which the offender might have a public assurance of their favour.

9. *For to this end did I write.* The apostle did not say that this was the *only* purpose of his writing, to induce them to excommunicate the offender. He does not say that he wished in an arbitrary manner to test their willingness to obey him, or to induce them to do a thing in itself wrong, in order to try their obedience. But the meaning is this: This was the main reason why he *wrote* to them, rather than to come personally among them.

of you, whether ye be obedient [a] in all things.

10 To whom ye forgive any thing, I *forgive* also : for if I forgave any thing, to whom I forgave *it*, for your sakes *forgave I it* in the [1] person of Christ.

11 Lest Satan should get an advantage of us: for we are not ignorant of his devices.

a chap. 7. 16.

1 or, *sight.*

The thing ought to have been done ; the offender ought to be punished ; and Paul says that he adopted the method of *writing* to them rather than of coming among them in person, in order to give them an opportunity to show whether they were disposed to be obedient. And the sense is, "You may now forgive him. He has not only been sufficiently punished, and he has not only evinced suitable penitence, but also another object which I had in view has been accomplished. I desired to see whether you were, as a church, disposed to be obedient. That object, also, has been accomplished. And now, since every thing aimed at in the case of discipline has been secured, you may forgive him, and should, without hesitation, again receive him to the bosom of the church."

10. *To whom ye forgive any thing.* The sense here is, " I have confidence in you as a Christian society and such confidence, that if you forgive an offence in one of your members, I shall approve the act, and shall also be ready to forgive." He refers, doubtless, to this particular case, but he makes his remark general. It is implied here, I think, that the Corinthians were disposed to forgive the offending brother ; and Paul here assures them that they had his hearty assent to this, and that if they did forgive him, he was ready to join them in the act, and to forgive him also. ¶ *For if I forgave any thing.* If I *forgive* any thing ; if I remit any of the punishments which have been inflicted by my authority. ¶ *For your sakes.* It is not on account of the offender alone ; it is in order to promote the happiness and purity of the church. ¶ *In the person of Christ.* Locke paraphrases this, " By the authority, and in the name of Christ." Doddridge, " As in the person of Christ, and by the high authority with which he has been pleased to invest me."

Tindal, " In the room of Christ." The word rendered *person* (Marg. *sight*, προσωπον, from προς and ὠψ), means properly the part towards, at, and around the eye. — *Robinson.* Then it means the face, visage, countenance ; then the presence, person, &c. Here it probably means, in the presence of Christ ; with his eye upon me, and conscious that I am acting before him, and must give account to him. It implies, undoubtedly, that Paul acted by his authority, and felt that he was doing that which Christ would approve.

11. *Lest Satan.* The devil. The name Satan denotes an adversary, an accuser, an enemy. It is the usual proper name which is given to the devil, the great adversary of God and man. ¶ *Should get an advantage of us.* The literal translation of the Greek would be, " That we may not be defrauded by Satan. " (Ἱνα μη πλεονεκτηθωμεν ὑπο του σατανα). The verb here used denotes *to have more than another ;* then to gain, to take advantage of one, to defraud. And the idea is, that they should at once re-admit the penitent offender to their communion, lest if they did not do it, Satan would take advantage of it to do injury to him and them. It is a *reason* given by Paul why they should lose no time in restoring him to the church. What the advantage was which Satan might gain, Paul does not specify. It might be this : That under pretence of duty, and seeking the purity of the church, Satan would tempt them to harsh measures ; to needless severity of discipline ; to an unkind and unforgiving spirit ; and thus, at the same time, injure the cause of religion, and ruin him who had been the subject of discipline. ¶ *For we are not ignorant of his devices.* We know his plans, his thoughts, his cunning, his skill. We are not ignorant of the great number

12 Furthermore, when *a* I came to Troas to *preach* Christ's gospel, and a *b* door was opened unto me of the Lord.

13 I had no rest *c* in my spirit, because I found not Titus my brother: but taking my leave of them I went from thence into Macedonia.

a Acts 16.8.   *b* 1 Cor. 16.9.

c chap. 7.5,6.

of stratagems which he is constantly using to injure us, and to destroy the souls of men. He is full of wiles; and Paul had had abundant occasion to be acquainted with the means which he had used to defeat his plans and to destroy the church. The church, at all times, has been subjected to the influence of those wiles, as well as individual Christians. And the church, therefore, as well as individual Christians, should be constantly on its guard against those snares. Even the best and purest efforts of the church are often perverted, as in the case of administering discipline, to the worst results; and by the imprudence and want of wisdom; by the rashness or overheated zeal; by the pretensions to great purity and love of truth; and by a harsh, severe, and censorious spirit, Satan often takes advantage of the church, and advances his own dark and mischievous designs.

12. *Furthermore.* But (δὲ). This particle is properly adversative; but frequently denotes transition, and serves to introduce *something else*, whether opposite to what precedes, or simply continuative or explanatory. Here, it is designed to *continue* or *explain* the statement before made of his deep affection for the church, and his interest in its affairs. He therefore tells them that when he came to Troas, and was favoured there with great success, and was engaged in a manner most likely of all others to interest his feelings and to give him joy, yet he was deeply distressed because he had not heard, as he expected, from them; but so deep was his anxiety that he left Troas and went into Macedonia. ¶ *When I came to Troas* This was a city of Phrygia, or Mysia, on the Hellespont, between Troy on the north, and Assos on the south; see Note on Acts xvi. 8. It was on the regular route from Ephesus

to Macedonia. Paul took that route because on his journey to Macedonia he had resolved, for the reasons above stated, not to go to Corinth. ¶ *To preach Christ's gospel.* Greek. "For (εἰς) the gospel of Christ;" that is, on account of his gospel; or to promote it. Why he selected Troas, or the region of the Troad (Note, Acts xvi. 8), as the field of his labours, he does not say. It is probable that he was waiting there to hear from Corinth by Titus, and while there he resolved not to be idle, but to make known as much as possible the gospel. ¶ *And a door was opened unto me;* see Note, 1 Cor. xvi. 9. There was an opportunity of doing good, and the people were disposed to hear the gospel. This was a work in which Paul delighted to engage, and in which he usually found his highest comfort. It was of all things the most adapted to promote his happiness.

13. *I had no rest in my spirit.* I was disappointed, sad, deeply anxious. Though the work in which I was engaged was that which usually gives me my highest joy, yet such was my anxiety to learn the state of things in Corinth, and the success of my letter, and to see Titus, whom I was expecting, that I had comparatively no peace, and no comfort. ¶ *But taking my leave of them.* Though so many considerations urged me to stay; though there was such a promising field of labour, yet such was my anxiety to hear from you, that I left them. ¶ *I went from thence into Macedonia;* see Note, Acts xvi. 9. I went over where I expected to find Titus, and to learn the state of your affairs. This is one of the few instances in which Paul left an inviting field of labour, and where there was a prospect of signal success, to go to another place. It is adduced *here* to show the deep interest which he had in the church at Corinth, and his

14 Now thanks *be* unto God, [a] which always causeth us to tri-

[a] Rom.8.37.

anxiety to learn what was their condition. It shows that there *may* be cases where it is proper for ministers to leave a field of great and inviting usefulness, to go to another field and to engage in another part of the great vineyard.

14. *Now thanks* be *unto God*, &c. There seem to have been several sources of Paul's joy on this occasion. The principal was, his constant and uniform success in endeavouring to advance the interests of the kingdom of the Redeemer. But in particular he rejoiced, (1.) Because Titus had come to him there, and had removed his distress; comp. ver. 13. (2.) Because he learned from him that his efforts in regard to the church at Corinth had been successful, and that they had hearkened to his counsels in his first letter; and, (3.) Because he was favoured with signal success in Macedonia. His being compelled, therefore, to remove from Troas and to go to Macedonia had been to him ultimately the cause of great joy and consolation. These instances of success Paul regarded as occasions of gratitude to God. ¶ *Which always causeth us.* Whatever may be our efforts, and wherever we are. Whether it is in endeavouring to remove the errors and evils existing in a particular church, or whether it be in preaching the gospel in places where it has been unknown, still success crowns our efforts, and we have the constant evidence of divine approbation. This was *Paul's* consolation in the midst of his many trials; and it proves that, whatever may be the external circumstances of a minister, whether poverty, want, persecution, or distress, he will have abundant occasion to give thanks to God if his efforts as a minister are crowned with success. ¶ *To triumph in Christ.* To triumph through the aid of Christ, or in promoting the cause of Christ. Paul had no joy which was not connected with Christ, and he had no success which he did not trace to him. The word which is here rendered

triumph (Θριαμβευοντι from Θριαμβευω) occurs in no other place in the New Testament, except in Col. ii. 15. It is there rendered "*triumphing* over them in it," that is, triumphing over the principalities and powers which he had spoiled, or plundered; and it there means that Christ led them in triumph after the manner of a conqueror. The word is here used in a causative sense — the sense of the Hebrew Hiphil conjugation. It properly refers to a triumph; or a triumphal procession. Originally the word Θριαμβος meant a hymn which was sung in honour of Bacchus; then the tumultuous and noisy procession which constituted the worship of the god of wine; and then any procession of a similar kind.—*Passow.* It was particularly applied among both the Greeks and the Romans to a public and solemn honour conferred on a victorious general on a return from a successful war in which he was allowed a magnificent entrance into the capital. In these triumphs, the victorious commander was usually preceded or attended by the spoils of war; by the most valuable and magnificent articles which he had captured; and by the princes, nobles, generals, or people whom he had subdued. The victor was drawn in a magnificent chariot, usually by two white horses. Other animals were sometimes used. "When Pompey triumphed over Africa, his chariot was drawn by elephants; that of Mark Antony by lions; that of Heliogabalus by tigers; and that of Aurelius by deer."—*Clark.* The people of Corinth were not unacquainted with the nature of a triumph. About one hundred and forty-seven years before Christ, Lucius Mummius, the Roman consul, had conquered all Achaia, and had destroyed Corinth, Thebes, and Colchis, and by order of the Roman senate was favoured with a triumph, and was surnamed *Achaicus.* Tindal renders this place, "Thanks be unto God which always giveth us the victory in Christ." Paul refers here to a victory which

umph in Christ, and maketh manifest the savour *a* of his knowledge by us in every place.

a Ca.1.3.

he had, and a triumph with which he was favoured by the Redeemer. It was a victory over the enemies of the gospel; it was success in advancing the interests of the kingdom of Christ; and he rejoiced in that victory, and in that success, with more solid and substantial joy than a Roman victor ever felt on returning from his conquests over nations, even when attended with the richest spoils of victory, and by humbled princes and kings in chains, and when the assembled thousands shouted *Io triumphe!* ¶ *And maketh manifest.* Makes known ; spreads abroad—as a pleasant fragrance is diffused through the air. ¶ *The savour* (ὀσμὴν). The smell; the fragrance. The word in the New Testament is used to denote a pleasant or fragrant odour, as of incense, or aromatics ; John xii. 3 ; see Eph. v. 2 ; Phil. iv. 18. There is an allusion here doubtless to the fact that in the triumphal processions fragrant odours were diffused around; flowers, diffusing a grateful smell, were scattered in the way ; and on the altars of the gods incense was burned during the procession, and sacrifices offered, and the whole city was filled with the smoke of sacrifices, and with perfumes. So Paul speaks of *knowledge* — the knowledge of Christ. In his triumphings, the knowledge of the Redeemer was diffused abroad, like the odours which were diffused in the triumphal march of the conqueror. And that odour or savour was acceptable to God—as the fragrance of aromatics and of incense was pleasant in the triumphal procession of the returning victor. The phrase "makes manifest the savour of his knowledge," therefore, means, that the knowledge of Christ was diffused everywhere by Paul, as the grateful smell of aromatics was diffused all around the triumphing warrior and victor. The effect of Paul's conquests everywhere was to diffuse the knowledge of the Saviour—and

15 For we are unto God a sweet savour of Christ, in them *b* that are saved, and in them that perish :

b 1Cor.1.18.

this was acceptable and pleasant to God—though there might be many who would not avail themselves of it, and would perish ; see ver. 15.

15. *For we are unto God.* We who are his ministers, and who thus triumph. It is implied here that Paul felt that ministers were labouring *for* God, and felt assured that their labours would be acceptable to him. —The *object* of Paul in the statement, in this and in the following verses, is undoubtedly to meet the charges of his detractors and enemies. He says, therefore, that whatever was the result of his labours in regard to the future salvation of men ; yet, that his well-meant endeavours, and labours, and self-denials in preaching the gospel, were acceptable to God. The measure of God's approbation in the case was not his *success*, but his fidelity, his zeal, his self-denial, whatever might be the reception of the gospel among those who heard it. ¶ *A sweet savour.* Like the smell of pleasant incense, or of grateful aromatics, such as were burned in the triumphal processions of returning conquerors. The meaning is, that their labours were acceptable to God; he was pleased with them, and would bestow on them the smiles and proofs of his approbation. The word here rendered "sweet savour" (εὐωδία) occurs only in this place, and in Eph. v. 2 ; Phil. iv. 18 ; and is applied to persons or things well-pleasing to God. It properly means good odour, or fragrance, and in the Septuagint it is frequently applied to the *incense* that was burnt in the public worship of God and to sacrifices in general ; Gen. viii. 21 ; Ex. xxix. 18, 25, 41 ; Lev. i. 9, 13, 17 ; ii. 2, 9, 12 ; iii. 5, 16 ; iv. 31, &c. &c. Here it means that the services of Paul and the other ministers of religion were *as* grateful to God as sweet incense, or acceptable sacrifices. ¶ *Of Christ.* That is, we are Christ's sweet savour to God : we are that which he has ap-

pointed, and which he has devoted and consecrated to God; we are the offering, so to speak, which he is continually making to God. ¶ *In them that are saved.* In regard to them who believe the gospel through our ministry and who are saved. Our labour in carrying the gospel to them, and in bringing them to the knowledge of the truth, is acceptable to God. Their salvation is an object of his highest desire, and he is gratified with our fidelity, and with our success. This reason why their work was acceptable to God is more fully stated in the following verse, where it is said that in reference to them they were the "savour of life unto life." The word "saved" here refers to all who become Christians, and who enter heaven ; and as the salvation of man is an object of such desire to God, it cannot but be that all who bear the gospel to men are engaged in an acceptable service, and that all their efforts will be pleasing to him, and approved in his sight In regard to *this* part of Paul's statement, there can be no difficulty. ¶ *And in them that perish.* In reference to them who reject the gospel, and who are finally lost.—It is implied here, (1.) That some *would* reject the gospel and perish, with whatever fidelity and self-denial the ministers of religion might labour. (2.) That though this would be the result, yet the labours of the ministers of religion would be acceptable to God. This is a fearful and awful declaration, and has been thought by many to be attended with difficulty. A few remarks may present the true sense of the passage, and remove the difficulty from it. (1.) It is not affirmed or implied here that the destruction of those who would reject the gospel, and who would perish, was *desired* by God or would be pleasing to him. This is no where affirmed or implied in the Bible. (2.) It is affirmed only that the labours of the ministers of religion in endeavouring to save them would be acceptable and pleasing to God. Their labours would be *in order* to save them, not to destroy them. *Their* desire was to bring all

to heaven—and this was acceptable to God. Whatever might be the result, whether successful or not, yet God would be pleased with self-denial, and toil, and prayer that was honestly and zealously put forth to save others from death. They would be approved by God in proportion to the amount of labour, zeal, and fidelity which they evinced. (3.) It would be by no fault of faithful ministers that men would perish. Their efforts would be to save them, and those efforts would be pleasing to God. (4.) It would be by no fault of the gospel that men would perish. The regular and proper tendency of the gospel is to save, not to destroy men ; as the tendency of medicine is to heal them, of food to support the body, of air to give vitality, of light to give pleasure to the eye, &c. It is provided for all, and is adapted to all. There is a sufficiency in the gospel. for all men, and in its nature it is as really fitted to save one as another. Whatever may be the manner in which it is received, it is always in itself the same pure and glorious system ; full of benevolence and mercy. *The bitterest enemy of the gospel cannot point to one of its provisions that is adapted or designed to make men miserable, and to destroy them.* All its provisions are adapted to salvation ; all its arrangements are those of benevolence ; all the powers and influences which it originates, are those which are fitted to save, not to destroy men. The gospel is what it is in itself—a pure, holy, and benevolent system, and is answerable only for effects which a pure, holy, and benevolent system is fitted to produce. To use the beautiful language of Theodoret, as quoted by Bloomfield, "We indeed bear the sweet odour of Christ's gospel to *all ;* but all who participate in it do not experience its salutiferous effects. Thus to diseased eyes even the light of heaven is noxious ; yet the sun does not bring the injury. And to those in a fever, honey is bitter ; yet it *is sweet* nevertheless. Vultures too, it is said, fly from sweet odours of myrrh ; yet myrrh is myrrh though the vultures avoid it. Thus,

16 To ^a the one *we are* the saviour of death unto death; and

a John 9.39; 1Pet.2.7,8.

if some be saved, though others perish, the gospel retains its own virtue, and we the preachers of it remain just as we are; and the gospel retains its odorous and salutiferous properties, though some may disbelieve and abuse it, and perish." Yet, (5.) It is implied that the gospel would be the occasion of heavier condemnation to some, and that they would sink into deeper ruin in consequence of its being preached to them. This is implied in the expression in ver. 16. " to the one we are a savour of death unto death." In the explanation of this, we may observe, (*a*) That those who perish would have perished at any rate. All were under condemnation whether the gospel had come to them or not. None will perish in consequence of the gospel's having been sent to them who would not have perished had it been unknown. Men do not perish because the gospel is sent to them, but for their own sins. (*b*) It is in fact by their own fault that men reject the gospel, and that they are lost. They are voluntary in this; and, whatever is their final destiny, they are not under compulsion. The gospel compels no one against his will either to go to heaven, or to hell. (*c*) Men under the gospel sin against greater light than they do without it. They have more to answer for. It increases their responsibility. If, therefore, they reject it, and go down to eternal death, they go from higher privileges; and they go, of course, to meet a more aggravated condemnation. For condemnation will always be in exact proportion to guilt; and guilt is in proportion to abused light and privileges. (*d*) The preaching of the gospel, and the offers of life, are often the occasion of the deeper guilt of the sinner. Often he becomes enraged. He gives vent to the deep malignity of his soul. He opposes the gospel with malice and infuriated anger. His eye kindles with indignation, and his lip curls with pride and scorn. He is profane and blasphemous; and the offering of

the gospel to him is the occasion of exciting deep and malignant passions against God, against the Saviour, against the ministers of religion. Against the gospel, men often manifest the same malignity and scorn which they did against the Saviour himself. Yet this is not the fault of the gospel, nor of the ministers of religion. It is the fault of sinners themselves; and while there can be no doubt that such a rejection of the gospel will produce their deeper condemnation, and that it is a savour of death unto death unto them; still the gospel is good and benevolent, and still God will be pleased with those who faithfully offer its provisions, and who urge it on the attention of men.

16. *To the one.* To those who perish. ¶ *We are the savour of death unto death.* We are the occasion of deepening their condemnation, and of sinking them lower into ruin. The expression here used means literally, " to the one class we bear a death-conveying odour leading to their death"— a savour, a smell which, under the circumstances, is destructive to life, and which leads to death. Mr. Locke renders this, " To the one my preaching is of ill savour, unacceptable and offensive, by their rejecting whereof they draw death on themselves." Grateful as their labours were to God, and acceptable as would be their efforts, whatever might be the results, yet Paul could not be ignorant that the gospel would in fact be the means of greater condemnation to many; see Notes on ver. 15. It was indeed by their own fault; yet wherever the gospel was preached, it would to many have this result. It is probable that the language here used is borrowed from similar expressions which were common among the Jews. Thus in Debarim Rabba, sec. 1, fol. 248, it is said, " As the bee brings home honey to the owner, but stings others, so it is with the words of the law." " They (the words of the law) are a savour of life to Israel, but a savour of death to the people of this world." Thus

to the other the savour of life unto life. And who *a is* sufficient for these things?

17 For we are not as many,

a chap.3.5,6.   1 or, *deal deceitfully with,*

which corrupt [1] the word of God : but as of sincerity, but as of God, in the sight *b* of God, speak we [2] in Christ.

chap.4.2.   *b* Heb.11.27.   2 or, *of.*

in Taarieth, fol. 7, 1, "Whoever gives attention to the law on account of the law itself, to him it becomes an aromatic of life (כם היריב), but to him who does not attend to the law on account of the law itself, to him it becomes an aromatic of death (מות כס)"—the idea of which is, that as medicines skilfully applied will heal, but if unskilfully applied will aggravate a disease, so it is with the words of the law. Again, "The word of the law which proceeds out of the mouth of God is an odour of life to the Israelites, but an odour of death to the Gentiles," see Rosenmüller, and Bloomfield. The sense of the passage is plain, that the gospel, by the wilful rejection of it, becomes the means of the increased guilt and condemnation of many of those who hear it. ¶ *And to the other.* To those who embrace it, and are saved. ¶ *The savour of life.* An odour, or fragrance producing life, or tending to life. It is a living, or life giving savour. It is in itself grateful and pleasant. ¶ *Unto life.* Tending to life ; or adapted to produce life. The word *life* here, as often elsewhere, is used to denote salvation. It is (1.) Life in opposition to the death in sin in which all are by nature ; (2.) In opposition to death in the grave—as it leads to a glorious resurrection ; (3.) In opposition to eternal death ; to the second dying, as it leads to life and peace and joy in heaven ; see the words "life" and "death" explained in the Notes on Rom. vi. 23. The gospel is "the savour of life unto life," because, (1.) It is its nature and tendency to produce life and salvation. It is adapted to that ; and is designed to that end. (2.) Because it actually results in the life and salvation of those who embrace it. It is the immediate and direct cause of their salvation ; of their recovery from sin ; of their glorious resurrection ; of their eternal life in heaven ;

¶ *And who is sufficient for these things?* For the arduous and responsible work of the ministry ; for a work whose influence *must* be felt either in the eternal salvation, or the eternal ruin of the soul. Who is worthy of so important a charge ? Who can undertake it without trembling ? Who can engage in it without feeling that he is in himself unfit for it, and that he needs constant divine grace ? This is an exclamation which any one may well make in view of the responsibilities of the work of the ministry. And we may remark, (1.) If *Paul* felt this, assuredly others should feel it also. If, with all the divine assistance which he had ; all the proofs of the peculiar presence of God, and all the mighty miraculous powers conferred on him, Paul had such a sense of unfitness for this great work, then a consciousness of unfitness, and a deep sense of responsibility, may well rest on all others. (2.) It was this sense of the responsibility of the ministry which contributed much to Paul's success. It was a conviction that the results of his work must be seen in the joys of heaven, or the woes of hell, that led him to look to God for aid, and to devote himself so entirely to his great work. Men will not feel much concern unless they have a deep sense of the magnitude and responsibility of their work. Men who feel as they should about the ministry will look to God for aid, and will feel that he alone can sustain them in their arduous duties.

17. *For we are not as many.* This refers doubtless to the false teachers at Corinth ; and to all who mingled human philosophy or tradition with the pure word of truth. Paul's *design* in the statement in this verse seems to be to affirm that he had such a deep sense of the responsibility of the ministerial office, and of its necessary influence on the eternal destiny of man, that it led him to preach the

simple gospel, the pure word of God. He did not dare to dilute it with any human mixture. He did not dare to preach philosophy, or human wisdom. He did not dare to mingle with it the crude conceptions of man. He sought to exhibit the simple truth as it was in Jesus ; and so deep was his sense of the responsibility of the office, and so great was his desire on the subject, that he had been enabled to do it. and to triumph always in Christ. So that, although he was conscious that he was in himself unfit for these things, yet by the grace of God he had been able always to exhibit the simple truth, and his labours had been crowned with constant and signal success. ¶ *Which corrupt the word of God.* Margin, " deal deceitfully with." The word here used (καπηλεύοντες) occurs no where else in the New Testament, and does not occur in the Septuagint. The word is derived from κάπηλος, which signifies properly a huckster, or a *retailer of wine*, a petty chapman ; a man who buys up articles for the purpose of selling them again. It also means sometimes a vintner, or an innkeeper. The proper idea is that of a small dealer and especially in wine. Such persons were notorious, as they are now, for diluting their wines with water (comp. Sept. in Isa. i. 22) ; and for compounding wines of other substances than the juice of the grape for purposes of gain. Wine, of all substances in trade, perhaps, affords the greatest facilities for such dishonest tricks ; and accordingly the dealers in that article have generally been most distinguished for fraudulent practices and corrupt and diluted mixtures. Hence the word comes to denote to adulterate ; to corrupt, &c. It is here applied to those who adulterated or corrupted the pure word of God in any way, and for any purpose. It probably has particular reference to those who did it either by Judaizing opinions, or by the mixtures of a false and deceitful philosophy. The latter mode would be likely to prevail among the subtle and philosophizing Greeks. It is in such ways that the gospel has been usually

corrupted. (1.) It is done by attempting to attach a philosophical explanation to the facts of revelation, and making *the theory* as important as *the fact.* (2.) By attempting to explain away the offensive points of revelation by the aid of philosophy. (3.) By attempting to make the facts of Scripture accord with the prevalent notions of philosophy, and by applying a mode of interpretation to the Bible which would fritter away its meaning, and make it mean any thing or nothing at pleasure. In these, and in various other ways, men have corrupted the word of God ; and of all the evils which Christianity has ever sustained in this world, the worst have been those which it has received from philosophy, and from those teachers who have corrupted the word of God. The fires of persecution it could meet, and still be pure ; the utmost efforts of princes, and monarchs, and of Satan to destroy it, it has outlived, and has shone purely and brightly amidst all these efforts ; but, when corrupted by philosophy, and by " science falsely so called," it has been dimmed in its lustre, paralyzed in its aims, and shorn of its power, and has ceased to be mighty in pulling down the strong holds of Satan's kingdom. Accordingly, the enemy of God has ceased to excite persecution, and now aims in various ways to *corrupt* the gospel by the admixture of philosophy, and of human opinions. Tindal renders this passage, " For we are not as many are which *choppe and chaunge* with the word of God "— an idea which is important and beautiful—but this is one of the few instances in which he mistook the sense of the original text. In general, the accuracy of his translation and his acquaintance with the true sense of the Greek text are very remarkable. ¶ *But as of sincerity.* Sincerely ; actuated by unmingled honesty and simplicity of aim ; see Note on chap. i. 12. ¶ *As of God.* As influenced by him ; as under his control and direction ; as having been sent by him ; as acting by his command ; see Note, chap. i. 12. ¶ *In the sight of God.* As if we felt that his eye was always on us. Nothing is better fitted to make a man sincere and honest, than this. ¶ *Speak we in Christ.* In the name, and in the service of Christ. We deliver our message with a deep consciousness that the eye of the all-seeing God is on us; that we can conceal nothing from him ; and that we must soon give up our account to him.

REMARKS.

1. In this chapter, and in the management of the whole case to which Paul here refers, we have an instance of his *tenderness* in administering discipline. This tenderness was manifested in many ways. (1.) He did nothing to wound the feelings of the offending party. (2.) He did nothing in the way of punishment which a stern sense of duty did not demand. (3.) He did it all with many tears. He wept at the necessity of administering discipline at all. He wept over the remissness of the church. He wept over the fall of the offending brother. (4.) He did not mention even the name of the offender. He did not blazon his faults abroad ; nor has he left any clue by which it can be known ; nor did he take any measures which were fitted to pain, unnecessarily, the feelings of his friends. If all discipline in the church were conducted in this manner, it would probably always be effectual and successful, ver. 1—10.

2. We ought cordially to receive and forgive an offending brother, as soon as he gives evidence of repentance. We should harbour no malice against him ; and if, by repentance, he has put away his sins, we should hasten to forgive him. This we should do as individuals, and as churches. God cheerfully forgives us, and receives us into favour on our repentance ; and we should hail *the privilege* of treating all our offending brethren in the same manner, ver. 7, 8.

3. *Churches* should be careful that Satan should not get an advantage over them, ver. 11. In every way possible he will attempt it ; and perhaps in few modes is it more often done than in administering discipline.

In such a case, Satan gains an advantage over a church in the following ways. (1.) In inducing it to *neglect* discipline. This occurs often because an offender is rich, or talented, or is connected with influential families ; because there is a fear of driving off such families from the church ; because the individual is of elevated rank, and the church suffers him to remain in her bosom. The laws of the church, like other laws, are often like cobwebs : Great flies break through, and the smaller ones are caught. The consequence is, that Satan gains an immense advantage. Rich and influential offenders remain in the church ; discipline is relaxed ; the cause of Christ is scandalized ; and the church at large feels the influence, and the work of God declines. (2.) Satan gains an advantage in discipline, sometimes, by too great *severity* of discipline. If he cannot induce a church to relax altogether, and to suffer offenders to remain, then he excites them to improper and needless severity. He drives them on to harsh discipline for small offences. He excites a spirit of persecution. He enkindles a false zeal on account of the Shibboleth of doctrine. He excites a spirit of party, and causes the church to mistake it for zeal for truth. He excites a spirit of persecution against some of the best men in the church, on account of pretended errors in doctrine, and kindles the flames of intestine war ; and breaks the church up into parties and fragments. Or he urges on the church, even in cases where discipline is proper, to needless and inappropriate severity ; drives the offender from its bosom ; breaks his spirit ; and prevents ever-onward his usefulness, his return, and his happiness. One of the chief arts of Satan has been to cause the church in cases of discipline to use *severity* instead of *kindness ;* to excite a spirit of persecution instead of love. Almost all the evils which grow out of attempts at discipline might have been prevented by a spirit of LOVE. (3.) Satan gains an advantage in cases of discipline, when the church is unwilling to re-admit to fellowship an offending but a penitent member. His spirit is broken; his usefulness is destroyed. The world usually takes sides with him against the church, and the cause of religion bleeds.

4. *Individual Christians*, as well as churches, should be careful that Satan does not get an advantage over them, ver. 11. Among the ways in which he does this are the following : (1.) By inducing them to conform to the world. This is done under the plea that religion is not gloomy, and morose, and ascetic. Thence he often leads professors into all the gayeties, and amusements, and follies of which the world partake. Satan gains an immense advantage to his cause when this is done—for all the influence of the professed Christian is with him. (2.) By producing laxness of opinion n regard to doctrine. Christ intends that his cause shall advance by the influence of truth ; and that his church shall be the witness of the truth. The cause of Satan advances by error and falsehood ; and when professed Christians embrace falsehood, or are indifferent to truth, their whole influence is on the side of Satan, and his advantage is immense when they become the advocates of error. (3.) By producing among Christians despondency, melancholy, and despair. Some of the best men are often thus afflicted and thrown into darkness, as Job was ; Job xxiii. 8—9. Indeed, it is commonly the best members of a church that have doubts in this manner, and that fall into temptation, and that are left to the buffetings of Satan. Your gay, and worldly, and fashionable Christians have usually no such troubles—except when they lie on a bed of death. They are not in the way of Satan. They do not oppose him, and he will not trouble them. It is your humble, praying, self-denying Christians that he dreads and hates ; and it is these that he is suffered to tempt, and to make sad, and to fill with gloom and doubt. And when this is done, it is an immense advantage to his cause. It produces the impression that religion is nothing but gloom

and melancholy, and the people of the world are easily led to hate and avoid it. Christians, therefore, *should be* cheerful, and benevolent, and happy —as they may be—lest Satan should get an advantage over them. (4.) By fanaticism. For when Satan finds that he can get no advantage over Christians by inducing them to do *nothing*, or to do any thing positively wrong or immoral, he drives them on with over-heated and ill-timed zeal ; he makes them unreasonably strenuous for some single opinion or measure ; he disposes them to oppose and persecute all who do not fall into their views, and feel as they feel. (5.) By contentions and strifes. Satan often gets an advantage in that way. No matter what the cause may be, whether it be for doctrines, or for any other cause, yet the very fact that there are contentions among the professed followers of "the Prince of peace" does injury, and gives Satan an advantage. No small part of his efforts, therefore, have been to excite contentions among Christians, an effort in which he has been, and is still, eminently successful.

5. Satan gets an advantage over sinners, and *they* should be on their guard. He does it, (1.) By producing a sense of security in their present condition ; and by leading them to indifference in regard to their eternal condition. In this he is eminently successful ; and when this is gained, all is gained that his cause demands. It is impossible to conceive of greater success in any thing than Satan has in producing a state of indifference to the subject of religion among men. (2.) By inducing them to *defer* attention to religion to some future time. This is an advantage, because, (*a*) It accomplishes all he wishes at present; (*b*) Because it is usually successful altogether. It is usually the same thing as resolving not to attend to religion at all. (3.) By producing false views of religion. He represents it at one time as gloomy, sad, and melancholy ; at another, as so easy, that it may be obtained, whenever they please ; at another, by persuading them that their sins are so

great that they cannot be forgiven. One great object of Satan is to blind the minds of sinners to the true nature of religion ; and in this he is usually successful. (4.) He deludes the aged by telling them it is too late; and the young by telling them that now is the time for mirth and pleasure, and that religion may be attended to at some future period of life. (5.) He gains an advantage by plunging the sinner deeper and deeper in sin ; inducing him to listen to the voice of temptation ; by making him the companion of the wicked ; and by deluding him with the promises of pleasure, honour, and gain in this world until it is too late, and he dies.

6. Ministers of the gospel *may* have occasion to triumph in the success of their work. Paul always met with success of some kind ; always had some cause of triumph. In all his trials, he had occasion of rejoicing, and always was assured that he was pursuing that course which would lead him ultimately to triumph, ver. 14.

7. The gospel may be so preached as to be successful, ver. 14. In the hands of Paul it was successful. So it was with the other apostles. So it was with Luther, Knox, Calvin. So it was with Whitefield, Edwards, Wesley, and Payson. If ministers are not successful, it is not the fault of the gospel. It is adapted to do good, and to save men ; and it *may be so* preached as to accomplish those great ends. If all ministers were as self-denying, and laborious, and prayerful as were these men, the gospel would be as successful now as it has ever been.

[There is much truth in this representation. Certainly no great revival of religion can rationally be expected when the ministers of the gospel are not self-denying, laborious, and prayerful. Yet we cannot *certainly* pronounce, that equal diligence in the use of means will in every case be attended with equal success. Allowance must be made for God's sovereignty, in dispensing his grace. Otherwise, wherever the word was preached under most favourable circumstances, as far as excellence of means is concerned, there also, we should expect, and find most success. But it has not been so in reality. Never did hearers enjoy a more favourable opportunity of conversion, than when more than the eloquence of angels fell from the lips of Jesus, and he taught the people as one having authority and not as the Scribes. Yet comparatively few, a solitary one here and there, listened to the voice of the charmer, though he charmed so wisely. Was it that he did not display the gospel in all its fulness, sufficiency, and loveliness? Was there any want of moral suasion, powerful argument, strong motive, touching appeal, in the Saviour's addresses? No! Yet immediately after the ascension of Jesus, the word of God subdued thousands on thousands, although employed by apostles only, whose ministrations, considered apart, must have been immeasurably inferior to those of Jesus. The same Jews that persisted in their unbelief, under the ministry of Christ, were disarmed of their prejudice, under the preaching of Peter! Whence the difference of efficacy? Whence the want of success, where most we should have expected to find it, and the command of it, where least we could have looked for it? One sentence solves the difficulty. "The Holy Ghost was not yet given, because that Jesus was not yet glorified."

Similar comparisons might be made between the ministrations of different individuals now. Men of the highest abilities, persevering diligence, and elevated piety, have been left to complain of comparative barrenness in the sphere which they occupied, while humbler instruments, in a field no way more promising, have been blessed with the harvest of souls. The comparison might even be made of different periods of the same ministry. All other circumstances being equal, or differing so slightly as not to affect the argument, the word spoken at one time seems to fall powerless to the ground, as the arrow on the breast of steel. No shaft hits the mark, no sinner retires like the stricken deer to bleed alone. At another time, the people are made willing in the day of power. Conviction spreads with the rapidity of contagion, and the Lord daily adds to his people such as shall be saved. Now this difference cannot be explained but by referring it to the different measures in which God is pleased to communicate his Spirit.]

8. Much of the work of the ministry is pleasant and delightful. It is the savour of life unto life, ver. 15, 16. There is no joy on earth of a higher and purer character than that which the ministers of the gospel have in the success of their work. There is no work more pleasant than that of imparting the consolations of religion to the sick, and the afflicted ; than that of directing inquiring sinners to the

Lamb of God; no joy on earth so pure and elevated as that which a pastor has in a revival of religion. In the evidence that God accepts his labours, and that to many his message is a savour of life unto life, there is a joy which no other pursuit can furnish; a joy, even on earth, which is more than a compensation for all the toils, self-denials, and trials of the ministry.

9. In view of the *happy* and *saving* results of the work of the ministry, we see the importance of the work. Those results are to be seen in heaven. They are to enter into the eternal destiny of the righteous. They are to be seen in the felicity and holiness of those who shall be redeemed from death. The very happiness of heaven, therefore, is dependent on the fidelity and success of the ministry. This work stretches beyond the grave. It reaches into eternity. It is to be seen in heaven. Other plans and labours of men terminate at death. But the work of the ministry reaches in its results into the skies; and is to be seen ever onward in eternity. Well might the apostle ask, "Who is sufficient for these things?"

10. The ministers of the gospel will be accepted of God, if faithful, whatever may be the result of their labours; whether seen in the salvation, or the augmented condemnation of those who hear them, ver. 15. They are a sweet savour to God. Their acceptance with him depends not on the measure of their success; but on their fidelity. If men reject the gospel, and make it the occasion of their greater condemnation, the fault is not that of ministers, but is their own. If men are faithful, God accepts their efforts; and even if many reject the message and perish, still a faithful ministry will not be to blame. That such results *should* follow from their ministry, indeed, increases their responsibility, and makes their office more awful, but it will not render them less acceptable in their labours in the sight of God.

11. We are to anticipate that the ministry will be the means of the deeper condemnation of many who hear the gospel, ver. 16. The gospel is to them a savour of death unto death. We are to expect that many will reject and despise the message, and sink into deeper sin, and condemnation, and wo. We are not to be disappointed, therefore, when we see such effects follow, and when the sinner sinks into a deeper hell from under the ministry of the gospel. It always *has* been the case, and we have reason to suppose it always will be. And painful as is the fact, yet ministers must make up their minds to witness this deeply painful result of their work.

12. The ministry is a deeply and awfully responsible work, ver. 16. It is connected with the everlasting happiness, or the deep and eternal condemnation of all those who hear the gospel. Every sermon that is preached is making an impression that will never be obliterated, and producing an effect that will never terminate. Its effects will never all be seen until the day of judgment, and in the awful solemnities of the eternal world. Well might Paul ask, "Who is sufficient for these things?"

13. It is a solemn thing to *hear* the gospel. If it is solemn for a minister to dispense it, it is not less solemn to hear it. It is connected with the eternal welfare of those who hear. And thoughtless as are multitudes who hear it, yet it is deeply to affect them hereafter. If they ever embrace it, they will owe their eternal salvation to it; if they continue to neglect it, it will sink them deep and for ever in the world of wo. Every individual, therefore, who hears the gospel dispensed, no matter by whom, should remember that he is listening to God's solemn message to men; and that it will and must exert a deep influence on his eternal doom.

14. A people should pray much for a minister. Paul often entreated the churches to which he wrote to pray for him. If *Paul* needed the prayers of Christians, assuredly Christians now do. Prayer for a minister is demanded because, (1.) He has the same infirmities, conflicts, and temptations which other Christians have. (2.)

CHAPTER III.

DO we begin again to commend ourselves? or need we, as

a chap. 5. 12.

some *others*, epistles [b] of commendation to you, or *letters* of commendation from you?

b Acts 18. 27.

He has those which are *peculiar*, and which grow out of the very nature of his office ; for the warfare of Satan is carried on mainly with the leaders of the army of God. (3.) He is engaged in a great and most responsible work —the greatest work ever committed to mortal man. (4.) His success will be generally in proportion as a people pray for him. The welfare of a people, therefore, is identified with their praying for their minister. He will preach better, and they will hear better, just in proportion as they pray for him. His preaching will be dull, dry, heavy ; will be without unction, spirituality, and life, unless they pray for him ; and their hearing will be dull, lifeless, and uninterested, unless they pray for him. No people will hear the gospel to much advantage who do not feel anxiety enough about it to pray for their minister.

15. The interview between a minister and his people in the day of judgment will be a very solemn one. Then the effect of his ministry will be seen. Then it will be known to whom it was a savour of life unto life, and to whom it was a savour of death unto death. Then the eternal destiny of all will be settled. Then the faithful minister will be attended to heaven by all to whom his ministry has been a savour of life unto life ; and then he will part for ever with all whom he so often warned and entreated in vain. In distant worlds—worlds for ever separated —shall be experienced the result of his labours. O ! how solemn must be the scene when *he* must give up his account for the manner in which he has preached; and *they*, for the manner in which they attended on his ministry!

16. Let all ministers, then, be careful that they do not corrupt the word of God, ver. 17. Let them preach it in simplicity and in truth. Let them not preach philosophy, or metaphysics, or their own fancy, or the tradition of men, or the teaching of the schools, but the simple truth as it is

in Jesus. Let them preach as sent *by* God ; as in the sight of God ; as commissioned by Christ to deliver a simple, plain, pure message to mankind, whether they will hear or forbear. Their *success* will be in proportion to the simplicity and purity of the gospel which they present ; their peace and joy in death and in heaven will be just as they shall have evidence then that in simplicity and sincerity they have endeavoured to present everywhere, and to all, the pure and simple gospel of Jesus Christ. As ministers, therefore, desire acceptance with God and success in the work, let them preach the pure gospel ; not adulterating it with foreign admixtures; not endeavouring to change it so as to be palatable to the carnal mind; not substituting philosophy for the gospel, and not withholding any thing in the gospel because men do not love it; and let the people of God everywhere sustain the ministry by their prayers, and aid them in their work by daily commending them to the God of grace. So shall they be able to perform the solemn functions of their office to divine acceptance; and so shall ministers and people find the gospel to be " a savour of life unto life.

CHAPTER III.

THIS chapter is closely connected in its design with the preceding. Paul had said in that chapter (ver. 14), that he had always occasion to triumph in the success which he had, and that God always blessed his labours ; and especially had spoken, in the close of the previous chapter (ver. 17), of his sincerity as contrasted with the conduct of some who corrupted the word of God. This *might* appear to some as if he designed to commend himself to them, or that he had said this for the purpose of securing their favour. It is probable also, that the false teachers at Corinth had been introduced there by letters of recommendation, perhaps from Judea. In reply to this, Paul intimates (ver.

1) that this was not his design ; (ver. 2) that he had no need of letters of recommendation to them, since (ver. 2, 3) *they* were his commendatory epistle ; they were themselves the best evidence of his zeal, fidelity, and success in his labours. He could appeal to them as the best proof that he was qualified for the apostolic office. His success among them, he says (ver. 4), was a ground of his trusting in God, an evidence of his acceptance. Yet, as if he should seem to rely on his own strength, and to boast of what he had done, he says (ver. 5) that his success was not owing to any strength which he had, or to any skill of his own, but entirely to the aid which he had received from God. It was God, he says (ver. 6), who had qualified him to preach, and had given him grace to be an able minister of the New Testament.

It is not improbable that the false teachers, being of Jewish origin, in Corinth, had commended the laws and institutions of Moses as being of superior clearness, and even as excelling the gospel of Christ. Paul takes occasion, therefore (ver. 7—11), to show that the laws and institutions of Moses were far inferior in this respect to the gospel. His was a ministration of death (ver. 7) ; though glorious it was to be done away (ver. 7) ; the ministration of the Spirit was therefore to be presumed to be far more glorious (ver. 8); the one was a ministration to condemnation, the other of righteousness (ver. 9) ; the one had comparatively no glory, being so much surpassed by the other (ver. 10 ;) and the former was to be done away, while the latter was to remain, and was therefore far more glorious, ver. 11.

This statement of the important difference between the laws of Moses and the gospel, is further illustrated by showing the *effect* which the institutions of Moses had had on the Jews themselves, ver. 12—15. That effect was to blind them. Moses had put a veil over his face (ver. 13), and the effect had been that the nation was blinded in reading the Old Testament, and had no just views of the

true meaning of their own Scriptures, ver. 14, 15.

Yet, Paul says, that that veil should be taken away, ver. 16—18. It was the *intention* of God that it should be removed. When that people should turn again to the Lord, it should be taken away, ver. 16. It *was* done where the Spirit of the Lord was, ver. 17. It was done *in fact* in regard to all true Christians, ver. 18. They were permitted to behold the glory of the Lord as in a glass, and they were changed into the same image. The same subject is continued in chap. iv., where Paul illustrates *the effect* of this clear revelation of the gospel, as compared with the institutions of Moses, on the Christian ministry.

1. *Do we begin again.* This is designed evidently to meet an objection. He had been speaking of his triumph in the ministry (chap. ii. 14), and of his sincerity and honesty, as contrasted with the conduct of many who corrupted the word of God, chap. ii. 17. It might be objected that he was magnifying *himself* in these statements, and designed to commend himself in this manner to the Corinthians. To this he replies in the following verses. ¶ *To commend ourselves ?* To recommend ourselves ; do we speak this in our own praise, in order to obtain your favour. ¶ *Or need we, as some* others. Probably some who had brought letters of recommendation to them from Judea. The false teachers at Corinth had been originally introduced there by commendatory letters from abroad. These were letters of introduction, and were common among the Greeks, the Romans, and the Jews, as they are now. They were usually given to persons who were about to travel, as there were no inns. and as travellers were dependent on the hospitality of those among whom they travelled. ¶ *Of commendation from you.* To other churches. It is implied here by Paul, that he sought no such letter ; that he travelled without them ; and that he depended on his zeal, and self-denial, and success to make him known, and to give him the affections of those to whom he

2 Ye *a* are our epistle, written in our hearts, known and read of all men :

a 1 Cor.9.2.

3 *Forasmuch as ye are* manifestly declared to be the epistle of Christ ministered by us, written

---

ministered—a much better recommendation than mere introductory letters. Such letters were, however, sometimes given by Christians, and are by no means improper, Acts xviii. 27. Yet, they do not appear to have been sought or used by the apostles generally. They depended on their miraculous endowments, and on the attending grace of God to make them known.

2. *Ye are our epistle;* comp. 1 Cor. ix. 2. This is a most beautiful and happy turn given to the whole subject. The sense is plain. It is, that the conversion of the Corinthians, under the faithful labours of the apostle, was a better testimonial of his character and fidelity than any letters could be. To see the force of this, it must be remembered, (1.) That Corinth was an exceedingly dissolute and abandoned place (see the Introduction to the first epistle); (2.) That a large number of them had been converted, and a church organized ; (3.) That their conversion, and the organization of a church in *such* a city were events that would be known abroad ; and, (4.) That it had been accomplished entirely under the labour of Paul and his companions. To their knowledge of him, therefore, and to his success there, he could confidently appeal as a testimonial of his character. The *characteristics* of this commendatory epistle, he proceeds immediately to state. The general sense is, that they were the letter of recommendation which God had given to him; and that their conversion under his ministry was the public testimonial of his character which all might see and read. ¶ *Written in our hearts.* A few MSS. and versions read thus, "your hearts;" and Doddridge has adopted this reading, and supposes that it means that the change produced not only in their external conduct, but in their inward temper, was so great, that all must see that it was an unanswerable attes-

tation to his ministry. But there is not sufficient authority for changing the text ; nor is it necessary. The sense is, probably, that this letter was, as it were, written on *his* heart. It was not merely that Paul had a tender affection for them, as Clarke supposes ; nor was it that he regarded them as "a copy of the letter of recommendation from Christ written in his heart," according to the fanciful conceit of Macknight ; but Paul's idea seems to have been this. He is speaking of the testimonial which he had from God. That testimonial consisted in the conversion of the Corinthians. This he says was written on his heart. It was not a cold letter of introduction, but it was such as, while it left him no room to doubt that God had sent him, also affected his feelings, and was engraven on his soul. It was to him, therefore, far more valuable than any mere letter of commendation or of introduction could be. It was a direct testimonial from God to his own heart of his approbation, and of his having appointed him to the apostolic office. All the difficulty, therefore, which has been felt by commentators in this passage, may be obviated by supposing that Paul here speaks of this testimonial or epistle as addressed to *himself*, and as satisfactory to *him*. In the other characteristics which he enumerates, he speaks of it as fitted to be a letter commendatory *of* himself to others. ¶ *Known and read of all men.* Corinth was a large, splendid, and dissipated city. Their conversion, therefore, would be known afar. All men would hear of it ; and their reformation, their subsequent life under the instruction of Paul, and the attestation which God had given among them to his labours, was a sufficient testimonial to the world at large, that God had called him to the apostolic office.

3. Forasmuch as ye are *manifestly declared.* You are made manifest as

not with ink, but with the Spirit of the living God ; not in tables

a Ex.24.12.

of stone, ^a but ^b in fleshly tables of the heart.

b Jer.31.33; Eze.11.19.

the epistle of Christ; or you, being made manifest, are the epistle, &c. They had been made manifest to be such by their conversion. The sense is, it is plain, or evident, that ye are the epistle of Christ. ¶ *To be the epistle of Christ.* That which Christ has sent to be our testimonial. He has given this letter of recommendation. He has converted you by our ministry, and that is the best evidence which *we* can have that we have been sent by him, and that our labour is accepted by him. Your conversion is his work, and it is his public attestation to our fidelity in his cause. ¶ *Ministered by us.* The idea here is, that Christ had employed their ministry in accomplishing this. They were Christ's letter, but it had been prepared by the instrumentality of the apostles. It had not been prepared by him independently of their labours, but in connection with, and as the result of those labours. Christ, in writing this epistle, so to speak, has used our aid; or employed us as amanuenses. ¶ *Written not with ink.* Paul continues and varies the image in regard to this "epistle," so that he may make the testimony borne to his fidelity and success more striking and emphatic. He says, therefore, that that it was not writtten as letters of introduction are, with ink—by traces drawn on a lifeless substance, and in lines that easily fade, or that may become easily illegible, or that can be read only by a few, or that may be soon destroyed. ¶ *But with the Spirit of the living God.* In strong contrast thus with letters written with ink. By the Spirit of God moving on the heart, and producing that variety of graces which constitute so striking and so beautiful an evidence of your conversion. If written by the Spirit of the living God, it was far more valuable, and precious, and permanent than any record which could be made by ink. Every trace of the Spirit's influences on the heart was an undoubted proof that God had sent

the apostles ; and was a proof which they would much more sensibly and tenderly feel than they could any letter of recommendation written in ink. ¶ *Not in tables of stone.* It is generally admitted that Paul here refers to the evidences of the divine mission of Moses which was given by the law engraven on tablets of stone, comp. ver. 7. Probably those who were false teachers among the Corinthians were Jews, and had insisted much on the divine origin and permanency of the Mosaic institutions. The law had been engraven on stone by the hand of God himself ; and had thus the strongest proofs of divine origin, and the divine attestation to its pure and holy nature. To this fact the friends of the law, and the advocates for the permanency of the Jewish institutions, would appeal. Paul says, on the other hand, that the testimonials of the divine favour through him were not on tablets of stone. *They* were frail, and easily broken. There was no life in them (comp. ver. 6 and 7) ; and valuable and important as they were, yet they could not be compared with the testimonials which God had given to those who successfully preached the gospel. ¶ *But in fleshly tables of the heart.* In truths engraven on the heart. This testimonial was of more value than an inscription on stone, because, (1.) No hand but that of God could reach the heart, and inscribe these truths there. (2.) Because it would be attended with a life-giving and living influence. It was not a mere dead letter. (3.) Because it would be permanent. Stones, even where laws were engraven by the finger of God, would moulder and decay, and the inscription made there would be destroyed. But not so with that which was made on the heart. It would live for ever. It would abide in other worlds. It would send its influence into all the relations of life; into all future scenes in this world ; and that influence would be seen and

4 And such trust have we through Christ to God-ward :

5 Not that we are sufficient

a John 15.5.

of *a* ourselves to think any thing, as of ourselves, but *b* our sufficiency *is* of God ;

b 1Cor.15.10; Phil.2.13.

felt in the world that shall never end. By all these considerations, therefore, the testimonials which Paul had of the divine approbation were more valuable than any mere letters of introduction, or human commendation could have been ; and more valuable even than the attestation which was given to the divine mission of Moses himself.

4. *And such trust have we.* Such confidence have we that we are appointed by God, and that he accepts our work. Such evidence have we in the success of our labours; such irrefragable proof that God blesses us ; that we have trust, or confidence, that we are sent by God, and are owned by him in our ministry. His confidence did not rest on letters of introduction from men, but in the evidence of the divine presence, and the divine acceptance of his work. ¶ *Through Christ.* By the agency of Christ. Paul had no success which he did not trace to him ; he had no joy of which he was not the source ; he had no confidence, or trust in God of which Christ was not the author ; he had no hope of success in his ministry which did not depend on him. ¶ *To God-ward.* Toward God, in regard to God (πρὸς τὸν Θεόν). Our confidence relates to God. It is confidence that he has appointed us, and sent us forth ; and confidence that he will still continue to own and to bless us.

5. *Not that we are sufficient of ourselves.* This is evidently designed to guard against the appearance of boasting, or of self-confidence. He had spoken of his confidence ; of his triumph ; of his success; of his undoubted evidence that God had sent him. He here says, that he did not mean to be understood as affirming that any of his success came from himself, or that he was able by his own strength to accomplish the great things which had been effected by his ministry. He well knew that he had no such self-sufficiency ; and he would not insinuate, in the slightest manner,

that he believed himself to be invested with any such power, comp. Note on John xv. 5. ¶ *To think any thing* (λογίσασθαί τι). The word here used means properly to reason, think, consider ; and then to reckon, count to, or impute to any one. It is the word which is commonly rendered *impute ;* see it explained more fully in the Note on Rom. iv. 5. Robinson (*Lexicon*) renders it in this place, " to reason out, to think out, to find out by thinking." Doddridge renders it, " to reckon upon any thing as from ourselves." Whitby renders it, " to reason : as if the apostle had said, We are unable by any reasoning of our own to bring men to conversion. Macknight gives a similar sense. Locke renders it, " Not as if I were sufficient of myself, to reckon upon any thing as from myself : " and explains it to mean that Paul was not sufficient of himself by any strength of natural parts to attain the knowledge of the gospel truths which he preached. The word may be rendered here, to reckon, reason, think, &c. ; *but it should be confined to the immediate subject under consideration.* It does not refer to thinking in general, or to the power of thought on any, and on all subjects—however true it may be in itself—but to the preaching the gospel. And the expression may be regarded as referring to the following points, which are immediately under discussion. (1.) Paul did not feel that he was sufficient of himself to have *reasoned* or *thought out* the truths of the gospel. They were communicated by God. (2.) He had no power by reasoning to convince or convert sinners. That was all of God. (3.) He had no right to *reckon* on success by any strength of his own. All success was to be traced to God. It is, however, also true, that all our powers of thinking and reasoning are from God; and that we have no ability to think clearly, to reason calmly, closely, and correctly, unless he shall

6 Who also hath made us able [a] ministers of the New [b] Testament ; not of the letter, [c]

a Eph 3.7; 1 Ti.1.12.
b Mat.26.28; Heb.8.6—10.

but of the spirit : for the [d] letter killeth, but [e] the spirit [1] giveth life.

c Rom.2.28.29.   *d* Rom.4.15; 7.9,10.
e John 6.63; Rom.8.2.   1 or, *quickeneth.*

preside over our minds and give us clearness of thought. How easy is it for God to disarrange all our faculties, and produce insanity ! How easy to suffer our minds to become unsettled, bewildered, and distracted with a multiplicity of thoughts ! How easy to cause every thing to appear cloudy, and dark, and misty ! How easy to affect our *bodies* with weakness, languor, disease, and through them to destroy all power of close and consecutive thought ! No one who considers *on how many things* the power of close thinking depends, can doubt that all our sufficiency in this is from God ; and that we owe to him every clear idea on the subjects of common life, and on scientific subjects, no less certainly than we do in the truths of religion, comp. the case of Bezaleel and Aholiab in common arts, Ex. xxxi. 1—6, and Job xxxii. 8.

6. *Who also hath made us able ministers*, &c. This translation does not *quite* meet the force of the original. It would seem to imply that Paul regarded himself and his fellow-labourers as men of talents, and of signal ability; and that he was inclined to boast of it. But this is not the meaning. It refers properly to his sense of the responsibility and difficulty of the work of the ministry; and to the fact that he did not esteem himself to be *sufficient* for this work in his own strength (chap. ii. 16 ; iii. 5) ; and he here says that God had made him *sufficient:* not able, talented, learned, but *sufficient* (ἱκάνωσεν ἡμᾶς) ; he has supplied our deficiency ; he has rendered us competent, or fit ;— if a word may be coined after the manner of the Greek here, " he has *sufficienced* us for this work." There is no assertion, therefore, here, that they were men of talents, or peculiar ability, but only that God had qualified them for their work, and made them by his grace sufficient to meet

the toils and responsibilities of this arduous office. ¶ *Of the New Testament.* Of the new covenant (Note, Matt. xxv. 28), in contradistinction from the old covenant, which was established through Moses. They were appointed to go forth and make the provisions of that new covenant known to a dying world. ¶ *Not of the letter.* Not of the literal, or verbal meaning, in contradistinction from the Spirit ; see Notes on Rom. ii. 27, 29 ; vii. 6. This is said, doubtless, in opposition to the Jews, and Jewish teachers. They insisted much on the letter of the law, but entered little into its real meaning. They did not seek out the true spiritual sense of the Old Testament ; and hence they rested on the mere literal observance of the rites and ceremonies of religion without understanding their true nature and design. Their service, though in many respects conformed to the letter of the law, yet became cold, formal, and hypocritical; abounding in mere ceremonies, and where the heart had little to do. Hence there was little pure spiritual worship offered to God ; and hence also they rejected the Messiah whom the old covenant prefigured, and was designed to set forth. ¶ *For the letter killeth*, comp. Notes on Rom. iv. 15 ; vii. 9, 10. The mere letter of the law of Moses. The effect of it was merely to produce condemnation ; to produce a sense of guilt, and danger, and not to produce pardon, relief, and joy. The law denounced death ; condemned sin in all forms ; and the effect of it was to produce a sense of guilt and condemnation. ¶ *But the spirit giveth life.* The spirit, in contradistinction from the mere literal interpretation of the Scriptures. The Spirit, that is, Christ, says Locke, comp. ver. 17. The spirit here means, says Bloomfield, that new spiritual system, the gospel. The Spirit of God speaking in us, says Doddridge.

7 But if the ministration of death, written *and* engraven in stones, was glorious, so that the children of Israel could not stead-

The spirit here seems to refer to the *New* Testament, or the new dispensation in contradistinction from the old. That was characterized mainly by its strictness of law, and by its burdensome rites, and by the severe tone of its denunciation for sin. It did not in itself provide a way of pardon and peace. Law condemns; it does not speak of forgiveness. On the contrary, the gospel, a spiritual system, is designed to impart life and comfort to the soul. It speaks peace. It comes not to condemn, but to save. It discloses a way of mercy, and it invites all to partake and live. It is called " spirit," probably because its consolations are imparted and secured by the Spirit of God—the source of all true life to the soul. It is the dispensation of the Spirit; and it demands a spiritual service—a service that is free, and elevated, and tending eminently to purify the heart, and to save the soul; see Note on ver. 17.

7. *But if the ministration of death.* In the previous verses, Paul had referred incidentally to the institutions of Moses, and to the superiority of the gospel. He had said that the former were engraven on stones, but the latter on the heart (ver. 3); that the letter of the former tended to death, but the latter to life (ver. 6). This sentiment he proceeds further to illustrate, by showing in what the superior glory of the gospel consisted. The *design* of the whole is, to illustrate the nature, and to show the importance of the ministerial office; and the manner in which the duties of that office were to be performed. That the phrase " ministration of death " refers to the Mosaic institutions, the connection sufficiently indicates, ver. 13—15. The word " ministration " (διακονία) means, properly, ministry; the office of ministering in divine things. It is usually applied to the officers of the church in the New Testament, Acts i. 17, 25; Rom. xi. 13; 1 Cor. xii. 5. The word here, however, seems to refer to the whole arrangement under the Mosaic econ-

omy, by which his laws were promulgated, and perpetuated. The expression " a ministration—written and engraven on stone," is somewhat harsh; but the *sense* evidently is, the ministration of a covenant, or of laws written on stones. The word " ministration " there refers to the arrangement, office, &c. by which the knowledge of these laws was maintained; the *ministering* under a system like that of the Jewish; or, *more strictly*, the act and occasion on which Moses himself *ministered*, or promulgated that system to the Jews, and when the glory of the work was irradiated even from his countenance. And the purpose of the apostle is to show that the ministry of the gospel is more glorious than *even* the ministry of Moses, when he was admitted near to God on the holy mount; and when such a glory attended his receiving and promulgating the law. It is called the " ministration of death," because it tended to condemnation; it did not speak of pardon; it was fitted only to deepen the sense of sin, and to produce alarm and dread; see Note on ver. 6. ¶ *Written* and *engraven in stones.* The ten commandments—the substance of all the Mosaic institutes, and the principal laws of his economy—were written, or engraven on tables of stone. ¶ *Was glorious.* Was attended with magnificence and splendour. The glory here referred to, consisted in the circumstance of sublimity and grandeur in which the law of Moses was given. It was, (1.) The glory of God as he was manifested on Mount Sinai, as the Lawgiver and Ruler of the people. (2.) The glory of the attending circumstances, of thunder, fire, &c. in which God appeared. The law was given in these circumstances. Its *giving*—called here the " ministration "—was amidst such displays of the glory of God. It was, (3.) A high honour and glory for Moses to be permitted to approach so near to God; to commune with him; and to receive at his hand the law for his

fastly behold the face of Moses for ^a the glory of his countenance; which *glory* was to be done away;

a Ex. 34. 1, 29—35.

people, and for the world. These were circumstances of imposing majesty and grandeur, which, however, Paul says were eclipsed and surpassed by the ministry of the gospel. ¶ *So that the children of Israel*, &c. In Ex. xxxiv. 29, 30, it is said, that " When Moses came down from Mount Sinai with the two tables of testimony in Moses' hand, when he came down from the mount, that Moses wist not that the skin of his face shone, while He talked with him. And when Aaron and all the children of Israel saw Moses, behold, the skin of his face shone ; and they were afraid to come nigh him." The word rendered " steadfastly behold" (ἀτενίσαι), means to gaze intently upon; to look steadily, or constantly, or fixedly ; see Note on Acts i. 10. There was a dazzling splendour, an irradiation ; a diffusion of light, such that they could not look intently and steadily upon it—as we cannot look steadily at the sun. *How* this was produced, is not known. It cannot be accounted for from natural causes, and was doubtless designed to be to the Israelites an attestation that Moses had been with God, and was commissioned by him. They would see, (1.) That it was unnatural, such as no known cause could produce ; and, (2.) Not improbably they would recognise a resemblance to the manner in which God usually appeared—the glory of the Shechinah in which he so frequently manifested himself to them. It would be to them, therefore, a demonstration that Moses had been with God. ¶ *Which* glory *was to be done away.* The splendour of that scene was transitory. It did not last. It was soon destroyed (τὴν καταργουμένην). It was not adapted or designed long to continue. This does not mean, as Doddridge supposes, " soon to be abolished in death;" or, as others, " ceasing with youth ;" but it means, that the shining or the splendour was transitory ; it was soon to cease ; it was not designed to be permanent.

8 How shall not the ministration of the Spirit be rather glorious ?

Neither the wonderful scenes accompanying the giving of the law on Sinai, nor the shining on the countenance of Moses, was designed to abide. The thunders of Sinai would cease to roll ; the lightenings to play ; the visible manifestations of the presence of God would all be gone ; and the supernatural illumination of the face of Moses also would soon cease —*perhaps* as Macknight, Bloomfield, and others suppose, as a prefiguration of the abrogation of the glory of the whole system of the Levitical law. Paul certainly means to say, that the glory of Moses, and of his dispensation, was a fading glory ; but that the glory of the gospel would be permanent, and increasing for ever.

8. *How shall not the ministration of the Spirit.* This is an argument from the less to the greater. Several things in it are worthy of notice. (1.) The proper contrast to the "ministration of death" (ver. 7), would have been ' ministration of life.' But Paul chose rather to call it the ' ministration of the spirit;' as the source of life ; or as conferring higher dignity on the gospel than to have called it simply the ministration of life. (2.) By the " Spirit" here is manifestly meant the Holy Spirit ; and the whole phrase denotes the gospel, or the preaching of the gospel, by which eminently the Holy Spirit is imparted. (3.) It is the high honour of the gospel ministry, that it is the means by which the Holy Spirit is imparted to men. It is designed to secure the salvation of men by his agency ; and it is through the ministry that the Holy Spirit is imparted, the heart renewed, and the soul saved. The work of the ministry is, therefore, the most important and honourable in which man can engage. ¶ *Be rather glorious.* (1.) Because that Moses tended to death ; this to life. (2.) Because that was engraven on stone ; this is engraved on the heart. (3.) Because that was the mere giving of a law ; this is con-

9 For if the ministration of condemnation *be* glory, much more
doth the ministration of righteousness exceed in glory.

10 For even that which was
made glorious had no glory in this
respect, by reason of the glory that
excelleth.

rected with the renovating influences
of the Holy Spirit. (4.) Because that
was soon to pass away. All the magnificence of the scene was soon to
vanish. But this is to remain. Its
influence and effect are to be everlasting. It is to stretch into eternity;
and its main glory is to be witnessed
in souls renewed and saved; and
amidst the splendours of heaven.
" The work of the Spirit of God on
the heart of a rational being, is much
more important than any dead characters which can be engraved on
insensible stones."—*Doddridge.*

9. *For if the ministration of condemnation.* Of Moses in giving the
law, the effect of which is to produce
condemnation.—Law condemns the
guilty; it does not save them. It
denounces punishment; it contains no
provisions of pardon. To *pardon* is
to depart from the law; and must be
done under the operation of another
system—since a law which contains
a provision for the pardon of offenders, and permits them to escape,
would be a burlesque in legislation.
The tendency of the Mosaic institutions, therefore, was to produce a
sense of condemnation. And so it
will be found by all who attempt to be
justified by the law. It will tend to,
and result in, their condemnation.
¶ Be *glory.* Be glorious; or be glory
itself.—It was glorious as a manifestation of the holiness and justice of
God; and glorious in the attending
circumstances. No event in our
world has been more magnificent in
the circumstances of external majesty
and splendour than the giving of the
law on Mount Sinai. ¶ *The ministration of righteousness.* The gospel;
the promulgation of the plan of mercy.
It is called "the ministration of
righteousness," in contradistinction
from the law of Moses, which was a
" ministration of condemnation."
The word "righteousness," however,
does not exactly express the force of
the original word. That word is δικ-

αιοσύνης, and it stands directly opposed
to the word καταχρισεως, *condemnation.* It should be rendered 'the
ministration of *justification*;' the
plan by which God justifies men; see
Note, Rom. i. 17. The law of Moses
condemns; the gospel is the plan by
which man is *justified.* And if that
which *condemns* could be glorious,
much more must that be by which
men can be justified, acquitted, and
saved. The superior glory of the
gospel, therefore, consists in the fact
that it is a scheme to justify and save
lost sinners. And this glory consists,
(1.) In *the fact* that it can be done
when all *law* condemns. (2.) In the
showing forth of the divine character
while it *is* done, as just, and merciful,
and benevolent in doing it—blending
all his great and glorious attributes
together—while the law disclosed only
one of his attributes—his justice. (3.)
In the *manner* in which it is done.
It is by the incarnation of the Son of
God—a far more glorious manifestation of deity than was made on Mount
Sinai. It is by the toils, and sufferings, and death of him who made the
atonement, and by the circumstances
of awful and imposing grandeur which
attended his death, when the sun was
darkened, and the rocks were rent—
far more grand and awful scenes than
occurred when the law was given. It
is by the resurrection and ascension
of the Redeemer—scenes far more
sublime than all the external glories
of Sinai when the law was given.
(4.) In the *effects*, or results. The
one condemns; the other justifies and
saves. The effect of the one is seen
in the convictions of conscience, in
alarm, in a sense of guilt, in the conscious desert of condemnation, and in
the apprehension of eternal punishment. The other is seen in sins forgiven; in peace of conscience; in the
joy of pardon; in the hope of heaven;
in comfort and triumph on the bed
of death, and amidst the glories of
heaven.

11 For if *a* that which is done away *was* glorious, much more that which remaineth *is* glorious.

a Rom. 5. 20, 21.

12 Seeing then that we have such hope, we use great ¹ plainness of speech :

1 Or, *boldness.*

10. *For even that which was made glorious* (τὸ δεδοξασμένον). That was splendid, excellent, or glorious. This refers doubtless, to the laws and institutions of Moses, especially to the primary giving of the law. Paul does not deny that *it* had an honour and majesty such, in some respects, as the Jews claimed for it. It was glorious in the manner in which it was given; it was glorious in the purity of the law itself; and it was glorious, or splendid in the magnificent and imposing ritual in which the worship of God was celebrated. But all this was surpassed in the brighter glory of the gospel. ¶ *Had no glory.* Gr. Was not glorious, or splendid (οὐδὲ δεδόξασται). Had comparatively no glory, or splendour. Its glory was all eclipsed. It was like the splendour of the moon and stars compared with the bright light of the sun. ¶ *By reason of the glory that excelleth.* In the gospel; in the incarnation, life, sufferings, death, and resurrection of the Lord Jesus; in the pardon of sin; in the peace and joy of the believer; and in the glories of the heavenly world to which the gospel elevates dying men.

11. *For if that which is done away,* &c. The splendour that attended the giving of the law; the bright shining of the face of Moses; and the ritual institutions of his religion. It was *to be* done away. It was never designed to be permanent. Every thing in it had a transient existence, and was so designed. Yet it was attended, Paul admits, with much that was magnificent and splendid. He had, in the previous verses, stated several important differences between the law and the gospel. He here states another. The law he calls (τὸ καταργούμενον) *the* thing which was to be made to cease; to be put an end to; to be done away with; to be abolished. It had no permanency; and it was designed to have none. Its glory, therefore, great as in many respects

it might be, could not be compared with that which was to be permanent —as the light of the stars fades away at the rising sun. It is implied here, that it was originally designed that the Mosaic institutions should not be permanent; that they should be mere shadows and types of better things; and that when the things which they adumbrated should appear, the shadows would vanish of course. This idea is one which prevails everywhere in the New Testament, and which the sacred writers are often at great pains to demonstrate. ¶ *Was glorious.* Gr. *By glory* (διὰ δόξης). That is, it was attended *by* glory; it was introduced by glory, it was encompassed *with* glory when it was established The idea here is, not that it was glorious *in itself*, but that it was accompanied *with* splendour and majesty. ¶ *That which remaineth.* The gospel (τὸ μένον). The thing that is to remain; that is permanent, abiding, perpetual; that has no principle of decay, and whose characteristic it is, that it is everlasting. The gospel is permanent, or abiding, (1.) Because it is designed to remain immutable through the remotest ages. It is not to be superseded by any new economy, or institution. It is *the* dispensation under which the affairs of the world are to be wound up, and under which the world is to close; see Note, 1 Cor. xv. 51. (2.) Its effects on the heart are permanent. It is complete in itself. It is not to be succeeded by any other system, and it looks to no other system in order to complete or perfect its operations on the soul. (3.) Its effects are to abide for ever. They will exist in heaven. They are to be seen in the soul that shall be recovered from sin, and that shall be glorious in the bosom of God for ever and ever. The Mosaic system— glorious as it was—shall be remembered as *introducing* the gospel; the gospel shall be remembered as directly fitting for heaven. Its most great and glorious results shall be seen in the permanent and eternal joys of heaven. The gospel contemplates a great, permanent, and eternal good, adapted to all ages, all climes, all people, and all worlds. It is, therefore, so much more glorious than the limited, temporary, and partial good of the Mosaic system, that that may be said in comparison to have had *no* glory.

12. *Seeing then that we have such hope.* Hope properly is a compound emotion, made up of a *desire* for an object, and an *expectation* of obtaining it. If there is no *desire* for it; or if the object is not pleasant and agreeable, there is no hope, though there may be expectation—as in the *expectation* of the pestilence, of famine, or sickness, or death. If there is no expectation of it, but a strong desire, there is no hope; as in cases where there is a strong desire of wealth, or fame, or pleasure; or where a man is condemned for murder, and has a strong desire but no prospect of pardon; or where a man is shipwrecked, and has a strong desire, but no expectation of again seeing his family and friends. In such cases, despondency or despair are the results. It is the union of the two feelings in proper proportions which constitutes hope. There has been considerable variety of views among expositors in regard to the proper meaning of the word in this place. Mr. Locke supposes that Paul here means the honourable employment of an apostle and minister of the gospel, or the glory belonging to the ministry in the gospel; and that his calling it "hope," instead of "glory," which the connection would seem to demand, is the language of modesty. Rosenmüller understands it of the hope of the perpetual continuance of the gospel dispensation. Macknight renders it "persuasion," and explains it as meaning the full persuasion or assurance that the gospel excels the law in the manner of its introduction; its permanency, &c. A few remarks may, perhaps, make it clear. (1.) It refers primarily to Paul, and the other ministers of the gospel. It is not properly the *Christian hope* as such to which he refers, but it is that which

the ministers of the gospel had. (2.) It refers to *all* that he had said before about the superiority of the gospel to the law; and it is designed to express the *result* of all that on his mind, and on the minds of his fellow-labourers. (3.) It refers to the *prospect*, confidence, persuasion, anticipation which he had as the effect of what he had just said. It is the prospect of eternal life; the clear expectation of acceptance, and the anticipation of heaven, based on the fact that this was a ministry of the Spirit (ver. 8): that it was a ministry showing the way of justification (ver. 9): and that it was never to be done away, but to abide for ever (ver. 11). On all these this strong hope was founded; and in view of these, Paul expressed himself clearly, not enigmatically; and not in types and figures, as Moses did. Every thing about the gospel was clear and plain; and this led to the confident expectation and assurance of heaven. The word *hope*, therefore, in this place will express the effect on the mind of Paul in regard to the work of the ministry, produced by the *group* of considerations which he had suggested, showing that the gospel was superior to the law; and that it was the ground of more clear and certain confidence and hope than any thing which the law could furnish. ¶ *We use.* We employ; we are accustomed to. He refers to the manner in which he preached the gospel, ¶ *Great plainness of speech.* Marg. *boldness.* We use the word "plainness" as applied to speech chiefly in two senses, (1.) To denote boldness, faithfulness, candour; in opposition to trimming, timidity, and unfaithfulness; and, (2.) To denote clearness, intelligibleness, and simplicity, in opposition to obscurity, mist, and highly-wrought and laboured forms of expression. The connection here shows that the *latter* is the sense in which the phrase here is to be understood; see ver. 13. It denotes openness, simplicity, freedom from the obscurity which arises from enigmatical and parabolical, and typical modes of speaking. This stands in opposition to figure, metaphor, and allegory—to

13 And not as Moses, *which* | put a vail over his face that the

an affected and laboured concealment of the idea in the manner which was common among the Jewish doctors and heathen philosophers, where their meaning was carefully concealed from the vulgar, and from all except the *initiated*. It stands opposed also to the necessary obscurity arising from typical institutions like those of Moses. And the doctrine of the passage is, that such is the clearness and fulness of the Christian revelation, arising from the fact, that it is the *last* economy, and that it does not look to the future, that its ministers may and should use clear and intelligible language. They should not use language abounding in metaphor and allegory. They should not use unusual terms. They should not draw their words and illustrations from science. They should not use mere technical language. They should not attempt to vail or cloak their meaning. They should not seek a refined and overwrought style. They should use expressions which other men use ; and express themselves as far as possible in the language of common life. What is preaching worth that is not understood? Why should a man talk at all unless he is intelligible? Who was ever more plain and simple in his words and illustrations than the Lord Jesus?

13. *And not as Moses*. Our conduct is not like that of Moses. We make no attempt to conceal any thing in regard to the nature, design, and duration of the gospel. We leave nothing designedly in mystery. ¶ *Which put a vail over his face*. That is, when he came down from Mount Sinai, and when his face shone. Ex. xxxiv. 33, " And till Moses had done speaking with them, he put a vail on his face." This vail he put off when he went to speak with God, but put on again when he delivered his commands to the people. What was the *design* of this, Moses has not himself declared. The statement which he makes in Exodus would lead us to suppose that it was on account of the exceeding brightness and dazzling splendour which shone around him, and which

made it difficult to look intently upon him ; and that this was in part the reason, even Paul himself seems to intimate in ver. 7. He, however, in this verse intimates that there was another design, which was that he might be, as Doddridge expresses it, "a kind of type and figure of his own dispensation." ¶ *That the children of Israel*. Mr. Locke understands this of the apostles, and supposes that it means, " We do not vail the light, so that the obscurity of what we deliver should hinder the children of Israel from seeing in the law which was to be done away, Christ who is the end of the law." But this interpretation is forced and unnatural. The phrase rendered " that " (πρὸς τὸ) evidently connects what is affirmed here with the statement about Moses ; and shows that the apostle means to say that Moses put the vail on his face *in order* that the children of Israel should not be able to see to the end of his institutions. That Moses had such a design, and that the putting on of the vail was emblematic of the nature of his institutions, Paul here distinctly affirms. No one can prove that this was *not* his design ; and in a land and time when types, and emblems, and allegorical modes of speech were much used, it is highly probable that Moses *meant* to intimate that the end and full purpose of his institutions were designedly concealed. ¶ *Could not stedfastly look*. Could not gaze intently upon (ἀτενίσαι) ; see Note on ver. 7. They could not clearly discern it ; there was obscurity arising from the fact of the designed concealment. He did not *intend* that they should clearly see the full purport and design of the institutions which he established. ¶ *To the end* (εἰς τὸ τέλος). Unto the end, purpose, design, or ultimate result of the law which he established. A great many different interpretations have been proposed of this. The meaning seems to me to be this : There was a glory and splendour in that which the institutions of Moses typified, which the children of Israel were not permitted then to be-

children of Israel could not stedfastly look to the end[a] of that which is abolished:

a Ro.10.4.

hold. There was a splendour and lustre in the face of Moses, which they could not gaze upon, and therefore he put a vail over it to diminish its intense brightness. In like manner there was a glory and splendour in the ultimate design and scope of his institutions, in that to which they referred, which they were not then *able, i. e.* prepared to look on, and the exceeding brightness of which he of design concealed. This was done by obscure types and figures, that resembled a vail thrown over a dazzling and splendid object. The word "end," then, I suppose, does not refer to termination, or close, but to the *design, scope*, or *purpose* of the Mosaic institutions ; to that which they were intended to introduce and adumbrate. THAT END was the Messiah, and the glory of his institutions ; see Note on Rom. x. "Christ is the *end* of the law." And the meaning of Paul, I take to be, is, that there was a splendour and a glory in the gospel which the Mosaic institutions were designed to typify, which was so great that the children of Israel were not fully prepared to see it, and that he designedly threw over that glory the vail of obscure types and figures; as he threw over his face a vail that partially concealed its splendour. Thus interpreted there is a consistency in the entire passage, and very great beauty. Paul, in the following verses, proceeds to state that the vail to the view of the Jews of his time was not removed ; that they still looked to the obscure types and institutions of the Mosaic law rather than on the glory which they were designed to adumbrate; *as if* they should choose to look on the *vail* on the face of Moses rather than on the splendour which it concealed. ¶ *Of that which is abolished.* Or rather *to be abolished*, (τοῦ καταργουμένου), whose nature, design, and intention it was that it should be abolished. It was never designed to be permanent ; and Paul speaks of it here as a thing that was

14 But their minds were blinded ; [a] for until this day remaineth the same vail untaken away in

a Ro.11.7,8,25.

known and indisputable that the Mosaic institutions were designed to be abolished.

14. *But their minds were blinded.* The word here used (πωρόω) means rather to harden; to make hard like stone ; and then to make dull or stupid. It is applied to the heart, in Mark vi. 52; viii. 17; to persons, in Rom. xi. 7; and to the eyes, in Job xvii. 7. Paul refers here to the fact that the understandings of the Jews were stupid, dull, and insensible, so that they did not see clearly the design and end of their own institutions. He states simply the fact, he does not refer to the cause of it. The fact that the Jews were thus stupid and dull is often affirmed in the New Testament. ¶ *For until this day,* &c. The sense of this is, that even to the time when Paul wrote, it was a characteristic of the great mass of the Jewish people, that they did not understand the true sense of their own Scriptures. They did not understand its doctrines in regard to the Messiah. A vail seems to be thrown over the Old Testament when they read it, as there was over the face of Moses, so that the glory of their own Scriptures is concealed from their view, as the glory of the face of Moses was hidden. ¶ *Of the Old Testament.* Greek, "of the old covenant." See this word "testament," or covenant, explained in the Notes on 1 Cor. xi. 25. This, I believe, is the only instance in which the Scriptures of the Jews are called the "Old Testament," or covenant, in the Bible. It was, of course, not a name which they used, or would use; but it is now with Christians the common appellation. No doubt can be entertained but that Paul uses the terms in the same manner in which we now do, and refers to all the inspired writings of the Jews. ¶ *Which* vail *is done away in Christ.* In the manifestation, or appearance of Jesus the Messiah, the vail is removed. The

the reading of the Old Testament; which *vail* is done away in Christ.

15 But even unto this day,

when Moses is read, the vail is upon their heart.

16 Nevertheless, when it shall

---

obscurity which rested on the prophecies and types of the former dispensation is withdrawn; and as the face of Moses could have been distinctly seen if the vail on his face had been removed, so it is in regard to the true meaning of the Old Testament by the coming of the Messiah. What was obscure is now made clear; and the prophecies are so completely fulfilled in him, that his coming has removed the covering, and shed a clear light over them all. Many of the prophecies, for example, until the Messiah actually appeared, appeared obscure, and almost contradictory. Those which spoke of him, for illustration, as man and as God; as suffering, and yet reigning; as dying, and yet as ever-living; as a mighty Prince, a conqueror, and a king, and yet as a man of sorrows; as humble, and yet glorious: all seemed difficult to be reconciled until they were seen to harmonise in Jesus of Nazareth. Then they were plain, and the vail was taken away. Christ is seen to answer all the previous descriptions of him in the Old Testament; and his coming casts a clear light on all which was before obscure.

15. *But even unto this day.* To the time when Paul wrote this epistle, about thirty years after Christ was put to death. But it is still as true as it was in the time of Paul; and the character and conduct of the Jews now so entirely accords with the description which he gives of them in his time, as to show that he drew from nature, and as to constitute one of the strong incidental proofs that the account in the New Testament is true. Of no other people on earth, probably, would a description be accurate eighteen hundred years *after* it was made. ¶ *When Moses is read.* When the five books of Moses are read, as they were regularly and constantly in their synagogues; see Note on Luke iv. 16. ¶ *The vail is upon their heart.* They do not see the true meaning and beauty of their own

Scriptures—a description as applicable to the Jews now as it was to those in the time of Paul.

16. *Nevertheless.* This is not always to continue. The time is coming when they shall understand their own Scriptures, and see their true beauty. ¶ *When it shall turn to the Lord.* When the Jewish people shall be converted. The word "it" here refers undoubtedly to "Israel" in ver. 13; and the sense is, that their blindness is not always to remain; there is to be a period when they shall turn to God, and shall understand his promises, and become acquainted with the true nature of their own religion. This subject the apostle has discussed at much greater length in the eleventh chapter of the epistle to the Romans; see Notes on that chapter. ¶ *The vail shall be taken away.* They shall then understand the true meaning of the prophecies, and the true nature of their own institutions. They shall see that they refer to the Lord Jesus, the incarnate Son of God, and the true Messiah. The genuine sense of their sacred oracles shall break upon their view with full and irresistible light. There may be an allusion in the *language* here to the declaration in Isa. xxv. 7, "And he will destroy in this mountain the face of the covering cast over all people, and the vail that is spread over all nations." This verse teaches, (1.) That the time will come when the Jews shall be converted to Christianity; expressed here by their turning unto the Lord, that is, the Lord Jesus; see Note, Acts i. 24. (2.) It seems to be implied that their conversion will be a conversion of *the people* at large; a conversion that shall be nearly simultaneous; a conversion *en masse.* Such a conversion we have reason to anticipate of the Jewish nation. (3.) The effect of this will be to make them acquainted with the true sense of their own Scriptures, and the light and beauty of the sayings of their own prophets. Now

turn to the Lord, the vail shall be taken away.*a*

17 Now the Lord *b* is that Spirit;

a Is. 25.7.   *b* 1 Cor. 15.45.

and where the *c* Spirit of the Lord *is*, there *is* liberty.

18 But we all, with open face

c Rom. 8.2.

they are in deep darkness on the subject; then they will see how entirely they meet and harmonise in the Lord Jesus. (4.) The true and only way of having a correct and full meaning of the Bible is by turning unto God. Love to him, and a disposition to do his will, is the best means of interpreting the Bible.

17. *Now the Lord is that Spirit.* The word "Lord" here evidently refers to the Lord Jesus; see ver. 16. It may be observed in general in regard to this word, that where it occurs in the New Testament unless the connection require us to understand it of God, it refers to the Lord Jesus. It was the common name by which he was known; see John xx. 13; xxi. 7, 12; Eph. iv. 1, 5. The design of Paul in this verse seems to be to account for the "liberty" which he and the other apostles had, or for the boldness, openness, and plainness (ver. 12) which they evinced in contradistinction from the Jews, who so little understood the nature of their institutions. He had said (ver. 6), that he was a minister "not of the letter, but of the Spirit;" and he had stated that the Old Testament was not understood by the Jews who adhered to the literal interpretation of the Scriptures. He here says, that the Lord Jesus was "the Spirit" to which he referred, and by which he was enabled to understand the Old Testament so as to speak plainly, and without obscurity. The sense is, that Christ was the Spirit; *i. e.* the sum, the substance of the Old Testament. The figures, types, prophecies, &c. all centered in him, and he was the end of all those institutions. If contemplated as having reference to him, it was easy to understand them. This I take to be the sentiment of the passage, though expositors have been greatly divided in regard to its meaning. Thus explained, it does not mean absolutely and abstractly that the Lord Jesus was "a Spirit," but

that he was the sum, the essence, the end, and the purport of the Mosaic rites, the spirit of which Paul had spoken in ver. 6, as contradistinguished from the letter of the law. ¶ *And where the Spirit of the Lord is, there is liberty.* This is a general truth designed to illustrate the particular sentiment which he had just advanced. The word "liberty" here (ἐλευθερία) refers, I think, to freedom in speaking; the power of speaking openly, and freely, as in ver. 12. It states the general truth, that the effect of the Spirit of God was to give light and clearness of view; to remove obscurity from a subject, and to enable one to see it plainly. This would be a truth that could not be denied by the Jews, who held to the doctrine that the Spirit of God revealed truth, and it must be admitted by all. Under the influence of that Spirit, therefore, Paul says, that he was able to speak with openness, and boldness; that he had a clear view of truth, which the mass of the Jews had not; and that the system of religion which he preached was open, plain, and clear. The word "freedom," would perhaps, better convey the idea. "There is freedom from the dark and obscure views of the Jews, freedom from their prejudices, and their superstitions; freedom from the slavery and bondage of sin; the freedom of the children of God, who have clear views of him as their Father and Redeemer, and who are enabled to express those views openly and boldly to the world."

18. *But we all.* All Christians. The discussion in the chapter has related mainly to the apostles; but this declaration seems evidently to refer to all Christians, as distinguished from the Jews. ¶ *With open face,* comp. Note on 1 Cor. xiii. 12. Tindal renders this, "and now the Lord's glory appeareth in us all as in a glass." The sense is, "with unvailed face," alluding to the fact (ver. 13) that the face of

beholding as in a glass *a* the glory of
the Lord, are changed into the same

a 1Cor.13.12.   *b* Rom.8.29.   *c* Ps 84.7.

b image from *c* glory to glory *even*
as [1] by the Spirit of the Lord.

1 or, *of the Lord the Spirit.*

Moses was vailed, so that the children of Israel could not stedfastly look on it. In contradistinction from that, Paul says that Christians are enabled to look upon the glory of the Lord in the gospel without a vail—without any obscure intervening medium. ¶ *Beholding as in a glass.* On the word *glass*, and the sense in which it is used in the New Testament, see Note on 1 Cor. xiii. 12. The word here used (κατοπτριζόμενοι) has been very variously rendered. Macknight renders it, " we all reflecting as mirrors the glory of the Lord." Doddridge, "beholding as by a glass." Locke, "with open countenances as mirrors, reflecting the glory of the Lord." The word κατοπτρίζω occurs nowhere else in the New Testament. It properly means to look in a mirror; to behold as in a mirror. The mirrors of the ancients were made of burnished metal, and they reflected images with great brilliancy and distinctness. And the meaning is, that the gospel reflected the glory of the Lord; it was, so to speak, the mirror —the polished, burnished substance in which the glory of the Lord shone, and where that glory was irradiated and reflected so that it might be seen by Christians. There was no vail over it; no obscurity; nothing to break its dazzling splendour, or to prevent its meeting the eye. Christians, by looking on the gospel, could see the glorious perfections and plans of God as bright, and clear, and brilliant as they could see a light reflected from the burnished surface of the mirror. So to speak, the glorious perfections of God shone from heaven; beamed upon the gospel, and were thence reflected to the eye and the heart of the Christian, and had the effect of transforming them into the same image. This passage is one of great beauty, and is designed to set forth the gospel as being *the reflection* of the infinite glories of God to the minds and hearts of men. ¶ *The glory of the Lord.* The splendour,

majesty, and holiness of God as manifested in the gospel, or of the Lord as incarnate. The idea is, that God was clearly and distinctly seen in the gospel. There was no obscurity, no vail, as in the case of Moses. In the gospel they were permitted to look on the full splendour of the divine perfections—the justice, goodness, mercy, and benevolence of God—to see him as he is with undimmed and unvailed glory. The idea is, that the perfections of God shine forth with splendour and beauty in the gospel, and that we are permitted to look on them clearly and openly. ¶ *Are changed into the same image.* It is possible that there may be an allusion here to the effect which was produced by looking into an ancient mirror. Such mirrors were made of burnished metal, and the reflection from them would be intense. If a strong light were thrown on them, the rays would be cast by reflection on the face of him who looked on the mirror, and it would be strongly illuminated. And the idea may be, that the glory of God, the splendour of the divine perfections, was thrown on the gospel, so to speak like a bright light on a polished mirror; and that that glory was reflected from the gospel on him who contemplated it, so that he appeared to be transformed into the same image. Locke renders it, " We are changed into his very image by a continued succession of glory, as it were, streaming upon us from the Lord." The figure is one of great beauty; and the idea is, that by placing ourselves within the light of the gospel; by contemplating the glory that shines there, we become changed into the likeness of the same glory, and conformed to that which shines there with so much splendour. By contemplating the resplendent face of the blessed Redeemer, we are changed into something of the same image. It is a law of our nature that we are moulded, in our moral feelings, by the persons with whom we associate, and by the objects which we contemplate. We become insensibly assimilated to those with whom we have intercourse, and to the objects with which we are familiar. We imbibe the opinions, we copy the habits, we imitate the manners, we fall into the customs of those with whom we have daily conversation, and whom we make our companions and friends. Their sentiments insensibly become our sentiments, and their ways our ways. It is thus with the *books* with which we are familiar. We are insensibly, but certainly moulded into conformity to the opinions, maxims, and feelings which are there expressed. Our own sentiments undergo a gradual change, and we are likened to those with which in this manner we are conversant. So it is in regard to the opinions and feelings which from any cause we are in the habit of bringing before our minds. It is the way by which men become corrupted in their sentiments and feelings, in their contact with the world; it is the way in which amusements, and the company of the gay and the dissipated possess so much power; it is the way in which the young and inexperienced are beguiled and ruined; and it is the way in which Christians dim the lustre of their piety, and obscure the brightness of their religion by their contact with the gay and fashionable world.— And it is on the same great principle that Paul says that by contemplating the glory of God in the gospel, we become insensibly, but certainly conformed to the same image, and made like the Redeemer. His image will be reflected on us. We shall imbibe his sentiments, catch his feelings, and be moulded into the image of his own purity. Such is the great and wise law of our nature; and it is on this principle, and by this means, that God designs we should be *made* pure on earth, and *kept* pure in heaven for ever. ¶ *From glory to glory.* From one degree of glory to another. "The more we behold this brilliant and glorious light, the more do we reflect back its rays; that is, the more we contemplate the great truths of the Christian religion, the more do

our minds become imbued with its spirit."—*Bloomfield.* This is said in contradistinction probably to Moses. The splendour on his face gradually died away. But not so with the light reflected from the gospel. It becomes deeper and brighter constantly.— This sentiment is parallel to that expressed by the psalmist; "They go from strength to strength" (Ps. lxxxiv. 7); *i. e.* they go from one degree of strength to another, or one degree of holiness to another, until they come to the full vision of God himself in heaven. The idea in the phrase before us is; that there is a continual increase of moral purity and holiness under the gospel until it results in the perfect glory of heaven. The *doctrine* is, that Christians advance in piety; and that this is done by the contemplation of the glory of God as it is revealed in the gospel. ¶ *As by the Spirit of the Lord.* Marg. "Of the Lord of the Spirit." Gr. "As from the Lord the Spirit." So Beza, Locke, Wolf, Rosenmüller, and Doddridge render it. The idea is, that it is by the Lord Jesus Christ the spirit of the law, the spirit referred to by Paul above, ver. 6, 17. It is done by the Holy Spirit procured or imparted by the Lord Jesus. This sentiment is in accordance with that which prevails everywhere in the Bible, that it is by the Holy Spirit alone that the heart is changed and purified. And the object of the observation here is, doubtless, to prevent the supposition that the change from "glory to glory" was produced in any sense by the *mere* contemplation of truth, or by any physical operation of such contemplation on the mind. It was by the Spirit of God alone that the heart was changed even under the gospel, and amidst the full blaze of its truth. Were it not for *his* agency, even the contemplation of the glorious truths of the gospel would be in vain, and would produce no saving effect on the human heart.

REMARKS.

1. The best of all evidences of a call to the office of the ministry is the divine blessing resting on our labours

ver. 1, 2. If sinners are converted; if souls are sanctified; if the interests of pure religion are advanced ; if by humble, zealous, and self-denying efforts, a man is enabled so to preach as that the divine blessing shall rest constantly on his labours, it is among the best of all evidences that he is called of God, and is approved by him. And though it may be true, and is true, that men who are self-deceived, or are hypocrites, are sometimes the means of doing good, yet it is still true, as a general rule, that eminent, and long-continued success in the ministry is an evidence of God's acceptance, and that he has called a minister to this office. *Paul* felt this, and often appealed to it ; and why may not others also ?

2. A minister may appeal to the effect of the gospel among his own people as a proof that it is from God, ver. 2, 3. Nothing else would produce such effects as were produced at Corinth, but the power of God. If the wicked are reclaimed ; if the intemperate and licentious are made temperate and pure ; if the dishonest are made honest ; and the scoffer learns to pray, under the gospel, it proves that it is from God. To such effects a minister may appeal as proof that the gospel which he preaches is from heaven. A system which will produce these effects must be true.

3. A minister should *so* live among a people as to be able to appeal to them with the utmost confidence in regard to the purity and integrity of his own character, ver. 1, 2. He should so live, and preach, and act, that he will be under no necessity of adducing testimonials from abroad in regard to his character. The effect of his gospel, and the tenor of his life, should be his best testimonial ; and to that he should be able to appeal. A man who is under a necessity, constantly, or often, of defending his own character ; of bolstering it up by testimonials from abroad ; who is obliged to spend much of his time in defending his reputation, or who chooses to spend much of his time in defending it, has usually a character

and reputation *not worth defending.* Let a man live as he ought to do, and he will, in the end, have a good reputation. Let him strive to do the will of God, and save souls, and he will have all the reputation which he *ought* to have. God will take care of his character ; and will give him just as much reputation as it is desirable that he should have ; see Ps. xxxvii. 5, 6.

4. The church is, as it were, an epistle sent by the Lord Jesus, to show his character and will, ver. 3. It is his representative on earth. It holds his truth. It is to imitate his example. It is to show how he lived. And it is to accomplish that which he would accomplish were he personally on earth, and present among men—as a letter is designed to accomplish some important purpose of the writer when absent. The church, therefore, *should* be such as shall appropriately express the will and desire of the Lord Jesus. It should resemble him. It should hold his truth; and it should devote itself with untiring diligence to the great purpose of advancing his designs, and spreading his gospel around the world.

5. Religion has its seat in the heart, ver. 3. It is engraven there. It is written not with ink, or engraven on stone, but it is written by the Spirit of God on the heart. That professed religion, therefore, which does not reach the heart, and which is not felt there, is false and delusive. There *is* no true religion which does not reach and affect the heart.

6. We should feel our dependence on God in all things, ver. 5. We are dependent on him, (1.) For revelation itself. Man had no power of originating the truths which constitute revelation. They are the free and pure gift of God. (2.) For success in saving souls. God only can change the heart. It is not done by human reasoning ; by any power of man ; by any eloquence of persuasion. It is by the power of God ; and if a minister of religion meets with any success, it will be by the presence and by the power of God alone. (3.) We are dependent on him for the power of thought at all ; for clearness of intel-

lect ; for such a state of bodily health as to permit us to think ; for bright conceptions ; for ability to arrange our thoughts; for the power of expressing them clearly ; for such a state of mind as shall be free from vain fancies, and vagaries, and eccentricities; and for such a state as shall mark our plans as those of common sense and prudence.   On such plans much of the comfort of life depends ; and on such plans depends also nearly all the success which men ever meet with in any virtuous and honourable calling. And if men *felt*, as they should do, how much they are dependent on God for the power of *clear thinking*, and for the characteristics of sound sense in their schemes, they would pray for it more than they do ; and would be more grateful that such a rich blessing is so extensively conferred on men.

7. Religion has a living power, ver. 6.   It is not the letter, but the spirit. It is not made up of forms and ceremonies.   It does not consist in cold, external rites, however regular they may be ; nor in formal prayer, or in stated seasons of devotion.   All these will be dead and vain unless the heart is given to God, and to his service. If these are all, there is no religion And if we have no better religion than that, we should at once abandon our hopes, and seek for that which does not kill, but which makes alive.

8. The office of the ministers of the gospel is glorious, and most honourable, ver. 7—9.   It is *far more* honourable than was the office of Moses ; and their work is far more glorious than was his.   *His* consisted in giving the law on tables of stone; in the external splendour which attended its promulgation ; and in introducing a system which must be soon done away.   His was a ministry "of death" and of "condemnation."   *Theirs* is a ministration by which the Holy Spirit is communicated to men— *through* them as channels, or organs by which the saving grace of that Spirit is imparted ; it is a work by which men are made righteous, justified, and accepted; it is a work whose effects are never to fade away, but which are to live amidst the splendours of heaven.

9. The responsibility and solemnity of the work of the ministry.   It was a solemn and responsible work for Moses to give the law amidst the thunders of Sinai to the children of Israel.   It is *much* more solemn to be the medium by which the eternal truths of the gospel are made known to men.   The one, imposing as it was, was designed to be temporary, and was soon to pass away.   The other is to be eternal in its effects, and is to enter vitally and deeply into the eternal destiny of man.   The one pertained to laws written on stone ; the other to influences that are deeply and for ever to affect the heart.   No work *can* be more solemn and responsible than that through which the Holy Spirit, with renewing and sanctifying power, is conveyed to man ; that which is connected with the justification of sinners ; and that which in its effects is to be permanent as the soul itself, and to endure as long as God shall exist.

10. We see the folly of attempting to be justified by the law, ver. 7, 9. It is the ministration of death and of condemnation.   It speaks only to condemn.   Law knows nothing of pardon. It is not given for that purpose ; and no perfect law can contain within itself provisions for pardon.   Besides, no one has ever complied with all the demands of the law; no one ever will. All have sinned.   But if ALL the demands of the law be not complied with, it speaks only to condemn, James ii. 10.   If a man in other respects has been ever so good a citizen, and yet has committed murder, he must die.   So says the law.   If a man has been ever so valiant, and fought ever so bravely, and yet is guilty of an act of treason, he must die.   The question is not what he has been in in other respects, or what else he may, or may not have done, but has he committed *this* offence ?   If he has, the law knows no forgiveness; and pronounces his condemnation.   If pardoned, it must be by some other system than by the regular operation of law.   So with the sinner against

God. If the law is violated, it speaks only to condemn. If he is pardoned, it can be only by the gospel of Jesus Christ.

11. The danger of grieving the Holy Spirit, ver. 8. The gospel is the field of the operations of the Holy Spirit in our world. It is the ministration of the Spirit. It is the channel by which his influences descend on man. To reject that gospel is to reject Him, *and to cut off the soul from all possibility of being brought under his saving influence and power for ever.* He strives with men only in connection with the gospel; and all hope, therefore, of being brought under his saving power, is in attending *to* that gospel, and embracing its provisions. The multitudes, therefore, who are rejecting or neglecting that gospel, are throwing themselves beyond his saving influences; and placing themselves beyond the possibility of salvation.

12. We see the *guilt* of neglecting or rejecting the gospel. It is the scheme, and the only scheme for pardon, ver. 8—10. It is a far more glorious manifestation of the goodness of God than the law of Moses. It is the glorious and benevolent manifestation of God through the incarnation, the sufferings, and the death of his Son. It is the ONLY plan of pardoning mercy that has been, or that will be revealed. If men are not pardoned through that, they are not pardoned at all. If they are not saved *by* that, they must die for ever. What guilt is there, therefore, in neglecting and despising it! What folly is there in turning away from its provisions of mercy, and neglecting to secure an interest in what it provides!

13. The gospel is to spread around the world, and endure to the end of time, ver. 11. It is not like the institutions of Moses, to endure for a limited period, and then to be done away. The cloud and tempest; the thunder and lightning on Mount Sinai which attended the giving of the law, soon disappeared. The unusual and unnatural splendour on the countenance of Moses soon vanished away.

All the magnificence of the Mosaic ritual also soon faded away. But not so the gospel. That abides. That is the *last* dispensation; the *permanent* economy: that under which the affairs of the world are to be brought to an end. That is to pervade all lands; to bless all people; to survive all revolutions; to outlive all the magnificence of courts, and all the splendour of mighty dynasties, and is to endure till this world shall come to an end, and live in its glorious effects for ever and ever. It is, therefore, to be the fixed principle on which all Christians are to act, that the gospel is to be permanent, and is to spread over all lands, and yet fill all nations with joy. And if so, how fervent and unceasing should be their prayers and efforts to accomplish this great and glorious result!

14. We learn from this chapter the duty of preaching in a plain, simple, intelligible manner, ver. 12. Preaching should always be characterised indeed by good sense, and ministers should show that they are not fools, and their preaching should be such as to interest thinking men—for there is no folly or nonsense in the Bible. But their preaching should not be obscure, metaphysical, enigmatical, and abstruse. It should be so simple that the unlettered may learn the plan of salvation; so plain that no one shall mistake it except by his own fault. The *hopes* of the gospel are so clear that there is no need of ambiguity or enigma; no need of abstruse metaphysical reasoning in the pulpit. Nor should there be an attempt to *appear* wise or profound, by studying a dry, abstruse, and cold style and manner. The preacher should be open, plain, simple, sincere; he should *testify* what he feels; should be able to speak as himself animated by *hope*, and to tell of a world of glory to which he is himself looking forward with unspeakable joy.

15. It is the privilege of the Christian to look on the unvailed and unclouded glory of the gospel, ver. 12, 13. He does not look at it through types and shadows. He does not contemplate it when a vail of obscurity is

drawn designedly over it. He sees it in its true beauty and splendour. The Messiah has come, and he may contemplate openly and plainly his glory, and the grandeur of his work. The Jews looked upon it in the light of *prophecy ;* to us it is history. They saw it only through obscure shadows, types, and figures ; we see it in open day, may survey at leisure its full beauty, and contemplate in the fulness of its splendour the gospel of the blessed God. For this we cannot be too thankful ; nor can we be too anxious lest we undervalue our privileges, and abuse the mercies that we enjoy.

16. In reading the Old Testament, we see the importance of suffering the reflected light of the New Testament to be thrown upon it, in order correctly to understand it, ver. 10, 14. It is our privilege to *know* what the institutions of Moses meant ; to see the *end* which he contemplated. And it is our privilege to see what they referred to, and how they prefigured the Messiah, and his gospel. In reading the Old Testament, therefore, there is no reason why we should not take with us the knowledge which we have derived from the New, respecting the character, work, and doctrines of the Messiah ; and to suffer them to influence our understanding of the laws and institutions of Moses. Thus shall we treat the Bible *as a whole,* and allow one part to throw light on another a privilege which we always concede to any book. There is no reason why Christians in reading the Old Testament should remain in the same darkness as the ancient, or the modern Jews.

17. Thus read, the Old Testament will be to us of inestimable value, ver. 14. It is of value not only as *introducing* the gospel ; as furnishing predictions whose fulfilment are full demonstration of the truth of religion ; as containing specimens of the sublimest and purest poetry in the world ; but it is of value as embodying, though amidst many types and shadows and much obscurity, all the great doctrines of the true religion. Though to the Jews, and to the world, there is a vail cast over it ; yet to the Christian there is a beauty and splendour on all its pages—for the coming of Christ has removed that vail, and the sense of those ancient writings is now fully seen. True piety will value the Old Testament, and will find there, in the sweetest poetry in the world, the expression of feelings which the religion of the Messiah only can produce ; and pure and elevated thoughts which could have been originated by nothing but his anticipated coming: It is no mark of piety or of wisdom to disparage the Jewish Scriptures. But the higher the attainments in Christian feeling, the more will the writings of Moses and the prophets be loved.

18. Men may have the Bible, and may read it long, and much, and yet not understand it, ver. 15. So it was, and is with the Jews. The Scriptures were attentively read by them, and yet they did not understand them. So it is still. There is a vail on their heart, and they are blinded. So it is often now with others. Men often read the Bible and see little beauty in it. They read, and they do not understand it. The reason is, the heart is not right. There should be a correspondence of feeling between the heart and the Bible, or a congeniality of view in order to appreciate its value and its truth. No man can understand or appreciate Milton or Cowper who has not a taste like theirs. No man can understand and appreciate a poem or an essay on patriotism, who is not a lover of his country ; or on chastity, who is impure ; or on temperance, who is intemperate ; or on virtue in general, who is a stranger to virtue in every form. And so in reading the Bible. To appreciate and understand fully the writings of David, Isaiah, Paul, or John, we must have their feelings : our hearts must glow with their love to God and the Redeemer ; we must feel as they did the guilt and burden of sin ; and we must rejoice as they did in the hope of deliverance, and in the prospect of heaven. Till men have these feelings, they are not to wonder that the Bible

CHAPTER IV.

THEREFORE, seeing we have this ministry, as we have received ^a mercy, we faint not ;

2 But have renounced the hidden things of ¹ dishonesty, not

a 1 Cor. 7.25.   1 shame.

walking in craftiness, nor handling the word of God deceitfully, ^b but by manifestation of the truth commending ourselves to every man's conscience in the sight of God.

b chap. 2.17.

is to them a dead letter, or a sealed book, and that they do not understand it, or see any beauty in its pages.

19. This chapter furnishes an argument for the fidelity and truth of the statement of Paul, ver. 15. The argument is, that his description is as applicable to the Jews now as it was in his own time—and that, therefore, it must have been drawn from nature. The same vail is on their hearts now as in his time ; there is the same blindness and darkness in regard to the true meaning of their Scriptures. The language of Paul will accurately express that blindness now ; and his description, therefore, is not drawn from fancy, but from fact. It is true now in regard to that singular people, and it was true in his own time ; and the lapse of eighteen hundred years has only served to confirm the truth of his description in regard to the people of his own nation and time.

20. That veil is to be removed only by their turning to God, ver. 16. It is only by true conversion that the mind can be brought to a full and clear understanding of the Scriptures ; and that event will yet take place in regard to the Jews. They shall yet be converted to the Messiah whom their fathers slew, and whom they have so long rejected ; and when that event shall occur, they shall see the beauty of their own Scriptures, and rejoice in the promises and glorious hopes which they hold out to the view.

21. The duty of *meditating* much on the glory of the gospel, ver. 18. It is by that we are purified. It is by keeping it constantly before the mind ; dwelling on its splendour ; thinking of its glorious truths, that we become transformed into the same image, and made like God. If the character is formed by the objects which we contemplate, and with which

we are familiar ; if we are insensibly moulded in our feelings and principles by that with which we constantly associate, then we should *think* much of the truths of the gospel. We should pray much—for thus we come in contact with God and his truth. We should read the Scripture much. We should commune with the good and the pure. We should make our companions of those who most love the Lord Jesus, and most decidedly bear his image. We should think much of a pure heaven. Thus shall we be moulded, insensibly it may be, but certainly, into the image of a holy God and Saviour, and be prepared for a pure and holy heaven.

CHAPTER IV.

THIS chapter is intimately connected with the preceding, and is indeed merely a statement of the consequences or results of the doctrine advanced there. In that chapter, Paul had stated the clearness and plainness of the gospel as contrasted with the institutions of Moses, and particularly that the Christian ministry was a ministration more glorious than that of Moses. It was more clear. It was a ministration of justification (ver. 9), and of the Spirit (ver. 8), and was a ministration where they were permitted to look upon the unvailed and unclouded glories of God, ver. 18. In this chapter he states some of the *consequences,* or *results* of their being called to this ministry ; and the design is, to magnify the office of the ministry ; to show the sustaining power of the truths which they preached ; the interest which the Corinthian Christians and all other Christians had in the ministry, and this to conciliate their favour ; and to show what there was to comfort them in the various trials to which as ministers they were exposed. Paul states therefore in this chapter—

1. That these clear and elevated views of the gospel sustained him; kept him from fainting; preserved him from deceit and all improper acts; made him open and honest; since he had no necessity for craft and guilt, but proclaimed a system of religion which *could* be commended to every man's conscience, and be seen to be true, ver. 1, 2.

2. That if any persons were lost, it was not the fault of the gospel, ver. 3, 4. That was clear, open, plain, glorious, and might be understood; and if they were lost, it was to be traced to the malign influence of the god of this world, and not to the gospel.

3. That the great purpose of Paul and his associates was to make known this clear and glorious truth of the gospel, and that, therefore, the apostles did not preach themselves, but Christ Jesus, the revealer and source of all this glory, ver. 5, 6. Their sole object was to show forth this pure and glorious light of the gospel.

4. That it was so arranged by God's appointment and providence that all the glory of the results of the ministry should be his, ver. 7—11. He had taken especial care that they should have no cause of self-exultation or glorying in preaching the gospel; and had taken effectual means that they should be humbled, and not lifted up with pride, from the fact that they were commissioned to make known such glorious truths, and had a ministry more honourable than that of Moses. He had, therefore, committed the treasure to earthen vessels; to frail, weak, dying men, and to men in humble life (ver. 7), and he had called them to submit to constant trials of persecution, poverty, peril, and want, in order that they might be humbled, and that God might manifestly have all the glory, ver. 8—11.

5. All this was for the sake of the church, a fact which was adapted to conciliate the favour of Christians, and excite their sympathy in the sufferings of the apostles, and to lead them to honour the ministry in a proper manner, ver. 12—15. It was not for their own welfare, happiness, honour, or emolument that they endured these trials in the ministry; it was that the church might be benefited, and thus abundant praise redound to God.

6. These considerations sustained them in their trials, ver. 16—18. They *had* comfort in all their afflictions. They felt that they were doing and suffering these things for the salvation of souls, and the glory of God, (ver. 16); they had inward strength given them every day, though the outward man perished (ver. 16); they knew that the result of this would be an eternal weight of glory (ver. 17); and they were enabled to look to another and a better world; to keep the eye on heaven, and to contemplate by faith the things which were unseen and eternal, ver. 18. These things supported them; and thus upheld they went cheerfully to their great work, and met with calmness and joy all the trials which it involved.

1. *Therefore* (Διὰ τοῦτο). On account of this. That is, because the light of the gospel is so clear; because it reveals so glorious truths, and all obscurity is taken away, and we are permitted to behold as in a mirror the glory of the Lord, chap. iii. 18. Since the glories of the gospel dispensation are so great, and its effects on the heart are so transforming and purifying. The object is, to show the effect of being intrusted with such a ministry, on the character of his preaching. ¶ *Seeing we have this ministry*. The gospel ministry, so much more glorious than that of Moses (chap. iii. 6); which is the ministry by which the Holy Spirit acts on the hearts of men (chap. iii. 8); which is the ministry of that system by which men are justified (chap. iii. 9); and which is the ministry of a system so pure and unclouded, chap. iii. 9—11, 18. ¶ *As we have received mercy*. Tindal renders this, "even as mercy is sure in us." The idea is, that it was by the mere mercy and favour of God, that he had been intrusted with the ministry, and the object of Paul is doubtless to prevent the *appearance* of arrogance and self-confidence by stating that it was to be traced entirely to God that he was put into the min-

istry. He doubtless had his eye on the fact that he had been a persecutor and blasphemer; and that it was by the mere favour of God that he had been converted and intrusted with the ministry, 1 Tim. i. 13. Nothing will more effectually humble a minister, and prevent his assuming any arrogant and self-confident airs, than to look over his past life; especially if his life was one of blasphemy, vice, or infidelity; and to remember that it is by the mere mercy of God that he is intrusted with the high office of an ambassador of Jesus Christ. Paul never forgot to trace his hope, his appointment to the ministerial office, and his success, to the mere grace of God. ¶ *We faint not.* This is one of the *effects* of being intrusted with such a ministry. The word here used (ἐκκακοῦμεν) means, properly, to turn out a coward; to lose one's courage; then to be faint-hearted, to faint, to despond, in view of trial, difficulty, &c.—*Robinson.* Here it means, that by the mercy of God, he was not disheartened by the difficulties which he met; his faith and zeal did not flag; he was enabled to be faithful, and laborious, and his courage always kept up, and his mind was filled with cheerfulness; see Note on chap. ii. 14. He was deterred by no difficulties; embarrassed by no opposition; driven from his purpose by no persecution; and his strength did not fail under any trials. The consciousness of being intrusted with *such* a ministry animated him; and the mercy and grace of God sustained him.

2. *But have renounced* (ἀπειπάμεθα from ἀπὸ and εἶπον). The word means properly to speak out or off; to refuse or deny; to interdict or forbid. Here it means, to renounce, or disown; to spurn, or scorn with aversion. It occurs no where else in the New Testament; and the sense here is, that the apostles had such a view of the truth of religion, and the glory of the Christian scheme (chap. iii. 13—18), as to lead them to discard every thing that was disguised, and artful, and crafty; every thing like deceit and fraud. The religions of the heathen were made up mainly of trick, and were supported by deception practised on the ignorant, and on the mass of men. Paul says, that he and his fellow-labourers had such views of the truth, and glory, and holiness of the Christian scheme, as to lead them solemnly to abjure and abhor all such dishonest tricks and devices. Truth never needs such arts; and no cause will long succeed by mere trick and cunning. ¶ *The hidden things of dishonesty.* Marg. *shame.* The Greek word most commonly means shame, or disgrace. The hidden things of shame here mean disgraceful conduct; clandestine and secret arts, which were in themselves shameful and disgraceful. They denote all *underhanded* dealings; all dishonest artifices and plans, such as were common among the heathen, and such probably as the false teachers adopted in the propagation of their opinions at Corinth. The expression here does not imply that the apostles ever had any thing to do with such arts; but that they solemnly abjured and abhorred them. Religion is open, plain, straight-forward. It has no alliance with cunning, and trick, and artifice. It should be defended openly; stated clearly; and urged with steady argument. It is a work of light, and not of darkness. ¶ *Not walking in craftiness.* Not acting craftily; not behaving in a crafty manner. The word here used (πανουργία from πᾶν, all, ἔργον, work, i. e. doing every thing, or capable of doing any thing) denotes shrewdness, cunning, and craft. This was common; and this was probably practised by the false teachers in Corinth. With this Paul says he had nothing to do. He did not adopt a course of carnal wisdom and policy (Note, chap. i. 12); he did not attempt to impose upon them, or to deceive them; or to make his way by subtile and deceitful arts. True religion can never be advanced by trick and craftiness. ¶ *Nor handling the word of God deceitfully* (δολοῦντες). Not falsifying; or deceitfully corrupting or disguising the truth of God. The phrase seems to be synonymous with that used in chap. ii. 17, and rendered "corrupt the word of God;" see Note on that verse. It

properly means to falsify, adulterate, corrupt, by Jewish traditions, &c. (Robinson, Bloomfield, Doddridge, &c.); or it may mean, as in our translation, to handle in a deceitful manner; to make use of trick and art in propagating and defending it. Tindal renders it, "neither corrupt we the word of God." ¶ *But by manifestation of the truth.* By making the truth manifest; *i. e.* by a simple exhibition of the truth. By stating it just as it is, in an undisguised and open manner. Not by adulterating it with foreign mixtures; not by mingling it with philosophy, or traditions; not by blunting its edge, or concealing any thing, or explaining it away; but by an open, plain, straight-forward exhibition of it as it is in Jesus. Preaching should consist in a simple exhibition of the truth. There is no deceit in the gospel itself; and there should be none in the manner of exhibiting it. It should consist of a simple statement of things as they are. The whole design of preaching is, to make known the truth. And this is done in an effectual manner only when it is simple, open, undisguised, without craft, and without deceit. ¶ *Commending ourselves to every man's conscience.* That is, so speaking the truth that every man's conscience shall approve it *as* true · every man shall see it to be true, and to be in accordance with what he knows to be right. Conscience is that faculty of the mind which distinguishes between right and wrong, and which prompts us to choose the former and avoid the latter; John viii. 9; Note, Rom. ii. 15; 1 Cor. x. 25, 27—29; 2 Cor. i. 12. It is implied here, (1.) That a course of life, and a manner of preaching that shall be free from dishonesty, and art, and trick, will be such as the consciences of men will approve. Paul sought such a course of life as should accord with their sense of *right,* and thus serve to commend the gospel to them. (2.) That the gospel may be so preached as to be seen by men to be true; so as to be approved as right; and so that every man's conscience shall bear testimony to its truth. Men do not *love* it, but they may see

that it is *true;* they may hate it, but they may see that the truth which condemns their practices is from heaven. This is an exceedingly important principle in regard to preaching, and vastly momentous in its bearing on the views which ministers should have of their own work. The gospel is reasonable. It may be seen to be true by every man to whom it is preached. And it should be the aim of every preacher *so* to preach it, as to enlist the consciences of his hearers in his favour. And it is a very material fact that *when* so preached the conscience and reason of every man *is* in its favour, and they know that it is true even when it pronounces their own condemnation, and denounces their own sins. This passage proves, therefore, the following things. (1.) That the gospel *may* be so preached as to be seen to be true by all men. Men are capable of seeing the truth, and even when they do not love it; they can perceive that it has demonstration that it is from God. It is a system so reasonable; so well established by evidence; so fortified by miracles, and the fulfilment of prophecies; so pure in its nature; so well-adapted to man; so fitted to his condition, and so well designed to make him better; and so happy in its influence on society, that men may be led to see that it is *true.* And this I take to be the case with almost all those men who habitually attend on the preaching of the gospel. Infidels do not *often* visit the sanctuary; and when they are in the habit of doing it, it is a fact that they gradually come to the conviction that the Christian religion is true. It is rare to find professed infidels in our places of worship; and the great mass of those who attend on the preaching of the gospel may be set down as *speculative* believers in the truth of Christianity. (2.) The consciences of men are on the side of truth, and the gospel may be so preached as to enlist their consciences in its favour. Conscience prompts to do right, and condemns us if we do wrong. It can never be made to approve of wrong, never **to** give a man peace if he does that which

3 But if our gospel be hid, it is hid to them *a* that are lost :

a 2 Th. 2.10.

4 In whom the god *a* of this world hath blinded the minds of

a John 12.31,40.

he knows to be evil. By no art or device ; by no system of laws, or bad government ; by no training or discipline, can it be made the advocate of sin. In all lands, at all times, and in all circumstances, it prompts a man to do what is right, and condemns him if he does wrong. It may be silenced for a time ; it may be " seared as with a hot iron," and for a time be insensible, but if it speak at all, it speaks to prompt a man to do what he believes to be right, and condemns him if he does that which is wrong. The consciences of men are on the side of the gospel ; and it is only their hearts which are opposed to it. Their consciences are in favour of the gospel in the following, among other respects. (*a*) They approve of it as a just, pure, holy, and reasonable system ; as in accordance with what they feel to be right ; as recommending that which ought to be done, and forbidding that which ought not to be done. (*b*) In its special requirements on themselves. Their consciences tell them that they *ought* to love God with all the heart ; to repent of their sins ; to trust in that Saviour who died for them ; and to lead a life of prayer and of devotedness to the service of God ; that they ought to be sincere and humble Christians, and prepare to meet God in peace. (*c*) Their consciences approve the truth that condemns them. No matter how strict it may seem to be ; no matter how loud its denunciation against their sins ; no matter how much the gospel may condemn their pride, avarice, sensuality, levity, dishonesty, fraud, intemperance, profaneness, blasphemy, or their neglect of their soul, yet their consciences approve of it as right, and proclaim that these things *ought* to be condemned, and ought to be abandoned. The heart may *love* them, but the conscience cannot be made to approve them. And the minister of the gospel may *always* approach his people, or an individual man, with the assurance that however

much they may *love* the ways of sin, yet that he has their *consciences* in his favour, and that in urging the claims of God on them, their consciences will *always* coincide with his appeals. (3.) The *way* in which a minister is to commend himself to the consciences of men, is that which was pursued by Paul. He must (*a*) Have a clear and unwavering conviction of the truth himself. On this subject he should have no doubt. He should be able to look on it as on a burnished mirror (Note, chap. iii. 18) ; and to see its glory as with open face. (*b*) It should be by the simple statement of the truth of the gospel. Not by preaching philosophy, or metaphysics, or the traditions of man, or the sentiments of theologians, but the simple truths of the gospel of Jesus Christ. Men may be made to see that these *are* truths, and God will take care that the reason and consciences of men shall be in their favour. (*c*) By the absence of all trick and cunning, and disguised and subtle arts. The gospel has nothing of these in itself, and it will never approve of them, nor will God bless them. A minister of Jesus should be frank, open, undisguised, and candid. He should make a sober and elevated appeal to the reason and conscience of man. The gospel is not " a cunningly-devised fable ;" it has no trick in itself, and the ministers of religion should solemnly abjure all the hidden things of dishonesty. ¶ *In the sight of God.* As in the immediate presence of God. We act as if we felt that his eye was upon us ; and this consideration serves to keep us from the hidden things of dishonesty, and from improper arts in spreading the true religion ; see Note on chap. ii. 17.

3. *But if our gospel be hid.* Paul here calls it *his* gospel, because it was that which he preached, or the message which he bore ; see Note, Rom. xvi. 25. The sense here is, " if the gospel which I preach is not understood ; if its meaning is obscure or hidden ; if its glory is not seen." It

them which believe not, lest the light of the glorious gospel of

Christ, who is the image *a* of God, should shine unto them.

is *implied* here, that to many the beauty and glory of the gospel was not perceived. This was undeniable, notwithstanding the plainness and fulness with which its truths were made known. The *object* of Paul here is, to state that this fact was not to be traced to any want of clearness in the gospel itself, but to other causes, and thus probably to meet an objection which might be made to his argument about the clearness and fulness of the revelation in the gospel. In the language which Paul uses here, there is undoubted allusion to what he had said respecting Moses, who put a vail on his face, chap. iii 13 He had hid, or concealed his face, as emblematic of the nature of his institutions (Note, chap. iii. 14) ; and here Paul says that it was not to be denied that the gospel was *vailed* also to some. But it was not from the nature of the gospel. It was not because God had purposely concealed its meaning. It was not from any want of clearness in itself. It was to be traced to other causes. ¶ *It is hid to them that are lost.* On the meaning of the word here rendered " lost ;" see Note, chap. ii. 15, there rendered "perish." It is hid among them who are about to perish ; who are perishing (*ἐν τοῖς ἀπολλυμένοις*); those who deserve to perish. It is concealed only among that class who may be designated *as* the perishing, or *as* the lost. Grotius explains this, " those who deserve to perish, who foster their vices, and will not see the truth which condemns those vices." And he adds, that this might very well be, for, " however conspicuous the gospel was in itself, yet like the sun it would not be visible to the blind." The cause was not in the gospel, but in themselves. This verse teaches, therefore, (1.) That the beauty of the gospel may be hidden from many of the human family. This is a matter of simple fact. There are thousands and millions to whom it is preached who see no beauty in it, and who regard it as foolishness. (2.)

That there is a class of men who may be called, even now, *the lost.* They are lost to virtue, to piety, to happiness, to hope. They deserve to perish ; and they are hastening to merited ruin. This class in the time of Paul was large ; and it is large now. It is composed of those to whom the gospel is hidden, or to whom it appears to be vailed, and who see no beauty in it. It is made up indeed of all the profane, polluted, and vile ; but their *characteristic* feature is, that the gospel is hidden from them, and that they see no beauty and glory in it. (3.) This is not the fault of the gospel. It is not the fault of the sun when men shut their eyes and will not see it. It is not the fault of a running stream, or a bubbling fountain, if men will not drink of it, but rather choose to die of thirst. The gospel does not obscure and conceal its own glory any more than the sun does. It is in itself a clear and full revelation of God and his grace ; and that glory is adapted to shed light upon the benighted minds of men.

1. *In whom.* In respect to whom ; among whom ; or in whose hearts. The design of this verse is *to account* for the fact that the glory of the gospel was not seen by them. It is to be traced entirely to the agency of him whom Paul here calls "the god of this world." ¶ *The god of this world.* There can be no doubt that Satan is here designated by this appellation ; though some of the fathers supposed that it means the true God, and *Clarke* inclines to this opinion. In John xii. 31, he is called " the prince of this world." In Eph. ii. 2, he is called " the prince of the power of the air." And in Eph. vi. 12, the same bad influence is referred to under the names of " principalities, and powers," " the rulers of the darkness of this world," and " spiritual wickedness in high places." The name "god" is here given to him, not because he has any divine attributes, but because he actually has the homage of the men of

this world *as* their god, as the being who is really worshipped, or who has the affections of their hearts in the same way as it is given to idols. By "this world" is meant the wicked world; or the mass of men. He has dominion over the world. They obey his will; they execute his plans; they further his purposes, and they are his obedient subjects. He has subdued the world to himself, and was really adored in the place of the true God; see Note on 1 Cor. x. 20. "They sacrificed to devils and not to God." Here it is meant by the declaration that Satan is the god of this world, (1.) That the world at large was under his control and direction. He secured the apostacy of man, and early brought him to follow his plans; and he has maintained his sceptre and dominion since. No more abject submission could be desired by him than has been rendered by the mass of men. (2.) The *idolatrous* world particularly is under his control, and subject to him; 1 Cor. x. 20. He is worshipped there; and the religious rites and ceremonies of the heathen are in general just such as a mighty being who hated human happiness, and who sought pollution, obscenity, wretchedness, and blood would appoint; and over all the heathen world his power is absolute. In the time of Paul all the world, except the Jews and Christians, was sunk in heathen degradation. (3.) He rules in the hearts and lives of all wicked men—and the world is full of wicked men. They obey him, and submit to his will in executing fraud, and rapine, and piracy, and murder, and adultery, and lewdness; in wars and fightings; in their amusements and pastimes; in dishonesty and falsehood. The dominion of Satan over this world has been, and is still almost universal and absolute; nor has the lapse of eighteen hundred years rendered the appellation improper as descriptive of his influence, that he is the god of this world. The world pursues his plans; yields to his temptations; neglects, or rejects the reign of God as he pleases; and submits to his sceptre, and is still full of abomina-

tion, cruelty, and pollution, as he desires it to be. ¶ *Hath blinded the minds of them which believe not.* Of all who discern no beauty in the gospel, and who reject it. It is implied here, (1.) That the minds of unbelievers are blinded; that they perceive no beauty in the gospel. This is often affirmed of those who reject the gospel, and who live in sin; see Note on chap. ii. 13; Mat. xxiii. 16, 17, 26; Luke iv. 18; John ix. 39; xii. 40; Rom. xi. 7. The sense is, that they did not *see* the spiritual beauty and glory of the plan of redemption. They act in reference to that as they would in reference to this world, if a bandage were over their eyes, and they saw not the light of the sun, the beauty of the landscape, the path in which they should go, or the countenance of a friend. All is dark, and obscure, and destitute of beauty to *them*, however much beauty may be seen in all these objects by others. (2.) That this is done by the agency of Satan; and that his dominion is secured by keeping the world in darkness. The affirmation is direct and positive, that it is by his agency that it is done. Some of the *modes* in which it is done are the following. (*a*) By a direct influence on the minds of men. I do not know why it is absurd to suppose that one intellect may, in some way unknown to us, have access to another, and have power to influence it; nor can it be proved that Satan may not have power to pervert the understanding; to derange its powers; to distract its attention; and to give in view of the mind a wholly delusive relative importance to objects. In the time of the Saviour it cannot be doubted that in the numerous cases of demoniacal possessions, Satan directly affected the minds of men; nor is there any reason to think that he has ceased to delude and destroy them. (*b*) By the false philosophy which has prevailed—a large part of which seems to have been contrived as if on purpose to deceive the world, and destroy the peace and happiness of men. (*c*) By the systems of superstition and idolatry. All these seem to be under the control of one master mind. They are so well conceived and adapted to prostrate the moral powers; to fetter the intellect; to pervert the will; to make men debased, sunken, polluted, and degraded; and they so uniformly accomplish this effect, that they have all the marks of being under the control of one mighty mind, and of having been devised to accomplish his purposes over men. (*d*) By producing in the minds of men a wholly disproportionate view of the value of objects. *A very small object held before the eye will shut out the light of the sun.* A piece of money of the smallest value laid on the eye will make every thing appear dark, and prevent all the glory of midday from reaching the seat of vision. And so it is with the things of this world. They are placed directly before us, and are placed directly between us and the glory of the gospel. And the trifles of wealth and of fashion; the objects of pleasure and ambition, are made to assume an importance in view of the mind which wholly excludes the glory of the gospel, and shuts out all the realities of the eternal world. And he does it (*e*) By the blinding influence of passion and vice. Before a vicious mind all is dark and obscure. There is no beauty in truth, in chastity, or honesty, or in the fear and love of God. Vice always renders the mind blind, and the heart hard, and shrouds every thing in the moral world in midnight. And in order to blind the minds of men to the glory of the gospel, Satan has only to place splendid schemes of speculation before men; to tempt them to climb the steeps of ambition; to entice them to scenes of gayety; to secure the erection of theatres, and gambling houses, and houses of infamy and pollution; to fill the cities and towns of a land with taverns and dram-shops; and to give opportunity everywhere for the full play and unrestrained indulgence of passion; and the glory of the gospel will be as effectually *unseen* as the glory of the sun is in the darkest night. ¶ *Lest the light*, &c. This passage states the *design* for which Satan blinds the minds of men. It is

because he *hates* the gospel, and wishes to prevent its influence and spread in the world. Satan has always hated and opposed it, and all his arts have been employed to arrest its diffusion on earth. The word *light* here means excellence, beauty, or splendour. Light is the emblem of knowledge, purity, or innocence; and is here and elsewhere applied to the gospel, because it removes the errors, and sins, and wretchedness of men, as the light of the sun scatters the shades of night. This purpose of preventing the light of the gospel shining on men, Satan will endeavour to accomplish by all the means in his power. It is his *grand* object in this world, because it is by the gospel only that men can be saved; by that that God is glorified on earth more than by any thing else; and because, therefore, if he can prevent sinners from embracing that, he will secure their destruction, and most effectually show his hatred of God. And it is to Satan a matter of little importance what men *may be*, or *are*, provided they are NOT Christians. They may be amiable, moral, accomplished, rich, honoured, esteemed by the world, because in the possession of all these he may be equally sure of their ruin, and *because*, also, these things may contribute somewhat to turn away their minds from the gospel. Satan, therefore, will not oppose plans of gain or ambition; he will not oppose purposes of fashion and amusement; he may not oppose schemes by which we desire to rise in the world; he will not oppose the theatre, the ball-room, the dance, or the song; he will not oppose thoughtless mirth; but the moment the gospel begins to shine on the benighted mind, that moment he will make resistance, and then all his power will be concentrated. ¶ *The glorious gospel.* Gr. ' The gospel of the glory of Christ,' a Hebraism for the glorious gospel. Mr. Locke renders it, " the glorious brightness of the light of the gospel of Christ," and supposes it means the brightness, or clearness, of the doctrine wherein Christ is manifested in the gospel.— It is all light, and splendour, and

5 For we preach not ourselves, but Christ Jesus the Lord ; and ourselves your servants for Jesus' sake.

beauty, compared with the dark systems of philosophy and heathenism. It is glorious, for it is full of splendour ; makes known the glorious God ; discloses a glorious plan of salvation ; and conducts ignorant, weak, and degraded man to a world of light. No two words in our language are so full of rich and precious meaning, as the phrase "glorious gospel." ¶ *Who is the image of God.* Christ is called the image of God, (1.) In respect to his divine nature, his exact resemblance to God in his divine attributes and perfections ; see Col. i. 15, and Heb. i. 3 ; and, (2.) In his moral attributes as Mediator, as showing forth the glory of the Father to men. He *resembles* God, and in him we see the divine glory and perfections embodied, and shine forth. It is from his *resemblance* to God in all respects that he is called his image ; and it is through him that the divine perfections are made known to men.—It is an object of especial dislike and hatred to Satan that the glory of Christ, who is the image of God, should shine on men, and fill their hearts. Satan hates that image ; he hates that men should become like God ; and he hates all that has a resemblance to the great and glorious Jehovah.

5. *For we preach not ourselves.* The connection here is not very apparent, and the design of this verse has been variously understood. The connection seems to me to be this. Paul gives here a reason for what he had said in the previous parts of the epistle respecting his conduct in the ministry. He had said that his course had been open, and pure, and free from all dishonest arts and tricks, and that he had not corrupted the word of God, or resorted to any artifice to accomplish his designs ; chap. ii. 17 ; iv. 1, 2. The *reason* of this he here says is, that he had not preached himself, or sought to advance his own interest. He regarded himself as sent to make known a Saviour ; himself as bound by all means to promote his cause, and to imitate him. Other

men—the false teachers, and the cunning priests of the heathen religion—sought to advance their own interest, and to perpetuate a system of delusion that would be profitable to themselves ; and they therefore resorted to all arts, and stratagems, and cunning devices to perpetuate their authority, and extend their influence. But the fact that Paul and his associates went forth to make known the Lord Jesus, was a reason why they avoided all such dishonest arts and artifices. " We are merely the *ambassadors* of another. We are not *principals* in this business, and do not despatch it as a business of our own, but we transact it as the *agents* for another, *i. e.* for the Lord Jesus, and we feel ourselves bound, therefore, to do it as he would have done it himself ; and as he was free from all trick, and dishonest art, we feel bound to be also." This seems to me to be the design of this passage. Ministers may be said to preach themselves in the following ways. (1.) When their preaching has a primary reference to their own interest ; and when they engage in it to advance their reputation, or to secure in some way their own advantage. When they aim at exalting their authority, extending their influence, or in any way promoting their own welfare (2.) When they proclaim their own opinions and not the gospel of Christ ; when they derive their doctrines from their own reasonings, and not from the Bible. (3.) When they put themselves forward ; speak much of themselves ; refer often to themselves ; are vain of their powers of reasoning, of their eloquence, and of their learning, and seek to make these known rather than the simple truths of the gospel. In one word, when self is primary, and the gospel is secondary ; when they prostitute the ministry to gain popularity ; to live a life of ease ; to be respected ; to obtain a livelihood ; to gain influence ; to rule over a people ; and to make the preaching of the gospel merely *an occasion* of advancing themselves in the world.—Such a plan, it is implied here, would lead to dishonest arts and devices, and to trick and stratagem to accomplish the end in view. And it is implied here, also, that to avoid all such tricks and arts the true way is not to preach ourselves, but Jesus Christ. ¶ *But Christ Jesus the Lord.* This Paul states to be the only purpose of the ministry. It is so far the sole design of the ministry that had it not been to make known the Lord Jesus, it would never have been established; and whatever other objects are secured by its appointment, and whatever other truths are to be illustrated and enforced by the ministry, yet, if this is not the primary subject, and if every other object is not made subservient to this, the design of the ministry is not secured. The word "Christ" properly means the anointed, *i. e.* the Messiah, the anointed of God for this great office (see Note, Mat. i. 1); but it is used in the New Testament as a proper name, the name that was appropriate to *Jesus.* Still it may be used with a reference to the fact of the Messiahship, and not merely as a proper name, and in this place it may mean that they preached Jesus *as* the Messiah, or the Christ, and defended his claims to that high appointment. The word "Lord" also is used to designate him (Mark xi. 3; John xx. 25); and when it stands by itself in the New Testament, it denotes the Lord Jesus (Note, Acts i. 24); but it properly denotes one who has rule or authority, or proprietorship; and it is used here not merely as a part of the appropriate title of the Saviour, but with reference to the fact that he had the supreme headship, or lordship over the church and the world. This important passage, therefore, means, that they made it their sole business to make known Jesus the Messiah, or the Christ, as the supreme head and Lord of people; *i. e.* to set forth the Messiahship and the lordship of Jesus of Nazareth, appointed to these high offices by God. To do this, or to preach Jesus Christ the Lord, implies the following things. (1.) To prove that he is the Messiah

so often predicted in the Old Testament, and so long expected by the Jewish people. To do this was a very vital part of the work of the ministry in the time of the apostles, and was essential to their success in all their attempts to convert the Jews; and to do this will be no less important in all attempts to bring the Jews now or in future times to the knowledge of the truth. No man *can* be successful among them who is not able to prove that Jesus is the Messiah.—It is not indeed so vital and leading a point now in reference to those to whom the ministers of the gospel usually preach; and it is probable that the importance of this argument is by many overlooked, and that it is not urged as it should be by those who "preach Christ Jesus the Lord." It involves the whole argument for the truth of Christianity. It leads to all the demonstrations that this religion is from God; and the establishment of the proposition that Jesus is the Messiah, is one of the most direct and certain ways of proving that his religion is from heaven. For (*a*) It contains the argument from the fulfilment of the prophecies—one of the main evidences of the truth of revelation; and (*b*) It involves an examination of all the evidences that Jesus gave that he was the Messiah sent from God, and of course an examination of all the miracles that he wrought in attestation of his divine mission. The first object of a preacher, therefore, is to demonstrate that Jesus is sent from God in accordance with the predictions of the prophets. (2.) To proclaim the truths that *he taught.* To make known his sentiments, and his doctrines, and not our own. This includes, of course, all that he taught respecting God, and respecting man; all that he taught respecting his own nature, and the design of his coming; all that he taught respecting the character of the human heart, and about human obligation and duty; all that he taught respecting death, the judgment, and eternity—respecting an eternal heaven, and an eternal hell. To explain, enforce, and vindicate his doctrines, is one great design of the ministry; and were there nothing else, this would be a field sufficiently ample to employ the life; sufficiently glorious to employ the best talents of man. The minister of the gospel is to teach the sentiments and doctrines of Jesus Christ, in contradistinction from all his own sentiments, and from all the doctrines of mere philosophy. He is not to teach science, or mere morals, but he is to proclaim and defend the doctrines of the Redeemer. (3.) He is to make known *the facts* of the Saviour's life. He is to show how he lived—to hold up his example in all the trying circumstances in which he was placed. For he came to show by his life what the law required; and to show how men *should* live. And it is the office of the Christian ministry, or a part of their work in preaching "Christ Jesus the Lord," to show how he lived, and to set forth his self-denial, his meekness, his purity, his blameless life, his spirit of prayer, his submission to the divine will, his patience in suffering, his forgiveness of his enemies, his tenderness to the afflicted, the weak, and the tempted; and the manner of his death. Were *this* all, it would be enough to employ the whole of a minister's life, and to command the best talents of the world. For he was the only perfectly pure model; and his example is to be followed by all his people, and his example is designed to exert a deep and wide influence on the world. Piety flourishes just in proportion as the pure example of Jesus Christ is kept before a people; and the world is made happier and better just as that example is kept constantly in view. To the gay and the thoughtless, the ministers of the gospel are to show how serious and calm was the Redeemer; to the worldly-minded, to show how he lived above the world; to the avaricious, how benevolent he was; to the profane and licentious, how pure he was; to the tempted, how he endured temptation; to the afflicted, how patient and resigned; to the dying, how he died:—to all, to show how holy, and heavenly-minded, and prayerful, and pure he was; in order

that they may be won to the same purity, and be prepared to dwell with him in his kingdom. (4.) To set forth the design of his death. To show why he came to die; and what was the great object to be effected by his sufferings and death. To exhibit, therefore, the sorrows of his life; to describe his many trials; to dwell upon his sufferings in the garden of Gethsemane, and on the cross. To show *why* he died, and what was to be the influence of his death on the destiny of man. To show *how* it makes an atonement for sin; how it reconciles God to man; how it is made efficacious in the justification and the sanctification of the sinner. And were there nothing else, *this* would be sufficient to employ all the time, and the best talents in the ministry. For the salvation of the soul depends on the proper exhibition of the design of the death of the Redeemer. There is no salvation but through his blood; and hence the nature and design of his atoning sacrifice is to be exhibited to every man, and the offers of mercy through that death to be pressed upon the attention of every sinner. (5.) To set forth the truth and the design of his resurrection. To *prove* that he rose from the dead, and that he ascended to heaven; and to show the influence of his resurrection on our hopes and destiny. The whole structure of Christianity is dependent on making out the fact that he rose; and *if* he rose, all the difficulties in the doctrine of the resurrection of the dead are removed at once, and his people will also rise. The influence of that fact, therefore, on our hopes and on our prospects for eternity, is to be shown by the ministry of the gospel; and were there nothing else, *this* would be ample to command all the time, and the best talents of the ministry. (6.) To proclaim him as "Lord." This is expressly specified in the passage before us. " For we preach Christ Jesus THE LORD;" we proclaim him *as* the Lord. That is, he is to be preached as having dominion over the conscience; as the supreme Ruler in his Church; as above all councils, and

6 For God, who commanded *a* the light to shine out of darkness,

a Gen. 1. 3.

synods, and conferences, and all human authority; as having a right to legislate for his people; a right to prescribe their mode of worship; a right to define and determine the doctrines which they shall believe. He is to be proclaimed also as ruling over all, and as exalted in his mediatorial character over all worlds, and as having all things put beneath his feet; Ps. ii. 6; Isa. ix. 6, 7; Mat. xxviii. 18; John xvii. 2; Eph. i. 20; Heb. ii. 8. ¶ *And ourselves your servants*, &c. So far as we make any mention of ourselves, it is to declare that we are your servants, and that we are bound to promote your welfare in the cause and for the sake of the Redeemer. That is, they were their servants in all things in which they could advance the interests of the Redeemer's kingdom among them. The doctrine is, that they regarded themselves as under obligation not to seek their own interest, or to build up their own reputation and cause, but to seek the welfare of the church; and promote its interests, as a servant does that of his master. They should not seek to lord it over God's heritage, and to claim supreme and independent authority. They were not masters but servants. The church at large was the master, and they were its servants. This implies the following things. (1.) That the *time* of ministers belongs to the church, and should be employed in its welfare. It is not their own; and it is not to be employed in farming, or in speculating, or in trafficking, or in idleness, or in lounging, or in unprofitable visiting, or in mere science, or in reading or making books that will not advance the interests of the church. The time of the ministry is not for ease, or ambition, or self-indulgence, but is to promote the interests of the body of Christ. So Paul felt, and so he lived. (2.) Their *talents* belong to the church. All their original talents, and all that they can acquire, should be honestly devoted to the welfare of the church of the Redeemer.

(3.) Their best efforts and plans, the avails of their best thoughts and purposes, belong to the church, and should be honestly devoted to it. Their strength and vigour, and influence should be devoted to it, as the vigour, and strength, and talent, and skill of a servant belong to the master; see Ps. cxxxvii. 5, 6. The language of the ministry, as of every Christian, should be:

I love thy church, O God,
　Her walls before thee stand,
Dear as the apple of thine eye,
　And graven on thy hand.

If e'er to bless thy sons
　My voice or hands deny,
These hands let useful skill forsake,
　This voice in silence die.

If e'er my heart forget
　Her welfare or her wo,
Let every joy this heart forsake,
　And every grief o'erflow.

For her my tears shall fall,
　For her my prayers ascend,
To her my cares and toils be given,
　Till toils and cares shall end.

And it implies, (4.) That they are the servants of the church in time of trial, temptation, and affliction. They are to devote themselves to the comfort of the afflicted. They are to be the guide to the perplexed. They are to aid the tempted. They are to comfort those that mourn, and they are to sustain and console the dying. They are to regard themselves as the servants of the church to accomplish these great objects; and are to be willing to deny themselves, and to take up their cross, and to consecrate their time to the advancement of these great interests. And they are, in all respects, to devote their time, and talents, and influence to the welfare of the church, with as much single-mindedness as the servant is to seek the interest of his master. It was in this way eminently that Paul was favoured with the success with which God blessed him in the ministry; and so every minister will be successful, just in proportion to the single-mindedness with which he devotes himself to the

¹ hath shined in our hearts, to *give* the light of the knowledge of the

glory of God in the face of Jesus Christ.

work of preaching Jesus Christ THE Lord.

6. *For God, who commanded*, &c. The design of this verse seems to be, to give a reason why Paul and his fellow-apostles did not preach themselves, but Jesus Christ the Lord, ver. 5. That reason was, that their minds had been so illuminated by that God who had commanded the light to shine out of darkness, that they had discerned the glory of the divine perfections shining in and through the Redeemer, and they therefore gave themselves, to the work of making him known among men. The doctrines which they preached they had not derived from men in any form. They had not been elaborated by human reasoning or science, nor had they been imparted by tradition. They had been communicated directly by the source of all light—the true God —who had shined into the hearts that were once benighted by sin. Having been thus illuminated, they had felt themselves bound to go and make known to others the truths which God had imparted to them. ¶ *Who commanded the light*, &c. Gen. i. 3. God caused it to shine by his simple command. He *said*, "let there be light, and there was light." The fact that it was produced by *his saying so* is referred to here by Paul by his use of the phrase (ὁ εἰπὼν) "Who *saying*," or speaking the light to shine from darkness. The passage in Genesis is adduced by Longinus as a striking instance of the sublime. ¶ *Hath shined in our hearts*. Marg. "It is he who hath." This is more in accordance with the Greek, and the sense is, "The God who at the creation bade the light to shine out of darkness, is he who has shined into our hearts; or it is the same God who has illuminated us, who commanded the light to shine at the creation." *Light* is every where in the Bible the emblem of knowledge, purity, and truth ; as darkness is the emblem of ignorance, error, sin, and wretched-

ness. See Note, John i. 4, 5. And the sense here is, that God had removed this ignorance, and poured a flood of light and truth on their minds. This passage teaches, therefore, the following important truths in regard to Christians—since it is as applicable to all Christians, as it was to the apostles. (1.) That the mind is by nature ignorant and benighted—to an extent which may be properly compared with the darkness which prevailed before God commanded the light to shine. Indeed, the darkness which prevailed before the light was formed, was a most striking emblem of the darkness which exists in the mind of man before it is enlightened by revelation, and by the Holy Spirit. For (*a*) In all minds by nature there is deep ignorance of God, of his law, and his requirements ; and (*b*) This is often greatly deepened by the course of life which men lead ; by their education ; or by their indulgence in sin, and by their plans of life ; and especially by the indulgence of evil passions. The tendency of man if left to himself is to plunge into deeper darkness, and to involve his mind more entirely in the obscurity of moral midnight. "Light is come into the world, and men loved darkness rather than light, because their deeds were evil," John iii. 19. (2.) This verse teaches the fact, that the minds of Christians are illuminated. They are enabled to see things as they are. This fact is often taught in the Scriptures; see 1 John ii. 20 ; 1 Cor. ii. 12—15. They have different views of things from their fellow-men, and different from what they once had. They perceive a beauty in religion which others do not see, and a glory in truth, and in the Saviour, and in the promises of the gospel, which they did not see before they were converted. This does not mean (*a*) That they are superior in their powers of understanding to other men—for the reverse is often the fact ; nor (*b*) That the effect of religion is at once to enlarge their own intellectual powers, and make them different from what they were before in this respect. But it means that they have clear and consistent views; they look at things as they are; they perceive a beauty in religion and in the service of God which they did not before. They see a beauty in the Bible, and in the doctrines of the Bible, which they did not before, and which sinners do not see. The temperate man will see a beauty in temperance, and in an argument for temperance, which the drunkard will not; the benevolent man will see a beauty in benevolence which the churl will not: and so of honesty, truth, and chastity. And especially will a man who is *reformed* from intemperance, impurity, dishonesty, and avarice, see a beauty in a virtuous life which he did not before see. There is indeed no *immediate* and *direct* enlargement of the intellect; but there is an effect on the heart which produces an appropriate and indirect effect on the understanding. It is at the same time true, that the practice of virtue, that a pure heart, and that the cultivation of piety all tend to regulate, strengthen, and expand the intellect, as the ways of vice and the indulgence of evil passions and propensities tend to enfeeble, paralyze, darken, and ruin the understanding; so that, other things being equal, the man of most decided virtue, and most calm and elevated piety, will be the man of the clearest and best regulated mind. His powers will be the most assiduously, carefully, and conscientiously cultivated, and he will feel himself bound to make the most of them.—The influence of piety in giving light to the mind is often strikingly manifested among unlettered and ignorant Christians. It often happens, as a matter of fact, that they have by far clearer, and more just and elevated views of truth than men of the most mighty intellects, and most highly cultivated by science and adorned with learning, but who have no piety; and a practical acquaintance with their own hearts, and a practical experience of the power of religion in the days of temptation and trial is a better enlightener of the mind on the subject of religion than all the learning of the schools. (3.) This verse teaches, that it is the *same God* who enlightens the mind of the Christian that commanded the light at first to shine. He is the source of all light. He formed the light in the natural world; he gives all light and truth on all subjects to the understanding; and he imparts all correct views of truth to the heart. Light is not originated by man; and man on the subject of religion no more creates the light which beams upon his benighted mind than he created the light of the sun when it first shed its beams over the darkened earth. "All truth is from the sempiternal source of light divine;" and it is no more the work of man to enlighten the mind, and dissipate the darkness from the soul of a benighted sinner, than it was of man to scatter the darkness that brooded over the creation, or than he can now turn the shades of midnight to noonday. All this work lies beyond the proper province of man; and is all to be traced to the agency of God—the great fountain of light. (4.) It is taught here that it is the *same power* that gives light to the mind of the Christian which at first commanded the light to shine out of darkness. It requires the exertion of the same Omnipotence; and the change is often *as* remarkable, and surprising.—Nothing can be conceived to be more grand than the first creation of light—when by one word the whole solar system was in a blaze. And nothing in the moral world is more grand than when by a word God commands the light to beam on the soul of a benighted sinner. Night is at once changed to day; and all things are seen in a blaze of glory. The works of God appear different; the word of God appears different; and a new aspect of beauty is diffused over all things.—If it be asked IN WHAT WAY God thus imparts light to the mind, we may reply, (1.) By his written and preached word. All spiritual and saving light to the minds of men has come through his revealed truth. Nor does the Spirit of God now give or reveal any light to the mind which is not to be found in the word of God.

and which is not imparted through that medium. (2.) God makes use of his providential dealings to give light to the minds of men. They are then, by sickness, disappointment, and pain, made to see the folly and vanity of the things of this world, and to see the necessity of a better portion. (3.) It is done especially and mainly by the influences of the Holy Spirit. It is directly by his agency that the heart becomes affected, and the mind enlightened. It is his province in the world to prepare the heart to receive the truth; to dispose the mind to attend to it : to remove the obstructions which existed to its clear perception; to enable the mind clearly to see the beauty of truth, and of the plan of salvation through a Redeemer. And whatever may be the means which may be used, it is still true that it is only by the Spirit of God that men are ever brought to see the truth clearly and brightly. The same Spirit that inspired the prophets and apostles also illuminates the minds of men now, removes the darkness from their minds, and enables them clearly to discover the truth as it is in Jesus. See Notes, 1 Cor. ii. 10—15. ¶ *To give the light of the knowledge of the glory of God.* This shows the *object,* or the *effect* of enlightening the mind. It is that Christians may behold the divine glory. The meaning is, that it is for the purpose of enlightening and instructing them *concerning* the knowledge of the glory of God.— *Bloomfield.* Doddridge renders it, " the lustre of the knowledge of God's glory." Tindal, "to give the light of the knowledge of the glorious God." The sense is, that the purpose of his shining into their hearts was to give light (πρὸς φωτισμὸν) *i. e.* unto the enlightening ; and the purpose of that light was to acquaint them with the knowledge of the divine glory. ¶ *In the face of Jesus Christ.* That is, that they might obtain the knowledge of the divine glory as it shines in the face of Jesus Christ ; or as it is reflected on the face, or the person of the Redeemer.—There is undoubted allusion here to what is said of Moses (chap. iii. 13) when the divine glory

was reflected on his face, and produced such a splendour and magnificence that the children of Israel could not steadfastly look upon it. The sense here is, that in the face or the person of Jesus Christ the glory of God shone clearly, and the divinity appeared without a vail. The divine perfections, as it were, illuminated him, as the face of Moses was illuminated ; or they shone forth through him, and were seen in him. The word rendered "face" here (προσώπον) may mean either face or person; see Note, chap. ii. 10. The sense is not materially affected which ever translation is preferred. It is, that the divine perfections shone in and through the Redeemer. This refers doubtless to the following truths. (1.) That the glory of the divine *nature* is seen in him, since he is "the brightness of his glory, and the express image of his person." Heb. i. 3. And it is in and through him that the glory of the divine perfections are made known, (2.) That the glory of the divine *attributes* are made known through him, since it is through him that the work of creation was accomplished (John i. 3, Col. i. 16); and it is by him that the mercy and goodness of God have been manifested to men. (3.) That the glory of the divine *moral character* is seen through him, since when on earth he manifested the embodied divine perfections; he showed what God is when incarnate; he lived as became the incarnate God—he was as pure and holy in human nature as God is in the heavens. And there is not, that we know of, one of the divine attributes or perfections which has not at some period, or in some form, been evinced by Jesus Christ. If it be the prerogative of God to be eternal, he was eternal ; Isa. ix. 6 ; Rev. i. 8, 18. If it be the prerogative of God to be the creator, he was also the creator (John i. 3); if to be omniscient, he was omniscient (Matt. xi. 27; Luke x. 22); if to be omnipresent, he is omnipresent (Matt. xviii. 20); if to be almighty, he was almighty (Isa. ix. 6); if to raise the dead, to give life, he did it (John v.

7 But we have this treasure in earthen vessels, that the ex-

21 ; xii. 43, 44; if to still waves and tempests, he did it (Mark iv. 39); if to be full of benevolence, to be perfectly holy, to be without a moral stain or spot, then all this is found in Jesus Christ. And as the wax bears the perfect image of the seal—perfect not only in the outline, and in the general resemblance, but in the filling up—in all the lines, and features, and letters on the seal, so it is with the Redeemer. There is not one of the divine perfections which has not the counterpart in him, and if the glory of the divine character is seen at all, it will be seen in and through him.

7. *But we have this treasure.* The treasure of the gospel ; the rich and invaluable truths which they were called to preach to others. The word " treasure " is applied to those truths on account of their inestimable worth. Paul in the previous verses had spoken of the gospel, the knowledge of Jesus Christ, as full of glory, and infinitely precious. This rich blessing had been committed to him and his fellow-labourers, to dispense it to others, and to diffuse it abroad. His purpose in this and the following verses is, to show that it had been so intrusted to them as to secure all the glory of its propagation to God, and so also as to show its unspeakable value. For this purpose, he not only affirms that it is a treasure, but says that it had been so entrusted to them as to show the power of God in its propagation ; that it had showed its value in sustaining them in their many trials ; and *they* had showed their sense of its worth by being willing to endure all kinds of trial in order to make it everywhere known, ver. 8—11. The expression here is similar to that which the Saviour uses when he calls the gospel "the pearl of great price," Matt. xiii. 46. ¶ *In earthen vessels.* This refers to the apostles and ministers of religion, as weak and feeble ; as having bodies decaying and dying ; as fragile, and liable to various accidents, and as being altogether unworthy to hold a treasure so invaluable ; as if valuable diamonds and gold

were placed in vessels of earth of coarse composition, easily broken, and liable to decay. The word *vessel* (σκεῦος) means properly any utensil or instrument ; and is applied usually to utensils of household furniture, or hollow vessels for containing things, Luke viii. 16 ; John xix. 29. It is applied to the human body, as made of clay, and therefore frail and feeble, with reference to its *containing* any thing, as, *e.g.*, treasure ; compare Note on Rom. ix. 22, 23. The word rendered earthen, (ὀστρακίνοις) means that which is made of shells (from ὄστρακινον), and then burnt clay, probably because vessels were at first made of burnt shells. It is fitted well to represent the human body ; frail, fragile, and easily reduced again to dust. The purpose of Paul here is, to show that it was by no excellency of his nature that the gospel was originated ; it was in virtue of no vigour and strength which he possessed that it was propagated, but that it had been, of design, committed by God to weak, decaying, and crumbling instruments, in order that it might *be seen* that it was by the power of God that such instruments were sustained in the trials to which they were exposed, and in order that it might be manifest to all that it was not originated and diffused by the power of those to whom it was intrusted. The idea is, that they were altogether insufficient of their own strength to accomplish what was accomplished by the gospel. Paul uses a metaphor similar to this in 2 Tim. ii. 20 ¶ *That the excellency of the power.* An elegant expression, denoting the exceeding great power. The great power referred to here was that which was manifested in connection with the labours of the apostles—the power of healing the sick, raising the dead, and casting out devils ; the power of bearing persecution and trial, and the power of carrying the gospel over sea and land, in the midst of danger, and in spite of all the opposition which men could make, whether as individuals or as combined ; and especially the power of converting the hearts of sin-

cellency *a* of the power may be of God, and not of us.

8 *We are* troubled *b* on every

a 1Co.2.5.

side, yet not distressed: *we are* perplexed, but not 1 in despair;

b chap.7.5.
1 or, *not altogether without help or means.*

ners, of humbling the proud, and leading the guilty to the knowledge of God, and the hope of heaven. The idea is, that all this was manifestly beyond human strength; and that God had of design chosen weak and feeble instruments *in order* that it might be everywhere seen that it was done not by human power but by his own. The instrumentality employed was altogether *disproportionate* in its nature to the effect produced. ¶ *May be of God.* May evidently appear to be of God; that it may be manifest to all that it is God's power and not ours. It was one great purpose of God that this should be kept clearly in view. And it is still done. God takes care that this shall be apparent. For, (1.) It is *always* true, whoever is employed, and however great may be the talents, learning, or zeal of those who preach, that it is by the power of God that men are converted. Such a work cannot be accomplished by man. It is not by might or by strength; and between the conversion of a proud, haughty, and abandoned sinner, and the power of him who is made the instrument, there is such a manifest disproportion, that it is evident it is the work of God. The conversion of the human heart is not to be accomplished by man. (2.) Ministers are frail, imperfect, and sinful, as they were in the time of Paul. When the imperfections of ministers are considered; when their frequent errors, and their not unfrequent moral obliquities are contemplated; when it is remembered how far many of them live from what they ought to do, and how few of them live in any considerable degree as becometh the followers of the Redeemer, it is wonderful that God blesses their labour as he does; and the matter of amazement is not that *no more* are converted under their ministry, but it is that *so many* are converted, or that *any* are converted; and it is manifest that it is the mere power of God. (3.) He often makes use of the most feeble,

and unlearned, and weak of his servants to accomplish the greatest effects. It is not splendid talents, or profound learning, or distinguished eloquence, that is always or even commonly most successful. Often the ministry of such is entirely barren; while some humble and obscure man shall have constant success, and revivals shall attend him wherever he goes. It is the man of faith, and prayer, and self-denial, that is blessed; and the purpose of God in the ministry, as in every thing else, is to "*stain the pride of all human glory,*" and to show that he is all in all.

8. We are *troubled.* We the apostles. Paul here refers to some of the *trials* to which he and his fellow-labourers were subjected in making known the gospel. The *design* for which he does it seems to be to show them, (1.) What they endured in preaching the truth; (2.) To show the sustaining power of that gospel in the midst of afflictions; and, (3.) To conciliate their favour, or to remind them that they had endured these things on their account, ver. 12—-15. Perhaps one leading design was to recover the affections of those of the Corinthians whose heart had been alienated from him, by showing them how much he had endured on their account. For this purpose he freely opens his heart to them, and tenderly represents the many and grievous pressures and hardships to which love to souls, and theirs among the rest, had exposed him.—*Doddridge.* The whole passage is one of the most pathetic and beautiful to be found in the New Testament. The word rendered troubled (Θλιβόμενοι, from Θλίβω) may have reference to *wrestling,* or to the contests in the Grecian games. It properly means, to press, to press together; then to press as in a crowd where there is a throng (Mark iii. 9); then to compress together (Matt. vii. 14); and then to oppress, or compress with evils, to distress, to afflict, 2

9 Persecuted, but not forsaken ; cast down, but not destroyed;

10 Always bearing *a* about in the body the dying of the Lord Je-

a Ga. 6. 17.

Thess. i. 6 ; 2 Cor. i. 6. Here it may mean, that he was encompassed with trials, or placed in the midst of them so that they pressed upon him as persons do in a crowd, or, possibly, as a man was close pressed by an adversary in the games. He refers to the fact that he was called to endure a great number of trials and afflictions. Some of those trials he refers to in chap. vii. 5. " When we were come into Macedonia, our flesh had no rest, but we were troubled on every side; without were fightings, within were fears." ¶ *On every side.* In every respect. In every way. We are subjected to all kinds of trial and affliction. ¶ *Yet not distressed.* This by no means expresses the force of the original ; nor is it possible perhaps to express it in a translation. Tindal renders it, " yet we are not without our shift." The Greek word here used (στενοχωρούμενοι) has a relation to the word which is rendered "troubled." It properly means to crowd into a narrow place ; to straiten as to room ; to be so straitened as not to be able to turn one's self. And the idea is, that though he was close pressed by persecutions and trials, yet he was not so hemmed in that he had no way to turn himself ; his trials did not wholly prevent motion and action He was not so closely pressed as a man would be who was so straitened that he could not move his body, or stir hand or foot. He had still resources ; he was permitted to move ; the energy of his piety, and the vigour of his soul could not be entirely cramped and impeded by the trials which encompassed him. The Syriac renders it, " In all things we are pressed, but are not suffocated." The idea is, he was not wholly discouraged, and disheartened, and overcome. He had resources in his piety which enabled him to bear up under these trials, and still to engage in the work of preaching the gospel. ¶ We are *perplexed* (ἀπορούμενοι). This word (from ἄπορος, without resource, which is derived from *α*, priv., and πόρος, way,

or exit) means to be without resource ; to know not what to do ; to hesitate ; to be in doubt and anxiety, as a traveller is, who is ignorant of the way, or who has not the means of prosecuting his journey. It means here, that they were often brought into circumstances of great embarrassment, where they hardly knew what to do, or what course to take. They were surrounded by foes ; they were in want ; they were in circumstances which they had not anticipated, and which greatly perplexed them. ¶ *But not in despair.* In the margin, " not altogether without help or means." Tindal renders this, " We are in poverty, but not utterly without somewhat." In the word here used, (ἐξαπορούμενοι) the preposition is intensive or emphatic, and means *utterly, quite.* The word means to be utterly without resource ; to despair altogether ; and the idea of Paul here is, that they were not left *entirely* without resource. Their wants were provided for ; their embarrassments were removed; their grounds of perplexity were taken away ; and unexpected strength and resources were imparted to them. When they did not know what to do ; when all resources seemed to fail them, in some unexpected manner they would be relieved and saved from absolute despair. How often does this occur in the lives of all Christians ! And how certain is it, that in all such cases God will interpose by his grace, and aid his people, and save them from absolute despair.

9. *Persecuted.* Often persecuted, persecuted in all places. The " Acts of the Apostles" show how true this was. ¶ *But not forsaken.* Not deserted ; nor left by God Though persecuted by men, yet they experienced the fulfilment of the divine promise that he would never leave nor forsake them. God always interposed to aid them ; always saved them from the power of their enemies ; always sustained them in the time of persecution. It is still true. His people

sus, that *a* the life also of Jesus might be made manifest in our body.

a 2 Ti. 2. 11, 12.

11 For we which live are *b* alway delivered unto death for Jesus' sake, that the life also of Jesus

b 1 Cor. 15. 31, 49.

have been often persecuted. Yet God has often interposed to save them from the hands of their enemies ; and where he has not saved them from their hands, and preserved their lives, yet he has never left them, but has sustained, upheld, and comforted them even in the dreadful agonies of death. ¶ *Cast down.* Thrown down by our enemies, perhaps in allusion to the contests of wrestlers, or of gladiators. ¶ *But not destroyed.* Not killed. They rose again ; they recovered their strength ; they were prepared for new conflicts. They surmounted every difficulty, and were ready to engage in new strifes, and to meet new trials and persecutions.

10. *Always bearing about in the body.* The expression here used is designed to show the great perils to which Paul was exposed. And the idea is, that he had on his body the marks, the stripes and marks of punishment and persecution, which showed that he was exposed to the same violent death which the Lord Jesus himself endured ; comp. Gal. vi. 17 : " I bear in my body the marks of the Lord Jesus." It is a strong energetic mode of expression, to denote the severity of the trials to which he was exposed, and the meaning is, that his body bore the marks of his being exposed to the same treatment as the Lord Jesus was ; and evidence that he was probably yet to die in a similar manner under the hands of persecutors ; comp. Col. i. 24. ¶ *The dying of the Lord Jesus.* The death ; the violent death. A death similar to that of the Lord Jesus. The idea is, that he was always exposed to death, and always suffering in a manner that was equivalent to dying. The expression is parallel to what he says in 1 Cor. xv. 31. " I die daily ;" and in 2 Cor. xi. 23, where he says, " in deaths oft." It does not mean that he bore about *literally* the dying of the Lord Jesus, but that he was exposed to a similar death, and had marks on his person

which showed that he was always exposed to the same violent death. This did not occur once only, or at distant intervals, but it occurred constantly, and wherever he was it was still true that he was exposed to violence, and liable to suffer in the same manner that the Lord Jesus did. ¶ *That the life also of Jesus,* &c. This passage has received a considerable variety of interpretation. Grotius renders it, " such a life as was that of Christ, immortal, blessed, heavenly." Locke, " That also the life of Jesus, risen from the dead, may be made manifest by the energy that accompanies my preaching in this frail body." Clarke supposes that it means, that he might be able in this manner to show that Christ was risen from the dead. But perhaps, Paul does not refer to one single thing in the life of the Lord Jesus, but means that he did this in order that in all things the same life, the same kind of living which characterized the Lord Jesus might be manifested in him ; or that he resembled him in his sufferings and trials, in order that in all things he might have the same life in his body. Perhaps, therefore, it may include the following things as objects at which the apostle aimed. (1.) A desire that his *life* might resemble that of the Lord Jesus. That there might be the same self-denial ; the same readiness to suffer ; the same patience in trials ; the same meekness, gentleness, zeal, ardour, love to God, and love to men evinced in his body which was in that of the Lord Jesus. Thus understood, it means that he placed the Lord Jesus before him as the model of his life, and deemed it an object to be attained even by great self-denial and sufferings to be conformed to him. (2.) A desire to attain to the same life in the resurrection which the Lord Jesus had attained to. A desire to be made like him, and that in his body which bore about the dying of the Lord Jesus, he might again

might be made manifest in our mortal flesh.

12 So then *a* death worketh in us, but life in you.

live after death as the Lord Jesus did. Thus understood, it implies an earnest wish to attain to the resurrection of the dead, and accords with what he says in Phil. iii. 8—11, which may perhaps be considered as Paul's own commentary on this passage, which has been so variously, and so little understood by expositors. " Yea, doubtless, and I count all things but loss, for the excellency of the knowledge of Jesus Christ my Lord ; for whom I have suffered the loss of all things, and do count them but dung that I may win Christ. That I may know him, and the power of his resurrection, and the fellowship of his sufferings, being made conformable unto his death ; if by any means I might attain unto the resurrection of the dead ;" comp. Col. i. 24. It intimates Paul's earnest desire and longing to be made like Christ in the resurrection (comp. Phil. iii. 21); his longing to rise again in the last day (comp. Acts xxvi. 7); his sense of the importance of the doctrine of the resurrection and his readiness to suffer anything if he might at last attain to the resurrection of the just, and be ready to enter with the Redeemer into a world of glory. The attainment of this is the high object before the Christian, and to be made like the Redeemer in heaven, to have a body like his, is the grand purpose for which they should live ; and sustained by this hope they should be willing to endure any trials, and meet any sufferings, if they may come to that same " life" and blessedness above.

11. *For we which live.* Those of us, the apostles and ministers of the Redeemer who still survive. James the brother of John had been put to death (Acts xii. 2); and it is probable also that some other of the apostles had been also. This verse is merely explanatory of the previous verse. ¶ *Are alway delivered unto death.* Exposed constantly to death. This shows what is meant in ver. 10, by bearing about in the body the dying

of the Lord Jesus; see Note on 1 Cor. xv. 31. ¶ *In our mortal flesh.* In our body. In our life on earth; and in our glorified body in heaven; see Note on ver. 10.

12. *So then death worketh in us.* We are exposed to death. The preaching of the gospel exposes us to trials which may be regarded as death working in us. Death has an energy over us (ἐνεργεῖται, is at work, is active, or operates); it is constantly employed in inflicting pains on us, and subjecting us to privation and trials. This is a strong and emphatic mode of saying that they were always exposed to death. We are called to serve and glorify the Redeemer, as it were, by repeated deaths and by constantly dying. ¶ *But life in you.* You live as the effect of our being constantly exposed to death. You reap the advantage of all our exposure to trials, and of all our sufferings. You are comparatively safe ; are freed from this exposure to death; and will receive eternal life as the fruit of our toils, and exposures. Life here may refer either to exemption from danger and death; or it may refer to the life of religion; the hopes of piety ; the prospect of eternal salvation. To me it seems most probable that Paul means to use it in the latter sense, and that he designs to say that while *he* was exposed to death and called to endure constant trial, the effect would be that *they* would obtain, in consequence of his sufferings, the blessedness of eternal life; comp. ver. 15. Thus understood, this passage means, that the sufferings and self-denials of the apostles were for the good of others, and would result in their benefit and salvation ; and the design of Paul here is to remind them of his sufferings in their behalf, in order to conciliate their favour and bind them more closely to him by the remembrance of his sufferings on their account.

13. *We having the same spirit of faith.* The same spirit that is ex-

13 We having the same *a* spirit of faith, according as it is written, *b* i believed, and therefore

a 2 Pe.1.1.   *b* Ps.116.10.

pressed in the quotation which he is about to make; the same faith which the psalmist had. We have the very spirit of faith which is expressed by David. The sense is, we have the same spirit of faith which he had who said, "I believed," &c. The phrase, "spirit of faith," means substantially the same as faith itself; a believing sense or impression of the truth. ¶ *According as it is written.* This passage is found in Ps. cxvi. 10. When the psalmist uttered the words, he was greatly afflicted; see ver. 3, 6—8. In these circumstances, he prayed to God, and expressed confidence in him, and placed all his reliance on him. In his affliction he spoke to God; he spoke of his confidence in him; he proclaimed his reliance on him; and his having spoken in this manner was the result of his belief, or of his putting confidence in God. Paul, in quoting this, does not mean to say that the psalmist had any reference to the preaching of the gospel; nor does he mean to say that his circumstances were in all respects like those of the psalmist. The circumstances resembled each other only in these respects, (1.) That Paul, like the psalmist, was in circumstances of trial and affliction; and, (2.) That the language which both used was that which was prompted by faith—faith, which led them to give utterance to the sentiments of their hearts; the psalmist to utter his confidence in God, and the hopes by which he was sustained, and Paul to utter *his* belief in the glorious truths of the gospel; to speak of a risen Saviour, and to show forth the consolations which were thus set before men in the gospel. The sentiments of both were the language of faith. Both, in afflictions, uttered the language of faith; and Paul uses here, as he often does, the language of the Old Testament, as *exactly* expressing his feelings, and the principles by

have I spoken; we also believe, and therefore speak;
14 Knowing *c* that he which

c chap.5.1—4.

which he was actuated. ¶ *We also believe,* &c. We believe in the truths of the gospel; we believe in God, in the Saviour, in the atonement, in the resurrection, &c. The sentiment is, that they had a firm confidence in these things, and that, as the result of that confidence they boldly delivered their sentiments. It prompted them to give utterance to their feelings. "Out of the abundance of the heart," said the Saviour, "the mouth speaketh," Matt. xii. 34. No man should attempt to preach the gospel who has not a firm belief of its truths; and he who *does* believe its truths will be prompted to make them known to his fellow-men. All successful preaching is the result of a firm and settled conviction of the truth of the gospel; and when such a conviction exists, it is natural to give utterance to the belief, and such an expression will be attended with happy influences on the minds of other men; see Note on Acts iv. 20.

14. *Knowing.* Being fully confident; having the most entire assurance. It was the assured hope of the resurrection which sustained them in all their trials. This expression denotes the full and unwavering belief, in the minds of the apostles, that the doctrines which they preached were true. They *knew* that they were revealed from heaven, and that all the promises of God would be fulfilled. ¶ *Shall raise up us also.* All Christians. In the hope of the resurrection they were ready to meet trials, and even to die. Sustained by this assurance, the apostles went forth amidst persecutions and opposition, for they knew that their trials would soon end, and that they would be raised up in the morning of the resurrection, to a world of eternal glory. ¶ *By Jesus.* By the power or the agency of Jesus. Christ will raise up the dead from their graves, John v. 25—29. ¶ *And shall present* us

raised up the Lord Jesus, shall raise up us also by Jesus, and shall present *us* with you.

15 For *a* all things *are* for your sakes, that the abundant grace

b might, through the thanksgiving of many, redound to the glory of God.

16 For which cause *c* we faint not; but though our outward

a 1 Co.3.21,22.   *b* chap.8.19.   *c* 1 Co.15.58.

with you. Will present us before the throne of glory with exceeding joy and honour. He will present us to God as those who have been redeemed by his blood. He will present us in the courts of heaven, before the throne of the eternal Father, as his ransomed people; as recovered from the ruins of the fall; as saved by the merits of his blood. They shall not only be raised up from the dead; but they shall be publicly and solemnly presented to God as his, as recovered to his service, and as having a title in the covenant of grace to the blessedness of heaven.

15. *For all things are for your sakes.* All these things; these glorious hopes, and truths, and prospects; these self-denials of the apostles, and these provisions of the plan of mercy. ¶ *For your sakes.* On your account. They are designed to promote your salvation. They are not primarily for the welfare of those who engage in these toils and self-denials; but the whole arrangement and execution of the plan of salvation, and all the self-denial evinced by those who are engaged in making that plan known, are in order that you might be benefitted. One object of Paul in this statement, doubtless, is, to conciliate their favour, and remove the objections which had been made to him by a faction in the church at Corinth. ¶ *That the abundant grace.* Grace abounding, or overflowing. The rich mercy of God that should be manifested by these means. It is *implied* here, that grace *would* abound by means of these labours and self-denials of the apostles. The grace referred to here is that which would be conferred on them in consequence of these labours. ¶ *Through the thanksgiving of many.* That many may have occasion of gratitude to God; that by these labours more persons may be

led to praise him. It was an object with Paul so to labour that as many as possible might be led to praise God, and have occasion to thank him to all eternity. ¶ *Redound to the glory of God.* That God may have augmented praise; that his glory in the salvation of men may abound. The sentiment of the passage is, that it would be for the glory of God that as many as possible should be brought to give praise and thanksgivings to him; and that, therefore, Paul endeavoured to make as many converts as possible. He denied himself; he welcomed toil; he encountered enemies; he subjected himself to dangers; and he sought by all means possible to bring as many as could be brought to praise God. The word "redound" ($\pi\epsilon\rho\iota\sigma\sigma\epsilon\acute{\upsilon}\eta$) here means abound, or be abundant; and the sense is, *that the overflowing grace thus evinced in the salvation of many would so abound as to promote the glory of God.*

16. *For which cause.* With such an object in view, and sustained by such elevated purposes and desires. The sense is, that the purpose of trying to save as many as possible would make toil easy, privations welcome, and would be so accompanied by the grace of God, as to gird the soul with strength, and fill it with abundant consolations. ¶ *We faint not.* For an explanation of the word here used, see Note on ver. 1. We are not exhausted, desponding, or disheartened. We are sustained, encouraged, emboldened by having such an object in view. ¶ *But though our outward man perish.* By outward man, Paul evidently means the body. By using the phrases, "the outward man," and the "inward man," he shows that he believed that man was made up of two parts, body and soul. He was no materialist. He has described two parts as constituting man, so distinct,

man perish, yet the inward *a man* is renewed day by day.

a Ro.7.22.

17 For *b* our light affliction, which is but for a moment,

b Rom.8.18,34.

that while the one perishes, the other is renewed; while the one is enfeebled, the other is strengthened; while the one grows old and decays, the other renews its youth and is invigorated. Of course, the soul is not dependent on the body for its vigour and strength, since it expands while the body decays; and of course the soul may exist independently of the body, and in a separate state. ¶ *Perish.* Grows old; becomes weak and feeble; loses its vigour and elasticity under the many trials which we endure, and under the infirmities of advancing years. It is a characteristic of the " outer man," that it thus perishes. Great as may be its vigour, yet it must decay and die. It cannot long bear up under the trials of life, and the wear and tear of constant action, but must soon sink to the grave. ¶ *Yet the inward* man. The soul; the undecaying, the immortal part. ¶ *Is renewed.* Is renovated, strengthened, invigorated. His powers of mind expanded; his courage became bolder; he had clearer views of truth; he had more faith in God. As he drew nearer to the grave and to heaven, his soul was more raised above the world, and he was more filled with the joys and triumphs of the gospel. The understanding and the heart did not sympathize with the suffering and decaying body; but, while that became feeble, the soul acquired new strength, and was fitting for its flight to the eternal world. This verse is an ample refutation of the doctrine of the materialist, and proves that there is in man something that is distinct from decaying and dying matter, and that there is a principle which may gain augmented strength and power, while the body dies; comp. Note, Rom. vii. 22. ¶ *Day by day.* Constantly. There was a daily and constant increase of inward vigour. God imparted to him constant strength in his trials, and sustained him with the hopes of heaven, as the body was decaying, and

tending to the grave. The sentiment of this verse is, that in an effort to do good, and to promote the salvation of man, the soul will be sustained in trials, and will be comforted and invigorated even when the body is weary, grows old, decays, and dies. It is the testimony of Paul respecting his own experience; and it is a fact which has been experienced by thousands in their efforts to do good, and to save the souls of men from death.

17. *For our light affliction.* This verse, with the following, is designed to show further the sources of consolation and support which Paul and his fellow-labourers had in their many trials. Bloomfield remarks on this passage, that " in energy and beauty of expression, it is little inferior to any in Demosthenes himself, to whom, indeed, and to Thucydides in his orations, the style of the apostle, when it rises to the oratorical, bears no slight resemblance." The passage abounds with intensive and emphatic expressions, and manifests that the mind of the writer was labouring to convey ideas which language, even after all the energy of expression which he could command, would very imperfectly communicate. The trials which Paul endured, to many persons would have seemed to be any thing else but light. They consisted of want, and danger, and contempt, and stoning, and toil, and weariness, and the scorn of the world, and constant exposure to death by land or by sea; see ver. 7—10, comp. chap. xi. 23—27. Yet these trials, though continued through many years, and constituting, as it were, his very life, he speaks of as the lightest conceivable thing when compared with that eternal glory which awaited him. He strives to get an expression as emphatic as possible, to show that in his estimation they were not worthy to be named in comparison with the eternal weight of glory. It is not sufficient to say that the affliction was " light" or was a mere trifle; but he

worketh for us a far more exceed- | **ing *and* eternal weight of glory ;**

says that it was to endure but for a moment. Though trials had followed him ever since he began to make known the Redeemer, and though he had the firmest expectation that they would follow him to the end of life and everywhere (Acts xx. 23), yet all this was a *momentary trifle* compared with the eternal glory before him. The word rendered "light" (ἐλαφρὸν) means that which is easy to bear, and is usually applied to a burden ; see Mat. xi. 30, comp. 2 Cor. i. 17. ¶ *Which is but for a moment.* The Greek word here used (παραυτίκα) occurs no where else in the New Testament. It is an adverb, from αὐτίκα, αὐτός, and means properly, *at this very instant; immediately* Here it seems to qualify the word "light," and to be used in the sense of momentary, transient. Bloomfield renders it, "for the at present lightness of our afflic-tion." Doddridge, "for this momen-tary lightness of our affliction, which passes off so fast, and leaves so little impression that it may be called levity itself." The apostle evidently wished to express two ideas in as emphatic a manner as possible ; first, that the affliction was *light*, and, secondly, that it was transient, momentary, and soon passing away. His object is to *contrast* this with the glory that awaited him, as being *heavy*, and as being also *eternal*, ¶ *Worketh for us;* see Note, ver. 12. Will produce, will result in. The effect of these af-flictions is to produce eternal glory. This they do, (1.) By their tendency to wean us from the world ; (2.) To purify the heart, by enabling us to break off from the sins on account of which God afflicts us ; (3.) By dis-posing us to look to God for consola-tion and support in our trials ; (4.) By inducing us to contemplate the glories of the heavenly world, and thus winning us to seek heaven as our home ; and, (5.) Because God has graciously promised to reward his people in heaven as the result of their bearing trials in this life. It is by affliction that he purifies them (Isa. xlviii. 10) ; and by trial that he

takes their affections from the objects of time and sense, and gives them a relish for the enjoyments which result from the prospect of perfect and eter-nal glory. ¶ *A far more exceeding* (καθ᾽ ὑπερβολὴν εἰς ὑπερβολὴν). There is not to be found any where a more energetic expression than this. The word (ὑπερβολή,) here used (whence our word *hyperbole*) means properly a throwing, casting, or throwing beyond. In the New Testament it means ex-cess, excellence, eminence ; see ver. 7. "The *excellency* of the power." The phrase καθ᾽ ὑπερβολὴν means ex-ceedingly, supereminently, Rom. vii. 13 ; 1 Cor. xii. 31 ; 2 Cor. i. 8 ; Gal. i. 13. This expression would have been by itself intensive in a high de-gree. But this was not sufficient to express Paul's sense of the glory which was laid up for Christians. It was not enough for him to use the ordinary highest expression for the superlative to denote the value of the object in his eye. He therefore coins an expression, and adds εἰς ὑπερβολὴν. It is not merely eminent ; but it is eminent *unto* eminence ; excess *unto* excess ; a hyperbole *unto* hyperbole —one hyperbole heaped on another; and the expression means that it is "exceeding exceedingly" glorious ; glorious in the highest possible degree, —*Robinson.* Mr. Slade renders it, "Infinitely exceeding." The expres-sion is the Hebrew form of denoting the highest superlative ; and it means that all hyperboles fail of expressing that eternal glory which remains for the just. It is infinite and boundless. You may pass from one degree to another ; from one sublime height to another ; but still an infinity remains beyond. Nothing can describe the uppermost height of that glory ; no-thing can express its infinitude. ¶ *Eternal.* This stands in contrast with the affliction that is for a mo-ment (παραυτίκα). The one is mo-mentary, transient ; so short, even in the longest life, that it may be said to be an instant ; the other has no limits to its duration. It is literally everlasting. ¶ *Weight* (βάρος). This

18 While we look not at the things which are seen, but at the

stands opposed to the (ἰλαφρὸν) *light* affliction. That was so light that it was a trifle. It was easily borne. It was like the most light and airy objects, which constitute no burden. It is not even here called *a burden*, or said to be heavy in any degree. This is so heavy as to be *a burden*. Grotius thinks that the image is taken from gold or silver articles, that are solid and heavy, compared with those that are mixed or plated. But why may it not refer to the insignia of glory and honour; a robe heavy with gold, or a diadem or crown, heavy with gold or diamonds: glory so rich, so profuse as to be heavy? The affliction was light; but the crown, the robe, the adornings in the glorious world were not trifles, or baubles, but solid, substantial, weighty. We apply the word weighty now to that which is valuable and important, compared with that which is of no value, probably because the precious metals and jewels are heavy; and it is by them that we usually estimate the value of objects. ¶ *Of glory* (δόξης). The Hebrew word כבד denotes weight as well as glory. And perhaps Paul had that use of the word in his eye in this strong expression. It refers here to the splendour, magnificence, honour, and happiness of the eternal world.—In this exceedingly interesting passage, which is worthy of the deepest study of Christians, Paul has set in most beautiful and emphatic contrast the trials of this life and the glories of heaven. It may be profitable to contemplate at a single glance the view which he had of them, that they may be brought distinctly before he mind.

THE ONE IS

1. AFFLICTION, θλίψις.
2. *Light*, ἐλαφρὸν.
3. For a moment, παραυτίκα

THE OTHER IS, by contrast,

(1.) GLORY, δόξη.
(2.) Weight, βάρος.
(3.) Eternal, αἰώνιον.

(4.) Eminent, or excellent, καθ᾽ ὑπερβολὴν.
(5.) Infinitely excellent, eminent in the highest degree, εἰς ὑπερβολὴν.

So the *account* stands in the view of Paul; and with this *balance* in favour of the eternal glory, he regarded afflictions as mere trifles, and made it the grand purpose of his life to gain the glory of the heavens. What wise man, looking at the account, would not do likewise?

18. *While we look*, &c. Or, rather, we not looking at the things which are seen. The design of this is, to show in what way the afflictions which they endured became in their view light and momentary. It was by looking to the glories of the future world, and thus turning away the attention from the trials and sorrows of this life. If we look directly at our trials; if the mind is fixed wholly on them, and we think of nothing else, they often appear heavy and long. Even comparatively light and brief sufferings will appear to be exceedingly difficult to bear. But if we can turn away the mind from them and contemplate future glory; if we can compare them with eternal blessedness, and feel that they will introduce us to perfect and everlasting happiness, they will appear to be transitory, and will be easily borne. And Paul here has stated the true secret of bearing trials with patience. It is to look at the things which are unseen. To anticipate the glories of the heavenly world. To fix the eye on the eternal happiness which is beyond the grave; and to reflect how short these trials *are*, compared with the eternal glories of heaven; and how short they will *seem* to be when we are there. ¶ *The things which are seen*. The things here below; the things of this life—poverty, want, care, persecution, trial, &c. ¶ *The things which are not seen*. The glories of heaven, comp. Heb. xi. 1. ¶ *The things which are seen are temporal*. This refers particularly to the things which they *suffered*. But

things which are not ^a seen : for the things which are seen *are*

a Heb.11.1.

it is *as* true of all things here below. Wealth, pleasure, fame, the three idols which the people of this world adore, are all to endure but for a little time. They will all soon vanish away. So it is with pain, and sorrow, and tears. All that we enjoy, and all that we suffer here, must soon vanish and disappear. The most splendid palace will decay ; the most costly pile will moulder to dust ; the most magnificent city will fall to ruins; the most exquisite earthly pleasures will soon come to an end ; and the most extended possessions can be enjoyed but a little time. So the acutest pain will soon be over; the most lingering disease will soon cease ; the evils of the deepest poverty, want, and suffering will soon be passed. There is nothing on which the eye can fix, nothing that the heart can desire here, which will not soon fade away ; or, it it survives, it is temporary in regard to us. We must soon leave it to others ; and *if* enjoyed, it will be enjoyed while *our bodies* are slumbering in the grave, and *our souls* engaged in the deep solemnities of eternity. How foolish then to make these our portion, and to fix our affections supremely on the things of this life ? How foolish also to be very deeply affected by the trials of this life, which at the furthest can be endured but a little longer before we shall be for ever beyond their reach ! ¶ *The things which are not seen are eternal.* Every thing which pertains to that state beyond the grave. (1.) God is eternal; not to leave us as our earthly friends do. (2.) The Saviour is eternal—to be our everlasting friend. (3.) The companions and friends there are eternal. The angels who are to be our associates, and the spirits of the just with whom we shall live, are to exist for ever. The angels never die ; and the pious dead shall die no more. There shall be then no separation, no death-bed, no grave, no sad vacancy and loss caused by the removal of a much-loved friend.

temporal ; but the things which are not seen *are* eternal.

(4.)The joys of heaven are eternal. There shall be no interruption ; no night ; no cessation ; no end. Heaven and all its joys shall be everlasting ; and he who enters there shall have the assurance that those joys shall endure and increase while eternal ages shall roll away. (5.) It may be added, also, that the woes of hell shall be eternal. They are now among the things which to us "are not seen ;' and they, as well as the joys of heaven, shall have no end. Sorrow there shall never cease ; the soul shall there never die ; the body that shall be raised up "to the resurrection of damnation " shall never again expire.—And when all these things are contemplated, well might Paul say of the things of this life— the sorrows, trials, privations, and persecutions which he endured, that they were " light," and were " for a moment." How soon will they pass away ; how soon shall we all be engaged amidst the unchanging and eternal realities of the things which are not seen !

REMARKS.

1. Ministers of the gospel have no cause to faint or to be discouraged, ver. 1. Whatever may be the reception of their message, and whatever the trials to which they may be subjected, yet there are abundant sources of consolation and support in the gospel which they preach. They have the consciousness that they preach a system of truth; that they are proclaiming that which God has revealed; and, if they are faithful, that they have his smiles and approbation. Even, therefore, if men reject, and despise their message, and if they are called to endure many privations and trials, they should not faint. It is enough for them that they proclaim the truth which God loves, and that they meet with his approbation and smiles. Trials will come in the ministry as every where else, but there are also peculiar consolations. There

may be much opposition and resistance to the message, but we should not faint or be discouraged. We should do our duty, and commit the result to God.

2. The gospel should be embraced by those to whom it comes, ver. 2. If it has their reason and conscience in its favour, then they should embrace it without delay. They are under the most sacred obligation to receive it, and to become decided Christians. Every man is bound, and may be urged to pursue, that course which his conscience approves; and the gospel may thus be pressed on the attention of all to whom it comes.

3. If men wish peace of conscience, they should embrace the gospel, ver. 2. They can never find it elsewhere. No man's *conscience* is at peace from the fact that he does not repent, and love God and obey the gospel. His *heart* may love sin; but his conscience cannot approve it. That is at peace only in doing the work of God; and that can find self-approbation only when it submits to him, and embraces the gospel of his Son. Then the conscience is at ease. *No man ever yet had a troubled conscience from the fact that he had embraced the gospel, and was an humble and decided Christian.* Thousands and millions have had a troubled conscience from the fact that they have neglected it. No man on a death-bed ever had a troubled conscience because he embraced religion too early in life. Thousands and millions have been troubled when they came to die, because they neglected it so long, or rejected it altogether. No man when death approaches has a troubled conscience because he has lived *too much* devoted to God the Saviour, and been too active as a Christian. But O how many have been troubled then because they have been worldly-minded, and selfish, and vain, and proud? The conscience gives peace just in proportion as we serve God faithfully; nor can all the art of man or Satan give peace to one conscience in the ways of sin, and in the neglect of the soul.

4. Ministers should preach the truth

—the simple truth—and nothing but the truth, ver. 2. They should make use of no false art, no deception, no trick, no disguise. They should be open, sincere, plain, pure in all their preaching, and in their manner of life. Such was the course of the Saviour; such the course of Paul; and such a course only will God approve and bless.

5. This is a deluded world, ver. 4. It is blinded and deceived by him who is here called the " god of this world." Satan rules in the hearts of men; and he rules by deceiving them, and in order to deceive them. Every thing which operates to prevent men from embracing the gospel has a tendency to blind the mind. The man who is seeking wealth as his only portion, is blinded and deceived in regard to its value. The man who is pursuing the objects of ambition as his main portion, is deceived in regard to the true value of things. And he, or she, who pursues pleasure as the main business of life, is deceived in regard to the proper value of objects. It is impossible to conceive of a world more deluded than this. We can conceive of a world more sinful, and more miserable, and such is hell; but there is no delusion and deception there. Things are seen as they are; and no one is deceived in regard to his character or prospects there. But here, every impenitent man is deceived and blinded. He is deceived about his own character; about the relative value of objects; about his prospects for eternity; about death, the judgment, heaven, hell. On none of these points has he any right apprehension; and on none is it possible for any human power to break the deep delusion, and to penetrate the darkness of his mind.

6. Men are in danger, ver. 4. They are under deep delusion, and they tread unconcerned near to ruin. They walk in darkness—blinded by the god of this world, and are very near a precipice, and nothing will rouse them from their condition. It is like children gathering flowers near a deep gulf, when the pursuit of *one* more flower may carry them too far, and

they will fall to rise no more. The delusion rests on every unsanctified mind; and it needs to remain but a little longer, and the soul will be lost. That danger deepens every day and every hour. If it is continued but a little longer it will be broken in upon by the sad realities of death, judgment, and hell. But then it will be too late. The soul will be lost—*deluded* in the world of probation; *sensible* of the truth only in the world of despair.

7. Satan will practise every device and art possible to prevent the gospel from shining upon the hearts of men. That light is painful and hateful to his eyes, and he will do all that can be done to prevent its being diffused. Every art which long-tried ingenuity and skill can devise, will be resorted to; every power which he can put forth will be exerted. If he can blind the minds of men, he will do it. If men *can* be hoodwinked, and gulled, it will be done. If error can be made to spread, and be embraced—error smooth, plausible, cunning—it will be diffused. Ministers will be raised up to preach it; and the press will be employed to accomplish it. If sinners can be deceived, and made to remain at ease in their sins, by novels and seductive poetry; by books false in sentiments, and perverse in morals, the press will be made to groan under the works of fiction. If theatres are necessary to cheat and beguile men, they will be reared; and the song, and the dance, the ball, and the splendid party will alike contribute to divert the attention from the cross of Christ, the worth of the soul, and the importance of a preparation to die. No art has been spared, or will be spared to deceive men; and the world is full of the devices of Satan to hoodwink and blind the perishing, and lead them down to hell.

8. Yet, Satan is not alone to blame for this. He does all he can, and he has consummate skill and art. Yet, let not the deluded sinner take comfort to himself because Satan is the tempter, and because he is deluded. The bitterness of death is not made sweet to a young man because he has been deluded by the arts of the veteran in temptation; and the fires of hell will not burn any the less fiercely because the sinner suffered himself to be deluded, and chose to go there through the ball-room or the theatre. The sinner is, after all, *voluntary* in his delusions. He does, or he might, know the truth. He goes voluntarily to the place of amusement; voluntarily forms the plans of gain and ambition which deceive and ruin the soul; goes voluntarily to the theatre, and to the haunts of vice; and *chooses* this course in the face of many warnings, and remonstrances. Who is to blame if he is lost! Who but himself?

9. Sinners should be entreated to rouse from this delusive and false security. They are now blinded, and deceived. Life is too short and too uncertain to be playing such a game as the sinner does. There are too many realities here to make it proper to pass life amidst deceptions and delusions. Sin is real, and danger is real, and death is real, and eternity is real; and man should rouse from his delusions, and look upon things as they are. Soon he will be on a bed of death, and then he will look over the follies of his life. Soon he will be at the judgment bar, and from that high and awful place look on the past and the future, and see things as they are. But, alas! it will be too late then to repair the errors of a life; and amidst the realities of those scenes, all that he may be able to do, will be to sigh unavailingly that he suffered himself to be deluded, deceived, and destroyed in the only world of probation, by the trifles and baubles which the great deceiver placed before him to beguile him of heaven, and to lead him down to hell!

10. The great purpose of the ministry is to make known in any and every way the Lord Jesus Christ, ver. 5. To this, the ministers of the gospel are to devote themselves. It is not to cultivate farms; to engage in traffic; to shine in the social circle; to be distinguished for learning; to become fine scholars; to be profoundly versed in science; or to be distinguished as authors, that they are

set apart ; but it is in every way possible to make known the Lord Jesus Christ. Whatever other men do, or not do ; however the world may choose to be employed, their work is simple and plain, and it is not to cease or be intermitted till death shall close their toils. Neither by the love of ease, of wealth, or pleasure are they to turn aside from their work, or to forsake the vocation to which God has called them.

11. We see the responsibility of the ministry, ver. 5. On the ministry devolves the work of making the Saviour known to a dying world. If they will not do it, the world will remain in ignorance of the Redeemer and will perish. *If there is one soul to whom they might make known the Saviour, and to whom they do not make him known, that soul will perish, and the responsibility will rest on the minister of the Lord Jesus.* And, O ! how great is this responsibility ! And who is sufficient for these things ?

12. Ministers of the gospel should submit to any self-denial in order that they may do good. Their Master did ; and Paul and the other apostles did. It is sufficient for the disciple that he be as the master ; and the ministers of the gospel should regard themselves as set apart to a work of self-denial, and called to a life of toil, like their Lord. Their rest is in heaven, and not on the earth. Their days of leisure and repose are to be found in the skies when their work is done, and not in a world perishing in sin.

13. The ministry is a glorious work, ver. 5. What higher honour is there on earth than to make known a Redeemer ? What pleasure more exquisite can there be than to speak of pardon to the guilty ? What greater comfort than to go to the afflicted and bind up their hearts ; to pour the balm of peace into the wounded spirit, and to sustain and cheer the dying ? The ministry has its own consolations amidst all its trials ; its own honour amidst the contempt and scorn with which it is often viewed by the world.

14. The situation of man would have been dreadful and awful had it not been for the light which is imparted by revelation, and by the Holy Spirit, ver. 6. Man would have ever remained like the dark night before God said, " Let there be light ;" and his condition would have been thick darkness, where not a ray of light would have beamed on his benighted way. Some idea of what this was, and would have continued to be, we have now in the heathen world, where thick darkness reigns over nations, though it has been somewhat broken in upon by the dim light which tradition has diffused there.

15. God has power to impart light to the most dark and benighted mind. There is no one to whom he cannot reveal himself and make his truth known, ver. 6. With as much ease as he commanded light to shine out of darkness at first can he command the pure light of truth to shine on the minds of men ; and on minds most beclouded by sin he can cause the sun of righteousness to shine with healing in his beams.

16. We should implore the enlightening influence of the Spirit of truth, ver. 6. If God is the source of light, we should seek it at his hands. Nothing to man is so valuable as the light of truth ; nothing of so much worth as the knowledge of the true God ; and with the deepest solicitude, and the most fervent prayer, should we seek the enlightening influences of his Spirit, and the guidance of his grace.

17. There is no true knowledge of God except that which shines in the face of Jesus Christ, ver. 6. He came to make known the true God. He is the exact image of God. He resembles him in all things. And he who does not love the character of Jesus Christ, therefore, does not love the character of God ; he who does not seek to be like Jesus Christ, does not desire to be like God. He who does not bear the image of the Redeemer, does not bear the image of God. To be a moral man merely, therefore, is not to be like God. To be amiable, and honest, merely, is not to be like God. Jesus Christ, the image of God, was more than this. He was *religious.* He was holy. He was, as a man, a man of prayer, and

filled with the love of God, and was always submissive to his holy will. He sought his honour and glory : and he made it the great purpose of his life and death to make known his existence, perfections, and name. To imitate him in this is to have the knowledge of the glory of God ; and no man is *like* God who does not bear the image of the Redeemer. No man is like God, therefore, who is not a Christian. Of course, no man can be prepared for heaven who is not a friend and follower of Jesus Christ.

18. God designs to secure the promotion of his own glory in the manner in which religion is spread in the world, ver. 7. For this purpose, and with this view, he did not commit it to angels, nor has he employed men of rank, or wealth, or profound scientific attainments to be the chief instruments in its propagation. He has committed it to frail, mortal men ; and often to men of humble rank, and even humble attainments—except attainments in piety. In fitting them for their work his grace is manifest ; and in all the success which attends their labours it is apparent that it is by the mere grace and mercy of God that it is done.

19. We see what our religion has cost, ver. 8, 9. Its extension in the world has been everywhere connected with sufferings, and toil, and tears. It began in the labours, sorrows, self-denials, persecutions, and dying agonies of the Son of God ; and to *introduce* it to the world cost his life. It was spread by the toils, and sacrafices, and sufferings of the apostles. It was kept up by the dying groans of martyrs. It has been preserved and extended on earth by the labours and prayers of the Reformers, and amidst scenes of persecution everywhere, and it is now extending through the earth by the sacrifices of those who are willing to leave country and home ; to cross oceans and deserts ; and to encounter the perils of barbarous climes, that they may make it known to distant lands. If estimated by what it has *cost*, assuredly no religion, no blessing is so valuable as Christianity. It is above all human valuation : and

it should be a matter of unfeigned thankfulness to us that God has been pleased to raise up men who have been *willing* to suffer so much that it might be perpetuated and extended on the earth ; and *we* should be willing also to imitate their example, and deny ourselves, that *we* may make its inestimable blessings known to those who are now destitute. To us, it is worth all it has cost—all the blood of apostles and martyrs ; to others, also, it would be worth all that it *would* cost to send it to them. How can we better express our sense of its worth, and our gratitude to the dying Redeemer, and our veneration for the memory of self-denying apostles and martyrs, than by endeavouring to diffuse the religion for which they died all over the world ?

20. We have in this chapter an illustration of the sustaining power of religion in trials, ver. 8, 9. The friends of Christianity have been called to endure every form of suffering. Poverty, want, tears, stripes, imprisonments, and deaths have been their portion. They have suffered under every form of torture which men could inflict on them. And yet the power of religion has never failed them. It has been amply tried ; and has shown itself able to sustain them always, and to enable them always to triumph. Though troubled, they have not been so close pressed that they had no room to turn ; though perplexed, they have not been without some resource ; though persecuted by men, they have not been forsaken by God ; though thrown down in the conflict, yet they have recovered strength, and been prepared to renew the strife, and to engage in new contentions with the foes of God. Who can estimate the value of a religion like this ? Who does not see that it is adapted to man in a state of trial, and that it furnishes him with just what he needs in this world ?

21. Christianity will live, ver. 8, 9. Nothing can destroy it. All the power that *could* be brought to bear on it to blot it from the earth *has* been tried, and yet it survives. No new attempt to destroy it can pre-

vail ; and it is now settled that this religion is to live to the end of time. It has *cost* much to obtain this demonstration ; but it is worth all it has cost, and the sufferings of apostles and martyrs, therefore, have not been for naught.

22. Christians should be willing to endure anything in order that they may become like Christ on earth, and be like him in heaven, ver. 10. It is worth all their efforts, and all their self-denials. It is the grand object before us; and we should deem no sufferings too severe, no self-denial or sacrifice too great, if we may become like him here below, and may live with him above, ver. 10, 11.

23. In order to animate us in the work to which God has called us; to encourage us in our trials; and to prompt us to a faithful discharge of our duties, especially those who like Paul are called to preach the gospel, we should have, like him, the following views and feelings—views and feelings adapted to sustain us in all our trials, and to uphold us in all the conflicts of life. (1.) A firm and unwavering belief of the truth of the religion which we profess, and of the truth which we make known to others, ver. 12. No man can preach successfully, and no man can do much good, whose mind is vacillating and hesitating ; who is filled with doubts, and who goes timidly to work, or who declares that of which he has no practical acquaintance, and no deep-felt conviction, and who knows not whereof he affirms. A man to do good must have a faith which never wavers ; a conviction of truth which is constant; a belief settled like the everlasting hills, which nothing can shake or overturn. With such a conviction of the truth of Christianity, and of the great doctrines which it inculcates, he *cannot but speak* of it, and make known his convictions. He that believes that men ARE in fact in danger of hell, WILL tell them of it; he that believes there is an awful bar of judgment, will tell them of it ; he that believes that the Son of God became incarnate and died for men, will tell them of it ; he that believes that there is a

heaven, will invite them to it. And one reason why professing Christians are so reluctant to speak of these things, is, that they have no very settled and definite conviction of their truth, and no correct view of their relative importance. (2.) We should have a firm assurance that God has raised up the Lord Jesus, and that we also shall be raised from the dead, ver. 14. The hope and expectation of the resurrection of the dead was one of the sustaining principles which upheld Paul in his labours, and to attain to this was one of the grand objects of his life, Acts xxiii. 6 ; Phil. iii. 11. Under the influence of this hope and expectation, he was willing to encounter any danger, and to endure any trial. The prospect of being raised up to eternal life and glory was all that was needful to make trials welcome, and to uphold him in the midst of privations and toils. And so we, if we are assured of this great truth, shall welcome trial also, and shall be able to endure afflictions and persecutions. They will soon be ended, and the eternal glory in the morning of the resurrection shall be more than a compensation for all that we shall endure in this life. (3.) We should have a sincere desire to promote the glory of God, and to bring as many as possible to join in his praise, and to celebrate his saving mercy, ver. 15. It was this which sustained and animated Paul ; and a man who has this as the leading object of his life, and his great purpose and aim, will be willing to endure much trial, to suffer much persecution, and to encounter many dangers. No object is so noble as that of endeavouring to promote the divine glory ; and he who is influenced by that will care little how many sufferings he is called to endure in this life.

24. Christians should have such a belief of the truth of their religion as to be willing to speak of it at all times, and in all places, ver. 13. If we *have* such a belief we shall be willing to speak of it. We cannot help it. We shall so see its value, and so love it, and our hearts will be so full of it,

and we shall see so much the danger of our fellow-men, that we shall be instinctively prompted to go to them and warn them of their danger, and tell them of the glories of the Redeemer.

25. Christians may expect to be supported and comforted in the trials and toils of life, ver. 16. The "outward man" will indeed perish and decay. The body will become feeble, weary, jaded, decayed, decrepit. It will be filled with pain, and will languish under disease, and will endure the mortal agony, and will be corrupted in the tomb. But the "inward man" will be renewed. The faith will be invigorated, the hope become stronger, the intellect brighter, the heart better, the whole soul be more like God. While the body, therefore, the less important part, decays and dies, the immortal part shall live and ripen for glory. Of what consequence is it, therefore, how soon or how much the body decays; or when, and where, and how it dies? Let the immortal part be preserved, let that live, and all is well. And while this is done, we should not, we shall not "faint." We shall be sustained, and shall find the consolations of religion to be fitted to all our wants, and adapted to all the necessities of our condition as weak, and frail, and dying creatures.

26. We learn from this chapter how to bear affliction in a proper manner, ver. 17, 18. It is by looking at eternity and comparing our trials with the eternal weight of glory that awaits us. In themselves afflictions often seem heavy and long. Human nature is often ready to sink under them. The powers of the body fail, and the mortal frame is crushed. The day seems long while we suffer; and the night seems often to be almost endless, Deut. xxviii. 67. But compared with eternity how short are all these trials! Compared with the weight of glory which awaits the believer, what a trifle are the severest sufferings of this life. Soon the ransomed spirit will be released, and will be admitted to the full fruition of the joys of the world above. In that world all these sorrows will seem like the sufferings of childhood, that we have now almost forgotten, and that now seem to us like trifles.

27. We should not look to the things which are seen as our portion, ver. 17, 18. They are light in their character, and are soon to fade away. Our great interests are beyond the grave. There all is weighty, and momentous, and eternal. Whatever great interests we have are there. Eternity is stamped upon all the joys and all the sorrows which are beyond this life. Here all is temporary, changing, decaying, dying. There all is fixed, settled, unchanging, immortal. It becomes us then as rational creatures *to look* to that world, to act with reference to it, to feel and act *as if* we felt that all our interests were there. Were this life all, every thing in relation to us would be trifling. But when we remember that there is an eternity; that we are near it; and that our conduct here is to determine our character and destiny there, life becomes invested with infinite importance. Who can estimate the magnitude of the interests at stake? Who can appreciate aright the importance of every step we take, and every plan we form?

28. All here below is temporary, decaying, dying; ver. 17, 18. Afflictions are temporary. They are but for a moment, and will soon be passed away. Our sorrows here will soon be ended. The last sigh on earth will soon be heaved; the last tear will have fallen on the cheek; the last pain will have shot across the seat of life! The last pangs of parting with a beloved friend will soon have been endured; and the last step which we are to take in "the valley of the shadow of death," will soon have been trod. And in like manner we shall soon have tasted the last cup of earthly joy. All our comforts here below will soon pass from us. Our friends will die. Our sources of happiness will be dried up. Our health will fail, and darkness will come over our eyes, and we shall go down to the dead. All our property

CHAPTER V.

FOR we know, that if our earthly house of *this* tabernacle *a* were

a Job 4.19; 2 Pet.1.13,14.

dissolved, we have a building of God, an house *b* not made with hands, eternal in the heavens.

b 1 Pet.1.4.

must be left, and all our honours be parted with for ever. In a little time —O, how brief! we shall have gone from all these, and shall be engaged in the deep and awful solemnities of the unchanging world. How vain and foolish, therefore, the attachment to earthly objects! How important to secure an interest in that future inheritance which shall never fade away!

29. Let it not be inferred, however, that *all* affliction shall be light, and for a moment, or that all earthly trial shall of course work out a far more exceeding and eternal weight of glory. There are sorrows beyond the grave compared with which the most heavy and most protracted woes this side the tomb, are " light," and are " but for a moment." And there are sorrows *in* this life, deep and prolonged afflictions—which by no means tend to prepare the soul for the " far more exceeding and eternal weight of glory." Such are those afflictions where there is no submission to the will of God; where there is murmuring, repining, impatience, and increased rebellion; where there is no looking to God for comfort, and no contemplation of eternal glory. Such are those afflictions where men look to philosophy, or to earthly friends to comfort them; or where they plunge deeper into the business, the gayety, or the vices of the world, to drown their sorrows and to obliterate the sense of their calamities. This is " the sorrow of the world, which worketh death," 2 Cor. vii. 10. In afflictions, therefore, it should be to us a matter of deep and anxious solicitude to know whether we have the right feelings, and whether we are seeking the right sources of consolation. And in such seasons it shall be the subject of our deep and earnest prayer to God that our trials *may*, by his grace, be made to work out for us " a far more exceeding and eternal weight of glory." All are afflicted; all suffer in various ways; and all *may* find

these trials terminate in eternal blessedness beyond the grave

CHAPTER V.

THIS chapter is closely connected with the former, and indeed has been improperly separated from it, as is manifest from the word " For " (γὰρ) with which it commences. It contains a further statement of *reasons* for what has been said in the previous chapter. The main subject there was the MINISTRY; the honesty and fidelity with which Paul and his fellow-labourers toiled (ver. 1—3); the trials and dangers which they encountered in the work of the ministry (ver. 7—12); and the consolations and supports which they had in its various trials, ver. 13—18. This chapter contains a continuation of the same subject, and a further statement of the motives which prompted them to their work, and of the supports which upheld them in the arduous duties to which they were called. It is a chapter full of exquisite beauties of sentiment and of language, and as well adapted to give consolation and support to all Christians now as it is to ministers; and the sentiments are as well adapted to sustain the humblest believer in his trials as they were to sustain the apostles themselves. The following are the points of consolation and support, and reasons for their zeal and self-denial, to which the apostle refers.

1. They had the assured prospect of the resurrection, and of eternal life, ver. 1—4. The body might decay, and be worn out; it might sigh and groan, but they had a better home, a mansion of eternal rest in the heavens. It was their earnest desire to reach heaven; though not such a desire as to make them unwilling to endure the toils and trials which God should appoint to them here below, but still an earnest, anxious wish to reach safely their eternal home in the skies. In the prospect of their heavenly home, and their eternal rest, they were willing

2 For in this we groan, *a* earnestly desiring to be clothed upon

a Rom.8.23.

with our house which is from heaven:

---

to endure all the trials which were appointed to them.

2. God had appointed them to this; he had fitted them for these trials; he had endowed them with the graces of his Spirit; and they were, therefore, willing to be absent from the body, and to be present with the Lord; ver. 5—8. They had such a view of heaven as their home that they were willing at any time to depart and enter the world of rest, and they did not, therefore, shrink from the trials and dangers which would be likely soon to bring them there.

3. They had a deep and constant conviction that they must soon appear before the judgment-seat of Christ; ver. 9—11. They laboured that they might be accepted by him (ver. 9); they knew that they must give a solemn account to him (ver. 10); they had a clear view, and a deep impression of the awful terrors of that day, and they laboured, therefore, to save as many as possible from the condemnation of the great Judge of all, and endeavoured to "persuade" them to be prepared for that scene; ver. 11.

4. Though to some they might appear to be under the influence of improper excitement, and even to be deranged (ver. 14), yet they were acting only under the proper influence of the love of Christ; ver. 14, 15. They were constrained and urged on by his love; they knew that he had died for all, and that all men were dead in sin; and they felt themselves the constraining influence of that love prompting them to deny themselves, and to devote their all to his service and cause.

5. Their views of all things had been changed; ver. 16, 17. They had ceased to act under the influences which govern other men; but their own hearts had been changed, and they had become new creatures in Christ, and in their lives they evinced the spirit which should govern those who were thus renewed.

6. They had been solemnly com-

missioned by God as his ambassadors in this cause. They had been sent to make known the terms and the way of reconciliation, and they felt it to be their duty to proclaim those terms on as wide a scale as possible, and with the utmost zeal and self-denial. It was God's glorious plan of reconciliation; and on the ground of the atonement made by the Redeemer, they could now offer salvation to all mankind, and as all *might* be saved, they felt themselves bound to offer the terms of salvation to as many as possible; ver. 18—21. The grand argument for urging sinners to be reconciled to God, is the fact that Christ has died for their sins, and, therefore, the apostles apprized of this fact, sought to urge as many as possible to become his friends; ver. 21.

1. *For we know.* We who are engaged in the work of the gospel ministry. Paul is giving a reason why he and his fellow-labourers did not become weary and faint in their work. The reason was, that they knew that even if their body should die, they had an inheritance reserved for them in heaven. The expression "we know" is the language of strong and unwavering assurance. They had no doubt on the subject. And it proves that there may be the assurance of eternal life; or such evidence of acceptance with God as to leave no doubt of a final admission into heaven. This language was often used by the Saviour in reference to the truths which he taught (John iii. 11; iv. 22); and it is used by the sacred writers in regard to the truths which they recorded, and in regard to their own personal piety; John xxi. 24; 1 John ii. 3, 5, 18; iii. 2, 14, 19, 24; iv. 6, 13; v. 2, 15, 19, 20. ¶ *That if our earthly house* The word "earthly" here (ἐπίγειος) stands opposed to "heavenly," or to the house eternal (ἐν τοῖς οὐρανοῖς) in the heavens." The word properly means "upon earth, terrestrial, belonging to the earth, or on the earth," and is applied to *bodies* (1

Cor. xv. 40); to earthly things (John iii. 12); to earthly, or worldly wisdom, James iii. 15. The word *house* here refers doubtless to the body, as the habitation, or the dwelling-place of the mind or soul. The soul dwells in it as we dwell in a house, or tent. ¶ *Of* this *tabernacle.* This word means a booth, or tent—a movable dwelling. The use of the word here is not a mere redundancy, but the idea which Paul designs to convey is, doubtless, that the body—the house of the soul—was not a *permanent* dwelling-place, but was of the same nature as a booth or tent, that was set up for a temporary purpose, or that was easily taken down in migrating from one place to another. It refers here to the body as the frail and temporary abode of the soul. It is not a permanent dwelling; a fixed habitation, but is liable to be taken down at any moment, and was fitted up with that view. Tindal renders it, "if our earthly mansion wherein we now dwell." The Syriac renders it, "for we know that if our house on earth, which is our body, were dissolved." The idea is a beautiful one, that the body is a mere unfixed, movable dwelling-place; liable to be taken down at any moment, and not designed, any more than a tent is, to be a permanent habitation. ¶ *Were dissolved* (καταλυθῇ). This word means properly to disunite the parts of any thing ; and is applied to the act of throwing down, or destroying a building. It is applied here to the body, regarded as a temporary dwelling that might be taken down, and it refers, doubtless, to the dissolution of the body in the grave. The idea is, that if this body should moulder back to dust, and be resolved into its original elements; or if by great zeal and labour it should be exhausted and worn out. Language like this is used by Eliphaz, the Temanite, in describing the body of man. "How much less in those that dwell in houses of clay," &c ; Job iv. 19; comp. 2 Pet. i. 13, 14. ¶ *We have a building of God.* Robinson (*Lexicon*) supposes that it refers to "the future spiritual body as the abode of the soul." Some have supposed that it refers to some "celestial vehicle" with which God invests the soul during the intermediate state. But the Scripture is silent about any such celestial vehicle. It is not easy to tell what was the precise idea which Paul here designed to convey. Perhaps a few remarks may enable us to arrive at the meaning. (1.) It was not to be temporary; not a tent or tabernacle that could be taken down. (2.) It was to be eternal in the heavens. (3.) It was to be such as to constitute a dwelling; *a clothing,* or such a protection as should keep the soul from being "naked." (4.) It was to be such as should constitute "life" in contradistinction from "mortality." These things will better agree with the supposition of its referring to the future *body* of the saints than any thing else ; and probably the idea of Paul is, that the body there will be incorruptible and immortal. When he says it is a "building of God" (ἐκ Θεοῦ), he evidently means that it is made *by* God; that he is the architect of that future and eternal dwelling. Macknight and some others, however, understood this of the mansions which God has fitted up for his people in heaven, and which the Lord Jesus has gone to prepare for them ; comp. John xiv. 2. But see Note on ver. 3. ¶ *An house.* A dwelling; an abode ; that is, according to the interpretation above, a celestial, pure, immortal body ; a body that shall have God for its immediate author, and that shall be fitted to dwell in heaven for ever. ¶ *Not made with hands.* Not constructed by man ; a habitation not like those which are made by human skill, and which are therefore easily taken down or removed, but one that is made by God himself. This does not imply that the "earthly house" which is to be superseded by that in heaven is made with hands, but the idea is, that the earthly dwelling has things about it which *resemble* that which is made by man, or *as if* it were made with hands ; *i. e.* it is temporary, frail, easily taken down or removed. But that which is in heaven is permanent, fixed, eternal, *as if* made by God.

3 If so be that being clothed we shall not be found naked. *a*

a Re.3.18; 16.15.

¶ *Eternal in the heavens.* Immortal; to live for ever. The future body shall never be taken down or dissolved by death. It is eternal, of course, only in respect to the future, and not in respect to the past. And it is not only eternal, but it is to abide for ever *in* the heavens—in the world of glory. It is never to be subjected to a dwelling on the earth ; never to be in a world of sin, suffering, and death. 2. *For in this.* In this tent, tabernacle, or dwelling. In our body here. ¶ *We groan;* comp. Note, Rom. viii. 22. The sense is, that we are subjected to so many trials and afflictions in the present body ; that the body is subjected to so many pains and to so much suffering, as to make us earnestly desire to be invested with that body which shall be free from all susceptibility to suffering. ¶ *Earnestly desiring to be clothed upon with our house,* &c. There is evidently here a change of the metaphor which gives an apparent harshness to the construction. One idea of the apostle is, that the body here, and the spiritual body hereafter, is a house or a dwelling. Here he speaks of it as *a garment* which may be put on or laid off; and of himself as earnestly desiring to put on the immortal clothing or vestment which was in heaven. Both these figures are common in ancient writings, and a change in this manner in the popular style is not unusual. The Pythagoreans compared the body to a tent, or hut, for the soul ; the Platonists liken it to a vestment.— *Bloomfield.* The Jews speak of a vestment to the soul in this world and the next. They affirm that the soul had a covering when it was under the throne of God, and before it was clothed with the body. This *vestment* they say was "the image of God" which was lost by Adam. After the fall, they say Adam and all his posterity were regarded as naked. In the future world they say the good will be clothed with a vestment for the soul which they speak of as lucid

4 For we that are in *this* tabernacle do groan, being burdened ;

and radiant, and such as no one on earth can attain.— *Schoettgen.* But there is no reason to think that Paul referred to any such trifles as the Jews have believed on this subject. He evidently regarded man as composed of body and soul. The soul was the more important part, and the body constituted its mere habitation or dwelling. Yet a body was essential to the idea of the complete man ; and since this was frail and dying, he looked forward to a union with the body that should be eternal in the heavens, as a more desirable and perfect habitation of the soul. Mr. Locke has given an interpretation of this in which he is probably alone, but which has so much appearance of plausibility that it is not improper to refer to it. He supposes that this whole passage has reference to the fact that at the coming of the Redeemer the body will be changed without experiencing death ; (comp. 1 Cor. xv. 51, 52); that Paul expected that this might soon occur ; and that he earnestly desired to undergo this transformation without experiencing the pains of dying. He therefore paraphrases it, "For in this tabernacle I groan, earnestly desiring, without putting off this mortal, earthly body by death, to have that celestial body superinduced, if so be the coming of Christ shall overtake me in this life, before I put off this body." ¶ *With our house.* The phrase "to be clothed upon with our house" seems to be harsh and unusual. The sense is plain, however, that Paul desired to be invested with that pure, spiritual, and undecaying body which was to be the eternal abode of his soul in heaven. That he speaks of as a house (οἰκητήριον), a more permanent and substantial dwelling than a *tent*, or tabernacle. 3. *If so be that being clothed.* This passage has been interpreted in a great many different ways. The view of Locke is given above. Rosenmüller renders it, " For in the other life we shall not be wholly destitute of a

not for that we would be un-clothed, but clothed upon, that mortality *a* might be swallowed up of life.

a 1 Cor.15.33.

body, but we shall have a body." Tindal renders it, "If it happen that we be found clothed, and not naked." Doddridge supposes it to mean, "since being so clothed upon, we shall not be found naked, and exposed to any evil and inconvenience, how entirely soever we may be stripped of every thing we can call our own here below." Hammond explains it to mean, "If, indeed, we shall, happily, be among the number of those faithful Christians, who will be found clothed upon, not naked." Various other exposi-tions may be seen in the larger com-mentaries. The meaning is probably this: (1.) The word "clothed" refers to the future spiritual body of believers; the eternal habitation in which they shall reside. (2.) The expression implies an earnest desire of Paul to be thus invested with that body. (3.) It is the language of humility and of deep solicitude, as if it were possible that they might fail, and as if it demanded their utmost care and anxiety that they *might* thus be clothed with the spiritual body in heaven. (4.) It means that in that future state, the soul will not be naked; *i. e.* destitute of any body, or covering. The present body will be laid aside. It will return to corruption, and the disembodied Spirit will ascend to God and to heaven. It will be disencum-bered of the body with which it has been so long clothed. But we are not thence to infer that it will be desti-tute of a body; that it will remain a naked soul. It will be clothed there in its appropriate glorified body; and will have an appropriate habitation there. This does not imply, as Bloom-field supposes, that the souls of the wicked will be destitute of any such habitation as the glorified body of the saints; which may be true—but it means simply that the soul shall not be destitute of an appropriate body in heaven, but that the union of body and soul there shall be known as well as on earth.

4. *For we.* We who are Chris-tians. All Christians. ¶ *That are in this tabernacle.* This frail and dying body; Note, ver. 1. ¶ *Do groan;* see ver. 2. This is a further explanation of what is said in ver. 2. It implies an ardent and earnest desire to leave a world of toil and pain, and to enter into a world of rest and glory. ¶ *Being burdened.* Being borne down by the toils, and trials, and calamities of this life; see Note, chap. iii. 7—10. ¶ *Not for that we would be unclothed.* Not that we are impatient, and unwilling to bear these burdens as long as God shall appoint. Not that we merely wish to lay aside this mortal body. We do not desire to die and depart merely because we suffer much, and because the body here is subjected to great trials. This is not the ground of our wish to depart. We are willing to bear trials. We are not impatient under afflictions. —The sentiment here is, that the mere fact that we may be afflicted much and long, should not be the principal reason why we should desire to depart. We should be willing to bear all this as long as God shall choose to appoint. The anxiety of Paul to enter the eternal world was from a higher motive than a mere desire to get away from trouble. ¶ *But clothed upon.* To be invested with our spiritual body. We desire to be clothed with that body. We desire to be in heaven, and to be clothed with immortality. We wish to have a body that shall be pure, undecaying, ever glorious. It was not, therefore, a mere desire to be released from sufferings; it was an earnest wish to be admitted to the glories of the future world, and partake of the happiness which we would enjoy there. This is *one* of the reasons why Paul wished to be in heaven. *Other* reasons he has stated elsewhere. Thus in Phil. i. 23, he says he had "a desire to depart and to *be with Christ.*" So in ver. 8 of this chapter, he says he was "willing rather to be absent from the body and to be pre-

5 Now he that hath wrought *a* us for the self-same thing, *is* God, who also hath given unto us the earnest *b* of the Spirit.

a Is.29.23; Ep.2.10.　　*b* Ep.1.14.

6 Therefore *we are* always confident, knowing that, whilst we are at home in the body, we are absent from the Lord :

sent with the Lord." In 2 Tim. iv. 6—8, he speaks of the "crown of righteousness" laid up for him as a reason why he was willing to die. ¶ *That mortality might be swallowed up of life.* On the meaning of the word rendered "swallowed up" (καταποθῇ); see Note on 1 Cor. xv. 54. The meaning here is, that it might be completely absorbed; that it might cease to be; that there might be no more mortality, but that he might pass to the immortal state—to the condition of eternal life in the heavens. The body here is mortal; the body there will be immortal; and Paul desired to pass away from the mortal state to one that shall be immortal, a world where there shall be no more death; comp. 1 Cor. xv. 53.

5. *Now he that hath wrought us for the self-same thing.* The phrase "self-same thing" here means *this very thing, i. e.* the thing to which he had referred—the preparation for heaven, or the heavenly dwelling. The word "wrought" here (κατεργασάμενος) means that God had *formed* or made them for this ; that is, he had by the influences of the Spirit, and by his agency on the heart, created them, as it were, for this, and adapted them to it. God has destined us to this change from corruption to incorruption ; he has adapted us to it ; he has formed us for it. It does not refer to the original creation of the body and the soul for this end, but it means that God, by his own renewing, and sanctifying, and sustaining agency, had formed them for this, and adapted them to it. The *object* of Paul in stating that it was done by God, is to keep this truth prominently before the mind. It was not by any native inclination, or strength, or power which they had, but it was all to be traced to God ; comp. Eph. ii. 10. ¶ *Who also hath given.* In addition to the fitting for eternal glory he has given us the earnest of the Spirit to sustain

us here. We are not only prepared to enter into heaven, but we have here also the support produced by the earnest of the Spirit. ¶ *The earnest of the Spirit.* On the meaning of this, see Note on chap. i. 22. He has given to us the Holy Spirit as the pledge or assurance of the eternal inheritance.

6. *Therefore we are always confident.* The word here used (θαρροῦντες) means to be of good cheer. To have good courage, to be full of hope. The idea is, that Paul was not dejected, cast down, disheartened, discouraged. He was cheerful and happy. He was patient in his trials, and diligent in his calling. He was full of hope, and of the confident expectation of heaven ; and this filled him with cheerfulness and with joy. Tindal renders it, "we are always of goud cheere." And this was not occasional and transitory, it was constant, it was uniform, it always (πάντοτε) existed.—This is an instance of the uniform *cheerfulness* which will be produced by the assured prospect of heaven. It is an instance too when the hope of heaven will enable a man to face danger with courage; to endure toil with patience; and to submit to trials in any form with cheerfulness. ¶ *Knowing ;* see ver. 1. This is another instance in which the apostle expresses undoubted assurance. ¶ *Whilst we are at home in the body.* The word here used (ἐνδημοῦντες) means literally to be among one's own people, to be at home ; to be present at any place. It is here equivalent to saying, "while we dwell in the body;" see ver. 1. Doddridge renders it, " sojourning in the body;" and remarks that it is improper to render it " at home in the body," since it is the apostle's design to intimate that this is *not* our home. But Bloomfield says that the word is never used in the sense of *sojourning*. The idea is not that of

7 (For *a* we walk by faith, not by sight:)

a Rom. 8.24,25.

8 We are confident, *I say*, and *b* willing rather to be absent

b Ph. 1.23.

being "at home"—for this is an idea which is the very opposite of that which the apostle wishes to convey. His purpose is not at all to represent the body here as our *home*, and the original word does not imply that. It means here simply to be *in* the body; to be present in the body; that is, while we are in the body. ¶ *We are absent from the Lord.* The Lord Jesus; see Notes, Acts i. 24; comp. Phil. i. 23. Here he was in a strange world, and among strangers. His great desire and purpose was to be *with* the Lord; and hence he cared little how soon the frail tabernacle of the body was taken down, and was cheerful amidst all the labours and sufferings that tended to bring it to the grave, and to release him to go to his eternal home where he would be present for ever with the Lord.

7. *For we walk.* To walk, in the Scriptures often denotes to live, to act, to conduct in a certain way; see Notes on Rom. iv. 12; vi. 4. It has reference to the fact that life is a journey, or a pilgrimage, and that the Christian is travelling to another country. The sense here is, that we conduct ourselves in our course of life with reference to the things which are unseen, and not with reference to the things which are seen. ¶ *By faith.* In the belief of those things which we do not see. We believe in the existence of objects which are invisible, and we are influenced by them. To walk by faith, is to live in the confident expectation of things that are to come; in the belief of the existence of unseen realities; and suffering them to influence us *as if* they were seen. The people of this world are influenced by the things that are *seen.* They live for wealth, honour, splendour, praise, for the objects which this world can furnish, and as if there were nothing which is unseen, or as if they ought not to be influenced by the things which are unseen. The Christian, on the contrary, has a firm conviction of the reality of the glories of

heaven; of the fact that the Redeemer is there; of the fact that there is a crown of glory; and he lives, and acts *as if* that were all real, and *as if* he saw it all. The simple account of faith, and of living by faith is, that we live and act *as if* these things were true, and suffer them to make an impression on our mind according to their real nature; see Note on Mark xvi. 16. It is contradistinguished from living simply under the influence of things that are seen. God is unseen—but the Christian lives, and thinks, and acts *as if* there were a God, and *as if* he saw him. Christ is unseen now by the bodily eye; but the Christian lives and acts as if he were seen, *i. e.* as if his eye were known to be upon us, and *as if* he was now exalted to heaven and was the only Saviour. The Holy Spirit is unseen; but he lives, and acts *as if* there were such a Spirit, and as if his influences were needful to renew, and purify the soul. Heaven is unseen; but the Christian lives, and thinks, and acts *as if* there were a heaven, and as if he now saw its glories. He has confidence in these, and in kindred truths, and he acts as if they were real.—Could man *see* all these; were they visible to the naked eye as they are to the eye of faith, no one would doubt the propriety of living and acting with reference to them. But *if* they exist, there is no more impropriety in acting with reference to them than if they were seen. Our seeing or not seeing them does not alter their nature or importance, and the fact that they are not seen does not make it improper to act with reference to them.—There are many ways of being convinced of the existence and reality of objects besides *seeing* them; and it may be as rational to be influenced by the reason, the judgment, or by strong confidence, as it is to be influenced by sight. Besides, all men are influenced by things which they have not seen. They hope for objects that are future.

from the body, and to be present with the Lord.

9 Wherefore we [1] labour, that,

[1] *endeavour.*

whether present or absent, we may be accepted of him.

10 For [a] we must all appear

[a] Rom. 14.10.

They aspire to happiness which they have not yet beheld. They strive for honour and wealth which are unseen, and which is in the distant future. They live, and act—influenced by strong faith and hope—*as if* these things were attainable; and they deny themselves, and labour, and cross oceans and deserts, and breathe in pestilential air to obtain those things which they have not seen, and which to them are in the distant future. And why should not the Christian endure *like* labour, and be willing to suffer in like manner, to gain the *unseen* crown which is incorruptible, and to acquire the *unseen* wealth which the moth does not corrupt?—And further still, the men of this world strive for those objects which they have not beheld, without any promise or any assurance that they shall obtain them. No being able to grant them has promised them; no one has assured them that their lives shall be lengthened out to obtain them. In a moment they may be cut off and all their plans frustrated; or they may be utterly disappointed and all their plans fail; or if they gain the object, it may be unsatisfactory, and may furnish no pleasure such as they had anticipated. But not so the Christian. He has, (1.) The promise of life. (2.) He has the assurance that sudden death cannot deprive him of it. It at once removes him *to* the object of pursuit, not *from* it. (3.) He has the assurance that *when* obtained, it shall not disgust, or satiate, or decay, but that it shall meet all the expectations of the soul, and shall be eternal. ¶ *Not by sight.* This may mean either that we are not influenced by a sight of these future glories, or that we are not influenced by the things which we see. The main idea is, that we are not influenced and governed by the sight. We are not governed and controlled by the things which we see, and we do not see those things which actually

influence and control us. In both it is *faith* that controls us, and not sight.

8. *We are confident,* ver. 6. We are cheerful, and courageous, and ready to bear our trial. Tindal renders it, "we are of good comfort." ¶ *And willing rather to be absent from the body.* We would prefer to die. The same idea occurs in Phil. i. 23. "Having a desire to depart and to be with Christ; which is far better." The sense is, that Paul would have *preferred* to die, and to go to heaven, rather than to remain in a world of sin and trial. ¶ *To be present with the Lord.* The Lord Jesus; see Note on Acts i. 24; comp. Phil. i. 23. The idea of Paul is, that the Lord Jesus would constitute the main glory of heaven, and that to be with him was equivalent to being in a place of perfect bliss. He had no idea of any heaven where the Lord Jesus was not; and to be with him was to be in heaven. That world where the Redeemer is, is heaven. This also proves that the spirits of the saints, when they depart, are with the Redeemer; *i. e.* are at once taken to heaven. It demonstrates (1.) That they are not annihilated. (2.) That they do not *sleep*, and remain in an unconscious state, as Dr. Priestley supposes. (3.) That they are not in some intermediate state, either in a state of purgatory, as the Papists suppose, or a state where all the souls of the just and the unjust are assembled in a common abode, as many Protestants have supposed; but, (4.) That they *dwell* WITH Christ; they are WITH the Lord (πρὸς τὸν Κύριον). They abide in his presence; they partake of his joy and his glory; they are permitted to sit with him in his throne; Rev. iii. 21. The same idea the Saviour expressed to the dying thief, when he said, "to-day shalt thou be with me in paradise;" Luke xxiii. 43.

9. *Wherefore* (Διὸ). In view of the facts stated above. Since we have the prospect of a resurrection and of

before the judgment - seat of Christ; that every one may receive *a* the things *done* in *his*

a chap. 7.3.

body, according to that he hath done, whether *it be* good or bad.

future glory; since we have the assurance that there is a house not made with hands, eternal in the heavens; and since God has given to us this hope, and has granted to us the earnest of the Spirit, we make it our great object so to live as to be accepted by him. ¶ *We labour.* The word here used (φιλοτιμούμεθα, from φίλος and τιμὴ, loving honour) means properly to love honour; to be ambitious. This is its usual classical signification. In the New Testament, it means to be ambitious to do any thing; to exert one's self; to strive, as if from a love or sense of honour. As in English, *to make it a point of honour* to do so and so.— *Robinson* (Lex.); see Rom. xv. 20; 1 Thess. iv. 11. It means here, that Paul made it a point of constant effort; it was his leading and constant aim to live so as to be acceptable to God, and to meet his approbation wherever he was. ¶ *Whether present or absent.* Whether present with the Lord (ver. 8), or absent from him (ver. 6); that is, whether in this world or the next; whether we are here, or removed to heaven. Wherever we are, or may be, it is, and will be our main purpose and object so to live as to secure his favour. Paul did not wish to live on earth regardless of his favour or without evidence that he would be accepted by him. He did not make the fact that he was absent from him, and that he did not see him with the bodily eye, an excuse for walking in the ways of ambition, or seeking his own purposes and ends. The idea is, that *so far as this point was concerned*, it made no difference with him whether he lived or died; whether he was on earth or in heaven; whether in the body or out of the body; it was the great fixed principle of his nature so to live as to secure the approbation of the Lord. And this is the true principle on which the Christian should act, and will act. The fact that he is now

absent from the Lord will be to him no reason why he should lead a life of sin and self-indulgence, any more than he would if he were in heaven; and the fact that he is soon to be with him is not the main reason why he seeks to live so as to please him. It is because this has become the fixed principle of the soul; the very purpose of the life; and this principle and this purpose will adhere to him, and control him wherever he may be placed, or in whatever world he may dwell. ¶ *We may be accepted of him.* The phrase here used (εὐάρεστοι εἶναι) means to be well-pleasing; and then to be acceptable, or approved; Rom. xii. 1; xiv. 18; Eph. v. 10; Phil. iv. 18; Tit. ii. 9. The sense here is, that Paul was earnestly desirous of so living as to please God, and to receive from him the tokens and marks of his favour. And the truth taught in this verse is, that this will be the great purpose of the Christian's life, and that it makes no difference as to the existence and operation of this principle whether a man is on earth or in heaven. He will equally desire it, and strive for it; and this is one of the ways in which religion makes a man conscientious and holy, and is a better guard and security for virtue than all human laws, and all the restraints which can be imposed by man.

10. *For we must* (δεῖ). It is proper, fit, necessary that we should all appear there. This fact, to which Paul now refers, is *another* reason why it was necessary to lead a holy life, and why Paul gave himself with so much diligence and self-denial to the arduous duties of his office. There is a necessity, or a fitness that we should appear there to give up our account, for we are here on trial; we are responsible moral agents; we are placed here to form characters for eternity. Before we receive our eternal allotment it is *proper* that we should render our account of the man-

ner in which we have lived, and of the manner in which we have improved our talents and privileges. In the nature of things, it is proper that we should undergo a trial before we receive our reward, or before we are punished; and God has made it necessary and certain, by his direct and positive appointment, that we should stand at the bar of the final judge; see Rom. xiv. 10. ¶ *All.* Both Jews and Gentiles; old and young; bond and free; rich and poor; all of every class, and every age, and every nation. None shall escape by being unknown; none by virtue of their rank, or wealth; none because they have a character too pure to be judged. All shall be arranged in one vast assemblage, and with reference to their eternal doom; see Rev. xx. 13. Rosenmuller supposes that the apostle here alludes to an opinion that was common among the Jews that the Gentiles only would be exposed to severe judgments in the future world, and that the Jews would be saved as a matter of course. But the idea seems rather to be, that as the trial of the great day was the most important that man could undergo, and as *all must* give account there, Paul and his fellow-labourers devoted themselves to untiring diligence and fidelity that they might be accepted in that great day. ¶ *Appear* (φανερω-θῆναι). This word properly means, to make apparent, manifest, known; to show openly, &c. Here it means that we must be manifest, or openly shown; *i. e.* we must be seen there, and be *publicly* tried. We must not only *stand* there, but our character will be seen, our desert will be known, our trial will be public. All will be brought from their graves, and from their places of concealment, and will *be seen* at the judgment-seat. The secret things of the heart and the life will all be made manifest and known. ¶ *The judgment-seat of Christ.* The tribunal of Christ, who is appointed to be the judge of quick and dead; see Note on John v. 25; Acts x. 42; xvii. 31. Christ is appointed to judge the world; and for this purpose he will assemble it before him, and

assign to all their eternal allotments; see Mat. xxv. ¶ *That every one may receive.* The word rendered *may receive* (κομίσηται) means properly to take care of, to provide for; and in the New Testament, to bear, to bring (Luke vii. 37); to acquire, to obtain, to receive. This is the sense here. Every individual shall take, receive, or *bear away* the appropriate reward for the transactions of this life of probation; see Eph. vi. 8; Col. iii. 25. ¶ *The things.* The appropriate *reward* of the actions of this life. ¶ Done *in* his *body.* Literally, "the things by or through (διὰ) the body." Tindal renders it, "the works of his body." The idea is, that every man shall receive an appropriate reward for the actions of this life. Observe here, (1.) That it is the works done *in* or *through* the body; not which the body itself has done. It is the *mind*, the man that has lived *in* the body, and acted by it, that is to be judged. (2.) It is to be for the deeds of this life; not for what is done *after death.* Men are not to be brought into judgment for what they do *after* they die. All beyond the grave is either reward or punishment; it is not probation. The destiny is to be settled for ever by what is done in this world of probation. (3.) It is to be for *all* the deeds done in the body; for all the thoughts, plans, purposes, words, as well as for all the *outward* actions of the man. All that has been thought or done must come into review, and man must give an account for all. ¶ *According to that he hath done.* As an exact retribution for all that has been done. It is to be a *suitable* and *proper* recompence. The retribution is to be measured by what has been done in this life. Rewards shall be granted to the friends, and punishments to the foes of God, just in proportion to, or suitably to their deeds in this life. Every man shall receive just what, under all the circumstances, he OUGHT to receive, and what will be impartial justice in the case. The judgment will be such that it will be capable of being *seen* to be right; and such as the universe at large, and as the individuals them-

11 Knowing therefore the terror *a* of the Lord, we persuade men; but *b* we are made manifest

a Heb. 10.31; Jude 23.

unto God, and I trust also are made manifest in your consciences.

b chap. 4.2.

selves will *see* ought to be rendered. ¶ *Whether* it be *good or bad.* Whether the life has been good or evil. The good will have no wish to escape the trial; the evil will not be able. No power of wickedness, however great, will be able to escape from the trial of that day; no crime that has been concealed in this life will be concealed there; no transgressor of law who may have long escaped the punishment due to his sins, and who may have evaded all human tribunals, will be able to escape there.

11. *Knowing therefore.* We who are apostles, and who are appointed to preach the gospel, having the fullest assurance of the terrors of the day of judgment, and of the wrath of God, endeavour to persuade men to be prepared to meet Him, and to give up their account. ¶ *The terror of the Lord.* This is, of the Lord Jesus, who will be seated on the throne of judgment, and who will decide the destiny of all men, ver. 10; comp. Mat. xxv. The sense is, knowing how much the Lord is to be feared; what an object of terror and alarm it will be to stand at the judgment-seat; how fearful and awful will be the consequences of the trial of that day. The Lord Jesus will be an object of terror and alarm, or it will be a subject inspiring terror and alarm to stand there on that day, because, (1.) He has all power, and is appointed to execute judgment; (2.) Because all must there give a strict and impartial account of all that they have done; (3.) Because the wrath of God will be shown in the condemnation of the guilty. It will be a day of awful wailing and alarm when all the living and the dead shall be arraigned on trial with reference to their eternal destiny; and when countless hosts of the guilty and impenitent shall be thrust down to an eternal hell. Who can describe the amazing terror of the scene? Who can fancy the horrors of the hosts of the guilty and the

wretched who shall then hear that their doom is to be fixed for ever in a world of unspeakable woe? The *influence* of the knowledge of the terror of the Lord on the mind of the apostle seems to have been two-fold; first, an apprehension of it as a personal concern, and a desire to escape it, which led him to constant self-denial and toil; and secondly, a desire to save others from being overwhelmed in the wrath of that dreadful day. ¶ *We persuade men.* We endeavour to persuade them to flee from the wrath to come; to be prepared to stand before the judgment-seat, and to be fitted to enter into heaven. Observe here the peculiarity of the statement. It is not, we drive men; or we endeavour to alarm men; or we frighten men; or we appeal merely to their fears, but it is, we persuade men, we endeavour to induce them by all the arts of persuasion and argument to flee from the wrath to come. The future judgment, and the scenes of future woe, are not proper topics for mere declamation. To declaim constantly on hell-fire and perdition; to appeal merely to the fears of men, is not the way in which Paul and the Saviour preached the gospel. The knowledge that there would be a judgment, and that the wicked would be sent to hell, was a powerful motive for Paul to endeavour to "persuade" men to escape from wrath, and was a motive for the Saviour to weep over Jerusalem, and to lament its folly, and its doom; Luke xix. 41 But they who fill their sermons with the denunciations of wrath; who dwell on the words hell and damnation, for the purpose of rhetoric or declamation, to round a period, or merely to excite alarm; and who "deal damnation around the land" as if they rejoiced that men were to be condemned, and in a tone and manner as if they would be pleased to execute it, have yet to learn the true nature of the way to win men to God, and the proper effect

12 For *a* we commend not ourselves again unto you, but give you occasion to glory on our

a chap. 3.1.

behalf, that ye may have some what to *answer* them which glory in ¹ appearance, and not in heart.

1 *in the face.*

of those awful truths on the mind. The true effect is, to produce tenderness, deep feeling, and love; to prompt to the language of persuasion and of tender entreaty; to lead men to weep over dying sinners rather than to denounce them; to pray to God to have mercy on them rather than to use the language of severity, or to assume tones as if they would be pleased to execute the awful wrath of God. ¶ *But we are made manifest unto God.* The meaning of this is, probably, that God sees that we are sincere and upright in our aims and purposes. He is acquainted with our hearts. All our motives are known to him, and he sees that it is our aim to promote his glory, and to save the souls of men. This is probably said to counteract the charge which might have been brought against him by some of the disaffected in Corinth, that he was influenced by improper motives and aims. To meet this, Paul says, that God knew that he was endeavouring to save souls, and that he was actuated by a sincere desire to rescue them from the impending terrors of the day of judgment. ¶ *And I trust also,* &c. And I trust also you are convinced of our integrity and uprightness of aim. The same sentiment is expressed in other words in chap. iv. 2. It is an appeal which he makes to them, and the expression of an earnest and confident assurance that they knew and felt that his aim was upright, and his purpose sincere.

12. *For we commend not ourselves again unto you.* This refers to what he had said in the previous verse. He had there said that he had such a consciousness of integrity that he could appeal to God, and that he was persuaded that the Corinthians also approved his course, or admitted that he was influenced by right motives. He here states the reason why he had said this. It was not to com-

mend himself to them. It was not to boast of his own character, nor was it in order to secure their praise or favour Some might be disposed to misrepresent all that Paul said of himself, and to suppose that it was said for mere vain-glory, or the love of praise. He tells them, therefore, that his sole aim was necessary self-defence, and in order that they might have the fullest evidence that he, by whom they had been converted, was a true apostle; and that he whom they regarded as their friend and father in the gospel was a man of whom they need not be ashamed. ¶ *But give you occasion.* This is a very happy turn of expression. The sense is, " You have been converted under my labours. You profess to regard me as your spiritual father and friend. I have no reason to doubt of your attachment to me. Yet you often hear my name slandered, and hear me accused of wanting the evidence of being an apostle, and of being vain-glorious, and self seeking. I know your desire to vindicate my character, and to show that you are my friends. I, therefore, say these things in regard to myself in order that you may be thus able to show your respect for me, and to vindicate me from the false and slanderous accusations of my enemies. Thus doing, you will be able to answer them; to show that the man whom you thus respect is worthy of your confidence and esteem." ¶ *On your behalf.* For your own benefit, or as it were in self-vindication for adhering to me, and evincing attachment to me. ¶ *That ye may have somewhat to* answer *them.* That you may be furnished with a ready reply when you are charged with adhering to a man who has no claims to the apostleship, or who is slandered in any other way. ¶ *Which glory in appearance.* The false teachers in Corinth. Probably they boasted of their rank, their eloquence, their talents, their external advantages; but

13 For whether we be be-side *a* ourselves, *it is* to God : or whether we be sober, *it is* for your cause.

a ch. 11. 1, 16, 17.

not in the qualities of the heart—in sincerity, honesty, real love for souls. Their consciences would not allow them to do this ; and they knew themselves that their boasting was mere vain pretence, and that there was no real and solid ground for it. The margin is, "in the face." The meaning is, probably, that their ground of boasting was external, and was such as can be seen of men, and was not rather the secret consciousness of right, which could exist only in the conscience and the heart. Paul, on the other hand, gloried mainly in his sincerity, his honesty, his desire for their salvation ; in his conscious integrity before God ; and not in any mere external advantages or professions, in his rank, eloquence, or talent. Accordingly all his argument here turns on his sincerity, his conscious uprightness, and his real regard for their welfare. And the truth taught here is, that sincerity and conscious integrity are more valuable than any or all external advantages and endowments.

13. *For whether we be beside ourselves.* This is probably designed to meet some of the charges which the false teachers in Corinth brought against him, and to furnish his friends there with a ready answer, as well as to show them the true principles on which he acted, and his real love for them. It is altogether probable that he was charged with being deranged ; that many who boasted themselves of prudence, and soberness, and wisdom, regarded him as acting like a mad-man. It has not been uncommon, by any means, for the cold and the prudent ; for formal professors and for hypocrites to regard the warm-hearted and zealous friends of religion as maniacs. Festus thought Paul was deranged, when he said, " Paul, thou art beside thyself; much learning doth make thee mad," (Acts xxvi. 24); and the Saviour himself was regarded by his immediate relatives and friends as beside himself, Mark iii. 21. And at all times there have been many, both in the church and out of it, who have regarded the friends of revivals, and of missions, and all those who have evinced any extraordinary zeal in religion, as deranged. The object of Paul here is to show, whatever might be the appearance or the estimate which they affixed to his conduct, what were the real principles which actuated him. These were zeal for God, love to the church, and the constraining influences of the love of Christ, ver. 14, 15. The word here rendered " be beside ourselves " (ἐξίστημεν, from ἐξίστημι) means properly, to put out of place ; to be put out of place ; and then to be put out of one's self, to astonish, to fill with wonder; Luke xxiv. 22; Acts viii. 9, 11; and then to be out of one's mind, to be deranged. Here it means that they were charged with being deranged, or that others esteemed, or professed to esteem Paul and his fellow-labourers deranged. ¶ It is *to God.* It is in the cause of God, and from love to him. It is such a zeal for him ; such an absorbing interest in his cause ; such love prompting to so great self-denial, and teaching us to act so much unlike other men as to lead them to think that we are deranged. The doctrine here is, that there may be such a zeal for the glory of God, such an active and ardent desire to promote his honour, as to lead others to charge us with derangement. It does not *prove* however that a man is deranged on the subject of religion because he is unlike others, or because he pursues a course of life that differs materially from that of other professors of religion, and from the man of the world. *He* may be the truly sane man after all ; and all the madness that may exist may be where there is a profession of religion without zeal ; a professed belief in the existence of God and in the realities of eternity, that produces no difference

14 For the love of *a* Christ con-
straineth us ; because we thus

a Cn. 8. 6.

judge, that if one died for all
then *b* were all dead.

b Ro. 5. 15; 14. 7, 9.

in the conduct between the professor
and other men ; or an utter unconcern
about eternal realities when a man is
walking on the brink of death and of
hell. There are few men that become
deranged *by* religion ; there are millions who act as madmen who have no
religion. And the highest instances
of madness in the world are those who
walk over an eternal hell without
apprehension or alarm. ¶ *Or whether
we be sober.* Whether we are sane,
or of sound mind ; comp. Mark v. 15.
Tindal renders this whole passage,
" For if we be too fervent, to God
we are too fervent ; if we keep measure, for our cause keep we measure."
The sense seems to be, " if we are
esteemed to be sane, and sober-
minded, as we trust you will admit us
to be, it is for your sake. Whatever
may be the estimate in which we are
held, we are influenced by love to
God, and love to man. In such a
cause, we cannot but evince zeal and
self-denial which may expose us to the
charge of mental derangement ; but
still we trust that by you we shall be
regarded as influenced by a sound
mind. We seek your welfare. We
labour for you. And we trust that
you will appreciate our motives, and
regard us as truly sober-minded."
  11. *For the love of Christ.* In this
verse, Paul brings into view *the principle* which actuated him ; the reason
of his extraordinary and disinterested
zeal. That was, that he was influenced by the love which Christ had
shown in dying for all men, and by
the argument which was furnished by
that death respecting the actual character and condition of man (in this
verse); and of the obligation of those
who professed to be his true friends,
ver. 15. The phrase " the love of
Christ " (ἀγάπη τοῦ Χριστοῦ) may denote either the love which Christ
bears *toward us,* and which he has
manifested, or our love *towards him.*
In the former sense the phrase " the
love of God " is used in Rom. v. 8 ;

2 Cor. xiii. 13, and the phrase "love
of Christ " in Eph. iii. 14. The phrase
is used in the latter sense in John
xv. 9, 10, and Rom. viii. 35. It is
impossible to determine the sense
with certainty, and it is only by the
view which shall be taken of the connection and of the argument which
will in any way determine the meaning. Expositors differ in regard to it.
It seems to me that the phrase here
means the love which Christ had toward us. Paul speaks of his dying
for all as the reason why he was urged
on to the course of self-denial which
he evinced. Christ died for all. All
were dead. Christ evinced his great
love for us, and for all, by giving himself to die ; and it was this love which
Christ had shown that impelled Paul
to his own acts of love and self-denial.
He gave himself to his great work
impelled by that love which Christ
had shown ; by the view of the ruined
condition of man which that work furnished ; and by a desire to emulate
the Redeemer, and to possess the
same spirit which he evinced. ¶ *Con-
straineth us* (συνέχει). This word
(συνέχω) properly means, to hold together, to press together, to shut up ;
then to press on, urge, impel, or excite. Here it means, that the impel-
ling, or exciting motive in the labours
and self-denials of Paul, was the love
of Christ—the love which he had
showed to the children of men.
Christ so loved the world as to give
himself for it. His love for the
world was a demonstration that men
were dead in sins. And we, being
urged by the same love, are prompted
to like acts of zeal and self-denial to
save the world from ruin. ¶ *Because
we thus judge.* Gr. " We judging this;"
that is, we thus determine in our
own minds, or we thus decide ; or this
is our firm conviction and belief—we
come to this conclusion. ¶ *That if
one died for all.* On the supposition
that one died for all ; or taking it for
granted that one died for all, then it

follows that all were dead. The "one" who died for all here is undoubtedly the Lord Jesus. The word "for" (ὑπὲρ) means in the place of, instead of; see Phil. 13 ; ver. 20. of this chapter. It means that Christ took the place of sinners, and died in their stead ; that he endured what was an ample equivalent for all the punishment which would be inflicted if they were to suffer the just penalty of the law ; that he endured so much suffering, and that God by his great substituted sorrows made such an expression of his hatred of sin, as to answer *the same end* in expressing his sense of the evil of sin, and in restraining others from transgression, *as if* the guilty were personally to suffer the full penalty of the law. If this was done, of course, the guilty might be pardoned and saved, since all the ends which could be accomplished by their destruction have been accomplished by the substituted sufferings of the Lord Jesus ; see Notes on Rom. iii. 25, 26, where this subject is considered at length.—The phrase " for all," (ὑπὲρ πάντων) obviously means for all mankind; for every man. This is an exceedingly important expression in regard to the extent of the atonement which the Lord Jesus made, and while it proves that his death was vicarious, *i. e.*, in the place of others, and for their sakes, it *demonstrates* also that the atonement was *general*, and had, in itself considered, no limitation, and no particular reference to any class or condition of men ; and no particular applicability to one class more than to another. There was nothing in the *nature* of the atonement that limited it to any one class or condition ; there was nothing in the design that made it, in itself, any more applicable to one portion of mankind than to another. And whatever may be true in regard to *the fact* as to its actual applicability, or in regard to *the purpose of God* to apply it, it is demonstrated by this passage that his death had an original applicability to all, and that the merits of that death were sufficient to save all. The argument in favour of the general atone-

ment, from this passage, consists in the following points. (1.) That Paul *assumes* this as a matter that was well known, indisputable, and universally admitted, that Christ died for all. He did not deem it necessary to enter into the argument to prove it, nor even to *state* it formally. It was so well known, and so universally admitted, that he made it a *first principle* — an elementary position — a maxim on which to base another important doctrine—to wit, that all were dead. It was a point which he assumed that no one would call in question ; a doctrine which might be laid down as the *basis* of an argument, like one of the first principles or maxims in science. (2.) It is the plain and obvious meaning of the expression—the sense which strikes *all* men, unless they have some theory to support to the contrary ; and it requires all the ingenuity which men can ever command to make it appear even *plausible*, that this is consistent with the doctrine of a limited atonement ; much more to make it out that it does not mean all. If a man is told that *all* the human family must die, the obvious interpretation is, that it applies to every individual. If told that all the passengers on board a steamboat were drowned, the obvious interpretation is, that every individual was meant. If told that a ship was wrecked, and that all the crew perished, the obvious interpretation would be that none escaped. If told that *all* the inmates of an hospital were sick, it would be understood that there was not an individual that was not sick. Such is the view which would be taken by nine hundred and ninety-nine persons out of a thousand, if told that Christ died for all ; nor could they conceive how this could be consistent with the statement that he died only for the elect, and that the elect was only a small part of the human family. (3.) This interpretation is in accordance with all the *explicit* declarations on the design of the death of the Redeemer. Heb. ii. 9, " That he, by the grace of God, should taste death for every man ;" comp. John iii. 16, "God so loved the world that he gave his only begotten Son, that *whosoever* believeth on him should not perish, but have everlasting life." 1 Tim. ii. 16, " Who gave himself a ransom for all." See Matt. xx. 28, " The Son of man came to give his life a ransom for many." 1 John ii. 2, " And he is the propitiation for our sins, and not for ours only, but also for the sins of the whole world." (4.) The fact also that on the ground of the atonement made by the Redeemer, salvation is offered to all men *by God*, is a proof that he died for all. The apostles were directed to go " into all the world and to preach the gospel *to every creature*," with the assurance that "he that believeth and is baptized shall be saved;" Mark xvi. 15, 16; and everywhere in the Bible the most full and free offers of salvation are made to all mankind ; comp. Isa. lv. 1; John vii. 37; Rev. xxii. 17. These offers are made on the ground that the Lord Jesus died for men ; John iii. 16. They are offers of salvation through the gospel, of the pardon of sin, and of eternal life to be made "to every creature." But if Christ died only for a part, if there is a large portion of the human family for whom he died in no sense whatever; if there is no provision of any kind made for them, then God must know this, and then the offers cannot be made with sincerity, and God is tantalising them with the offers of that which does not exist, and which he knows does not exist. It is of no use here to say that the preacher does not know who the elect are, and that he is obliged to make the offer to all in order that the elect may be reached. For it is not the preacher only who offers the gospel. It is God who does it, and he knows who the elect are, and yet *he* offers salvation to all. And if there is no salvation provided for all, and no possibility that all to whom the offer comes should be saved, then God is insincere ; and there is no way possible of vindicating his character. (5.) If this interpretation is not correct, and if Christ did not die for all, then the argument of Paul here is a *non sequitur*, and is worthless. The demonstration that all are

dead, according to him is, that Christ died for all. But suppose that he meant, or that he knew, that Christ died only for a part, for the elect, then how would the argument stand, and what would be its force? " Christ died only for a portion of the human race, *therefore* ALL are sinners. Medicine is provided only for a part of mankind, therefore all are sick. Pardon is offered to part only, therefore all are guilty." But Paul never reasoned in this way. He believed that Christ died for all mankind, and on the ground of that he inferred at once that all needed such an atonement ; that all were sinners, and that all were exposed to the wrath of God. And the argument is in this way, and in this way only, sound. But still it may be asked, What is the force of this argument? How does the fact that Christ died for all, prove that all were sinners, or dead in sin ?—I answer, (*a*) In the same way that to provide medicine for all, proves that all are sick, or liable to be sick ; and to offer pardon to all who are in a prison, proves that all there are guilty. What insult is it to offer medicine to a man in health ; or pardon to a man who has violated no law ! And there would be the same insult in offering salvation to a man who was not a sinner, and who did not need forgiveness. (*b*) The dignity of the sufferer, and the extent of his sufferings, prove that all were under a deep and dreadful load of guilt. Such a being would not have come to die unless *the race* had been apostate ; nor would he have endured so great sorrows unless a deep and dreadful malady had spread over the world. The deep anxiety ; the tears ; the toils ; the sufferings, and the groans of the Redeemer, show what was *his* sense of the condition of man, and prove that *he* regarded them as degraded, fallen, and lost. And if the Son of God, who knows all hearts, regarded them as lost, they *are* lost. He was not mistaken in regard to the character of man, and he did not lay down his life under the influence of delusion and error. If to the view which has been taken of this important passage it be objected that the work of the atonement must have been to a large extent in vain; that it has actually been applied to but comparatively a small portion of the human family, and that it is unreasonable to suppose that God would suffer so great sorrows to be endured for naught, we may reply, (1.) That it may not have been in vain, though it may have been rejected by a large portion of mankind. There may have been other purposes accomplished by it besides the direct salvation of men. It was doing much when it rendered it consistent for God to offer salvation to all; it is much that God could be seen to be just and yet pardoning the sinner; it was much when his determined hatred of sin, and his purpose to honour his law, was evinced; and in regard to the benevolence and justice of God to other beings and to other worlds, much, very much was gained, though all the human race had rejected the plan and been lost, and in regard to *all* these objects, the plan was not in vain, and the sufferings of the Redeemer were not for naught. But, (2.) It is in accordance with what we see everywhere, when much that God does seems to our eyes, though not to his, to be in vain. How much rain falls on ever sterile sands or on barren rocks, to our eyes in vain! What floods of light are poured each day on barren wastes, or untraversed oceans, to our eyes in vain! How many flowers shed forth their fragrance in the wilderness, and 'waste their sweetness on the desert air," to us apparently for naught! How many pearls lie useless in the ocean; how much gold and silver in the earth; how many diamonds amidst rocks to us unknown, and apparently in vain! How many lofty trees rear their heads in the untraversed wilderness, and after standing for centuries fall on the earth and decay, to our eyes in vain! And how much *medicinal virtue* is created by God each year in the vegetable world that is unknown to man, and that decays and is lost without removing any disease, and that seems to be created in vain! And how long has it been before the most valuable medicines have been

found out, and applied to alleviating pain, or removing disease! Year after year, and age after age, they existed in a suffering world, and men died perhaps within a few yards of the medicine which would have relieved or saved them, but it was unknown, or if known disregarded. But times were coming when their value would be appreciated, and when they would be applied to benefit the sufferer. So with the plan of salvation. It may be rejected, and the sufferings of the Redeemer may seem to have been for naught. But they will yet be of value to mankind; and when the time shall come for the whole world to embrace the Saviour, there will be found no want of sufficiency in the plan of redemption, and in the merits of the Redeemer to save all the race.

[A measure of truth is, doubtless, involved in this controversy concerning the universality of atonement; and the discussion of the subject in America, and more recently in this country, cannot fail ultimately to produce the most beneficial results. Yet we must express our conviction, that the seeming difference of opinion among evangelical men, has arisen from mutual misunderstanding, and that misunderstanding from the use of ambiguous phraseology. One says, Christ died for all men. No, says another, for the elect only. The dispute goes on and on, till at last the discovery is made, that while the same words were used by the disputants, each attached his own meaning to them. This ambiguity is painfully felt in the treatise of a distinguished writer, who has recently appeared on the limited side of the question. He does not explain, till he has advanced very far in the discussion, what sense he attaches to the common phraseology of "Christ dying for all men." He tells us afterwards, however, that he understands it in the highest sense of securing salvation for them; when we are convinced, that much of the argument might have been spared, or at all events better directed, than against a position which few or none maintain. The author is himself sensible of this. "The question," says he, "might, perhaps, have been settled at the outset by a careful definition of terms; but I have purposely deferred doing so, judging, that it might be done with better effect as the discussion proceeded. In speaking of the Saviour's dying for men, or dying for sinners, I have u·ed the expression in what I conceive to be the strict and proper meaning, viz. as signifying his dying with an *intention* to save them. This, however, is not the only meaning the expression will bear.

For all men, for sinners in general, the Saviour died. He died in their *nature*, he died in their *stead*, he died doing honour to the law which they had violated; in other words, he died removing every legal obstruction that lay in the way of their obtaining life."—*The Death of Christ the Redemption of his People, p.* 70. Now, it is only in this last sense, that any rational advocate of general aspect in the atonement will maintain that Christ died for all men. Nor could he desire better language in which to express his views, than that which is furnished in the above quotation. That the atonement has certain general aspects is now nearly admitted on all hands. "General it must be in some sense," says the author already quoted, "if in some sense it be applicable to all, and that this is the case the foregoing statement undeniably proves," p. 68. The general aspect of the atonement is argued, from those well-known passages in which it is declared to have a reference to men, all men, the world, and the whole world. The reader will find some of these passages quoted above in the commentary. Of this universal phraseology various explanations have been given. Some have supplied the qualifying adjective " elect " in these places, where the design of atonement is said to embrace the " world." Modern writers of the highest name, however, and on both sides of the question, have vied with each other in their indignant repudiation of any such expletive. " I have felt myself," says Dr. Wardlaw, " far from satisfied with a common way of interpreting some of those texts which express the extent of the atonement in universal terms by means of a convenient supplement. According to this method of explanation, the world is, in such occurrences of it, made to signify the ' elect world,' the word ' elect ' being inserted as a supplement, conceived to be necessary for the consistency of scripture. An ' elect world' indeed, has become a phrase in common use with a particular class of commentators and divines; being employed with as much matter of course freedom, as if it had actually had the sanction of ordinary usage in the sacred volume; but it is not to be found there." And subjoins Dr. Marshall, writing on the limited side of the question, " It certainly is not to be found there, and with every word of this well-deserved censure I cordially agree." Here then is one principle of interpretation fairly exploded, and few nowadays will have the hardihood to espouse it. Again, the phraseology has been explained of the world of Jews and Gentiles indiscriminately, Gentiles as well as Jews; and those who adopt this view tell us, that the Jewish system was narrow and exclusive, embracing only one people, the progeny of Abraham; that it was the design of God, in the fulness of time, to enlarge his church and to receive within her am-

ple arms men of all nations, Jew and Gentile, Barbarian and Scythian, bond and free; that the death of Christ was at once the fulfilment and abrogation of the typical system with all its peculiar and exclusive rites; that by it the middle wall of partition between the Jew and the rest of the world was thrown down; that, therefore, it was natural to represent it as having a reference to all men and to the world, even when absolute universality was not and could not be intended. Such a vast enlargement of the scale on which spiritual blessings were now to be conferred, in consequence of the death of Christ, could not well have been expressed, it is alleged, in any other or in less universal terms. *See this view of the subject well exhibited in Hill's System*, vol. ii. chap. v. 3d. edit.

To this principle of interpretation we have no great objection. There is doubtless much truth in it. It lends valuable assistance in the investigation of many passages. But is there not some sense in which that atonement has an aspect absolutely to all, and every man? As much as we have seen admitted above. Now, if the Saviour "died in the nature and stead of all, removing every legal obstruction that lay in the way of their obtaining life," how comes it to pass, that this universal aspect cannot be found in any of those confessedly the most universal passages in the Bible? If it be true, it must be found somewhere in the scriptures, and nowhere so likely, as in this class of texts; and the language, moreover, is just such as is naturally fitted to express this sense. While then we allow, that the phraseology in question may be in part explained by the admission of Gentiles as well as Jews into the kingdom of God; we maintain at the same time, that there is nothing in it which prevents us from including *all* in each of those divisions of mankind. Nay, if the apostles had wished to express this idea, how otherwise could they have done it? " Say if you will," says Dr. Wardlaw, commenting on John iii. 16, 17, "that the ' world' means Jews and Gentiles, still if it is not any definite number of Jews and Gentiles, it is Jews and Gentiles as together composing the world of mankind."

That the atonement, indeed, has a certain benign aspect towards all men, appears from its very nature. The exact equivalent view, as it has been not inappropriately termed, is now nearly abandoned. Rarely do we find any one affirming, that Christ endured exactly what the elect would have suffered and deserved, and that, therefore, there can be sufficiency in his death for that favoured number and for none besides. What then is the light in which the atonement of Christ ought to be viewed? We think the only rational and scriptural account of it, is that which regards it as a great remedial scheme, which rendered it consistent with the divine honour and all the interests of the divine administration, to extend mercy to *guilty men at large*, and which would have been equally requisite, had there been an intention to save one only, or millions; numbers indeed not forming any part of the question. Here then is something done, which removes legal obstructions and thereby opens the way to heaven for all. And if any do not enter in, their inability is moral, and lies not in any insufficiency of the divine provision. This view, however, seems to furnish a just foundation for the universality of gospel invitations, while it fastens the guilt of rejecting gospel provision on the sinner himself.

Thus far we feel disposed to agree with our author in his commentary, or rather dissertation on the verse and the subject it involves. We maintain, however, that the atonement has a *special* as well as a *general* aspect; that while it is gloriously true that it looks to all men, it has at the same time a special regard to some. We object, therefore, to the statement, "that the atonement in itself considered had no limitation and no particular reference to any class or condition of men, and no particular applicability to one class more than to another." This is similar to certain rash assertions that have recently been current in our own country; as that "while the atonement opens the door of mercy to all, it secures salvation to none;" that "Christ died as much for those who perish, as for those who are saved." We cannot envy that reputation for acuteness which may be gained by the free use of such language. Is it not God's design to save his people? Is not the atonement the means by which he does so, the means by which the purpose of electing love is fulfilled? And yet has that atonement no special reference to the elect? Further, if it be the means of saving *them*, does it not *secure* their salvation? Certainly, amongst men, if any effectual means were devised to accomplish a particular end, that end would be said to be secured by such means. The writer is aware of the ingenious evasion, that it is God's gracious purpose to apply the atonement, and not the atonement itself, that connects it with the elect, and secures their salvation. We are told, moreover, that we should look on the atonement by itself, and consider it in a philosophical way. The purpose to apply is an after arrangement. But *first*, a purpose to apply the atonement to a special class, differs in nothing from an original design to save such class by it, for that purpose must have been present to the mind of God in determining on atonement. To say that God saves a certain number by the atonement, and that yet in making it he had no special design in their favour, however it may recommend itself to philosophical refinement, will always be rejected by the common sense of mankind.

Second. If we must consider the atonement apart from any special purpose connected with it, why not divest it also of any general purpose, that we may look on it steadily *per se*, and in this way reduce it to a mere abstraction, about which nothing could be either affirmed or denied?

The advocates of universal atonement, or some of the more forward among them, have recently carried out their views so far, as to deny that God in providing the atonement, or Christ in making it, had any special *love* to the elect. An eminent writer on that side, however, to whom reference has already been made, while he goes the length of denying special *design*, maintains the existence of special *love*, and administers a reproof to those of his own party, who go to this extreme. This is indeed an important concession, for *special love* is not very different from *special design*, nor is it easy to see how, in the mind of God, the one could subsist without the other. "The love of the Father is the same thing as election. Election is nothing but the love of the Father formed into a purpose."— *Marshall.* Or the point may be put in this way. Had God in providing the atonement special love to the elect? Where is the proof of it? Doubtless in that very provision. But if God in making it had no *design* to save them by it, the proof is not only weakened but destroyed. Special love, therefore, necessarily involves special design.

To do away with any thing like speciality of design, much has been said on the order of the divine decrees, especially as to whether the decree of atonement, or that of election, be first in order of nature. If that of atonement be first, it is asserted speciality is out of the question, as that is secured only by election, which is a posterior arrangement. On this subject it is more easy to darken counsel by words without knowledge, than to speak intelligibly. It may be fairly questioned, if those who have written most on it, fully understand themselves. Nor can we help lamenting, that so great a part of the controversy should have been made to turn on this point, which has hitherto eluded the grasp of the most profound, and drawn the controvertists into regions of thought, too high for the boldest flights of human intellect. After all that can be said on the subject, it must be allowed that the whole arrangement connected with the salvation of man, existed *simultaneously* in the mind of God, nor will any one rise much wiser from inquiries into which was first and which last.

The truth on the whole subject, then, seems to be, that while the atonement has a general reference towards all, it has at the same time a special reference to the elect of God, or as it is well expressed in a recent synodical decision, "The Saviour in making the atonement, bore special covenant relation to the elect; had a special love to them, and infallibly secured their everlasting salvation, whilst his obedience unto death, afforded such a satisfaction to the justice of God, as that on the ground of it, in consistency with his character and law, the door of mercy is open to all men, and a full and free salvation is presented for their acceptance." The special aspect, indeed, ought no more to be denied than the general. It rests on a large number of what may be called *special* texts; as, " Christ also loved *the Church* and gave himself for it, that he might sanctify and cleanse it," &c. " For the transgression of *my people* was he stricken." " I lay down my life for *the sheep*," Eph. v. 25; Isa. liii. 8; John x. 15. Nor will it do to say of this numerous class of passages, that they find a sufficient explanation in the purpose of application, which is connected with the remedy for sin, since most of them are of a kind that connect the salvation of the elect *directly with the atonement itself*, and not with any after design of applying it. This idea seems but an ingenious shift to sustain a favourite theory. How direct, for example, is this connection in the following passage : "who loved me and gave himself for me." No one who had not a theory to support, would ever think of introducing an after design of application to explain this. Indeed, as an able reviewer in one of our periodicals observes of the scheme that excludes a special design, "it separates too much the atonement from the salvation of man. It does not connect those that are saved, those that are regenerated by divine grace, at all specially with the sacrifice of Christ." Another important branch of evidence on this point, lies in the special relation which Christ in dying sustained towards his people, as that of shepherd, husband, surety, &c., and which cannot be explained on any other principle than that of special design.

If the question were put, how we preserve our consistency, in thus maintaining both the general and special view, we reply, first, that if *both* views are found in scripture, it matters not whether we can explain the consistency between them or no. But second, it is not so difficult as some would imagine, to conceive of God appointing a remedy with a general aspect towards the race, but specially intended to secure the salvation of his chosen people.]

¶ *Then were all dead.* All dead in sin; that is, all were sinners. The fact that he died for all proves that all were transgressors. The word "dead" is not unfrequently used in the scriptures to denote the condition of sinners; see Eph. ii. 1. It means not that sinners are in *all* senses, and in all respects like a lifeless corpse,

for they are not. They are still moral agents, and have a conscience, and are capable of thinking, and speaking, and acting. It does not mean that they have no more power than one in the grave, for they *have* more power. But it means that there is a striking similarity, in some respects, between one who is dead and a sinner. That similarity does not extend to every thing, but in many respects it is very striking. (1.) The sinner is as insensible to the glories of the heavenly world, and the appeals of the gospel, as a corpse is to what is going on around or above it. The body that lies in the grave is insensible to the voice of friendship, and the charms of music, and the hum of business, and the plans of gain and ambition ; and so the sinner is insensible to all the glories of the heavenly world, and to all the appeals that are made to him, and to all the warnings of God. He lives as though there were no heaven and no hell ; no God and no Saviour. (2.) There is need of the same divine power to convert a sinner which is needful to raise up the dead. The same cause does not exist, making the existence of that power necessary, but it *is a fact* that a sinner *will* no more be converted by his own power than a dead man will rise from the grave by his own power. No man ever yet was converted without direct divine agency, any more than Lazarus was raised without divine agency. And there is no more just or melancholy description which can be given of man, than to say that he is *dead in sins.* He is insensible to all the appeals that God makes to him ; he is insensible to all the sufferings of the Saviour, and to all the glories of heaven ; he lives as though these did not exist, or as though he had no concern in them ; his eyes see no more beauty in them than the sightless eyeballs of the dead do in the material world ; his ear is as inattentive to the calls of God and the gospel as the ear of the dead is to the voice of friendship or the charms of melody ; and in a world that is full of God, and that might be full of hope, he is living without God and without hope.

15 And *that* he died for all, that *a* they which live should not henceforth live unto themselves, but

unto him which died for them, and rose again.

16 Wherefore henceforth know

a 1 Cor. 6. 19, 20.

15. *And* that *he died for all,* &c. This verse is designed still further to explain the reasons of the conduct of the apostle.   He had not lived for himself.   He had not lived to amass wealth, or to enjoy pleasure, or to obtain a reputation.   He had lived a life of self-denial, and of toil; and he here states the reason why he had done it. It was because he felt that the great purpose of the death of the Redeemer was to secure this result.   To that Saviour, therefore, who died for all, he consecrated his talents and his time, and sought in every way possible to promote *his* glory.   ¶ *That they which live.*   They who are true Christians, who are made alive unto God as the result of the dying love of the Redeemer.   Sinners are dead in sins. Christians are alive to the worth of the soul, the presence of God, the importance of religion, the solemnities of eternity; *i. e.* they act and feel as if these things had a real existence, and as if they should exert a constant influence upon the heart and life.

[" *They which live.*"   This spiritual life, doubtless, implies that a man is alive to the worth of the soul, the presence of God, &c.; but it intimates something deeper too, which is the *foundation* of those things, and without which they could not exist.   Scott paraphrases thus, " were *quickened* and pardoned, and so passed from death to life ;" and Guyse still more explicitly, " were made supernaturally alive by his quickening spirit and by faith in him."   *This* is the root ; the things mentioned in the comment, the fruit ; this the cause, these only the effects.]

It is observable that Paul makes a distinction here between those for whom Christ died and those who actually " live," thus demonstrating that there may be many for whom he died who do not live to God, or who are not savingly benefited by his death.   The atonement was for all, but only a part are actually made alive to God.   Multitudes reject it; but the fact that he died for all; that he tasted death for every man, that he not only died for the elect but

for all others, that his benevolence was so great as to embrace the whole human family in the design of his death, is a reason why they who are actually made alive to God should consecrate themselves entirely to his service.   The fact that he died for all evinced such unbounded and infinite benevolence that it should induce us who are actually benefited by his death, and who have any just views of it, to devote all that we have to his service.   ¶ *Should not henceforth live unto ourselves.*   Should not seek our own ease and pleasure; should not make it our great object to promote our own interest, but should make it the grand purpose of our lives to promote *his* honour, and to advance *his* cause.   This is a vital principle in religion, and it is exceedingly important to know what is meant by living to ourselves, and whether we do it. It is done in the following, and perhaps in some other ways.   (1.) When men seek pleasure, gain, or reputation as the controlling principle of their lives.   (2.) When they are regardless of the *rights* of others, and sacrifice all the claims which others have on them in order to secure the advancement of their own purposes and ends. (3.) When they are regardless of the *wants* of others, and turn a deaf ear to all the appeals which charity makes to them, and have no time to give to serve them, and no money to spare to alleviate their wants ; and especially when they turn a deaf ear to the appeals which are made for the diffusion of the gospel to the benighted and perishing.   (4.) When their main purpose is the aggrandizement of their own families, for their families are but a diffusion of self.   And, (5.) When they seek their own salvation only from selfish motives, and not from a desire to honour God.   Multitudes are selfish even in their religion ; and the main purpose which they have in view, is to promote their own objects, and not the honour of the Master whom they profess to serve. They seek and profess religion only because they desire to escape from wrath, and to obtain the happiness of heaven, and not from any love to the Redeemer or any desire to honour him. Or they seek to build up the interests of their own church and party, and all their zeal is expended on that and that alone, without any real desire to honour the Saviour. Or though *in* the church, they are still selfish, and live wholly to themselves. They live for fashion, for gain, for reputation. They practice no self-denial; they make no effort to advance the cause of God the Saviour. ¶ *But unto him*, &c. Unto the Lord Jesus Christ. To live to him is the opposite to living unto ourselves. It is to seek his honour ; to feel that we belong to him ; that all our time and talents ; all our strength of intellect and body ; all the avails of our skill and toil, all belong to him, and should be employed in his service. If we have talents by which we can influence other minds, they should be employed to honour the Saviour. If we have skill, or strength to labour by which we can make money, we should feel that it all belongs to him, and should be employed in his service. If we have property, we should feel that it is his, and that he has a claim upon it all, and that it should be honestly consecrated to his cause. And if we are endowed with a spirit of enterprise, and are fitted by nature to encounter perils in distant and barbarious climes, as Paul was, we should feel like him that we are bound to devote all entirely to his service, and to the promotion of his cause. A servant, a slave, does not live to himself but to his master. His person, his time, his limbs, his talents, and the avails of his industry are not regarded as his own. He is judged incapable of holding any property which is not at the disposal of his master. If he has strength, it is his master's. If he has skill, the avails of it are his master's. If he is an ingenious mechanic, or labours in any department ; if he is amiable, kind, gentle, and faithful, and adapted to be useful in an eminent degree, it is regarded as all the property of his master. He is bound to go where his master chooses ; to execute the task which he assigns ; to deny himself at his master's will ; and to come and lay the avails of all his toil and skill at his master's feet. He is regarded as having been purchased with money ; and the purchase money is supposed to give a right to his time, his talents, his services, and his soul. Such as the slave is supposed to become by purchase, and by the operation of human laws, the Christian becomes by the purchase of the Son of God, and by the voluntary recognition of him as the master, and as having a right to all that we have and are. To him all belongs ; and all should be employed in endeavouring to promote his glory, and in advancing his cause. ¶ *Which died for them, and rose again.* Paul here states the grounds of the obligation under which he felt himself placed, to live not unto himself but unto Christ. (1.) The first is, the fact that Christ had *died* for him, and for all his people. The effect of that death was the same as a purchase. It *was* a purchase ; see Note, 1 Cor. vi. 20 ; vii. 23 ; comp. 1 Pet. i. 18, 19. (2.) The second is, that he had risen again from the dead. To this fact Paul traced all his hopes of eternal life, and of the resurrection from the dead ; see Rom. iv. 25. As we have the hope of the resurrection from the dead only from the fact that he rose ; as he has " brought life and immortality to light," and hath in this way " abolished death " (2 Tim. i. 10) ; as all the prospect of entering a world where there is no death and no grave is to be traced to the resurrection of the Saviour, so we are bound by every obligation of gratitude to devote ourselves without any reserve to him. To him, and him alone should we live ; and in his cause our lives should be, as Paul's was, a living sacrifice, holy and acceptable in his sight.

16. *Wherefore henceforth.* In view of the fact that the Lord Jesus died for all men, and rose again. The effect of that has been to change all our feelings, and to give us entirely new views of men, of ourselves, and of

we no man after the flesh: yea, though we have known Christ after | the flesh, yet now henceforth know we *him* no more.

the Messiah, so that we have become new creatures. The word "henceforth" (ἀπὸ τοῦ νῦν) means properly from the present time; but there is no impropriety in supposing that Paul refers to the time when he first obtained correct views of the Messiah, and that he means from that time. His mind seems to have been thrown back to the period when these new views burst upon his soul; and the sentiment is, that from the time when he obtained those new views, he had resolved to know no one after the flesh. ¶ *Know we no man.* The word *know* here (οἴδαμεν) is used in the sense of, we form our estimate of; we judge; we are influenced by. Our estimate of man is formed by other views than according to the flesh. ¶ *According to the flesh.* A great many different interpretations have been proposed of this expression, which it is not needful here to repeat. The meaning is, probably, that in his estimate of men he was not influenced by the views which are taken by those who are unrenewed, and who are unacquainted with the truths of redemption. It may include a great many things, and perhaps the following. (1.) He was not influenced in his estimate of men by a regard to their birth, or country. He did not form an attachment to a Jew because he was a Jew, or to a Gentile because he was a Gentile. He had learned that Christ died for all, and he felt disposed to regard all alike. (2.) He was not influenced in his estimate of men by their rank, and wealth, and office. Before his conversion he had been, but now he learned to look on their moral character, and to regard that as making the only permanent, and really important distinction among men. He did not esteem one man highly because he was of elevated rank, or of great wealth, and another less because he was of a different rank in life. (3.) It may also include the idea, that he had left his own kindred and friends on account of superior attachment to Christ. He had

parted from them to preach the gospel. He was not restrained by their opinions; he was not kept from going from land to land by love to them. It is probable that they remained Jews. It may be, that they were opposed to him, and to his efforts in the cause of the Redeemer. It may be that they would have dismissed him from a work so self-denying, and so arduous, and where he would be exposed to so much persecution and contempt. It may be that they would have set before him the advantages of his birth and education; would have reminded him of his early brilliant prospects; and would have used all the means possible to dissuade him from embarking in a cause like that in which he was engaged. The passage here means that Paul was influenced by none of these considerations. In early life he had been. He had prided himself on rank, and on talent. He was proud of his own advantages as a Jew; and he estimated worth by rank, and by national distinction, Phil. iii. 4—6. He had despised Christians on account of their being the followers of the man of Nazareth; and there can be no reason to doubt that he partook of the common feelings of his countrymen and held in contempt the whole Gentile world. But his views were changed—so much changed as to make it proper to say that he was a new creature, ver. 17. When converted, he did not confer with flesh and blood (Gal. i. 16); and in the school of Christ, he had learned that if a man was his disciple, he must be willing to forsake father and mother, and sister and brother, and to hate his own life that he might honour him, Luke xiv. 26. He had formed his principle of action now from a higher standard than any regard to rank, or wealth, or national distinction; and had risen above them all, and now estimated men not by these external and factitious advantages, but by a reference to their personal character and moral worth. ¶ *Yea, though we have known Christ after the flesh.*

Though in common with the Jewish nation we expected a Messiah who would be a temporal prince, and who would be distinguished for the distinctions which are valued among men, yet we have changed our estimate of him, and judge of him in this way no longer. There can be no doubt that Paul, in common with his countrymen, had expected a Messiah who would be a magnificent temporal prince and conqueror, one who they supposed would be a worthy successor of David and Solomon. The coming of such a prince, Paul had confidently expected. He expected no other Messiah. He had fixed his hopes on that. This is what is meant by the expression ' to know Christ after the flesh.' It does not mean that he had seen him in the flesh, but that he had formed, so to speak, carnal views of him, and such as men of this world regard as grand and magnificent in a monarch and conqueror. He had had no correct views of his spiritual character, and of the pure and holy purposes for which he would come into the world. ¶ *Yet now henceforth know we him no more.* We know him no more in this manner. Our conceptions and views of him are changed. We no more regard him according to the flesh ; we no longer esteem the Messiah who was to come as a temporal prince and warrior; but we look on him as a spiritual Saviour, a Redeemer from sin. The idea is, that his views of him had been entirely changed. It does not mean, as our translation would seem to imply, that Paul would have no further acquaintance with Christ, but it means that from the moment of his conversion he had laid aside all his views of his being a temporal sovereign, and all his feelings that he was to be honoured only because he supposed that he would have an elevated rank among the monarchs of the earth. Locke and Macknight, it seems to me, have strangely mistaken this passage. The former renders it, " For if I myself have gloried in this, that Christ was himself circumcised as I am, and was of my blood and nation, I do so now no more any longer." The same substantially is the view of Macknight. Clarke as strangely mistakes it, when he says that it means that Paul could not prize now a man who was a sinner because he was allied to the royal family of David, nor prize a man because he had seen Christ in the flesh. The correct view, as it seems to me, is given above. And the *doctrine* which is taught here is, that at conversion, the views are essentially changed, and that the converted man has a view of the Saviour entirely different from what he had before. He may not, like Paul, have regarded him as a temporal prince ; he may not have looked to him as a mighty monarch, but his views in regard to his person, character, work, and loveliness will be entirely changed. He will see a beauty in his character which he never saw before. Before, he regarded him as a root out of dry ground ; as the despised man of Nazareth ; as having nothing in his character to be desired, or to render him lovely (Isa. liii) ; but at conversion the views are changed. He is seen to be the chief among ten thousand and altogether lovely ; as pure, and holy, and benevolent ; as mighty, and great, and glorious ; as infinitely benevolent ; as lovely in his precepts, lovely in his life, lovely in his death, lovely in his resurrection, and as most glorious as he is seated on the right hand of God. He is seen to be a Saviour exactly adapted to the condition and wants of the soul ; and the soul yields itself to him to be redeemed by him alone. There is no change of view so marked and decided as that of the sinner in regard to the Lord Jesus Christ at his conversion ; and it is a clear proof that we have never been born again if our views in reference to him have never undergone any change. " What think ye of Christ?" is a question the answer to which will determine any man's character, and demonstrate whether he is or is not a child of God. Tindal has more correctly expressed the sense of this than our translation. " Though we have known Christ after the flesh, now henceforth know we him so no more."

17 Therefore if any man *be* in Christ, *he is* ¹ a new *a* creature:

1 *let him be.*   *a* John. 3. 3; Gal. 6. 15.

old things are passed away; behold, *b* all things are become new.

b Is. 65. 17; Re. 21. 5.

---

17. *Therefore if any man* be *in Christ.* The phrase to "be *in* Christ," evidently means to be united to Christ by faith ; or to be in him as the branch is in the vine—that is, so united to the vine, or so in it, as to derive all its nourishment and support from it, and to be sustained entirely by it. John xv. 2, "Every branch *in* me." ver. 4, "Abide *in* me, and I in you." "The branch cannot bear fruit of itself except it abide *in* the vine ; no more can ye except ye abide *in* me." See also ver. 5—7, see Note on John xv. 2. To be "in Christ" denotes a more tender and close union ; and implies that all our support is from him. All our strength is derived from him ; and denotes further that we shall partake of his fulness, and share in his felicity and glory, as the branch partakes of the strength and vigour of the parent vine. The word "therefore" (Ὥστε) here implies that the reason why Paul infers that any one is a new creature who is in Christ is that which is stated in the previous verse ; to wit, the change of views in regard to the Redeemer to which he there refers, and which was so great as to constitute a change like a new creation. The affirmation here is universal, "if any man be in Christ ;" that is, all who become true Christians—undergo such a change in their views and feelings as to make it proper to say of them that they are new creatures. No matter what they have been before, whether moral or immoral ; whether infidels or speculative believers ; whether amiable, or debased, sensual and polluted, yet if they become Christians they all experience such a change as to make it proper to say they are a new creation. ¶ *A new creature.* Marg. "Let him be." This is one of the instances in which the margin has given a less correct translation than is in the text. The idea evidently is, not that he *ought* to be a new creature, but that he is in fact ; not that he *ought* to

live as becomes a new creature—which is true enough—but that he will in fact live in that way, and manifest the characteristics of the new creation. The phrase " a new creature " (καινὴ κτίσις) occurs also in Gal. vi. 15. The word rendered " creature " (κτίσις) means properly in the New Testament, *creation*. It denotes, (1.) The act of creating (Rom. i. 20); (2.) A created thing, a creature (Rom. i. 25); and refers (*a*) To the universe, or creation in general ; Mark x. 6 ; xiii. 9—11; 1 Pet. iii. 4. (*b*) To man, mankind ; Mark xvi. 15 ; Col. i. 23. Here it means a new creation in a moral sense, and the phrase new creature is equivalent to the expression in Eph. iv. 24, "The new man, which after God is created in righteousness and true holiness." It means, evidently, that there is a change produced in the renewed heart of man that is equivalent to the act of creation, and that bears a strong resemblance to it—a change, so to speak, as if the man was made over again, and had become new. The mode or manner in which it is done is not described, nor should the words be pressed to the quick, as if the process were the same in both cases—for the words are here evidently figurative. But the phrase implies evidently the following things. (1.) That there is an exertion of divine power in the conversion of the sinner as really as in the act of creating the world out of nothing, and that this is as indispensable in the one case as in the other. (2.) That a change is produced so great as to make it proper to say that he is a new man. He has new views, new motives, new principles, new objects and plans of life. He seeks new purposes, and he lives for new ends. If a drunkard becomes reformed, there is no impropriety in saying that he is a new man. If a man who was licentious becomes pure, there is no impropriety in saying that he is not the same man that he was

18 And all things *are* of God, who hath reconciled *a* us to himself by

a Col. 1. 20.

Jesus Christ, and hath given to us the ministry of reconciliation;

before. Such expressions are common in all languages, and they are as proper as they are common. There *is* such a change as to make the language proper. And so in the conversion of a sinner. There *is* a change so deep, so clear, so entire, and so abiding, that it is proper to say, here is a new creation of God—a work of the divine power as decided and as glorious as when God created all things out of nothing. There is no other moral change that takes place on earth so deep, and radical, and thorough as the change at conversion. And there is no other where there is so much propriety in ascribing it to the mighty power of God. ¶ *Old things are passed away.* The old views in regard to the Messiah, and in regard to men in general, ver. 16. But Paul also gives this a general form of expression, and says that old things in general have passed away—referring to every thing. It was true of all who were converted that old things had passed away. And it may include the following things. (1.) In regard to the Jews—that their former prejudices against Christianity, their natural pride, and spirit of seducing others; their attachment to their rites and ceremonies, and dependence on them for salvation had all passed away. They now renounced that independence, relied on the merits of the Saviour, and embraced all as brethren who were of the family of Christ. (2.) In regard to the Gentiles—their attachment to idols, their love of sin and degradation, their dependence on their own works, had passed away, and they had renounced all these things, and had come to mingle their hopes with those of the converted Jews, and with all who were the friends of the Redeemer. (3.) In regard to all, it is also true that old things pass away. Their former prejudices, opinions, habits, attachments pass away. Their supreme love of self passes away.

Their love of sins passes away. Their love of the world passes away. Their supreme attachment to their earthly friends rather than God passes away. Their love of sin, their sensuality, pride, vanity, levity, ambition, passes away. There is a deep and radical change on all these subjects,—a change which *commences* at the new birth; which is *carried on* by progressive sanctification; and which is *consummated* at death and in heaven. ¶ *Behold, all things are become new.* That is, all things in view of the mind. The purposes of life, the feelings of the heart, the principles of action, all become new. The understanding is consecrated to new objects, the body is employed in new service, the heart forms new attachments. Nothing can be more strikingly descriptive of the facts in conversion than this; nothing more entirely accords with the feelings of the new-born soul. All is new. There are new views of God, and of Jesus Christ; new views of this world and of the world to come; new views of truth and of duty; and every thing is seen in a new aspect and with new feelings. Nothing is more common in young converts than such feelings, and nothing is more common than for them to say that all things are new. The Bible seems to be a new book, and though they may have often read it before, yet there is a beauty about it which they never saw before, and which they wonder they have not before perceived. The whole face of nature seems to them to be changed, and they seem to be in a new world. The hills, and vales, and streams; the sun, the stars, the groves, the forests, seem to be new. A new beauty is spread over them all; and they now see them to be the work of God, and his glory is spread over them all, and they can *now* say,

"My Father made them all."

The heavens and the earth are filled with new wonders, and all things seem now to speak forth the praise of God. Even the very countenances of friends seem to be new; and there are new feelings towards all men; a new kind of love to kindred and friends; and a love before unfelt for enemies; and a new love for all mankind.

18. *And all things* are *of God*. This refers particularly to the things in question, the renewing of the heart, and the influences by which Paul had been brought to a state of willingness to forsake all, and to devote his life to the self-denying labours involved in the purpose of making the Saviour known. He makes the statement *general*, however, showing his belief that not only these things were produced by God, but that *all* things were under his direction, and subject to his control. Nothing that he had done was to be traced to his own agency or power, but God was to be acknowledged everywhere. This great truth Paul never forgot; and he never suffered himself to lose sight of it. It was in his view a cardinal and glorious truth; and he kept its influence always before his mind and his heart. In the important statement which follows, therefore, about the ministry of reconciliation, he deeply feels that the whole plan, and all the success which has attended the plan, was to be traced not to his zeal, or fidelity, or skill, but to the agency of God; see Note on 1 Cor. iii. 6, 7. ¶ *Who hath reconciled us to himself.* The word *us* here includes, doubtless, all who were Christians—whether Jews or Gentiles, or whatever was their rank. They had all been brought into a state of reconciliation, or agreement with God through the Lord Jesus Christ. Before they were opposed to God. They had violated his laws. They were his enemies. But by the means of the plan of salvation they had been brought into a state of agreement, or harmony, and were united in feeling and in aim with him. Two men who have been alienated by prejudice, by passion, or by interest, are reconciled when the cause of the alienation is removed, on whichever side it may have existed, or if on both sides, and

when they lay aside their enmity and become friends. Thenceforward they are agreed, and live together without alienation, heart-burnings, jealousies, and strife. So between God and man. There was a variance; there was an alienation. Man was alienated from God. He had no love for him. He disliked his government and laws. He was unwilling to be restrained. He sought his own pleasure. He was proud, vain, self-confident. He was not pleased with the character of God, or with his claims, or his plans. And in like manner, God was *displeased* with the pride, the sensuality, the rebellion, the haughtiness of man. He was displeased that his law had been violated, and that man had cast off his government. Now reconciliation could take place only when these causes of alienation should be laid aside, and when God and man should be brought to harmony; when man should lay aside his love of sin, and should be pardoned, and when, therefore, God could consistently treat him as a friend. The Greek word which is here used (καταλλάσσω) means properly to change against any thing; to exchange for any thing, for money, or for any article.—*Robinson.* In the New Testament it means to change one person towards another; that is, to reconcile *to* any one; see Note on Rom. v. 10. It conveys the idea of producing a *change*, so that one who is alienated should be brought to friendship. Of course, all the *change* which takes place must be on the part of man, for God will not change, and the purpose of the plan of reconciliation is to effect such a *change* in man as to make him *in fact* reconciled to God, and at agreement with him. There were indeed obstacles to reconciliation on the part of God, but they did not arise from any unwillingness to be reconciled; from any reluctance to treat his creature as his friend; but they arose from the fact that man had sinned, and that God was just; that such is the perfection of God that he *cannot* treat the good and evil alike; and that, therefore, if he should treat man as his friend, it was necessary that in some proper way he should maintain the honour of his law, and show his hatred of sin, and should secure the conversion and future obedience of the offender. All this God proposed to secure by the atonement made by the Redeemer, rendering it consistent for him to exercise the benevolence of his nature, and to pardon the offender. But God is not changed. The plan of reconciliation has made no change in his character. It has not made him a different being from what he was before. There is often a mistake on this subject; and men seem to suppose that God was *originally* stern, and unmerciful, and inexorable, and that he has been *made* mild and forgiving by the atonement. But it is not so. No change has been made in God; none needed to be made; none could be made. He was *always* mild, and merciful, and good; and the gift of a Saviour and the plan of reconciliation *is just an expression of his original willingness to pardon.* When a father sees a child struggling in the stream, and in danger of drowning, the peril and the cries of the child make no *change* in the character of the father, but such was his former love for the child that he would plunge into the stream at the hazard of his own life to save him. So it is with God. Such was his original love for man, and his disposition to show mercy, that he would submit to *any* sacrifice, except that of truth and justice, in order that he might save him. Hence he sent his only Son to die—not to change his own character; not to make himself a different being from what he was, but *in order* to show his love and his readiness to forgive when it could be consistently done. " *God so loved the world* THAT he sent his only begotten Son," John iii. 16. ¶ *By Jesus Christ.* By the agency, or medium of Jesus Christ. He was the mediator to interpose in the work of reconciliation. And he was abundantly qualified for this work, and was the *only* being that has lived in this world who was qualified for it. For, (1.) He was endowed with a divine and human nature—the nature of

both the parties at issue—God and man, and thus, in the language of Job, could "lay his hand upon both," Job ix. 33. (2.) He was intimately acquainted with both the parties, and knew what was needful to be done. He knew God the Father so well that he could say, "No man knoweth the Father but the Son," Mat. xi. 27. And he knew man so well that it could be said of him, he "needed not that any should testify of man, for he knew what was in man," John ii. 25. No one can be a mediator who is not acquainted with the feelings, views, desires, claims, or prejudices of both the parties at issue. (3.) He was the *friend* of both the parties. *He loved God.* No man ever doubted this, or had any reason to call it in question, and he was always desirous of *securing* all that God claimed, and of vindicating him, and he never abandoned any thing that God had a right to claim. And *he loved man.* He showed this in all his life. He sought *his* welfare in every way possible, and gave himself for him. Yet no one is qualified to act the mediator's part who is not the common friend of both the parties at issue, and who will not seek the welfare, the right, or the honour of both. (4.) He was willing to suffer any thing from either party in order to produce reconciliation. From the hand of God he was willing to endure all that he deemed to be necessary, in order to show his hatred of sin by his vicarious sufferings, and to make an atonement; and from the hand of man he was willing to endure all the reproach, and contumely, and scorn which could be possibly involved in the work of inducing man to be reconciled to God.—And, (5.) He has removed all the obstacles which existed to a reconciliation. On the part of God, he has made it consistent for him to pardon. He has made an atonement, so that God can be just while he justifies the sinner. He has maintained his truth, and justice, and secured the stability of his moral government while he admits offenders to his favour. And on the part of man, he, by the agency of his Spirit, overcomes the unwillingness of the

19 To wit, that God was in Christ, reconciling the world

unto himself, not imputing their trespasses *a* unto them; and hath

a Ro. 3. 21, 25.

sinner to be reconciled, humbles his pride, shows him his sin, changes his heart, subdues his enmity against God, and secures *in fact* a harmony of feeling and purpose between God and man, so that they shall be *reconciled* for ever. ¶ *And hath given to us.* To us the apostles and our fellow-labourers. ¶ *The ministry of reconciliation.* That is, of announcing to men the nature and the conditions of this plan of being reconciled. We have been appointed to make this known, and to press its acceptance on men; see ver. 20.

19. *To wit* (Greek, 'Ως ότι), *namely.* This verse is designed further to state the nature of the plan of reconciliation, and of the message with which they were intrusted. It contains an abstract, or an epitome of the whole plan; and is one of those emphatic passages in which Paul compresses into a single sentence the substance of the whole plan of redemption. ¶ *That God was in Christ.* That God was *by* Christ (ἐν Χριστῷ), by means of Christ; *by* the agency, or mediatorship of Christ. Or it may mean that God was united to Christ, and manifested himself by him. So Doddridge interprets it. Christ was the mediator by means of whom God designed to accomplish the great work of reconciliation. ¶ *Reconciling the world unto himself.* The *world* here evidently means the human race generally, without distinction of nation, age, or rank. The whole world was alienated from him, and he sought to have it reconciled. This is one *incidental* proof that God designed that the plan of salvation should be adapted to all men; see Note on ver. 14. It may be observed further, that *God* sought that the world should be reconciled. Man did not seek it He had no plan for it. He did not desire it. He had no way to effect it. It was the *offended* party, not the *offending*, that sought to be reconciled; and this shows the strength of his love. It was love for enemies and

alienated beings, and love evinced to them by a most earnest desire to become their friend, and to be at agreement with them; comp. Note on Rom. v. 8. Tindal renders this very accurately, "For God was in Christ, and made agreement between the world and himself, and imputed not their sins unto them." ¶ *Not imputing their trespasses.* Not reckoning their transgressions to them; that is, forgiving them, pardoning them. On the meaning of the word *impute*, see Note, Rom. iv. 3. The idea here is, that God did not charge on them with inexorable severity and stern justice their offences, but graciously provided a plan of pardon, and offered to remit their sins on the conditions of the gospel. The plan of reconciliation demonstrated that he was not *disposed* to impute their sins to them, as he might have done, and to punish them with unmitigated severity for their crimes, but was more disposed to pardon and forgive. And it may be here asked, if God was not disposed to charge with unrelenting severity *their own sins* to their account, but was rather disposed to pardon them, can we believe that he is disposed to charge on them *the sin of another?* If he does not charge on them with inexorable and unmitigated severity *their own transgressions*, will he charge on them with unrelenting severity—*or at all*—the sin of Adam? see Note on Rom. v. 19. The sentiment here is, that God is not disposed or inclined to charge the transgressions of men upon them; he has no pleasure in doing it; and *therefore* he has provided a plan by which they may be pardoned. At the same time it is true that unless their sins *are* pardoned, justice will charge or impute their sins to them, and will exact punishment to the uttermost.

[See also the supplementary Notes on Romans v. 12, 19, where the subject of imputed sin is considered at length. The argument by which the author attempts here to set aside

1 committed unto us the word of reconciliation.

1 *put in us.*

that doctrine, is not of great force. Because God " graciously provided a plan of pardon," in consequence of which he can consistently remit or not reckon transgression, he cannot be supposed to hold us guilty of Adam's sin! This is substantially the argument. We might just reverse the matter, and would then certainly argue more conclusively thus : God does impute the first sin to us, and we are guilty, moreover, of actual sin, therefore in love he has provided a plan by which he can consistently deliver us from this accumulated load of sin. The deeper our guilt, the greater the necessity for the provision. But how the providing of atonement disproves the doctrine of imputed sin, it is impossible to see. Besides the non-imputation of trespasses here spoken of, can only be applied to such as accept the provision in the gospel, and can therefore be no reason for the denial of imputed sin. Neither this nor actual sin will be charged against the believer, and the glory of Christ's work is that it delivers him from both. Mr. Scott thus interprets, " When, therefore, sinners were brought to God, as ' in Christ reconciling the world unto himself' in humble faith, he no more imputed their trespasses unto them, but blotted them out by a free forgiveness." Nor can the language mean any thing else ; for while by the atonement all legal obstructions are removed, sinners are still charged with guilt, till they receive it. It ought also to be noticed, that the author changes the idea in the text into a mere *disposition* on the part of God not to charge trespasses, whereas the apostle speaks of their actual non-imputation. This last certainly cannot be strictly *universal.* If that he intended, there should have accompanied it some explanation of the difficulties with which such an opinion is surrounded, and of the manner in which the passage can be reconciled with other passages which speak of non-imputation of guilt, as a privilege exclusively confined to believers. If the universality of the non-imputation could be made out, there might be something like foundation for the argument against imputed sin ; though *even in that case*, it would not follow, that, because God had remitted the sins of all, or determined not to reckon them, imputed sin had not existed and been remitted too, as well as actual transgressions]

¶ *And hath committed unto us the word of reconciliation.* Margin, " put in us." Tindal renders this, " and hath committed unto us the preaching of the atonement." The meaning is, that the office of making known the

20 Now then we are *a* ambassadors for Christ ; as though God

a Job 33.23; Mal. 2.7; Eph. 6.20.

nature of this plan, and the conditions on which God was willing to be reconciled to man, had been committed to the ministers of the gospel.

20. *Now then we are ambassadors for Christ.* We are the ambassadors whom Christ has sent forth to negotiate with men in regard to their reconciliation to God. Tindal renders this, " Now then are we messengers in the room of Christ." The word here used ($\pi\rho\epsilon\sigma\beta\epsilon\acute{\upsilon}o\mu\epsilon\nu$, from $\pi\rho\epsilon\sigma\beta\upsilon\varsigma$, an aged man, an elder, and then an ambassador) means to act as an ambassador, or sometimes merely to deliver a message for another, without being empowered to do any thing more than to explain or enforce it.— *Bloomfield.* See Thucyd. 7. 9. An ambassador is a minister of the highest rank, employed by one prince or state at the court of another, to manage the concerns of his own prince or state, and representing the dignity and power of his sovereign.— *Webster.* He is sent to do what the sovereign would himself do were he present. They are sent to make known the will of the sovereign, and to negotiate matters of commerce, of war, or of peace, and in general every thing affecting the interests of the sovereign among the people to whom they are sent. At all times, and in all countries, an ambassador is a sacred character, and his person is regarded as inviolable. He is bound implicitly to obey the instructions of his sovereign, and as far as possible to do only what the sovereign would do were he himself present. Ministers are ambassadors for Christ, as they are sent to do what he would do were he personally present. They are to make known, and to explain, and enforce the terms on which God is willing to be reconciled to men. They are not to negotiate on any new terms, nor to change those which God has proposed, nor to follow their own plans or devices, but they are simply to urge, explain, state, and enforce the terms on which God is willing to be reconciled. Of course

did beseech *you* by us, we pray *you* in Christ's stead, be ye reconciled to God.

21 For *a* he hath made him *to*

a Is. 53.6,9,12; Ga. 3.13; 1 Fe. 2.22,24; 1 John 3.5.

they are to seek the honour of the sovereign who has sent them forth, and to seek to do only his will. They go not to promote their own welfare; not to seek honour, dignity, or emolument; but they go to transact the business which the Son of God would engage in were he again personally on the earth. It follows that their office is one of great dignity, and great responsibility, and that respect should be showed them as the ambassadors of the King of kings. ¶ *As though God did beseech* you *by us.* Our message is to be regarded as the message of God. It is God who speaks. What we say to you is said in his name and on his authority, and should be received with the respect which is due to a message directly from God. The gospel message is God speaking to men through the ministry, and entreating them to be reconciled. This invests the message which the ministers of religion bear with infinite dignity and solemnity; and it makes it a fearful and awful thing to reject it. ¶ *We pray* you *in Christ's stead* (ὑπὲρ Χριστοῦ). In the place of Christ; or doing what he did when on earth, and what he would do were he where we are. ¶ *Be ye reconciled to God.* This is the sum and burden of the message which the ministers of the gospel bear to their fellow-men; see Note on ver. 19. It implies that *man* has something to do in this work. *He* is to be reconciled to God. He is to give up his opposition. He is to submit to the terms of mercy. All the change in the case is to be in him, for God cannot change. God has removed all the obstacles to reconciliation which existed on *his* part. He has done all that he will do, all that needed to be done, in order to render reconciliation easy as possible. And now it remains that man should lay aside his hostility, abandon his sins, embrace the terms of mercy, and become in

be sin for us, who knew no sin; that we might be made *b* the righteousness of God in him.

b Ro. 5.19.

fact reconciled to God. And the great object of the ministers of reconciliation is to urge this duty on their fellow-men. They are to do it in the name of Christ. They are to do it as if Christ were himself present, and were himself urging the message. They are to use the arguments which he would use; evince the zeal which he would show; and present the motives which he would present to induce a dying world to become in fact reconciled to God.

21. *For he hath made him* to be *sin for us.* The Greek here is, 'for him who knew no sin, he hath made sin, or a sin-offering for us.' The *design* of this very important verse is, to urge the strongest possible reason for being reconciled to God. This is implied in the word (γὰρ) *for.* Paul might have urged other arguments, and presented other strong considerations. But he chooses to present this fact, that Christ has been made sin for us, as embodying and concentrating all. It is the most affecting of all arguments; it is the one that is likely to prove most effectual. It is not indeed improper to urge on men every other consideration to induce them to be reconciled to God. It is not improper to appeal to them by the conviction of duty; to appeal to their reason and conscience; to remind them of the claims, the power, the goodness, and the fear of the Creator; to remind them of the awful consequences of a continued hostility to God; to persuade them by the hope of heaven, and by the fear of hell (ver. 11.) to become his friends: but, after all, the strongest argument, and that which is most adapted to melt the soul, is the fact that the Son of God has become incarnate for our sins, and has suffered and died in our stead. When all other appeals fail this is effectual; and this is in fact the strong argument by which the mass of those who

become Christians are induced to abandon their opposition and to become reconciled to God. ¶ To be *sin*. The words 'to be' are not in the original. Literally it is, 'he has made him sin, or a sin-offering' (*ἁμαρτίαν ἐποίησεν*). But what is meant by this? What is the exact idea which the apostle intended to convey? I answer, it cannot be, (1.) That he was literally *sin* in the abstract, or sin as such. No one can pretend this. The expression must be, therefore, in some sense, figurative. Nor, (2.) Can it mean that he was *a sinner*, for it is said in immediate connection that he "knew no sin," and it is everywhere said that he was holy, harmless, undefiled. Nor, (3.) Can it mean that he was, in any proper sense of the word, *guilty*, for no one is truly guilty who is not personally a transgressor of the law; and if he was, in any proper sense, *guilty*, then he deserved to die, and his death could have no more merit than that of any other guilty being; and if he was properly *guilty* it would make no difference in this respect whether it was by his own fault or by imputation: a *guilty* being *deserves* to be punished; and where there is desert of punishment there can be no merit in sufferings. But all such views as go to make the holy Redeemer a sinner, or guilty, or deserving of the sufferings which he endured, border on blasphemy, and are abhorrent to the whole strain of the Scriptures. In no form, in no sense possible, is it to be maintained that the Lord Jesus was sinful or guilty. It is a corner stone of the whole system of religion, that in all conceivable senses of the expression he was holy, and pure, and the object of the divine approbation. And every view which *fairly leads* to the statement that he was in any sense guilty, or which implies that he deserved to die, is *prima facie* a false view, and should be at once abandoned. But, (4.) If the declaration that he was made "sin" (*ἁμαρτίαν*) does not mean that he was sin itself, or a sinner, or guilty, then it must mean that he was a *sin-offering*,—an offering or a sacrifice for sin; and this is the interpretation which is

now generally adopted by expositors; or it must be taken as an abstract for the concrete, and mean that God *treated him as if he were a sinner*. The former interpretation, that it means that God made him a sin-offering, is adopted by Whitby, Doddridge, Macknight, Rosenmüller, and others; the latter, that it means that God treated him as a sinner, is adopted by Vorstius, Schoettgen, Robinson (*Lex.*), Bishop Bull, and others. There are many passages in the Old Testament where the word "sin" (*ἁμαρτία*) is used in the sense of sin-offering, or a sacrifice for sin. Thus, Hos. iv. 8, "They eat up the sin of my people;" *i. e.* the sin-offerings; see Ezek. xliii. 22, 25; xliv. 29; xlv. 22, 23, 25. See Whitby's Note on this verse. But whichever meaning is adopted, whether it means that he was a sacrifice for sin, or that God treated him *as if* he were a sinner, *i. e.* subjected him to sufferings which, if he had been personally a sinner, would have been a proper expression of his hatred of transgression, and a proper punishment for sin, in either case it means that he made an atonement; that he died for sin; that his death was not merely that of a martyr; but that it was designed by substituted sufferings to make reconciliation between man and God. Locke renders this, probably expressing the true sense, "For God hath made him subject to suffering and death, the punishment and consequence of sin, as if he had been a sinner, though he were guilty of no sin." To me, it seems probable that the sense is, that God treated him *as if* he had been a sinner; that he subjected him to such pains and woes as would have been a proper punishment *if* he had been guilty; that while he was, in fact, in all senses perfectly innocent, and while God knew this, yet that in consequence of the voluntary assumption of the place of man which the Lord Jesus took, it pleased the Father to lay on him the deep sorrows which would be the proper expression of his sense of the evil of sin; that he endured so much suffering, as would answer the same great ends in maintaining the truth, and honour, and justice of God, as if the guilty had themselves endured the penalty of the law. This, I suppose, is what is usually meant when it is said "our sins were imputed to him;" and though this language is not used in the Bible, and though it is liable to great mis-apprehension and perversion, yet if this is its meaning, there can be no objection to it.

[Certainly Christ's being made sin, is not to be explained of his being made sin in the ab-stract, nor of his having actually become a sin-ner; yet it does imply, that sin was charged on Christ, or that it was imputed to him, and that he became answerable for it. Nor can this idea be excluded, even if we admit that "sin-offering" is the proper rendering of ἁμαρτία in the passage. "That Christ," says an old divine commenting on this place, "was made sin for us, because he was a sacrifice for sin, we confess; but therefore was he a sacrifice for sin because our sins were imputed to him, and punished in him." The doctrine of imputa-tion of sin to Christ is here, by plain enough inference at least. The rendering in our Bibles, however, asserts it in a more direct form. Nor, after all the criticism that has been expended on the text, does there seem any necessity for the abandonment of that rendering, on the part of the advocate of im-putation. For first ἁμαρτία in the Septuagint, and the corresponding אָשָׁם in the Hebrew, denote both the sin and the sin-offering, the piacular sacrifice and the crime itself. Second, the antithesis in the passage, so obvious and beautiful, is destroyed by the adoption of "sin-offering." Christ was made sin, we righte-ousness.

There seems in our author's comment on this place, and also on the fifth of the Romans, an attempt to revive the oft refuted objection against imputation, viz., that it involves some-thing like a transference of moral character, an infusion, rather than an imputation of sin or righteousness. Nothing of this kind is at all implied in the doctrine. Its advocates with one voice disclaim it; and the reader will see the objection answered at length in the sup-plementary Notes on the fourth and fifth chap-ters of Romans. What then is the value of such arguments or insinuations as these: " All such views as go to make the holy Redeemer a sinner, or guilty, or deserving of the suffer-ings he endured, border on blasphemy," &c. Nor is it wiser to affirm that "if Christ was properly guilty, it would make no difference in this respect, whether it was by his own fault or by imputation." What may be meant in this connection by "properly guilty," we know not. But this is certain, that there is an immense difference between Christ's having

the *guilt* of *our* iniquities charged on him, and having the guilt of his own so charged.

It is admitted in the commentary, that God "treated Christ as if he had been a sinner," and this is alleged as the probable sense of the passage. But this treatment of Christ on the part of God, must have some *ground*, and where shall we find it, unless in the imputa-tion of sin to him? If the guilt of our iniquities, or which is the same thing, the law obligation to punishment, be not charged on Christ, how in justice can he be subjected to the punish-ment? If he had not voluntarily come under such obligation, what claim had law on him? That the very words "sin imputed to Christ" are not found in scripture, is not a very for-midable objection. The words in this text are stronger and better " He was *made sin*," and says Isaiah, according to the rendering of Bishop Lowth, " The Lord made to meet upon him the iniquities of us all. It was required of him, and he was made answerable." Isa. liii. 6.]

¶ *Who knew no sin.* He was not guilty. He was perfectly holy and pure. This idea is thus expressed by Peter (1 Pet. ii. 22): " who did no sin, neither was guile found in his mouth;" and in Heb. vii. 26, it is said he was " holy, harmless, undefiled, separate from sinners." In all re-spects, and in all conceivable senses, the Lord Jesus was pure and holy. If he had not been, he would not have been qualified to make an atonement. Hence the sacred writers are every-where at great pains to keep this idea prominent, for on this depends the whole superstructure of the plan of salvation. The phrase " *knew* no sin," is an expression of great beauty and dignity. It indicates his entire and perfect purity. He was altogether unacquainted with sin ; he was a stranger to transgression ; he was conscious of no sin ; he committed none. He had a mind and heart per-fectly free from pollution, and his whole life was perfectly pure and holy in the sight of God. ¶ *That we might be made the righteousness of God.* This is a Hebraism, meaning the same as *divinely righteous*. It means that we are made righteous in the sight of God; that is, that we are accepted as righteous, and treated as righteous by God on account of what the Lord Jesus has done. There is here an evident and beautiful contrast between what is said of Christ, and what is said of us. He was made *sin ;* we are made *righteousness ;* that is, he was treated *as if* he were a sinner, though he was perfectly holy and pure ; we are treated *as if* we were righteous, though we are defiled and depraved. The idea is, that on account of what the Lord Jesus has endured in our behalf we are treated as if we had ourselves entirely fulfilled the law of God, and had never become exposed to its penalty. In the phrase "righteousness *of God,*" there is a reference to the fact that this is *his* plan of making men righteous, or of justifying them. They who thus become righteous, or are justified, are justified on his plan, and by a scheme which he has devised. Locke renders this, "that we, in and by him, might be made righteous, by a righteousness imputed to us by God." The idea is, that all our righteousness in the sight of God we receive in and through a Redeemer. All is to be traced to him. This verse contains a beautiful epitome of the whole plan of salvation, and the peculiarity of the Christian scheme. On the one hand, one who was perfectly innocent, by a voluntary substitution, is treated AS IF he were guilty , that is, is subjected to pains and sorrows which *if he were* guilty would be a proper punishment for sin : and on the other, they who *are* guilty and who deserve to be punished, are treated, through his vicarious sufferings, *as if* they were perfectly innocent ; that is, in a manner which would be a proper expression of God's approbation if he had not sinned. The whole plan, therefore, is one of substitution ; and without substitution, there can be no salvation. Innocence voluntarily suffers for guilt, and the guilty are thus made pure and holy, and are saved. The greatness of the divine compassion and love is thus shown for the guilty ; and on the ground of this it is right and proper for God to call on men *to be* reconciled to him. It is the strongest argument that can be used. When God has given his only Son to the bitter suffering of death on the cross *in order* that we may be reconciled, it

is the highest possible argument which can be used why we *should* cease our opposition to him, and become his friends.

[See the supplementary Notes on Rom. i. 17 ; iii. 21. See also the additional Note above, on the first clause of the verse. The "righteousness of God," is doubtless that righteousness which the divine Saviour wrought out, in his active and passive obedience, and if ever any of the guilty race of Adam are "treated as righteous" by God, it must be solely on the ground of its imputation.]

REMARKS.

1. It is possible for Christians to have the assurance that they shall enter into heaven, ver. 1. Paul said that *he* knew this ; John knew this (see Note on ver. 1), and there is no reason why others should not know it. If a man hates sin he may know that as well as any thing else ; if he loves God, why should he not know that as well as to know that he loves an earthly friend ? If he desires to be holy, to enter heaven, to be eternally pure, why should we have any doubt about that ? If he loves to pray, to read the Bible, to converse of heaven —if his heart is truly in these things, he may *know* it, as well as know any thing else about his own character or feelings.

2. If a Christian *may* know it, he *should* know it. No other knowledge is so desirable as this. Nothing will produce so much comfort as this. Nothing will contribute so much to make him firm, decided, and consistent in his Christian walk as this. No other knowledge will give him so much support in temptation ; so much comfort in trial ; so much peace in death. And *if* a man is a Christian, he should give himself no rest till he obtains assurance on this subject ; if he is *not* a Christian he cannot know *that* too soon, or take too early measures to flee from the wrath to come.

3. The body will soon be dissolved in death, ver. 1. It is a frail crumbling, decaying dwelling, that must soon be taken down. It has none of the properties of a permanent abode. It *can* be held together but a little

time. It is like a hut or cottage, that is shaken by every gust of wind; like a tent when the pins are loose, and the cords unstranded, or rotten, and when the wind will soon sweep it away. And since this is the fact, we may as well know it, and not attempt to conceal it from the mind. All truth may be looked at calmly, and should be, and a man who is residing in a frail and shattered dwelling, should be looking out for one that is more permanent and substantial. Death should be looked at. The fact that this tabernacle shall be taken down should be looked at; and every man should be asking with deep interest the question whether there is not a more permanent dwelling for him in a better world.

4. This life is burdened, and is full of cares, ver. 2, 4. It is such as is fitted to make us desire a better state. We groan here under sin, amidst temptation, encompassed by the cares and toils of life. We are burdened with duties, and we are oppressed by trials; and under all we are sinking to the grave. Soon, under the accumulated burdens, the body will be crushed, and sink back to the dust. Man cannot endure the burden long, and ne must soon die. These accumulated trials and cares are such as are adapted to make him desire a better inheritance, and to look forward to a better world. God designs that this shall be a world of care and anxiety, in order that we may be led to seek a better portion beyond the grave.

5. The Christian has a permanent home in heaven, ver. 1, 2, 4. There is a house not made with hands; an eternal home; a world where mortality is unknown. There is his home; that is his eternal dwelling. Here he is a stranger, among strangers, in a strange world. In heaven is his home. The body here may be sick, feeble, dying; there it shall be vigorous, strong, immortal. He may have no comfortable dwelling here; he may be poor, and afflicted; there he shall have an undecaying dwelling, an unchanging home. Who in a world like this should not desire to be a Christian? What

other condition of life is so desirable as that of the man who is *sure* that after a few more days he shall be admitted to an eternal home in heaven, where the body never dies, and where sin and sorrow are known no more?

6. The Christian should be willing to bear all the pain and sorrow which God shall appoint, ver. 1—4. Why should he not? He knows not only that God is good in all this; but he knows that it is but for a moment; that he is advancing toward heaven, and that he will soon be at home. Compared with that eternal rest what trifles are all the sufferings of this mortal life!

7. We should not desire to die merely to get rid of pain, or to be absent from the body, ver. 4. It is not merely in order that we may be "unclothed," or that we may get away from a suffering body, that we should be willing to die. Many a sinner suffers so much here that he is willing to plunge into an awful eternity, as he supposes, to get rid of pain, when, alas! he plunges only into deeper and eternal woe. We should be willing to bear as much pain, and to bear it as long as God shall be pleased to appoint. We should submit to all without a murmur. We should be anxious to be relieved only when God shall judge it best for us to be away from the body, and to be present with the Lord.

8. In a mere readiness to die there is no evidence that we are prepared for heaven; comp. ver. 4. Many a man supposes that because he is ready to die, that, therefore, he is prepared. Many a one takes comfort because a dying friend was ready and willing to die. But in a mere willingness to die there is no evidence of a preparation for death, because a hundred causes may conspire to produce this besides piety. And let us not be deceived by supposing that because we have no alarm about death, and are willing to go to another world, that therefore we are prepared. It may be either stupidity, or insensibility; it may be a mere desire to get rid of suffering; it may be because we are cherishing a

hope of heaven which is altogether vain and illusive.

9. The Christian should, and may desire to depart and to be in heaven, ver. 2. Heaven is his home ; and it is his privilege to desire to be there. Here he is in a world of trial and of sin. There he shall be in a world of joy and of holiness. Here he dwells in a frail, suffering, decaying body. There he shall be clothed with immortality. It is his privilege, therefore, to desire, as soon as it shall be the will of God, to depart, and to enter on his eternal inheritance in heaven. He should have a strong, fixed, firm desire for that world ; and should be ready at the shortest notice to go and to be for ever with the Lord.

10. The hopes and joys of Christians, and all their peace and calmness in the prospect of death, are to be traced to God, ver. 5. It is not that they are not naturally as timid and fearful of dying as others ; it is not that they have any native courage or strength, but it is to be traced entirely to the mercy of God, and the influence of his Spirit, that they are enabled to look calmly at death, at the grave, at eternity. With the assured prospect of heaven, they have nothing to fear in dying ; and if we have the " earnest of the Spirit "—the pledge that heaven is ours—we have nothing to fear in the departure from this world.

11. The Christian should be, and may be, always cheerful, ver. 6. Paul said that he was always confident, or cheerful. Afflictions did not depress him ; trials did not cast him down. He was not disheartened by opposition ; he did not lose his courage by being reviled and persecuted. In all this he was cheerful and bold. There is nothing in religion to make us melancholy and sad. The assurance of the favour of God, and the hope of heaven, should have, and will have, just the opposite effect. A sense of the presence of God, a conviction that we are sinners, a deep impression of the truth that we are to die, and of the infinite interest of the soul at stake, will indeed make us serious and solemn, and should do so. But this is

not inconsistent with *cheerfulness*, but is rather fitted to produce it. It is favourable to a state of mind where all irritability is suppressed, and where the mind is made calm and settled ; and this is favourable to cheerfulness. Besides, there is much, very much in religion to *prevent* sadness, and to remove gloom from the soul. The hope of heaven, and the prospect of dwelling with God and with holy beings for ever, is the best means of expelling the gloom which is caused by the disappointments and cares of the world. And much as many persons suppose that religion *creates* gloom, it is certain that nothing in this world has done so much to lighten care, to break the force of misfortune and disappointment, to support in times of trial, and to save from despair, as the religion of the Redeemer. And it is moreover certain that there are no persons so habitually calm in their feelings, and cheerful in their tempers, as consistent and devout Christians. If there are some Christians, like David Brainerd, who are melancholy and sad, as there are undoubtedly, it should be said, (1.) That they are few in number ; (2.) That their gloom is to be traced to constitutional propensity, and not to religion ; (3.) That they have, even with all their gloom, joys which the world never experiences, and which can never be found in sin ; and, (4.) That their gloom is not produced *by* religion, but *by the want of more of it.*

12. It is noble to act with reference to things unseen and eternal, ver. 7. It elevates the soul ; lifts it above the earth ; purifies the heart ; and gives to man a new dignity. It prevents all the grovelling effect of acting from a view of present objects, and with reference to the things which are just around us. " Whatever withdraws us," says Dr. Johnson, " from the power of our senses ; whatever makes the past, the distant, or the future, predominate over the present, advances us in the dignity of thinking beings."— *Tour to the Hebrides,* p. 322, ed. Phil. 1810. Whatever directs the eye and the heart to heaven ; whatever may make man feel and believe

that there is a God, a Saviour, a heaven, a world of glory, elevates him with the consciousness of his immortality, and raises him above the grovelling objects that wither and debase the soul. Man should act with reference to eternity. He should be conscious of immortality. He should be deeply impressed with that high honour that awaits him of standing before God. He should feel that he *may* partake in the glories of the resurrection; that he may inherit an eternal heaven. Feeling thus, what trifles are the things of the earth! How little should he be moved by its trials! How little should he be influenced by its wealth, its pleasures, and its honours!

13. The Christian, when he leaves the body, is at once with the Lord Jesus, ver. 8. He rushes, as it were instinctively, to his presence, and casts himself at his feet. He has no other home than where the Saviour is; he thinks of no future joy or glory but that which is to be enjoyed with him. Why then should we fear death? Lay out of view, as we may, the momentary pang, the chilliness, and the darkness of the grave, and think of that which will be the moment *after* death—the view of the Redeemer, the sight of the splendours of the heavenly world, the angels, the spirits of the just made perfect, the river of the paradise of God, and the harps of praise, and what has man to fear in the prospect of dying?

Why should I shrink at pain or woe,
  Or feel at death dismay?
I've Canaan's goodly land in view,
  And realms of endless day.

Apostles, martyrs, prophets there,
  Around my Saviour stand;
And soon my friends in Christ below
  Will join the glorious band.

Jerusalem! my happy home!
  My soul still pants for thee;
When shall my labours have an end
  In joy, and peace, and thee!
          C. Wesley.

14. We should act feeling that we are in the immediate presence of God, and so as to meet his acceptance and approbation, whether we remain on earth, or whether we are removed to eternity, ver. 9. The prospect of being with him, and the consciousness that his eye is fixed upon us, should make us diligent, humble, and laborious. It should be the great purpose of our lives to secure his favour, and meet with his acceptance; and it should make no difference with us in this respect, where we are — whether on earth or in heaven; with the prospect of long life, or of an early death; in society or in solitude; at home or abroad; on the land or on the deep; in sickness or in health; in prosperity or in adversity, it should be our great aim so to live as to be "accepted of him." And the Christian *will* so act. To act in this manner is the very nature of true piety; and where this desire does not exist, there can be no true religion.

15. We must appear before the judgment-seat, ver. 10. We must *all* appear there. This is inevitable. There is not one of the human family that can escape. Old and young; rich and poor; bond and free; all classes, all conditions, all nations must stand there, and give an account for all the deeds done in the body, and receive their eternal doom. How solemn is the thought of being *arraigned!* How deeply affecting the idea that on the issue of *that one trial* will depend our eternal weal or woe! How overwhelming the reflection that from that sentence there can be no appeal; no power of reversing it; no possibility of afterwards changing our destiny!

16. We shall soon be there, ver. 10. No one knows when he is to die; and death when it comes will remove us at once to the judgment-seat. A disease that may carry us off in a few hours may take us there; or death that may come in an instant shall bear us to that awful bar. How many are stricken down in a moment; how many are hurried without *any* warning to the solemnities of the eternal world! So we may die. No one can *insure* our lives; no one can guard us from the approach of the invisible king of terrors.

17. We should be ready to depart

If we *must* stand at the awful bar ; and if we may be summoned there any moment, assuredly we should lose no time in being ready to go. It is our great business in life; and it should claim our first attention, and all other things should be postponed that we may be ready to die. It should be the first inquiry every morning, and the last subject of thought every evening—for who knows when he rises in the morning but that before night he may stand at the judgment-seat ! Who, when he lies down on his bed at night, knows but that in the silence of the night-watches he may be summoned to go alone—to leave his family and friends, his home and his bed, to answer for all the deeds done in the body ?

18. We should endeavour to save others from eternal death, vor. 11. If we have ourselves any just views of the awful terrors of the day of judgment, and if we have any just views of the wrath of God, we should endeavour " to persuade " others to flee from the wrath to come. We should plead with them ; we should entreat them; we should weep over them ; we should pray for them, that they may be saved from going up to meet the awful wrath of God. If our friends are unprepared to meet God; if they are living in impenitence and sin, and if we have *any* influence over others in any way, we should exert it all to induce them to come to Christ, and to save themselves from the awful terrors of that day. Paul deemed no self-denial and no sacrifice too great, if he might persuade them to come to God, and to save their souls. And who that has any just views of the awful terrors of the day of judgment ; of the woes of an eternal hell, and of the glories of an eternal heaven; can deem that labour too great which shall be the means of saving immortal souls? Not to frighten them should we labour, not to alarm them merely should we plead with them, but we should endeavour by all means to *persuade* them to come to the Redeemer. We should not use tones of harshness and denunciation ; we should not speak of hell as if we would rejoice to execute the sentence,

but we should speak with tenderness, earnestness, and with tears (comp. Acts xx. 31), that we may induce our friends and fellow-sinners to be reconciled to God.

19. We should not deem it strange or remarkable if we are charged with being deranged for being active and zealous in the subject of religion, ver. 13. There will always be enough, both *in* the church and *out* of it, to charge us with over-heated zeal; with want of prudence ; or with decided mental alienation. But we are not to forget that Paul was accused of being "mad ;" and even the Redeemer was thought to be "beside himself." " It is sufficient for the disciple that he be as his master, and the servant as his Lord ;" and if the Redeemer was charged with derangement on account of his peculiar views and his zeal, we should not suppose that any strange thing had happened to us if we are accused in like manner.

20. The gospel should be offered to all men, ver. 14. If Christ died for all, then salvation is provided for all ; and then it should be offered to all freely and fully. It should be done without any mental reservation, for God has no such mental reservation ; without any hesitation or misgiving ; without any statements that would break the force, or weaken the power of such an offer on the consciences of men. If they reject it, they should be left to see that they reject that which is in good faith offered to them, and that for this they must give an account to God. Every man who preaches the gospel should feel that he is not only *permitted* but REQUIRED to preach the gospel " to every creature ;" nor should he embrace any opinion whatever which will in form or in fact cramp him or restrain him in thus offering salvation to all mankind. The fact that Christ died for all, and that all may be saved, should be a fixed and standing point in all systems of theology, and should be allowed to shape every other opinion, and to shed its influence over every other view of truth.

21 All men by nature are dead in sins, ver. 14. They are insensible to

their own good; to the appeals of God; to the glories of heaven, and to the terrors of hell. They do not act for eternity; they are without concern in regard to their everlasting destiny. They are as insensible to all these things, until aroused by the Spirit of God, as a dead man in his grave is to surrounding objects. And there is nothing that ever did arouse such a man, or ever could, but the same power that made the world, and the same voice that raised Lazarus from his grave. This melancholy fact strikes us everywhere; and we should be deeply humbled that it is *our* condition by nature, and should mourn that it is the condition of our fellowmen everywhere.

22. We should form our estimate of objects and of their respective value and importance by other considerations than those which are derived from their temporal nature, ver. 16. It should not be simply according to the flesh. It should not be as they estimate them who are living for this world. It should not be by their rank, their splendour, or their fashion. It should be by their reference to eternity, and their bearing on the state of things there.

23. It should be with us a very serious inquiry whether our views of Christ are such as they have who are living after the flesh, or such only as the unrenewed mind takes, ver. 16. The carnal mind has no just views of the Redeemer. To every impenitent sinner he is "a root out of a day ground." There is no beauty in him. And to every hypocrite, and every deceived professor of religion, there is really no beauty seen in him. There is no spontaneous, elevated, glowing attachment to him. It is all forced and unnatural. But to the true Christian there is a beauty seen in his character that is not seen in any other; and the whole soul loves him, and embraces him. His character is seen to be most pure and lovely; his benevolence boundless; his ability and willingness to save, infinite. The renewed soul desires no other Saviour; and rejoices that he is just what he is—rejoices in his humiliation as

well as his exaltation; in his poverty as well as his glory; rejoices in the privilege of being saved by him who was spit upon, and mocked, and crucified, as well as by him who is at the right hand of God. One thing is certain, unless we have just views of Christ we can never be saved.

24. The new birth is a great and most important change, ver. 17. It is not in name or in profession merely, but it is a deep and radical change of the heart. It is so great that it may be said of each one that he is *a new creation* of God; and in relation to each one, that old things are passed away, and all things are become new. How important it is that we examine our hearts and see whether this change has taken place, or whether we are still living without God and without hope. It is indispensable that we be born again; John iii. If we are not born again, and if we are not new creatures in Christ, we must perish for ever. No matter what our wealth, talent, learning, accomplishment, reputation, or morality; unless we have been so changed that it may be said, and that we can say, " old things are passed away, and all things are become new," we must perish for ever. *There is no power in the universe that can save a man who is not born again.*

25. The gospel ministry is a most responsible and important work, ver. 18, 19. There is no other office of the same importance; there is no situation in which man can be placed more solemn than that of making known the terms on which God is willing to bestow favour on apostate man.

26. How amazing is the divine condescension, that God should have ever proposed such a plan of reconciliation, ver. 20, 21. That he should not only have been *willing* to be reconciled, but that he should have *sought*, and have been so *anxious* for it as to be willing to send his own Son to die to secure it! It was pure, rich, infinite benevolence. God was not to be *benefited* by it. He was infinitely blessed and happy even though man should have been lost. He was pure, and just, and holy, and it was not *necessary* to resort to this in order to

CHAPTER VI.

WE then, *as* workers *a* together *with him*, beseech *you*

a chap.5.20.

also that ye receive not the grace of
God in vain.*b*

2 (For he saith,*c* I have heard

b He. 12.15.   *c* Is. 49.8.

vindicate his own character. He had
done man no wrong ; and if man had
perished in his sins, the throne of God
would have been pure and spotless.
It was love ; mere love. It was pure,
holy, disinterested, infinite benevolence. It was worthy of a God ; and
it has a claim to the deepest gratitude
of man.

Let us then, in view of this whole
chapter, seek to be reconciled to God.
Let us lay aside all our opposition to
him. Let us embrace his plans. Let
us be willing to submit to him, and to
become his ETERNAL FRIENDS. Let us
seek to heaven to which he would
raise us ; and though our earthly house
of this tabernacle *must* be dissolved,
let us be prepared, as we may be, for
that eternal habitation which he has
fitted up for all who love him in the
heavens.

CHAPTER VI.

THIS chapter, closely connected in
sense with the preceding, is designed
as an address to the Corinthian Christians, exhorting them to act worthily
of their calling, and of their situation
under such a ministry as they had enjoyed. In the previous chapters, Paul
had discoursed at length of the design
and of the labours of the ministry. The
main drift of all this was to show them
the nature of reconciliation, and the
obligation to turn to God, and to live
to him. This idea is pursued in this
chapter ; and in view of the labours
and self-denials of the ministry, Paul
urges on the Corinthian Christians
the duty of coming out from the world,
and of separating themselves entirely
from all evil. The chapter may be
conveniently contemplated in the following parts :

I. Paul states that he and his associates were fellow-labourers with God,
and he exhorts the Corinthians not to
receive the grace of God in vain. To
induce them to make a wise improvement of the privileges which they enjoyed, he quotes a passage from Isaiah,
and applies it as meaning that it was

then an acceptable time, and that
they might avail themselves of mercy,
ver. 1, 2.

II. He enumerates the labours and
self-denials of the ministry. He refers
to their sincerity, zeal, and honesty of
life. He shows how much they had
been willing to endure in order to
convey the gospel to others, and how
much they had in fact endured, and
how much they had benefited others.
He speaks of their afflictions in a most
tender and beautiful manner, and of
the happy results which had followed
from their self-denying labours, ver.
3 10. The design of this is, evidently, to remind them of what their
religion had cost, and to appeal to
them in view of all this to lead holy
and pure lives.

III. Paul expresses his ardent attachment for them, and says that *if*
they were straitened—if they did not
live as they should do, it was not because he and his fellow-labourers had
not loved them, and sought their welfare, but from a defect in themselves,
ver. 11, 12.

IV. As a *reward* for all that he had
done and suffered for them, he now
asked only that they should live as
became Christians, ver. 13—18. He
sought not silver, or gold, or apparel.
He had not laboured as he had done
with any view to a temporal reward.
And he now asked simply that they
should come out from the world, and
be dissociated from every thing that
was evil. He demanded that they
should be separated from all idolatry,
and idolatrous practices ; assures them
that there can be no union between
light and darkness ; righteousness and
unrighteousness ; Christ and Belial ;
that there can be no agreement between the temple of God and idols ;
reminds them of the fact that they are
the temple of God ; and encourages
them to do this by the assurance that
God would be their God, and that they
should be his adopted sons and daughters. The chapter is one of great

thee in a time accepted, and in the day of salvation have I succoured thee : behold, now *is* the accepted

time ; behold, now *is* the day of salvation.)

3 Giving no *a* offence in any

a 1 Co. 10. 32.

beauty ; and the argument for a holy life among Christians is one that is exceedingly forcible and tender.

1. *We then,* as *workers together* with him. On the meaning of this expression, see Note, 1 Cor. iii. 9. The Greek here is (συνεργοῦντες) " working together," and may mean either that the apostles and ministers to whom Paul refers were joint-labourers in entreating them not to receive the grace of God in vain ; or it may mean that they *co-operated* with God, or were engaged *with* him in endeavouring to secure the reconciliation of the world to himself. Tindal renders it, " we as helpers." Doddridge, " we then as the joint-labourers of God." Most expositors have concurred in this interpretation. The word properly means, to work together ; to co-operate in producing any result. Macknight supposes that the word here is in the vocative, and is an address to the fellow-labourers of Paul, entreating *them* not to receive the grace of God in vain. In this opinion he is probably alone, and has manifestly departed from the scope and design of the passage. Probably the most *obvious* meaning is that of our translators, who regard it as teaching that Paul was a joint-worker with God in securing the salvation of men. ¶ *That ye receive not the grace of God in vain.* The " grace of God " here means evidently the gracious offer of reconciliation and pardon. And the sense is, " We entreat you not to neglect or slight this offer of pardon, so as to lose the benefit of it, and be lost. It is offered freely and fully. It may be partaken of by all, and all may be saved. But it may also be slighted, and all the benefits of it will then be lost." The sense is, that it was possible that this offer might be made to them, they might hear of a Saviour, be told of the plan of reconciliation, and have the offers of mercy pressed on their attention and acceptance, and yet all be in vain. They might

notwithstanding all this be lost, for simply *to hear* of the plan of salvation or the offers of mercy, will no more save a sinner than *to hear* of medicine will save the sick. It must be embraced and applied, or it will be in vain. It is true that Paul probably addressed this to those who were professors of religion ; and the sense is, that they should use all possible care and anxiety lest these offers should have been made in vain. They should examine their own hearts ; they should inquire into their own condition ; they should guard against self-deception. The same persons (chap. v. 20) Paul had exhorted also to be reconciled to God ; and the idea is, that he would earnestly entreat even professors of religion to give all diligence to secure an interest in the saving mercy of the gospel, and to guard against the possibility of being self-deceived and ruined.

2. *For he saith ;* see Isaiah xlix. 8. In that passage the declaration refers to the Messiah, and the design is there to show that God would be favourable to him ; that he would hear him when he prayed, and would make him the medium of establishing a covenant with his own people, and of spreading the true religion around the earth ; see my Note on that place. Paul quotes the passage here not as affirming that he used it in exactly the same sense, or with reference to the same design for which it was originally spoken, but as expressing the idea which he wished to convey, or in accordance with the general *principle* implied in its use in Isaiah. The general idea there, or the principle involved, was, that under the Messiah God would be willing to hear ; that is, that he would be disposed to show mercy to the Jew and to the Gentile. This is the main idea of the passage as used by Paul. Under the Messiah, it is said by Isaiah, God would be willing to show mercy. That would be an acceptable time. That time,

says Paul, has arrived. The Messiah has come, and now God is willing to pardon and save. And the doctrine in this verse is, *that under the Messiah, or in the time of Christ, God is willing to show mercy to men.* In him alone is the throne of grace accessible, and now that he has come, God is willing to pardon, and men should avail themselves of the offers of mercy. ¶ *I have heard thee.* The Messiah. I have listened to thy prayer for the salvation of the heathen world. The *promise* to the Messiah was, that the heathen world should be given to him; but it was a promise that it should be in answer to *his* prayers and intercessions. " Ask of me, and I shall give thee the heathen for thine inheritance, and the uttermost parts of the earth for thy possession ;" Ps. ii. 8. The salvation of the heathen world, and of all who are saved, is to be in answer to the prevalent intercession of the Lord Jesus. ¶ *In a time accepted.* In Isaiah, " in an acceptable time." The idea is, that he had prayed in a time when God was *disposed* to show mercy ; the time when in his wise arrangements he had designed that his salvation should be extended to the world. It is a time which he had *fixed* as the appropriate period for extending the knowledge of his truth and his salvation ; and it proves that there *was* to be a period which was the *favourable* period of salvation, that is, which God esteemed to be the proper period for making his salvation known to men. At such a period the Messiah would pray, and the prayer would be answered. ¶ *In the day of salvation.* In the time when I am disposed to show salvation. ¶ *Have I succoured thee.* The Messiah. I have sustained thee, that is, in the effort to make salvation known. God here speaks of there being an accepted time, a limited period, in which petitions in favour of the world would be acceptable to him. That time Paul says had come ; and the idea which he urges is, that men should avail themselves of that, and embrace now the offers of mercy. ¶ *Behold, now is the accepted time,* &c. The meaning of this passage is, the " Mes-

siah is come. The time referred to by Isaiah has arrived. It is now a time when God is ready to show compassion, to hear prayer, and to have mercy on mankind. Only through the Messiah, the Lord Jesus, does he show mercy, and men should therefore now embrace the offers of pardon." The doctrine taught here, therefore, is, that through the Lord Jesus, and where he is preached, God is willing to pardon and save men ; and this is true *wherever* he is preached, and as long as men live under the sound of the gospel. The world is under a dispensation of mercy, and God is willing to show compassion, and while this exists, that is, while men live, the offers of salvation are to be freely made to them. The time *will* come when it will not be an acceptable time with God. The day of mercy will be closed ; the period of trial will be ended ; and men will be removed to a world where no mercy is shown, and where compassion is unknown. This verse, which should be read as a parenthesis, is designed to be connected with the argument which the apostle is urging, and which he presented in the previous chapter. The general doctrine is, that men should seek reconciliation with God. To enforce that, he here says, that it was *now* the acceptable time, the time when God was willing to be reconciled to men. The general sentiment of this passage may be thus expressed (1) Under the gospel it is an acceptable time, a day of mercy, a time when God is willing to show mercy to men. (2.) There may be special seasons which may be peculiarly called the acceptable, or accepted time. (*a*) When the gospel is pressed on the attention by the faithful preaching of his servants, or by the urgent entreaties of friends ; (*b*) When it is brought to our attention by any striking dispensation of Providence ; (*c*) When the Spirit of God strives with us, and brings us to deep reflection, or to conviction for sin ; (*d*) In a revival of religion, when many are pressing into the kingdom—it is at all such seasons an accepted time, a day of salvation, a day which we should improve. It

thing, that the ministry be not blamed :

1 *commending.*

is "NOW" such a season, because, (1.) The time of mercy will pass by, and God will not be willing to pardon the sinner who goes unprepared to eternity. (2.) Because we cannot calculate on the future. We have no assurance, no evidence that we shall live another day, or hour. (3.) It is taught here, that the time *will* come when it will *not* be an accepted time. *Now* is the accepted time ; at some future period it will NOT be. If men grieve away the Holy Spirit ; if they continue to reject the gospel ; if they go unprepared to eternity, no mercy can be found. God does not design to pardon beyond the grave. He has made no provision for forgiveness there ; and they who are not pardoned in this life, must be unpardoned for ever.

3. *Giving no offence in any thing.* We the ministers of God, ver. 1. The word rendered *offence* means, properly, *stumbling;* then offence, or cause of offence, a falling into sin. The meaning here is, " giving no occasion for contemning or rejecting the gospel ;" and the idea of Paul is, that he and his fellow-apostles so laboured as that no one who saw or knew them, should have occasion to reproach the ministry, or the religion which they preached ; but so that in their pure and self-denying lives, the strongest argument should be seen for embracing it ; comp. Matt. x. 16 ; 1 Cor. viii. 13 ; x. 32, 33. Notes, Phil. ii. 15 ; 1 Thes. ii. 10 ; v. 22. *How* they conducted so as to give no offence he states in the following verses. ¶ *That the ministry be not blamed.* The phrase, " the ministry," refers here not merely to the ministry of Paul, that is, it does not mean merely that *he* would be subject to blame and reproach, but that the *ministry itself* which the Lord Jesus had established would be blamed, or would be reproached by the improper conduct of any one who was engaged in that work. The idea is, that the misconduct of one minister of the gospel would bring

4 But in all *things* approving ¹ ourselves as the ministers ᵃ of

a 1 Co. 4. 1.

a reproach upon the profession itself, and would prevent the usefulness and success of others, just as the misconduct of a physician exposes the profession to reproach, or the bad conduct of a lawyer reflects itself in some degree on the entire profession. And it is so everywhere. The errors, follies, misconduct, or bad example of one minister of the gospel brings a reproach upon the sacred calling itself, and prevents the usefulness of many others. Ministers do not stand alone. And though no one can be responsible for the errors and failings of others, yet no one can avoid suffering in regard to his usefulness by the sins of others. Not only, therefore, from a regard to his personal usefulness should every minister be circumspect in his walk, but from respect to the usefulness of all others who sustain the office of the ministry, and from respect to the success of religion all over the world. Paul made it one of the principles of his conduct so to act that no man should have cause to speak reproachfully of the ministry on his account. In order to this, he felt; it to be necessary not only to *claim* and *assert* honour for the ministry, but to lead such a life as should deserve the respect of men. If a man wishes to secure respect for his calling, it must be by living in the manner which that calling demands, and then respect and honour will follow as a matter of course ; see *Calvin.*

4. *But in all* things. In every respect. In all that we do. In every way, both by words and deeds. *How* this was done, Paul proceeds to state in the following verses. ¶ *Approving ourselves as the ministers of God.* Marg. " Commending." Tindal renders it, " In all things let us behave ourselves as the ministers of God." The idea is, that Paul and his fellow-labourers endeavoured to live as *became* the ministers of God, and so as to commend the ministry to the confidence and affection of men. They endeavoured to live as was appropri-

God, in much patience, in af- | 5 In stripes, *a* in imprisonments,
flictions, in necessities, in dis- | ¹ in tumults, in labours, in watch-
tresses, | ings, in fastings.

a ch. 11. 23, &c. | 1 or *in tossings to and fro.*

ate to those who were the ministers of God, and so that the world would be disposed to do honour to the ministry. ¶ *In much patience.* In the patient endurance of afflictions of all kinds. Some of his trials he proceeds to enumerate. The idea is, that a minister of God, in order to do good and to commend his ministry, should set an example of patience. He preaches this as a duty to others ; and if, when he is poor, persecuted, oppressed, calumniated, or imprisoned, he should murmur, or be insubmissive, the consequence would be that he would do little good by all his preaching. And no one can doubt, that God often places his ministers in circumstances of peculiar trial, among other reasons, in order that they may illustrate their own precepts by their example, and show to their people with what temper and spirit they may and ought to suffer. Ministers often do a great deal more good by their example in suffering than they do in their preaching. It is easy to preach to others ; it is not so easy to manifest just the right spirit in time of persecution and trial. Men too can resist preaching, but they cannot resist the effect and power of a good example in times of suffering. In regard to the manner in which Paul says that the ministry may commend itself, it may be observed, that he *groups* several things together ; or mentions several *classes* of influences or means. In this and the next verse he refers to various kinds of afflictions. In the following verses he groups several things together, pertaining to a holy life, and a pure conversation. ¶ *In afflictions.* In all our afflictions ; referring to *all* the afflictions and trials which they were called to bear. The following words, in the manner of a climax, specify more particularly the kinds of trials which they were called to endure. ¶ *In necessities.* This is a stronger term than afflictions, and denotes the

distress which arose from *want.* He everywhere endured adversity. It denotes *unavoidable* distress and calamity. ¶ *In distresses.* The word here used (στενοχωρία) denotes properly *straitness of place,* want of room ; then straits, distress, anguish. It is a stronger word than either of those which he had before used. See it explained in the Notes on Rom. ii. 9. Paul means that in all these circumstances he had evinced patience, and had endeavoured to act as became a minister of God.

5. *In stripes.* In this verse, Paul proceeds to *specifications* of what he had been called to endure. In the previous verse, he had spoken of his afflictions in general terms. In this expression, he refers to the fact that he and his fellow-labourers were scourged in the synagogues and cities as if they had been the worst of men. In 2 Cor. xi. 23—25, Paul says that he had been scourged five times by the Jews, and had been thrice beaten with rods. See Notes on that place. ¶ *In imprisonments.* As at Philippi ; Acts xvi. 24. seq. It was no uncommon thing for the early preachers of Christianity to be imprisoned. ¶ *In tumults.* Marg. *Tossing to and fro.* The Greek word (ἀκαταστασία) denotes properly *instability,* thence disorder, tumult, commotion. Here it means that in the various tumults and commotions which were produced by the preaching of the gospel, Paul endeavoured to act as became a minister of God. Such tumults were excited at Corinth (Acts xviii. 6) ; at Philippi (Acts xvi. 19, 20) ; at Lystra and Derbe (Acts xiv. 19) ; at Ephesus (Acts xix.), and in various other places. The idea is, that if the ministers of religion are assailed by a lawless mob, they are to endeavour to show the spirit of Christ there, and to evince all patience, and to *do good* even in such a scene. Patience and the Christian spirit may often do more good in such scenes than much

6 By pureness, by knowledge, by long-suffering, by kindness, by the Holy Ghost, by love unfeigned,

preaching would do elsewhere. ¶ *In labours.* Referring probably to the labours of the ministry, and its incessant duties, and perhaps also to the labours which they performed for their own support, as it is well known that Paul and probably also the other apostles, laboured often to support themselves. ¶ *In watchings.* In wakefulness, or want of sleep. He probably refers to the fact that in these arduous duties, and in his travels, and in anxious cares for the churches, and for the advancement of religion, he was often deprived of his ordinary rest. He refers to this again in chap. xi. 27. ¶ *In fastings.* Referring probably not only to the somewhat frequent fasts to which he voluntarily submitted as acts of devotion, but also to the fact that in his travels, when abroad and among strangers, he was often destitute of food. To such trials, those who travelled as Paul did, among strangers, and without property, would be often compelled to submit ; and *such* trials, almost without number, the religion which we now enjoy has cost. It at first cost the painful life, the toils, the anxieties, and the sufferings of the Redeemer ; and it has been propagated and perpetuated amidst the deep sorrows, the sacrifices, and the tears and blood of those who have contributed to perpetuate it on earth. For such a religion, originated, extended, and preserved in such a manner, we can never express suitable gratitude to God. Such a religion we cannot overestimate in value ; and for the extension and perpetuity of such a religion, *we* also should be willing to practise unwearied self-denial.

6. *By pureness.* Paul, having in the previous verses, grouped together some of the sufferings which he endured, and by which he had endeavoured to commend and extend the true religion, proceeds here to group together certain other influences by which he had sought the same object. The substance of what he here says is, that it had not only been done by sufferings and trials, but by a holy life, and by entire consecration to the great cause to which he had devoted himself. He begins by stating that it was by *pureness,* that is, by integrity, sanctity, a holy and pure life. All preaching, and all labours would have been in vain without this ; and Paul well knew that if he succeeded in the ministry, he must be a good man. The same is true in all other professions. One of the essential requisites of an orator, according to Quintilian, is, that he must be a good man ; and no man may expect ultimately to succeed in any calling of life unless he is *pure.* But however this may be in other callings, no one will doubt it in regard to the ministry of the gospel. ¶ *By knowledge.* Interpreters have differed much in the interpretation of this. Rosenmüller and Schleusner understand by it *prudence.* Grotius interprets it as meaning a knowledge of the law. Doddridge supposes that it refers to a solicitude to improve in the knowledge of those truths which they were called to communicate to others. Probably the idea is a very simple one. Paul is showing how he endeavoured to commend the gospel to others, ver. 4. He says, therefore, that one way was by communicating knowledge, true knowledge. He proclaimed that which was true, and which was real knowledge, in opposition to the false science of the Greeks, and in opposition to those who would substitute declamation for argument, and the mere ornaments of rhetoric for truth. The idea is, that the ministry should not be *ignorant,* but that if they wished to commend their office, they should be well informed, and should be men of good sense. Paul had no belief that an ignorant ministry was preferable to one that was characterized by true knowledge ; and *he* felt that if he was to be useful it was to be by his imparting to others truth that would be useful. " The priest's lips should keep knowledge ;" Mal. ii. 7. ¶ *By*

7 By the word *a* of truth, by
the *b* power of God, by the

a ch. 4. 2.　　　　*b* 1 Co. 2. 4.

armour *c* of righteousness on the
right hand and on the left,

c Eph 6. 11, &c.

long-suffering. By patience in our
trials, and in the provocations which
we meet with. We endeavour to obtain and keep a control over our
passions, and to keep them in subjection. See this word explained in the
Notes on 1 Cor. xiii. 4. ¶ *By kindness;* see Note, 1 Cor. xiii. 4. By
gentleness of manner, of temper, and
of spirit. By endeavouring to evince
this spirit to all, whatever may be their
treatment of us, and whatever may
be our provocations. Paul felt that
if a minister would do good he must
be *kind*, and gentle to all. ¶ *By the
Holy Ghost.* By the sanctifying influences of the Holy Spirit. By those
graces and virtues which it is his office
peculiarly to produce in the heart ;
comp. Gal. v. 22, 23. Paul here evidently refers not to the miraculous
agency of the Holy Spirit, but he is
referring to the Spirit which he and
his fellow-ministers manifested, and
means here, doubtless, that they
evinced such feelings as the Holy
Spirit produced in the hearts of the
children of God. ¶ *By love unfeigned.*
Sincere, true, ardent love to all. By
undissembled, pure, and genuine affection for the souls of men. What
good can a minister do if he does not
love his people, and the souls of men?
The prominent characteristic in the
life of the Redeemer was *love*—love to
all. So if we are like him, and if we
do any good, we shall have love to
men. No man is useful without it ;
and ministers, in general, are useful
just in proportion as they have it. It
will prompt to labour, self-denial, and
toil ; it will make them patient,
ardent, kind ; it will give them zeal,
and will give them access to the
heart ; it will accomplish what no
eloquence, labour, or learning will do
without it. He who shows that he
loves me has access at once to my
heart; he who does not, cannot *make*
a way there by any argument, eloquence, denunciation, or learning. No
minister is useful without it ; no one
with it can be otherwise than useful.

7. *By the word of truth.* That is,
by making known the truths of the
gospel. It was his object to make
known the simple truth. He did not
corrupt it by false mixtures of philosophy and human wisdom, but communicated it as it had been revealed
to him. The object of the appointment of the Christian ministry is to
make known the truth, and when that
is done it cannot but be that they will
commend their office and work to the
favourable regards of men. ¶ *By the
power of God.* By the divine power
which attended the preaching of the
gospel. Most of the ancient commentators explain this of the power
of working miracles. *Bloomfield.*
But it probably includes *all* the displays of divine power which attended
the propagation of the gospel, whether
in the working of miracles, or in the
conversion of men. If it be asked
how Paul used this power so as to
give no offence in the work of the
ministry, it may be replied, that the
miraculous endowments bestowed
upon the apostles, the power of speaking foreign languages, &c., seem to
have been bestowed upon them to be
employed in the same way as were
their natural faculties ; see Notes on
1 Cor. xiv. 32. The idea here is, that
they used the great powers intrusted
to them by God, not as impostors
would have done, for the purposes of
gain and ambition, or for vain display,
but solely for the furtherance of the
true religion, and the salvation of
men. They thus showed that they
were sent from God, as well by the
nature of the powers with which they
were intrusted, as by the manner in
which they used them. ¶ *By the
armour of righteousness on the right
hand and on the left.* Interpreters have
varied much in the exposition of this
passage; and many have run into utter
wildness. Grotius says, that it refers
to the manner in which the ancient
soldiers were armed. They bore a
spear in their right hand, and a shield
in the left. With the former they

8 By honour and dishonour, by evil report and good report : as deceivers, *a* and *yet* true ;

a John. 7. 12, 17.

attacked their foes, with the latter they made defence. Some have supposed that it refers to the fact that they were taught to use the sword with the left hand as well as with the right. The simple idea is, that they were completely armed. To be armed on the right hand and on the left is to be well armed, or entirely equipped. They went forth to conflict. They met persecution, opposition, and slander. As the soldier went well armed to battle, so did they. But the armour with which *they* met their foes, and which constituted their entire panoply, was a holy life. With that they met all the assaults of their enemies ; with that all slander and persecution. That was their defence, and by that they hoped and expected to achieve their conquests. They had no swords, and spears, and helmets, and shields ; no carnal weapons of offence and defence ; but they expected to meet all their assaults, and to gain all their victories, by an upright and holy life.

8. *By honour and dishonour.* The apostle is still illustrating the proposition that he and his fellow-labourers endeavoured to give no offence (ver. 3), and to commend themselves as the ministers of God, ver. 4. He here (ver. 8—10) introduces another *group* of particulars in which it was done. The main idea is, that they endeavoured to act in a manner so as to commend the ministry and the gospel, whether they were in circumstances of honour or dishonour, whether lauded or despised by the world. The word rendered "by" (διὰ) does not here denote the *means* by which they commended the gospel, but the *medium.* In the midst of honour and dishonour ; whatever might be the esteem in which they were held by the world, they gave no offence. The first is, "by honour." They were not everywhere honoured, or treated with respect. Yet they *were* sometimes honoured by men. The churches which they founded would

honour them, and as the ministers of religion they would be by them treated with respect. Perhaps occasionally also they might be treated with great attention and regard by the men of the world on account of their miraculous powers ; comp. Acts xxviii. 7. So now, ministers of the gospel are often treated with great respect and honour. They are beloved and venerated ; caressed and flattered, by the people of their charge. As ministers of God, as exercising a holy function, their office is often treated with great respect by the world. If they are eloquent or learned, or if they are eminently successful, they are often highly esteemed and loved. It is difficult in such circumstances to "commend themselves as the ministers of God." Few are the men who are not injured by honour ; few who are not corrupted by flattery. Few are the ministers who are proof against this influence, and who in such circumstances can honour the ministry. If done, it is by showing that they regard such things as of little moment ; by showing that they are influenced by higher considerations than the love of praise ; by not allowing this to interfere with their duties, or to make them less faithful and laborious ; but rather by making this the occasion of increased fidelity and increased zeal in their master's cause. Most ministers do more to "give offence" in times when they are greatly honoured by the world than when they are despised. Yet it is possible for a minister who is greatly honoured to make it the occasion of commending himself more and more as a minister of God. And he should do it ; as Paul said he did.—The other situation was "in dishonour." It is needless to say, that the apostles were often in situations where they had opportunity thus to commend themselves as the ministers of God. If *sometimes* honoured, they were *often* dishonoured. If the world sometimes flattered and caressed them, it often despised them, and cast out their names as evil ; see Note, 1 Cor. iv. 13. And perhaps it is so substantially now with those who are faithful. In such circumstances, also, Paul sought to commend himself as a minister of God. It was by receiving all expressions of contempt with meekness ; by not suffering them to interfere with the faithful discharge of his duties ; by rising above them, and showing the power of religion to sustain him ; and by returning good for evil, prayers for maledictions, blessings for curses, and by seeking to save, not injure and destroy those who thus sought to overwhelm him with disgrace. It may be difficult to do this, but it can be done ; and *when* done, a man always does good. ¶ *By evil report.* The word here used (δυσφημίας), means, properly, ill omened language, malediction, reproach, contumely. It refers to the fact that they were often slandered and calumniated. Their motives were called in question, and their names aspersed. They were represented as deceivers and impostors, &c. The statement here is, that in such circumstances, and when thus assailed and reproached, they endeavoured to commend themselves as the ministers of God. Evidently they endeavoured to do this by not slandering or reviling in return ; by manifesting a Christian spirit ; by *living down* the slanderous accusation, and by doing good if possible even to their calumniators. It is more difficult, says Chrysostom, to bear such reports than it is pain of body ; and it is consequently more difficult to evince a Christian spirit then. To human nature it is trying to have the name slandered and cast out as evil when we are conscious only of a desire to do good. But it is sufficient for the disciple that he be as his master, and if they called the master of the house Beelzebub, we must expect they will also those of his household. It is a fine field for a Christian minister, or any other Christian, to do good when his name is unjustly slandered. It gives him an opportunity of showing the true excellency of the Christian spirit ; *and it gives him the inexpres-*

sible privilege of being like Christ— like him in his suffering and in the moral excellence of character. A man should be willing to be anything if it will make him like the Redeemer— whether it be in suffering or in glory ; see Phil. iii. 10 ; 1 Pet. iv. 13. ¶ *And good report.* When men speak well of us ; when we are commended, praised, or honoured. To honour the gospel then, and to commend the ministry, is, (1.) To show that the heart is not set on this, and does not seek it ; (2.) To keep the heart from being puffed up with pride and self-estimation ; (3.) *Not* to suffer it to interfere with our fidelity to others, and with our faithfully presenting to them the truth. Satan often attempts to *bribe* men by praise, and to neutralize the influence of ministers by flattery. It seems hard to go and proclaim to men painful truths who are causing the incense of praise to ascend around us. And it is commonly much easier for a minister of the gospel to commend himself as a minister of God when he is slandered than when he is praised, when his name is cast out as evil than when the breezes of popular favour are wafted upon him. Few men can withstand the influence of flattery, but many men can meet persecution with a proper spirit ; few men comparatively can always evince Christian fidelity to others when they live always amidst the influence of " good report," but there are many who can be faithful when they are poor, and despised, and reviled. Hence it has happened, that God has so ordered it that his faithful servants have had but little of the " good report" which this world can furnish, but that they have been generally subjected to persecution and slander. ¶ *As deceivers.* That is, we are regarded and treated as if we were deceivers, and as if we were practising an imposition on mankind, and as if we would advance our cause by any trick or fraud that would be possible. We are regarded and treated as deceivers. Perhaps this refers to some charges which had been brought against them by the opposing faction at Corinth (*Locke*), or perhaps to the opinion

9 As *a* unknown and *yet* well known ; as dying, and, be-

a 1 Cor. 4. 9.

hold, we live ; *b* as chastened, and not killed ;

b Ps. 118. 18.

which the Jewish priests and heathen philosophers entertained of them. The idea is, that though they were extensively regarded and treated as impostors, yet they endeavoured to live as became the ministers of God. They bore the imputation with patience, and they applied themselves diligently to the work of saving souls. Paul seldom turned aside to vindicate himself from such charges, but pursued his master's work, and evidently felt that if he *had* a reputation that was worth any thing, or deserved any reputation, God would take care of it ; comp. Ps. xxxvii. 1—4. A man, especially a minister, who is constantly endeavouring to vindicate his own reputation, usually has a reputation which is not worth vindicating. A man who deserves a reputation will ultimately obtain just as much as is good for him, and as will advance the cause in which he is embarked. ¶ *And yet true.* We are *not* deceivers and impostors. Though we are regarded as such, yet we show ourselves to be true and faithful ministers of Christ.

9. *As unknown.* As those who are deemed to be of an obscure and ignoble rank in life, unknown to the great, unknown to fame. The idea, I think, is, that they went as *strangers*, as persons unknown, in preaching the gospel. Yet, though thus unknown, they endeavour to commend themselves as the ministers of God. Though among strangers ; though having no introduction from the great and the noble, yet they endeavoured so to act as to convince the world that they were the ministers of God. This could be done only by a holy life, and by the evidence of the divine approbation which would attend them in their work. And by this, the ministers of religion, if they are faithful, may make themselves known even among those who were strangers, and may live so as to "give no offence." Every minister and every Christian, even when they are " unknown", and when among strangers, should remem-

ber their high character as the servants of God, and should so live as to commend the religion which they profess to love, or which they are called on to preach. And yet how often is it that ministers when among strangers seem to feel themselves at liberty to lay aside their ministerial character, and to engage in conversation, and even partake of amusements which they themselves would regard as wholly improper if it were known that they were the ambassadors of God ! And how often is it the case that professing Christians when travelling, when among strangers, when in foreign lands, forget their high calling, and conduct in a manner wholly different from what they did when surrounded by Christians ; and when restrained by the sentiments and by the eyes of a Christian community ! ¶ *And yet well known.* Our sentiments and our principles are well known. We have no concealments to make. We practise no disguise. We attempt to impose on no one. Though obscure in our origin ; though without rank, or wealth, or power, or patronage, to commend ourselves to favour, yet we have succeeded in making ourselves known to the world. Though obscure in our origin, we are not obscure now. Though suspected of dark designs, yet our principles are all well known to the world. No men of the same obscurity of birth ever succeeded in making themselves more extensively known than did the apostles. The world at large became acquainted with them ; and by their self-denial, zeal, and success, they extended their reputation around the globe. ¶ *As dying.* That is, regarded by others as dying. As condemned often to death ; exposed to death ; in the midst of trials that expose us to death, and that are ordinarily followed by death ; see Note on 1 Cor. xv. 31, on the phrase, " I die daily." They passed through so many trials that it might be said that they were constantly dying. ¶ *And, behold, we live.* Strange

10 As sorrowful, yet alway rejoicing ; as poor, yet mak-

as it may seem, we still survive. Through all our trials we are preserved, and though often exposed to death, yet we still live. The idea here is, that in all these trials, and in these exposures to death, they endeavoured to commend themselves as the ministers of God. They bore their trials with patience; submitted to these exposures without a murmur ; and ascribed their preservation to the interposition of God. ¶ *As chastened.* The word *chastened* (παιδευόμενοι) means *corrected, chastised.* It is applied to the chastening which God causes by afflictions and calamities ; 1 Cor. xi. 32 ; Rev. iii. 19 ; Heb. xii. 6. It refers here, not to the scourgings to which they were subjected in the synagogues and elsewhere, but to the chastisements which *God* inflicted ; the trials to which *he* subjected them. And the idea is, that in the midst of these trials, they endeavoured to act as became the ministers of God. They bore them with patience. They submitted to them as coming from his hand. They felt that they were right ; and they submitted without a murmur. ¶ *And not killed.* Though severely chastened, yet we are not put to death. We survive them — preserved by the interposition of God.

10. *As sorrowful* (λυπούμενοι). Grieving, afflicted, troubled, sad. Under these sufferings we seem always to be cast down and sad. We endure afflictions that usually lead to the deepest expressions of grief. If the world looks only upon our trials, we must be regarded as always suffering, and always sad. The world will suppose that we have cause for continued lamentation (*Doddridge*), and they will regard us as among the most unhappy of mortals. Such, perhaps, is the estimate which the world usually affixes to the Christian life. They regard it as a life of sadness and of gloom ; of trial and of melancholy. They see little in it that is cheerful, and they suppose that a heavy burden presses constantly on the heart of the Christian. Joy they think

pertains to the gayeties and pleasures of this life ; sadness to religion. And perhaps a more comprehensive statement of the feelings with which the gay people of the world regard Christians cannot be found than in this expression, " *as sorrowful.*" True, they are not free from sorrow. They are tried like others. They have peculiar trials arising from persecution, opposition, contempt, and from the conscious and deep-felt depravity of their hearts. They ARE serious ; and their seriousness is often interpreted as gloom. But there is another side to this picture, and there is much in the Christian character and feelings unseen or unappreciated by the world. For they are ¶ *Alway rejoicing.* So Paul was, notwithstanding the fact that he always appeared to have occasion for grief. Religion had a power not only to sustain the soul in trial, but to fill it with positive joy. The sources of his joy were doubtless the assurances of the divine favour and the hopes of eternal glory. And the same is true of religion always. There is an *internal peace* and joy which the world may not see or appreciate, but which is far more than a compensation for all the trials which the Christian endures. ¶ *As poor.* The idea is, we are poor, yet in our poverty we endeavour " to give no offence, and to commend our selves as the ministers of God." This would be done by their patience and resignation ; by their entire freedom from every thing dishonest and dishonourable, and by their readiness, when necessary, to labour for their own support. There is no doubt that the apostles were poor ; comp. Acts iii. 6. The little property which some of them had, had all been forsaken in order that they might follow the Saviour, and go and preach his gospel. And there is as little doubt that the mass of ministers are still poor, and that God designs and desires that they should be. It is in such circumstances that he designs they should illustrate the beauty and the sustaining power of

ing many rich ; as having no-thing, and *yet* possessing all *a* things.

a Ps. 84. 11.

11 O *ye* Corinthians, our mouth is open unto you, our *b* heart is enlarged.

b Ep. 6. 8; Re. 22. 12.

religion, and be examples to the world. ¶ *Yet making many rich.* On the meaning of the word rich see Note, Rom. ii. 4. Here the apostle means that he and his fellow-labourers, though poor themselves, were the instruments of conferring durable and most valuable possessions on many persons. They had bestowed on them the true riches. They had been the means of investing them with treasures infinitely more valuable than any which kings and princes could bestow. They to whom they ministered were made partakers of the treasure where the moth doth not corrupt, and where thieves do not break through nor steal. ¶ *As having nothing.* Being utterly destitute. Having no property. This was true, doubtless, in a literal sense, of most of the apostles. ¶ *And yet possessing all things.* That is, (1.) Possessing a portion of all things that may be necessary for our welfare, as far as our heavenly Father shall deem to be necessary for us. (2.) Possessing an interest in all things, so that we can enjoy them. We can derive pleasure from the works of God—the heavens, the earth, the hills, the streams, the cattle on the mountains or in the vales, as the works of God. We have a *possession* in them so that we can enjoy them as his works, and can say, " Our Father made them all." They are given to man to enjoy. They are a part of the inheritance of man. And though we cannot call them our own in the legal sense, yet we can call them ours in the sense that we can derive pleasure from their contemplation, and see in them the proofs of the wisdom and the goodness of God. The child of God that *looks* upon the hills and vales ; upon an extensive and beautiful farm or landscape, *may* derive more *pleasure* from the contemplation of them as the work of God and his gift to men, than the real owner does, if irreligious, from contemplating all this

as his own. And so far as mere happiness is concerned, the friend of God who sees in all this the proofs of God's beneficence and wisdom, may have a more valuable *possession* in those things than he who holds the title-deeds. (3.) Heirs of all things. We have a title to immortal life—a promised part in all that the universe can furnish that can make us happy. (4.) In the possession of pardon and peace ; of the friendship of God and the knowledge of the Redeemer, we have the possession of all things. This comprises all. He that has this, what need has he of more ? This meets all the desires ; satisfies the soul ; makes the man happy and blessed. He that has God for his portion, may be said to have all things, for he is " all in all." He that has the Redeemer for his friend has all things that he needs, for " he that spared not his own Son, but gave him up for us all, how shall he not with him also freely give us all things ?" Rom. viii. 32.

11. *O ye Corinthians, our mouth is open unto you.* We speak freely, and fully. This is an affectionate address to them, and has reference to what he had just said. It means that, when the heart was full on the subject, words would flow freely, and that he had given vent to the fervid language which he had just used because his heart was full. He loved them ; he felt deeply ; and he spoke to them with the utmost freedom of what he had thought, and purposed, and done. ¶ *Our heart is enlarged.* We have deep feelings, which naturally vent themselves in fervent and glowing language. The main idea here is, that he had a strong affection for them; a heart which embraced and loved them all, and which expressed itself in the language of deep emotion. He had loved them so that he was willing to be reproached, and to be persecuted, and to be poor, and to have his name cast out

12 Ye are not straitened in us, but ye are straitened in your own bowels.

13 Now for a recompence in the same, (I speak as unto *my* children,) be ye also enlarged.

14 Be [a] ye not unequally yoked together with unbelievers ; for

a De. 7. 2, 3; 1 Cor. 7. 39.

as evil. " I cannot be silent. I conceal or dissemble nothing. I am full of ardent attachment, and that naturally vents itself in the strong language which I have used." True attachment will find means of expressing itself. A heart full of love will give vent to its feelings. There will be no dissembling and hypocrisy there. And if a minister loves the souls of his people he will pour out the affections of his heart in strong and glowing language.

12. *Ye are not straitened in us.* That is, you do not possess a narrow or contracted place in our affections. We love you fully, ardently, and are ready to do all that can be done for your welfare. There is no want of room in our affections towards you. It is not narrow, confined, pent up. It is ample and free. ¶ *But ye are straitened in your own bowels.* That is, in the affections of your hearts. The word here used ($\sigma\pi\lambda\acute{\alpha}\gamma\chi\nu\alpha$) commonly means in the Bible the tender affections. The Greek word properly denotes the *upper* viscera ; the heart, the lungs, the liver. It is applied by Greek writers to denote those parts of victims which were eaten during or after the sacrifice.—*Robinson (Lex.).* Hence it is applied to the *heart*, as the seat of the emotions and passions ; and especially the gentler emotions, the tender affections, compassion, pity, love, &c. *Our* word " bowels" is applied usually to the lower viscera, and by no means expresses the idea of the word which is used in Greek. The idea here is, that they were straitened, or were *confined* in their affections for him. It is the language of reproof, meaning that he had not received from them the demonstrations of attachment which he had a right to expect, and which was a fair and proportionate return for the love bestowed on them. Probably he refers to the fact that they had formed parties ; had admitted false teachers ;

and had not received his instructions as implicitly and as kindly as they ought to have done.

13. *Now for a recompence in the same.* " By way of recompence, open your hearts in the same manner towards me as I have done toward you. It is all the reward or compensation which I ask of you ; all the return which I desire. I do not ask silver or gold, or any earthly possessions. I ask only a return of love, and a devotedness to the cause which I love, and which I endeavour to promote." ¶ *I speak as unto* my *children.* I speak as a parent addressing his children. I sustain toward you the relation of a spiritual father, and I have a right to require and expect a return of affection. ¶ *Be ye also enlarged.* Be not straitened in your affections. Love me as I love you. Give to me the same proofs of attachment which I have given you. The idea in this verse is, that the only compensation or remuneration which he expected for all the love which he had shown them, and for all his toils and self-denials in their behalf (ver. 4, 5), was, that they would love him, and yield obedience to the laws of the gospel requiring them to be separate from the world, ver. 11 16. One ground of the claim which he had to their affection was, that he sustained toward them the relation of a father, and that he had a right to require and to expect such a return of love. The Syriac renders it well, " Enlarge your love towards me." Tindal renders it, " I speak unto you as unto children, which have like reward with us ; stretch yourselves therefore out ; bear not the yoke with unbelievers."

14. *Be ye not unequally yoked together with unbelievers.* This is closely connected in sense with the previous verse. The apostle is there stating the nature of the remuneration or recompence which he asks for all the love which he had shown to

what fellowship hath righteousness with unrighteousness? and

what communion hath light with darkness?

---

them. He here says, that one mode of remuneration would be to yield obedience to his commands, and to separate themselves from all improper alliance with unbelievers. " Make me this return for my love. Love me also, and as a proof of your affection, be not improperly united with unbelievers. Listen to me as a father addressing his children, and secure your own happiness and piety by not being unequally yoked with those who are not Christians." The word which is here used (ἑτεροζυγέω) means properly, to bear a different yoke, to be yoked heterogeneously. — *Robinson* (*Lex.*). It is applied to the custom of yoking animals of different kinds together (*Passow*); and as used here means not to mingle together, or be united with unbelievers. It is implied in the use of the word that there is a dissimilarity between believers and unbelievers so great that it is as improper for them to mingle together as it is to yoke animals of different kinds and species. The ground of the injunction is, that there is a difference between Christians and those who are not, so great as to render such unions improper and injurious. The direction here refers doubtless to all kinds of improper connections with those who were unbelievers. It has been usually supposed by commentators to refer particularly to marriage. But there is no reason for confining it to marriage. It doubtless includes that, but it may as well refer to any other intimate connection, or to intimate friendships, or to participation in their amusements and employments, as to marriage. The radical idea is, that they were to abstain from *all* connections with unbelievers — with infidels, and heathens, and those who were not Christians, which would *identify* them with them; or they were to have no connection with them *in any thing as* unbelievers, heathens, or infidels; they were to partake with them in nothing that was *peculiar* to them as such. They were to have no part with them in their heathenism,

unbelief, and idolatry, and infidelity; they were not to be united with them in any way or sense where it would necessarily be understood that they were partakers with them in those things. This is evidently the principle here laid down, and this principle is as applicable now as it was then. In the remainder of this verse and the following verses (15, 16), he states *reasons* why they should have no such intercourse. There is no principle of Christianity that is more important than that which is here stated by the apostle; and none in which Christians are more in danger of erring, or in which they have more difficulty in determining the exact rule which they are to follow. The questions which arise are very important. Are we to have no intercourse with the people of the world? Are we cut loose from all our friends who are not Christians? Are we to become monks, and live a recluse and unsocial life? Are we never to mingle with the people of the world in business, in innocent recreation, or in the duties of citizens, and as neighbours and friends? It is important, therefore, in the highest degree, to endeavour to ascertain what are the principles on which the New Testament requires us to act in this matter. And in order to a correct understanding of this, the following principles may be suggested. I. There is a large field of action, pursuit, principle, and thought, over which infidelity, sin, heathenism, and the world as such, have the entire control. It is wholly without the range of Christian law, and stands opposed to Christian law. It pertains to a different kingdom; is conducted by different principles, and tends to destroy and annihilate the kingdom of Christ. It cannot be reconciled with Christian principle, and cannot be conformed to but in entire violation of the influence of religion. Here the prohibition of the New Testament is absolute and entire. Christians are not to mingle with the people of the world *in* these things;

and are not to partake of them. This prohibition, it is supposed, extends to the following, among other things. (1.) To idolatry. This was plain. On no account or pretence were the early Christians to partake of that, or to countenance it. In primitive times, during the Roman persecutions, all that was asked was that they should cast a little incense on the altar of a heathen god. They refused to do it, and because they refused to do it, thousands perished as martyrs. They judged rightly; and the world has approved their cause. (2.) Sin, vice, licentiousness. This is also plain. Christians are in no way to patronise them, or to lend their influence to them, or to promote them by their name, their presence, or their property. "Neither be partakers of other men's sins;" 1 Tim. v. 22; 2 John 11. (3.) Arts and acts of dishonesty, deception, and fraud in traffic and trade. Here the prohibition also must be absolute. No Christian can have a right to enter into partnership with another where the business is to be conducted on dishonest and unchristian principles, or where it shall lead to the violation of any of the laws of God. If it involves deception and fraud in the principles on which it is conducted; if it spreads ruin and poverty as the distilling and vending of ardent spirits does; if it leads to the necessary violation of the Christian Sabbath, then the case is plain. A Christian is to have no "fellowship with such unfruitful works of darkness, but is rather to reprove them;" Eph. v. 11. (4.) The amusements and pleasures that are entirely worldly, and sinful in their nature; that are wholly under worldly influence, and which cannot be brought under Christian principles. Nearly all amusements are of this description. The true principle here seems to be, that if a Christian in such a place is expected to lay aside his Christian principles, and if it would be deemed indecorous and improper for him to introduce the subject of religion, or if religion would be regarded as entirely inconsistent with the nature of the amusement then he is not to be found

there. The world reigns there, and if the principles of his Lord and Master would be excluded, he should not be there. This applies of course to the theatre, the circus, the ballroom, and to large and splendid parties of pleasure. We are not to associate with idolaters *in* their idolatry; nor with the licentious *in* their licentiousness; nor with the infidel *in* his infidelity; nor with the proud *in* their pride; nor with the gay *in* their gayety; nor with the friends of the theatre, or the ball-room, or the circus *in* their attachment to these places and pursuits. And whatever *other* connection we are to have with them as neighbours, citizens, or members of our families, we are not to participate with them IN *these things.* Thus far all seems to be clear; and the rule is a plain one, whether it applies to marriage, or to business, or to religion, or to pleasure; comp. Note. 1 Cor. v. 10. II. There is a large field of action, thought, and plan which may be said to be *common* with the Christian and the world; that is, where the Christian is not expected to abandon his own principles, and where there will be, or need be, no compromise of the sternest views of truth, or the most upright, serious, and holy conduct. He may carry his principles with him; may always manifest them if necessary; and may even commend them to others. A few of these may be referred to. (1.) Commercial transactions and professional engagements that are conducted on honest and upright principles, even when those with whom we act are not Christians. (2.) Literary and scientific pursuits, which never, when pursued with a right spirit, interfere with the principles of Christianity, and never are contrary to it. (3.) The love and affection which are due to relatives and friends. Nothing in the Bible assuredly will prohibit a pious son from uniting with one who is not pious in supporting an aged and infirm parent, or a much loved and affectionate sister. The same remark is true also respecting the duty which a wife owes to a husband, a husband to a wife, or a parent to a child, though

15 And what concord hath | Christ with Belial? or what

one of them should not be a Christian. And the same observation is true also of neighbours, who are not to be prohibited from uniting *as* neighbours in social intercourse, and in acts of common kindness and charity, though all not Christians. (4.) As citizens. We owe duties to our country, and a Christian need not refuse to act with others in the elective franchise, or in making or administering the laws. Here, however, it is clear that he is not at liberty to violate the laws and the principles of the Bible. He *cannot* be at liberty to unite with them in political schemes that are contrary to the law of God, or in elevating to office men whom he cannot vote for with a good conscience as qualified for the station. (5.) In plans of public improvement, in schemes that go to the advancement of the public welfare, when the schemes do not violate the laws of God. But *if* they involve the necessity of violating the Sabbath, or any of the laws of God, assuredly he cannot consistently participate in them. (6.) In doing good to others. So the Saviour was with sinners; so he ate, and drank, and conversed with them. So we may mingle with them, without partaking of their wicked feelings and plans, so far as we can do them good, and exert over them a holy and saving influence. In all the situations here referred to, and in all the duties growing out of them, the Christian may maintain his principles, and may preserve a good conscience. Indeed the Saviour evidently contemplated that his people would have *such* intercourse with the world, and that in it they would do good. But in none of these is there to be any compromise of principle; in none to be any yielding to the opinions and practices that are contrary to the laws of God. III. There is a large field of action, conduct, and plan, where Christians only will act together. These relate to the peculiar duties of religion—to prayer, Christian fellowship, the ordinances of the gospel, and most of the plans of Christian beneficence. Here the world will not intrude; and here assuredly there will be no necessity of any compromise of Christian principle. ¶ *For what fellowship.* Paul proceeds here to state *reasons* why there should be no such improper connection with the world. The main reason, though under various forms, is that there can be no fellowship, no communion, nothing *in common* between them; and that therefore they should be separate. The word fellowship (μετοχή) means partnership, participation. What is there in common; or how can the one partake with the other? The interrogative form here is designed to be emphatic, and to declare in the strongest terms that there can be no such partnership. ¶ *Righteousness.* Such as you Christians are required to practise; implying that all were to be governed by the stern and uncompromising principles of honesty and justice. ¶ *With unrighteousness.* Dishonesty, injustice, sin; implying that the world is governed by such principles. ¶ *And what communion* (κοινωνία). Participation; communion; that which is *in common.* What is there in common between light and darkness? What common principle is there of which they both partake? There is none. There is a total and eternal separation. ¶ *Light.* The emblem of truth, virtue, holiness; see Note, Mat. iv. 16; v. 16; John i. 4; Rom. ii. 19; 2 Cor. iv. 4, 6. It is implied here that Christians are enlightened, and walk in the light. Their principles are pure and holy—principles of which light is the proper emblem. ¶ *Darkness.* The emblem of sin, corruption, ignorance; implying that the world to which Paul refers was governed and influenced by these. The idea is, that as there is an entire separation between light and darkness in their nature; as they have nothing in common, so it is and should be, between Christians and sinners. There should be a separation. There can be nothing in common between holiness and sin; and Christians should have nothing to do "with the unfruitful works of darkness;" Eph. v. 11.

part hath he that believeth with an infidel?

16 And what agreement hath

a 1 Cor. 3.16,17; 6.19; Ep. 2.21,22.

15. *And what concord* ($\sigma\nu\mu\phi\acute{\omega}\nu\eta\sigma\iota\varsigma$). Sympathy, unison. This word refers properly to the unison or harmony produced by musical instruments, where there is *a chord*. What accordance, what unison is there; what strings are there which being struck will produce a chord or harmony? The idea is, then, there is *as much* that is discordant between Christ and Belial as there is between instruments of music that produce only discordant and jarring sounds. ¶ *Hath Christ*. What is there in common between Christ and Belial, implying that Christians are governed by the principles, and that they follow the example of Christ. ¶ *Belial*. B$\iota\lambda\iota\alpha\lambda$ or B$\iota\lambda\iota\alpha\rho$, as it is found in some of the late editions. The form Beliar is Syriac. The Hebrew word (בְּלִיַּעַל) means literally *without profit; worthlessness; wickedness.* It is here evidently applied to Satan. The Syriac translates it "Satan." The idea is, that the persons to whom Paul referred, the heathen, wicked, unbelieving world, were governed by the principles of Satan, and were "taken captive by him at his will" (2 Tim. ii. 26; comp. John viii. 44), and that Christians should be separate from the wicked world, as Christ was separate from all the foolings, purposes, and plans of Satan. He had no participation in them; he formed no union with them; and so it should be with the followers of the one in relation to the followers of the other. ¶ *Or what part* ($\mu\epsilon\rho\iota\varsigma$). Portion, share, participation, fellowship. This word refers usually to a division of an estate; Luke x. 42; Note, Acts viii. 21; Col. i. 12. There is no participation; nothing in common. ¶ *He that believeth*. A Christian; a man the characteristic of whom it is that he believes on the Lord Jesus. ¶ *With an infidel*. A man who does not believe—whether a heathen idolater, a profane man, a scoffer, a philosopher,

the temple of God with idols? for ye *a* are the temple of the living God; as God hath said, *b* I will

b Ex. 29.45; Le. 26.12; Je. 31.1,33; 32.38 Ez. 11.20; 36.28; 37. 26, 27.

a man of science, a moral man, or a son or daughter of gayety. The idea is, that on the subject of religion there is no union; nothing in common; no participation. They are governed by different principles; have different feelings; are looking to different rewards; and are tending to a different destiny. The believer, therefore, should not select his partner in life and his chosen companions and friends from this class, but from those with whom he has sympathy, and with whom he has common feelings and hopes.

16. *And what agreement* ($\sigma\nu\gamma\kappa\alpha$-$\tau\acute{\alpha}\vartheta\epsilon\sigma\iota\varsigma$). Assent, accord, agreement: what *putting or laying down together* is there? What is there in one that resembles the other? ¶ *The temple of God*. What has a temple of God to do with idol worship? It is erected for a different purpose, and the worship of idols in it would not be tolerated. It is implied here that Christians are themselves the temple of God, a fact which Paul proceeds immediately to illustrate; and that it is as absurd for them to mingle with the infidel world as it would be to erect the image of a heathen god in the temple of JEHOVAH. This is strong language, and we cannot but admire the energy and copiousness of the expressions used by Paul, "which cannot," says Bloomfield, "be easily paralleled in the best classical writers." ¶ *With idols*. Those objects which God hates, and on which he cannot look but with abhorrence. The sense is, that for Christians to mingle with the sinful world; to partake of their pleasures, pursuits, and follies, is as detestable and hateful in the sight of God as if his temple were profaned by erecting a deformed, and shapeless, and senseless block in it as an object of worship. And, assuredly, if Christians had such a sense of the abomination of mingling with the world, they would feel the obligation to be separate and pure. ¶ *For ye are the*

dwell in them, and walk in *them ;* and I will be their God, and they shall be my people.

17 Wherefore[a] come out from among them, and be ye separate, saith the Lord, and touch not the

a Is. 52.11; chap. 7.1: Re. 18.4.

temple of the living God ; see this explained in the Notes on 1 Cor. iii. 16, 17. The idea is, that as God dwells with his people, they ought to be separated from a sinful and polluted world. ¶ *As God hath said.* The words here quoted are taken substantially from Ex. xxxix. 45; Lev. xxvi. 12; Ezek. xxxvii. 27. They are not literally quoted, but Paul has thrown together the substance of what occurs in several places. The sense, however, is the same as occurs in the places referred to. ¶ *I will dwell in them* (ἐνοικήσω). I will take up my indwelling in them. There is an allusion doubtless to the fact that he would be present among his people by the *Sechinah,* or the visible symbol of his presence; see Note on 1 Cor. iii. 16, 17. It implies, when used with reference to Christians, that the Holy Spirit would abide with them, and that the blessing of God would attend them; see Rom. viii; Col. iii. 16; 2 Tim. i. 14. ¶ *And walk in* them. That is, I will walk among them. I will be one of their number. He was present among the Jews by the public manifestation of his presence by a symbol; he is present with Christians by the presence and guidance of his Holy Spirit. ¶ *And I will be their God.* Not only the God whom they worship, but the God who will protect and bless them. I will take them under my peculiar protection, and they shall enjoy my favour. This is certainly *as* true of Christians as it was of the Jews, and Paul has not departed from the spirit of the promise in applying it to the Christian character. His object in quoting these passages is, to impress on Christians the solemnity and importance of the truth that God dwelt among them and with them; that they were under his care and protection; that they belonged to him, and that they therefore should be separate from the world.

17. *Wherefore.* Since you are a peculiar people. Since God, the holy

and blessed God, dwells with you and among you. ¶ *Come out from among them.* That is, from among idolaters and unbelievers; from a gay and vicious world. These words are taken, by a slight change, from Isaiah lii. 11. They are there applied to the Jews in Babylon, and are a solemn call which God makes on them to leave the place of their exile, to come out from among the idolaters of that city and return to their own land; see my Note on that place. Babylon, in the Scriptures, is the emblem of whatever is proud, arrogant, wicked, and opposed to God; and Paul, therefore, applies the words here with great beauty and force to illustrate the duty of Christians in separating themselves from a vain, idolatrous, and wicked world. ¶ *And be ye separate.* Separate from the world, and all its corrupting influences. ¶ *Saith the Lord ;* see Isaiah lii. 11. Paul does not use this language as if it had original reference to Christians, but he applies it as containing an important principle that was applicable to the case which he was considering, or as language that would appropriately express the idea which he wished to convey. The language of the Old Testament is often used in this manner by the writers of the New. ¶ *And touch not the unclean* thing. In Isaiah, "touch no unclean thing;" that is, they were to be pure, and to have no connection with idolatry in any of its forms. So Christians were to avoid all unholy contact with a vain and polluted world. The sense is, "Have no close connection with an idolater, or an unholy person. Be pure; and feel that you belong to a community that is under its own laws, and that is to be distinguished in moral purity from all the rest of the world." ¶ *And I will receive you.* That is, I will receive and recognise you as my friends and my adopted children. This could not be done until they were separated from an unclean *thing;* and I will receive you,

18 And*a* will be a Father un-

a Je. 31.9; Re. 21.7.

to you, and ye shall be my sons and daughters, saith the Lord Almighty.

idolatrous and wicked world. The fact of their being received by God, and recognised as his children, depended on their coming out from the world. These words with the verses following, though used evidently somewhat in the form of a quotation, yet are not to be found in any single place in the Old Testament. In 2 Sam. vii. 14, God says of Solomon, " I will be his Father, and he shall be my son." In Jer. xxxi. 9, God says, " For I am a Father to Israel, and Ephraim is my first-born." It is probable that Paul had such passages in his eye, yet he doubtless designed rather to express the general sense of the promises of the Old Testament than to quote any single passage. Or why may it not be that we should regard Paul here himself as speaking as an inspired man directly, and making a promise then first communicated immediately from the Lord ? Paul was inspired as well as the prophets; and it may be that he meant to communicate a promise directly from God. Grotius supposes that it was not taken from any particular place in the Old Testament, but was a part of a hymn that was in use among the Hebrews.

18. *And I will be a Father unto you.* A father is the protector, counsellor, and guide of his children. He instructs them, provides for them, and counsels them in time of perplexity. No relation is more tender than this. In accordance with this, God says, that he will be to his people their protector, counsellor, guide, and friend. He will cherish towards them the feeling of a father ; he will provide for them, he will acknowledge them as his children. No higher honour can be conferred on mortals than to be adopted into the family of God, and to be permitted to call the Most High *our Father.* No rank is so elevated as that of being the sons and the daughters of the Lord Almighty. Yet this is the common appellation by which God addresses his people ; and

the most humble in rank, the most poor and ignorant of his friends on earth, the most despised among men, may reflect that they are the children of the ever-living God, and have the Maker of the heavens and the earth as their Father and their eternal Friend. How poor are all the honours of the world compared with this ! ¶ *The Lord Almighty.* The word here used ($\pi\alpha\nu\tau o\kappa\rho\acute{\alpha}\tau\omega\rho$) occurs nowhere except in this place and in the Book of Revelation; Rev. i. 8 ; iv. 8 ; xi. 17; xv. 3 ; xvi. 7, 14 ; xix. 6. 16 ; xxi. 22. It means one who has all power ; and is applied to God in contradistinction from idols that are weak and powerless. God is able to protect his people, and they who put their trust in him shall never be confounded. What has he to fear who has a friend of almighty power ?

REMARKS.

1. It is right and proper to exhort Christians not to receive the grace of God in vain, ver. 1. Even they sometimes abuse their privileges ; become neglectful of the mercy of God ; undervalue the truths of religion, and do not make as much as they should do of the glorious truths that are fitted to sanctify and to save. *Every Christian should endeavour to make just as much as possible of his privileges, and to become just as eminent as he can possibly be in his Christian profession.*

2. The benefits of salvation to this world come through the intercession of Jesus Christ, ver. 2. It is because God is pleased to hear him ; because *he* calls on God in an accepted time that *we* have any hope of pardon. The sinner enjoys no offer of mercy, and no possibility of pardon except what he owes to Jesus Christ. Should he cease to plead for men, the offers of salvation would be withdrawn, and the race would perish for ever.

3. The world is under a dispensation of mercy, ver. 2. Men may be

saved: God is willing to show compassion, and to rescue them from ruin.

4. How important is the present moment ! ver. 2. How important is *each* moment! It may be the *last* period of mercy. No sinner can calculate with any certainty on another instant of time. God holds his breath, and with infinite ease he can remove him to eternity. Eternal results hang on the present—the fleeting moment, and yet how unconcerned are the mass of men about their present condition ; how unanxious about what may possibly or probably occur the next moment ! Now, the sinner may be pardoned. The next moment he may be beyond the reach of forgiveness. This instant, the bliss of heaven is offered him ; the next, he may be solemnly excluded from hope and heaven !

5. The ministers of the gospel should give no occasion of offence to any one, ver. 3. On each one of them depends a portion of the honour of the ministry in this world, and of the honour of Jesus Christ among men. How solemn is this reponsibility ! How pure, and holy, and unblameable should they be !

6. Ministers and all Christians should be willing to suffer in the cause of the Redeemer, ver. 4, 5. If the early ministers and other Christians were called to endure the pains of imprisonment and persecution for the honour of the gospel, assuredly we should be willing also to suffer. Why should there be any more reason for their suffering than for ours ?

7. We see what our religion has cost, ver. 4, 5. It has come down to us through suffering. *All* the privileges that we enjoy have been the fruit of toil, and blood, and tears, and sighs. The best blood in human veins has flowed to procure these blessings ; the holiest men on earth have wept, and been scourged, and tortured, that we might possess these privileges. What thanks should we give to God for all this ! How highly should we prize the religion that has cost so much !

8. In trial we should evince such a spirit as not to dishonour, but to honour our religion, ver. 3—5. This is as incumbent on all Christians as it is on ministers of the gospel. It is in such scenes that the reality of religion is tested. It is then that its power is seen. It is then that its value may be known. Christians and Christian ministers often do good in circumstances of poverty, persecution, and sickness, which they never do in health, and in popular favour, and in prosperity. And God often places his people in trial that they may do good then, expecting that they will accomplish more then than they could in prosperous circumstances. They whose aim it is to do good have often occasion to bless God that they were subjected to trial. Bunyan wrote the " Pilgrim's Progress " in a dungeon : and almost all the works of Baxter were written when he was suffering under persecution, and forbidden to preach the gospel. The devil is often foiled in this way. He persecutes and opposes Christians ; and on the rack and at the stake they do most to destroy his kingdom ; he throws them into dungeons, and they make books which go down even to the millennium, making successful war on the empire of darkness. Christians, therefore, should esteem it a privilege to be permitted *to suffer* on account of Christ ; Phil. i. 29.

9. If ministers and other Christians do any good they must be pure, ver. 6, 7. The gospel is to be commended by pureness, and knowledge, and the word of truth, and the armour of righteousness. It is in this way that they are to meet opposition ; in this way that they are to propagate their sentiments. No man need expect to do good in the ministry or as a private Christian, who is not a holy man. No man who *is* a holy man can help doing good. It will be a matter of course that he will shed a healthful moral influence around him. And he will no more live without effect than the sun sheds its steady beams on the earth without effect. His influence may be very noiseless and still, like the sunbeams or the dew, but it will be felt in the world. Wicked men can resist any thing else better than they can a holy example. They can make a

mock of preaching; they can deride exhortation; they can throw away a tract; they can burn the Bible; but what can they do against a holy example? No more than they can against the vivifying and enlightening beams of the sun; and a man who leads a holy life cannot help doing good, and cannot be prevented from doing good.

10. They who are Christians must expect to meet with much dishonour, and to be subjected often to the influence of evil report, ver. 8. The world is unfriendly to religion, and its friends must never be surprised if their motives are impeached, and their names calumniated.

11. Especially is this the case with ministers, ver. 8. They should make up their minds to it, and they should not suppose that any strange thing had happened to them if they are called thus to suffer.

12. They who are about to make a profession of religion, and they who are about to entering on the work of the ministry, or who are agitating the question whether they should be ministers, should ask themselves whether they are prepared for this. They should count the cost; nor should they either make a profession of religion or think of the ministry as a profession, unless they are willing to meet with dishonour, and to go through evil report; to be poor (ver. 10), and to be despised and persecuted, or to die in the cause which they embrace.

13. Religion has power to sustain the soul in trials, ver. 10. Why should he be sad who has occasion to rejoice always? Why should he deem himself poor, though he has slender earthly possessions, who is able to make many rich? Why should he be melancholy as if he had nothing, who has Christ as his portion, and who is an heir of all things? Let not the poor, who are rich in faith, despond as though they had nothing. They have a treasure which gold cannot purchase, and which will be of infinite value when all other treasure fails. He that has an everlasting inheritance in heaven cannot be called a poor man. And he that can look to such an inherit-

ance should not be unwilling to part with his earthly possessions. Those who seem to be most wealthy are often the poorest of mortals; and those who seem to be poor, or who are in humble circumstances, often have an enjoyment of even this world which is unknown in the palaces and at the tables of the great. They look on all things as the work of their Father; and in their humble dwellings, and with their humble fare, they have an enjoyment of the bounties of their heavenly Benefactor, which is not experienced often in the dwellings of the great and the rich.

14. A people should render to a minister and a pastor a return of love and confidence that shall be proportionate to the love which is shown to them, ver. 12. This is but a reasonable and fair requital, and this is necessary not only to the comfort, but to the success of a minister. What good can he do unless he has the affections and confidence of his people?

15. The compensation or recompence which a minister has a right to expect and require for arduous toil is, that his people should be "enlarged" in love towards him, and that they should yield themselves to the laws of the Redeemer, and be separate from the world, ver. 13. And this is an ample reward. It is what he seeks, what he prays for, what he most ardently desires. If he is worthy of his office, he will seek not theirs but them (2 Cor. xii. 14), and he will be satisfied for all his toils if he sees them walking in the truth (3 John 4), and showing in their lives the pure and elevated principles of the gospel which they profess to love.

16. The welfare of religion depends on the fact that Christians should be separate from a vain, and gay, and wicked world, ver. 14—16. Why should they partake of those things in which they can, if Christians, have nothing in common? Why attempt to mingle light with darkness? to form a compact between Christ and Belial? or to set up a polluted idol in the temple of the living God? The truth is, there are great and eternal principles in the gospel which should not be sur-

CHAPTER VII.

HAVING therefore these *a* promises, dearly beloved, let us

a chap.6.17,18 ;1John 3.3.

cleanse *b* ourselves from all filthiness of the flesh and spirit, perfecting holiness in the fear of God.

b Ps.51.10 ;Eze.36.25,26 ;1 John 1.7, 9.

rendered, and which cannot be broken down. Christ intended to set up a kingdom that should be unlike the kingdoms of this world. And he designed that his people should be governed by different principles from the people of this world.

17. They who are about to make a profession of religion should resolve to separate themselves from the world, ver. 14, 15. Religion cannot exist where there is no such separation, and they who are unwilling to forsake infidel companions and the gay amusements and vanities of life, and to find their chosen friends and pleasures among the people of God, can have no evidence that they are Christians. The world with all its wickedness and its gay pleasures must be forsaken, and there must be an effectual line drawn between the friends of God and the friends of sin.

Let us, then, who profess to be the friends of the Redeemer remember how pure and holy we should be. It should not be indeed with the spirit of the Pharisee ; it should not be with a spirit that will lead us to say, "stand by, for I am holier than thou;" but it should be, while we discharge all our duties to our impenitent friends, and while in all our intercourse with the world we should be honest and true, and while we do not refuse to mingle with them as neighbours and citizens as far as we can without compromitting Christian principles, still our chosen friends and our dearest friendships should be with the people of God. For, his friends should be our friends ; our happiness should be with them, and the world should see that we *prefer* the friends of the Redeemer to the friends of gayety, ambition, and sin.

18. Christians are the holy temple of God, ver. 16. How pure should they be ! How free should they be from sin ! How careful to maintain consciences void of offence !

19. What an inestimable privilege it is to be a Christian ! (ver. 18) ; to be a child of God ! to feel that he is a Father and a Friend ! to feel that though we may be forsaken by all others ; though poor and despised, yet there is one who never forsakes ; one who never forgets that he has sons and daughters dependent on him, and who need his constant care. Compared with this, how small the honour of being permitted to call the rich our friends, or to be regarded as the sons or daughters of nobles and of princes ! Let the Christian then most highly prize his privileges, and feel that he is raised above all the elevations of rank and honour which this world can bestow. All these shall fade away, and the highest and the lowest shall meet on the same level in the grave, and alike return to dust. But the elevation of the child of God shall only begin to be visible and appreciated when all other honours fade away.

20. Let all seek to become the sons and daughters of the Lord Almighty. Let us aspire to this rather than to earthly honours ; let us seek this rather than to be numbered with the rich and the great. All cannot be honoured in this world, and few are they who can be regarded as belonging to elevated ranks here. But *all* may be the children of the living God, and be permitted to call the Lord Almighty their Father and their Friend. O ! if men could as easily be permitted to call themselves the sons of monarchs and princes; if they could as easily be admitted to the palaces of the great and sit down at their tables *as they can enter heaven*, how greedily would they embrace it ! And yet how poor and paltry would be such honour and pleasure compared with that of feeling that we are the adopted children of the great and the eternal God !

CHAPTER VII.

THE first verse of this chapter properly belongs to the previous chapter, and should have been attached to that.

It is an exhortation made in view of the promises there referred to, to make every effort to obtain perfect purity, and to become entirely holy.

In ver. 2, 3, he entreats the Corinthians, in accordance with the wish which he had expressed in chap. vi. 13, to receive him as a teacher and a spiritual father; as a faithful apostle of the Lord Jesus. To induce them to do this, he assures them that he had given them, at no time, any occasion of offence. He had injured no man; he had wronged no man. Possibly some might suppose that he had injured them by the sternness of his requirements in forbidding them to contract friendships and alliances with infidels; or in the case of discipline in regard to the incestuous person. But he assures them that all his commands had been the fruit of most tender love for them, and that he was ready to live and die with them.

The remainder of the chapter (ver. 4—15) is occupied mainly in stating the joy which he had at the evidence which they had given that they were ready to obey his commands. He says, therefore (ver. 4), that he was full of comfort and joy; and that in all his tribulation, the evidence of their obedience had given him great and unfeigned satisfaction. In order to show them the extent of his joy, he gives a pathetic description of the anxiety of mind which he had on the subject in his troubles in Macedonia, and particularly his distress on not meeting with Titus as he had expected, ver. 5. But this distress had been relieved by his coming, and by the evidence which was furnished through him that they were ready to yield obedience to his commands, ver. 6, 7. This joy was greatly increased by his hearing from Titus the effect which his former epistle to them had produced, ver. 8—13. He had felt deep anxiety in regard to that. He had even regretted, it would seem (ver. 8), that he had sent it. He had been deeply pained at the necessity of giving them pain, ver. 8. But the effect had been all that he had desired; and when he learned from Titus the effect which it had produced—the

deep repentance which they had evinced, and the thorough reformation which had occurred (ver. 9—11), he had great occasion to rejoice that he had sent the epistle to them. This new and distinguished instance of their obedience had given him great joy, and confirmed him in the proof that they were truly attached to him. The apostle adds, in the conclusion of the chapter, that his jo was greatly increased by the joy which Titus manifested, and his entire satisfaction in the conduct of the Corinthians and the treatment which he had received from them (ver. 13), so that though he, Paul, had often had occasion to speak in the kindest terms of the Corinthians, all that he had ever said in their favour Titus had realized in his own case (ver. 14), and the affection of Titus for them had been greatly increased by his visit to them, ver. 15. The whole chapter, therefore, is eminently adapted to produce good feeling in the minds of the Corinthians toward the apostle, and to strengthen the bonds of their mutual attachment.

1. *Having therefore these promises.* The promises referred to in chap. vi 17, 18; the promise that God would be a Father, a protector, and a friend The idea is, that as we have a promise that God would dwell in us, that he would be our God, that he would be to us a Father, we should remove from us whatever is offensive in his sight, and become perfectly holy. ¶ *Let us cleanse ourselves.* Let us purify ourselves. Paul was not afraid to bring into view the agency of Christians themselves in the work of salvation. He, therefore, says, 'let us purify ourselves,' as if Christians had much to do; as if their own agency was to be employed; and as if their purifying was dependent on their own efforts. While it is true that all purifying influence and all holiness proceeds from God, it is also true that the effect of all the influences of the Holy Spirit is to excite us to diligence to purify our own hearts, and to urge us to make strenuous efforts to overcome our own sins. He who expects to be made pure without any effort of his own, will never become pure; and

he who ever becomes holy will become so in consequence of strenuous efforts to resist the evil of his own heart, and to become like God. The *argument* here is, that we have the promises of God to aid us. We do not go about the work in our own strength. It is not a work in which we are to have no aid. But it is a work which God desires, and where he will give us all the aid which we need. ¶ *From all filthiness of the flesh.* The noun here used (μολυσμὸς) occurs nowhere else in the New Testament. The *verb* occurs in 1 Cor. viii. 7; Rev. iii. 4 ; xiv. 4, and means to stain, defile, pollute, as a garment; and the word here used means *a soiling*, hence defilement, pollution, and refers to the defiling and corrupting influence of fleshly desires and carnal appetites. The filthiness of the flesh here denotes evidently the gross and corrupt appetites and passions of the body, including all such actions of all kinds as are inconsistent with the virtue and purity with which the body, regarded as the temple of the Holy Ghost, should be kept holy—all such passions and appetites as the Holy Spirit of God would not produce. ¶ *And spirit.* By "filthiness of the spirit," the apostle means, probably, all the thoughts or mental associations that defile the man. Thus the Saviour (Mat. xv. 19) speaks of evil thoughts, &c. that proceed out of the heart, and that pollute the man. And probably Paul here includes all the sins and passions which appertain particularly to mind or to the soul rather than to carnal appetites, such as the desire of revenge, pride, avarice, ambition, &c. These are in themselves as polluting and defiling as the gross sensual pleasures. They stand as much in the way of sanctification, they are as offensive to God, and they prove as certainly that the heart is depraved as the grossest sensual passions. The main difference is, that they are more *decent* in the external appearance; they can be better concealed; they are usually indulged by a more elevated class in society; but they are not the less offensive to God. It may be added, also, that they are often conjoined in the same

person; and that the man who is defiled in his "spirit" is often a man most corrupt and sensual in his "flesh." Sin sweeps with a desolating influence through the whole frame, and it usually leaves no part unaffected, though some part may be more deeply corrupted than others. ¶ *Perfecting.* This word (ἐπιτελοῦντες) means properly to bring to an end, to finish, complete. The idea here is, that of carrying it out to the completion. Holiness had been commenced in the heart, and the exhortation of the apostle is, that they should make every effort that it might be complete in all its parts. He does not say that this work of perfection had ever been accomplished—nor does he say that it had not been. He only urges the obligation to make an effort to be entirely holy; and this obligation is not affected by the inquiry whether any one has been or has not been perfect. It is an obligation which results from the nature of the law of God and his unchangeable claims on the soul. The fact that no one has been perfect does not relax the claim; the fact that no one will be in this life does not weaken the obligation. It proves only the deep and dreadful depravity of the human heart, and should humble us under the stubbornness of guilt. The obligation to be perfect is one that is unchangeable and eternal ; see Mat. v. 48; 1 Pet. i. 15. Tindal renders this, "and grow up to full holiness in the fear of God." The unceasing and steady aim of every Christian should be perfection—perfection in all things—in the love of God, of Christ, of man ; perfection of heart, and feeling, and emotion ; perfection in his words, and plans, and dealings with men ; perfection in his prayers, and in his submission to the will of God. No man can be a Christian who does not sincerely desire it, and who does not constantly aim at it. No man is a friend of God who can acquiesce in a state of sin, and who is satisfied and contented that he is not as holy as God is holy. And any man who has no desire to be perfect as God is, and who does not make it his daily and constant aim to be as

2 Receive us; we have wronged no man, we have corrupted no man, *a* we have defrauded no man.

a 1 Sa.12.3,4 ; Ac.20.33 ,chap.12.17.

3 I speak not *this* to condemn *you;* for I have said *b* before, that ye are in our hearts to die and live with *you.*

b chap.6.11,12.

perfect as God, may set it down as demonstrably certain that he has no true religion. How can a man be a Christian who is willing to acquiesce in a state of sin, and who does not desire to be just like his Master and Lord ? ¶ *In the fear of God.* Out of fear and reverence of God. From a regard to his commands, and a reverence for his name. The idea seems to be, that we are always in the presence of God ; we are professedly under his law ; and we should be awed and restrained by a sense of his presence from the commission of sin, and from indulgence in the pollutions of the flesh and spirit. There are many sins that the presence of a child will restrain a man from committing ; and how should the conscious presence of a holy God keep us from sin ! If the fear of man or of a child will restrain us, and make us attempt to be holy and pure, how should the fear of the all-present and the all-seeing God keep us not only from outward sins, but from polluted thoughts and unholy desires !

2. *Receive us.* Tindal renders this, " understand us." The word here used (χωρησατε) means properly, give space, place, or room ; and it means here evidently, make place or room for us in your affections; that is, admit or receive us as your friends. It is an earnest entreaty that they would do what he had exhorted them to do in chap. vi. 13 ; see Note on that verse. From that he had digressed in the close of the last chapter. He here returns to the subject. and asks an interest in their affections and their love. ¶ *We have wronged no man.* We have done injustice to no man. This is given as a reason why they should admit him to their full confidence and affection. It is not improbable that he had been charged with injuring the incestuous person by the severe discipline which he had found it necessary to inflict on him ; Note 1 Cor. v. 5. This charge would

not improbably be brought against him by the false teachers in Corinth. But Paul here says, that whatever was the severity of the discipline, he was conscious of having done injury to no member of that church. It is possible, however, that he does not here refer to any such charge, but that he says in general that he had done no injury, and that there was no reason why they should not receive him to their entire confidence. It argues great consciousness of integrity when a man who has spent a considerable time, as Paul had, with others, is able to say that he had wronged no man in any way. Paul could not have made this solemn declaration unless he was certain he had lived a very blameless life ; comp. Acts xx. 33. ¶ *We have corrupted no man.* This means that he had corrupted no man in his morals, either by his precept or his example. The word (φθειρω) means in general to bring into a worse state or condition, and is very often applied to morals. The idea is, here, that Paul had not by his precept or example made any man the worse. He had not corrupted his principles or his habits, or led him into sin. ¶ *We have defrauded no man.* We have taken no man's property by cunning, by trick, or by deception. The word πλεονεκτεω means literally to have more than another, and then to take advantage, to seek unlawful gain, to circumvent, defraud, deceive. The idea is, that Paul had taken advantage of no circumstances to extort money from them, to overreach them, or to cheat them. It is the conviction of a man who was conscious that he had lived honestly, and who could appeal to them all as full proof that his life among them had been blameless.

3. *I speak not* this *to condemn* you. I do not speak this with any desire to reproach you. I do not complain of you for the purpose of condemning, or because I have a desire to find fault,

4 Great *is* my boldness of speech toward you, great *a* *is* my glorying of you: I am filled with com-

a 1 Co.1.4 ;chap.1.14.

fcrt, I am exceeding joyful *b* in all our tribulation.

5 For, when we were come into

b Ph.2.17 ;Col.1.24.

though I am compelled to speak in some respect of your want of affection and liberality towards me. It is not because I have no love for you, and wish to have occasion to use words implying complaint and condemnation. ¶ *For I have said before;* chap. vii. 11, 12. ¶ *That ye are in our hearts.* That is, we are so much attached to you; or you have such a place in our affections. ¶ *To die and live with* you. If it were the will of God, we would be glad to spend our lives among you, and to die with you; an expression denoting most tender attachment. A similar well-known expression occurs in Horace :

Tecum vivere amem, tecum obeam libens.
            Odes, B. III. IX. 24.
With the world I live, with the world I die.

This was an expression of the tenderest attachment. It was true that the Corinthians had not shown themselves remarkably worthy of the affections of Paul, but from the beginning he had felt towards them the tenderest attachment. And if it had been the will of God that he should cease to travel, and to expose himself to perils by sea and land to spread the knowledge of the Saviour, he would gladly have confined his labours to them, and there have ended his days.

4. *Great* is *my boldness of speech toward you.* This verse seems designed to soften the apparent harshness of what he had said (chap. vi. 12), when he intimated that there was a want of love in them towards him (*Bloomfield*), as well as to refer to the plainness which he had used all along in his letters to them. He says, therefore, that he speaks freely; he speaks as a friend; he speaks with the utmost openness and frankness; he conceals nothing from them. He speaks freely of their faults, and he speaks freely of his love to them; and he as frankly commends them and praises them. It is the open, undisguised language of a friend, when he

throws open his whole soul and conceals nothing. ¶ *Great* is *my glorying of you.* I have great occasion to commend and praise you, and I do it freely. He refers here to the fact that he had boasted of their liberality in regard to the proposed collection for the poor saints of Judea (chap. ix. 4); that he had formerly boasted much of them to Titus, and of their readiness to obey his commands (ver. 14); and that now he had had abundant evidence, by what he had heard from Titus (ver. 5. seq.), that they were disposed to yield to his commands, and obey his injunctions. He had probably often had occasion to boast of their favourable regard for him. ¶ *I am filled with comfort.* That is, by the evidence which I have received of your readiness to obey me. ¶ *I am exceeding joyful.* I am overjoyed. The word here used occurs nowhere else in the New Testament except in Rom. v. 20. It is not found in the classic writers ; and is a word which Paul evidently compounded (from ὑπὲρ and περισσεύω), and means to *superabound over,* to superabound greatly, or exceedingly. It is a word which would be used only when the heart was full, and when it would be difficult to find words to express its conceptions. Paul's heart was full of joy; and he pours forth his feelings in the most fervid and glowing language. I have joy which cannot be expressed. ¶ *In all our tribulation;* see Note, chap. i. 4.

5. *For when we were come into Macedonia.* For the reasons which induced Paul to go into Macedonia; see Notes on chap. i. 16 ; comp. Notes, chap. ii. 12, 13. ¶ *Our flesh had no rest.* We were exceedingly distressed and agitated. We had no rest. The causes of his distress he immediately states. ¶ *But we were troubled on every side.* In every way. We had no rest in any quarter. We were obliged to enter into harassing labours and strifes there, and we were full of

Macedonia, our flesh had no rest, but we were troubled on every side; without *a* *were* fightings, within *were* fears.

6 Nevertheless God, that comforteth those that are cast down,

a De.32.25.

comforted us by the coming of Titus; *b*

7 And not by his coming only, but by the consolation wherewith he was comforted in you, when he told us your earnest desire, your

b chap.2.13.

anxiety in regard to you. ¶ *Without were fightings.* Probably he here refers to fierce opposition, which he met with in prosecuting his work of preaching the gospel. He met there, as he did everywhere, with opposition from Pagans, Jews, and false brethren. Tumults were usually excited wherever he went; and he preached the gospel commonly amidst violent opposition. ¶ *Within were fears.* Referring probably to the anxiety which he had in regard to the success of the epistle which he had sent to the church at Corinth. He felt great solicitude on the subject. He had sent Titus there to see what was the state of the church and to witness the effect of his instructions. Titus had not come to him as he had expected, at Troas (chap. ii. 13), and he felt the deepest anxiety in regard to him and to the success of his epistle. His fears were probably that they would be indisposed to exercise the discipline on the offender; or lest the severity of the discipline required should alienate them from him; or lest the party under the influence of the false teachers should prevail. All was uncertainty, and his mind was filled with the deepest apprehension.

6. *God that comforteth those that are cast down.* Whose characteristic is, that he gives consolation to those who are anxious and depressed. All his consolation was in God; and by whatever instrumentality comfort was administered, he regarded and acknowledged God as the author; see Note, chap. i. 4. ¶ *By the coming of Titus.* To Macedonia. He rejoiced not only in again seeing him, but especially in the intelligence which he brought respecting the success of his epistle, and the conduct of the church at Corinth.

7. *And not by his coming only.*

Not merely by the fact that he was restored to me, and that my anxieties in regard to him were now dissipated. It is evident that Paul, not having met with Titus as he had expected, at Troas, had felt much anxiety on his account, perhaps apprehending that he was sick, or that he had died. ¶ *But by the consolation wherewith he was comforted in you.* Titus was satisfied and delighted with his interview with you. He had been kindly treated, and he had seen all the effect produced by the letter which he had desired. He had, therefore, been much comforted by his visit to Corinth, and this was a source of additional joy to Paul. He rejoiced at what he had witnessed among you, and he imparted the same joy to me also. The joy of one friend will diffuse itself through the heart of another. Joy is diffusive, and one Christian cannot well be happy without making others happy also. ¶ *When he told us of your earnest desire.* Either to rectify what was amiss (*Doddridge, Clarke*); or to see me.—*Macknight, Rosenmuller, Bloomfield.* It seems to me that the connection requires us to understand it of their desire, their anxiety to comply with his commands, and to reform the abuses which existed in the church, and which had given him so much pain. ¶ *Your mourning.* Produced by the epistle. Your deep repentance over the sins which had prevailed in the church. ¶ *Your fervent mind toward me.* Greek, ' Your *zeal* for me.' It denotes that they evinced great *ardour* of attachment to him, and an earnest desire to comply with his wishes. ¶ *So that I rejoiced the more.* I not only rejoiced at his coming, but I rejoiced the more at what he told me of you. Under any circumstances the coming of Titus would have been an occasion

mourning, your fervent mind toward me ; so that I rejoiced the more.

8 For though I made you sorry with a letter, I do not repent,

though I a did repent : for I perceive that the same epistle hath made you sorry, though it were but for a season.

9 Now I rejoice, not that ye

a chap. 2. 4.

of joy ; but it was especially so from the account which he gave me of you.

8. *For though I made you sorry*, &c. That is, in the first epistle which he had sent to them. In that epistle he had felt it necessary to reprove them for their dissensions and other disorders which had occurred and which were tolerated in the church. That epistle was fitted to produce pain in them—as severe and just reproof always does; and Paul felt very anxious about its effect on them. It was painful to him to write it, and he was well aware that it must cause deep distress among them to be thus reproved. ¶ *I do not repent.* I have seen such happy effects produced by it ; it has so completely answered the end which I had in view; it was so kindly received, that I do not regret now that I wrote it. It gives me no pain in the recollection, but I have occasion to rejoice that it was done. ¶ *Though I did repent.* Doddridge renders this, " however anxious I may have been." The word here used does not denote repentance in the sense in which that word is commonly understood, as if any wrong had been done. It is not the language of remorse. It can denote here nothing more than " that uneasiness which a good man feels, not from the consciousness of having done wrong, but from a tenderness for others, and a fear lest that which, prompted by duty, he had said, should have too strong an effect upon them."—*Campbell*, diss. vi. part iii. § 9. See the meaning of the word further illustrated in the same dissertation. The word (μεταμέλομαι) denotes properly to change one's purpose or mind after having done any thing (*Robinson*) ; or an uneasy feeling of regret for what has been done without regard either to duration or effects.— *Campbell*. Here it is not to be understood that Paul meant to say he had done any thing wrong. He was an

inspired man, and what he had said was proper and right. But he was a man of deep feeling, and of tender affections. He was pained at the necessity of giving reproof. And there is no improbability in supposing that after the letter had been sent off, and he reflected on its nature and on the pain which it would cause to those whom he tenderly loved, there might be some misgiving of heart about it, and the deepest anxiety, and regret at the necessity of doing it. What parent is there who has not had the same feeling as this? He has felt it necessary to correct a beloved child, and has formed the purpose, and has executed it. But is there no misgiving of heart ? No question asked whether it might not have been dispensed with ? No internal struggle; no sorrow ; no emotion which may be called *regret* at the resolution which has been taken ? Yet there is no *repentance* as if the parent had done wrong. He feels that he has done what was right and necessary. He approves his own course, and has occasion of rejoicing at the good effects which follow. Such appears to have been the situation of the apostle Paul in this case; and it shows that he had a tender heart, that he did not delight in giving pain, and that he had no desire to overwhelm them with grief. When the effect was seen, he was not unwilling that they should be apprized of the pain which it had cost him. When a parent has corrected a child, no injury is done if the child becomes acquainted with the strugglings which it has cost him, and the deep pain and anxiety caused by the necessity of resorting to chastisement. ¶ *For I perceive*, &c. I perceive the good effect of the epistle. I perceive that it produced the kind of sorrow in you which I desired. I see that it has produced permanent good results. The sorrow which it caused in you is

were made sorry, but that ye sorrowed to repentance : for ye were made sorry, [1] after a godly manner,

1 or, *according to God.*

that ye might receive damage by us in nothing.

10 For godly sorrow [a] worketh

a Je.31.9;Ez.7.16.

only for a season ; the good effects will be abiding. I have,therefore, great occasion to rejoice that I sent the epistle. It produced permanent repentance and reformation (ver. 9), and thus accomplished all that I wished or desired.

9. *Now I rejoice, not that ye were made sorry, &c.* I have no pleasure in giving pain to any one, or in witnessing the distress of any. When men are brought to repentance under the preaching of the gospel, the ministers of the gospel do not find pleasure *in* their grief as such. They are not desirous of making men unhappy by calling them to repentance, and they have no pleasure in the deep distress of mind which is often produced by their preaching, in itself considered. It is only because such sorrow is an indication of their return to God, and will be followed by happiness and by the fruits of good living, that they find any pleasure in it, or that they seek to produce it. ¶ *But that ye sorrowed to repentance.* It was not mere grief ; it was not sorrow producing melancholy, gloom, or despair ; it was not sorrow which led you to be angry at him who had reproved you for your errors—as is sometimes the case with the sorrow that is produced by reproof ; but it was sorrow that led to a change and reformation. It was sorrow that was followed by a putting away of the evil for the existence of which there had been occasion to reprove you. The word here rendered "repentance" (μετάνοιαν) is a different word from that which, in ver. 8, is rendered " I did repent," and indicates a different state of mind. It properly means a change of mind or purpose ; comp. Heb. xii. 7. It denotes a change for the better ; a change of mind that is durable and productive in its consequences ; a change which amounts to a permanent reformation ; see Campbell's Diss. ut supra. The sense here is, that it produced a change, a reformation. It was such sorrow for their sin as to lead them to

reform and to put away the evils which had existed among them. It was this fact, and not that they had been made sorry, that led Paul to rejoice. ¶ *After a godly manner.* Marg. " according to God ;" see Note on the next verse. ¶ *That ye might receive damage by us in nothing.* The Greek word rendered " receive damage " (ζημιωθῆτε) means properly to bring loss upon any one ; to receive loss or detriment ; see Note on 1 Cor. iii. 15 ; comp. Phil. iii. 8. The sense here seems to be, " So that on the whole no real injury was done you in any respect by me. You were indeed put to pain and grief by my reproof. You sorrowed. But it has done you no injury on the whole. It has been a benefit to you. If you had not reformed, if you had been pained without putting away the sins for which the reproof was administered, if it had been *mere* grief without any proper fruit, you might have said that you would have suffered a loss of happiness, or you might have given me occasion to inflict severer discipline. But now you are gainers in happiness by all the sorrow which I have caused." Sinners are gainers in happiness in the end by all the pain of repentance produced by the preaching of the gospel. No man suffers loss by being told of his faults if he repents ; and men are under the highest obligations to those faithful ministers and other friends who tell them of their errors, and who are the means of bringing them to true repentance.

10. *For godly sorrow.* " Sorrow according to God " ('Η γὰρ κατὰ Θεὸν λύπη). That is, such sorrow as has respect to God, or is according to his will, or as leads the soul to him. This is a very important expression in regard to true repentance, and shows the exact nature of that sorrow which is connected with a return to God. The phrase may be regarded as implying the following things. (1.) Such sorrow as God *approves*, or such as is

suitable to, or conformable to his will and desires. It cannot mean that it is such sorrow or grief as God has, for he has none ; but such as shall be in accordance with what God *demands* in a return to him. It is a sorrow which his truth is fitted to produce on the heart; such a sorrow as shall *appropriately* arise from viewing sin as God views it ; such sorrow as exists in the mind when our views accord with his in regard to the existence, the extent, the nature, and the ill-desert of sin. Such views will lead to sorrow that it has ever been committed ; and such views will be " according to God." (2.) Such sorrow as shall be exercised *towards* God in view of sin ; which shall arise from a view of the evil of sin as committed against a holy God. It is not mainly that it will lead to pain; that it will overwhelm the soul in disgrace ; that it will forfeit the favour or lead to the contempt of man; or that it will lead to an eternal hell ; but it is such as arises from a view of the evil of sin as committed against a holy and just God, deriving its *main* evil from the fact that it is an offence against his infinite Majesty. Such sorrow David had (Ps. li. 4), when he said, " against thee, thee only have I sinned ;" when the offence regarded as committed against man, enormous as it was, was lost and absorbed in its greater evil when regarded as committed against God. So all true and genuine repentance is that which regards sin as deriving its main evil from the fact that it is committed *against God.* (3.) That which leads *to God.* It leads *to* God to obtain forgiveness ; to seek for consolation. A heart truly contrite and penitent seeks God, and implores pardon from him. Other sorrow in view of sin than that which is genuine repentance, leads the person *away* from God. He seeks consolation in the world; he endeavours to drive away his serious impressions or to drown them in the pleasures and the cares of life. But genuine sorrow for sin leads the soul *to* God, and conducts the sinner, through the Redeemer, to him to obtain the pardon and peace which he only can give to a wounded spirit. In

God alone can pardon and true peace be found ; and godly sorrow for sin will seek them there. ¶ *Worketh repentance.* Produces a change that shall be permanent; a reformation. It is not mere regret ; it does not soon pass away in its effects, but it produces permanent and abiding changes. A man who mourns over sin as committed against God, and who seek *to* God for pardon, will reform his life and truly repent. He who has grief for sin only because it will lead to disgrace or shame, or because it will lead to poverty or pain, will not necessarily break off from it and reform. It is only when it is seen that sin is committed against God and is evil in his sight, that it leads to a change of life. ¶ *Not to be repented of* (ἀμεταμέλητον); see Note on ver. 8. Not to be regretted. It is permanent and abiding. There is no occasion to mourn over such repentance and change of life. It is that which the mind approves, and which it will always approve. There will be no reason for regretting it, and it is so. Who ever yet repented of having truly repented of sin? Who is there, who has there ever been, who became a true penitent, and a true Christian, who ever regretted it ? Not an individual has ever been known who regretted his having become a Christian. Not one who regretted that he had become one too soon in life, or that he had served the Lord Jesus too faithfully or too long. ¶ *But the sorrow of the world.* All sorrow which is not toward God, and which does not arise from just views of sin as committed against God, or lead to God. Probably Paul refers here to the sorrow which arises from worldly causes and which does not lead to God for consolation. Such may be the sorrow which arises from the loss of friends or property ; from disappointment, or from shame and disgrace, Perhaps it may include the following things. (1.) Sorrow arising from losses of property and friends, and from disappointment. (2.) Sorrow for sin or vice when it overwhelms the mind with the consciousness of guilt, and when it does not lead to God, and when there is no

repentance to salvation not to be repented of : but the sorrow of the world *a* worketh death.

a Pr.17.22.

11 For behold this self-same thing, that ye sorrowed after a godly *b* sort, what carefulness *c* it

b Is.66.2.   *c* Tit.3.8.

contrition of soul from viewing it as an offence against God. Thus a female who has wandered from the paths of virtue, and involved her family and herself in disgrace ; or a man who has been guilty of forgery, or perjury, or any other disgraceful crime, and who is detected ; a man who has violated the laws of the land, and who has involved himself and family in disgrace, will often feel regret, and sorrow, and also remorse, but it arises wholly from worldly considerations, and does not lead to God. (3.) When the sorrow arises from a view of worldly consequences merely, and when there is no looking to God for pardon and consolation. Thus men, when they lose their property or friends, often pine in grief without looking to God. Thus when they have wandered from the path of virtue and have fallen into sin, they often look merely to the *disgrace* among men, and see their names blasted, and their comforts gone, and pine away in grief. There is no looking to God for pardon or for consolation. The sorrow arises from this world, and it terminates there. It is the loss of what they valued pertaining to this world, and it is all which they had, and it produces death. It is sorrow such as the men of this world have, begins with this world, and terminates with this world. ¶ *Worketh death.* Tends to death, spiritual, temporal, and eternal. It does not tend to life. (1.) It produces distress only. It is attended with no consolation. (2.) It tends to break the spirit, to destroy the peace, and to mar the happiness. (3.) It often leads to death itself. The spirit is broken, and the heart pines away under the influence of the unalleviated sorrow ; or under its influence men often lay violent hands on themselves and take their lives. Life is *often* closed under the influence of such sorrow. (4.) It tends to eternal death. There is no looking to God ; no looking for pardon. It produces murmur-

ing, repining, complaining, fretfulness against God, and thus leads to his displeasure and to the condemnation and ruin of the soul.

11. *For behold this self-same thing.* For see in your own case the happy effects of godly sorrow. See the effects which it produced ; see an illustration of what it is fitted to produce. The construction is, "For lo ! this very thing, to wit, your sorrowing after a godly manner, wrought carefulness, clearing of yourselves," &c. The object of Paul is to illustrate the effects of godly sorrow, to which he had referred in ver. 10. He appeals, therefore, to their own case, and says that it was beautifully illustrated among themselves. ¶ *What carefulness* (σπουδήν). This word properly denotes *speed, haste ;* then diligence, earnest effort, forwardness. Here it is evidently used to denote the diligence and the great anxiety which they manifested to remove the evils which existed among them. They went to work to remove them. They did not sit down to mourn over them merely, nor did they *wait* for God to remove them, nor did they plead that they could do nothing, but they set about the work as though they believed it might be done. When men are thoroughly convinced of sin, they will set about removing it with the utmost diligence. They will feel that this can be done, and must be done, or that the soul will be lost. ¶ What *clearing of yourselves* (ἀπολογίαν). Apology. This word properly means a plea or defence before a tribunal or elsewhere ; Acts xxii. 1 ; 2 Tim. iv. 16. Tindal renders it, "Yea, it caused you to clear yourselves." The word here properly means *apology* for what had been done ; and it probably refers here to the effort which would be made by the sounder part of the church to clear themselves from blame in what had occurred. It does not mean that the guilty, when convicted of sin, will attempt to

.vrought in you, yea, *what* clearing *a* of yourselves, yea, *what* indignation, *b* yea, *what* fear, *c* yea, *what* vehement desire, *d* yea, *what* zeal, yea, *what* revenge! *e*

a Ep.5.11.　　b Ep.4 26.　　c He.4.1.
d Ps.42.1; 130.6.

In all *things* ye have approved yourselves *f* to be clear in this matter.

12 Wherefore, though I wrote unto you, *I did it* not for his

e Re.3.19; Mat.5.29,30.　　f Ro.14.18.

vindicate themselves and to apologize to God for what they had done ; but it means that the church at Corinth were anxious to state to Titus all the mitigating circumstances of the case: they showed great solicitude to free themselves, as far as could be done, from blame ; they were anxious, as far as could be, to show that they had not approved of what had occurred, and perhaps that it had occurred only because it could not have been prevented. We are not to suppose that all the things here referred to occurred in the same individuals, and that the same persons precisely evinced diligence, and made the apology, &c. It was done by the church ; all evinced deep feeling ; but some manifested it in one way, and some in another. The whole church was roused, and all felt, and all endeavoured in the proper way to free themselves from the blame, and to remove the evil from among them. ¶ *Yea*, what *indignation*. Indignation against the sin, and perhaps against the persons who had drawn down the censure of the apostle. One effect of true repentance is to produce decided *hatred* of sin. It is not mere regret, or sorrow, it is positive *hatred*. There is a deep indignation against it as an evil and a bitter thing. ¶ *Yea*, what *fear*. Fear lest the thing should be repeated. Fear lest it should not be entirely removed. Or it may possibly mean fear of the displeasure of Paul, and of the punishment which would be inflicted if the evil were not removed. But it more probably refers to the anxious state of mind that the whole evil might be corrected, and to the dread of having any vestige of the evil remaining among them. ¶ *Yea*, what *vehement desire*. This may either mean their fervent wish to remove the cause of complaint, or their anxious desire to see the apostle. It is used in the latter sense in

ver. 7, and according to Doddridge and Bloomfield this is the meaning here. Locke renders it, "desire of satisfying me." It seems to me more probable that Paul refers to their anxious wish to remove the sin, since this is the topic under consideration. The point of his remarks in this verse is not so much their affection for him as their indignation against their sin, and their deep grief that sin had existed and had been tolerated among them. ¶ *Yea*, what *zeal*. Zeal to remove the sin, and to show your attachment to me. They set about the work of reformation in great earnest. ¶ *Yea*, what *revenge !* Tindal renders this, "it caused punishment." The idea is, that they immediately set about the work of inflicting punishment on the offender. The word here used (ἐκδίκησις) probably denotes *maintenance of right, protection ;* then it is used in the sense of *avengement*, or *vengeance ;* and then of penal retribution or punishment ; see Luke xxi. 22 ; 2 Thess. i. 8 ; 1 Pet. ii. 14. ¶ *In all* things, &c. The sense of this is, "You have entirely acquitted yourselves of blame in this business." The apostle does not mean that none of them had been to blame, or that the church had been free from fault, for a large part of his former epistle is occupied in reproving them for their faults in this business, but he means that by their zeal and their readiness to take away the cause of complaint, they had removed all necessity of further blame, and had pursued such a course as entirely to meet his approbation. They had cleared themselves of any further blame in this business, and had become, so far as this was concerned, " clear" (ἀγνούς) or pure.

12. *Wherefore, though I wrote unto you,* &c. In this verse Paul states the main reason why he had written to them on the subject. It was not

cause that had done the wrong, nor for his cause that suffered wrong, but that our care *a* for you in the sight of God might appear unto you.

13 Therefore we were comforted in your comfort : yea, and

exceedingly the more joyed we for the joy of Titus, because his spirit was refreshed *b* by you all.

14 For if I have boasted any thing to him of you, I am not ashamed ; but as we spake all things to you in truth, even so

principally on account of the man who had done the wrong, or of him who had been injured ; but it was from tender anxiety for the whole church, and in order to show the deep interest which he had in their welfare. ¶ *Not for his cause that had done the wrong.* Not mainly, or principally on account of the incestuous person ; 1 Cor. v. 1. It was not primarily with reference to him as an individual that I wrote, but from a regard to the whole church. ¶ *Nor for his cause that had suffered wrong.* Not merely that the wrong which he had suffered might be rectified, and that his rights might be restored, valuable and desirable as was that object. The offence was that a man had taken his father's wife as his own (1 Cor. v. 1), and the person injured, therefore, was his father. It is evident from this passage, I think, that the father was living at the time when Paul wrote this epistle. ¶ *But that our care, &c.* I wrote mainly that I might show the deep interest which I had in the church at large, and my anxiety that it might not suffer by the misconduct of any of its members. It is from a regard to the welfare of the whole earth that discipline should be administered, and not simply with reference to an individual who has done wrong, or an individual who is injured. In church discipline such *private* interests are absorbed in the general interest of the church at large.

13. *Therefore we were comforted in your comfort.* The phrase "your comfort," here seems to mean the happiness which they had, or might reasonably be expected to have in obeying the directions of Paul, and in the repentance which they had manifested. Paul had spoken of no other consolation or comfort than this ; and

the idea seems to be that they were a happy people, and would be happy by obeying the commands of God. This fact gave Paul additional joy, and he could not but rejoice that they had removed the cause of the offence, and that they would not thus be exposed to the displeasure of God. Had they not repented and put away the evil, the consequences to them must have been deep distress. As it was, they would be blessed and happy. ¶ *And exceedingly the more, &c.* Titus had been kindly received, and hospitably entertained, and had become much attached to them. This was to Paul an additional occasion of joy ; see ver. 7.

14. *For if I have boasted any thing to him, &c.* This seems to imply that Paul had spoken most favourably to Titus of the Corinthians before he went among them. He had probably expressed his belief that he would be kindly received ; that they would be disposed to listen to him, and to comply with the directions of the apostle; perhaps he had spoken to him of what he anticipated would be their liberality in regard to the collection which he was about to make for the poor saints at Jerusalem. ¶ *I am not ashamed.* It has all turned out to be true. He has found it as I said it would be. All my expectations are realized; and you have been as kind, and hospitable, and benevolent as I assured him you would be. ¶ *As we spake all things to you in truth.* Every thing which I said to you was said in truth. All my promises to you, and all my commands, and all my reasonable expectations expressed to you, were sincere. I practised no disguise, and all that I have said thus far turned out to be true. ¶ *Even so our boasting, &c.* My boasting of your character, and

our boasting, which *I made* before Titus, is found a truth.

15 And his [1] inward affection is more abundant toward you, whilst he remembereth the obedience of

you all, how with fear [a] and trembling ye received him.

16 I rejoice, therefore, that I have confidence [b] in you in all *things*.

---

[1] bowels.   [a] Ph.2.12.

[b] 2 Th.3.4; Phile.8.21.

---

of your disposition to do right, which I made before Titus has turned out to be true. It was as I said it would be. I did not commend you too highly to him, as I did not overstate the matter to you in my epistle.

15. *And his inward affection*, &c. He has become deeply and tenderly attached to you. His affectionate regard for you has been greatly increased by his visit. On the meaning of the word here rendered "inward affection" (σπλαγχια, Marg. *bowels*) see Note on chap. vi. 12. It denotes here deep, tender attachment, or love. ¶ *How with fear and trembling ye received him.* With fear of offending, and with deep apprehension of the consequences of remaining in sin. He saw what a fear there was of doing wrong, and what evidence there was, therefore, that you were solicitous to do right.

16. *I rejoice, therefore, that I have confidence*, &c. I have had the most ample proof that you are disposed to obey God, and to put away every thing that is offensive to him. The address of this part of the epistle, says Doddridge, is wonderful. It is designed, evidently, not merely to commend them for what they had done, and to show them the deep attachment which he had for them, but in a special manner to prepare them for what he was about to say in the following chapter, respecting the collection which he had so much at heart for the poor saints at Jerusalem. What he here says was admirably adapted to introduce that subject. They had thus far showed the deepest regard for him. They had complied with all his directions. All that he had said of them had proved to be true. And as he had boasted of them to Titus (ver. 14), and expressed his entire confidence that they would comply with his requisitions, so he had also boasted of them to the churches of Macedonia,

and expressed the utmost confidence that they would be liberal in their benefactions, chap. ix. 2. All that Paul here says in their favour, therefore, was eminently adapted to excite them to liberality, and prepare them to comply with his wishes in regard to that contribution.

REMARKS.

1. Christians are bound by every solemn and sacred consideration to endeavour to purify themselves, ver. 1. They who have the promises of eternal life, and the assurance that God will be to them a father, and evidence that they are his sons and daughters, should not indulge in the filthiness of the flesh and spirit.

2. Every true Christian will aim at perfection, ver. 1. He will desire to be perfect; he will strive for it; he will make it a subject of unceasing and constant prayer. No man can be a Christian to whom it would not be a pleasure to be at once as perfect as God. And if any man is conscious that the idea of being made *at once* perfectly holy would be unpleasant or painful, he may set it down as certain evidence that he is a stranger to religion.

3. No man can be a Christian who voluntarily indulges in sin, or in what he knows to be wrong, ver. 1. A man who does that cannot be aiming at perfection. A man who does that shows that he has no real desire to be perfect.

4. How blessed will be heaven, ver. 1. There we shall be perfect. And the crowning glory of heaven is not that we shall be *happy*, but that we shall be *holy*. Whatever there is in the heart that is good shall there be perfectly developed; whatever there is that is evil shall be removed, and the whole soul will be like God. The Christian desires heaven because he will be there perfect. He desires no other

heaven. He could be induced to accept no other if it were offered to him. He blesses God day by day that there *is* such a heaven, and that there is no other ; that there is *one* world which sin does not enter, and where evil shall be unknown.

5. What a change will take place at death, ver. 1. The Christian will be there made perfect. *How* this change will be there produced we do not know. Whether it will be by some extraordinary influence of the Spirit of God on the heart, or by the mere removal from the body, and from a sinful world to a world of glory, we know not. The fact seems to be clear, that at death the Christian will be made at once as holy as God is holy, and that he will ever continue to be in the future world.

6. What a desirable thing it is to die, ver. 1. Here, should we attain to the age of the patriarchs, like them we should continue to be imperfect. Death only will secure our perfection ; and death, therefore, is a desirable event. The perfection of our being could not be attained but for death ; *and every Christian should rejoice that he is to die.* It is better to be in heaven than on earth ; better to be with God than to be away from him ; better to be made perfect than to be contending here with internal corruption, and to struggle with our sins. " I would not live always," was the language of holy Job ; " I desire to depart and to be with Christ," was the language of holy Paul.

7. It is often painful to be compelled to use the language of reproof, ver. 8. Paul deeply regretted the necessity of doing it in the case of the Corinthians, and expressed the deepest anxiety in regard to it. No man, no minister, parent, or friend can use it but with deep regret that it is necessary But the painfulness of it should not prevent our doing it. It should be done tenderly but faithfully. If done with the deep feeling, with the tender affection of Paul, it will be done right ; and when so done, it will produce the desired effect, and do good. No man should use the language of reproof with a hard heart, or

with severity of feeling. If he is, like Paul, ready to weep when he does it, it will do good. If he does it because he *delights* in it, it will do evil.

8. It is a subject of rejoicing where a people exercise repentance, ver. 8. A minister has pleasure not *in* the pain which his reproofs cause ; not in the deep anxiety and distress of the sinner, and not in the pain which Christians feel under his reproofs, but he has joy in the happy results or the fruits which follow from it. It is only from the belief that those tears will produce abundant joy that he has pleasure in causing them, or in witnessing them.

9. The way to bring men to repentance is to present to them the simple and unvarnished truth, ver. 8, 9. Paul stated simple and plain truths to the Corinthians. He did not abuse them ; he did not censure them in general terms ; he stated things just as they were, and *specified* the things on account of which there was occasion for repentance. So if ministers wish to excite repentance in others, they must *specify* the sins over which others should weep ; if we wish, as individuals, to feel regret for our sins, and to have true repentance toward God, we must dwell on those *particular* sins which we have committed, and should endeavour so to reflect on them that they may make an appropriate impression on the heart. No man will truly repent by *general* reflections on his sin ; no one who does not endeavour so to dwell on his sins as that they shall make the proper impression which each one is fitted to produce on the soul. Repentance is that state of mind which a view of the truth in regard to our own depravity is fitted to produce.

10. There is a great difference between godly sorrow and the sorrow of the world, ver. 10. All men feel sorrow. All men, at some period of their lives, grieve over their past conduct. Some in their sorrow are pained because they have offended God, and go to God, and find pardon and peace in him. That sorrow is unto salvation. But the mass do not look to God. They turn away from him even in their

CHAPTER VIII.

MOREOVER, brethren, we do you to wit of the grace of God bestowed on the churches of Macedonia; [a]

2 How that, in a great trial

a chap.9.2,4.

disappointments, and in their sorrows, and in the bitter consciousness of sin. They seek to alleviate their sorrows in worldly company, in pleasure, in the intoxicating bowl; and such sorrow works death. It produces additional distress, and deeper gloom here, and eternal woe hereafter.

11. We may learn what constitutes true repentance, ver. 11. There should be, and there will be, deep feeling. There will be "carefulness," deep anxiety to be freed from the sin; there will be a desire to remove it; "indignation" against it; "fear" of offending God; "earnest desire" that all that has been wrong should be corrected; "zeal" that the reformation should be entire; and a wish that the appropriate "revenge," or expression of displeasure, should be excited against it. The true penitent hates nothing so cordially as he does his sin. He hates nothing but sin. And his warfare with that is decided, uncompromising, inexorable, and eternal.

12. It is an evidence of mercy and goodness in God that the sorrow which is felt about sin *may* be made to terminate in our good, and to promote our salvation, ver. 10, 11. If sorrow for sin had been suffered to take its own course, and had proceeded unchecked, it would in all cases have produced death. If it had not been for the merciful interposition of Christianity, by which even sorrow might be turned to joy, this world would have been everywhere a world of sadness and of death. Man would have suffered. Sin always produces, sooner or later, woe. Christianity has done nothing to make men wretched, but it has done every thing to bind up broken hearts. It has revealed a way by which sorrow may be turned into joy, and the bitterness of grief may be followed by the sweet calm and sunshine of peace.

13. The great purpose of Christian discipline is to benefit the whole church, ver. 12. It is not merely on account of the offender, nor is it merely that the injured may receive a just recompense. It is primarily that the church may be pure, and that the cause of religion may not be dishonoured. When the work of discipline is entered on from any private and personal motives, it is usually attended with bad feeling, and usually results in evil. When it is entered on with a desire to honour God, and to promote the purity of the church, when the whole aim is to deliver the church from opprobrium and scandal, and to have just such a church as Jesus Christ desires, then it will be prosecuted with good temper, and with right feeling, and then it will lead to happy results. Let no man institute a process of discipline on an offending brother from private, personal, and revengeful feelings. Let him first examine his own heart, and let him be sure that his aim is solely the glory of Christ, before he attempts to draw down the censure of the church on an offending brother. How many cases of church discipline would be arrested if this simple rule were observed! And while the case before us shows that it is important in the highest degree that discipline should be exercised on an offending member of the church; while no consideration should prevent us from exercising that discipline; and while every man should feel desirous that the offending brother should be reproved or punished, yet this case also shows that it should be done with the utmost tenderness, the most strict regard to justice, and the deepest anxiety that the general interests of religion should not suffer by the manifestation of an improper spirit, or by improper motives in inflicting punishment on an offending brother.

CHAPTER VIII.

IN the previous chapter the apostle had expressed his entire confidence in the ready obedience of the Corinth-

of affliction, the abundance of their joy and their deep *a* poverty

a Mar.12.44.

abounded unto the riches of their [1] liberality.

[1] *simplicity.*

ians in all things. To this confidence he had been led by the promptitude with which they had complied with his commands in regard to the case of discipline there, and by the respect which they had shown to Titus, whom he had sent to them. All that he had ever said in their favour had been realized ; all that had ever been asked of them had been accomplished The object of his statement in the close of chap. vii. seems to have been to excite them to diligence in completing the collection which they had begun for the poor and afflicted saints of Judea. On the consideration of that subject, which lay so near his heart, he now enters; and this chapter and the following are occupied with suggesting arguments, and giving directions for a liberal contribution.

Paul had given directions for taking up this collection in the first epistle ; see chap. xvi. 1. seq.; comp. Rom. xv. 26. This collection he had given Titus direction to take up when he went to Corinth ; see ver. 6—17 of this chapter. But from some cause it had not been completed, ver. 10, 11. What that cause was, is not stated, but it may have been possibly the disturbances which had existed there, or the opposition of the enemies of Paul, or the attention which was necessarily bestowed in regulating the affairs of the church. But in order that the contribution might be made, and might be a liberal one, Paul presses on their attention several considerations designed to excite them to give freely. The chapter is, therefore, of importance to us, as it is a statement of the duty of giving liberally to the cause of benevolence, and of the motives by which it should be done. In the presentation of this subject, Paul urges upon them the following considerations.

He appeals to the very liberal example of the churches of Macedonia, where, though they were exceedingly poor, they had contributed with great

cheerfulness and liberality to the object, ver. 1—5.

From their example he had been induced to desire Titus to lay the subject before the church at Corinth, and to finish the collection which he had begun, ver. 6.

He directs them to abound in this, not as a matter of commandment, but excited by the example of others, ver. 7, 8.

He appeals to them by the love of the Saviour; reminds them that though he was rich yet he became poor, and that they were bound to imitate his example, ver. 9.

He reminds them of their intention to make such a contribution, and of the effort which they had made a year before ; and though they had been embarrassed in it, and might find it difficult still to give as much as they had intended, or as much as they would wish, still it would be acceptable to God. For if there was a willing mind, God accepted the offering, ver. 10—12.

He assures them that it was not his wish to burden or oppress them. All that he desired was that there should be an equality in all the churches, ver. 13—15.

To show them how much he was interested in this, he thanks God that he had put it into the heart of Titus to engage in it. And in order more effectually to secure it, he says that he had sent with Titus a brother who was well known, and whose praise was in all the churches. He had done this in order that the churches might have entire confidence that the contribution would be properly distributed. Paul did not wish it to be intrusted to himself. He would leave no room for suspicion in regard to his own character; he would furnish the utmost security to the churches that their wishes were complied with. He desired to act honestly not only in the sight of the Lord, but to furnish evidence of his entire honesty to men, ver. 16—21.

To secure the same object he had also sent *another* brother, and these three brethren he felt willing to recommend as faithful and tried; as men in whom the church at Corinth might repose the utmost confidence, ver. 22—24.

1. *Moreover, brethren, we do you to wit.* We make known to you; we inform you. The phrase "we do you to wit," is used in Tindal's translation, and means "we cause you to know." The *purpose* for which Paul informed them of the liberality of the churches of Macedonia was to excite them to similar liberality. ¶ *Of the grace of God,* &c. The favour which God had shown them in exciting a spirit of liberality, and in enabling them to contribute to the fund for supplying the wants of the poor saints at Jerusalem. The word "grace" ($\chi\acute{\alpha}\rho\iota\varsigma$) is sometimes used in the sense of *gift,* and the phrase "gift of God" some have supposed *may* mean *very great gift,* where the words "of God" may be designed to mark any thing very eminent or excellent, as in the phrase "cedars of God," "mountains of God," denoting very great cedars, very great mountains. Some critics (as Macknight, Bloomfield, Locke, and others) have supposed that this means that the churches of Macedonia had been able to contribute largely to the aid of the saints of Judea. But the more obvious and correct interpretation, as I apprehend, is that which is implied in the common version, that the phrase "grace of God," means that God had bestowed on them grace to give according to their ability in this cause. According to this it is implied, (1.) That a disposition to contribute to the cause of benevolence is to be traced to God. He is its author. He excites it. It is not a plant of native growth in the human heart, but a large and liberal spirit of benevolence is one of the effects of his grace, and is to be traced to him. (2.) It is a *favour* bestowed on a church when God excites in it a spirit of benevolence. It is one of the evidences of his love. And indeed there cannot be a higher proof of the favour of God than when by his grace he inclines and enables us to contribute

largely to meliorate the condition, and to alleviate the wants of our fellowmen. Perhaps the apostle here meant delicately to hint this. He did not therefore say coldly that the churches of Macedonia had contributed to this object, but he speaks of it as *a favour* shown to them by God that they were able to do it. And he meant, probably, gently to intimate to the Corinthians that it would be an evidence that they were enjoying the favour of God if they should contribute in like manner. ¶ *The churches of Macedonia.* Philippi, Thessalonica, Berea. For an account of Macedonia, see Notes, Acts xvi. 9; Rom. xv. 26. Of these churches, that at Philippi seems to have been most distinguished for liberality (Phil. iv. 10, 15, 16, 18), though it is probable that other churches contributed according to their ability, as they are commended (comp. chap. ix. 2) without distinction.

2. *How that, in a great trial of affliction.* When it might be supposed they were unable to give; when many would suppose they needed the aid of others; or when it might be supposed their minds would be wholly engrossed with their own concerns. The trial to which the apostle here refers was doubtless some persecution which was excited against them, probably by the Jews; see Acts xvi. 20; xvii. 5. ¶ *The abundance of their joy.* Their joy arising from the hopes and promises of the gospel. Notwithstanding their persecutions, their joy has abounded, and the effect of their joy has been seen in the liberal contribution which they have made. Their joy could not be repressed by their persecution, and they cheerfully contributed largely to the aid of others. ¶ *And their deep poverty.* Their very low estate of poverty was made to contribute liberally to the wants of others. It is implied here, (1.) That they were very poor—a fact arising probably from the consideration that the poor generally embraced the gospel first, and also because it is probable that they were molested and stripped of their property in persecutions (comp. Heb. x. 34); (2.) That notwithstanding this they were enabled to make a

3 For to *their* power, (I bear record,) yea, and beyond *their* power, *they were* willing of themselves;

4 Praying us with much entreaty that we would receive the gift, and *take upon us* the fellowship [a] of the ministering to the saints.

5 And *this they did*, not as we hoped, but first gave their ownselves to the Lord, and unto us by the will of God.

a Acts 11,29 ; Ro. 15.25, 26.

liberal contribution—a fact demonstrating that a people *can* do much even when poor if all feel disposed to do it, and that afflictions are favourable to the effort ; and, (3.) That one cause of this was the *joy* which they had even in their trials. If a people have the joys of the gospel ; if they have the consolations of religion themselves, they will somehow or other find means to contribute to the welfare of others. They will be willing to labour with reference to it, or they will find something which they can sacrifice or spare. Even their deep poverty will abound in the fruits of benevolence. ¶ *Abounded.* They contributed liberally. Their joy was manifested in a large donation, notwithstanding their poverty. ¶ *Unto the riches of their liberality.* Marg. " Simplicity." The word (ἁπλότης) here used means properly sincerity, candour, probity; then Christian simplicity, integrity; then liberality; see Rom. xii. 8 (Marg.); 2 Cor. ix. 11, 13. The phrase "riches of liberality," is a Hebraism, meaning rich, or abundant liberality. The sense is, their liberality was much greater than could be expected from persons so poor; and the object of the apostle is, to excite the Corinthians to give liberally by their example.

3. *For to* their *power.* To the utmost of their ability ¶ *I bear record.* Paul had founded those churches and had spent much time with them. He was therefore well qualified to bear testimony in regard to their condition. ¶ *Yea, and beyond* their *power.* Beyond what could have been expected; or beyond what it would have been thought possible in their condition. Doddridge remarks that this is a noble hyperbole, similar to that used by Demosthenes when he says, " I have performed all, even with an industry beyond my power." The sense is, they were willing to give more than they were well able. It shows the strong interest which they had in the subject, and the anxious desire which they had to relieve the wants of others. ¶ *Of themselves* (αὐθαίρετοι). Acting from choice, self-moved, voluntarily, of their own accord. They did not wait to be urged and pressed to do it. They rejoiced in the opportunity of doing it. They came forward of their own accord and made the contribution. " God loveth a cheerful giver" (chap. ix. 7); and from all the accounts which we have of these churches in Macedonia it is evident that they were greatly distinguished for their cheerful liberality.

4. *Praying us with much entreaty.* Earnestly entreating me to receive the contribution and convey it to the poor and afflicted saints in Judea. ¶ *And* take upon us *the fellowship of the ministering to the saints.* Greek, " that we would take the gift and the fellowship of the ministering to the saints." They asked of us to take part in the labour of conveying it to Jerusalem. The occasion of this distress which made the collection for the saints of Judea necessary, was probably the famine which was predicted by Agabus, and which occurred in the time of Claudius Cæsar; see Note on Acts xi. 28. Barnabas was associated with Paul in conveying the contribution to Jerusalem; Acts vi. 30. Paul was unwilling to do it unless they particularly desired it, and he seems to have insisted that some person should be associated with him; ver. 20; 1 Cor. xvi. 3, 4.

5. *And this they did*, &c. They did not give what we expected only. We knew their poverty, and we expected only a small sum from them. ¶ *Not as we hoped.* Not according to the utmost of our hopes. We were

6 Insomuch that we desired Titus, that as he had begun, so he would also finish in you the same [1] grace also.

7 Therefore, as ye abound [a] in every *thing, in* faith, and utterance,

1 or *gift.*   *a* 1 Cor.1.5.

and knowledge, and *in* all diligence, and *in* your love to us, *see* that ye abound in this grace also.

8 I speak not [b] by commandment, but by occasion of the for-

b 1 Cor.7.6.

greatly disappointed in the amount which they gave, and in the manner in which it was done. ¶ *But first gave their ownselves to the Lord.* They first made an entire consecration of themselves and all that they had to the Lord. They kept nothing back. They felt that all they had was his. And where a people honestly and truly devote *themselves* to God, they will find no difficulty in having the means to contribute to the cause of charity. ¶ *And unto us by the will of God.* That is, they gave themselves to us to be directed in regard to the contribution to be made. They complied with our wishes and followed our directions. The phrase " by the will of God," means evidently that God moved them to this, or that it was to be traced to his direction and providence. It is one of the instances in which Paul traces every thing that is right and good to the agency and direction of God.

6. *Insomuch.* The sense of this passage seems to be this, " We were encouraged by this unexpected success among the Macedonians. We were surprised at the extent of their liberality. And encouraged by this, we requested Titus to go among you and finish the collection which you had proposed and which you had begun. Lest you should be outstripped in liberality by the comparatively poor Macedonian Christians, we were anxious that you should perform what you had promised and contemplated, and we employed Titus, therefore, that he might go at once and finish the collection among you." ¶ *The same grace also.* Marg. " *Gift ;*" see Note on ver. 1. The word refers to the contribution which he wished to be made.

7. *Therefore as ye abound in every* thing; see Note, 1 Cor. i. 5. Paul

never hesitated to commend Christians where it could be done with truth; and the fact that they were eminent in some of the Christian duties and graces, he makes the ground of the exhortation that they would abound in all. From those who had so many eminent characteristics of true religion he had a right to expect much; and he therefore exhorts them to manifest a symmetry of Christian character. ¶ In *faith.* In the full belief of the truth and obligation of the gospel. ¶ *And utterance.* In the ability to instruct others; perhaps referring to their power of speaking foreign languages; 1 Cor. xiv. ¶ *And knowledge.* The knowledge of God, and of his truth. ¶ *And* in *all diligence.* Diligence or readiness in the discharge of every duty. Of this, Paul had full evidence in their readiness to comply with his commands in the case of discipline to which so frequent reference is made in this epistle. ¶ *And* in *your love to us.* Manifested by the readiness with which you received our commands; see chap. vii. 4, 6, 7, 11, 16. ¶ See *that ye abound in this grace also.* The idea here is, that eminence in spiritual endowments of any kind, or in any of the traits of the Christian character should lead to great benevolence, and that the character is not complete unless benevolence be manifested toward every good object that may be presented.

8. *I speak not by commandment.* This does not mean that he had no express command of God in the case, but that he did not mean *to command* them; he did not speak authoritatively; he did not intend to prescribe what they should give. He used only moral motives, and urged the considerations which he had done to *persuade* rather than to *command* them to give; see ver. 10. He was endeavouring to

wardness of others, and to prove the sincerity of your love.

9 For ye know the grace of our Lord Jesus Christ, that,

though he was [a] rich, yet for your sakes he became poor, [b] that ye through his poverty might be rich. [c]

a John 1.1.　　*b* Luke 9.58; Phil.2.6, 7.　　*c* Rev.3.18.

induce them to give liberally, not by abstract command and law, but by showing them what others had given who had much less ability and much fewer advantages than they had. Men cannot be induced to give to objects of charity by command, or by a spirit of dictation and authority. The only successful, as well as the only lawful appeal, is to their hearts and consciences, and sober judgments. And if an apostle did not take upon himself the language of authority and command in matters of Christian benevolence, assuredly ministers and ecclesiastical bodies now have no right to use any such language. ¶ *But by occasion of the forwardness of others.* I make use of the example of the churches of Macedonia as an argument to induce you to give liberally to the cause. ¶ *And to prove the sincerity of your love.* The apostle does not specify here what "love" he refers to, whether love to God, to Christ, to himself, or to the church at large. It may be that he designedly used the word in a general sense, to denote love to any good object; and that he meant to say that liberality in assisting the poor and afflicted people of God would be the best evidence of the sincerity of their love to God, to the Redeemer, to him, and to the church. Religion is love; and that love is to be manifested by doing good to all men as we have opportunity. The most *substantial* evidence of that love is when we are willing to part with our property, or with whatever is valuable to us, to confer happiness and salvation on others.

9. *For ye know,* &c. The apostle Paul was accustomed to illustrate every subject, and to enforce every duty where it could be done, by a reference to the life and sufferings of the Lord Jesus Christ. The design of this verse is apparent. It is, to show the duty of giving liberally to

the objects of benevolence, from the fact that the Lord Jesus was willing to become poor in order that he might benefit others. The idea is, that he who was Lord and proprietor of the universe, and who possessed all things, was willing to leave his exalted station in the bosom of the Father and to become poor, in order that we might become rich in the blessings of the gospel, in the means of grace, and as heirs of all things; and that we who are thus benefited, and who have such an example, should be willing to part with our earthly possessions in order that we may benefit others. ¶ *The grace.* The benignity, kindness, mercy, goodness. His coming in this manner was a proof of the highest benevolence. ¶ *Though he was rich.* The riches of the Redeemer here referred to, stand opposed to that poverty which he assumed and manifested when he dwelt among men. It implies, (1.) His pre-existence, for he *became* poor. He had been rich. Yet not in this world. He did not lay aside wealth here on earth after he had possessed it, for he had none. He was not first rich and then poor on earth, for he had no earthly wealth. The Socinian interpretation is, that he was "rich in power and in the Holy Ghost;" but it was not true that he laid these aside, and that he became poor in either of them. He *had* power, even in his poverty, to still the waves, and to raise the dead, and he was always full of the Holy Ghost. His family was poor; and his parents were poor; and he was himself poor all his life. This then *must* refer to a state of antecedent riches before his assumption of human nature; and the expression is strikingly parallel to that in Phil. ii. 6, seq. "Who being in the form of God, thought it not robbery to be equal with God, but made himself of no reputation," &c. (2.) He was rich as the Lord and proprietor of all things.

He was the Creator of all (John i. 3; Col. i. 16), and as Creator he had a right to all things, and the disposal of all things. The most absolute right which can exist is that acquired by the act of creation; and this right the Son of God possessed over all gold, and silver, and diamonds, and pearls; over all earth and lands; over all the treasures of the ocean, and over all worlds. The extent and amount of his riches, therefore, is to be measured by the extent of his dominion over the universe; and to estimate his riches, therefore, we are to conceive of the sceptre which he sways over the distant worlds. What wealth has man that can compare with the riches of the Creator and Proprietor of all? How poor and worthless appears all the gold that man can accumulate compared with the wealth of him whose are the silver, and the gold, and the cattle upon a thousand hills? ¶ *Yet for your sakes.* That is, for your sakes as a part of the great family that was to be redeemed. In what respect it was for their sake, the apostle immediately adds when he says, it was that they might be made rich. It was not for his own sake, but it was for ours. ¶ *He became poor.* In the following respects. (1.) He chose a condition of poverty, a rank of life that was usually that of poverty. He "took upon himself the form of a servant;" Phil. ii. 7. (2.) He was connected with a poor family. Though of the family and lineage of David (Luke ii. 4), yet the family had fallen into decay, and was poor. In the Old Testament he is beautifully represented as a shoot or sucker that starts up from the root of a decayed tree; see my Note on Isa. xi. 1. (3.) His whole life was a life of poverty. He had no home; Luke ix. 58. He chose to be dependent on the charity of the few friends that he drew around him, rather than to *create* food for the abundant supply of his own wants. He had no farms or plantations; he had no splendid palaces; he had no money hoarded in useless coffers or in banks; he had no property to distribute to his friends. His mother he commended when he died to the charitable attention of one of his disciples (John xix. 27), and all his personal property seems to have been the raiment which he wore, and which was divided among the soldiers that crucified him. Nothing is more remarkable than the difference between the plans of the Lord Jesus and those of many of his followers and professed friends. He formed no plan for becoming rich, and he always spoke with the deepest earnestness of the dangers which attend an effort to accumulate property. He was among the most poor of the sons of men in his life; and few have been the men on earth who have not had *as much* as he had to leave to surviving friends, or to excite the cupidity of those who should fall heirs to their property when dead. (4.) He died poor. He made no will in regard to his property, for he had none to dispose of. He knew well enough the effect which would follow if he had amassed wealth, and had left it to be divided among his followers. They were *very* imperfect; and even around the cross there might have been anxious discussion, and perhaps strife about it, as there is often now over the coffin and the unclosed grave of a rich and foolish father who has died. Jesus intended that his disciples should never be turned away from the great work to which he called them by any wealth which he would leave them; and he left them not even a *keepsake* as a memorial of his name. All this is the more remarkable from two considerations. (*a*) That he had it in his power to choose the manner in which he would come. He might have come in the condition of a splendid prince. He might have rode in a chariot of ease, or have dwelt in a magnificent palace. He might have lived with more than the magnificence of an oriental prince, and might have bequeathed treasures greater than those of Crœsus or Solomon to his followers. But he *chose* not to do it. (*b*) It would have been as right and proper for *him* to have amassed wealth, and to have sought princely possessions, as for any of his followers. What is right for them would have been right for him. Men often mistake on this

10 And herein I give *my* advice: for this is expedient for you, who have begun before, not only to do, but also to be [1] forward a year ago.

1 *willing.*

---

subject; and though it cannot be demonstrated that all his followers should aim to be as poor as he was, yet it is undoubtedly true that he meant that his example should operate constantly to check their desire of amassing wealth. In him it was *voluntary;* in us there should be always a *readiness to be poor* if such be the will of God; nay, there should be rather a *preference* to be in moderate circumstances that we may thus be like the Redeemer. ¶ *That ye through his poverty might be rich.* That is, might have durable and eternal riches, the riches of God's everlasting favour. This includes, (1.) The present possession of an interest in the Redeemer himself. "Do you see these extended fields?" said the owner of a vast plantation to a friend. "They are mine. All this is mine." "Do you see yonder poor cottage?" was the reply of the friend as he directed his attention to the abode of a poor widow. "She has more than all this. She has CHRIST as her portion; and that is more than all." He who has an interest in the Redeemer has a possession that is of more value than all that princes can bestow. (2.) The heirship of an eternal inheritance, the prospect of immortal glory; Rom. viii. 17. (3.) Everlasting treasures in heaven. Thus the Saviour compares the heavenly blessings to *treasures;* Mat. vi. 20. Eternal and illimitable wealth is theirs in heaven; and to raise us to that blessed inheritance was the design of the Redeemer in consenting to become poor. This, the apostle says, was to be secured by his poverty. This includes probably the two following things, viz. (1.) That it was to be by the *moral influence* of the fact that he was poor that men were to be blessed. He designed by his example to counteract the effect of wealth; to teach men that this was not the thing to be aimed at; that there were more important purposes of life than to obtain money; and to furnish a perpetual reproof of those who are aiming to amass riches. The example of the Redeemer thus stands before the whole church and the world as a living and constant memorial of the truth that men need other things than wealth; and that there are objects that demand their time and influence other than the accumulation of property. It is well to have such an example; well to have before us the example of one who *never* formed any plan for gain, and who constantly lived above the world. In a world where gain is the great object, where all men are forming plans for it, it is well to have one great model that shall continually demonstrate the folly of it, and that shall point to better things. (2.) The word "poverty" here may include more than a mere want of property. It may mean all the circumstances of his low estate and humble condition; his sufferings and his woes. The whole train of his privations was included in this; and the idea is, that he gave himself to this lowly condition in order that by his sufferings he might procure for us a part in the kingdom of heaven. His *poverty* was a part of the sufferings included in the work of the atonement. For it was not the sufferings of the garden merely, or the pangs of the cross, that constituted the atonement, it was the series of sorrows and painful acts of humiliation which so thickly crowded his life. By all these he designed that we should be made rich; and in view of all these the argument of the apostle is, we should be willing to deny ourselves to do good to others.

10. *And herein I give my advice.* Not undertaking to *command* them, or to prescribe how much they should give. Advice will go much farther than commands on the subject of charities. ¶ *For this is expedient for you* (συμφέρει). That is, this will be of advantage to you; it will be profitable; it will be becoming. The idea is, that they were bound by a regard to consistency and to their own

11 Now therefore perform *a* the doing *of it;* that as *there was* a readiness to will, so *there may be* a

a 1 Ti.6.19 ; Heb.13.16 ; James 2.15,16.

performance also out of that which ye have.

12 For if *b* there be first a

b Luke 21.3.

welfare, to perform what they had purposed. It became them; it was proper, and was demanded ; and there would have been manifest disadvantages if it had not been done. ¶ *Who have begun before.* Who commenced the collection a year before; see ver. 6. It had been commenced with fair prospects of success, but had been interrupted probably by the dissensions which arose in the church there. ¶ *Not only to do.* Not merely to accomplish it as if by constraint, or as a matter of compulsion and drudgery. ¶ *But also to be forward.* Marg. " *Willing.*" So the Greek (τὸ ϑέλειν). They were voluntary in this, and they set about it with vigorous and determined zeal and courage. There was a resolute determination in the thing, and a willingness and heartiness in it which showed that they were actuated by Christian principle. Consistency, and their own reputation and advantage, now demanded that they should complete what they had begun.

11. *As* there was *a readiness to will.* Now accomplish the thing, and be not satisfied with having begun it. Do not suppose that the intention was sufficient, or that you are now released from the obligation. A year indeed has elapsed; but the necessity of the aid for the poor has not ceased. The sentiment here is, that if we have felt it our duty to aid in a cause of benevolence, and have commenced it, and have then been interrupted in executing our purpose, we should seize the first favourable opportunity to accomplish what we had designed. We should not regard ourselves as released from our obligation, but should, from a regard to consistency and our obligation to God, accomplish what we had intended. ¶ *Out of that which ye have.* According to your ability; see ver. 12. It should be in proportion to your means.

12. *For if there be first a willing mind.* If there is a *readiness* (προ-ϑυμία), a disposition to give ; if the

heart is in it, then the offering will be acceptable to God, whether you be able to give much or little. A willing mind is the first consideration. No donation, however large, can be acceptable where that does not exist ; none, however small, can be otherwise than acceptable where that is found. This had relation as used by Paul to the duty of almsgiving ; but the *principle* is as applicable to every thing in the way of duty. A willing mind is the first and main thing. It is that which God chiefly desires, and that without which every thing else will be offensive, hypocritical, and vain ; see Note, chap. ix. 7. ¶ It is *accepted.* Doddridge, Rosenmüller, Macknight, and some others apply this to the person, and render it, " *he* is accepted ;" but the more usual, and the more natural interpretation is to apply it to the gift—*it* is accepted. God will approve of it, and will receive it favourably. ¶ *According to that a man hath,* &c. He is not required to give what he has not. His obligation is proportioned to his ability. His offering is acceptable to God according to the largeness and willingness of his heart, and not according to the narrowness of his fortune.— *Locke.* If the means are small, if the individual is poor, and if the gift shall be, therefore, small in amount, yet it may be proof of a larger heart and of more true love to God and his cause than when a much more ample benefaction is made by one in better circumstances. This sentiment the Saviour expressly stated and defended in the case of the poor widow ; Mark xii. 42—44 ; Luke xxi. 1—4. She who had cast in her two mites into the treasury had put in more than all which the rich men had contributed, for they had given of their abundance, but she had cast in all that she had, even all her living. The great and obviously just and equal principle here stated, was originally applied by Paul to the duty of giving alms. But it is

willing mind, *it is* accepted according to that a man hath, *and* not according to that he hath not.

---

equally true and just as applied to all the duties which we owe to God. He demands, (1.) A willing mind, a heart disposed to yield obedience. He claims that our service should be voluntary and sincere, and that we should make an unreserved consecration of what we have. Secondly, he demands only what we have power to render. He requires a service strictly according to our ability, and to be measured by that. He demands no more than our powers are fitted to produce; no more than we are able to render. *Our obligations in all cases are limited by our ability.* This is obviously the rule of equity, and this is all that is anywhere demanded in the Bible, and this *is* everywhere demanded. Thus our love to him is to be in proportion to *our* ability, and not to be graduated by the ability of angels or other beings. " And thou shalt love the Lord thy God with ALL THY heart, and with *all* THY soul, and with *all* THY mind, and with *all* THY strength;" Mark xii. 30. Here the obligation is limited by the ability, and the love is to be commensurate with the ability. So of repentance, faith, and of obedience in any form. None but a tyrant ever demands more than can be rendered; and to demand more is the appropriate description of a tyrant, and cannot appertain to the ever-blessed God. Thirdly, if there is any service rendered to God, according to the ability, it is accepted of him. It may not be as much or as valuable as may be rendered by beings of higher powers; it may not be as much as we would desire to render, but it is all that God demands, and is acceptable to him. The poor widow was not able to give as much as the rich man; but her offering was equally acceptable, and *might* be more valuable, for it would be accompanied with her prayers. The service which *we* can render to God may not be equal to that which the angels render; but it may be equally appropriate to

13 For *I mean* not that other men be eased, and ye burdened :

14 But by an equality, *that* now at this time your abundance

---

our condition and our powers, and may be equally acceptable to God. God may be *as well pleased* with the sighings of penitence as the praises of angels; with the offerings of a broken and a contrite heart as with the loud hallelujahs of unfallen beings in heaven.

13. *For* I mean *not that other men be eased,* &c. I do not intend that others should be eased in order to relieve you. Literally, " Not that there should be *rest* (ἄνεσις, *a letting loose; remission, relaxation*) to others, but *affliction* (θλίψις) to you." Probably the Corinthians were able to contribute more than many other churches, certainly more than the churches of Macedonia (ver. 2), and Paul therefore presses upon them the duty of giving according to their means, yet he by no means intended that the entire burden should come on them.

14. *But by an equality.* On just and equal principles. ¶ *That now at this time,* &c. That at the present time your abundance may be a supply for their wants, so that at some future time, if there should be occasion for it, their abundance may be a supply for your wants. The idea is this. Corinth was then able to give liberally, but many of the other churches were not. They were poor, and perhaps persecuted and in affliction. But there might be great reverses in their condition. Corinth might be reduced from its affluence, and might itself become dependent on the aid of others, or might be unable to contribute any considerable amount for the purposes of charity. The members of the church in Corinth, therefore, should so act in their circumstances of prosperity, that others would be disposed to aid them should their condition ever be such as to demand it. And the doctrine here taught is, (1.) That the support of the objects of benevolence should be on *equal* principles. The rich should bear an equal

may be a supply for their want, that their abundance also may be *a supply* for your want, that there may be equality :

15 As it is written, *a* He that *had gathered* much had nothing over ; and he that *had gathered* little had no lack.

a Ex.16.18.

and fair proportion, and if more frequent demands are made on their benefaction than on others they should not complain. (2.) Christians should contribute liberally while they have the means. In the vicissitudes of life no one can tell how soon he may be unable to contribute, or may even be dependent on the charity of others himself. A change in the commercial world ; losses by fire or at sea ; want of success in business ; loss of health, and the failure of his plans, may soon render him unable to aid the cause of benevolence. While he is prospered he should embrace every opportunity to do good to all. Some of the most painful regrets which men ever have, arise from the reflection that when prospered they were indisposed to give to benefit others, and when their property is swept away they become unable. God often sweeps away the property which they were *indisposed* to contribute to aid others, and leaves them to penury and want. Too late they regret that they were not the liberal patrons of the objects of benevolence when they were able to be. ¶ *That there may be equality.* That all may be just and equal. That no unjust burden should be borne by any one portion of the great family of the redeemed. Every Christian brother should bear his due proportion.

15. *As it is written;* see Ex. xvi. 18. ¶ *He that* had gathered *much,* &c. This passage was originally applied to the gathering of manna by the children of Israel. The manna which fell around the camp of Israel was gathered every morning. All that were able were employed in gathering it ; and when it was collected it was distributed in the proportion of an omer, or about five pints to each man. Some would be more active and more successful than others. Some by age or infirmity would collect little ; probably many by being confined to the camp would collect

none. They who had gathered more than an omer, therefore, would in this way contribute to the wants of others, and would be constantly manifesting a spirit of benevolence. And such was their willingness to do good in this way, such their readiness to collect more than they knew would be demanded for their own use, and such the arrangement of Providence in furnishing it, that there was no want ; and there was no more gathered than was needful to supply the demands of the whole. Paul applies this passage, therefore, in the very spirit in which it was originally penned. He means to say that the rich Christians at Corinth should impart freely to their poorer brethren. They had gathered more wealth than was immediately necessary for their families or themselves. They should, therefore, impart freely to those who had been less successful. Wealth, like manna, is the gift of God. It is like that spread by his hand around us every day. Some are able to gather much more than others. By their skill, their health, their diligence, or by providential arrangements, they are eminently successful. Others are feeble, or sick, or aged, or destitute of skill, and are less successful. All that is obtained is by the arrangement of God. The health, the strength, the skill, the wisdom by which we are enabled to obtain it, are all his gift. That which is thus honestly obtained, therefore, should be regarded as *his* bounty, and we should esteem it a privilege daily to impart to others less favoured and less successful. Thus society will be bound more closely together. There will be, as there was among the Israelites, the feelings of universal brotherhood. There will be on the one hand the happiness flowing from the constant exercise of the benevolent feelings ; on the other the strong ties of gratitude. On the one hand the evils of poverty will be prevented,

16 But thanks *be* to God, which put the same earnest care into the heart of Titus for you.

17 For indeed he accepted the exhortation; *a* but being more for-

a ver.6.

and on the other the not less, though different evils resulting from superabundant wealth. Is it a forced and unnatural analogy also to observe, that wealth, like manna, corrupts by being kept in store? Manna if kept more than a single day became foul and loathsome. Does not wealth hoarded up when it might be properly employed; wealth that *should* have been distributed to relieve the wants of others, become corrupting in its nature, and offensive in the sight of holy and benevolent minds? comp. James v. 2—4. Wealth, like manna, should be employed in the service which God designs—employed to diffuse everywhere the blessings of religion, comfort, and peace.

16. *But thanks* be *to God.* Paul regarded every right feeling, and every pure desire; every inclination to serve God or to benefit a fellow mortal, as the gift of God. He, therefore, ascribes the praise to him that Titus was disposed to show an interest in the welfare of the Corinthians. ¶ *The same earnest care.* The earnest care here referred to was that the Corinthians might complete the collection, and finish what they had proposed. Titus was willing to undertake this, and see that it was done. ¶ *For you.* For your completing the collection. Paul represents it as being done *for* them, or for their welfare. The poor saints in Judea indeed were to have the immediate benefit of the contribution, but it was a privilege for them to give, and Paul rejoiced that they had that privilege. A man who presents to Christians a feasible object of benevolence, and who furnishes them an opportunity of doing good to others, is doing good to them, and they should esteem it an act of kindness done to them.

17. *For indeed he accepted the exhortation.* He cheerfully complied with the exhortation which I gave

ward, of his own accord he went unto you.

18 And we have sent with him the brother, *b* whose praise *is* in the gospel throughout all the churches:

b chap.12 18.

him, to wit, to visit you, and excite you to this good work. ¶ *But being more forward.* More disposed to do this than I had supposed. The idea here is, that he was very ready to engage in this; he was more ready to engage in it than Paul was to exhort him to it; he anticipated his request; he had already resolved to engage in it. ¶ *Of his own accord he went,* &c. He went voluntarily and without urging. The ground of Paul's thankfulness here seems to have been this. He apprehended probably some difficulty in obtaining the collection there. He was acquainted with the distracted state of the church, and feared that Titus might have some reluctance to engage in the service. He was therefore very agreeably surprised when he learned that Titus was willing to make another journey to Corinth and to endeavour to complete the collection.

18. *And we have sent with him the brother.* It has been generally supposed that this anonymous brother was Luke. Some have supposed however that it was Mark, others that it was Silas or Barnabas. It is impossible to determine with certainty who it was, nor is it material to know. Whoever it was, it was some one well known, in whom the church at Corinth could have entire confidence. It is remarkable that though Paul mentions him again (chap. xii. 18), he does it also in the same manner, without specifying his name. The only circumstances that can throw any light on this are, (1.) That Luke was the companion and intimate friend of Paul, and attended him in his travels. From Acts xvi. 10, 11, where Luke uses the term "*we*," it appears that he was with Paul when he first went into Macedonia, and from ver. 15 it is clear that he went with Paul to Philippi. From Acts xvii. 1, where Luke alters his style and uses the term "they," it is evident that he did

19 And not *that* only, but who was also chosen *a* of the churches to travel with us with this [1] grace, which is administered by us to *b*

a 1 Cor.16.3,4.   1 or, *gift.*

the glory of the same Lord, and *declaration of* your ready mind :

20 Avoiding this, that no man should blame us in this abun-

b chap.4.15.

not accompany Paul and Silas when they went to Thessalonica, but either remained at Philippi or departed to some other place. He did not join them again until they went to Troas on the way to Jerusalem; Acts xx. 5. In what manner Luke spent the interval is not known. Macknight supposes that it might have been in multiplying copies of his gospel for the use of the churches. Perhaps also he might have been engaged in preaching, and in services like that in the case before us. (2.) It seems probable that Luke is the person referred to by the phrase "whose praise is in the gospel throughout all the churches." This would be more likely to be applied to one who had written a gospel, or a life of the Redeemer that had been extensively circulated, than to any other person. Still it is by no means *certain* that he is the person here referred to, nor is it of material consequence. ¶ *Whose praise.* Who is well known and highly esteemed. ¶ Is *in the gospel.* Either for writing the gospel, or for preaching the gospel. The Greek will bear either construction. In some way he was celebrated for making known the truths of the gospel.

19. *And not* that *only.* Not only is he esteemed on account of other services which he has rendered by his preaching and writings; but he has had a new mark of the confidence of the churches in being appointed to convey the collection to Jerusalem. ¶ *Chosen of the churches.* Chosen by the churches. Many concurred in the choice, showing that they had entire confidence in him. Paul had been unwilling to have charge of this contribution alone (1 Cor. xvi. 3, 4 ; comp. ver. 20), and he had procured the appointment of some one to undertake it. Probably he expected that the church at Corinth would concur in this appointment. ¶ *With this* ϒrace. Marg. " *Gift;*" see ver. 1.

The word here refers to the alms, or the collection which had been made. ¶ *Which is administered by us.* That is, which is undertaken by us. Paul had been the instrument of procuring it. ¶ *To the glory of the same Lord.* The Lord of us all. The design was to promote the glory of the Lord by showing the influence of religion in producing true benevolence. ¶ *And declaration of your ready mind.* That is, to afford you an opportunity of evincing your readiness to do good to others, and to promote their welfare.

20. *Avoiding this.* That is, I intend to prevent any blame from being cast upon me in regard to the management of these funds. For this purpose Paul had refused to have the entire management of the funds (see 1 Cor. xii. 3, 4), and had secured the appointment of one who had the entire confidence of all the churches. ¶ *That no man should blame us.* That no one should have any occasion to say that I had appropriated it to my own use or contrary to the will of the donors. Paul felt how dangerous it was for ministers to have much to do with money matters. He had a very deep impression of the necessity of keeping his own character free from suspicion on this subject. He knew how easy it might be for his enemies to raise the charge that he had embezzled the funds and appropriated them to his own use. He therefore insisted on having associated with him some one who had the entire confidence of the churches, and who should be appointed by them, and thus he was certain of being for ever free from blame on the subject. A most important example for all ministers in regard to the pecuniary benefactions of the churches. ¶ *In this abundance,* &c. In this large amount which is contributed by the churches and committed to our disposal. Large sums of money are in our time committed to the ministers of the gospel in the

dance which is administered by us:

21 Providing for honest *a* things,

a Ro.12.17; Ph.4.8; 1 Pe.2.12.

not only in the sight of the Lord, but also in the sight of men.

22 And we have sent with them

execution of the objects of Christian benevolence. Nothing can be more wise than the example of Paul here, that they should have associated with them others who have the entire confidence of the churches, that there may not be occasion for slander to move her poisonous tongue against the ministers of religion.

21. *Providing for honest things.* The expression here used occurs in Rom. xii. 17; see the Note on that place. In that place, however, it refers to the manner in which we are to treat those who injure us; here it refers to the right way of using property; and it seems to have been a kind of maxim by which Paul regulated his life, a *vade mecum* that was applicable to every thing. The sentiment is, that we are to see to it beforehand that all our conduct shall be comely or honest. The word rendered "providing for" (προνοούμενοι) means foreseeing, or perceiving beforehand; and the idea is, that we are to make it a matter of previous calculation, a settled plan, a thing that is to be attended to of set design. In the middle voice, the form in which it occurs here, it means to provide for in one's own behalf; to apply oneself to any thing; to practise diligently. *Robinson.* The word rendered "things honest" (καλά) means properly beautiful, or, comely. The idea which is presented here is, that we are to see beforehand, or we are to make it a matter of set purpose that what we do shall be comely, *i. e.* just, honourable, correct, not only in the sight of the Lord, but in the sight of men. Paul applies this in his own case to the alms which were to be intrusted to him. His idea is, that he meant so to conduct in the whole transaction as that his conduct should be approved by God, but that it should also be regarded as *beautiful* or correct in the sight of men. He knew how much his own usefulness depended on an irreproachable character. He, there-

fore, procured the appointment of one who had the entire confidence of the churches to travel with him. But there is no reason for confining this to the particular case under consideration. It seems to have been the leading maxim of the life of Paul, and it should be of ours. The maxim may be applied to every thing which we have to do; and should constantly regulate us. It may be applied to the acquisition and use of property; to the discharge of our professional duties; to our intercourse with others; to our treatment of inferiors and dependents; to our charities, &c.—in all of which we should make it a matter of previous thought, of earnest diligence, that our conduct should be perfectly honest and comely before God and man. Let us learn from this verse also, that ministers of the gospel should be especially careful that their conduct in money matters, and especially in the appropriation of the charities of the church, should be above suspicion. Much is often intrusted to their care, and the churches and individual Christians often commit much to their discretion. Their conduct in this should be without reproach; and in order to this, it is well to follow the example of Paul, and to insist that others who have the entire confidence of the churches should be associated with them. Nothing is easier than to raise a slanderous report against a minister of the gospel; and nothing gratifies a wicked world more than to be able to do it—and perhaps especially if it pertains to some improper use of money. It is not easy to meet such reports when they are started; and a minister, therefore, should be guarded, as Paul was, at every possible point, that he may be freed from that "whose breath outvenoms all the worms of Nile"—SLANDER.

22. *And we have sent with them our brother.* Who this was is wholly unknown, and conjecture is useless.

our brother, whom we have often-times proved diligent in many things, but now much more diligent, upon the great confidence which [1] *I have* in you.

23 Whether *any do inquire*

1 or, *he hath.*

of Titus, *he is* my partner and fellow-helper concerning you; or our brethren *be inquired of*, *they are* the messengers [a] of the churches, *and* the glory of Christ.

a Ph.2.25.

Some have supposed that it was Apollos, others Silas, others Timothy. But there are no means of ascertaining who it was; nor is it material. It was some one in whom Paul had entire confidence. ¶ *Whom we have oftentimes proved diligent.* Of whom we have evidence that he has been faithful. It is evident, therefore, that he had been the companion and fellow-labourer of Paul. ¶ *But now much more diligent,* &c. Who will now prove himself much more diligent than ever before. ¶ *Upon the confidence,* &c. Marg. "he hath." The margin is doubtless the more correct reading here. The idea is, that this brother had great confidence in the Corinthians that they would give liberally, and that he would, therefore, evince special diligence in the business.

23. *Whether* any do inquire *of Titus.* It is to be observed that the words " any do inquire " are not in the original; nor is it clear that these are the most proper words to be introduced here. The Greek may mean either, " if any do inquire about Titus," or it may mean " if any thing is to be said about Titus." The sense of the passage may either be, that some of the faction at Corinth might be disposed to inquire about the authority of Titus to engage in this work, or that Paul having said so much in commendation of the persons who went with Titus, it seemed proper also to say something in his favour also. The idea is, " If any inquiry is made from any quarter about him, or if it is necessary from any cause to say any thing about him, I would say he is my partner," &c. ¶ He is *my partner,* &c. He partakes with me in preaching the gospel, and in establishing and organizing churches; comp. Tit. i 5. To the Corinthians this fact would be a sufficient commendation of Titus.

¶ *Or our brethren* be inquired of. That is, the brethren who accompanied Titus. If any inquiry was made about their character, or if it was necessary to say any thing in regard to them. ¶ They are *the messengers of the churches.* They have the entire confidence of the churches, having been selected and appointed by them to a work of labour and responsibility; comp. Phil. ii. 25. The words here rendered "messengers of the churches," are in the original " apostles of the churches," (ἀπόστολοι ἐκκλησιῶν). The word *apostles* here is used evidently in its proper sense, to denote one who is sent out to transact any business for others, or as an agent or legate. These persons were not *apostles* in the technical sense, and this is an instance where the word is applied in the New Testament to those who had no claim to the apostolic office. It is also applied in a similar way to Apollos and Barnabas, though neither, strictly speaking, were apostles. ¶ And *the glory of Christ.* That is, they have a character so well known and established for piety; they are so eminent Christians and do such honour to the Christian name and calling, that they may be called the glory of Christ. It is an honour to Christ that he has called such persons into his church, and that he has so richly endowed them. Every Christian should so live as that it would appear to all the world that it was an honour and glory to the Redeemer that he had such followers; an honour to his gospel that it had converted such and brought them into his kingdom. It is sufficient honour, moreover, to any man to say that he is "the glory of Christ." Such a character should be, and will be, as it was here, a recommendation sufficient for any to secure them the confidence of others.

24 Wherefore shew ye to them, and before the churches, the proof of your love, and of our boasting[a] on your behalf.

a chap.7.14.

24. *Wherefore show ye to them, &c.* By a liberal contribution in the cause in which they are engaged and for which they have come among you now, furnish the evidence that you love me and the Christian cause, and show that I have not boasted of you in vain. ¶ *The proof of your love.* Your love to me, to God, to the cause of religion; see Note on ver. 8. ¶ *And of our boasting, &c.* My boasting that you would give liberally to the object; see Note, chap. vii. 14. Let it now be seen that my boasting was well founded, and that I properly understood your character, and your readiness to contribute to the objects of Christian benevolence.

REMARKS.

1. Let us bear in mind that a disposition to be liberal proceeds only from God, ver. 1. The human heart is by nature selfish, and indisposed to benevolence. It is only by the grace of God that men are excited to liberality; and we should therefore *pray* for this as well as for all other graces. We should beseech God to remove selfishness from our minds; to dispose us to feel as we should feel for the wants of others, and to incline us to give just what we *ought* to give to relieve them in trouble, and to promote their temporal and eternal welfare.

2. It is an inestimable blessing when God gives a spirit of liberality to the church, ver. 1. It should be regarded as a proof of his special favour; and as an evidence of the prevalence of the principles of true religion.

3. Men are often most liberal when in circumstances of distress, perplexity, and affliction, ver. 2. Prosperity often freezes the heart, but adversity opens it. Success in life often closes the hand of benevolence, but adversity opens it. We are taught to feel for the sufferings of others by suffering ourselves; and in the school of adversity we learn invaluable lessons of benevolence which we should never

acquire in prosperity. If you want the tear of sympathy: if you want aid in a good cause, go to a man in affliction, and his heart is open. And hence it is that God often suffers his people to pass through trials in order that they may possess the spirit of large and active benevolence.

4. If Christians desire to be liberal they must *first* devote themselves to God, ver. 5. If this is not done they will have no heart to give, and they will not give. They will have a thousand excuses ready, and there will be no ground of appeal which we can make to them. True liberality is always based on the fact that we have given ourselves wholly to God.

5. When Christians have honestly devoted *themselves* to God, it will be easy to contribute liberally to the cause of benevolence, ver. 5. They will find *something* to give; or if they have nothing now they will labour and deny themselves in order that they may have something to give. If every professed Christian on earth had honestly given *himself* to God, and should act in accordance with this, the channels of benevolence would never be dry.

6. We should compare ourselves in the matter of benevolence with the churches here referred to, ver. 3. They were poor; they were in deep affliction, and yet they contributed all in their power, and beyond their power. Do we do this? Do we give according to our ability? Do we deny ourselves of one comfort? withhold one gratification? curtail one expense which fashion demands, in order that we may have the means of doing good? O! if every Christian would give according to his ability to the sacred cause of charity, how soon would the means be ample to place the Bible in every family on the globe, to preach the gospel in every country, and to maintain all the institutions which the cause of humanity needs in this and in other lands.

7. The Christian character is in-

complete unless there is a spirit of large and liberal beneficence, ver. 7. This is indispensable to the proper symmetry of the Christian graces, and this should be cultivated in order to give beauty and completeness to the whole. Yet it cannot be denied that there are true Christians where this is wanting. There are those who give every other evidence of piety ; who are men of prayer, and who evince humility, and who are submissive in trials, and whose conversation is that of Christians, who are yet sadly deficient in this virtue. Either by an original closeness of disposition, or by a defect of education, or by want of information in regard to the objects of Christian benevolence, they are most stinted in their benefactions, and often excite the amazement of others that they give so little to the cause of benevolence. Such persons should be entreated to carry out their Christian character to completion. As they abound in other things, they should abound in this grace also. They are depriving themselves of much comfort, and are bringing much injury on the cause of the Redeemer while they refuse to sustain the great objects of Christian charity. No Christian character is symmetrical or complete unless it is crowned with the spirit of large and comprehensive benevolence towards every object that tends to promote the temporal and eternal welfare of man.

8. The sincerity of our love should be tested, and will be, by our readiness to deny ourselves to do good to others, ver. 8. The love of the Lord Jesus was tested in that way ; and there can be no true love to God or man where there is not a readiness to contribute of our means for the welfare of others. If we love the Redeemer we shall devote all to his service ; if we love our fellow-men we shall evince our "sincerity" by being willing to part with our earthly substance to alleviate their woes, enlighten their ignorance, and save their souls.

9. Let us imitate the example of the Lord Jesus, ver. 9. He was rich, yet he became poor ; and, O ! how

poor ! Let the rich learn to copy his example, and be willing to part with their abundant and superfluous wealth in order that they may relieve and benefit others. That man is most happy as well as most useful, who most resembles the Redeemer ; that man will be most happy who stoops from the highest earthly elevation to the lowest condition that he may minister to the welfare of others.

10. Charity should be voluntary, ver. 12. It should be the free and spontaneous offering of the heart ; and the first promptings of the heart, before the pleadings of avarice come in, and the heart grows cold by the influence of returning covetousness, are likely to be the most correct.

11. Charity should be in an honest proportion to our means, ver. 12. It should be according to what a man hath. God hath left the determination of this proportion to every individual, responsible to him alone. He has not told us how much we shall give, or in what proportion we shall give ; but he has left it for every individual to decide what he *may* give, and what he *ought* to give.

12. If men do not give according to their means they must answer for it to God. Every man may have opportunity to contribute to relieve others if he will open his heart and ears to the cries of a suffering and a dying world. No man can complain that he has no opportunity to give ; or that he may not procure for his own soul all the blessings which can be produced by the most large and liberal benevolence.

13. Men have no excuse for being lost, ver. 12. If God required more of them than they could render they would have excuse. They would not be to blame. They might be sufferers and martyrs in hell, but no one would blame them. But the sinner can never have any such excuse. God never required any more of him than he had power to render ; and if he dies it will be his own fault, and the throne of God will still be spotless and pure.

14. God's government is an equal, and just, and good government, ver. 12. What can be more equitable than

CHAPTER IX.

FOR as touching the minister-ing *a* to the saints, it is

a chap.8.4, &c.

the principle that a man is accepted according to what he has? What ground of complaint can the sinner have in regard to this administration?

15. The churches should bear their just proportion in the cause of Christian beneficence, ver. 13—15. There *are* great interests of charity which MUST be sustained. The world cannot do without them. Not only must the poor be provided for, but the cause of temperance, and of Sabbath-schools, and of missions must be sustained. Bibles *must* be distributed, and men must be educated for the ministry, and the widow and the fatherless must be the objects of Christian benevolence. These burdens, if they are burdens, should be equally distributed. The rich should furnish *their fair propor-tion* in sustaining them; and those in more moderate circumstances must do *their* fair proportion also in sustaining them. If this were done, all the objects of Christian benevolence could be sustained, and they would in fact not be burdensome to the churches. With infinite ease all might be contributed that is necessary to send the gospel around the world.

16. Ministers of the gospel should have as little as possible to do with money matters, ver. 19—21. While they should be willing, if it is necessary, to be the almoners of the churches, and should esteem it a privilege to be the means of conveying to the poor and needy, and to the great cause of benevolence, what the churches may choose to commit to them, yet they should not covet this office; they should not show any particular desire for it; nor should they do it unless, like Paul, they have the most ample security that the voice of slander can never be raised in regard to their management. Let them see to it that they have persons associated with them who have the entire confidence of the churches; men who will be re-sponsible also, and who will be com-petent witnesses of the manner in

superfluous for me to write to you:

2 For I know the forwardness

which they discharge their duty. In all things ministers should be pure. On few points is there more danger that the enemy will endeavour to take advantage, and to injure their char-acter, than in regard to their abuse of funds intrusted to their care.

17. Let all Christians so live that it may be honestly said of them they are "the glory of Christ," ver. 23. Let them aim so to live that it will be esteemed to be an honour to the Re-deemer that he called them into his kingdom, and that he so richly en-dowed them by his grace. *This* would be a commendation to all men where they might go; to say this is enough to say of any man. None can have a higher character than to have it said with truth of him "he is the glory of Christ; he is an honour to his Re-deemer and to his cause."

CHAPTER IX.

IN this chapter the apostle con-tinues the subject which he had dis-cussed in chap. viii.—the collection which he had purposed to make for the poor saints in Judea. The deep anxiety which he had that the collec-tion should be liberal; that it should not only be such as to be really an aid to those who were suffering, but be such as would be an expression of tender attachment to them on the part of the Gentile converts, was the rea-son, doubtless, why Paul urged this so much on their attention. His primary wish undoubtedly was, to furnish aid to those who were suffering. But in connection with that, he also wished to excite a deep interest among the Gentile converts in behalf of those who had been converted to Christian-ity among the Jews. He wished that the collection should be so liberal as to show that they felt that they were united as brethren, and that they were grateful that they had received the true religion from the Jews. And he doubtless wished to cement as much as possible the great body of the Christian brotherhood, and to impress

of your mind, for which I boast of you to them of Macedonia, that Achaia was ready a year ago ; and your zeal hath provoked very many.

3 Yet have I sent the brethren, lest our boasting of you should be in vain in this behalf ; that, as I said, ye may be ready :

4 Lest haply if they of Macedonia come with me, and find you unprepared, we (that we say not, ye) should be ashamed in this same confident boasting. *a*

---

a chap. 8. 24.

---

on their minds the great truths that whatever was their national origin, and whatever were their national distinctions, yet in Christ they were one. For this purpose he presses on their attention a great variety of considerations why they should give liberally, and this chapter is chiefly occupied in stating reasons for that in addition to those which had been urged in the previous chapter. The following view will present the main points in the chapter.

(1.) He was aware of their readiness to give, and knowing this, he had boasted of it to others, and others had been excited to give liberally from what the apostle had said of them, ver. 1, 2. The *argument* here is, that Paul's veracity and their own character were at stake and depended on their now giving liberally.

(2.) He had sent the brethren to them in order that there might by no possibility be a *failure,* ver. 3—5. Though he had the utmost confidence in them, and fully believed that they were disposed to give liberally, yet he knew also that something might prevent it unless messengers went to secure the contributions, and that the consequence might be, that he and they would be " ashamed " that he had boasted so much of their readiness to give.

(3.) To excite them to give liberally, Paul advances the great principles that the reward in heaven will be in proportion to the liberality evinced on earth, and that God loves one who gives cheerfully, ver. 6, 7. By the prospect, therefore, of an ample reward, and by the desire to meet with the approbation of God, he calls upon them to contribute freely to aid their afflicted Christian brethren.

(4.) He further excites them to lib-eral giving by the consideration that if they contributed liberally, God was able to furnish them abundantly with the means of doing good on a large scale in time to come, ver. 8—11. In this way he would enable them to do good hereafter in proportion as they were disposed to do good now, and the result of all would be, that abundant thanks would be rendered to God— thanks from those who were aided, and thanks from those who had aided them that they had been enabled to contribute to supply their wants.

(5.) As a final consideration inducing them to give, the apostle states that not only would they thus do good, but would show the power of the gospel, and the affection which they had for the Jewish converts, and would thus contribute much in promoting the glory of God. The Jewish converts would see the power of the gospel on their Gentile brethren ; they would feel that they now appertained to one great family; they would praise God for imparting his grace in this manner ; and they would be led to pray much for those who had thus contributed to alleviate their wants, ver. 12—14.

(6.) Paul closes the whole chapter, and the whole discussion respecting the contribution about which he had felt so deep an interest, by rendering thanks to God for his " unspeakable gift," JESUS CHRIST, ver. 15. Paul was ever ready, whatever was the topic before him, to turn the attention to him. He here evidently regards him as the author of all liberal feeling, and of all true charity ; and seems to imply that all that *they* could give would be small compared with the " unspeakable gift " of God, and that the fact that God had imparted *such* a gift to the world was a reason why *they* should be willing to devote all they had to his service.

1. *For as touching the ministering to the saints.* In regard to the collection that was to be taken up for the aid of the poor Christians in Judea; see Notes on Rom. xv. 26; 1 Cor. xvi. 1; 2 Cor. viii. ¶ *It is superfluous,* &c. It is needless to urge that matter on you, because I know that you acknowledge the obligation to do it, and have already purposed it. ¶ *For me to write to you.* That is, to write more, or to write largely on the subject. It is unnecessary for me to urge arguments why it should be done; and all that is proper is to offer some suggestions in regard to the *manner* in which it shall be accomplished.

9. *For I know the forwardness of your mind.* I know your promptitude, or your readiness to do it; see chap. viii. 10. Probably Paul here means that he had had opportunity before of witnessing their readiness to do good, and that he had learned in particular of Titus that they had formed the plan to aid in this contribution. ¶ *For which I boast of you to them of Macedonia.* To the church in Macedonia; see chap. viii. 1. So well assured was he that the church at Corinth would make the collection as it had proposed, that he boasted of it to the churches of Macedonia as if it were already done, and made use of this as an argument to stimulate them to make an effort. ¶ *That Achaia was ready a year ago.* Achaia was that part of Greece of which Corinth was the capital; see Note, Acts xviii. 12. It is probable that there were Christians in other parts of Achaia besides Corinth, and indeed it is known that there was a church in Cenchrea (see Rom. xvi. 1.) which was one of the ports of Corinth. Though the contribution would be chiefly derived from Corinth, yet it is probable that the others also would participate in it. The phrase "was ready" means that they had been preparing themselves for this collection, and doubtless Paul had stated that the collection was already made and was waiting. He had directed them (1

Cor. xvi. 1.) to make it on the first day of the week, and to lay it by in store, and he did not doubt that they had complied with his request. ¶ *And your zeal.* Your ardour and promptitude. The readiness with which you entered into this subject, and your desire to relieve the wants of others. ¶ *Hath provoked.* Has roused, excited, impelled to give. We use the word *provoke* commonly now in the sense of *to irritate,* but in the Scriptures it is confined to the signification of *exciting,* or rousing. The ardour of the Corinthians would excite others not only by their promptitude, but because Corinth was a splendid city, and their example would be looked up to by Christians at a distance. This is one instance of the effect which will be produced by the example of a church in a city.

3. *Yet have I sent the brethren.* The brethren referred to in chap. viii. 18, 22, 23. ¶ *Lest our boasting of you.* That you were disposed to contribute, and that you were already prepared, and that the contribution was ready. ¶ *Should be in vain.* Lest any thing should have occurred to prevent the collection. I have sent them that they may facilitate it, and that it may be secure and certain. ¶ *In this behalf.* In this respect. That is, lest our boasting of you, in regard to your readiness to contribute to relieve the wants of others, should be found to have been ill-grounded.

4. *Lest haply if they of Macedonia.* If any of the Macedonians should happen to come with me, and should find that you had done nothing. He does not say that they *would* come with him, but it was by no means improbable that they would. It was customary for some of the members of the churches to travel with Paul from place to place, and the intercourse was constant between Macedonia and Achaia. Paul had, therefore, every reason to suppose that some of the Macedonians would accompany him when he should go to Corinth. At all events it was probable that the Macedonians would learn from some quarter whether the

5 Therefore I thought it necessary to exhort the brethren, that they would go before unto you, and make up beforehand your [1] bounty, [2] whereof ye had notice before, that the same might be ready, as *a mat-*

[1] *blessing.*   [2] or, *which hath been so much spoken of before.*

ter of bounty, and not as *of* covetousness.

6 But this *I say,* He [a] which soweth sparingly shall reap also sparingly ; and he which soweth bountifully shall reap also bountifully.

[a] Ps.41.1—3 ; Pr.11.24,25 ; 19.17 ; 22.9 ; Ga. 6.7,9.

Corinthians were or were not ready when Paul should go to them ¶ *We (that we say not ye) should be ashamed,* &c. " In this," says Bloomfield, " one cannot but recognise a most refined and delicate turn, inferior to none of the best classical writers." Paul had boasted confidently that the Corinthians would be ready with their collection. He had excited and stimulated the Macedonians by this consideration. He had induced them in this way to give liberally, chap. viii. 1—4. If now it should turn out after all that the Corinthians had given nothing, or had given stintedly, the character of Paul would suffer. His veracity and his judgment would be called in question, and he would be accused of trick, and artifice, and fraud in inducing them to give. Or if he should not be charged with dishonesty, yet he would be humbled and mortified himself that he had made representations which had proved to be so unfounded. But this was not all. The character of the Corinthians was also at stake. They had purposed to make the collection. They had left the impression in the mind of Paul that it would be done. They had hitherto evinced such a character as to make Paul confident that the collection would be made. If now by any means this should fail, their character would suffer, and they would have occasion to be ashamed that they had excited so confident expectations of what they would do.

5. *Therefore I thought it necessary,* &c. In order to *secure* the collection, and to avoid all unpleasant feeling on all hands. ¶ *That they would go before unto you.* Before I should come. ¶ *And make up beforehand your bounty.* Prepare it before I come. The word " bounty" is in the Marg. rendered " blessing." The Greek

(εὐλογία) means properly commendation, *eulogy.* Then it means blessing, praise applied to God. Then *that which blesses*—a gift, donation, favour, bounty—whether of God to men, or of one man to another. Here it refers to their contribution as that which would be adapted to confer *a blessing* on others, or fitted to produce happiness. ¶ *That the same might be ready as* a matter of *bounty.* That it may truly appear as a liberal and voluntary offering ; as an act of generosity and not as *wrung* or extorted from you. That it may be truly a *blessing*—a *thank-offering* to God and adapted to do good to men. ¶ *And not as of covetousness.* " And not like a sort of extortion, wrung from you by mere dint of importunity."—*Doddridge.* The word here used (πλεονεξία) means usually covetousness, greediness of gain, which leads a person to defraud others. The idea here is, that Paul would have them give this as an act of bounty, or liberality on their part, and not as an act of covetousness on his part, not as extorted by him from them.

6. *But this* I say. This I say in order to induce you to give liberally. This I say to prevent your supposing that because it is to be a voluntary offering you may give only from your superfluity, and may give sparingly. ¶ *He which soweth sparingly.* This expression has all the appearance of a proverb, and doubtless is such. It does not occur indeed elsewhere in the Scriptures, though substantially the same sentiment exciting to liberality often occurs ; see Ps. xli. 1—3 ; Prov. xi. 24, 25 ; xix. 17 ; xxii. 9. Paul here says that it is in giving as it is in agriculture. A man that sows little must expect to reap little. If he sows a small piece of land he will reap a small harvest ; or if he is niggardly in sowing and wishes to *save* his seed and

will not commit it to the earth, he must expect to reap little. So it is in giving. Money given in alms, money bestowed to aid the poor and needy, or to extend the influence of virtue and pure religion, is money bestowed in a way similar to the act of committing seed to the earth. It will be returned again in some way with an abundant increase. It shall not be lost. The seed may be buried long. It may lie in the ground with no indication of a return or of increase. One who knew not the arrangements of Providence might suppose it was lost and dead. But in due time it shall spring up and produce an ample increase. So with money given to objects of benevolence. To many it may seem to be a waste, or may appear to be thrown away. But in due time it will be repaid in some way with abundant increase. And the man who wishes to make the most out of his money for future use and personal comfort will give liberally to deserving objects of charity—just as the man who wishes to make the most out of his grain will not suffer it to lie in his granary, but will commit the seed to the fertile earth. " Cast thy bread upon the waters : for thou shalt find it again after many days" (Eccl. xi. 1); that is, when the waters as of the Nile have overflown the banks and flooded the whole adjacent country, then is the time to cast abroad thy seed. The waters will retire, and the seed will sink into the accumulated fertile mud that is deposited, and will spring up in an abundant harvest. So it is with that which is given for objects of benevolence. ¶ *Shall reap also sparingly.* Shall reap in proportion to what he sowed. This every one knows is true in regard to grain that is sowed. It is also no less true in regard to deeds of charity. The idea is, that God will bestow rewards in proportion to what is given. These rewards may refer to results in this life, or to the rewards in heaven, or both. All who have ever been in the habit of giving liberally to the objects of benevolence can testify that they have lost nothing, but have reaped in proportion to their liberality. This follows in various ways. (1.) In the *comfort* and peace which results from giving. If a man wishes to *purchase* happiness with his gold, he can secure the most by bestowing it liberally on objects of charity. It will produce him more immediate peace than it would to spend it in sensual gratifications, and far more than to hoard it up useless in his coffers. (2.) In reflection on it hereafter. It will produce more happiness in remembering that he has done good with it, and promoted the happiness of others, than it will to reflect that he has hoarded up useless wealth, or that he has squandered it in sensual gratification. The one will be unmingled pleasure when he comes to die ; the other will be unmingled self-reproach and pain. (3.) In subsequent life, God will in some way repay to him far more than he has bestowed in deeds of charity. By augmented prosperity, by health and future comfort, and by raising up for us and our families, when in distress and want, friends to aid us, God can and often does abundantly repay the liberal for all their acts of kindness and deeds of beneficence. (4.) God can and will reward his people in heaven abundantly for all their kindness to the poor, and all their self-denials in endeavouring to diffuse the influence of truth and the knowledge of salvation. Indeed the rewards of heaven will be in no small degree apportioned in this manner, and determined by the amount of benevolence which we have shown on earth ; see Mat. xxv. 34—40. On all accounts, therefore, we have every inducement to give liberally. As a farmer who desires an ample harvest scatters his seed with a liberal hand ; as he does not grudge it though it falls into the earth ; as he scatters it with the expectation that in due time it will spring up and reward his labours, so should we give with a liberal hand to aid the cause of benevolence, nor should we deem what we give to be lost or wasted though we wait long before *we* are recompensed, or though *we* should be in no other way rewarded than by the comfort which arises from the act of doing good.

7 Every man according as he purposeth in his heart, *so let him give;*

a De.15.7,8.

not *a* grudgingly, or of necessity : for God loveth a cheerful *b* giver.

b Ex.35 5 ; Ro.12 8.

7. *Every man according as he purposeth in his heart,* &c. The main idea in this verse is, that the act of giving should be voluntary and cheerful. It should not seem to be extorted by the importunity of others (ver. 6) ; nor should it be given from urgent necessity, but it should be given as an offering of the heart. On this part of the verse we may remark, (1.) That the heart is usually more concerned in the business of giving than the head. If liberality is evinced, it will be the heart which prompts to it ; if it is not evinced, it will be because the heart has some bad passions to gratify, and is under the influence of avarice, or selfishness, or some other improper attachment. Very often a man is convinced he *ought* to give liberally, but a narrow heart and a parsimonious spirit prevents it. (2.) We should follow the dictates of the heart in giving. I mean that a man will usually give more correctly who follows the first promptings of his heart when an object of charity is presented, than he will if he takes much time to deliberate. The instinctive prompting of a benevolent heart is to give liberally. And the *amount* which should be given will usually be suggested to a man by the better feelings of his heart. But if he resolves to deliberate much, and if he suffers the heart to grow cold, and if he defers it, the pleadings of avarice will come in, or some object of attachment or plan of life will rise to view, or he will begin to compare himself with others, and he will give much *less* than he would have done if he had followed the first impulse of feeling. God implanted the benevolent feelings in the bosom that they should prompt us to do good ; and he who acts most in accordance with them is most likely to do what he ought to do ; and in general it is the safest and best rule for a man to give just what *his heart* prompts him to give when an object of charity is presented. Man at best is too selfish to be likely to give too much or to go beyond his

means ; and if in a few instances it should be done, more would be gained in value in the cultivation of benevolent feeling than would be lost in money. I know of no better rule on the subject, than to cultivate as much as possible the benevolent feelings, and then to throw open the soul to every proper appeal to our charity, and to give just according to the instinctive prompting of the heart. (3.) Giving should be voluntary and cheerful. It should be from the heart. Yet there is much, very much that is not so, and there is, therefore, much benevolence that is *spasmodic* and spurious ; that cannot be depended on, and that will not endure. No dependence can be placed on a man in regard to giving who does not do it from the steady influences of a benevolent heart. But there is much obtained in the cause of benevolence that is produced by a kind of *extortion* It is given because others give, and the man would be ashamed to give less than they do. Or, it is given because he thinks his rank in life demands it, and he is prompted to do it by pride and vanity. Or, he gives from respect to a pastor or a friend, or because he is warmly importuned to give ; or because he is shut up to a kind of necessity to give, and must give or he would lose his character and become an object of scorn and detestation. In all this there is nothing cheerful and voluntary ; and there can be nothing in it acceptable to God. Nor can it be depended on permanently. The heart is not in it, and the man will evade the duty as soon as he can, and will soon find excuses for not giving at all. ¶ *Not grudgingly.* Greek, " Not of grief" (μὴ ἐκ λύπης). Not as if he were sorry to part with his money. Not as if he were constrained to do a thing that was extremely painful to him. ¶ *Or of necessity.* As if he were compelled to do it. Let him do it cheerfully. ¶ *For God loveth a cheerful giver.* And who does not? Valuable

8 And *a* God *is* able to make all grace abound toward you : that ye, always having all sufficiency

a Ph.4.19.

in all *things*, may abound to every good work :

9 (As it is written, *b* He hath

b Ps.112.9.

as any gift may be in itself, yet if it is forced and constrained ; if it can be procured only after great importunity and persevering effort, who can esteem it as desirable ? God desires the heart in every service. No service that is not cheerful and voluntary ; none that does not arise from true love to him can be acceptable in his sight. God loves it because it shows a heart like his own—a heart disposed to give cheerfully and do good on the largest scale possible ; and because it shows a heart attached from principle to his service and cause. The expression here has all the appearance of a proverb, and expressions similar to this occur often in the Scriptures. In an uninspired writer, also, this idea has been beautifully expanded. " In all thy gifts show a cheerful countenance, and dedicate thy tithes with gladness. Give unto the Most High according as he hath enriched thee : and as thou hast gotten give with a cheerful eye. For the Lord recompenseth, and will give thee seven times as much."—Wisdom of the Son of Sirach, chap. xxxv. 9—11. In nothing, therefore, is it more important than to examine the motives by which we give to the objects of benevolence. However liberal may be our benefactions, yet God may see that there is no sincerity, and may hate the spirit with which it is done.

8. *And God is able,* &c. Do not suppose that by giving liberally you will be impoverished and reduced to want. You should rather confide in God, who is able to furnish you abundantly with what is needful for the supply of your necessities. Few persons are ever reduced to poverty by liberality. Perhaps in the whole circle of his acquaintance it would be difficult for an individual to point out *one* who has been impoverished or made the poorer in this way. Our selfishness is generally a sufficient guard against this ; but it is also to be added, that the divine blessing rests

upon the liberal man, and that God keeps him from want. But in the mean time there are multitudes who are made poor by the want of liberality. They are parsimonious in giving, but they are extravagant in dress, and luxury, and in expenses for amusement or vice, and the consequence is poverty and want. " There is that withholdeth more than is meet, and it tendeth to poverty ;" Prov. xi. 24. The divine blessing rests upon the liberal ; and while every person should make a proper provision for his family, every one should give liberally, confiding in God that he will furnish the supplies for our future wants. Let this maxim be borne in mind, that no one is usually made the poorer by being liberal. ¶ *All grace.* All kinds of favour. He is able to impart to you those things which are needful for your welfare. ¶ *That ye always,* &c. The sense is, " If you give liberally you are to expect that God will furnish you with the means, so that you will be able to abound more and more in it." You are to expect that he will abundantly qualify you for doing good in every way, and that he will furnish you with all that is needful for this. The man who gives, therefore, should have faith in God. He should expect that God will bless him in it ; and the experience of the Christian world may be appealed to in proof that men are *not* made poor by liberality.

9. *As it is written.* Ps. cxii. 9. The idea is, " in this way will the saying in the Scriptures be verified, or the promise confirmed." The psalmist is describing the character of the righteous man. One of his characteristics, he says, is, that he has scattered abroad, he has given liberally to the poor. On such a man a blessing is pronounced (ver. 1) ; and one of the blessings will be that he shall be prospered. Some difficulty has been felt by commentators to see how the quotation here made sustains the position of Paul that the liberal man

dispersed abroad ; he hath given to the poor : his righteousness remaineth for ever.

10 Now he [a] that ministereth seed to the sower both minister

a Is.55.10.   b Hos.10.12.

would be blessed of God, and would receive an increase according to his liberality. In order to this, they have supposed (see Doddridge, Bloomfield, and Clarke) that the word "righteousness" means the same as almsgiving, or that "he would always have something to bestow." But I would suggest that perhaps Paul quoted this, as quotations are frequently made in the Scriptures, where a passage was familiar. He quotes only a part of the passage, meaning that the whole passage confirms the point under consideration. Thus the whole passage in the psalm is, "He hath dispersed ; he hath given to the poor ; his righteousness endureth for ever ; *his horn shall be exalted with honour;*" that is, he shall be abundantly blessed with prosperity and with the favour of God. Thus the entire promise sustains the position of Paul, that the liberal man would be abundantly blessed. The phrase "he hath dispersed" ('Εσκόρπισεν), may refer either to the act of sowing, as a man scatters seed on the earth ; or there may be an allusion to the oriental custom of scattering money among an assembled company of paupers ; comp. Prov. xi. 24. ¶ *His righteousness.* His deeds of beneficence. ¶ *Remaineth.* In its fruits and consequences ; that is, either in its effects on others, or on himself. It *may* mean that the sums so distributed will remain with him for ever, inasmuch as he will be supplied with all that is needful to enable him to do good to others. This interpretation accords with the connection.

10. *Now he that ministereth seed to the sower.* This is an expression of an earnest wish. In the previous verses he had stated the promises, or had shown what we had a right to *expect* as a consequence of liberality. He here unites the expression of an earnest desire that they might experience this themselves. The allusion

bread for *your* food, and multiply your seed sown, and increase the fruits [b] of your righteousness ;)

11 Being enriched in every thing to all bountifulness, [1] which

1 *simplicity,* or *liberality.*

is to the act of sowing seed. The idea is, that when a man scatters seed in his field God provides him with the means of *sowing again.* He not only gives him a harvest to supply his wants, but he blesses him also *in giving him the ability to sow again.* Such was the benevolent wish of Paul. He desired not only that God would supply their returning wants, but he desired also that he *would give them the ability to do good again;* that he would furnish them the means of future benevolence. He acknowledges God as the source of all increase, and wishes that they may experience the results of such increase. Perhaps in this language there is an allusion to Isa. lv. 10 ; and the idea is, that it is God who furnishes by his providence the seed to the sower. In like manner he will furnish you the means of doing good. ¶ *Minister bread for your food.* Furnish you with an ample supply for your wants. ¶ *Multiply your seed sown.* Greatly increase your means of doing good ; make the result of all your benefactions so to abound that you may have the means of doing good again, and on a larger scale, as the seed sown in the earth is so *increased* that the farmer may have the means of sowing more abundantly again. ¶ *And increase the fruits of your righteousness.* This evidently means, the results and effects of their benevolence. The word "righteousness" here refers to their liberality ; and the wish of the apostle is, that the results of their beneficence might greatly abound, that they might have the means of doing extensive good, and that they might be the means of diffusing happiness from afar.

11. *Being enriched in every thing,* &c. In all respects your riches are conferred on you for this purpose. The design of the apostle is to state to them the true reason why wealth was

a causeth through us thanksgiving to God.

12 For the administration of this service not only supplieth *b* the want of the saints, but is abun-

a chap.1.11; 4.15.   *b* chap.8.14.

bestowed. It was not for the purposes of luxury and self-gratification ; not to be spent in sensual enjoyment, not for parade and display ; it was that it might be distributed to others in such a way as to cause thanksgiving to God. At the same time, this implies the expression of an earnest wish on the part of Paul. He did not desire that they should be rich for their own gratification or pleasure ; he desired it only as the means of their doing good to others. Right feeling will desire properly only as the means of promoting happiness and producing thanksgiving to God. They who truly love their children and friends will wish them to be successful in acquiring wealth only that they may have the means and the disposition to alleviate misery, and promote the happiness of all around them. No one who has true benevolence will desire that any one in whom he feels an interest should be enriched for the purpose of living amidst luxury, and encompassing himself with the indulgences which wealth can furnish. If a man has not a disposition to do good with money, it is not true benevolence to desire that he may not possess it. ¶ *To all bountifulness.* Marg. Simplicity, or liberality. The word (ἁπλότης) means properly sincerity, candour, probity; then also simplicity, frankness, fidelity, and especially as manifesting itself in liberality ; see Rom. xii. 8 ; 2 Cor. viii. 2. Here it evidently means *liberality,* and the idea is, that property is given for this purpose, in order that there may be liberality evinced in doing good to others. ¶ *Which causeth through us,* &c. That is, we shall so distribute your alms as to cause thanksgiving to God. The result will be that by our instrumentality, thanks will be given to the great Source and Giver of all wealth. Property should *always* be so employed as to produce thanks-

dant also by many thanksgivings unto God ;

13 Whiles by the experiment of this ministration they glorify *c* God for your professed subjection

c Mat.5.16.

giving. If it is made to contribute to our own support and the support of our families, it should excite thanksgiving. If it is given to others, it should be *so* given, if it is possible, that the recipient should be more grateful *to God* than *to us ;* should feel that though we may be the honoured instrument in distributing it, yet the true benefactor is God.

12. *For the administration of this service.* The distribution of this proof of your liberality. The word *service* here, says Doddridge, intimates that this was to be regarded not merely as an act of *humanity,* but *religion.* ¶ *The want of the saints.* Of the poor Christians in Judea on whose behalf it was contributed. ¶ *But is abundant also by many thanksgivings unto God.* Will abound unto God in producing thanksgivings. The result will be that it will produce abundant thanksgiving in their hearts to God.

13. *Whiles by the experiment,* &c. Or rather, by the *experience* of this ministration ; the proof (δοκιμῆς), the evidence here furnished of your liberality. They shall in this ministration have *experience* or *proof* of your Christian principle. ¶ *They glorify God.* They will praise God as the source of your liberality, as having given you the means of being liberal, and having inclined your hearts to it. ¶ *For your professed subjection,* &c. Literally, " For the obedience of your profession of the gospel." It does not imply merely that there was a profession of religion, but that there was a *real* subjection to the gospel which they professed. This is not clearly expressed in our translation. Tindal has expressed it better, " Which praise God for your obedience in acknowledging the gospel of Christ." There was a real and sincere submission to the gospel of Christ, and that was manifested by their giving liberally to supply the wants of

unto the gospel of Christ, and for *your* liberal distribution unto them, and unto all *men ;*

14 And by their prayer for you,

a chap.8.1.

which long after you for the ex ceeding grace *a* of God in you.

15 Thanks *b be* unto God for his unspeakable gift.*c*

b James 1.17.　　　*c* John 3.16.

others. The doctrine is, that one evidence of true subjection to the gospel ; one proof that our profession is sincere and genuine, is a willingness to contribute to relieve the wants of the poor and afflicted friends of the Redeemer. *And unto all* men. That is, all others whom you may have the opportunity of relieving.

14. *And by their prayer for you.* On the grammatical construction of this difficult verse, Doddridge and Bloomfield may be consulted. It is probably to be taken in connection with ver. 12, and ver. 13 is a parenthesis. Thus interpreted, the sense will be, " The administration of this service (ver. 12) will produce abundant thanks to God. It will also (ver. 14) produce *another effect.* It will tend to excite the prayers of the saints for *you,* and thus produce important benefits to yourselves. They will earnestly desire your welfare, they will anxiously pray to be united in Christian friendship with those who have been so signally endowed with the grace of God." The sentiment is, that charity should be shown to poor and afflicted Christians because it will lead them to pray for us and to desire our welfare. The prayers of the poorest Christian for us are worth more than all we usually bestow on them in charity ; and he who has secured the pleadings of a child of God, however humble, in his behalf, has made a good use of his money. ¶ *Which long after you.* Who earnestly desire to see and know you. Who will sincerely desire your welfare, and who will thus be led to pray for you. ¶ *For the exceeding grace of God in you.* On account of the favour which God has shown to you ; the strength and power of the Christian principle, manifesting itself in doing good to those whom you have never seen. The apostle supposes that the exercise of a charitable disposition is to be traced entirely to **God.** God is the author of all grace ;

he alone excites in us a disposition to do good to others.

15. *Thanks* be *unto God.* Whitby supposes that this refers to the charitable disposition which they had manifested, and that the sense is, that God was to be adored for the liberal spirit which they were disposed to manifest, and the aid which they were disposed to render to others. But this, it is believed, falls far below the design of the apostle. The reference is rather to the inexpressible gift which God had granted to them in bestowing his Son to die for them ; and this is one of the most striking instances which occur in the New Testament, showing that the mind of Paul was *full* of this subject ; and that wherever he *began,* he was sure to *end* with a reference to the Redeemer. The invaluable gift of a Saviour was so familiar to his mind, and he was so accustomed to dwell on that in his private thoughts, that the mind naturally and easily glanced on that whenever any thing occurred that by the remotest allusion would suggest it. The idea is, " Your benefactions are indeed valuable ; and for them, for the disposition which you have manifested, and for all the good which you will be enabled thus to accomplish, we are bound to give thanks to God. All this will excite the gratitude of those who shall be benefited. But how small is all this compared with the *great gift* which *God* has imparted in bestowing a Saviour ! That is unspeakable. No words can express it, no language convey an adequate description of the value of the gift, and of the mercies which result from it." ¶ *His unspeakable gift.* The word here used ($\dot{\alpha}\nu\varepsilon\kappa\delta\iota\eta\gamma\dot{\eta}\tau\omega$) means, what cannot be related, unutterable. It occurs nowhere else in the New Testament. The idea is, that no words can properly express the greatness of the gift thus bestowed on man. It is higher than the mind

can conceive; higher than language can express. On this verse we may observe, (1.) That the Saviour is a *gift* to men. So he is uniformly represented; see John iii. 16; Gal. i. 4; ii. 20; Eph. i. 22; Tim. ii. 6; Tit. ii. 14. Man had no claim on God. He could not *compel* him to provide a plan of salvation; and the whole arrangement—the selection of the Saviour, the sending him into the world, and all the benefits resulting from his work, are all an undeserved gift to man. (2.) This is a gift unspeakably great, whose value no language can express, no heart fully conceive. It is so because, (a) Of his own greatness and glory; (b) Because of the inexpressible love which he evinced; (c) Because of the unutterable sufferings which he endured; (d) Because of the inexpressibly great benefits which result from his work. No language can do justice to this work in either of these respects; no heart in this world fully conceives the obligation which rests upon man in virtue of his work. (3.) Thanks should be rendered to God for this. We *owe* him our highest praises for this. This appears, (a) Because it was *mere benevolence* in God. We had no claim; we could not compel him to grant us a Saviour. The gift might have been withheld, and his throne would have been spotless. We owe no thanks where we have a claim; where we deserve nothing, then he who benefits us has a *claim on* our thanks. (b) Because of the benefits which we have received from him. Who can express this? All our peace and hope; all our comfort and joy in this life; all our prospect of pardon and salvation; all the offers of eternal glory are to be traced to him. Man has *no* prospect of being happy when he dies but in virtue of the "unspeakable gift" of God. And when he thinks of his sins, which may now be freely pardoned; when he thinks of an agitated and troubled conscience, which may now be at peace; when he thinks of his soul, which may now be unspeakably and eternally happy; when he thinks of the hell from which he is delivered, and of the

heaven to whose eternal glories he may now be raised up by the gift of a Saviour, his heart should overflow with gratitude, and the language should be continually on his lips and in his heart, "THANKS BE UNTO GOD FOR HIS UNSPEAKABLE GIFT." Every other mercy should seem small compared with this; and every manifestation of right feeling in the heart should lead us to contemplate the source of it, and to feel, as Paul did, that *all* is to be traced to the unspeakable gift of God.

REMARKS.

1. This chapter, with the preceding, derives special importance from the fact that it contains the most extended discussion of the principles of Christian charity which occurs in the Bible. No one can doubt that it was intended by the Redeemer that his people should be distinguished for benevolence. It was important, therefore, that there should be some portion of the New Testament where the principles on which charity should be exercised, and the motives by which Christians should be induced to give, should be fully stated. Such a discussion we have in these chapters; and they therefore demand the profound and prayerful attention of all who love the Lord Jesus.

2. We have here a striking specimen of the manner in which the Bible is written. Instead of abstract statements and systematic arrangement, the principles of religion are brought out in connection *with a case* that actually occurred. But it follows that it is important to study attentively the Bible, and to be familiar with every part of it. In some part of the Scriptures, statements of the principles which should guide us in given circumstances will be found; and Christians should, therefore, be familiar with every part of the Bible.

3. These chapters are of special importance to the ministers of religion, and to all whose duty it is to press upon their fellow Christians the duty of giving liberally to the objects of benevolence. The principles on which it should be done are fully developed

CHAPTER X.

NOW I Paul myself beseech *a* you by the meekness and gen-

a Ro.12.1.

tleness of Christ, who [1] in presence *b am* base among you, but being absent am bold toward you :

1 or, *in outward appearance.*
b ver.10.

here. The motives which it is lawful to urge are urged here by Paul. It may be added, also, that the chapters are worthy of our profound study on account of the admirable tact and address which Paul evinces in inducing others to give. Well he knew human nature. Well he knew the motives which would influence others to give. And well he knew exactly how to shape his arguments and adapt his reasoning to the circumstances of those whom he addressed.

4. The *summary* of the motives presented in this chapter contains still the most important argument which can be urged to produce liberality. We cannot but admire the felicity of Paul in this address—a felicity not the result of craft and cunning, but resulting from his amiable feelings, and the love which he bore to the Corinthians and to the cause of benevolence. He reminds them of the high opinion which he had of them, and of the honourable mention which he had been induced to make of them (ver. 1, 2) ; he reminds them of the painful result to his own feelings and theirs if the collection should in any way fail, and it should appear that his confidence in them had been misplaced (ver. 3—5) ; he refers them to the abundant reward which they might anticipate as the result of liberal benefactions, and of the fact that God loved those who gave cheerfully (ver. 6, 7) ; he reminds them of the abundant grace of God, who was able to supply all their wants and to give them the means to contribute liberally to meet the wants of the poor (ver. 8) ; he reminds them of the joy which their liberality would occasion, and of the abundant thanksgiving to God which would result from it (ver. 12, 13); and he refers them to the unspeakable gift of God, Jesus Christ, as an example, and an argument, and as urging the highest claims in them, ver. 15. "Who," says Doddridge,

"could withstand the force of such oratory?" No doubt it was effectual in that case, and it should be in all others.

5. May the motives here urged by the apostle be effectual to persuade us all to liberal efforts to do good! Assuredly there is no *less* occasion for Christian liberality now than there was in the time of Paul. There are still multitudes of the poor who need the kind and efficient aid of Christians. And the whole world now is a field in which Christian beneficence may be abundantly displayed, and every land may, and should experience the benefits of the charity to which the gospel prompts, and which it enjoins. Happy are they who are influenced by the principles of the gospel to do good to all men ! Happy they who have any opportunity to illustrate the power of Christian principle in this ; any ability to alleviate the wants of one sufferer, or to do any thing in sending that gospel to benighted nations which alone can save the soul from eternal death !

6. Let us especially thank God for his unspeakable gift, Jesus Christ. Let us remember that to him we owe every opportunity to do good : that it was because he came that there is any possibility of benefiting a dying world ; and that all who profess to love him are bound to imitate his example and to show their sense of their obligation to God for giving a Saviour. How poor and worthless are all our gifts compared with the great gift of God ; how slight our expressions of compassion, even at the best, for our fellow-men, compared with the compassion which he has shown for us ! When God has given his Son to die for us, what should we not be willing to give that we may show our gratitude, and that we may benefit a dying world !

CHAPTER X.

PAUL, having finished the subject of

the duty of alms-giving in the previous chapter, enters into this on a vindication of himself from the charges of his enemies. His general design is to vindicate his apostolic authority, and to show that he had a right, as well as others, to regard himself as sent from God. This vindication is continued through chap. xi. and xii. In this chapter the stress of the argument is, that he did not depend on any thing *external* to recommend him —on any " carnal weapons ;" on any thing which commended itself by the outward appearance; or on any thing that was so much valued by the admirers of human eloquence and learning. He seems willing to admit all that his enemies could say of him on that head, and to rely on other proofs that he was sent from God. In chap. xi. he pursues the subject, and shows by a comparison of himself with others, that he had as good a right certainly as they to regard himself as sent by God. In chap. xii. he appeals to another argument, to which none of his accusers were able to appeal, that he had been permitted to see the glories of the heavenly world, and had been favoured in a manner unknown to other men.

It is evident that there was one or more false teachers among the Corinthians who called in question the divine authority of Paul. These teachers were native Jews (chap. xi 10, 22), and they boasted much of their own endowments. It is impossible, except from the epistle itself, to ascertain the nature of their charges and objections against him. From the chapter before us it would seem that one principal ground of their objection was, that though he was bold enough in his letters and had threatened to exercise discipline, yet that he would not dare to do it. They accused him of being, when present with them, timid, weak, mild, pusillanimous, of lacking moral courage to inflict the punishment which he had threatened in his letters. To this he replies in this chapter.

(1.) He appeals to the meekness and gentleness of Christ; thus indirectly and delicately vindicating his own mildness from their objections, and entreats them not to give him occasion to show the boldness and severity which he had purposed to do. He had no *wish* to be bold and severe in the exercise of discipline, ver. 1, 2.

(2.) He assures them that the weapons of his warfare were not carnal, but spiritual. He relied on the truth of the gospel and on the power of motives ; and these weapons were mighty by the aid of God to cast down all that offend him. Yet he was ready to revenge and punish all disobedience by severe measures if it were necessary, ver. 3—6.

(3.) They looked on the outward appearance. He cautioned them to remember that he had as good claims to be regarded as belonging to Christ at they had, ver. 7. He had given proofs that he was an apostle, and the false teachers should look at those proofs lest they should be found to be opposing God. He assured them that *if* he had occasion to exercise his power he would have no reason to be ashamed of it, ver. 8. It would be found to be ample to execute punishment on his foes.

(4.) The false teachers had said that Paul was terrible only in his letters. He boasted of his power, but it was, they supposed, only *epistolary bravery*. He would not dare to execute his threatening. In reply to this, Paul, in a strain of severe irony, says that he would not seem to terrify them by mere letters. It would be by something far more severe. He advised such objectors, therefore, to believe that he would prove himself to be such as he had shown himself to be in his letters ; to look at the *evidence*, since they boasted of their talent for reasoning, that he would show himself in fact to be what he had threatened to be, ver. 9—12.

(5.) He pursues the strain of severe irony by secretly comparing himself with them, ver. 12—16. They boasted much, but it was only by comparing themselves with one another, and not with any elevated standard of excellence. Paul admitted that he had not the *courage* to do that, ver. 12. Nor did he *dare* to boast of things wholly

2 But I beseech *you*, that I may | not be bold when I am present

beyond his ability as they had done. He was contented to act only within the proper limits prescribed to him by his talents and by the appointment of God. Not so they. They had boldness and courage to go far *beyond* that, and to boast of things wholly *beyond* their ability, and beyond the proper measure, ver. 13, 14. Nor had he courage to boast of entering into other men's labours. It required more courage than he had, to make a boast of what he had done if he had availed himself of things made ready to his hand as if they were the fruit of his own labours, implying that *they* had done this; that they had come to Corinth, a church founded by his labours, and had quietly set themselves down there, and then, instead of going into other fields of labour, had called in question the authority of him who had founded the church, and who was labouring indefatigably elsewhere, ver. 15, 16. Paul adds, that such was not *his* intention. He aimed to preach the gospel beyond, to carry it to regions where it had not been spread. Such was the nature of *his* courage; such the kind of boldness which *he* had, and he was not ambitious to join them in *their* boasting.

(6.) He concludes this chapter with a very serious admonition. Leaving the strain of irony, he seriously says that if any man were disposed to boast, it should be only in the Lord. He should glory not in self-commendation, but in the fact that he had evidence that the Lord approved him; not in his own talents or powers, but in the excellence and glory of the Lord, ver. 17, 18.

1. *Now I Paul myself beseech you.* I entreat you who are members of the church not to give me occasion for the exercise of severity in discipline. I have just expressed my confidence in the church in general, and my belief that you will act in accordance with the rules of the gospel. But I cannot thus speak of all. There are some among you who have spoken with contempt of my authority and my claims as an apostle. Of them I

cannot speak in this manner; but instead of *commanding* them I *entreat* them not to give me occasion for the exercise of discipline. ¶ *By the meekness and gentleness of Christ.* In view of the meekness and mildness of the Redeemer; or desiring to imitate his gentleness and kindness. Paul wished to imitate that. He did not wish to have occasion for severity. He desired at all times to imitate, and to exhibit the gentle feelings of the Saviour. He had no pleasure in severity; and he did not desire to exhibit it. ¶ *Who in presence.* Marg. *In outward appearance.* It may either mean that when present among them he appeared, according to their representation, to be humble, mild, gentle (ver. 10); or that in his external appearance he had this aspect; see on ver. 10. Most probably it means that they had represented him as *timid* when among them, and afraid to exercise discipline, however much he had threatened it. ¶ *Am base among you.* The word here used (ταπεινὸς) usually means low, humble, poor. Here it means *timid, modest,* the opposite of boldness. Such was formerly the meaning of the English word *base.* It was applied to those of low degree or rank; of humble birth; and stood opposed to those of elevated rank or dignity. Now it is commonly used to denote that which is degraded or worthless; of mean spirit; vile; and stands opposed to that which is manly and noble. But Paul did not mean to use it here in that sense. He meant to say that they regarded him as *timid* and afraid to execute the punishment which he had threatened, and as manifesting a spirit which was the opposite of boldness. This was doubtless a *charge* which they brought against him; but we are not necessarily to infer that it was true. All that it proves is, that he was modest and unobtrusive, and that they interpreted this as timidity and want of spirit. ¶ *But being absent am bold toward you.* That is, in my letters; see on ver. 10. This they charged him with, that he was bold enough when away from

with that confidence, wherewith *a* I think to be bold against some, which 1 think of us as if we walked according to the flesh.

a 1 Cor.4.21 ; chap.13.2,10.   1 *or, reckon.*

them, but that he would be tame enough when he should meet them face to face, and that they had nothing to fear from him.

2. *That I may not be bold.* I entreat you so to act that I may not have occasion to exercise the severity which I fear I shall be compelled to use against those who accuse me of being governed wholly by worldly motives and policy. ¶ *That I may not be bold.* That I may not be compelled to be bold and decisive in my measures by your improper conduct. ¶ *Which think of us.* Marg. *Reckon.* They suppose this; or, they accuse me of it. By the word "us" here Paul means himself, though it is possible also that he speaks in the name of his fellow-apostles and labourers who were associated with him, and the objections *may* have referred to all who acted with him. ¶ *As if we walked.* As if we lived or acted. The word "walk" in the Scriptures is often used to denote the course or manner of life; Notes, Rom. iv. 12; 2 Cor. v. 7. ¶ *According to the flesh;* see Note on chap. i. 17. As if we were governed by the weak and corrupt principles of human nature. As if we had no higher motive than carnal and worldly policy. As if we were seeking our own advantage and not the welfare of the world. The charge was, probably, that he was not governed by high and holy principles, but by the principles of mere worldly policy ; that he was guided by personal interests, and by worldly views—by ambition, or the love of dominion, wealth, or popularity, and that he was destitute of every supernatural endowment and every evidence of a divine commission.

3. *For though we walk in the flesh.* Though we are mortal like other men ; though we dwell like them in mortal bodies, and necessarily must devote some care to our temporal wants ; and though, being in the flesh, we are con-

3 For though we walk in the flesh, we do not war after *a* the flesh :

4 (For the weapons *b* of our

a Ro.8.13.   *b* Ep.6.13; 1 Th.5.8.

scious of imperfections and frailties like others. The sense is, that he did not claim exemption from the common wants and frailties of nature. The best of men are subject to these wants and frailties; the best of men are liable to err. ¶ *We do not war after the flesh.* The warfare in which he was engaged was with sin, idolatry, and all forms of evil. He means that in conducting this he was not actuated by worldly views or policy, or by such ambitious and interested aims as controlled the men of this world. This refers primarily to the warfare in which Paul was himself engaged as an apostle ; and the idea is, that he went forth as a soldier under the great Captain of his salvation to fight his battles and to make conquests for him. A similar allusion occurs in 2 Tim. ii. 3, 4. It is true, however, that not only all ministers, but all Christians are engaged in a warfare ; and it is equally true that they do not maintain their conflict "after the flesh," or on the principles which govern the men of this world. The warfare of Christians relates to the following points. (1.) It is a warfare with the corrupt desires and sensual propensities of the heart ; with eternal corruption and depravity, with the remaining unsubdued propensities of a fallen nature. (2.) With the powers of darkness ; the mighty spirits of evil that seek to destroy us ; see Eph. vi. 11—17. (3.) With sin in all forms ; with idolatry, sensuality, corruption, intemperance, profaneness, wherever they may exist. The Christian is opposed to all these, and it is the aim and purpose of his life as far as he may be able to resist and subdue them. He is a soldier enlisted under the banner of the Redeemer to oppose and resist all forms of evil. But his warfare is not conducted on worldly principles. Mahomet propagated his religion with the sword ; and the men of this world seek for victory by arms and violence;

warfare *a* *arc* not carnal, but mighty 1 through *b* God to the pulling down *c* of strong holds;)

a 1 Ti.1.18.   1 or, *to.*   *b* chap.13.3,4.
         c Jer.1.10.

The Christian looks for his conquests only by the force and the power of truth, and by the agency of the Spirit of God.

4. *For the weapons of our warfare.* The means by which we hope to achieve our victory. ¶ Are *not carnal.* Not those of the flesh. Not such as the men of the world use. They are not such as are employed by conquerors; nor are they such as men in general rely on to advance their cause. We do not depend on eloquence, or talent, or learning, or wealth, or beauty, or any of the external aids on which the men of this world rely. They are not such as derive advantage from any power inherent in themselves. Their strength is derived from God alone. ¶ *But mighty through God.* Marg. "*to.*" They are rendered mighty or powerful by the agency of God. They depend on him for their efficacy. Paul has not here specified the weapons on which he relied; but he had before specified them (chap. vi. 6, 7), so that there was no danger of mistake. The weapons were such as were furnished by truth and righteousness, and these were rendered mighty by the attending agency of God. The sense is, that God is the author of the doctrines which we preach, and that he attends them with the agency of his Spirit, and accompanies them to the hearts of men. It is important for all ministers to feel that *their* weapons are mighty ONLY through God. Conquerors and earthly warriors go into battle depending on the might of their own arm, and on the wisdom and skill which plans the battle. The Christian goes on his warfare, feeling that however well adapted the truths which he holds are to accomplish great purposes, and however wisely his plans are formed, yet that the efficacy of all depends on the agency of God. He has no hope of victory but in God. And if God does not attend him, he is sure of in-

5 Casting down 2 imaginations, *d* and every high *e* thing that exalteth itself against the knowledge

2 or, *reasonings.*   *d* 1 Co.1.19.
         e Ps.18.27; Ez.17.24.

evitable defeat. ¶ *To the pulling down of strongholds.* The word here rendered "strongholds" (ὀχύρωμα) means properly a fastness, fortress, or strong fortification. It is here beautifully used to denote the various obstacles *resembling* a fortress which exist, and which are designed and adapted to oppose the truth and the triumph of the Christian's cause. All those obstacles are strongly *fortified.* The sins of his heart are fortified by long indulgence and by the hold which they have on his soul. The wickedness of the world which he opposes is strongly fortified by the fact that it has seized on strong human passions; that one point strengthens another; that great numbers are united. The idolatry of the world was strongly fortified by prejudice, and long establishment, and the protection of laws, and the power of the priesthood; and the opinions of the world are entrenched behind false philosophy and the power of subtle argumentation. The whole world is fortified against Christianity; and the nations of the earth have been engaged in little else than in raising and strengthening such strongholds for the space of six thousand years. The Christian religion goes forth against all the combined and concentrated powers of resistance of the whole world; and the warfare is to be waged against every strongly fortified place of error and of sin. These strong fortifications of error and of sin are to be battered down and laid in ruins by our spiritual weapons.

5. *Casting down imaginations.* Marg. *reasonings.* The word is probably used here in the sense of *device,* and refers to all the plans of a wicked world; the various systems of false philosophy; and the reasonings of the enemies of the gospel. The various systems of false philosophy were so intrenched that they might be called the stronghold of the enemies of God. The foes of Christianity pretend to a

of God, and bringing into captivity [a] every thought to [b] the obedience of Christ;

6 And having in a readiness to

revenge all disobedience, when your obedience [c] is fulfilled.

7 Do ye look on things after the outward [d] appearance? If any man

a Mat.11.29.30.
b Ge.8.21 ; Mat.15.19 ; He.4.12.

c chap.7.15.   d John 7.24.

great deal of *reason*, and rely on that in resisting the gospel. ¶ *And every high thing*, &c. Every exalted opinion respecting the dignity and purity of human nature ; all the pride of the human heart and of the understanding. All this is opposed to the knowledge of God, and all exalts itself into a vain self-confidence. Men entertain vain and unfounded opinions respecting their own excellency, and they feel that they do not need the provisions of the gospel and are unwilling to submit to God. ¶ *And bringing into captivity*, &c. The figure here is evidently taken from military conquests. The idea is, that all the strongholds of heathenism, and pride, and sin would be demolished ; and that when this was done, like throwing down the walls of a city or making a breach, all the plans and purposes of the soul, the reason, the imagination, and all the powers of the mind would be subdued or led in triumph by the gospel, like the inhabitants of a captured city. Christ was the great Captain in this warfare. In his name the battle was waged, and by his power the victory was won. The captives were made for him and under his authority ; and all were to be subject to his control. Every power of thought in the heathen world ; all the systems of philosophy and all forms of opinion among men ; all the purposes of the soul; all the powers of reason, memory, judgment, fancy in an individual, were all to come under the laws of Christ. All *doctrines* were to be in accordance with his will ; philosophy should no longer control them, but they should be subject to the will of Christ. All the *plans of life* should be controlled by the will of Christ, and formed and executed under his control—as captives are led by a conqueror. All *the emotions and feelings of the heart* should be controlled by him, and led by him as a

captive is led by a victor. The sense is, that it was the aim and purpose of Paul to accomplish this, and that it would certainly be done. The strongholds of philosophy, heathenism, and sin should be demolished, and all the opinions, plans, and purposes of the world should become subject to the all-conquering Redeemer.

6. *And having in a readiness*, &c. I am ready to punish all disobedience, notwithstanding all that is said to the contrary ; see Notes on ver. 1, 2. Clothed as I am with this power; aiming to subdue all things to Christ, though the weapons of my warfare are not carnal, and though I am modest or timid (ver. 1) when I am with you, I am prepared to take any measures of severity required by my apostolic office, in order that I may inflict deserved punishment on those who have violated the laws of Christ. The design of this is, to meet the objection of his enemies, that he would not *dare* to execute his threatenings. ¶ *When your obedience is fulfilled.* Doddridge renders this, " now your obedience is fulfilled, and the sounder part of your church restored to due order and submission." The idea seems to be, that Paul was ready to inflict discipline when the church had showed a readiness to obey his laws, and to do its own duty—delicately intimating that the reason why it was not done was the want of entire promptness in the church itself, and that it could not be done on any offender as long as the church itself was not prepared to sustain him. The church was to discountenance the enemies of the Redeemer ; to show an entire readiness to sustain the apostle, and to unite with him in the effort to maintain the discipline of Christ's house.

7. *Do ye look on things after the outward appearance ?* This is addressed evidently to the members of the church, and with reference to the

trust to himself that he is Christ's, let him of himself think this again, that, as he *is* Christ's, even so *are* we Christ's.

8 For though I should boast somewhat more of our authority,

a which the Lord hath given us for edification, *b* and not for your destruction, I should not be ashamed :

9 That I may not seem as if I would terrify you by letters.

a chap. 13. 2, 3.　　　*b* chap. 13. 8.

claims which had been set up by the false teachers. There can be no doubt that they valued themselves on their external advantages, and laid claim to peculiar honour in the work of the ministry, because they were superior in personal appearance, in rank, manners, or eloquence to Paul. Paul reproves them for thus judging, and assures them that this was not a proper criterion by which to determine on qualifications for the apostolic office. Such things were highly valued among the Greeks, and a considerable part of the effort of Paul in these letters is to show that these things constitute no evidence that those who possessed them were sent from God. ¶ *If any man trust to himself,* &c. This refers to the false teachers who laid claims to be the followers of Christ by way of eminence. Whoever these teachers were, it is evident that they claimed to be on the side of Christ, and to be appointed by him. They were probably Jews, and they boasted of their talents and eloquence, and possibly that they had seen the Saviour. The phrase "trust to himself," seems to imply that they relied on some special merit of their own, or some special advantage which they had.—*Bloomfield.* It may have been that they were of the same tribe that he was, or that they had seen him, or that they confided in their own talents or endowments as a proof that they had been sent by him. It is not an uncommon thing for men to have such confidence in their own gifts, and particularly in a power of fluent speaking, as to suppose that this is a sufficient evidence that they are sent to preach the gospel. ¶ *Let him of himself think this again.* Since he relies so much on himself ; since he has such confidence in his own powers, let him look at the evidence that I also am of Christ. ¶ *That as*

he is Christ's, even so are *we Christ's.* That I have given as much evidence that I am commissioned by Christ as they can produce. It may be of a different kind. It is not in eloquence, and rank, and the gift of a rapid and ready elocution, but it may be superior to what they are able to produce. Probably Paul refers here to the fact that he had seen the Lord Jesus, and that he had been directly commissioned by him. The sense is, that no one could produce more proofs of being called to the ministry than he could.

8. *For though I should boast,* &c. If I should make even higher claims than I have done to a divine commission. I could urge higher evidence than I have done that I am sent by the Lord Jesus. ¶ *Of our authority.* Of my authority as an apostle, my power to administer discipline, and to direct the affairs of the church. ¶ *Which the Lord hath given us for edification.* A power primarily conferred to build up his people and save them and not to destroy. ¶ *I should not be ashamed.* It would be founded on good evidence and sustained by the nature of my commission. I should also have no occasion to be ashamed of the manner in which it has been exercised—a power that has in fact been employed in extending religion and edifying the church, and not in originating and sustaining measures fitted to destroy the soul.

9. *That I may not seem,* &c. The meaning of this verse seems to be this. " I say that I might boast more of my power in order that I may not appear disposed to terrify you with my letters merely. I do not threaten more than I can perform. I have it in my power to execute all that I have threatened, and to strike an awe not only by my letters, but by the infliction of extraordinary miraculous punishments. And if I should boast that I had done

10 For *his* letters, ¹ say they, *are* weighty and powerful; but

his bodily presence *is* weak, and *his* speech contemptible

this, and could do it again, I should have no reason to be ashamed. It would not be vain and empty boasting; not boasting which is not well-founded."

10.*For his letters.* The letters which he has sent to the church when absent. Reference is had here probably to the first epistle to the Corinthians. They might also have seen some of Paul's other epistles, and been so well acquainted with them as to be able to make the general remark that he had the power of writing in an authoritative and impressive manner. ¶ *Say they.* Marg. *Said he.* Greek (φησί) in the singular. This seems to have referred to some one person who had uttered the words—perhaps some one who was the principal leader of the faction opposed to Paul. ¶ *Are weighty and powerful.* Tindal renders this, "Sore and strong." The Greek is, "heavy and strong" (βαρεῖαι καὶ ἰσχυραί). The sense is, that his letters were energetic and powerful. They abounded with strong argument, manly appeals, and impressive reproof. This even his enemies were compelled to admit, and this no one can deny who ever read them. Paul's letters comprise a considerable portion of the New Testament; and some of the most important doctrines of the New Testament are those which are advocated and enforced by him; and his letters have done more to give shape to the theological doctrines of the Christian world than any other cause whatever. He wrote fourteen epistles to churches and individuals on various occasions and on a great variety of topics; and his letters soon rose into very high repute among even the inspired ministers of the New Testament (see 2 Pet. iii. 15, 16), and were regarded as inculcating the most important doctrines of religion. The general characteristics of Paul's letters are, (1.) They are strongly argumentative. See especially the epistles to the Romans and the Hebrews. (2.) They are distinguished for bold-

ness and vigour of style. (3.) They are written under great energy of feeling and of thought—a rapid and impetuous torrent that bears him forcibly along. (4.) They abound more than most other writings in parentheses, and the sentences are often involved and obscure. (5.) They often evince rapid transitions and departures from the regular current of thought. A thought strikes him suddenly, and he pauses to illustrate it, and dwells upon it long, before he returns to the main subject. The consequence is, that it is often difficult to follow him. (6.) They are powerful in reproof—abounding with strokes of great boldness of denunciation, and also with specimens of most withering sarcasm and most delicate irony. (7.) They abound in expressions of great tenderness and pathos. Nowhere can be found expressions of a heart more tender and affectionate than in the writings of Paul. (8.) They dwell much on great and profound doctrines, and on the application of the principles of Christianity to the various duties of life. (9.) They abound with references to the Saviour. He illustrates every thing by his life, his example, his death, his resurrection. It is not wonderful that letters composed on such subjects and in such a manner by an inspired man produced a deep impression on the Christian world; nor that they should be regarded now as among the most important and valuable portions of the Bible. Take away Paul's letters, and what a chasm would be made in the New Testament! What a chasm in the religious opinions and in the consolations of the Christian world! ¶ *But* his *bodily presence.* His personal appearance. ¶ *Is weak.* Imbecile, feeble (ἀσθενὴς)—a word often used to denote infirmity of body, sickness, disease; Mat. xxv. 39, 43, 44; Luke x. 9; Acts iv. 9; v. 15, 16; 1 Cor. xi. 30. Here it is to be observed that this is a mere charge which was brought against him, and it is not of necessity to be supposed that it was

11 Let such an one think this, that, such as we are in word by letters when we are absent, such

will we be also in deed when we are present.

12 For *a* we dare not make our-

a chap.3.1.

true, though the presumption is, that there was some foundation for it. It is supposed to refer to some bodily imperfections, and possibly to his diminutive stature. Chrysostom says that his stature was low, his body crooked, and his head bald. Lucian, in his *Philopatris*, says of him, Corpore erat parvo, contracto, incurvo, tricubitali —probably an exaggerated description, perhaps a caricature—to denote one very diminutive and having no advantages of personal appearance. According to Nicephorus, Paul "was a little man, crooked, and almost bent like a bow ; with a pale countenance, long and wrinkled ; a bald head; his eyes full of fire and benevolence ; his beard long, thick, and interspersed with gray hairs, as was his head," &c. But there is no certain evidence of the truth of these representations. Nothing in the Bible would lead us to suppose that Paul was remarkably diminutive or deformed ; and though there may be some foundation for the charge here alleged that his bodily presence was weak, yet we are to remember that this was the accusation of his enemies, and that it was doubtless greatly exaggerated. Nicephorus was a writer of the sixteenth century, and his statements are worthy of no regard. That Paul was eminently an eloquent man may be inferred from a great many considerations ; some of which are, (1.) His recorded discourses in the Acts of the Apostles, and the effect produced by them. No one can read his defence before Agrippa or Felix and not be convinced that as an orator he deserves to be ranked among the most distinguished of ancient times. No one who reads the account in the Acts can believe that he had any remarkable impediment in his speech or that he was remarkably deformed. (2.) Such was somehow his grace and power as an orator that he was taken by the inhabitants of Lycaonia as *Mercury*, the god of eloquence; Acts xvi. 12. Assuredly the evidence

here is, that Paul was not deformed. (3.) It may be added, that Paul is mentioned by Longinus among the principal orators of antiquity. From these circumstances, there is no reason to believe that Paul was remarkably deficient in the qualifications requisite for an orator, or that he was in any way remarkably deformed. ¶ *And* his *speech contemptible.* To be despised. Some suppose that he had an impediment in his speech. But conjecture here is vain and useless. We are to remember that this is a charge made by his adversaries, and that it was made by the fastidious Greeks, who professed to be great admirers of eloquence, but who in his time confided much more in the mere art of the rhetorician than in the power of thought, and in energetic appeals to the reason and conscience of men. Judged by their standard it may be that Paul had not the graces in voice or manner, or in the knowledge of the Greek language which they esteemed necessary in a finished orator ; but judged by his power of thought, and his bold and manly defence of truth, and his energy of character and manner, and his power of impressing truth on mankind, he deserves, doubtless, to be ranked among the first orators of antiquity. No man has left the impress of his own mind on more other minds than Paul.

11. *Let such an one think this,* &c. Let them not flatter themselves that there will be any discrepancy between my words and my deeds. Let them feel that all which has been threatened will be certainly executed unless there is repentance. Paul here designedly contradicts the charge which was made against him ; and means to say that all that he had threatened in his letters would be certainly executed unless there was a reform. I think that the evidence here is clear that Paul does not intend to admit what they said about his bodily presence to

selves of the number, or compare ourselves with some that commend themselves : but they measuring

1 *understand it not.*

bc true ; and most probably all that has been recorded bout his deformity is mere fable.

12. *For we dare not make ourselves of the number.* We admit that we are not bold enough for that. They had accused him of a want of boldness and energy when present with them, ver. 1, 10. Here in a strain of severe but delicate irony, he says he was *not* bold enough to do things which they had done. He did not *dare* to do the things which had been done among them. To such boldness of character, present or absent, he could lay no claim. ¶ *Or compare ourselves, &c.* I am not bold enough for that. That requires a stretch of boldness and energy to which I can lay no claim. ¶ *That commend themselves.* That put themselves forward, and that boast of their endowments and attainments. It is probable that this was commonly done by those to whom the apostle here refers ; and it is certain that it is everywhere the characteristic of pride. To do this, Paul says, required greater boldness than he possessed, and on this point he yielded to them the palm. The satire here is very delicate, and yet very severe, and was such as would doubtless be felt by them. ¶ *But they measuring themselves by themselves.* Whitby and Clarke suppose that this means that they compare themselves with each other ; and that they made the false apostles particularly their standard. Doddridge, Grotius, Bloomfield, and some others suppose the sense to be, that they made themselves the standard of excellence. They looked continually on their own accomplishments, and did not look at the excellences of others. They thus formed a disproportionate opinion of themselves, and undervalued all others. Paul says that he had not boldness enough for that. It required a moral courage to which he could lay no claim. Horace (Epis. i. 7. 98) has an expression similar to this :—

themselves by themselves, and comparing themselves among themselves, [1] are not wise.[a]

a Pr.26.12.

Metiri se quemque suo modulo ac pede verum est.

The sense of Paul is, that they made themselves the standard of excellence ; that they were satisfied with their own attainments ; and that they overlooked the superior excellence and attainments of others. This is a graphic description of pride and self-complacency ; and, alas ! it is what is often exhibited. How many there are, and it is to be feared even among professing Christians, who have no other standard of excellence than themselves. Their views are the standard of orthodoxy ; their modes of worship are the standard of the proper manner of devotion ; their habits and customs are in their own estimation perfect ; and their own characters are the models of excellence, and they see little or no excellence in those who differ from them. They look on themselves as the true measure of orthodoxy, humility, zeal, and piety ; and they condemn all others, however excellent they may be, who differ from them. ¶ *And comparing themselves with themselves.* Or rather comparing themselves *with* themselves. Themselves they make to be the standard, and they judge of everything by that. ¶ *Are not wise.* Are stupid and foolish. Because, (1.) They had no such excellence as to make themselves the standard. (2.) Because this was an indication of pride. (3.) Because it made them blind to the excellences of others. It was to be presumed that others *had* endowments not inferior to theirs. (4.) Because the requirements of God, and the character of the Redeemer, were the proper standard of conduct. Nothing is a more certain indication of folly than for a man to make himself the standard of excellence. Such an individual must be blind to his own *real* character ; and the only thing certain about his attainments is, that he is inflated with pride. And yet how common ! How self-satisfied are most persons ! How

13 But we will not boast of things without *our* measure, but according to the measure of the

1 rule which God hath distributed to us, a measure to reach even unto you.

1 or, *line.*

pleased with their own character and attainments! How grieved at any comparison which is made with others implying their inferiority! How prone to undervalue all others simply because they differ from them!—The margin renders this, " understand it not," that is, they do not understand their own character or their inferiority.

13. *But we will not boast of things without our measure.* Tindal renders this, " But we will not rejoice above measure." There is great obscurity in the language here, arising from its brevity. But the general idea seems to be plain. Paul says that he had not boldness as they had to boast of things wholly *beyond* his proper rule and his actual attainments and influence : and, especially, that he was not disposed to enter into other men's labours ; or to boast of things that had been done by the mere influence of his name, and beyond the proper limits of his personal exertions. He made no boast of having done any thing where he had not been himself on the ground and laboured assiduously to secure the object. *They,* it is not improbable, had boasted of what had been done in Corinth as though it were really their work though it had been done by the apostle himself. Nay more, it is probable that they boasted of what had been done by the mere influence of their name. Occupying a central position, they supposed that their reputation had gone abroad, and that the mere influence of their *reputation* had had an important effect. Not so with Paul. He made no boast of any thing but what God had enabled him to do by his evangelical labours, and by personal exertions. He entered into no other men's labours. and claimed nothing that others had done as his own. He was not bold enough for that. ¶ *But according to the measure of the rule,* &c. Marg. Or, *line.* The word rendered " rule" (Greek, κανὼν, whence our English word *canon*) means properly

a *reed, rod,* or *staff* employed to keep any thing stiff, erect, asunder (Hom. Il. 8. 103) ; then a measuring rod or line ; then any standard or rule—its usual meaning in the New Testament, as, *e. g.,* of life and doctrine, Gal. vi. 16 ; Phil. iii. 16.—*Robinson's Lex.* Here it means the limit, boundary line, or sphere of action assigned to any one. Paul means to say that God had appropriated a certain line or boundary as the proper limit of his sphere of action ; that his appropriate sphere extended to them ; that in going to them, though they were far distant from the field of his early labours, he had confined himself within the proper limits assigned him by God ; and that in boasting of his labours among them he was not boasting of any thing which did not properly fall within the sphere of labour assigned to him. The meaning is, that Paul was especially careful not to boast of any thing beyond his proper bounds. ¶ *Which God hath distributed to us.* Which in assigning our respective fields of labour God has assigned unto me and my fellowlabourers. The Greek word here rendered " distributed " (ἐμεϱίσεν) means properly to measure ; and the sense is, that God had measured out or apportioned their respective fields of labour ; that by his providence he had assigned to each one his proper sphere, and that in the distribution Corinth had fallen to the lot of Paul. In going there he had kept within the proper limits ; in boasting of his labours and success there he did not boast of what did not belong to him. ¶ *A measure to reach even unto you.* The sense is, " the limits assigned me include you, and I may therefore justly boast of what I have done among you as within my proper field of labour." Paul was the apostle to the Gentiles (Acts xxvi. 17, 18) ; and the whole country of Greece therefore he regarded as falling within the limits assigned to him. No one therefore

14 For we stretch not ourselves beyond *our measure*, as though we reached unto you, for we are come as far as to you also in *preaching* the gospel of Christ :

a Ro.15.20.

15 Not boasting of things without *our* measure, *that is*, of [a] other men's labours ; but having hope when your faith is increased, that we shall be [1] enlarged by

1 or. *magnified in you*.

could blame him for going there as if he was an intruder ; no one assert that he had gone beyond the proper bounds.

14. *For we stretch not ourselves beyond* our measure. In coming to preach to you we have not gone beyond the proper limits assigned us. We have not endeavoured to enlarge the proper boundaries, to *stretch the line* which limited us, but have kept honestly within the proper limits. ¶ *As though we reached not unto you.* That is, as if our boundaries did not extend so far as to comprehend you. We have not overstepped the proper limits, as if Greece was not within the proper sphere of action. ¶ *For we are come as far as to you*, &c. In the regular work of preaching the gospel we have come to you. We have gone from place to place preaching the gospel where we had opportunity ; we have omitted no important places, until in the regular discharge of our duties in preaching we have reached you and have preached the gospel to you. We have not omitted other places in order to come to you and enter into the proper field of labour of others, but in the regular work of making the gospel known as far as possible to all men we have come to Corinth. Far as it is, therefore, from the place where we started, we have approached it in a regular manner, and have not gone out of our proper province in doing it.

15. *Not boasting of things without* our *measure.* There is here probably an allusion to the false teachers at Corinth. They had come *after* Paul had been there, and had entered into his labours. When he had founded the church ; when he had endured trials and persecutions in order to reach Corinth ; when he had laboured there for a year and a half (Acts xviii. 11), *they* came and entered the quiet and easy field, formed parties, and

claimed the field as their own. Paul says that he had not courage to do that ; see Note, ver. 12. That requires a species of boldness to which he could lay no claim ; and he did not assume honour to himself like that. ¶ *That is, of other men's labours.* Not intruding into churches which we did not establish, and claiming the right to direct their affairs, and to exclude the founders from all proper honours and all influence, and endeavouring to alienate the affections of Christians from their spiritual father and guide. ¶ *But having hope*, &c. So far from this ; so far from a desire to enter into the labours of others and quietly enjoying the avails of their industry ; and so far even from a desire to sit down ourselves and enjoy the fruit of our own labours, I desire to penetrate other untrodden regions ; to encounter new dangers ; to go where the gospel has not been planted, and to rear other churches there. I do not, therefore, make these remarks as if I wished even to dispossess the teachers that have entered into my labours. I make them because I wish to be aided by you in extending the gospel further ; and I look to your assistance in order that I may have the means of going into the regions where I have not made known the name of the Redeemer. ¶ *When your faith is increased.* When you become so strong as not to need my presence and my constant care ; and when you shall be able to speed me on my way and to aid me on my journey. He expected to be assisted by them in his efforts to carry the gospel to other countries. ¶ *That we shall be enlarged.* Marg. *Magnified by you.* Bloomfield supposes that this means. " to gain fame and glory by you ;" that is, as the teacher may justly by his pupils. So Robinson renders it, " to make great, to praise." But to me the idea seems to be that he wished them to enlarge

you according to our rule abundantly.

16 To preach the gospel in the *regions* beyond you, *and* not to boast in another man's line [1] of things made ready to our hand.

17 But *a* he that glorieth, let him glory in the Lord.

1 or, *rule*.　　　　　　*a* Je.9.24.

or magnify him by introducing him to larger fields of action ; by giving him a wider sphere of labour. It was not that he wished to be magnified by obtaining a wider reputation, not as a matter of praise or ambition, but he wished to have his work and success greatly enlarged. This he hoped to be enabled to do partly by the aid of the church at Corinth. When they became able to manage their own affairs ; when his time was not demanded to superintend them ; when their faith became so strong that his presence was not needed ; and when they should assist him in his preparations for travel, then he would enter on his wider field of labour. He had no intention of sitting down in ease as the false teachers in Corinth seem disposed to have done. ¶ *According to our rule.* Greek, "According to our canon ;" see on ver. 13. The sense is, according to the rule by which the sphere of his labours had been marked out. His rule was to carry the gospel as far as possible to the heathen world. He regarded the regions lying far beyond Corinth as coming properly within his limits ; and he desired to occupy that field. ¶ *Abundantly.* Greek, Unto abundance. So as to abound ; that is, to occupy the field assigned as far as possible.

16. *To preach the gospel in the* regions *beyond you.* What regions are referred to here can be only a matter of conjecture. It may be that he wished to preach in other parts of Greece, and that he designed to go to Arcadia or Lacedæmon. Rosenmüller supposes that as the Corinthians were engaged in commerce, the apostle hoped that by them some tidings of the gospel would reach the countries with which they were engaged in traffic. But I think it most probable that he alludes to Italy and Spain. It is certain that he had formed the design of visiting Spain

(Rom. xv. 24, 28) ; and he doubtless wished the Corinthians to aid him in that purpose, and was anxious to do this as soon as the condition of the eastern churches would allow it. ¶ And *not to boast in another man's line of things,* &c. Marg. *Rule,* the same word (*κανών*) which occurs in ver. 13. The meaning is, that Paul did not mean to boast of what properly belonged to others. He did not claim what they had done as his own. He did not intend to labour within what was properly their bounds, and then to claim the field and the result of the labour as his. He probably means here to intimate that this had been done by the false teachers of Corinth ; but so far was he from designing to do this, that he meant soon to leave Corinth, which was properly within his limits, and the church which he had founded there, to go and preach the gospel to other regions. Whether Paul ever went to Spain has been a question (see Note on Rom. xv. 24) ; but it is certain that he went to Rome, and that he preached the gospel in many other places after this besides Corinth.

17. *But he that glorieth.* He that boasts. Whatever may be the occasion of his boasting, whether in planting churches or in watering them ; whether in his purposes, plans, toils, or success. Paul himself did not deem it improper on some occasions to boast (chap. xi. 16 ; xii. 5), but it was not of his own power, attainments, or righteousness. He was disposed to trace all to the Lord, and to regard him as the source of all blessing and all success. ¶ *Let him glory in the Lord.* In this serious and weighty admonition, Paul designs, doubtless, to express the manner in which *he* was accustomed to glory, and to furnish an admonition to the Corinthians. In the previous part of the chapter there had been some severe irony. He closes the chapter with the utmost

18 For not he that commendeth himself is approved, but *a* whom the Lord commendeth.

a Ro.2.29.

seriousness and solemnity of manner, in order to show on his part that he was not disposed to glory in his own attainments and to admonish them not to boast of theirs. If they had any thing valuable they should regard the Lord as the author of it. In this admonition it is probable that Paul had in his eye the passage in Jer. ix. 23, 24; though he has not expressly quoted it. "Let not the wise man glory in his wisdom, neither let the mighty man glory in his might, let not the rich man glory in his riches; but let him that glorieth glory in this, that he understandeth and knoweth me, that I am the LORD which exercise loving-kindness, judgment, and righteousness in the earth." The sentiment is a favourite one with Paul, as it should be with all Christians; see Note on 1 Cor. i. 31. On this verse we may *here* remark, I. That nothing is more common than for men to boast or glory. Little as they really have in which to glory, yet there is no one probably who has not *something* of which he is proud, and of which he is disposed to boast. It would be difficult or impossible to find a person who had not something on which he prided himself; something in which he esteemed himself superior to others. II. The things of which they boast are very various. (1.) Many are proud of their personal beauty; many, too, who would be unwilling to be thought proud of it. (2.) Many glory in their accomplishments; or, what is more likely, in the accomplishments of their children. (3.) Many glory in their talents; talents for any thing, valuable or not, in which they suppose they surpass others. They glory in their talent for eloquence, or science, or gaining knowledge; or in their talent for gaining property or keeping it; for their skill in their professions or callings; for their ability to run, to leap, or to practise even any trick or sleight of hand. There is nothing so worthless that it does not constitute a subject of glorying, *provided it be ours.* If it belong to others it may be valueless. (4.) Many glory in their property; in fine houses, extended plantations, or in the reputation of being rich; or in gorgeous dress, equipage, and furniture. In short, there is nothing which men possess in which they are not prone to glory. Forgetful of God the giver; forgetful that all may be soon taken from them, or that they soon must leave all; forgetful that none of these things can constitute a distinction in the grave or beyond, they boast as if these things were to remain for ever, and as if they had been acquired independently of God. How prone is the man of talents to forget that God has given him his intellect, and that for its proper use he must give account! How prone is the rich man to forget that he must die! How prone the gay and the beautiful to forget that they will lie undistinguished in the grave; and that death will consume them as soon as the most vile and worthless of the species! III. If we glory it should be in the Lord. We should ascribe our talents, wealth, health, strength, and salvation to him. We should rejoice, (1.) That we *have* such a Lord, so glorious, so full of mercy, so powerful, so worthy of confidence and love. (2.) We should rejoice in our endowments and possessions as his gift. We should rejoice that we may come and lay every thing at his feet, and whatever may be our rank, or talents, or learning, we should rejoice that we may come with the humblest child of poverty, and sorrow, and want, and say, "Not unto us, not unto us, but unto thy name give glory, for thy mercy and for thy truth's sake;" Ps. cxv. 1; see Note on 1 Cor. i. 31.

18. *For not he who commendeth himself,* &c. Not he who boasts of his talents and endowments. He is not to be judged by the estimate which he shall place on himself, but by the estimate which God shall form and express. ¶ *Is approved.* By God.

It is no evidence that we shall be saved that we are prone to commend ourselves ; see Rom. xvi. 10. ¶ *But whom the Lord commendeth :* see Note on Rom. ii. 29. The idea here is, that men are to be approved or rejected by God. He is to pass judgment on them, and that judgment is to be in accordance with his estimate of their character, and not according to their own If he approves them they will be saved ; if he does not, vain will be all their empty boasting ; vain all their reliance on their wealth, eloquence. learning, or earthly honours. None will save them from condemnation ; not all these things can purchase for them eternal life. Paul thus seriously shows that we should be mainly anxious to obtain the divine favour. It should be the grand aim and purpose of our life ; and we should repress all disposition for vain-glory or self-confidence ; all reliance on our talents, attainments, or accomplishments for salvation. OUR BOAST IS THAT WE HAVE SUCH A REDEEMER ; AND IN THAT WE ALL MAY GLORY.

REMARKS.

1. We should have no *desire* to show off any peculiar boldness or energy of character which we may have ; ver. 1, 2. We should greatly prefer to evince the gentleness and meekness of Christ. Such a character is in itself of far more value than one that is merely energetic and bold ; that is rash, authoritative, and fond of display.

2. They who are officers in the church should have no *desire* to administer discipline ; ver. 2. Some men are so fond of power that they always love to exercise it. They are willing to show it even by inflicting punishment on others ; and " dressed in a little brief authority" they are constantly seeking occasion to show their consequence ; they magnify trifles ; they are unwilling to pass by the slightest offences. The reason is not that they love the truth, but that they love their own consequence, and they seek every opportunity to show it.

3. All Christians and all Christian ministers are engaged in a warfare ;

ver. 3. They are at war with sin in their own hearts, and with sin wherever it exists on earth, and with the powers of darkness. With foes so numerous and so vigilant, they should not expect to live a life of ease or quietness. Peace, perfect peace, they may expect in heaven, not on earth. Here they are to fight the good fight of faith and thus to lay hold on eternal life. It has been the common lot of all the children of God to maintain such a war, and shall *we* expect to be exempt ?

> " Shall *I* be carried to the skies
>   On flowery beds of ease,
>   While others fought to win the prize,
>   And sailed through bloody seas ?
>
> " Are there no foes for me to face,
>   Must I not stem the flood ?
>   Is this vile world a friend to grace,
>   To help me on to God ? "

4. The weapons of the Christian are not to be carnal, but are to be spiritual ; ver. 4. He is not to make his way by the exhibition of human passion ; in bloody strife ; and by acting under the influence of ambitious feelings. Truth is his weapon ; and armed with truth, and aided by the Spirit of God, he is to expect the victory. How different is the Christian warfare from others ! How different is Christianity from other systems ! Mahomet made his way by arms, and propagated his religion amidst the din of battle. But not so Christianity. That is to make its way by the silent, but mighty operation of truth ; and there is not a rampart of idolatry and sin that is not yet to fall before it.

5. The Christian should be a man of a pure spirit ; ver. 4. He is to make his way by the truth. He should therefore love the truth, and he should seek to diffuse it as far as possible. In propagating or defending it, he should be *always* mild, gentle, and kind Truth is never advanced, and an adversary is never convinced, where passion is evinced ; where there is a haughty manner or a belligerent spirit. The apostolic precepts are *full of wisdom,* " speaking the truth in love" Eph. iv. 1), " in MEEKNESS INSTRUCTING those that oppose themselves ; if

God peradventure will give them repentance to the acknowledging of the truth;" 2 Tim. ii. 25.

6. In his warfare the Christian shall conquer; ver. 4, 5. Against the truth of Christianity nothing has been able to stand. It made its way against the arrayed opposition of priests and emperors; against customs and laws; against inveterate habits and opinions; against all forms of sin, until it triumphed, and "the banners of the faith floated from the palaces of the Cesars." So it will be in all the conflicts with evil. Nothing is more certain than that the powers of darkness in this world are destined to fall before the power of Christian truth, and that every stronghold of sin shall yet be demolished. So it is in the conflicts of the individual Christian. He may struggle long and hard. He may have many foes to contend with. But he shall gain the victory. His triumph shall be secure; and he shall yet be enabled to say, " I have fought a good fight—*henceforth there is laid up for me* A CROWN."

" The saints in all this glorious war
Shall conquer though they die;
They see the triumph from afar,
And seize it with their eye."

7. Yet all should feel their dependence on God; ver. 4. It is only through him and by his aid that we have any power. Truth itself has no power except as it is attended and directed by God; and we should engage in our conflict feeling that none but God can give us the victory. If forsaken by him, we shall fall; if supported by him, we may face without fear a "frowning world," and all the powers of the "dark world of hell."

8. We should not judge by the outward appearance; ver. 7. It is the heart that determines the character; and by that God shall judge us, and by that we should judge ourselves.

9. We should aim to extend the gospel as far as possible; ver. 14—16. Paul aimed to go beyond the regions where the gospel had been preached, and to extend it to far distant lands. So the "field" still "is the world." A large portion of the earth is yet unevangelized. Instead, therefore, of sitting down quietly in enjoyment and ease, let us, like him, earnestly desire to extend the influence of pure religion, and to bring distant nations to the saving knowledge of the truth.

10. Let us not boast in ourselves; ver. 17. Not of our talents, wealth, learning, or accomplishments let us glory. But let us glory that we have such a God as JEHOVAH. Let us glory that we have such a Redeemer as Jesus Christ. Let us glory that we have such a sanctifier as the Holy Spirit. Let us acknowledge God as the source of all our blessings, and to him let us honestly consecrate our hearts and our lives.

11. What a reverse of judgment there will yet be on human character! ver. 17, 18. How many now commend themselves who will be *condemned* in the last day. How many men boast of their talents and morals, and even their religion, who will then be involved in indiscriminate condemnation with the most vile and worthless of the race. How anxious should we be, therefore, to secure the approbation of God; and whatever our fellow-men may say of us, how infinitely desirable is it to be commended then by our heavenly Father.

CHAPTER XI.

This chapter is connected in its general design with the preceding. The object of Paul is to vindicate himself from the charges which had been brought against him, and especially to vindicate his claims to the apostolic office. It is *ironical* in its character, and is of course severe upon the false teachers who had accused him in Corinth. The main purpose is to state his claims to the office of an apostle, and especially to show that when he mentioned those claims, or even boasted of his labours, he had ground for doing so. It would seem that they had charged him with "*folly*" in boasting as he had done. Probably the false teachers were loud in proclaiming their own praise, but represented Paul as guilty of folly in praising himself. He therefore (ver. 1) asks them if they could bear with him a little further in his folly, and entreats them to do it. This verse contains the scope of the chapter; and the remainder of the chapter is an enumeration of the causes which he had for his boasting, though probably each reason is adapted to some form of accusation brought against him.

Having entreated them to bear with him a little further, he states the *reasons* why he was disposed to go into this subject at all; ver. 2—4. It was not because he was disposed to sound his own praise, but it was from love to them. He had espoused them as a chaste virgin to Christ. He was afraid that their affections would be alienated from the Redeemer. He reminded them of the manner in which Eve was tempted; and he reminded them that by the same smooth and plausible arts their affections might also be stolen away, and that they might be led into sin. He reminds them that there was danger of their receiving another gospel, and expresses the apprehension that they had done it, and that they had embraced a deceiver; ver. 4.

Having made this general statement of his design, Paul now goes more into detail in answering the objections against him, and in showing the reasons which he had for boasting as he had done. The statement in answer to their objections relates to the following points.

(1.) He had supposed that he was not behind the chiefest of the apostles. He had supposed that he had claims to the apostolic office of as high an order as any of them. Called to the work as he had been, and labouring as he had done, he had regarded himself as having an indisputable claim to the office of an apostle. True, they had charged him with being rude in speech, a charge which he was not disposed to deny, but in a far more important point than that he had showed that he was not disqualified for the apostolic office. In *knowledge*, the main qualification, he had not been deficient, as probably even his opponents were disposed to admit; ver. 5, 6.

(2.) **He** had not deprived himself of the claims to the office and honours of an apostle by declining to receive from them a compensation, and by preaching the gospel without charge; ver. 7—9. Probably they had alleged that this was a proof that he *knew* that he had no claim to the honours of an apostle. He, therefore, states exactly how this was. He had *received* a support, but he had robbed other churches to do it. And even when he was with them, he had received supplies from a distant church in order that he might not be burdensome to them. The charge was therefore groundless, that he *knew* that he had no right to the support due to an apostle.

(3.) He declares it to be his fixed purpose that no one should prevent his boasting in that manner. And this he did because he loved them, and because he would save them from the snares of those who would destroy them. He therefore stated the true character of those who attempted to deceive them. They were the ministers of Satan, appearing as the ministers of righteousness, as Satan himself was transformed into an angel of light; ver 10—15.

(4.) Paul claims the privilege of boasting as a fool a little further; ver. 16. And he claims that as others boasted, and as they were allowed to do so by the Corinthians, he had also a right to do the same thing. They suffered them to boast; they allowed them to do it even if they devoured them, and smote them, and took their property. It was but fair, therefore, that he should be allowed to boast a little of what he was and of what he had done; ver. 17—20.

(5.) He goes, therefore, into an extended and most tender description of what he had suffered, and of his claims to their favourable regard. He had all the personal advantages arising from birth which they could pretend to. He was a Hebrew, of the seed of Abraham, and a minister of Christ; ver. 21—23. He had endured far more labours and dangers than they had done; and in order to set this before them he enumerates the trials through which he had pas-

CHAPTER XI.

WOULD to God ye could bear with me a little in *my* folly : and indeed bear [1] with me.

2 For I am jealous over you

sed, and states the labours which constantly came upon him ; ver. 23—30. Of these things, of his sufferings, and trials, and infirmities, he felt that he had a right to speak, and these constituted a far higher claim to the confidence of the Christian church than the endowments of which his adversaries boasted.

(6.) As another instance of peril and suffering, he refers to the fact that his life was endangered when he was in Damascus, and that he barely escaped by being lowered down from the wall of the city, ver. 31—33. The conclusion which Paul doubtless intends should be derived from all this is, that he had far higher grounds of claim to the office of an apostle than his adversaries would admit, or than they could furnish themselves. He admitted that he was weak and subject to infirmities ; he did not lay claim to the graces of a polished elocution, as they did ; but if a life of self-denial and toil, of an honest devotion to the cause of truth at imminent and frequent hazard of life, constituted an evidence that he was an apostle, he had that evidence. They appealed to their birth, their rank, their endowments as public speakers. In the quiet and comfort of a congregation and church established to their hands ; in reaping the avails of the labours of others ; and in the midst of enjoyments, they coolly laid claims to the honours of the ministerial office, and denied his claims. In trial, and peril, and labour, and poverty ; in scourges, and imprisonments, and shipwrecks ; in hunger and thirst ; in unwearied travelling from place to place ; and in the care of all the churches, were *his* claims to their respect and confidence, and he was willing that any one that chose should make the comparison between them. Such was *his* "foolish" boasting ; such his claims to their confidence and regard.

1. *Would to God.* Greek, " I would " (Ὄφελον). This expresses earnest desire, but in the Greek there is no appeal to God. The sense would be well expressed by " O that," or " I earnestly wish." ¶ *Ye could bear with me.* That you would bear patiently with me ; that you would hear me patiently, and suffer me to speak of myself. ¶ *In my folly.* Folly in boasting. The idea seems to be, " I know that boasting is generally foolish, and that it is not to be indulged in. But though it is to be generally regarded as folly, yet circumstances compel me to it, and I ask your indulgence in it." It is possible also that his opponents accused him of folly in boasting so much of himself. *And indeed bear with me.* Marg. *Ye do bear.* But the text has probably the correct rendering. It is the expression of an earnest wish that they would tolerate him a little in this. He entreats them to bear with him because he was constrained to it.

2. *For I am jealous over you.* This verse expresses the reason why he was disposed to speak of his attainments, and of what he had done. It was because he loved them, and because he feared that they were in danger of being seduced from the simplicity of the gospel. The phrase " I am jealous " (Ζηλῶ) means properly, I ardently love you ; I am full of tender attachment to you. The word was usual among the Greeks to denote an ardent affection of any kind (from ζίω, to boil, to be fervid or fervent). The precise meaning is to be determined by the connection ; see Note on 1 Cor. xii. 31. The *word* may denote the jealousy which is felt by an apprehension of departure from fidelity on the part of those whom we love ; or it may denote a fervid and glowing attachment. The meaning here probably is, that Paul had a strong attachment to them. ¶ *With godly jealousy.* Greek, "with the zeal of God " (Θεοῦ ζήλῳ). That is, with very great or vehement zeal—in accordance with the Hebrew custom when

with godly jealousy : for I have espoused you *a* to one husband, that I may present *you as* a chaste virgin *b* to Christ.

3 But I fear, lest by any

means, as the serpent beguiled Eve through his subtilty, so your minds should be corrupted from the simplicity that is in Christ.

a Hos. 2. 19, 20.　　　　*b* Le. 21. 13.

the name God is used to denote any thing signally great, as the phrase "mountains of God," meaning very elevated or lofty mountains. The mention of this ardent attachment suggested what follows. His mind reverted to the tenderness of the marriage relation, and to the possibility that in that relation the affections might be estranged. He makes use of this figure, therefore, to apprize them of the change which he apprehended. ¶ *For I have espoused you,* &c. The word here used (άρμόζω) means properly to adapt, to fit, to join together. Hence to join in wedlock, to marry. Here it means to marry to another; and the idea is, that Paul had been the agent employed in forming a connection, similar to the marriage connection, between them and the Saviour. The *allusion* here is not certain. It may refer to the custom which prevailed when friends made and procured the marriage for the bridegroom ; or it may refer to some custom like that which prevailed among the Lacedemonians where persons were employed to form the lives and manners of virgins and prepare them for the duties of the married life. The sense is clear. Paul claims that it was by *his* instrumentality that they had been united to the Redeemer. Under him they had been brought into a relation to the Saviour similar to that sustained by the bride to her husband ; and he felt all the interest in them which naturally grew out of that fact and from a desire to present them blameless to the pure Redeemer. The relation of the Church to Christ is often represented by marriage ; see Eph. v. 23—33 ; Rev. xix. 7 ; xxi. 9. ¶ *To one husband.* To the Redeemer. ¶ *That I may present* you *as a chaste virgin to Christ.* The allusion here, according to Doddridge, is, to the custom among the Greeks " of having an

officer whose business it was to educate and form young women, especially those of rank and figure, designed for marriage, and then to *present* them to those who were to be their husbands, and if this officer through negligence permitted them to be corrupted between the espousals and the consummation of the marriage, great blame would fall upon him." Such a responsibility Paul felt. So anxious was he for the entire purity of that church which was to constitute " the bride, the Lamb's wife ;" so anxious that all who were connected with that church should be presented pure in heaven.

3. *But I fear.* Paul had just compared the church to a virgin, soon to be presented as a bride to the Redeemer. The mention of this seems to have suggested to him the fact that the first woman was deceived and led astray by the tempter, and that the same thing might occur in regard to the church which he was so desirous should be preserved pure. The grounds of his fear were, (1.) That Satan had seduced the first woman, thus demonstrating that the most holy were in danger of being led astray by temptation ; and, (2.) That special efforts were made to seduce them from the faith. The persuasive arts of the false teachers ; the power of philosophy ; and the attractive and corrupting influences of the world, he had reason to suppose might be employed to seduce them from simple attachment to Christ. ¶ *Lest by any means.* Lest somehow (μήπως). It is implied that many means would be used ; that all arts would be tried; and that in some way, which perhaps they little suspected, these arts would be successful, unless they were constantly put upon their guard. ¶ *As the serpent beguiled Eve ;* see Gen. iii. 1—11. The word serpent here refers doubtless to Satan, who was the agent by whom Eve was

beguiled; see John viii. 44; 1 John iii. 8; Rev. xii. 9; xx. 2. Paul did not mean that they were in danger of being corrupted in the same way, but that similar efforts would be made to seduce them. Satan adapts his temptations to the character and circumstances of the tempted. He varies them from age to age, and applies them in such a way as best to secure his object. Hence all should be on their guard. No one knows the mode in which he will approach him, but all may know that he will approach them in *some* way. ¶ *Through his subtilty;* see Gen. iii. 1. By his craft, art, wiles (ἐν τῇ πανουργίᾳ). The word implies that shrewdness, cunning, craft was employed. A tempter always employs cunning and art to accomplish his object. The precise *mode* in which Satan accomplished his object is not certainly known. *Perhaps* the cunning consisted in assuming an attractive form—a fascinating manner—a manner fitted to charm; perhaps in the idea that the eating of the forbidden fruit had endowed a serpent with the power of reason and speech above all other animals, and that it might be expected to produce a similar transformation in Eve. At all events there were false pretences and appearances, and such Paul apprehended would be employed by the false teachers to seduce and allure them, see on ver. 13, 14. ¶ *So your minds should be corrupted.* So your thoughts should be perverted. So your hearts should be alienated. The mind is corrupted when the affections are alienated from the proper object, and when the soul is filled with unholy plans, and purposes, and desires. ¶ *From the simplicity that is in Christ.* (1.) From simple and single-hearted *devotedness* to him—from pure and unmixed attachment to him. The fear was that their affections would be fixed on other objects, and that the *singleness* and *unity* of their devotedness to him would be destroyed. (2.) From his *pure doctrines.* By the admixture of philosophy; by the opinions of the world there was danger that their minds should be turned away from their hold on the simple truths which Christ had taught. (3.) From that simplicity of mind and heart; that childlike candour and docility; that freedom from all guile, dishonesty, and deception which so eminently characterized the Redeemer. Christ had a single aim; was free from all guile; was purely honest; never made use of any improper arts; never resorted to false appearances; and never deceived. His followers should in like manner be artless and guileless. There should be no mere cunning, no trick, no craft in advancing their purposes. There should be nothing but honesty and truth in all that they say. Paul was afraid that they would lose this beautiful simplicity and artlessness of character and manner; and that they would insensibly be led to adopt the maxims of mere cunning, of policy, of expediency, of seductive arts which prevailed so much in the world—a danger which was imminent among the shrewd and cunning people of Greece; but which is confined to no time and no place. Christians should be more guileless than even children are; *as* pure and free from trick, and from art and cunning as was the Redeemer himself. (4.) From the simplicity *in worship* which the Lord Jesus commended and required. The worship which the Redeemer designed to establish was simple, unostentatious, and pure—strongly in contrast with the gorgeousness and corruption of the pagan worship, and even with the imposing splendour of the Jewish temple service. He intended that it should be adapted to all lands, and such as could be offered by all classes of men—a pure worship, claiming first the homage of the heart, and then such simple external expressions as should best exhibit the homage of the heart. How easily might this be corrupted! What temptations were there to attempt to corrupt it by those who had been accustomed to the magnificence of the temple service, and who would suppose that the religion of the Messiah *could* not be less gorgeous than that which was designed to shadow forth his coming; and by those who had been accustomed to

4 For if he that cometh preacheth another Jesus, whom

we have not preached, or *if* ye receive another spirit, which ye

the splendid rites of the pagan worship, and who would suppose that the true religion *ought* not to be less costly and splendid than the false religion had been. If so much expense had been lavished on false religions, how natural to suppose that equal costliness at least should be bestowed on the true religion. Accordingly the history of the church for a considerable part of its existence has been little more than a record of the various forms in which the simple worship instituted by the Redeemer has been corrupted, until all that was gorgeous in pagan ceremonies and splendid in the Jewish ritual has been introduced as a part of Christian worship. (5.) From simplicity in dress and manner of living. The Redeemer's dress was simple. His manner of living was simple. His requirements demand great simplicity and plainness of apparel and manner of life ; 1 Pet. iii. 3—6 ; 1 Tim. ii. 9, 10. Yet how much proneness is there at all times to depart from this ! What a besetting sin has it been in all ages to the church of Christ ! And how much pains should there be that the very simplicity that is in Christ should be observed by all who bear the Christian name !

4. *For if he that cometh,* &c. There is much difficulty in this verse in ascertaining the true sense, and expositors have been greatly perplexed and divided in opinion, especially with regard to the true sense of the last clause, "ye might well bear with *him*." It is difficult to ascertain whether Paul meant to speak ironically or seriously ; and different views will prevail as different views are taken of the design. If it be supposed that he meant to speak seriously, the sense will be, " If the false teacher could recommend a better Saviour than I have done, or a Spirit better able to sanctify and save, then there would be a propriety in your receiving him and tolerating his doctrines." If the former, then the sense will be, " You cannot well bear with *me ;* but if a man

comes among you preaching a false Saviour, and a false Spirit, and a false doctrine, then you bear with him without any difficulty." Another interpretation still has been proposed, by supposing that the word "me" is to be supplied at the close of the verse instead of " him," and then the sense would be, " If you receive so readily one who preaches another gospel, one who comes with far less evidence that he is sent from God than I have, and if you show yourselves thus ready to fall in with any kind of teaching that may be brought to you, you might at least bear with *me* also." Amidst this variety it is not easy to ascertain the true sense. To me it seems probable, however, that Paul spoke *seriously,* and that our translation has expressed the true sense. The main idea doubtless is, that Paul felt that there was danger that they would be corrupted. If they could bring a better gospel, a more perfect system, and proclaim a more perfect Saviour, there would be no such change. But that could not be expected. It could not be done. If therefore they preached *any other* Saviour or any other gospel ; if they departed from the truths which *he* had taught them, *it would be for the worse.* It could not be otherwise. The Saviour whom he preached was perfect, and was able to save. The Spirit which he preached was perfect, and able to sanctify. The gospel which he preached was perfect, and there was no hope that it could be improved. Any change must be for the worse ; and as the false teachers varied from his instructions, there was every reason to apprehend that their minds would be corrupted from the simplicity that was in Christ. The principal idea, therefore, is, that the gospel which *he* preached was as perfect as it could be, and that any change would be for the worse. No doctrine which others brought could be recommended *because* it was better. By the phrase " he that cometh " is meant doubtless the false teacher in Corinth. ¶ *Preacheth another Jesus.*

have not received, or another *a* gospel, which ye have not accepted, ye might well bear ¹ with *him*.

a Ga.1.7,8.
1 or, *with me.*

Proclaims one who is more worthy of your love and more able to save. If he that comes among you and claims your affections can point out another Christ who is more worthy of your confidence, then I admit that you do well to receive him. It is *implied* here that this could not be done. The Lord Jesus in his character and work is perfect. No Saviour superior to him has been provided; none but he is necessary. ¶ *Whom we have not preached.* Let them show, if they can, that they have any Saviour to tell of whom we have not preached. We have given all the evidence that we are sent by God, and have laid all the claim to your confidence, which they can do for having made known the Saviour. They with all their pretensions have no Saviour to tell you of with whom we have not already made you acquainted. They have no claims, therefore, from this quarter which we have not also. ¶ *Or if ye receive another spirit,* &c. If they can preach to you another Sanctifier and Comforter; or if under their ministry you have received higher proofs of the power of the Spirit in performing miracles; in the gift of tongues; in renewing sinners and in comforting your hearts. The idea is, that Paul had proclaimed the existence and agency of the same Holy Spirit which they did; that his preaching had been attended with as striking proofs of the presence and power of that Spirit; that he had all the evidence of a divine commission from such an influence attending his labours which they could possibly have. They could reveal no spirit better able to sanctify and save; none who had more power than the Holy Spirit which they had received under the preaching of Paul, and there was therefore no reason why they should be "corrupted" or seduced from the simple doctrines which they had received,

5 For I suppose I *b* was not a whit behind the very chiefest apostles.

6 But though *c* I be rude in

b 1 Co.15.10; chap.12.11.
c 1 Co.1.17;2.1,13.

and follow others. ¶ *Or another gospel,* &c. A gospel more worthy of your acceptance—one more free, more full, more rich in promises; one that revealed a better plan of salvation, or that was more full of comfort and peace. ¶ *Ye might well bear with him.* Marg. *"with me."* The word *him* is not in the Greek; but is probably to be supplied. The sense is, there would then be some excuse for your conduct. There would be some reason why you should welcome such teachers. But if this cannot be done; if they can preach no other and no better gospel and Saviour than I have done, then there is no excuse. There is no reason why you should follow such teachers and forsake those who were your earliest guides in religion. —Let us never forsake the gospel which we have till we are sure we can get a better. Let us adhere to the simple doctrines of the New Testament until some one can furnish better and clearer doctrines. Let us follow the rules of Christ in our opinions and our conduct; our plans, our mode of worship, our dress, and our amusements, engagements, and company, until we can *certainly* ascertain that there are better rules. A man is foolish for making any change until he has evidence that he is likely to better himself; and it remains yet to be proved that any one has ever bettered himself or his family by forsaking the simple doctrines of the Bible, and embracing a philosophical speculation; by forsaking the scriptural views of the Saviour as the incarnate God, and embracing the views which represent him as a mere man; by forsaking the simple and plain rules of Christ about our manner of life, our dress, and our words and actions, and embracing those which are recommended by mere fashion and by the customs of a gay world.

5. *For I suppose,* &c. I think that

speech, yet not *a* in knowledge ; but we have been thoroughly made manifest *b* among you in all things.

7 Have I committed an offence in abasing myself that ye might be exalted, because I have preached to you the gospel of God freely ?

I gave as good evidence that I was commissioned by God as the most eminent of the apostles. In the miracles which I performed ; in the abundance of my labours, and in my success, I suppose that I did not fall behind any of them. If so, I ought to be regarded and treated as an apostle ; and if so, then the false teachers should not be allowed to supplant me in your affections, or to seduce you from the doctrines which I have taught. On the evidence that Paul was equal to others in the proper proof of a commission from God ; see Notes on ver. 21—30.

6. But though I be *rude in speech ;* see Note, chap. x. 10. The word rendered *rude* here (ἰδιώτης) means properly a private citizen, in opposition to one in a public station ; then a plebeian, or one unlettered or unlearned, in opposition to one of more elevated rank, or one who is learned ; see Notes on Acts iv. 13 ; 1 Cor. xiv. 16. The idea is, my language is that of a plain unlettered person. This was doubtless charged upon him by his enemies, and it may be that he designed in part to admit the truth of the charge. ¶ *Yet not in knowledge.* I do not admit that I am ignorant of the religion which I profess to teach. I claim to be acquainted with the doctrines of Christianity. It does not appear that they charged him with ignorance. If it be asked how the admission that he was rude in speech consists with the fact that he was endowed by the Holy Spirit with the power of speaking languages, we may observe that Paul had undoubtedly learned to speak Greek in his native place (Tarsus in Cilicia). and that the Greek which he had learned there was probably a corrupt kind, such as was spoken in that place. It was this Greek which he probably continued to speak ; for there is no more reason to suppose that the Holy Spirit would aid him

in speaking a language which he had thus early learned than he would in speaking Hebrew. The endowments of the Holy Spirit were conferred to enable the apostles to speak languages which they had never learned, not in perfecting them in languages with which they were before acquainted. It may have been true, therefore, that Paul may have spoken some languages which he never learned with more fluency and perfection than he did those which he had learned to speak when he was young. See the remarks of the Archbishop of Cambray, as quoted by Doddridge *in loc.* It may be remarked, also, that some estimate of the manner of Paul on this point may be formed from his writings. Critics profoundly acquainted with the Greek language remark, that while there is great energy of thought and of diction in the writings of Paul ; while he chooses or *coins* most expressive words, yet that there is everywhere a want of Attic elegance of manner, and of the smoothness and beauty which were so grateful to a Grecian ear. ¶ *But we have been thoroughly made manifest, &c.* You have known all about me. I have concealed nothing from you, and you have had ample opportunity to become thoroughly acquainted with me. The meaning is, " I need not dwell on this. I need speak no more of my manner of speech or knowledge. With all that you are well acquainted."

7. *Have I committed an offence.* Have I done wrong. Greek, " Have I committed a sin." There is here a somewhat abrupt transition from the previous verse ; and the connection is not very apparent. *Perhaps* the connection is this. " I admit my inferiority in regard to my manner of speaking. But this does not interfere with my full understanding of the doctrines which I preach, nor does it interfere with the numerous evidences

8 I robbed other churches, taking wages *of them,* to do you service.

9 And when I was present with you, and wanted, I ^a was chargeable to no man : for that

which I have furnished that I am called to the office of an apostle. What then *is* the ground of offence ? In what *have* I erred ? Wherein have I shown that I was not qualified to be an apostle ? Is it in the fact that I have not chosen to press my claim to a support, but have preached the gospel without charge ?" There can be no doubt that they urged this as an objection to him, and as a proof that he was *conscious* that he had no claim to the office of an apostle ; see Notes on 1 Cor. ix. 3—18. Paul here answers this charge ; and the sum of his reply is, that he *had* received a support, but that it had come from others, a support which they had furnished because the Corinthians had neglected to do it. ¶ *In abasing myself.* By labouring with my own hands ; by submitting to voluntary poverty, and by neglecting to urge my reasonable claims for a support. ¶ *That ye might be exalted.* In spiritual blessings and comforts. I did it because I could thus better promote religion among you. I could thus avoid the charge of aiming at the acquisition of wealth ; could shut the mouths of gainsayers, and could more easily secure access to you. Is it now to be seriously urged as a fault that I have sought your welfare, and that in doing it I have submitted to great self-denial and to many hardships? See Notes on 1 Cor. ix. 18, seq.

8. *I robbed other churches.* The churches of Macedonia and elsewhere, which had ministered to his wants. Probably he refers especially to the church at Philippi (see Phil. iv. 15, 16), which seems to have done more than almost any other church for his support. By the use of the word "robbed" here Paul does not mean that he had obtained any thing from them in a violent or unlawful manner, or any thing which they did not give voluntarily. The word (ἐσύλησα) means properly, " I spoiled, plundered, robbed," but the idea of Paul here

is, that he, *as it were,* robbed them, because he did not render an equivalent for what they gave him. They supported him when he was labouring for another people. A conqueror who plunders a country gives *no equivalent* for what he takes. In this sense only could Paul say that he had plundered the church at Philippi. His general principle was, that " the labourer was worthy of his hire," and that a man was to receive his support from the people for whom he laboured (see 1 Cor. ix. 7—14), but this rule he had not observed in this case. ¶ *Taking wages* of them. Receiving a support from them. They bore my expenses. ¶ *To do you service.* That I might labour among you without being supposed to be striving to obtain your property, and that I might not be compelled to labour with my own hands, and thus to prevent my preaching the gospel as I could otherwise do. The supply from other churches rendered it unnecessary in a great measure that his time should be taken off from the ministry in order to obtain a support.

9. *And when I was present with you.* When I was labouring in order to build up the church in Corinth. ¶ *I was chargeable to no man.* I was burdensome to no one ; or more literally, " I did not lie as a dead weight upon you." The word here used, which occurs nowhere else in the New Testament (κατενάρκησα), means, literally, *to become torpid against, i. e.* to the detriment of any one ; and hence to be burdensome. According to Jerome, its use here is a Cilicism of Paul. The idea is that he did not lead a torpid, inactive life at the expense of others. He did not expect a support from them when he was doing nothing ; nor did he demand support which would in any sense be a burden to them. By his own hands (Acts xviii. 3), and by the aid which he received from abroad, he was supported without deriving aid from the people

which was lacking to me, the *a* brethren which came from Macedonia supplied : and in all *things* I have kept myself from being burdensome unto you, and *so* will I keep *myself.*

10 As the truth of Christ is in me, [1] no man shall stop me of this boasting in the regions of Achaia.

11 Wherefore? because I love you not? God knoweth.

12 But what I do, that I will do,

i *this boasting shall not be stopped in me.*

---

of Corinth. ¶ *And in all* things, &c. In all respects I have carefully kept myself from being a burden on the church. Paul had no idea of living at other men's expense when he was doing nothing. He did not, as a general thing, mean to receive any thing for which he had not rendered a fair equivalent; a just principle for ministers and for all other men ; see chap. xii. 13.

10. *As the truth of Christ is in me.* That is, I solemnly declare this as in the presence of Christ. As I am a Christian man ; as I feel bound to declare the truth, and as I must answer to Christ. It is a solemn form of asseveration, equal to an oath ; see Note on Rom. ix. 1 ; comp. 1 Tim. ii. 7. ¶ *No man shall stop me,* &c. Marg. *This boasting shall not be stopped in me;* see Note on 1 Cor. ix. 15. The idea here is, that Paul was solemnly determined that the same thing should continue. He had not been burdensome to any, and he was resolved that he would not be. Rather than be burdensome he had laboured with his own hands, and he meant to do it still. No man in all Achaia should ever have reason to say that he had been an idler, and had been supported by the churches when he was doing nothing. It was the fixed and settled purpose of his life never to be burdensome to any man. What a noble resolution ! How fixed were the principles of his life ! And what an instance of magnanimous self-denial and of elevated purpose ! Every man, minister or otherwise, should adopt a similar resolution. He should resolve to receive nothing for which he has not rendered a fair equivalent, and resolve if he has health *never* to be a burden to his friends or to the church of God. And even if sick he may yet feel that

he is not burdensome to others. If he is gentle and grateful ; if he makes no unnecessary care ; and especially if he furnishes an example of patience and piety, and seeks the blessing of God on his benefactors, he furnishes them what they will usually esteem an ample equivalent. No man *need* be burdensome to his friends; and all should resolve that by the grace of God they never will be. There is considerable variety in the MSS. here (see Mill on the place), but in regard to the general sense there can be no doubt. Nothing should ever hinder this boasting ; nothing should deprive him of the privilege of saying that he had not been a burden. ¶ *In the regions of Achaia.* Achaia was that part of Greece of which Corinth was the capital ; see Note on Acts xviii. 12.

11. *Wherefore,* &c. It is not because I do not love you. It is not from pride, or because I would not as willingly receive aid from you as from any other. It is not because I am more unwilling to be under obligation to you than to others. I have a deep and tender attachment to you; but it is because I can thus best promote the gospel and advance the kingdom of the Redeemer. Possibly it might have been thought that his unwillingness to receive aid from *them* was some proof of reserve towards them or want of affection, and this may have been urged against him. This he solemnly denies.

12. *But what I do.* The course of life which I have been pursuing I will continue to pursue. That is, I will continue to preach as I have done without demanding a support. I will labour with my own hands if necessary ; I will preach without *demanding* rigidly what I might be entitled to. ¶ *That I may cut off occasion* That I might give them no opportun-

that I may cut off occasion from them *a* which desire occasion; that wherein they glory, they may be found even as we.

a Ga.1.7; Ph.1.15,&c.
b Ga.2.4; 2 Pet.2.1; 1 John 4.1; Re.2.2.

ity of accusing me of desiring to grow rich, and of calumniating me. Paul meant that they should have no plausible pretext even for accusing him; that no man should be able to say that he was preaching merely for the hire. ¶ *Which desire occasion.* No doubt his enemies eagerly sought opportunities of accusing him, and greatly wished for some plausible reason for charging him with that which would be disgraceful and ruinous to his character. Or it may mean that they desired opportunity from the example of Paul to justify themselves in their course; that they took wages from the church at Corinth largely, and desired to be able to say that they had his example. ¶ *That wherein they glory.* Probably meaning that they boasted that they preached the gospel gratis; that they received nothing for their labours. Yet while they did this, it is not improbable that they received presents of the Corinthians, and under various pretences contrived to get from them an ample support, perhaps much more than would have been a reasonable compensation. Men who *profess* to preach the gospel *gratis,* usually contrive in various ways to get more from the people than those who receive a regular and stipulated compensation. By taxing pretty liberally their hospitality; by accepting liberal presents; by frequent proclamation of their self-denial and their poverty, they usually filch large amounts from the people. No people were ever louder in praise of poverty, or in proclamation of their own self-denials than some orders of monks, and that when it might be said almost that the richest possessions of Europe were passing into their hands. At all events, Paul meant that these men should have no opportunity from *his* course to take any such advantage. He knew what he had a right to (1 Cor. ix.), but he

13 For such *are* false *b* apostles, deceitful *c* workers, transforming themselves into the apostles of Christ.

c Ph.3.2; Tit.1.10,11.

had not urged the right. He had received nothing from the church at Corinth, and he meant to receive nothing. He had honestly preached the gospel to them without charge, and he meant still to do it, 1 Cor. ix. 18. They should, therefore, have no opportunity from his conduct either to accuse him of preaching for money, or of sheltering themselves under his example in pretending to preach for nothing when they were in fact obtaining large sums from the people. ¶ *They may be found even as we.* That they may be compelled honestly to pursue such a course as I do, and be found to be in fact what they pretend to be. The sense is, " I mean so to act that if they follow my example, or plead my authority, they may be found to lead an honest life; and that if they boast on this subject, they shall boast strictly according to truth. There shall be no trick; nothing underhanded or deceptive in what they do so far as my example can prevent it."

13. *For such are false apostles.* They have no claim to the apostolic office. They are deceivers. They *pretend* to be apostles; but they have no divine commission from the Redeemer. Paul had thus far argued the case without giving them an explicit designation as deceivers. But here he says that men who had conducted thus; who attempted to impose on the people; who had brought another gospel, whatever pretences they might have—and he was not disposed to deny that there was much that was plausible,—were really impostors and the enemies of Christ. It is morally certain, from ver. 22, that these men were Jews; but why they had engaged in the work of preaching, or why they had gone to Corinth, cannot with certainty be determined. ¶ *Deceitful workers.* Impostors. Men who practise various

14 And no marvel ; for Satan [a] himself is transformed into an angel of light.

a Ge.3.1,5; Re.12.9.

arts to impose on others. They were crafty, and fraudulent, and hypocritical. It is probable that they were men who saw that great advantage might be taken of the new religion ; men who saw the power which it had over the people, and who saw the confidence which the new converts were inclined to repose in their teachers ; perhaps men who had seen the disciples to the Christian faith commit all their property to the hands of the apostles, or who had heard of their doing it (comp. Acts iv. 34, 35), and who supposed that by pretending to be apostles also they might come in for a share of this confidence, and avail themselves of this disposition to commit their property to their spiritual guides. To succeed, it was needful as far as possible to undermine the influence of the true apostles, and take their place in the confidence of the people. Thence they were " *deceitful* (δόλιοι) workers," full of trick, and cunning, and of plausible arts to impose on others. ¶ *Transforming themselves*, &c. Pretending to be apostles. Hypocritical and deceitful, they yet pretended to have been sent by Christ. This is a direct charge of hypocrisy. They knew they were deceivers; and yet they assumed the high claims of apostles of the Son of God.

14. *And no marvel.* And it is not wonderful, ver. 15. Since Satan himself is capable of appearing to be an angel of light, it is not to be deemed strange that those who are in his service also should resemble him. ¶ *For Satan himself is transformed*, &c. That is, he who is an apostate angel ; who is malignant and wicked ; who is the prince of evil, assumes the appearance of a holy angel. Paul assumes this as an indisputable and admitted truth, without attempting to prove it, and without referring to any particular instances. Probably he had in his eye cases where Satan put on false and delusive appearances for the purpose of deceiving, or where he assumed the appearance of great sanctity and re-

verence for the authority of God. Such instances occurred in the temptation of our first parents (Gen. iii. 1 —6), and in the temptation of the Saviour, Mat. iv. The phrase " an angel of light," means a pure and holy angel, light being the emblem of purity and holiness. Such are all the angels that dwell in heaven ; and the idea is, that Satan assumes such a form as to appear to be such an angel. Learn here, (1.) His power. He can *assume* such an aspect as he pleases. He can dissemble and appear to be eminently pious. He is the prince of duplicity as well as of wickedness ; and it is the consummation of bad power for an individual to be able to assume any character which he pleases. (2.) His art. He is long practised in deceitful arts. For six thousand years he has been practising the art of delusion. And with him it is perfect. (3.) We are not to suppose that all that *appears* to be piety is piety. Some of the most plausible appearances of piety are assumed by Satan and his ministers. None ever professed a profounder regard for the authority of God than Satan did when he tempted the Saviour. And if the prince of wickedness can *appear* to be an angel of light, we are not to be surprised if those who have the blackest hearts appear to be men of most eminent piety. (4.) We should be on our guard. We should not listen to suggestions merely because they *appear* to come from a pious man, nor because they *seem* to be prompted by a regard to the will of God. We may be *always* sure that, if we are to be tempted, it will be by some one having a great appearance of virtue and religion. (5.) We are not to expect that Satan will *appear* to man to be as bad as he is. He never shows himself openly to be a spirit of pure wickedness ; or black and abominable in his character; or full of evil and hateful. He would thus defeat himself. It is for this reason that wicked men do not believe that there is such a being as Satan. Though continually under

15 Therefore *it is* no great thing if his ministers also be transformed as the ministers of righteousness ; whose end *a* shall be according to their works.

a Ph.3.19.

16 I say again, Let no man think me a fool ; *b* if otherwise, yet as a fool ¹ receive me, that I may boast myself a little.

17 That which I speak, I

b chap. 12.6,11.   1 or, *suffer.*

his influence and "led captive by him at his will," yet they neither see him nor the chains which lead them, nor are they willing to believe in the existence of the one or the other.

15. *Therefore* it is *no great thing,* &c. It is not to be deemed surprising. You are not to wonder if men of the basest, blackest character put on the appearance of the greatest sanctity, and even become eminent as professed preachers of righteousness. ¶ *Whose end shall be,* &c. Whose final destiny. Their doom in eternity shall not be according to their fair professions and plausible pretences, for they cannot deceive God ; but shall be according to their real character, and their works. Their work is a work of deception, and they shall be judged according to that. What revelations there will be in the day of judgment, when all impostors shall be unmasked, and when all hypocrites and deceivers shall be seen in their true colours ! And how desirable is it that there should be such a day to disclose all beings in their true character, and FOR EVER to remove imposture and delusion from the universe !

16. *I say again.* I repeat it. He refers to what he had said in ver. 1. The sense is, " I have said much respecting myself which may seem to be foolish. I admit that to boast in this manner of one's own self in general is folly. But circumstances compel me to it. And I entreat you to look at those circumstances and not regard me as a fool for doing it." ¶ *If otherwise.* If you think otherwise. If I cannot obtain this of you that you will not regard me as acting prudently and wisely. If you *will* think me foolish, still I am constrained to make these remarks in vindication of myself. ¶ *Yet as a fool receive me.* Marg. "Suffer ;" see ver. 1. Bear with me as you do with others.

Consider how much I have been provoked to this ; how necessary it is to my character ; and do not reject and despise me because I am constrained to say that of myself which is usually regarded as foolish boasting. ¶ *That I may boast myself a little.* Since others do it and are not rebuked, may I be permitted to do it also ; see ver. 18, 19. There is something sarcastic in the words " *a little.*" The sense is, " Others are allowed to boast a great deal. Assuredly I may be allowed to boast *a little* of what I have done."

17. *That which I speak.* In praise of myself. ¶ *I speak* it *not after the Lord ;* see Note on 1 Cor. vii. 12. The phrase here may mean either, I do not speak this by inspiration or claiming to be inspired by the Lord ; or more probably it may mean, I do not speak this imitating the example of the Lord Jesus or strictly as becomes his follower. He was eminently modest, and never vaunted or boasted. And Paul probably means to say, " I do not in this profess to follow him entirely. I admit that it is a departure from his pure example in this respect. But circumstances have compelled me , and much as I would prefer another strain of remark, and sensible as I am in general of the folly of boasting, yet a regard to my apostolic office and authority urges me to this course." Bloomfield supposes that the apostle is not speaking seriously, but that he has an allusion to their view of what he was saying. "Be it so, if you think that what I speak, I speak not as I profess to do according to the Lord, or with a view to subserve the purposes of his religion, but *as it were* in folly, in the confidence of boasting, yet permit me to do it notwithstanding, since you allow others to do it." It is not easy to settle which is the true sense of the passage. I see no

speak *it* ^a not after the Lord, but as it were foolishly, in this confidence ^b of boasting.

18 Seeing ^c that many glory after the flesh, I will glory also.

a 1 Co.7.12.　　*b* chap.9.4.

19 For ye suffer fools gladly, seeing ye *yourselves* are wise.

20 For ye suffer, if a man bring you into bondage, if a man devour *you*, if a man take *of you*, if a man

c Ph.3.3,4; 1 Co.4.10.

conclusive evidence against either. But the former seems to me to be most in accordance with the scope of the whole. Paul admitted that what he said was not in exact accordance with the spirit of the Lord Jesus; and in admitting this he designed probably to administer a delicate hint that all *their* boasting was a wide departure from that spirit. ¶ *As it were foolishly.* As in folly. It is to be admitted that to boast is in general foolish; and I admit that my language is open to this general charge ¶ *In this confidence of boasting.* In confident boasting. I speak confidently and I admit in the spirit of boasting.

18. *Seeing that many glory*, &c. The false teachers in Corinth. They boasted of their birth, rank, natural endowments, eloquence, &c.; see ver. 22. Comp. Phil. iii. 3, 4. ¶ *I will glory also.* I also will boast of my endowments, which though somewhat different yet pertain in the main to the *flesh* also; see ver. 23, seq. *His* endowments *in the flesh*, or what he had to boast of pertaining to the flesh, related not so much to birth and rank, though not inferior to them in these, but to what *the flesh* had endured—to stripes and imprisonments, and hunger and peril. This is an exceedingly delicate and happy turn given to the whole subject.

19. *For ye suffer fools gladly.* You tolerate or endure those who are really fools. This is perhaps, says Dr. Bloomfield, the most sarcastic sentence ever penned by the apostle Paul. Its sense is, " You profess to be wondrous wise. And yet you who are so wise a people, freely tolerate those who are foolish in their boasting; who proclaim their own merits and attainments. You may allow me, therefore, to come in for my share, and boast also, and thus obtain your favour." Or it may mean, " You are

so profoundly wise as easily to. see who are fools. You have great power of discernment in this, and have found out that I am a fool, and also that other boasters are fools. Yet knowing this, you bear patiently with such fools; have admitted them to your favour and friendship, and I may come in among the rest of the fools, and partake also of your favours." They *had* borne with the false apostles who had boasted of their endowments, and yet they claimed to be eminent for wisdom and discernment.

20. *For ye suffer*, &c. You bear patiently with men who impose on you in every way, and who are constantly defrauding you, though you profess to be so wise, and you may bear with me a little, though I have no such intention. Seriously, if you bear with boasters who intend to delude and deceive you in various ways, you may bear with one who comes to you with no such intention, but with an honest purpose to do good. ¶ *If a man bring you into bondage* (καταδουλοῖ). If a man, or if any one (εἰ τις) *make a slave of you*, or reduce you to servitude. The idea is, doubtless, that the false teachers set up a lordship over their consciences; destroyed their freedom of opinion; and made them subservient to their will. They really took away their Christian freedom as much as if they had been slaves. In what way this was done is unknown. It may be that they imposed on them rites and forms, commanded expensive and inconvenient ceremonies, and required arduous services merely at their own will. A false religion always makes slaves. It is only true Christianity that leaves perfect freedom. All heathens are slaves to their priests; all fanatics are slaves to some fanatical leader; all those who embrace error are slaves to those who claim to be their guides. The papist every-

exalt himself, if a man smite you on the face.

21 I speak as concerning reproach, as though we had been

---

where is the slave of the priest, and the despotism there is as great as in any region of servitude whatever. ¶ *If a man devour* you. This is exceedingly sarcastic. The idea is, " Though you are so wise, yet you in fact tolerate men who impose on you —no matter though they eat you up, or consume all that you have. By their exorbitant demands they would consume all you have—or, as we would say, eat you out of house and home." All this they took patiently; and freely gave all that they demanded. False teachers are always rapacious. They seek the *property,* not the *souls* of those to whom they minister. Not satisfied with a maintenance, they aim to obtain *all,* and their plans are formed to secure as much as possible of those to whom they minister. ¶ *If a man take* of you. If he take and seize upon your possessions. If he comes and takes what he pleases and bears it away as his own. ¶ *If a man exalt himself.* If he set himself up as a ruler and claim submission. No matter how arrogant his claims, yet you are ready to bear with him. You *might* then bear with me in the very moderate demands which I make on your obedience and confidence. ¶ *If a man smite you on the face.* The word here rendered " smite " (δέρω) means properly to skin, to flay; but in the New Testament it means to beat, to scourge—especially so as to take off the skin; Mat. xxi. 35 ; Mark xii. 3, 5. The idea here is, if any one treats you with contumely and scorn —since there can be no higher expression of it than to smite a man on the face ; Mat. xxvi. 67. It is not to be supposed that this occurred literally among the Corinthians ; but the idea is, that the false teachers really treated them with as little respect as if they smote them on the face. In what way this was done is unknown; but probably it was by their domineering manners, and the little respect which they showed for the opinions and feelings of the Corinthian Chris-

tians. Paul says that as they bore this very patiently, they might allow *him* to make some remarks about himself in self-commendation.

21. *I speak as concerning reproach.* I speak of disgrace. That is, says Rosenmüller, " I speak of your disgrace, or, as others prefer it, of the disgrace of the false apostles." Doddridge regards it as a question. " Do I speak this by way of dishonour, from an envious desire to derogate from my superiors so as to bring them down to my own level?" But to me it seems that Paul refers to what he had been admitting respecting himself—to what he had evinced in rudeness of speech (ver. 6), and to his not having urged his claims to the support which an apostle had a right to receive—to things, in short, which *they* esteemed to be disgraceful or reproachful. And his idea, it seems to me, is this : " I have been speaking of reproach or disgrace *as if* I was weak, *i. e.* as if I was disposed to admit as true all that has been said of me as reproachful or disgraceful ; all that has been said of my want of qualifications for the office, of my want of talent, or elevated rank, or honourable birth, &c. I have not pressed my claims, but have been reasoning as if all this were true—*as if* all that was honourable in birth and elevated in rank belonged to them—all that is mean and unworthy pertained to me. But it is not so. Whatever *they* have *I* have. Whatever they can boast of, I can boast of in a more eminent degree. Whatever advantage there is in birth is mine ; and I can tell of toils, and trials, and sufferings in the apostolic office which far surpass theirs." Paul proceeds, therefore, to a full statement of his advantages of birth and of his labours in the cause of the Redeemer. ¶ *As though we had been weak.* As if I had no claims to urge ; as if I had no just cause of boldness, but must submit to this reproach. ¶ *Howbeit* (δέ). *But.* The sense is, if any one is disposed to boast, I am ready for him. I can

weak. Howbeit whereinsoever any is bold, (I speak foolishly,) I am bold also.

22 Are they Hebrews? so *am* I.

Are they Israelites? so *am* I. Are they the seed of Abraham? so *am* I.

23 Are they ministers of Christ?

tell also of things that have as high claims to confidence as they can. If they are disposed to go into a comparison on the points which qualify a man for the office of an apostle, I am ready to compare myself with them. ¶ *Whereinsoever* (ἰν ᾧ). In what. Whatever they have to boast of I am prepared also to show that I am equal to them. Be it pertaining to birth, rank, education, labours, they will find that I do not shrink from the comparison. ¶ *Any is bold* (τις τολμᾷ). Any one *dares* to boast; any one is bold. ¶ *I speak foolishly.* Remember now that I speak as a fool. I have been charged with this folly. Just now keep that in mind; and do not forget that it is only a fool who is speaking. Just recollect that I have no claims to public confidence: that I am destitute of all pretensions to the apostolic office; that I am given to a vain parade and ostentation, and to boasting of what does not belong to me, and when you recollect this let me tell my story. The whole passage is ironical in the highest degree. The sense is, "It is doubtless all nonsense and folly for a man to boast who has only the qualifications which I have. But there is a great deal of wisdom in *their* boasting who have so much more elevated endowments for the apostolic office." ¶ *I am bold also.* I can meet them on their own ground, and speak of qualifications not inferior to theirs.

22. *Are they Hebrews?* This proves that the persons who had made the difficulty in Corinth were those who were of Hebrew extraction, though it may be that they had been born in Greece and had been educated in the Grecian philosophy and art of rhetoric. It is also clear that they prided themselves on being Jews—on having a connection with the people and land from whence the religion which the Corinthian church now professed had emanated. Indications are apparent everywhere in the New

Testament of the superiority which the Jewish converts to Christianity claimed over those converted from among the heathen. Their boast would probably be that they were the descendants of the patriarchs; that the land of the prophets was theirs; that they spake the language in which the oracles of God were given; that the true religion had proceeded from them, &c. ¶ *So* am *I.* I have as high claims as any of them to distinction on this head. Paul had all their advantages of birth. He was an Israelite; of the honoured tribe of Benjamin; a Pharisee, circumcised at the usual time (Phil. iii. 5), and educated in the best manner at the feet of one of their most eminent teachers; Acts xxii. 3. ¶ *Are they Israelites?* Another name, signifying substantially the same thing. The only difference is, that the word " Hebrew " signified properly one who was from beyond (יִבְרִי from עָבַר, to pass, to pass over—hence applied to Abraham, because he had come from a foreign land; and the word denoted properly *a foreigner*—a man from the land or country *beyond*, עֵבֶר) the Euphrates. The name *Israelite* denoted properly one descended from Israel or Jacob, and the difference between them was, that the name *Israelite*, being a patronymic derived from one of the founders of their nation, was in use among themselves; the name *Hebrew* was applied by the Canaanite to them as having come from *beyond* the river, and was the current name among foreign tribes and nations. See Gesenius's Lexicon on the word (יִבְרִי) *Hebrew.* Paul in the passage before us means to say that he had as good a claim to the honour of being a native born descendant of Israel as could be urged by any of them. ¶ *Are they the seed of Abraham?* Do they boast that they are descended from Abraham? This with all the Jews was regarded as a distinguished honour (see Mat. iii. 9;

(1 speak as a fool) I *am* more ; in labours *a* more abundant, in stripes *b* above measure, in prisons more frequent, in deaths *c* oft.

a 1 Co.15.10.   b Ac.9.16; 20.23; 21.11.
              c 1 Co.15.30,32.

John viii. 39), and no doubt the false teachers in Corinth boasted of it as eminently qualifying them to engage in the work of the ministry. ¶ *So am I.* Paul had the same qualification. He was a Jew also by birth. He was of the tribe of Benjamin ; Phil. iii. 5.

23. *Are they ministers of Christ ?* Though Jews by birth yet they claimed to be the ministers of the Messiah. ¶ *I speak as a fool.* As if he had said, " Bear in mind, in what I am now about to say, that he who speaks is accused of being a fool in boasting. Let it not be deemed improper that I should act in this character, and since you regard me as such, let me speak like a fool." His frequent reminding them of this charge was eminently fitted to humble them that they had ever made it, especially when they were reminded by an enumeration of his trials, of the character of the man against whom the charge was brought. ¶ *I am more.* Paul was not disposed to deny that they were true ministers of Christ. But he had higher claims to the office than they had. He had been called to it in a more remarkable manner, and he had shown by his labours and trials that he had more of the true spirit of a minister of the Lord Jesus than they had. He therefore goes into detail to show what he had endured in endeavouring to diffuse the knowledge of the Saviour ; trials which he had borne probably while they had been dwelling in comparative ease, and in a comfortable manner, free from suffering and persecution. ¶ *In labours more abundant.* In the kind of labour necessary in propagating the gospel. Probably he had now been engaged in the work a much longer time than they had, and had been far more indefatigable in it. ¶ *In stripes.* In receiving stripes ; *i. e.,* I have been more frequently scourged ; ver. 24.

24 Of the Jews five times received I forty *stripes* *d* save one.

25 Thrice was I beaten *e* with rods, once was I *f* stoned, thrice

d De. 25.3.   e Ac.16.22.
              f Ac.14.19.

This was a proof of his being a minister of Christ, because eminent devotedness to him at that time, of necessity subjected a man to frequent scourging. The ministry is one of the very few places, perhaps it stands alone in this, where it is proof of peculiar qualification for office that a man has been treated with all manner of contumely, and has even been often publicly whipped. What other office admits such a qualification as this ? ¶ *Above measure.* Exceedingly ; far exceeding them. He had received far more than they had, and he judged, therefore, that this was one evidence that he had been called to the ministry. ¶ *In prisons more frequent.* Luke, in the Acts of the Apostles, mentions only one imprisonment of Paul before the time when this epistle was written. That was at Philippi with Silas, Acts xvi. 23, seq. But we are to remember that many things were omitted by Luke. He does not profess to give an account of *all* that happened to Paul ; and an omission is not a contradiction. For any thing that Luke says, Paul may have been imprisoned often. He *mentions* his having been in prison once ; he does not *deny* that he had been in prison many times besides ; see on ver. 24. ¶ *In deaths oft.* This is, exposed to death ; or suffering pain equal to death ; see on chap. i. 9. No one familiar with the history of Paul can doubt that he was often in danger of death.

24. *Of the Jews,* &c. On this verse and the following verse it is of importance to make a few remarks preliminary to the explanation of the phrases. (1.) It is admitted that the particulars here referred to cannot be extracted out of the Acts of the Apostles. A few can be identified, but there are many more trials referred to here than are specified there. (2.) This *proves* that this epistle was

not framed from the history, but that they are written independently of one another.—*Paley.* (3.) Yet they are not inconsistent one with the other. For there is no article in the enumeration here which is contradicted by the history, and the history, though silent with respect to many of these transactions, has left *space* enough to suppose that they may have occurred. (*a*) There is no *contradiction* between the accounts. Where it is said by Paul that he was *thrice* beaten with rods, though in the Acts but *one* beating is mentioned, yet there is no contradiction. It is only the *omission* to record *all* that occurred to Paul. But had the history, says Paley, contained an account of *four* beatings with rods, while Paul mentions here but *three*, there would have been a contradiction. And so of the other particulars. (*b*) Though the Acts of the Apostles be silent concerning many of the instances referred to, yet that silence may be accounted for on the plan and design of the history. The date of the epistle synchronizes with the beginning of the twentieth chapter of the Acts. The part, therefore, which precedes the twentieth chapter is the only place in which can be found any notice of the transactions to which Paul here refers. And it is evident from the Acts that the author of that history was not with Paul until his departure from Troas, as related in chap. xvi. 10 ; see Note on that place. From that time Luke attended Paul in his travels. From that period to the time when this epistle was written occupies but four chapters of the history, and it is here if anywhere that we are to look for the minute account of the life of Paul. But here much may have occurred to Paul before Luke joined him. And as it was the design of Luke to give an account of Paul mainly *after* he had joined him, it is not to be wondered at that many things may have been omitted of his previous life. (*c*) The period of time after the conversion of Paul to the time when Luke joined him at Troas is very succinctly given. That period embraced sixteen years, and is comprised in a few chapters. Yet in that

time Paul was constantly travelling. He went to Arabia, returned to Damascus, went to Jerusalem, and then to Tarsus, and from Tarsus to Antioch, and thence to Cyprus, and then through Asia Minor, &c. In this time he must have made many voyages, and been exposed to many perils. Yet all this is comprised in a few chapters, and a considerable portion of them is occupied with an account of public discourses. In that period of sixteen years, therefore, there was ample opportunity for all the occurrences which are here referred to by Paul ; see Paley's Horæ Paulinæ on 2 Cor. No. ix. (*d*) I may add, that from the account which *follows* the time when Luke joined him at Troas (from Acts xvi. 10), it is altogether probable that he *had* endured much before. After that time there is mention of *just such* transactions of scourging, stoning,&c., as are here specified, and it is altogether probable that he had been called to suffer them before. When Paul says " of the Jews," &c., he refers to this because this was a Jewish mode of punishment. It was usual with them to inflict but thirty-nine blows. The Gentiles were not limited by law in the number which they inflicted. ¶ *Five times.* This was doubtless in their synagogues and before their courts of justice. They had not the power of capital punishment, but they had the power of inflicting minor punishments. And though the *instances* are not specified by Luke in the Acts, yet the statement here by Paul has every degree of probability. We know that he often preached in their synagogues (Acts ix. 20 ; xiii. 5, 14, 15 ; xiv. 1 ; xvii. 17 ; xviii. 4); and nothing is more probable than that they would be enraged against him, and would vent their malice in every way possible. They regarded him as an apostate, and a ringleader of the Nazarenes, and they would not fail to inflict on him the severest punishment which they were permitted to inflict. ¶ *Forty* stripes *save one.* The word *stripes* does not occur in the original, but is necessarily understood. The law of Moses (Deut. xxv.

I suffered shipwreck, a night [a] and a day I have been in the deep;

a Ac.xxvii.

26 *In* journeyings often, *in* perils of waters, *in* perils of rob-

---

3) expressly limited the number of stripes that might be inflicted to forty. In no case might this number be exceeded. This was a humane provision, and one that was not found among the heathen, who inflicted any number of blows at discretion. Unhappily it is not observed among professedly Christian nations where the practice of whipping prevails, and particularly in slave countries, where the master inflicts any number of blows at his pleasure. In practice among the Hebrews, the number of blows inflicted was in fact limited to thirty-nine, lest by any accident in counting, the criminal should receive more than the number prescribed in the law. There was another reason still for limiting it to thirty-nine. They usually made use of a scourge with three thongs, and this was struck thirteen times. That it was usual to inflict but thirty-nine lashes is apparent from Josephus, Ant. book IV. chap. viii. § 21.

25. *Thrice was I beaten with rods.* In the Acts of the Apostles there is mention made of his being beaten in this manner but once before the time when this epistle was written. That occurred at Philippi ; Acts xvi. 22, 23. But there is no reason to doubt that it was more frequently done. This was a frequent mode of punishment among the ancient nations, and as Paul was often persecuted, he would be naturally subjected to this shameful punishment. ¶ *Once I was stoned.* This was the usual mode of punishment among the Jews for blasphemy. The instance referred to here occurred at Lystra ; Acts xiv. 19. Paley (Horæ Paulinæ) has remarked that this, when confronted with the history, furnished the nearest approach to a contradiction without a contradiction being actually incurred, that he ever had met with. The history (Acts xiv.19) contains but one account of his being actually stoned. But prior to this (Acts xiv. 5), it mentions that "an assault was made both of the

Gentiles, and also of the Jews with their rulers, to use them despitefully and to stone them, but they were aware of it, and fled to Lystra and Derbe." "Now," Paley remarks, "had the assault been completed ; had the history related that a stone was thrown, as it relates that preparations were made both by Jews and Gentiles to stone Paul and his companions; or even had the account of this transaction stopped without going on to inform us that Paul and his companions were aware of their danger and fled, a contradiction between the history and the epistle would have ensued. Truth is necessarily consistent, but it is scarcely possible that independent accounts, not having truth to guide them, should thus advance to the very brink of contradiction without falling into it." ¶ *Thrice I suffered shipwreck.* On what occasions, or where, is now unknown, as these instances are not referred to in the Acts of the Apostles. The instance of shipwreck recorded there (chap. xxvii.), which occurred when on his way to Rome, happened *after* this epistle was written, and should not be supposed to be one of the instances referred to here. Paul made many voyages in going from Jerusalem to Tarsus, and to Antioch, and to various parts of Asia Minor, and to Cyprus; and shipwrecks in those seas were by no means such unusual occurrences as to render this account improbable. ¶ *A night and a day,* &c. The word here used (νυχθημερον) denotes a complete natural day, or twenty-four hours. ¶ *In the deep.* To what this refers we do not now certainly know. It is probable, however, that Paul refers to some period when, having been shipwrecked, he was saved by supporting himself on a plank or fragment of the vessel until he obtained relief. Such a situation is one of great peril, and he mentions it, therefore, among the trials which he had endured. The supposition of some commentators

bers, *in* perils *a* by *mine own* countymen, *in* perils by the heathen, *in* pearls in the city, *in* perils in the wilderness, *in* perils in the sea, *in* perils among false brethren ;

27 In weariness and painfulness, in watchings *b* often, in hunger *c* and thirst, in fastings often, in cold and nakedness.

28 Besides those things that

a Ac.14.5.

b Ac.20.31.   *c* 1 Cor.4.11.

that he spent his time on some rock in the deep ; or of others that this means some deep dungeon; or of others that he was swallowed by a whale, like Jonah, shows the extent to which the fancy is often indulged in interpreting the Bible.

26. *In journeyings often.* Of course subject to the fatigue, toil, and danger which such a mode of life involves. ¶ In *perils of waters.* In danger of losing my life at sea, or by floods, or by crossing streams. ¶ *Of robbers.* Many of the countries, especially Arabia, through which he travelled, were then infested, as they are now, with robbers. It is not impossible or improbable that he was often attacked and his life endangered. It is still unsafe to travel in many of the places through which he travelled. ¶ *By* mine own *countrymen.* The Jews. They often scourged him ; laid wait for him and were ready to put him to death. They had deep enmity against him as an apostate, and he was in constant danger of being put to death by them. ¶ *By the heathen.* By those who had not the true religion. Several instances of his danger from this quarter are mentioned in the Acts. ¶ *In the city.* In cities, as in Derbe, Lystra, Philippi, Jerusalem, Ephesus, &c. ¶ *In the wilderness.* In the desert, where he would be exposed to ambushes, or to wild beasts, or to hunger and want. Instances of this are not recorded in the Acts, but no one can doubt that they occurred. The idea here is, that he had met with constant danger wherever he was, whether in the busy haunts of men or in the solitude and loneliness of the desert. ¶ *In the sea ;* see ver. 25. ¶ *Among false brethren.* This was the crowning danger and trial to Paul, as it is to all others. A man can better bear danger by land and water, among robbers and in deserts,

than he can bear to have his confidence abused, and to be subjected to the action and the arts of spies upon his conduct. *Who* these were he has not informed us. He mentions it as the chief trial to which he had been exposed, that he had met those who pretended to be his friends, and who yet had sought every possible opportunity to expose and destroy him. Perhaps he has here a delicate reference to the danger which he apprehended from the false brethren in the church at Corinth.

27. *In weariness.* Resulting from travelling, exposure, labour, and want. The word κόπος (from κόπτω, to beat, to cut) means, properly, wailing and grief, accompanied with beating the breast. Hence the word means toil, labour, wearisome effort. ¶ *And painfulness.* This word (μόχθις) is a stronger term than the former. It implies painful effort; labour producing sorrow, and in the New Testament is uniformly connected with the word rendered " weariness" (1 Thess. ii. 9 ; 2 Thess. iii. 8), rendered in both those places "travail." ¶ *In watchings often.* In loss of sleep, arising from abundant toils and from danger; see Note on chap. vi. 5. ¶ *In hunger and thirst.* From travelling among strangers, and being dependent on them and on his own personal labours; see Note, 1 Cor. iv. 11. ¶ *In fastings often.* Either voluntary or involuntary ; see Note on chap. vi. 5. ¶ *In cold and nakedness;* see Note, 1 Cor. iv. 11.

28. *Besides those things that are without.* In addition to these external trials, these trials pertaining to the body, I have mental trials and anxieties resulting from the necessary care of all the churches. But on the meaning of these words commentators are not agreed. Rosenmüller supposes that the phrase means " besides

are without, that which cometh upon me daily, the care *a* of all the churches.

a Ac.15.36,40.

29 Who *b* is weak, and I am not weak? who is offended, and I burn not?

b 1 Co.9.22.

those things that come from other sources," "that I may omit other things." Beza, Erasmus, Bloomfield, and some others suppose that the passage means those things out of the regular routine of his office. Doddridge, "besides foreign affairs." Probably the sense is, "Apart from the things beside" (Χωρὶς τῶν παρεκτὸς); "not to mention other matters; or if other matters should be laid aside, there is this continually rushing anxiety arising from the care of all the churches." That is, this would be enough in itself. Laying aside all that arises from hunger, thirst, cold, &c., this continual care occupies my mind and weighs upon my heart. ¶ *That which cometh upon me daily.* There is great force in the original here. The phrase rendered "that which cometh upon me" means properly, "that which *rushes* upon me." The word (ἐπισύστασις) means properly a concourse, a crowd, hence a tumult; and the idea here is, that these cares rushed upon him, or pressed upon him like a crowd of men or a mob that bore all before it. This is one of Paul's most energetic expressions, and denotes the incessant anxiety of mind to which he was subject. ¶ *The care of all the churches.* The care of the numerous churches which he had established, and which needed his constant supervision. They were young; many of them were feeble; many were made up of heterogeneous materials; many composed of Jews and Gentiles mingled together, with conflicting prejudices, habits, preferences; many of them were composed of those who had been gathered from the lowest ranks of life; and questions would be constantly occurring relating to their order and discipline in which Paul would feel a deep interest, and which would naturally be referred to him for decision. Besides this, they had many trials. They were persecuted, and would suffer much. In their sufferings Paul would feel deep sympathy,

and would desire, as far as possible, to afford them relief. In addition to the churches which *he* had planted, he would feel an interest in all others, and doubtless many cases would be referred to him as an eminent apostle for counsel and advice. No wonder that all this came rushing on him like a tumultuous assembly ready to overpower him.

29. *Who is weak,* &c. I sympathize with all. I feel where others feel, and their sorrows excite deep sympathetic emotions in my bosom. Like a tender and compassionate friend I am affected when I see others in circumstances of distress. The word *weak* here may refer to any want of strength, any infirmity or feebleness arising either from body or mind. It may include all who were feeble by persecution or by disease; or it may refer to the weak in faith and doubtful about their duty (see 1 Cor. ix. 22), and to those who were burdened with mental sorrows. The idea is, that Paul had a deep sympathy in all who *needed* such sympathy from any cause. And the statement here shows the depth of feeling of this great apostle; and shows what should be the feeling of every pastor; see Note on Rom. xii. 15. ¶ *And I am not weak?* I share his feelings and sympathize with him. If he suffers, I suffer. Bloomfield supposes that Paul means that in the case of those who were weak in the faith he *accommodated* himself to their weakness and thus became all things to all men; see my Note on 1 Cor. ix. 22. But it seems to me probable that he uses the phrase here in a more *general* sense, as denoting that he sympathized with those who were weak and feeble in all their circumstances. ¶ *Who is offended* (σκανδαλίζεται). Who is *scandalized.* The word means properly to cause to stumble and fall; hence to be a stumbling-block to any one; to give or cause offence to any one. The idea here seems to be, "who is liable to be led astray; who

30 If I must needs glory, I will *a* glory of the things which concern mine infirmities.

31 The God *b* and Father of

our Lord Jesus Christ, which *c* is blessed for evermore, knoweth *d* that I lie not.

32 In Damascus *e* the governor

a chap.12.5,9,10.   b Ga.1.3.

c Ro.9.5.   d 1 Th.2.5.   e Ac.9.24,25.

has temptations and trials that are likely to lead him to sin or to cause him to fall, and I do not burn with impatience to restore him, or with indignation against the tempter?" In all such cases Paul deeply sympathized with them, and was prompt to aid them. ¶ *And I burn not?* That is, with anger or with great agitation of mind at learning that any one had fallen into sin. This may either mean that he would burn with indignation against those who had led them into sin, or be deeply excited in view of the disgrace which would be thus brought on the Christian cause. In either case it means that his mind would be in a glow of emotion; he would feel deeply; he could not look upon such things with indifference or without being deeply agitated. With all he sympathized; and the condition of all, whether in a state of feeble faith, or feeble body, or falling into sin, excited the deepest emotions in his mind. The truth here taught is, that Paul felt a deep sympathy for all others who bore the Christian name, and this sympathy for others greatly increased the cares and toils of the apostolic office which he sustained. But having given this exposition, candour compels me to acknowledge that the whole verse *may* mean, "Who is feeble in the faith in regard to certain observances and rites and customs (1 Cor. ix. 22), and I do not also evince the same? I do not rouse their prejudices, or wound their feelings, or alarm them. On the other hand, who is scandalized, or led into sin by the example of others in regard to such custom; who is led by the example of others into transgression, and I do not burn with indignation?" In either case, however, the general sense is, that he sympathized with all others.

30. *If I must needs glory.* It is unpleasant for me to boast, but circumstances have compelled me. But since I am compelled, I will not boast

of my rank, or talents, but of that which is regarded by some as an infirmity. ¶ *Mine infirmities.* Greek, "The things of my weakness." The word here used is derived from the same word which is rendered weak," in ver. 29. He intends doubtless to refer here to what had preceded in his enumeration of the trials which he had endured. He had spoken of *sufferings.* He had endured much. He had also spoken of that tenderness of feeling which prompted him to sympathize so deeply when others suffered. He admitted that he often wept, and trembled, and glowed with strong feelings on occasions which perhaps to many would not seem to call for such strong emotions, and which they might be disposed to set down as a weakness or infirmity. This might especially be the case among the Greeks, where many philosophers, as the Stoics, were disposed to regard *all* sympathetic feeling, and all sensitiveness to suffering as an infirmity. But Paul admitted that he was disposed to glory in this alone. He gloried that he *had* *suffered* so much; that he had endured so many trials on account of Christianity, and that he *had* a mind that was capable of feeling for others and of entering into their sorrows and trials. Well might he do this, for there is no more lovely feature in the mind of a virtuous man, and there is no more lovely influence of Christianity than this, that it teaches us to "bear a brother's woes," and to sympathize in all the sorrows and joys of others. Philosophy and infidelity may be dissocial, cheerless, cold; but it is not so with Christianity. Philosophy may snap asunder all the cords which bind us to the living world, but Christianity strengthens these cords; cold and cheerless atheism and scepticism may teach us to look with unconcern on a suffering world, but it is the glory of Christianity that it teaches us to feel an interest in the weal or woe of

under Aretas the king kept the city of the Damascenes with a

garrison, desirous to apprehend me:

---

the obscurest man that lives, to rejoice in his joy, and to weep in his sorrows.

31. *The God and Father,* &c. Paul was accustomed to make solemn appeals to God for the truth of what he said, especially when it was likely to be called in question; see ver. 10; comp. Rom. ix. 1. The solemn appeal which he here makes to God is made in view of what he had just said of his sufferings, not of what follows— for there was nothing in the occurrence at Damascus that demanded so solemn an appeal to God. The *reason* of this asseveration is probably that the transactions to which he had referred were known to but few, and perhaps not all of them to even his best friends; that his trials and calamities had been so numerous and extraordinary that his enemies would say that they were improbable, and that all this had been the mere fruit of exaggeration; and as he had no *witnesses* to appeal to for the truth of what he said, he makes a solemn appeal to the ever-blessed God. This appeal is made with great *reverence.* It is not rash, or bold, and is by no means irreverent or profane. He appeals to God as the Father of the Redeemer whom he so much venerated and loved, and as himself blessed for evermore. If all appeals to God were made on as important occasions as this, and with the same profound veneration and reverence, such appeals would never be improper, and we should never be shocked as we are often now when men appeal to God. This passage *proves* that an appeal to God on great occasions is not improper; it proves also that it should be done with profound veneration.

32. *At Damascus.* This circumstance is mentioned as an additional trial. It is evidently mentioned as an instance of peril which had escaped his recollection in the rapid account of his dangers enumerated in the previous verses. It is designed to show what imminent danger he was in, and how narrowly he escaped with his life. On the situation of Damascus, see

Note, Acts ix. 2. The transaction here referred to is also related by Luke (Acts ix. 24, 25), though without mentioning the name of the king, or referring to the fact that the governor kept the city with a garrison. ¶ *The governor.* Greek, ὁ ἐθνάρχης, *The ethnarch;* properly a ruler of the people, a prefect, a ruler, a chief. Who he was is unknown, though he was evidently some officer under the king. It is not improbable that he was a Jew, or at any rate he was one who could be influenced by the Jews, and he was doubtless excited by the Jews to guard the city, and if possible to take Paul as a malefactor. Luke informs us (Acts ix. 23, 24) that the Jews took counsel against Paul to kill him, and that they watched the gates night and day to effect their object. They doubtless represented Paul as an apostate, and as aiming to overthrow their religion. He had come with an important commission to Damascus and had failed to execute it; he had become the open friend of those whom he came to destroy; and they doubtless claimed of the civil authorities of Damascus that he should be given up and taken to Jerusalem for trial. It was not difficult, therefore, to secure the co-operation of the governor of the city in the case, and there is no improbability in the statement. ¶ *Under Aretas the king.* There were three kings of this name who are particularly mentioned by ancient writers. The first is mentioned in 2 Mac. v. 8, as the "king of the Arabians." He lived about 170 years before Christ, and of course could not be the one referred to here. The second is mentioned in Josephus, Ant. b. xiii. chap. xv. § 2. He is first mentioned as having reigned in Cœlo-Syria, but as being called to the government of Damascus by those who dwelt there, on account of the hatred which they bore to Ptolemy Meneus. Whiston remarks in a note on Josephus, that this was the first king of the Arabians who took Damascus and reigned there, and that this name

33 And through a window | by the wall, and escaped his
in a basket was I let down | hands.

afterwards became common to such Arabian kings as reigned at Damascus and at Petra; see Josephus, Ant. b. xvi. chap. ix. § 4. Of course this king reigned some time before the transaction here referred to by Paul. A third king of this name, says Rosenmüller, is the one mentioned here. He was the father-in-law of Herod Antipas. He made war with his son-in-law Herod because he had repudiated his daughter, the wife of Herod. This he had done in order to marry his brother Philip's wife; see Note, Mat. xiv. 3. On this account Aretas made war with Herod, and in order to resist him, Herod applied to Tiberius the Roman emperor for aid. Vitellius was sent by Tiberius to subdue Aretas, and to bring him dead or alive to Rome. But before Vitellius had embarked in the enterprise, Tiberius died, and thus Aretas was saved from ruin. It is supposed that in this state of things, when thus waging war with Herod, he made an incursion to Syria and seized upon Damascus, where he was reigning when Paul went there; or if not reigning there personally, he had appointed an *ethnarch* or governor who administered the affairs of the city in his place. ¶ *Kept the city*, &c. Luke (Acts ix. 24) says that they watched the gates day and night to kill him. This was probably the Jews. Meantime the ethnarch guarded the city, to prevent his escape. The Jews would have killed him at once; the ethnarch wished to apprehend him and bring him to trial. In either case Paul had much to fear, and he, therefore, embraced the only way of escape. ¶ *With a garrison*. The word which is used here in the original (φρουρέω) means simply to watch; to guard; to keep. Our translation would seem to imply that there was a body of men *stationed* in order to guard the city. The true idea is, that there were men who were appointed to guard the gates of the city and to keep watch lest he should escape them. Damascus was surrounded, as all ancient cities were, with high walls, and it did not occur

to them that he could escape in any other way than by the gates.

33. *And through a window.* That is, through a little door or aperture in the wall; perhaps something like an embrasure, that might have been large enough to allow a man to pass through it. Luke says (Acts ix. 25) that they let him down "by the wall." But there is no inconsistency. They doubtless first passed him *through* the embrasure or loop-hole in the wall, and then let him down gently by the side of it. Luke does not say it was *over* the top of the wall, but merely that he descended *by* the wall. It is not probable that an embrasure or opening would be near the bottom, and consequently there would be a considerable distance for him to descend by the side of the wall after he had passed through the window. Bloomfield, however, supposes that the phrase employed by Luke and rendered "*by* the wall," means properly "*through* the wall." But I prefer the former interpretation. ¶ *In a basket.* The word here used (σαργάνη) means anything braided or twisted; hence a rope-basket, a net-work of cords, or a wicker hamper. It might have been such an one as was used for catching fish, or it might have been made for the occasion. The word used by Luke (Acts ix. 25) is σπυρίς,—a word usually meaning a basket for storing grain, provisions, &c. Where Paul went immediately after he had escaped them, he does not here say. From Gal. i. 17, it appears that he went into Arabia, where he spent some time, and then returned to Damascus, and after three years he went up to Jerusalem. It would not have been safe to have gone to Jerusalem at once, and he therefore waited for the passions of the Jews to have time to cool, before he ventured himself again in their hands.

REMARKS.

1. There may be circumstances, but they are rare, in which it may be proper to speak of our own attainments,

and of our own doings; ver. 1. Boasting is in general nothing but folly—the fruit of pride—but there may be situations when to state what we have done may be necessary to the vindication of our own character, and may tend to honour God. Then we should do it; not to trumpet forth our own fame, but to glorify God and to advance his cause. Occasions occur however but rarely in which it is proper to speak in this manner of ourselves.

2. The church should be pure. It is the bride of the Redeemer; the "Lamb's wife;" ver. 2. It is soon to be presented to Christ, soon to be admitted to his presence. How holy should be that church which sustains such a relation! How anxious to be worthy to appear before the Son of God!

3. All the individual members of that church should be holy; ver. 2. They as individuals are soon to be presented in heaven as the fruit of the labours of the Son of God, and as entitled to his eternal love. How pure should be the lips that are soon to speak his praise in heaven; how pure the eyes that are soon to behold his glory; how holy the feet that are soon to tread his courts in the heavenly world!

4. There is great danger of being corrupted from the simplicity that is in Christ; ver. 3. Satan desires to destroy us; and his great object is readily accomplished if he can seduce Christians from simple devotedness to the Redeemer; if he can secure corruption in doctrine or in the manner of worship, and can produce conformity in dress and in the style of living to this world. Formerly he excited persecution. But in that he was foiled. The more the church was persecuted the more it grew. Then he changed his ground. What he could not do by persecution he sought to do by corrupting the church; and in this he has been by far more successful. This can be done slowly but certainly; effectually but without exciting suspicion. And it matters not to Satan whether the church is crippled by persecution or its zeal destroyed by false doctrine and by con-

formity to the world. *His* aim is secured; and the power of the church destroyed. The form in which he *now* assails the church is by attempting to seduce it from simple and hearty attachment to the Saviour. And, O! in how many instances is he successful.

5. Our religion has cost much suffering. We have in this chapter a detail of extraordinary trials and sorrows in establishing it; and we have reason to be thankful, in some degree, that the enemies of Paul made it necessary for him to boast in this manner. We have thus some most interesting details of facts of which otherwise we should have been ignorant; and we see that the life of Paul was a life of continual self-denial and toil. By sea and land; at home and abroad; among his own countrymen and strangers, he was subjected to continued privations and persecution. So it has been always in regard to the establishment of the gospel. It began its career in the sufferings of its great Author, and the foundation of the church was laid in his blood. It progressed amidst sufferings, for all the apostles, except John, it is supposed were martyrs. It continued to advance amidst sufferings—for ten fiery persecutions raged throughout the Roman empire, and thousands died in consequence of their professed attachment to the Saviour. It has been always propagated in heathen lands by self-denials and sacrifices, for the life of a missionary is that of sacrifice and toil. How many such men as David Brainerd and Henry Martyn have sacrificed their lives in order to extend the true religion around the world!

6. All that *we* enjoy is the fruit of the sufferings, toils, and sacrifices of others. We have not one Christian privilege or hope which has not cost the life of many a martyr. How thankful should we be to God that he was pleased to raise up men who would be *willing* thus to suffer, and that he sustained and kept them until their work was accomplished!

7. We may infer the *sincerity* of the men engaged in propagating the Christian religion. What had Paul to

gain in the sorrows which he endured? Why did he not remain in his own land and reap the honours which were then fully within his grasp? The answer is an easy one. It was because he believed that Christianity was true; and believing that, he believed that it was of importance to make it known to the world. Paul did not endure these sorrows, and encounter these perils for the sake of pleasure, honour, or gain. No man who reads this chapter can doubt that he was sincere, and that he was an honest man.

8. The Christian religion is, therefore, true. Not because the first preachers were sincere—for the advocates of error are often sincere, and are willing to suffer much or even to die as martyrs; but because this was a case when their sincerity proved *the facts* in regard to the truth of Christianity. It was not sincerity in regard *to opinions* merely, it was in regard *to facts.* They not only *believed* that the Messiah had come and died and risen again, but they *saw him—saw* him when he lived; *saw* him die; *saw* him after he was risen; and it was in relation to these *facts* that they were sincere. But how could they be deceived here? Men may be deceived in their opinions; but how could *John, e. g.,* be deceived in affirming that he was intimately acquainted— the bosom friend—with Jesus of Nazareth; that he saw him die; and that he conversed with him *after* he had died? In this he could not be mistaken; and sooner than deny this, John would have spent his whole life in a cave in Patmos, or have died on the cross or at the stake. But if John *saw* all this, then the Christian religion is true.

9. We should be willing to suffer now. If Paul and the other apostles were willing to endure so much, why should not we be? If they were willing to deny themselves so much in order that the gospel should be spread among the nations, why should not we be? It is now just as important that it should be spread as it was then; and the church should be just as willing to sacrifice its comforts to make the gospel known as it was in the days of Paul. We may add, also, that if there was the same devotedness to Christ evinced by all Christians now which is described in this chapter; if there was the same zeal and self-denial, the time would not be far distant when the gospel would be spread all around the world. May the time soon come when all Christians shall have the same self-denial as Paul; and especially when all who enter the ministry shall be WILLING to forsake country and home, and to encounter peril in the city and the wilderness; on the sea and the land; to meet cold, and nakedness, hunger, thirst, persecution, and death in any way in order that they may make known the name of the Saviour to a lost world.

CHAPTER XII.

THIS chapter is a continuation of the same general subject which was discussed in the two previous chapters. The general design of the apostle is, to defend himself from the charges brought against him in Corinth, and especially, as it would appear, from the charge that he had no claims to the character of an apostle. In the previous chapters he had met these charges, and had shown that he had just cause to be bold towards them; that he had in his life given evidence that he was called to this work, and especially that by his successes and by his sufferings he had showed that he had evidence that he had been truly engaged in the work of the Lord Jesus.

This chapter contains the following subjects.

1. Paul appeals to another evidence that he was engaged in the apostolic office—an evidence to which none of his accusers could appeal—that he had been permitted to behold the glories of the heavenly world; ver. 1 —10. In the previous chapter he had mentioned his trials. Here he says (ver. 1), that as they had compelled him to boast, he would mention the revelation which he had had of the Lord. He details, therefore, the remarkable vision which he had had several years before (ver. 2—4), when he was caught up to heaven, and permitted to behold the wonders there.

CHAPTER XII.

IT is not expedient for me doubtless to glory. ¹ I will

1 *For I will.*

come to visions and revelations of the Lord.

2 I knew a man in *a* Christ

a Rom.16.7.

Yet he says, that lest such an extraordinary manifestation should exalt him above measure, he was visited with a sore and peculiar trial—a trial from which he prayed earnestly to be delivered, but that he received answer that the grace of God would be sufficient to support him; ver. 5—9. It was in view of this, he says (ver. 10) that he had pleasure in infirmities and sufferings in the cause of the Redeemer.

2. He then (ver. 11, 12) sums up what he had said; draws the conclusion that he had given every sign or evidence that he was an apostle; that in all that pertained to toil, and patience, and miracles, he had shown that he was commissioned by the Saviour; though with characteristic modesty he said *he was nothing.*

3. He then expresses his purpose to come again and see them, and his intention then not to be burdensome to them; ver. 13—15. He was willing to labour for them, and to exhaust his strength in endeavouring to promote their welfare without receiving support from them, for he regarded himself in the light of a father to them, and it was not usual for children to support their parents.

4. In connection with this, he answers another charge against himself. Some accused him of being crafty; that though he did not burden them, yet he knew well how to manage so as to secure what he wanted without burdening them, or seeming to receive any thing from them; ver. 16. To this he answers by an appeal to fact. Particularly he appeals to the conduct of Titus when with them, in full proof that he had no such design; ver. 17 —19.

5. In the conclusion of the chapter, he expresses his fear that when he should come among them he would find much that would humble them, and give him occasion for severity of discipline; ver. 20, 21. This apprehension is evidently expressed in order

that they might be led to examine themselves, and to put away whatever was wrong.

1. *It is not expedient.* It is not well; it does not become me. This may either mean that he felt and admitted that it did not become him to boast in this manner; that there was an impropriety in his doing it though circumstances had compelled him, and in this sense it is understood by nearly, or quite, all expositors; or it may be taken ironically. "Such a man as I am ought not to boast. So you say, and so it would seem. A man who has done no more than I have; who has suffered nothing; who has been idle and at ease as I have been, ought surely not to boast. And since there is such an evident impropriety in *my* boasting and speaking about myself, I will turn to another matter, and inquire whether the same thing may not be said about visions and revelations. I will speak, therefore, of a man who had some remarkable revelations, and inquire whether *he* has any right to boast of the favours imparted to him." This seems to me to be the probable interpretation of this passage. ¶ *To glory.* To boast; chap. x. 8, 13; xi. 10. One of the charges which they alleged against him was, that he was given to boasting without any good reason. After the enumeration in the previous chapter of what he had done and suffered, he says that this was doubtless very true. Such a man has nothing to boast of. ¶ *I will come.* Marg. "For I will." Our translators have omitted the word (γὰρ) *for* in the text, evidently supposing that it is a mere expletive. Doddridge renders it, "nevertheless." But it seems to me that it contains an important sense, and that it should be rendered by THEN. "Since it is not fit that I should glory, *then* I will refer to visions, &c. I will turn away then from that subject, and come to another." Thus the word (γὰρ) is used in John vii. 41. "Shall THEN

about fourteen [1] years ago, (whether in the body, I cannot tell ; or whether out of the body,

I cannot tell : God knoweth ; such an one caught up to the third heaven.

1 *A.D.*46; Acts 22.17.

(μὴ γὰρ) Christ come out of Galilee?" Acts viii. 31. "How can I THEN (πῶς γὰρ) except some man should guide me?" see also Acts xix. 35 ; Rom. iii. 3 ; Phil. i. 18. ¶ *To visions.* The word *vision* is used in the Scriptures often to denote the mode in which divine communications were usually made to men. This was done by causing some scene to appear to pass before the mind as in a landscape, so that the individual seemed to *see* a representation of what was to occur in some future period. It was usually applied to *prophecy*, and is often used in the Old Testament ; see my Note on Isa. i. 1, and also on Acts ix. 10. The vision which Paul here refers to was that which he was permitted to have of the heavenly world ; ver. 4. He was permitted to *see* what perhaps no other mortal had seen, the glory of heaven. ¶ *And revelations of the Lord.* Which the Lord had made. Or it may mean manifestations which the Lord had made of himself to him. The word rendered *revelations* means properly an *uncovering* (ἀποκάλυψις, from ἀποκαλύπτω, to uncover), and denotes a removal of the veil of ignorance and darkness, so that an object may be clearly seen ; and is thus applied to truth revealed, because the obscurity is removed and the truth becomes manifest.

2. *I knew a man in Christ.* I was acquainted with a Christian ; the phrase " in Christ" meaning nothing more than that he was united to Christ or was a Christian ; see Rom. xvi. 7. The reason why Paul did not speak of this directly as a vision which he had himself seen was probably that he was accused of boasting, and he had admitted that it did not become *him* to glory. But though it did not become *him* to boast directly, yet he could tell them of a man concerning whom there would be no impropriety evidently in boasting. It is not uncommon, moreover, for a man to speak of him-

self in the third person. Thus Cesar in his Commentaries uniformly speaks of himself. And so John in his Gospel speaks of himself, chap. xiii. 23, 24 ; xix. 26 ; xxi. 20. John did it on account of his modesty, because he would not appear to put himself forward, and because the mention of his own name as connected with the friendship of the Saviour in the remarkable manner in which he enjoyed it, might have savoured of pride. For a similar reason Paul may have been unwilling to mention his own name here ; and he may have abstained from referring to this occurrence elsewhere, because it might savour of pride, and might also excite the envy or ill-will of others. Those who have been most favoured with spiritual enjoyments will not be the most ready to proclaim it. They will cherish the remembrance in order to excite gratitude in their own hearts and support them in trial ; they will not blazon it abroad as if they were more the favourites of heaven than others are. That this refers to Paul himself is evident for the following reasons. (1.) His argument required that he should mention something that had occurred to himself. Any thing that had occurred to another would not have been pertinent. (2.) He applies it directly to himself (ver. 7), when he says that God took effectual measures that he should not be unduly exalted in view of the abundant revelations bestowed on him. ¶ *About fourteen years ago.* On what occasion or where this occurred, or why he concealed the remarkable fact so long, and why there is no other allusion to it, is unknown ; and conjecture is useless. If this epistle was written, as is commonly supposed, about the year 58, then this occurrence must have happened about the year 44. This was several years after his conversion, and of course this does not refer to the *trance* mentioned in Acts ix. 9, at the time when he was converted. Dr. Benson supposes that this vision was made to him when he was praying in the temple after his return to Jerusalem, when he was directed to go from Jerusalem to the Gentiles (Acts xxii. 17), and that it was intended to support him in the trials which he was about to endure. There can be little danger of error in supposing that its object was to support him in those remarkable trials, and that God designed to impart to him such views of heaven and its glory, and of the certainty that he would soon be admitted there, as to support him in his sufferings, and make him willing to bear all that should be laid upon him. God often gives to his people some clear and elevated spiritual comforts *before* they enter into trials as well as while in them ; he prepares them for them before they come. This vision Paul had kept secret for fourteen years. He had doubtless *often* thought of it ; and the remembrance of that glorious hour was doubtless one of the reasons why he bore trials so patiently and was willing to endure so much. But before this he had had no occasion to mention it. He had other proofs in abundance that he was called to the work of an apostle ; and to mention this would savour of pride and ostentation. It was only when he was *compelled* to refer to the evidences of his apostolic mission that he refers to it here. ¶ *Whether in the body, I cannot tell.* That is, I do not pretend to explain it. I do not know how it occurred. With the *fact* he was acquainted ; but *how* it was brought about he did not know. Whether the body was caught up to heaven ; whether the soul was for a time separated from the body ; or whether the scene passed before the mind in a vision, so that he *seemed* to have been caught up to heaven, he does not pretend to know. The evident idea is, that at the time he was in a state of insensibility in regard to surrounding objects, and was unconscious of what was occurring, as if he had been dead. Where Paul confesses his own ignorance of what occurred to himself it would be vain for

us to inquire ; and the question *how* this was done is immaterial. No one can doubt that God had power if he chose to transport the body to heaven ; or that he had power for a time to separate the soul from the body ; or that he had power to represent to the mind so clearly the view of the heavenly world that he would appear to see it ; see Acts vii. 56. It is clear only that he lost all consciousness of any thing about him at that time, and that he saw only the things in heaven. It may be added here, however, that Paul evidently supposed that his soul *might* be taken to heaven without the body, and that it might have separate consciousness and a separate existence. He was not, therefore, a materialist, and he did not believe that the existence and consciousness of the soul was dependent on the body. ¶ *God knoweth.* With the mode in which it was done God only could be acquainted. Paul did not attempt to explain that. That was to him of comparatively little consequence, and he did not lose his time in a vain attempt to explain it. How happy would it be if all theologians were as ready to be satisfied with the knowledge of *a fact,* and to leave the mode of explaining it with God, as this prince of theologians was. Many a man would have busied himself with a vain *speculation* about the way in which it was done ; Paul was contented with the *fact* that it had occurred. ¶ *Such an one caught up.* The word which is here used ($\dot{\alpha}\rho\pi\acute{\alpha}\zeta\omega$) means, to seize upon, to snatch away, as wolves do their prey (John xii. 10) ; or to seize with avidity or eagerness (Mat. xi. 12) ; or to carry away, to hurry off by force or involuntarily ; see John vi. 15 ; Acts vii. 39 ; xxiii. 10. In the case before us there is implied the idea that Paul was conveyed by a foreign force ; or that he was suddenly seized and snatched up to heaven. The word expresses the suddenness and the rapidity with which it was done. Probably it was instantaneous, so that he appeared at once to be in heaven. Of the mode in which it was done Paul has given no explanations ; and conjecture would

3 And I knew such a man, (whether in the body, or out of the body, I cannot tell: God knoweth;)

4 How that he was caught up into paradise, *a* and heard unspeakable words, which it is not [1] lawful for a man to utter.

a Lu.23.43 ; Re.2.7.   1 or, *possible.*

be useless. ¶ *To the third heaven.* The Jews sometimes speak of seven heavens, and Mahomet has borrowed this idea from the Jews. But the Bible speaks of but three heavens, and among the Jews in the apostolic ages also the heavens were divided into three. (1.) The aerial, including the clouds and the atmosphere, the heavens above us, *until* we come to the stars. (2.) The starry heavens, the heavens in which the sun, moon, and stars appear to be situated. (3.) The heavens *beyond* the stars. That heaven was supposed to be the residence of God, of angels, and of holy spirits. It was this upper heaven, the dwelling-place of God, to which Paul was taken, and whose wonders he was permitted to behold—this region where God dwelt ; where Christ was seated at the right hand of the Father, and where the spirits of the just were assembled. The fanciful opinions of the Jews about seven heavens may be seen detailed in Schoettgen or in Wetstein, by whom the principal passages from the Jewish writings relating to the subject have been collected. As their opinions throw no light on this passage, it is unnecessary to detail them here.

3. *And I knew such a man.* It is not uncommon to repeat a solemn affirmation in order that it may be made more emphatic. This is done here. Paul repeats the idea, that he was intimately acquainted with such a man, and that he did not know whether he was in the body or out of the body. All that was known to God.

4. *Into paradise.* The word paradise (παράδισος) occurs but three times in the New Testament ; Luke xxiii. 43 ; 2 Cor. xii. 4 ; Rev. ii. 7. It occurs often in the Septuagint, as the translation of the word *garden* ; Gen. ii. 8—10, 15, 16 ; iii. 1—3, 8, 16, 23, 24 ; xiii. 10 ; Num. xxiv. 6 ; Isa. li. 3 ; Ezek. xxviii. 13 ; xxxi. 8, 9 ; Joel ii. 3. And also Isa. i. 30 ; Jer. xxix. 5 ; and

of the word (פרדס) *Pardes* in Neh. ii. 8 ; Eccl. ii. 5 ; Cant. ii. 13. It is a word which had its origin in the language of eastern Asia, and which has been adopted in the Greek, the Roman, and other western languages. In Sanscrit the word *paradêsha* means a land elevated and cultivated ; in Armenian, *pardes* denotes a garden around the house planted with trees, shrubs, grass for use and ornament. In Persia, the word denotes the *pleasure gardens* and *parks* with wild animals around the country residences of the monarchs and princes. Hence it denotes in general a garden of pleasure ; and in the New Testament is applied to the abodes of the blessed after death, the dwelling-place of God and of happy spirits ; or to heaven as a place of blessedness. Some have supposed that Paul here by the word "paradise" means to describe a different place from that denoted by the phrase "the third heaven ;" but there is no good reason for this supposition. The only difference is that this word implies the idea of a place of blessedness ; but the same place is undoubtedly referred to. ¶ *And heard unspeakable words.* The word which is here rendered "unspeakable" (ἄῤῥητα) may either mean what *cannot* be spoken, or what *ought* not to be spoken. The word means unutterable, ineffable ; and whichever idea we attach to it, Paul meant to say that he could not attempt by words to do justice to what he saw and heard. The use of the word "*words*" here would seem to imply that he heard the *language* of exalted praise ; or that there were truths imparted to his mind which he could not hope to convey in any language spoken by men. ¶ *Which it is not lawful for a man to utter.* Marg. "*Possible.*" Witsius supposes that the word ἐξὸν may include both, and Doddridge accords with the interpretation. See also Robinson's Lex. The word is most commonly used in the signification of *lawful*. Thus, Mat. xiv. 4, " It is not *lawful* for thee to have her." Acts xvi. 21, " Which it is not *lawful* for us to observe ;" xxii. 25, " Is it *lawful* for you to scourge a man that is a Roman," &c. In the same sense of *lawful* it is used in Mat. xii. 2, 10, 12 ; xx. 15 ; Mark ii. 26 ; x. 2. When it refers to *possibility* it probably means *moral* possibility; that is, propriety, or it means that it is right. It seems to me, therefore, that the word here rather means that it was not *proper* to give utterance to those things ; it would not be *right* to attempt it. It might be also true that it would not have been possible for language to convey clearly the ideas connected with the things which Paul was then permitted to see ; but the main thought is, that there was some reason why it would not be *proper* for him to have attempted to communicate those ideas to men at large. The Jews held that it was unlawful to pronounce the *Tetragrammaton, i. e.* the name of four letters (יהוה), JEHOVAH ; and whenever that name occurred in their scriptures, they substituted the name *Adonai* in its place. They maintain indeed that the true pronunciation is utterly lost, and none of them to this day attempt to pronounce it. But this was mere superstition : and it is impossible that Paul should have been influenced by any such reason as this.

The transaction here referred to is very remarkable. It is the only instance in the scriptures of any one who was taken to heaven, either in reality or in vision, and who returned again to the earth and was then qualified to communicate important truths about the heavenly world from personal observation. Enoch and Elijah were taken to heaven ; but they returned not to converse with men. Elijah appeared with Moses in conversation with Jesus on the mount of transfiguration ; but they conversed with him only about his decease, which he was about to accomplish at Jerusalem ; Luke ix. 31. There would have been no propriety for them to have spoken to Jesus of heaven, for he came down from heaven and was *in* heaven (John iii. 13), and they were not permitted to speak to the disciples of heaven. Lazarus was raised from the dead (John xi.), and many of the saints which had slept in their graves arose at the death of Jesus (Mat. xxvii. 52), but there is no intimation that they communicated any thing to the living about the heavenly world. Of all the millions who have been taken to heaven, not one has been permitted to return to bear his testimony to its glories ; to witness for God that he is faithful to his promises ; to encourage his pious friends to persevere ; or to invite his impenitent friends to follow him to that glorious world. And so fixed is the law ; so settled is the principle, that even Lazarus was not permitted to go, though at the earnest request of the rich man in hell, and warn his friends not to follow him to that world of woe ; Luke xvi. 27—31. Mahomet indeed feigned that he had made a journey to heaven, and he attempts to describe what he saw ; and the difference between *true inspiration* and *false* or *pretended inspiration* is strikingly evinced by the difference between Paul's dignified silence—*verba sacro digna silentio* (*Horace*) and the puerilities of the prophet of Mecca. See the Koran, chap. xvii. As the difference between the true religion and imposture is strikingly illustrated by this, we may recur to the principal events which happened to the Impostor on his celebrated journey. The whole account may be seen in Prideaux's Life of Mahomet, p. 43. seq. He solemnly affirmed that he had been translated to the heaven of heavens ; that on a white beast, less than a mule, but larger than an ass, he had been conveyed from the temple of Mecca to that of Jerusalem ; had successively ascended the seven heavens with his companion Gabriel, receiving and returning the salutations of its blessed inhabitants ; had then proceeded alone within two bow-shots of the throne of the Almighty, when he felt a cold which pierced him to the heart, and was touched on the shoulder by the hand of God, who commanded him to pray fifty times a day, but with the advice of Moses he was prevailed on to have the number reduced to five ; and that he then returned to Jerusalem and to Mecca, having performed a journey of thousands of years in the tenth part of a night.

The fact that Paul was not permitted to communicate what he had seen is very remarkable. It is natural to ask why it is so ? Why has not God sent down departed saints to *tell* men of the glories of heaven? Why does he not permit them to come and bear testimony to what they have seen and enjoyed ? Why not come and clear up the doubts of the pious ; why not come and convince a thoughtless world ; why not come and bear honourable testimony for God that he is faithful to reward his people ? And especially why did he not suffer Paul, whom he had permitted to behold the glories of paradise, to testify simply to what he had seen, and tell us what was there ?

To these questions, so obvious, it is impossible to give an answer that we can demonstrate to be the true one. But we may suggest *some* reasons which may furnish a *plausible* answer, and which may serve to remove some of the perplexity in the case. I would, therefore, suggest that the following may have been some of the reasons why Paul was not permitted to communicate what he saw to men. (1.) It was designed for the support of Paul himself in view of the very remarkable trials which he was about to endure. God had called him to great toils and self-denials. He was to labour much alone ; to go to foreign lands ; to be persecuted, and ultimately put to death ; and it was his purpose to qualify him for this work by some peculiar manifestation of his favour. He accordingly gave him such views of heaven that he would be supported in his trials by a conviction of the undoubted truth of what he taught, and by the prospect of certain glory when his labours should end. It was one instance when God gave peculiar views to prepare for trials, as he often does to his people now, preparing them in a peculiar manner for peculiar trials. Christians, from some cause, often have more elevated views and deeper feeling *before* they are called to endure trials than they have at other times—peculiar grace to prepare them for suffering. But as this was designed in a peculiar manner for Paul alone, it was not proper for him to communicate what he saw to others. (2.) It is probable that if there were a full revelation of the glories of heaven we should not be able to comprehend it ; or even if we did, we should be incredulous in regard to it. So unlike what we see ; so elevated above our highest comprehension ; probably so unlike what we now anticipate is heaven, that we should be slow to receive the revelation. It is always difficult to describe what we have not seen, even on earth, so that we shall have *any* very clear idea of it : how much more difficult must it be to describe heaven. We are often incredulous about what is reported to exist in foreign lands on earth which we have not seen, and a long time is often necessary before we will believe it. The king of Siam, when told by the Dutch ambassador that water became so hard in his country that men might walk on it, said, " I have often suspected you of falsehood, but now I *know* that you lie." So incredulous might we be, with our weak faith, if we were told what actually exists in heaven. We should not improbably turn away from it as wholly incredible. (3.) There are great truths which it is not the design of God to reveal to men. The object is to communicate *enough* to win us, to comfort us, to support our faith, not to reveal *all*. In eternity there must be boundless truths and glories which are not *needful* for us to know now, and which, on many accounts, it would not be proper to be revealed to men. The question is not, do we know *all*, but have we *enough* safely to guide us to heaven, and to comfort us in the trials of life. (4.) There *is* enough revealed of heaven for our guidance and comfort in this world. God has told us what it will be in general. It will be a world without sin ; without tears ;

5 Of such an one will I glory :
yet *a* of myself I will not glory,
but in mine infirmities.

a chap.11.30; ver.9,10.

without wrong, injustice, fraud, or
wars ; without disease, pestilence,
plague, death ; and it is easy to fill
up the picture sufficiently for all our
purposes. Let us think of a world
where all shall be pure and holy ; of a
world free from all that we now behold
that is evil ; free from pain, disease,
death ; a world where "friends never
depart, foes never come ;" a world
where all shall be harmony and love
—and where all this shall be ETERNAL,
and we shall see that God has revealed *enough* for our welfare here. The
highest *hopes* of man are met when
we anticipate AN ETERNAL HEAVEN ;
the heaviest trials may be cheerfully
borne when we have the prospect of
EVERLASTING REST. (5.) One other
reason may be assigned why it was not
proper for Paul to disclose what he
saw, and why God has withheld more
full revelations from men about heaven. It is, that his purpose is that
we shall here walk by faith and not
by sight. We are not to see the reward, nor to be told fully what it is.
We are to have such confidence in
God that we shall assuredly believe
that he will fully reward and bless us,
and under this confidence we are to
live and act here below. God designs,
therefore, to try our faith, and to
furnish an abundant evidence that his
people are *disposed* to obey his commands and to put their trust in his
faithfulness. Besides, if *all* the glories of heaven were revealed ; if all
were told that might be ; and if heaven were made as attractive to mortal view as possible, then it might
appear that his professed people were
influenced *solely* by the hope of the
reward. As it is, there is enough to
support and comfort ; not enough to
make it the main and only reason why
we serve God. It may be added, (*a*)
That we have *all* the truth which we
shall ever have about heaven here
below. No other messenger will
come ; none of the pious dead will
return. If men, therefore, are not

6 For though I would desire
to glory, I shall not be a fool ;
for I will say the truth : but *now*

willing to be saved in view of the
truth which they have, they must be
lost. God will communicate no
more. (*b*) The Christian will soon
know all about heaven. He will *soon*
be there. He begins no day with any
certainty that he may not close it in
heaven ; he lies down to rest at no
time with any assurance that he will
not wake in heaven amidst its full and
eternal splendours. (*c*) The sinner
will soon know fully what it is *to lose
heaven*. A moment may make him
fully sensible of his loss—for he may
die ; and a moment may put him for
ever beyond the possibility of reaching a world of glory.

5. *Of such an one will I glory.* Of
such a man it would be right to boast.
It would be admitted that it is right
to exult in such a man, and to esteem
him to be peculiarly favoured by God.
I will boast of him as having received
peculiar honour from the Lord.
Bloomfield, however, supposes that
the words rendered "of such an one "
should be translated "of such a thing,"
or of such a transaction ; meaning " I
can indeed justly boast of my being
caught up to heaven as of a thing the
whole glory of which pertains to him
who has thus exalted me ; but of myself, or of any thing in me, I will not
boast." So Rosenmüller explains it.
But it seems to me that the connection requires that we should understand it of a person, and that the passage is partly ironical. Paul speaks
in the third person. He chooses to
keep himself *directly* out of view.
And though he refers really to himself, yet he would not say this directly,
but says that of such a man they
would admit it would be proper to
boast. ¶ *Yet of myself.* Directly.
It is not expedient for me to boast of
myself. " You would allow me to
boast of such a man as I have referred
to ; I admit that it is not proper for
me to boast directly of myself." ¶ *But
in mine infirmities.* My weaknesses,
trials, pains, sufferings ; such as many

I forbear, lest any man should think of me above that which he | seeth me *to be,* or *that* he heareth of me.

---

regard as infirmities ; see Note on chap. xi. 30.

6. *For though I would desire to glory.* I take this to be a solemn and serious declaration of the *irony* which precedes ; and that Paul means to say seriously, that if he had a wish to boast as other men boasted, if he chose to make much of his attainments and privileges, he would have enough of which to make mention. It would not be mere empty boasting without any foundation or any just cause, for he had as much of which to speak in a confident manner pertaining to his labours as an apostle, and his evidence of the divine favour, as could be urged by any one. "I might go on to speak much more than I have done, and to urge claims which all would admit to be well-founded." ¶ *I shall not be a fool.* "It would not be foolish boasting; for it would be according to truth. I could urge much more than I have done ; I could speak of things which no one would be disposed to call in question as laying the foundation of just claims to my being regarded as eminently favoured of God ; I could seriously state what all would admit to be such." ¶ *For I will say the truth.* That is, "Whatever I should say on this subject would be the simple truth. I should mention nothing which has not actually occurred. But I forbear, lest some one should form an improper estimate of me." The apostle seems to have intended to have added something more, but he was checked by the apprehension to which he here refers. Or perhaps he means to say that if he should boast of the vision to which he had just referred ; if he should go on to say how highly he had been honoured and exalted by it, there would be no impropriety in it. It was so remarkable that if he confined himself strictly to the truth, as he would do, still it would be regarded by all as a very extraordinary honour, and one to which no one of the false teachers could refer as laying a foundation for *their* boasting. ¶ *Lest any man should*

think of me, &c. The idea in this part of the verse I take to be this. "I desire and expect to be estimated by my public life. I expect to be judged of men by my deeds, by what they see in me, and by my general reputation in respect to what I have done in establishing the Christian religion. I am willing that my character and reputation, that the estimate in which I shall be held by mankind, shall rest on that. I do not wish that my character among men shall be determined by my *secret* feelings ; or by any secret extraordinary communication from heaven which I may have, and which cannot be subjected to the observation of my fellow-men. I am willing to be estimated by my public life ; and however valuable such extraordinary manifestations may be to me as an individual ; or however much they may comfort me, I do not wish to make the basis of my public reputation. I expect to stand and be estimated by my public deeds ; by what all men see and hear of me ; and I would not have them form even a favourable opinion of me beyond that." This is the noble language of a man who was willing to enjoy such a reputation as his public life entitled him to. He wished to have the basis of his reputation such that all men could see and examine it. Unlike enthusiasts and fanatics, he appealed to no secret impulses ; did not rest his claims for public confidence on any peculiar communications from heaven ; but wished to be estimated by his public deeds. And the important truth taught is, that however much the communion we may have with God ; however much comfort and support in prayer and in our favoured moments of fellowship with God ; or however much we may fancy in this way that we are the favourites of heaven ; and however much this may support us in trial : still this should not be made the foundation of claim to the favourable opinions of our fellow-men. By our public character ; by our well-known actions ; by

7 And lest I should be exalted above measure through the abundance of the revelations, there was given to me a thorn *a* in the flesh,

a Eze.28. 24; Ga.4.14.

our lives as seen by men, we should desire to be estimated, and we should be *satisfied* with such a measure of public esteem as our deportment shall fairly entitle us to. We should seldom, perhaps, refer to our moments of secret, happy, and most favoured communion with God. Paul kept his most elevated joys in this respect, secret *for fourteen years :*—what an example to those who are constantly blazoning their Christian experience abroad, and boasting of what they have enjoyed ! We should *never* refer to such moments as a foundation for the estimate in which our character shall be held by our fellow men. We should never make this the foundation of a claim to the public confidence in us. For all such claims; for all the estimate in which we shall be held by men, we should be willing to be tried by our lives. Paul would not even make *a vision of heaven ;* not even *the privilege of having beheld the glories of the upper world, though a favour conferred on no other living man,* a ground of the estimate in which his character should be held ! What an example to those who wish to be estimated by secret raptures, and by special communications to their souls from heaven ! No. Let us be willing to be estimated *by men* by what they see in us ; to enjoy such a reputation as our conduct shall fairly entitle us to. Let our communion with God cheer our own hearts ; but let us not obtrude this on men as furnishing a claim for an exalted standard in their estimation.

7. *And lest I should be exalted.* Lest I should be spiritually proud ; lest I should become self-confident and vain, and suppose that I was a special favourite of Heaven. If Paul was in danger of spiritual pride, who is not ? If it was necessary for God to adopt some special measures to keep him humble, we are not to be surprised that the same thing should occur in other cases. There is abundant reason to believe that Paul was naturally a proud man. He was by nature self-confident ; trusting in his own talents and attainments, and eminently ambitious. When he became a Christian, therefore, one of his besetting sins would be pride ; and as he had been peculiarly favoured in his call to the apostleship ; in his success as a preacher ; in the standing which he had among the other apostles, and in the revelations imparted to him, there was also peculiar danger that he would become self-confident and proud of his attainments. There is no danger that more constantly besets Christians, and even eminent Christians, than pride. There is no sin that is more subtile, insinuating, deceptive ; none that lurks more constantly around the heart and that finds a more ready entrance, than pride. He who has been characterized by pride before his conversion will be in special danger of it afterwards ; he who has eminent gifts in prayer, or in conversation, or in preaching, will be in special danger of it ; he who is eminently successful will be in danger of it ; and he who has any extraordinary spiritual comforts will be in danger of it. Of this sin he who lives nearest to God may be in most special danger ; and he who is most eminent in piety should feel that he also occupies a position where the enemy will approach him in a sly and subtile manner, and where he is in peculiar danger of a fall. Possibly the fear that he might be in danger of being made proud by the flattery of his friends may have been one reason why Paul kept this thing concealed for fourteen years ; and if men wish to keep themselves from the danger of this sin, they should not be forward to speak even of the most favoured moments of their communion with God. ¶ *Through the abundance of the revelations.* By my being raised thus to heaven, and by being permitted to behold the wonders of the heavenly world, as well as by the

the [a] messenger of Satan, to buffet me, lest I should be exalted above measure.

a Job 2.7; Lu.13,16.

numerous communications which God had made to me at other times. ¶ *There was given to me.* That is, God was pleased to appoint me. The word which Paul uses is worthy of special notice. It is that this "thorn in the flesh" was *given* to him, implying that it was a favour. He does not complain of it; he does not say it was sent in cruelty; he does not even speak of it as an affliction; he speaks of it as a *gift*, as any man would of a favour that had been bestowed. Paul had so clear a view of the *benefits* which resulted from it that he regarded it as a favour, as Christians should every trial. ¶ *A thorn in the flesh.* The word here used (σκόλοψ) occurs nowhere else in the New Testament. It means properly any thing pointed or sharp, *e. g.* a stake or palisade (Xen. Anab. v. 2, 5); or the point of a hook. The word is used in the Septuagint to denote a *thorn* or prickle, as a translation of רּיִּכ (*sir*), in Hos. ii. 6, " I will hedge up thy way with *thorns ;*" to denote a pricking briar in Ezek. xxviii. 24, as a translation of בֹלֹון (*sillon*), meaning a thorn or prickle, such as is found in the shoots and twigs of the palm-tree; and to denote "pricks in the eyes" (Num. xxxiii. 55), as a translation of שׂכִּים (*sikkim*), thorns or prickles. So far as the *word* here used is concerned, it means a sharp thorn or prickle; and the idea is, that the trial to which he refers was as troublesome and painful as such a thorn would be in the flesh. But whether he refers to some infirmity or pain in the flesh or the body is another question, and a question in which interpreters have been greatly divided in opinion. Every one who has become familiar with commentaries knows that almost every expositor has had his own opinion about this, and also that no one has been able to give any good reason for his own. Most of them have been fanciful; and many of them eminently ridiculous. Even Baxter, who was

8 For this [a] thing I besought the Lord thrice, that it might depart from me.

a De.3.23,27; Ps 77.2,11; La.3.8; Mat.26.44.

subject himself to some such disorder, supposes that it might be the stone or gravel; and the usually very judicious Doddridge supposes that the view which he had of the glories of heavenly objects so affected his nerves as to produce a *paralytic* disorder, and particularly a stammering in his speech, and perhaps also a ridiculous distortion of the countenance. This opinion was suggested by Whitby, and has been adopted also by Benson, Macknight, Slade, and Bloomfield. But though sustained by most respectable names, it would be easy to show that it is mere conjecture, and perhaps quite as improbable as any of the numerous opinions which have been maintained on the subject. If Paul's speech had been affected, and his face distorted, and his nerves shattered by such a sight, how could he doubt whether he was in the body or out of it when this occurred? Many of the Latin fathers supposed that some unruly and ungovernable lust was intended. Chrysostom and Jerome suppose that he meant the headache; Tertullian an earache; and Rosenmüller supposes that it was the gout in the head, *kopfgicht*, and that it was a periodical disorder such as affected him when he was with the Galatians; Gal. iv. 13. But all conjecture here is vain; and the numerous strange and ridiculous opinions of commentators is a melancholy attestation of their inclination to fanciful conjecture where it is *impossible* in the nature of the case to ascertain the truth. All that can be known of this is, that it was some infirmity of the flesh, some bodily affliction or calamity, that was *like* the continual piercing of the flesh with a thorn (Gal. iv. 13); and that it was something that was *designed* to prevent spiritual pride. It is not indeed an improbable supposition that it was something that could be seen by others, and that thus tended to humble him when with them. ¶ *The messenger of Satan.* Among the Hebrews it was customary to attribute severe and painful diseases to Satan ; comp. Job ii. 6, 7 ; comp. Note on Luke xiii. 16. In the time of the Saviour malignant spirits are known to have taken possession of the body in numerous cases, and to have produced painful bodily diseases, and Paul here says that Satan was permitted to bring this calamity on him. ¶ *To buffet me.* To buffet, means to smite with the hand ; then to maltreat in any way. The meaning is, that the effect and design of this was deeply to afflict him. Doddridge and Clarke suppose that the reference is here to the false teacher whom Satan had sent to Corinth, and who was to him the source of perpetual trouble. But it seems more probable to me that he refers to some bodily infirmity. The general truth taught in this verse is, that God will take care that his people shall not be unduly exalted by the manifestations of his favour, and by the spiritual privileges which he bestows on them. He will take measures to humble them ; and a large part of his dealings with his people is designed to accomplish this. Sometimes it will be done, as in the case of Paul, by bodily infirmity or trial, by sickness, or by long and lingering disease ; sometimes by great poverty and by an humble condition of life ; sometimes by *reducing* us from a state of affluence where we were in danger of being exalted above measure ; sometimes by suffering us to be slandered and calumniated, by suffering foes to rise up against us who shall blacken our character and in such a manner that we cannot meet it ; sometimes by persecution ; sometimes by want of success in our enterprises, and if in the ministry, by withholding his Spirit ; sometimes by suffering us to fall into sin, and thus greatly humbling us before the world. Such was the case with David and with Peter ; and God often permits us to see in this manner our own weakness, and to bring us to a sense of our dependence and to proper humility by suffering us to perform some act that should be ever after-

ward *a standing source* of our humiliation ; some act so base, so humiliating, so evincing the deep depravity of our hearts as *for ever* to make and keep us humble. How could David be lifted up with pride after the murder of Uriah ? How could Peter after having denied his Lord with a horrid oath ? Thus many a Christian is *suffered* to fall by the temptation of Satan to show him his weakness and to keep him from pride ; many a fall is made the occasion of the permanent benefit of the offender. And perhaps every Christian who has been much favoured with elevated spiritual views and comforts can recall something which shall be to him a standing topic of regret and humiliation in his past life. We should be thankful for *any* calamity that will humble us ; and we should remember that clear and elevated views of God and heaven are, after all, *more* than a compensation for all the sufferings which it may be necessary to endure in order to make us humble.

8. *For this thing.* On account of this ; in order that this calamity might be removed. ¶ *I besought the Lord.* The word " Lord" in the New Testament, when it stands without any other word in connection to limit its signification, commonly denotes the Lord Jesus Christ ; see Note on Acts i. 24. The following verse here shows conclusively that it was the Lord Jesus to whom Paul addressed this prayer. The answer was that his grace was sufficient for him ; and Paul consoled himself by saying that it was a sufficient support if the power of Christ implied in that answer, should rest on him. He would glory in trials if *such* was their result. Even Rosenmüller maintains that it was the Lord Jesus to whom this prayer was addressed, and says that the Socinians themselves admit it. So Grotius (on ver. 9) says that the answer was given by Christ. But if this refers to the Lord Jesus, then it proves that it is right to go to him in times of trouble, and that it is right to worship him. Prayer is the most solemn act of adoration which we can perform ; and no better authority can be required

9 And he said unto me, My grace is sufficient for thee : for my strength is made perfect in weakness. Most gladly therefore

for paying divine honours to Christ than the fact that Paul worshipped him and called upon him to remove a severe and grievous calamity. ¶ *Thrice.* This may either mean that he prayed for this *often*, or that he sought it on three set and solemn occasions. Many commentators have supposed that the former is meant. But to me it seems probable that Paul on three special occasions earnestly prayed for the removal of this calamity. It will be recollected that the Lord Jesus prayed three times in the garden of Gethsemane that the cup might be removed from him, Mat. xxvi. 44. At the third time he ceased, and submitted to what was the will of God. There is some reason to suppose that the Jews were in the habit of praying three times for any important blessing or for the removal of any calamity ; and Paul in this would not only conform to the usual custom, but especially he would be disposed to imitate the example of the Lord Jesus. Among the Jews *three* was a sacred number, and repeated instances occur where an important transaction is mentioned as having been done thrice ; see Num. xxii. 28 ; xxiv. 10 ; 1 Sam. iii. 8 ; xx. 41 ; 1 Kings xviii. 44 ; Prov. xxii. 20 ; Jer. vii. 4 ; xxii. 29 ; John xxi. 17. The probability, therefore, is, that Paul on three different occasions earnestly besought the Lord Jesus that this calamity might be removed from him. It might have been exceedingly painful, or it might, as he supposed, interfere with his success as a preacher ; or it might have been of such a nature as to expose him to ridicule ; and he prayed, therefore, if it were possible that it might be taken away. The passage proves that it is *right* to pray earnestly and repeatedly for the removal of any calamity. The Saviour so prayed in the garden ; and Paul so prayed here. Yet it also proves that there should be a *limit* to such prayers. The Saviour prayed three times ; and Paul limited himself to the same number of petitions and

then submitted to the will of God. This does not prove that we should be limited to exactly this number in our petitions; but it proves that there should be a limit ; that we should not be over-anxious, and that when it is plain from any cause that the calamity will not be removed, we should submit to it. The Saviour in the garden knew that the cup would not be removed, and he acquiesced. Paul was *told* indirectly that *his* calamity would not be removed, and he submitted. *We* may expect no such revelation from heaven, but we may know in other ways that the calamity will not be removed ; and *we* should submit. The child or other friend for whom we prayed may die ; or the calamity, as, *e. g.* blindness, or deafness, or loss of health, or poverty, may become permanent, so that there is no hope of removing it ; and we should then cease to pray that it may be removed, and we should cheerfully acquiesce in the will of God. So David prayed most fervently for his child when it was alive ; when it was deceased, and it was of no further use to pray for it, he bowed in submission to the will of God, 2 Sam. xii. 20.

9. *And he said unto me.* The Saviour replied. In what way this was done, or whether it was done at the time when the prayer was offered, Paul does not inform us. It is possible, as Macknight supposes, that Christ appeared to him again and spake to him in an audible manner. Grotius supposes that this was done by the בת קיל (*Bath-qol*)—" daughter of the voice," so frequently referred to by the Jewish writers, and which they suppose to be referred to in 1 Kings xix. 12, by the phrase, " a still small voice." But it is impossible to determine in what way it was done, and it is not material. Paul was in habits of communion with the Saviour, and was accustomed to receive revelations from him. The material fact here is, that the request was *not* granted in the exact form in which he presented it, but that he received as-

surance of grace to support him in his trial. It is one of the instances in which the fervent prayer of a good man, offered undoubtedly in faith, was not answered in the form in which he desired, though substantially answered in the assurance of grace sufficient to support him. It furnishes, therefore, a very instructive lesson in regard to prayer, and shows us that we are not to expect as a matter of course that all our prayers will be literally answered, and that we should not be disappointed or disheartened if they are not. It is *a matter of fact* that not all the prayers even of the pious, and of those who pray having faith in God as a hearer of prayer, are literally answered. Thus the prayer of David (2 Sam. xii. 16—20) was not literally answered; the child for whose life he so earnestly prayed died. So the Saviour's request was not literally answered, Mark xiv. 36. The cup of suffering which he so earnestly desired should be taken away was not removed. So in the case before us; comp. also Deut. iii. 23—27; Job xxx. 20; Lam. iii. 8. So in numerous cases now, Christians pray with fervour and with faith for the removal of some calamity which is not removed; or for something which they regard as desirable for their welfare which is withheld. Some of the *reasons* why this is done are obvious. (1.) The grace that will be imparted if the calamity is not removed will be of greater value to the individual than would be the direct answer to his prayer. Such was the case with Paul; so it was doubtless with David; and so it is often with Christians now. The removal of the calamity might be apparently a blessing, but it might also be attended with danger to our spiritual welfare; the grace imparted may be of permanent value and may be connected with the development of some of the loveliest traits of Christian character. (2.) It might not be for the good of the individual who prays that the exact thing should be granted. When a parent prays with great earnestness and with *insubmission* for the life of a child, he knows not what he is doing. If the child lives, he may be the occasion of much more grief to him than if he had died. David had far more trouble from Absalom than he had from the death of the child for which he so earnestly prayed. At the same time it may be better for the child that he should be removed. If he dies in infancy he will be saved. But who can tell what will be his character and destiny should he live to be a man? So of other things. (3.) God has often some better thing in store for us than would be the immediate answer to our prayer. Who can doubt that this was true of Paul? The promised grace of Christ as sufficient to support us is of more value than would be the mere removal of any bodily affliction. (4.) It would not be well for us, probably, should our petition be literally answered. Who can tell what is best for himself? If the thing were obtained, who can tell how soon we might forget the benefactor and become proud and self-confident? It was the design of God to *humble* Paul; and this could be much better accomplished by continuing his affliction and by imparting the promised grace, than by withdrawing the affliction and withholding the grace. The very thing to be done was to keep him humble; and this affliction could not be withdrawn without also foregoing the benefit. It is true, also, that where things are in themselves proper to be asked, Christians sometimes ask them in an improper manner, and this is one of the reasons why *many* of their prayers are not answered. But this does not pertain to the case before us. ¶ *My grace is sufficient for thee.* A much better answer than it would have been to have removed the calamity; and one that seems to have been entirely satisfactory to Paul. The meaning of the Saviour is, that he would support him; that he would not suffer him to sink exhausted under his trials; that he had nothing to fear. The infliction was not indeed removed; but there was a promise that the favour of Christ would be shown to him constantly, and that he would find his support to be ample. If Paul

will I rather glory *a* in my infirmities, that the power *b* of Christ may rest upon me.

a ver.5.   b 1Pe.4 14

had this support, he might well bear the trial ; and if we have this assurance, as we may have, we may welcome affliction, and rejoice that calamities are brought upon us. It is a sufficient answer to our prayers if we have the solemn promise of the Redeemer that we shall be upheld and never sink under the burden of our heavy woes. ¶ *My strength is made perfect in weakness.* That is, the strength which I impart to my people is more commonly and more completely manifested when my people feel that they are weak. It is not imparted to those who feel that they are strong and who do not realize their need of divine aid. It is not so completely manifested to those who *are* vigorous and strong as to the feeble. It is when we are conscious that we are feeble, and when we feel our need of aid, that the Redeemer manifests his power to uphold, and imparts his purest consolations. Grotius has collected several similar passages from the classic writers which may serve to illustrate this expression. Thus Pliny, vii. Epis. 26, says, " We are best where we are weak." Seneca says, " Calamity is the occasion of virtue." Quintilian, " All temerity of mind is broken by bodily calamity. " Minutius Felix, " Calamity is often the discipline of virtue." There are few Christians who cannot bear witness to the truth of what the Redeemer here says, and who have not experienced the most pure consolations which they have known, and been most sensible of his comforting presence and power in times of affliction. ¶ *Most gladly, therefore,* &c. I count it a privilege to be afflicted, if my trials may be the means of my more abundantly enjoying the favour of the Redeemer. His presence and imparted strength are more than a compensation for all the trials that I endure. ¶ *That the power of Christ.* The strength which Christ imparts ; his power manifested

10 Therefore I take pleasure in infirmities, in reproaches, in necessities, in persecutions, in

in supporting me in trials. ¶ *May rest upon me* (ἐπισκηνώσῃ). The word properly means *to pitch a tent upon ;* and then to dwell in or upon. Here it is used in the sense of abiding upon, or remaining with. The sense is, that the power which Christ manifested to his people rested with them, or abode with them in their trials, and *therefore* he would rejoice in afflictions, in order that he might partake of the aid and consolation thus imparted. Learn hence, (1.) That a Christian never *loses* any thing by suffering and affliction. If he may obtain the favour of Christ by his trials he is a gainer. The favour of the Redeemer is more than a compensation for all that we endure in his cause. (2.) The Christian is a *gainer* by trial. I never knew a Christian that was not ultimately benefited by trials. I never knew one who did not find that he had *gained* much that was valuable to him in scenes of affliction. I do not know that I have found one who would be willing to exchange the advantages he has gained in affliction for all that the most uninterrupted prosperity and the highest honours that the world could give would impart. (3.) Learn to bear trials with joy. They are good for us. They develope some of the most lovely traits of character. They injure no one if they are properly received. And a Christian should *rejoice* that he *may* obtain what he *does* obtain in affliction, cost what it may. It is worth more than it costs ; and when we come to die, the things that we shall have most occasion to thank God for will be our afflictions. And, O ! if they are the means of raising us to a higher seat in heaven, and placing us nearer the Redeemer there who will not rejoice in his trials ?

10. *Therefore I take pleasure.* Since so many benefits result from trials ; since my afflictions are the occasion of obtaining the favour of Christ in

distresses for Christ's sake: for when I am weak, then am I strong.

11 I am become a fool in

so eminent a degree, I rejoice in the privilege of suffering. There is often real *pleasure* in affliction, paradoxical as it may appear. Some of the happiest persons I have known are those who have been deeply afflicted ; some of the purest joys which I have witnessed have been manifested on a sick-bed, and in the prospect of death. And I have no doubt that Paul, in the midst of all his infirmities and reproaches, had a joy above that which all the wealth and honour of the world could give. See here the power of religion. It not only supports, it comforts. It not only enables one to bear suffering with resignation, but it enables him to *rejoice*. Philosophy blunts the feelings; infidelity leaves men to murmur and repine in trial ; the pleasures of this world have no power even to support or comfort in times of affliction ; but Christianity furnishes positive pleasure in trial, and enables the sufferer to smile through his tears. ¶ *In infirmities*. In my weaknesses; see Note on chap. xi. 30. ¶ *In reproaches.* In the contempt and scorn with which I meet as a follower of Christ, Note, chap. xi. 21. ¶ *In necessities*. In want ; see Notes on chap. vi. 4, 5, ¶ *In distresses for Christ's sake;* Note, chap. vi. 4. In the various wants and difficulties to which I am exposed on account of the Saviour, or which I suffer in his cause. ¶ *For when I am weak, then am I strong*. When I feel weak ; when I am subjected to trial, and nature faints and fails, then strength is imparted to me, and I am enabled to bear all. The more I am borne down with trials, the more do I feel my need of divine assistance, and the more do I feel the efficacy of divine grace. Such was the promise in Deut. xxxiii. 25 : " As thy days, so shall thy strength be." So in Heb. xi. 24 : " Who out of weakness were made strong." What Christian has not experienced this, and been able to

glorying : ye have compelled me : for I ought to have been commended of you : for [a] in nothing am I behind the very

say that when he felt himself weak and felt like sinking under the accumulation of many trials, he has found his strength according to his day, and felt an arm of power supporting him ? It is then that the Redeemer manifests himself in a peculiar manner ; and then that the excellency of the religion of Christ is truly seen and its power appreciated and felt.

11. *I am become a fool in glorying.* The meaning of this expression I take to be this. " I have been led along in speaking of myself until I admit I appear foolish in this kind of boasting. It is folly to do it, and I would not have entered on it unless I had been driven to it by my circumstances and the necessity which was imposed on me of speaking of myself." Paul doubtless desired that what he had said of himself should not be regarded as an example for others to follow. Religion repressed all vain boasting and self-exultation ; and to prevent others from falling into a habit of boasting, and then pleading his example as an apology, he is careful to say that he regarded it as folly ; and that he would by no means have done it if the circumstances of the case had not constrained him. If any one, therefore, is disposed to imitate Paul in speaking of himself and what he has done, let him do it only when he is in circumstances like Paul, and when the honour of religion and his usefulness imperiously demand it ; and let him not forget that it was the deliberate conviction of Paul that boasting was the characteristic of a fool! ¶ *Ye have compelled me*. You have made it necessary for me to vindicate my character and to state the evidence of my divine commission as an apostle. ¶ *For I ought to have been commended of you*. By you. Then this boasting, so foolish, would have been unnecessary. What a delicate reproof ! All the fault of this

chiefest apostles, though ^a I be nothing.

a Lu.17.10; 1Co.3.7; Ep.3.7.

12 Truly the signs ^b of an apostle were wrought among you in all

b 1 Col.9.2.

foolish boasting was theirs. They knew him intimately. They had derived great benefits from his ministry, and they were bound in gratitude and from a regard to right and truth to vindicate him. But they had not done it ; and hence, through their fault, he had been compelled to go into this unpleasant vindication of his own character. ¶ *For in nothing am I behind the very chiefest apostles.* Neither in the evidences of my call to the apostolic office (see 1 Cor. ix. 1, seq.) ; nor in the endowments of the Spirit ; nor in my success ; nor in the proofs of a divine commission in the power of working miracles ; see Note on chap. xi. 5. ¶ *Though I be nothing.* This expression was either used in sarcasm or seriously. According to the former supposition it means, that he was regarded as nothing ; that the false apostles spoke of him as a mere nothing, or as having no claims to the office of an apostle. This is the opinion of Clarke, and many of the recent commentators. Bloomfield inclines to this. According to the latter view, it is an expression of humility on the part of Paul, and is designed to express his deep sense of his unworthiness in view of his past life—a conviction deepened by the exalted privileges conferred on him, and the exalted rank to which he had been raised as an apostle. This was the view of most of the early commentators. Doddridge unites the two. It is not possible to determine with certainty which is the true interpretation ; but it seems to me that the latter view best accords with the scope of the passage, and with what we have reason to suppose the apostle *would* say at this time. It is true that in this discussion (chap. x. seq.) there is much that is sarcastic. But in the whole strain of the passage before us he is serious. He is speaking of his sufferings, and of the evidences that he was raised to elevated rank as an apostle, and it is not quite natural to

suppose that he would throw in a sarcastic remark just in the midst of this discussion. Besides, this interpretation accords exactly with what he says, 1 Cor. xv. 9 : "For I am the least of all the apostles, that am not meet to be called an apostle." If this be the correct interpretation, then it teaches, (1.) That the highest attainments in piety are not inconsistent with the deepest sense of our nothingness and unworthiness. (2.) That the most distinguished favours bestowed on us by God are consistent with the lowest humility. (3.) That those who are most favoured in the Christian life, and most honoured by God, should not be unwilling to take a low place, and to regard and speak of themselves as nothing. Compared with God, what are they ?—Nothing. Compared with the angels, what are they?—Nothing. As creatures compared with the vast universe, what are we ?—Nothing. An atom, a speck. Compared with other Christians, the eminent saints who have lived before us, what are we ? Compared with what we ought to be, and might be, what are we ?—Nothing. Let a man look over his past life, and see how vile and unworthy it has been; let him look at God, and see how great and glorious he is; let him look at the vast universe, and see how immense it is ; let him think of the angels, and reflect how pure they are ; let him think of what he might have been, of how much more he might have done for his Saviour ; let him look at his body, and think how frail it is, and how soon it must return to the dust ; and no matter how elevated his rank among his fellow-worms, and no matter how much God has favoured him as a Christian or a minister, he will feel, if he feels right, that he is nothing. The most elevated saints are distinguished for the deepest humility ; those who are nearest to God feel most their distance ; they who are to occupy the highest place in

patience, in signs, and wonders, and mighty deeds.

13 For what is it wherein you were inferior to other churches, except *it be* that I *a* myself was not burdensome to you? forgive we this wrong.

14 Behold, the third time I

a chap.11.9.

---

heaven feel most deeply that they are unworthy of the lowest.

12. *Truly the signs of an apostle.* Such miracles as the acknowledged apostles worked. Such "signs" or evidences that they were divinely commissioned; see Note on Mark xvi. 17; Acts ii. 22; Rom. xv. 19. ¶ *Were wrought among you.* That is, by me; see Note, 1 Cor. ix. 2. ¶ *In all patience.* I performed those works notwithstanding the opposition which I met with. I patiently persevered in furnishing the evidence of my divine commission. There was a succession of miracles demonstrating that I was from God, notwithstanding the unreasonable opposition which I met with, until I *convinced* you that I was called to the office of an apostle. ¶ *In signs and wonders.* In working miracles; comp. Note, Acts ii. 22. What these miracles at Corinth were, we are not distinctly informed. They probably, however, were similar to those wrought in other places, in healing the sick, &c.; the most *benevolent* as it was one of the most *decisive* proofs of the divine power.

13. *For what is it, &c.* This verse contains a striking mixture of sarcasm and irony, not exceeded, says Bloomfield, by any example in Demosthenes. The sense is, "I have given among you the most ample proof of my apostolic commission. I have conferred on you the highest favours of the apostolic office. In these respects you are superior to all other churches. In one respect only are you *inferior* —it is in this, that you have not been *burdened* with the privilege of supporting me. If you had had this, you would have been inferior to no others. But this was owing to me; and I pray that you will forgive me this. I might have urged it; I might have claimed it; I might have given you the privilege of becoming equal to the most favoured in all respects. But I have

not pressed it, and you have not done it, and I ask your pardon." There is a delicate insinuation that they had not contributed to his wants (see Note, chap. xi. 8); an intimation that it was a privilege to contribute to the support of the gospel, and that Paul *might* have been "burdensome to them" (see Notes on 1 Cor. ix. 1— 12); and an admission that he was in part to blame for this, and had not in this respect given them an opportunity to equal other churches in all respects. ¶ *Was not burdensome to you,* see this explained in the Notes on chap. x. 8. ¶ *Forgive me this wrong.* "If it be a fault, pardon it. Forgive me that I did not give you this opportunity to be equal to other churches. It is a privilege to contribute to the support of the gospel, and they who are permitted to do it should esteem themselves highly favoured. I pray you to pardon me for depriving you of any of your Christian privileges." What the feelings of the Corinthians were about forgiving Paul for this we know not; but most churches would be as ready to forgive a minister for this as for any other offence.

14. *Behold, the third time I am ready to come to you.* That is, this is the third time that I have *purposed* to come and see you, and have made preparation for it. He does not mean that he had been twice with them and was now coming the third time, but that he had twice before intended to go and had been disappointed; see 1 Cor. xvi. 5; 2 Cor. i. 15, 16. His purpose had been to visit them on his way to Macedonia, and again on his return from Macedonia. He had now formed a third resolution, which he had a prospect of carrying into execution. ¶ *And I will not be burdensome to you.* I resolve still, as I have done before, not to receive a compensation that shall be oppressive to you,

am ready to come to you ; and I will not be burdensome to you : for *a* I seek not yours, but you : for the children ought not to lay

a 1 Co.10 33; 1 Th.2.8.

see Notes on chap. xi. 9, 10. ¶ *For I seek not yours, but you.* I desire not to obtain your property, but to save your souls. This was a noble resolution ; and it is the resolution which should be formed by every minister of the gospel. While a minister of Christ has a claim to a competent support, his main purpose should not be to obtain such a support. It should be the higher and nobler object of winning souls to the Redeemer. See Paul's conduct in this respect explained in the Notes on Acts xx. 33. ¶ *For the children,* &c. There is great delicacy and address in this sentiment. The meaning is, " It is not natural and usual for children to make provisions for their parents. The common course of events and of duty is, for parents to make provision for their offspring. I, therefore, your spiritual father, choose to act in the same way. I make provision for your spiritual wants ; I labour and toil for you as a father does for his children. I seek your welfare, as he does, by constant self-denial. In return, I do not ask you to provide for me, any more than a father ordinarily expects his children to provide for him. I am willing to labour as he does, content with doing my duty, and promoting the welfare of those under me." The words rendered " ought out" (*οὐ ὀφεί-λει*) are to be understood in a *comparative* sense. Paul does not mean that a child ought *never* to provide for his parents, or to lay any thing up for a sick, a poor, and an infirm father, but that the duty of doing that was slight and unusual compared with the duty of a parent to provide for his children. The one was of comparatively rare occurrence ; the other was constant and was the ordinary course of duty It *is* a matter of obligation for a child to provide for an aged and helpless parent ; but commonly the duty is that of a parent to provide for

up for the parents, but the parents for the children.

15 And I will very gladly spend and be spent for [1] you ; though

1 your souls.

his children. Paul felt like a father toward the church in Corinth ; and he was willing, therefore, to labour for them without compensation.

15. *And I will very gladly spend.* I am willing to spend my strength, and time, and life, and all that I have, for your welfare, as a father cheerfully does for his children. Any expense which may be necessary to promote your salvation I am willing to submit to. The labour of a father for his children is cheerful and pleasant. Such is his love for them that he delights in toil for their sake, and that he may make them happy. The toil of a pastor for his flock should be cheerful. He should be willing to engage in unremitted efforts for their welfare ; and if he has any right feeling he will find *a pleasure* in that toil He will not grudge the time demanded ; he will not be grieved that it exhausts his strength, or his life, any more than a father will who toils for his family. And as the pleasures of a father who is labouring for his children are among the purest and most pleasant which men ever enjoy, so it is with a pastor. Perhaps, on the whole, the pleasantest employment in life is that connected with the pastoral office; the happiest moments known on earth are the duties, arduous as they are, of the pastoral relation. God thus, as in the relation of a father, tempers toil and pleasure together ; and accompanies most arduous labours with present and abundant reward. ¶ *Be spent.* Be exhausted and worn out in my labours. So the Greek word means. Paul was willing that his powers should be entirely exhausted and his life consumed in this service. ¶ *For you.* Marg. as in the Greek, for *your souls.* So it should have been rendered. So Tindal renders it. The sense is, that he was willing to become wholly exhausted if by it he might secure the salvation of their

the more abundantly I love you, the less I be loved.

16 But be it so, I did not burden

you : nevertheless, being crafty, I caught you with guile.

17 Did I make a gain of you by

---

souls. ¶ *Though the more abundantly I love you,* &c. This is designed doubtless as a gentle reproof. It refers to the fact that notwithstanding the tender attachment which he had evinced for them, they had not manifested the love in return which' he had a right to expect. It is *possible* that there may be an allusion to the case of a fond, doting parent. It sometimes happens that a parent fixes his affections with undue degree on some one of his children ; and in such cases it is not uncommon that the child evinces *special* ingratitude and want of love. Such *may* be the allusion here—that Paul had fixed his affections on them like a fond, doting father, and that he had met with a return by no means corresponding with the fervour of his attachment ; yet still he was willing, like such a father, to exhaust his time and strength for their welfare. The doctrine is, that we should be willing to labour and toil for the good of others, even when they evince great ingratitude. The proper end of labouring for their welfare is not to excite their gratitude, but to obey the will of God ; and no matter whether others are grateful or not ; whether they love us or not ; whether we can promote our popularity with them or not, let us do them good always. It better shows the firmness of our Christian principle to endeavour to benefit others when they love us the less for all our attempts, than it does to attempt to do good on the swelling tide of popular favour.

16. *But be it so.* This is evidently a charge of his enemies ; or at least a charge which it might be supposed they would make. Whether they ever in fact made it, or whether the apostle merely anticipates an objection, it is impossible to determine. It is clearly to be regarded as *the language* of objectors ; for, (1.) It can never be supposed that Paul would state as a serious matter that he had

caught them with deceit or fraud. (2.) He *answers* it as an objection in the following verse. The meaning is, " We admit that you did not burden us. You did not exact a support from us. But all this was mere trick. You accomplished the same thing in another way. You professed when with us not to seek our property but our souls. But in various ways you contrived to get our money, and to secure your object. You made others the agents for doing this, and sent them among us under various pretexts to gain money from us." It will be remembered that Paul had sent Titus among them to take up the collection for the poor saints in Judea (chap viii. 6), and it is not at all improbable that some there had charged Paul with making use of this pretence only to obtain money for his own private use. To guard against this charge, was one of the reasons why Paul was so anxious to have some persons appointed by the church to take charge of the contribution ; see 1 Cor. xvi. 3 ; comp. Notes on 2 Cor. viii. 19— 21. ¶ *Being crafty.* Being cunning That is, by sending persons to obtain money on different pretences. ¶ *I caught you with guile.* I took you by deceit or fraud. That is, making use of fraud in pretending that the money was for poor and afflicted saints, when in reality it was for my own use. It is impossible that Paul should have ever admitted this of himself ; and they greatly pervert the passage who suppose that it applies to him, and then plead that it is right to make use of guile in accomplishing their purposes. Paul never carried his measures by dishonesty, nor did he ever justify fraud ; comp. Notes on Acts xxiii. 6.

17. *Did I make a gain,* &c. In refuting this slander, Paul appeals boldly to the facts, and to what they knew. " Name the man," says he, " who has thus defrauded you under my instructions. If the charge is

any of them whom I sent unto you?

18 I desired Titus, *a* and with *him* I sent a brother: *b* Did Titus make a gain of you? walked we not in the same spirit? *walked we* not in the same steps?

a chap.7.2.   *b* chap.8.6.

19 Again, think ye that we excuse ourselves *c* unto you? we speak before God in Christ: but *we do* all things, dearly beloved, for your edifying.

20 For I fear, lest, when *d* I come, I shall not find you such as I would, and *that* I shall be found unto you

c chap.5.12.   *d* 1 Co.4 21; chap.13.2.10.

well-founded, let him be specified, and let the mode in which it was done be distinctly stated." The phrase "make a gain" (from πλεονεκτέω), means properly to have an advantage; then to take advantage, to seek unlawful gain. Here Paul asks whether he had defrauded them by means of any one whom he had sent to them.

18. *I desired Titus.* To go and complete the collection which you had commenced; see chap. viii. C. ¶ *And with* him *I sent a brother;* see Note on chap. viii. 18. ¶ *Did Titus make a gain of you?* They knew that he did not. They had received him kindly, treated him with affection, and sent him away with every proof of confidence and respect; see chap. vii. 7. How then could they now pretend that he had defrauded them? ¶ *Walked we not in the same spirit?* Did not all his actions resemble mine? Was there not the same proof of honesty, sincerity, and love which I have ever manifested? This is a very delicate turn. Paul's course of life when *with* them they admitted was free from guile and from any attempt to get money by improper means. They charged him only with attempting it by means of others. He now boldly appeals to them and asks whether Titus and he had not *in fact* acted in the same manner; and whether they had not alike evinced a spirit free from covetousness and deceit?

19. *Again, think ye that we excuse ourselves unto you?* see Note on chap. v. 12. The sense is, Do not suppose that this is said from mere anxiety to obtain your favour, or to ingratiate ourselves into your esteem. This is said doubtless to keep himself

from the suspicion of being actuated by improper motives. He had manifested great solicitude certainly in the previous chapter to vindicate his character; but he here says that it was not from a mere desire to show them that his conduct was right; it was from a desire to honour Christ. ¶ *We speak before God in Christ.* We declare the simple and undisguised truth as in the presence of God. I have no mere desire to palliate my conduct; I disguise nothing; I conceal nothing; I say nothing for the mere purpose of self-vindication, but I can appeal to the Searcher of hearts for the exact truth of all that I say. The phrase "before God in Christ," means probably, "I speak as in the presence of God, and as a follower of Christ, as a Christian man." It is the solemn appeal of a Christian to his God for the truth of what he said, and a solemn asseveration that what he said was not for the mere purpose of excusing or *apologizing for* (Greek) his conduct. ¶ *But* we do *all things, dearly beloved, for your edifying.* All that I have done has been for your welfare. My vindication of my character, and my effort to disabuse you of your prejudices, has been that you might have unwavering confidence in the gospel and might be built up in holy faith. On the word *edify*, see Notes on Rom. xiv. 19; 1 Cor. viii. 1; x. 23.

20. *For I fear lest, when I come;* see ver. 14. ¶ *I shall not find you such as I would.* That is, walking in the truth and order of the gospel. He had feared that the disorders would not be removed, and that they would not have corrected the errors which prevailed, and for which he had rebuked them. It was on this ac-

such as ye would not ; lest *there be* debates, envyings, wraths, strifes, backbitings, whisperings, swellings, tumults :

21 *And* lest, when I come again, my God will humble *a* me

among you, and *that* I shall bewail many which have sinned already, and have not repented *b* of the uncleanness, and fornication, *c* and lasciviousness which they have committed.

a chap.2.1.   *b* Re.2.21.   *c* 1 Co.5.1.

count that he had said so much to them. His desire was that all these disorders might be removed, and that he might be saved from the necessity of exercising severe discipline when he should come among them. ¶ *And that I shall be found unto you such as ye would not.* That is, that I shall be compelled to administer discipline, and that my visit may not be as pleasant to you as you would desire. For this reason he wished all disorder corrected, and all offences removed ; that every thing might be pleasant when he should come ; see 1 Cor. iv. 21 ; comp. Note on chap. x 2. ¶ *Lest* there be *debates.* I fear that there may be existing there debates, &c., which will require the interposition of the authority of an apostle. On the meaning of the word *debate,* see Note on Rom. i. 29. ¶ *Envyings ;* see Note on 1 Cor. iii. 3. ¶ *Wraths.* Anger or animosities between contending factions, the usual effect of forming parties. ¶ *Strifes.* Between contending factions ; see Note on 1 Cor. iii. 3. ¶ *Backbitings ;* see Note on Rom. i. 30. ¶ *Whisperings ;* see Note on Rom. i. 29. ¶ *Swellings.* Undue elation ; being puffed up (see Note on chap viii. 1 ; 1 Cor. iv. 6, 18, 19 ; v. 2)—such as would be produced by vain self-confidence. ¶ *Tumults.* Disorder and confusion arising from this existence of parties. Paul, deeply sensible of the evil of all this, had endeavoured in this correspondence to suppress it, that all things might be pleasant when he should come among them.

21. And *lest, when I come again, my God will humble me,* &c. Lest I should be compelled to inflict punishment on those whom I suppose to have been converted under my ministry. I had rejoiced in them as true converts: I had counted them as

among the fruit of my ministry. Now to be compelled to inflict punishment on them as having no religion would mortify me and humble me. The infliction of punishment on members of the church is a sort of punishment to him who inflicts it as well as to him who is punished. Members of the church should walk uprightly, lest they overwhelm the ministry in shame. ¶ *And that I shall bewail many,* &c. If they repented of their sin he could still rejoice in them. If they continued in their sin till he came, it would be to him a source of deep lamentation. It is evident from the word "many" here that the disorders had prevailed very extensively in the church at Corinth. The word rendered "have sinned already" means "who have sinned *before,*" and the idea is, that they were old offenders, and that they had not yet repented. ¶ *The uncleanness ;* see Note, Rom. i. 24. ¶ *And fornication and lasciviousness,* &c. ; see Notes on 1 Cor. v. 1 , vi. 18. This was *the* sin to which they were particularly exposed in Corinth, as it was *the* sin for which that corrupt city was particularly distinguished. See the Introduction to the first epistle. Hence the frequent cautions in these epistles against it ; and hence it is not to be wondered at that some of those who had become professing Christians had fallen into it. It may be added that it is still the sin to which converts from the corruptions and licentiousness of paganism are particularly exposed.

CHAPTER XIII.

THIS closing chapter of the epistle relates to the following subjects.

I. The assurance of Paul that he was about to come among them (ver. 1—4), and that he would certainly inflict punishment on all who deserved it. His enemies had reproached him

CHAPTER XIII.

THIS *is* the third *time* I am coming to you. In *a* the

a De.19.15 ; He.10.28,29

mouth of two or three witnesses shall every word be established.

---

as being timid and pusillanimous ; see Notes on chap. x. 1, 2, 10, 11. They had said that he was powerful to threaten, but afraid to execute. It is probable that they had become more bold in this from the fact that he had twice proposed to go there and had failed. In reply to all this, he now in conclusion solemnly assures them that he was coming, and that in *all* cases where an offence was proved by two or three witnesses, punishment would be inflicted ; ver. 1. He assures them (ver. 2) that he would not spare ; and that since they sought a proof that Christ had sent him, they should *witness* that proof in the punishment which he would inflict (ver. 3) ; for that Christ was now clothed with power and was able to execute punishment, though he had been crucified ; ver. 4.

II. Paul calls on them solemnly to examine themselves and to see whether they had any true religion ; ver. 5, 6. In the state of things which existed there ; in the corruption which had abounded in the church, he solemnly commands them to institute a faithful inquiry, to know whether they had not been deceived ; at the same time expressing the hope that it would appear as the result of their examination that they were not reprobates.

III. He earnestly prays to God that they might do no evil ; that they might be found to be honest and pure, whatever might be thought of Paul himself or whatever might become of him ; ver. 7. Their repentance would save Paul from exerting his miraculous power in their punishment, and might thus prevent the proof of his apostolic authority which they desired, and the consequence might be that they *might* esteem him to be a reprobate, for he could not exert his miraculous power except in the cause of truth ; ver. 8. Still he was willing to be esteemed an impostor if *they* would do no evil.

IV. He assures them that he earnestly wished their perfection, and that the design of his writing to them severe as he had appeared, was their edification ; ver. 9, 10.

V. Then he bids them an affectionate and tender farewell, and closes with the usual salutations and benedictions ; ver. 11—14.

1. *This* is *the third* time, &c. ; see Note on chap. xii. 14. For an interesting view of this passage, see Paley's Horæ Paulinæ on this epistle, No. xi. It is evident that Paul had been to Corinth but once before this, but he had resolved to go before a second time, but had been disappointed. ¶ *In the mouth of two or three witnesses*, &c. This was what the law of Moses required ; Deut. xx. 16 ; see Note on John viii. 17 ; comp. Mat. xviii. 16. But in regard to its application here, commentators are not agreed. Some suppose that Paul refers to his own epistles which he had sent to them as the two or three witnesses by which his promise to them would be made certain ; that he had purposed it and promised it two or three times, and that as this was all that was required by the law, it would certainly be established. This is the opinion of Bloomfield, Rosenmüller, Grotius, Hammond, Locke, and some others. But, with all the respect due to such great names, it seems to me that this would be trifling and childish in the extreme. Lightfoot supposes that he refers to Stephanas, Fortunatus, and Achaicus, who would be witnesses to them of his purpose ; see 1 Cor. xvi. 17. But the more probable opinion, it seems to me, is that of Doddridge, Macknight, and others, that he anticipated that there would be necessity for the administration of discipline there, but that he would feel himself under obligation in administering it to adhere to the reasonable maxim of the Jewish law. No one should be condemned or punished where there was not at least two

2 I told you before, and foretell you, as if I were present, the second time ; and being absent now I write to them *a* which heretofore have sinned, and to all other, that, if I come again, I will not spare :

a chap.12.21.

3 Since ye seek a proof of Christ speaking in me, which to you-ward is not weak, but is mighty *b* in you.

4 For though *c* he was crucified through weakness, yet he liveth

b 1 Co.9.2.   *c* Ph.2.7,8; 1 Pe.3.18.

---

or three witnesses to prove the offence. But where there were, discipline would be administered according to the nature of the crime.

2. *I told you before.* That I would not spare offenders ; that I would certainly punish them. He had intimated this before in the first Epis. chap. iv. 21 ; chap. v. ¶ *And foretell you.* Now apprise you of my fixed determination to punish every offender as he deserves. ¶ *As if I were present the second time.* The mention of the second time here proves that Paul had been with them but *once* before. He had formed the resolution to go to them, but had been disappointed. The time when he had been with them is recorded in Acts xviii. 1, seq. He now uses the same language to them which he says he would use if he were with them, as he had expected to be, the second time. See the remarks of Paley on this passage, referred to above. ¶ *And being absent ;* see Note on 1 Cor. v. 3. ¶ *To them which have heretofore sinned.* To all the offenders in the church. They had supposed that he would not come to them (1 Cor. iv. 18), or that if he came he would not dare to inflict punishment, 2 Cor. 9—11. They had, therefore, given themselves greater liberty, and had pursued their own course, regardless of his authority and commands. ¶ *I will not spare.* I will punish them. They shall not escape.

3. *Since ye seek a proof of Christ speaking in me ;* see the Notes on the previous chapters. They had called in question his apostolic authority ; they had demanded the evidence of his divine commission. He says that he would now furnish such evidence by inflicting just punishment on all offenders, and they should have abundant proof that Christ spoke by him, or that he was inspired. ¶ *Which to*

you-ward *is not weak.* Or *who,* that is, Christ, is not weak, &c. Christ has manifested his power abundantly towards you, that is, either by the miracles that had been wrought in his name; or by the diseases and calamities which they had suffered on account of their disorders and offences (see Note on 1 Cor. xi. 30; v.); or by the force and efficacy of his doctrine. The connection, it seems to me, requires that we should understand it of the calamities which had been inflicted by Christ on them for their sins, and which Paul says would be inflicted again if they did not repent. The idea is, that they had had ample demonstration of the power of Christ to inflict punishment, and they had reason to apprehend it again.

4. *For though he was crucified through weakness.* Various modes have been adopted of explaining the phrase " through weakness." The most probable explanation is that which refers it to the human nature which he had assumed (Phil. ii. 7, 8 ; 1 Pet. iii. 18), and to the *appearance* of weakness which he manifested. He did not choose to exert his power. He appeared to his enemies to be weak and feeble. This idea would be an *exact* illustration of the point before the apostle. He is illustrating his own conduct, and especially in the fact that he had not exerted his miraculous powers among them in the punishment of offenders ; and he does it by the example of Christ, who though abundantly *able* to have exerted his power and to have rescued himself from his enemies, yet was willing to *appear* weak, and to be crucified. It is very clear, (1.) That the Lord Jesus *seemed* to his enemies to be weak and incapable of resistance. (2.) That he did not put forth his power to protect his life. He in

by the power of God. For we also are weak ¹ in him, but we shall live with him by the power of God towards you.

5 Examine ᵃ yourselves, whether

ye be in the faith; prove your own selves. Know ye not your own selves, how that Jesus Christ ᵇ is in you, except ye be reprobates? ᶜ

1 or, *with.*
a 1 Cor.11.28; 1 John 3.20,21.

b Ro.8.10; Ga.4.19.
c 1 Co.9.27; 2 Ti.3.8.

fact offered no resistance, *as if* he had no power. (3.) He had a human nature that was peculiarly sensitive, and sensible to suffering; and that was borne down and crushed under the weight of mighty woes; see my Notes on Isa. liii. 2, 3. From all these causes he *seemed* to be weak and feeble; and these appear to me to be the principal ideas in this expression. ¶ *Yet he liveth.* He is not now dead. Though he was crucified, yet he now lives again, and is now capable of exerting his great power He furnishes proof of his being alive, in the success which attends the gospel, and in the miracles which are wrought in his name and by his power. There is a *living* Redeemer in heaven; a Redeemer who is able to exert all the power which he ever exerted when on earth; a Redeemer, therefore, who is able to save the soul; to raise the dead; to punish all his foes. ¶ *By the power of God.* In raising him from the dead and placing him at his own right hand; see Eph. i. 19—21. Through the power of God he was brought from the tomb, and has a place assigned him at the head of the universe. ¶ *For we also are weak in him.* Marg. "*with* him." We his apostles, also, are weak in virtue of our connection with him. We are subject to infirmities and trials; we seem to have no power; we are exposed to contempt; and we appear to our enemies to be destitute of strength. Our enemies regard us as feeble; and they despise us. ¶ *But we shall live with him,* &c. That is, we shall show to you that we are *alive.* By the aid of the power of God we shall show that we are *not* as weak as our foes pretend; that we *are* invested with power; and that we are able to inflict the punishment which we threaten. This is one of the numerous instances in which Paul illustrated the case

before him by a reference to the example and character of Christ. The idea is, that Christ did not exert *his* power, and appeared to be weak, and was put to death. So Paul says that he had not exerted *his* power, and seemed to be weak. But, says he, Christ lives, and is clothed with strength; and so we, though we appear to be weak, shall exert among you, or toward you, the power with which he has invested us, in inflicting punishment on our foes.

5. *Examine yourselves;* see Note on 1 Cor. xi. 28. The particular reason why Paul calls on them to examine themselves was, that there was occasion to fear that many of them had been deceived. Such had been the irregularities and disorders in the church at Corinth; so ignorant had many of them shown themselves of the nature of the Christian religion, that it was important, in the highest degree, for them to institute a strict and impartial examination to ascertain whether they had not been altogether deceived. This examination, however, is never unimportant or useless for Christians; and an exhortation to do it is *always* in place. So important are the interests at stake, and so liable are the best to deceive themselves, that all Christians should be often induced to examine the foundation of their hope of eternal salvation. ¶ *Whether ye be in the faith.* Whether you are true Christians. Whether you have any true faith in the gospel. Faith in Jesus Christ, and in the promises of God through him, is one of the distinguishing characteristics of a true Christian; and to ascertain whether we have any true faith, therefore, is to ascertain whether we are sincere Christians. For some reasons for such an examination, and some remarks on the mode of doing it; see Note

or. 1 Cor. xi. 28. ¶ *Prove your own selves.* The word here used (δοκιμάζετε) is stronger than that before used, and rendered "examine" (πειράζετε). This word, *prove*, refers to assaying or trying metals by the powerful action of heat ; and the idea here is, that they should make the *most thorough* trial of their religion, to see whether it would stand the test ; see Note on 1 Cor. iii. 13. The *proof* of their piety was to be arrived at by a faithful examination of their own hearts and lives ; by a diligent comparison of their views and feelings with the word of God ; and especially by making *trial* of it in life. The best way to *prove* our piety is to subject it to *actual trial* in the various duties and responsibilities of life. A man who wishes to *prove* an axe to see whether it is good or not, does not sit down and look at it, or read all the treatises which he can find on axe-making, and on the properties of iron and steel, valuable as such information would be ; but he shoulders his axe and goes into the woods, and puts it to the trial there. If it cuts well ; if it does not break ; if it is not soon made dull, he understands the quality of his axe better than he could in any other way. So if a man wishes to know what his religion is worth, let him *try* it in the places where religion is of any value. Let him go into the world with it. Let him go and *try* to do good ; to endure affliction in a proper manner ; to combat the errors and follies of life ; to admonish sinners of the error of their ways ; and to urge forward the great work of the conversion of the world, and he will soon see there what his religion is worth—as easily as a man can test the qualities of an axe. Let him not merely sit down and think, and compare himself with the Bible and look at his own heart—valuable as this may be in many respects —but let him treat his religion as he would any thing else—let him subject it to actual experiment. That religion which will enable a man to imitate the example of Paul or Howard, or the great Master himself, *in doing good*, is genuine. That religion which will enable a man to endure persecu-

tion for the name of Jesus ; to bear calamity without murmuring ; to submit to a long series of disappointments and distresses for Christ's sake, is genuine. That religion which will prompt a man unceasingly to a life of prayer and self-denial ; which will make him ever conscientious, industrious, and honest ; which will enable him to warn sinners of the errors of their ways, and which will dispose him to seek the friendship of Christians, and the salvation of the world, is pure and genuine. *That will answer the purpose.* It is like the good axe with which a man can chop all day long, in which there is no flaw, and which does not get dull, *and which answers all the purposes of an axe.* Any other religion than this is worthless. ¶ *Know ye not your own selves.* That is, "Do you not know yourselves ?" This does not mean, as some may suppose, that they might know *of* themselves, without the aid of others, what their character was ; or that they might themselves ascertain it ; but it means that they might know *themselves,* i. e. their character, principles, conduct. This *proves* that Christians *may know* their true character. If they are Christians, they may know it with as undoubted certainty as they may know their character on any other subject. Why should not a man be as able to determine whether he loves God as whether he loves a child, a parent, or a friend ? What greater difficulty need there be in understanding the character on the subject of religion than on any other subject ; and why should there be any more reason for doubt on this than on any other point of character ? And yet it is remarkable, that while a child has no doubt that he loves a parent, or a husband a wife, or a friend a friend, almost all Christians are in very great doubt about their attachment to the Redeemer and to the great principles of religion. Such was not the case with the apostles and early Christians. "I KNOW," says Paul, "whom I have believed, and am persuaded that he is able to keep that which I have committed to him," &c.; 2 Tim. i. 12. "We KNOW,' says

6 But I trust that ye shall know that we are not reprobates.

7 Now I pray to God that ye do no evil; not that we should appear approved, but that ye

John, speaking in the name of the body of Christians, "that we have passed from death unto life;" 1 John iii. 14. "We KNOW that we are of the truth;" 19. "We KNOW that he abideth in us;" 24. "We KNOW that we dwell in him;" 1 John iv. 13 ; see also v. 2, 19, 20. So Job said, " I KNOW that my Redeemer liveth, and that he shall stand in the latter day upon the earth," &c.; Job xix. 25. Such is the current language of scripture. Where, in the Bible, do the sacred speakers and writers express doubts about their attachment to God and the Redeemer ? Where is such language to be found as we hear from almost all professing Christians, expressing entire *uncertainty* about their condition ; absolute doubt whether they love God or hate him; whether they are going to heaven or hell; whether they are influenced by good motives or bad ; and even *making it a matter of merit* to be in such doubt, and thinking it wrong *not* to doubt ? What would be thought of a husband that should make it a matter of merit to doubt whether he loved his wife ; or of a child that should think it wrong *not* to doubt whether he loved his father or mother ? Such attachments *ought* to be doubted—but they do not occur in the common relations of life. On the subject of religion men often act as they do on no other subject ; and if it is right for one to be satisfied of the sincerity of his attachments to his best earthly friends, and to *speak* of such attachment without wavering or misgiving, it cannot be wrong to be satisfied with regard to our attachment to God, and to *speak* of that attachment, as the apostles did, in language of undoubted confidence. ¶ *How that Jesus Christ is in you.* To be in Christ, or for Christ to be in us, is a common mode in the scriptures of expressing the idea that we are Christians. It is language derived from the close union which subsists between the Redeemer and his people; see the phrase ex-

plained in the Note on Rom. viii. 10. ¶ *Except ye be reprobates ;* see Note on Rom. i. 28. The word rendered " reprobates " (ἀδόκιμοι) means properly *not approved, rejected :* that which will not stand the trial. It is properly applicable to metals, as denoting that they will not bear the tests to which they are subjected, but are found to be base or adulterated. The sense here is, that they might know that they were Christians, unless their religion was base, false, adulterated ; or such as would not bear the test. There is no allusion here to the sense which is sometimes given to the word *reprobate,* of being cast off or abandoned by God, or doomed by him to eternal ruin in accordance with an eternal purpose. Whatever may be the truth on that subject, nothing is taught in regard to it here. The simple idea is, that they might know that they were Christians, unless their religion was such as would not stand the test, or was worthless.

6. *But I trust,* &c. The sense of this verse is, " Whatever may be the result of your examination of yourselves, I trust (Gr. *I hope*) you will not find us false and to be rejected ; that is, I trust you will find in me evidence that I am commissioned by the Lord Jesus to be his apostle." The idea is, that they would find when he was among them, that he was endowed with all the qualifications needful to confer a claim to the apostolic office.

7. *Now I pray to God that ye do no evil.* I earnestly desire that you may do right, and only right ; and I beseech God that it may be so, whatever may be the result in regard to me, and whatever may be thought of my claims to the apostolic office. This is designed to mitigate the apparent severity of the sentiment in ver. 6. There he had said that they would find him fully endowed with the power of an apostle. They would see that he was able abundantly to punish

should do that which is honest, though we be as reprobates.

8 For *a* we can do nothing

a Pr.21.30.

the disobedient. They would have ample demonstration that he was endowed by Christ with all the powers appropriate to an apostle, and that all that he had claimed had been well-founded, all that he threatened would be executed. But this *seemed* to imply that he *desired* that there should be occasion for the exercise of that power of administering discipline; and he, therefore, in this verse, removes all suspicion that such was his wish, by saying solemnly, that he prayed to God that they might never do wrong; that they might never give him occasion for the exercise of his power in that way, though as a consequence he would be regarded as a reprobate, or as having no claims to the apostolic office. He would rather be regarded as an impostor; rather lie under the reproach of his enemies that he had no claims to the apostolic character, than that they, by doing wrong, should give him occasion to show that he was not a deceiver. ¶ *Not that we should appear approved.* My great object, and my main desire, is not to urge my claims to the apostolic office and clear up my own character; it is that you should lead honest lives, whatever may become of me and my reputation. ¶ *Though we be as reprobates.* I am willing to be regarded as rejected, disapproved, worthless, like base metal, provided you lead honest and holy lives. I prefer to be so esteemed, and to have you live as becomes Christians, than that you should dishonour your Christian profession, and thus afford me the opportunity of demonstrating, by inflicting punishment, that I am commissioned by the Lord Jesus to be an apostle. The sentiment is, that a minister of the gospel should desire that his people should walk worthy of their high calling, whatever may be the estimate in which he is held. He should never desire that they should do wrong—how *can* he do it?—in order that he may take occasion from

against the truth, but for the truth.

9 For we are glad, when we

their wrong-doing to vindicate, in any way, his own character, or to establish a reputation for skill in administering discipline or in governing a church. What a miserable condition it is—and as wicked as it is miserable—for a man to wish to take advantage of a state of disorder, or of the faults of others, in order to establish his own character, or to obtain reputation. Paul spurned and detested such a thought; yet it is to be feared it is sometimes done.

8. *For we.* That is, we the apostles. ¶ *Can do nothing against the truth,* &c. That is, we who are under the influence of the Spirit of God; who have been commissioned by him as apostles, can do nothing that shall be against the great system of truth which we are appointed to promulgate and defend. You need, therefore, apprehend no partial or severe discipline from us; no unjust construction of your conduct. Our aim is to promote the truth, and to do what is right; and we cannot, therefore, by any regard to our own reputation, or to any personal advantage, do what is wrong, or countenance, or desire what is wrong in others. We must wish that which is right to be done by others, whatever may be the effect on us—whether we are regarded as apostles or deceivers. I suppose, therefore, that this verse is designed to qualify and confirm the sentiment in the previous verse, that Paul meant to do only right; that he wished all others to do right; and that whatever might be the effect on his own reputation, or however he might be regarded, he *could not* go against the great system of gospel truth which he preached, or even *desire* that others should ever do wrong, though it might in any way be for his advantage. It was a *fixed principle* with him to act only in accordance with truth; to do what was right.

9. *For we are glad when we are weak,* &c. We rejoice in your wel-

are weak, and ye are strong : and this also we wish, *even* your perfection.*a*

10 Therefore I write these things being absent, lest being present I should use sharpness, *b* according *c*

a 1 Th.3.10; He.6.1. *b* Tit.1.13. *c* chap.10.8.

to the power which the Lord hath given me to edification, and not to destruction.

11 Finally, brethren, farewell. Be perfect, *d* be of good comfort, be *e* of one mind, live in peace ;

d ver.9.
e Ro.12.16 ; 15.5 ; Ep.4.3 ; Ph.2.2 ; 1 Pe.3.8.

fare, and are willing to submit to self-denial and to infirmity if it may promote your spiritual strength. In the connection in which this stands it seems to mean, " I am content to appear *weak,* provided you do no wrong ; I am willing *not* to have occasion to exercise my power in punishing offenders, and had rather lie under the reproach of being actually weak, than to have occasion to exercise my power by punishing you for wrongdoing ; and provided you are strong in the faith and in the hope of the gospel, I am very willing, nay, I rejoice that I am under this necessity of appearing weak." ¶ *And this also we wish.* I desire this in addition to your doing no evil. ¶ Even *your perfection.* The word here used (*καταρτισις*) occurs nowhere else in the New Testament, though the verb from which it is derived (*καταρτιζω*) occurs often ; Mat. iv. 21; xxi. 16; Mark i. 19; Luke vi. 40 ; Rom. ix. 22 ; 1 Cor. i. 10 ; 2 Cor. xiii. 11; Gal. vi. 1; 1 Thess. iii. 10, *et al.* ; see Note on ver. 11. On the meaning of the word see Rom. ix. 22. The idea of *restoring,* putting in order, fitting, repairing, is involved in the word always, and hence the idea of making perfect ; *i. e.* of *completely restoring* any thing to its proper place. Here it evidently means that Paul wished their *entire* reformation—so that there should be no occasion for exercising discipline. Doddridge renders it, "perfect good order." Macknight, "restoration." For this restoration of good order Paul had diligently laboured in these epistles ; and this was an object near to his heart.

10. *Therefore I write these things, &c.* This is a kind of apology for what he had said, and especially for the apparently harsh language which he had felt himself constrained to use.

He had reproved them; he had admonished them of their faults ; he had threatened punishment, all of which was designed to prevent the necessity of severe measures when he should be with them. ¶ *Lest being present I should use sharpness.* In order that when I come I may not have occasion to employ severity ; see the sentiment explained in the Note on chap. x. 2. ¶ *According to the power, &c.* That I may not use the power with which Christ has invested me for maintaining discipline in his church. The same form of expression is found in chap. x. 8 ; see Note on that place.

11. *Finally, brethren* (*λοιπον*). The remainder; all that remains is for me to bid you an affectionate farewell. The word here rendered "farewell" (*χαιρετε*), means usually to joy and rejoice, or to be glad ; Luke i. 14; John xvi. 20, 22 ; and it is often used in the sense of "joy to you," "hail !" as a salutation ; Mat. xxvi. 49; xxvii. 29. It is also used as a salutation at the beginning of an epistle, in the sense of *greeting ;* Acts xv. 23 ; xxiii. 26; James i. 1. It is generally agreed, however, that it is here to be understood in the sense of *farewell,* as a parting salutation, though it may be admitted that there is included in the word an expression of a wish for their happiness. This was among the last words which Cyrus, when dying, addressed to his friends. ¶ *Be perfect.* See this word explained in the Notes on ver. 9, and Rom. ix. 22 It was a wish that every disorder might be removed ; that all that was *out of joint* might be restored ; that every thing might be in its proper place ; and that they might be just what they ought to be: A command to be perfect, however, does not prove that it has ever in fact been obeyed : and an earnest wish on the part of an apostle that

and the God of love and peace shall be with you.

12 Greet *a* one another with an holy kiss.

a Ro.16.16.

13 All the saints salute you.

14 The *b* grace of the Lord Jesus Christ, and the love ot God, and the *c* communion of the

b Ro.16.24. *c* Ph.2.1.

others *might* be perfect, does not demonstrate that they were ; and this passage should not be adduced to prove that any *have* been free from sin. It may be adduced, however, to prove that an obligation rests on Christians to be perfect, and that there is no natural obstacle to their becoming such, since God never can command us to do an impossibility. Whether any one, but the Lord Jesus, *has been* perfect, however, is a question on which different denominations of Christians have been greatly divided. It is incumbent on the advocates of the doctrine of sinless perfection to produce *some one instance* of a perfectly sinless character. This has not *yet* been done. ¶ *Be of good comfort.* Be consoled by the promises and supports of the gospel. Take comfort from the hopes which the gospel imparts. Or the word may possibly have a reciprocal sense, and mean, *comfort one another ;* see Schleusner. Rosenmüller renders it, "receive admonition from all with a grateful mind, that you may come to greater perfection." It is, at any rate, the expression of an earnest wish on the part of the apostle, that they might be happy. ¶ *Be of one mind.* They had been greatly distracted, and divided into different parties and factions. At the close of the epistle he exhorts them as he had repeatedly done before, to lay aside these strifes, and to be united, and manifest the same spirit ; see Note on Rom. xii. 16 ; xv. 5 ; see Note also on 1 Cor. i. 10. The sense is, that Paul desired that dissensions should cease, and that they should be united in opinion and feeling as Christian brethren. ¶ *Live in peace.* With each other. Let contentions and strifes cease. To promote the restoration of peace had been the main design of these epistles. ¶ *And the God of love and peace.* The God who is all love, and who is the author of all peace. What a glo-

rious appellation is this ! There can be no more beautiful expression, and it is as true as it is beautiful, that God is a God of *love* and of *peace.* He is infinitely benevolent ; he delights in exhibiting his love ; and he delights in the love which his people evince for each other. At the same time he is the author of peace, and he delights in peace among men. When Christians love each other they have reason to expect that the God of love will be with them ; when they live in peace, they may expect the God of peace will take up his abode with them. In contention and strife we have no reason to expect his presence ; and it is only when we are willing to lay aside all animosity that we may expect the God of peace will fix his abode with us.

12. *Greet.* Salute, see Note, Rom. xvi. 3. ¶ *With an holy kiss.* Note, Rom. xvi. 16.

13. *All the saints salute you.* That is, all who were with Paul, or in the place where he was. The epistle was written from Macedonia, probably from Philippi. See Intro. § 3.

14. *The grace of our Lord Jesus Christ ;* see Note, Rom xvi. 20. This verse contains what is usually called *the apostolic benediction ;* the form which has been so long, and which is almost so universally used, in dismissing religious assemblies. It is properly *a prayer,* and it is evident that the Optative *εἴη,* "*May* the grace," &c., is to be supplied. It is the expression of a desire that the favours here referred to may descend on all for whom they are thus invoked. ¶ *And the love of God.* May the love of God *towards* you be manifest. This must refer peculiarly to the *Father,* as the Son and the Holy Spirit are mentioned in the other members of the sentence. The " love of God" here referred to is the manifestation of his goodness and favour in the pardon of sin, in the communi-

Holy Ghost, *be* with you all. Amen.

The second *epistle* to the Co-

rinthians was written from Philippi, *a city* of Macedonia, by Titus and Lucas.

cation of his grace, in the comforts and consolations which he imparts to his people, in all that constitutes an expression of love. The love of God brings salvation ; imparts comfort ; pardons sin ; sanctifies the soul ; fills the heart with joy and peace ; and Paul here prays that all the blessings which are the fruit of that love may be with them. ¶ *And the communion of the Holy Ghost ;* comp. Note, 1 Cor. x. 16. The word *communion* (χιινωνία) means properly participation, fellowship, or having any thing *in common;* Acts ii. 42 ; Rom. xv. 26 ; 1 Cor. i. 9 ; x. 16 ; 2 Cor. vi. 14 ; viii. 4 ; ix. 13 ; Gal. ii. 9 ; Eph. iii. 9 ; 1 John i. 3. This is also a wish or prayer of the apostle Paul ; and the desire is either that they might partake of the views and feelings of the Holy Ghost ; that is, that they might have fellowship *with him ;* or that they might all in common partake of the gifts and graces which the Spirit of God imparts. He gives love, joy, peace, long-suffering, gentleness, goodness, faith (Gal. v. 22), as well as miraculous endowments ; and Paul prays that these things might be imparted freely to *all* the church *in common*, that all might participate in them : all might share them. ¶ *Amen.* This word is wanting, says Clarke, in almost every MS. of any authority. It was however early affixed to the epistle.

In regard to this closing verse of the epistle, we may make the following remarks. (1.) It is *a prayer;* and if it is a prayer addressed to God, it is no less so to the Lord Jesus and to the Holy Spirit. If so, it is right to offer worship to the Lord Jesus and to the Holy Spirit. (2.) There is a distinction in the divine nature ; or there is the existence of what is usually termed three persons in the Godhead. If not, why are they mentioned in this manner ? If the Lord Jesus is not divine and equal with the Father, why is he mentioned in this connection ? How strange it

would be for Paul, an inspired man, to pray in the same breath, "the grace of a man or an angel" and "the love of God" be with you ! And if the "Holy Spirit" be merely an *influence* of God or an *attribute* of God, how strange to pray that the "love of God" and the participation or fellowship of an "influence of God," or an "attribute of God" might be with them ! (3.) The Holy Spirit is *a person*, or has a distinct personality. He is not an attribute of God, nor a mere divine influence. How could prayer be addressed to *an attribute*, or *an influence ?* But here, nothing can be plainer than that there were favours which the Holy Ghost, as an intelligent and conscious agent, was expected to bestow. And nothing can be plainer than that they were favours in some sense *distinct* from those which were conferred by the Lord Jesus, and by the Father. Here is a *distinction* of some kind *as real* as that between the Lord Jesus and the Father; here are favours expected from him distinct from those conferred by the Father and the Son ; and there is, therefore, here all the proof that there can be, that there is in some respects a distinction between the persons here referred to, and that the Holy Spirit is an intelligent, conscious agent. (4.) The Lord Jesus is not *inferior* to the Father, that is, he has an equality with God. If he were *not* equal, how could he be mentioned, as he here is, as bestowing favours like God, and especially why is he mentioned *first ?* Would Paul, in invoking blessings, mention the name of a mere man or an angel before that of the eternal God ? (5.) The passage, therefore, furnishes a proof of the doctrine of the Trinity that has not yet been answered, and, it is believed, cannot be. On the supposition that there are three persons in the adorable Trinity, united in essence and yet distinct in some respects, all is plain and clear. But on the supposition that the Lord

Jesus is a mere man, an angel, or an archangel, and that the Holy Spirit is an attribute, or an influence from God, how unintelligible, confused, strange does all become ! That Paul, in the solemn close of the epistle, should at the same time invoke blessings from a mere creature, and from God, and from an *attribute*, surpasses belief. But that he should invoke blessings from him who was the equal with the Father, and from the Father himself, and from the Sacred Spirit sustaining the same rank, and in like manner imparting important bles sings, is in accordance with all that we should expect, and makes all harmonious and appropriate. (6.) Nothing could be a more proper close of the epistle ; nothing is a more appropriate close of public worship, than such an invocation. It is a prayer to the ever-blessed God, that all the rich influences which he gives as Father, Son, and Holy Ghost, may be imparted ; that all the benefits which God confers in the interesting relations in which he makes himself known to us may descend and bless us. What more appropriate prayer can be offered at the close of public worship ? How seriously should it be pronounced, as a congregration is about to separate, perhaps to come together no more ! With what solemnity should all join in it, and how devoutly should all pray, as they thus separate, that these rich and inestimable blessings may rest upon them ! With hearts uplifted to God it should be pronounced and heard ; and every worshipper should leave the sanctuary deeply feeling that what he most needs as he leaves the place of public worship ; as he travels on the journey of life ; as he engages in its duties or meets its trials ; as he looks at the grave and eternity, is the grace of the Lord Jesus Christ, the love of God, and the blessings which the Holy Spirit imparts in renewing, and sanctifying, and comforting his people. What more appropriate prayer than this for the writer and reader of these Notes ! May that blessing rest alike upon us, though we may be strangers in the flesh, and may those divine and heavenly influences guide us alike to the same everlasting kingdom of glory

In regard to the subscription at the end of this epistle, it may be observed, that it is wanting in a great part of the most ancient MSS., and is of no authority whatever ; see Notes at the end of the epistle to the Romans, and 1 Corinthians. In this case, however, this subscription is in the main correct, as there is evidence that it was written from Macedonia, and not improbably from Philippi. See the Introduction to the epistle.

THE EPISTLE OF PAUL THE APOSTLE

TO THE

GALATIANS

INTRODUCTION.

§ 1. *The Situation of Galatia, and the Character of the People.*

Galatia was a province of Asia Minor, having Pontus on the east, Bithynia and Paphlagonia north, Cappadocia and Phrygia south, and Phrygia west. See the map prefixed to the Acts of the Apostles. In Tanner's Classical Atlas, however, it extends on the north to the Euxine or Black sea. It was probably about two hundred miles in its greatest extent from east to west, and varied in breadth from twelve to an hundred and fifty miles. It was one of the largest provinces of Asia Minor, and covered an extent of country almost as large as the State of New Jersey. It is probable, however, that the boundaries of Galatia varied at different times as circumstances dictated. It had no *natural* boundary, except on the north ; and of course the limits may have been varied by conquests, or by the will of the Roman emperor, when it was erected into a province.

The name *Galatia* is derived from the word *Gaul*, and was given to it because it had been conquered by the Gauls, who, having subdued the country, settled in it.—*Pausanias*, Attic. cap. iv. These were mixed with various Grecian families, and the country was also called *Gallogræcia.—Justin.* lib. xxiv. 4 ; xxv. 2 ; xxvii. 3. This invasion of Asia Minor was made, according to Justin (lib. xxv. cap. 2), about the four hundred and seventy-ninth year after the founding of Rome, and, of course, about 272 years before Christ. They invaded Macedonia and Greece ; and subsequently invaded Asia Minor, and became an object of terror to all that region. This expedition issued from Gaul, passed over the Rhine, along the Danube, through Noricum, Pannonia, and Mœsia, and at its entrance into Germany, carried along with it many of the Tectosages. On their arrival in Thrace, Lutarius took them with him, crossed the Bosphorus, and effected the conquest of Asia Minor.—Liv. lib. xxxviii. c. 16. Such was their number, that Justin says, "they filled all Asia (*i. e.* all Asia Minor) like swarms of bees. Finally, they became so numerous that no kings of the east could engage in war without an army of Gauls ; neither when driven from their kingdom could they flee to any other than to the Gauls. Such was the terror of the name of Gauls, and such the invincible felicity of their arms—*et armorum invicta felicitas erat*—that they supposed that in no other way could their own majesty be protected, or being lost, could be recovered, without the aid of Gallic courage. Their being called in by the king of B'thynia for aid, when they had gained the victory, they divided the kingdom with him, and called that region *Gallogræcia.*"—Justin, xxv. 2. Under the reign of Augustus Cesar, about 26 years before the birth of Christ, this region was reduced into the form of a Roman colony, and was governed by a *proprætor*, appointed by the emperor.

Their original Gaulish language they retained so late as the fifth century, as appears from the testimony of Jerome, who says that their dialect was nearly the same as that of the Treviri.—Tom. iv. p. 256. ed. Benedict. At the same time, they also spoke the Greek language in common with all the inhabitants of Lesser Asia, and therefore the epistle to them was written in Greek, and was intelligible to them as well as to others.

The Galatians, like the inhabitants of the surrounding country, were heathens, and their religion was of a gross and debasing kind. They are said to have worshipped " the mother of the gods," under the name of *Agdistis.* Callimachus, in his hymns, calls them " a foolish people." And Hillary, himself a Gaul, calls them *Gallos indociles*—expressions which, says Calmet, may well excuse Paul's addressing them as " foolish," chap. iii. 1. There were few cities to be found among them, with the exception of Ancyra, Tavium, and Pessinus, which carried on some trade.

The possessors of Galatia were of three different nations or tribes of Gauls ; the Tolistobogi, the Trocmi, and the Tectosagi. There are imperial medals extant, on which these names are found. It is of some importance to bear in mind these distinctions. It is possible that while Peter was making converts in one part of Galatia, the apostle Paul was in another; and that some, claiming authority as from Peter, propagated opinions not conformable to the views of Paul, to correct and expose which was one design of this epistle.—*Calmet.*

The Gauls are mentioned by ancient historians as a tall and valiant people. They went nearly naked. Their arms were only a sword and buckler. The impetuosity of their attack, it is said, was irresistible, and hence they became so formidable, and were usually so victorious.

It is not possible to ascertain the number of the inhabitants of Galatia, at the time when the gospel was preached there, or when this epistle was written. In 2 Macc. viii. 20, it is said that Judas Maccabeus, exhorting his followers to fight manfully against the Syrians, referred to several instances of divine interposition to encourage them ; and among others, " he told them of the battle which they had in Babylon with the *Galatians ;* how they came but eight thousand in all to the business, with four thousand Macedonians ; and that the Macedonians being perplexed, the eight thousand destroyed an hundred and twenty thousand, because of the help which they had from heaven, and so received a great booty." But it is not certain that this refers to those who dwelt in Galatia. It may refer to *Gauls* who at that time had overrun Asia Minor ; the Greek word here used, (Γαλάτας) being taken equally for either. It is evident, however, that there was a large population that went under this general name ; and it is probable that Galatia was thickly settled at the time when the gospel was preached there. It was in the central part of Asia Minor, then one of the most densely populated parts of the world, and was a region singularly fertile.—Strabo, lib. xii. p. 567, 568, ed. Casaub. Many persons, also, were attracted there for the sake of commerce. That there were many Jews also, in all the provinces of Asia Minor, is apparent not only from the Acts of the Apostles, but is expressly declared by Josephus, Ant. xvi. 6.

§ 2. *The time when the Gospel was preached in Galatia.*

There is no certain information as to the time when the gospel was first preached in Galatia, or the persons by whom it was done. There is mention, however, of Paul's having preached there several times, and several circumstances lead us to suppose that those churches were established by him, or that he was the first to carry the gospel to them, or that he and Barnabas together preached the gospel there on the *mission* on which they were sent from Antioch, Acts xiii. 2. seq.   In Acts xvi. 5, 6, it is expressly said that they went " throughout Phrygia and the region of Galatia."   This journey was for the purpose of confirming the churches, and was undertaken at the suggestion of Paul (Acts xv. 36), with the design of visiting their brethren in every city where they had preached the word of the Lord.   It is true, that in the account of the mission of Paul and Barnabas (Acts xiv.), it is not expressly said that they went into Galatia ; but it is said (Acts xiv. 5, 6), that when they were in Iconium, an assault was made on them, or a purpose formed to stone them, and that, being apprized of it, they fled unto Lystra and Derbe, cities of Lycaonia, " and unto the region that lieth round about."   Pliny, lib. v. c. 27, says, that a part of Lycaonia bordered on Galatia, and contained fourteen cities, of which Iconium was the most celebrated.   Phrygia also was contiguous to Galatia, and to Lycaonia, and these circumstances render it probable that when Paul proposed to Barnabas to visit again the churches where they had preached, Galatia was included, and that they had been there before this visit referred to in Acts xvi. 6.

It may be, also, that Paul refers to himself in the epistle (chap. i. 6), where he says, " I marvel that ye are so soon removed from him that CALLED YOU into the grace of Christ unto another gospel ," and if so, then it is plain that he preached to them first, and founded the churches there.   The same thing may be evinced also from the expression in chap. iv. 15, where he says, " I bear you record, that if it had been possible, ye would have plucked out your own eyes, and have given them to me ;" an expression which leads us to suppose that they had formed for him a peculiar attachment, because he had first preached the gospel to them, and that there had existed all the ardour of attachment implied in their *first love*.   It is quite evident, therefore, I think, that the gospel was preached among the Galatians first by Paul, either alone or in company with some other one of the apostles.   It is possible, however, as has been intimated above, that Peter also may have preached in one part of Galatia at the time that Paul was preaching in other parts.   It is a circumstance also of some importance on this point, that Paul speaks in this epistle in a tone of authority, and with a severity of reproof which he would hardly have used unless he had at first preached there, and had a right to be regarded as the founder of the church, and to address it as its father   In this respect the tone here is quite different, as Mr. Locke has remarked, from what is observable in the epistle to the Romans.   Paul had not been at Rome when he addressed the church there by letter, and his language differs materially from that which occurs in the epistles to the Corinthians and Galatians.   It was to them the very respectful and mild language of a stranger ; here it is respectful, but it is the authoritative language of a father having a right to reprove.

§ 3. *The date of this Epistle.*

Many have supposed that this was the first epistle which Paul wrote. Tertullian maintained this (see Lardner, vol. vi. p. 7. ed. Lond. 1829), and Epiphanius also.   Theodoret and others suppose it was written at Rome, and was consequently written near the close of the life of Paul, and was one of his last epistles.   Lightfoot supposes also that it was written from Rome, and that it was among the first which Paul wrote there.   Chrysostom says that this epistle was written before that to the Romans.   Lewis Capellus, Witsius, and Wall suppose that it was written from Ephesus after the apostle had been a second time in Galatia.   This also was the opinion of Pearson, who places it in the year 57, after the first epistle to the Corinthians, and before

Paul left Ephesus. Grotius thought it difficult to assign the date of the epistle, but conjectures that it was written about the same time as that to the Romans. Mill supposes that it was not written until after that to the Romans, probably at Troas, or some other place in Asia, as Paul was going to Jerusalem. He dates the epistle in the year 58. Dr. Benson supposes that it was written at Corinth, when the apostle was first there, and made a long stay of a year and six months. While there, he supposes that Paul received tidings of the instability of the converts in Galatia, and wrote this epistle and sent it by one of his assistants. See these opinions examined in Lardner as quoted above. Lardner himself supposes that it was written from Corinth about the year 52, or the beginning of the year 53. Macknight supposes it was written from Antioch, after the council at Jerusalem, and before Paul and Silas undertook the journey in which they delivered to the churches the decrees which were ordained at Jerusalem ; Acts xvi. 4. Hug, in his Introduction, supposes that it was written at Ephesus in the year 57, and after the I. and II. Thess., and the epistle to Titus had been written. Mr. Locke supposes that Paul established churches in Galatia, in the year 51; and that this epistle was written between that time and the year 57. These opinions are mostly mere conjecture ; and amidst such a variety of sentiment, it is evidently impossible to determine exactly at what time it was written. The only mark of time in the epistle itself occurs in chap. i. 6, where the apostle says, " I marvel that ye are *so soon* (οὕτω ταχίως) removed from him that called you," &c.; where the words " so soon" would lead us to suppose that it was at no distant period after he had been among them. Still it might have been several years. The date assigned to it in the Polyglott Bible (Bagster's) is the year 58.

The exact date of the epistle is of very little importance. In regard to the time when it was written the only arguments which seem to me to be of much weight, are those advanced by Paley in his Horæ Paulinæ. " It will hardly be doubted," says he, " but that it was written whilst the dispute concerning the circumcision of Gentile converts was fresh in men's minds ; for even supposing it to have been a forgery, the only credible motive that can be assigned for the forgery, was to bring the name and authority of the apostle into this controversy. No design can be so insipid, or so unlikely to enter into the thoughts of any man, as to produce an epistle written earnestly and pointedly on one side of a controversy, when the controversy itself was dead, and the question no longer interesting to any class of readers whatever. Now the controversy concerning the circumcision of Gentiles was of such a nature, that, if it arose at all, it must have arisen in the beginning of Christianity." Paley then goes on to show that it was natural that the Jews, and converts from the Jews, should start this question, and agitate it ; and that this was much more likely to be insisted on while the temple was standing, and they continued as a nation, and sacrifices were offered, than after their city and temple were destroyed. It is therefore clear that the controversy must have been started, and the epistle written *before* the invasion of Judea, by Titus, and the destruction of Jerusalem. The *internal* evidence leads to this conclusion. On the whole, it is probable that the epistle was written somewhere about the year 53, or between that and 57 ; and was evidently designed to settle an important controversy in the churches of Galatia. The *place* where it was written, must be, I think, wholly a matter of conjecture. The subscription at the end that it was written from Rome is of no authority whatever; and there are no internal circumstances, which, so far as I can see, throw any light on the subject.

§ 4. *The design of the Epistle.*

It is easy to discern from the epistle itself that the following circumstances existed in the churches of Galatia, and that it was written with reference to them.

(1.) That they had been at first devotedly attached to the apostle Paul, and had received his commands and instructions with implicit confidence when he was among them ; chap. iv. 14, 15 ; comp. chap. i. 6.

(2.) That they had been perverted from the doctrine which he taught them soon after he had left them ; chap. i. 6.

(3.) That this had been done by persons who were of Jewish origin, and who insisted on the observance of the rites of the Jewish religion.

(4.) That they claimed to have come directly from Jerusalem, and to have derived their views of religion and their authority from the apostles there.

(5.) That they taught that the apostle Paul was inferior to the apostles there ; that he had been called more recently into the apostolic office ; that the apostles at Jerusalem must be regarded as the source of authority in the Christian church ; and that, therefore, the teaching of Paul should yield to that which was derived directly from Jerusalem.

(6.) That the laws of Moses were binding, and were necessary in order to justification. That the rite of circumcision especially was of binding obligation ; and it is probable (chap. vi. 12), that they had prevailed on many of the Galatians to be circumcised, and certain that they had induced them to observe the Jewish festivals ; chap. iv. 10.

(7.) It would seem, also, that they urged that Paul himself had changed his views since he had been among the Galatians, and now maintained the necessity of circumcision ; chap. v. 11. Perhaps they alleged this, from the undoubted fact that Paul, when at Jerusalem (Acts xxi. 26), had complied with some of the customs of the Jewish ritual.

(8.) That they urged that all the promises of God were made to Abraham, and that whoever would partake of those promises, must be circumcised as Abraham was. This Paul answers, chap. iii. 7; iv. 7.

(9.) That in consequence of the promulgation of these views, great dissensions had arisen in the church, and strifes of an unhappy nature existed, greatly contrary to the spirit which should be manifested by those who bore the Christian name.

From this description of the state of things in the churches of Galatia, the design of the epistle is apparent, and the scope of the argument will be easily seen. Of this state of things the apostle had been undoubtedly apprised, but whether by letters, or by messengers from the churches there, is not declared. It is not improbable, that some of his friends in the churches there had informed him of it, and he immediately set about a remedy to the evils existing there.

I. The first object, therefore, was to show that he had received his commission as an apostle, *directly from God*. He had not received it at all from man ; he had not even been instructed by the other apostles ; he had not acknowledged their superiority ; he had not even consulted them. He did not acknowledge, therefore, that the apostles at Jerusalem possessed any superior rank or authority. His commission, though he had not seen the Lord Jesus before he was crucified, he had, nevertheless, derived immediately from him. The doctrine, therefore, which he had taught them, that the Mosaic laws were not binding, and that there was no necessity of being circumcised, was a doctrine which had been derived directly from God. In proof of this, he goes into an extended statement (chap. i.), of the manner in which he had been called, and of the fact; that he had not consulted with the apostles at Jerusalem, or confessed his inferiority to them ; of the fact that when they had become acquainted with the manner in which he preached, they approved his course (chap. i. 24 ; ii. 1—10); and of the fact that on one occasion, he had actually been constrained to differ from Peter, the oldest of the apostles, on a point in which he was manifestly wrong, and on one of the very points then under consideration.

II. The second great object, therefore, was to show the real nature and design of the law of Moses, and to prove that the peculiar rites of the Mosaic ritual, and especially the rite of circumcision, were not necessary to justification and salvation ; and that they who observed that rite, did in fact renounce the Scripture method of justification ; make the sacrifice of Christ of no value, and make slaves of themselves. This leads him into a consideration of the true nature of the doctrine of justification, and of the way of salvation by a Redeemer.

This point he shows in the following way,

(1.) By showing that those who lived before Christ, and especially Abraham, were in fact justified, not by obedience to the ritual law of Moses, but by faith in the promises of God ; chap. iii. 1—18.

(2.) By showing that the design of the Mosaic ritual was only temporary, and that it was intended to lead to Christ; chap. iii. 19—29 ; iv. 1—8.

(3.) In view of this, he reproves the Galatians for having so readily fallen into the observance of these customs ; chap. iv. 9—21.

(4.) This view of the design of the Mosaic law, and of its tendency, he illustrates by an allegory drawn from the case of Hagar ; chap. iv. 21—31.

This whole discourse is succeeded by an affectionate exhortation to the Galatians, to avoid the evils which had been engendered ; reproving them for the strifes existing in consequence of the attempt to introduce the Mosaic rites, and earnestly entreating them to stand firm in the liberty which Christ had vouchsafed to them from the servitude of the Mosaic institutions, chap. v. vi.

The design of the whole epistle, therefore, is to state and defend the true doctrine of justification, and to show that it did not depend on the observance of the laws of Moses. In the general purpose, therefore, it accords with the design of the epistle to the Romans. In one respect, however, it differs from the design of that epistle. That was written, to show that man could not be justified by *any works of the law*, or by conformity to *any* law, moral or cere-monial ; the object of this is, to show that justification cannot be obtained by *conformity to the ritual* or *ceremonial law ;* or that the observance of the ceremonial law is not necessary to salvation. In this respect, therefore, this epistle is of less general interest than that to the Romans. It is also, in some respects, more difficult. The argument, if I may so express myself, is more *Jewish.* It is more in the Jewish manner ; is designed to meet a Jew in his own way, and is, therefore, somewhat more difficult for all to follow. Still it contains great and vital statements on the doctrines of salvation, and, as such, demands the profound and careful attention of all who desire to be saved, and who would know the way of acceptance with God

EPISTLE TO THE GALATIANS

CHAPTER I.

PAUL, an apostle, (not of men, neither by man, but *a* by Jesus Christ, and God the Father, who *b* raised him from the dead ;)

a Ac.9.6,15.   *b* Ac.2.24.

CHAPTER I.

ANALYSIS.

THE main design of Paul in this chapter, is to show that he had received his call to the apostleship, not from man, but from God. It had been alleged (see the Introduction above) that the apostles at Jerusalem possessed the most elevated rank, and the highest authority in the Christian church ; that they were to be regarded as the fountains and the judges of the truth ; that Paul was inferior to them as an apostle ; and that they who inculcated the necessity of circumcision, and the observance of the rites of Moses, were sustained by the authority and the examples of the apostles at Jerusalem.

To meet this statement was the design of this first chapter. Paul's grand object was to show that he was not appointed by men ; that he had not been commissioned by men ; that he had not derived his instructions from men ; that he had not even consulted with them ; but that he had been commissioned and taught expressly by Jesus Christ, and that when the apostles at Jerusalem had become acquainted with him, and with his views and plans of labour, long after he had begun to preach, they had fully concurred with him. This argument comprises the following parts :

I. The solemn declaration that he was not commissioned by men, and that he was not, in any sense, an apostle of man, together with the general salutation to the churches in Galatia ; ver. 1—5.

II. The expression of his astonish-ment that the Galatians had so soon forsaken his instruction, and embraced another gospel ; and a solemn declaration that whoever preached another gospel was to be held accursed ; ver. 6—10. Twice he anathematizes those who attempt to declare any other way of justification than that which consisted in faith in Christ, and says that it was no gospel at all. It was to be held as a great and fixed principle, that there was but one way of salvation ; and no matter who attempted to preach any other, he was to be held accursed.

III. To show, therefore, that *he* was not appointed by men, and that he had not received his instructions from men, but that he had preached the truth directly revealed to him by God, and that which was, therefore, immutable and eternal, he goes into a statement of the manner in which he was called into the ministry, and made acquainted with the gospel ; ver. 11—21.

(*a*) He affirms, that he was not taught it by man, but by the express revelation of Jesus Christ ; ver. 11, 12.

(*b*) He refers to his former well-known life, and his zeal in the Jewish religion ; showing how much he had been formerly opposed to the gospel ; ver. 13, 14.

(*c*) He says that he had been separated, by the divine purpose, from his mother's womb, to be a preacher of the gospel, and that when he was called to the ministry, he had no conference with any human being, as to what he was to preach ; he did not go up to Jerusalem to consult with those who were older apostles, but he retired far from them into Arabia, and thence again returned to Damascus ; ver. 15—17.

(d) After three years. he says, he did indeed go to Jerusalem; but he remained there but fifteen days, and saw none of the apostles but Peter and James; ver. 18, 19. His views of the gospel were formed before that; and that he did not submit implicitly to Peter, and learn of him, he shows in ch. ii., where he says, he "withstood him to the face."

(e) After that, he says, he departed into the regions of Cilicia, in Asia Minor, and had no opportunity of conference with the churches which were in Judea. Yet they heard that he who had been formerly a persecutor, had become a preacher, and they glorified God for it ; ver. 20—24. Of course, he had had no opportunity of deriving his views of religion from them ; he had been in no sense dependent on them ; but so far as they were acquainted with his views, they concurred in them. The sum of the argument, therefore, in this chapter is, that when Paul went into Cilicia and the adjacent regions, he had never seen but two of the apostles, and that but for a short time ; he had never seen the apostles together ; and he had never received any instructions from them. His views of the gospel, which he had imparted to the Galatians, he had derived directly from God.

1. *Paul an apostle ;* see Note, Rom. i. 1. This is the usual form in which he commences his epistles ; and it was of special importance to commence this epistle in this manner, because it was one design to vindicate his apostleship, or to show that he had received his commission directly from the Lord Jesus. ¶ *Not of men.* "Not from (ἀπ') men." That is, he was not *from* any body of men, or commissioned by men. The word apostle means *sent,* and Paul means to say, that he was not *sent* to execute any purpose of men, or commissioned by them. His was a higher calling ; a calling of God, and he had been sent directly *by* him. Of course, he means to exclude here all classes of men as having had any thing to do in sending

him forth ; and, especially, he means to affirm, that he had not been sent out by the body of apostles at Jerusalem. This, it will be remembered (see the Introduction), was one of the charges of those who had perverted the Galatians from the faith which Paul had preached to them. ¶ *Neither by man.* "Neither *by* or *through* (δι') the instrumentality of any man." Here he designs to exclude all men from having had any agency in his appointment to the apostolic office. He was neither sent out *from* any body of men to execute their purposes ; nor did he receive his commission, authority, or ordination through the medium of any man. A minister of the gospel now receives his call from God, but he is ordained or set apart to his office by man. Matthias, the apostle chosen in the place of Judas (Acts i. 26), received his call from God, but it was by the vote of the body of the apostles. Timothy was also called of God, but he was appointed to his office by the laying on the hands of the presbytery ; 1 Tim. iv. 14. But Paul here says, that *he* received no such commission as that from the apostles. They were not the means or the medium of ordaining him to his work. He had, indeed, together with Barnabas, been set apart at Antioch, by the brethren there (Acts xiii. 1—3), for a *special mission* in Asia Minor ; but this was not an appointment to the apostleship. He had been restored to sight after the miraculous blindness produced by seeing the Lord Jesus on the way to Damascus, by the laying on of the hands of Ananias, and had received important instruction from him (Acts ix. 17), but his commission as an apostle had been received directly from the Lord Jesus, without any intervening medium, or any form of human authority, Acts ix. 15 ; xxii. 17—21 ; 1 Cor. ix. 1. ¶ *But by Jesus Christ.* That is, directly by Christ. He had been called by him, and commissioned by him, and sent by him, to engage in the work of the gospel. ¶ *And God the Father.* These words were omitted by Marcion, because, says Jerome he

2 And all the brethren which are with me, unto the churches of Galatia: *a*

3 Grace *b be* to you, and peace, from God the Father, and *from* our Lord Jesus Christ,

a Ac.16.6; 18.23.   *b* Ro.1.7,&c.

4 Who gave *c* himself for our sins, that he might deliver us *d* from this present evil *e* world, according *f* to the will of God and our Father:

c John 10.17,18; Tit.2.14.   *d* John 17.14.
e 1 John 2.16.   *f* Ro.8.27.

held that Christ raised himself from the dead. But there is no authority for omitting them. The sense is, that he had the highest possible authority for the office of an apostle; he had been called to it by God himself, who had raised up the Redeemer. It is remarkable here, that Paul associates Jesus Christ and God the Father, as having called and commissioned him. We may ask here, of one who should deny the divinity of Christ, how Paul could mention him as being equal with God in the work of commissioning him? We may further ask, how could he say that he had not received his call to this office from a man, if Jesus Christ was a mere man? That he was called by Christ, he expressly says, and strenuously maintains as a point of great importance. And yet, the very point and drift of his argument is, to show that he was not called by *man.* How could this be if Christ was a mere man? ¶ *Who raised him from the dead:* see Notes on Acts ii. 24, 32. It is not quite clear, why Paul introduces this circumstance here. It may have been, (1.) Because his mind was full of it, and he wished on all occasions to make that fact prominent; (2.) Because this was the distinguishing feature of the Christian religion, that the Lord Jesus had been raised up from the dead, and he wished, in the outset, to present the superiority of that religion which had brought life and immortality to light; and, (3.) Because he wished to show that he had received his commission from that same God who had raised up Jesus, and who was, therefore, the author of the true religion. His commission was from the source of life and light, the God of the living and the dead; the God who was the author of the glorious scheme which revealed life and immortality.

2. *And all the brethren which are with me.* It was usual for Paul to associate with him the ministers of the gospel, or other Christians who were with him, in expressing friendly salutations to the churches to which he wrote, or as uniting with him, and concurring in the sentiments which he expressed. Though Paul claimed to be inspired, yet it would do much to conciliate favour for what he advanced, if others also concurred with what he said, and especially if they were known to the churches to which the epistles were written. Sometimes the names of others were associated with his in the epistle; see Note, 1 Cor. i. 1; Phil. i. 1; Col. i. 1; 1 Thess. i. 1. As we do not know where this epistle was written, of course we are ignorant who the "brethren" were, who are here referred to. They may have been ministers with Paul, or they may have been the private members of the churches. Commentators have been much divided in opinion on the subject; but all is conjecture. It is obviously impossible to determine. ¶ *Unto the churches.* How many churches there were in Galatia, is unknown. There were several *cities* in Galatia, as Ancyria, Tavia, Pessinus, &c. It is not improbable that a church had been established in each of the cities, and as they were not far distant from each other, and the people had the same general character and habits, it is not improbable that they had fallen into the same errors. Hence the epistle is directed to them in common.

3. *Grace be unto you,* &c. This is the usual apostolic salutation, imploring for them the blessing of God. See it fully explained in the Notes on Rom. i. 7.

4. *Who gave himself for our sins.* The reason why Paul so soon introduces this important doctrine, and

makes it here so prominent, probably is, that this was the cardinal doctrine of the Christian religion, the great truth which was ever to be kept before the mind, and because this truth had been in fact lost sight of by them. They had embraced doctrines which tended to obscure it, or to make it void. They had been led into error by the Judaizing teachers, who held that it was necessary to be circumcised, and to conform to the whole Jewish ritual. Yet the tendency of all this was to obscure the doctrines of the gospel, and particularly the great truth that men can be justified only by faith in the blood of Jesus; chap. v. 4 ; comp. chap. ĭ. 6, 7. Paul, therefore, wished to make this prominent—the very *starting point* in their religion; a truth never to be forgotten, that Christ gave himself for their sins, that he might deliver them from all the bad influences of this world, and from all the false systems of religion engendered in this world. The expression "*who gave*" (τοῦ δόντος) is one that often occurs in relation to the work of the Redeemer, where it is represented as a *gift*, either on the part of God, or on the part of Christ himself; see Note on John iii. 16 ; comp. John iv. 10 ; Rom. iv. 25 ; 2 Cor. ix. 15 ; Gal. ii. 20 ; Eph. v. 25 ; Tit. ii. 14. This passage proves, (1.) That it was wholly *voluntary* on the part of the Lord Jesus. No one compelled him to come ; no one could compel him. It is not too much to say, that God *could* not, and *would* not COMPEL any innocent and holy being to undertake the great work of the atonement, and endure the bitter sorrows which were necessary to redeem man. God will *compel* the guilty to suffer, but he never will compel the innocent to endure sorrows, even in behalf of others. The whole work of redemption must be *voluntary*, or it could not be performed. (2.) It evinced great benevolence on the part of the Redeemer. He did not come to take upon himself unknown and unsurveyed woes. He did not go to work in the dark. He knew what was to be done. He knew just what sorrows were to be endured—how long,

how keen, how awful. And yet, knowing this, he came resolved and prepared to endure all those woes, and to drink the bitter cup to the dregs. (3.) If there had not been this benevolence in his bosom, man must have perished for ever. He could not have saved himself; and he had no power or right to compel another to suffer in his behalf; and even God would not lay this mighty burden on any other, unless he was entirely willing to endure it. How much then do we owe to the Lord Jesus ; and how entirely should we devote our lives to him who loved us, and gave himself for us. The word *himself*, is rendered by the Syriac, *his life* (*Nӑphsh'*); and this is in fact the sense of the Greek, that he gave his *life* for our sins, or that he died in our stead. He gave his *life* up to toil, tears, privation, sorrow, and death, that he might redeem us. The phrase, "*for our sins*" (ὑπὲρ τῶν ἁμαρτιῶν ἡμῶν), means the same as *on account of ;* meaning, that the cause or reason why he gave himself to death, was our sins ; that is, he died because we are sinners, and because we could be saved only by his giving himself up to death. Many MSS. instead of ὑπὲρ, here read περὶ, but the sense is not materially varied. The Syriac translates it, "who gave himself *instead of*," by a word denoting that there was a *substitution* of the Redeemer in our place. The sense is, that the Lord Jesus became a vicarious offering, and died in the stead of sinners. It is not possible to express this idea more distinctly and unambiguously than Paul has done, in this passage. Sin was the procuring cause of his death ; to make expiation for sin was the design of his coming ; and sin is pardoned and removed only by his substituted suffering. ¶ *That he might deliver us*. The word here used (ἐξέληται) properly means, to pluck out, to tear out ; to take out from a number, to select ; then to rescue or deliver. This is the sense here. He came and gave himself that he might *rescue* or *deliver* us from this present evil world. It does not mean to take away by death, or to remove to another world, but that he might

5 To whom *be* glory for ever and ever. Amen.

6 I marvel that ye are so soon removed *a* from him that called you into the grace of Christ unto another gospel;

a chap.5.4,7,8.

effect a separation between us and what the apostle calls here, "this present evil world." The grand purpose was, to rescue sinners from the dominion of this world, and separate them unto God. ¶ *This present evil world ;* see John xvii. 15, 16. Locke supposes, that by this phrase is intended the Jewish institutions, or the Mosaical age, in contradistinction from the age of the Messiah. Bloomfield supposes, that it means "the present state of being, this life, filled as it is with calamity, sin, and sorrow ; or, rather, the *sin itself,* and the misery consequent upon it." Rosenmüller understands by it, "the men of this age, Jews, who reject the Messiah ; and Pagans, who are devoted to idolatry and crime." The word rendered *world* ($\alpha i \grave{\omega} \nu$), means properly *age,* an indefinitely long period of time ; then eternity, for ever. It then comes to mean the world, either present or future ; and then the present world, as it is, with its cares, temptations, and desires ; the idea of evil, physical and moral, being everywhere implied —*Robinson, Lex.;* Mat. xiii. 22 ; Luke xvi. 8 ; xx. 34 ; Rom. xii. 2. Here it means the world as it is, without religion, a world of bad passions, false opinions, corrupt desires ; a world full of ambition, and of the love of pleasure, and of gold, a world where God is not loved or obeyed ; a world where men are regardless of right, and truth, and duty; where they live for themselves, and not for God ; in short, that great community, which in the Scriptures is called THE WORLD, in contradistinction from the kingdom of God. That world, that evil world, is full of sin ; and the object of the Redeemer was to *deliver* us from that ; that is, to effect a separation between his followers and that. It follows, therefore, that his followers constitute a peculiar community, not governed by the prevailing maxims, or influenced by the peculiar feelings of the people of this world.

And it follows, also, that if there is not *in fact* such a separation, then the purpose of the Redeemer's death, in regard to us, has not been effected, and we are still a part of that great and ungodly community, *the world.* ¶ *According to the will of God,* &c. Not by the will of man, or by his wisdom, but in accordance with the will of God. It was his purpose that the Lord Jesus should thus give himself ; and his doing it was in accordance with his will, and was pleasing in his sight. The whole plan originated in the divine purpose, and has been executed in accordance with the divine will. If in accordance with *his* will, it is good, and is worthy of universal acceptation.

5. *To whom* be *glory,* &c. Let him have all the praise and honour of the plan and its execution. It is not uncommon for Paul to introduce an ascription of praise in the midst of an argument: see Note on Rom. i. 25. It results from the strong desire which he had, that all the glory should be given to God, and showed that he believed that all blessings had their origin in him, and that he should be always acknowledged.

6 *I marvel.* I wonder. It is remarked by Luther (Comm. in loco), that Paul here uses as mild a word as possible. He does not employ the language of severe reproof, but he expresses his astonishment that the thing should have occurred. He was deeply affected and amazed, that such a thing could have happened. They had cordially embraced the gospel ; they had manifested the tenderest attachment for him ; they had given themselves to God, and yet in a very short time they had been led wholly astray, and had embraced opinions which tended wholly to pervert and destroy the gospel. They had shown an instability and inconstancy of character, which was to him. perfectly surprising. ¶ *That ye are so soon.* This proves that the epistle was written not long

after the gospel was first preached to them. According to the general supposition, it could not have been more than from two to five years. Had it been a long and gradual decline ; had they been destitute for years of the privileges of the gospel; or had they had time to forget him who had first preached to them, it would not have been a matter of surprise. But when it occurred in a few months ; when their once ardent love for Paul, and their confidence in him had so soon vanished, or their affections become alienated, and when they had so soon embraced opinions tending to set the whole gospel aside, it could not but excite his wonder. Learn hence, that men, professedly pious, and apparently ardently attached to the gospel, *may* become soon perverted in their views, and alienated from those who had called them into the gospel, and whom they professed tenderly to love. The ardour of the affections becomes cool, and some artful, and zealous, and plausible teachers of error seduce the mind, corrupt the heart, and alienate the affections. Where there is the ardour of the first love to God, there is also an effort soon made by the adversary, to turn away the heart from him ; and young converts are commonly *soon* attacked in some plausible manner, and by art and arguments adapted to turn away their minds from the truth, and to alienate the affections from God. ¶ *So soon removed.* This also, Luther remarks, is a mild and gentle term. It implies that *foreign* influence had been used, to turn away their minds from the truth. The word here used ($\mu\epsilon\tau\alpha\tau\iota$-$\theta\epsilon\sigma\theta\epsilon$) means, to transpose, put in another place; and then, to go over from one party to another. Their affections had become transferred to other doctrines than those which they had at first embraced, and they had moved off from the only true foundation, to one which would give them no support. ¶ *From him that called you.* There has been great difference of opinion in regard to the sense of this passage. Some have supposed, that it refers to God ; others to Christ ; others to Paul himself. Either sup-

position makes good sense, and conveys an idea not contrary to the Scriptures in other places. Doddridge, Chandler, Clarke, Macknight, Locke, and some others refer it to Paul ; Rosenmüller, Koppe, and others, suppose it refers to God ; and others refer it to the Redeemer. The Syriac renders it thus : " I marvel that ye are so soon turned away from that Messiah (Christ) who has called you." &c. It is not possible, perhaps, to determine the true sense. It does not seem to me to refer to Paul, as the main object of the epistle is, not to show that they had removed from *him*, but from the *gospel*—a far more grievous offence ; and it seems to me that it is to be referred to God. The reasons are, (1.) That he who had called them, is said to have called them "into the grace of Christ," which would be hardly said of Christ himself; and, (2.) That the work cf calling men is usually in the Scriptures attributed to God ; 1 Thess. ii. 12 ; v. 24 ; 2 Thess. ii. 14 ; 2 Tim. i. 9. ¶ *Into the grace of Christ.* Locke renders this, "into the covenant of grace which is by Christ." Doddridge understands it of the method of salvation which is *by* or *through* the grace of Christ. There is no doubt that it refers to the plan of salvation which is by Christ, or in Christ ; and the main idea is, that the scheme of salvation which they had embraced under his instruction, was one which contemplated salvation only by the grace or favour of Christ ; and that from that they had been removed to another scheme, essentially different, where the grace of Christ was made useless and void. It is Paul's object to show that the true plan makes Christ the great and prominent object ; and that the plan which they had embraced was in this respect wholly different. ¶ *Unto another gospel.* A gospel which destroys the grace of Christ ; which proclaims salvation on other terms than simple dependence on the merits of the Lord Jesus ; and which has introduced the Jewish rites and ceremonies as essential, in order to obtain salvation. The apostle calls that scheme the *gospel.*

7 Which *a* is not another; but there be some that trouble you, and would pervert *b* the gospel of Christ.

8 But though we, or an angel from heaven, preach any other gospel unto you than that which we have preached unto you, let *c* him be accursed.

a 2 Co.11.4.   *b* Ac.15.1,24; 2 Co.2.17;   chap.5.10,12.   *c* 1 Co.16.22.

because it pretended to be; it was preached by those who claimed to be preachers of the gospel; who alleged that they had come direct from the apostles at Jerusalem, and who pretended to declare the method of salvation. It claimed to be the gospel, and yet it was essentially unlike the plan which he had preached as constituting the gospel. That which *he* preached, inculcated the entire dependence of the sinner on the merits and grace of Christ; that system had introduced dependence on the observance of the rites of the Mosaic system, as necessary to salvation.

7. *Which is not another.* There is also a great variety of views in regard to the meaning of this expression. Tindal translates it, "which is nothing else but there be some that trouble you." Locke, "which is not owing to any thing else but only this, that ye are troubled with a certain sort of men who would overturn the gospel of Christ." But Rosenmüller, Koppe, Bloomfield, and others, give a different view; and according to them the sense is, "which, however, is not another gospel, nor indeed the gospel at all, or true," &c. According to this, the design was to state, that what they taught had none of the elements or characteristics of the gospel. It was a different system, and one which taught an entirely different method of justification before God. It seems to me that this is the true sense of the passage, and that Paul means to teach them that the system, though it was called the gospel, was essentially different from that which he had taught, and which consisted in simple reliance on Christ for salvation. The system which *they* taught, was in fact the Mosaic system; the Jewish mode, depending on the rites and ceremonies of religion; and which, therefore, did not deserve to be called the *gospel.* It would load them again with burden-some rites, and with cumbrous institutions, from which it was the great purpose of the gospel to relieve them.

¶ *But there be some that trouble you.* Though this is most manifestly another system, and not the gospel at all, yet there are some persons who are capable of giving trouble and of unsettling your minds, by making it plausible. They pretend that they have come direct from the apostles at Jerusalem; that they have received their instructions from them, and that they preach the true gospel as they teach it. They pretend that Paul was called into the office of an apostle after them; that he had never seen the Lord Jesus; that he had derived his information only from others; and thus they are able to present a plausible argument, and to unsettle the minds of the Galatians. ¶ *And would prevent.* That is, the tendency of their doctrine is wholly to *turn away* (μετασρέψαι), to destroy, or render useless the gospel of Christ. It would lead to the denial of the necessity of dependence on the merits of the Lord Jesus for salvation, and would substitute dependence on rites and ceremonies. This does not of necessity mean that such was the design of their teaching, for they might have been in the main honest; but that such was the *tendency* and *result* of their teaching. It would lead men to *rely* on the Mosaic rites for salvation.

8. *But though we.* That is, we the apostles. Probably, he refers particularly to himself, as the plural is often used by Paul when speaking of himself. He alludes here, possibly, to a charge which was brought against him by the false teachers in Galatia, that he had changed his views since he came among them, and now preached differently from what he did then; see the Introduction. They endeavoured probably to fortify their own opinions in regard to the obligations of the

Mosaic law, by affirming, that though Paul when he was among them had maintained that the observance of the law was not necessary to salvation, yet that he had changed his views, and now held the same doctrine on the subject which they did. What they relied on in support of this opinion is unknown. It is certain, however, that Paul *did*, on some occasions (see Note on Acts xxi. 21—26), comply with the Jewish rites, and it is not improbable that they were acquainted with that fact, and interpreted it as proving that he had changed his sentiments on the subject. At all events, it would make their allegation plausible that Paul was *now* in favour of the observance of the Jewish rites, and that if he had ever taught differently, he must now have changed his opinion. Paul therefore begins the discussion by denying this in the most solemn manner. He affirms that the gospel which he had at first preached to them was the true gospel. It contained the great doctrines of salvation. It was to be regarded by them as a fixed and settled point, that there was no other way of salvation but by the merits of the Saviour. No matter who taught any thing else ; no matter though it be alleged that he had changed his mind ; no matter even though he *should* preach another gospel ; and no matter though an angel from heaven should declare any other mode of salvation, it was to be held as a fixed and settled position, that the true gospel had been preached to them at first. We are not to suppose that Paul admitted that he had changed his mind, or that the inferences of the false teachers there were well-founded, but we are to understand this as affirming in the most solemn manner that the true gospel, and the only method of salvation, had been preached among them at first. ¶ *Or an angel from heaven.* This is a very strong rhetorical mode of expression. It is not to be supposed that an angel from heaven would preach any other than the true gospel. But Paul wishes to put the strongest possible case, and to affirm in the strongest manner possible, that the true gospel had been preached to them. The great system of salvation had been taught ; and no other was to be admitted, no matter who preached it ; no matter what the character or rank of the preacher : and no matter with what imposing claims he came. It follows from this, that the mere rank, character, talent, eloquence, or piety of a preacher does not of necessity give his doctrine a claim to our belief, or prove that his gospel is true. Great talents may be prostituted ; and great sanctity of manner, and even holiness of character, may be in error ; and no matter what may be the rank, and talents, and eloquence, and piety of the preacher, if he does not accord with the gospel which was first preached, he is to be held accursed. ¶ *Preach any other gospel, &c.* ; see Note on ver. 6. Any gospel that differs from that which was first preached to you, any system of doctrines which goes to deny the necessity of simple dependence on the Lord Jesus Christ for salvation. ¶ *Let him be accursed.* Gr. ἀνάθεμα (*anathema*). On the meaning of this word, see Notes on 1 Cor. xii. 3 ; xvi. 22. It is not improperly here rendered "accursed," or "devoted to destruction." The object of Paul is to express the greatest possible abhorrence of any other doctrine than that which he had himself preached. So great was his detestation of it, that, says Luther, " he casteth out very flames of fire, and his zeal is so fervent, that he beginneth almost to curse the angels." It follows from this, (1.) That any other doctrine than that which is proclaimed in the Bible on the subject of justification, is to be rejected and treated with abhorrence, no matter what the rank, talent, or eloquence of him who defends it. (2.) That we are not to patronise or countenance such preachers. No matter what their zeal or their apparent sincerity, or their apparent sanctity, or their apparent success, or their real boldness in rebuking vice, we are to withdraw from them. " Cease, my son," said Solomon, " to hear the instruction that causes to err from the words of know-

9 As we said before, so say I now again, If any *man* preach any other ^a gospel unto you than that ye have received, let him be accursed.

10 For do I now persuade

a De.4.2; Re.22.18.

ledge; Prov. xix. 27. Especially are we to withdraw wholly from that instruction which goes to deny the great doctrines of salvation ; that pure gospel which the Lord Jesus and the apostle taught. If Paul would regard even an angel as doomed to destruction, and as held accursed, should he preach any other doctrine, assuredly *we* should not be found to lend our countenance to it, nor should we patronise it by attending on such a ministry. Who would desire to attend on the ministry of even an angel if he was to be held accursed? How much less the ministry of a man preaching the same doctrine !—It does not follow from this, however, that we are to treat others with severity of language or with the language of *cursing.* They must answer to God. *We* are to withdraw from their teaching; we are to regard the *doctrines* with abhorrence ; and we are not to lend our countenance to them. To their own master they stand or fall; but what *must* be the doom of a teacher whom an inspired man. has said should be regarded as "ACCURSED !"—It may be added, how responsible is the ministerial office ! How fearful the account which the ministers of religion must render ! How much prayer, and study, and effort are needed that they may be able to understand the true gospel, and that they may not be led into error, or lead others into error.

9. *As we said before.* That is, in the previous verse. It is equivalent to saying, "as I have just said ;" see 2 Cor. vii. 3. It cannot be supposed that he had said this when he was with them, as it cannot be believed that he then anticipated that his doctrines would be perverted, and that another gospel would be preached to them. The sentiment of ver. 8 is here repeated on account of its importance. It is common in the scriptures, as indeed it is everywhere else, to *repeat* a declaration in order to deepen the impression of its importance and its

truth. Paul would not be misunderstood on this point. He would leave no doubt as to his meaning. He would not have it supposed that he had uttered the sentiment in ver. 8 hastily; and he therefore repeats it with emphasis. ¶ *Than that ye have received.* In the previous verse, it is, "that which we have preached." By this change in the phraseology he designs, probably, to remind them that they had once solemnly professed to embrace that system. It had not only been *preached* to them, it had been *embraced* by them. The teachers of the new system, therefore, were really in opposition to the once avowed sentiments of the Galatians ; to what they knew to be true. They were not only to be held accursed, therefore, because Paul so declared, but because they preached what the Galatians themselves knew to be false, or what was contrary to that which they had themselves professed to be true.

10. *For do I now persuade men, or God?* The word "now" (ἄρτι) is used here, evidently, to express a contrast between his present and his former purpose of life. Before his conversion to Christianity, he impliedly admits, that it *was* his object to conciliate the favour of men ; that he derived his authority from them (Acts ix. 1, 2); that he endeavoured to act so as to please them and gain their good esteem. But *now* he says, this was not his object. He had a higher aim. It was to please God, and to conciliate his favour. The object of this verse is obscure ; but it seems to me to be connected with what follows, and to be designed to introduce that by showing that he had not *now* received his commission from men, but had received it from God. *Perhaps* there may be an allusion to an implied allegation in regard to him. It *may* have been alleged (see Notes on the previous verses) that even *he* had changed his mind, and was now himself an observer of the laws of Moses

men, or God? or do I seek *a* to please men? for if I yet pleased

men, I should not *b* be the servant of Christ.

a 2 Co.12.19; 1 Th.2.4.

b Ja.4.4.

To this, perhaps, he replies, by this question, that such conduct would not have been inconsistent in his view, when it was his main purpose to please *men*, and when he derived his commission from them; but that *now* he had a higher aim. His purpose was to please God; and he was not aiming in any way to gratify men. The word which is rendered "persuade" here (πείθω), has been very variously interpreted. Tindal renders it, "seek now the favour of men or of God?" Doddridge: "Do I now solicit the favour of men or of God?" This also is the interpretation of Grotius, Hammond, Elsner, Koppe, Rosenmüller, Bloomfield, &c. and is undoubtedly the true explanation. The word properly means to *persuade*, or to *convince;* Acts xviii. 4; xxviii. 23; 2 Cor. v. 11. But it also means, to bring over to kind feelings, to conciliate, to pacify, to quiet. Sept. 1 Sam. xxiv. 8; 2 Macc. iv. 25; Acts xii. 20; 1 John iii. 19. By the *question* here, Paul means to say, that his great object was now to *please God.* He desired his favour rather than the favour of man. He acted with reference to his will. He derived his authority from him, and not from the Sanhedrim or any earthly council. And the purpose of all this is to say, that he had not received his commission to preach from man, but had received it directly from God. ¶ *Or do I seek to please men?* It is not my aim or purpose to please men, and to conciliate their favour; comp. 1 Thess. ii. 4. ¶ *For if I yet pleased men.* If I made it my aim to please men; if this was the regulating principle of my conduct. The word "*yet*" here (ἔτι) has reference to his former purpose. It implies that this had once been his aim. But he says if he had *pursued* that purpose to please men; if this had *continued* to be the aim of his life, he would not *now* have been a servant of Christ. He had been constrained to *abandon* that purpose in order that he might be a servant of

Christ; and the sentiment is, that in order that a man may become a Christian, it is necessary for him to abandon the purpose of pleasing men as the rule of his life. It may be implied also that if *in fact* a man makes it his aim to please men, or if this is the purpose for which he lives and acts, and if he shapes his conduct with reference to that, he cannot be a Christian or a servant of Christ. A Christian *must* act from higher motives than those, and he who aims supremely at the favour of his fellowmen has full evidence that he is not a Christian. A friend of Christ must do his duty, and must regulate his conduct by the will of God, whether men are pleased with it or not. And it may be further implied that the life and deportment of a sincere Christian *will not* please men. It is not that which they love. A holy, humble, spiritual life they do not love. It is true, indeed, that their consciences tell them that such a life is right; that they are often constrained to speak well of the life of Christians, and to commend it; it is true that they are constrained to respect a man who is a sincere Christian, and that they often repose confidence in such a man; and it is true also that they often speak with respect of them when they are dead; but the life of an humble, devoted, and zealous Christian they do not *love.* It is contrary to their views of life. And especially if a Christian so lives and acts as to reprove them either by his words or by his life; or if a Christian makes his religion so prominent as to interfere with their pursuits or pleasures, they do not love it. It follows from this, (1.) That a Christian is not to *expect* to please men. He must not be disappointed, therefore, if he does not. His Master did not please the world; and it is enough for the disciple that he be as his master. (2.) A professing Christian, and especially a minister, should be alarmed when the world flatters and caresses him. He

11 But I certify you, brethren, that the gospel which was
preached of me, is not after
man.

a 1 Co.15.1—3

12 For [a] I neither received it
of man, neither was I taught *it*,
but by the revelation [b] of Jesus
Christ.

b Ep.3.3.

should fear either, (*a*) That he is not living as he ought to do, and that sinners love him *because* he is so much like them, and keeps them in countenance; or, (*b*) That they *mean* to make him betray his religion and become conformed to them. It is a great point gained for the gay world, when it can, by its caresses and attentions, get a Christian to forsake a prayer-meeting for a party, or surrender his deep spirituality to engage in some political project. " Woe unto you," said the Redeemer, " when all men speak well of you," Luke vi. 26. (3.) One of the main differences between Christians and the world is, that others *aim* to please men; the Christian *aims* to please God. And this is a *great* difference. (4.) It follows that if men would become Christians, they must cease to make it their object to please men. They must be willing to be met with contempt and a frown; they must be willing to be persecuted and despised; they must be willing to lay aside all hope of the praise and the flattery of men, and be content with an honest effort to please God. (5.) True Christians must differ from the world. Their aims, feelings, purposes must be unlike the world. They are *to be* a peculiar people; and they should be willing to be esteemed such. It does not follow, however, that a true Christian should not desire the good esteem of the world, or that he should be indifferent to an honourable reputation (1 Tim. iii. 7); nor does it follow that a consistent Christian will not often command the respect of the world. In times of trial, the world will repose confidence in Christians; when any work of benevolence is to be done, the world will instinctively look to Christians; and notwithstanding sinners will not *love* religion, yet they will secretly feel assured that some of the brightest ornaments of society are Christians, and that they have a *claim* to the confidence and esteem of their

fellow-men. ¶ The *servant of Christ.* A Christian.

11. *But I certify you.* I make known to you; or, I declare to you; see 1 Cor. xv. 1. Doubtless this had been known to them before, but he now assures them of it, and goes into an extended illustration to show them that he had not received his authority from *man* to preach the gospel To state and prove this is the main design of this chapter. ¶ *Is not after man.* Gr. Not according to man; see ver. 1. That is, he was not appointed by man, nor had he any human instructor to make known to him what the gospel was. He had neither received it from man, nor had it been debased or adulterated by any human admixtures. He had received it directly from the Lord Jesus.

12. *For I neither received it of man.* This is very probably said in reply to his opponents, who had maintained that Paul had derived his knowledge of the gospel from other men, as he had not been personally known to the Lord Jesus, or been of the number of those whom he called to be his apostles. In reply to this, he says, that he did not receive his gospel in any way from man. ¶ *Neither was I taught it.* That is, by man He was not taught it by any written account of it, or by the instruction of man in any way. The only plausible objection to this statement which could be urged would be the fact that Paul had an interview with Ananias (Acts ix. 17) before his baptism, and that he would probably receive instructions from him. But to this it may be replied, (1.) That there is no evidence that Ananias went into an explanation of the nature of the Christian religion in his interview with Paul; (2.) Paul had *before* this been taught what Christianity was by his interview with the Lord Jesus on the way to Damascus (Acts ix. 5; xxvi. 14—18); (3.) The purpose for which Ananias

13 For ye have heard of my conversation in time past in the Jews' religion, how that beyond

measure I persecuted the church *a* of God, and wasted it.

14 And profited in the Jews'

was sent to him in Damascus was that he might receive his sight, and be filled with the Holy Ghost, Acts ix. 17. Whatever instructions he may have received through Ananias, it is still true that his call was *directly* from the Lord Jesus, and his information of the nature of Christianity from *his* revelation. ¶ *But by the revelation of Jesus Christ.* On his way to Damascus, and subsequently in the temple, Acts xxii. 17—21. Doubtless he received communications at various times from the Lord Jesus with regard to the nature of the gospel and his duty. The sense here is, that he was not indebted to *men* for his knowledge of the gospel, but had derived it entirely from the Saviour.

13. *For ye have heard of my conversation.* My conduct, my mode of life, my deportment ; see Note on 2 Cor. i. 12. Probably Paul had himself made them acquainted with the events of his early years. The *reason* why he refers to this is, to show them that he had not derived his knowledge of the Christian religion from any instruction which he had received in his early years, or any acquaintance which he had formed with the apostles. He had at first been decidedly opposed to the Lord Jesus, and had been converted only by his wonderful grace. ¶ *In the Jews' religion.* In the belief and practice of *Judaism ;* that is, as it was understood in the time when he was educated. It was not merely in the religion of Moses, but it was in that religion as understood and practised by the Jews in his time, when opposition to Christianity constituted a very material part of it. In *that* religion Paul proceeds to show that he had been more distinguished than most persons of his time. ¶ *How that beyond measure.* In the highest possible degree ; beyond all limits or bounds ; exceedingly. The phrase which Paul here uses (καθ᾽ ὑπερβολὴν), *by hyperbole,* is one which he frequently employs to denote any thing

that is *excessive,* or that cannot be expressed by ordinary language ; see the Greek in Rom. vii. 13 ; 1 Cor. xii. 31 ; 2 Cor. i. 8 ; iv. 7, 17. ¶ *I persecuted the church ;* see Acts viii. 3 ; ix. 1, seq. ¶ *And wasted it.* Destroyed it. The word which is here used, means properly to waste or destroy, as when a city or country is ravaged by an army or by wild beasts. His *purpose* was utterly to root out and destroy the Christian religion.

14. *And profited.* Made advances and attainments. He made advances not only in the knowledge of the Jewish religion, but also he surpassed others in his zeal in defending its interests. He had had better advantages than most of his countrymen ; and by his great zeal and characteristic ardour he had been able to make higher attainments than most others had done. ¶ *Above many my equals.* Marg. *Equal in years.* This is the true sense of the original. It means that he surpassed those of the same age with himself. Possibly there may be a reference here to those of the same age who attended with him on the instructions of Gamaliel. ¶ *Being more exceedingly zealous.* More studious of; more ardently attached to them ; more anxious to distinguish himself in attainments in the religion in which he was brought up. All this is fully sustained by all that we know of the character of Paul, as at all times a man of singular and eminent zeal in all that he undertook. ¶ *Of the traditions of my fathers.* Or the traditions of the Jews ; see Note, Mat. xv. 2. A large part of the doctrines of the Pharisees depended on mere tradition ; and Paul doubtless made this a special matter of study, and was particularly tenacious in regard to it. It was to be learned, from the very nature of it, only by *oral* teaching, as there is no evidence that it was then recorded. Subsequently these traditions were recorded in the *Mishna,* and are found in the Jewish

religion above many my [1] equals in mine own nation, being [a] more exceedingly zealous of the traditions [b] of my fathers.

[1] *equal in years.*   [a] Ac.22,3, Ph.3.6.
        [b] Mar.7.5—13.

writings. But in the time of Paul they were to be learned as they were handed down from one to another; and hence the utmost diligence was requisite to obtain a knowledge of them. Paul does not here say that he was zealous then for the practice of the new religion, nor for the study of the Bible. His object in going to Jerusalem and studying at the feet of Gamaliel was doubtless to obtain a knowledge of the traditions of the sect of the Pharisees. Had he been studying the Bible all that time, he would have kept from the fiery zeal which he evinced in persecuting the church, and would, if he had studied it right, been saved from much trouble of conscience afterwards.

15. *But when it pleased God.* Paul traced all his hopes of eternal life, and all the good influences which had ever borne upon his mind, to God. ¶ *Who separated me,* &c. That is, who destined me; or who purposed from my very birth that I should be a preacher and an apostle. The meaning is, that God had in his secret purposes set him apart to be an apostle. It does not mean that he had actually called him in his infancy to the work, for this was not so, but that he designed him to be an important instrument in his hands in spreading the true religion. Jeremiah (i. 5) was thus set apart, and John the Bapist was thus early designated for the work which they afterwards performed. It follows from this, (1.) That God often, if not always, has *purposes* in regard to men from their very birth. He *designs* them for some important field of labour, and endows them at their creation with talents adapted to that. (2.) It does not follow that because a young man has gone far astray; and has become even a blasphemer and a persecutor, that God has not destined him to some important and holy work in his service. How many men have

15 But when it pleased God, [c] who separated me from my mother's womb, and called *me* by his grace,

[c] Is.49.1; Je.1.5.

been called, like Paul, and Newton, and Bunyan, and Augustine, from a life of sin to the service of God. (3.) God is often training up men in a remarkable manner for future usefulness. His eye is upon them, and he watches over them, until the time comes for their conversion. His providence was concerned in the education and training of Paul. It was by the divine intention with reference to his future work that he had so many opportunities of education, and was so well acquainted with the "traditions" of that religion which he was yet to demonstrate to be unfounded and false. He gave him the opportunity to cultivate his mind, and prepare to grapple with the Jew in argument, and show him how unfounded were his hopes. So it is often now. He gives to a young man an opportunity of a finished education. Perhaps he suffers him to fall into the snares of infidelity, and to become familiar with the arguments of sceptics, that he may thus be better prepared to meet their sophisms, and to enter into their feelings. His eye is upon them in their wanderings, and they are suffered often to wander far; to range the fields of science; to become distinguished as scholars, as Paul was; until the time comes for their conversion, and then, in accordance with the purpose which set them apart from the world, God converts them, and consecrates all their talents and attainments to his service. (4.) We should never despair of a young man who has wandered far from God. If he has risen high in attainments; if his whole aim is ambition; or if he has become an infidel, still we are not to despair of him. It is *possible* still that God "separated" that talent to his service from the very birth, and that he means yet to call it all to his service. How easy it was to convert Saul of Tarsus when the proper period

16 To reveal *a* his Son in me, | that *b* I might preach him among

a 2 Co.4.6. | b Ac.9.15.

arrived. So it is of the now unconverted and unconsecrated, but cultivated talent among the young men of our land Far as they may have wandered from God and virtue, yet much of that talent has been devoted to him in baptism, and by parental purposes and prayers ; and, it may be—*as is morally certain from the history of the past*—that much of it is consecrated also by the divine purpose and intention for the noble cause of virtue and pure religion. In that now apparently wasted talent; in that learning now apparently devoted to other aims and ends, there is much that *will* yet adorn the cause of virtue and religion; and how fervently should we pray that it may be "called" by the grace of God and actually devoted to his service. ¶ *And called me by his grace.* On the way to Damascus. It was special *grace*, because he was then engaged in bitterly opposing him and his cause.

16. *To reveal his Son in me.* This is to be regarded as connected with the first part of ver. 15, " When it pleased God to reveal his Son in me," *i. e.* on the way to Damascus. The phrase evidently means, to make me acquainted with the Lord Jesus, or to reveal his Son *to* me ; comp. the Greek in Mat. x. 32, for a similar expression. The *revelation* here referred to was the miraculous manifestation which was made to Paul on his way to Damascus ; comp. 2 Cor. iv. 6. That revelation was in order to convince him that he was the Messiah ; to acquaint him with his nature, rank, and claims ; and to qualify him to be a preacher to the heathen. ¶ *That I might preach him.* In order that I might so preach him ; or with a view to my being appointed to this work. This was the leading purpose for which Paul was converted, Acts ix. 15 ; xxii. 21. ¶ *The heathen.* The Gentiles ; the portion of the world that was not Jewish, or that was destitute of the true religion. ¶ *Immediately.* Koppe supposes that this is to be connected with " I went into Arabia" (ver. 17). Rosenmüller sup-

poses it means, " Immediately *I consented.*" Dr. Wells and Locke suppose that it refers to the fact that he immediately went to Arabia. But this seems to me to be an unnatural construction. The words are too remote from each other to allow of it. The evident sense is, that he was at once *decided.* He did not take time to deliberate whether he should or should not become a Christian. He made up his mind at once and on the spot. He did not consult with any one ; he did not ask advice of any one ; he did not wait to be instructed by any one. He was convinced by the vision in an overpowering manner that Jesus was the Messiah, and he yielded at once. The main idea is, that there was no delay, no consultation, no deferring it, that he might see and consult with his friends, or with the friends of Christianity. The object for which he dwells on this is, to show he did not receive his views of the gospel from man. ¶ *I conferred not.* I did not *lay the case* (προσανεθέμην) before any man ; I did not confer with any one. ¶ *Flesh and blood.* Any human being, for so the phrase properly signifies ; see Note, Mat. xvi. 17. This does not mean here, that Paul did not consult his own ease and happiness ; that he was regardless of the sufferings which he might be called to endure ; that he was willing to suffer, and was not careful to make provision for his own comfort—which was true in itself—but that he did not lay the case before any man, or any body of men for instruction or advice. He acted promptly and decisively. He was not disobedient to the heavenly vision (Acts xxvi. 19), but resolved at once to obey. Many suppose that this passage means that Paul did not take counsel of the evil passions and suggestions of his own heart, or of the feelings which would have prompted him to lead a life of ambition, or a life under the influence of corrupt desires. But however true this was in fact, no such thing is intended here.

the heathen : immediately I conferred not with flesh and ^a blood :

a 2 Co.5.16.

17 Neither went I up to Jerusalem to them which were apostles

---

It means simply that he did not take
counsel of any human being. He resolved at once to follow the command
of the Saviour, and at once to obey
him. The passage shows, (1.) That
when the Lord Jesus calls us to follow him we should promptly and decidedly obey. (2.) We should not
delay even to take counsel of earthly
friends, or wait for human advice, or
consult their wishes, but should *at
once* resolve to follow the Lord Jesus.
Most persons, when they are awakened
to see their guilt, and their minds are
impressed on the subject of religion,
are prone to *defer* it ; to resolve to
think of it at some future time ; or to
engage in some other business before
they become Christians ; or, at least,
they wish to finish what they have on
hand before they yield to God. Had
Paul pursued this course, he would
probably never have become a Christian. It follows, therefore, (3.) That
when the Lord Jesus calls us, we
should at once abandon any course of
life, however pleasant, or any plan of
ambition, however brilliant, or any
scheme of gain, however promising,
in order that we may follow him.
What a brilliant career of ambition
did Paul abandon ! and how promptly
and decidedly did he do it ! He did
not pause or hesitate a moment ; but
brilliant as were his prospects, he at
once forsook all ; paused in mid-
career in his ambition ; and without
consulting a human being, at once
gave his heart to God. Such a course
should be pursued by all. Such a
promptness and decision will prepare
one to become an eminent Christian,
and to be eminently useful.

17. *Neither went I up to Jerusalem.*
That is, I did not go there at once.
I did not go to consult with the apostles there, or to be instructed by them
in regard to the nature of the Christian religion. The design of this
statement is, to show that in no sense
did he derive his commission from
man. ¶ *To them which were apostles
before me.* This implies that Paul *then*

regarded himself to be an apostle.
They were, he admits, apostles *before*
he was ; but he felt also that he had
original authority with them, and he
did not go to them to receive instruction, or to derive his commission from
them. Several of the apostles remained in Jerusalem for a considerable
time after the ascension of the Lord
Jesus, and it was regarded as the
principal place of authority ; see
Acts xv. ¶ *But I went into Arabia.*
Arabia was south of Damascus, and
at no great distance. The line indeed
between Arabia Deserta and Syria
is not very definitely marked, but it is
generally agreed that Arabia extends
to a considerable distance into the great
Syrian desert. To what part of Arabia,
and for what purpose Paul went, is
wholly unknown. Nothing is known of
the circumstances of this journey ; nor
is the time which he spent there
known. It is known indeed (ver. 18)
that he did not go to Jerusalem until
three years after his conversion, but
how large a part of this time was spent
in Damascus, we have no means of
ascertaining. It is probable that
Paul was engaged during these three
years in preaching the gospel in Damascus and the adjacent regions, and
in Arabia ; comp. Acts ix. 20, 22, 27.
The account of this journey into
Arabia is wholly omitted by Luke
in the Acts of the Apostles, and this
fact, as has been remarked by Paley
(Horæ Paulinæ, chap. v. No. 2), demonstrates that the Acts and this
epistle were not written by the same
author, or that the one is independent
of the other ; because "if the Acts
of the Apostles had been a forged history made up from the epistle, it is
impossible that this journey should
have been passed over in silence ; if
the epistle had been composed out of
what the author had read of St. Paul's
history in the Acts, it is unaccountable
that it should have been inserted."
As to the reason why Luke omitted
to mention the journey into Arabia,
nothing is known. Various conjec-

before me ; but I went into Arabia, and returned again into Damascus.

18 Then *a* after three years I

a Ac.9.26.

went ¹ up to Jerusalem to see Peter, and abode with him fifteen days.

19 But other of the apostles

¹ or, *returned.*

tures have been entertained, but they are *mere* conjectures. It is sufficient to say, that Luke has by no means recorded *all* that Paul or the other apostles did, nor has he pretended to do it. He has given the leading events in the public labours of Paul ; and it is not at all improbable that he has omitted not a few short excursions made by him for the purpose of preaching the gospel. The journey into Arabia, probably, did not furnish any incidents *in regard to the success of the gospel there* which required particular record by the sacred historian, nor has Paul himself referred to it for any such reason, or intimated that it furnished any incidents, or any facts, that required particularly the notice of the historian. He has mentioned it for a different purpose altogether, to show that he did not receive his commission from the apostles, and that he did not go at once to consult them. He went directly the other way. As Luke, in the Acts, had no occasion to illustrate this ; as he had no occasion to refer to this *argument,* it did not fall in with the design to mention the fact. Nor is it known *why* Paul went into Arabia. Bloomfield supposes that it was in order to recover his health after the calamity which he suffered on the way to Damascus. But every thing in regard to this is mere conjecture. I should rather think it was more in accordance with the general character of Paul that he made this short excursion for the purpose of preaching the gospel. ¶ *And returned again unto Damascus.* He did not go to Jerusalem to consult with the apostles after his visit to Arabia, but returned again to the place where he was converted and preached there, showing that he had not derived his commission from the other apostles.

18. *Then after three years.* Probably three years after his departure from Jerusalem to Damascus, not

after his return to Arabia. So most commentators have understood it. ¶ *Went up to Jerusalem.* More correctly, as in the margin, *returned.* ¶ *To see Peter.* Peter was the oldest and most distinguished of the apostles. In chap. ii. 9, he, with James and John, is called a *pillar.* But why Paul went particularly to see *him* is not known. It was probably, however, from the celebrity and distinction which he knew Peter had among the apostles that he wished to become particularly acquainted with him. The word which is here rendered *to see* (ἰστορῆσαι) is by no means that which is commonly employed to denote that idea. It occurs nowhere else in the New Testament ; and properly means to ascertain by personal inquiry and examination, and then to *narrate,* as a historian was accustomed to do, whence our word *history.* The notion of personally seeing and examining, is one that belongs essentially to the word, and the idea here is that of seeing or visiting Peter in order to a personal acquaintance. ¶ *And abode with him fifteen days.* Probably, says Bloomfield, including three Lord's-days. Why he departed then is unknown. Beza supposes that it was on account of the plots of the Grecians against him, and their intention to destroy him (Acts ix. 29) ; but this is not assigned by Paul himself as a reason. It is probable that the purpose of his visit to Peter would be accomplished in that time, and he would not spend more time than was necessary with him. It is clear that in the short space of *two weeks* he could not have been very extensively taught by Peter the nature of the Christian religion, and probably the time is mentioned here to show that he had not been under the teaching of the apostles.

19. *Save James the Lord's brother* That the James here referred to was an apostle, is clear. The whole con-

saw I none, save James [a] the Lord's brother.

a Mar.6.3.

struction of the sentence demands this supposition. In the list of the apostles in Mat. x. 2,3, two of this name are mentioned, James the son of Zebedee and brother of John, and James the son of Alpheus. From the Acts of the Apostles, it is clear that there were two of this name in Jerusalem. Of these, James the brother of John was slain by Herod (Acts xii. 2), and the other continued to reside in Jerusalem, Acts xv. 13 ; xxi. 13. This latter James was called James the Less (Mark xv. 40), to distinguish him from the other James, probably because he was the younger. It is probable that this was the James referred to here, as it is evident from the Acts of the Apostles that he was a prominent man among the apostles in Jerusalem. Commentators have not been agreed as to what is meant by his being the brother of the Lord Jesus. Doddridge understands it as meaning that he was " the near kinsman " or cousin-german to Jesus, for he was, says he, the son of Alpheus and Mary, the sister of the virgin ; and if there were but two of this name, this opinion is undoubtedly correct. In the Apostolical Constitutions (see Rosenmüller) three of this name are mentioned as apostles or eminent men in Jerusalem ; and hence many have supposed that one of them was the son of Mary the mother of the Lord Jesus. It is said (Mat. xiii. 55) that the brothers of Jesus were James and Joses, and Simon, and Judas ; and it is remarkable that three of the apostles bear the same names ; James the son of Alpheus, Simon Zelotes, and Judas ; John xiv. 22. It is indeed *possible*, as Bloomfield remarks, that three brothers of our Lord and three of his apostles might bear the same names, and yet be different persons ; but such a coincidence would be very remarkable, and not easily explained. But if it were not so, then the James here was the son of Alpheus, and consequently a cousin of the Lord Jesus. The word *brother* may, according to

20 Now the things which I write unto you, behold, before God, I lie not.

scripture usage, be understood as denoting a *near kinsman*. See Schleusner (Lex. 2) on the word αδελφός. After all, however, it is not quite certain who is intended. Some have supposed that neither of the apostles of the name of James is intended, but another James who was the son of Mary the mother of Jesus. See Koppe *in loc.* But it is clear, I think, that one of the apostles is intended. Why James is particularly mentioned here is unknown. As, however, he was a prominent man in Jerusalem, Paul would naturally seek his acquaintance. It is possible that the other apostles were absent from Jerusalem during the fifteen days when he was there.

20. *Behold, before God I lie not.* This is an oath, or a solemn appeal to God ; see Note, Rom. ix. 1. The design of this oath here is to prevent all suspicion of falsehood. It may seem to be remarkable that Paul should make this solemn appeal to God in this argument, and in the narrative of a plain fact, when his statement could hardly be called in question by any one. But we may remark, (1.) That the oath here refers not only to the fact that he was with Peter and James but fifteen days, but to the *entire group* of facts to which he had referred in this chapter. " The things which I wrote unto you." It included, therefore, the narrative about his conversion, and the direct revelation which he had from the Lord Jesus. (2.) There were no *witnesses* which he could appeal to in this case, and he could, therefore, only appeal to God. It was probably not practicable for him to appeal to Peter or James, as neither of them were in Galatia, and a considerable part of the transactions here referred to occurred where there were no witnesses. It pertained to the direct revelation of truth from the Lord Jesus. The only way, therefore, was for Paul to appeal directly to God for the truth of what he said. (3.) The importance of the truth here affirmed

21 Afterwards I *a* came into the regions of Syria and Cilicia ;

22 And was unknown by face unto the churches *b* of Judea which were in Christ :

a Ac.9.30.　　　　　*b* 1 Th.2.14.

23 But they had heard *c* only, That he which persecuted us in times past, now preacheth the faith which once he destroyed.

24 And they glorified*d* God in me.

c Ac.9.13,26.　　　　　*d* Ac.21.19,20.

was such as to justify this solemn appeal to God. It was an extraordinary and miraculous revelation of the truth by Jesus Christ himself. He received information of the truth of Christianity from no human being. He had consulted no one in regard to its nature. That fact was so extraordinary, and it was so remarkable that the system thus communicated to him should harmonize so entirely with that taught by the other apostles with whom he had had no intercourse, that it was not improper to appeal to God in this solemn manner. It was, therefore, no trifling matter in which Paul appealed to God ; and a solemn appeal of the same nature and in the same circumstances can never be improper.

21. *Afterwards I came,* &c. In this account he has omitted a circumstance recorded by Luke (Acts ix. 29), of the controversy which he had with the Grecians or Hellenists. It was not material to the purpose which he has here in view, which is to state that he was not indebted to the apostles for his knowledge of the doctrines of Christianity. He therefore merely states that he left Jerusalem soon after he went there, and travelled to other places. ¶ *The regions of Syria.* Syria was between Jerusalem and Cilicia. Antioch was the capital of Syria, and in that city and the adjacent places he spent considerable time ; comp. Acts xv. 23, 41. ¶ *Cilicia.* This was a province of Asia Minor, of which Tarsus, the native place of Paul, was the capital ; see Note on Acts vi. 9.

22. *And was unknown by face,* &c. Paul had visited Jerusalem only, and he had formed no acquaintance with any of the churches in the other parts of Judea. He regarded himself at the first as called to preach particularly to the Gentiles, and he did not remain even to form an acquaintance

with the Christians in Judea. ¶ *The churches of Judea.* Those which were out of Jerusalem. Even at the early period of the conversion of Paul there were doubtless many churches in various parts of the land. ¶ *Which were in Christ.* United to Christ ; or which were Christian churches. The *design* of mentioning this is, to show that he had not derived his views of the gospel from any of them. He had neither been instructed by the apostles, nor was he indebted to the Christians in Judea for his knowledge of the Christian religion.

23. *But they had heard only,* &c. They had not seen me ; but the remarkable fact of my conversion had been reported to them. It was a fact that could hardly be concealed ; see Note, Acts xxvi. 26.

24. *And they glorified God in me.* They praised God on my account. They regarded me as a true convert and a sincere Christian ; and they praised God that he had converted such a persecutor, and had made him a preacher of the gospel. The *design* for which this is mentioned is, to show that though he was personally unknown to them, and had not derived his views of the gospel from them, yet that he had their entire confidence. They regarded him as a convert and an apostle, and they were disposed to praise God for his conversion. This fact would do much to conciliate the favour of the Galatians, by showing them that he had the confidence of the churches in the very land where the gospel was first planted, and which was regarded as the source of ecclesiastical authority. In view of this we may remark, (1.) That it is the duty of Christians kindly and affectionately to receive among their number those who have been converted from a career of persecution or of sin in any form. And it is always done by true Christians. It is easy to forgive a

man who has been actively engaged in persecuting the church, or a man who has been profane, intemperate, dishonest, or licentious, if he becomes a true penitent, and confesses and forsakes his sins. No matter what his life has been; no matter how abandoned, sensual, or devilish; if he manifests true sorrow and gives evidence of a change of heart, he is cordially received into any church, and welcomed as a fellow-labourer in the cause which he once destroyed. Here, at least, is one place where forgiveness is cordial and perfect. His former life is not remembered, except to praise God for his grace in recovering a sinner from such a course; the evils that he has done are forgotten; and he is henceforward regarded as entitled to all the privileges and immunities of a member of the household of faith. There is not on earth an infuriated persecutor or blasphemer who would not be cordially welcomed to any Christian church on the evidence of his repentance; not a man so debased and vile that the most pure, and elevated, and learned, and wealthy Christians would not rejoice to sit down with him at the same communion table on the evidence of his conversion to God. (2.) We should "glorify" or praise God for all such instances of conversion. We should do it because, (a) Of the abstraction of the talents of the persecutor from the cause of evil. Paul could have done, and would have done immense service to the enemies of Christianity if he had pursued the career which he had commenced. But when he was converted, all that bad influence ceased. So when an infidel or a profligate man is converted now, (b) Because now his talents will be consecrated to a better service. They will be employed in the cause of truth and salvation. All the power of the matured and educated talent will now be devoted to the interests of religion; and it is a fact for which we should thank God, that he often takes educated talent, and commanding influence, and an established reputation for ability, learning, and zeal, and devotes it to his own service. (c) Because there

will be a change of destiny; because the enemy of the Redeemer will now be saved. The moment when Saul of Tarsus was converted, was the moment which determined a change in his eternal destiny. Before, he was in the broad way to hell; henceforward he walked in the path of life and salvation. Thus we should always rejoice over a sinner returning from the error of his ways; and should praise God that he who was in danger of eternal ruin is now an heir of glory. Christians are not jealous in regard to the *numbers* who shall enter heaven. They feel that there is "room" for all; that the feast is ample for all; and they rejoice when *any* can be induced to come with them and partake of the happiness of heaven. (3.) *We* may still glorify and praise God for the grace manifested in the conversion of Saul of Tarsus. What does not the world owe to him! What do we not owe to him! No man did as much in establishing the Christian religion as he did; no one among the apostles was the means of converting and saving so many souls; no one has left so many and so valuable writings for the edification of the church. To him we owe the invaluable epistles—so full of truth, and eloquence, and promises, and consolations—on which we are commenting; and to him the church owes, under God, some of its most elevated and ennobling views of the nature of Christian doctrine and duty. After the lapse, therefore, of eighteen hundred years, we should not cease to glorify God for the conversion of this wonderful man, and should feel that *we* have cause of thankfulness that he changed the infuriated persecutor to a holy and devoted apostle. (4.) Let us remember that God has the same power now. There is not a persecutor whom he could not convert with the same ease with which he changed Saul of Tarsus. There is not a vile and sensual man that he could not make pure; not a dishonest man that his grace could not make honest; not a blasphemer that he could not teach to venerate his name; not a lost and abandoned sinner that he cannot receive to himself. Let us

CHAPTER II.

THEN, fourteen years after, *a* I went up again to Jerusalem

then without ceasing cry unto him that his grace may be continually manifested in reclaiming such sinners from the error of their ways, and bringing them to the knowledge of the truth, and to a consecration of their lives to his service.

CHAPTER II.

ANALYSIS.

THE second chapter is closely connected *in sense* with the first, and is indeed a part of the same argument. Injury has been done by the division which is made. The proper division would have been at the close of the 10th verse of this chapter. The general scope of the chapter, like the first, is to show that he did not receive the gospel from man; that he had not derived it from the apostles; that he did not acknowledge his indebtedness to them for his views of the Christian religion; that they had not even set up *authority* over him; but that they had welcomed him as a fellow-labourer, and acknowledged him as a coadjutor in the work of the apostleship. In confirmation of this he states (ver. 1) that he had indeed gone to Jerusalem, but that he had done it by express revelation (ver. 2); that he was cordially received by the apostles there —especially by those who were pillars in the church; and that so far from regarding himself as inferior to the other apostles, he had resisted Peter to his face at Antioch on a most important and vital doctrine.

The chapter, therefore, may be regarded as divided into two portions, viz. :—

I. *The account of his visit to Jerusalem and of what occurred there,* ver. 1—10.

(*a*) He had gone up fourteen years after his conversion, after having laboured long among the Gentiles in his own way, and without having felt his dependence on the apostles at Jerusalem, ver. 1, 2.

(*b*) When he was there, there was no attempt made to compel him to submit to the Jewish rites and cus-

with Barnabas, and took Titus with *me* also.

a Ac.15.2,&c.

toms; and what was conclusive in the case was, that they had not even required Titus to be circumcised, thus proving that they did not assert jurisdiction over Paul, and that they did not intend to impose the Mosaic rites on the converts from among the Gentiles, ver. 3—5.

(*c*) The most distinguished persons among the apostles at Jerusalem, he says, received him kindly, and admitted him to their confidence and favour without hesitation. They added no heavy burdens to him (ver. 6); they saw evidence that he had been appointed to bear the gospel to the Gentiles (ver. 7, 8); they gave to him and Barnabas the right hand of fellowship (ver. 9); and they asked only that they should remember and show kindness to the poor saints in Judea, and thus manifest an interest in those who had been converted from Judaism, or contribute their proper proportion to the maintenance of all, and show that they were not disposed to abandon their own countrymen, ver. 10. In this way they gave the fullest proof that they approved the course of Paul, and admitted him into entire fellowship with them as an apostle.

II. *The scene at Antioch, where Paul rebuked Peter for his dissimulation;* ver 11—21. The main object of mentioning this seems to be to show, first, that he did not regard himself as inferior to the other apostles, or that he had not derived his views of the gospel from them; and, secondly, to state that the observance of the Jewish rites was not necessary to salvation, and that he had maintained that from the beginning. He had strongly urged it in a controversy with Peter, and in a case where Peter was manifestly wrong; and it was no new doctrine on the subject of justification which he had preached to the Galatians. He states, therefore,

(*a*) That he had opposed Peter at Antioch, because he had dissembled there, and that even Barnabas had been carried away with the course which Peter had practised; ver. 11—14.

(*b*) That the Jews must be justified by faith, and not by dependence on their own law; ver. 15, 16.

(*c*) That they who are justified by faith should act consistently, and not attempt to build again the things which they had destroyed; ver. 17, 18.

(*d*) That the effect of justification by faith was to make one dead to the law that he might live unto God; that the effect of it was to make one truly alive and devoted to the cause of true religion; and to show this, he appeals to the effect of his own heart and life (ver. 19, 20).

(*e*) And that if justification could be obtained by the law, then Christ had died in vain; ver. 21. He thus shows that the effect of teaching the necessity of the observance of the Jewish rites was to destroy the gospel, and to render it vain and useless.

1. *Then fourteen years after.* That is, fourteen years after his first visit there subsequent to his conversion. Some commentators, however, suppose that the date of the fourteen years is to be reckoned from his conversion. But the more obvious construction is, to refer it to the time of his visit there, as recorded in the previous chapter; ver 18. This time was spent in Asia Minor chiefly in preaching the gospel. ¶ *I went up again to Jerusalem.* It is commonly supposed that Paul here refers to the visit which he made as recorded in Acts xv. The circumstances mentioned are substantially the same; and the object which he had at that time in going up was one whose mention was entirely pertinent to the argument here. He went up with Barnabas to submit a question to the assembled apostles and elders at Jerusalem, in regard to the necessity of the observance of the laws of Moses. Some persons who had come among the Gentile converts from Judea had insisted on the necessity of being circumcised in order to be saved. Paul and Barnabas had opposed them; and the dispute had become so warm that it was agreed to submit the subject to the apostles and elders at Jerusalem. For that

purpose Paul and Barnabas had been sent, with certain others, to lay the case before all the apostles. As the question which Paul was discussing in this epistle was about the necessity of the observance of the laws of Moses in order to justification, it was *exactly in point* to refer to a journey when this very question had been submitted to the apostles. Paul indeed had made another journey to Jerusalem before this with the collection for the poor saints in Judea (Acts xi. 29, 30; xii. 25), but he does not mention that here, probably because he did not then see the other apostles, or more probably because that journey furnished no illustration of the point now under debate. On the occasion here referred to (Acts xv.), the very point under discussion here constituted the main subject of inquiry, and was definitely settled. ¶ *And took Titus with me also.* Luke, in the Acts of the Apostles (xv. 2), says, that there were others with Paul and Barnabas on that journey to Jerusalem. But who they were he does not mention. It is by no means certain that Titus was *appointed* by the church to go to Jerusalem; but the contrary is more probable. Paul seems to have taken him with him as a private affair; but the reason is not mentioned. It may have been to show his Christian liberty, and his sense of what he had a right to do; or it may have been *to furnish a case* on the subject of inquiry, and submit the matter to them whether Titus was *to be* circumcised. He was a Greek; but he had been converted to Christianity. Paul had not circumcised him; but had admitted him to the full privileges of the Christian church. Here then was *a case in point;* and it may have been important to have had such a case before them, that they might fully understand it. This, as Doddridge properly remarks, is the first mention which occurs of Titus. He is not mentioned by Luke in the Acts of the Apostles, and though his name occurs several times in the second epistle to the Corinthians (ii. 13; vii. 6; viii. 6, 16, 23; xii. 18), yet it is to be remembered that that epistle was written a consid-

2 And I went up by revelation, and communicated unto them that gospel which I preach among the Gentiles; but ¹ pri-

erable time after this to the Galatians. Titus was a Greek, and was doubtless converted by the labours of Paul, for he calls him his own son, Tit. i. 4. He attended Paul frequently in his travels; was employed by him in important services (see 2 Cor. in the places referred to above); was left by him in Crete to set in order the things that were wanting, and to ordain elders there (Tit. i. 5); subsequently he went into Dalmatia (2 Tim. iv. 10), and is supposed to have returned again to Crete, whence it is said he propagated the gospel in the neighbouring islands, and died at the age of 94.—*Calmet.*

2. *And I went up by revelation.* Not for the purpose of receiving instruction from the apostles there in regard to the nature of the Christian religion. It is to be remembered that the design for which Paul states this is, to show that he had not received the gospel from men. He is careful, therefore, to state that he went up by the express command of God. He did not go up to receive instructions from the apostles there in regard to his own work, or to be confirmed by them in his apostolic office, but he went to submit an important question pertaining to the church at large. In Acts xv. 2, it is said that Paul and Barnabas went up by the appointment of the church at Antioch. But there is no discrepancy between that account and this, for though he was designated by the church there, there is no improbability in supposing that he was directed by a special revelation to comply with their request. The reason why he says that he went up by direct revelation seems to be, to show that he did not *seek* instruction from the apostles; he did not go of his own accord to consult with them as if he were dependent on them; but even in a case when he went to advise with them he was under the influence of express and direct revelation, proving that he was as much commissioned by God as they were. ¶ *And*

communicated unto them that gospel, &c. Made them acquainted with the doctrines which he preached among the heathen. He stated fully the principles on which he acted; the nature of the gospel which he taught; and his doctrine about the exemption of the Gentiles from the obligations of the law of Moses. He thus satisfied them in regard to his views of the gospel; and showed them that he understood the system of Christianity which had been revealed. The result was, that they had entire confidence in him, and admitted him to entire fellowship with them; ver. 9. ¶ *But privately.* Marg. *Severally.* Gr. κατ' ἰδίαν. The phrase means that he did it not in a public manner; not before a promiscuous assembly; not even before all the apostles collected together, but in a private manner to a few of the leaders and chief persons. He made a private explanation of his motives and views, that they might understand it before it became a matter of public discussion. The *point* on which Paul made this private explanation was not whether the gospel was to be preached to the Gentiles, for on that they had no doubt after the revelation to Peter (Acts x.); but whether the rites of the Jews were to be imposed on the Gentile converts. Paul explained his views and his practice on that point, which were that he did not *impose* those rites on the Gentiles; that he taught that men might be justified without their observance; and that they were not necessary in order to salvation. The *reasons* why he sought this private interview with the leading men in Jerusalem he has not stated. But we may suppose that they were something like the following. (1.) The Jews in general had very strong attachment to their own customs, and this attachment was found in a high degree among those who were converted from among them to the Christian faith. They would be strongly excited, therefore, by the doctrine that those customs were not necessary

vately to them which were of reputation, lest by any means I

a should run, or had run, in vain.

a Ph.2.16.

to be observed. (2.) If the matter were submitted to a promiscuous assembly of converts from Judaism, it could not fail to produce great excitement. They could not be made readily to understand the reasons why Paul acted in this manner; there would be no possibility in an excited assemblage to offer the explanations which might be desirable; and after every explanation which could be given in this manner, they might have been unable to understand all the circumstances of the case. (3.) If a few of the principal men were made to understand it, Paul felt assured that their influence would be such as to prevent any great difficulty. He therefore sought an early opportunity to lay the case before them in private, and to secure their favour; and this course contributed to the happy issue of the whole affair; see Acts xv. There was indeed much disputation when the question came to be submitted to "the apostles and elders" (Acts xv. 7); many of the sect of the Pharisees in that assembly maintained that it was needful to teach the Gentiles that the law of Moses was to be kept (Acts xv. 5); and no one can tell what would have been the issue of that discussion among the excitable minds of the converts from Judaism, had not Paul taken the precaution, as he here says, to have submitted the case in private to those who were of "reputation," and if Peter and James had not in this manner been satisfied, and had not submitted the views which they did, as recorded in Acts xv. 7—21, and which terminated the whole controversy. We may just remark here that this fact furnishes an argument such as Paley has dwelt so much on in his Horæ Paulinæ— though he has not referred to this— of what he calls *undesigned coincidences.* The affair in Acts xv. and the course of the debate, *looks very much* as if Peter and James had had some conference with Paul in private, and had had an opportunity of under-

standing fully his views on the subject before the matter came before the "apostles and elders" in public, though no such private conference is there referred to by Luke. But on turning to the epistle to the Galatians, we find in fact that he had on one occasion before seen the same Peter and James (chap. i. 18, 19); and that he had had a private interview with those "of reputation" on these very points, and particularly that James, Peter, and John had approved his course, and given to him and Barnabas the right hand of fellowship; chap. ii. 9. Thus understood, the case here referred to was one of the most consummate instances of prudence that occurred in the life of Paul; and from this case we may learn, (1.) That when a difficulty is to be settled involving great principles, and embracing a great many points, it is better to seek an opportunity *of private explanation* than to submit it to a promiscuous multitude or to public debate. It is not well to attempt to settle important points when the passions of a promiscuous assembly may be excited, and where prejudices are strong. It is better to do it by private explanations, when there is an opportunity coolly to ask questions and to state the facts just as they are. (2.) The importance of securing the countenance of influential men in a popular assembly; of having men *in* the assembly who would understand the whole case. It was morally certain that if such men as Peter and James were made to understand the case, there would be little difficulty in arriving at an amicable adjustment of the difficulty. (3.) Though this passage does not refer to preaching the gospel in general, since the gospel here submitted to the men of reputation was the question referred to above, yet we may remark, that great prudence should be used in preaching; in stating truths that may excite prejudices, or when we have reason to apprehend prejudices; and that it is

3 But neither Titus, who was with me, being a Greek, was compelled to be circumcised:

4 And that because of false [a] brethren unawares brought in, who came in privily to spy out our

a Ac.15.1,24.

often best to preach the gospel to men of reputation (κατ' ἰδίαν) *separately*, or *privately*. In this way the truth can be made to bear on the conscience; it may be better adapted to the character of the individual; he may put himself less in a state of defence, and guard himself less against the proper influences of truth. And especially is this true in *conversing* with persons on the subject of religion. It should be if possible *alone*, or *privately*. Almost any man may be approached on the subject of religion if it be done when he is alone; when he is at leisure, and if it be done in a kind spirit. Almost any man will become irritated if you address him personally in a promiscuous assembly, or even with his family around him. I have never in more than in one or two instances been unkindly treated when I have addressed an individual on the subject of religion if he was alone; and though a minister should never shrink from stating the truth, and should never be afraid of man, however exalted his rank, or great his talents, or vast his wealth, yet he will probably meet with most success when he discourses *privately* to "them which are of reputation." ¶ *To them which were of reputation.* Meaning here the leading men among the apostles. Tindal renders this, "which are counted chefe." Doddridge, "those of greatest *note* in the church." The Greek is, literally, "those who seem," more fully in ver. 6; "who seem to be something," *i. e.* who are persons of note, or who are distinguished. ¶ *Lest by any means I should run, or had run in vain.* Lest the effects of my labours and journeys should be lost. Paul feared that if he did not take this method of laying the case before them privately, they would not understand it. Others might misrepresent him, or their prejudices might be excited, and when the case came before the assembled apostles and elders, a decision might

be adopted which would go to prove that he had been entirely wrong in his views, or which would lead those whom he had taught, to believe that he was, and which would greatly hinder and embarrass him in his future movements. In order to prevent this, therefore, and to secure a just decision, and one which would not hinder his future usefulness, he had sought this private interview, and thus his object was gained.

3. *But neither Titus, who was with me.* Paul introduces this case of Titus undoubtedly to show that circumcision was not necessary to salvation. It was a case just in point. He had gone up to Jerusalem with express reference to this question. Here was a man whom he had admitted to the Christian church without circumcising him. He claimed that he had a right to do so; and that circumcision was not *necessary* in order to salvation. If it were necessary, it would have been proper that Titus should have been compelled to submit to it. But Paul says this was not demanded; or if demanded by any, the point was yielded, and he was not compelled to be circumcised. It is to be remembered that this was at Jerusalem; that it was a case submitted to the apostles there; and that consequently the determination of this case settled the whole controversy about the obligation of the Mosaic laws on the Gentile converts. It is quite evident from the whole statement here, that Paul did not intend that Titus should be circumcised; that he maintained that it was not necessary; and that he resisted it when it was demanded; ver. 4, 5. Yet on another occasion he himself performed the act of circumcision on Timothy; Acts xvi. 3. But there is no inconsistency in his conduct. In the case of Titus it was *demanded* as a matter of right and as obligatory on him, and he resisted the principle as dangerous. In the case of Timothy, it was a voluntary

liberty *a* which we have in Christ Jesus, that they might bring us into bondage: *b*

a chap.5.1,13.   *b* 2 Co.11.20; chap.4.3,9.

compliance on his part with the usual customs of the Jews, where it was not pressed as a matter of obligation, *and where it would not be understood as indispensable to salvation.* No danger would follow from compliance with the custom, and it might do much to conciliate the favour of the Jews, and he therefore submitted to it. Paul would not have hesitated to have circumcised Titus in the same circumstances in which it was done to Timothy; but the circumstances were different; and when it was insisted on as a matter of principle and of obligation, it became a matter of principle and of obligation with him to oppose it. ¶ *Being a Greek.* Born of Gentile parents, of course he had not been circumcised. Probably both his parents were Greeks. The case with Timothy was somewhat different. His mother was a Jewess, but his father was a Greek; Acts xvi. 3. ¶ *Was compelled to be circumcised.* I think it is implied here that this was demanded and insisted on by some that he should be circumcised. It is also implied that Paul resisted it, and the point was yielded, thus settling the great and important principle that it was not necessary in order to salvation; see ver. 5.

4. *And that because of false brethren.* Who these false brethren were is not certainly known, nor is it known whether he refers to those who were at Jerusalem or to those who were at Antioch. It is probable that he refers to *Judaizing Christians*, or persons who claimed to be Christians and to have been converted from Judaism. Whether they were dissemblers and hypocrites, or whether they were so imperfectly acquainted with Christianity, and so obstinate, opinionated, and perverse, though really in some respects good men, that they were conscientious in this, it is not easy to determine. It is clear, however, that they opposed the apostle Paul; that they regarded him as teaching dangerous doctrines; that they perverted and misstated his views; and that they claimed to have clearer views of the nature of the true religion than he had. Such adversaries he met everywhere (2 Cor. xi. 26); and it required all his tact and skill to meet their plausible representations. It is evident here that Paul is assigning a *reason* for something which he had done, and that reason was to counteract the influence of the "false brethren" in the case. But what is the thing concerning which he assigns a reason? It is commonly supposed to have been on account of the fact that he did not submit to the circumcision of Titus, and that he means to say that he resisted that in order to counteract their influence, and defeat their designs. But I would submit whether ver. 3 is not to be regarded as a parenthesis, and whether the fact for which he assigns *a reason* is not that he sought a private interview with the leading men among the apostles? ver. 2. The *reason* of his doing that would be obvious. In this way he could more easily counteract the influence of the false brethren. He could make a full statement of his doctrines. He could meet their inquiries, and anticipate the objections of his enemies. He could thus secure the influence of the leading apostles in his favour, and effectually prevent all the efforts of the false brethren to impose the Jewish rites on Gentile converts. ¶ *Unawares brought in.* The word rendered "unawares" (παρεισάκτους) is derived from a verb meaning to lead in by the side of others, to introduce along with others; and then to lead or bring in by stealth, to smuggle in.—*Robinson, Lex.* The verb occurs nowhere in the New Testament but in 2 Pet. ii. 1, where it is applied to heresies, and is rendered "Who privily shall bring in." Here it refers probably to men who had been artfully introduced into the ministry, who made pretensions to piety, but who were either strangers to it, or who were greatly ignorant of the true nature of the Christian system; and who were disposed to take

5 To whom we gave place by subjection, no, not for an hour; that the truth of the gospel might continue with you.

---

every advantage, and to impose on others the observance of the peculiar rites of the Mosaic economy. *Into what* they were brought, the apostle does not say. It may have been that they had been introduced into the ministry in this manner (*Doddridge*); or it may be that they were introduced into the "assembly" where the apostles were collected to deliberate on the subject.—*Chandler.* I think it probable that Paul refers to the occurrences in Jerusalem, and that these false brethren had been introduced *from* Antioch or some other place where Paul had been preaching, or that they were persons whom his adversaries had introduced to *demand* that Titus should be circumcised, under the plausible pretence that the laws of Moses required it, but really in order that there might be such proof as they desired that this rite was to be imposed on the Gentile converts. If Paul was compelled to submit to this; if they could carry this point, it would be just such an instance as they needed, and would settle the whole inquiry, and prove that the Mosaic laws were to be imposed on the Gentile converts. This was the reason why Paul so strenuously opposed it. ¶ *To spy out our liberty which we have in Christ Jesus.* In the practice of the Christian religion. The liberty referred to was, doubtless, the liberty from the painful, expensive, and onerous rites of the Jewish religion; see chap. v. 1. Their object in spying out the liberty which Paul and others had, was, undoubtedly, to be witnesses of the fact that they did not observe the peculiar rites of the Mosaic system; to make report of it; to insist on their complying with those customs, and thus to secure the imposition of those rites on the Gentile converts. Their first object was to satisfy themselves of *the fact* that Paul did not insist on the observance of their customs; and then to secure, by the authority of the apostles, an injunction or order that Titus should be circumcised, and

that Paul and the converts made under his ministry should be required to comply with those laws. ¶ *That they might bring us into bondage.* Into bondage to the laws of Moses; see Note, Acts xv. 10.

5. *To whom we gave place by subjection, no, not for an hour.* We did not submit to this at all. We did not yield even for the shortest time. We did not waver in our opposition to their demands, or in the slightest degree become subject to their wishes. We steadily opposed their claims, in order that the great principle might be forever settled, that the laws of Moses were not to be imposed as obligatory on the Gentile converts. This I take to be the clear and obvious sense of this passage, though there has been a great variety of opinions on it. A considerable number of MSS. omit the words οἷς οὐδὲ, "to whom neither" (see Mill, Koppe, and Griesbach), and then the sense would be reversed, that Paul *did* yield to them for or after a short time, in order that he might in this way better consult the permanent interests of the gospel. This opinion has been gaining ground for the last century, that the passage here has been corrupted; but it is by no means confirmed. The ancient versions, the Syriac, the Vulgate, and the Arabic, accord with the usual reading of the text. So also do by far the largest portion of MSS., and such, it seems to me, is the sense demanded by the connection. Paul means, in the whole passage, to say, that a *great principle* was settled. That the question came up fairly whether the Mosaic rites were to be imposed on Gentile converts. That false brethren were introduced who demanded it; and that he steadily maintained his ground. He did not yield a moment. He felt that a great principle was involved; and though on all proper occasions he was willing to yield and to become all things to all men, yet here he did not court them, or temporize with them in the least. The phrase "by subjec-

6 But of those who seemed ^a to be somewhat, whatsoever they were, it maketh no matter to me: God ^b accepteth no man's person: for they who seemed *to be*

a chap.6.3.

somewhat, in conference added nothing to me ;

7 But contrariwise, when they saw that the gospel of the uncircumcision was committed unto me,

b Ac.10.34; Ro.2.1.

tion" here means, that he did not suffer himself to be *compelled* to yield. The phrase " for an hour " is equivalent to the shortest period of time. He did not waver, or yield at all. ¶ *That the truth of the gospel might continue with you.* That the great principle of the Christian religion which had been taught you might continue, and that you might enjoy the full benefit of the pure gospel, without its being intermingled with any false views. Paul had defended these same views among the Galatians, and he now sought that the same views might be confirmed by the clear decision of the college of apostles at Jerusalem.

6. *But of those who seemed to be somewhat;* see ver. 2. This undoubtedly refers to those who were the most eminent among the apostles at Jerusalem. There is an apparent harshness in our common translation which is unnecessary. The word here used (δοκούντων) denotes those who were thought to be, or who were of reputation ; that is, men who were of note and influence among the apostles. The object of referring to them here is, to show that he had the concurrence and approbation of the most eminent of the apostles to the course which he had pursued. ¶ *Whatsoever they were, it maketh no matter to me.* Tindal renders this, " What they were in time passed, it maketh no matter to me." The idea seems to be this. Paul means to say that whatever was their real rank and standing, it did not in the least affect his authority as an apostle, or his argument. While he rejoiced in their concurrence, and while he sought their approbation, yet he did not admit for a moment that he was inferior to them as an apostle, or dependent on them for the justness of his views What they were, or what they might be thought to be, was immaterial to his claims as an apostle,

and immaterial to the authority of his own views as an apostle. He had derived his gospel from the Lord Jesus ; and he had the fullest assurance that his views were just. Paul makes this remark evidently *in keeping* with all that he had said, that he did not regard himself as in any manner dependent on them for his authority. He did not treat them with disrespect; but he did not regard them as having a *right* to claim an authority over him. ¶ *God accepteth no man's person ;* see Notes, Acts x. 34 ; Rom. ii. 11. This is a general truth, that God is not influenced in his judgment by a regard to the rank, or wealth, or external condition of any one. Its *particular* meaning here is, that the authority of the apostles was not to be measured by their external rank, or by the measure of reputation which they had among men. If, therefore, it were to be admitted that he himself was not in circumstances of so much external honour as the other apostles, or that they were esteemed to be of more elevated rank than he was, still he did not admit that this gave them a claim to any higher authority. God was not influenced in *his* judgment by any such consideration ; and Paul therefore claimed that all the apostles were in fact on a level in regard to their authority. ¶ *In conference.* When I conferred with them, ver. 2. They did not then impose on me any new obligations ; they did not communicate any thing to me of which I was before ignorant.

7. *The gospel of the uncircumcision.* The duty of preaching the gospel to the uncircumcised part of the world ; that is, to the Gentiles Paul had received this as his peculiar office when he was converted and called to the ministry (see Acts ix. 15 ; xxii. 21) ; and they now perceived that he had been specially intrusted with this office, from the remarkable success

a as *the gospel* of the circumcision *was* unto Peter ;

8 (For he that wrought effectually in Peter to the apostleship

a 1 Th.2.4 ; 1 Ti.2.7.

of the circumcision, the same was mighty in me toward the Gentiles ;)

9 And when James, Cephas,

---

which had attended his labours. It is evidently not meant here that Paul was to preach *only* to the Gentiles and Peter *only* to the Jews, for Paul often preached in the synagogues of the Jews, and Peter was the first who preached to a Gentile (Acts x.) ; but it is meant that it was the *main* business of Paul to preach to the Gentiles, or that this was especially intrusted to him. ¶ *As* the gospel *of the circumcision.* As the office of preaching the gospel to the Jews. ¶ *Was unto Peter.* Peter was to preach principally to the circumcised Jews. It is evident that until this time Peter had been principally employed in preaching to the Jews. Paul selects Peter here particularly, doubtless because he was the oldest of the apostles, and in order to show that he was himself regarded as on a level in regard to the apostleship with the most aged and venerable of those who had been called to the apostolic office by the personal ministry of the Lord Jesus.

8. *For he that wrought effectually in Peter,* &c. Or by the means or agency of Peter. The argument here is, that the same effects had been produced under the ministry of Paul among the Gentiles which had been under the preaching of Peter among the Jews. It is inferred, therefore, that God had called both to the apostolic office ; see this argument illustrated in the Notes on Acts xi. 17. ¶ *The same was mighty in me,* &c. In enabling me to work miracles, and in the success which attended the ministry.

9. *And when James, Cephas, and John, who seemed to be pillars* That is, pillars or supports in the church. The word rendered *pillars* (στύλοι) means properly firm support ; then persons of influence and authority, as in a church, or that support a church as a pillar or column does an edifice. In regard to James, see Note on chap. i. 19 ; comp. Acts xv. 13. Cephas or

Peter was the most aged of the apostles, and regarded as at the head of the apostolical college. John was the beloved disciple, and his influence in the church must of necessity have been great. Paul felt that if he had the countenance of these men, it would be an important proof to the churches of Galatia that he had a right to regard himself as an apostle. Their countenance was expressed in the most full and decisive manner. ¶ *Perceived the grace that was given unto me.* That is, the favour that had been shown to me by the great Head of the church, in so abundantly blessing my labours among the Gentiles. ¶ *They gave unto me and Barnabas the right-hands of fellowship.* The right-hand in token of fellowship or favour. They thus publicly acknowledged us as fellow-labourers, and expressed the utmost confidence in us. To give the right-hand with us is a token of friendly salutation, and it seems that it was a mode of salutation not unknown in the times of the apostles. They were thus recognised as associated with the apostles in the great work of spreading the gospel around the world. Whether this was done in a public manner is not certainly known ; but it was probably in the presence of the church, or possibly at the close of the council referred to in Acts xv. ¶ *That we should go unto the heathen.* To preach the gospel, and to establish churches. In this way the whole matter was settled, and settled as Paul desired it to be. A delightful harmony was produced between Paul and the apostles at Jerusalem ; and the result showed the wisdom of the course which he had adopted. There had been no harsh contention or strife. No jealousies had been suffered to arise. Paul had sought an opportunity of a full statement of his views to them in private (ver. 2), and they had been entirely satisfied that God had called him and

and John, who seemed to be pillers, *a* perceived the grace *b* that was given unto me, they gave to me and Barnabas the right-hands

a Mat.16.18; Ep.2.20.

of fellowship; that we *should go* unto the heathen, and they unto the circumcision.

10 Only *they would* that we

b Ro.1.5; 12.3,6.

Barnabas to the work of making known the gospel among the heathen. Instead of being jealous at their success, they had rejoiced in it; and instead of throwing any obstacle in their way, they cordially gave them the right-hand. How easy would it be always to prevent jealousies and strifes in the same way! If there was, on the one hand, the same readiness for a full and frank explanation; and if, on the other, the same freedom from envy at remarkable success, how many strifes that have disgraced the church might have been avoided! The true way to avoid strife is just that which is here proposed. Let there be on both sides perfect frankness; let there be a willingness to explain and state things just as they are; and let there be a disposition to rejoice in the talents, and zeal, and success of others, even though it should far outstrip our own, and contention in the church would cease, and every devoted and successful minister of the gospel would receive the right-hand of fellowship from all —however venerable by age or authority—who love the cause of true religion.

10. *Only they would that we should remember the poor.* That is, as I suppose, the poor Christians in Judea. It can hardly be supposed that it would be necessary to make this an express stipulation in regard to the converts from among the Gentiles, and it would not have been very pertinent to the case before them to have done so. The object was, to bind together the Christians from among the heathen and from among the Jews, and to prevent alienation and unkind feeling. It might have been alleged that Paul was disposed to forget his own countrymen altogether; that he regarded himself as so entirely the apostle of the Gentiles that he would become wholly alienated from those who were his " kinsmen according to

the flesh," and thus it might be apprehended that unpleasant feelings would be engendered among those who had been converted from among the Jews. Now nothing could be better adapted to allay this than for him to pledge himself to feel a deep interest in the poor saints among the Jewish converts; to remember them in his prayers; and to endeavour to secure contributions for their wants. Thus he would show that he was not alienated from his countrymen; and thus the whole church would be united in the closest bonds. It is probable that the Christians in Judea were at that time suffering the ills of poverty arising either from some public persecution, or from the fact that they were subject to the displeasure of their countrymen. All who know the peculiar feelings of the Jews at that time in regard to Christians, must see at once that many of the followers of Jesus of Nazareth would be subjected to great inconveniences on account of their attachment to him. Many a wife might be disowned by her husband; many a child disinherited by a parent, many a man might be thrown out of employment by the fact that others would not countenance him; and hence many of the Christians would be poor. It became, therefore, an object of special importance to provide for them; and hence this is so often referred to in the New Testament. In addition to this, the church in Judea was afflicted with famine; comp. Acts xi. 30; Rom. xv. 25—27; 1 Cor. xvi. 1, 2; 2 Cor. viii. 1—7. ¶ *The same which I also was forward to do.* See the passages just referred to. Paul interested himself much in the collection for the poor saints at Jerusalem, and in this way he furnished the fullest evidence that he was not alienated from them, but that he felt the deepest interest in those who were his kindred. One of the proper ways of securing *union*

should remember the poor; the same which I *a* also was forward to do.

11 But when Peter was come

a Ac.11.30; Ro.15.25.

in the church is to have the poor with them and depending on them for support; and hence every church has some poor persons as one of the bonds of union. The best way to unite *all* Christians, and to prevent alienation, and jealousy, and strife, is to have *a great common object of charity*, in which all are interested and to which all may contribute. Such a common object for all Christians is a sinful world. All who bear the Christian name may unite in promoting its salvation, and nothing would promote union in the now divided and distracted church of Christ like a deep and common interest in the salvation of all mankind.

11. *But when Peter was come to Antioch.* On the situation of Antioch, see Note, Acts xi. 19. The *design* for which Paul introduces this statement here is evident. It is to show that he regarded himself as on a level with the chief apostles, and that he did not acknowledge his inferiority to any of them. Peter was the eldest, and probably the most honoured of the apostles. Yet Paul says that he did not hesitate to resist him in a case where Peter was manifestly wrong, and thus showed that he was an apostle of the same standing as the others. Besides, what he said to Peter on that occasion was exactly pertinent to the strain of the argument which he was pursuing with the Galatians, and he therefore introduces it (ver. 14—21) to show that he had held the same doctrine all along, and that he had defended it in the presence of Peter, and in a case where Peter did not reply to it. The *time* of this journey of Peter to Antioch cannot be ascertained; nor the occasion on which it occurred. I think it is evident that it was after this visit of Paul to Jerusalem, and the occasion *may* have been to inspect the state of the church at Antioch, and to compose any differences of opinion which may have

to *b* Antioch, I withstood him to the face, because he was to be blamed.

12 For before that certain

b Ac.15.35.

existed there. But every thing in regard to this is mere conjecture; and it is of little importance to know when it occurred. ¶ *I withstood him to the face.* I openly opposed him, and reproved him. Paul thus showed that he was equal with Peter in his apostolical authority and dignity. The instance before us is one of faithful public reproof; and every circumstance in it is worthy of special attention, as it furnishes a most important illustration of the manner in which such reproof should be conducted. The *first* thing to be noted is, that it was done openly, and with candour. It was reproof addressed to the offender himself. Paul did not go to others and whisper his suspicions; he did not seek to undermine the influence and authority of another by slander; he did not calumniate him and then justify himself on the ground that what he had said was no more than true: he went to him at once, and he frankly stated his views and reproved him in a case where he was manifestly wrong. This too was a case so public and well known that Paul made his remarks before the church (ver. 14) because the church was interested in it, and because the conduct of Peter led the church into error. ¶ *Because he was to be blamed.* The word used here may either mean because he had *incurred* blame, or because he *deserved* blame. The essential idea is, that he had done wrong, and that he was by his conduct doing injury to the cause of religion.

12. *For before that certain came.* Some of the Jews who had been converted to Christianity. They evidently observed in the strictest manner the rites of the Jewish religion. ¶ *Came from James;* see Note on chap. i. 19. Whether they were sent by James, or whether they came of their own accord, is unknown. It is evident only that they had been intimate with James at Jerusalem, and

came from James, he did eat ^a with the Gentiles: but when they were come, he withdrew and separated himself, fearing

a Ac.11.3.

they doubtless pleaded his authority. James had nothing to do with the course which they pursued ; but the sense of the whole passage is, that James was a leading man at Jerusalem, and that the rites of Moses were observed there. When they came down to Antioch, they of course observed those rites, and insisted that others should do it also. It is very evident that at Jerusalem the peculiar rites of the Jews were observed for a long time by those who became Christian converts. They would not at once cease to observe them, and thus needlessly shock the prejudices of their countrymen ; see Notes on Acts xxi. 21—25. ¶ *He did eat with the Gentiles.* Peter had been taught that in the remarkable vision which he saw as recorded in Acts x. He had learned that God designed to break down the wall of partition between the Jews and the Gentiles, and he familiarly associated with them, and partook with them of their food. He evidently disregarded the peculiar laws of the Jews about meats and drinks, and partook of the common food which was in use among the Gentiles. Thus he showed his belief that all the race was henceforward to be regarded as on a level, and that the peculiar institutions of the Jews were not to be considered as binding, or to be imposed on others. ¶ *But when they were come, he withdrew and separated himself.* He withdrew from the Gentiles, and probably from the Gentile converts to Christianity. The reason why he did this is stated. He feared those who were of the circumcision, or who had been Jews. Whether they demanded this of him ; whether they encountered him in debate ; or whether he silently separated himself from the Gentiles without their having said any thing to him, is unknown. But he feared the effect of their opposition ; he feared their reproaches ; he feared the report

them which were of the circumcision.

13 And the other Jews dissembled likewise with him ; in-

which would be made to those at Jerusalem ; and perhaps he apprehended that a tumult would be excited and a persecution commenced at Antioch by the Jews who resided there. This is a melancholy illustration of Peter's characteristic trait of mind. We see in this act the same Peter who trembled when he began to sink in the waves ; the same Peter who denied his Lord. Bold, ardent, zealous, and forward ; he was at the same time timid and often irresolute ; and he often had occasion for the deepest humility, and the most poignant regrets at the errors of his course. No one can read his history without loving his ardent and sincere attachment to his Master ; and yet no one can read it without a tear of regret that he was left thus to do injury to his cause. No man loved the Saviour more sincerely than he did, yet his constitutional timidity and irresoluteness of character often led him to courses of life fitted deeply to wound his cause.

13 *And the other Jews.* That is, those who had been converted to Christianity. It is probable that they were induced to do it by the example of Peter, as they would naturally regard him as a leader. ¶ *Dissembled likewise with him.* Dissembled or concealed their true sentiments. That is, they attempted to conceal from those who had come down from James the fact that they had been in the habit of associating with the Gentiles, and of eating with them. From this it would appear that they intended to conceal this wholly from them, and that they withdrew from the Gentiles before any thing had been said to them by those who came down from James. ¶ *Insomuch that Barnabas also was carried away,* &c. Concerning Barnabas, see Note, Acts iv. 36. Barnabas was the intimate friend of Paul. He had been associated with him in very important labours ; and the fact,

somuch that Barnabas also was carried away with their dissimulation.

14 But when I saw that they

a ver.5.

therefore, that the conduct of Peter was exciting so unhappy an influence as even to lead so worthy and good a man as he was into hypocrisy and error, made it the more proper that Paul should publicly notice and reprove the conduct of Peter. It could not but be a painful duty, but the welfare of the church and the cause of religion demanded it, and Paul did not shrink from what was so obvious a duty.

14. *But when I saw that they walked not uprightly.* To *walk*, in the Scriptures, is usually expressive of conduct or deportment ; and the idea here is, that their conduct in this case was not honest. ¶ *According to the truth of the gospel.* According to the true spirit and design of the gospel. That requires perfect honesty and integrity; and as that was the rule by which Paul regulated his life, and by which he felt that all ought to regulate their conduct, he felt himself called on openly to reprove the principal person who had been in fault. The spirit of the world is crafty, cunning, and crooked. The gospel would correct all that wily policy, and would lead man in a path of entire honesty and truth. ¶ *I said unto Peter before them all.* That is, probably, before all the church, or certainly before all who had offended with him in the case. Had this been a *private affair*, Paul would doubtless have sought a private interview with Peter, and would have remonstrated with him in private on the subject. But it was public. It was a case where many were involved, and where the interests of the church were at stake. It was a case where it was very important to establish some fixed and just principles, and he therefore took occasion to remonstrate with him in public on the subject. This might have been at the close of public worship ; or it may have been that the subject came up for debate in some of their public meetings, whether

walked not uprightly, according to the truth *a* of the gospel, I said unto Peter *b* before *them* all, If thou, being a Jew, livest after the

b 1 Ti.5.20.

the rites of the Jews were to be imposed on the Gentile converts. This was a question which agitated all the churches where the Jewish and Gentile converts were intermingled; and it would not be strange that it should be the subject of public debate at Antioch. The fact that Paul reproved Peter before "them all," proves, (1.) That he regarded himself, and was so regarded by the church, as on an equality with Peter, and as having equal authority with him. (2.) That public reproof is right when an offence has been public, and when the church at large is interested, or is in danger of being led into error ; comp. 1 Tim. v. 20, " Them that sin rebuke before all, that others also may fear." (3.) That it is a duty to reprove those who err. It is a painful duty, and one much neglected ; still it is a duty often enjoined in the Scriptures, and one that is of the deepest importance to the church. He does a favour to another man who, in a kind spirit, admonishes him of his error, and reclaims him from a course of sin. He does another the deepest injury, who suffers sin unrebuked to lie upon him, and who sees him injuring himself and others, and who is at no pains to admonish him for his faults. (4.) If it is the duty of one Christian to admonish another who is an offender, and to do it in a kind spirit, it is the duty of him who has offended to *receive* the admonition in a kind spirit, and with thankfulness. Excitable as Peter was by nature, yet there is no evidence that he became angry here, or that he did not receive the admonition of his brother Paul with perfect good temper, and with an acknowledgment that Paul was right and that he was wrong. Indeed, the case was so plain,—as it usually is if men would be honest,—that he seems to have felt that it was right, and to have received the rebuke as became a Christian. Peter, unhappily, was accustomed to

manner of Gentiles, and not as do the Jews, why compellest thou the Gentiles to live as do the Jews?

a Ep.2.3,12.

rebukes; and he was at heart too good a man to be offended when he was admonished that he had done wrong. A good man is willing to be reproved when he has erred, and it is usually proof that there is much that is wrong when we become excited and irritable if another admonishes us of our faults. It may be added here, that nothing should be inferred from this in regard to the *inspiration* or apostolic authority of Peter. The fault was not that he taught error *of doctrine*, but that he sinned *in conduct*. Inspiration, though it kept the apostles from teaching error, did not keep them necessarily from sin. A man may always *teach* the truth, and yet be far from perfection in practice. The case here proves that Peter was not perfect, a fact proved by his whole life; it proves that he was sometimes timid, and even, for a period, timeserving, but it does not prove that what he wrote for our guidance was false and erroneous. ¶ *If thou, being a Jew.* A Jew by birth. ¶ *Livest after the manner of the Gentiles.* In eating, &c., as he had done before the Judaizing teachers came from Jerusalem, ver. 12. ¶ *And not as do the Jews.* Observing their peculiar customs, and their distinctions of meals and drinks. ¶ *Why compellest thou the Gentiles, &c.* As he would do, if he insisted that they should be circumcised, and observe the peculiar Jewish rites. The charge against him was gross inconsistency in doing this. " Is it not at least as lawful for them to neglect the Jewish observances, as it was for thee to do it but a few days ago?"—*Doddridge.* The word here rendered "compellest," means here *moral* compulsion or persuasion The idea is, that the conduct of Peter was such as to lead the Gentiles to the belief that it was necessary for them to be circumcised in order to be saved. For a similar use of the word, see Mat.

15 We *who are* Jews by nature, and not sinners *a* of the Gentiles,

16 Knowing that *b* a man is

b Ac.13.38,39; Ro.3.20.

xiv. 22; Luke xiv. 23; Acts xxviii 19.

15. *We* who are *Jews by nature.* It has long been a question whether this and the following verses are to be regarded as a part of the address of Paul to Peter, or the words of Paul as a part of the epistle to the Galatians. A great variety of opinion has prevailed in regard to this. Grotius says, " Here the narrative of Paul being closed, he pursues his argument to the Galatians." In this opinion Bloomfield and many others concur. Rosenmüller and many others suppose that the address to Peter is continued to ver. 21. Such *seems* to be the most obvious interpretation, as there is no break or change in the style, nor any vestige of a transfer of the argument to the Galatians. But, on the other hand, it may be urged, (1.) That Paul in his writings often changes his mode of address without indicating it. —*Bloomfield.* (2.) That it is rather improbable that he should have gone into so long a discourse with Peter on the subject of justification. His purpose was answered by the reproof of Peter for his dissimulation; and there is something incongruous, it is said, in his instructing Peter at such length on the subject of man's justification. Still it appears to me probable that this is to be regarded as a part of the discourse of Paul to Peter, to the close of ver. 21. The following reasons seem to me to require this interpretation:—(1.) It is the most natural and obvious—usually a safe rule of interpretation. The discourse proceeds *as if* it were an address to Peter. (2.) There *is* a change at the beginning of the next chapter, where Paul expressly addresses himself to the Galatians. (3.) As to the impropriety of Paul's addressing Peter at length on the subject of justification, we are to bear in mind that he did not address him *alone.* The *reproof* was addressed to Peter particularly,

not justified by the works of the law, but by the faith *a* of Jesus Christ, even we have believed in Jesus Christ, that we might be

a Ro.5.1; chap.3.11,24.

but it was "before them all" (ver. 14) ; that is, before the assembled church, or before the persons who had been led astray by the conduct of Peter, and who were in danger of error on the subject of justification. Nothing, therefore, was more proper than for Paul to continue his discourse for *their* benefit, and to state to them fully the doctrine of justification. And nothing was more pertinent or proper for him now than to report this to the Galatians as a part of his argument to them, showing that he had *always*, since his conversion, held and defended the same doctrine on the subject of the way in which men are to be justified in the sight of God. It is, therefore, I apprehend, to be regarded as an address to Peter and the other Jews who were present. "*We* who were born Jews." ¶ *By nature.* By birth ; or, we were born Jews. We were not born in the condition of the Gentiles. ¶ *And not sinners of the Gentiles.* This cannot mean that Paul did not regard the Jews as sinners, for his views on that subject he has fully expressed in Rom. ii. iii. But it must mean that the Jews were not born under the disadvantages of the Gentiles in regard to the true knowledge of the way of salvation. They were not left wholly in ignorance about the way of justification, as the Gentiles were. They knew, or they might know, that men could not be saved by their own works. It was also true that they were under more restraint than the Gentiles were, and though they were sinners, yet they were not abandoned to so gross and open sensuality as was the heathen world. They were not idolaters, and wholly ignorant of the law of God.

16. *Knowing.* We who are Jews by nature, or by birth. This cannot mean that *all* the Jews knew this, or that he who was a Jew knew it as a matter of course, for many Jews were ignorant of it, and many opposed it.

justified by the faith of Christ, and not by the works of the law : for *b* by the works of the law shall no flesh be justified.

b Ps.143.2; He.7.18,19.

But it means that the persons here referred to, those who had been born Jews, and who had been converted to Christianity, had had an opportunity to learn and understand this, which the Gentiles had not. This gospel had been preached to them, and they had professedly embraced it. They were not left to the gross darkness and ignorance on this subject which pervaded the heathen world, and they had had a better opportunity to learn it than the converts from the Gentiles. They ought, therefore, to act in a manner becoming their superior light, and to show in all their conduct that they fully believed that a man could not be justified by obedience to the law of Moses. This rendered the conduct of Peter and the other Jews who "dissembled" with him so entirely inexcusable. They could not plead ignorance on this vital subject, and yet they were pursuing a course, the tendency of which was to lead the Gentile converts to believe that it was indispensable to observe the laws of Moses, in order to be justified and saved. ¶ *That a man is not justified by the works of the law;* see Notes on Rom. i. 17 ; iii. 20, 26 ; iv. 5. ¶ *But by the faith of Jesus Christ.* By believing on Jesus Christ ; see Notes, Mark xvi. 16 ; Rom. iii. 22. ¶ *Even we have believed in Jesus Christ.* We are therefore justified. The object of Paul here seems to be to show, that as they had believed in the Lord Jesus, and thus had been justified, there was no necessity of obeying the law of Moses with any view to justification. The thing had been fully done without the deeds of the law, and it was now unreasonable and unnecessary to insist on the observance of the Mosaic rites. ¶ *For by the works of the law,* &c ; see Notes on Rom. iii. 20, 27. In this verse, the apostle has stated in few words the important doctrine of justification by faith—the doctrine which

Luther so justly called, *Articulus stantis, vel cadentis ecclesiæ.* In the notes referred to above, particularly in the Notes on the Epistle to the Romans, I have stated in various places what I conceive to be the true doctrine on this important subject. It may be useful, however, to throw together in one connected view, as briefly as possible, the leading ideas on the subject of justification, as it is revealed in the gospel.   I. Justification is properly a word applicable to courts of justice, but is used in a similar sense in common conversation among men. An illustration will show its nature. A man is charged, *e. g.* with an act of trespass on his neighbour's property. Now there are two ways which he may take *to justify himself*, or to meet the charge, so as to be regarded and treated as innocent. He may, (*a*) Either *deny* that he performed the act charged on him, or he may, (*b*) Admit that the deed was done, and set up as a defence, that he *had a right* to do it, In either case, if the point be made out, he will be *just* or *innocent* in the sight of the law.   The law will have nothing against him, and he will be regarded and treated in the premises as an innocent man ; or he has justified himself in regard to the charge brought against him. II. Charges of a very serious nature are brought against man by his Maker. He is charged with violating the law of God ; with a want of love to his Maker ; with a corrupt, proud, sensual heart ; with being entirely alienated from God by wicked works ; in one word, with being entirely depraved. This charge extends to all men ; and to the entire life of every unrenewed man. It is not a charge merely affecting the external conduct, nor merely affecting the heart ; it is a charge of entire alienation from God ; a charge, in short, of total depravity ; see, especially, Rom. i., ii., iii. That this charge is a very serious one, no one can doubt. That it deeply affects the human character and standing, is as clear. It is a charge brought in the Bible ; and God appeals in proof of it to the history of the world, to every

man's conscience, and to the life of every one who has lived ; and on these facts, and on his own power in searching the hearts, and in knowing what is in man, he rests the proofs of the charge. III. It is impossible for man to vindicate himself from this charge. *He can neither show that the things charged have not been committed, nor that, having been committed, he had a right to do them.* He cannot *prove* that God is not right in all the charges which he has made against him in his word ; and he cannot prove that it was right for him to do as he has done. The charges against him are facts which are undeniable, and the facts are such as cannot be vindicated. But if he can do neither of these things, then he cannot be justified by the law. The law will not acquit him. It holds him guilty. It condemns him. No *argument* which he can use will show that he is right, and that God is wrong. No *works* that he can perform will be any compensation for what he has already done. No *denial* of the existence of the facts charged will alter the case ; and he must stand condemned by the law of God. In the legal sense he cannot be justified ; and justification, if it ever exist at all, must be in a mode that is a departure from the regular operation of law, and in a mode which the law did not contemplate, for no *law* makes any provision for the *pardon* of those who violate it. It must be by some system which is distinct from the law, and in which man may be justified on different principles than those which the law contemplates. IV. This other system of justification is that which is revealed in the gospel by the faith of the Lord Jesus. It does NOT consist in either of the following things. (1.) It is *not* a system or plan where the Lord Jesus takes the part of the sinner *against* the law or *against* God. He did not come to show that the sinner was right, and that God was wrong. He admitted most fully, and endeavoured constantly *to* show, that God was right, and that the sinner was wrong ; nor can an instance be referred to where the Saviour took the part of the sinner against God in any such sense that he endeavoured to show that the sinner had not done the things charged on him, or that he had a right to do them. (2.) It is not that we *are* either innocent, or are declared to be innocent. God justifies the "ungodly," Rom. iv. 5. We are not innocent; we never have been; we never shall be; and it is not the design of the scheme to declare any such *untruth* as that we are not personally undeserving. It will be *always* true that the justified sinner has no claims to the mercy and favour of God. (3.) It is not that we cease to be undeserving personally. He that is justified by faith, and that goes to heaven, will go there admitting that he *deserves* eternal death, and that he is saved wholly by favour and not by desert. (4.) It is *not* a declaration on the part of God that *we* have wrought out salvation, or that *we* have any claim for what the Lord Jesus has done. Such a declaration would not be true, and would not be made. (5.) It is not that the righteousness of the Lord Jesus is *transferred* to his people. Moral character cannot be transferred. It adheres to the moral agent as much as colour does to the rays of light which cause it. It is not true that *we* died for sin, and it cannot be so reckoned or imputed. It is not true that *we* have any merit, or any claim, and it cannot be so reckoned or imputed. All the imputations of God are according to truth; and he will always reckon us to be personally undeserving and sinful. But if justification be none of these things, it may be asked, what is it? I answer—*It is the declared purpose of God to regard and treat those sinners who believe in the Lord Jesus Christ as if they had not sinned, on the ground of the merits of the Saviour.* It is not mere pardon. The main difference between pardon and justification respects the sinner contemplated in regard to his *past* conduct, and to God's *future dealings* with him. Pardon is a free forgiveness of past offences. It has reference to those sins *as* forgiven and blotted out. It is an act of remission on the part of God. Justifi-

cation has respect to the law, and to God's *future dealings* with the sinner. It is an act by which God determines to treat him hereafter *as* a righteous man, or *as if* he had not sinned. The ground or reason of this is, the merit of the Lord Jesus Christ; merit such that we can plead it *as if* it were our own. The *rationale* of it is, that the Lord Jesus has accomplished by his death the same happy effects in regard to the law and the government of God, which would have been accomplished by the death of the sinner himself. In other words, nothing would be gained to the universe by the everlasing punishment of the offender himself, which will not be secured by his salvation on the ground of the death of the Lord Jesus. He has taken our place, and died in our stead; and he has met the descending stroke of justice, which would have fallen on our own head if he had not interposed (see my Notes on Isa. liii.) and now the great interests of justice will be as firmly secured if we are saved, as they would be if we were lost. The law has been fully obeyed by one who came to save us, and *as much* honour has been done to it by his obedience as could have been by our own; that is, it *as much* shows that the law is *worthy* of obedience to have it perfectly obeyed by the Lord Jesus, as it would if it were obeyed by us. It *as much* shows that the law of a sovereign is worthy of obedience to have it obeyed by an only son and an heir to the crown, as it does to have it obeyed by his subjects. And it has *as much* shown the evil of the violation of the law to have the Lord Jesus suffer death on the cross, as it would if the guilty had died themselves. If transgression whelm the innocent in calamity; if it extends to those who are perfectly *guiltless*, and inflicts pain and woe on them, it is as certainly an expression of the evil of transgression *as if* the guilty themselves suffer. And an impression as deep has been made of the evil of sin by the sufferings of the Lord Jesus in our stead, *as if* we had suffered ourselves. He endured on the cross as intense agony as we can conceive it possible for a sinner ever to endure; and the dignity of the person who suffered, THE INCARNATE GOD, is more than an equivalent for the more lengthened sorrows which the penalty of the law exacts in hell. Besides, from the very dignity of the sufferer in our place, an impression has gone abroad on the universe more deep and important than would have been by the sufferings of the individual himself in the world of woe. The sinner who is lost will be unknown to other worlds. His *name* may be unheard beyond the gates of the prison of despair. The *impression* which will be made on distant worlds by his individual sufferings will be as a part of *the aggregate of woe*, and his individual sorrows may make *no* impression on distant worlds. But not so with him who took our place. He stood in the centre of the universe. The sun grew dark, and the dead arose, and angels gazed upon the scene, and from his cross an *impression* went abroad to the farthest part of the universe, showing the tremendous effects of the violation of law, when not one soul could be saved from its penalty without such sorrows of the Son of God. In virtue of all this, the offender, by believing on him, may be treated *as if* he had not sinned; and this constitutes justification. God admits him to favour *as if* he had himself obeyed the law, or borne its penalty, since as many good results will now follow from his salvation as could be derived from his punishment; and since all the additional happy results will follow which can be derived from the exercise of pardoning mercy. The character of God is thus revealed. His mercy is shown. His determination to maintain his law is evinced. The truth is maintained; and yet he shows the fulness of his mercy and the richness of his benevolence.

[The reader will find the above objections to the doctrine of imputation fully considered in the supplementary Notes on Rom. iv. 5; see especially the Note on Rom. iv. 3, in which it is observed, that almost every objection against the imputation of righteousness may be traced to two sources. The first of

these is the idea that Christ's righteousness becomes ours, in the same sense that it is his, viz., of personal achievement; an idea continually rejected by the friends, and as often proceeded on by the enemies, of imputation. The second source is the idea that imputation involves a transference of moral character, whereas the *imputing* and the *infusing* of righteousness are allowed to be two very different things. Now, in this place, the commentator manifestly proceeds on these mistaken views. What does he mean by " transference of the righteousness of Christ" when he says, "justification is not that the righteousness of the Lord Jesus is transferred to his people?" What follows, at once explains. " Moral character," he continues, " cannot be transferred. It adheres to the moral agent, as much as colour does to the rays of light which cause it." But this is quite aside from the subject, and proves what never had been denied. The same remarks apply with equal force to what is said about our being " always personally undeserving," and never regarded as having ourselves actually " wrought out salvation." These objections belong to the first source of misconception noticed above.

It has been asked a thousand times, and the question is most pertinent, How can God treat believers as innocent, if there be not some sense in which they are so? " The imputations of God are according to truth," so is his treatment. The author tells us, that the ground of justification is the "merits of the Saviour," which phrase he prefers throughout, to the more scriptural and more appropriate one of the righteousness of Christ; more appropriate, because the subject is forensic, belonging to judicature and dealing in matters of law; see Hervey's reply to Wesley, vol. iv. p. 33. Yet if these merits, or this righteousness, be not imputed to us—held as ours – *how can we be justified on any such ground ?* "I would further observe," says Mr. Hervey, replying to Wesley in the publication just quoted, " that you have dropt the word imputed," which inclines me to suspect you would cashier the thing. But let me ask, Sir, how can we be justified by the merits of Christ, unless they are imputed to us? Would the payment made by a surety procure a discharge for the debtor, unless it were placed to his account? It is certain the sacrifices of old could not make an atonement, unless they were imputed to each offerer respectively. This was an ordinance settled by Jehovah himself, Lev. vii. 18. And were not the sacrifices, was not their imputation, typical of Christ and things pertaining to Christ, the former prefiguring his all-sufficient expiation; the latter shadowing forth the way whereby we are partakers of its efficacy?

The language of President Edwards, the prince of American divines, indeed of theolo-

17 But if, while we seek to be | justified by Christ, we *a* ourselves

a 1 John 3.9,10.

gians universally, is decisive enough, and one would think that the opinion of this master in reasoning should have its weight on the other side of the Atlantic. "It is absolutely necessary," says he, "that in order to a sinner's being justified, the righteousness of some other should be reckoned to his account; for it is declared, that the person justified is looked on as, in himself, ungodly: but God neither will nor can justify a person without a righteousness; for justification is manifestly a forensic term, as the word is used in scripture, and a judicial thing or the act of a judge; so that if a person should be justified without a righteousness, the judgment would not be according to truth. The sentence of justification would be a false sentence, unless there be a righteousness performed, that is, by the judge properly looked upon as his."

Nor are we sure, if our author's distinction between pardon and justification be altogether accurate. By those who deny imputed righteousness, justification is frequently said to consist in the *mere remission of sin*. In a recent American publication, the views of the "new school party" are thus given: "Though they retain the word justification, they make it consist in mere pardon. In the eye of the law, the believer, according to their views, is not justified at all, and never will be throughout eternity. Though on the ground of what Christ has done, God is pleased to forgive the sinner upon his believing, Christ's righteousness is not reckoned in any sense as his, or set down to his account. He believes, and his *faith or act of believing* is accounted to him for righteousness; that is, faith is so reckoned to his account that God *treats* him as if he were righteous."—*Old and New Theology*, by *James Wood.* Now Mr. Barnes does not exactly say that justification and pardon are the same, for he makes a distinction. "The main difference between the two respects the sinner contemplated in regard to his *past* conduct, and to God's *future* dealings with him." "Pardon is a free forgiveness of *past* offences. Justification has respect to the law and to God's *future* dealings." But this difference is not respecting the *nature* of the things. It is simply a matter of time, of past and future; and justification, after all, is neither more nor less than pardon of sins past and to come. A criminal is often pardoned while yet his guilt is allowed. To exalt pardon to justification, there must be supposed a righteousness, on the ground of which not only is sin forgiven, but *the person accepted and declared legally righteous.* And in this lies the main difference between the two. In the case of the believer however these are never found

apart. Whoever is pardoned is at the same time justified. Earthly princes sometimes remit the punishment of crime, but seldom or never dream of honouring the criminal; but wherever God pardons, he dignifies and ennobles.]

17. *But if, while we seek to be justified by Christ.* The connection here is not very clear, and the sense of the verse is somewhat obscure. Rosenmüller supposes that this is an objection of a Jew, supposing that where the law of Moses is not observed there is no rule of life, and that therefore there must be sin; and that since the doctrine of justification by faith taught that there was no necessity of obeying the ceremonial law of Moses, therefore Christ, who had introduced that system, must be regarded as the author and encourager of sin. To me it seems probable that Paul here has reference to an objection which has in all ages been brought against the doctrine of justification by faith, and which seems to have existed in his time, that the doctrine leads to licentiousness. The objections are, that it does not teach the necessity of the observance of the law in order to acceptance with God. That it pronounces a man justified and accepted who is a violator of the law. That his acceptance does not depend on moral character. That it releases him from the obligation of law, and that it teaches that a man may be saved though he does not conform to law. These objections existed early, and have been found everywhere where the doctrine of justification by faith has been preached. I regard this verse, therefore, as referring to these objections, and not as being peculiarly the objection of a Jew. The idea is, "You seek to be justified by faith without obeying the law. You professedly reject that, and do not hold that it is necessary to yield obedience to it. If now it shall turn out that you are sinners; that your lives are not holy; that you are free from the wholesome restraint of the law, and are given up to lives of sin, will it not follow that Christ is

also are found sinners, *is* therefore Christ the minister of sin? God forbid.

18 For if I build again the things which I destroyed, I make myself a transgressor.·

a Ro.7.4,10; 8.2.　　*b* Ro.6.11,14.

the cause of it; that he taught it; and that the system which he introduced is responsible for it? And is not the gospel therefore responsible for introducing a system that frees from the restraint of the law, and introduces universal licentiousness?" To this Paul replies by stating distinctly that the gospel has no such tendency, and particularly by referring in the following verses to his own case, and to the effect of the doctrine of justification on his own heart and life. ¶ *We ourselves are found sinners.* If it turns out that we are sinners, or if others discover by undoubted demonstration that we lead lives of sin; if they see us given up to a lawless life, and find us practising all kinds of evil; if it shall be seen not only that we are not pardoned and made better by the gospel, but are actually made worse, and are freed from all moral restraint. ¶ Is *therefore Christ the minister of sin?* Is it to be traced to him? Is it a fair and legitimate conclusion that this is the tendency of the gospel? Is it to be charged on him, and on the plan of justification through him, that a lax morality prevails, and that men are freed from the wholesome restraints of law? ¶ *God forbid.* It is not so. This is not the proper effect of the gospel of Christ, and of the doctrine of justification by faith. The system is not fitted to produce such a freedom from restraint, and if such a freedom exists, it is to be traced to something else than the gospel.

18. *For if I build again the things which I destroyed.* Paul here uses the first person; but he evidently intends it as a general proposition, and means that if *any one* does it he becomes a transgressor. The sense is, that if a man, having removed or destroyed that which was evil, again introduces it or establishes it, he does wrong, and is a transgressor of the

19 For I *a* through the law am dead to the law, that I might live *b* unto God.

20 I am crucified *c* with Christ: nevertheless I live; yet not I, but Christ liveth in *d* me: and the

c chap.5.24; 6.14.　　*d* 1 Th.5.10; 1 Pe.4.2.

law of God. The particular application here, as it seems to me, is to the subject of circumcision and the other rites of the Mosaic law. They had been virtually abolished by the coming of the Redeemer, and by the doctrine of justification by faith. It had been seen that there was no necessity for their observance, and of that Peter and the others had been fully aware. Yet they were lending their influence again to establish them or to "build" them up again. They complied with them, and they insisted on the necessity of their observance. Their conduct, therefore, was that of building up again that which had once been destroyed, destroyed by the ministry, and toils, and death of the Lord Jesus, and by the fair influence of his gospel. To rebuild that again; to re-establish those customs, was wrong, and now involved the guilt of a transgression of the law of God. Doddridge supposes that this is an address to the Galatians, and that the address to Peter closed at the previous verse. But it is impossible to determine this; and it seems to me more probable that this is all a part of the address to Peter, or rather perhaps to the assembly when Peter was present; see Note on ver. 15.

19. *For I through the law.* On this passage the commentators are by no means agreed. It is agreed that in the phrase "am dead to the law," the law of Moses is referred to, and that the meaning is, that Paul had become dead to that as a ground or means of justification. He acted as though it were not; or it ceased to have influence over him. A dead man is insensible to all around him. He hears nothing; sees nothing; and nothing affects him. So when we are said to be dead to any thing, the meaning is, that it does not have an influence over us. In this sense Paul

life which I now live in the flesh, I live by the faith of the Son of God, who loved me, and gave himself [a] for me.

a John 10.11; Ep.5.2.

was dead to the law of Moses. He ceased to observe it as a ground of justification. It ceased to be the grand aim and purpose of his life, as it had been formerly, to obey it. He had higher purposes than that, and truly lived to God ; see Note, Rom. vi. 2. But on the meaning of the phrase " through the law " (διὰ νόμου) there has been a great variety of opinion. Bloomfield, Rosenmüller, and some others suppose that he means the Christian religion, and that the meaning is, " by one law, or doctrine, I am dead to another ;" that is, the Christian doctrine has caused me to cast aside the Mosaic religion. Doddridge, Clarke, Chandler, and most others, however, suppose that he here refers to the law of Moses, and that the meaning is, that by contemplating the true character of the law of Moses itself; by considering its nature and design ; by understanding the extent of its requisitions, he had become dead to it ; that is, he had laid aside all expectations of being justified by it. This seems to me to be the correct interpretation. Paul had formerly expected to be justified by the law. He had endeavoured to obey it. It had been the object of his life to comply with all its requisitions in order to be saved by it ; Phil. iii. 4— 6. But all this while he had not fully understood its nature ; and when he was made fully to feel and comprehend its spiritual requirements, then all his hopes of justification by it died, and he became dead to it ; see this sentiment more fully explained in the Note on Rom. vii. 9. ¶ That I might live unto God. That I might be truly alive, and might be found engaged in his service. He was dead to the law, but not to every thing. He had not become literally inactive and insensible to all things, like a dead man, but he had become truly sensible to the commands and appeals of God, and had consecrated himself to his service; see Note, Rom. vi. 11.

20. I am crucified with Christ. In the previous verse, Paul had said that he was dead. In this verse he states what he meant by it, and shows that he did not wish to be understood as saying that he was inactive, or that he was literally insensible to the appeals made to him by other beings and objects. In respect to one thing he was dead ; to all that was truly great and noble he was alive. To understand the remarkable phrase, " I am crucified with Christ," we may remark, (1.) That this was the way in which Christ was put to death. He suffered on a cross, and thus became literally dead. (2.) In a sense similar to this, Paul became dead to the law, to the world, and to sin. The Redeemer by the death of the cross became insensible to all surrounding objects, as the dead always are. He ceased to see, and hear, and was as though they were not. He was laid in the cold grave, and they did not affect or influence him. So Paul says that he became insensible to the law as a means of justification ; to the world ; to ambition and the love of money ; to the pride and pomp of life, and to the dominion of evil and hateful passions. They lost their power over him ; they ceased to influence him. (3.) This was with Christ, or by Christ. It cannot mean literally that he was put to death with him, for that is not true. But it means that the effect of the death of Christ on the cross was to make him dead to these things, in like manner as he, when he died, became insensible to the things of this busy world. This may include the following things. (a) There was an intimate union between Christ and his people, so that what affected him, affected them ; see John xv. 5, 6. (b) The death of the Redeemer on the cross involved as a consequence the death of his people to the world and to sin ; see chap. v. 24 ; vi. 14. It was like a blow at the root of a vine or a tree, which would affect every branch and tendril or like a blow at

the head which affects every member of the body. (c) Paul felt *identified* with the Lord Jesus; and he was willing to share in all the ignominy and contempt which was connected with the idea of the crucifixion. He was willing to regard himself as one with the Redeemer. If there was disgrace attached to the manner in which he died, he was willing to share it with him. He regarded it as a matter to be greatly desired to be made *just like Christ* in all things, and even in the manner of his death. This idea he has more fully expressed in Phil. iii. 10, " That I may know him, [*i. e.* I desire earnestly to know him,] and the power of his resurrection, and the fellowship of his sufferings, *being made conformable unto his death;*" see also Col. i. 24; comp. 1 Pet. iv. 13. ¶ *Nevertheless I live.* This expression is added, as in ver. 19, to prevent the possibility of mistake. Paul, though he was crucified with Christ, did not wish to be understood that he felt himself to be *dead*. He was not inactive; not insensible, as the dead are, to the appeals which are made from God, or to the great objects which ought to interest an immortal mind. Ho was still actively employed, and the more so from the fact that he was crucified with Christ. The object of all such expressions as this is, to show that it was no design of the gospel to make men inactive, or to annihilate their energies. It was not to cause men to do nothing. It was not to paralyse their powers, or stifle their own efforts. Paul, therefore, says, " I am not dead. I am truly alive ; and I live a better life than I did before." Paul was *as* active after conversion as he was before. Before, he was engaged in persecution ; now, he devoted his great talents with as much energy, and with as untiring zeal, to the cause of the great Redeemer. Indeed the whole narrative would lead us to suppose that he was *more* active and zealous *after* his conversion than he was before. The effect of religion is not to make one dead in regard to the putting forth of the energies of the soul. True religion never made one

lazy man ; it has converted many a man of indolence, and effeminacy, and self-indulgence to a man actively engaged in doing good. If a professor of religion is *less* active in the service of God than he was in the service of the world ; less laborious, and zealous, and ardent than he was before his supposed conversion, he ought to set it down as full proof that he is an utter stranger to true religion. ¶ *Yet not I.* This is also designed to prevent misapprehension. In the previous clause he had said that he lived, or was actively engaged. But lest this should be misunderstood, and it should be inferred that he meant to say it was by his own energy or powers, he guards it, and says it was not at all from himself. It was by no native tendency ; no power of his own ; nothing that could be traced to himself. He assumed no credit for any zeal which he had shown in the true life. He was disposed to trace it all to another. He had ample proof in his past experience that there was no tendency in himself to a life of true religion, and he therefore traced it all to another. ¶ *Christ liveth in me.* Christ was the *source* of all the life that he had. Of course this cannot be taken literally that Christ had a residence in the apostle, but it must mean that his grace resided in him ; that his principles actuated him ; and that he derived all his energy, and zeal, and life from his grace. The union between the Lord Jesus and the disciple was so close that it might be said the one lived in the other. So the juices of the vine are in each branch, and leaf, and tendril, and live in them and animate them ; the vital energy of the brain is in each delicate nerve—no matter how small—that is found in any part of the human frame. Christ was in him as it were the vital principle. All his life and energy were derived from him. ¶ *And the life which I now live in the flesh.* As I now live on the earth surrounded by the cares and anxieties of this life, I carry the life-giving principles of my religion to all my duties and all my trials. ¶ *I live by the faith of the Son of God.* By confidence in the

21 I do not frustrate the grace of God : for if *a* righteousness *come* by the law, then Christ is dead in vain.

a He.7.11.

CHAPTER III.

O FOOLISH *b* Galatians, who *c* hath bewitched you, that

b Mat.7.26.   *c* chap.5.7.

Son of God, looking to him for strength, and trusting in his promises, and in his grace. *Who loved me, &c.* He felt under the highest obligation to him from the fact that he had loved him, and given himself to the death of the cross in his behalf. The conviction of obligation on this account Paul often expresses ; see Notes on Rom. vi. 8—11 ; Rom. viii. 35—39 ; 2 Cor. v. 15. There is no higher sense of obligation than that which is felt towards the Saviour ; and Paul felt himself bound, as we should, to live entirely to him who had redeemed him by his blood.

21. *I do not frustrate the grace of God.* The word rendered "frustrate" (ἀθετῶ) means properly to displace, abrogate, abolish ; then to make void, to render null ; Mark vii. 9 ; Luke vii. 30 ; 1 Cor. i. 19. The phrase " the grace of God," here refers to the favour of God manifested in the plan of salvation by the gospel, and is another name for the gospel. The sense is, that Paul would not take any measures or pursue any course that would render that vain or inefficacious. Neither by his own life, by a course of conduct which would show that it had no influence over the heart and conduct, nor by the observance of Jewish rites and customs, would he do any thing to render that inefficacious. The design is to show that he regarded it as a great principle that the gospel was efficacious in renewing and saving man, and he would do nothing that would tend to prevent that impression on mankind. A life of sin, of open depravity and licentiousness, would do that. And in like manner a conformity to the rites of Moses as a ground of justification would tend to frustrate the grace of God, or to render the method of salvation solely by the Redeemer nugatory. This is to be regarded, therefore as at the same time a reproof of Peter for complying with customs which tended to frustrate the plan of

the gospel, and a declaration that he intended that his own course of life should be such as to confirm the plan, and show its efficacy in pardoning the sinner and rendering him alive in the service of God. ¶ *For if righteousness* come *by the law.* If justification can be secured by the observance of *any* law—ceremonial or moral—then there was no need of the death of Christ as an atonement. This is plain. If man by conformity to *any* law could be justified before God, what need was there of an atonement? The work would then have been wholly in his own power, and the merit would have been his. It follows from this, that man cannot be justified by his own morality, or. his alms-deeds, or his forms of religion, or his honesty and integrity. If he can, he needs no Saviour, he can save himself. It follows also that when men depend on their own amiableness, and morality, and good works, they would feel no need of a Saviour ; and this is the true reason why the mass of men reject the Lord Jesus. They suppose they do not deserve to be sent to hell. They have no deep sense of guilt. They confide in their own integrity, and feel that God *ought* to save them. Hence they feel no need of a Saviour ; for why should a man in health employ a physician ? And confiding in their own righteousness, they reject the grace of God, and despise the plan of justification through the Redeemer. To feel the need of a Saviour it is necessary to feel that we are lost and ruined sinners ; that we have no merit on which we can rely ; and that we are entirely dependent on the mercy of God for salvation. Thus feeling, we shall receive the salvation of the gospel with thankfulness and joy, and show that in regard to us Christ is not " dead in vain."

CHAPTER III.

ANALYSIS.

THE address of Paul to Peter, as I suppose, was closed at the last verse

ye should not obey the truth, before whose eyes Jesus Christ hath been evidently set forth, crucified among you?

---

of chapter ii. The apostle in this chapter, in a direct address to the Galatians, pursues the argument on the subject of justification by faith. In the previous chapters he had shown them fully that he had received his views of the gospel directly from the Lord Jesus, and that he had the concurrence of the most eminent among the apostles themselves. He proceeds to state more fully what his views were; to confirm them by the authority of the Old Testament; and to show the necessary effect of an observance of the laws of Moses on the great doctrine of justification by faith. This subject is pursued through this chapter and the following. This chapter comprises the following subjects.

(1.) A severe reproof of the Galatians for having been so easily seduced by the arts of cunning men from the simplicity of the gospel, ver. 1. He says that Christ had been plainly set forth crucified among them, and it was strange that they had so soon been led astray from the glorious doctrine of salvation by faith.

(2.) He appeals to them to show that the great benefits which *they* had received had not been in consequence of the observance of the Mosaic rites, but had come solely by the hearing of the gospel, ver. 2—5. Particularly the Holy Spirit, with all his miraculous and converting and sanctifying influences, had been imparted only in connection with the gospel. This was the most rich and most valuable endowment which they had ever received; and this was solely by the preaching of Christ and him crucified.

(3.) In illustration of the doctrine of justification by faith, and in proof of the truth of it, he refers to the case of Abraham, and shows that he was justified in this manner, and that the scripture had promised that others would be justified in the same way, ver. 6—9.

(4.) He shows that the law pronounced a curse on all those who were under it, and that consequently it was impossible to be justified by it. But Christ had redeemed us from that curse, having taken the curse on himself, so that now we might be justified in the sight of God. In this way, says he, the blessing of Abraham might come on the Gentiles, and they all might be saved in the same manner that he was, ver. 10—14.

(5.) This view he confirms by showing that the promise made to Abraham was made *before* the giving of the law. It was a mode of justification in existence *before* the law of Moses was given. It was of the nature of a solemn compact or covenant on the part of God. It referred particularly to the Messiah, and to the mode of justification in him. And as it was of the nature of a covenant, it was impossible that the law given many years after could disannul it, or render it void, ver. 15—18.

(6.) It might then be asked, what was the use of the law? Why was it given? It was *added*, Paul says, on account of transgressions, and was designed to restrain men from sin, and to show them their guilt. It was, further, not *superior* to the promise of a Mediator, or to the Mediator, for it was appointed by the instrumentality of *angels*, and it was in the hand of the Mediator himself, *under him*, and subject to him. It could not therefore be *superior* to him, and to the plan of justification through him, ver. 19, 20.

(7.) Yet Paul answers an important objection here, and a very obvious and material inquiry. It is, whether he means to teach that the law of God is contradictory to his promises? Whether the law and the gospel are rival systems? Whether it is necessary, in order to hold to the excellency of the one to hold that the other is contradictory, evil, and worthless? To all this he answers; and says, by no means. He says the fault was not in the law. The view which he had taken, and which was revealed in the Bible, arose from the nature of the case. The law was as good a law as could be made, and it answered all the purposes of law. It was *so* excellent, that if it had been possible that men could be justified by law at all, that was the law by which it would have been done. But it was not possible. The effect of the law, therefore, was to show that all men were sinners, and to shut them up to the plan of justification by the work of a Redeemer. It was appointed, therefore, not to justify men, but to lead them to the Saviour, ver. 21—24.

(8.) The effect of the plan of justification by faith in the Lord Jesus was to make the mind free. It was no longer under a schoolmaster. They who are justified in this way become the children of God. They all become one in the Redeemer. There is neither Jew nor Greek, but they constitute one great family, and are the children of Abraham, and heirs according to the promise, ver. 25—29.

1. *O foolish Galatians.* That is, foolish for having yielded to the influence of the false teachers, and for having embraced doctrines that tended to subvert the gospel of the Redeemer. The original word here used (ἀνόητοι) denotes void of understanding; and they had shown it in a remarkable manner in rejecting the doctrine of the apostles, and in embracing the errors into which they had fallen. It will be remembered that this is an expression similar to what was applied to them by others; see the Introduction, § I. Thus Callimachus in his hymns calls them " a foolish people," and Hillary, himself a Gaul, calls them *Gallos indociles,* expressions remarkably in accordance with that used here by Paul. It is implied that they were without stability of character. The particular thing to which Paul refers here is, that they were so easily led astray by the arguments of the false teachers. ¶ *Who hath bewitched you.* The word here used (ἐβάσκανε) properly means, to prate about any one ; and then to mislead by pretences, as if by magic arts ; to fascinate ; to influence by a charm. The idea here is, that they had not been led by *reason* and by *sober judgment,* but that there

must have been some charm or fascination to have taken them away in this manner from what they had embraced as true, and what they had the fullest evidence was true. Paul had sufficient confidence in them to believe that they had not embraced their present views under the unbiassed influence of judgment and reason, but that there must have been some fascination or charm by which it was done. It was in fact accomplished by the arts and the plausible pretences of those who came from among the Jews. ¶ *That ye should not obey the truth.* The truth of the gospel. That you should yield your minds to falsehood and error. It should be observed, however, that this phrase is wanting in many MSS. It is omitted in the Syriac version ; and many of the most important Greek and Latin Fathers omit it. Mill thinks it should be omitted ; and Griesbach has omitted it. It is not essential to the passage in order to the sense ; and it conveys no truth which is not elsewhere taught fully. It is apparently added to show what was the effect of their being bewitched or enchanted. ¶ *Before whose eyes.* In whose very presence. That is, it has been done so clearly that you may be said to have *seen* it. ¶ *Jesus Christ hath been evidently set forth.* By the preaching of the gospel. He has been so fully and plainly preached that you may be said to have seen him. The effect of his being preached in the manner in which it has been done, ought to have been as great as if you had seen him crucified before your eyes. The word rendered " hath been evidently set forth " (προεγράφη), means properly *to write before ;* and then to announce beforehand in writing; or *to announce by posting up on a tablet.* The meaning here is, probably, that Christ has been announced among them crucified, as if the doctrine was set forth in a public written tablet—*Robinson's Lex.* There was the utmost clearness and distinctness of view, so that they need not make any mistake in regard to him. The Syriac renders it, " Christ has been crucified before your eyes as if he had been represented by paint-

2 This only would I learn of you, Received [a] ye the Spirit by

a Ep.1.13.

the works of the law, or [b] by the hearing of faith?

b Rom.10.17.

ing." According to this, the idea is, that it was as plain as if there had been a representation of him by a picture. This has been done chiefly by preaching. I see no reason, however, to doubt that Paul means also to include the celebration of the Lord's supper, in which the Lord Jesus is so clearly exhibited as a crucified Saviour. ¶ *Crucified among you.* That is, represented among you *as* crucified. The words "among you," however, are wanting in many MSS. and obscure the sense. If they are to be retained, the meaning is, that the representations of the Lord Jesus as crucified had been as clear and impressive among them as if they had seen him with their own eyes. The *argument* is, that they had so clear a representation of the Lord Jesus, and of the design of his death, that it was strange that they had so soon been perverted from the belief of it. Had they *seen* the Saviour crucified; had they stood by the cross and witnessed his agony in death on account of sin, how could they doubt what was the design of his dying, and how could they be seduced from faith in his death, or be led to embrace any other method of justification? How could they *now* do it, when, although they had not *seen* him die, they had the fullest knowledge of the object for which he gave his precious life? The doctrine taught in this verse is, that a faithful exhibition of the sufferings and death of the Saviour *ought* to exert an influence over our minds and hearts *as if* we had seen him die ; and that they to whom such an exhibition has been made should avoid being led astray by the blandishments of false doctrines, and by the arts of man. Had we *seen* the Saviour expire, we could never have forgotten the scene. Let us endeavour to cherish a remembrance of his sufferings and death *as if* we had seen him die.

2. *This only would I learn of you.* I would ask this of you; retaining still the language of severe reproof. The

design here, and in the following verses, is, to *prove* to them that the views which they had at first embraced were correct, and that the views which they *now* cherished were false To show them this, he asks them the simple question, by what means they had obtained the exalted privileges which they enjoyed? Whether they had obtained them by the simple gospel, or whether by the observance of the law? The word "only" here ($\mu\acute{o}\nu o\nu$) implies that this was enough to settle the question. The argument to which he was about to appeal was *enough* for his purpose. He did not need to go any further. They had been converted, They had received the Holy Spirit. They had had abundant evidence of their acceptance with God, and the simple matter of inquiry now was, whether this had occurred as the regular effect of the gospel, or whether it had been by obeying the law of Moses? ¶ *Received ye the Spirit.* The Holy Spirit. He refers here, doubtless, to *all* the manifestations of the Spirit which had been made to them, in renewing the heart, in sanctifying the soul, in comforting them in affliction, and in his miraculous agency among them. The Holy Spirit had been conferred on them at their conversion (comp. Acts x. 44; xi. 17) and this was to them proof of the favour of God, and of their being accepted by him. ¶ *By the works of the law.* By obeying the law of Moses or of *any* law. It was in no way connected with their obeying the law. This must have been so clear to them that no one could have any doubt on the subject. The inestimably rich and precious gift of the Holy Spirit had *not* been conferred on them in consequence of their obeying the law. ¶ *Or by the hearing of faith.* In connection with hearing the gospel requiring faith as a condition of salvation. The Holy Spirit was sent down only in connection with the preaching of the gospel. It was a matter of truth, and which could not be denied,

3 Are ye so foolish? having *a* begun in the Spirit, are ye now
made perfect *b* by the flesh?

that those influences had not been imparted under the law, but had been connected with the gospel of the Redeemer; comp. Acts ii. The doctrine taught in this verse is, that the benefits resulting to Christians from the gift of the Holy Spirit are enough to prove that the gospel is from God, and therefore true. This was the case with regard to the miraculous endowments communicated in the early ages of the church by the Holy Spirit; for the miracles which were wrought, the knowledge of languages imparted, and the conversion of thousands from the error of their ways, proved that the system was from heaven; and it is true now. Every Christian has had ample proof, from the influences of the Spirit on his heart and around him, that the system which is attended with such benefits is from heaven. His own renewed heart; his elevated and sanctified affections; his exalted hopes; his consolations in trial; his peace in the prospect of death, and the happy influences of the system around him in the conversion of others, and in the intelligence, order, and purity of the community, are ample proof that the religion is true. Such effects do not come from any attempt to keep the law; they result from no other system. No system of infidelity produces them; no mere system of infidelity can produce them. It is only by that pure system which proclaims salvation by the grace of God; which announces salvation by the merits of the Lord Jesus, that such effects are produced. The Saviour promised the Holy Spirit to descend after his ascension to heaven to apply his work; and everywhere, under the faithful preaching of the simple gospel, that Spirit keeps up the evidence of the truth of the system by his influences on the hearts and lives of men.

3. *Are ye so foolish?* Can it be that you are so unwise? The idea is, that Paul hardly thought it credible that they could have pursued such a course. They had so cordially embraced the gospel when he preached to them, they had given such evidences that they were under its influence, that he regarded it as hardly possible that they should have so far abandoned it as to embrace such a system as they had done. ¶ *Having begun in the Spirit.* That is, when the gospel was first preached to them. They had commenced their professedly Christian life under the influence of the Holy Spirit, and with the pure and spiritual worship of God. They had known the power and spirituality of the glorious gospel. They had been renewed by the Spirit; sanctified in some measure by him; and had submitted themselves to the spiritual influences of the gospel. ¶ *Are ye now made perfect.* Tindal renders this, "ye would now end." The word here used (ἐπιτελέω) means properly, to bring through to an end, to finish; and the sense here has probably been expressed by Tindal. The idea of *perfecting,* in the sense in which we now use that word, is not implied in the original. It is that of finishing, ending, completing; and the sense is: "You began your Christian career under the elevated and spiritual influences of Christianity, a system so pure and so exalted above the carnal ordinances of the Jews. Having begun thus, can it be that you are *finishing* your Christian course, or carrying it on to completion by the observance of those ordinances, as if they were more pure and elevating than Christianity? Can it be that you regard them as *an advance* on the system of the gospel?" ¶ *By the flesh.* By the observance of the carnal rites of the Jews, for so the word here evidently means. This has not ever been an uncommon thing. Many have been professedly converted by the Spirit, and have soon fallen into the observance of mere rites and ceremonies, and depended mainly on them for salvation. Many *churches* have commenced their career in an elevated and spiritual manner, and have *ended* in the observance of mere forms. So

4 Have ye suffered so ¹ many things in vain? *a* if *it be* yet in vain.

5 He therefore that ministereth

1 or, *great.*   a 2 John 8.

b to you the Spirit, and worketh miracles among you, *doeth he it* by the works of the law, or by the hearing of faith?

b 2 Cor. 3. 8.

many Christians begin their course in a spiritual manner, and end it "in the flesh" in another sense. They soon conform to the world. They are brought under the influence of worldly appetites and propensities. They forget the spiritual nature of their religion; and they live for the indulgence of ease, and for the gratification of the senses. They build them houses, and they "plant vineyards," and they collect around them the instruments of music, and the bowl and the wine is in their feasts, and they surrender themselves to the luxury of living; and it seems as if they intended to *perfect* their Christianity by drawing around them as much of the world as possible. The beautiful simplicity of their early piety is gone. The blessedness of those moments when they lived by simple faith has fled. The times when they sought all their consolation in God are no more; and they now seem to differ from the world only in form. I dread to see a Christian inherit much wealth, or even to be thrown into very prosperous business. I see in it a temptation to build himself a splendid mansion, and to collect around him all that constitutes luxury among the people of the world. How natural for him to feel that if he has wealth like others, he should show it in a similar manner! And how easy for the most humble and spiritually-minded Christian, in the beginning of his Christian life, to become conformed to the world (such is the weakness of human nature in its best forms); and having begun in the spirit, to end in the flesh!

4. *Have ye suffered so many things in vain?* Paul reminds them of what they had endured on account of their attachment to Christianity. He assures them, that if the opinions on account of which they had suffered were false, then their sufferings had been in vain. They were of no use to them—for what advantage was it to

suffer for a false opinion? The opinions for which they had suffered had not been those which they now embraced. They were not those connected with the observance of the Jewish rites. They had suffered on account of their having embraced *the gospel,* the system of justification by a crucified Redeemer; and now, if those sentiments were wrong, why, their sufferings had been wholly in vain; see this argument pursued at much greater length in 1 Cor. xv. 18, 19, 29—32. *If it be yet in vain.* That is, I trust it is not in vain. I hope you have not so far abandoned the gospel, that all your sufferings in its behalf have been of no avail. I believe the system is true; and if true, and you are sincere Christians, it will not be in vain that you have suffered in its behalf, though you have gone astray. I trust, that although your principles have been shaken, yet they have not been wholly overthrown, and that you will not reap the reward of your having suffered so much on account of the gospel.

5. *He therefore that ministereth, &c.* This verse contains substantially a repetition of the argument in ver. 2. The argument is, that the gift of the Holy Spirit to them was not imparted in consequence of the observance of the law of Moses, but in connection with the preaching of the gospel. By the word "he" in this place, Clarke, Doddridge, Bloomfield, Chandler, Locke and many others, suppose that the apostle means himself. Bloomfield says, that it is the common opinion of "all the ancient commentators." But this seems to me a strange opinion. The obvious reference, it seems to me, is to God, who had furnished or imparted to them the remarkable influences of the Holy Spirit, and this had been done in connection with the preaching of the gospel, and not by the observance of the law. If, however, it refers to Paul, it means that

6 Even as Abraham *a* believed God, and it was[1] accounted to him for righteousness.

7 Know ye therefore, that they

a Ge.15.6.　　1 or, *imputed.*

he had been made the agent or instrument in imparting to them those remarkable endowments, and that this had been done by one who had not enforced the necessity of obeying the law of Moses, but who had preached to them the simple gospel.

6. *Even as Abraham believed God,* &c.; see this passage fully explained in the Notes on Rom. iv. 3. The passage is introduced here by the apostle to show that the most eminent of the patriarchs was not saved by the deeds of the law. He was saved by faith, and this fact showed that it was possible to be saved in that way, and that it was the design of God to save men in this manner. Abraham believed God, and was justified, *before* the law of Moses was given. It could not, therefore, be pretended that the law was *necessary* to justification ; for if it had been, Abraham could not have been saved. But if not necessary in his case, it was in no other ; and this instance demonstrated that the false teachers among the Galatians were wrong even according to the Old Testament.

7. *Know ye therefore,* &c. Learn from this case. It is an inference which follows, that all they who believe are the children of Abraham. ¶ *They which are of faith.* Who believe, and who are justified in this manner. ¶ *Are the children of Abraham.* Abraham was the "father of the faithful." The most remarkable trait in his character was his unwavering confidence in God. They who evinced the same trait, therefore, were worthy to be called his children. They would be justified in the same way, and in the same manner meet the approbation of God. It is *implied* here, that it was sufficient for salvation to have a character which would render it proper to say that we are the children of Abraham. If we are like him, if we evince the same spirit and character, we may be sure of salvation.

which are of faith, the same are the children *b* of Abraham.

8 And the Scripture, foreseeing that God would justify *c* the

b John 8.39; Ro.4.11—16.　　*c* ver.22.

8. *And the Scripture.* The word Scripture refers to the Old Testament; see Note, John v. 39. It is here personified, or spoken of as *foreseeing.* The idea is, that he by whom the scriptures were inspired, foresaw that. It is agreeable, the meaning is, to the account on the subject in the Old Testament. The Syriac renders this, " Since God foreknew that the Gentiles would be justified by faith, he before announced to Abraham, as the scripture saith, In thee shall all nations be blessed." ¶ *Foreseeing.* That is, this doctrine is contained in the Old Testament. It was foreseen and predicted that the heathen would be justified by faith, and not by the works of the law. ¶ That *God would justify the heathen.* Gr. The nations—τὰ ἔθνη—the Gentiles. The fact that the heathen, or the Gentiles would be admitted to the privileges of the true religion, and be interested in the benefits of the coming of the Messiah, is a fact which is everywhere abundantly predicted in the Old Testament. As an instance, see Isa. xlix. 6, 22, 23 ; lx. I do not know that it is anywhere distinctly foretold that the heathen would be justified by *faith,* nor does the argument of the apostle require us to believe this. He says that the scriptures, *i. e.* he who inspired the scriptures, *foresaw* that fact, and that the scriptures were written *as if* with the knowledge of that fact ; but it is not directly affirmed. The whole structure and frame of the Old Testament, however, proceeds on the supposition that it would be so; and this is all that the declaration of the apostle requires us to understand. ¶ *Preached before the gospel.* This translation does not convey quite the idea to us, which the language of Paul, in the original, would to the people to whom he addressed it. We have affixed a *technical sense* to the phrase " to preach the gospel." It is applied to the formal

heathen through faith, preached before the gospel unto Abraham, *saying,* [a] In thee shall all nations be blessed.

a Ge.12,3; 22.18; Ac.3.25.

and public annunciation of the truths of religion, especially the " good news" of a Saviour's birth, and of redemption by his blood. But we are not required by the language used here to suppose that this was done to Abraham, or that "the gospel" was preached to him in the sense in which we all now use that phrase. The expression, in Greek (προευηγγελίσατο), means merely, " the joyful news was announced beforehand to Abraham ;" *scil.* that in him should all the nations of the earth be blessed. It was *implied,* indeed, that it would be by the Messiah ; but the distinct point of the " good news " was not the " *gospel* " as we understand it, but it was that somehow through him all the nations of the earth would be made happy. Tindal has well translated it, " Showed beforehand glad tidings unto Abraham." This translation should have been adopted in our common version. ¶ *In thee shall all nations be blessed ;* see Notes on Acts iii. 25 ; Rom. iv. 13. All nations should be made happy in him, or through him. The sense is, that the Messiah was to be descended from him, and the religion of the Messiah, producing peace and salvation, was to be extended to all the nations of the earth ; see Gen. xii. 3; comp. Note on ver. 16 of this chapter.

[Εὐαγγελίζω doubtless here, as elsewhere, signifies to announce glad tidings. And in all the passages where this word occurs, even in those where the author might be disposed to allow that the "gospel technically" was meant, the translation which he proposes here would be very suitable and exact. It was certainly the same gospel that was preached to Abraham, that is now preached to us, *though not with the same fulness of revelation,* in his case. The apostle here affirms that the gospel, *i. e.,* the way of justification through Christ, in opposition to the legal system he had been condemning—was, *in few words,* preached to Abraham, being contained in that promise, " in thee shall all nations be blessed;" see Gen. xxii. 17. The full meaning of the promise, indeed, could not be gathered from

9 So then [b] they which be of faith are blessed with faithful Abraham.

10 For as many as are of the

b chap.4.28.

the words themselves, but Abraham must have understood their application in a far more extensive sense than that " somehow through him all the nations of the earth would be made happy." Whether the true import were made known to him directly by the Spirit of God, or discerned by him in typical representation, it is certain that Abraham's faith terminated on the promised Seed, *i. e.,* Christ whose day he desired to see, and seeing it afar, was glad, John viii. 56. " Hereof it followeth," says Luther on the place, " that the blessing and faith of Abraham is the same that ours is, that Abraham's Christ is our Christ, that Christ died as well for the sins of Abraham as for us."]

9, *So then they which be of faith.* They whose leading characteristic it is that they *believe.* This was the leading trait in the character of Abraham, and this is the leading thing required of those who embrace the gospel, and in the character of a true Christian. ¶ *Are blessed with faithful Abraham.* In the same manner they are interested in the promises made to him, and they will be treated as he was. They are justified in the same manner, and admitted to the same privileges on earth and in heaven.

10 *For as many as are of the works of the law.* As many as are seeking to be justified by yielding obedience to the law—whether the moral law, or the ceremonial law. The proposition is general ; and it is designed to show that, from the nature of the case, it is impossible to be justified by the works of the law, since, under all circumstances of obedience which we can render, we are still left with its heavy curse resting on us. ¶ *Are under the curse.* The curse which the law of God denounces. Having failed by all their efforts to yield perfect obedience, they must, of course, be exposed to the curse which the law denounces on the guilty. The word rendered curse (κατάρα) means, as with us, properly, *imprecation,* or *cursing.* It is used in the Scriptures particularly in the sense of the Hebrew

works of the law, are under the curse: for it is written, ^a Cursed *is* every one that continueth not in

a De.27.26.

אלה, malediction, or execration (Job xxxi. 30; Jer. xxix. 18; Dan. ix. 11); of the word מארה (Mal. ii. 2; Rev. iii. 33); and especially of the common Hebrew word קללה, a curse; Gen. xxvii. 12, 13; Deut. xi. 26, 28, 29; xxiii. 5; xxvii. 13, *et sæpe al.* It is here used evidently in the sen:e of devoting to punishment or destruction; and the idea is, that all who attempt to secure salvation by the works of the law, must be exposed to its penalty. It denounces a curse on all who do not yield entire obedience; and no partial compliance with its demands can save from the penalty. ¶ *For it is written.* The substance of these words is found in Deut. xxviii. 26: "Cursed be he that confirmeth not all the words of this law to do them." It is the solemn close of a series of maledictions, which Moses denounces in that chapter on the violators of the law. In this quotation, Paul has given the sense of the passage, but he has quoted literally neither from the Hebrew nor from the Septuagint. The *sense*, however, is retained. The word "cursed" here means, that the violator of the law shall be devoted to punishment or destruction. The phrase "that continueth not," in the Hebrew is "that confirmeth not"—that does not establish or confirm by his life. He would *confirm* it by *continuing* to obey it; and thus the sense in Paul and in Moses is substantially the same. The word "all" is not expressed in the Hebrew in Deuteronomy, but it is evidently implied, and has been inserted by the English translators. It is found, however, in six MSS. of Kennicott and De Rossi; in the Samaritan text; in the Septuagint; and in several of the Targums.—*Clarke.* ¶ *The book of the law.* That is, in the law. This phrase is not found in the passage in Deuteronomy. The expression there is, "the words of this law." Paul gives it a somewhat larger sense, and applies it to the whole of the law of God. The mean-

all things which are written in the book of the law to do them.

11 But that no man is justified

ing is, that the *whole* law must be obeyed, or man cannot be justified by it, or will be exposed to its penalty and its curse. This idea is expressed more fully by James (ii. 10); "Whosoever shall keep the whole law, and yet offend in one point, he is guilty of all;" that is, he is guilty of breaking the law *as a whole*, and must be held responsible for such violation. The sentiment here is one that is common to *all* law, and must be, from the nature of the case. The idea is, that a man who does not yield compliance to a whole law, is subject to its penalty, or to a curse. All law is sustained on this principle. A man who has been honest, and temperate, and industrious, and patriotic, if he commits a single act of murder, is subject to the curse of the law, and must meet the penalty. A man who has been honest and honourable in all his dealings, yet if he commit a single act of forgery, he must meet the curse denounced by the laws of his country, and bear the penalty. So, in all matters pertaining to law : no matter what the integrity of the man ; no matter how upright he has been, yet, for *the one offence* the law denounces a penalty, and he must bear it. It is out of the question for him to be justified by it. He cannot plead as a reason why he should not be condemned for the act of murder or forgery, that he has in all other respects obeyed the law, or even that he has been guilty of no such offences before. Such is the idea of Paul in the passage before us. It was clear to his view that man had not in all respects yielded obedience to the law of God. If he had not done this, it was impossible that he should be justified by the law, and he must bear its penalty.

11. *But that no man is justified,* &c. The argument which Paul has been pursuing he proceeds to confirm by an express declaration of the Bible. The argument is this : " It is impos-

by the law in the sight of God, *it is* evident : for, The *a* just shall live by faith.

12 And the law *b* is not of faith :

---

a Hab.2.4.　　　　b Rom.10.5,6.

---

sible that a man should be justified by the law, because God has appointed another way of justification." But there cannot be two ways of obtaining life, and as he has appointed *faith* as the condition on which men shall *live*, he has precluded from them the possibility of obtaining salvation in any other mode. ¶ *For, The just shall live by faith.* This is quoted from Hab. ii. 4. This passage is also quoted by Paul in Rom. i. 17 ; see it explained in the Note on that verse. The sense here is, that life is promised to man only in connection with faith. It is not by the works of the law that it is done. The condition of life is faith : and he lives who believes. The meaning is not, I apprehend, that the man who is justified by faith shall live, but that life is promised and exists only in connection with faith, and that the just or righteous man obtains it only in this way. Of course it cannot be obtained by the observance of the law, but must be by some other scheme.

12. *And the law is not of faith.* The law is not a matter of faith ; it does not relate to faith; it does not require faith ; it deals in other matters, and it pertains to another system than to faith. ¶ *But, The man, &c.* This is the language of the law, and this is what the law teaches. It does not make provision for faith, but it requires unwavering and perpetual obedience, if man would obtain life by it ; see this passage explained in the Notes on Rom. x. 5.

13. *Christ hath redeemed us.* The word used here (ἐξηγόρασεν) is not that which is usually employed in the New Testament to denote redemption. That word is λυτρόω. The difference between them mainly is, that the word used here more usually relates to *a purchase* of any kind; the other is used strictly with reference to *a ransom.* The word here used is more *general* in its meaning; the other is

but, The *c* man that doeth them shall live in them.

13 Christ *d* hath redeemed us from the curse of the law, being

---

c Le.18.5; Eze.20.11.　　d 2 Co.5.21; chap.4.5.

---

strictly appropriated to a ransom. This distinction is not observable here, however, and the word here used is employed in the proper sense of redeem. It occurs in the New Testament only in this place, and in chap. iv. 5 ; Eph. v. 16 ; Col. iv. 5. It properly means, to purchase, to buy up; and then to purchase any one, to redeem, to set free. Here it means, that Christ had purchased, or set us free from the curse of the law, by his being made a curse for us. On the meaning of the words redeem and ransom, see my Notes on Rom. iii. 25; Isa. xliii. 3 ; comp 2 Cor. v. 21. ¶ *From the curse of the law.* The curse which the law threatens, and which the execution of the law would inflict ; the punishment due to sin. This must mean, that he has rescued us from the consequences of transgression in the world of woe ; he has saved us from the punishment which our sins have deserved. The word, " us " here, must refer to *all* who are redeemed; that is, to the Gentiles as well as the Jews. The curse of the law is a curse which is due to sin, and cannot be regarded as applied particularly to any one class of men. All who violate the law of God, however that law may be made known, are exposed to its penalty. The word "law" here, relates to the law of God in general, to all the laws of God made known to man. The law of God denounced death as the wages of sin. It threatened punishment in the future world for ever. That would certainly have been inflicted, but for the coming and death of Christ. The world is lying by nature under this curse, and it is sweeping the race on to ruin. ¶ *Being made a curse for us.* This is an exceedingly important expression. Tindal renders it, " And was made a curse for us." The Greek word is κατάρα, the same word which is used in ver. 10 ; see Note on that verse. There is scarcely any

made a curse for us : for it is writ-
a De.21.23.
ten, ^a Cursed is every one that hangeth on a tree :

passage in the New Testament on which it is more important to have correct views than this ; and scarcely any one on which more erroneous opinions have been entertained. In regard to it, we may observe that it does not mean, (1.) That by being made a curse, his character or work were in any sense displeasing to God. He approved always of what the Lord Jesus did, and he regarded his whole character with love and approbation. The passage should never be so interpreted as to leave the impression that he was in any conceivable sense the object of the divine displeasure. (2.) He was not ill-deserving. He was not blame-worthy. He had done no wrong. He was holy, harmless, undefiled. No crime charged upon him was proved ; and there is no clearer doctrine in the Bible than that in all his character and work the Lord Jesus was perfectly holy and pure. (3.) He was not guilty in any proper sense of the word. The word guilty means, properly, to be bound to punishment for crime. It does not mean properly, to be exposed to suffering, but it always, when properly used, implies the notion of personal crime. I know that theologians have used the word in a somewhat different sense, but it is contrary to the common and just apprehensions of men. When we say that a man is guilty, we instinctively think of his having committed a crime, or having done something wrong. When a jury finds a man guilty, it implies that the man has committed a crime, and ought to be punished. But in this sense, and in no conceivable sense, where the word is properly used, was the Lord Jesus guilty. (4.) It cannot be meant that the Lord Jesus properly bore the penalty of the law. His sufferings were in the place of the penalty, not the penalty itself. They were a substitution for the penalty, and were, therefore, strictly and properly vicarious, and were not the identical sufferings which the sinner would himself have endured. There are some things

in the penalty of the law, which the Lord Jesus did not endure, and which a substitute or a vicarious victim could not endure. Remorse of conscience is a part of the inflicted penalty of the law, and will be a vital part of the sufferings of the sinner in hell—but the Lord Jesus did not endure that. Eternity of sufferings is an essential part of the penalty of the law—but the Lord Jesus did not suffer for ever. Thus there are numerous sorrows connected with the consciousness of personal guilt, which the Lord Jesus did not and cannot endure. (5.) He was not sinful, or a sinner, in any sense. He did not so take human guilt upon him, that the words sinful and sinner could with any propriety be applied to him. They are not applied to him any way in the Bible ; but the language there is undeviating. It is, that in all senses he was holy and undefiled. And yet language is often used on this subject which is horrible and but little short of blasphemy, as if he was guilty, and as if he was even the greatest sinner in the universe. I have heard language used which sent a thrill of horror to my heart ; and language may be found in the writings of those who hold the doctrine of imputation in the strictest sense, which is but little short of blasphemy. I have hesitated whether I should copy expressions here on this subject from one of the greatest and best of men,—I mean LUTHER,—to show the nature of the views which men sometimes entertain on the subject of the imputation of sin to Christ. But as Luther deliberately published them to the world in his favourite book, which he used to call his "Catharine de Bora," after the name of his wife ; and as similar views are sometimes entertained now ; and as it is important that such views should be held up to universal abhorrence,— no matter how respectable the source from which they emanate,—I will copy a few of his expressions on this subject. " And this, no doubt, all the prophets did foresee in spirit, that

Christ should become the greatest transgressor, murderer, adulterer, thief, rebel, and blasphemer, THAT EVER WAS OR COULD BE IN THE WORLD. For he being made a sacrifice for the sins of the whole world, is not now an innocent person and without sins ; is not now the Son of God, born of the Virgin Mary ; but a sinner which hath and carrieth the sin of Paul, who was a blasphemer, an oppressor, and a persecutor ; of Peter, which denied Christ ; of David, which was an adulterer, a murderer, and caused the Gentiles to blaspheme the name of the Lord ; and, briefly, which hath and beareth all the sins of all men in his body ; not that he himself committed them, but for that he received them, being committed or done of us, and laid them upon his own body, that he might make satisfaction for them with his own blood. Therefore, this general sentence of Moses comprehendeth him also (albeit in his own person he was innocent), because it found him amongst sinners and transgressors ; like as the magistrate taketh him for a thief, and punisheth him whom he findeth among other thieves and transgressors, though he never committed any thing worthy of death. When the law, therefore, found him among thieves it condemned and killed him as a thief." " If thou wilt deny him to be a sinner and accursed, deny, also, that he was crucified and dead." " But if it be not absurd to confess and believe that Christ was crucified between two thieves, then it is not absurd to say that he was accursed, and OF ALL SINNERS, THE GREATEST."* " God, our most merciful Father, sent his only Son into the world, and laid upon him all the sins of all men, saying, be thou Peter, that denier ; Paul, that persecutor, blasphemer, and cruel oppressor ; David, that adulterer ; that sinner which did eat the apple in paradise ; that thief which hanged upon the cross ; and, briefly, be thou the person which hath committed the sins of all men ; see, therefore, that thou pay and satisfy for them."—*Luther on the Galatians,* chap. iii. 13. [pp. 213 —215. Ed. Lond. 1838.] Luther was

* The underscoring is mine.

a great and holy man. He held, as firmly as any one can, to the personal holiness of the Redeemer. But this language shows how imperfect and erroneous views may warp the language of holy men ; and how those sentiments led him to use language which is little less than blasphemy. Indeed, we cannot doubt that if Luther had heard this very language used by one of the numerous enemies of the gospel in his time, as applicable to the Saviour, he would have poured out the full torrent of his burning wrath, and all the stern denunciations of his most impassioned eloquence, on the head of the scoffer and the blasphemer. It is singular, it is one of the remarkable facts in the history of mind, that a man with the New Testament before him, and accustomed to contemplate daily its language, could ever have allowed himself to use expressions like these of the holy and unspotted Saviour. But what *is* the meaning of the language of Paul, it will be asked, when he says that he was "made a curse for us?" In reply, I answer, that the meaning must be ascertained from the passage which Paul quotes in support of his assertion, that Christ was " made a curse for us." That passage is, " Cursed is every one that hangeth on a tree." This passage is found in Deut. xxi. 20. It occurs in a law respecting one who was hanged for a " sin worthy of death," ver. 22. The law was, that he should be buried the same day, and that the body should not remain suspended over the night, and it is added, as a reason for this, that " he that is hanged is accursed of God ;" or, as it is in the margin, " the curse of God." The meaning is, that when one was executed for crime in this manner, he was the object of the Divine displeasure and malediction. Regarded thus as an object accursed of God, there was a propriety that the man who was executed for crime should be *buried* as soon as possible, that the offensive object should be hidden from the view In quoting this passage, Paul leaves out the words " of God," and simply says, that the one who was hanged or a tree was held accursed. The sense of the passage before us is, therefore, that Jesus was subjected to what was regarded as an accursed death. *He was treated in his death* as if *he had been a criminal.* He was put to death in the same manner as he would have been if he had himself been guilty of the violation of the law. Had he been a thief or a murderer; had he committed the grossest and the blackest crimes, this would have been the punishment to which he would have been subjected. This was the mode of punishment adapted to those crimes, and he was treated *as if* all these had been committed by him. Or, in other words, had he been guilty of all these, or any of these, he could not have been treated in a more shameful and ignominious manner than he was ; nor could he have been subjected to a more cruel death. As has already been intimated, it does not mean that he was guilty, nor that he was not the object of the approbation and love of God, but that his death was the same that it would have been if he had been the vilest of malefactors, and that that death was regarded by the law as accursed. It was by such substituted sorrows that we are saved ; and he consented to die the most shameful and painful death, *as if* he were the vilest malefactor, in order that the most guilty and vile of the human race might be saved. In regard to the way in which his death is connected with our justification, see Note on chap. ii. 16. It may be observed, also, that the punishment of the cross was unknown to the Hebrews in the time of Moses, and that the passage in Deut. xxi. 23, did not refer originally to that. Nor is it known that hanging criminals alive was practised among the Hebrews. Those who were guilty of great crimes were first stoned or otherwise put to death, and then their bodies were suspended for a few hours on a gibbet. In many cases, however, merely the *head* was suspended after it had been severed from the body, Gen. xl. 17—19 ; Num. xxv. 4, 5. Crucifixion was not known in the time of the giving of the law ; but the Jews gave such an extent to the law in Deut. xxi. 23, as to include

this mode of punishment ; see John xix. 31, seq. The force of the argument here, as used by the apostle Paul, is, that if to be suspended on a gibbet after having been put to death, was regarded as a curse, it should not be regarded as a curse in a less degree to be suspended alive on a cross, and to be put to death in this manner. If this interpretation of the passage be correct, then it follows that this should never be used as implying, *in any sense*, that Christ was guilty, or that he was ill-deserving, or that he was an object of the divine displeasure, or that he poured out on him all his wrath. He was, throughout, an object of the divine love and approbation. God never loved him more, or approved what he did more, than when he gave himself to death on the cross. He had no hatred towards him ; he had no displeasure to express towards him. And it is this which makes the atonement so wonderful and so glorious. Had he been displeased with him ; had the Redeemer been properly an object of his wrath ; had he in any sense *deserved* those sorrows, there would have been no merit in his sufferings ; there would have been no atonement. What merit can there be when one suffers only what he deserves ? But what made the atonement so wonderful, so glorious, so benevolent ; what made it *an atonement at all*, was, that innocence was treated as if it were guilt ; that the most pure, and holy, and benevolent, and lovely being on earth should *consent* to be treated, and should be treated by God and man, as if he were the most vile and ill-deserving. This is the mystery of the atonement ; this shows the wonders of the divine benevolence ; this is the nature of substituted sorrow ; and this lays the foundation for the offer of pardon, and for the hope of eternal salvation.

[The curse of the law is doubtless the sentence of condemnation it has pronounced against sinners. Christ being made a curse for us signifies, therefore, his appointment of God to endure the penalty denounced by the law, in our room. *He* intercepted the curse that must have fallen on us, and ruined us for ever. This quotation, and the original passage in Deuteronomy, certainly do intimate something like *wrath* or *displeasure* in the divine mind. Our author's criticism, here, seems to have but a slender foundation. He affirms, that though Moses in Deut. xxi. 23, speaks of the criminal that hung on a tree being "accursed of God," Paul leaves out "of God," thereby intimating "that Jesus was subjected to what was regarded (by man) as an accursed death." This criticism is employed to get rid of the idea that the Holy Jesus was the object of the divine malediction, and gives opportunity for affirming, what is indeed true, that never was Jesus regarded with greater complacency by his Father, than when he hung on the cross and died in the room of sinners. Yet some meaning must be attached to those scriptures which allege, or seem to allege, that the wrath of God was the bitterest ingredient in the Saviour's cup; see his complaints in the xxii. xl. lxix. and lxxx. Psalms. Nor can the agony in the garden, and the exclamation on the cross, be otherwise accounted for. Speaking of this last, an author of whom America has some reason to boast, says, In the language of the psalmist, God hid his face from him, that is, if I mistake not, withdrew from him wholly, those manifestations of supreme complacency in his character and conduct, which he had always before made. As this was in itself a most distressing testimony of the divine anger against sin, so it is naturally imagined, and I think, when we are informed that it pleased Jehovah to bruise him, directly declared in the scriptures, that this manifestation was accompanied by other disclosures of the anger of God against sin, and against him as the substitute of sinners."— *Dwight's sermon on the Priesthood of Christ.* It is not with very much reason or modesty therefore, that the commentator objects to the passage being understood as *in any sense* implying that God "poured out on Christ all his wrath;" such certainly was the fact. And the simple omission by Paul here of the words "of God" is too slender ground for the assertion, that that awful truth is not only not affirmed by him, but tacitly denied.

But this extraordinary criticism is by no means new. Luther thus speaks of it as an objection in his day, "that Paul omitted this word (of God) which is in Moses"—therefore they ask this question, how this sentence may be applied to Christ, that he is accursed of God, and hanged on a tree, seeing that he is no malefactor or thief, but righteous and holy? "This," says the reformer—and the language may be held as his reply to much that is said of him above—"this may peradventure move the simple and the ignorant, thinking that the Sophisters do speak it not only wittily, but also very godly, and thereby do defend the honour and glory of Christ, and give warning to all Christians to beware that they think not

so wickedly of Christ, that he should be made a curse."—*Luther's comment in loco.*

The passage certainly does intimate, if there be any meaning in language, that Christ, *as the substitute of sinners*, was accursed of God. "We cannot but consider his choosing to hang upon a tree, a situation declared by the ceremonial law to be accursed of God, as intended to demonstrate to the world, that although he himself continued in all things written in the law to do them, his death was not merely the infliction of human law upon an innocent man, but a suffering which in the sight of God was penal."—*Hill*, vol. ii. p. 117, 3d edit. Indeed all the objections and difficulties which Mr. Barnes has stated on this verse, would disappear, if the distinction in the above quotation, and carefully marked also by Luther, were duly attended to, viz., *that*, between Christ, viewed in his own person, and viewed as the substitute of sinners. By overlooking this distinction in such passages as that before us, we not only stumble at the doctrine of imputation, but play into the hands of the Socinians, and well nigh yield the fortress to them; it being just about as difficult to suppose that an innocent being can suffer for sin, as that sin should be imputed to him. "Many expositors," Mr. Scott has well observed, "who contend against the imputation of Christ's righteousness to believers, in disputing against Socinians argue for the vicarious sufferings of Christ in our stead. Now what is this but imputation? *He*, though perfectly holy, paid the debt which *we* sinners had contracted. It was exacted and he became answerable; we sinners, on believing, are made the righteousness of God in him, and receive the inheritance which *he* merited. This then is a reciprocal imputation."—*Comment in loco.* The objections which our author has again in this place urged against the doctrine of imputation, have already been considered, in previous supplementary Notes; see on 2 Cor. v. 21; Rom. iv. v. throughout. It is never supposed, for a moment, by the advocates of that doctrine, that Christ was personally guilty, or that he was guilty in any other sense than having sin charged on him, and being in consequence thereof under obligation to suffer the penalty.

A word now on Luther's language, which sends such a thrill of horror to the commentator's heart, although he knew all the while that the reformer was as zealous for the spotless purity of the Redeemer as himself. Luther was the great reviver of a forgotten, though vital, doctrine; a doctrine which he believed to be "articulus stantis vel cadentis ecclesiæ," viz. the doctrine of justification by faith, through the imputed righteousness of Christ. With this was inseparably connected the imputation of our sin to him. Considering the importance of this doctrine, and the almost

14 That *a* the blessing of Abraham might come on the Gentiles through Jesus Christ ; that we

a Ro.4.9,16.

might receive the promise *b* of the Spirit through faith.

15 Brethren, I speak after the

b Is.44.3; Eze.36.27; Joel 2.28,29.

universal neglect into which it had fallen, it is not to be wondered at, that Luther should express himself strongly on the subject, nor do those authors increase their claim on our confidence, who depart very far from the doctrine of the reformation on this subject. Luther's expressions may possibly be *too* strong, but might the same charge not be brought against the words of that apostle, who has ventured to affirm, not that Christ has been made a *sinner* but *sin* itself, in the very abstract, as if no force of language could be too much on such a subject; see 2 Cor. v. 21, supplementary Note, in which the common rendering of "sin-offering," by which this passage is weakened, is shown to be inadmissable. To the same effect, we are entitled to cite this very passage, notwithstanding every attempt to distort it, in which Paul not only says that Christ was accursed, but a curse, *καταρα* for *καταρατος*, as in the other place *'αμαρτια* for *'αμαρτωλος*. Moreover, the reader will find, if he choose to consult Luther's commentary, that he takes great care to affirm "that Christ is innocent as concerning his own person," so that mistake is impossible. It is worthy of notice, too, that the reason why he has introduced such names as thief, malefactor, &c., is that such were the parties who were hanged on a tree under the law, and the "Sophisters" had asked how this sentence could be applied to Christ, who was no thief or malefactor? He resolves it by a reference to the doctrine of imputation, and affirms that Christ "sustained the person" or stood in the room of such. Nor does our author do great justice to the reformer in his second and third quotation. Immediately before the sentence beginning "if thou wilt deny," &c., Luther has, "But some man will say it is very absurd and slanderous to call the Son of God accursed sinner;" and to this the sentence quoted is an answer—an answer to the very objection in the commentary, and therefore ought in justice to have been placed in that light, when it affirms no more than that the fact of Christ being crucified and dead, necessarily implied that sin was charged to his account, otherwise, under the administration of a just God, these things never could have happened to him. The same remarks apply to the third quotation, which is but part of one and the same sentence with the second, and the reader has only to consult the commentary of Luther to be satisfied on the point.]

14. *That the blessing of Abraham.* The blessing which Abraham enjoyed, to wit, that of being justified by faith.

¶ *Might come on the Gentiles.* As well as on the Jews. Abraham was blessed in this manner *before* he was circumcised (Rom. iv. 11), and the same blessing might be imparted to others also who were not circumcised; see this argument illustrated in the Notes on Rom. iv. 10—12. ¶ *Through Jesus Christ.* Since he has been made a curse for all, and since he had no exclusive reference to the Jews or to any other class of men, all may come and partake alike of the benefits of his salvation. ¶ *That we might receive the promise of the Spirit.* That all we who are Christian converts. The promise of the Spirit, or the promised Spirit, is here put for all the blessings connected with the Christian religion. It includes evidently the miraculous agency of the Holy Spirit ; and all his influences in renewing the heart, in sanctifying the soul, and in comforting the people of God. These influences had been obtained in virtue of the sufferings and death of the Lord Jesus in the place of sinners, and these influences were the sum of all the blessings promised by the prophets.

15. *Brethren, I speak after the manner of men.* I draw an illustration from what actually occurs among men. The illustration is, that when a contract or agreement is made by men involving obligations and promises, no one can add to it or take from it. It will remain as it was originally made. So with God. He made a solemn promise to Abraham. That promise pertained to his posterity. The blessing was connected with that promise, and it was of the nature of a compact with Abraham. But if so, then this could not be effected by the law which was four hundred years after, and the law must have been given to secure some different object from that designed by the promise made to Abraham, ver. 19. But the promise made to Abraham was designed to secure the "in-

manner of men ; Though *it be* but a man's [1] covenant, yet *if it be*

1 *testament.*

confirmed, no man **disannulleth**, or addeth thereto.

---

heritance," or the favour of God ; and if so, then the same thing could not be secured by the observance of the law, since there could not be two ways so unlike each other of obtaining the same thing. God cannot have two ways of justifying and saving men ; and if he revealed a mode to Abraham, and that mode was by faith, then it could not be by the observance of the law which was given so long after. The main design of the argument and the illustration here (ver. 15, seq.) is to show that the promise made to Abraham was by no means made void by the giving of the law. The law had another design, which did not interfere with the promise made to Abraham. That stood on its own merits, irrespective of the demands and the design of the law. It is possible, as Rosenmüller suggests, that Paul may have had his eye on an objection to his view. The objection may have been that there were important acts of legislation which succeeded the promise made to Abraham, and that that promise must have been superseded by the giving of the law. To this he replies that the Mosaic law given at a late period could not take away or nullify a solemn promise made to Abraham, but that it was intended for a different object. ¶ *Though it be but a man's covenant.* A compact or agreement between man and man. Even in such a case no one can add to it or take from it. The *argument* here is, that such a covenant or agreement must be much less important than a promise made by God. But even that could not be annulled. How much less, therefore, could a covenant made by God be treated as if it were vain. The word covenant here (διαθήκη) is in the margin rendered " Testament ;" *i. e.* will. So Tindal renders it. Its proper classical signification is will or testament, though in the Septuagint and in the New Testament it is the word which is used to denote a covenant or compact; see Note, Acts iii. 25. Here it is

used in the proper sense of the word covenant, or compact ; a mutual agreement between man and man. The idea is, that where such a covenant exists ; where the faith of a man is solemnly pledged in this manner, no change can be made in the agreement. It is ratified, and firm, and final. ¶ *If it be confirmed.* By a seal or otherwise. ¶ *No man disannulleth,* &c. It must stand. No one can change it. No new conditions can be annexed ; nor can there be any drawing back from its terms. It binds the parties to a faithful fulfilment of all the conditions. This is well understood among men ; and the apostle says that the same thing must take place in regard to God.

16. *Now to Abraham and his seed.* To him and his posterity. ¶ *Were the promises made.* The promise here referred to was that which is recorded in Gen. xxii. 17, 18. " In blessing I will bless thee, and in multiplying I will multiply thy seed as the stars of heaven, and as the sand which is upon the sea-shore ; and in thy seed shall all the nations of the earth be blessed." ¶ *He saith not, And to seeds, as of many, but as of one,* &c. He does not use the plural term, as if the promise extended to many persons, but he speaks in the singular number, as if but one was intended ; and that one must be the Messiah. Such is Paul's interpretation ; such is evidently the sentiment which he intends to convey, and the argument which he intends to urge. He designs evidently to be understood as affirming that in the use of the *singular* number σπέρμα (seed), instead of the plural σπέρματα (seeds), there is a fair ground of argument to demonstrate that the promise related to Christ or the Messiah, and to him primarily if not exclusively. Now no one ever probably read this passage without feeling a difficulty, and without asking himself whether this argument is sound, and is worthy a man of candour, and especially of an inspired man. Some of the difficulties in the

16 Now to Abraham *a* and his seed were the promises made. He

a Ge.12.3,7; 17.7.

saith not, And to seeds, as of many; but as of one, And to thy seed which is Christ.

passage are these. (1.) The promise referred to in Genesis seems to have related to the posterity of Abraham at large, without *any* particular reference to an individual. It is to his seed ; his descendants ; to all his seed or posterity. Such would be the fair and natural interpretation should it be read by hundreds or thousands of persons who had never heard of the interpretation here put upon it by Paul. (2.) The argument of the apostle seems to proceed on the supposition that the word "seed" (σπέρμα), *i. e.* posterity, here cannot refer to more than one person. If it had, says he, it would be in the plural number. But the fact is, that the word *is* often used to denote posterity at large ; to refer to descendants without limitation, just as the word posterity is with us ; and it is a fact, moreover, that the word is not used in the plural at all to denote a posterity, the singular form being constantly employed for that purpose. Any one who will open Tromm's Concordance to the Septuagint, or Schmids' on the New Testament, will see the most ample confirmation of this remark. Indeed the *plural* form of the word is never used except in this place in Galatians. The difficulty, therefore, is, that the remark here of Paul appears to be a *trick* of argument, or a *quibble* more worthy of a trifling Jewish Rabbi, than of a grave reasoner or an inspired man. I have stated this difficulty freely, just as I suppose it has struck hundreds of minds, because I do not wish to shrink from any real difficulty in examining the Bible, but to see whether it can be fairly met. In meeting it, expositors have resorted to various explanations, most of them, as it seems to me, unsatisfactory, and it is not necessary to detail them. Bishop Burnet, Doddridge, and some others suppose that the apostle means to say that the promises made to Abraham were *not only* appropriated to one class of his descendants, that is, to those by Isaac, but that they cen-

tred in *one illustrious* person, through whom all the rest are made partakers of the blessings of the Abrahamic covenant. This Doddridge admits the apostle says in " *bad Greek,*" but still he supposes that this is the true exposition. Noessett and Rosenmüller suppose that by the word σπέρμα (*seed*) here, is not meant the Messiah, but Christians in general ; the body of believers. But this is evidently in contradiction of the apostle, who expressly affirms that Christ was intended. It is also liable to another objection that is fatal to the opinion. The very point of the argument of the apostle is, that the singular and not the plural form of the word is used, and that therefore an *individual*, and not a *collective body* or a number of individuals, is intended. But according to this interpretation the reference *is*, in fact, to a numerous body of individuals, to the whole body of Christians. Jerome affirms that the apostle made use of a false argument, which, although it might appear well enough to the stupid Galatians, would not be approved by wise or learned men. —*Chandler.* Borger endeavours to show that this was in accordance with the mode of speaking and writing among the Hebrews, and especially that the Jewish Rabbis were accustomed to draw an argument like this from *the singular number*, and that the Hebrew word (זרע) *seed* is often used by them in this manner ; see his remarks as quoted by Bloomfield *in loc.* But the objection to this is, that though this might be common, yet it is not the less a quibble on the word, for certainly the very puerile reasoning of the Jewish Rabbis is no good authority on which to vindicate the authority of an apostle. Locke and Clarke suppose that this refers to Christ as the spiritual head of the mystical body, and to all believers in him. Le Clerc supposes that it is an allegorical kind of argument, that was fitted to convince the Jews only, who were accustomed to this kind of reasoning. I do not know but this solution may be satisfactory to many minds, and that it is capable of vindication, since it is not easy to say how far it is proper to make use of methods of argument used by an adversary in order to convince them. The *argumentum ad hominem* is certainly allowable to a certain extent, when designed to show the legitimate tendency of the principles advanced by an opponent. But here there is no evidence that Paul was reasoning with an adversary. He was showing the Galatians, not the Jews, what was the truth, and justice to the character of the apostle requires us to suppose that he would make use of only such arguments as are in accordance with the eternal principles of truth, and such as may be seen to be true in all countries and at all times. The question then is, whether the argument of the apostle here drawn from the use of the singular word *σπέρμα* (*seed*), is one that can be seen to be sound? or is it a mere quibble, as Jerome and Le Clerc suppose? or is it to be left to be *presumed* to have had a force which we cannot now trace? for *this* is possible. Socrates and Plato may have used arguments of a subtile nature, based on some nice distinctions of words which were perfectly sound, but which we, from our necessary ignorance of the delicate shades of meaning in the language, cannot now understand. Perhaps the following remarks may show that there is *real* force and propriety in the position which the apostle takes here. If not, then I confess my inability to explain the passage. (1.) There can be no reasonable objection to the opinion that the promise originally made to Abraham *included* the Messiah, and the promised blessings were to descend through him. This is so often affirmed in the New Testament, that to deny it would be to deny the repeated declarations of the sacred writers, and to make war on the whole structure of the Bible; see particularly Rom. iv.; comp. John viii. 56. If this general principle be admitted, it will remove much perplexity from the controversy. (2.) The pro-

mise made to Abraham (Gen. xxii 18), "and in thy seed (בזרעך, Sept. ἐν τῷ σπέρματί σου, where the words both in Heb. and in Gr. are in the singular number) shall all the nations of the earth be blessed," cannot refer to *all* the seed or the posterity of Abraham taken collectively. He had two sons, Isaac by Rebecca, and Ishmael by Hagar, besides numerous descendants by Keturah; Gen. xxv. 1, seq. Through a large part of these no particular blessings descended on the human family, and there is no sense in which all the families of the earth are particularly blessed in them. On any supposition, therefore, there must have been *some* limitation of the promise; or the word "seed" was intended to include only *some* portion of his descendants, whether a particular branch or an individual, does not yet appear. It must have referred to *a part* only of the posterity of Abraham, but to what part is to be learned only by subsequent revelations. (3.) It was the *intention* of God to confine the blessing to one branch of the family, to *Isaac* and his descendants. The *peculiar* promised blessing was to be through him, and not through the family of Ishmael. This intention is often expressed, Gen. xvii. 19—21; xxi. 12; xxv. 11; comp. Rom. ix. 7; Heb. xi. 18. Thus the original promise of a blessing through the posterity of Abraham became somewhat *narrowed down*, so as to show that there was to be a limitation of the promise to a particular portion of his posterity. (4.) If the promise had referred to the two branches of the family; if it had been intended to include Ishmael as well as Isaac, then some term would have been used that would have expressed this. So unlike were Isaac and Ishmael; so different in the circumstances of their birth and their future life; so dissimilar were the prophecies respecting them, that it might be said that their descendants were two races of men; and in scripture the race of Ishmael ceased to be spoken of as the descendants or the posterity of Abraham. There was a sense in which the posterity of Isaac was regarded as the seed or posterity of Abraham in which the descendants of Ishmael were not ; and the term σπίρμα or " seed " therefore properly designated the posterity of Isaac. It might be said, then, that the promise " to thy seed " did not refer to the *two* races, as if he had said σπίρματα, " seeds," but to *one* (σπίρμα), " the seed " of Abraham, by way of eminence. (5.) This promise was subsequently *narrowed down* still more, so as to include only one portion of the descendants of Isaac. Thus it was limited to the posterity of *Jacob*, Esau being excluded ; subsequently the peculiar blessing was promised to the family of *Judah*, one of the twelve sons of Jacob (Gen. xlix. 10) ; in subsequent times it was still further narrowed down or limited to the family of Jesse ; then to that of David ; then to that of Solomon, until it terminated in the Messiah. The original intention of the promise was that there *should be* a limitation, and that limitation was made from age to age, until it terminated in the Messiah, the Lord Jesus Christ. By being thus narrowed down from age to age, and limited by successive revelations, it was shown that the Messiah was eminently intended,—which is what Paul says here. The promise was indeed at first general, and the term used was of the most general nature ; but it was shown from time to time that God *intended* that it should be applied only to one branch or portion of the family of Abraham ; and that limitation was finally so made as to terminate in the Messiah. This I take to be the meaning of this very difficult passage of scripture ; and though it may not be thought that *all* the perplexities are removed by these remarks, yet I trust they will be seen to be so far removed as that it will appear that there is real force in the argument of the apostle, and that it is not a mere trick of argument, or a quibble unworthy of him as an apostle and a man.

[Whatever may be thought of this solution of the difficulty, the author has certainly given more than due prominence to the objections that are supposed to lie against the apostle's argument. Whatever license a writer in the American Biblical Repository, or such like

work, might take, it certainly is not wise in a commentary intended for Sabbath Schools to affirm, that the great difficulty of the passage is "that the remark here of Paul appears to be a trick of argument, or a quibble more worthy of a trifling Jewish Rabbi than of a grave reasoner and an inspired man," and then to exhibit such a formidable array of objection, and behind it a defence comparatively feeble, accompanied with the acknowledgment that if that be not sufficient the author can do no more ! These objections, moreover, are not only stated "fairly" but strongly, and something more than strongly ; so that while in the end the authority of the apostle is apparently vindicated, the effect is such, that the reader, unaccustomed to such treatment of inspired men, is tempted to exclaim, "non tali auxilio, nec defensoribus istis, tempus eget." Indeed we are surprised that, with Bloomfield and Borger before him, the author should ever have made some of the assertions which are set down under this text. As to objection *first*, it does not matter what interpretation hundreds and thousands of persons would naturally put on the passage in Genesis, since the authority of an inspired apostle must be allowed to settle its meaning against them all. The *second* objection affirms, that "the word σπιρμα is not used in the plural at all to denote a posterity," on which Bloomfield thus remarks, "it has been denied that the word ירﬠ is ever used in the plural, except to denote the seeds of vegetables. And the same assertion has been made respecting σπιρμα. But the former position merely extends to the Old Testament, which only contains a fragment and small part of the Hebrew language. So that it cannot be proved that ירﬠ was *never* used in the *plural* to denote *sons, races.* As to the latter assertion it is unfounded ; for though σπιρμα is used in the singular as a noun of multitude, to denote several children, yet it is sometimes used in the plural to signify several sons of the same family ; as in Soph. Œd. Col. 599, γῆς ἐμῆς ἀπηλάθην Προς τῶν ἐμαυτοῦ σπιρμάτων."
The elaborate Latin Note of Borger, part of which is quoted in Bloomfield, will give complete satisfaction to the student who may wish thoroughly to examine this place. He maintains, 1st. That though the argument of the apostle may not be founded exactly on the use of the singular number, yet the absurdity of his application of the passage in Genesis to the Messiah, would have been obvious if, instead of the singular the plural had been used, "si non σπιρματος sed σπιρματων mentio fuisset facta;" from which he justly concludes, that at all events "numerum cum hac explicatione non pugnare." 2nd. The word ירﬠ is in certain places understood of one man only (de uno homine) and therefore may be so here. 3rd. The apostle, arguing with Jews, employs an argu-

17 And this I say, *That* the covenant that was confirmed before of God in Christ, the law which *a*

a Ex.12.40,41.

ment to which they were accustomed to attach importance; for they laid great stress on the respective use of the singular and plural number; which argument, indeed, would be liable to the objections stated against it by Mr. Barnes, if the thing to be proven rested entirely on this ground, and had not, besides, its foundation in the actual truth of the case. If the singular number in this place *really had that force attached to it* which the apostle declares, and if the Jews were influenced in other matters by arguments of this kind, it was certainly both lawful and wise to reason with them after their own fashion. 4th. What is still more to the point, the Jewish writers themselves frequently use the word ערז, *not only of one man,* but especially of the *Messiah,* "non tantum *de uno homine,* sed imprimis etiam de *Messia eanmoere* solent."

On the whole, the objections against the reasoning on this passage, are raised in defiance of apostolical interpretation. But, as has been well observed, "the apostle, to say nothing of his inspiration, might be supposed to be better qualified to decide on a point of this kind, than any modern philologist."— *Bloomfield in loco.*

17. *The covenant which was confirmed before of God.* By God, in his promise to Abraham. It was confirmed *before* the giving of the law. The confirmation was the solemn promise which God made to him. ¶ *In Christ.* With respect to the Messiah, a covenant relating to him, and which promised that he should descend from Abraham. The word "in," in the phrase "in Christ," does not quite express the meaning of the Greek εἰς Χριστόν. That means rather "*unto* Christ;" or *unto* the Messiah; that is, the covenant had respect to him. This is a common signification of the preposition εἰς. ¶ *The law.* The law given by God to Moses on mount Sinai. ¶ *Which was four hundred and thirty years after.* In regard to the difficulties which have been felt respecting the chronology referred to here; see the Note on Acts vii. 6. The exact time here referred to was probably when Abraham was called, and when the promise was first made to him. Assuming that as the time referred to, it is not difficult to make

was four hundred and thirty years after, cannot disannul, that it should make the promise of none effect.

out the period of four hundred and thirty years. That promise was made when Abraham was seventy-five years old; Gen. xii. 3, 4. From that time to the birth of Isaac, when Abraham was a hundred years old, was twenty-five years; Gen. xxi. 5. Isaac was sixty when Jacob was born; Gen. xxv. 26. Jacob went into Egypt when he was one hundred and thirty years old; Gen. xlvii. 9. And the Israelites sojourned there, according to the Septuagint (Ex. xii. 40), two hundred and fifteen years, which completes the number; see Doddridge, Whitby, and Bloomfield. This was doubtless the common computation in the time of Paul; and as his argument did not depend at all on the *exactness* of the reckoning, he took the estimate which was in common use, without pausing or embarrassing himself by an inquiry whether it was strictly accurate or not. His argument was the same, whether the law was given four hundred and thirty years after the promise, or only two hundred years. The argument is, that a law given *after* the solemn promise which had been made and confirmed, could not make that promise void. It would still be binding according to the original intention; and the law must have been given for some purpose entirely different from that of the promise. No one can doubt the soundness of this argument. The promise to Abraham was of the nature of a compact. But no law given by one of the parties to a treaty or compact can disannul it. Two nations make a treaty of peace, involving solemn promises, pledges, and obligations. No *law* made afterwards by one of the nations can disannul or change that treaty. Two men make a contract with solemn pledges and promises. No act of *one* of the parties can change that, or alter the conditions. So it was with the covenant between God and Abraham. God made to him solemn promises which *could* not be affected by

18 For if *a* the inheritance *be* of the law, *it is* no more of promise : but God gave *it* to Abraham by promise.

19 Wherefore then *serveth* the

a Rom.4.14.   *b* Ro.5.20.   *c* ver.16.

law? *b* It was added because of transgressions, till the seed *c* should come to whom the promise was made; *and it was* ordained by angels *d* in the hand *e* of a Mediator.

d Ac.7.53; He.2.2.   *e* Ex.20.19—22; De. 5.22—31.

a future giving of a law. God would feel himself to be under the most solemn obligation to fulfil *all* the promises which he had made to him.

18. *For if the inheritance.* The inheritance promised to Abraham. The sum of the promise was, that "he should be the heir of the world;" see Rom. iv. 13, and the Note on that verse. To that heirship or inheritance Paul refers here, and says that it was an essential part of it that it was to be in virtue of the promise made to him, and not by fulfilling the law. ¶ *Be of the law.* If it be by observing the law of Moses; or if it come in any way by the fulfilling of law. This is plain. Yet the Jews contended that the blessings of justification and salvation were to be in virtue of the observance of the law of Moses. But if so, says Paul, then it could not be by the promise made to Abraham, since there could not be two ways of obtaining the same blessing. ¶ *But God gave* it *to Abraham by promise.* That, says Paul, is a settled point. It is perfectly clear ; and that is to be held as an indisputable fact, that the blessing was given to Abraham by a promise. That promise was confirmed and ratified hundreds of years before the law was given, and the giving of the law could not affect it. But that promise was, that he would be the ancestor of the Messiah, and that in him all the nations of the earth should be blessed. Of course, if they were to be blessed in this way, then it was not to be by the observance of the law, and the law must have been given for a different purpose. What that was, he states in the following verses.

19. *Wherefore then* serveth *the law?* This is obviously an objection which might be urged to the reasoning which the apostle had pursued. It was very obvious to ask, if the principles which he had laid down were

correct, of what use was the law? Why was it given at all? Why were there so many wonderful exhibitions of the Divine power at its promulgation? Why were there so many commendations of it in the Scriptures? And why were there so many injunctions to obey it? Are all these to be regarded as nothing; and is the law to be esteemed as worthless? To all this, the apostle replies that the law was not useless, but that it was given by God for great and important purposes, and especially for purposes closely connected with the fulfilment of the promise made to Abraham and the work of the Mediator. ¶ *It was added* (προσετίθη). It was *appended* to all the previous institutions and promises. It was an *additional* arrangement on the part of God for great and important purposes. It was an arrangement *subsequent* to the giving of the promise, and was intended to secure important advantages until the superior arrangement under the Messiah should be introduced, and was with reference to that. ¶ *Because of transgressions.* On account of transgressions, or with reference to them. The meaning is, that the law was given to show the true nature of transgressions, or to show what was sin. It was not to reveal a way of justification, but it was to disclose the true nature of sin ; to deter men from committing it ; to declare its penalty ; to convince men of it, and thus to be " ancillary" to, and preparatory to the work of redemption through the Redeemer. This is the true account of the law of God as given to apostate man, and this use of the law still exists. This effect of the law is accomplished, (1.) By showing us what God requires, and what is duty. It is the straight rule of what is right; and to depart from that is the measure of wrong. (2.) It shows us the nature and extent of transgression by showing us how far we have departed from it. (3.) It shows what is the just penalty of transgression, and is thus fitted to reveal its true nature. (4.) It is fitted to produce *conviction* for sin, and thus shows how evil and bitter a thing transgression is; see Notes on Rom. iv. 15; vii. 7—11. (5.) It thus shows its own inability to justify and save men, and is a preparatory arrangement to lead men to the cross of the Redeemer; see Note on ver. 24. At the same time, (6.) The law was given with reference to transgressions in order to keep men from transgression. It was designed to restrain and control them by its denunciations, and by the fear of its threatened penalties. When Paul says that the law was given on account of transgressions, we are not to suppose that this was the *sole* use of the law; but that this was a main or leading purpose. It may accomplish many other important purposes (*Calvin*), but this is one leading design. And this design it still accomplishes. It shows men their duty. It reminds them of their guilt. It teaches them how far they have wandered from God. It reveals to them the penalty of disobedience. It shows them that justification by the law is impossible, and that there *must be* some other way by which men must be saved. And since these advantages are derived from it, it is of importance that that law should be still proclaimed, and that its high demands and its penalties should be constantly held up to the view of men. ¶ *Till the seed should come*, &c. The Messiah, to whom the promise particularly applied; see ver. 16. It is not implied here that the law would be of no use *after* that, but that it would accomplish important purposes *before* that. A large portion of the laws of Moses would then indeed cease to be binding. They were given to accomplish important purposes among the Jews until the Messiah should come, and then they would give way to the more important institutions of the gospel. But the moral law would continue to accomplish valuable objects *after* his

advent, in showing men the nature of transgression and leading them to the cross of Christ. The essential idea of Paul here is, that the whole arrangement of the Mosaic economy, including all his laws, was with reference to the Messiah. It was a part of a great and glorious whole. It was not an independent thing. It did not stand by itself. It was incomplete and in many respects unintelligible until he came—as one part of a tally is unmeaning and useless until the other is found. In itself it did not justify or save men, but it served to introduce a system by which they could be saved. It contained no provisions for justifying men, but it was in the design of God an essential part of a system by which they could be saved. It was not a whole in itself, but it was a part of a glorious whole, and led to the completion and fulfilment of the entire scheme by which the race could be justified and brought to heaven. ¶ And it was *ordained by angels*. That is, the law was ordained by angels. The word ordained here ($\delta\iota\alpha\tau\alpha\gamma\epsilon\iota\varsigma$) usually means to arrange; to dispose in order; and is commonly used with reference to the marshalling of an army. In regard to the sentiment here that the law was ordained by angels, see the Note on Acts vii. 53. The Old Testament makes no mention of the presence of angels at the giving of the law, but it was a common opinion among the Jews that the law was given by the instrumentality of angels, and arranged by them; and Paul speaks in accordance with this opinion; comp. Heb. ii. 2. The sentiment here is that the law was prescribed, ordered, or arranged by the instrumentality of the angels; an opinion, certainly, which none can prove *not* to be true. In itself considered, there is no more absurdity in the opinion that the law of God should be given by the agency of angels, than there is that it should be done by the instrumentality of man. In the Septuagint (Deut. xxxiii. 2) there is an allusion of the same kind. The Hebrew is, "From his right hand went a fiery law for them." The LXX. render this, "His angels with him on his right-hand;" comp. Joseph. Ant. xv. 5, 3. That angels were present at the giving of the law is more than implied, it is believed, in two passages of the Old Testament. The one is that which is referred to above, and a part of which the translators of the Septuagint expressly apply to angels; Deut. xxxiii. 2. The Hebrew is, " JEHOVAH came from Sinai, and rose up from Seir unto them; he shined forth from mount Paron, and he came [literally] with ten thousands of holiness;" that is, with his holy ten thousands, or with his holy myriads (קדש מרבבת). By the holy myriads here mentioned what can be meant but *the angels?* The word "holy" in the Scriptures is not given to storms and winds and tempests; and the natural interpretation is, that he was attended with vast hosts of intelligent beings. The same sentiment is found in Ps. lxviii. 17: " The chariots of God are myriads, thousands repeated; the Lord is in the midst of them, as in Sinai, as in his sanctuary." Does not this evidently imply that when he gave the law on Mount Sinai he was surrounded by a multitude of angels? see Stuart on the Hebrews, Excursus viii. pp. 565—567. It may be added, that in the fact itself there is no improbability. What is more natural than to suppose that when the law of God was promulgated in such a solemn manner on mount Sinai *to a world,* that the angels should be present? If any occasion on earth has ever occurred where their presence was allowable and proper, assuredly that was one. And yet the Scriptures abound with assurances that the angels are interested in human affairs, and that they have had an important agency in the concerns of man. ¶ *In the hand.* That is, under the direction, or control of. To be in the hand of one is to be under his control; and the idea is, that while this was done by the ordering of the angels or by their disposition, it was under the control of a Mediator Rosenmüller, however, and others suppose that this means simply *by* (*per*); that is, that it was done by the instrumentality of a Mediator. But it seems to me to

imply more than this; that the Mediator here referred to had some jurisdiction or control over the law thus given; or that it was subject to him, or with reference to him. The interpretation however will be affected by the view which is taken of the meaning of the word Mediator. ¶ *Of a Mediator.* The word Mediator (Μεσίτης;) means properly one who intervenes between two parties, either as an interpreter or *internuncius,* or as an intercessor or reconciler. In the New Testament, in all the places where it occurs, unless the passage before us be an exception, it is applied to the Lord Jesus, the great Mediator between God and man; 1 Tim. ii. 5; Heb. viii. 6; ix. 15; xii. 24. There has been some difference of opinion as to the reference of the word here. Rosenmüller, Grotius, Doddridge, Bloomfield, Robinson (*Lex.*), Chandler, and many others suppose that it refers to Moses. Calvin and many others suppose that the reference is to Christ. The common sentiment among expositors undoubtedly is, that the reference is to Moses; and it is by no means easy to show that that is not the correct opinion. But to me it seems that there are reasons why it should be regarded as having reference to the great Mediator between God and man. Some of the reasons which incline me to this opinion are, (1.) That the name Mediator is not, so far as I know, applied to Moses elsewhere in the Scriptures. (2.) The name is appropriated to the Lord Jesus. This is certainly the case in the New Testament, unless the passage before us be an exception; and the name is not found in the Old Testament. (3.) It is difficult to see the pertinency of the remark here, or the bearing on the argument, on the supposition that it refers to Moses. How would it affect the drift and purport of the apostle's reasoning? How would it bear on the case? But on the supposition that it refers to the Lord Jesus, that would be a material fact in the argument. It would show that the law was subordinate to the Messiah, and was with reference to him. It was not only subservient by

20 Now a mediator is not a *mediator* of one, but God [a] is
one.

a De.6.4.

being ordained by angels, but as being under the Mediator, and with reference to him until he, the "promised seed," should come. (4.) It is only by such an interpretation that the following "vexed" verse can be understood. If that be applied to Moses, I see not that *any* sense can be affixed to it that shall be pertinent or intelligible. These reasons may not appear satisfactory to others ; and I admit they are not as clear as would be desirable that reasons should be in the exposition of the Bible, but they may be allowed perhaps to have *some* weight. If they *are* of weight, then the sentiment of the passage is, that the law was wholly subordinate, and could not make the promise of no effect. For, (1.) It was given hundreds of years after the promise. (2.) It was under the direction of angels, who must themselves be inferior to, and subordinate to the Messiah, the Mediator between God and man. If given by their agency and instrumentality, however important it might be, it could not interfere with a direct promise made by God himself, but must be subordinate to that promise. (3.) It was under the Mediator, the promised Messiah. It was in his hand, and subject to him. It was a part of the great plan which was contemplated in the promise, and was tributary to that, and must be so regarded. It was not an independent scheme ; not a thing that stood by itself ; but a scheme subordinate and tributary, and wholly under the control of the Mediator, and a part of the plan of redemption, and of course to be modified or abrogated just as that plan should require, and to be regarded as wholly tributary to it. This view will accord certainly with the argument of Paul, and with his design in showing that the law could by no means, and in no way, interfere with the promise made to Abraham, but must be regarded as wholly subordinate to the plan of redemption.

20. *Now a mediator is not a media-tor of one, &c.* This verse has given great perplexity to commentators. "There is, unquestionably," says Bloomfield, "no passage in the New Testament that has so much, and to so little purpose, exercised the learning and ingenuity of commentators as the present, which seems to defy all attempts to elicit any satisfactory sense, except by methods so violent as to be almost the same thing as writing the passage afresh." In regard, however, to the truth of the declarations here—that "a mediator is not a mediator of one," and that " God is one " —there can be no doubt, and no difficulty. The very idea of a mediator supposes that there are two parties or persons between whom the mediator comes either to reconcile them or to bear some message from the one to the other ; and it is abundantly affirmed also in the Old Testament that there is but one God ; see Deut. vi. 4. But the difficulty is, to see the pertinency or the bearing of the remark on the argument of the apostle. What does he intend to illustrate by the declaration ? and how do the truths which he states, illustrate the point before him ? It is not consistent with the design of these Notes to detail the numerous opinions which have been entertained of the passage. They may be found in the larger commentaries, and particularly may be seen in Koppe, Excursus vii. on the Galatians. After referring to a number of works on the passage, Rosenmüller adopts the following interpretation, proposed by Noessett, as expressing the true sense. But he (*i. e.* Moses) is not a mediator of one race (to wit, the Abrahamic), but God is the same God of them and of the Gentiles. The sense according to this is, that Moses had not reference in his office as mediator or as *internuncius* to the descendants of Abraham, or to that *one seed* or race, referred to in the promise. He added the hard conditions of the law ; required its stern and severe observances ; his institutions pertained to the Jews mainly. They indeed might obtain the favour of

God, but by compliance with the severe laws which he had ordained. But to the *one seed*, the whole posterity of Abraham, they concerning whom the promise was made, the Gentiles as well as the Jews, he had no reference in his institutions : all their favours, therefore, must depend on the fulfilment of the *promise* made to Abraham. But God is one and the same in reference to all. His promise pertains to all. He is the common God to the Jews and the Gentiles. There is great difficulty in embracing this view of the passage, but it is not necessary for me to state the difficulty or to attempt to show that the view here proposed cannot be defended. Whitby has expressed substantially the same interpretation of this passage. " But this mediator (namely, Moses) was only the mediator of the Jews, and so was only the mediator of one party, to whom belonged the blessing of Abraham, ver. 8, 14. But God, who made the promise, ' That in one should all the families of the earth be blessed,' is one ; the God of the other party, the Gentiles as well as the Jews, and so as ready to justify the one as the other." According to this interpretation, the sense is, that Moses was mediator of *one part* of Abraham's seed, the Israelites ; but was not the mediator of the *other part* of that seed, the Gentiles; yet there was the same God to both parties, who was equally ready to justify both. Locke has expressed a view of the passage which differs somewhat from this, but which has quite as much plausibility. According to his exposition it means, that God was but one of the parties to the promise. The Jews and the Gentiles made up the promise. But at the giving of the law Moses was a mediator only between God and *the Israelites*, and, therefore, could not transact any thing which would tend to the disannulling of the promise which was between God and *the Jews and Gentiles together*, the other party to the promise. Or in other words, at the covenant made on mount Sinai, there was really present but one of the parties, and consequently nothing could be

done that would affect the other. Moses did not appear in behalf of the Gentiles. They had no representative there. He was engaged only for the Jews, for *a part* only of the one party, and that part could not transact any thing for the whole. The giving of the law, therefore, could not affect the promise which was made to Abraham, and which related to the Jews and the Gentiles as together constituting one party. This view is plausible. It has been adopted by Doddridge, and perhaps *may* be the true interpretation. No one can deny, however, that it is forced, and that it is far from being obvious. It seems to be *making a meaning* for the apostle, or furnishing him with an argument, rather than *explaining* the one which he has chosen to use ; and it may be doubted whether Paul would have used an argument that *required* so much explanation as this before it could be understood. All these expositions proceed on the supposition that the word "mediator" here refers to Moses, and that the transaction here referred to was that on mount Sinai. I would suggest a sense of the passage which I have found in none of the commentaries which I have consulted, and which I would, therefore, propose with diffidence. All that I can claim for it is, that it *may* possibly be the meaning. According to the view which I shall submit, the *words* here are to be regarded as used in their usual signification ; and the simplest interpretation possible is to be given to the propositions in the verse. One proposition is, that a mediator is not appointed with reference to one party, but to two. This proposition is universal. Wherever there is a mediator there are *always* two parties. The other proposition is, that God is one ; that is, that he is *the same one God*, in whatever form his will may be made known to men, whether by a promise as to Abraham, or by the law as to Moses. The interpretation which I would propose embraces the following particulars (1.) The *design* of the apostle is, to show that the giving of the law could not abrogate or affect the promise made to Abraham ; and to show at the same time what *is* its true object. It could not *annul* the promises, says Paul. It was given long after, and could not affect them, ver. 17. It was an *addition*, an *appendage*, a subsequent enactment for a specific purpose, yet a part of the same general plan, and subordinate to the Mediator, ver. 19. It was to be shown also that the law was not *against* the promises of God. It was a good law (ver. 21); and was not designed to be an *opposing* system, or intended to *counteract* the promise, or the scheme of salvation *by* promise, but was a part of the *same* great plan. (2.) A mediator *always* supposes two parties. In *all* the transactions, therefore, where a mediator is employed, there is supposed to be two parties. When, therefore, the promise was made to Abraham with reference to the Messiah, the great Mediator; and when the law was given in the hand of the Mediator, and under his control, there is *always* supposed to be two parties. (3.) The *whole* arrangement here referred to is under the Mediator, and with reference to him. The promise made to Abraham had reference to him and to those who should believe on him; and the law given by Moses was also under him, and with reference to him. He was the grand object and agent of all. He was the Mediator with reference to both. Each transaction had reference to him, though in different ways; the transaction with Abraham relating to him in connection with a promise; the transaction at the giving of the law being under his control *as* Mediator, and being a part of the one great plan. There was an *identity* of plan; and the plan had reference to the Messiah, the great Mediator. (4.) God is one and the same. He is throughout one of the parties; *and he does not change.* However the arrangements may vary, whether in giving the law or imparting a promise, he is the same. There is but one God in all the transaction; and he, throughout, constitutes one of the parties. The other party is man, at first receiving the promise from this one God with reference to the Media-

ator through Abraham, and then receiving the law through the same Mediator on mount Sinai. He is still the one party unchanged; and there is the same Mediator; implying all along that there are two parties. (5.) It follows, therefore, agreeably to the argument of the apostle, that the law given so long after the promise, could not abrogate it, because they pertained to the same plan, were under the same one God, who was one unchanging party in all this transaction, and had reference to the same Mediator and were alike under his control. It followed, also, that the law was temporary (ver. 19); *interposed* for important purposes until the "seed should come," because it was a part of the same general arrangement, and was under the control of the same Mediator, and directed by the same one God, the unchanging one party in all these transactions. It followed, further, that the one could not be against the other (ver. 21), because they were a part of the same plan, under the control of the same Mediator, and where the same God remained unchanged as the one party. All that is assumed in this interpretation is, (*a*) That there was but *one* plan or arrangement; or that the transaction with Abraham and with Moses were parts of one great scheme; and, (*b*) That the Mediator here referred to was not Moses, but the Messiah, the Son of God. The following paraphrase will express the sense which I have endeavoured to convey. "The giving of the law could not annul or abrogate the promise made to Abraham. It was long after that, and it was itself subservient to that. It was given by the instrumentality of angels, and it was entirely under the control of the Mediator, the Messiah. The plan was one; and all the parts of it, in the promise made to Abraham and in the giving of the law, were subordinate to him. A mediator always supposes two parties, and the reference to the Mediator, alike in the promise to Abraham and in the giving of the law, supposes that there *were* two parties. God is one party, the same unchanging God in all the forms

21 *Is* the law then against *a* the promises of God? God forbid: for if *b* there had been a law given which could have given life, verily

a Mat.5.17.   b chap.2.21.

righteousness should have been by the law.

22 But the Scripture hath concluded all *c* under sin, that the

c Ro.4.11,12,16.

of the promise and of the law. In this state of things, it is impossible that the law should clash with the promise, or that it should supersede or modify it. It was *a part* of the one great plan; appointed with reference to the work which the Mediator came to do; and in accordance with the promise made to Abraham; and therefore they could not be contradictory and inconsistent." It is assumed in all this that the Messiah was contemplated in the whole arrangement, and that it was entered into with reference to him. That this *may* be assumed no one can deny who believes the scriptures. The whole arrangement in the Old Testament, it is supposed, was designed to be ancillary to redemption; and the interpretation which has been submitted above is based on that supposition.

21. Is *the law then against the promises of God?* Is the law of Moses to be regarded as opposed to the promises made to Abraham? Does this follow from any view which can be taken of the subject? The object of the apostle in asking this question is, evidently, to take an opportunity to deny in the most positive manner that there can be any such clashing or contradiction. He shows, therefore, what was the design of the law, and declares that the object was to further the plan contemplated in the promise made to Abraham. It was an auxiliary to that. It was as good as a law could be; and it was designed to prepare the way for the fulfilment of the promise made to Abraham. ¶ *God forbid.* It cannot be. It is impossible. I do not hold such an opinion. Such a sentiment by no means follows from what has been advanced; comp. Note, Rom. iii. 4. ¶ *For if there had been a law given which could have given life.* The law of Moses is as good as a law can be. It is pure, and holy, and good. It is not the design to insinuate any thing against the law

in itself, or to say that as a law it is defective. But law *could not* give life. It is not its nature; and man cannot be justified by obedience to it. No man ever has yielded perfect compliance with it, and no man, therefore, can be justified by it; comp Notes on chap. ii. 16; iii. 10. ¶ *Verily righteousness should have been by the law.* Or justification would have been secured by the law. The law of Moses was as well adapted to this as a law could be. No better law could have been originated for this purpose, and if men were to *attempt* to justify themselves before God by their own works, the law of Moses would be *as* favourable for such an undertaking as any law which could be revealed. It is as reasonable, and equal, and pure. Its demands are as just, and its terms as favourable as could be any of the terms of mere law. And *such* a law has been given in part in order to show that justification by the law is out of the question. If men could not be justified by a law so pure, and equal, and just; so reasonable in all its requirements and so perfect, how could they expect to be justified by conformity to any *inferior* or *less perfect* rule of life? The fact, therefore, that no one can be justified by the pure law revealed on mount Sinai, for ever settles the question about the possibility of being justified by law.

22. *But the Scripture.* The Old Testament (Note, John v. 39), containing the law of Moses. ¶ *Hath concluded all under sin.* Has *shut up* (συνέκλεισεν) all under the condemnation of sin; that is, has declared all men, no matter what their rank and external character, to be sinners. Of course, they cannot be justified by that law which declares them to be guilty, and which condemns them, any more than the law of the land will acquit a murderer, and pronounce him innocent, at the same time that it holds him to be guilty. In regard to

promise ^a by faith of Jesus Christ might be given to them that believe.

23 But before faith came, we

a Ro.3.9,19,23.

the meaning of the expression here used; see Note on Rom. xi. 32; comp. Rom. iii. 9, 19. *That the promise by faith of Jesus Christ, &c.* That the promise referred to in the transaction with Abraham, the promise of justification and life by faith in the Messiah. Here we see *one* design of the law. It was to show that they could not be justified by their own works, to *hedge up their way* in regard to justification by their own righteousness, and to show them their need of a better righteousness. The law accomplishes the same end now. It shows men that they are guilty, and it does it in order that they may be brought under the influence of the pure system of the gospel, and become interested in the promises which are connected with eternal salvation. 23. *But before faith came.* That is, the system of salvation by faith in the Lord Jesus. Faith here denotes the Christian religion, because faith is its distinguishing characteristic. ¶ *We were kept under the law.* We, who were sinners; we, who have violated the law. It is a general truth, that before the gospel was introduced, men were under the condemning sentence of the law ¶ *Shut up unto the faith.* Enclosed by the law with reference to the full and glorious revelation of a system of salvation by faith. The design and tendency of the law was to shut us up to that as the only method of salvation. All other means failed. The law condemned every other mode, and the law condemned all who attempted to be justified in any other way. Man, therefore, was shut up to that as his last hope; and could look only to that for any possible prospect of salvation. The word which in this verse is rendered "were kept" (ἐφρουρούμεθα), usually means to guard or watch, as in a castle, or as prisoners are guarded; and though the word should not be pressed too far in the interpretation,

were kept under the law, shut up unto the faith which should afterwards be revealed.

24 Wherefore the law ^b was our

b Col.2.17 ; He.9.9,10.

yet it implies that there was *a rigid scrutiny* observed; that the law guarded them; that there was no way of escape; and that they were shut up, as prisoners under sentence of death, to the only hope, which was that of *pardon.* ¶ *Unto the faith, &c.* That was the only hope. The law condemned them, and offered no hope of escape. Their only hope was in that system which was to be revealed through the Messiah, the system which extended forgiveness on the ground of faith in his atoning blood.

24. *Wherefore the law was our schoolmaster.* The word rendered *schoolmaster* (παιδαγωγὸς, whence the word *pedagogue*), referred originally to a slave or freedman, to whose care boys were committed, and who accompanied them to the public schools. The idea here is not that of *instructor*, but there is reference to the office and duty of the *pædagogus* among the ancients. The office was usually intrusted to slaves or freedmen. It is true, that when the *pædagogus* was properly qualified, he assisted the children committed to his care in preparing their lessons. But still his main duty was not *instruction*, but it was to watch over the boys; to restrain them from evil and temptation; and to conduct them to the schools, where they might receive instruction. See, for illustrations of this, Wetstein, Bloomfield, &c. In the passage before us, the proper notion of *pedagogue* is retained. In our sense of the word *schoolmaster*, Christ is the schoolmaster, and not the law. The law performs the office of the ancient pedagogue, to *lead us to* the teacher or the instructor. That teacher or instructor is Christ. The ways in which the law does this may be the following:—(1.) It *restrains* us and rebukes us, and keeps us as the ancient pedagogue did his boys. (2.) The whole law was designed to be introductory to Christ. The sacrifices and

schoolmaster *to bring us* unto Christ, that we might be justified by faith.

25 But after that faith is come, we are no longer under a schoolmaster.

a John 1.12; 1 John 3.1,2.

26 For ye are all the children *a* of God by faith in Christ Jesus.

27 For *b* as many of you as have been baptized into Christ, have put on Christ.

28 There is *c* neither Jew nor

b Ro.6.3.   c Col.3.11.

offerings were designed to shadow forth the Messiah, and to introduce him to the world. (3.) The moral law—the law of God—shows men their sin and danger, and thus leads them to the Saviour. It condemns them, and thus prepares them to welcome the offer of pardon through a Redeemer. (4.) It *still* does this. The whole economy of the Jews was designed to do this; and under the preaching of the gospel it is still done. Men see that they are condemned; they are convinced by the law that they cannot save themselves, and thus they are led to the Redeemer. The effect of the preached gospel is to show men their sins, and thus to be preparatory to the embracing of the offer of pardon. Hence the importance of preaching the law still; and hence it is needful that men should be made to feel that they are sinners, in order that they may be prepared to embrace the offers of mercy; comp. Note on Rom. x. 4.

25. *But after that faith is come.* The scheme of salvation by faith. After that is revealed; see Note on ver. 23. ¶ *We are no longer under a schoolmaster.* Under the *pædagogus*, or pedagogue. We are not kept in restraint, and under bondage, and led along *to* another to receive instruction. We are directly under the great Teacher, the Instructor himself; and have a kind of freedom which we were not allowed before. The bondage and servitude have passed away; and we are free from the burdensome ceremonies and expensive rites (comp. Note on Acts xv. 10) of the Jewish law, and from the sense of condemnation which it imposes. This was true of the converts from Judaism to Christianity—that they became free from the burdensome rites of the law; and it is true of all converts to the faith of Christ, that, having been made to see their sin by the law, and

having been conducted by it to the cross of the Redeemer, they are now made free.

26. *For ye are all the children of God,* &c. All who bear the Christian name—the converts from among the Jews and Gentiles alike; see Note on John i. 12. The idea here is, that they are no longer under tutors and governors; they are no longer subject to the direction and will of the *pædagogus;* they are arrived *at age,* and are admitted to the privileges of sons; see Note on chap. iv. 1. The language here is derived from the fact, that until the son arrived at age, he was in many respects not different from a servant. He was under laws and restraints; and subject to the will of another. When of age, he entered on the privileges of heirship, and was free to act for himself. Thus, under the law, men were under restraints, and subject to heavy exactions. Under the gospel, they are free, and admitted to the privileges of the sons of God.

27. *For as many of you.* Whether by nature Jews or Gentiles. ¶ *As have been baptized into Christ.* Or unto (εἰς—the same preposition which in ver. 24 is rendered *unto*) Christ. That is, they were baptized *with reference* to him, or receiving him as the Saviour; see this explained in the Note on Rom. vi. 3. ¶ *Have put on Christ.* That is, they have put on his sentiments, opinions, characteristic traits, &c., as a man clothes himself. This language was common among the ancient writers; see it explained in the Note on Rom. xiii. 14.

28. *There is neither Jew nor Greek.* All are on a level; all are saved in the same way; all are entitled to the same privileges. There is no favouritism on account of birth, beauty, or blood All confess that they are sinners; all are saved by the merits of the same Saviour; all are admitted to

Greek, there is neither bond nor free, there is neither male nor fe- | male : for ye are all one in Christ Jesus.

the same privileges as children of God. The word "Greek" here is used to denote the Gentiles generally; since the whole world was divided by the Jews into "Jews and Greeks"— the Greeks being the foreign nation best known to them. The Syriac renders it here "*Aramean*,"—using the word to denote the Gentiles generally. The meaning is, that whatever was the birth, or rank, or nation, or colour, or complexion, all under the gospel were on a level. They were admitted to the same privileges, and endowed with the same hopes of eternal life. This does not mean that all the civil distinctions among men are to be disregarded. It does not mean that no respect is to be shown to those in office, or to men in elevated rank. It does not mean that all are on a level in regard to talents, comforts, or wealth; but it means *only* that all men are on a level *in regard to religion*. This is the sole point under discussion; and the interpretation should be limited to this. It is not a fact that men are on a level in all things, nor is it a fact that the gospel designs to break down all the distinctions of society. Paul means to teach that no man has any preference or advantage in the kingdom of God because he is a rich man, or because he is of elevated rank; no one is under any disadvantage because he is poor, or because he is ignorant, or a slave. All at the foot of the cross are sinners; all at the communion table are saved by the same grace; all who enter into heaven, will enter clothed in the same robes of salvation, and arranged, not as princes and nobles, and rich men and poor men, in separate orders and ranks, but mingling together as redeemed by the same blood, and arranged in ranks according to their eminence in holiness; comp. my Notes on Isa. lvi. 8. ¶ *There is neither bond nor free.* The condition of a free man does not give him any peculiar claims or advantages in regard to religion; and the condition of a slave does not ex-

clude him from the hope of heaven, or from being regarded as a child of God, on the same terms, and entitled to the same privileges as his master. In regard to religion, they are on the same level. They are alike sinners, and are alike saved by grace. They sit down at the same communion table; and they look forward to the same heaven. Christianity does not admit the one to favour because he is free, or exclude the other because he is a slave. Nor, when they are admitted to favour, does it give the one a right to lord it over the other, or to feel that he is of any more value in the eye of the Redeemer, or any nearer to his heart. The essential idea is, that they are on a level, and that they are admitted to the favour of God without respect to their external condition in society. I do not see any evidence in *this* passage that the Christian religion designed to abolish slavery, any more than I do in the following phrase, "there is neither male nor female," that it was intended to abolish the distinction of the sexes; nor do I see in this passage any evidence that there should not be proper respect shown by the servant to his master, though both of them are Christians, any more than there is in the following phrase, that suitable respect should not be shown in the intercourse with the sexes; comp. 1 Tim. vi. 1—6. But the proof is explicit, that masters and slaves may alike become Christians on the same terms, and are, in regard to their religious privileges and hopes, on a level. No peculiar favour is shown to the one, in the matter of salvation, because he is free, nor is the other excluded because he is a slave. And from this it follows :—(1.) That they should sit down to the same communion table. There should be no invidious and odious distinctions there. (2.) They should be regarded alike as Christian brethren in the house of God, and should be addressed and treated accordingly. (3.) The slave should excite the interest, and receive the watchful care of the pastor, as well as his master. Indeed, he may need it more; and from his ignorance, and the fewness of his opportunities, it may be proper that special attention should be bestowed on him. In regard to this doctrine of Christianity, that there is neither "bond nor free" among those who are saved, or that all are on a level in regard to salvation, we may remark further, (1.) That it is peculiar to Christianity. All other systems of religion and philosophy *make* different ranks, and endeavour to promote the distinctions of *caste* among men. They teach that certain men are the favourites of heaven, in virtue of their birth or their rank in life, or that they have peculiar facilities for salvation. Thus, in India the Brahmin is regarded as, by his birth, the favourite of heaven, and all others are supposed to be of a degraded rank. The great effort of men, in their systems of religion and philosophy, has been to show that there are favoured ranks and classes, and to make permanent distinctions on account of birth and blood. Christianity regards all men as made of one blood to dwell on all the face of the earth (see Note, Acts xvii. 26), and esteems them all to be equal in the matter of salvation; and whatever notions of *equality* prevail in the world are to be traced to the influence of the Christian religion. (2.) If men are regarded as equal before God, and as entitled to the same privileges of salvation; if there is in the great work of redemption "neither bond nor free," and those who are in the church are on a level, then such a view will induce a master to treat his slave with kindness, when that relation exists. The master who has any right feelings, will regard his servant as a Christian brother, redeemed by the same blood as himself, and destined to the same heaven. He will esteem him not as "a chattel" or "a thing," or as a piece "of property," but he will regard him as an immortal being, destined with himself to the same heaven, and about to sit down with him in the realms of glory. How can he treat such a brother with unkindness or severity? How can he rise from the same communion table with him, and give way to violent feelings against him, and regard him and treat him as if he were a brute? And Christianity, by the same principle that "the slave is a brother in the Lord," will do more to mitigate the horrors of slavery, than all the enactments that men can make, and all the other views and doctrines which can be made to prevail in society; see Philem. 16. (3.) This doctrine would lead to universal emancipation. All are on a level before God. In the kingdom of Jesus there is neither bond nor free. One is as much an object of favour as another. With this feeling, how can a Christian hold his fellow Christian in bondage? How can he regard as "a chattel" or "a thing," one who, like himself, is an heir of glory? How can he *sell* him on whom the blood of Jesus has been sprinkled? Let him feel that his slave is his equal in the sight of God; that with himself he is an heir of glory; that together they are soon to stand on Mount Zion above; that the slave is an immortal being, and has been redeemed by the blood of Calvary, and how *can* he hold such a being in bondage, and how *can* he transfer him from place to place and from hand to hand for gold? If all masters and all slaves were to become Christians, slavery would at once cease; and the prevalence of the single principle before us would put an end to all the ways in which man oppresses his fellow-man. Accordingly, it is well known that in about three centuries the influence of Christianity banished slavery from the Roman empire. ¶ *There is neither male nor female.* Neither the male nor the female have any peculiar advantages for salvation. There are no favours shown on account of sex. Both sexes are, in this respect, on a level. This does not mean, of course, that the sexes are to be regarded as in all respects equal; nor can it mean that the two sexes may not have peculiar duties and privileges in other respects. It does not prove that one of the sexes may not perform important offices in the church, which would not

29 And if ye *be* Christ's, then *a* are ye Abraham's seed, and heirs *b* according to the promise.

a ver.7.　　　　*b* Ro.8.17.

be proper for the other. It does not prove that the duties of the ministry are to be performed by the female sex, nor that the various duties of domestic life, nor the various offices of society, should be performed without any reference to the distinction of sex. The interpretation should be confined to the matter under consideration; and the passage proves only that *in regard to salvation* they are on a level. One sex is not to be regarded as peculiarly the favourite of heaven, and the other to be excluded. Christianity thus elevates the female sex to an equality with the male, on the most important of all interests; and it has in this way made most important changes in the world wherever it has prevailed. Everywhere but in connection with the Christian religion, woman has been degraded. She has been kept in ignorance. She has been treated as an inferior in all respects. She has been doomed to unpitied drudgery, and ignorance, and toil. So she was among the ancient Greeks and Romans; so she is among the savages of America; so she is in China, and India, and in the islands of the sea; so she is regarded in the Koran, and in all Mohammedan countries. It is Christianity alone which has elevated her; and nowhere on earth does man regard the mother of his children as an intelligent companion and friend, except where the influence of the Christian religion has been felt. At the communion table, at the foot of the cross, and in the hopes of heaven, she is on a level with man; and this fact diffuses a mild, and purifying, and elevating influence over all the relations of life. Woman has been raised from deep degradation by the influence of Christianity; and, let me add, she has everywhere acknowledged the debt of gratitude, and devoted herself, as under a deep sense of obligation, to lessening the burdens of humanity, and to the work of elevating the degraded, instructing the ig-

CHAPTER IV.

NOW I say, *That* the heir, as long as he is a child, differeth

norant, and comforting the afflicted, all over the world. Never has a debt been better repaid, or the advantages of elevating one portion of the race been more apparent. ¶ *For ye are all one in Christ Jesus.* You are all equally accepted through the Lord Jesus Christ; or you are all on the same level, and entitled to the same privileges in your Christian profession. Bond and free, male and female, Jew and Greek, are admitted to equal privileges, and are equally acceptable before God. And the church of God, no matter what may be the complexion, the country, the habits, or the rank of its members, is one. Every man on whom is the image and the blood of Christ, is A BROTHER to every other one who bears that image, and should be treated accordingly. What an influence would be excited in the breaking up of the distinctions of rank and *caste* among men; what an effect in abolishing the prejudice on account of colour and country, if this were universally believed and felt!

29. *And if ye* be *Christ's*. If you belong to the Messiah, and are interested in his work. ¶ *Then are ye Abraham's seed.* The promise made to Abraham related to the Messiah. It was a promise that in him all should be blessed. Abraham believed in that Messiah, and was distinguished for his faith in him who was to come. If they believed in Christ, therefore, they showed that they were the spiritual descendants of Abraham. No matter whether they were Jews or Gentiles; whether they had been circumcised or not, they had the same spirit which he evinced, and were interested in the promises made to him. ¶ *And heirs according to the promise;* see Rom. viii. 17. Are heirs of God. You inherit the blessings promised to Abraham, and partake of the felicity to which he looked forward. You have become truly heirs of God, and this is in accordance with the promise

nothing from a servant, though he be lord of all;

made to Abraham. It is not by the obedience of the law ; it is by faith—in the same way that Abraham possessed the blessing ;—an arrangement *before* the giving of the law, and therefore one that may include *all*, whether Jews or Gentiles. All are on a level ; and all are alike the children of God, and in the same manner, and on the same terms that Abraham was.

CHAPTER IV.

ANALYSIS.

THE design of this chapter is, to show the effect of being under the law, and the inconsistency of that kind of bondage or servitude with the freedom which is vouchsafed to the true children of God by the gospel. It is, in accordance with the whole drift of the epistle, to recall the Galatians to just views of the gospel ; and to convince them of their error in returning to the practice of the Mosaic rites and customs. In the previous chapter he had shown them that believers in the gospel were the true children of Abraham ; that they had been delivered from the curse of the law ; that the law was a schoolmaster to lead them to Christ, and that they were all the children of God. To illustrate this further, and to show them the true nature of the freedom which they had as the children of God, is the design of the argument in this chapter. He therefore states :

(1.) That it was under the gospel only that they received the full advantages of freedom; ver. 1—5. Before Christ came, indeed, there were true children of God, and heirs of life. But they were in the condition of *minors ;* they had not the privileges of *sons.* An heir to a great estate, says the apostle (ver. 1, 2), is treated substantially as if he were a servant. He is under tutors and governors ; he is not permitted to enter on his inheritance ; he is kept under the restraint of law. So it was with the people of God under the law of Moses. They were under restraints, and were admitted to comparatively

2 But is under tutors and governors until the time appointed of the father.

few of the privileges of the children of God. But Christ came to redeem those who were under the law, and to place them in the elevated condition of adopted sons; ver. 4, 5. They were no longer servants ; and it was as unreasonable that they should conform again to the Mosaic rites and customs, as it would be for the heir of full age, and who has entered on his inheritance, to return to the condition of minorship, and to be placed again under tutors and governors, and to be treated as a servant.

(2.) As sons of God, God had sent forth the Spirit of his Son into their hearts, and they were enabled to cry Abba, Father. They were no longer servants ; but heirs of God, and should avail themselves of the privileges of heirs; ver. 6, 7.

(3.) Sustaining this relation, and being admitted to these privileges, the apostle remonstrates with them for returning again to the " weak and beggarly elements" of the former dispensation—the condition of servitude to rites and customs in which they were before they embraced the gospel; ver. 8—11. When they were ignorant of God, they served those who were no gods, and there was some excuse for that; ver. 8. But now they had known God, they were acquainted with his laws ; they were admitted to the privileges of his children ; they were made free, and there could be no *no* excuse for returning again to the bondage of those who had no true knowledge of the liberty which the gospel gave. Yet they observed days and times as though these were binding, and they had never been freed from them (ver. 10) ; and the apostle says, that he is afraid that his labours bestowed on them, to make them acquainted with the plan of redemption, had been in vain.

(4.) To bring them to a just sense of their error, he reminds them of their former attachment to him, ver 12—20. He had indeed preached to them amidst much infirmity, and much that was fitted to prejudice them against him (ver. 13) ; but they had disregarded that, and had evinced towards him the highest proofs of attachment—so, much so, that they had received him as an angel of God (ver. 14), and had been ready to pluck out their own eyes to give them to him, ver. 15. With great force, therefore, he asks them why they had changed their views towards him so far as to forsake his doctrines ? Had he become their enemy by telling the truth? ver. 16. He tenderly addresses them, therefore, as little children, and says, that he has the deepest solicitude for their welfare, and the deepest anxiety on account of their danger—a solicitude which he compares (ver. 19,) with the pains of child-birth.

(5.) In order to enforce the whole subject, and to show the true nature of the conformity to the law compared with the liberty of the gospel, he allegorizes an interesting part of the Mosaic history—the history of the two children of Abraham; ver. 21—31. The condition of Hagar—a slave—under the command of a master—harshly treated—cast out and disowned, was an apt illustration of the condition of those who were under the servitude of the law. It would strikingly represent Mount Sinai, and the law that was promulgated there, and the condition of those who were under the law. That, too, was a condition of servitude. The law was stern, and showed no mercy. It was like a master of a slave, and would treat those who were under it with a rigidness that might be compared with the condition of Hagar and her son; ver. 24, 25. That same Mount Sinai also was a fair representation of Jerusalem as it was then—a city full of rites and ceremonies, where the law reigned with rigour, where there was a burdensome system of religion, and where there was none of the freedom which the gospel would furnish ; ver. 25. On the other hand, the children of the free woman were an apt illustration of those who were made free from the oppresive ceremonies of the law by the gospel ; ver. 22. That Jerusalem was free. The new system from heaven was one of liberty and rejoicing ; ver.

26, 27. Christians were, like Isaac, the children of promise, and were not slaves to the law ; ver. 28, 31. And as there was a command (ver. 30) to cast out the bondwoman and her son, so the command now was to reject all that would bring the mind into ignoble servitude, and prevent its enjoying the full freedom of the gospel. The whole argument is, that it would be as unreasonable for those who were Christians to submit again to the Jewish rites and ceremonies, as it would be for a freeman to sell himself into slavery. And the design of the whole is, to recall them from the conformity to Jewish rites and customs, and from their regarding them as now binding on Christians.

1. *Now I say.* He had before said (ch. iii. 24, 25) that while they were under the law they were in a state of minority. This sentiment he proceeds further to illustrate by showing the true condition of one who was a minor. ¶ That *the heir.* Any heir to an estate, or one who has a prospect of an inheritance. No matter how great is the estate ; no matter how wealthy his father ; no matter to how elevated a rank he may be raised on the moment that he enters on his inheritance, yet till that time he is in the condition of a servant. ¶ *As long as he is a child.* Until he arrives at the age. The word rendered " child " (νήπιος) properly means an *infant ;* literally, *one not speaking* (*in* luuop. *un,* *Voos*), and henee a child or babe, but without any definite limitation.—*Rob.* It is used as the word infant is with us in law, to denote a *minor.* ¶ *Differeth nothing from a servant,* That is, he has no more control of his property ; he has it not at his command. This does not mean that he does not differ *in any respect,* but only that *in the matter under consideration* he does not differ. He differs in his prospects of *inheriting* the property, and in the affections of the father, and usually in the advantages of education, and in the respect and attention shown him. but in regard to property, he does not differ, and he is like a servant, under the control and direction of others. ¶ *Though he be lord*

3 Even so we, when we were

of all. That is, in prospect. He has a prospective right to all the property, which no one else has. The word "lord" here (κύριος), is used in the same sense in which it is often in the Scriptures, to denote master or owner. The idea which this is designed to illustrate is, that the condition of the Jews before the coming of the Messiah was inferior in many respects to what the condition of the friends of God would be under him—as inferior as the condition of an heir was before he was of age,to what it would be when he should enter on his inheritance. The Jews claimed, indeed, that they were the children or the sons of God, a title which the apostle would not withhold from the pious part of the nation ; but it was a condition in which they had not entered on the full inheritance, and which was far inferior to that of those who had embraced the Messiah, and who were admitted to the full privileges of sonship. They were indeed heirs. They were interested in the promises. But still they were in a condition of comparative servitude, and could be made free only by the gospel.

2. *But is under.* Is subject to their control and direction. ¶ *Tutors.* The word *tutor* with us properly means *instructor.* But this is not quite the sense of the original. The word ɛπίτροπος properly means a steward, manager, agent ; Matt. xx. 8; Luke viii. 3. As used here, it refers to one—usually a slave or a freedman —to whose care the boys of a family were committed, who trained them up, accompanied them to school, or sometimes instructed them at home; comp. Note on ch. iii. 24. Such a one would have the control of them. ¶ *And governors.* This word (οικόνομος) means a house-manager, an overseer, a steward. It properly refers to one who had authority over the slaves or servants of a family, to assign them their tasks and portions. They generally, also, had the management of the affairs of the household, and of the accounts. They were commonly

children, were in bondage under the 1 elements of the world :

slaves, who were intrusted with this office as a reward for fidelity ; though sometimes free persons were employed ; Luke xvi. 1, 3, 8. These persons had also charge of the sons of a family, probably in respect to their *pecuniary* matters, and thus differed from those called *tutors.* It is not necessary, however, to mark the difference in the words with great accuracy. The general meaning of the apostle is, that the heir was under government and restraint. ¶ *Until the time appointed of the father.* The time fixed for his entering on the inheritance. The time when he chose to give him his portion of the property. The law with us fixes the age at twenty-one when a son shall be at liberty to manage for himself. Other countries have affixed other times. But still, the time when the son shall inherit the father's property must be fixed by the father himself if he is living, or may be fixed by his will if he is deceased. The son cannot *claim* the property when he comes of age.

3. *Even so we.* We who were Jews—for so I think the word here is to be limited, and not extended to the heathen, as Bloomfield supposes. The reasons for limiting it are, (1). That the heathens in no sense sustained such a relation to the law and promises of God as is here supposed; (2.) Such an interpretation would not be pertinent to the design of Paul. He is stating reasons why there should not be subjection to the laws of Moses, and his argument is, that that condition was like that of bondage or minorship. ¶ *When we were children* (νήπιοι). Minors ; see Note on ver. 1. The word is not υἱοι, sons ; but the idea is, that they were in a state of nonage ; and though heirs, yet were under severe discipline and regimen. They were under a kind of government that was fitted to that state, and not to the condition of those who had entered on their inheritance. ¶ *Were in bondage.* In a state of servitude. Treated as servants or slaves. ¶ *Under the ele-*

4 But when the fulness of the time was come, God sent forth his Son, made of a woman, made under the law,

---

ments of the world. Marg. *Rudiments.* The word rendered *elements* (sing. στοιχεῖον), properly means a row or series ; a little step ; a pin or peg, as the gnomen of a dial; and then any thing *elementary*, as a sound, a letter. It then denotes the elements or rudiments of any kind of instruction, and in the New Testament is applied to the first lessons or principles of religion; Heb. v. 15. It is applied to the elements or component parts of the physical world ; 2 Pet. iii. 10, 12. Here the figure is kept up of the reference to the infant (ver. 1, 3) ; and the idea is, that lessons were taught under the Jewish system adapted to their nonage—to a state of childhood. They were treated as children under tutors and governors. The phrase "the elements of the world," occurs also in Col. ii. 8, 20. In ver. 9 of this chapter, Paul speaks of these lessons as "beggarly elements," referring to the same thing as here. Different opinions have been held as to the reason why the Jewish institutions are here called "the elements *of the world.*" Rosenmüller supposes it was because many of those rites were common to the Jews and to the heathen – as they also had altars, sacrifices, temples, libations, &c. Doddridge supposes it was because those rites were adapted to the low conceptions of children, who were most affected with sensible objects, and have no taste for spiritual and heavenly things. Locke supposes it was because those institutions led them not beyond this world, or into the possession and taste of their heavenly inheritance. It is probable that there is allusion to the Jewish manner of speaking, so common in the Scriptures, where this world is opposed to the kingdom of God, and where it is spoken of as transient and worthless compared with the future glory. The world is fading, unsatisfactory, temporary. In allusion to this common use of the word, the Jewish institutions are called the *worldly rudiments.* It is not that they were in themselves evil—for that

is not true ; it is not that they were adapted to foster a worldly spirit— for that is not true; it is not that they had their origin from this world—for that is not true ; nor is it from the fact that they resembled the institutions of the heathen world—for that is as little true ; but it is, that, like the things of the world, they were transient, temporary, and of little value. They were unsatisfactory in their nature, and were soon to pass away, and to give place to a better system— as the things of this world are soon to give place to heaven.

4. *But when the fulness of the time was come.* The full time appointed by the Father ; the completion (*filling up,* ...) of the designated period for the coming of the Messiah, see Notes on Isa. xlix. 7, 8 ; 2 Cor. vi. 2. The sense is, that the time which had been predicted, and when it was proper that he should come, was complete. The exact period had arrived when all things were ready for his coming. It is often asked why he did not come sooner, and why mankind did not have the benefit of his incarnation and atonement immediately after the fall? Why were four thousand dark and gloomy years allowed to roll on, and the world suffered to sink deeper and deeper in ignorance and sin ? To these questions perhaps no answer entirely satisfactory can be given. God undoubtedly saw reasons which we cannot see, and reasons which we shall approve if they are disclosed to us. It may be observed, however, that this delay of redemption was in entire accordance with the whole system of divine arrangements, and with all the divine interpositions in favour of men. Men are suffered long to pine in want, to suffer from disease, to encounter the evils of ignorance, before interposition is granted. On all the subjects connected with human comfort and improvement, the same questions may be asked as on the subject of redemption. Why was the invention of the art of printing so long delayed,

and men suffered to remain in ignorance? Why was the discovery of vaccination delayed so long, and millions suffered to die who might have been saved? Why was not the bark of Peru sooner known, and why did so many millions die who might have been saved by its use? So of most of the medicines, and of the arts and inventions that go to ward off disease, and to promote the intelligence, the comfort, and the salvation of man. In respect to *all* of these, it may be true that they are made known *at the very best time*, the time that will on the whole most advance the welfare of the race. And so of the incarnation and work of the Saviour. It was seen by God to be the *best* time, the time when on the whole the race would be most benefited by his coming. Even with our limited and imperfect vision, *we* can see the following things in regard to its being the most fit and proper time. (1.) It was just the time when all the prophecies centred in him, and when there could be no doubt about their fulfilment. It was important that such an event should be predicted in order that there might be full evidence that he came from heaven; and yet in order that prophecy may be seen to have been uttered by God, it must be so far before the event as to make it impossible to have been the result of mere human conjecture. (2.) It was proper that the world should be brought to see its need of a Saviour, and that a fair and satisfactory opportunity should be given to men to try all other schemes of salvation that they might be prepared to welcome this. This had been done. Four thousand years were sufficient to show to man his own powers, and to give him an opportunity to devise some scheme of salvation. The opportunity had been furnished under every circumstance that could be deemed favourable. The most profound and splendid talent of the world had been brought to bear on it, especially in Greece and Rome; and ample opportunity had been given to make a fair trial of the various systems of religion devised on national happiness and individual welfare; their

power to meet and arrest crime; to purify the heart; to promote public morals, and to support man in his trials; their power to conduct him to the true God, and to give him a well-founded hope of immortality. All had failed; and then it was a proper time for the Son of God to come and to reveal a better system. (3.) It was a time when the world was at peace. The temple of Janus, closed only in times of peace, was then shut, though it had been but once closed before during the Roman history. What an appropriate time for the "Prince of Peace" to come! The world was, to a great extent, under the Roman sceptre. Communications between different parts of the world were then more rapid and secure than they had been at any former period, and the gospel could be more easily propagated. Further, the Jews were scattered in almost all lands, acquainted with the promises, looking for the Messiah, furnishing facilities to their own countrymen the apostles to preach the gospel in numerous synagogues, and qualified, if they embraced the Messiah, to become most zealous and devoted missionaries. The same language, the Greek, was, moreover, after the time of Alexander the Great, the common language of no small part of the world, or at least was spoken and understood among a considerable portion of the nations of the earth. At no period before had there been so extensive a use of the same language. (4.) It was a proper period to make the new system known. It accorded with the benevolence of God, that it should be delayed no longer than that the world should be in a suitable state for receiving the Redeemer. When that period, therefore, had arrived, God did not delay, but sent his Son on the great work of the world's redemption. ¶ *God sent forth his Son.* This implies that the Son of God had an existence before his incarnation; see John xvi. 28. The Saviour is often represented as *sent* into the world, and as *coming forth* from God. ¶ *Made of a woman.* In human nature; born of a woman, This also implies that he had another

5 To redeem them that were under the law, that we might receive the adoption of sons.

6 And because ye are sons, God hath sent forth the Spirit *a* of his

a Ro.8.15,17.

Son into your hearts, crying, Abba, Father.

7 Wherefore thou art no more a servant, but a son ; and if a son, then an heir of God through Christ.

---

nature than that which was derived from the woman. On the supposition that he was a mere man, how unmeaning would this assertion be ! How natural to ask, in what other way could he appear than to be born of a woman ? Why was *he* particularly designated as coming into the world in this manner ? How strange would it sound if it were said, " In the sixteenth century came Faustus Socinus preaching Unitarianism, *made of a woman !*" or, " In the eighteenth century came Dr. Joseph Priestley, *born of a woman*, preaching the doctrines of Socinus !" How else could they appear ? would be the natural inquiry. What was there peculiar in their birth and origin that rendered such language necessary ? The *language* implies that there were other ways in which the Saviour might have come ; that there was something peculiar in the fact that *he* was born of a woman ; and that there was some special reason why that fact should be made prominently a matter of record. The promise was (Gen. iii. 15) that the Messiah should be the "seed" or the descendant of woman; and Paul probably here alludes to the fulfilment of that promise. ¶ *Made under the law.* As one of the human race, partaking of human nature, he was subject to the law of God. As a man he was bound by its requirements, and subject to its control. He took his place under the law that he might accomplish an important purpose for those who were under it. He made himself subject to it that he might become one of them, and secure their redemption.

5. *To redeem them.* By his death as an atoning sacrifice ; see Note on chap. iii. 13. ¶ *Them that were under the law.* Sinners, who had violated the law, and who were exposed to its dread penalty. ¶ *That*

we might receive the adoption of sons Be adopted as the sons or the children of God ; see Notes, John i. 12 ; Rom. viii. 15.

6. *And because ye are sons.* As a consequence of your being adopted into the family of God, and being regarded as his sons. It follows as a part of his purpose of adoption that his children shall have the spirit of the Lord Jesus. ¶ *The Spirit of his Son.* The spirit of the Lord Jesus ; the spirit which animated him, or which he evinced. The idea in that as the Lord Jesus was enabled to approach God with the language of endearment and love, so they would be. He, being the true and exalted Son of God, had the spirit appropriate to such a relation ; they being adopted, and made like him, have the same spirit. The "spirit" here referred to does not mean, as I suppose, the Holy Spirit as such ; nor the miraculous endowments of the Holy Spirit, but the spirit which made them like the Lord Jesus ; the spirit by which they were enabled to approach God as his children, and use the reverent, and tender, and affectionate language of a child addressing a father. It is that language used by Christians when they have evidence of adoption ; the expression of the warm, and elevated, and glowing emotions which they have when they can approach God as their God, and address him as *their* Father. ¶ *Crying.* That is, the spirit thus cries, Πνεῦμα—κράζον. Comp. Notes, Rom. viii. 26, 27. In Rom. viii. 15 it is, "wherewith we cry." ¶ *Abba, Father ;* see Note, Rom. viii. 15. It is said in the Babylonian Gemara, a Jewish work, that it was not permitted slaves to use the title of *Abba* in addressing the master of the family to which they belonged. If so, then the language which Christians are

8 Howbeit then, when ye knew not God, ye did service unto them which by nature are no gods.

1 or, *back.*

9 But now, after that ye have known God, or rather are known of God, how turn ye [1] again to the weak and beggarly [2] elements,

2 *rudiments.*

---

here represented as using is the language of freemen, and denotes that they are not under the servitude of sin. 7. *Wherefore.* In consequence of this privilege of addressing God as your Father. ¶ *Thou art no more.* You who are Christians. ¶ *A servant.* In the servitude of sin ; or treated as a servant by being bound under the oppressive rites and ceremonies of the law ; comp. Note on ver. 3. ¶ *But a son.* A child of God, adopted into his family, and to be treated as a son. ¶ *And if a son,* &c. Entitled to all the privileges of a son, and of course to be regarded as an heir through the Redeemer, and with him. See the sentiment here expressed explained in the Note on Rom. viii. 17.

8. *Howbeit.* But, ’Ἀλλὰ. The address in this verse and the following is evidently to the portion of the Galatians who had been heathen. This is probably indicated by the particle ἀλλὰ, *but* denoting a transition. In the previous verses Paul had evidently had the Jewish converts more particularly in his eye, and had described their former condition as one of servitude to the Mosaic rites and customs, and had shown the inconveniences of that condition, compared with the freedom imparted by the gospel. To complete the description, he refers also to the Gentiles, as a condition of worse servitude still, and shows (ver. 9) the absurdity of *their* turning back to a state of bondage of any kind, after the glorious deliverance which they had obtained from the degrading servitude of pagan rites. The sense is, " If the Jews were in such a state of servitude, how much more galling and severe was that of those who had been heathens. Yet from *that* servitude the gospel had delivered them, and made them freemen. How absurd now to go back to a state of vassalage, and to become servants under the oppressive rites of the Jewish law ! " ¶ *When*

ye knew not God. In your state of heathenism, when you had no knowledge of the true God and of his service. The object is not to apologize for what they did, because they did not know God ; it is to state the fact that they were in a state of gross and galling *servitude.* ¶ *Ye did service.* This does not express the force of the original. The meaning is, " Ye were *slaves* to (ἐδουλεύσατε) ; you were in a condition of *servitude,* as opposed to the freedom of the gospel ;" comp. ver. 3, where the same word is used to describe the state of the Jews. The drift of the apostle is, to show that the Jews and Gentiles, before their conversion to Christianity, were in a state of vassalage or servitude, and that it was absurd in the highest degree to return to that condition again. ¶ *Unto them which by nature are no gods.* Idols, or false gods. The expression " by nature," φύσει, according to Grotius, means, *in fact, re ipsa.* The sense is, that they *really* had no pretensions to divinity. Many of them were imaginary beings ; many were the objects of creation, as the sun, and winds, and streams ; and many were departed heroes that had been exalted to be objects of worship. Yet the *servitude* was real. It fettered their faculties ; controlled their powers ; bound their imagination, and commanded their time and property, and made them slaves. Idolatry is always slavery ; and the servitude of sinners to their passions and appetites, to lust. and gold, and ambition, is not less galling and severe than was the servitude to the pagan gods or the Jewish rites, or than is the servitude of the African now to a harsh and cruel master. Of all Christians it may be said that before their conversion they "did service," or were *slaves* to harsh and cruel masters ; and nothing but the gospel has made them free. It may be added, that the chains of idolatry all over the world are as

whereunto ye desire again to be in bondage?

10 Ye observe days, and months, and times, and years.

fast riveted and as galling as they were in Galatia, and that nothing but the same gospel which Paul preached there can break those chains and restore man to freedom.

9. *But now, &c.* The sense is, that since they had been made free from their ignoble servitude in the worship of false gods, and had been admitted to the freedom found in the worship of the true God, it was absurd that they should return again to that which was truly slavery or bondage, the observance of the rites of the Jewish law. ¶ *That ye have known God.* The true God, and the ease and freedom of his service in the gospel. ¶ *Or rather are known of God.* The sense is, " Or, to speak more accurately or precisely, are known by God." The *object* of this correction is to avoid the impression which might be derived from the former phrase that their acquaintance with God was owing *to themselves.* He therefore states, that it was rather that they were known of God ; that it was all owing to him that they had been brought to an acquaintance with himself. Perhaps, also, he means to bring into view the idea that it was a favour and privilege to be known by God, and that therefore it was the more absurd to turn back to the weak and beggarly elements. ¶ *How turn ye again.* Marg. *Back.* " How is it that you are returning to such a bondage?" The question implies surprise and indignation that they should do it. ¶ *To the weak and beggarly elements.* To the rites and ceremonies of the Jewish law, imposing a servitude really not less severe than the customs of paganism. On the word *elements,* see Note on ver. 3. They are called "weak" because they had no power to save the soul ; no power to justify the sinner before God. They are called " beggarly" (Gr. πτωχὰ, *poor*), because they could not impart spiritual riches. They really could confer few benefits on man. Or it may be, as Locke supposes, because the law kept men in the poor estate of pupils from

the full enjoyment of the inheritance; ver. 1—3. ¶ *Whereunto ye desire again to be in bondage. As if* you had a wish to be under servitude. The absurdity is as great as it would be for a man who had been freed from slavery to desire again his chains. They had been freed by the gospel from the galling servitude of heathenism, and they now again had sunk into the Jewish observances, *as if they preferred slavery to freedom,* and were willing to go from one form of it to another. The main idea is, that it is absurd for men who have been made free by the gospel to go back again into any kind of servitude or bondage. We may apply it to Christians now. Many sink into a kind of servitude not less galling than was that to sin before their conversion. Some become the slaves of mere ceremonies and forms in religion. Some are slaves to fashion, and the world yet rules them with the hand of a tyrant. They have escaped, it may be, from the galling chains of ambition, and degrading vice, and low sensuality ; but they became slaves to the love of money, or of dress, or of the fashions of the world, *as if they loved slavery and chains ;* and they seem no more able to break loose than the slave is to break the bonds which bind him. And some are slaves to some expensive and foolish habit. Professed Christians, *and Christian ministers too,* become slaves to the disgusting and loathsome habit of using *tobacco,* bound by a servitude as galling and as firm as that which ever shackled the limbs of an African. I grieve to add also that many professed Christians are slaves to the habit of " sitting long at the wine" and indulging in it freely. O that such knew the liberty of Christian freedom, and would break away from all such shackles, and *show* how the gospel frees men from *all* foolish and absurd customs !

10. *Ye observe.* The object of this verse is to *specify* some of the things to which they had become enslaved ¶ *Days.* The days here referred to

11 I am afraid of you, lest I have bestowed upon you labour in vain.

12 Brethren, I beseech you, be as I *am;* for I *am* as *ye are;* ye have not injured me at all.

are doubtless the days of the Jewish festivals. They had numerous days of such observances, and in addition to those specified in the Old Testament, the Jews had added many others as days commemorative of the destruction and rebuilding of the temple, and of other important events in their history. It is not a fair interpretation of this to suppose that the apostle refers to the *Sabbath,* properly so called, for this was a part of the Decalogue; and was observed by the Saviour himself, and by the apostles also. It *is* a fair interpretation to apply it to all those days which are not commanded to be kept holy in the Scriptures; and hence the passage is as applicable to the observance of saints' days, and days in honour of particular events in sacred history, as to the days observed by the Galatians. There is as real *servitude* in the observance of the numerous festivals, and fasts in the Papal communion and in some Protestant churches, as there was in the observance of the days in the Jewish ecclesiastical calendar, and for any thing that I can see, such observances are as inconsistent now with the freedom of the gospel as they were in the time of Paul. We should observe as seasons of holy time what it can be proved God has commanded us, and no more. ¶ *And months.* The festivals of the new moon, kept by the Jews. Num. x. 10; xxviii. 11—14. On this festival, in addition to the daily sacrifice, two bullocks, a ram, and seven sheep of a year old were offered in sacrifice. The appearance of the new-moon was announced by the sound of trumpets. See Jahn, Archae. § 352. ¶ *And times.* Stated times; festivals returning periodically, as the Passover, the feast of Pentecost, and the feast of Tabernacles. See Jahn, Archae. chap. 3. § 346—360. ¶ *And years.* The sabbatical year, or the year of jubilee. See Jahn as above.

11. *I am afraid of you,* &c. I have fears respecting you. His fears were that they had no genuine Christian principle. They had been so easily perverted and turned back to the servitude of ceremonies and rites, that he was apprehensive that there could be no real Christian principle in the case. What pastor has not often had such fears of his people, when he sees them turn to the weak and beggarly elements of the world, or when, after having "run well," he sees them become the slaves of fashion, or of some habit inconsistent with the simplicity of the gospel?

12. *Brethren, I beseech you, be as I* am, &c. There is great brevity in this passage, and no little obscurity, and a great many different interpretations have been given of it by commentators. The various views expressed may be seen in Bloomfield's Crit. Dig. Locke renders it, "Let you and I be as if we were all one, Think yourselves to be very me; as I in my own mind put no difference at all between you and myself." Koppe explains it thus: Imitate my example; for I, though a Jew by birth, care no more for Jewish rites than you." Rosenmüller explains it, "Imitate my manner of life in rejecting the Jewish rites; as I, having renounced the Jewish rites, was much like you when I preached the gospel to you." Other interpretations may be seen in Chandler, Doddridge, Calvin, &c. In our version there seems to be an impropriety of expression; for if he was as they were it would seem to be a matter of course that they would be like him, or would resemble him. The sense of the passage, however, it seems to me cannot be difficult. The reference is doubtless to the Jewish rites and customs, and to the question whether they were binding on Christians. Paul's object is to persuade them to abandon them. He appeals to them, therefore, by his own example. And it means evidently, "Imitate me in this thing. Follow my example, and yield no conformity to those rites and customs." The *ground* on which he

13 Ye know how, through *a* infirmity of the flesh I preached the gospel unto you at the first:

14 And my temptation which

was in my flesh ye despised not nor rejected ; but received me as an angel *b* of God, *even* as Christ *c* Jesus.

a 1 Co.2.3. *b* 2 Sa.19.27 ; Mal.2.7. *c* Mat.10.40.

asks them to imitate him may be either, (1.) That *he* had abandoned them or, (2.) Because he asks them *to yield a point* to him. He had done so in many instances for their welfare, and had made many sacrifices for their salvation, and he now aks them to yield this *one* point, and to become as he was, and to cease these Jewish observances, as he had done. ¶ *For I am as ye are.* Gr. "For I as ye." This means, I suppose, "For I have conformed to your customs in many things. I have abandoned my own peculiarities ; given up my customs as far as possible ; conformed to you as Gentiles as far as I could do, in order to benefit and save you. I have laid aside the peculiarity of the Jew on the principle of becoming all things to all men (Notes, 1 Cor. ix. 20—22), in order that I might save you. I ask in return only the slight sacrifice that you will now become like me in the matter under consideration." ¶ *Ye have not injured me at all.* "It is not a personal matter. I have no cause of complaint. You have done me no personal wrong. There is no variance between us ; no unkind feeling; no injury done as individuals. I may, therefore, with the more freedom, ask you to yield this point, when I assure you that I do not feel personally injured. I have no wrong to complain of, and I ask it on higher grounds than would be an individual request: it is for your good, and the good of the great cause." When Christians turn away from the truth, and disregard the instructions and exhortations of pastors, and become conformed to the world, it is not a personal matter, or a matter of personal offence to them, painful as it may be to them. They have no peculiar reason to say that they are personally injured. It is a higher matter. The cause suffers. The interests of religion are injured. The church at large is offended, and the Saviour is "wounded in the house of

his friends." Conformity to the world, or a lapse into some sin, is a public offence, and should be regarded as an injury done to the cause of the Redeemer. It shows the magnanimity of Paul, that though they had abandoned his doctrines, and forgotten his love and his toils in their welfare, he did not regard it as a *personal* offence, and did not consider himself personally injured. An ambitious man or an impostor would have made that the main, if not the only thing.

13. *Ye know how.* To show them the folly of their embracing the new views which they had adopted, he reminds them of past times, and particularly of the strength of the attachment which they had evinced for him in former days. ¶ *Through infirmity of the flesh.* Gr. *Weakness* (ἀσθένειαν); comp. Notes on 1 Cor. ii. 3; 2 Cor. x. 10 ; xii. 7.

14. *And my temptation. My trial,* the thing which was to me a trial and calamity. The meaning is, that he was afflicted with various calamities and infirmities, but that this did not hinder their receiving him as an angel from heaven. There is, however, a considerable variety in the MSS. on this verse. Many MSS., instead of "*my* temptation," read "*your* temptation," and Mill maintains that this is the true reading. Griesbach hesitates between the two. But it is not very important to determine which is the true reading. If it should be "*your,*" then it means that they were tempted by his infirmities to reject him ; and so it amounts to about the same thing. The general sense is, that he had some bodily infirmity, perhaps some periodically returning disease, that was a great trial to him, which they bore with, with great patience and affection. What that was, he has not informed us, and conjecture is vain. ¶ *But received me as an angel of God.* With the utmost respect, as if I had been an angel sent from God. ¶ Even

15 Where [1] is then the blessedness ye spake of? for I bear you
record, that, if *it had been* possible,
ye would have plucked out your

1 or, *what was.*

own eyes, and have given them to
me.

16 Am I therefore become your
enemy, because I tell you the truth?

---

as Christ Jesus. As you would have
done the Redeemer himself. Learn
hence, (1.) That the Lord Jesus is
superior to an angel of God. (2.)
That the highest proof of attachment
to a minister, is to receive him as the
Saviour would be received. (3.) It
showed their attachment to the Lord
Jesus, that they received his apostle
as they would have received the Saviour himself; comp. Mat. x. 40.

15. *Where is then the blessedness.*
Marg. " What was"—in accordance
with the Greek. The words " ye
spake of" are not in the Greek, and
should have been printed in Italic.
But they obscure the sense at any
rate. This is not to be regarded as a
question, asking what had become of
the blessedness, implying that it had
departed; but it is rather to be regarded as an *exclamation,* referring
to the happiness of that moment, and
their affection and joy when they thus
received him. " What blessedness
you had then! How happy was that
moment! What tenderness of affection! What overflowing joy !" It
was a time full of joy, and love, and
affectionate confidence. So Tindal
well renders it, " How happy were ye
then !" In this interpretation, Doddridge, Rosenmüller, Bloomfield,
Koppe, Chandler, and others concur.
Locke renders it, " What benedictions did you then pour out on me !"
¶ *For I bear you record.* I testify.
¶ *Ye would have plucked out your own
eyes,* &c. No higher proof of attachment could have been given. They
loved him so much, that they would
have given to him *any* thing, however
dear; they would have done any thing
to contribute to his welfare. How
changed, now that they had abandoned
his doctrines, and yielded themselves
to the guidance of those who taught a
wholly different doctrine !

16. *Am I therefore become your
enemy,* &c. Is my telling you the
truth in regard to the tendency of the

doctrines which you have embraced,
and the character of those who have
led you astray, and your own error, a
proof that I have ceased to be your
friend? How apt are we to feel that
the man who tells us of our faults is
our enemy! How apt are we to treat
him coldly, and to "cut his acquaintance," and to regard him with dislike!
The *reason* is, he gives us pain; and
we cannot have pain given us, even by
the stone against which we stumble,
or by any of the brute creation, without momentary indignation, or regarding them for a time as our enemies.
Besides, we do not like to have another person acquainted with our
faults and our follies; and we naturally
avoid the society of those who are
thus acquainted with us. Such is
human nature; and it requires no
little grace for us to overcome this,
and to regard the man who tells us of
our faults, or the faults of our families,
as our friend. We love to be flattered,
and to have our friends flattered; and
we shrink with pain from any exposure, or any necessity for repentance.
Hence we become alienated from him
who is faithful in reproving us for our
faults. Hence men become offended
with their ministers when they reprove
them for their sins. Hence they become offended at the truth. Hence
they resist the influences of the Holy
Spirit, whose office it is to bring the
truth to the heart, and to reprove
men for their sins. There is nothing
more difficult than to regard with
steady and unwavering affection the
man who faithfully tells us the truth
at all times, when that truth is painful. Yet he is our best friend. " Faithful are the wounds of a friend, but the
kisses of an enemy are deceitful,"
Prov. xxvii. 6. If I am in danger of
falling down a precipice, he shows to
me the purest friendship who tells me
of it; if I am in danger of breathing
the air of the pestilence, and it can
be avoided, he shows to me pure kind-

17 They zealously affect you, *but* *a* not well ; yea, they would exclude [1] you, that ye might affect them.

a Ro.10.2.   1 or, *us.*

18 But *it is* good to be zealously affected always *b* in *a* good *thing*, and not only when I am present with you.

b 1 Co.15.58.

ness who tells me of it. So still more, if I am indulging in a course of conduct that may ruin me, or cherishing error that may endanger my salvation, he shows me the purest friendship who is most faithful in warning me, and apprising me of what must be the termination of my course.

17. *They zealously affect you ;* see 1 Cor. xii. 31 (Gr.) ; xiv. 39. The word here used (Ζηλόω), means to be zealous towards, *i. e.,* for or against any person or thing ; usually, in a good sense, to be eager for. Here it means, that the false teachers made a show of zeal towards the Galatians, or professed affection for them in order to gain them as their followers. They were full of ardour, and professed an extraordinary concern for their welfare — as men always do who are demagogues, or who seek to gain proselytes. The object of the apostle in this is, probably, to say, that it was not wholly owing to themselves that they had become alienated from the doctrines which he had taught. Great pains had been taken to do it ; and there had been a show of zeal which would be likely to endanger any person. ¶ *But not well.* Not with good motives, or with good designs. ¶ *Yea, they would exclude you.* Marg. *Us.* A few printed editions of the New Testament have ἡμᾶς, *us,* instead of ὑμᾶς, *you.—Mill.* The word *exclude* here probably means, that they endeavoured to exclude the Galatians from the love and affection of Paul. They would shut them out from that, in order that they might secure them for their own purposes. If the reading in the margin, however, should be retained, the sense would be clearer. " They wish to exclude *us, i. e.,* me, the apostle, in order that they may have you wholly to themselves. If they can once get rid of your attachment to me, then they will have no difficulty in securing you for themselves." This reading, says

Rosenmüller, is found " in many of the best codices, and versions, and fathers." It is adopted by Doddridge, Locke, and others. The main idea is clear : Paul stood in the way of their designs. The Galatians were truly attached to him, and it was necessary, in order to accomplish their ends, to withdraw their affections from him. When false teachers have designs on a people, they begin by alienating their confidence and affections from their pastors and teachers. They can hope for no success until this is done ; and hence the efforts of errorists, and of infidels, and of scorners, is to undermine the confidence of a people in the ministry, and when this is done there is little difficulty in drawing them over to their own purposes. ¶ *That ye might affect them.* The same word as in the former part of the verse,—" that ye might zealously affect them"—*i. e.,* that ye might show ardent attachment to them. Their *first* work is to manifest *special interest* for your welfare ; their *second,* to alienate you from him who had first preached the gospel to you ; their *object,* not your salvation, or your real good, but to secure your zealous love for themselves.

18. *But it is good to be zealously affected.* The meaning of this is, " Understand me : I do not speak against zeal. I have not a word to say in its disparagement. In itself, it is good ; and *their* zeal would be good if it were in a good cause." Probably, they relied much on their zeal ; perhaps they maintained, as errorists and deceivers are very apt to do, that *zeal* was sufficient evidence of the goodness of their cause, and that persons who are *so very zealous* could not possibly be bad men. How often is this plea set up by the friends of errorists and deceivers ! ¶ *And not only when I am present with you.* It seems to me that there is great adroitness and great delicacy of irony in

19 My *a* little children, of whom I travail in birth again until Christ be formed in you,

20 I desire to be present with

you now, and to change my voice ; for [1] I stand in doubt of you.

21 Tell me, ye that desire to be under the law, do ye not hear the law?

a 1 Co.4.15.

[1] or, *I am perplexed for you.*

this remark ; and that the apostle intends to remind them as gently as possible, that it would have been as well for them to have shown their zeal in a *good* cause when he was absent, as well as when he was with them. The sense may be, " You *were* exceedingly zealous in a good cause when I was with you. You loved the truth ; you loved me. Since I left you, and as soon almost as I was out of your sight, your zeal died away, and your ardent love for me was transferred to others. Suffer me to remind you, that it would be well to be zealous of good when I am away, as well as when I am with you. There is not much true affection in that which dies away as soon as a man's back is turned." The *doctrine* is, that true zeal or love will live alike when the object is near and when it is removed; when our friends are present with us, and when they leave us; when their eye is upon us, and when it is turned away.

19. *My little children.* The language of tender affection, such as a parent would use towards his own offspring ; see Note, 1 Cor. iv. 15; comp. Mat. xviii. 3 ; John xiii. 33 ; 1 John ii. 1, 12, 13 ; iv. 4 ; v. 21. The idea here is, that Paul felt that he sustained towards them the relation of a father, and he had for them the deep and tender feelings of a parent. ¶ *Of whom I travail in birth again.* For whose welfare I am deeply anxious : and for whom I endure deep anguish ; comp. 1 Cor. iv. 15. His anxiety for them he compares to the deepest sufferings which human nature endures ; and his language here is a striking illustration of what ministers of the gospel should feel, and do sometimes feel, in regard to their people. ¶ *Until Christ be formed in you.* The name *Christ* is often used to denote his religion, or the principles of his gospel ; see Note on Rom. xiii. 14. Here it means, until Christ reigns wholly in your

hearts ; till you wholly and entirely embrace his doctrines ; and till you become wholly imbued with his spirit; see Col. i. 27.

20. *I desire to be present with you now.* They had lost much by his absence ; they had changed their views ; they had in some measure become alienated from him ; and he wishes that he might be again with them, as he was before. He would hope to accomplish much more by his personal presence than he could by letter. ¶ *And to change my voice.* That is, from complaint and censure, to tones of entire confidence. ¶ *For I stand in doubt of you.* Marg. " *I am perplexed for you.*" On the meaning of the word here used, see Note on 2 Cor. iv. 8. The sense is plain. Paul had much reason to doubt the sincerity and the solidity of their Christian principles, and he was deeply anxious on that account.

21. *Tell me,* &c. In order to show fully the nature and the effect of the law, Paul here introduces an illustration from an important fact in the Jewish history. This *allegory* has given great perplexity to expositors. and, in some respects, it is attended with real difficulty. An examination of the difficulties will be found in the larger commentaries. My object, without examining the expositions which have been proposed, will be to state, in as few words as possible, the simple meaning and design of the allegory. The *design* it is not difficult to understand. It is *to show the effect of being under the bondage or servitude of the Jewish law, compared with the freedom which the gospel imparts.* Paul had addressed the Galatians as having a real desire to be under bondage, or to be servants; Note on ver. 9. He had represented Christianity as a state of freedom, and Christians as the sons of God—not servants, but freemen. To show the difference of the two conditions, he appeals to two

22 For it is written, That Abraham had two sons; the one *a* by a bond-maid, the other *b* by a free woman.

a Ge.16.15.   b Ge.21.1,2.

23 But he *who was* of the *c* bond-woman was born after the flesh; but he of the free woman *was* by promise.

c Ro.9.7,8.

cases which would furnish a striking illustration of them. The one was the case of Hagar and her son. The effect of *bondage* was well illustrated there. She and her son were treated with severity, and were cast out and persecuted. This was *a fair illustration* of bondage under the law; of the servitude to the laws of Moses; and was a fit representation of Jerusalem as it was in the time of Paul. The other case was that of Isaac. He was the son of a free woman, and was treated accordingly. He was regarded as a son, not as a servant. And he was *a fair illustration* of the case of those who were made free by the gospel. They enjoyed a similar freedom and sonship, and should not seek a state of servitude or bondage. The condition of Isaac was a fit illustration of the New Jerusalem; the heavenly city; the true kingdom of God. But Paul does not mean to say, as I suppose, that the history of the son of Hagar and of the son of Rebecca was *mere* allegory, or that the narrative by Moses was *designed* to represent the different condition of those who were under the law and under the gospel. He uses it simply, *as showing the difference between servitude and freedom, and as a striking* ILLUSTRATION *of the nature of the bondage to the Jewish law, and of the freedom of the gospel*, just as any one may use a striking historical fact to illustrate a principle. These general remarks will constitute the *basis* of my interpretation of this celebrated allegory. The expression "tell me," is one of affectionate remonstrance and reasoning; see Luke vii. 42, "Tell me, therefore, which of these will love him most?" Comp. Isa. i. 18, "Come, now, and let us reason together, saith the Lord." ¶ *Ye that desire to be under the law;* Note, ver. 9. You who wish to yield obedience to the laws of Moses. You who maintain that conformity to those laws is neces-

sary to justification. ¶ *Do ye not hear the law?* Do you not understand what the law says? Will you not listen to its own admonitions, and the instruction which may be derived from the law on the subject? The word "law" here refers not to the commands that were uttered on mount Sinai, but to the *book* of the law. The passage to which reference is made is in the Book of Genesis; but all the five books of Moses were by the Jews classed under the general name of the law; see Note on Luke xxiv. 44. The sense is, "Will you not listen to a narrative found in one of the books of the law itself, fully illustrating the nature of that servitude which you wish?"

22. *For it is written;* Gen. xvi. xxi. ¶ *Abraham had two sons.* Ishmael and Isaac. Abraham subsequently had several sons by Keturah after the death of Sarah; Gen. xxvi. 1—6. But the two sons by Hagar and Sarah were the most prominent, and the events of their lives furnished the particular illustration which Paul desired. ¶ *The one by a bond-maid.* Ishmael, the son of Hagar. Hagar was an Egyptian slave, whom Sarah gave to Abraham in order that he might not be wholly without posterity; Gen. xvi. 3. ¶ *The other by a free woman.* Isaac, the son of Sarah; Gen. xxi. 1, 2.

23. *But he* who was *of the bond-woman was born after the flesh.* In the ordinary course of nature, without any special promise, or any unusual divine interposition, as in the case of Isaac. ¶ *But he of the free woman,* &c. The birth of Isaac was in accordance with a special promise, and by a remarkable divine interposition; see Gen. xviii. 10; xxi. 1, 2; Heb. xi. 11, 12; comp. Notes on Rom. iv. 19—21. The idea here of Paul is, that the son of the slave was in a humble and inferior condition from his very birth. There was no special promise

24 Which things are an allegory: *a* for these are the two
1 covenants ; the one from the

mount 2 Sinai, *b* which gendereth
to bondage, which is Agar.

a 1 Co.10.11.   1 or, *testaments.*
2 *Sina.*   b De.33.2.

attending him. He was *born* into a
state of inferiority and servitude
which attended him through his whole
life. Isaac, however, was met with
promises as soon as he was born, and
was under the benefit of those promises as long as he lived. The *object*
of Paul is, to state the truth in regard
to a condition of servitude and slavery.
It is attended with evils from beginning to end ; from the birth to the
grave. By this illustration he means
to show them the folly of becoming
the voluntary slaves of the law after
they had once been made free.

24. *Which things.* The different
accounts of Ishmael and Isaac. ¶ *Are
an allegory.* May be regarded alle-
gorically, or as illustrating great principles in regard to the condition of
slaves and freemen ; and may therefore be used to illustrate the effect of
servitude to the law of Moses compared with the freedom of the gospel.
He does not mean to say that the
historical record of Moses was not
true, or was merely allegorical ; nor
does he mean to say that Moses *meant*
this to be an allegory, or that he *intended* that it should be applied to the
exact purpose to which Paul applied
it. No such design is apparent in the
narrative of Moses, and it is evident
that he had no such intention. Nor
can it be shown that Paul means to be
understood as saying that Moses had
any such design, or that his account
was not a record of a plain historical
fact. Paul uses it as he would any
other historical fact that would illustrate the same principle, and he makes
no more use of it than the Saviour did
in his parables of real or fictitious
narratives to illustrate an important
truth, or than we always do of real
history to illustrate an important
principle. The word which is here
used by Paul (ἀλληγορέω) is derived
from ἄλλος, another, and ἀγορεύω, to
speak, to speak openly or in public.—
Passow. It properly means to speak
any thing otherwise than it is understood (*Passow*) ; to speak allegori-

cally ; to allegorize. The word does
not occur elsewhere in the New Testament, nor is it found in the Septuagint, though it occurs often in the
classic writers. An allegory is a continued metaphor ; see Blair's Lectures, xv. It is a figurative sentence
or discourse, in which the principal
object is described by another subject
resembling it in its properties and
circumstances.—*Webster.* Allegories
are in words what hieroglyphics are
in painting. The distinction between
a *parable* and an *allegory* is said to
be, that a parable is a *supposed* history to illustrate some important truth,
as the parable of the good Samaritan,
&c.; an allegory is based on *real facts.*
It is not probable, however, that this
distinction is always carefully observed. Sometimes the allegory is based
on the resemblance to some inanimate
object, as in the beautiful allegory in
the eightieth psalm. Allegories, parables, and metaphors abound in the
writings of the East. Truth was more
easily treasured up in this way, and
could be better preserved and transmitted when it was connected with an
interesting story. The lively fancy
of the people of the East also led them
to this mode of communicating truth ;
though a love for it is probably founded in human nature. The best sustained allegory of any considerable
length in the world is, doubtless, Bunyan's Pilgrim's Progress ; and yet
this is among the most popular of all
books. The ancient Jews were exceedingly fond of allegories, and even
turned a considerable part of the Old
Testament into allegory. The ancient
Greek philosophers also were fond of
this mode of teaching. Pythagoras
instructed his followers in this manner, and this was common among the
Greeks, and was imitated much by
the early Christians.—*Calmet.* Many
of the Christian fathers, of the school
of Origen, made the Old Testament
almost wholly allegorical, and found
mysteries in the plainest narratives.
The Bible became thus with them a

25 For this Agar is mount Sinai in Arabia, and [1] answereth to Jerusalem which now is, and is in bondage with her children.

1 or, *is in the same rank with.*

book of enigmas, and exegesis consisted in an ingenious and fanciful accommodation of all the narratives in the scriptures to events in subsequent times. The most fanciful, and the most ingenious man, on this principle, was the best interpreter ; and as any man might attach any hidden mystery which he chose to the scriptures, they became wholly useless as an infallible guide. Better principles of interpretation now prevail ; and the great truth has gone forth, never more to be recalled, that the Bible is to be interpreted on the same principle as all other books ; that its language is to be investigated by the same laws as language in all other books ; and that no more liberty is to be taken in allegorizing the scriptures than may be taken with Herodotus or Livy. It is lawful to use narratives of real events to illustrate important principles always. Such a use is often made of history ; and such a use, I suppose, the apostle Paul makes here of an important fact in the history of the Old Testament. ¶ *For these are.* These may be used to represent the two covenants. The apostle *could not mean that the sons of Sarah and Hagar were literally the two covenants ;* for this could not be true, and the declaration would be unintelligible. In what sense could Ishmael be called *a covenant ?* The meaning, therefore, must be, that they furnished an apt illustration or representation of the two covenants ; they would show what the nature of the two covenants was. The words " are " and " is " are often used in this sense in the Bible, to denote that one thing *represents* another. Thus in the institution of the Lord's supper ; " Take, eat, this is my body " (Matt. xxvi. 26); *i. e.,* this *represents* my body. The bread was not the living body that was then before them. So in ver. 28. " This is my blood of the new covenant ;" *i. e.,* this represents my blood. The wine in the cup *could not* be the living blood of the Redeemer that was then flowing in his

veins ; see Note on that place ; comp Gen. xli. 26. ¶ *The two covenants* Marg. *Testaments.* The word means here, covenants or compacts ; see Note on 1 Cor. xi. 25. The two covenants here referred to, are the one on mount Sinai made with the Jews, and the other that which is made with the people of God in the gospel. The one resembles the condition of bondage in which Hagar and her son were ; the other the condition of freedom in which Sarah and Isaac were. ¶ *The one from the mount Sinai.* Marg. *Sina.* The Greek is *Sina,* though the word may be written either way. ¶ *Which gendereth to bondage.* Which tends to produce bondage or servitude That is, the laws are stern and severe ; and the observance of them costly, and onerous like a state of bondage ; see Note on Acts xv. 10. ¶ *Which is Agar.* Which Hagar would appropriately represent. The condition of servitude produced by the law had a strong resemblance to her condition as a slave.

25. *For this Agar is mount Sinai.* This Hagar well represents the law given on mount Sinai. No one can believe that Paul meant to say that Hagar was *literally* mount Sinai. A great deal of perplexity has been felt in regard to this passage, and Bentley proposed to cancel it altogether as an interpolation. But there is no good authority for this. Several MSS. and versions read it, " For this Sinai is a mountain in Arabia ;" others, " to this Hagar Jerusalem answereth," &c. Griesbach has placed these readings in the margin, and has marked them as not to be rejected as certainly false, but as worthy of a more attentive examination ; as sustained by some plausible arguments, though not in the whole satisfactory. The word Hagar in Arabic is said to signify *a rock ;* and it has been supposed that the name was appropriately given to mount Sinai, because it was a pile of rocks, and that Paul had allusion to this meaning of the word here. So

26 But Jerusalem *a* which is above is free, which is the mother of us all.

a He.12.22; Re.21.2,10.

27 For it is written, *b* Rejoice *thou* barren that bearest not ; break forth and cry, thou that travailest

b Isa.54.1.

Chandler, Rosenmüller, and others interpret it. But I cannot find in Castell or Gesenius that the word Hagar in Arabic has this signification; still less is there evidence that the name was ever given to mount Sinai by the Arabs, or that such a signification was known to Paul. The plainest and most obvious sense of a passage is generally the true sense ; and the obvious sense here is, that Hagar was *a fair representation* of mount Sinai, and of the law given there. ¶ *In Arabia.* Mount Sinai is situated in Arabia Petræa, or the Rocky. Rosenmüller says that this means "in the Arabic language;" but probably in this interpretation he stands alone. ¶ *And answereth to Jerusalem.* Marg. *Is in the same rank with.* The margin is the better translation. The meaning is, it is just like it, or corresponds with it. Jerusalem as it is now (*i. e.*, in the days of Paul), is like mount Sinai. It is subject to laws, and rites, and customs ; bound by a state of servitude, and fear, and trembling, such as existed when the law was given on mount Sinai. There is no freedom ; there are no great and liberal views ; there is none of the liberty which the gospel imparts to men. The word συστοιχεῖ, *answereth to,* means properly to advance in order together ; to go together with, as soldiers march along in the same rank ; and then to correspond to. It means here that mount Sinai and Jerusalem as it then was would be fitted *to march together* in the same platoon or rank. In marshalling an army, care is taken to place soldiers of the same height, and size, and skill, and courage, if possible, together. So here it means that they were *alike.* Both were connected with bondage, like Hagar. On the one, a law was given that led to bondage ; and the other was in fact under a miserable servitude of rites and forms. ¶ *Which now is.* As it exists now ; that is, *a slave* to rites

and forms, as it was in fact in the time of Paul. ¶ *And is in bondage.* To laws and customs. She was under hard and oppressive rites, like slavery. She was also in bondage to sin (John viii. 33, 34) ; but this does not seem to be the idea here. ¶ *With her children.* Her inhabitants. She is represented as a mother, and her inhabitants, the Jews, are in the condition of the son of Hagar. On this passage comp. Notes on 1 Cor. x. 4, for a more full illustration of the principles involved here.

26. *But Jerusalem which is above.* The spiritual Jerusalem ; the true church of God. Jerusalem was the place where God was worshipped, and hence it became synonymous with the word *church,* or is used to represent the people of God. The word rendered "above," (ἄνω) means properly *up above,* that which is above ; and hence heavenly, celestial ; Col. iii. 1, 2 ; John viii. 23. Here it means the heavenly or celestial Jerusalem ; Rev. xxi. 2, " And I John saw the holy city, new Jerusalem, coming down from God, out of heaven." Heb. xii. 22, " Ye are come unto mount Zion, and unto the city of the living God, the heavenly Jerusalem." Here it is used to denote the church, as being of heavenly origin. ¶ *Is free.* The spirit of the gospel is that of freedom. It is freedom from sin, freedom from the bondage of rites and customs, and it tends to promote universal freedom ; see Note on ver. 7 ; comp. John viii. 32, 36 ; Note, 2 Cor. iii. 17. ¶ *Which is the mother of us all.* Of all who are true Christians, whether we are by birth Jews or Gentiles. We should not, therefore, yield ourselves to any degrading and debasing servitude of any kind ; comp. Note, 1 Cor. vi. 12.

27. *For it is written.* This passage is found in Isa. liv. 1. For an exposition of its meaning as it occurs there, see my Notes on Isaiah. The *object* of the apostle in introducing it here seems to be to prove that the

not; for the desolate hath many more children than she which hath an husband.

a Ac.3.25; chap.3.29.

28 Now we, *a* brethren, as Isaac was, are the children of promise.

29 But as then he *b* that was

b Ge.21.9.

Gentiles as well as the Jews would partake of the privileges connected with the heavenly Jerusalem. He had in the previous verse spoken of the Jerusalem from above as the common mother of ALL true Christians, whether by birth Jews or Gentiles. This might be disputed or doubted by the Jews; and he therefore adduces this proof from the Old Testament. Or if it was not doubted, still the quotation was pertinent, and would illustrate the sentiment which he had just uttered. The mention of Jerusalem as *a mother* seems to have suggested this text. Isaiah had spoken of Jerusalem as a female that had been long desolate and childless, now rejoicing by a large accession from the Gentile world, and increased in numbers like a female who should have more children than one who had been long married. To this Paul appropriately refers when he says that the whole church, Jews and Gentiles, were the children of the heavenly Jerusalem, represented here as a rejoicing mother. He has not quoted literally from the Hebrew, but he has used the Septuagint version, and has retained the sense. The sense is, that the accession from the Gentile world would be far more numerous than the Jewish people had ever been; a prophecy that has been already fulfilled. ¶ *Rejoice* thou *barren that bearest not.* As a woman who has had no children would rejoice. This represents probably the heathen world as having been apparently forsaken and abandoned, and with whom there had been none of the true children of God. ¶ *Break forth and cry.* Or "break forth and exclaim;" *i. e.* break out into loud and glad exclamations at the remarkable accession. The *cry* here referred to was to be a *joyful* cry or shout; the language of exultation. So the Hebrew word in Isa. liv. 1 (צהל) means. ¶ *For the desolate.* She who was desolate and apparently forsaken. It literally re-

fers to a woman who had seemed to be desolate and forsaken, who was unmarried. In Isaiah it may refer to Jerusalem, long forsaken and desolate, or as some suppose to the Gentile world; see my Note on Isa. liv. 1. ¶ *Than she which hath an husband.* Perhaps referring to the Jewish people as in covenant with God, and often spoken of as *married* to him; Isa. lxii. 4, 5; liv. 5.

28. *Now we, brethren.* We who are Christians. ¶ *Are the children of the promise.* We so far resemble Isaac, that there are great and precious promises made to us. We are not in the condition of Ishmael, to whom no promise was made.

29. *But as then he that was born after the flesh.* Ishmael; see ver. 23. ¶ *Persecuted him* that was born *after the Spirit.* That is, Isaac. The phrase, "after the Spirit," here, is synonymous with "according to the promise" in the previous verse. It stands opposed to the phrase "after the flesh," and means that his birth was by the special or miraculous agency of God; see Rom. iv. It was not in the ordinary course of events. The *persecution* here referred to, was the injurious treatment which Isaac received from Ishmael, or the opposition which subsisted between them. The *particular* reference of Paul is doubtless to Gen. xxi. 9, where it is said that "Sarah saw the son of Hagar the Egyptian, which she had born unto Abraham, mocking." It was on account of this, and at the special request of Sarah, that Hagar and her son were expelled from the house of Abraham; Gen. xxi. 10. ¶ *Even so it is now.* That is, Christians, the children of the promise, are persecuted by the Jews, the inhabitants of Jerusalem, "as it now is," and who are uninterested in the promises, as Ishmael was. For an illustration of this, see Paley's *Horæ Paulinæ,* on this Epistle, No. V. Dr. Paley has remarked that it does not appear that

born after the flesh, persecuted him *that was born* after the Spirit, even so, ^a *it is* now.

30 Nevertheless, what saith ^b the Scripture? Cast out the bond-woman and her son: for the son of

the apostle Paul was ever set upon by the Gentiles, unless they were first stirred up by the Jews, except in two instances. One of these was at Philippi, after the cure of the Pythoness (Acts xvi. 19); and the other at Ephesus, at the instance of Demetrius; Acts xix. 24. The persecutions of the Christians arose, therefore, mainly from the Jews, from those who were in bondage to the law, and to rites and customs; and Paul's allusion here to the case of the persecution which Isaac the free-born son endured, is exceedingly pertinent and happy.

30. *Nevertheless.* But ('Αλλά). ¶ *What saith the Scripture?* What does the Scripture teach on the subject? What lesson does it convey in regard to the bondman? ¶ *Cast out the bondwoman and her son.* This was the language of Sarah, in an address to Abraham, requesting him to cast out Hagar and Ishmael; Gen. xxi. 10. That was done. Paul uses it here as applicable to the case before him. As used by him the meaning is, that every thing like servitude in the gospel is to be rejected, as Hagar and Ishmael were driven away. It does not mean, as it seems to me, that they were to expel the Jewish *teachers* in Galatia, but that they were to reject every thing like servitude and bondage; they were to adhere only to that which was free. Paul cannot here mean that the passage in Gen. xxi. 10, originally had reference to the gospel, for nothing evidently was farther from the mind of Sarah than any such reference; nor can it be shown that he meant to approve of or vindicate the conduct of Sarah; but he finds a passage applicable to his purpose, and he conveys his ideas in that language as exactly expressing his meaning. We all use language in that way wherever we find it.

[Yet God *confirmed* the sentence of Sarah; Gen. xxi. 12. Hence Mr. Scott thus para-

the bond-woman shall not be heir with the son of the free woman.

31 So then, brethren, we are not children of the bond-woman, but of the free.

a John 15.19.   *b* Ge.21.10,12.

phrases, " But as the Galatians might read in the Scriptures that *God himself* had *commanded* Hagar and Ishmael to be sent away from Abraham's family, that the son of the bondwoman might not share the inheritance with Isaac; even so the Jewish nation would soon be cast out of the church, and all who continued under the legal covenant excluded from heaven."]

31. *So then, brethren.* It follows from all this. Not from the allegory regarded as *an argument*—for Paul does not use it thus—but from the considerations suggested on the whole subject. Since the Christian religion is so superior to the Jewish; since we are by it freed from degrading servitude, and are not in bondage to rites and ceremonies; since it was designed to make us truly free, and since by that religion we are admitted to the privileges of sons, and are no longer under laws, and tutors, and governors, as if we were minors; from all this it follows, that we should feel and act, not as if we were children of a bondwoman, and born in slavery, but as if we were children of a free-woman, and born to liberty. It is the birthright of Christians to think, and feel, and act like freemen, and they should not allow themselves to become the slaves of customs, and rites, and ceremonies, but should feel that they are the adopted children of God.

Thus closes this celebrated allegory—an allegory that has greatly perplexed most expositors, and most readers of the Bible. In view of it, and of the exposition above, there are a few remarks which may not inappropriately be made.

(1.) It is by no means affirmed, that the history of Hagar and Sarah in Genesis, had any original reference to the gospel. The account there is a plain historical narrative, not *designed* to have any such reference.

(2.) The narrative contains important *principles*, that may be used as illustrating truth, and is so used by the apostle Paul. There are parallel points between the history and the truths of religion, where the one may be *illustrated* by the other.

(3.) The apostle does not use it at all in the way of *argument,* or as if that *proved* that the Galatians were not to submit to the Jewish rites and customs. It is an illustration of the comparative nature of servitude and freedom, and would, therefore, illustrate the difference between a servile compliance with Jewish rites, and the freedom of the gospel.

(4.) This use of an historical fact by the apostle does not make it proper for *us* to turn the Old Testament into allegory, or even to make a very free use of this mode of illustrating truth. That an allegory may be used sometimes with advantage, no one can doubt while the "Pilgrim's Progress" shall exist. Nor can any one doubt that Paul has here derived, in this manner, an important and striking illustration of truth from the Old Testament. But no one acquainted with the history of interpretation can doubt that vast injury has been done by a fanciful mode of explaining the Old Testament ; by making every fact in its history an allegory ; and every pin and pillar of the tabernacle and the temple a *type.* Nothing is better fitted to bring the whole science of interpretation into contempt; nothing more dishonours the Bible, than to make it a book of enigmas, and religion to consist in puerile conceits The Bible is a book of sense ; and all the doctrines essential to salvation are plainly revealed. It should be interpreted, not by mere conceit and by fancy, but by the sober laws according to which are interpreted other books. It should be explained, not under the influence of a vivid imagination, but under the influence of a heart imbued with a love of truth, and by an understanding disciplined to investigate the meaning of words and phrases, and capable of rendering *a reason* for the interpretation which is proposed. Men may abundantly use the facts in the Old Testament to illustrate human nature, as Paul did; but far distant be the day, when the principles of Origen

and of Cocceius shall **again** prevail, and when it shall be assumed, that "the Bible means every thing that it can be made to mean."

[These are excellent remarks, and the caution which the author gives against extravagant and imaginative systems of interpreting scripture cannot be too often repeated. It is allowed, however, nearly on all hands, that this allegory is brought forward by way of *illustration* only, and not of argument. This being the case, the question, as to whether the history in Genesis were *originally* intended to represent the matter, to which Paul here applies it, is certainly not of very great importance, notwithstanding the learned labour that has been expended on it, and to such an extent as to justify the critic's remark, "vexavit interpretes vehementer vexatus ab iis et ipse." Whatever be the original design of the passage, the apostle *has* employed it as an illustration of his subject, and was guided by the Spirit of inspiration in so doing. But certainly we should not be very far wrong, if since an apostle has *affirmed* such spiritual representation, we should suppose it originally intended by the Spirit ; nor are we in great danger of making types of every pin and pillar, *so long as we strictly confine ourselves to the admission of such only as rest upon apostolic authority.* "This transaction," says the eminently judicious Thomas Scott, "was so remarkable, the coincidence so exact, and the illustration so instructive, that we cannot doubt it *originally was intended,* by the Holy Spirit, as an allegory and type of those things to which the inspired apostle referred it."]

CHAPTER V.
ANALYSIS.

This chapter is properly a continuation of the argument in the previous chapter, and is designed to induce the Galatians to renounce their conformity to the Jewish law, and to become entirely conformed to the gospel. In particular, it seems to be designed to meet a charge that had been brought against him, that he had preached the necessity of circumcision, or that he had so practised it as to show that he believed that it was obligatory on others. Under his example, or pleading his authority, it seems the false teachers there had urged the necessity of its observance; see ver. 11. The argument and the exhortation consist of the following parts.

I. He exhorts them to stand firm in the liberty of Christianity, and not to be brought again under bondage; ver. 1.

II. He solemnly assures them, that if they depended on circumcision for salvation, they could derive no benefit from Christ. They put themselves into a perfect legal state, and must

CHAPTER V.

STAND *a* fast therefore in the *b* liberty wherewith Christ

a Ep.6.14.
b John 8.32,36; Ro.6.18; Ac.15.10.

depend on that alone; and that was equivalent to renouncing Christ altogether, or to falling from grace; ver. 2—6.

III. He assures them that their present belief could not have come from him by whom they were originally brought to the knowledge of the truth; but must have been from some foreign influence, operating like leaven; ver. 7—9.

IV. He says he had confidence in them, on the whole, that they would obey the truth, and that they would suffer him who had troubled them to bear his proper judgment, gently insinuating that he should be disowned or cut off; ver. 10, 12.

V. He vindicates himself from the charge that he preached the necessity of circumcision. His vindication was, that if he had done that, he would have escaped persecution, for then the offence of the cross would have ceased; ver. 11.

VI. He assures them that they had been called unto liberty; that the gospel had made them free. Yet Paul felt how easy it was to abuse this doctrine, and to pretend that Christ had freed them from *all* restraint, and from the bondage of *all* law. Against this he cautions them. Their liberty was not licentiousness. It was not freedom from all the restraints of the law. It was not that they might give indulgence to the passions of the flesh. It was designed that they should serve one another; and not fall into the indulgence of raging passions, producing strife and mutual hatred; ver. 13—15.

VII. To illustrate this, and to show them the evils of giving indulgence to their appetites under the pretence that they were *free*, he proceeds to show what *were* the passions to which carnal indulgence would give rise, or what were the works of the flesh; ver. 16—21.

VIII. On the other hand, the Spirit produces a train of most lovely vir-

hath made us free, and be not entangled again with the yoke of bondage.

2 Behold, I Paul say unto you,

tues, feelings, and affections, against which there could be no law; v. 22, 23.

IX. They who were Christians had in fact crucified the flesh. They were bound to live after the teachings of the Spirit, and Paul, therefore, exhorts them to lay aside all vain-glory and envy, and to live in peace; ver. 24—26.

1. *Stand fast, therefore.* Be firm and unwavering. This verse properly belongs to the previous chapter, and should not have been separated from it. The sense is, that they were to be firm and unyielding in maintaining the great principles of Christian liberty. They had been freed from the bondage of rites and ceremonies; and they should by no means, and in no form, yield to them again. ¶ *In the liberty,* &c.; comp. John viii. 32, 36; Rom. vi. 18; Notes, chap. iv. 3—5. ¶ *And be not entangled again.* Tindal renders this, "And wrap not yourselves again." The sense is, do not again allow such a yoke to be put on you; do not again become slaves to any rites, and customs, and habits. ¶ *The yoke of bondage.* Of servitude to the Jewish laws; see Note, Acts xv. 10.

2. *Behold, I Paul say unto you.* I, who at first preached the gospel to you; I, too, who have been circumcised, and who was formerly a strenuous assertor of the necessity of observing the laws of Moses; and I, too, who am charged (see ver. 11) with still preaching the necessity of circumcision, now solemnly say to you, that if you are circumcised with a view to being justified by that in whole or in part, it amounts to a rejection of the doctrine of justification by Christ, and an entire apostacy from him. He is to be "a whole Saviour." No one is to share with him in the honour of saving men; and no rite, no custom, no observance of law, is to divide the honour with his death. The design of Paul is to give them the most solemn assurance on this point; and

that if ye be circumcised, Christ shall profit you nothing.

3 For I testify again to every

by his own authority and experience to guard them from the danger, and to put the matter to rest. ¶ *That if ye be circumcised.* This must be understood with reference to the subject under consideration. If you are circumcised with such a view as is maintained by the false teachers that have come among you; that is, with an idea that it is necessary in order to your justification. He evidently did not mean that if any of them *had* been circumcised before their conversion to Christianity; nor could he mean to say, that circumcision in all cases amounted to a rejection of Christianity, for he had himself procured the circumcision of Timothy, Acts xvi. 3. If it was done, as it was then, for prudential considerations, and with a wish not necessarily to irritate the Jews, and to give one a more ready access to them, it was not to be regarded as wrong. But if, as the false teachers in Galatia claimed, as a thing *essential* to salvation, as *indispensable* to justification and acceptance with God, then the matter assumed a different aspect; and then it became in fact a renouncing of Christ as *himself sufficient* to save us. So with any thing else. Rites and ceremonies in religion may be in themselves well enough, if they are *held* to be matters not essential; but the moment they are regarded as vital and essential, that moment they begin to infringe on the doctrine of justification by faith alone, and that moment they are to be rejected; and it is because of the danger that this *will* be the case, that they are to be used sparingly in the Christian church. Who does not know the danger of depending upon prayers, and alms, and the sacraments, and extreme unction, and penance, and empty forms for salvation? And who does not know how much in the papal communion the great doctrine of justification has been obscured by numberless such rites and forms? ¶ *Christ shall profit you nothing.* Will be of no advantage to

man that is circumcised, that he is a debtor to do the whole law.

4 Christ is become of no ef-

you. Your dependence on circumcision, in these circumstances, will in fact amount to a rejection of the Saviour, and of the doctrine of justification by him.

3. *For I testify again.* Probably he had stated this when he had preached the gospel to them first, and he now solemnly bears witness to the same thing *again.* Bloomfield, however, supposes that the word *again* here (πάλιν) means, on the other hand, or, *furthermore*, or, as we would say, "and again." ¶ *That he is a debtor to do the whole law.* He binds himself to obey all the law of Moses. Circumcision was the distinguishing badge of the Jews, as baptism is of Christians. A man, therefore, who became circumcised became *a professor of the Jewish religion*, and bound himself to obey all its peculiar laws. This must be understood, of course, with reference to the point under discussion; and means, if he did it with a view to justification, or as a thing that was necessary and binding. It would not apply to such a case as that of Timothy, where it was a matter of mere expediency or prudence; see Note on ver. 2.

4. *Christ is become of no effect unto you.* You will derive no advantage from Christ. His work in regard to you is needless and vain. If you can be justified in any other way than by him, then of course you do not need him, and your adoption of the other mode is in fact a renunciation of him. Tindal renders this, "Ye are gone quite from Christ." The word here used (καταργέω), means properly, to render inactive, idle, useless; to do away, to put an end to; and here it means that they had withdrawn from Christ, if they attempted to be justified by the law. They would not need him if they could be thus justified; and they could derive no benefit from him. A man who can be justified by his own obedience, does not need the aid or the merit of another; and if it was true, as they seemed to suppose,

fect *a* unto you, whosoever of you are justified by the law : ye are fallen *b* from grace.

5 For we through the Spirit wait *c*

that they could be justified by the law, it followed that the work of Christ was in vain so far as they were concerned. ¶ *Whosoever of you are justified by the law.* On the supposition that any of you are justified by the law; or if, as you seem to suppose, any are justified by the law. The apostle does not say that this had in fact ever occurred; but he merely makes a supposition. If such a thing should or could occur, it would follow that you had fallen from grace. ¶ *Ye are fallen from grace.* That is, this would amount to apostasy from the religion of the Redeemer, and would be in fact a rejection of the grace of the gospel. That this had ever in fact occurred among true Christians the apostle does not affirm *unless* he affirmed that men can in fact be justified by the law, since he makes the falling from grace a consequence of that. But did Paul mean to teach that? Did he mean to affirm that any man in fact had been, or could be justified by his own obedience to the law ? Let his own writings answer ; see, especially, Rom. iii. 20. But unless he held that, then this passage does not prove that any one who has ever been a true Christian has fallen away. The fair interpretation of the passage does not demand that. Its simple and obvious meaning is, that if a man who has been a professed Christian *should be* justified by his own conformity to the law, and adopt that mode of justification, then that would amount to a rejection of the mode of salvation by Christ, and would be a renouncing of the plan of justification by grace. The two systems cannot be united. The adoption of the one is, in fact, a rejection of the other. Christ will be "a whole Saviour," or none. This passage, therefore, *cannot* be adduced to prove that any true Christian has in fact fallen away from grace, unless it proves also that man may be justified by the deeds of the law, contrary to the repeated dec-

for the hope of righteousness *d* by faith.

6 For in Jesus Christ neither

a Ro.9.31.32.   *b* He.12.15.   *c* Ro.8.25
                    d 2Ti.4.8.

larations of Paul himself. The word " grace " here, does not mean grace in the sense of *personal religion,* it means the *system* of salvation by grace, in contradistinction from that by merit or by works—the system of the gospel.

5. For we. We who are Christians. It is a characteristic of the true Christian. ¶ *Through the Spirit.* The Holy Spirit. We expect salvation only by his aid. ¶ *Wait for.* That is, we *expect* salvation in this way. The main idea is, not that of *waiting* as if the thing were *delayed;* it is that of *expecting.* The sense is, that true Christians have no other hope of salvation than by faith in the Lord Jesus. It is not by their own works, nor is it by any conformity to the law. The object of Paul is, to show them the true nature of the Christian hope of eternal life, and to recall them from dependence on their conformity to the law. ¶ *The hope of righteousness.* The hope of justification. They had no other hope of justification than by faith in the Redeemer ; see Note on Rom. i. 17.

6. For in Jesus Christ. In the religion which Christ came to establish. ¶ *Neither circumcision,* &c. It makes no difference whether a man is circumcised or not. He is not saved *because* he is circumcised, nor is he condemned *because* he is not. The design of Christianity is to abolish these rites and ceremonies, and to introduce a way of salvation that shall be applicable to all mankind alike ; see Notes on ch. iii. 28; 1 Cor. vii. 19; comp. Rom. ii. 29. ¶ *But faith which worketh by love.* Faith that evinces its existence by love to God, and benevolence to men. It is not a mere *intellectual* belief, but it is that which reaches the heart, and controls the affections. It is not a *dead* faith, but it is that which is operative, and which is seen in Christian kindness and affection. It is not mere belief of the truth, or mere *orthodoxy,* but it is that which produces true at-

" circumcision availeth any thing, nor uncircumcision ; but faith which *b* worketh by love.

7 Ye did run well ; who did hinder you, that ye should not obey the truth ?

a 1 Co.7.19.   b 1 Ti.1.3 ; Ja.2.18—22.

8 This persuasion *cometh* not or him that calleth you.

9 A little *c* leaven leaveneth the whole lump.

10 I have confidence in you through the Lord, that ye will

1 or, *drive you back.*   c Mat.13.33 ; 1 Co.5.6.

tachment to others. A mere intellectual assent to the truth may leave the heart cold and unaffected ; mere orthodoxy, however bold and self-confident, and "sound," may not be inconsistent with contentions, and strifes, and logomachies, and divisions. The true faith is that which is seen in benevolence, in love to God, in love to all who bear the Christian name ; in a readiness to do good to all mankind. This shows that the *heart* is affected by the faith that is held ; and this in the nature and design of all genuine religion. Tindal renders this, "faith, which by love is mighty in operation."

7. *Ye did run well.* The Christian life is often represented as a race ; see Notes on 1 Cor. ix. 24—26. Paul means here, that they began the Christian life with ardour and zeal ; comp. chap. iv. 15. ¶ *Who did hinder you.* Marg. *Drive you back.* The word used here (ἀνακόπτω) means properly to beat or drive back. Hence it means to hinder, check, or retard. Dr. Doddridge remarks that this is "an Olympic expression, and properly signifies *coming across the course* while a person is running in it, in such a manner as to *jostle,* and throw him out of the way." Paul asks, with emphasis, who it could have been that retarded them in their Christian course, implying that it could have been done only by their own consent, or that there was really no cause why they should not have continued as they began. ¶ *That ye should not obey the truth.* The true system of justification by faith in the Redeemer. That you should have turned aside, and embraced the dangerous errors in regard to the necessity of obeying the laws of Moses.

8. *This persuasion.* This belief that it is necessary to obey the laws of Moses, and to intermingle the observance of Jewish rites with the belief of the Christian doctrines in order to be saved. ¶ *Not of him that calleth you.* That is, of God, who had called them into his kingdom. That it refers to God and not to Paul is plain. They knew well enough that Paul had not persuaded them to it, and it was important now to show them that it could not be traced to God, though they who taught it pretended to be commissioned by him.

9. *A little leaven,* &c. This is evidently a proverbial expression ; see it explained in the Notes on 1 Cor. v. 6. Its meaning here is, that the embracing of the errors which they had adopted was to be traced to some influence existing among themselves, and acting like leaven. It may either mean that there was existing among them from the first a slight *tendency* to conform to rites and customs, and that this had now like leaven pervaded the mass ; or it may mean that the false teachers there might be compared to leaven, whose doctrines, though *they* were few in number, had pervaded the mass of Christians ; or it may mean, as many have supposed, that *any* conformity to the Jewish law was like leaven. If they practised circumcision, it would not stop there. The tendency to conform to Jewish rites would spread from that until it would infect all the doctrines of religion, and they would fall into the observance of *all* the rites of the Jewish law. It seems to me that the *second* interpretation referred to above is the correct one ; and that the apostle means to say, that the influence which had brought this change about was at first small and unimportant ; that there might have been but a few teachers of that kind, and it might have not been deemed worthy of particular attention or alarm ; but that the doctrines thus infused into the churches,

be none otherwise minded : but he
that troubleth you shall bear his *a*
judgment, whosoever he be.

11 And I, brethren, if I yet

preach circumcision, why do I
yet suffer persecution? *b* then
is the offence *c* of the cross
ceased.

a 2 Co.10.6.

b chap.6.12.   *c* 1 Co.1.23.

had spread like leaven, until the whole
mass had become affected.

10. *I have confidence in you,* &c.
Though they had been led astray, and
had embraced many false opinions,
yet, on the whole, Paul had confidence
in their piety, and believed they would
yet return and embrace the truth.
¶ *That ye will be none otherwise
minded.* That is, than you have been
taught by me ; or than I think and
teach on the subject. Paul doubtless
means to say, that he had full confidence that they would embrace the
views which he was inculcating on the
subject of justification, and he makes
this remark in order to modify the
severity of his tone of reprehension,
and to show that, notwithstanding all
he had said, he had confidence still in
their piety. He believed that they
would concide with him in his opinion,
alike on the general subject of justification, and in regard to the cause of
their alienation from the truth. He,
therefore, gently insinuates that it was
not to be traced to themselves that
they had departed from the truth, but
to the "little leaven " that had leavened the mass ; and he adds, that
whoever had done this, should be held
to be responsible for it. ¶ *But he
that troubleth you.* By leading you
into error. ¶ *Shall bear his judgment.* Shall be responsible for it,
and will receive proper treatment from
you. He gently states this general
principle, which is so obvious ; states
that he does not believe that the de-
fection is to be traced to themselves ;
and designs to prepare their minds for
a proposition which he intends to submit (ver. 12), that the offending person or persons should be disowned and
cut off. ¶ *Whosoever he be.* " I do
not know who he is. I mention no
names ; accuse no one by name ; and
advise no severe measures against any
particular individual. I state only the
obvious principle that every man
should bear his own burden, and be

held responsible for what he has done
—no matter who he is."

11. *And I, brethren.* Paul here proceeds to vindicate himself from giving
countenance to the doctrines which
they had advanced there. It is evident that the false teachers in Galatia
appealed to Paul himself, and alleged
that *he* insisted on the necessity of
circumcision, and that they were teaching no more than he taught. On
what they founded this is unknown.
It *may* have been mere slander ; or it
may have arisen from the fact that he
had circumcised Timothy (Acts xvi.
3), and, possibly, that he may have
encouraged circumcision in some other
similar cases. Or it may have been
inferred from the fact (which was undoubtedly true) that Paul in general
complied with the customs of the Jews
when he was with them. But his
conduct and example had been greatly
perverted. He had *never* enjoined
circumcision as necessary to salvation ; and had never complied with
Jewish customs where there was danger that it would be understood that
he regarded them as at all indispensable, or as furnishing a ground of acceptance with God. ¶ *If I yet preach
circumcision.* If I preach it as necessary to salvation ; or if I enjoin it
on those who are converted to Christianity. ¶ *Why do I yet suffer persecution?* That is, from the Jews.
" Why do they oppose me ? Circumcision is the peculiar badge of the
Jewish religion ; it implies all the rest
(see ver. 2) ; and if I preach the necessity of that, it would satisfy the
Jews, and save me from persecution.
They would never persecute one who
did that as they do me ; and the fact
that I *am* thus persecuted by them is
full demonstration that I am not regarded as preaching the necessity of
circumcision." It is remarkable that
Paul does not expressly deny the
charge. The reason may be, that his
own word would be called in question,

12 I would they were even cut off which trouble you.

13 For, brethren, ye have been called unto liberty ; only *use* not

or that it might require much explanation to show *why* he had recommended circumcision in any case, as in the case of Timothy; Acts xvi. 3. But the fact that he was persecuted by the Jews settled the question, and showed that he did not preach the necessity of circumcision in any such sense as to satisfy them, or in any such sense as was claimed by the false teachers in Galatia. In regard to the fact that Paul was persecuted by the Jews ; see Acts xiv. 1, 2, 19 ; xvii. 4, 5, 13 ; comp. Paley, *Horæ Paulinæ*, Galat. No. V. ¶ *Then is the offence of the cross ceased.* "For if I should preach the necessity of circumcision, as is alleged, the offence of the cross of Christ would be removed. The necessity of depending on the merits of the sacrifice made on the cross would be taken away, since then men could be saved by conformity to the laws of Moses. The very thing that I have so much insisted on, and that has been such a stumbling-block to the Jews (Note, 1 Cor. i. 23), that conformity to their rites was of no avail, and that they must be saved only by the merits of a crucified Saviour, would be done away with." Paul means that if this had been done, he would have saved himself from giving offence, and from the evils of persecution. He would have preached that men could be saved by conformity to Jewish rites, and that would have saved him from all the persecutions which he had endured in consequence of preaching the necessity of salvation by the cross.

12. *I would they were even cut off.* That is, as I understand it, from the communion of the church. So far am I, says Paul, from agreeing with them, and preaching the necessity of circumcision as they do, that I sincerely wish they were excluded from the church as unworthy a place among the children of God. For a very singular and monstrous interpretation of this passage, though adopted by Chrysostom, Theodoret, Theophylact, Jerome, Grotius, Rosenmüller, Koppe, and others, the learned reader may consult Koppe on this verse. To my amazement, I find that this interpretation has also been adopted by Robinson in his Lexicon, on the word *ἀποκόπτω*. I will state the opinion in the words of Koppe. *Non modo circumcidant se, sed, si velint, etiam mutilant se—ipsa genitalia resecent.* The simple meaning is, I think, that Paul wished that the authors of these errors and disturbances were excluded from the church. ¶ *Which trouble you.* Who pervert the true doctrines of salvation, and who thus introduce error into the church. Error always sooner or later causes trouble ; comp. Note, 1 Cor. v. 7.

13. *For, brethren, ye have been called unto liberty.* Freedom from Jewish rites and ceremonies ; see the Notes on chap. iii. 28 ; iv. 9, 21—31. The meaning here is, that Paul wished the false teachers removed *because* true Christians had been called unto liberty, and they were abridging and destroying that liberty. They were not in subjection to the law of Moses, or to any thing else that savoured of bondage. They were free ; free from the servitude of sin, and free from subjection to expensive and burdensome rites and customs. They were to remember this as a great and settled principle ; and so vital a truth was this, and so important that it should be maintained, and so great the evil of forgetting it, that Paul says he earnestly wishes (ver. 12) that all who would reduce them to that state of servitude were cut off from the Christian church. ¶ *Only use not liberty,* &c. The word *use* here introduced by our translators, obscures the sense. The idea is, "You are called to liberty, but it is not liberty for an occasion to the flesh. It is not freedom from virtuous restraints, and from the laws of God. It is liberty from the servitude of sin, and religious rites and ceremonies, not freedom from the necessary restraints of virtue." It was necessary to give this caution, because, (1.) There was

a liberty for an occasion to the flesh, but by love serve *b* one another.

14 For all the law is fulfilled in one word, *even* in this,

a 1 Co.8.9 ; 1 Pe.2.16.   *b* 1 John 3.18.

c Thou shalt love thy neighbour as thyself.

15 But if ye bite and devour one another, take heed that ye be not consumed one of another.

c Le.19.18 ; Mat.22.39,40 ; James 2.8.

a strong tendency in all converts from heathenism to relapse again into their former habits. Licentiousness abounded, and where they had been addicted to it before their conversion, and where they were surrounded by it on every hand, they were in constant danger of falling into it again. A bare and naked declaration, therefore, that they had been called to *liberty*, to freedom from restraint, might have been misunderstood, and some might have supposed that they were free from *all* restraints. (2.) It is needful to guard the doctrine from abuse at all times. There has been a strong tendency, as the history of the church has shown, to abuse the doctrine of grace. The doctrine that Christians are "free;" that there is liberty to them from restraint, has been perverted always by Antinomians, and been made the occasion of their indulging freely in sin. And the result has shown that nothing was more important than to guard the doctrine of *Christian liberty*, and to show exactly what Christians are *freed from*, and what laws are still binding on them. Paul is, therefore, at great pains to show that the doctrines which he had maintained did not lead to licentiousness, and did not allow the indulgence of sinful and corrupt passions. ¶ *An occasion*. As allowing indulgence to the flesh, or as a furtherance or help to corrupt passions ; see the word explained in the Notes on Rom. vii. 8. ¶ *To the flesh*. The word flesh is often used in the writings of Paul to denote corrupt and gross passions and affections ; see Notes on Rom. vii. 18 ; viii. 1. ¶ *But by love serve one another*. By the proper manifestation of love one to another strive to promote each other's welfare. To do this will not be inconsistent with the freedom of the gospel. When there is *love* there is no servitude. Duty is pleasant, and offices of kindness agree-

able. Paul does not consider them as freed from *all* law and *all* restraint; but they are to be governed by the law of love. They were not to feel that they were *so* free that they might lawfully give indulgence to the desires of the flesh, but they were to regard themselves as under the law to love one another ; and thus they would fulfil the law of Christian freedom.

14. *For all the law is fulfilled, &c.* That is, this expresses the substance of the whole law ; it embraces and comprises all. The apostle of course here alludes to the law in regard to our duty to our fellow-men, since that was the point which he particularly enforces. He is saying that this law would counteract all the evil workings of the flesh, and if this were fulfilled, all our duty to others would be discharged. A similar sentiment he has expressed in Rom. xiii. 8—10 ; see Notes on that passage. The *turn* here in the discussion is worthy of particular notice. With great skill he changes the subject from a doctrinal argument to a strain of practical remark, and furnishes most important lessons for the right mode of overcoming our corrupt and sensual passions, and discharging our duty to others. ¶ *Thou shalt love thy neighbour, &c* ; see this explained in the Note on Mat. xix. 19.

15. *But if ye bite*. The word here used (δάκνω), means, properly, to bite, to sting ; and here seems to be used in the sense of contending and striving—a metaphor not improbably taken from dogs and wild beasts. ¶ *And devour one another*. As wild beasts do. The sense is, "if you contend with each other ;" and the reference is, probably, to the strifes which would arise between the two parties in the churches—the Jewish and the Gentile converts. ¶ *Take heed that ye be not consumed, &c*. As wild beasts contend sometimes until both are

16 *This* I say then, Walk *a* in the Spirit, and *1* ye shall not fulfil the lust of the flesh.

17 For *b* the flesh lusteth against the Spirit, and the Spirit against the flesh: and these are contrary *c* the one to the other ; so that *d* ye cannot do the things that ye would.

a Ro.8.1,4,13.   1 or, *fulfil not.*

b Ro.7.21—23.   c Ro.8.6,7.
d Ro.7.15,19.

slain. Thus, the idea is, in their contentions they would destroy the spirituality and happiness of each other ; their characters would be ruined ; and the church be overthrown. The readiest way to destroy the spirituality of a church, and to annihilate the influence of religion, is to excite a spirit of contention.

16. This *I say then.* This is the true rule about overcoming the propensities of your carnal natures, and of avoiding the evils of strife and contention. ¶ *Walk.* The Christian life is often represented as a journey, and the word *walk*, in the scripture, is often equivalent to *live ;* Mark vii. 5 ; Notes, Rom. iv. 12 ; vi. 4 ; viii. 1. ¶ *In the Spirit.* Live under the influences of the Holy Spirit ; admit those influences fully into your hearts. Do not resist him, but yield to all his suggestions ; see Note, Rom. viii. 1. What the Holy Spirit would produce, Paul states in ver. 22, 23. If a man would yield his heart to those influences, he would be able to overcome all his carnal propensities ; and it is because he resists that Spirit, that he is ever overcome by the corrupt passions of his nature. Never was a better, a safer, or a more easy rule given to overcome our corrupt and sensual desires than that here furnished ; comp. Notes, Rom. viii. 1—13. *And ye shall not fulfil, &c.* Marg. *Fulfil not*—as if it were a command. So Tindal renders it. But the more common interpretation, as it is the more significant, is that adopted by our translators. Thus it is not merely a command, *it* is the statement of an important and deeply interesting truth—that the only way to overcome the corrupt desires and propensities of our nature, is by submitting to the influences of the Holy Spirit. It is not by philosophy ; it is not by mere resolutions to resist them ; it is not by the force of education and laws ; it is

only by admitting into our souls the influence of religion, and yielding ourselves to the guidance of the Holy Spirit of God. If we live under the influences of that Spirit, we need not fear the power of the sensual and corrupt propensities of our nature.

17. *For the flesh lusteth against the Spirit.* The inclinations and desires of the flesh are contrary to those of the Spirit. They draw us away in an opposite direction, and while the Spirit of God would lead us one way, our carnal nature would lead us another, and thus produce the painful controversy which exists in our minds. The word "Spirit" here refers to the Spirit of God, and to his influences on the heart. ¶ *And these are contrary, &c.* They are opposite in their nature. They never can harmonize ; see Rom. viii. 6, 7 ; comp. below ver. 19—23. The *contrariety* Paul has illustrated by showing what each produces ; and they are as opposite as adultery, wrath, strife, murders, drunkenness, &c., are to love, joy, goodness, gentleness, and temperance. ¶ *So that ye cannot do the things that ye would ;* see this sentiment illustrated in the Notes on Rom. vii. 15—19. The expression "cannot do" is stronger by far than the original, and it is doubted whether the original will bear this interpretation. The literal translation would be, " Lest what ye will, those things ye should do " (ἵνα μὴ ἃ ἂν θέλητε, ταῦτα ποιῆτε). It is rendered by Doddridge, " So that ye do not the things that ye would." By Locke, " You do not the things that you propose to yourselves ;" and Locke remarks on the passage, " Ours is the only translation that I know which renders it cannot." The Vulgate and the Syriac give a literal translation of the Greek, " So that you do not what you would." This is undoubtedly the true rendering ; and, in the original, there is no declaration about the possibility or

the impossibility, the ability or the inability to do these things. It is simply a statement *of a fact*, as it is in Rom. vii. 15, 19. That statement is, that in the mind of a renewed man there is a contrariety in the two influences which bear on his soul—the Spirit of God inclining him in one direction, and the lusts of the flesh in another ; that one of these influences is so great as in fact to restrain and control the mind, and prevent its doing what it would otherwise do; that when there is an inclination in one direction, there is a controlling and over-powering influence in another, producing a conflict, which prevents it, and which finally checks and restrains the mind. There is no reason for interpreting this, moreover, as seems always to be the case, of the over-powering tendency in the mind to evil, as if it taught that the Christian was desirous of doing good, but *could not*, on account of his indwelling corruption. So far as the language of Paul or the fact is concerned, it may be understood of just the opposite, and may mean, that such are the restraints and influences of the Holy Spirit on the heart, that the Christian *does not* the evil which he otherwise would, and to which his corrupt nature inclines him. He (Paul) is exhorting them (ver. 16) to walk in the Spirit, and assures them that thus they would not fulfil the lusts of the flesh. To encourage them to this, he reminds them that there were contrary principles in their minds, the influences of the Spirit of God, and a carnal and downward tendency of the flesh. These are contrary one to the other ; and such are, in fact, the influences of the Spirit on the mind, that the Christian does not do the things which he otherwise would. So understood, or understood in any fair interpretation of the original, it makes no assertion about the ability or inability of man to do right or wrong. It affirms *as a fact*, that where these opposite principles exist, a man does not do the things which otherwise he would. If a man *could* not do otherwise than he actually does, he would not be to blame. Whether a Christian *could* not resist

the influences of the Holy Spirit, and yield to the corrupt desires of the flesh ; or whether he *could* not overcome these evil propensities and do right always, are points on which the apostle here makes no affirmation. His is the statement of *a mere fact*, that where these counteracting propensities exist in the mind, there is a conflict, and that the man does not do what he otherwise would do.

[The translation of this clause which the author has given, may be allowed. It is certainly adopted by many Calvinists, and by Mr. Scott among the number. Yet Bloomfield, who cannot be suspected of any great leaning towards that class of theologians, defends the common translation. "I am surprised," says he, "that Mr. Locke should think our common version is singular in the sense it assigns. The Latin versions are indeed dubious, but most of the early commentators were inclined to adopt the sense 'cannot do,' and so almost all eminent Biblical critics for the last century." Nor would we object to the meaning which the author has attached to the clause, viz. that such are the restraints and influences of the Holy Spirit on the heart, that the Christian *does not* the evil which he otherwise would. This sense is ably advocated by Dr. Wardlaw, in his Discourses on the Socinian controversy. He contends, that in this view, the connection is simple and obvious ; and affirms "that the Spirit's opposition to the flesh, for the purpose of preventing the indulgence of its inclinations, is either assigned as a reason for the statement, that if they 'walked in the Spirit,' the lust of the flesh would not be fulfilled, or is presented as an encouragement to compliance with the admonition, so to walk;" otherwise, he thinks no legitimate sequence can be found in the apostle's exhortation; 5th edit. p. 398. Yet, were we disposed to insist on the other sense, might not the terrible contest between the fleshly and the spiritual nature be alleged as the apostle's reason for the exhortation, continually to abide, to *walk* in the Spirit as the only remedy for this perpetual malady ? And, in this way, the sequence is just as natural and obvious as in the other view. Mr. Scott and many other commentators combine both senses. "Believers do not the things which they would. They are not so holy as they long to be; nor yet do they indulge those corrupt inclinations which still rise up in their hearts, and cause them much trouble."—Comment in loco. Our author's assertion, therefore, that this passage "seems *always* to be interpreted of the overpowering tendency in the mind to evil," admits of many exceptions, even on the Calvinistic side ; and the implied censure, that passages are violently strained to support opinion, on the subject of human inability, different from his own, falls to the ground. The *new* sense, which, by implication, he affirms *never* to be mentioned by those of opposite views, is by them frequently asserted and vindicated !

But apart altogether from the proposed translation of the clause, and the meaning attached to it in its amended form—admitting both; it may, notwithstanding, be observed, on

18 But if *a* ye be led of the Spirit, ye are not under the law.

19 Now the works of the flesh

b are manifest; which are *these*, Adultery, fornication, uncleanness, lasciviousness,

---

a Ro.6.14; 8.2.

b Mat.15.19; Ep.5.3—6; Col.3.5,6; Re.22.15.

---

the whole passage, that if it contains nothing *directly* on the subject of human ability, yet the struggle it asserts between two opposite principles, the flesh and the spirit, in the renewed mind, is not over-favourable to *great* views as to what man *can* do, or *could* do. If in the renewed mind this can least prevail, and prevail to such an extent, as the passage intimates, what must be the state of the unrenewed mind? The answer is too obvious. Allow, that the apostle states no more than the *fact*, that, in consequence of this struggle, the Christian " does not do the things which otherwise he would *do*," and *even* take this in the sense of not doing the *evil* he otherwise would have done, still it follows, and with all the conviction of direct assertion, that, independently of spiritual aid, the man or the Christian *could not* or *would not* have acted rightly.

Mr. Barnes has expressed himself somewhat plainly on this subject under Rom. viii. 7, where the reader will find, in a supplementary Note on that passage, much that is applicable to what occurs here. "Whether," he there says, "the *man himself* might not obey the law, whether *he* has, or has not ability to do it, is a question which the apostle does not touch." He is careful, however, not directly to assert the affirmative, but leaves the reader to draw the inference in regard to the author's opinion. And in this place, especially, have we reason to complain of disingenuous ambiguity. The phraseology connected with this dispute, *can*, *could*, &c., should have been explained. If it had been affirmed that God requires nothing of us which is *physically* or *naturally* impossible for us to do; *e. g.*, He does not require us to transport ourselves from earth to heaven, and from heaven to earth, as angels do at his bidding, *because* for such service we have no *natural* powers—there could have been no disputing of this position. But if it be *natural* or *physical* power to which the author alludes under the term *can* and *could*, why not say so, and by a brief explanation relieve his unthinking readers from their perplexity? If men can and could discharge duty only in so far as natural ability is concerned, but *morally* are allowed to be unable to think a good thought, all that sound Calvinists desire on this subject is conceded. Nor, remains there the slightest force in the objection, that "if a man *could not* do otherwise than he actually does, he would not be to blame." Men will not be taken to account for natural inabilities, for certainly they are not to blame that they have not the faculties of angels. But *moral* inability is *sin*, and for it we must answer. It is *rooted aversion* to that which is good. Meantime, statements, such as that quoted above, without explanation, have done unmeasureable mischief to certain classes of readers; and furnishing them with an argument against the doctrine of accountability, are fitted to harden them in sin.

There seems too much truth in the censure passed on the New School Divines of America, that *even* when they "retain the term *natural* in connection with ability, and thus *appear* to accord with those who are in the

habit of making the distinction (of natural and moral ability) in reality, they occupy very different ground. Though when they speak of ability, they frequently annex to it the word "natural," they seldom speak of inability at all; *but produce the impression, that the ability which they preach is fully adequate to enable the sinner, independently of divine grace, to do all that God requires.*"—Old and New Views by James Wood, Philadelphia, p. 162. The same author asserts, and with some appearance of reason, that "though Mr. Barnes expresses himself with much more caution than Messrs. Finney and Duffield, it is apparent that he favours their sentiments." Ibid. page 168.

18. *But if ye be led of the Spirit.* If you submit to the teachings and guidance of the Holy Spirit. ¶ *Ye are not under the law.* You are under a different dispensation—the dispensation of the Spirit. You are free from the restraints and control of the Mosaic law, and are under the control of the Spirit of God.

19. *Now the works of the flesh.* What the flesh, or what corrupt and unrenewed human nature produces. ¶ *Are manifest.* Plain, well-known. The world is full of illustrations of what corrupt human nature produces, and as to the existence and nature of those works, no one can be ignorant. It is evident here that the word σάρξ, *flesh*, is used to denote *corrupt human nature*, and not merely the *body*; since many of the vices here enumerated are the passions of the *mind* or the *soul*, rather than of the body. Such are "wrath," "strife," "heresies," "envyings," &c., which cannot be said to have their seat in the body. If the word, therefore, is used to denote *human nature*, the passage furnishes a sad commentary on its tendency, and on the character of man. It is closely parallel to the declaration of the Saviour in Matt. xv. 19. Of the *nature* of most of these sins, or works of the flesh, it is unnecessary to offer any comment. They are not so rare as not to be well known, and the meaning of the words requires little exposition. In regard to the *existence* of these vices as the result

20 Idolatry, witchcraft, hatred, variance, emulations, wrath, strife, seditions, heresies,

21 Envyings, murders, drunkenness, revellings, and such like :

of the which I tell you before, as I have also told *you* in time past, that they which do such things shall not inherit the kingdom of God.

of human nature, the Notes on Rom. i. may be examined ; or a single glance at the history of the past, or at the present condition of the heathen and a large part of the Christian world, would furnish an ample and a painful demonstration.

20. *Witchcraft.* Pretending to witchcraft. The apostle does not vouch for the actual existence of witchcraft ; but he says that what was known as such was a proof of the corrupt nature of man, and was one of the fruits of it. No one can doubt it. It was a system of imposture and falsehood throughout ; and nothing is a better demonstration of the depravity of the human heart than an extended and systematized attempt to impose on mankind. The word which is here used (φαρμακία, whence our word *pharmacy*, from φάρμακον, a medicine, poison, magic potion) means, properly, the preparing and giving of medicine. Then it means also poisoning, and also magic art, or enchantment ; because in savage nations pharmacy or medicine consisted much in magical incantations. Thence it means sorcery or enchantment, and it is so used uniformly in the New Testament. It is used only in Gal. v. 20; Rev. ix. 21 ; xviii. 23 ; xxi. 8. Some have supposed that it means here *poisoning*, a crime often practised ; but the more correct interpretation is, to refer it to the black art, or to pretensions to witchcraft, and the numerous delusions which have grown out of it, as a striking illustration of the corrupt and depraved nature of man. ¶ *Hatred.* Gr. *Hatreds*, in the plural. Antipathies, and want of love, producing contentions and strifes. ¶ *Variance.* Contentions ; see Note, Rom. i. 29. ¶ *Emulations* (ζήλοι). In a bad sense, meaning heart-burning, or jealousy, or perhaps inordinate ambition. The sense is ardour or zeal *in a bad cause*, leading to strife, &c. ¶ *Wrath.* This also is plural

in the Greek (θυμοί), meaning passions, *bursts of anger ;* Note, 2 Cor. xii. 20. ¶ *Strife.* Also plural in the Greek ; see Note, 2 Cor. xii. 20 ¶ *Seditions ;* see Note, Rom. xvi. 17. ¶ *Heresies;* see Note, Acts v. 17 ; 1 Cor. xi. 19.

21. *Envyings ;* Note, 2 Cor. xii. 20. ¶ *Revellings;* Notes, 2 Cor. xii. 20 ; Rom. xiii. 13. ¶ *And such like.* This class of evils, without attempting to specify all. ¶ *Of which I tell you before.* In regard to which I forewarn you. ¶ *As I have also told* you *in time past.* When he was with them. ¶ *Shall not inherit the kingdom of God.* Cannot possibly be saved ; see Notes on 1 Cor. vi. 9—11. In regard to this passage, we may remark ; (1.) That it furnishes the most striking and unanswerable proof of human depravity. Paul represents these things as "the works of the flesh," the works of the unrenewed nature of man. They are such as human nature, when left to itself, everywhere produces. The world shows that such is the fact; and we cannot but ask, is a nature producing this to be regarded as pure ? Is man an unfallen being? Can he save himself? Does he need no Saviour ? (2.) This passage is full of fearful admonition to those who indulge in any or all of these vices. Paul, inspired of God, has solemnly declared, that such cannot be saved. They *cannot* enter into the kingdom of heaven as they are. Nor is it *desirable* that they should. What would heaven be if filled up with adulterers, and fornicators, and idolaters, with the proud and envious, and with murderers, and drunkards? To call such a place *heaven*, would be an abuse of the word. No one could wish to dwell there; and such men *cannot* enter into heaven. (3.) The human heart must be changed, or man cannot be saved. This follows of course. If such is its tendency, then there is a

22 But the fruit *a* of the Spirit is love, joy, peace, long-suffering gentleness, goodness, faith,

a John 15.5; Ep.5.9.

necessity for such a change as that in regeneration, in order that man may be happy and be saved. (4.) We should rejoice that such men *cannot*, with their present characters, be admitted to heaven. We should rejoice that there *is* one world where these vices are unknown, a world of perfect and eternal purity. When we look at the earth ; when we see how these vices prevail ; when we reflect that every land is polluted, and that we cannot traverse a continent or an island, visit a nook or corner of the earth, dwell in any city or town, where these vices do not exist, O how refreshing and invigorating is it to look forward to a pure heaven ! How cheering the thought that there is one world where these vices are unknown ; one world, all whose ample plains may be traversed, and the note of blasphemy shall never fall on the ear ; one world, where virtue shall be safe from the arts of the seducer ; one world where we may for ever dwell, and not one reeling and staggering drunkard shall ever be seen ; where there shall be not one family in want and tears from the vice of its unfaithful head ! With what joy should we look forward to that world ! With what ardour should we pant that it may be our own !

22. *But the fruit of the Spirit.* That which the Holy Spirit produces. It is not without design, evidently, that the apostle uses the word "Spirit" here, as denoting that these things do not flow from our own nature. The vices above enumerated are the proper "works" or result of the operations of the human heart ; the virtues which he enumerates are produced by a foreign influence—the agency of the Holy Spirit. Hence Paul does not trace them to our own hearts, *even when renewed.* He says that they are to be regarded as the proper result of the Spirit's operations on the soul. ¶ *Is love.* To God and to men. Probably the latter here is particularly intended, as the fruits of the Spirit are placed in contradistinction

from those vices which lead to strife among men. On the meaning of the word *love,* see Notes on 1 Cor. xiii. 1 ; and for an illustration of its operations and effects, see the Notes on that whole chapter. ¶ *Joy.* In the love of God ; in the evidences of pardon ; in communion with the Redeemer, and in his service ; in the duties of religion, in trial, and in the hope of heaven ; see Notes, Rom. v. 2 ; comp. 1 Pet. i. 8. ¶ *Peace.* As the result of reconciliation with God ; see Notes, Rom. v. 1. ¶ *Long-suffering.* In affliction and trial, and when injured by others ; see Note, 1 Cor. xiii. 4. ¶ *Gentleness.* The same word which is translated *kindness* in 2 Cor. vi. 6 ; see Note on that place. The word means goodness, kindness, benignity ; and is opposed to a harsh, crabbed, crooked temper. It is a disposition to be pleased ; it is mildness of temper, calmness of spirit, an unruffled disposition, and a disposition to treat all with urbanity and politeness. This is one of the regular effects of the Spirit's operations on the heart. Religion makes no one crabbed, and morose, and sour. It sweetens the temper ; corrects an irritable disposition ; makes the heart kind ; disposes us to make all around us as happy as possible. This is true politeness ; a kind of politeness which can far better be learned in the school of Christ than in that of Chesterfield ; by the study of the New Testament than under the direction of the dancing-master. ¶ *Goodness ;* see Note on Rom. xv. 14. Here the word seems to be used in the sense of *beneficence,* or a disposition to do good to others. The sense is, that a Christian must be a good man. ¶ *Faith.* On the meaning of the word faith, see Note on Mark xvi. 16. The word here may be used in the sense of *fidelity,* and may denote that the Christian will be a *faithful man,* a man faithful to his word and promises ; a man who can be trusted or confided in. It is probable that the word is used in this sense because the object

23 Meekness, temperance: against *a* such there is no law.

24 And they that are Christ's

a 1 Ti. 1.9.   1 or, *passions*.   b Ro. 8. 4, 5.

have crucified the flesh with the *i* affections and lusts.

25 If *b* we live in the Spirit, let us also walk in the Spirit.

---

of the apostle is not to speak of the feelings which we have towards God so much as to illustrate the influences of the Spirit in directing and controlling our feelings towards men. True religion makes a man *faithful*. The Christian is faithful as a man; faithful as a neighbour, friend, father, husband, son. He is faithful to his contracts; faithful to his promises. No man can be a Christian who is not thus faithful, and all pretensions to being under the influences of the Spirit when such fidelity does not exist, are deceitful and vain.

23. *Meekness;* see Note, Mat. v. 5. ¶ *Temperance.* The word here used, (ἐγκράτεια), means properly *self-control, continence.* It is derived from ἐν and κράτος, *strength,* and has reference to the *power* or ascendancy which we have over exciting and evil passions of all kinds. It denotes the self-rule which a man has over the evil propensities of his nature. Our word *temperance* we use now in a much more limited sense, as referring mainly to abstinence from intoxicating drinks. But the word here used is employed in a much more extended signification. It includes the dominion over all evil propensities, and may denote continence, chastity, self-government, moderation in regard to all indulgences as well as abstinence from intoxicating drinks. See the word explained in the Notes on Acts xxiv. 25. The sense here is, that the influences of the Holy Spirit on the heart make a man *moderate* in all indulgences; teach him to restrain his passions, and to govern himself; to control his evil propensities, and to subdue all inordinate affection. The Christian will not only abstain from intoxicating drinks, but from all exciting passions; he will be temperate in his manner of living, and in the government of his temper. This *may* be applied to temperance properly so called with us; but it should not be limited to that. A Christian *must be*

a temperate man; and if the effect of his religion is not to produce this, it is false and vain. Abstinence from intoxicating drinks, as well as from all improper excitement, is demanded by the very genius of his religion, and on this subject there is no danger of drawing the cords too close. No man was ever injured by the strictest temperance, by total abstinence from ardent spirits, and from wine as a beverage; no man is certainly safe who does not abstain; no man, it is believed, can be in a proper frame of mind for religious duties who indulges in the habitual use of intoxicating drinks. Nothing does more scandal to religion than such indulgences; and, other things being equal, he is the most under the influence of the Spirit of God who is the most thoroughly a man of temperance. ¶ *Against such there is no law.* That is, there is no law to condemn such persons. These are not the things which the law denounces. These, therefore, are the true freemen; free from the condemning sentence of the law, and free in the service of God. Law condemns sin; and they who evince the spirit here referred to are free from its denunciations.

24. *And they that are Christ's.* All who are true Christians. ¶ *Have crucified the flesh.* The corrupt passions of the soul have been put to death; *i. e.,* destroyed. They are as though they were dead, and have no power over us; see Note, chap. ii. 20. ¶ *With the affections.* Marg. *Passions.* All corrupt desires. ¶ *And lusts;* see Note, Rom. i. 24.

25. *If we live in the Spirit.* Note, ver. 16. The sense of this verse probably is, "We who are Christians profess to be under the influences of the Holy Spirit. By his influences and agency is our spiritual life. We profess not to be under the dominion of the flesh; not to be controlled by its appetites and desires. Let us then act in this manner, and as if we be-

26 Let *a* us not be desirous of vainglory, provoking one another, envying one another.

a Ph. 2. 3.

lieved this. Let us yield ourselves to his influences, and show that we are controlled by that Spirit." It is an earnest exhortation to Christians to yield wholly to the agency of the Holy Spirit on their hearts, and to submit to his guidance ; see Notes, Rom. viii. 5, 9.

26. *Let us not be desirous of vainglory.* The word here used (κενοδοξοι) means proud or vain of empty advantages, as of birth, property, eloquence, or learning. The reference here is probably to the paltry competitions which arose on account of these supposed advantages. It is possible that this might have been one cause of the difficulties existing in the churches of Galatia, and the apostle is anxious wholly to check and remove it. The Jews prided themselves on their birth, and men are everywhere prone to overvalue the supposed advantages of birth and blood. The doctrines of Paul are, that on great and most vital respects men are on a level ; that these things contribute nothing to salvation (Notes, chap. iii. 28); and that Christians should esteem them of little importance, and that they should not be suffered to interfere with their fellowship, or to mar their harmony and peace. ¶ *Provoking one another.* The sense is, that they who *are* desirous of vainglory, *do* provoke one another. They provoke those whom they regard as inferiors by a haughty carriage and a contemptuous manner towards them. They look upon them often with contempt ; pass them by with disdain ; treat them as beneath their notice ; and this *provokes* on the other hand hard feeling, and hatred, and a disposition to take revenge. When men regard themselves as equal in their great and vital interests ; when they feel that they are fellow-heirs of the grace of life ; when they feel that they belong to one great family, and are in their great interests on a level ; deriving no advantage from birth and blood ; on a level as descendants of the same apostate father ; as being themselves sinners ; on a level at the foot of the cross, at the communion table, on beds of sickness, in the grave, and at the bar of God ; when they feel this, then the consequences here referred to will be avoided. There will be no haughty carriage such as to provoke opposition ; and on the other hand there will be no envy on account of the superior rank of others. ¶ *Envying one another.* On account of their superior wealth, rank, talent, learning. The true way to cure envy is to make men feel that in their great and important interests they are on a level. Their great interests are beyond the grave. The distinctions of this life are temporary, and are comparative trifles. Soon all will be on a level in the grave, and at the bar of God and in heaven. Wealth, and honour, and rank do not avail there. The poorest man will wear as bright a crown as the rich ; the man of most humble birth will be admitted as near the throne as he who can boast the longest line of illustrious ancestors. Why should a man who is soon to wear a " crown incorruptible and undefiled and that fadeth not away," envy him who has a ducal coronet here, or a royal diadem—baubles that are soon to be laid aside for ever ? Why should he, though poor here, who is soon to inherit the treasures of heaven where " moth and rust do not corrupt," envy him who can walk over a few acres as his own, or who has accumulated a glittering pile of dust, soon to be left for ever ? Why should he who is soon to wear the robes of salvation, made " white in the blood of the Lamb," envy him who is " clothed in purple and fine linen," or who can adorn himself and his family in the most gorgeous attire which art and skill can make, soon to give place to the winding-sheet ; soon to be succeeded by the simple garb which the most humble wears in the grave ? If men feel that their great interests are beyond the tomb : that in the important matter of salvation they are on a level ; that soon they are to be undistinguish-

CHAPTER VI.

BRETHREN, [1] if a man be overtaken in a fault, ye which

are spiritual restore [a] such an one in the spirit of meekness; con-

1 or, *although.*   a Ja.5.19,20.

---

ed beneath the clods of the valley, how unimportant comparatively would it seem to adorn their bodies, to advance their name and rank and to improve their estates! The rich and the great would cease to look down with contempt on those of more humble rank, and the poor would cease to envy those above them, for they are soon to be their equals in the grave; their equals, perhaps their superiors in heaven!

CHAPTER VI.

ANALYSIS.

This chapter is composed entirely of affectionate exhortation, and the expression of the apostle's earnest solicitude in the behalf of the Christians in Galatia. He exhorts them (ver. 1) to bring back to the ways of virtue any one who through the strength of strong temptation had been led astray. He entreats them (ver. 2) to bear one another's burdens, and thus to show that they were true friends of Christ, and governed by his laws. He entreats them not to be lifted up with pride, and not to affix an inordinate estimate to any thing that they possessed, assuring them that their true estimate was to be formed from the character of their own works; ver. 3—5. He exhorts them to minister to the wants of their public teachers, the preachers of the gospel; ver. 6. In ver. 7—10, he reminds them of the solemn day of judgment, when all will be tried; assures them that men will be judged and rewarded according to their works; and entreats them not to be weary in well-doing, but to labour on patiently in doing good, with the assurance that they should reap in due season. In ver. 11, he shows them the interest which he felt in them by his having done what was unusual for him, and what perhaps he had done in no other instance—writing an entire letter in his own hand. He then states the true reason why others wished them to be circumcised. It was the dread of persecution, and not any real love to the cause of religion.

They did not themselves keep the law, and they only desired to glory in the number of converts to their views; ver. 12, 13. But Paul says that *he* would glory in nothing but in the cross of Christ. By that he had been crucified to the world, and the world had been crucified to him (ver. 14); and he repeats the solemn assurance that in the Christian religion neither circumcision nor uncircumcision was of any importance whatever; ver. 15. This was the true rule of life, and on as many as walked according to this principle, he invokes the blessing of God; ver. 16. He closes the epistle by entreating them to give him no more trouble. He bore in his body already the marks or sufferings which he had received in the cause of the Lord Jesus. His trials already were sufficient; and he entreats them to spare him from future molestation (ver. 17), and closes with the benediction; ver. 18.

1. *Brethren, if a man be overtaken.* Marg. *Although.* It is a case which the apostle supposes might happen. Christians were not perfect; and it was possible that they who were true Christians might be surprised by temptation, and fall into sin. The word rendered *be overtaken* ($\pi\varrho o\lambda\eta\phi\vartheta\eta$ from $\pi\varrho o\lambda\alpha\mu\beta\acute{\alpha}\nu\omega$), means properly to take before another, to anticipate (1 Cor. xi. 21); then to be before taken or caught; and may here mean either that one had been *formerly* guilty of sin or had been recently *hurried on* by his passions or by temptations to commit a fault. It is probable that the latter here is the true sense, and that it means, if a man is found to be overtaken by any sin; if his passions, or if temptation get the better of him. Tindal renders it, "If any man be fallen by chance into any fault." It refers to cases of surprise, or of sudden temptation. Christians do not commit sin deliberately, and as a part of the plan of life; but they may be surprised by sudden temptation, or urged on by impetuous or head-strong pas-

sidering thyself, lest thou also be tempted.

2 Bear *a* ye one another's burdens, and so fulfil the law of Christ.

a Ro.15.1.

sion, as David and Peter were. Paul does not speak of the possibility of restoring one who deliberately forms the plan of sinning; he does not suppose that such a man could be a Christian, and that it would be proper to speak of *restoring* such a man. ¶ *Ye which are spiritual.* Who are under the influences of the Holy Spirit; see Note on chap. v. 22, 23. The apostle, in this verse, refers evidently to those who have fallen into some sensual indulgence (chap. v. 19 —21), and says that they who have escaped these temptations, and who are under the influences of the Spirit, should recover such persons. It is a very important qualification for those who would recover others from sin, that they should not bo guilty of the same sin themselves. Reformers should be holy men; men who exercise discipline in the church should be "spiritual" men—men in whom implicit confidence may be properly reposed. ¶ *Restore such an one.* On the meaning of the word here used, see Note on 2 Cor. xiii. 11. Here it means, not to restore him to the church after he has been excluded, but *set him right,* bring him back, recover him from his errors and his faults. The apostle does not say in what manner this is to be done; but it is usually to be done doubtless by affectionate admonition, by faithful instruction, and by prayer. Discipline or punishment should not be resorted to until the other methods are tried in vain; Mat. xviii. 15—17. ¶ *In the spirit of meekness.* With a kind, forbearing, and forgiving spirit; Note, Mat. v. 5. Not with anger; not with a lordly and overbearing mind; not with a love of finding others in fault, and with a desire for inflicting the discipline of the church; not with a harsh and unforgiving temper, but with love, and gentleness, and humility, and patience, and with a readiness to forgive when wrong has been done. This is an essential qualification for restoring and recovering an offending

brother. No man should attempt to rebuke or admonish another who cannot do it in the spirit of meekness; no man should engage in any way in the work of reform who has not such a temper of mind. ¶ *Considering thyself,* &c. Remembering how liable you are yourself to err; and how much kindness and indulgence should therefore be shown to others. You are to act as if you felt it possible that you might also be overtaken with a fault; and you should act as you would wish that others should do towards you. Pliny (Epis. viii. 22) has expressed a similar sentiment in the following beautiful language. " Atque ego optimum et emendatissimum existimo, qui caeteris ita ignoscit, tanquam ipse quotidie peccet; ita peccatis abstinet, tanquam nemini ignoscat. Proinde hoc domi, hoc foris, hoc in omni vitæ genere teneamus, ut nobis implacabiles simus, exorabiles istis etiam, qui dare veniam nisi sibi nesciunt." The doctrine taught by Paul is, that such is human infirmity, and such the strength of human depravity, that no one knows into what sins he may himself fall. He may be tempted to commit the same sins which he endeavours to amend in others; he may be left to commit even worse sins. If this is the case, we should be tender while we are firm; forgiving while we set our faces against evil; prayerful while we rebuke, and compassionate when we are compelled to inflict on others the discipline of the church. Every man who has any proper feelings, when he attempts to recover an erring brother should pray for him and for himself also; and will regard his duty as only half done, and that very imperfectly, if he does not " consider also that he himself may be tempted."

2. *Bear ye one another's burdens;* see Note, Rom. xv. 1. Bear with each other; help each other in the divine life. The sense is, that every man has peculiar temptations and easily besetting

3 For if a man think himself to be something, when he is nothing, he deceiveth himself.

z 2 Co.13.5.

sins, which constitute a heavy burden. We should aid each other in regard to these, and help one another to overcome them. ¶ *And so fulfil the law of Christ.* The peculiar law of Christ, requiring us to love one another ; see Note on John xiii. 34. This was the distinguishing law of the Redeemer ; and they could in no way better fulfil it than by aiding each other in the divine life. The law of Christ would not allow us to reproach the offender, or to taunt him, or to rejoice in his fall. We should help him to take up his load of infirmities, and sustain him by our counsels, our exhortations, and our prayers. Christians, conscious of their infirmities, have *a right* to the sympathy and the prayers of their brethren. They should not be cast off to a cold and heartless world ; a world rejoicing over their fall, and ready to brand them as hypocrites. They should be pressed to the warm bosom of brotherly kindness ; and prayer should be made to ascend without ceasing around an erring and a fallen brother. Is this the case in regard to all who bear the Christian name ?

3. *For if a man think himself to be something,* &c.; see chap. v. 26. This is designed, evidently, to be another reason why we should be kind and tender to those who have erred. It is, that even those who are most confident may fall. They who feel secure, and think it impossible that they should sin, are not safe. They may be wholly deceived, and may be nothing, when they have the highest estimate of themselves. They may themselves fall into sin, and have need of all the sympathy and kindness of their brethren. ¶ *When he is nothing.* When he has no strength, and no moral worth. When he is not such as he apprehends, but is lifted up with vain self-conceit. ¶ *He deceiveth himself.* He understands not his own character. " The worst part of the fraud falls on his own head."—*Doddridge.* He does

4 But let every man prove *a* his own work, and then shall he have rejoicing in himself *b* alone, and not in another :

b Pr.14.14.

not accomplish what he expected to do; and instead of acquiring reputation from others, as he expected, he renders himself contemptible in their sight.

4. *But let every man prove.* That is, try or examine in a proper manner. Let him form a proper estimate of what is due to himself, according to his real character. Let him compare himself with the word of God, and the infallible rule which he has given, and by which we are to be judged in the last great day ; comp. Note, Rom. xii. 3 ; 1 Cor. xi. 28 ; 2 Cor. xiii. 5. ¶ *His own work.* What he does. Let him form a fair and impartial estimate of his own character. ¶ *And then shall he have rejoicing.* That is, he will be appropriately rewarded, and will meet with no disappointment. The man who forms an improper estimate of his own character will be sure to be disappointed. The man who examines himself, and who forms no extravagant expectation in regard to what is due to himself, will be appropriately rewarded, and will be made happy. If, by the careful examination of himself, he finds his life to be virtuous, and his course of conduct pure ; if he has done no wrong to others, and if he finds evidence that he is a child of God, then he will have cause of rejoicing. ¶ *In himself alone;* comp. Prov. xiv. 14 : " A good man shall be satisfied from himself." The sentiment is, that he will find in himself a source of pure joy. He will not be dependent on the applause of others for happiness. In an approving conscience ; in the evidence of the favour of God ; in an honest effort to lead a pure and holy life, he will have happiness. The source of his joys will be within ; and he will not be dependent, as the man of ambition, and the man who thinks of himself more highly than he ought, will, on the favours of a capricious multitude, and on the breath of popular applause. ¶ *And not in another.* He will not be dependent

5 For every man shall bear his own burden.

6 Let *a* him that is taught in the

word communicate unto him that teacheth in all good things.

7 Be not deceived ; God is not

a 1 Co.9.11—14.

on others for happiness. Here is the true secret of happiness. It consists, (1.) In not forming an improper estimate of ourselves ; in knowing just what we are, and what is due to us ; in not thinking ourselves to be something, when we are nothing. (2.) In leading such a life that it may be examined *to the core*, that we may know exactly what we are without being distressed or pained. That is, in having a good conscience, and in the honest and faithful discharge of our duty to God and man. (3.) In not being dependent on the fickle applause of the world for our comfort. The man who has no internal resources, and who has no approving conscience ; who is happy only when others smile, and miserable when they frown, is a man who can have no security for enjoyment. The man who has a good conscience, and who enjoys the favour of God, and the hope of heaven, carries with him the source of perpetual joy. He cannot be deprived of it. His purse may be taken, and his house robbed, but the highwayman cannot rob him of his comforts. He carries with him an unfailing source of happiness when abroad, and the same source of happiness abides with him at home ; he bears it into society, and it remains with him in solitude ; it is his companion when in health, and when surrounded by his friends, and it is no less his companion when his friends leave him, and when he lies upon a bed of death.

5. *For every man shall bear his own burden.* This seems to be a kind of proverbial saying ; and it means here, every man shall have his proper reward. If he is a virtuous man, he will be happy ; if a vicious man, he will be miserable. If a virtuous man, he will have the source of happiness in himself ; if a sinner, he must bear the proper penalty of his sin. In the great day every man shall be properly rewarded. Knowing this, we should be little anxious about the sentiments

of others, and should seek to maintain a good conscience towards God and man. The design of this passage is, to prevent men from forming an improper estimate of themselves, and of the opinions of others. Let a man feel that he is soon to stand at the judgment-seat, and it will do much to keep him from an improper estimate of his own importance ; let him feel that he must give an account to God, and that his great interests are to be determined by the estimate which *God* will affix to his character, and it will teach him that the opinion of the world is of little value. This will restrain his vanity and ambition. This will show him that the great business of life is to secure the favour of God, and to be prepared to give up his account ; and there is no way so effectual of checking ambition, and subduing vanity and the love of applause, as to feel that we are soon to stand at the awful bar of God.

6. *Let him that is taught in the word.* In the word of God ; *i. e.* the gospel. ¶ *Communicate unto him.* Let him *share* with him who teaches; let there be a *common* participation of all good things ¶ *In all good things.* In every thing that is needful for their comfortable subsistence. On the duty here enjoined, see Notes on 1 Cor. ix. 11—13.

7. *Be not deceived.* That is, in regard to your character, and your hopes for eternity. This is a formula of introduction to some admonition that is peculiarly weighty and important. It implies that there was *danger* that they would be deceived in reference to their character. The *sources* of the danger were the corruption of their own hearts, the difficulty of knowing their true character, the instructions of false teachers, &c. ; see Note on 1 Cor. vi. 9. ¶ *God is not mocked.* He cannot be imposed on, or mocked. He knows what our real character is, and he will judge us accordingly. The word rendered *mocked*

mocked : for whatsoever a man soweth, that shall he also reap.

8 For he that soweth to his [a] flesh shall of the flesh reap corrup-

a Job 4.8; Pr.22.8; Ho.8.7.

($μυκτηρίζω$), means, properly, to turn up the nose in scorn; hence to mock, or deride, or insult. The sense is, that God could not be imposed on, or could not be insulted with impunity, or successfully. To *mock* is, properly, (1.) To imitate, to mimic : to imitate in contempt or derision. (2.) To deride, to laugh at, to ridicule. (3.) To defeat, or to illude, or to disappoint. (4.) To fool, to tantalize.— *Webster.* Here it cannot mean to *imitate*, or to *mimic*, but it refers to the principles of the divine administration, and must mean that they could not be treated with contempt, or successfully evaded. They could not hope to illude or impose on God. His principles of government were settled, and they could not impose on him. To what the reference is here, is not perfectly plain. In the connection in which it stands, it seems to refer to the support of the ministers of the gospel ; and Paul introduces the general principle, that as a man sows he will reap, to show them what will be the effect of a liberal and proper use of their property. If they made a proper use of it; if they employed it for benevolent purposes ; if they appropriated what they should to the support of religion, they would reap accordingly. God could not be imposed on in regard to this. They could not make him think that they had true religion when they were sowing to the flesh, and when they were spending their money in purchasing pleasure, and in luxury and vanity. No zeal, however ardent ; no prayers, however fervent or long, no professions, however loud, would impose on God. And to make such prayers, and to manifest such zeal and such strong professions, while the heart was with the world, and they were spending their money for every thing else but religion, was mocking God. Alas, how much mockery of God like this still prevails ! How much, when men *seem* disposed to make God believe that they are exceedingly zealous and devoted, while their heart is truly

with the world ! How many long prayers are offered ; how much zeal is shown ; how many warm professions are made, *as if* to make God and man believe that the heart was truly engaged in the cause of religion, while little or nothing is given in the cause of benevolence ; while the ministers of religion are suffered to starve ; and while the "loud professor" rolls in wealth, and is distinguished for luxury of living, for gayety of apparel, for splendour of equipage, and for extravagance in parties of pleasure ! Such professors attempt to mock God. They are really sowing to the flesh ; and of the flesh they must reap corruption. ¶ *For whatsoever a man soweth*, &c.; see Note, 2 Cor. ix. 6. This figure is taken from agriculture. A man who sows wheat, shall reap wheat ; he who sows barley, shall reap barley ; he who sows cockle, shall reap cockle. Every kind of grain will produce grain like itself. So it is in regard to our works. He who is liberal, shall be dealt with liberally; he who is righteous, shall be rewarded; he who is a sinner, shall reap according to his deeds.

8. *For he that soweth to his flesh* That makes provision for the indulgence of fleshly appetites and passions; see Notes on chap. v. 19—21. He who makes use of his property to give indulgence to licentiousness, intemperance, and vanity. ¶ *Shall of the flesh.* From the flesh, or as that which indulgence in fleshly appetites properly produces. Punishment, under the divine government, is commonly in the line of offences. The punishment of licentiousness and intemperance in this life is commonly loathsome and offensive disease ; and when long indulged, the sensualist becomes haggard, and bloated, and corrupted, and sinks into the grave. Such, also, is often the punishment of luxurious living, of a pampered appetite, of gluttony, as well as of intemperate drinking. But if the punishment does not follow in this life, it will be sure to overtake the sensualist in the world

tion; but he that soweth to the Spirit, *a* shall of the Spirit reap life everlasting.

9 And let *b* us not be weary in

a Pr.11.18; Ja.3.18. *b* 1 Co.15.58.

well-doing; for in due season we shall reap, if *c* we faint not.

10 As we have therefore opportunity, *d* let us do good unto all *e*

c He.10.36; Re.2.10.
d Ec.9.10. *e* Mat.5.43; Tit.3.8.

---

to come. There he shall reap ruin final and everlasting. ¶ *Corruption.* (1.) By disease. (2.) In the grave—the home to which the sensualist rapidly travels. (3.) In the world of woe. There all shall be corrupt. His virtue—even the semblance of virtue, shall all be gone. His understanding, will, fancy—his whole soul shall be debased and corrupt. No virtue will linger and live on the plains of ruin, but all shall be depravity and woe. Every thing in hell is debased and corrupt; and the whole harvest of sensuality in this world and the world to come, is degradation and defilement. ¶ *But he that soweth to the Spirit.* He who follows the leadings and cultivates the affections which the Holy Spirit would produce; see Notes on chap. v. 22, 23. ¶ *Shall of the Spirit.* As the result of following the leadings of the Spirit. ¶ *Reap life everlasting;* see Note on Rom. ii. 7.

9. *And let us not be weary in well-doing;* see Note on 1 Cor. xv. 58. The reference here is particularly to the support of the ministers of religion (ver. 6), but the apostle makes the exhortation general. Christians sometimes become weary. There is so much opposition to the best plans for doing good; there is so much to be done; there are so many calls on their time and their charities; and there is often so much ingratitude among those whom they endeavour to benefit, that they become disheartened. Such Paul addresses, and exhorts them not to give over, but to persevere. ¶ *For in due season.* At the day of judgment. Then we shall receive the full reward of all our self-denials and charities. ¶ *We shall reap, if we faint not.* If we do not give over, exhausted and disheartened. It is *implied* here, that unless a man perseveres in doing good to the end of life, he can hope for no reward. He who becomes disheartened, and who

gives over his efforts; he that is appalled by obstacles, and that faints on account of the embarrassments thrown in his way; he that pines for ease, and withdraws from the field of benevolence, shows that he has no true attachment to the cause, and that his heart has never been truly in the work of religion. He who becomes a true Christian, becomes such FOR ETERNITY. He has enlisted, never to withdraw. He becomes pledged to do good and to serve God *always.* No obstacles are to deter, no embarrassments are to drive him from the field. With the vigour of his youth, and the wisdom and influence of his riper years; with his remaining powers when enfeebled by age; with the last pulsation of life here, and with his immortal energies in a higher world, he is to do good. For that he is to live. In that he is to die; and when he awakes in the resurrection with renovated powers, he is to awake to an everlasting service of doing good, as far as he may have opportunity, in the kingdom of God.

10. *As we have therefore opportunity, let us do good unto all men.* This is the true rule about doing good. "The opportunity to do good," says Cotton Mather, "imposes the obligation to do it." The simple rule is, that we are favoured with the opportunity, and that we have the power. It is not that we are to do it when it is convenient; or when it will advance the interest of a party; or when it may contribute to our fame; the rule is, that we are to do it when we have the opportunity. No matter how often that occurs; no matter how many objects of benevolence are presented —the more the better; no matter how much self-denial it may cost us; no matter how little *fame* we may get by it; still, if we have the *opportunity* to do good, we are to do it, and should be thankful for the privilege. And it is to be done *to all men.* Not

men, especially to them *a* who are of the household of faith.

11 Ye see how large a letter I

a 1 John 3.14.

have written unto you with mine own hand.

12 As many as desire to make

---

to our family only; not to our party; not to our neighbours; not to those of our own colour; not to those who live in the same land with us, but to all mankind. If we can reach and benefit a man who lives on the other side of the globe, whom we have never seen, and *shall* never see in this world or in the world to come, still we are to do him good. Such is Christianity. And in this, as in all other respects, it differs from the narrow and selfish spirit of *clanship* which prevails all over the world. ¶ *Especially*. On the same principle that a man is bound particularly to benefit his own family and friends. In his large and expansive zeal for the world at large, he is not to forget or neglect them. He is to feel that they have peculiar claims on him. They are near him. They are bound to him by tender ties. They may be particularly dependent on him. Christianity does not relax the ties which bind us to our country, our family, and our friends. It makes them more close and tender, and excites us more faithfully to discharge the duties which grow out of these relations. But, in addition to that, it excites us to do good to all men, and to bless the stranger as well as the friend; the man who has a different colour from our own, as well as he who has the same; the man who lives in another clime, as well as he who was born in the same country in which *we* live. ¶ *Of the household of faith*. Christians are distinguished from other men primarily by their *believing* the gospel, and by its influence on their lives.

11. *Ye see*. This might be rendered *see*, in the imperative. So Tindal renders it, "Behold." But it is more commonly supposed that it should be rendered in the indicative. The sense is not materially different whichever translation is adopted. The *object* of the apostle is, to direct their attention to the special proof of his love, which he had manifested in writing such a letter. ¶ *How large a letter*.

Considerable variety has existed in regard to the interpretation of this phrase. The word here used and translated *how large* (πηλίκος), means, properly, *how great*. Some have supposed that it refers to the *size of the letters* which Paul made in writing the epistle—the length and crudeness of the characters which he used. Such interpreters suppose that he was not well versed in writing Greek, and that he used large letters, and those somewhat rudely made, like the Hebrew. So Doddridge and Whitby interpret it; and so Theodoret, Jerome, Theophylact, and some others. He might not, says Doddridge, have been well versed in the Greek characters; or "this inaccuracy of his writings might have been owing to the infirmity or weakness of his nerves, which he had hinted at before." Jerome says, that Paul was a Hebrew, and that he was unacquainted with the mode of writing Greek letters; and that because necessity demanded that he should write a letter in his own hand, contrary to his usual custom, he was obliged to form his characters in this crude manner. According to this interpretation, it was, (1.) A pledge to the Galatians that the epistle was genuine, since it bore the marks of his own handwriting; and, (2.) It was proof of special affection for them that he was willing to undergo this labour on their account. Others suppose that he means to refer to the size *of the epistle* which he had written. Such is the interpretation of Grotius, Koppe, Bloomfield, Clarke, Locke, Chandler, and is, indeed, the common interpretation, as it is the obvious one. According to this, it was proof of special interest in them, and regard for them, that he had written to them a whole letter with his own hand. Usually he employed an amanuensis, and added his name, with a brief benediction or remark at the close; see Notes, Rom. xvi. 22; 1 Cor. xvi. 21. What *induced* him to depart from his

a fair show in the flesh, they constrain you to be circumcised ; only lest they should suf-

fer persecution for the cross of Christ.

13 For neither they themselves

usual custom here is unknown. Jerome supposes that he refers here to *what follows* from this verse to the end of the epistle, as that which he had written with his own hand, but the word *ἔγραψα*, says Rosenmüller, refers rather to what he *had* written, than to that which he intended to write. On this verse, the reader may consult with advantage, Tholuck on the Life and Writings of Paul: German Selections, by Edwards and Park, Andover, 1839, pp. 35, 64, 65.

12. *As many as desire to make a fair show in the flesh.* To be distinguished for their conformity to external rites and customs. To be known for their zeal in this cause. They sought to show their zeal by making converts, and by inducing others also to conform to those customs. Paul here refers, doubtless, to the Jewish teachers, and he says that their main object was to evince their zeal in the observance of rites and ceremonies. ¶ *They constrain you.* You who are Gentiles. They insist on circumcision as indispensable to salvation. ¶ *Only lest they should suffer persecution.* It is not from any true love for the cause of religion. It is, that they may avoid persecution from the Jews. If they should renounce the doctrine which taught that circumcision was indispensable, they would be exposed to the rage of the Jews, and would suffer persecution. Rather than do this, they make a show of great zeal in inducing others to be circumcised. ¶ *For the cross of Christ.* From attachment to the cause of a crucified Saviour. If they insisted on entire dependence on the merits of his blood, and renounced all dependence on rites and ceremonies, they would suffer persecution. This verse shows the true cause of the zeal which the Judaizing teachers evinced. It was the fear of persecution. It was the want of independence and boldness in maintaining the doctrine that men were to be saved only by the merits of the Lord Jesus. By attempting to

blend together the doctrines of Judaism and Christianity; by maintaining that the observance of the Jewish rites was necessary, and yet that Jesus was the Messiah, they endeavoured to keep in with both parties ; and thus to escape the opposition of the Jews. It was an unhallowed compromise. It was an attempt to blend things together which could not be united. One *must* really displace the other. If men depended on the rites of Moses, they had no need of dependence on the Messiah ; if they professed to depend on him, then to rely on any thing else was in fact to disown and reject him. Embracing the one system was in fact renouncing the other. Such is the argument of Paul ; and such his solemn remonstrance against embracing any doctrine which would obscure the glory of simple dependence on the cross of Christ.

13. *For neither they themselves who are circumcised.* The Jewish teachers, or perhaps *all* Jews. It was true in general that the Jews did not wholly and entirely obey the law of Moses, but it is probable that the apostle refers particularly here to the judaizing teachers in Galatia. ¶ *Keep the law.* The law of Moses, or the law of God. Paul's idea is, that if they were circumcised they brought themselves under obligation to keep the *whole* law of God; see Note, ch. v. 3. But *they* did not do it. (1.) No man *perfectly* observes the whole law of God. (2.) The Jewish nation as such were very far from doing it. (3.) It is probable that these persons did not *pretend* even to keep the whole law of Moses. Paul insists on it that if they were circumcised, and depended on that for salvation, they were under obligation to keep the whole law. But *they* did not. Probably they did not offer sacrifice, or join in any of the numerous observances of the Jewish nation, except some of the more prominent, such as circumcision. This, says Paul, is inconsistent in the highest degree ; and they thus

who are circumcised keep the law ; but desire to have you circumcised, that they may glory in your flesh.

14 But *a* God forbid that I should glory, save in the cross of our Lord Jesus Christ, [1] by

a Ph.3.3,7,8.   1 or, *whereby.*

---

show their insincerity and hypocrisy. ¶ *That they may glory in your flesh.* In having you as converts, and in persuading you to be circumcised, that they may show their zeal for the law, and thus escape persecution. The phrase " in your flesh" here, is equivalent to " in your circumcision ;" making use of your circumcision to promote their own importance, and to save themselves from persecution.

14. *But God forbid.* Note, Rom. iii. 4. " For me it is not to glory except in the cross of Christ." The *object* of Paul here is evidently to place himself in contrast with the judaizing teachers, and to show his determined purpose to glory in nothing else but the cross of Christ. Well they knew that he had as much occasion for glorying in the things pertaining to the flesh, or in the observance of external rites and customs, as any of them. He had been circumcised. He had had all the advantages of accurate training in the knowledge of the Jewish law. He had entered on life with uncommon advantages. He had evinced a zeal that was not surpassed by any of them ; and his life, so far as conformity to the religion in which he had been trained was concerned, was blameless; Phil. iii. 4—8. This must have been to a great extent known to the Galatians; and by placing his own conduct in strong contrast with that of the judaizing teachers, and showing that *he* had no ground of confidence in himself, he designed to bring back the minds of the Galatians to simple dependence on the cross. ¶ *That I should glory.* That I should boast ; or that I should rely on any thing else. Others glory in their conformity to the laws of Moses ; others in their zeal, or their talents, or their learning, or their orthodoxy ; others in their wealth, or their accomplishments ; others in their family alliances, and their birth ; but the supreme boast and glorying of a Christian is in the cross of Christ. ¶*In the*

cross of our Lord Jesus Christ. In Jesus the crucified Messiah. It is a subject of rejoicing and glorying that we have *such* a Saviour. The world looked upon him with contempt; and the cross was a stumblingblock to the Jew, and folly to the Greek. Notes, 1 Cor. i. 23. But to the Christian, that cross is the subject of glorying. It is so because, (1.) Of the love of him who suffered there ; (2.) Of the purity and holiness of his character, for the innocent died there for the guilty ; (3.) Of the honour there put on the law of God by his dying to maintain it unsullied ; (4.) Of the reconciliation there made for sin, accomplishing what could be done by no other oblation, and by no power of man ; (5.) Of the pardon there procured for the guilty ; (6.) Of the fact that through it we become dead to the world, and are made alive to God; (7.) Of the support and consolation which goes from that cross to sustain us in trial ; and, (8.) Of the fact that it procured for us admission into heaven, a title to the world of glory. All is glory around the cross. It was a glorious Saviour who died ; it was glorious love that led him to die ; it was a glorious object to redeem a world ; and it is unspeakable glory to which he will raise lost and ruined sinners by his death. O who would not glory in such a Saviour ! Compared with this, what trifles are all the objects in which men usually boast ! And what a lesson is here furnished to the true Christian ! Let us not boast of our wealth. It will soon leave us, or we shall be taken from it, and it can aid us little in the great matters that are before us. It will not ward off disease ; it will not enable us to bear pain ; it will not smooth the couch of death ; it will not save the soul. Let us not glory in our strength, for it will soon fail; in our beauty, for we shall soon be undistinguished in the corruptions of the tomb ; in our accomplishments, for they will not save

whom the world is crucified *a* unto me, and I unto the world.

15 For *b* in Christ Jesus neither circumcision availeth any thing, nor uncircumcision, but a *c* new creature.

16 And as many as walk ac-

a ch.2.20.　　*b* ch.5.6.　　*c* 2 Co.5.17.

cording to this rule, peace *d be* on them, and mercy, and upon the Israel of God.

17 From henceforth let no man trouble me : for *e* I bear in my body the marks of the Lord Jesus.

d Ps.125.5.　　*e* Col.1.24.

us ; in our learning, for it is not that by which we can be brought to heaven. But *let* us glory that we have for a Saviour the eternal Son of God—that glorious Being who was adored by the inhabitants of heaven ; who made the worlds ; who is pure, and lovely, and most holy ; and who has undertaken our cause and died to save us. I desire no higher honour than to be saved by the Son of God. It is the exaltation of my nature, and shows me more than any thing else its true dignity, that one so great and glorious sought my redemption. That cannot be an object of temporary value which he sought by coming from heaven, and if there is any object of real magnitude in this world, it is the soul which the eternal Son of God died to redeem. ¶ *By whom the world is crucified unto me,* &c. ; see Notes on ch. ii. 20.

15. *For in Christ Jesus.* In his religion; see Note on ch. v. 6. ¶ *But a new creature.* The fact that a man is created anew, or born again, constitutes the real difference between him and other men. This is what Christ requires ; this is the distinction which he designs to make. It is not by conformity to certain rites and customs that a man is to be accepted; it is not by elevated rank, or by wealth, or beauty, or blood ; it is not by the colour of the complexion ; but the grand inquiry is, whether a man is born again, and is in fact a new creature in Christ Jesus ; see Note on 2 Cor. v. 17, for an explanation of the phrase " a new creature."

16. *And as many as walk.* As many as *live,* for so the word *walk* is used in the Scriptures. *According to this rule.* Gr. This *canon* ; see the word explained in the Notes on 2 Cor. x. 13. ¶ *Peace* be *on them ;* see Note, Rom. xv. 33. ¶ *And upon the Israel of God.* The true church of

God; all who are his true worshippers; see Notes on Rom. ii. 28, 29 ; ix. 6.

17. *From henceforth.* For the remaining time ; that is, during the remainder of my life. ¶ *Let no man trouble me.* This implies that he had had trouble of some kind, and that he earnestly desires that he may have no more. What particular trouble he here refers to, is not certainly known, and commentators have not been agreed. It seems to me that the connection requires us to understand it of the molestation which he had in regard to his call to the apostolic office, and his authority to explain and defend the religion of the Redeemer. This had been one principal subject of this epistle. His authority had been called in question. He had felt it necessary to go into a vindication of it. His instructions had been departed from on the ground that he was not one of the original apostles, and that he differed from others ; see ch. i. 11. Hence all the anxiety and trouble which he had had in regard to their departure from the doctrines which he had taught them. He closes the whole subject of the epistle by this tender and affecting language, the sense of which has been well expressed by Crellius: " I have shown my apostolic authority, and proved that I am commissioned by the Lord Jesus. I have stated and vindicated the great doctrine of justification by faith, and shown that the Mosaic law is not necessarily binding. On these points may I have no more trouble. I have enough for my nature to bear of other kinds. I bear in my body the impressive proofs that I *am* an apostle, and the sufferings that require all my fortitude to sustain them. These marks, received in the service of the Lord Jesus, and so strongly resembling those which *he* himself received, prove

18 Brethren, the [a] grace of our Lord Jesus Christ be with your spirit. Amen.

Unto the Galatians, written from Rome.

a 2 Ti.4.22; Phil.8.25.

that I am truly engaged in his cause, and am commissioned by him. These wounds and sorrows are so many, that I have need of the kindness and prayers of Christians rather than to be compelled to vindicate myself, and to rebuke them for their own wanderings."

¶ *For I bear in my body the marks of the Lord Jesus.* The word here rendered "marks" (στίγματα), means properly the marks or brands which are pricked or burnt in upon the body. So slaves were sometimes branded by their masters to prevent their escape; and so devotees to an idol god sometimes caused to be impressed on themselves the name or image of the divinity which they adored. Herodotus (ii. 113) mentions a temple of Hercules in Egypt, in which if any slave took refuge, and had the sacred *brands* or marks impressed on him (στίγματα), he thereby devoted himself to the god, and it was not lawful for any one to injure him. Many have supposed that Paul here says, in allusion to such a custom, that he had the name of the Redeemer impressed on his body, and that he regarded himself as devoted to him and his cause. It seems to me that by these *marks* or brands he refers to the *weals* which he had received in his body ; the marks of stripes and sufferings which he endured in the service of the Redeemer. Comp. 2 Cor. xi. 24, 25. He had repeatedly been scourged. He bore the marks of that on his person now. They were the evidences that he was devoted to the Saviour. He had received them in his cause ; and they were the proofs that he belonged to the Lord Jesus. He had suffered for him, and had suffered much. Having thus suffered, and having thus the evidence that he belonged to the Saviour, and having by his sufferings given ample proof of that to others, he asks to be freed from further molestation. Some had in their body the marks of circumcision, the evidence that they

were disciples of the law of Moses ; others had perhaps in their persons the image and name of an idol to which they were devoted ; but the marks which *he* bore were the *weals* which he had received by being again and again whipped publicly in the cause of the Redeemer. To that Redeemer, therefore, he felt himself united, and from that attachment he would not allow himself to be diverted. How often has an old soldier shown his *scars* with pride and exultation as a proof of his attachment to his country ! Numerous scars ; the loss of an arm, an eye, or a leg, are thus the much valued and vaunted pledges of attachment to liberty, and a passport to the confidence of every man who loves his country. "I prize this wound," said Lafayette, when struck in the foot by a musket ball at Germantown, "as among the most valued of my honours." So Paul felt in regard to the scourges which he had received in the cause of the Lord Jesus. They were his boast and his glory ; the pledge that he had been engaged in the cause of the Saviour, and a passport to all who loved the Son of God. Christians now are not subjected to such stripes and scourgings. But let us have *some* marks of our attachment to the Lord Jesus. By a holy life ; by self-denial ; by subdued animal affections ; by zeal in the cause of truth ; by an imitation of the Lord Jesus; and by the marks of suffering in our body, if we should be called to it, let us have *some* evidence that we are his, and be able to say, when we look on death and eternity, "we bear with us the evidence that we belong to the Son of God." To us that will be of more value than any ribbon or star indicating elevated rank; more valuable than a ducal coronet ; more valuable than the brightest jewel that ever sparkled on the brow of royalty.

18. *Brethren, the grace, &c.* ; see Note, Rom. xvi. 20.